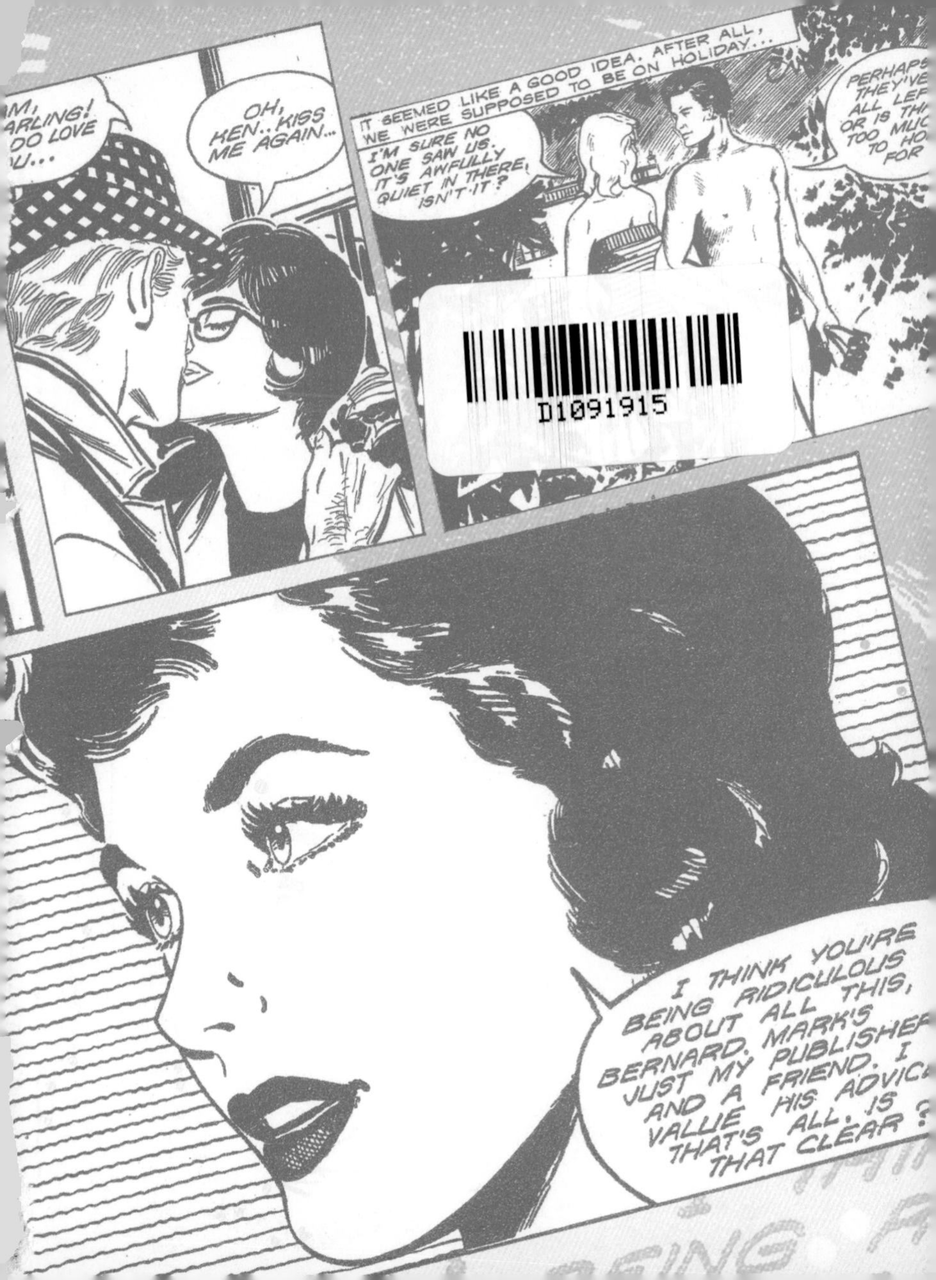
OH, KEN.. KISS ME AGAIN...
IT SEEMED LIKE A GOOD IDEA. AFTER ALL, WE WERE SUPPOSED TO BE ON HOLIDAY...
I'M SURE NO ONE SAW US. IT'S AWFULLY QUIET IN THERE, ISN'T IT?
I THINK YOU'RE BEING RIDICULOUS ABOUT ALL THIS, BERNARD. MARK'S JUST MY PUBLISHER AND A FRIEND. I VALUE HIS ADVICE, THAT'S ALL. IS THAT CLEAR?

Valentine

PICTURE STORY
LIBRARY

True
Love

For the lovely Julie…

The publishers would like to thanks the team at IPC Media Ltd and DC Comics for their help in compiling this book, particularly David Abbott and Linda Lee.

Published in 2008 by Prion
An imprint of the Carlton Publishing Group
20 Mortimer Street
London W1T 3JW

A catalogue record for this book is available from the British Library.

ISBN 978-1-85375-645-0

Edited and compiled by Lara Maiklem

Design: Stephen Cary and Emily Clarke
Production: Claire Hayward

Printed and bound in Dubai
10 9 8 7 6 5 4 3 2 1

Valentine

PICTURE STORY
LIBRARY

True
Love

SIX DRAMATIC PICTURE STORY ROMANCES
INSPIRED BY CLASSIC HITS FROM THE
50'S AND 60'S

PRION

CONTENTS

INTRODUCTION

These days it's almost impossible to imagine a world without teenagers, but before the 1950s the transition from childhood to adulthood took place without the luxury of teenage years. The affluence of the 1950s, however, changed all that. Children stayed at school longer and earned money from part-time jobs to spend on clothes, that weren't as square as their parents', and records, by hip newcomers like Cliff Richard, Adam Faith, Elvis Presley and Billy Fury.

The weekly comic *Valentine*, launched in 1957, and its monthly spin off, *Valentine Picture Story Library*, exploited this new teenage phenomenon brilliantly with its stories written around the hot hits of the day. Here, romantic ballads with a groovy beat were transformed into heart pounding picture love-stories. Such hits as 'You Made Me Love You', 'Say It With Music', 'Treat Me Nice', even Cliff's 'Livin' Lovin' Doll' all inspired tales that sent teenage hearts aflutter because pop songs, more than anything else, were about 'Love' with a capital 'L'.

Envy of another girl's good looks and her effortless comfort around boys was common in the heroines of these stories and rivalry for the hand of the hottest boy in town was the most popular plot. Blondes had more fun, but brunettes in glasses who proved their honesty and devotion always seemed to end the story in a clinch with their man. The heroines also tended to be a little older than the audience the stories were aimed at – they had their own pad, but had to work hard for their independence. Their rivals, on the other hand, moved in the glamorous circles of the movie industry or the world of pop, or just did nothing at all yet remained remarkably unworried financially.

Cool cat or hellcat, the girls from these strips were slim, beautiful and curvaceous, full-lipped and never seen with a hair out of place, even if they were stuck in a lifeboat for weeks – as you'll see in one of the stories that follow! The artists, mostly Spanish, certainly knew how to make a girl look good without resorting to making them look like stick thin pre-pubescent boys with long hair.

Whilst the weekly *Valentine* catered for a quick hit, the monthly *Valentine Picture Story Library* contained longer stories where there was room for some real soul searching as girl meets boy, girl loses boy to attractive rival, or gets confused when another boy arrives, or thinks her boy is two-timing her when he's not. Even if there was a formula to the stories it had a thousand variations, just as you can get a thousand songs out of 12 bars and a backbeat.

So curl up on the sofa and travel back to the days when romance involved rocket spies, problems with 50 grand pianos, twins changing places and where you'll learn just what to do when you find your pretty young cousin in your boyfriend's lap after you've been busted by the police for jiving in the street.

Steve Holland, classic comics collector and historian.

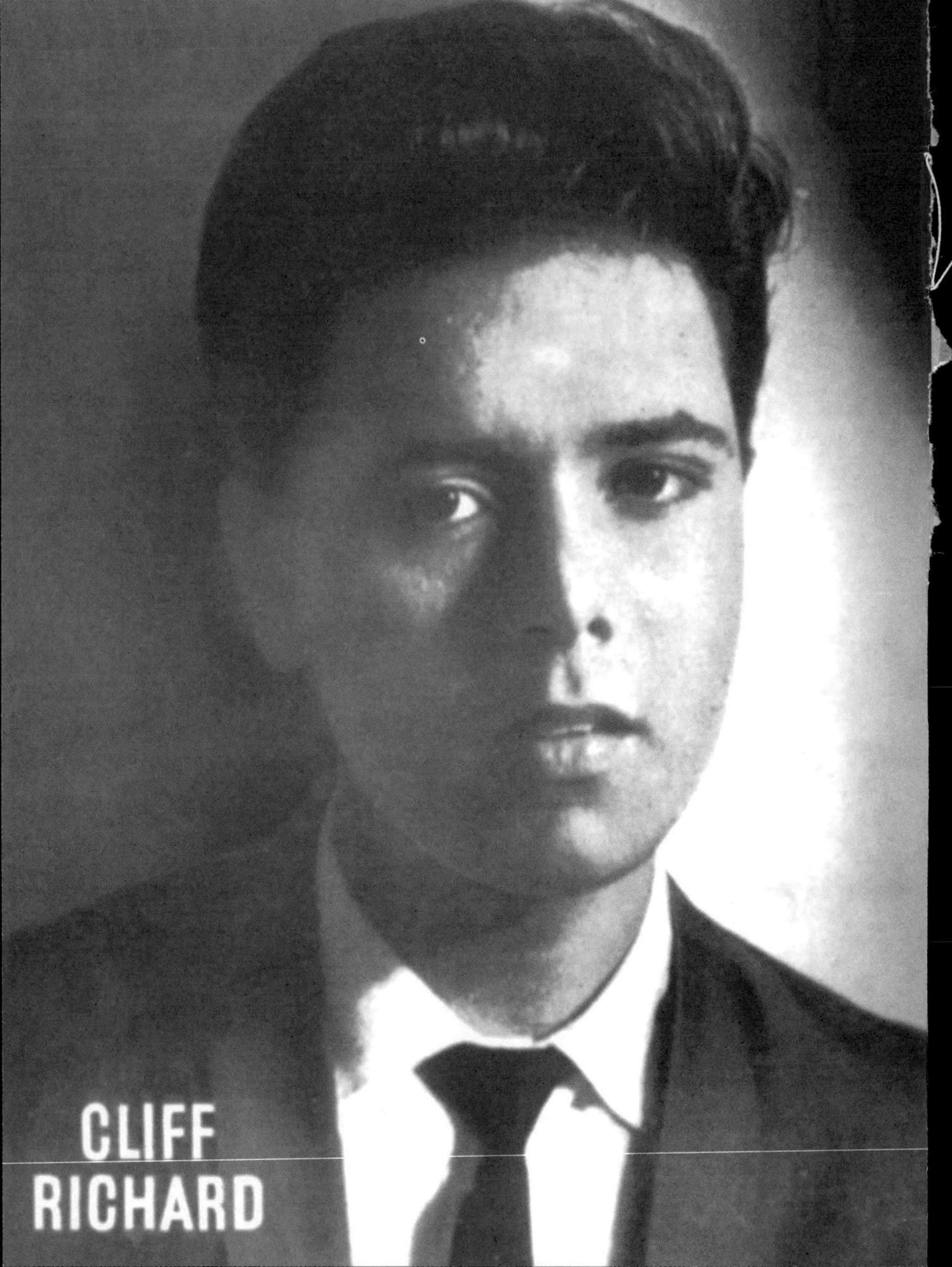
CLIFF
RICHARD

Valentine

PICTURE STORY LIBRARY

Nº 20
1/-

LIVIN' LOVIN' DOLL

sung by **CLIFF RICHARD**

This song title inspires our fascinating picture love-story

A FLEETWAY LIBRARY

ALL IN PICTURES INSIDE

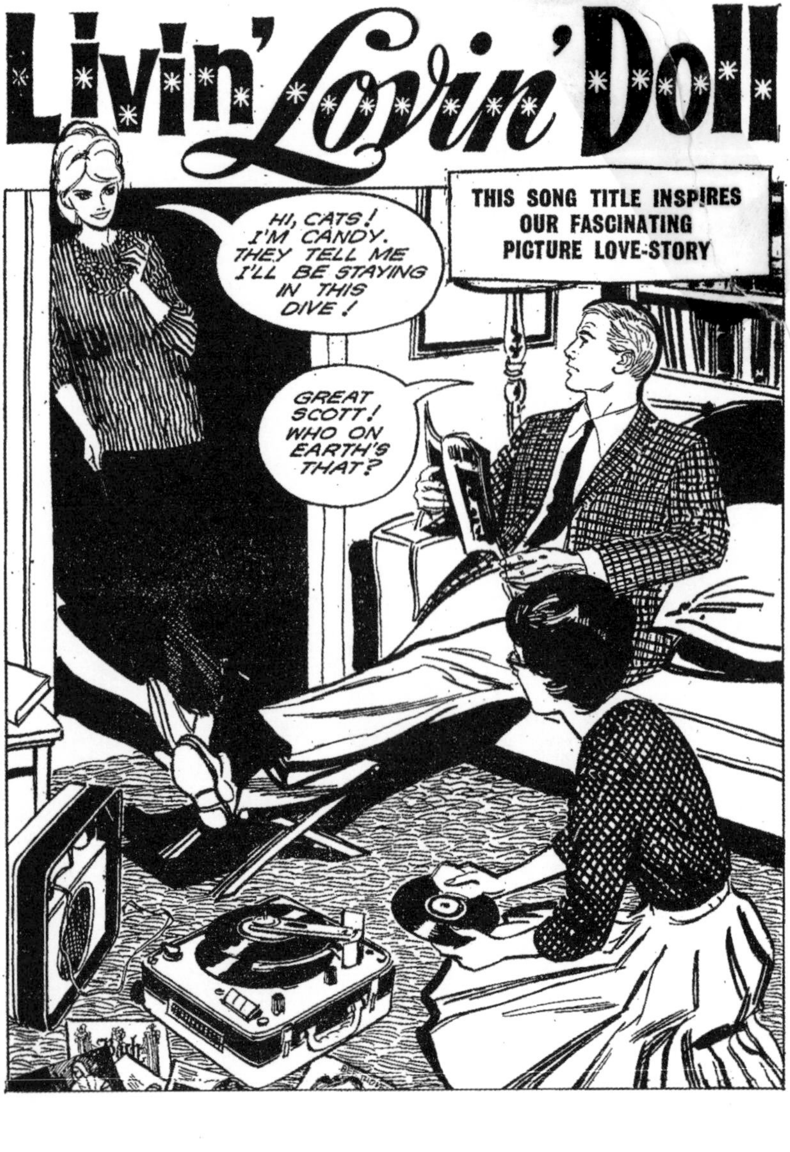
Livin' Lovin' Doll
THIS SONG TITLE INSPIRES OUR FASCINATING PICTURE LOVE-STORY
HI, CATS! I'M CANDY. THEY TELL ME I'LL BE STAYING IN THIS DIVE!
GREAT SCOTT! WHO ON EARTH'S THAT?

INTRODUCTION

These days it's almost impossible to imagine a world without teenagers, but before the 1950s the transition from childhood to adulthood took place without the luxury of teenage years. The affluence of the 1950s, however, changed all that. Children stayed at school longer and earned money from part-time jobs to spend on clothes, that weren't as square as their parents', and records, by hip newcomers like Cliff Richard, Adam Faith, Elvis Presley and Billy Fury.

The weekly comic *Valentine*, launched in 1957, and its monthly spin off, *Valentine Picture Story Library*, exploited this new teenage phenomenon brilliantly with its stories written around the hot hits of the day. Here, romantic ballads with a groovy beat were transformed into heart pounding picture love-stories. Such hits as 'You Made Me Love You', 'Say It With Music', 'Treat Me Nice', even Cliff's 'Livin' Lovin' Doll' all inspired tales that sent teenage hearts aflutter because pop songs, more than anything else, were about 'Love' with a capital 'L'.

Envy of another girl's good looks and her effortless comfort around boys was common in the heroines of these stories and rivalry for the hand of the hottest boy in town was the most popular plot. Blondes had more fun, but brunettes in glasses who proved their honesty and devotion always seemed to end the story in a clinch with their man. The heroines also tended to be a little older than the audience the stories were aimed at – they had their own pad, but had to work hard for their independence. Their rivals, on the other hand, moved in the glamorous circles of the movie industry or the world of pop, or just did nothing at all yet remained remarkably unworried financially.

Cool cat or hellcat, the girls from these strips were slim, beautiful and curvaceous, full-lipped and never seen with a hair out of place, even if they were stuck in a lifeboat for weeks – as you'll see in one of the stories that follow! The artists, mostly Spanish, certainly knew how to make a girl look good without resorting to making them look like stick thin pre-pubescent boys with long hair.

Whilst the weekly *Valentine* catered for a quick hit, the monthly *Valentine Picture Story Library* contained longer stories where there was room for some real soul searching as girl meets boy, girl loses boy to attractive rival, or gets confused when another boy arrives, or thinks her boy is two-timing her when he's not. Even if there was a formula to the stories it had a thousand variations, just as you can get a thousand songs out of 12 bars and a backbeat.

So curl up on the sofa and travel back to the days when romance involved rocket spies, problems with 50 grand pianos, twins changing places and where you'll learn just what to do when you find your pretty young cousin in your boyfriend's lap after you've been busted by the police for jiving in the street.

Steve Holland, classic comics collector and historian.

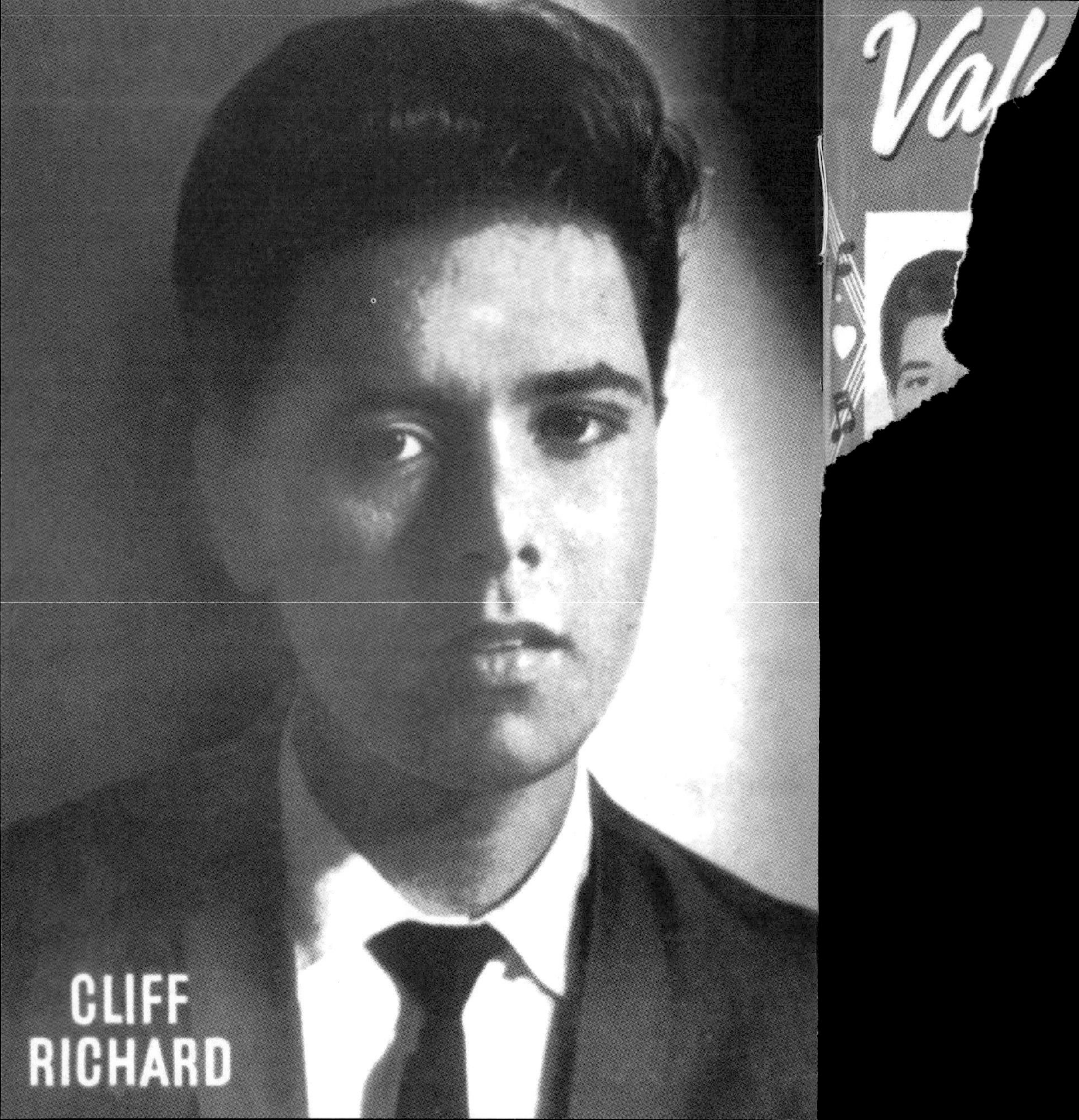
CLIFF
RICHARD

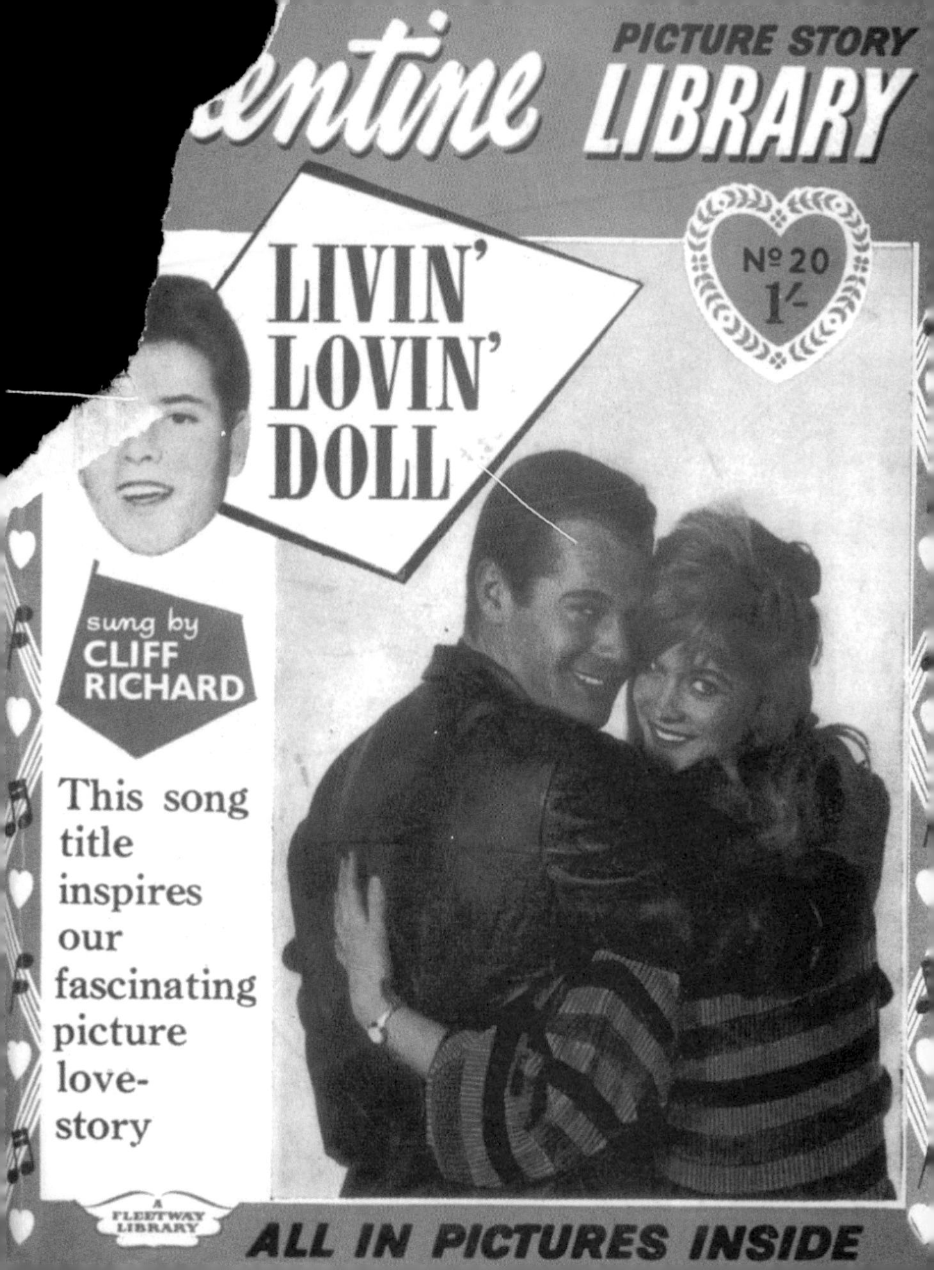
entine
PICTURE STORY
LIBRARY
№ 20
1/-
LIVIN'
LOVIN'
DOLL
sung by
CLIFF
RICHARD
This song
title
inspires
our
fascinating
picture
love-
story
A
FLEETWAY
LIBRARY
ALL IN PICTURES INSIDE

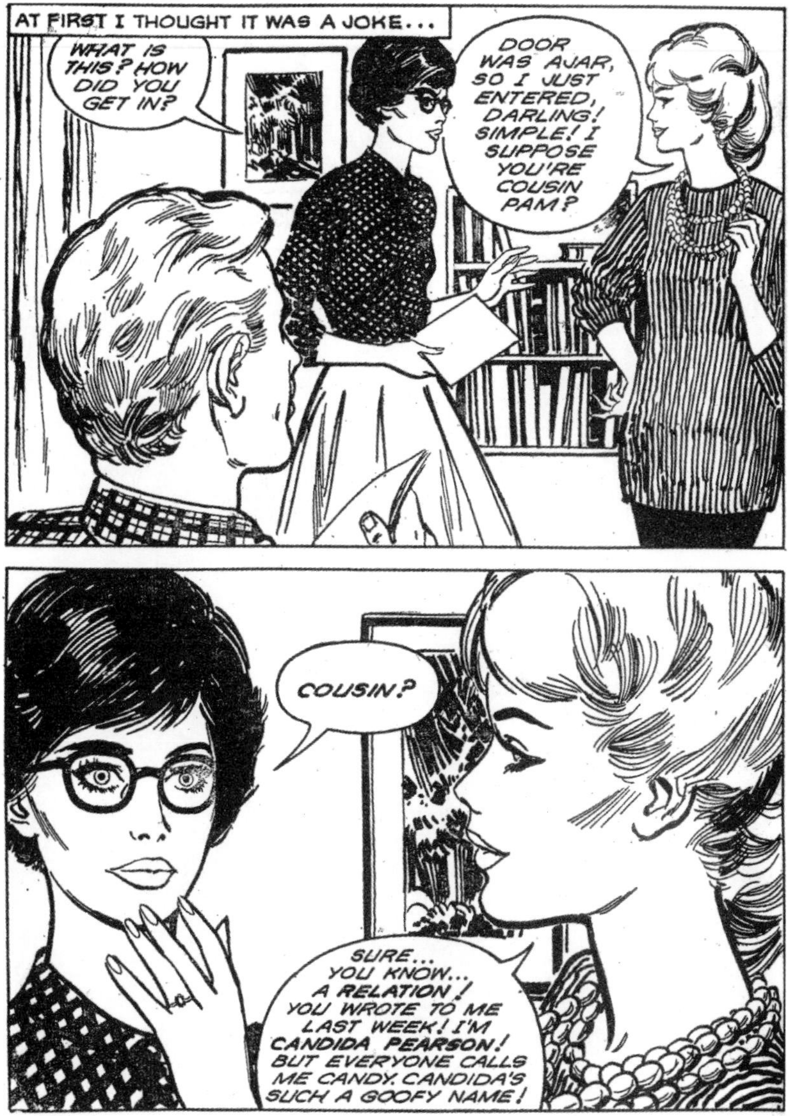
AT FIRST I THOUGHT IT WAS A JOKE...
WHAT IS THIS? HOW DID YOU GET IN?
DOOR WAS AJAR, SO I JUST ENTERED, DARLING! SIMPLE! I SUPPOSE YOU'RE COUSIN PAM?
COUSIN?
SURE... YOU KNOW... A RELATION! YOU WROTE TO ME LAST WEEK! I'M CANDIDA PEARSON! BUT EVERYONE CALLS ME CANDY. CANDIDA'S SUCH A GOOFY NAME!

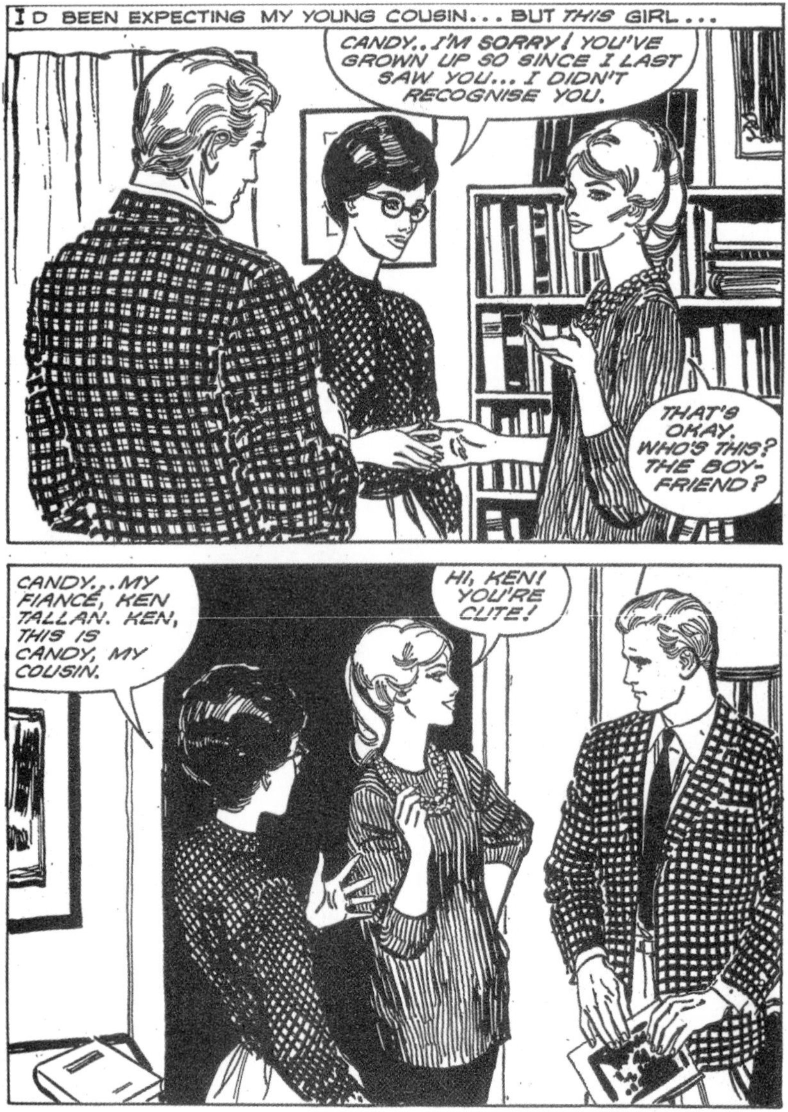
I'D BEEN EXPECTING MY YOUNG COUSIN... BUT THIS GIRL...
CANDY..I'M SORRY! YOU'VE GROWN UP SO SINCE I LAST SAW YOU... I DIDN'T RECOGNISE YOU.
THAT'S OKAY. WHO'S THIS? THE BOY-FRIEND?
CANDY...MY FIANCÉ, KEN TALLAN. KEN, THIS IS CANDY, MY COUSIN.
HI, KEN! YOU'RE CUTE!

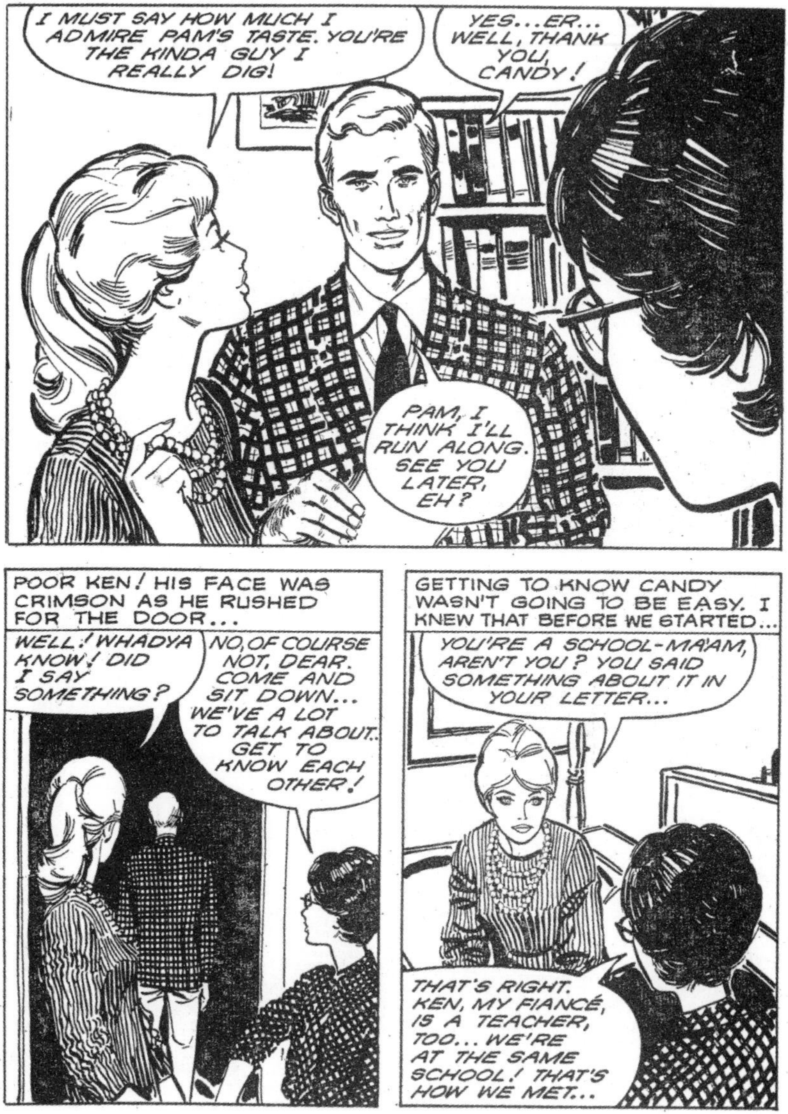
I MUST SAY HOW MUCH I ADMIRE PAM'S TASTE. YOU'RE THE KINDA GUY I REALLY DIG!
YES...ER... WELL, THANK YOU, CANDY!
PAM, I THINK I'LL RUN ALONG. SEE YOU LATER, EH?
POOR KEN! HIS FACE WAS CRIMSON AS HE RUSHED FOR THE DOOR...
WELL! WHADYA KNOW! DID I SAY SOMETHING?
NO, OF COURSE NOT, DEAR. COME AND SIT DOWN... WE'VE A LOT TO TALK ABOUT.. GET TO KNOW EACH OTHER!
GETTING TO KNOW CANDY WASN'T GOING TO BE EASY. I KNEW THAT BEFORE WE STARTED...
YOU'RE A SCHOOL-MA'AM, AREN'T YOU? YOU SAID SOMETHING ABOUT IT IN YOUR LETTER...
THAT'S RIGHT. KEN, MY FIANCÉ, IS A TEACHER, TOO... WE'RE AT THE SAME SCHOOL! THAT'S HOW WE MET...

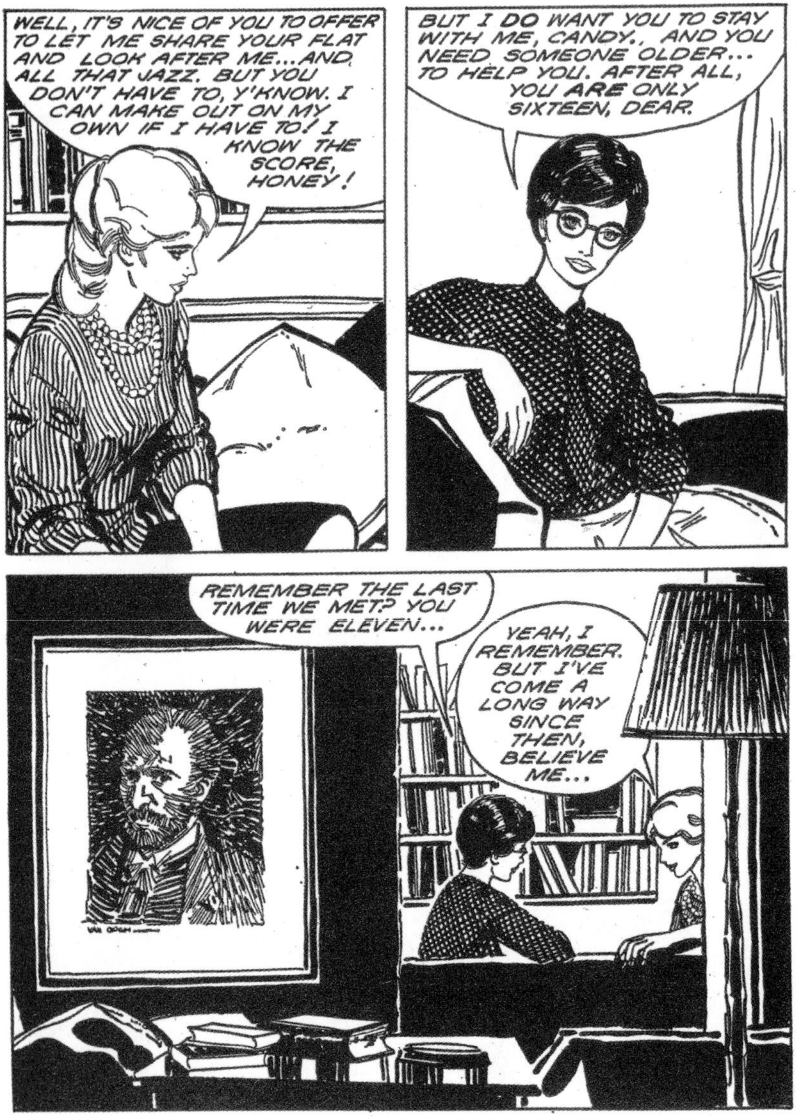
WELL, IT'S NICE OF YOU TO OFFER TO LET ME SHARE YOUR FLAT AND LOOK AFTER ME...AND ALL THAT JAZZ. BUT YOU DON'T HAVE TO, Y'KNOW. I CAN MAKE OUT ON MY OWN IF I HAVE TO! I KNOW THE SCORE, HONEY!
BUT I DO WANT YOU TO STAY WITH ME, CANDY., AND YOU NEED SOMEONE OLDER... TO HELP YOU. AFTER ALL, YOU ARE ONLY SIXTEEN, DEAR.
REMEMBER THE LAST TIME WE MET? YOU WERE ELEVEN...
YEAH, I REMEMBER. BUT I'VE COME A LONG WAY SINCE THEN, BELIEVE ME...

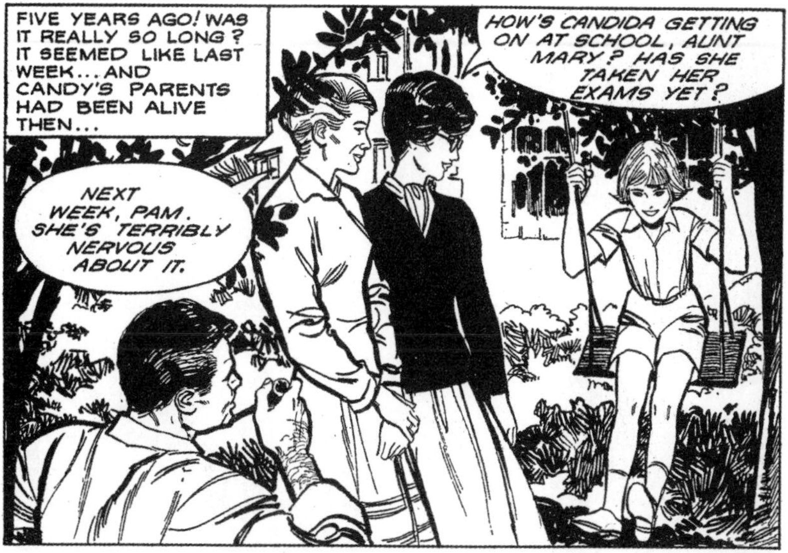
FIVE YEARS AGO! WAS IT REALLY SO LONG? IT SEEMED LIKE LAST WEEK... AND CANDY'S PARENTS HAD BEEN ALIVE THEN...
HOW'S CANDIDA GETTING ON AT SCHOOL, AUNT MARY? HAS SHE TAKEN HER EXAMS YET?
NEXT WEEK, PAM. SHE'S TERRIBLY NERVOUS ABOUT IT.

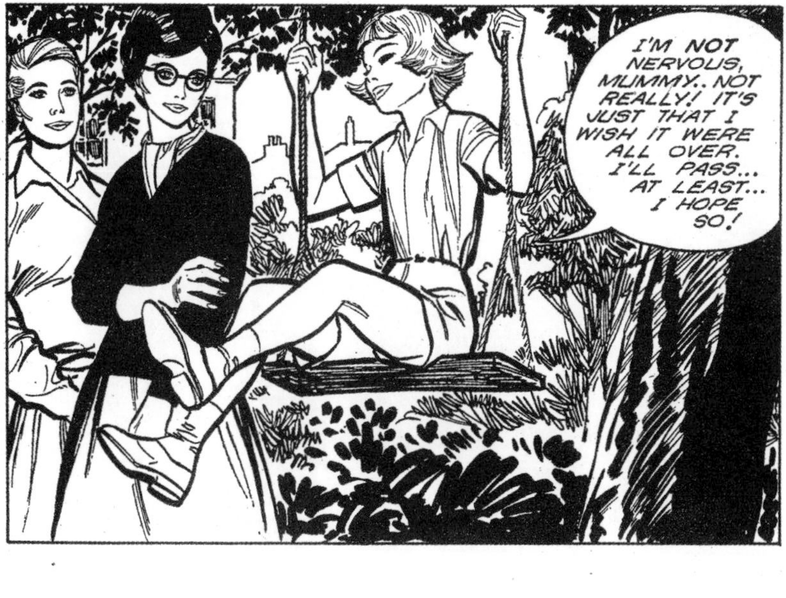
I'M NOT NERVOUS, MUMMY.. NOT REALLY! IT'S JUST THAT I WISH IT WERE ALL OVER. I'LL PASS... AT LEAST... I HOPE SO!

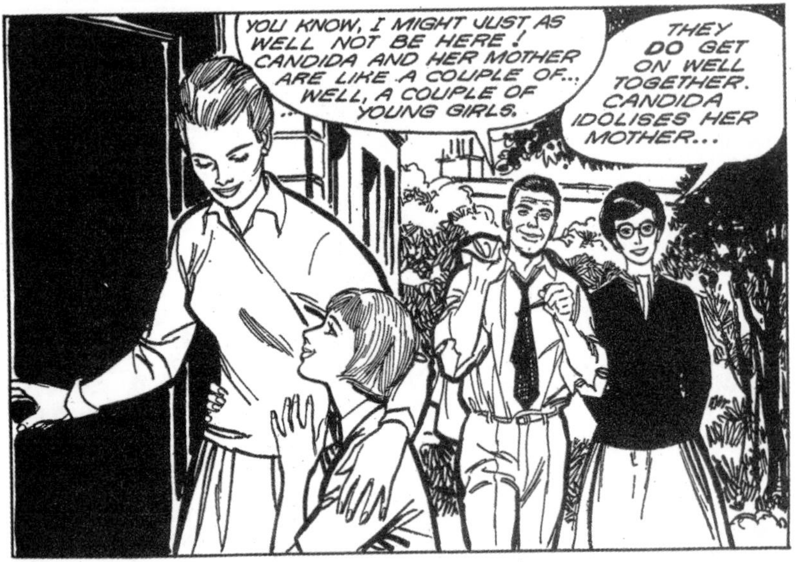
YOU KNOW, I MIGHT JUST AS WELL NOT BE HERE! CANDIDA AND HER MOTHER ARE LIKE A COUPLE OF... WELL, A COUPLE OF YOUNG GIRLS.
THEY DO GET ON WELL TOGETHER. CANDIDA IDOLISES HER MOTHER...

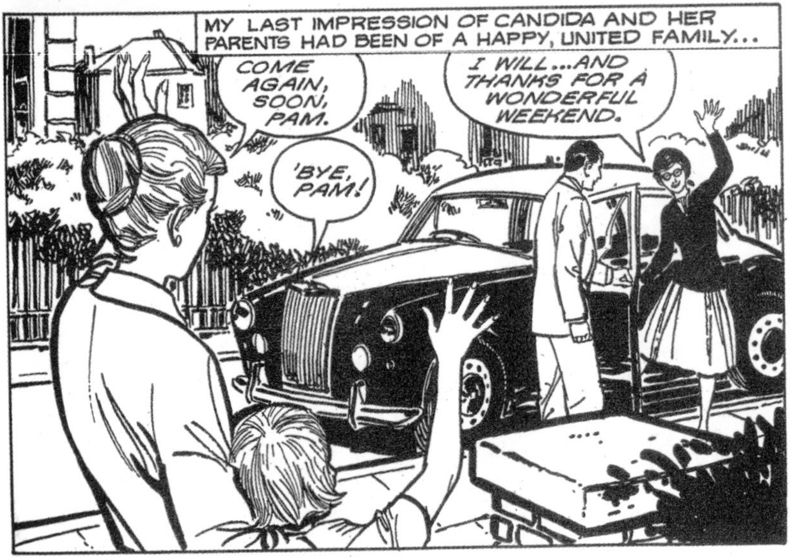
MY LAST IMPRESSION OF CANDIDA AND HER PARENTS HAD BEEN OF A HAPPY, UNITED FAMILY...
COME AGAIN, SOON, PAM.
'BYE, PAM!
I WILL...AND THANKS FOR A WONDERFUL WEEKEND.

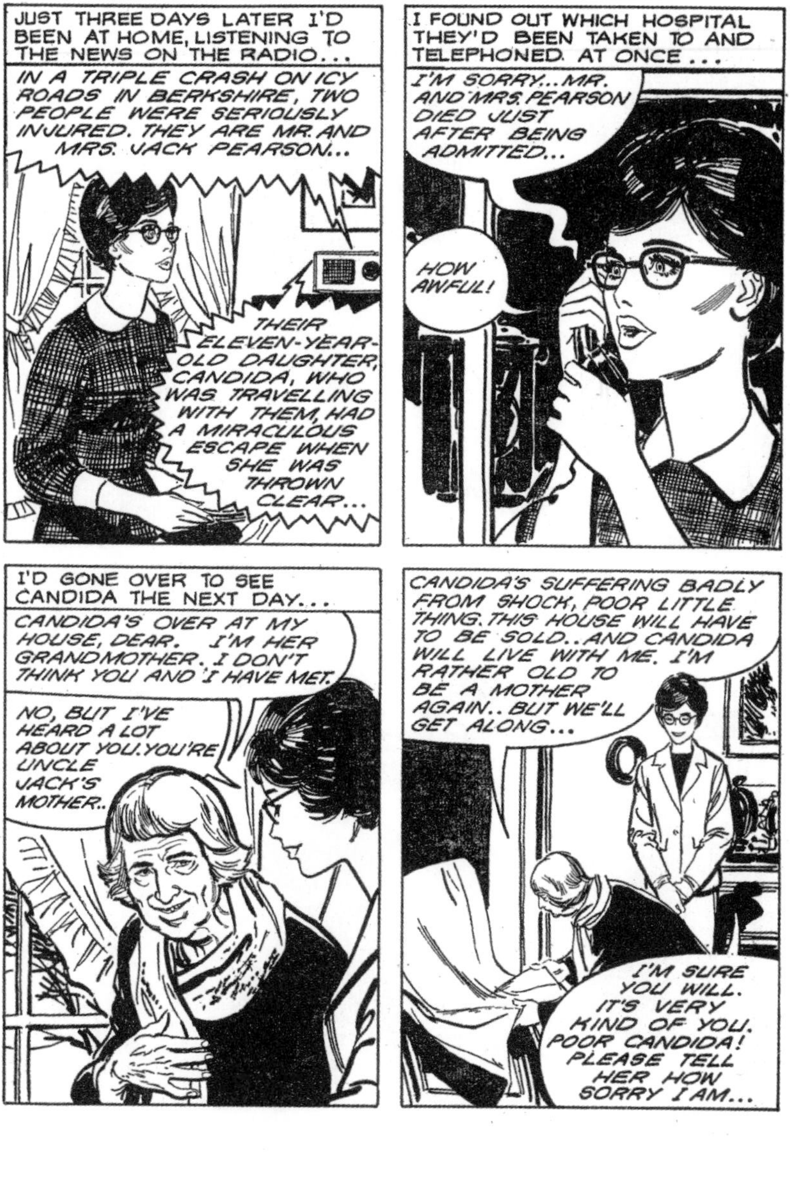
JUST THREE DAYS LATER I'D BEEN AT HOME, LISTENING TO THE NEWS ON THE RADIO...
IN A TRIPLE CRASH ON ICY ROADS IN BERKSHIRE, TWO PEOPLE WERE SERIOUSLY INJURED. THEY ARE MR. AND MRS. JACK PEARSON...
THEIR ELEVEN-YEAR-OLD DAUGHTER, CANDIDA, WHO WAS TRAVELLING WITH THEM, HAD A MIRACULOUS ESCAPE WHEN SHE WAS THROWN CLEAR...
I FOUND OUT WHICH HOSPITAL THEY'D BEEN TAKEN TO AND TELEPHONED AT ONCE...
I'M SORRY... MR. AND MRS. PEARSON DIED JUST AFTER BEING ADMITTED...
HOW AWFUL!
I'D GONE OVER TO SEE CANDIDA THE NEXT DAY...
CANDIDA'S OVER AT MY HOUSE, DEAR. I'M HER GRANDMOTHER.. I DON'T THINK YOU AND I HAVE MET.
NO, BUT I'VE HEARD A LOT ABOUT YOU. YOU'RE UNCLE JACK'S MOTHER..
CANDIDA'S SUFFERING BADLY FROM SHOCK, POOR LITTLE THING. THIS HOUSE WILL HAVE TO BE SOLD.. AND CANDIDA WILL LIVE WITH ME. I'M RATHER OLD TO BE A MOTHER AGAIN.. BUT WE'LL GET ALONG...
I'M SURE YOU WILL. IT'S VERY KIND OF YOU. POOR CANDIDA! PLEASE TELL HER HOW SORRY I AM...

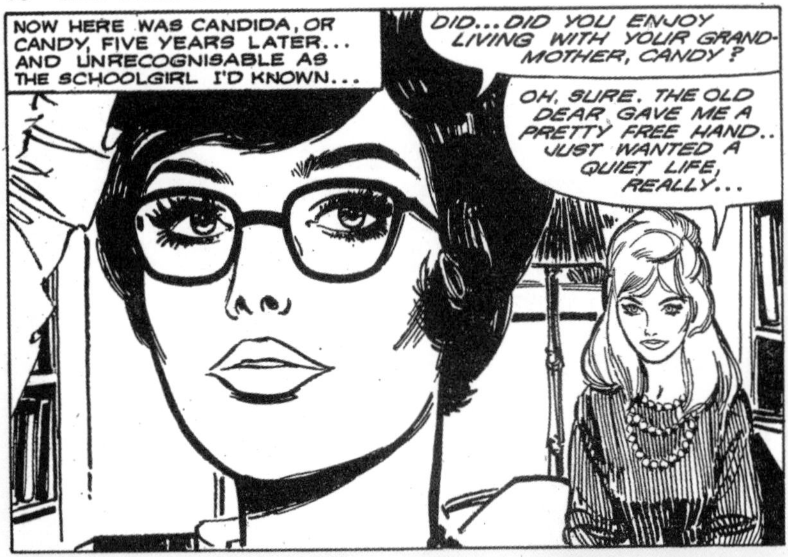
NOW HERE WAS CANDIDA, OR CANDY, FIVE YEARS LATER... AND UNRECOGNISABLE AS THE SCHOOLGIRL I'D KNOWN...
DID...DID YOU ENJOY LIVING WITH YOUR GRAND-MOTHER, CANDY?
OH, SURE. THE OLD DEAR GAVE ME A PRETTY FREE HAND.. JUST WANTED A QUIET LIFE, REALLY...

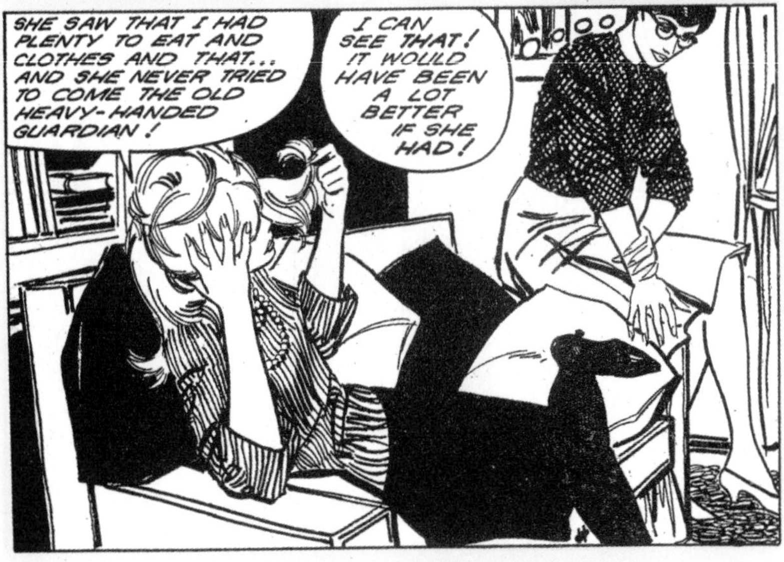
SHE SAW THAT I HAD PLENTY TO EAT AND CLOTHES AND THAT... AND SHE NEVER TRIED TO COME THE OLD HEAVY-HANDED GUARDIAN!
I CAN SEE THAT! IT WOULD HAVE BEEN A LOT BETTER IF SHE HAD!

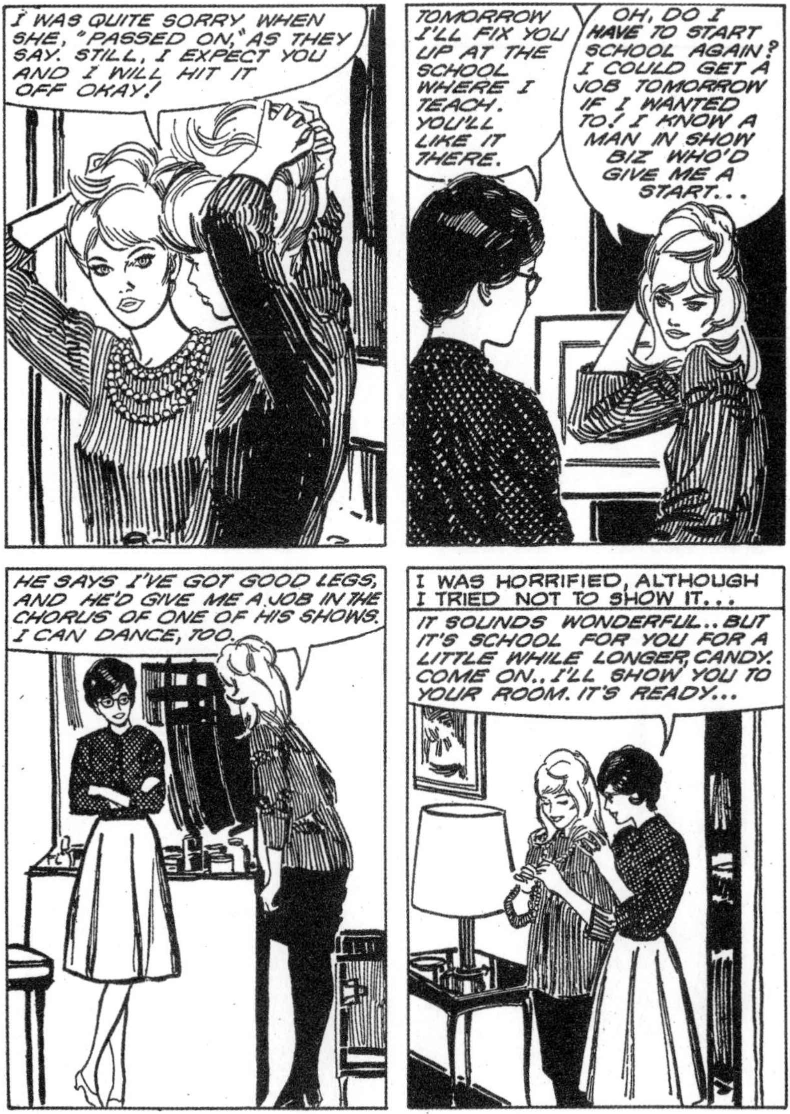
I WAS QUITE SORRY WHEN SHE, "PASSED ON," AS THEY SAY. STILL, I EXPECT YOU AND I WILL HIT IT OFF OKAY!
TOMORROW I'LL FIX YOU UP AT THE SCHOOL WHERE I TEACH. YOU'LL LIKE IT THERE.
OH, DO I HAVE TO START SCHOOL AGAIN? I COULD GET A JOB TOMORROW IF I WANTED TO! I KNOW A MAN IN SHOW BIZ WHO'D GIVE ME A START...
HE SAYS I'VE GOT GOOD LEGS, AND HE'D GIVE ME A JOB IN THE CHORUS OF ONE OF HIS SHOWS. I CAN DANCE, TOO.
I WAS HORRIFIED, ALTHOUGH I TRIED NOT TO SHOW IT...
IT SOUNDS WONDERFUL.. BUT IT'S SCHOOL FOR YOU FOR A LITTLE WHILE LONGER, CANDY. COME ON.. I'LL SHOW YOU TO YOUR ROOM. IT'S READY...

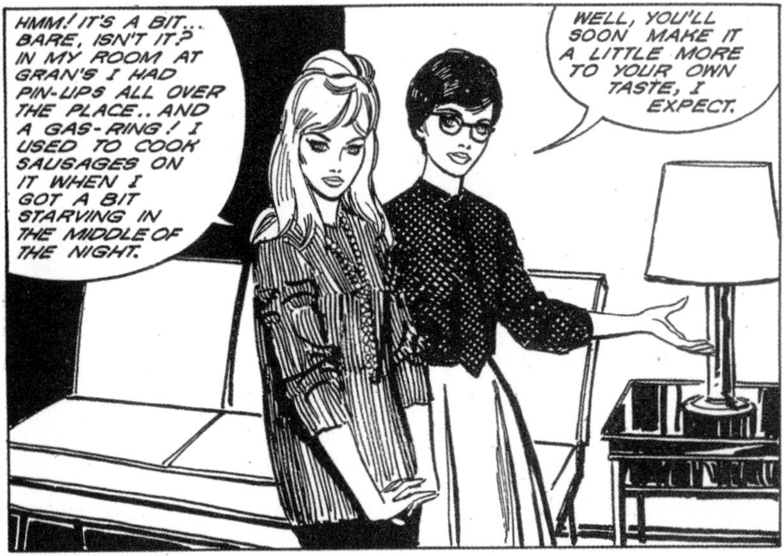
HMM! IT'S A BIT.. BARE, ISN'T IT? IN MY ROOM AT GRAN'S I HAD PIN-UPS ALL OVER THE PLACE.. AND A GAS-RING! I USED TO COOK SAUSAGES ON IT WHEN I GOT A BIT STARVING IN THE MIDDLE OF THE NIGHT.
WELL, YOU'LL SOON MAKE IT A LITTLE MORE TO YOUR OWN TASTE, I EXPECT.

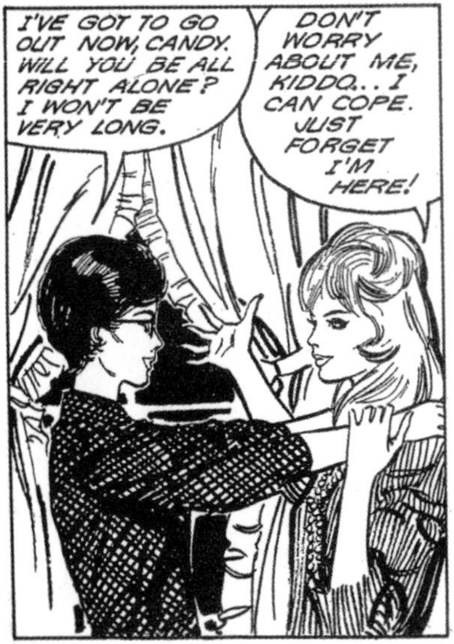
I'VE GOT TO GO OUT NOW, CANDY. WILL YOU BE ALL RIGHT ALONE? I WON'T BE VERY LONG.
DON'T WORRY ABOUT ME, KIDDO... I CAN COPE. JUST FORGET I'M HERE!

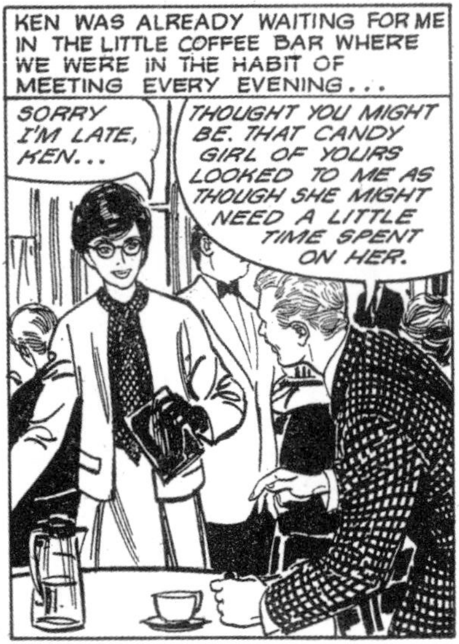
KEN WAS ALREADY WAITING FOR ME IN THE LITTLE COFFEE BAR WHERE WE WERE IN THE HABIT OF MEETING EVERY EVENING...
SORRY I'M LATE, KEN...
THOUGHT YOU MIGHT BE. THAT CANDY GIRL OF YOURS LOOKED TO ME AS THOUGH SHE MIGHT NEED A LITTLE TIME SPENT ON HER.

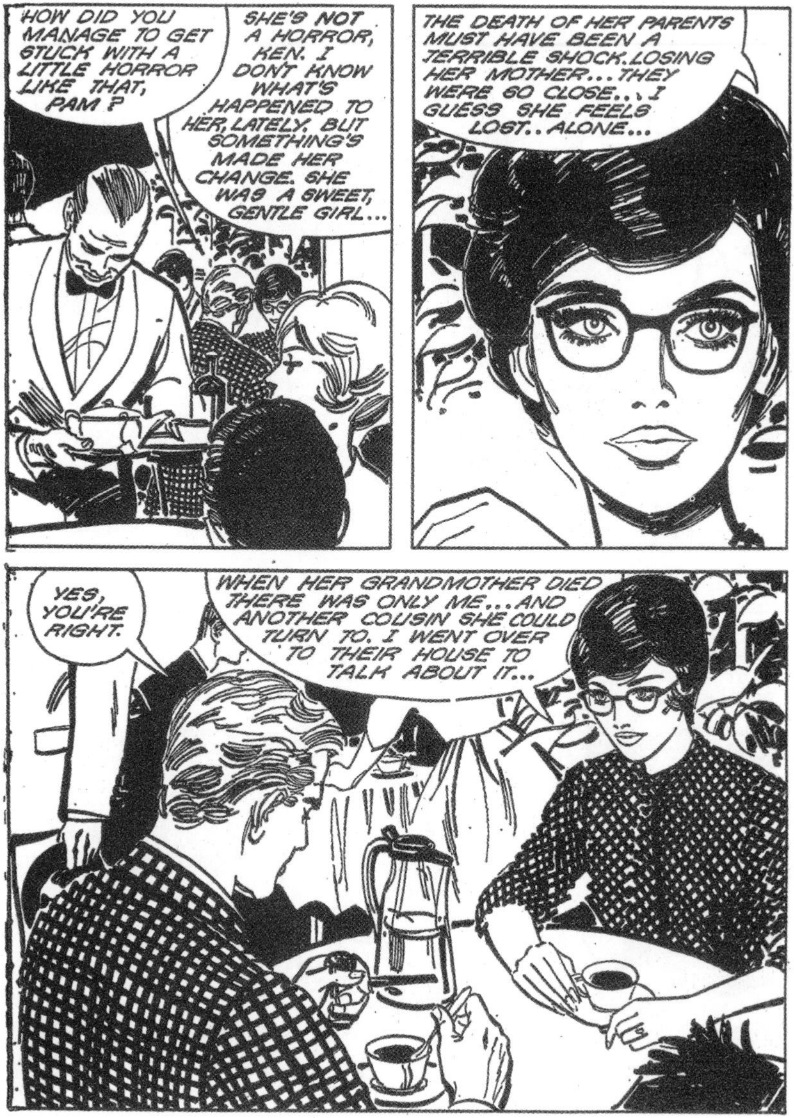
HOW DID YOU MANAGE TO GET STUCK WITH A LITTLE HORROR LIKE THAT, PAM?
SHE'S NOT A HORROR, KEN. I DON'T KNOW WHAT'S HAPPENED TO HER, LATELY, BUT SOMETHING'S MADE HER CHANGE. SHE WAS A SWEET, GENTLE GIRL...
THE DEATH OF HER PARENTS MUST HAVE BEEN A TERRIBLE SHOCK. LOSING HER MOTHER... THEY WERE SO CLOSE... I GUESS SHE FEELS LOST.. ALONE...
YES, YOU'RE RIGHT.
WHEN HER GRANDMOTHER DIED THERE WAS ONLY ME... AND ANOTHER COUSIN SHE COULD TURN TO. I WENT OVER TO THEIR HOUSE TO TALK ABOUT IT...

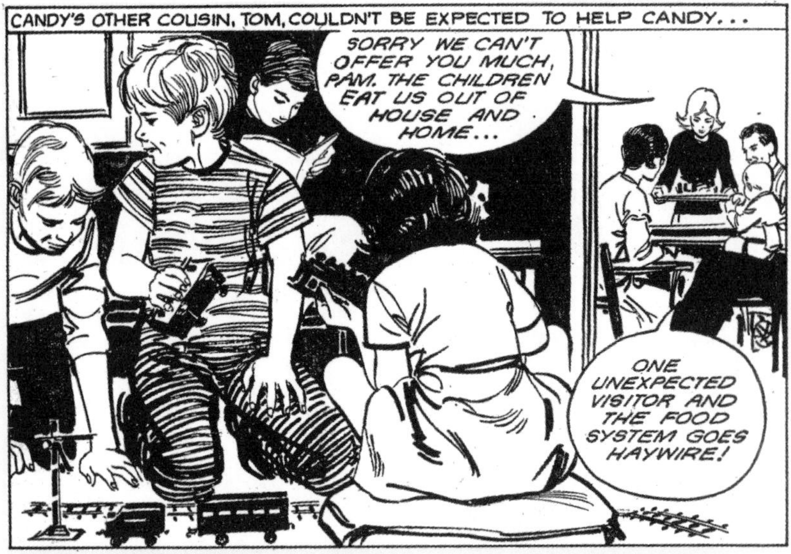
CANDY'S OTHER COUSIN, TOM, COULDN'T BE EXPECTED TO HELP CANDY...
SORRY WE CAN'T OFFER YOU MUCH, PAM. THE CHILDREN EAT US OUT OF HOUSE AND HOME...
ONE UNEXPECTED VISITOR AND THE FOOD SYSTEM GOES HAYWIRE!

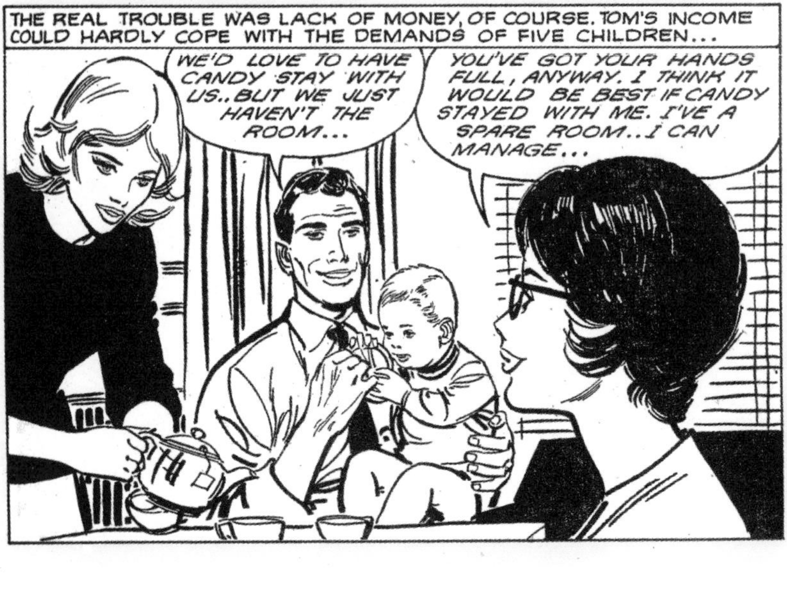
THE REAL TROUBLE WAS LACK OF MONEY, OF COURSE. TOM'S INCOME COULD HARDLY COPE WITH THE DEMANDS OF FIVE CHILDREN...
WE'D LOVE TO HAVE CANDY STAY WITH US.. BUT WE JUST HAVEN'T THE ROOM...
YOU'VE GOT YOUR HANDS FULL, ANYWAY. I THINK IT WOULD BE BEST IF CANDY STAYED WITH ME. I'VE A SPARE ROOM.. I CAN MANAGE...

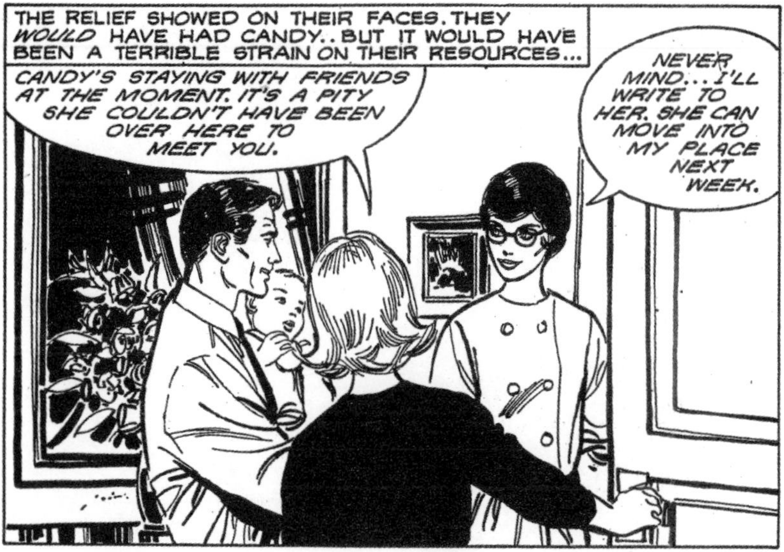
THE RELIEF SHOWED ON THEIR FACES. THEY *WOULD* HAVE HAD CANDY.. BUT IT WOULD HAVE BEEN A TERRIBLE STRAIN ON THEIR RESOURCES...
CANDY'S STAYING WITH FRIENDS AT THE MOMENT. IT'S A PITY SHE COULDN'T HAVE BEEN OVER HERE TO MEET YOU.
NEVER MIND... I'LL WRITE TO HER. SHE CAN MOVE INTO MY PLACE NEXT WEEK.

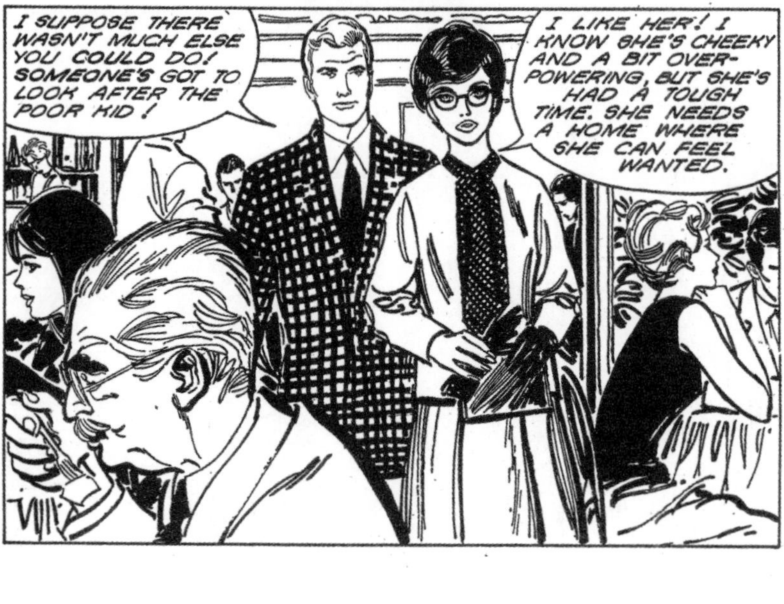
I SUPPOSE THERE WASN'T MUCH ELSE YOU COULD DO! SOMEONE'S GOT TO LOOK AFTER THE POOR KID!
I LIKE HER! I KNOW SHE'S CHEEKY AND A BIT OVER-POWERING, BUT SHE'S HAD A TOUGH TIME. SHE NEEDS A HOME WHERE SHE CAN FEEL WANTED.

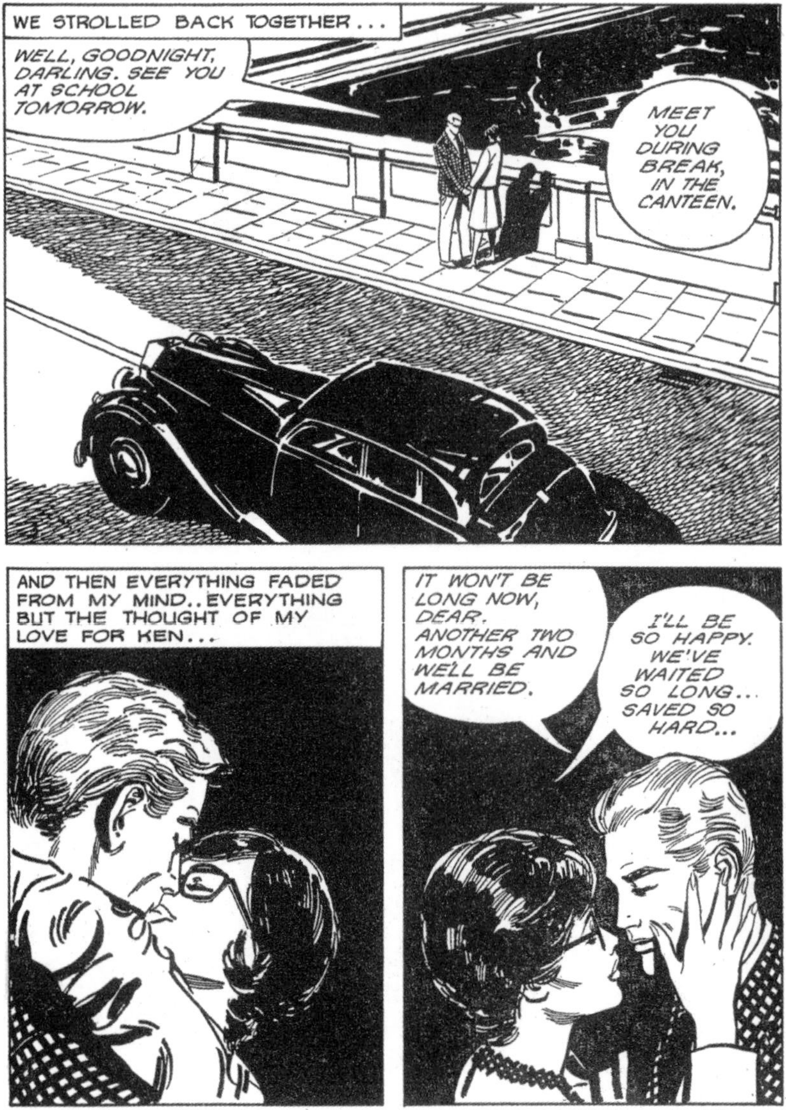
WE STROLLED BACK TOGETHER . . .
WELL, GOODNIGHT, DARLING. SEE YOU AT SCHOOL TOMORROW.
MEET YOU DURING BREAK, IN THE CANTEEN.
AND THEN EVERYTHING FADED FROM MY MIND..EVERYTHING BUT THE THOUGHT OF MY LOVE FOR KEN . . .
IT WON'T BE LONG NOW, DEAR. ANOTHER TWO MONTHS AND WE'LL BE MARRIED.
I'LL BE SO HAPPY. WE'VE WAITED SO LONG... SAVED SO HARD...

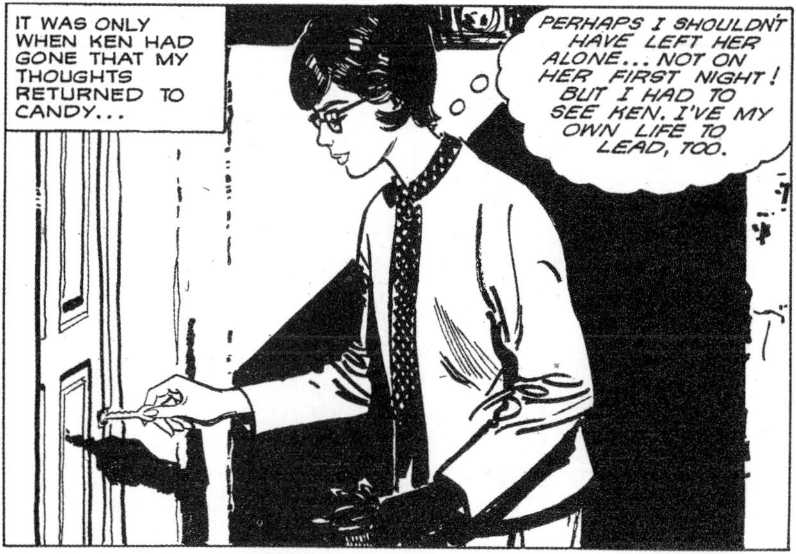
IT WAS ONLY WHEN KEN HAD GONE THAT MY THOUGHTS RETURNED TO CANDY...
PERHAPS I SHOULDN'T HAVE LEFT HER ALONE... NOT ON HER FIRST NIGHT! BUT I HAD TO SEE KEN. I'VE MY OWN LIFE TO LEAD, TOO.

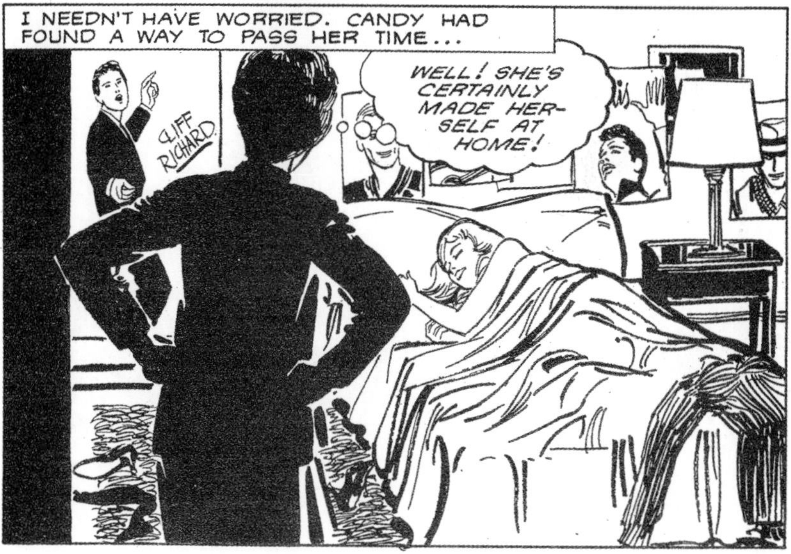
I NEEDN'T HAVE WORRIED. CANDY HAD FOUND A WAY TO PASS HER TIME...
CLIFF RICHARD
WELL! SHE'S CERTAINLY MADE HER-SELF AT HOME!

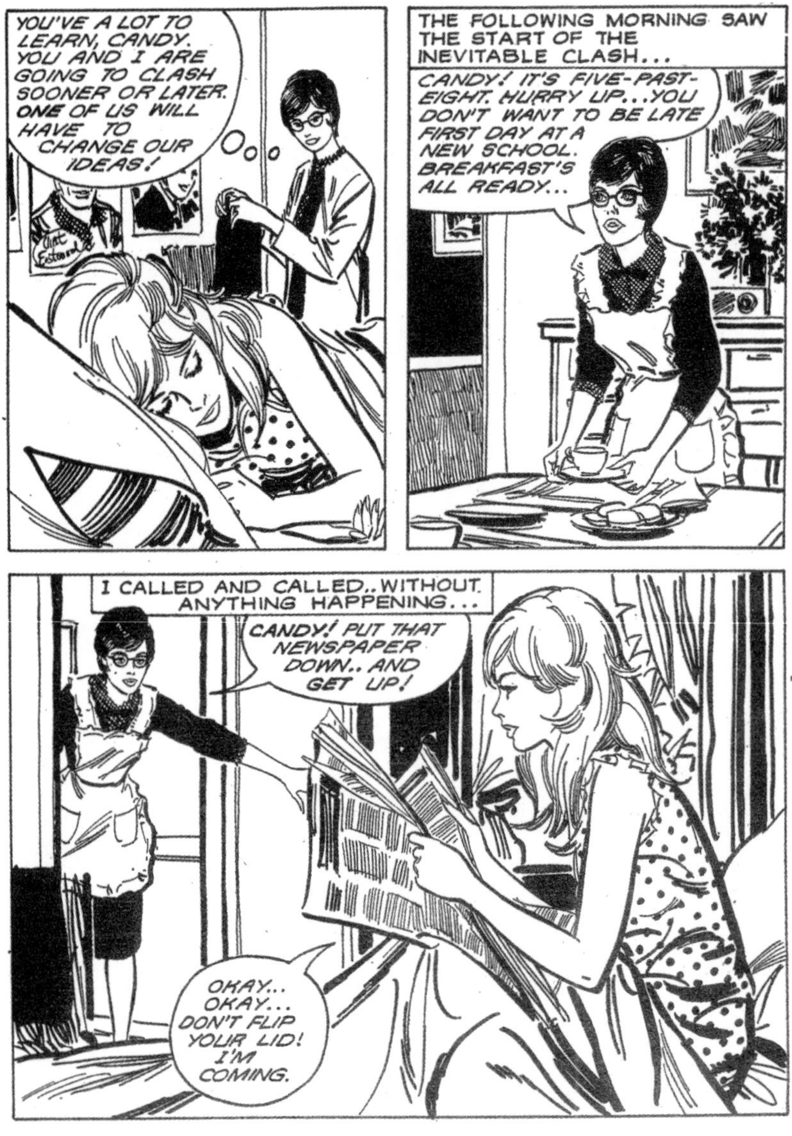
YOU'VE A LOT TO LEARN, CANDY. YOU AND I ARE GOING TO CLASH SOONER OR LATER. ONE OF US WILL HAVE TO CHANGE OUR IDEAS!
THE FOLLOWING MORNING SAW THE START OF THE INEVITABLE CLASH...
CANDY! IT'S FIVE-PAST-EIGHT. HURRY UP...YOU DON'T WANT TO BE LATE FIRST DAY AT A NEW SCHOOL. BREAKFAST'S ALL READY...
I CALLED AND CALLED.. WITHOUT ANYTHING HAPPENING...
CANDY! PUT THAT NEWSPAPER DOWN.. AND GET UP!
OKAY... OKAY... DON'T FLIP YOUR LID! I'M COMING.

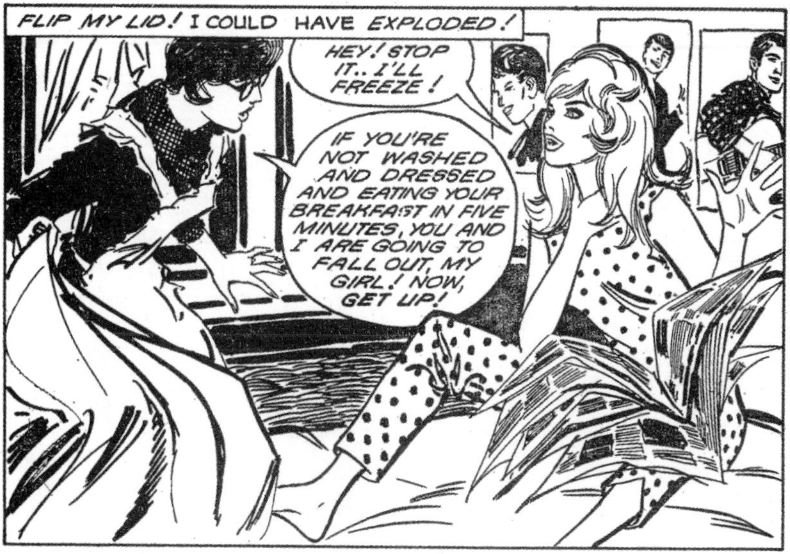
FLIP MY LID! I COULD HAVE EXPLODED!
HEY! STOP IT.. I'LL FREEZE!
IF YOU'RE NOT WASHED AND DRESSED AND EATING YOUR BREAKFAST IN FIVE MINUTES, YOU AND I ARE GOING TO FALL OUT, MY GIRL! NOW, GET UP!

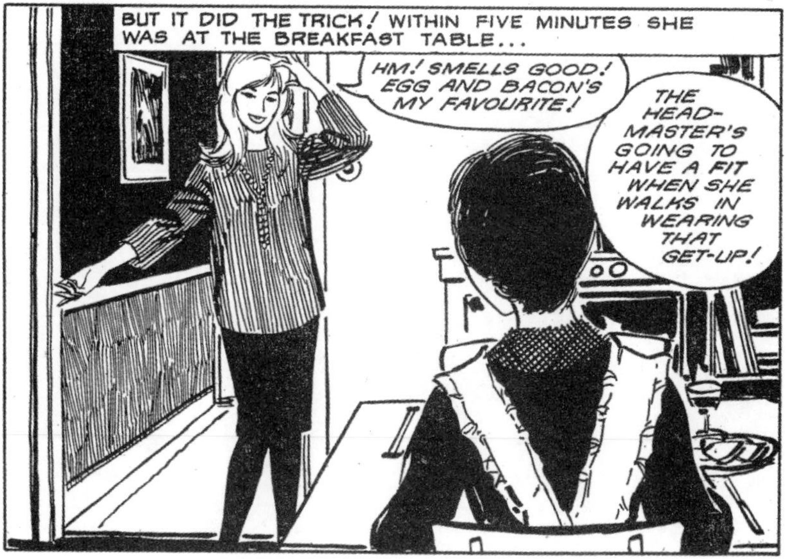
BUT IT DID THE TRICK! WITHIN FIVE MINUTES SHE WAS AT THE BREAKFAST TABLE...
HM! SMELLS GOOD! EGG AND BACON'S MY FAVOURITE!
THE HEAD-MASTER'S GOING TO HAVE A FIT WHEN SHE WALKS IN WEARING THAT GET-UP!

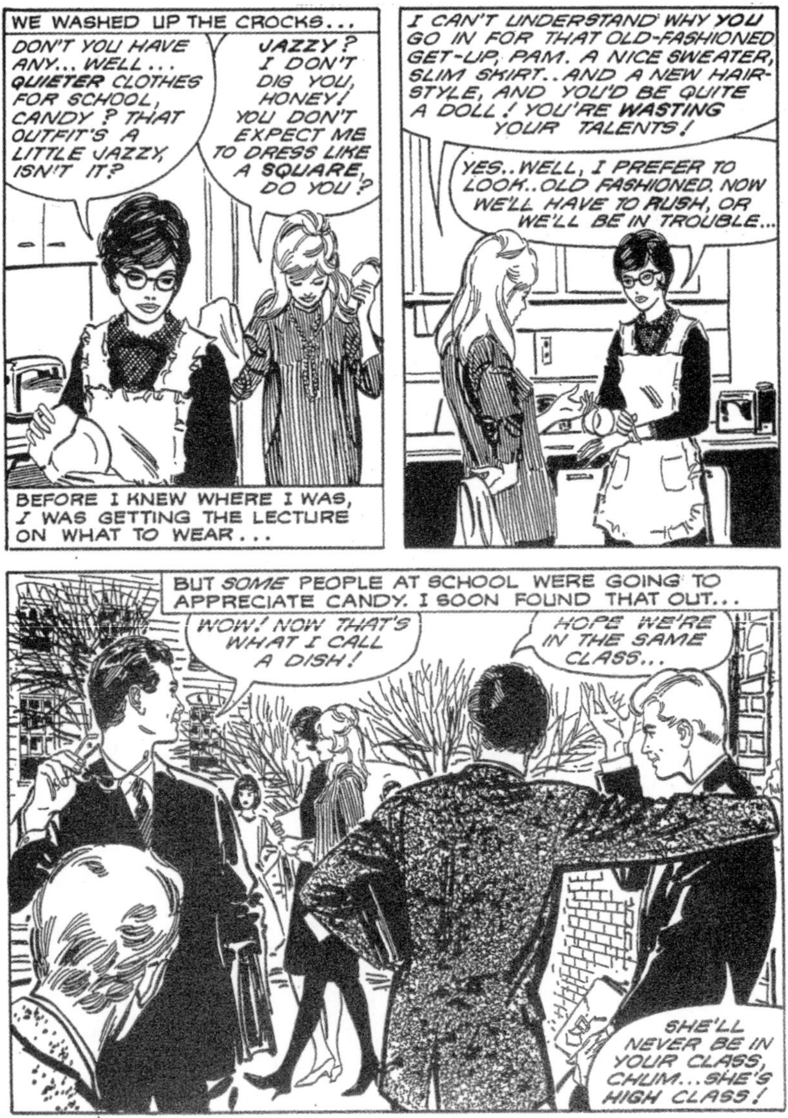
WE WASHED UP THE CROCKS...
DON'T YOU HAVE ANY... WELL... QUIETER CLOTHES FOR SCHOOL, CANDY? THAT OUTFIT'S A LITTLE JAZZY, ISN'T IT?
JAZZY? I DON'T DIG YOU, HONEY! YOU DON'T EXPECT ME TO DRESS LIKE A SQUARE, DO YOU?
BEFORE I KNEW WHERE I WAS, I WAS GETTING THE LECTURE ON WHAT TO WEAR...
I CAN'T UNDERSTAND WHY YOU GO IN FOR THAT OLD-FASHIONED GET-UP, PAM. A NICE SWEATER, SLIM SKIRT.. AND A NEW HAIR-STYLE, AND YOU'D BE QUITE A DOLL! YOU'RE WASTING YOUR TALENTS!
YES.. WELL, I PREFER TO LOOK.. OLD FASHIONED. NOW WE'LL HAVE TO RUSH, OR WE'LL BE IN TROUBLE...
BUT SOME PEOPLE AT SCHOOL WERE GOING TO APPRECIATE CANDY. I SOON FOUND THAT OUT...
WOW! NOW THAT'S WHAT I CALL A DISH!
HOPE WE'RE IN THE SAME CLASS...
SHE'LL NEVER BE IN YOUR CLASS, CHUM... SHE'S HIGH CLASS!

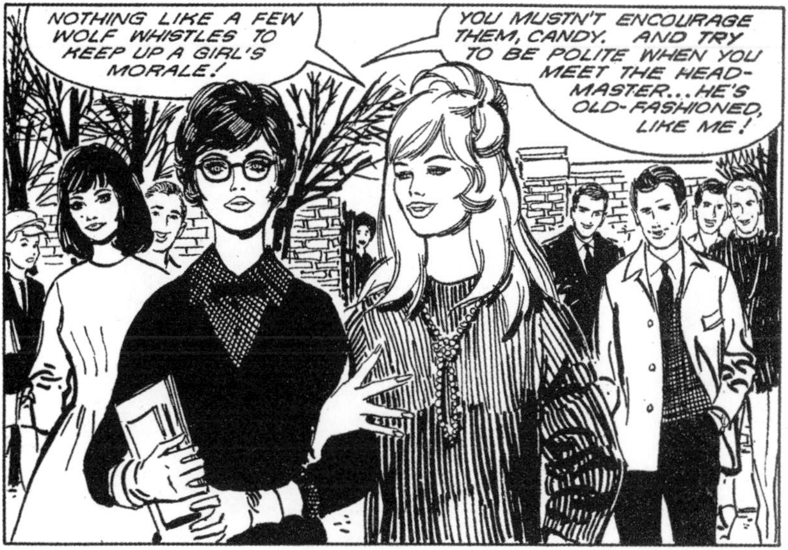
NOTHING LIKE A FEW WOLF WHISTLES TO KEEP UP A GIRL'S MORALE!
YOU MUSTN'T ENCOURAGE THEM, CANDY. AND TRY TO BE POLITE WHEN YOU MEET THE HEAD-MASTER...HE'S OLD-FASHIONED, LIKE ME!

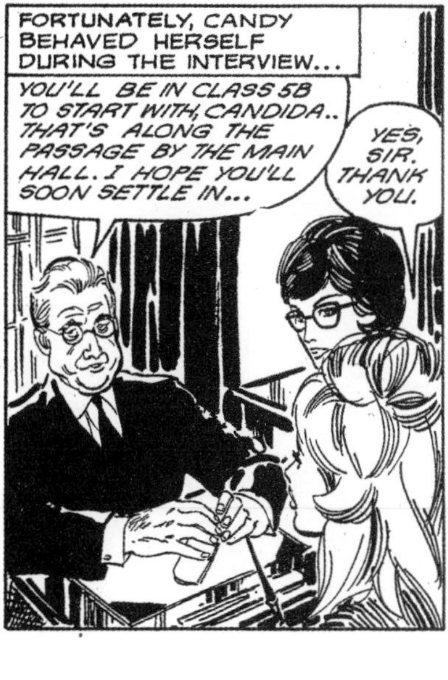
FORTUNATELY, CANDY BEHAVED HERSELF DURING THE INTERVIEW...
YOU'LL BE IN CLASS 5B TO START WITH, CANDIDA.. THAT'S ALONG THE PASSAGE BY THE MAIN HALL. I HOPE YOU'LL SOON SETTLE IN...
YES, SIR. THANK YOU.

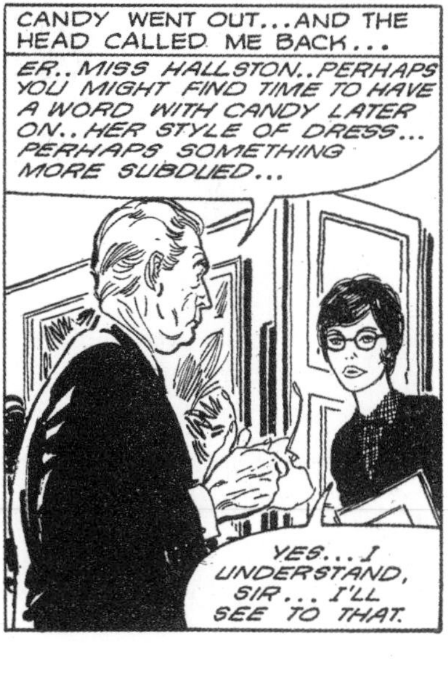
CANDY WENT OUT...AND THE HEAD CALLED ME BACK...
ER.. MISS HALLSTON.. PERHAPS YOU MIGHT FIND TIME TO HAVE A WORD WITH CANDY LATER ON.. HER STYLE OF DRESS... PERHAPS SOMETHING MORE SUBDUED...
YES... I UNDERSTAND, SIR... I'LL SEE TO THAT.

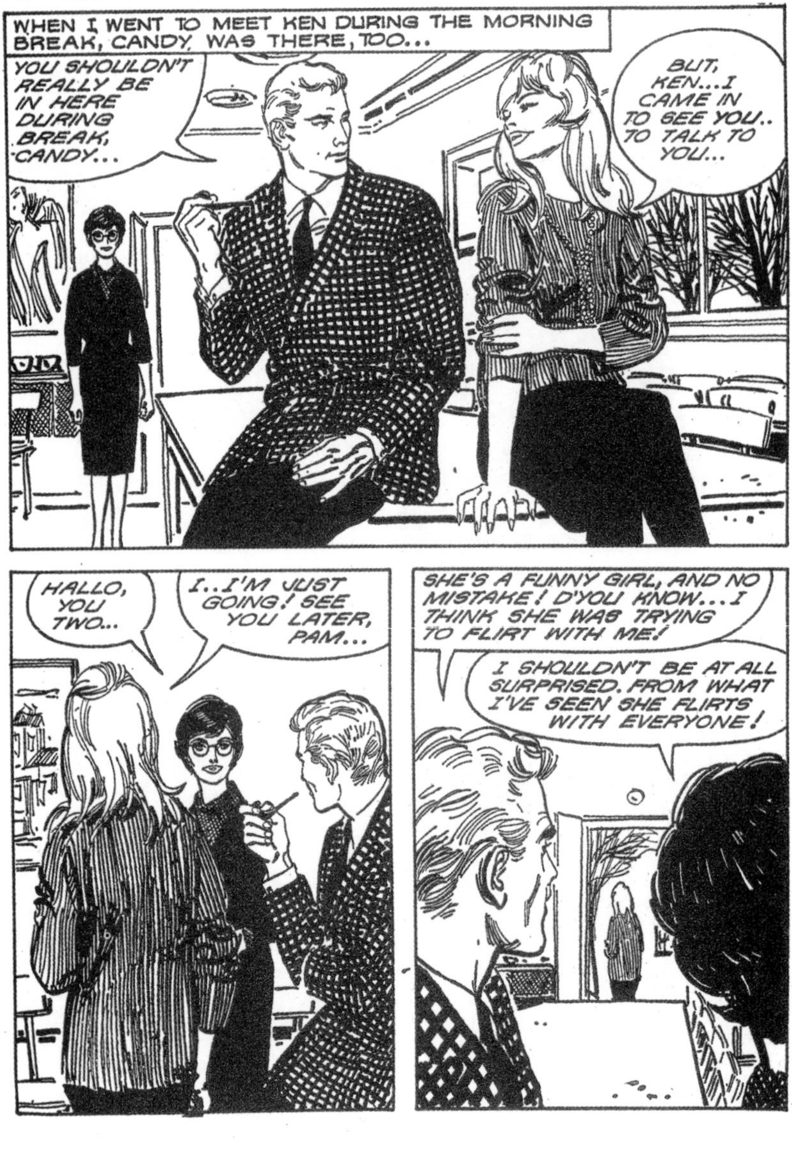
WHEN I WENT TO MEET KEN DURING THE MORNING BREAK, CANDY WAS THERE, TOO...
YOU SHOULDN'T REALLY BE IN HERE DURING BREAK, CANDY...
BUT, KEN...I CAME IN TO SEE YOU.. TO TALK TO YOU...
HALLO, YOU TWO...
I..I'M JUST GOING! SEE YOU LATER, PAM...
SHE'S A FUNNY GIRL, AND NO MISTAKE! D'YOU KNOW...I THINK SHE WAS TRYING TO FLIRT WITH ME!
I SHOULDN'T BE AT ALL SURPRISED. FROM WHAT I'VE SEEN SHE FLIRTS WITH EVERYONE!

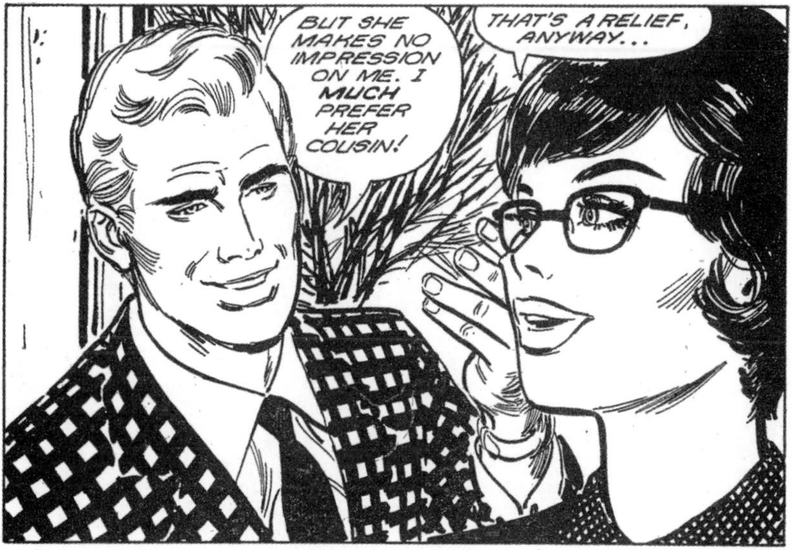
BUT SHE MAKES NO IMPRESSION ON ME. I **MUCH** PREFER HER COUSIN!
THAT'S A RELIEF, ANYWAY...

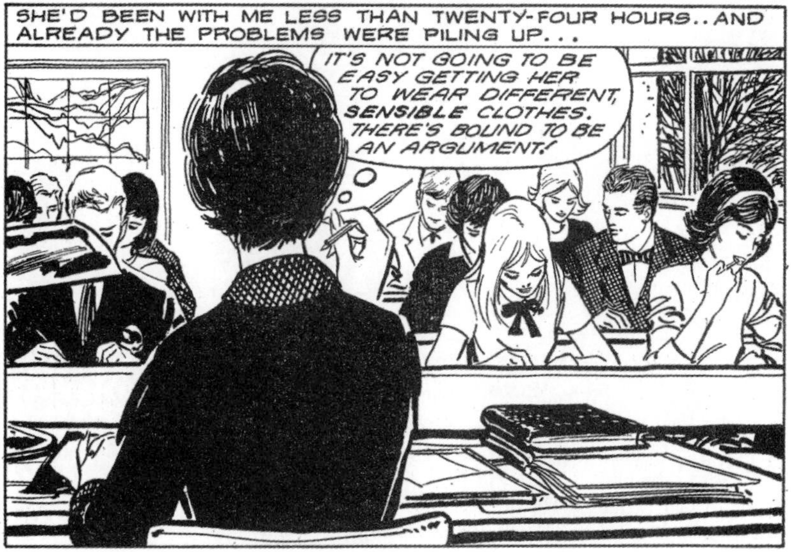
SHE'D BEEN WITH ME LESS THAN TWENTY-FOUR HOURS..AND ALREADY THE PROBLEMS WERE PILING UP...
IT'S NOT GOING TO BE EASY GETTING HER TO WEAR DIFFERENT, **SENSIBLE** CLOTHES. THERE'S BOUND TO BE AN ARGUMENT!

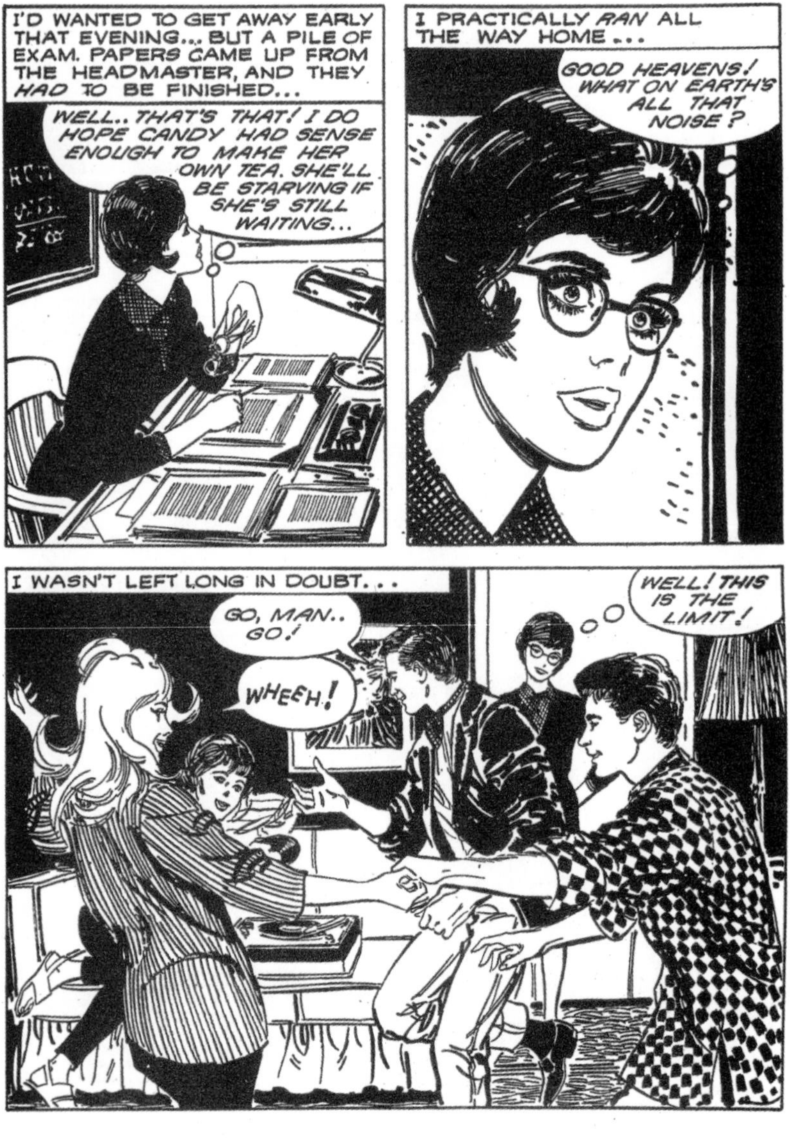
I'D WANTED TO GET AWAY EARLY THAT EVENING... BUT A PILE OF EXAM. PAPERS CAME UP FROM THE HEADMASTER, AND THEY HAD TO BE FINISHED...
WELL.. THAT'S THAT! I DO HOPE CANDY HAD SENSE ENOUGH TO MAKE HER OWN TEA. SHE'LL BE STARVING IF SHE'S STILL WAITING...
I PRACTICALLY RAN ALL THE WAY HOME...
GOOD HEAVENS! WHAT ON EARTH'S ALL THAT NOISE?
I WASN'T LEFT LONG IN DOUBT...
GO, MAN.. GO!
WHEEH!
WELL! THIS IS THE LIMIT!

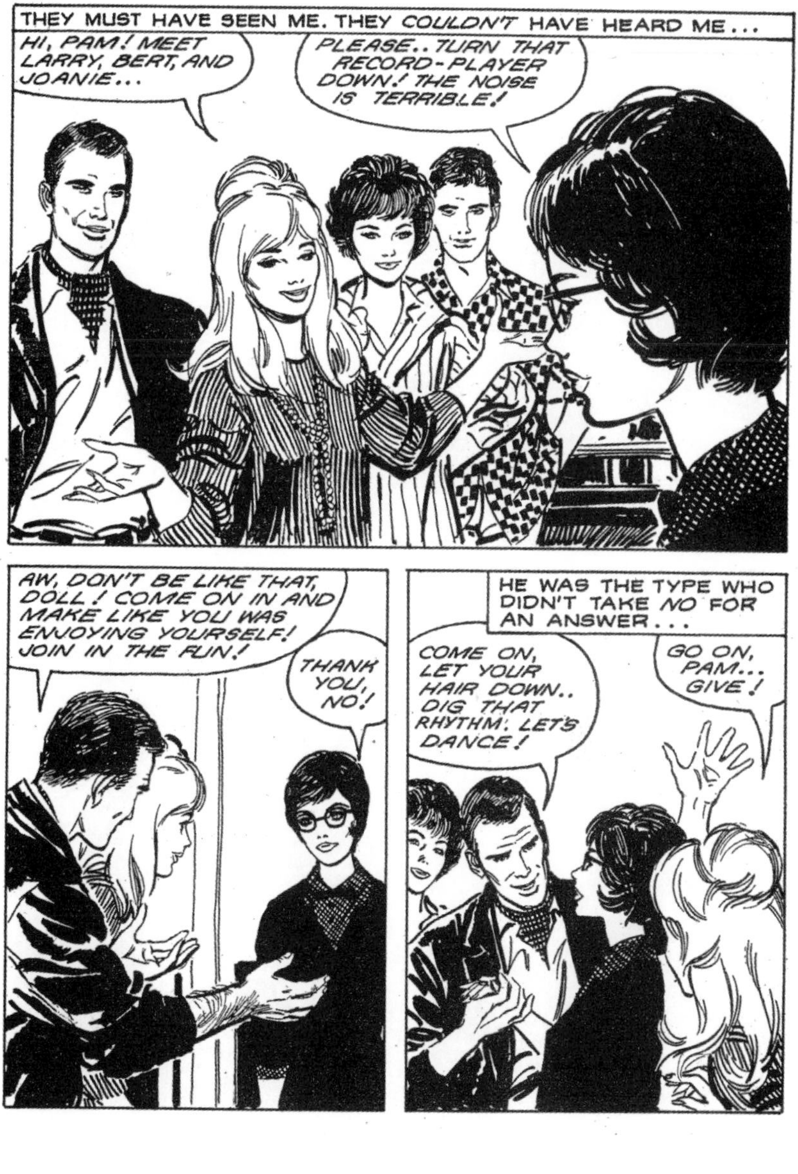
THEY MUST HAVE SEEN ME. THEY COULDN'T HAVE HEARD ME...
HI, PAM! MEET LARRY, BERT, AND JOANIE...
PLEASE.. TURN THAT RECORD-PLAYER DOWN! THE NOISE IS TERRIBLE!
AW, DON'T BE LIKE THAT, DOLL! COME ON IN AND MAKE LIKE YOU WAS ENJOYING YOURSELF! JOIN IN THE FUN!
THANK YOU, NO!
HE WAS THE TYPE WHO DIDN'T TAKE NO FOR AN ANSWER...
COME ON, LET YOUR HAIR DOWN.. DIG THAT RHYTHM. LET'S DANCE!
GO ON, PAM... GIVE!

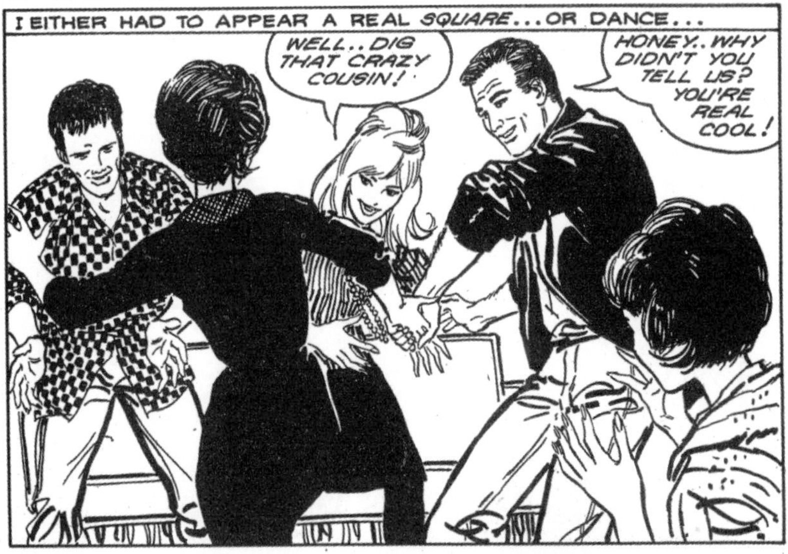
I EITHER HAD TO APPEAR A REAL SQUARE...OR DANCE...
WELL..DIG THAT CRAZY COUSIN!
HONEY..WHY DIDN'T YOU TELL US? YOU'RE REAL COOL!

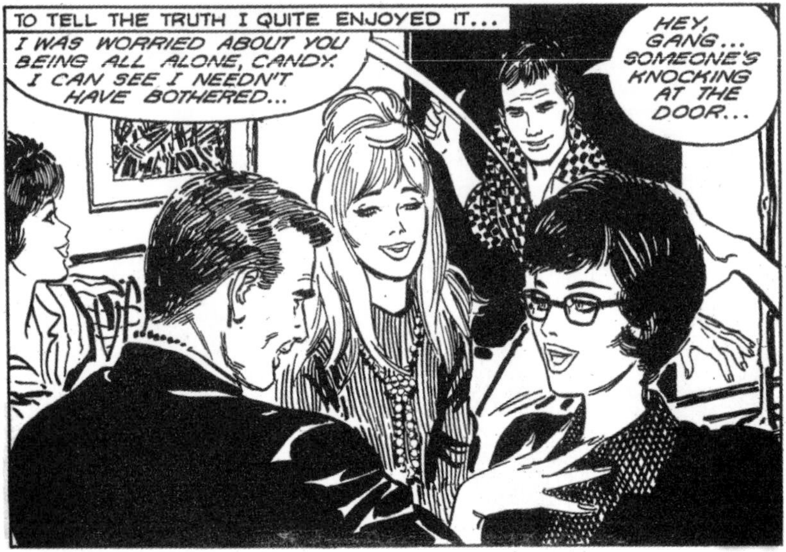
TO TELL THE TRUTH I QUITE ENJOYED IT...
I WAS WORRIED ABOUT YOU BEING ALL ALONE, CANDY. I CAN SEE I NEEDN'T HAVE BOTHERED...
HEY, GANG... SOMEONE'S KNOCKING AT THE DOOR...

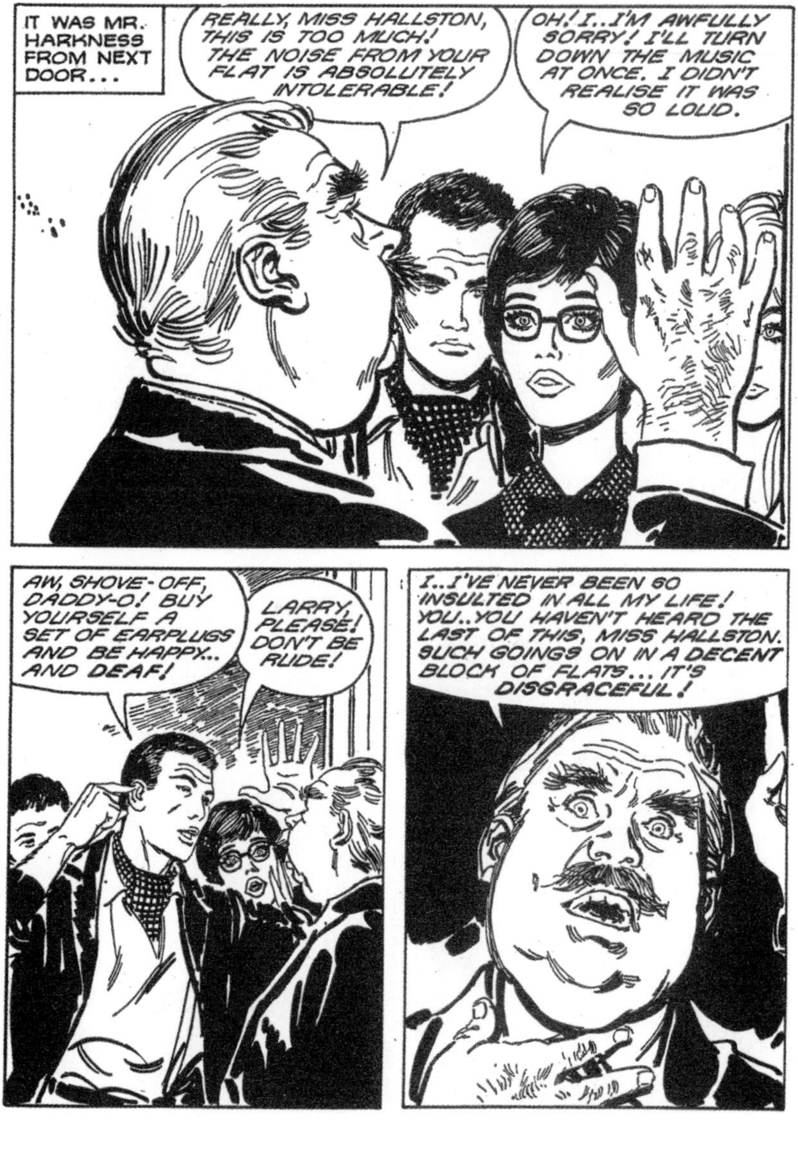
IT WAS MR. HARKNESS FROM NEXT DOOR...
REALLY, MISS HALLSTON, THIS IS TOO MUCH! THE NOISE FROM YOUR FLAT IS ABSOLUTELY INTOLERABLE!
OH! I..I'M AWFULLY SORRY! I'LL TURN DOWN THE MUSIC AT ONCE. I DIDN'T REALISE IT WAS SO LOUD.
AW, SHOVE-OFF, DADDY-O! BUY YOURSELF A SET OF EARPLUGS AND BE HAPPY... AND DEAF!
LARRY, PLEASE! DON'T BE RUDE!
I..I'VE NEVER BEEN SO INSULTED IN ALL MY LIFE! YOU..YOU HAVEN'T HEARD THE LAST OF THIS, MISS HALLSTON. SUCH GOINGS ON IN A DECENT BLOCK OF FLATS... IT'S DISGRACEFUL!

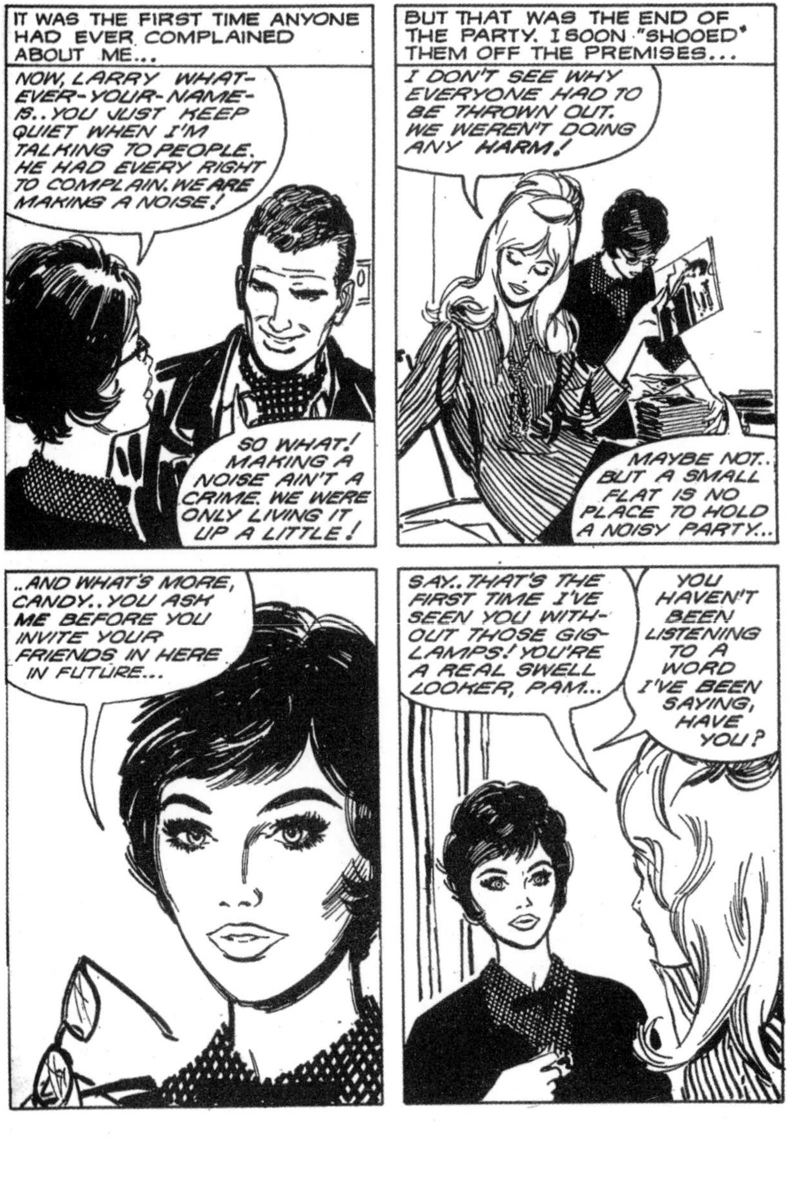
IT WAS THE FIRST TIME ANYONE HAD EVER COMPLAINED ABOUT ME...
NOW, LARRY WHAT-EVER-YOUR-NAME-IS.. YOU JUST KEEP QUIET WHEN I'M TALKING TO PEOPLE. HE HAD EVERY RIGHT TO COMPLAIN. WE ARE MAKING A NOISE!
SO WHAT! MAKING A NOISE AIN'T A CRIME. WE WERE ONLY LIVING IT UP A LITTLE!
BUT THAT WAS THE END OF THE PARTY. I SOON "SHOOED" THEM OFF THE PREMISES...
I DON'T SEE WHY EVERYONE HAD TO BE THROWN OUT. WE WEREN'T DOING ANY HARM!
MAYBE NOT.. BUT A SMALL FLAT IS NO PLACE TO HOLD A NOISY PARTY...
..AND WHAT'S MORE, CANDY.. YOU ASK ME BEFORE YOU INVITE YOUR FRIENDS IN HERE IN FUTURE...
SAY.. THAT'S THE FIRST TIME I'VE SEEN YOU WITH-OUT THOSE GIG-LAMPS! YOU'RE A REAL SWELL LOOKER, PAM...
YOU HAVEN'T BEEN LISTENING TO A WORD I'VE BEEN SAYING, HAVE YOU?

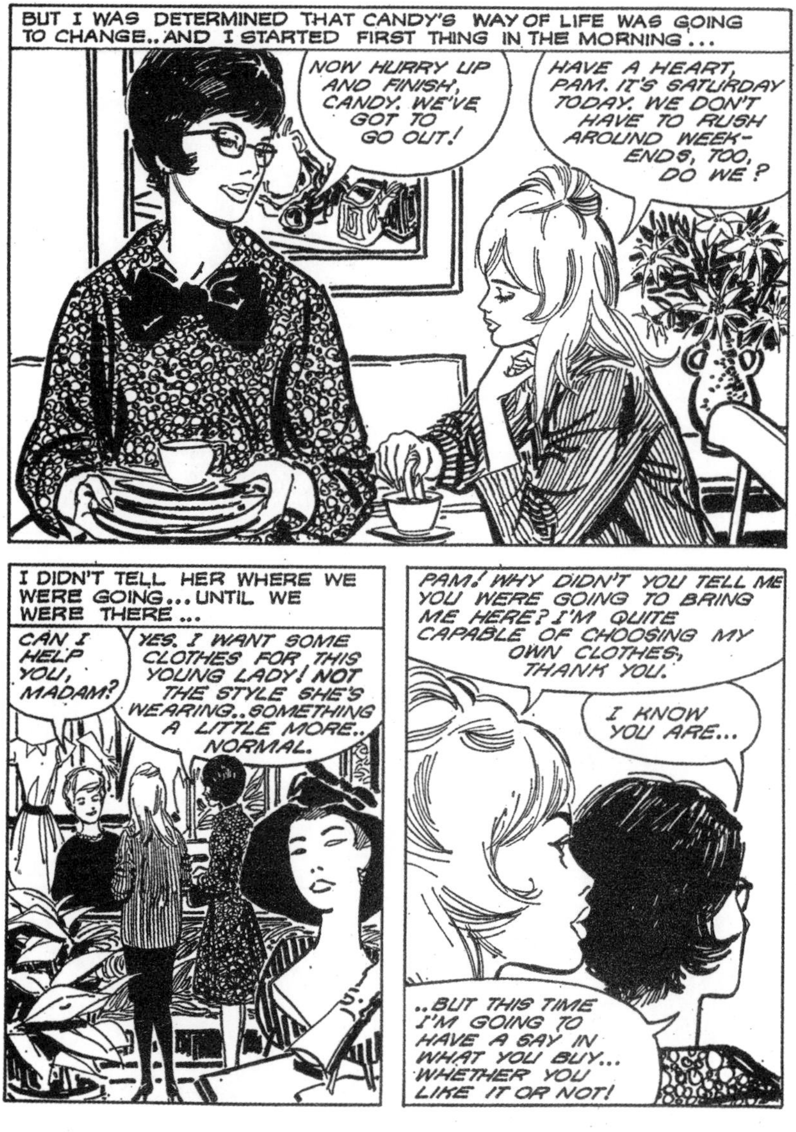
BUT I WAS DETERMINED THAT CANDY'S WAY OF LIFE WAS GOING TO CHANGE.. AND I STARTED FIRST THING IN THE MORNING...
NOW HURRY UP AND FINISH, CANDY. WE'VE GOT TO GO OUT!
HAVE A HEART, PAM. IT'S SATURDAY TODAY. WE DON'T HAVE TO RUSH AROUND WEEK-ENDS, TOO, DO WE?
I DIDN'T TELL HER WHERE WE WERE GOING... UNTIL WE WERE THERE...
CAN I HELP YOU, MADAM?
YES. I WANT SOME CLOTHES FOR THIS YOUNG LADY! NOT THE STYLE SHE'S WEARING.. SOMETHING A LITTLE MORE.. NORMAL.
PAM! WHY DIDN'T YOU TELL ME YOU WERE GOING TO BRING ME HERE? I'M QUITE CAPABLE OF CHOOSING MY OWN CLOTHES, THANK YOU.
I KNOW YOU ARE...
..BUT THIS TIME I'M GOING TO HAVE A SAY IN WHAT YOU BUY... WHETHER YOU LIKE IT OR NOT!

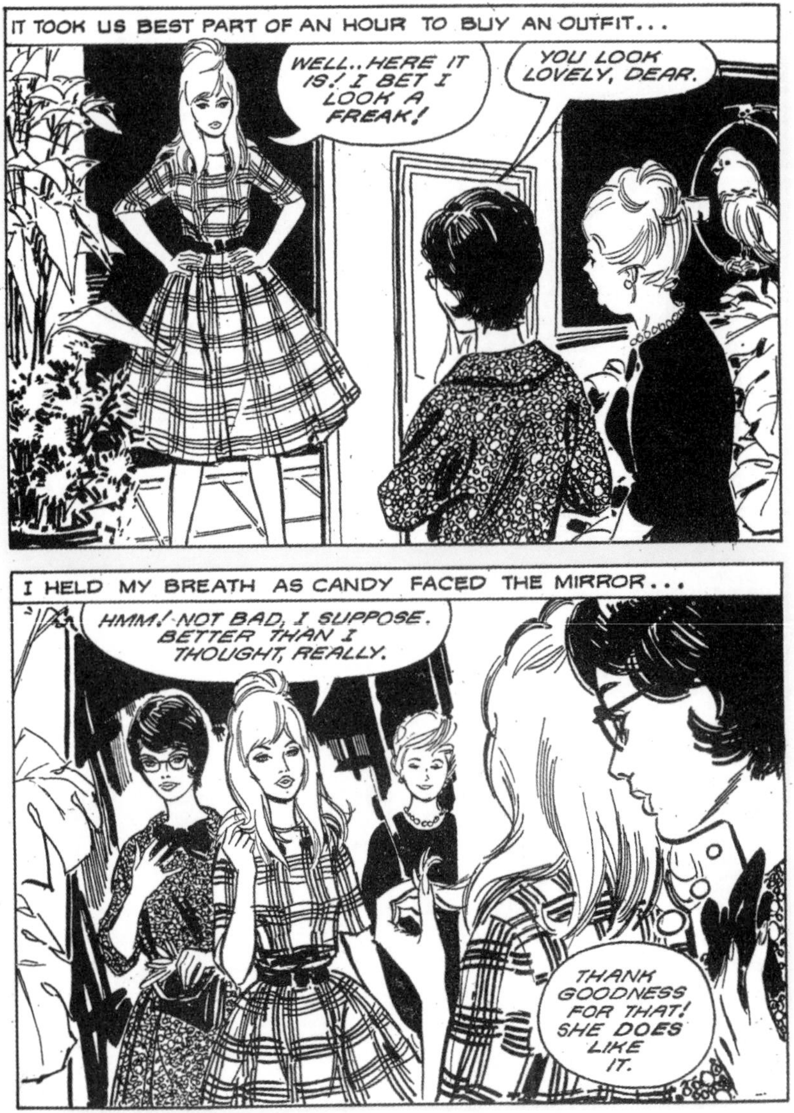
IT TOOK US BEST PART OF AN HOUR TO BUY AN OUTFIT...
WELL..HERE IT IS! I BET I LOOK A FREAK!
YOU LOOK LOVELY, DEAR.
I HELD MY BREATH AS CANDY FACED THE MIRROR...
HMM! NOT BAD, I SUPPOSE. BETTER THAN I THOUGHT, REALLY.
THANK GOODNESS FOR THAT! SHE DOES LIKE IT.

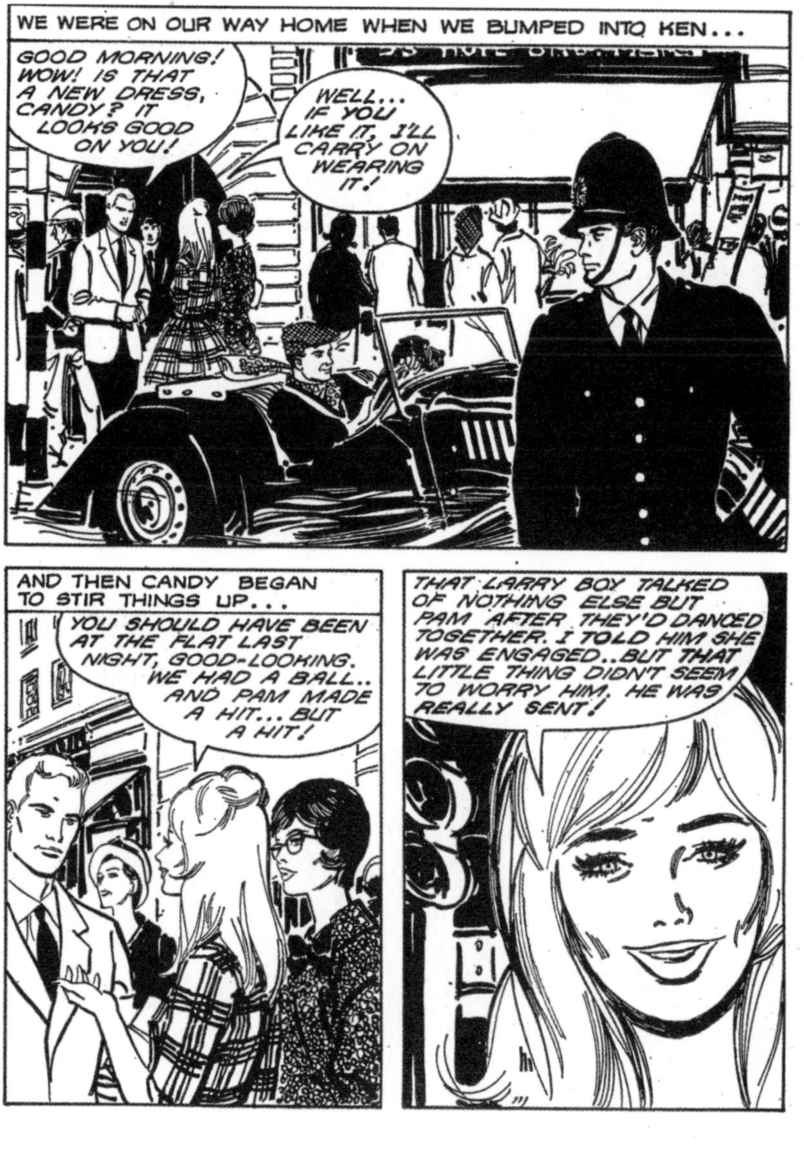
WE WERE ON OUR WAY HOME WHEN WE BUMPED INTO KEN...
GOOD MORNING! WOW! IS THAT A NEW DRESS, CANDY? IT LOOKS GOOD ON YOU!
WELL... IF YOU LIKE IT, I'LL CARRY ON WEARING IT!
AND THEN CANDY BEGAN TO STIR THINGS UP...
YOU SHOULD HAVE BEEN AT THE FLAT LAST NIGHT, GOOD-LOOKING. WE HAD A BALL.. AND PAM MADE A HIT... BUT A HIT!
THAT LARRY BOY TALKED OF NOTHING ELSE BUT PAM AFTER THEY'D DANCED TOGETHER. I TOLD HIM SHE WAS ENGAGED..BUT THAT LITTLE THING DIDN'T SEEM TO WORRY HIM. HE WAS REALLY SENT!

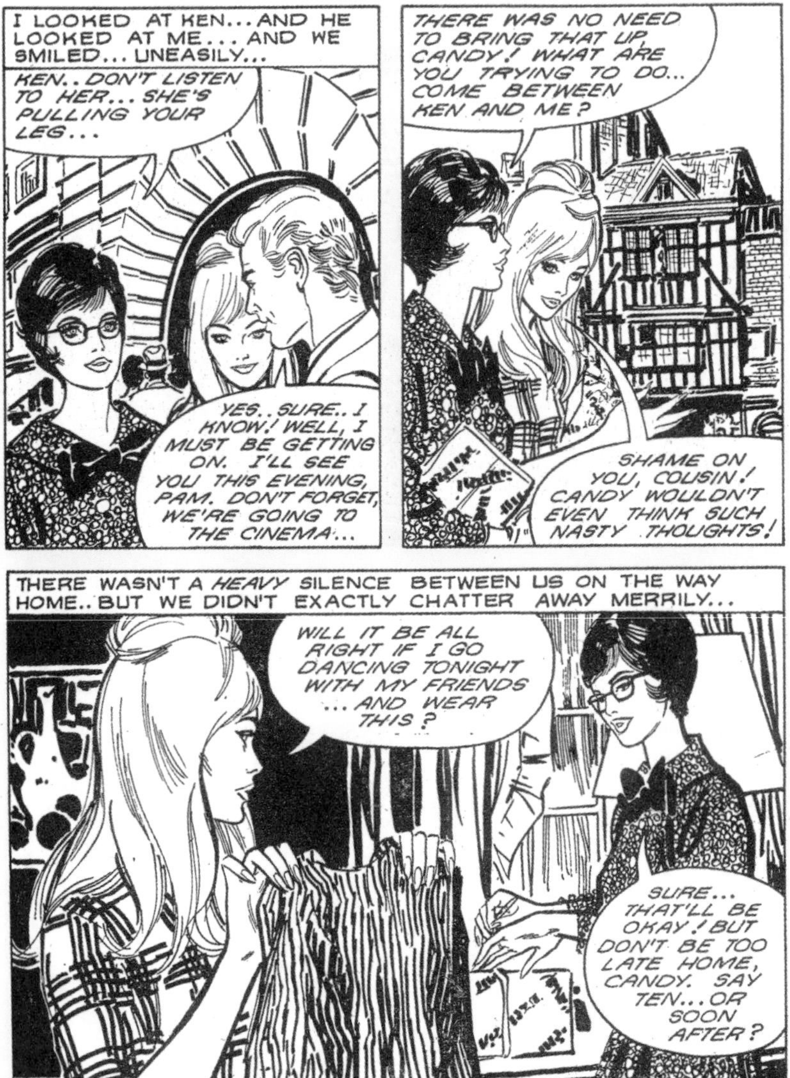
I LOOKED AT KEN... AND HE LOOKED AT ME... AND WE SMILED... UNEASILY...
KEN.. DON'T LISTEN TO HER... SHE'S PULLING YOUR LEG...
YES.. SURE.. I KNOW! WELL, I MUST BE GETTING ON. I'LL SEE YOU THIS EVENING, PAM. DON'T FORGET, WE'RE GOING TO THE CINEMA...
THERE WAS NO NEED TO BRING THAT UP, CANDY! WHAT ARE YOU TRYING TO DO... COME BETWEEN KEN AND ME?
SHAME ON YOU, COUSIN! CANDY WOULDN'T EVEN THINK SUCH NASTY THOUGHTS!
THERE WASN'T A HEAVY SILENCE BETWEEN US ON THE WAY HOME.. BUT WE DIDN'T EXACTLY CHATTER AWAY MERRILY...
WILL IT BE ALL RIGHT IF I GO DANCING TONIGHT WITH MY FRIENDS ... AND WEAR THIS?
SURE... THAT'LL BE OKAY! BUT DON'T BE TOO LATE HOME, CANDY. SAY TEN... OR SOON AFTER?

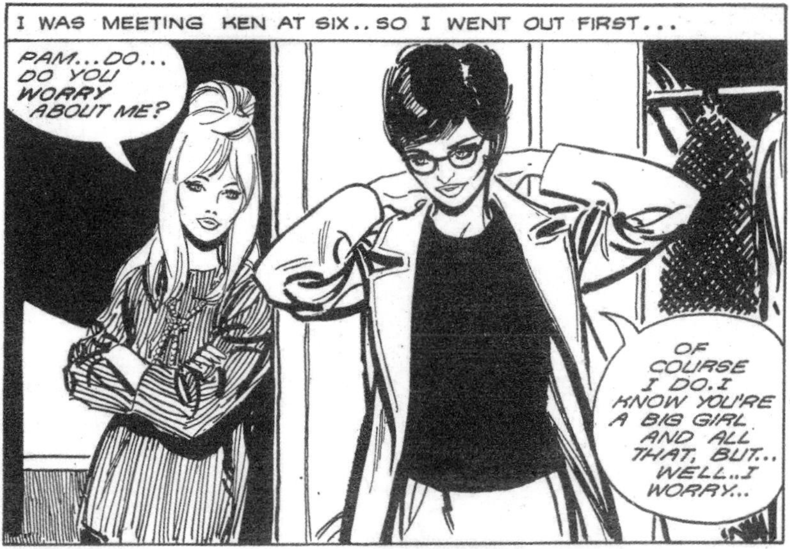
I WAS MEETING KEN AT SIX.. SO I WENT OUT FIRST...
PAM...DO... DO YOU WORRY ABOUT ME?
OF COURSE I DO. I KNOW YOU'RE A BIG GIRL AND ALL THAT, BUT... WELL.. I WORRY...

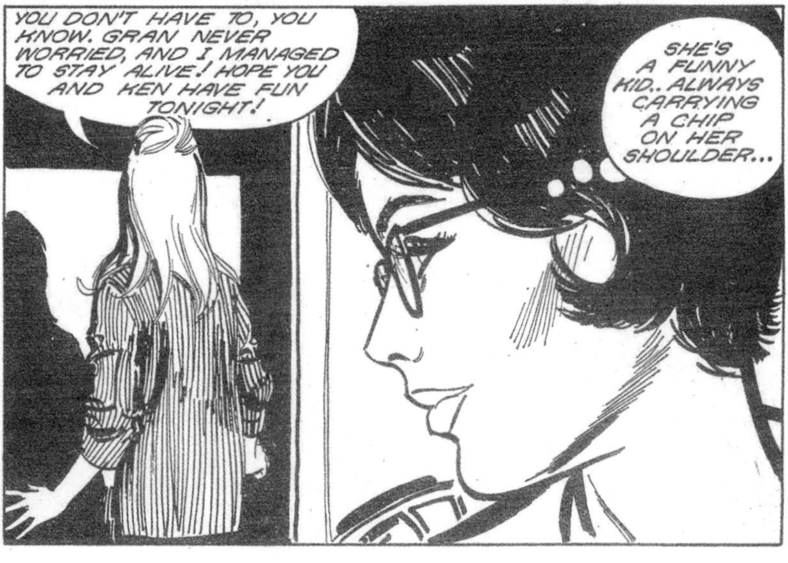
YOU DON'T HAVE TO, YOU KNOW. GRAN NEVER WORRIED, AND I MANAGED TO STAY ALIVE! HOPE YOU AND KEN HAVE FUN TONIGHT!
SHE'S A FUNNY KID.. ALWAYS CARRYING A CHIP ON HER SHOULDER...

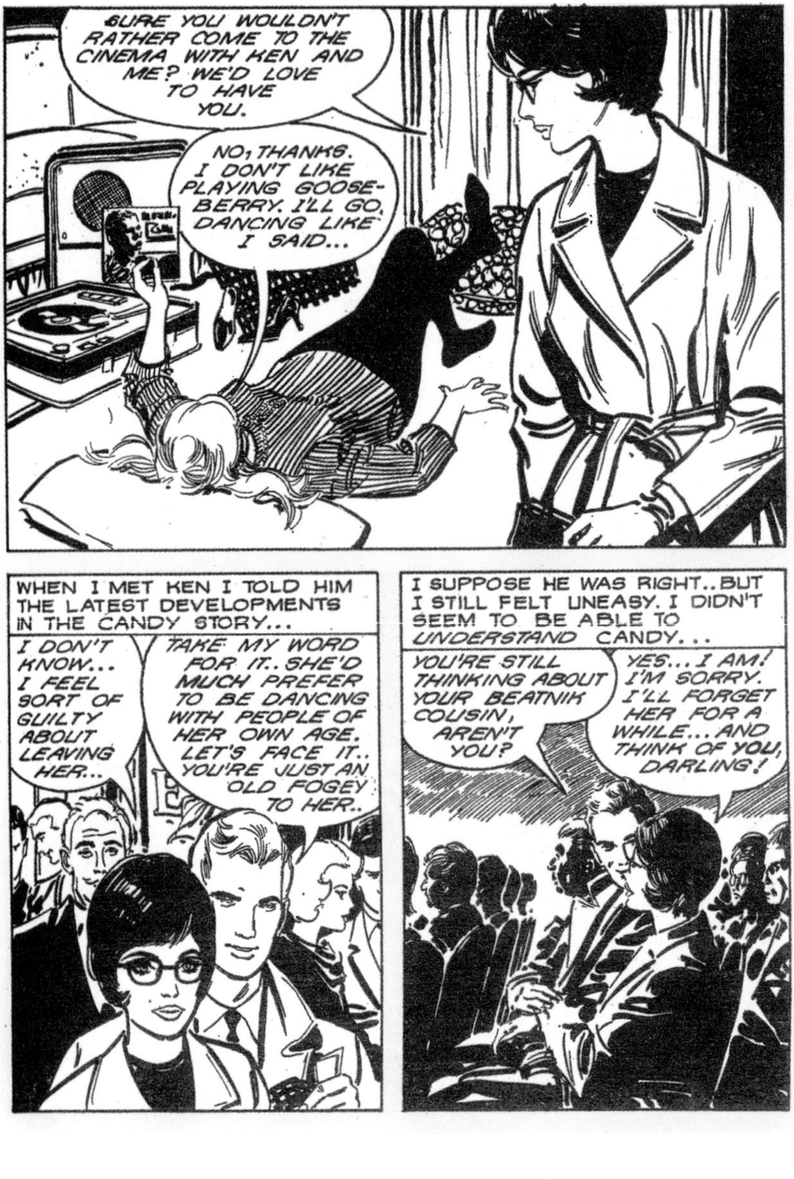
SURE YOU WOULDN'T RATHER COME TO THE CINEMA WITH KEN AND ME? WE'D LOVE TO HAVE YOU.
NO, THANKS. I DON'T LIKE PLAYING GOOSE-BERRY. I'LL GO DANCING LIKE I SAID...
WHEN I MET KEN I TOLD HIM THE LATEST DEVELOPMENTS IN THE CANDY STORY...
I DON'T KNOW... I FEEL SORT OF GUILTY ABOUT LEAVING HER...
TAKE MY WORD FOR IT.. SHE'D MUCH PREFER TO BE DANCING WITH PEOPLE OF HER OWN AGE. LET'S FACE IT.. YOU'RE JUST AN OLD FOGEY TO HER..
I SUPPOSE HE WAS RIGHT.. BUT I STILL FELT UNEASY. I DIDN'T SEEM TO BE ABLE TO UNDERSTAND CANDY...
YOU'RE STILL THINKING ABOUT YOUR BEATNIK COUSIN, AREN'T YOU?
YES... I AM! I'M SORRY. I'LL FORGET HER FOR A WHILE... AND THINK OF YOU, DARLING!

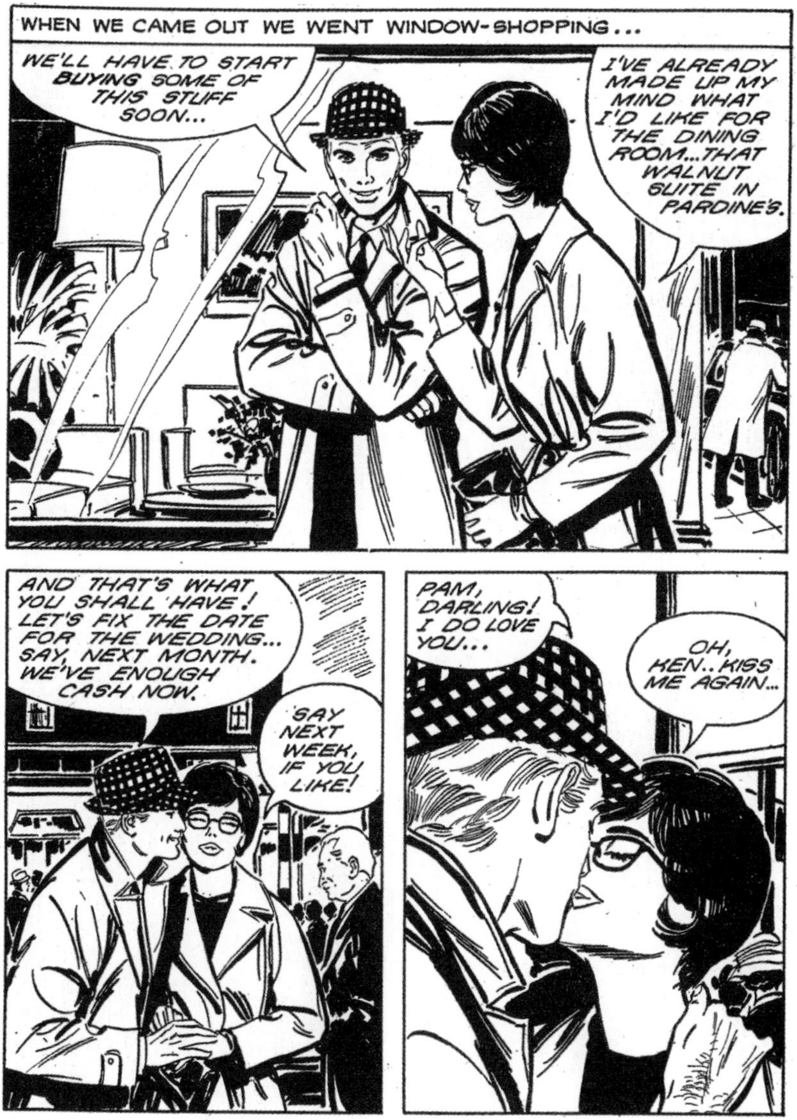
WHEN WE CAME OUT WE WENT WINDOW-SHOPPING...
WE'LL HAVE TO START BUYING SOME OF THIS STUFF SOON...
I'VE ALREADY MADE UP MY MIND WHAT I'D LIKE FOR THE DINING ROOM...THAT WALNUT SUITE IN PARDINE'S.
AND THAT'S WHAT YOU SHALL HAVE! LET'S FIX THE DATE FOR THE WEDDING... SAY, NEXT MONTH. WE'VE ENOUGH CASH NOW.
SAY NEXT WEEK, IF YOU LIKE!
PAM, DARLING! I DO LOVE YOU...
OH, KEN.. KISS ME AGAIN...

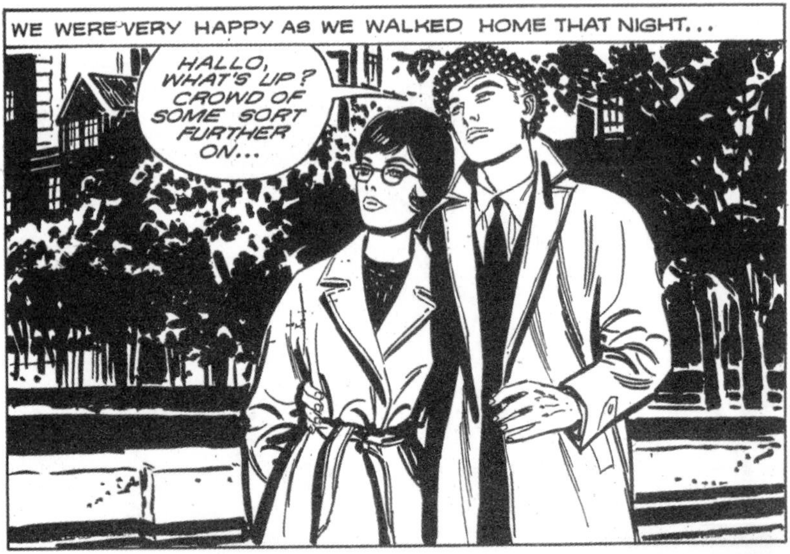
WE WERE VERY HAPPY AS WE WALKED HOME THAT NIGHT...
HALLO, WHAT'S UP? CROWD OF SOME SORT FURTHER ON...

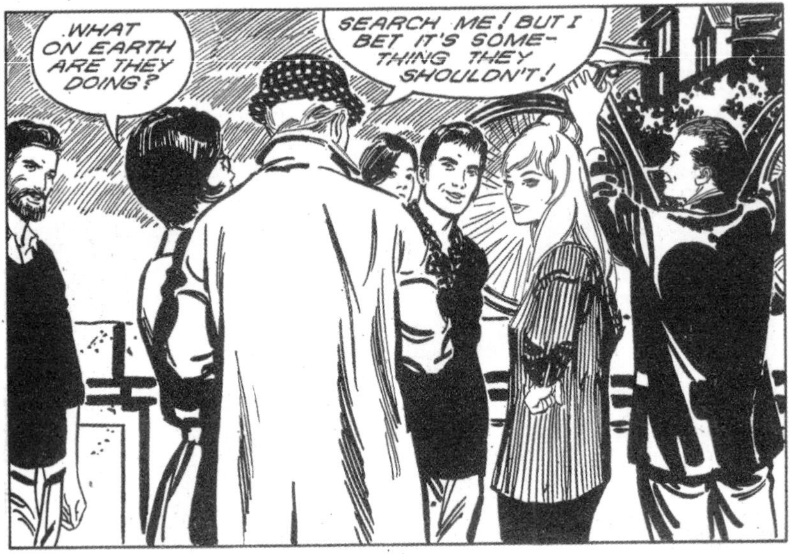
WHAT ON EARTH ARE THEY DOING?
SEARCH ME! BUT I BET IT'S SOME-THING THEY SHOULDN'T!

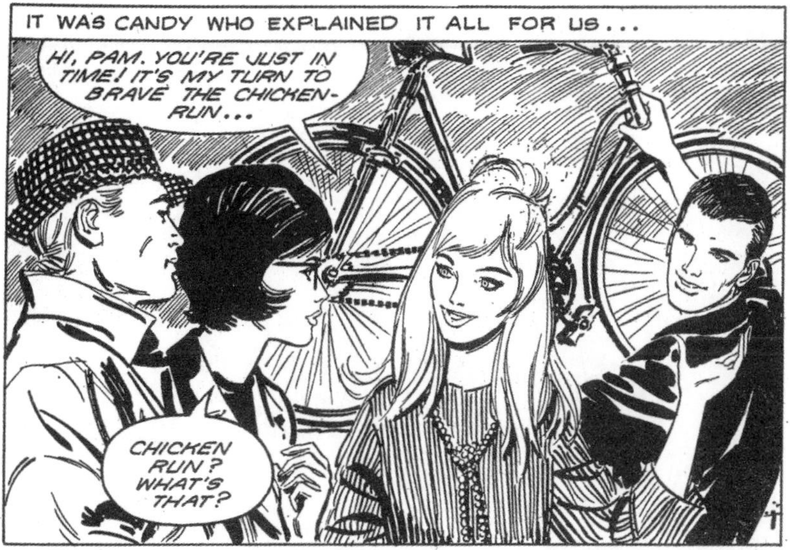
IT WAS CANDY WHO EXPLAINED IT ALL FOR US...
HI, PAM. YOU'RE JUST IN TIME! IT'S MY TURN TO BRAVE THE CHICKEN-RUN...
CHICKEN RUN? WHAT'S THAT?

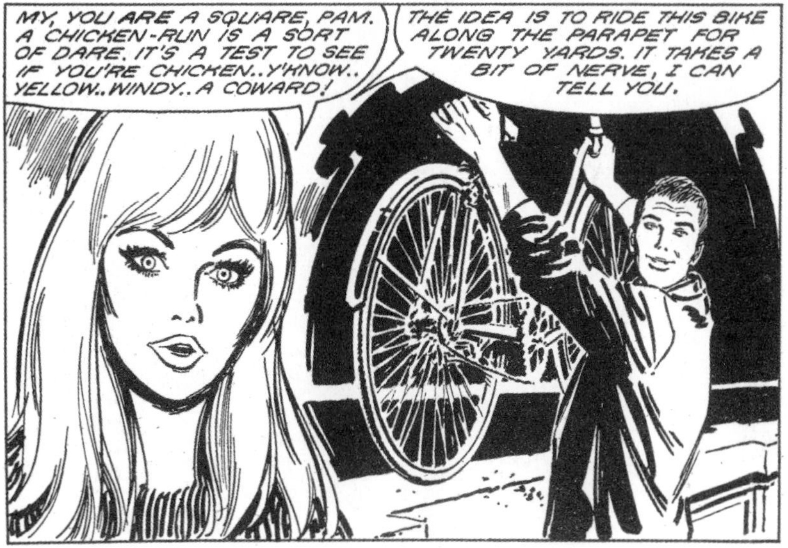
MY, YOU ARE A SQUARE, PAM. A CHICKEN-RUN IS A SORT OF DARE. IT'S A TEST TO SEE IF YOU'RE CHICKEN..Y'KNOW.. YELLOW..WINDY..A COWARD!
THE IDEA IS TO RIDE THIS BIKE ALONG THE PARAPET FOR TWENTY YARDS. IT TAKES A BIT OF NERVE, I CAN TELL YOU.

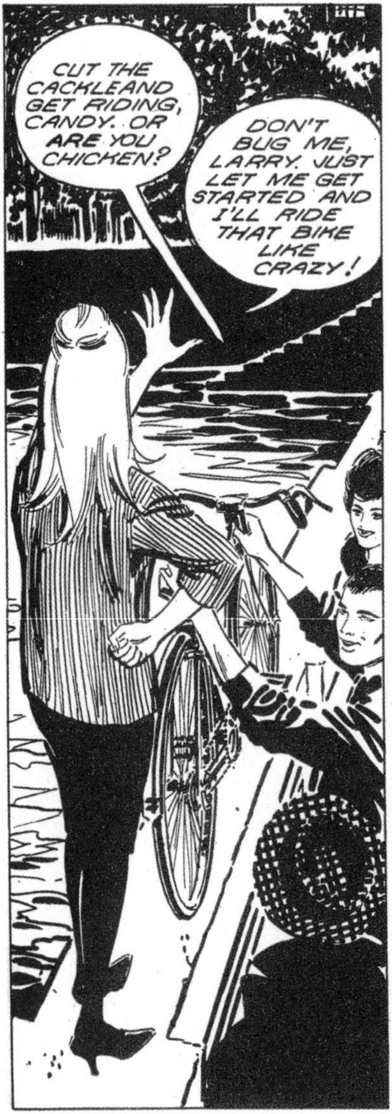
CUT THE CACKLEAND GET RIDING, CANDY. OR ARE YOU CHICKEN?
DON'T BUG ME, LARRY. JUST LET ME GET STARTED AND I'LL RIDE THAT BIKE LIKE CRAZY!

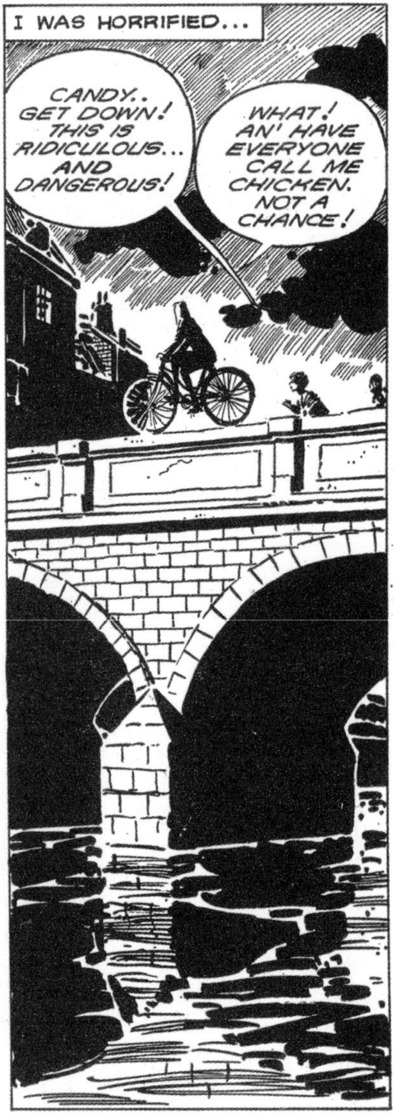
I WAS HORRIFIED...
CANDY.. GET DOWN! THIS IS RIDICULOUS... AND DANGEROUS!
WHAT! AN' HAVE EVERYONE CALL ME CHICKEN. NOT A CHANCE!

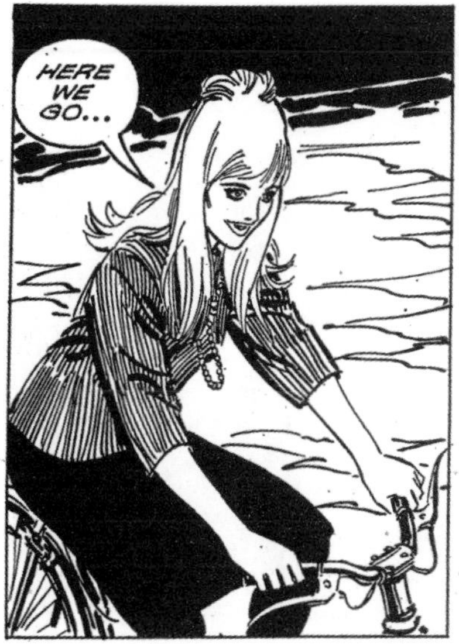
HERE WE GO...

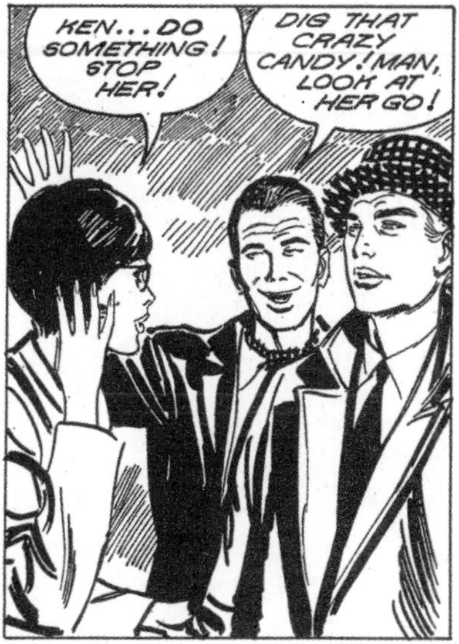
KEN...DO SOMETHING! STOP HER!
DIG THAT CRAZY CANDY! MAN, LOOK AT HER GO!

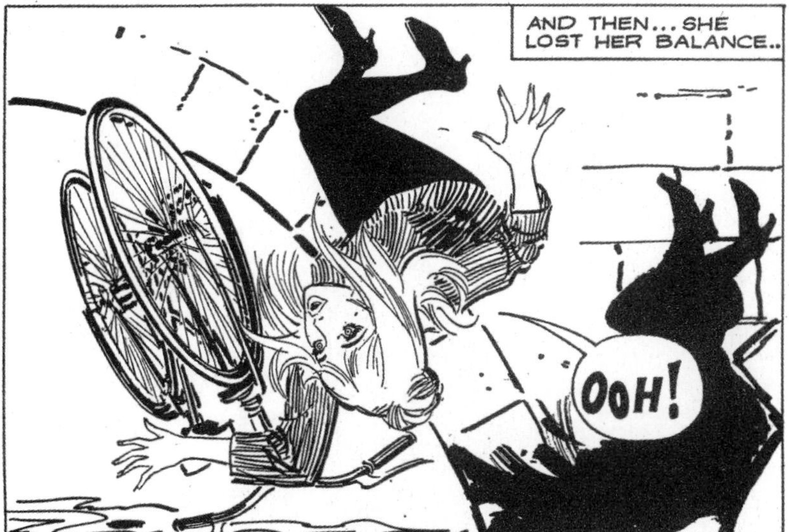
AND THEN...SHE LOST HER BALANCE..
OOH!

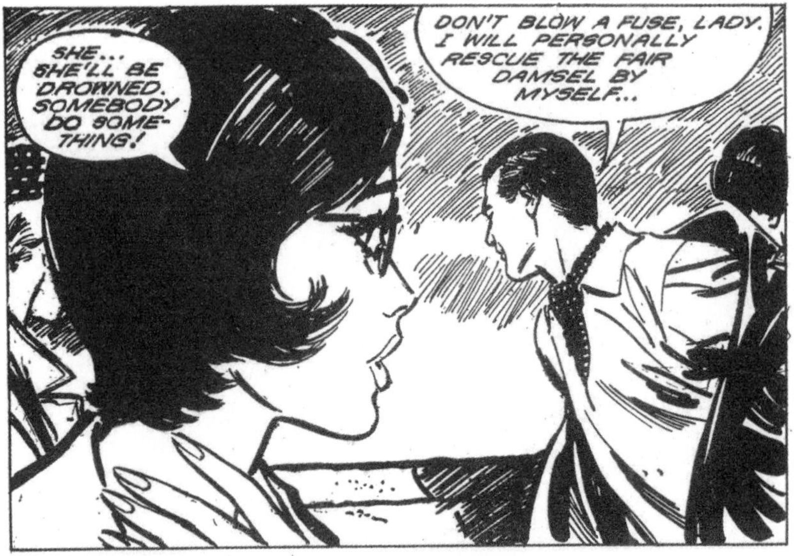
SHE... SHE'LL BE DROWNED. SOMEBODY DO SOME-THING!
DON'T BLOW A FUSE, LADY. I WILL PERSONALLY RESCUE THE FAIR DAMSEL BY MYSELF...

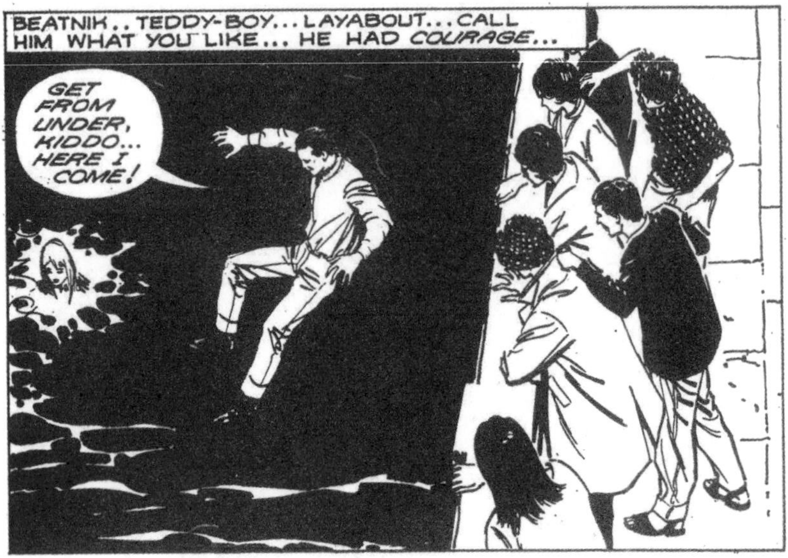
BEATNIK.. TEDDY-BOY... LAYABOUT... CALL HIM WHAT YOU LIKE... HE HAD COURAGE...
GET FROM UNDER, KIDDO... HERE I COME!

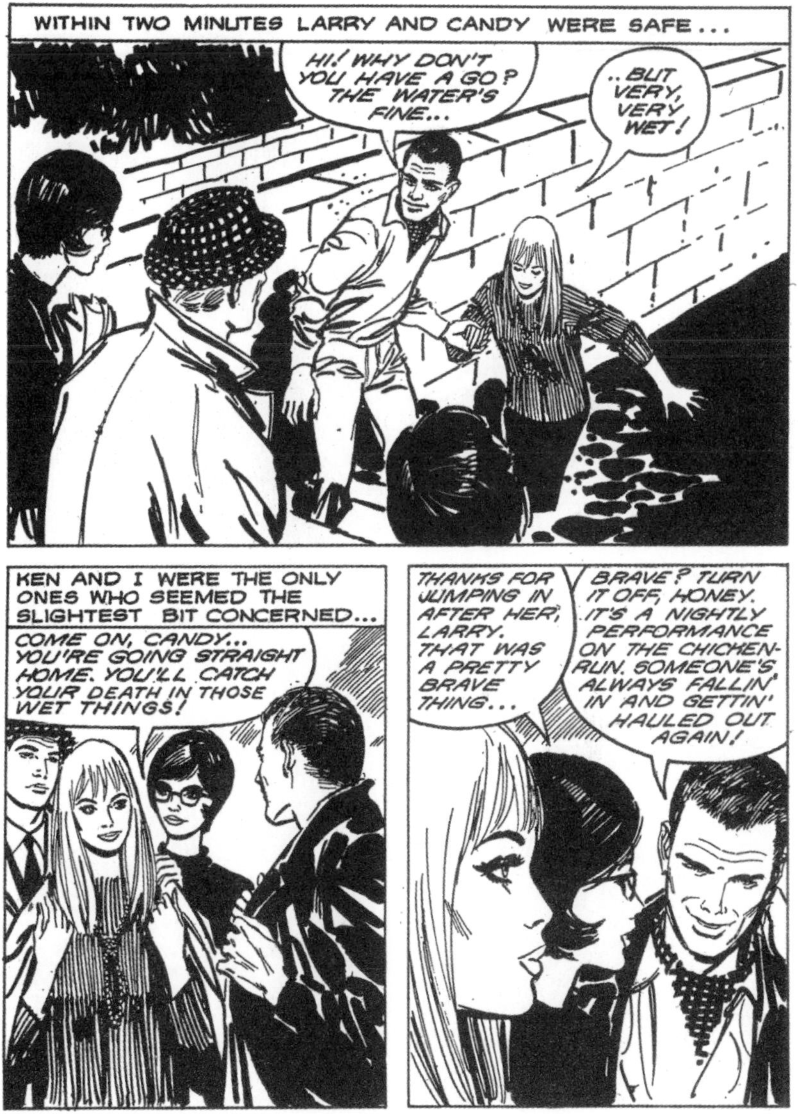
WITHIN TWO MINUTES LARRY AND CANDY WERE SAFE...
HI! WHY DON'T YOU HAVE A GO? THE WATER'S FINE...
..BUT VERY, VERY WET!
KEN AND I WERE THE ONLY ONES WHO SEEMED THE SLIGHTEST BIT CONCERNED...
COME ON, CANDY... YOU'RE GOING STRAIGHT HOME. YOU'LL CATCH YOUR DEATH IN THOSE WET THINGS!
THANKS FOR JUMPING IN AFTER HER, LARRY. THAT WAS A PRETTY BRAVE THING...
BRAVE? TURN IT OFF, HONEY. IT'S A NIGHTLY PERFORMANCE ON THE CHICKEN-RUN. SOMEONE'S ALWAYS FALLIN' IN AND GETTIN' HAULED OUT AGAIN!

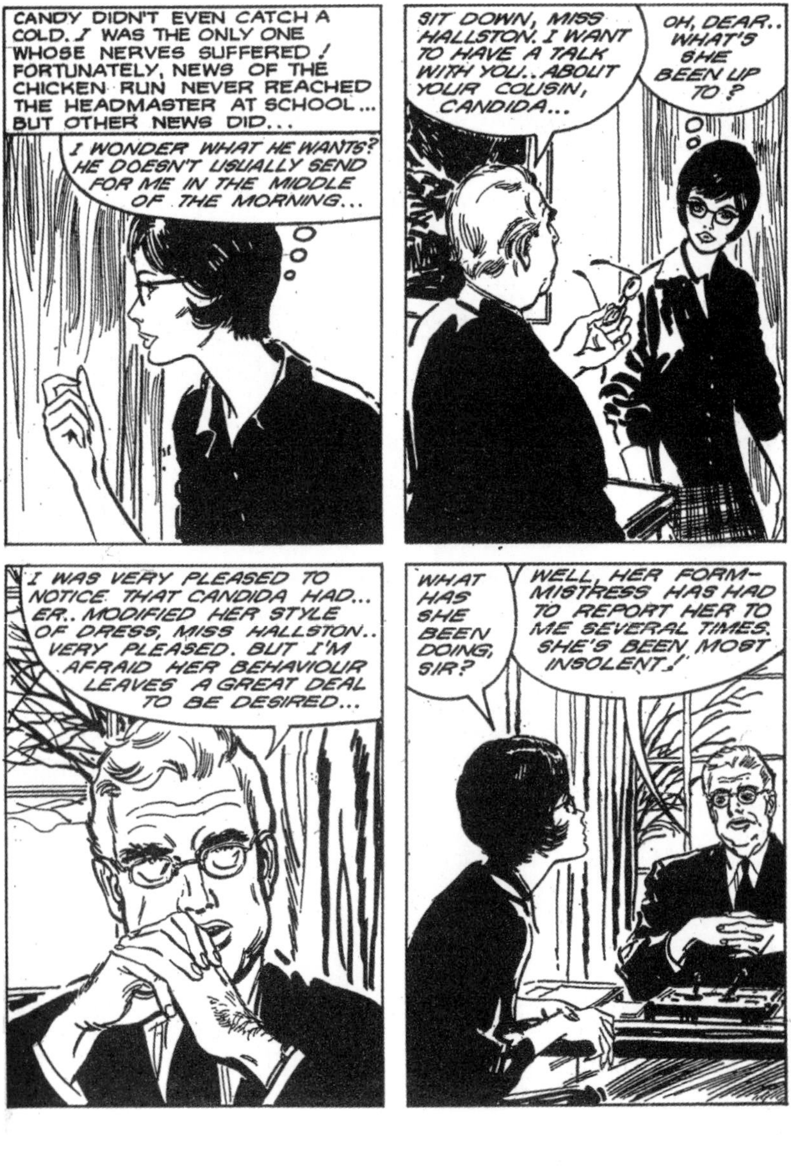
CANDY DIDN'T EVEN CATCH A COLD. I WAS THE ONLY ONE WHOSE NERVES SUFFERED! FORTUNATELY, NEWS OF THE CHICKEN RUN NEVER REACHED THE HEADMASTER AT SCHOOL... BUT OTHER NEWS DID...
I WONDER WHAT HE WANTS? HE DOESN'T USUALLY SEND FOR ME IN THE MIDDLE OF THE MORNING...
SIT DOWN, MISS HALLSTON. I WANT TO HAVE A TALK WITH YOU.. ABOUT YOUR COUSIN, CANDIDA...
OH, DEAR.. WHAT'S SHE BEEN UP TO?
I WAS VERY PLEASED TO NOTICE THAT CANDIDA HAD... ER.. MODIFIED HER STYLE OF DRESS, MISS HALLSTON.. VERY PLEASED. BUT I'M AFRAID HER BEHAVIOUR LEAVES A GREAT DEAL TO BE DESIRED...
WHAT HAS SHE BEEN DOING, SIR?
WELL, HER FORM-MISTRESS HAS HAD TO REPORT HER TO ME SEVERAL TIMES. SHE'S BEEN MOST INSOLENT!

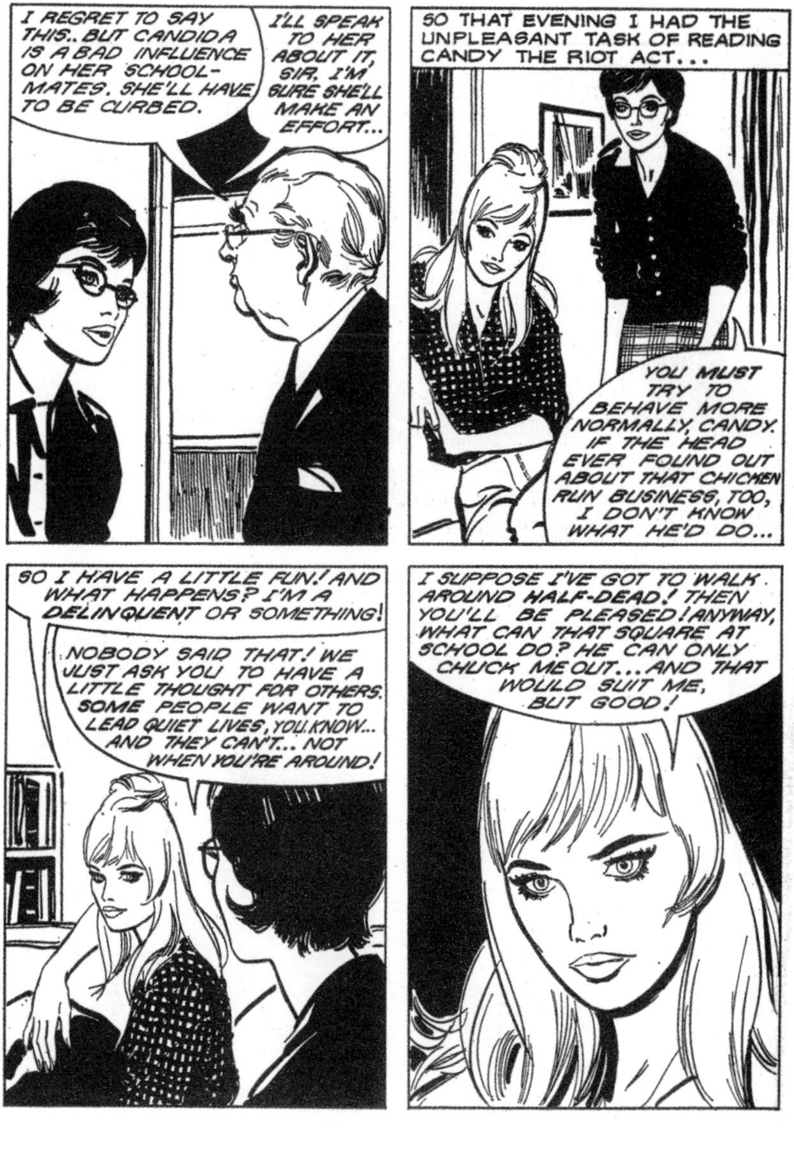
I REGRET TO SAY THIS.. BUT CANDIDA IS A BAD INFLUENCE ON HER SCHOOL-MATES. SHE'LL HAVE TO BE CURBED.
I'LL SPEAK TO HER ABOUT IT, SIR. I'M SURE SHE'LL MAKE AN EFFORT...
SO THAT EVENING I HAD THE UNPLEASANT TASK OF READING CANDY THE RIOT ACT...
YOU MUST TRY TO BEHAVE MORE NORMALLY, CANDY. IF THE HEAD EVER FOUND OUT ABOUT THAT CHICKEN RUN BUSINESS, TOO, I DON'T KNOW WHAT HE'D DO...
SO I HAVE A LITTLE FUN! AND WHAT HAPPENS? I'M A DELINQUENT OR SOMETHING!
NOBODY SAID THAT! WE JUST ASK YOU TO HAVE A LITTLE THOUGHT FOR OTHERS. SOME PEOPLE WANT TO LEAD QUIET LIVES, YOU KNOW... AND THEY CAN'T... NOT WHEN YOU'RE AROUND!
I SUPPOSE I'VE GOT TO WALK AROUND HALF-DEAD! THEN YOU'LL BE PLEASED! ANYWAY, WHAT CAN THAT SQUARE AT SCHOOL DO? HE CAN ONLY CHUCK ME OUT... AND THAT WOULD SUIT ME, BUT GOOD!

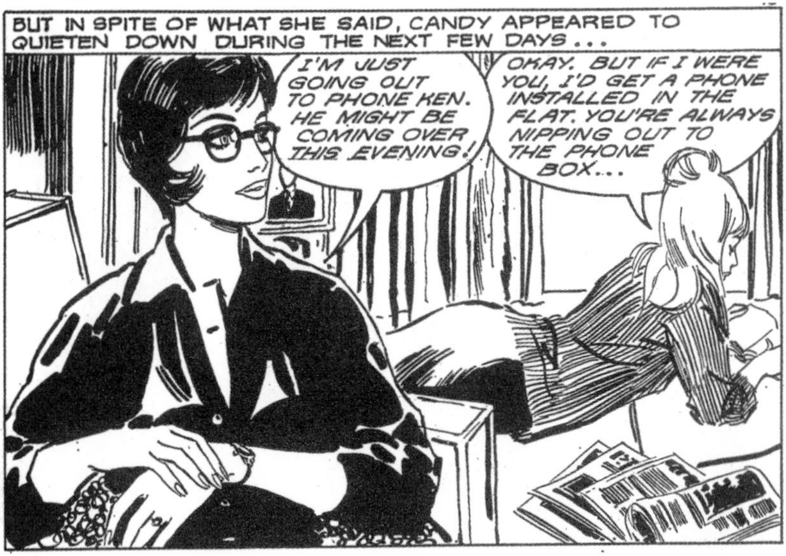
BUT IN SPITE OF WHAT SHE SAID, CANDY APPEARED TO QUIETEN DOWN DURING THE NEXT FEW DAYS...
I'M JUST GOING OUT TO PHONE KEN. HE MIGHT BE COMING OVER THIS EVENING!
OKAY. BUT IF I WERE YOU, I'D GET A PHONE INSTALLED IN THE FLAT. YOU'RE ALWAYS NIPPING OUT TO THE PHONE BOX...

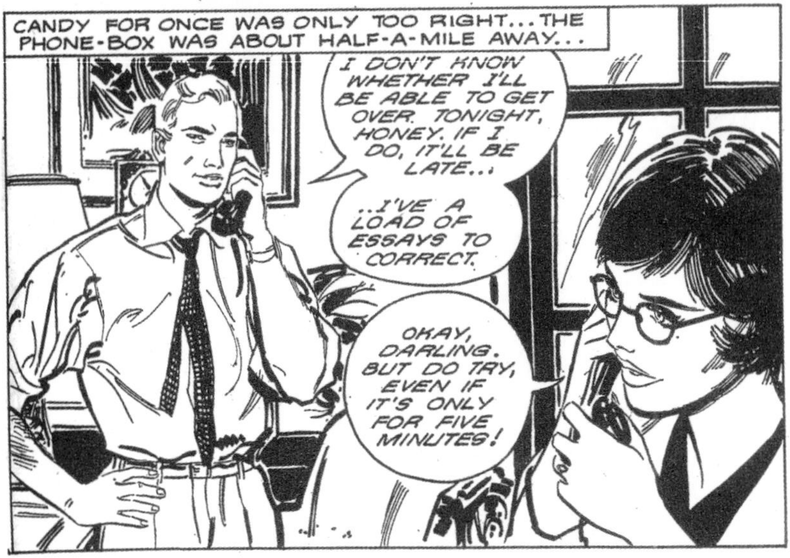
CANDY FOR ONCE WAS ONLY TOO RIGHT... THE PHONE-BOX WAS ABOUT HALF-A-MILE AWAY...
I DON'T KNOW WHETHER I'LL BE ABLE TO GET OVER TONIGHT, HONEY. IF I DO, IT'LL BE LATE...
..I'VE A LOAD OF ESSAYS TO CORRECT.
OKAY, DARLING. BUT DO TRY, EVEN IF IT'S ONLY FOR FIVE MINUTES!

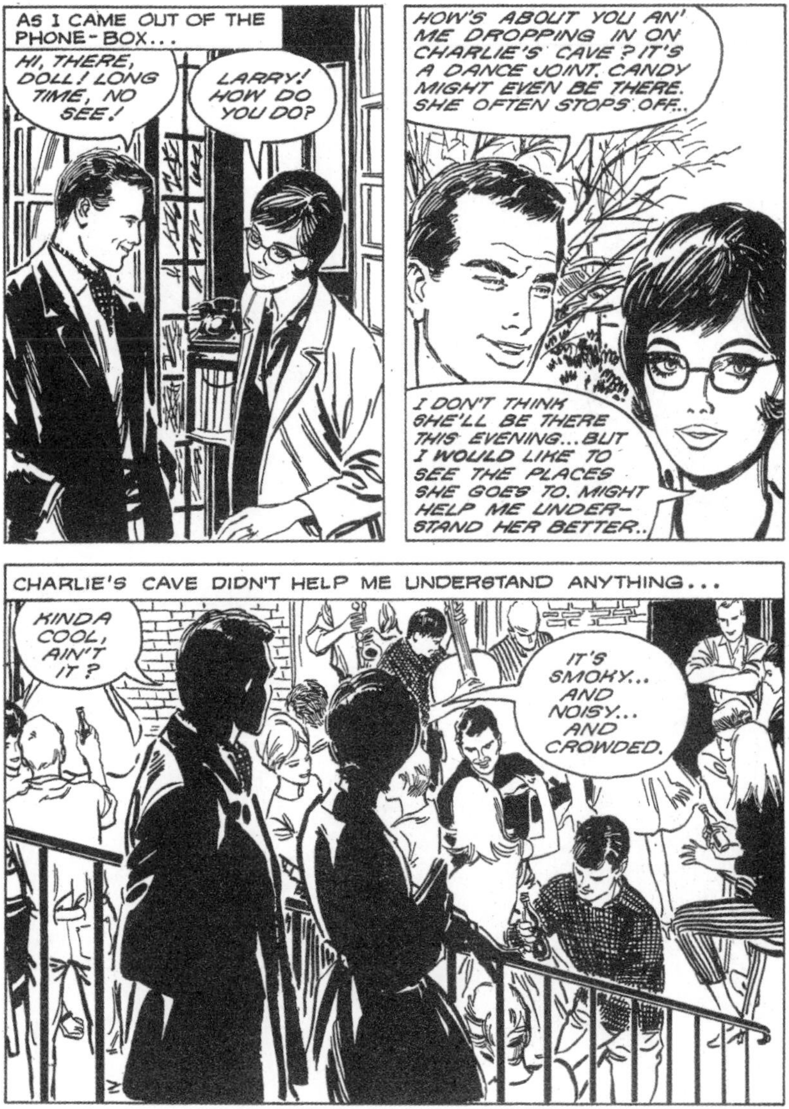
AS I CAME OUT OF THE PHONE-BOX...
HI, THERE, DOLL! LONG TIME, NO SEE!
LARRY! HOW DO YOU DO?
HOW'S ABOUT YOU AN' ME DROPPING IN ON CHARLIE'S CAVE? IT'S A DANCE JOINT. CANDY MIGHT EVEN BE THERE. SHE OFTEN STOPS OFF..
I DON'T THINK SHE'LL BE THERE THIS EVENING...BUT I WOULD LIKE TO SEE THE PLACES SHE GOES TO. MIGHT HELP ME UNDER-STAND HER BETTER..
CHARLIE'S CAVE DIDN'T HELP ME UNDERSTAND ANYTHING...
KINDA COOL, AIN'T IT?
IT'S SMOKY... AND NOISY... AND CROWDED.

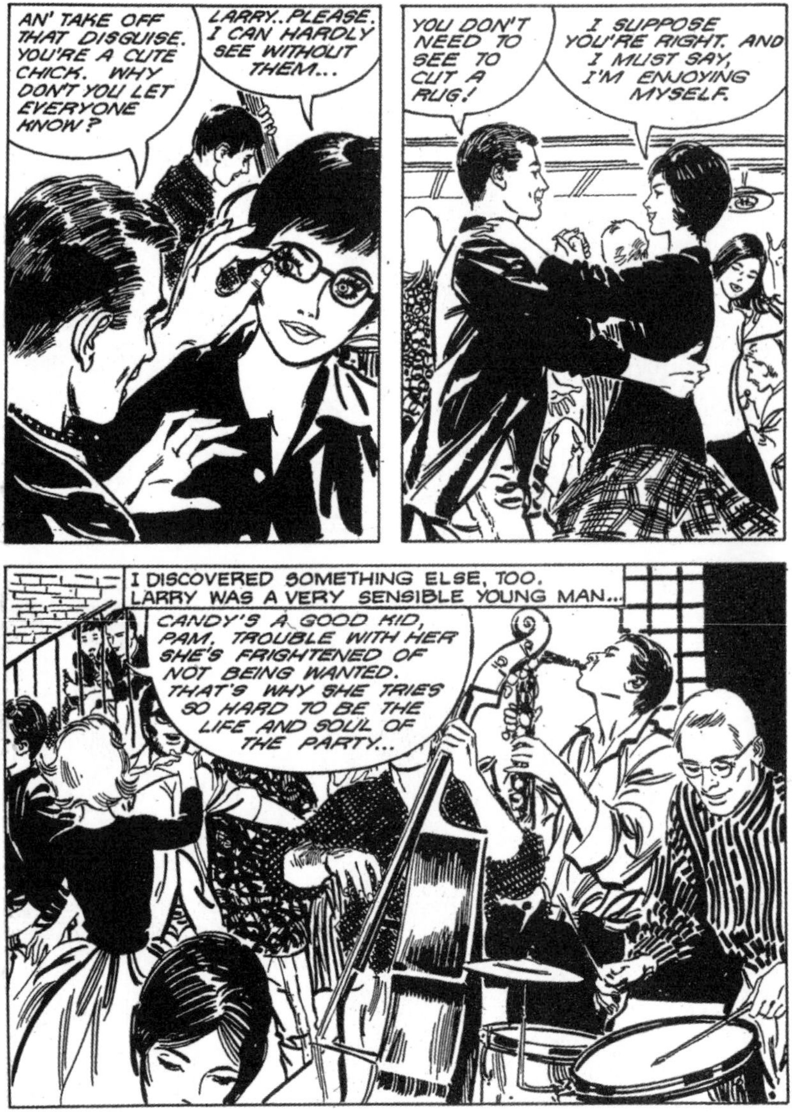
AN' TAKE OFF THAT DISGUISE. YOU'RE A CUTE CHICK. WHY DON'T YOU LET EVERYONE KNOW?
LARRY..PLEASE. I CAN HARDLY SEE WITHOUT THEM...
YOU DON'T NEED TO SEE TO CUT A RUG!
I SUPPOSE YOU'RE RIGHT. AND I MUST SAY, I'M ENJOYING MYSELF.
I DISCOVERED SOMETHING ELSE, TOO. LARRY WAS A VERY SENSIBLE YOUNG MAN...
CANDY'S A GOOD KID, PAM. TROUBLE WITH HER SHE'S FRIGHTENED OF NOT BEING WANTED. THAT'S WHY SHE TRIES SO HARD TO BE THE LIFE AND SOUL OF THE PARTY...

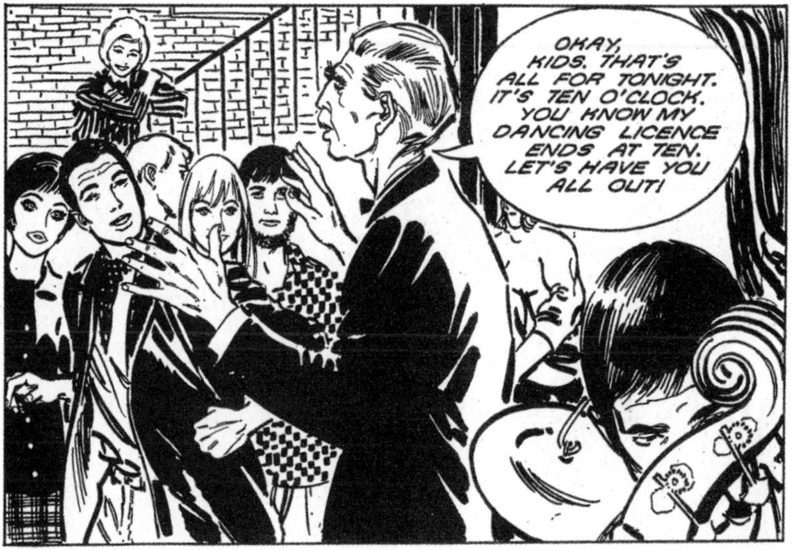
OKAY, KIDS. THAT'S ALL FOR TONIGHT. IT'S TEN O'CLOCK. YOU KNOW MY DANCING LICENCE ENDS AT TEN. LET'S HAVE YOU ALL OUT!

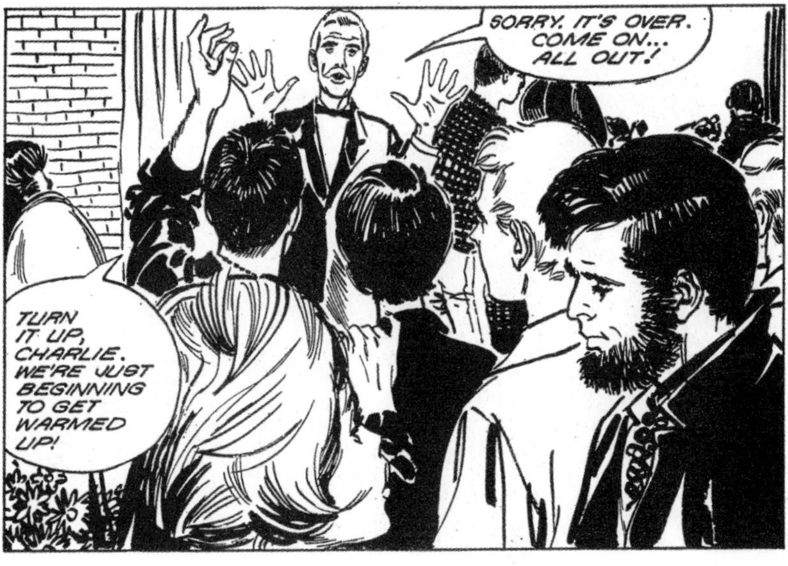
SORRY. IT'S OVER. COME ON... ALL OUT!
TURN IT UP, CHARLIE. WE'RE JUST BEGINNING TO GET WARMED UP!

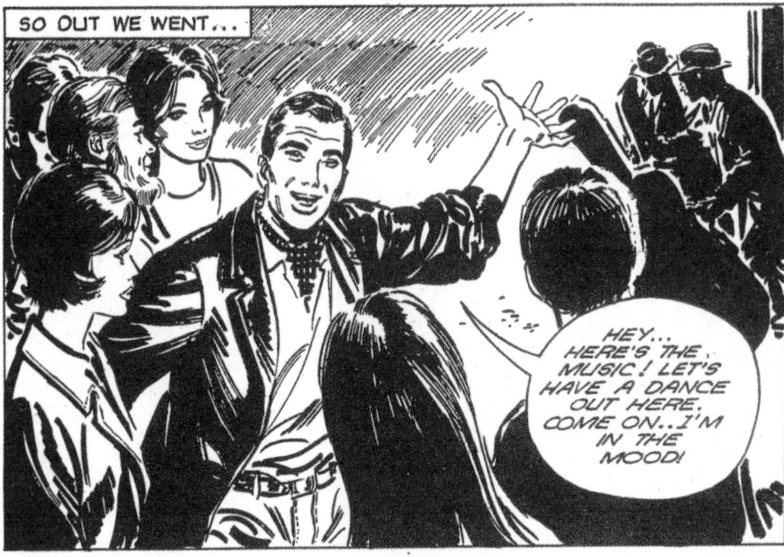
SO OUT WE WENT...
HEY... HERE'S THE MUSIC! LET'S HAVE A DANCE OUT HERE. COME ON..I'M IN THE MOOD!

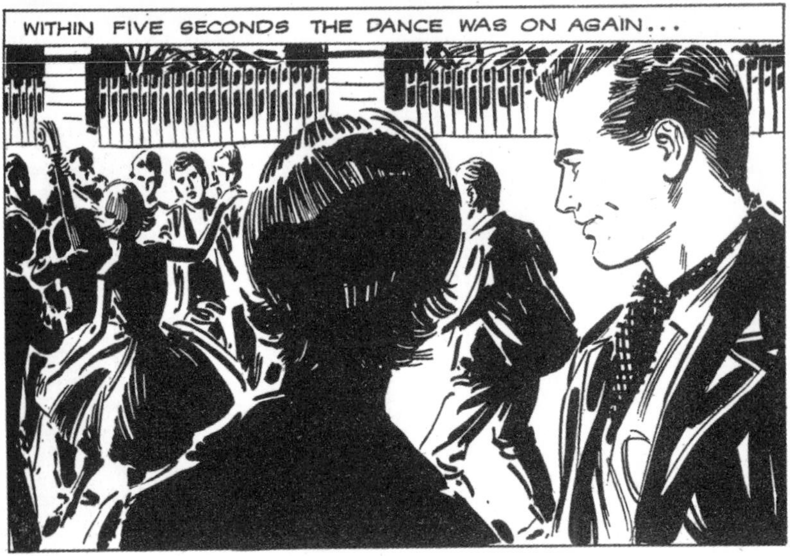
WITHIN FIVE SECONDS THE DANCE WAS ON AGAIN...

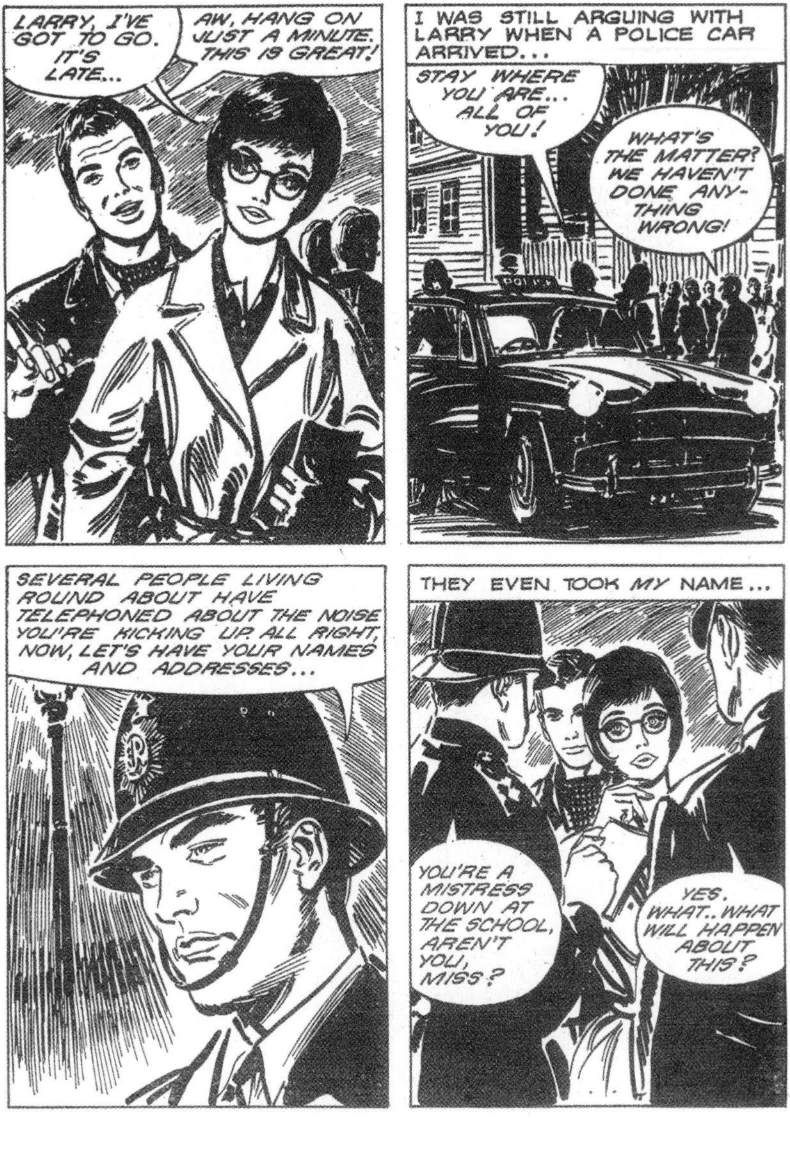
LARRY, I'VE GOT TO GO. IT'S LATE...
AW, HANG ON JUST A MINUTE. THIS IS GREAT!
I WAS STILL ARGUING WITH LARRY WHEN A POLICE CAR ARRIVED...
STAY WHERE YOU ARE... ALL OF YOU!
WHAT'S THE MATTER? WE HAVEN'T DONE ANY-THING WRONG!
SEVERAL PEOPLE LIVING ROUND ABOUT HAVE TELEPHONED ABOUT THE NOISE YOU'RE KICKING UP. ALL RIGHT, NOW, LET'S HAVE YOUR NAMES AND ADDRESSES...
THEY EVEN TOOK MY NAME...
YOU'RE A MISTRESS DOWN AT THE SCHOOL, AREN'T YOU, MISS?
YES. WHAT.. WHAT WILL HAPPEN ABOUT THIS?

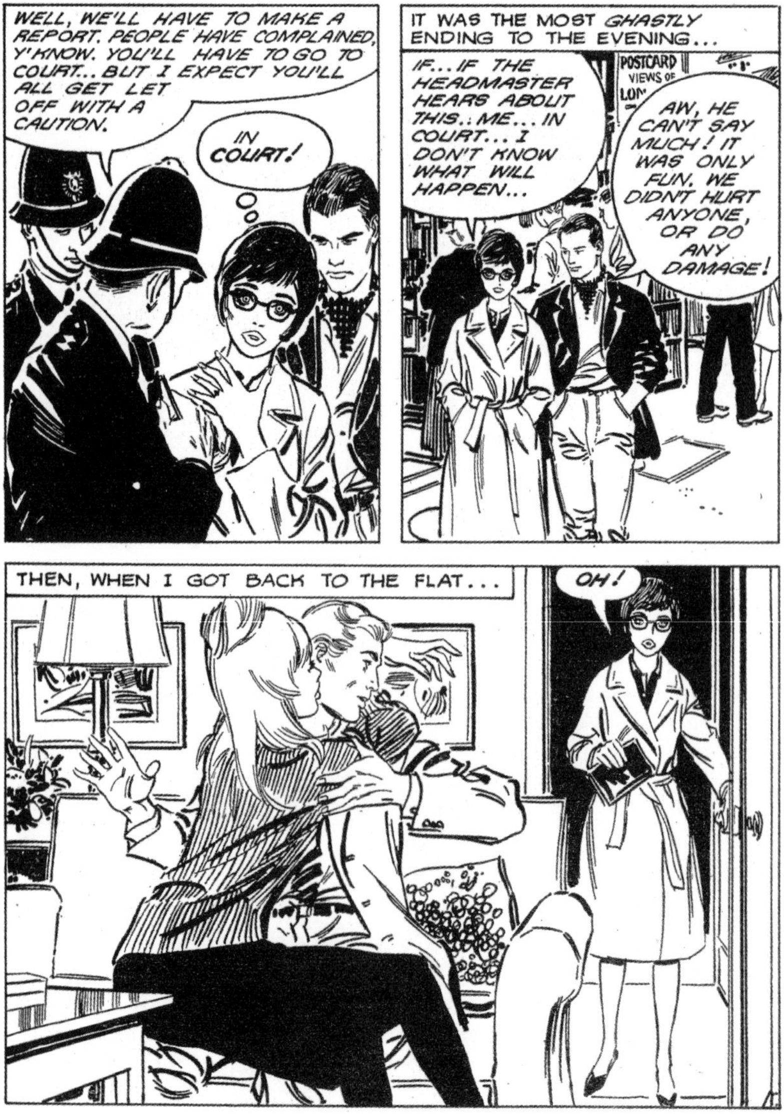
WELL, WE'LL HAVE TO MAKE A REPORT. PEOPLE HAVE COMPLAINED, Y'KNOW. YOU'LL HAVE TO GO TO COURT... BUT I EXPECT YOU'LL ALL GET LET OFF WITH A CAUTION.
IN COURT!
IT WAS THE MOST GHASTLY ENDING TO THE EVENING...
IF... IF THE HEADMASTER HEARS ABOUT THIS.. ME... IN COURT... I DON'T KNOW WHAT WILL HAPPEN...
POSTCARD
AW, HE CAN'T SAY MUCH! IT WAS ONLY FUN. WE DIDN'T HURT ANYONE, OR DO ANY DAMAGE!
THEN, WHEN I GOT BACK TO THE FLAT...
OH!

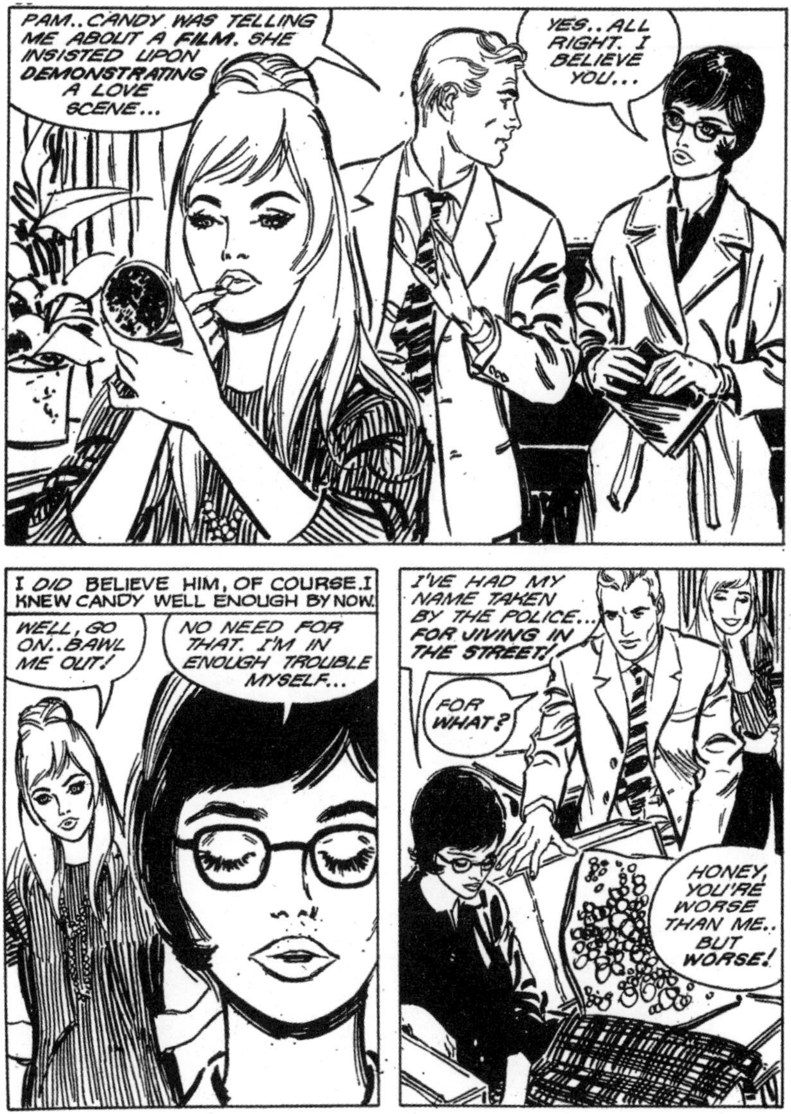
PAM..CANDY WAS TELLING ME ABOUT A FILM. SHE INSISTED UPON DEMONSTRATING A LOVE SCENE...
YES..ALL RIGHT. I BELIEVE YOU...
I DID BELIEVE HIM, OF COURSE. I KNEW CANDY WELL ENOUGH BY NOW.
WELL, GO ON..BAWL ME OUT!
NO NEED FOR THAT. I'M IN ENOUGH TROUBLE MYSELF...
I'VE HAD MY NAME TAKEN BY THE POLICE... FOR JIVING IN THE STREET!
FOR WHAT?
HONEY, YOU'RE WORSE THAN ME.. BUT WORSE!

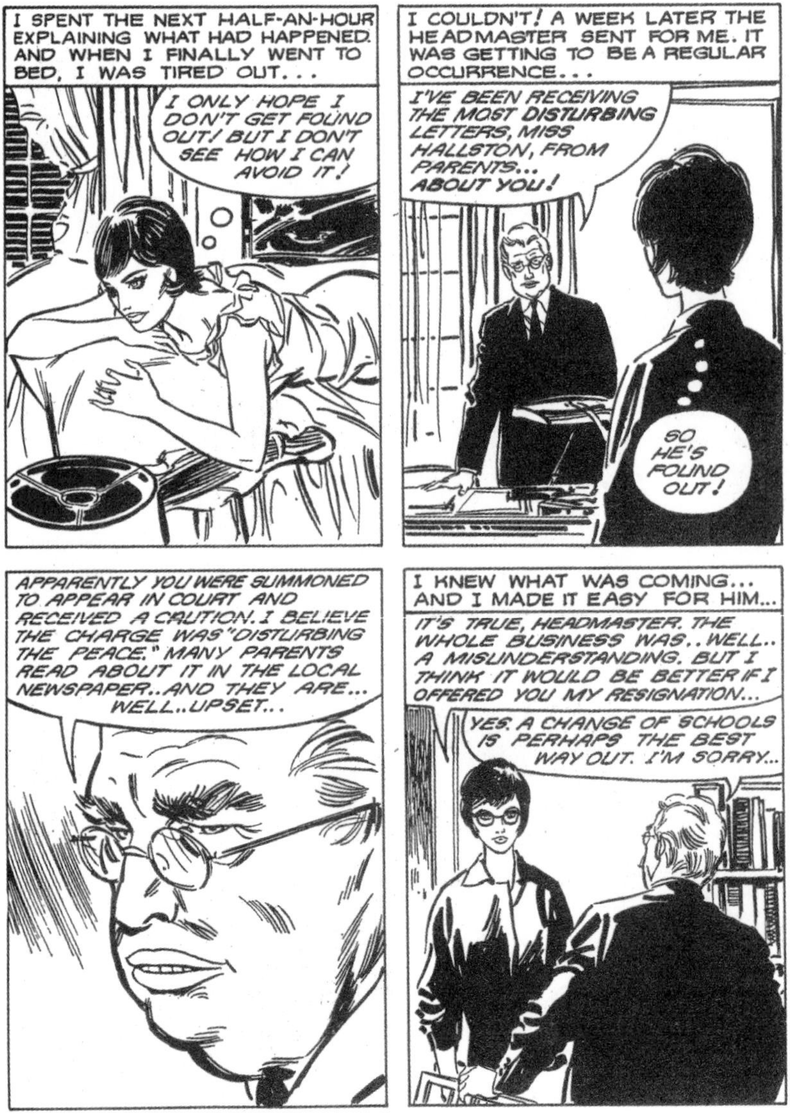
I SPENT THE NEXT HALF-AN-HOUR EXPLAINING WHAT HAD HAPPENED. AND WHEN I FINALLY WENT TO BED, I WAS TIRED OUT...
I ONLY HOPE I DON'T GET FOUND OUT! BUT I DON'T SEE HOW I CAN AVOID IT!
I COULDN'T! A WEEK LATER THE HEADMASTER SENT FOR ME. IT WAS GETTING TO BE A REGULAR OCCURRENCE...
I'VE BEEN RECEIVING THE MOST DISTURBING LETTERS, MISS HALLSTON, FROM PARENTS... ABOUT YOU!
SO HE'S FOUND OUT!
APPARENTLY YOU WERE SUMMONED TO APPEAR IN COURT AND RECEIVED A CAUTION. I BELIEVE THE CHARGE WAS "DISTURBING THE PEACE." MANY PARENTS READ ABOUT IT IN THE LOCAL NEWSPAPER.. AND THEY ARE... WELL.. UPSET...
I KNEW WHAT WAS COMING... AND I MADE IT EASY FOR HIM...
IT'S TRUE, HEADMASTER. THE WHOLE BUSINESS WAS.. WELL.. A MISUNDERSTANDING. BUT I THINK IT WOULD BE BETTER IF I OFFERED YOU MY RESIGNATION...
YES. A CHANGE OF SCHOOLS IS PERHAPS THE BEST WAY OUT. I'M SORRY...

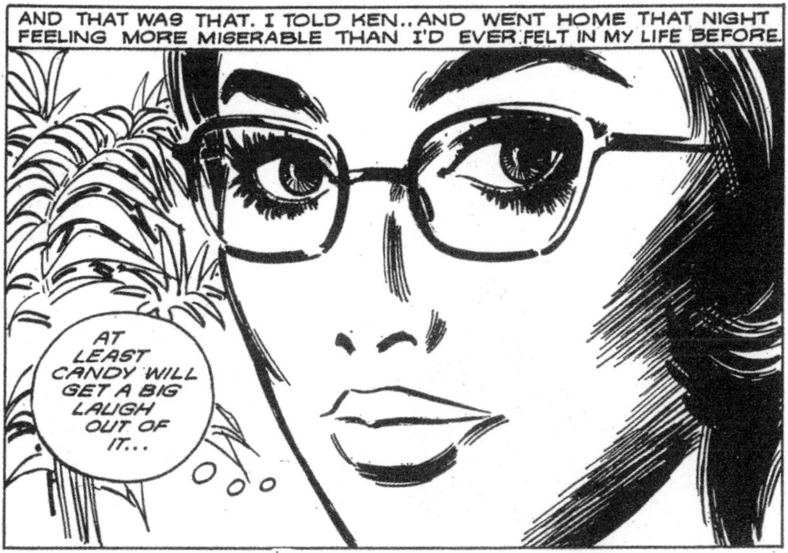
AND THAT WAS THAT. I TOLD KEN.. AND WENT HOME THAT NIGHT FEELING MORE MISERABLE THAN I'D EVER FELT IN MY LIFE BEFORE.
AT LEAST CANDY WILL GET A BIG LAUGH OUT OF IT...

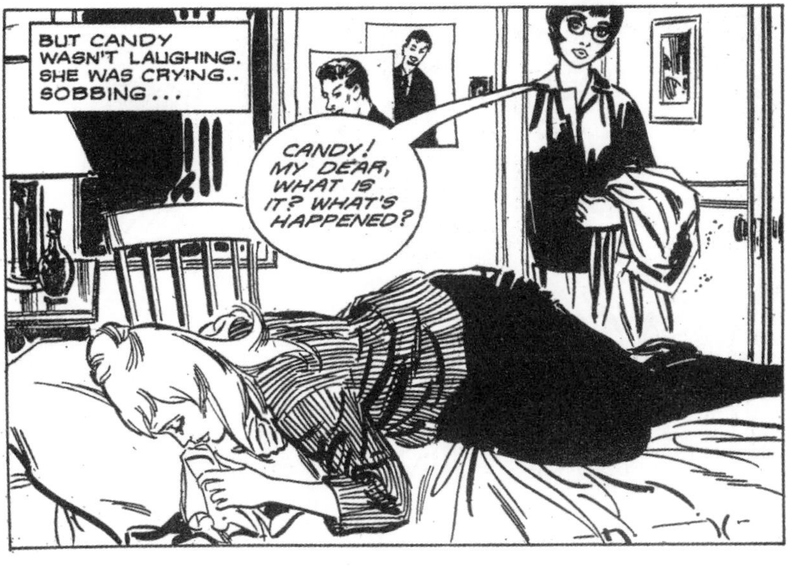
BUT CANDY WASN'T LAUGHING. SHE WAS CRYING.. SOBBING...
CANDY! MY DEAR, WHAT IS IT? WHAT'S HAPPENED?

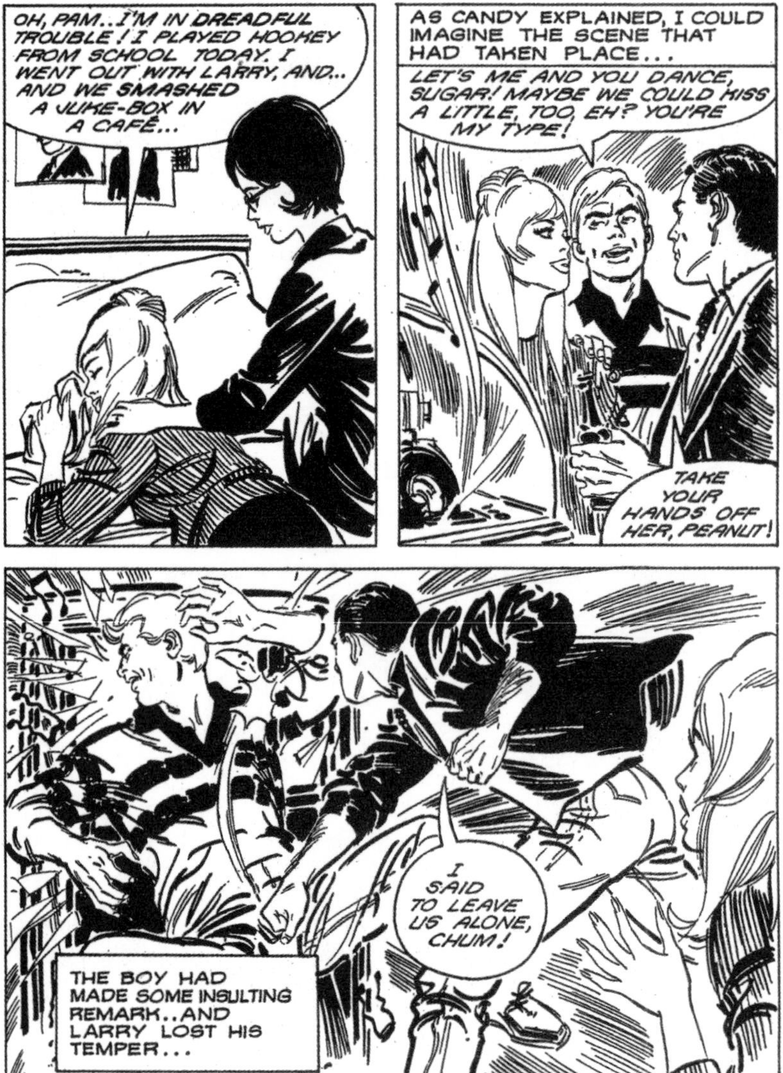
OH, PAM..I'M IN DREADFUL TROUBLE! I PLAYED HOOKEY FROM SCHOOL TODAY. I WENT OUT WITH LARRY, AND... AND WE SMASHED A JUKE-BOX IN A CAFÉ...
AS CANDY EXPLAINED, I COULD IMAGINE THE SCENE THAT HAD TAKEN PLACE...
LET'S ME AND YOU DANCE, SUGAR! MAYBE WE COULD KISS A LITTLE, TOO, EH? YOU'RE MY TYPE!
TAKE YOUR HANDS OFF HER, PEANUT!
I SAID TO LEAVE US ALONE, CHUM!
THE BOY HAD MADE SOME INSULTING REMARK..AND LARRY LOST HIS TEMPER...

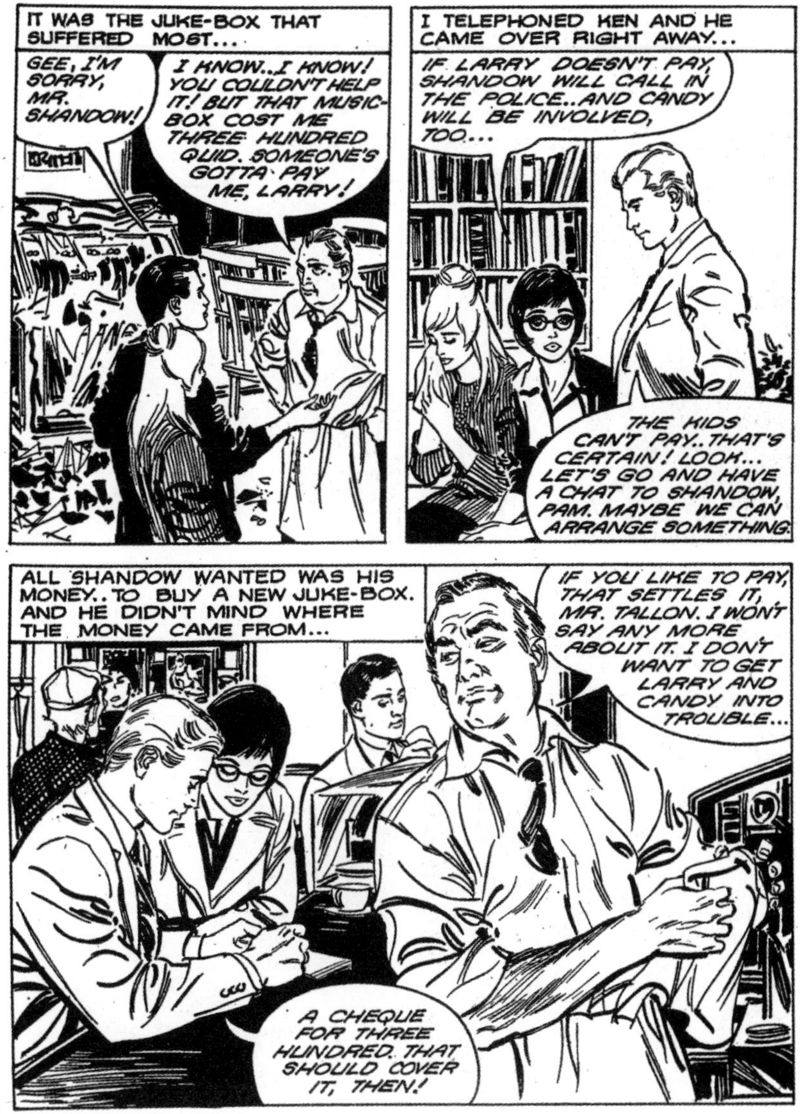
IT WAS THE JUKE-BOX THAT SUFFERED MOST...
GEE, I'M SORRY, MR. SHANDOW!
I KNOW..I KNOW! YOU COULDN'T HELP IT! BUT THAT MUSIC-BOX COST ME THREE HUNDRED QUID. SOMEONE'S GOTTA PAY ME, LARRY!
I TELEPHONED KEN AND HE CAME OVER RIGHT AWAY...
IF LARRY DOESN'T PAY, SHANDOW WILL CALL IN THE POLICE..AND CANDY WILL BE INVOLVED, TOO...
THE KIDS CAN'T PAY..THAT'S CERTAIN! LOOK... LET'S GO AND HAVE A CHAT TO SHANDOW, PAM. MAYBE WE CAN ARRANGE SOMETHING.
ALL SHANDOW WANTED WAS HIS MONEY..TO BUY A NEW JUKE-BOX. AND HE DIDN'T MIND WHERE THE MONEY CAME FROM...
IF YOU LIKE TO PAY, THAT SETTLES IT, MR. TALLON. I WON'T SAY ANY MORE ABOUT IT. I DON'T WANT TO GET LARRY AND CANDY INTO TROUBLE...
A CHEQUE FOR THREE HUNDRED. THAT SHOULD COVER IT, THEN!

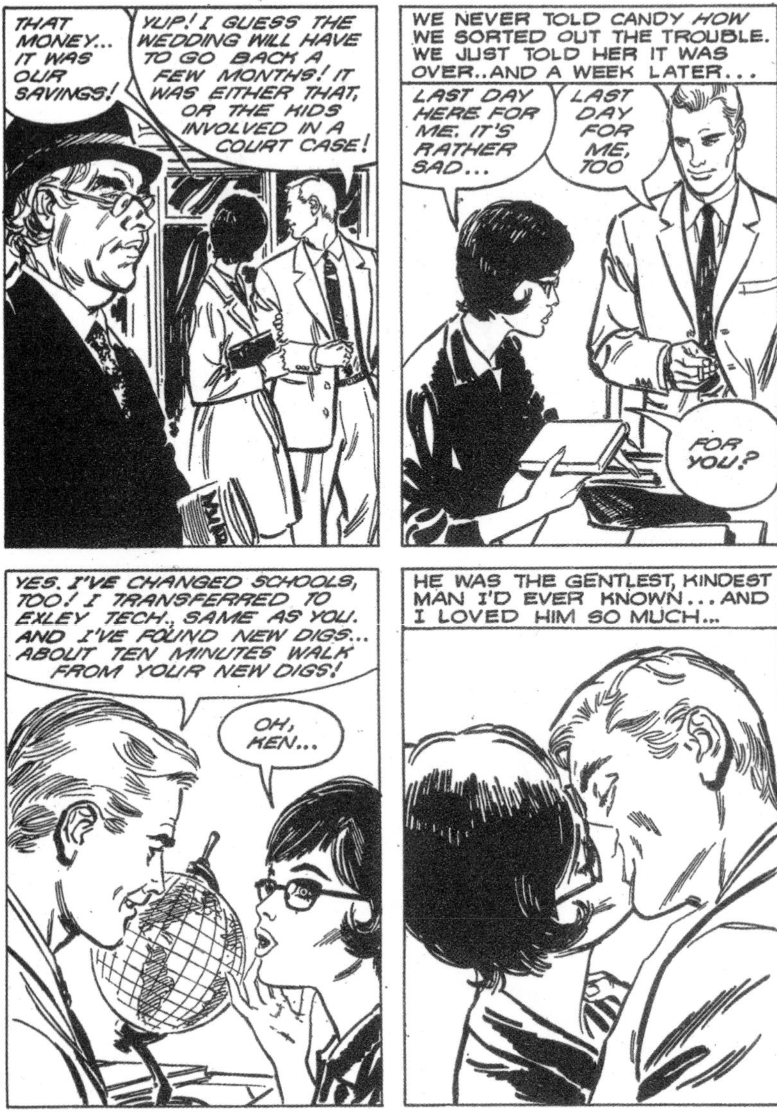
THAT MONEY... IT WAS OUR SAVINGS!
YUP! I GUESS THE WEDDING WILL HAVE TO GO BACK A FEW MONTHS! IT WAS EITHER THAT, OR THE KIDS INVOLVED IN A COURT CASE!
WE NEVER TOLD CANDY HOW WE SORTED OUT THE TROUBLE. WE JUST TOLD HER IT WAS OVER..AND A WEEK LATER...
LAST DAY HERE FOR ME. IT'S RATHER SAD...
LAST DAY FOR ME, TOO
FOR YOU?
YES. I'VE CHANGED SCHOOLS, TOO! I TRANSFERRED TO EXLEY TECH., SAME AS YOU. AND I'VE FOUND NEW DIGS... ABOUT TEN MINUTES WALK FROM YOUR NEW DIGS!
OH, KEN...
HE WAS THE GENTLEST, KINDEST MAN I'D EVER KNOWN... AND I LOVED HIM SO MUCH...

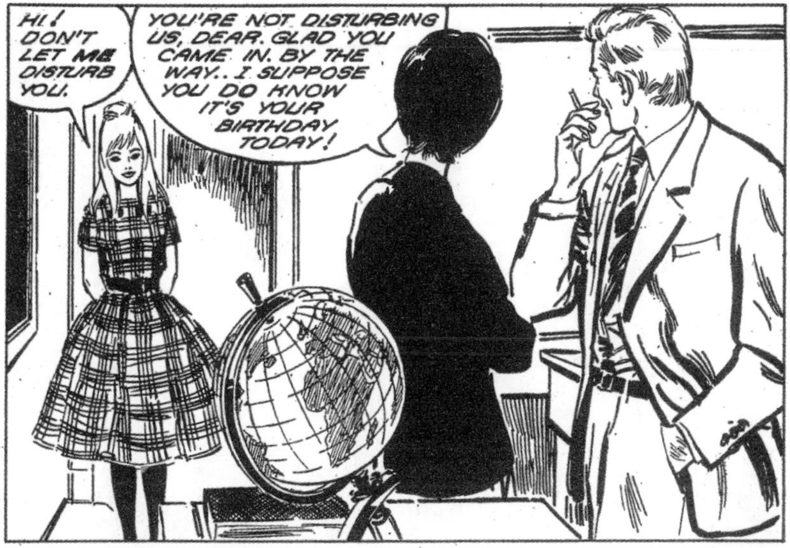
HI! DON'T LET ME DISTURB YOU.
YOU'RE NOT DISTURBING US, DEAR. GLAD YOU CAME IN. BY THE WAY.. I SUPPOSE YOU DO KNOW IT'S YOUR BIRTHDAY TODAY!

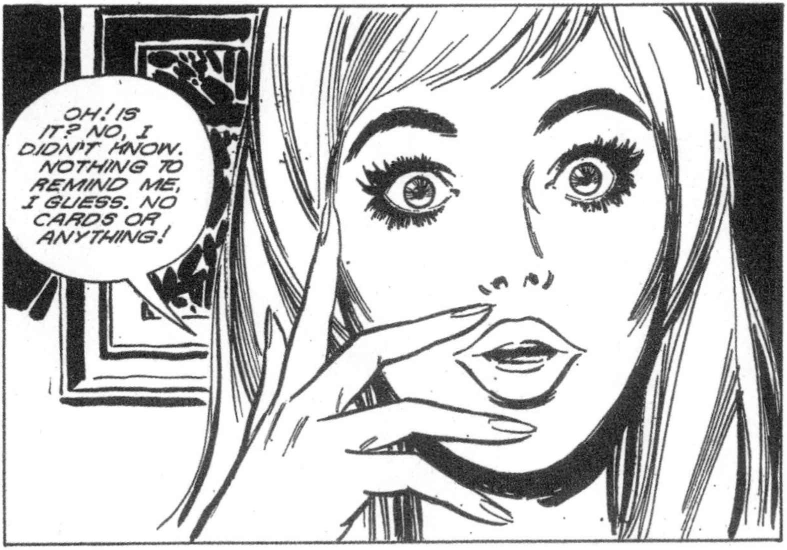
OH! IS IT? NO, I DIDN'T KNOW. NOTHING TO REMIND ME, I GUESS. NO CARDS OR ANYTHING!

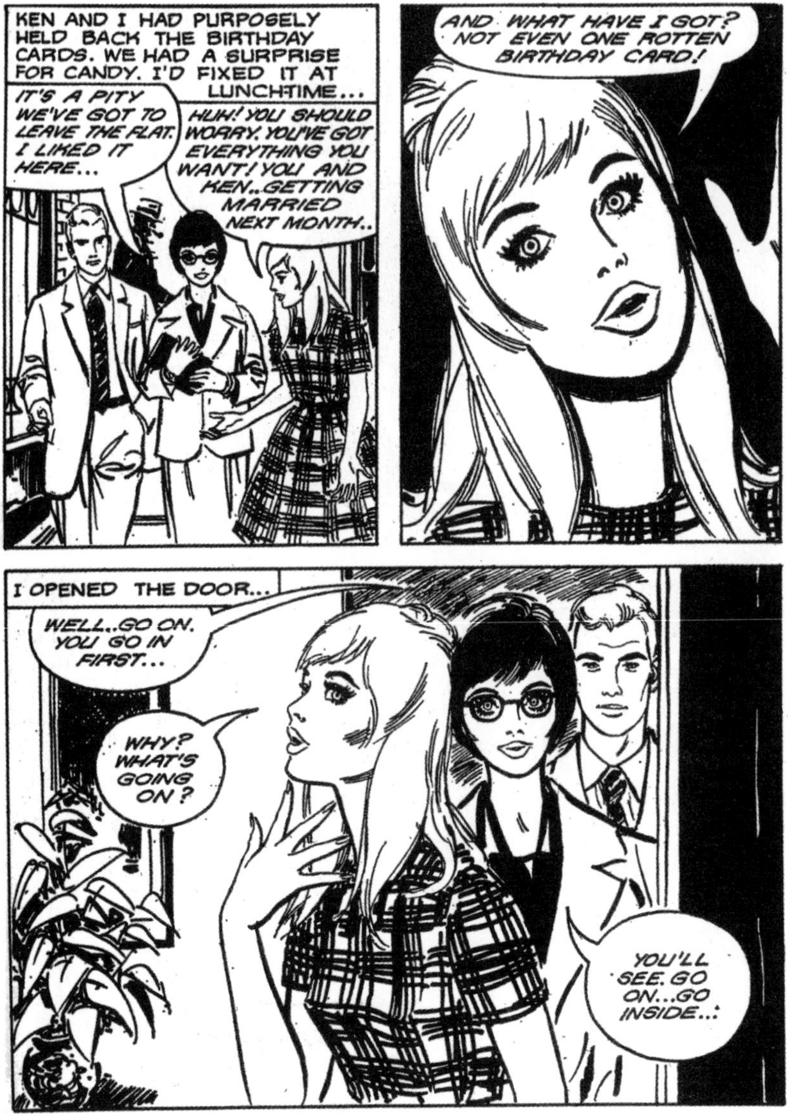
KEN AND I HAD PURPOSELY HELD BACK THE BIRTHDAY CARDS. WE HAD A SURPRISE FOR CANDY. I'D FIXED IT AT LUNCHTIME...
IT'S A PITY WE'VE GOT TO LEAVE THE FLAT. I LIKED IT HERE...
HUH! YOU SHOULD WORRY. YOU'VE GOT EVERYTHING YOU WANT! YOU AND KEN..GETTING MARRIED NEXT MONTH..
AND WHAT HAVE I GOT? NOT EVEN ONE ROTTEN BIRTHDAY CARD!
I OPENED THE DOOR...
WELL..GO ON. YOU GO IN FIRST...
WHY? WHAT'S GOING ON?
YOU'LL SEE. GO ON...GO INSIDE..!

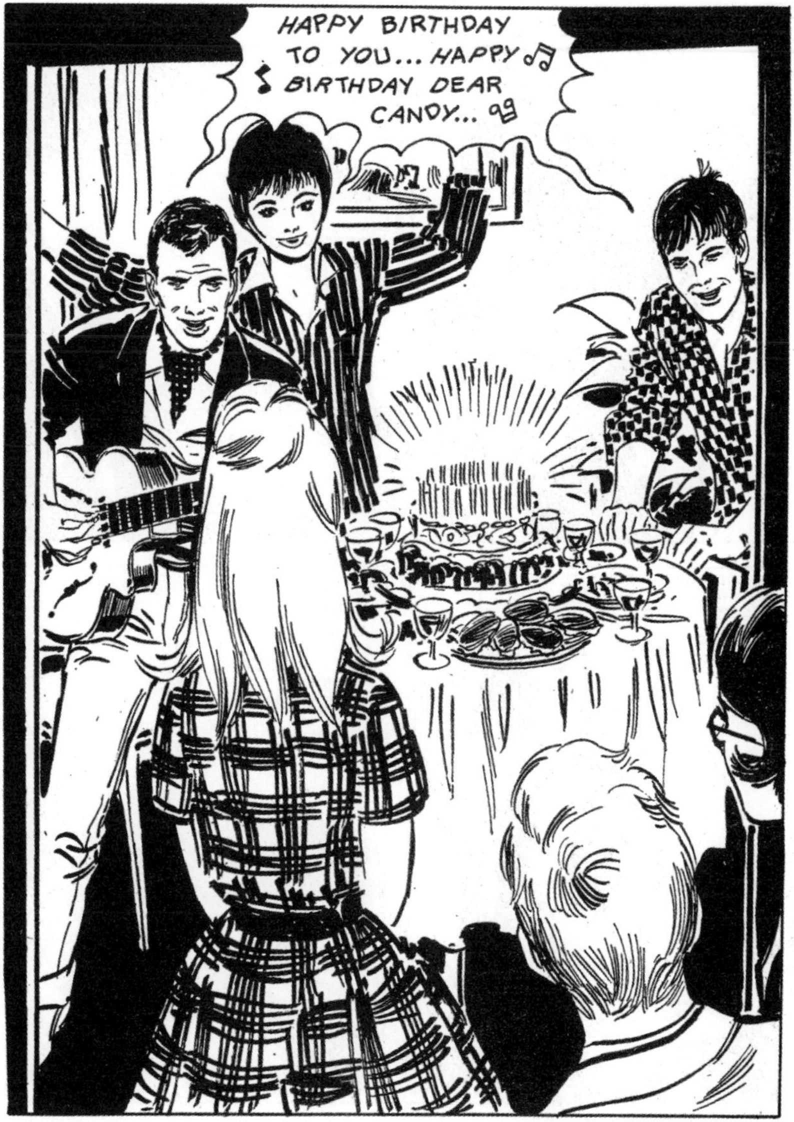
HAPPY BIRTHDAY TO YOU... HAPPY BIRTHDAY DEAR CANDY...

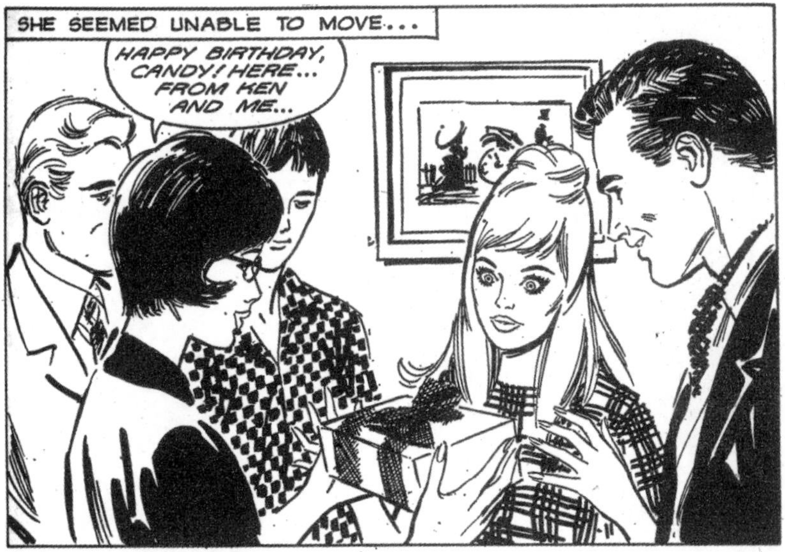
SHE SEEMED UNABLE TO MOVE...
HAPPY BIRTHDAY, CANDY! HERE... FROM KEN AND ME...

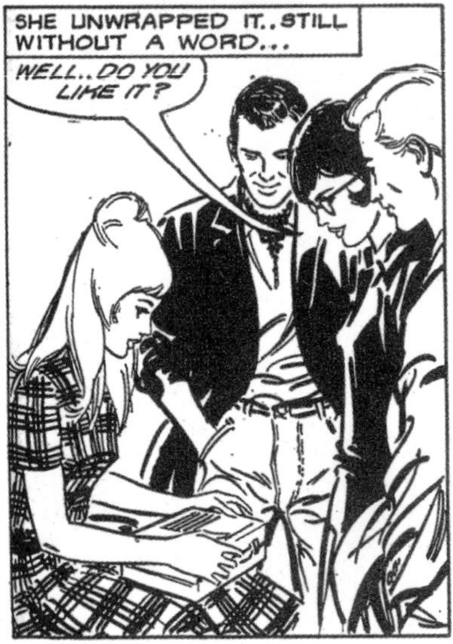
SHE UNWRAPPED IT..STILL WITHOUT A WORD...
WELL..DO YOU LIKE IT?

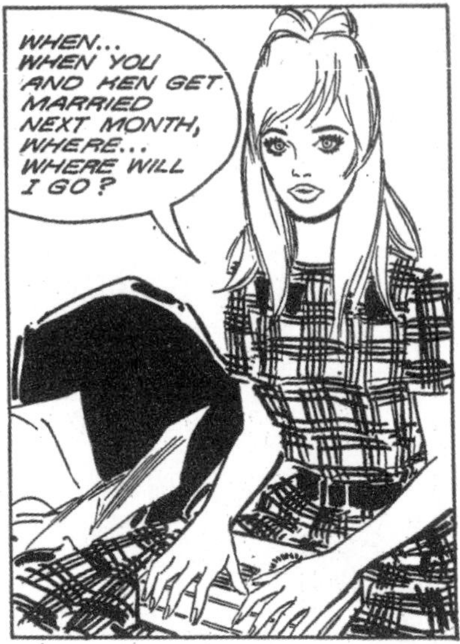
WHEN... WHEN YOU AND KEN GET MARRIED NEXT MONTH, WHERE... WHERE WILL I GO?

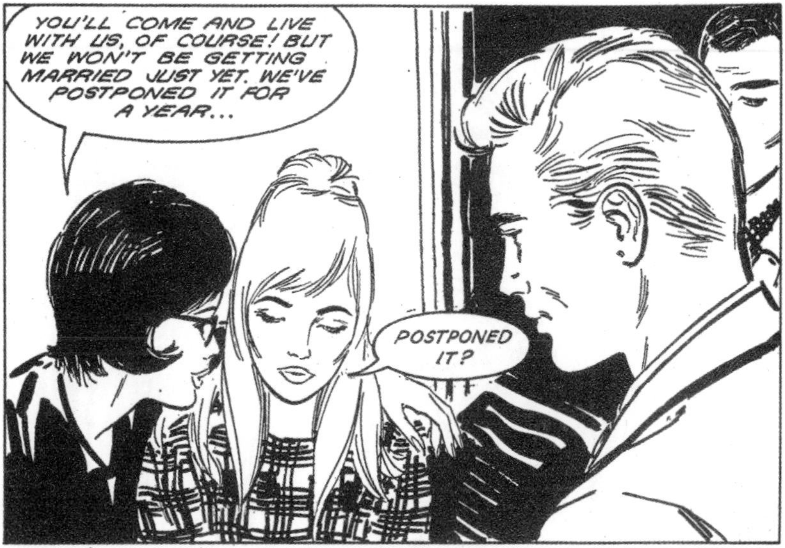
YOU'LL COME AND LIVE WITH US, OF COURSE! BUT WE WON'T BE GETTING MARRIED JUST YET. WE'VE POSTPONED IT FOR A YEAR...
POSTPONED IT?

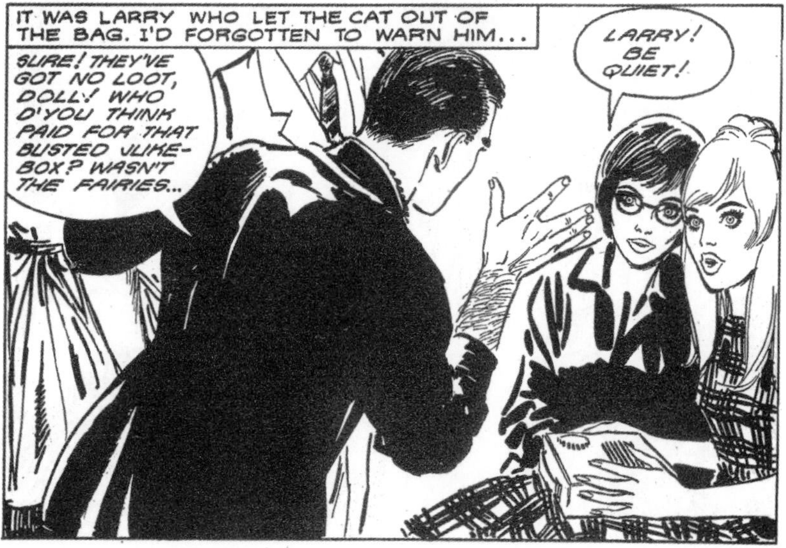
IT WAS LARRY WHO LET THE CAT OUT OF THE BAG. I'D FORGOTTEN TO WARN HIM...
SURE! THEY'VE GOT NO LOOT, DOLL! WHO D'YOU THINK PAID FOR THAT BUSTED JUKE-BOX? WASN'T THE FAIRIES...
LARRY! BE QUIET!

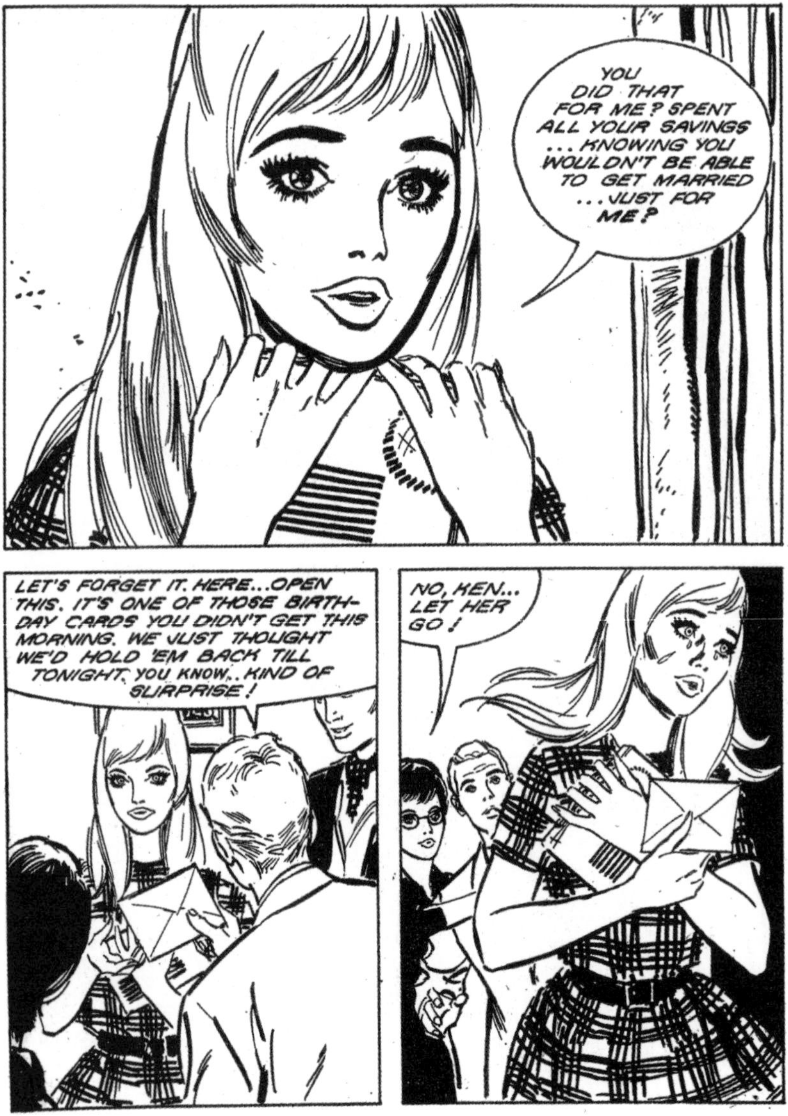
YOU DID THAT FOR ME? SPENT ALL YOUR SAVINGS ... KNOWING YOU WOULDN'T BE ABLE TO GET MARRIED ... JUST FOR ME?
LET'S FORGET IT. HERE...OPEN THIS. IT'S ONE OF THOSE BIRTH-DAY CARDS YOU DIDN'T GET THIS MORNING. WE JUST THOUGHT WE'D HOLD 'EM BACK TILL TONIGHT. YOU KNOW.. KIND OF SURPRISE!
NO, KEN... LET HER GO!

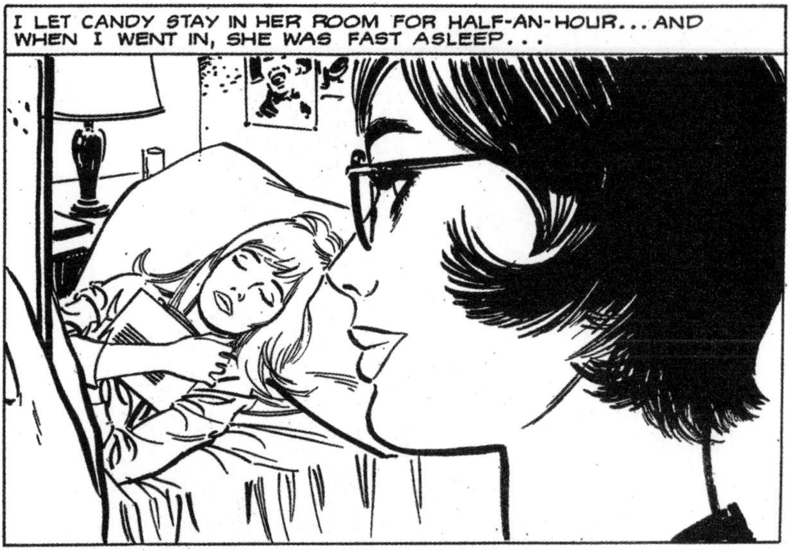
I LET CANDY STAY IN HER ROOM FOR HALF-AN-HOUR... AND WHEN I WENT IN, SHE WAS FAST ASLEEP...

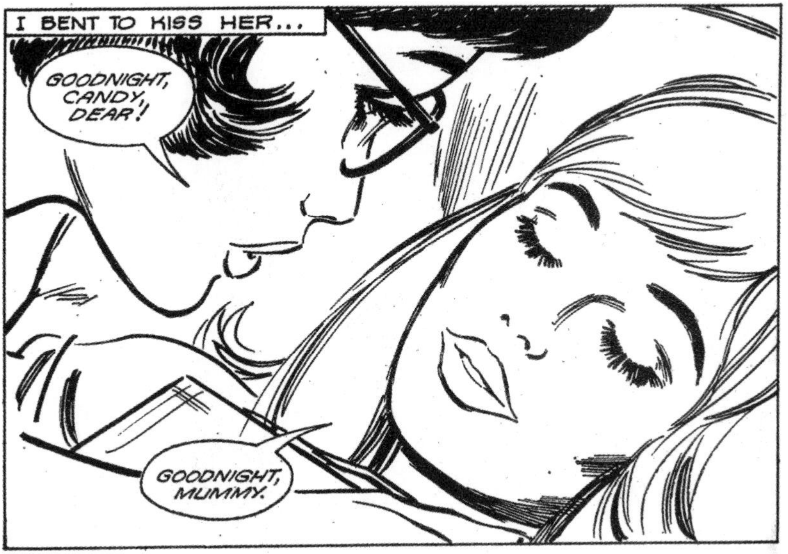
I BENT TO KISS HER...
GOODNIGHT, CANDY, DEAR!
GOODNIGHT, MUMMY.

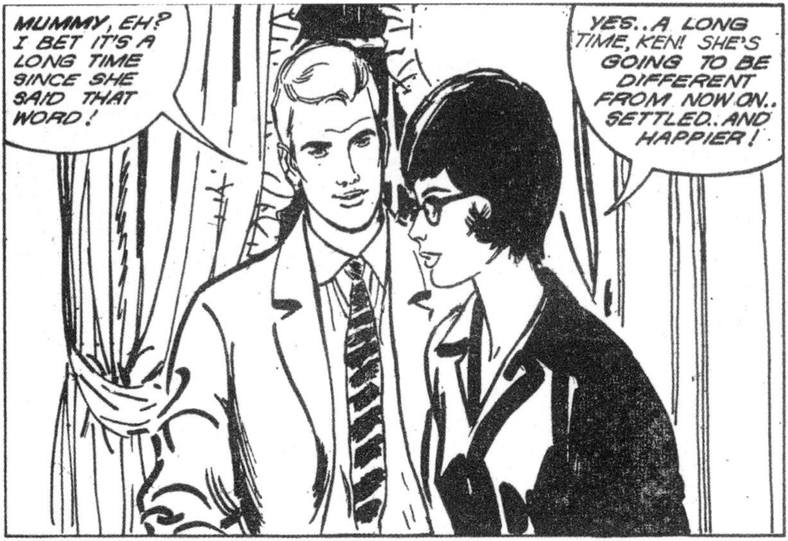
MUMMY, EH? I BET IT'S A LONG TIME SINCE SHE SAID THAT WORD!
YES..A LONG TIME, KEN! SHE'S GOING TO BE DIFFERENT FROM NOW ON.. SETTLED..AND HAPPIER!

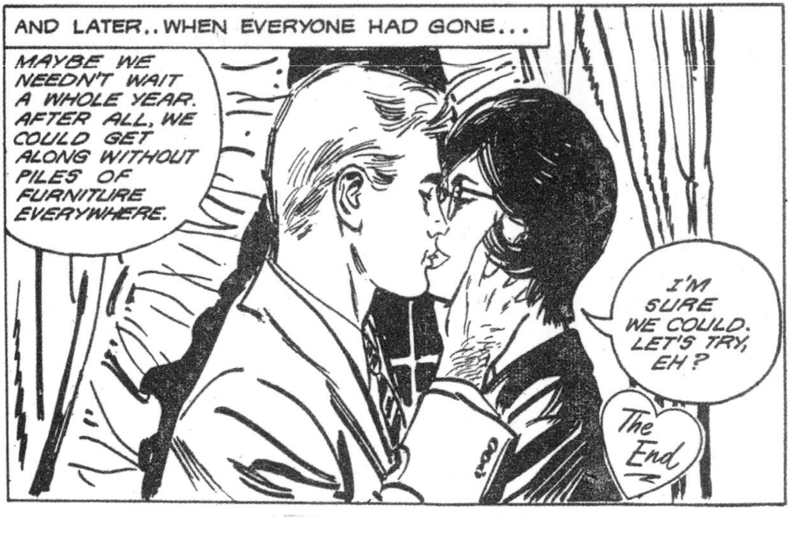
AND LATER..WHEN EVERYONE HAD GONE...
MAYBE WE NEEDN'T WAIT A WHOLE YEAR. AFTER ALL, WE COULD GET ALONG WITHOUT PILES OF FURNITURE EVERYWHERE.
I'M SURE WE COULD. LET'S TRY, EH?
The End

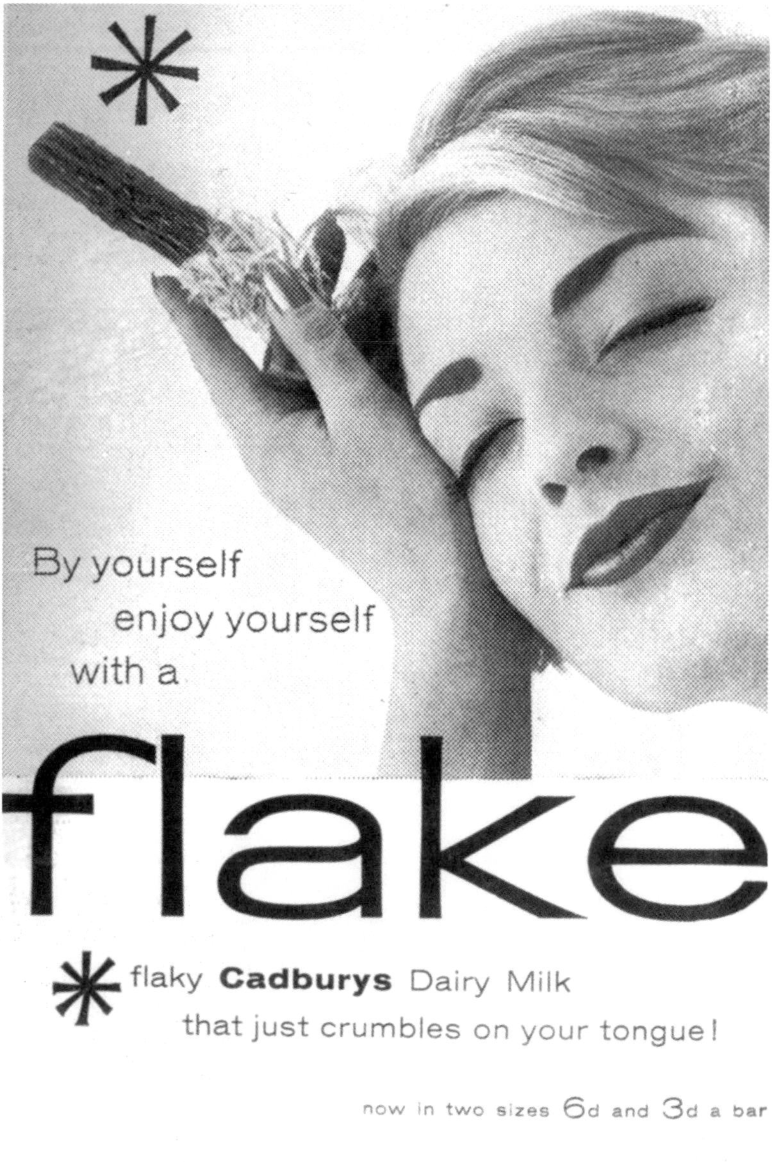
By yourself
enjoy yourself
with a
flake
flaky Cadburys Dairy Milk
that just crumbles on your tongue!
now in two sizes 6d and 3d a bar

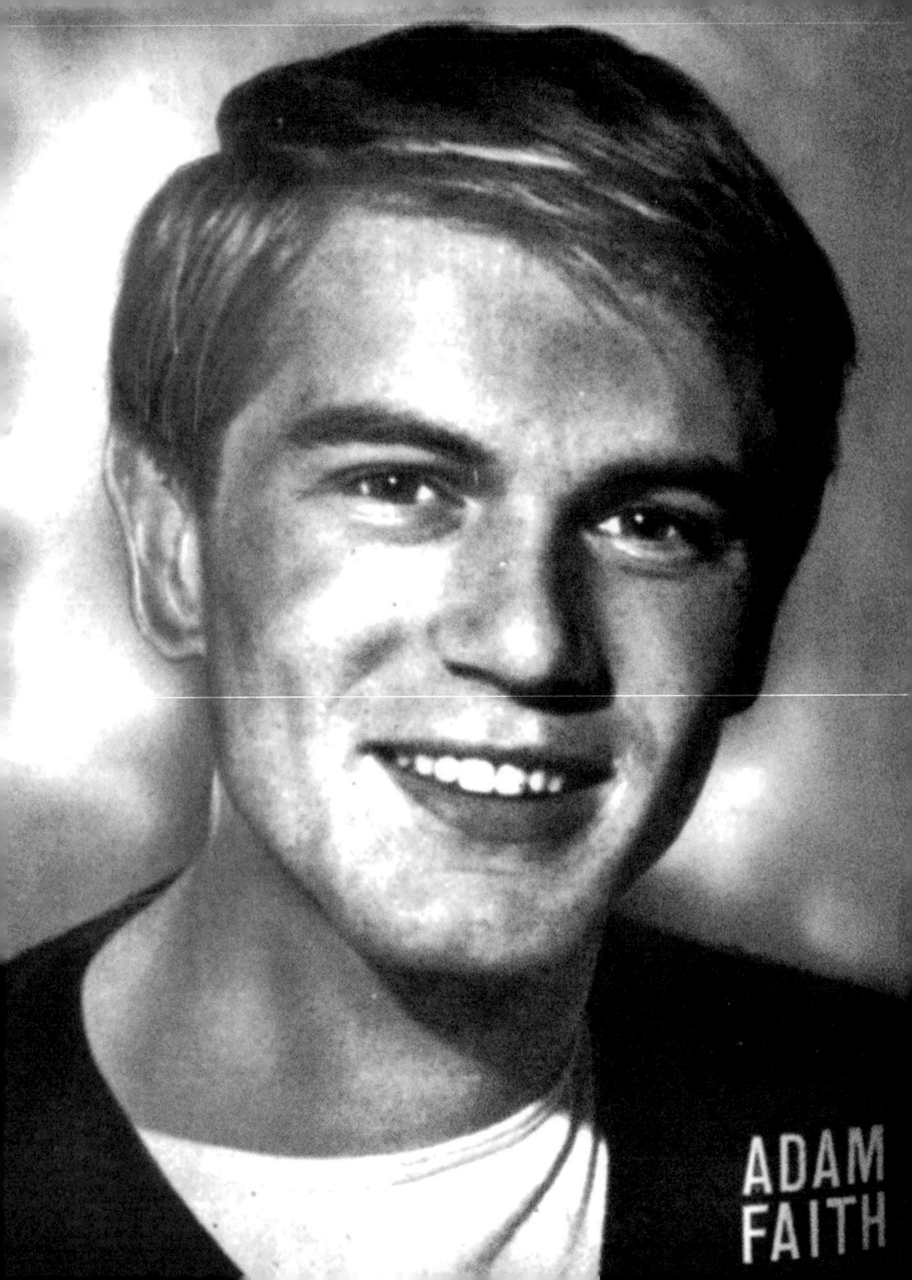
ADAM
FAITH

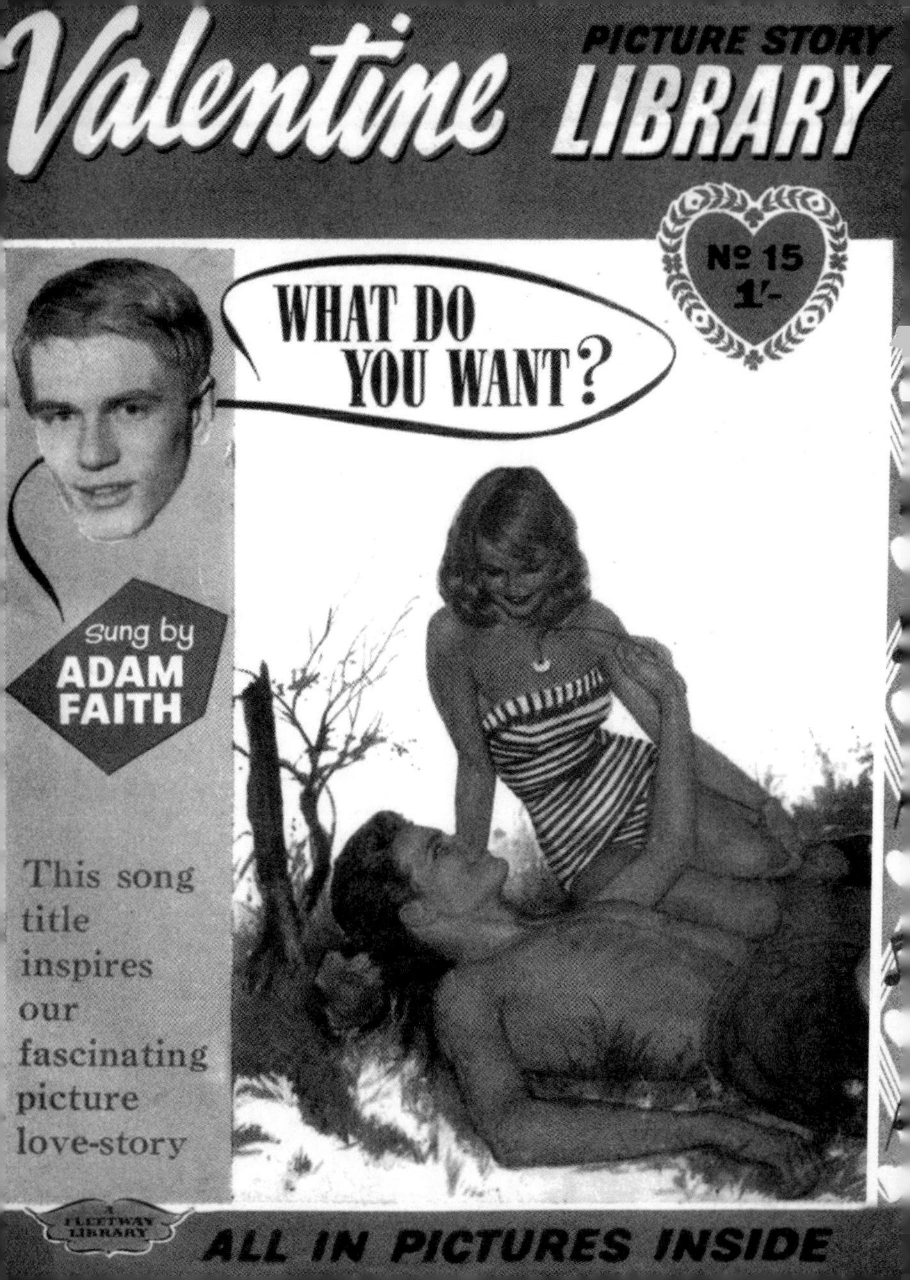
Valentine
PICTURE STORY LIBRARY
No 15
1/-
WHAT DO YOU WANT?
Sung by ADAM FAITH
This song title inspires our fascinating picture love-story
A FLEETWAY LIBRARY
ALL IN PICTURES INSIDE

What Do You Want?

a gay picture-story inspired by this intriguing song title

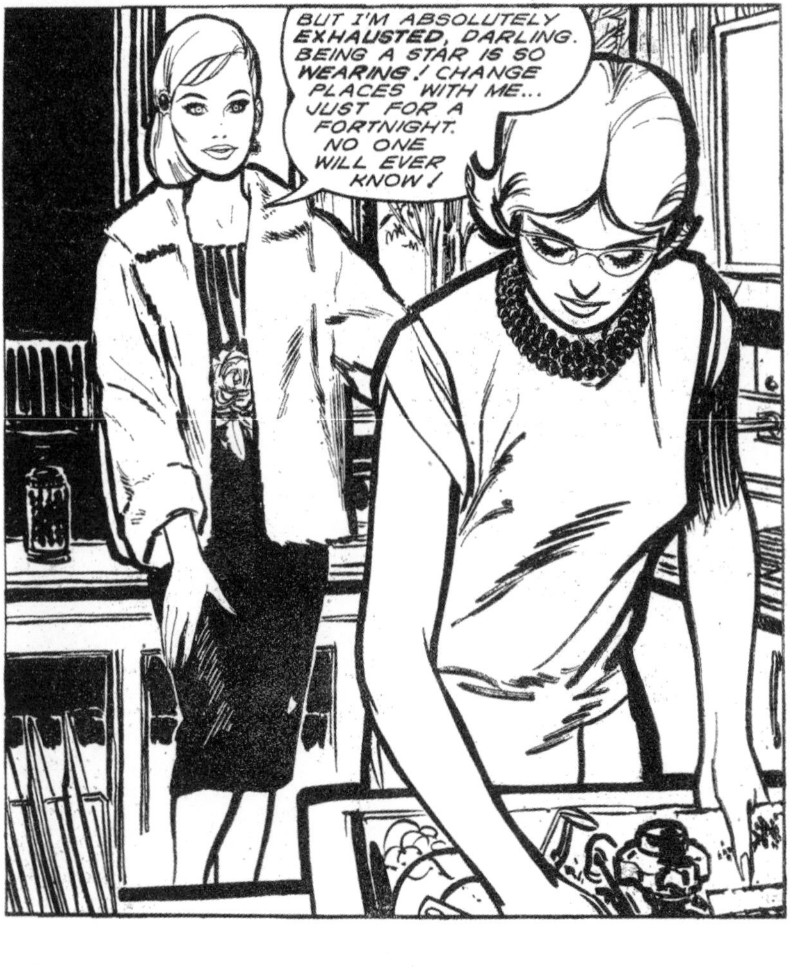
BUT I'M ABSOLUTELY EXHAUSTED, DARLING. BEING A STAR IS SO WEARING! CHANGE PLACES WITH ME... JUST FOR A FORTNIGHT. NO ONE WILL EVER KNOW!

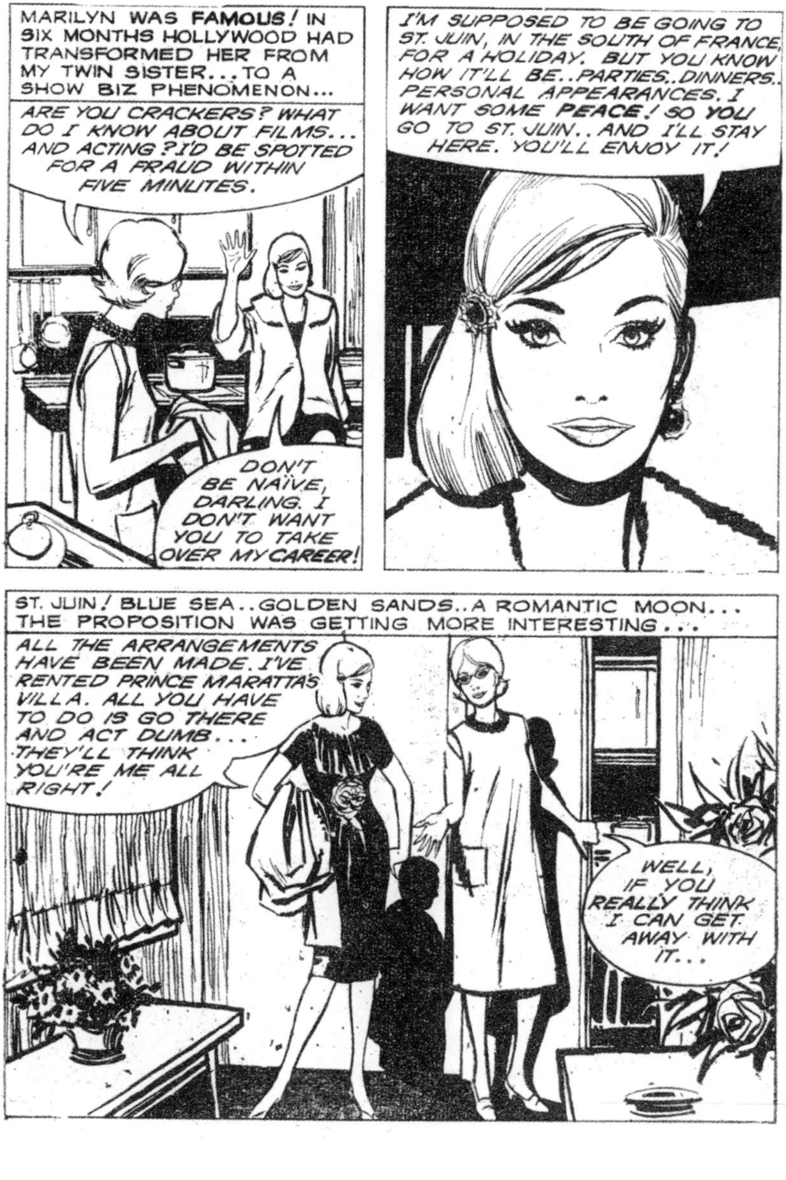
MARILYN WAS FAMOUS! IN SIX MONTHS HOLLYWOOD HAD TRANSFORMED HER FROM MY TWIN SISTER...TO A SHOW BIZ PHENOMENON...
ARE YOU CRACKERS? WHAT DO I KNOW ABOUT FILMS... AND ACTING? I'D BE SPOTTED FOR A FRAUD WITHIN FIVE MINUTES.
DON'T BE NAÏVE, DARLING. I DON'T WANT YOU TO TAKE OVER MY CAREER!
I'M SUPPOSED TO BE GOING TO ST. JUIN, IN THE SOUTH OF FRANCE, FOR A HOLIDAY. BUT YOU KNOW HOW IT'LL BE..PARTIES..DINNERS.. PERSONAL APPEARANCES. I WANT SOME PEACE! SO YOU GO TO ST. JUIN..AND I'LL STAY HERE. YOU'LL ENJOY IT!
ST. JUIN! BLUE SEA..GOLDEN SANDS..A ROMANTIC MOON... THE PROPOSITION WAS GETTING MORE INTERESTING...
ALL THE ARRANGEMENTS HAVE BEEN MADE. I'VE RENTED PRINCE MARATTA'S VILLA. ALL YOU HAVE TO DO IS GO THERE AND ACT DUMB... THEY'LL THINK YOU'RE ME ALL RIGHT!
WELL, IF YOU REALLY THINK I CAN GET AWAY WITH IT...

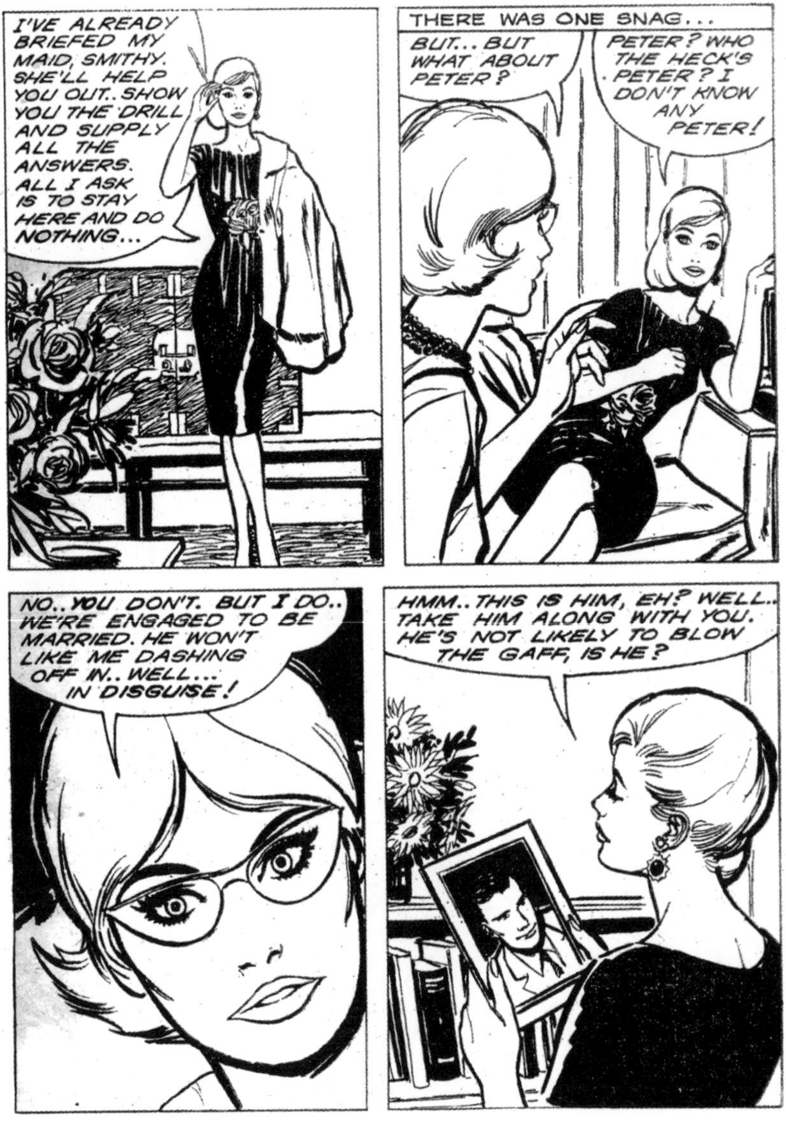
I'VE ALREADY BRIEFED MY MAID, SMITHY. SHE'LL HELP YOU OUT.. SHOW YOU THE DRILL AND SUPPLY ALL THE ANSWERS. ALL I ASK IS TO STAY HERE AND DO NOTHING...
THERE WAS ONE SNAG...
BUT... BUT WHAT ABOUT PETER?
PETER? WHO THE HECK'S PETER? I DON'T KNOW ANY PETER!
NO.. YOU DON'T. BUT I DO.. WE'RE ENGAGED TO BE MARRIED. HE WON'T LIKE ME DASHING OFF IN.. WELL... IN DISGUISE!
HMM.. THIS IS HIM, EH? WELL.. TAKE HIM ALONG WITH YOU. HE'S NOT LIKELY TO BLOW THE GAFF, IS HE?

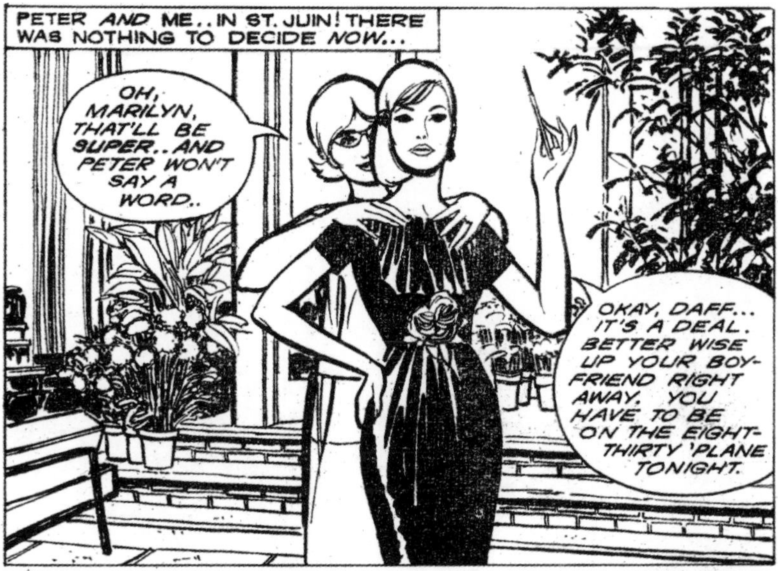
PETER AND ME.. IN ST. JUIN! THERE WAS NOTHING TO DECIDE NOW...
OH, MARILYN, THAT'LL BE SUPER.. AND PETER WON'T SAY A WORD..
OKAY, DAFF... IT'S A DEAL. BETTER WISE UP YOUR BOY-FRIEND RIGHT AWAY. YOU HAVE TO BE ON THE EIGHT-THIRTY 'PLANE TONIGHT.

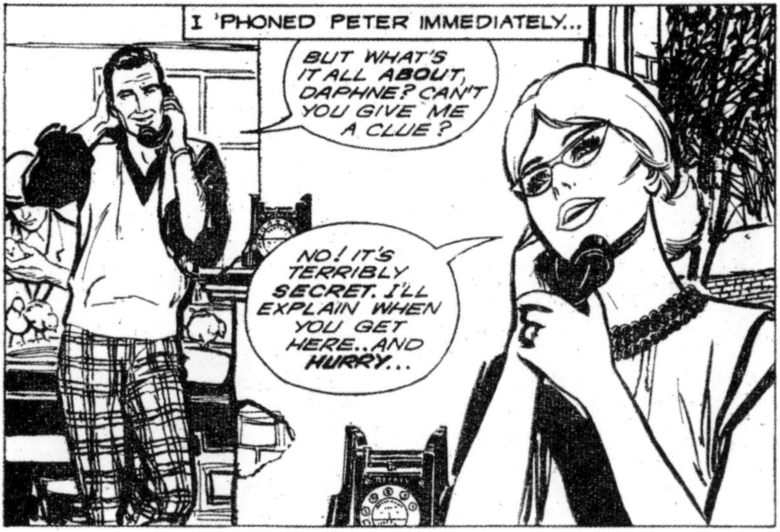
I 'PHONED PETER IMMEDIATELY...
BUT WHAT'S IT ALL ABOUT, DAPHNE? CAN'T YOU GIVE ME A CLUE?
NO! IT'S TERRIBLY SECRET. I'LL EXPLAIN WHEN YOU GET HERE.. AND HURRY...

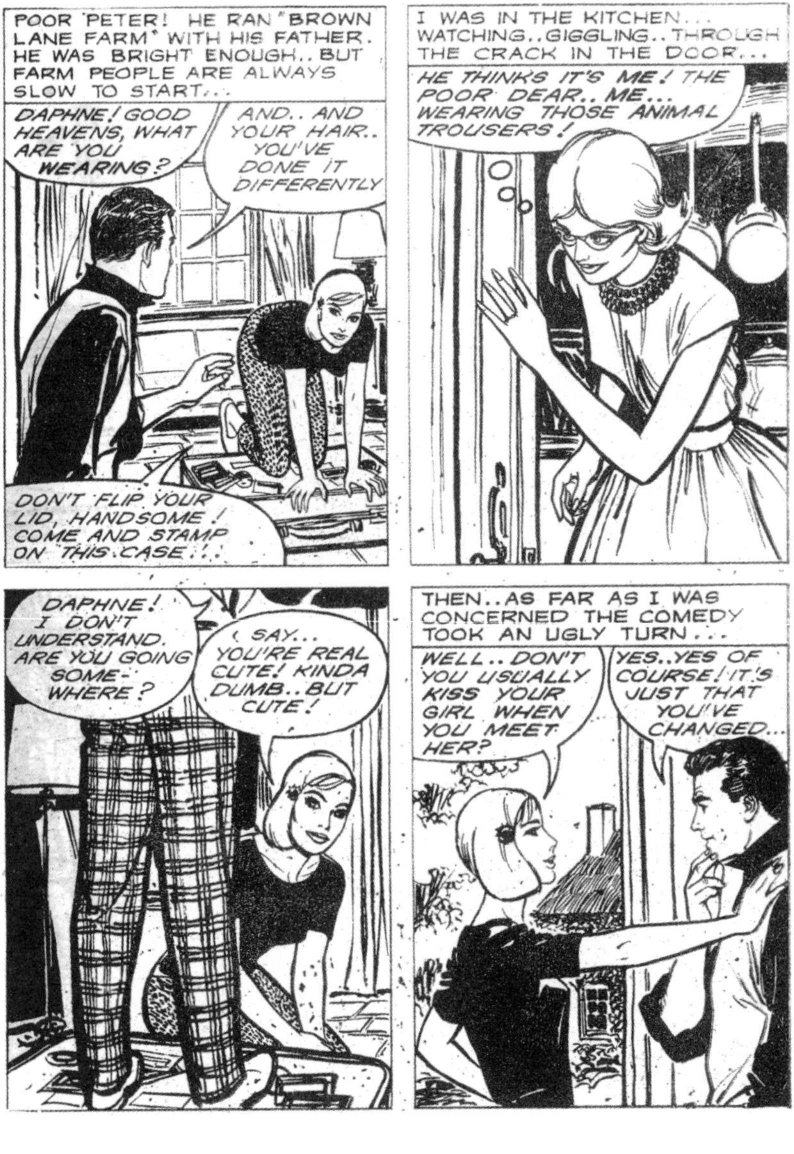
POOR PETER! HE RAN "BROWN LANE FARM" WITH HIS FATHER. HE WAS BRIGHT ENOUGH.. BUT FARM PEOPLE ARE ALWAYS SLOW TO START...
DAPHNE! GOOD HEAVENS, WHAT ARE YOU WEARING?
AND.. AND YOUR HAIR.. YOU'VE DONE IT DIFFERENTLY
DON'T FLIP YOUR LID, HANDSOME! COME AND STAMP ON THIS CASE!
I WAS IN THE KITCHEN... WATCHING..GIGGLING..THROUGH THE CRACK IN THE DOOR...
HE THINKS IT'S ME! THE POOR DEAR.. ME... WEARING THOSE ANIMAL TROUSERS!
DAPHNE! I DON'T UNDERSTAND. ARE YOU GOING SOME-WHERE?
I SAY... YOU'RE REAL CUTE! KINDA DUMB.. BUT CUTE!
THEN..AS FAR AS I WAS CONCERNED THE COMEDY TOOK AN UGLY TURN...
WELL.. DON'T YOU USUALLY KISS YOUR GIRL WHEN YOU MEET HER?
YES..YES OF COURSE! IT'S JUST THAT YOU'VE CHANGED...

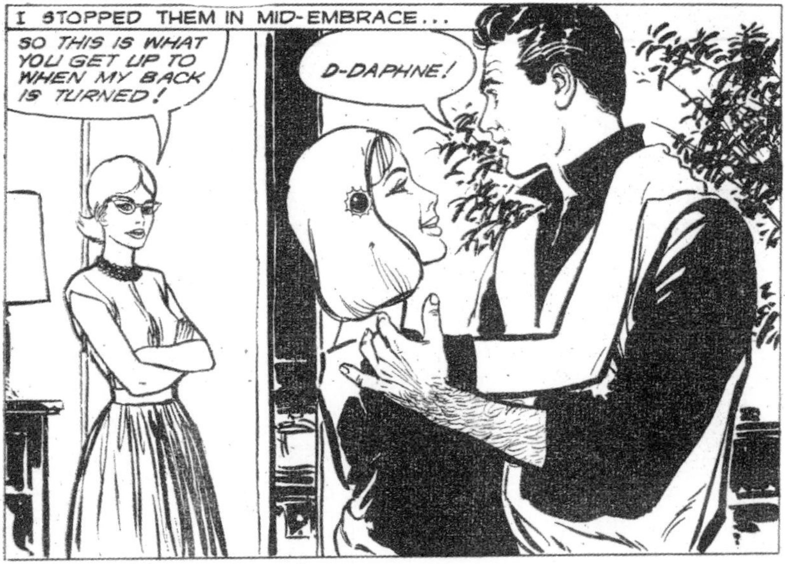
I STOPPED THEM IN MID-EMBRACE...
SO THIS IS WHAT YOU GET UP TO WHEN MY BACK IS TURNED!
D-DAPHNE!

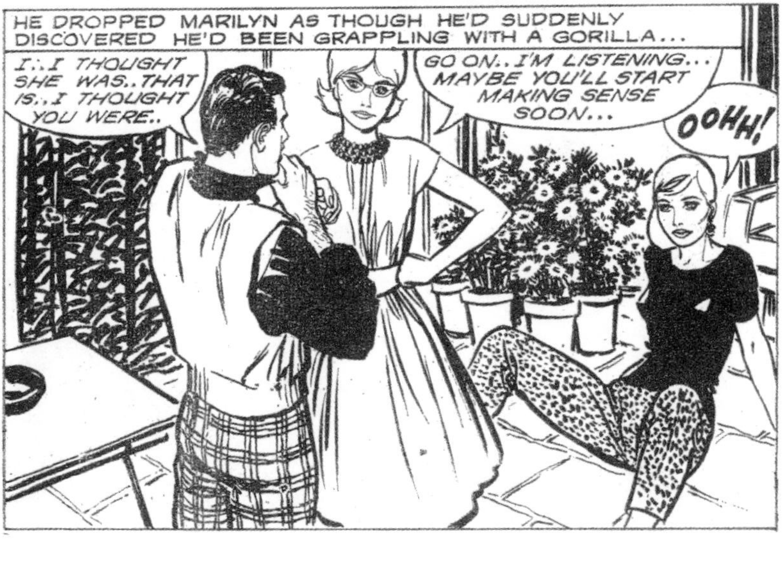
HE DROPPED MARILYN AS THOUGH HE'D SUDDENLY DISCOVERED HE'D BEEN GRAPPLING WITH A GORILLA...
I..I THOUGHT SHE WAS..THAT IS..I THOUGHT YOU WERE..
GO ON..I'M LISTENING... MAYBE YOU'LL START MAKING SENSE SOON...
OOHH!

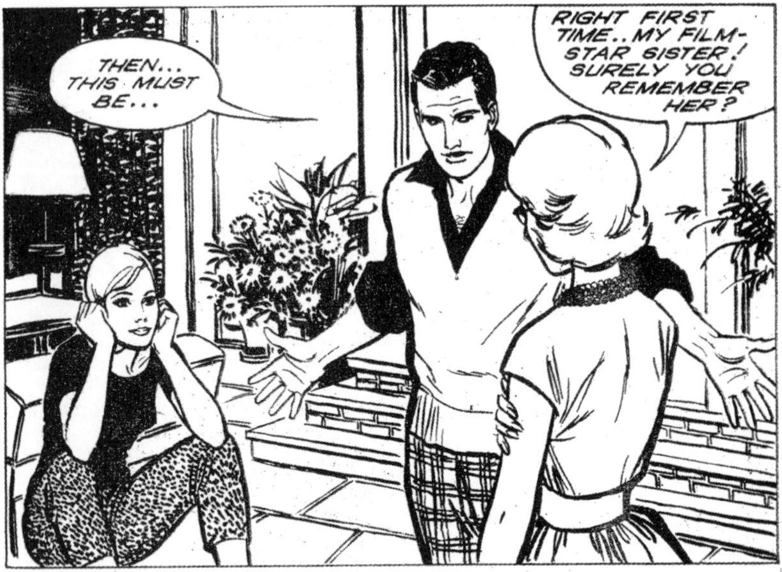
THEN... THIS MUST BE...
RIGHT FIRST TIME..MY FILM-STAR SISTER! SURELY YOU REMEMBER HER?

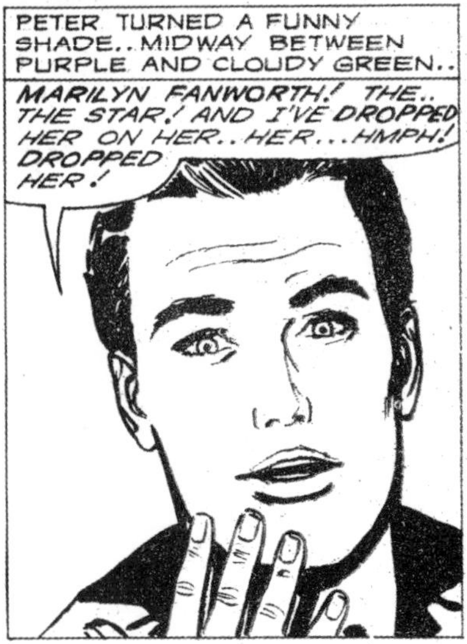
PETER TURNED A FUNNY SHADE..MIDWAY BETWEEN PURPLE AND CLOUDY GREEN..
MARILYN FANWORTH! THE.. THE STAR! AND I'VE DROPPED HER ON HER..HER...HMPH! DROPPED HER!

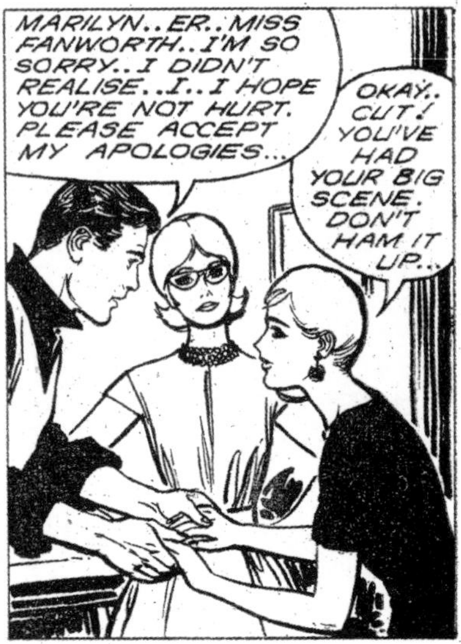
MARILYN..ER..MISS FANWORTH..I'M SO SORRY..I DIDN'T REALISE..I..I HOPE YOU'RE NOT HURT. PLEASE ACCEPT MY APOLOGIES...
OKAY.. CUT! YOU'VE HAD YOUR BIG SCENE. DON'T HAM IT UP...

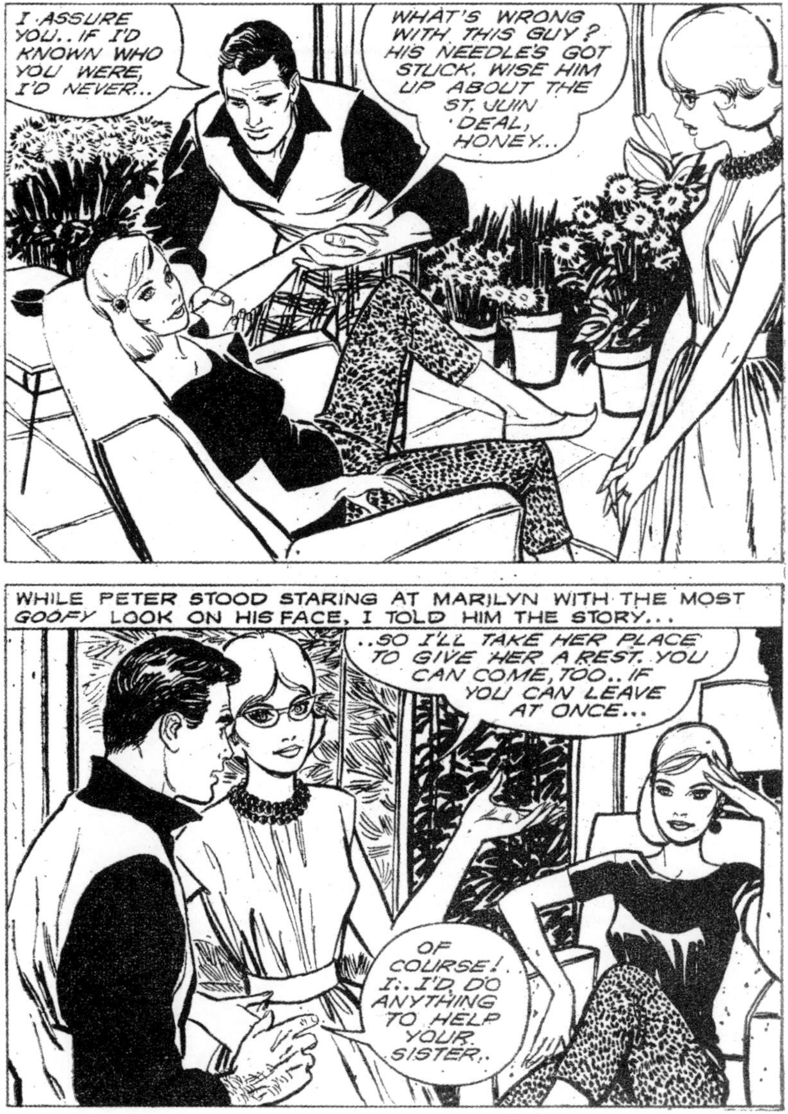
I ASSURE YOU.. IF I'D KNOWN WHO YOU WERE, I'D NEVER...
WHAT'S WRONG WITH THIS GUY? HIS NEEDLE'S GOT STUCK. WISE HIM UP ABOUT THE ST. JUIN DEAL, HONEY...
WHILE PETER STOOD STARING AT MARILYN WITH THE MOST GOOFY LOOK ON HIS FACE, I TOLD HIM THE STORY...
..SO I'LL TAKE HER PLACE TO GIVE HER A REST. YOU CAN COME, TOO.. IF YOU CAN LEAVE AT ONCE...
OF COURSE! I..I'D DO ANYTHING TO HELP YOUR SISTER..

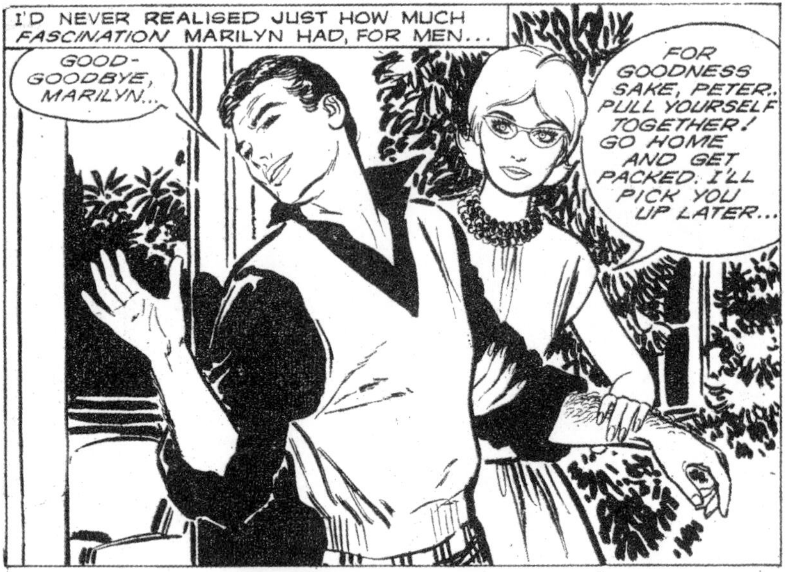
I'D NEVER REALISED JUST HOW MUCH FASCINATION MARILYN HAD, FOR MEN...
GOOD-GOODBYE, MARILYN...
FOR GOODNESS SAKE, PETER.. PULL YOURSELF TOGETHER! GO HOME AND GET PACKED. I'LL PICK YOU UP LATER...

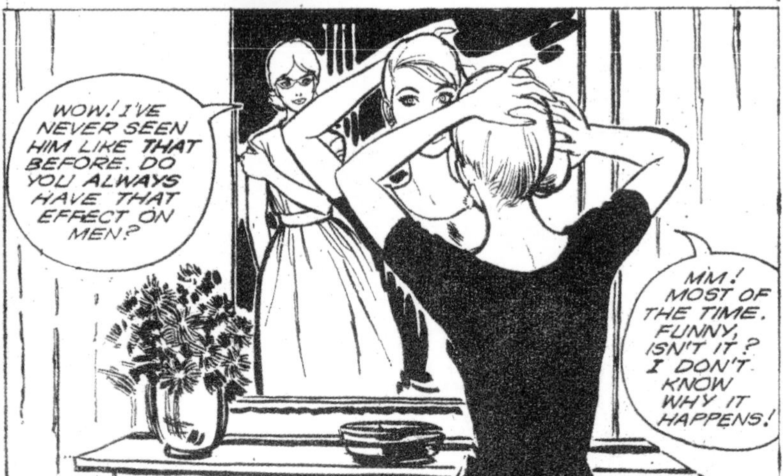
WOW! I'VE NEVER SEEN HIM LIKE THAT BEFORE. DO YOU ALWAYS HAVE THAT EFFECT ON MEN?
MM! MOST OF THE TIME. FUNNY, ISN'T IT? I DON'T KNOW WHY IT HAPPENS!

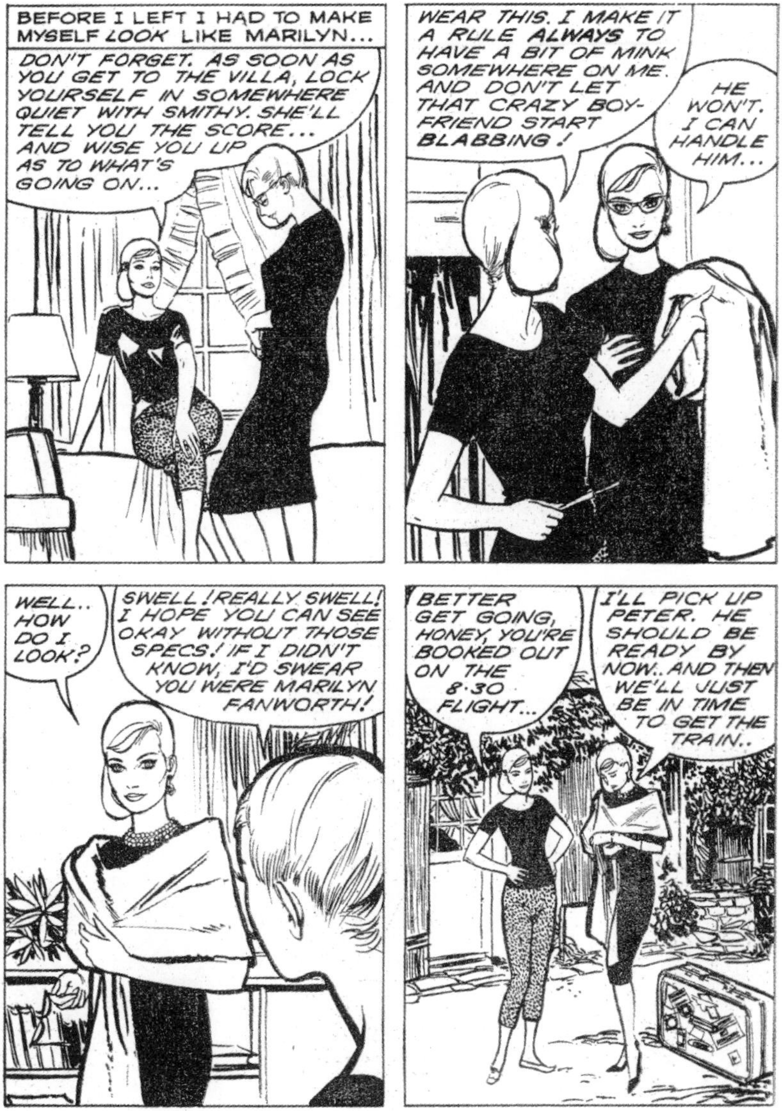
BEFORE I LEFT I HAD TO MAKE MYSELF LOOK LIKE MARILYN...
DON'T FORGET. AS SOON AS YOU GET TO THE VILLA, LOCK YOURSELF IN SOMEWHERE QUIET WITH SMITHY. SHE'LL TELL YOU THE SCORE... AND WISE YOU UP AS TO WHAT'S GOING ON...
WEAR THIS. I MAKE IT A RULE ALWAYS TO HAVE A BIT OF MINK SOMEWHERE ON ME. AND DON'T LET THAT CRAZY BOY-FRIEND START BLABBING!
HE WON'T. I CAN HANDLE HIM...
WELL.. HOW DO I LOOK?
SWELL! REALLY SWELL! I HOPE YOU CAN SEE OKAY WITHOUT THOSE SPECS! IF I DIDN'T KNOW, I'D SWEAR YOU WERE MARILYN FANWORTH!
BETTER GET GOING, HONEY, YOU'RE BOOKED OUT ON THE 8·30 FLIGHT...
I'LL PICK UP PETER. HE SHOULD BE READY BY NOW.. AND THEN WE'LL JUST BE IN TIME TO GET THE TRAIN..

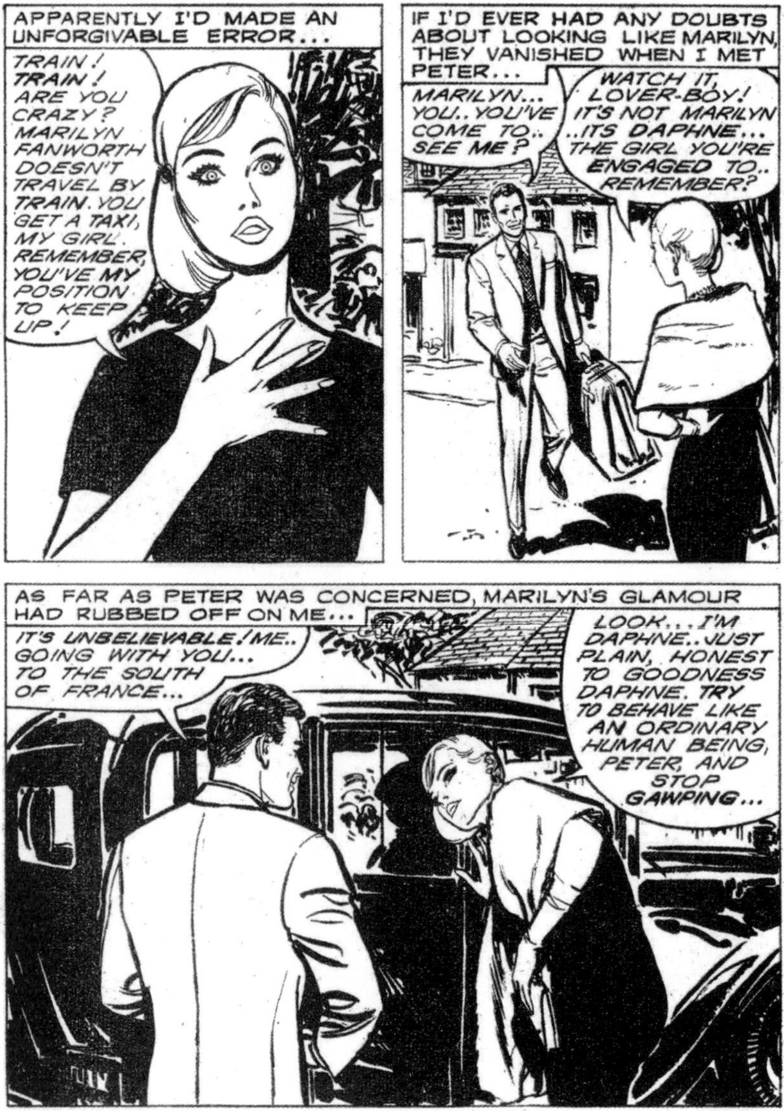
APPARENTLY I'D MADE AN UNFORGIVABLE ERROR...
TRAIN! TRAIN! ARE YOU CRAZY? MARILYN FANWORTH DOESN'T TRAVEL BY TRAIN. YOU GET A TAXI, MY GIRL. REMEMBER, YOU'VE MY POSITION TO KEEP UP!
IF I'D EVER HAD ANY DOUBTS ABOUT LOOKING LIKE MARILYN, THEY VANISHED WHEN I MET PETER...
MARILYN... YOU.. YOU'VE COME TO.. SEE ME?
WATCH IT, LOVER-BOY! IT'S NOT MARILYN ..ITS DAPHNE... THE GIRL YOU'RE ENGAGED TO.. REMEMBER?
AS FAR AS PETER WAS CONCERNED, MARILYN'S GLAMOUR HAD RUBBED OFF ON ME...
IT'S UNBELIEVABLE! ME.. GOING WITH YOU... TO THE SOUTH OF FRANCE...
LOOK... I'M DAPHNE.. JUST PLAIN, HONEST TO GOODNESS DAPHNE. TRY TO BEHAVE LIKE AN ORDINARY HUMAN BEING, PETER, AND STOP GAWPING...

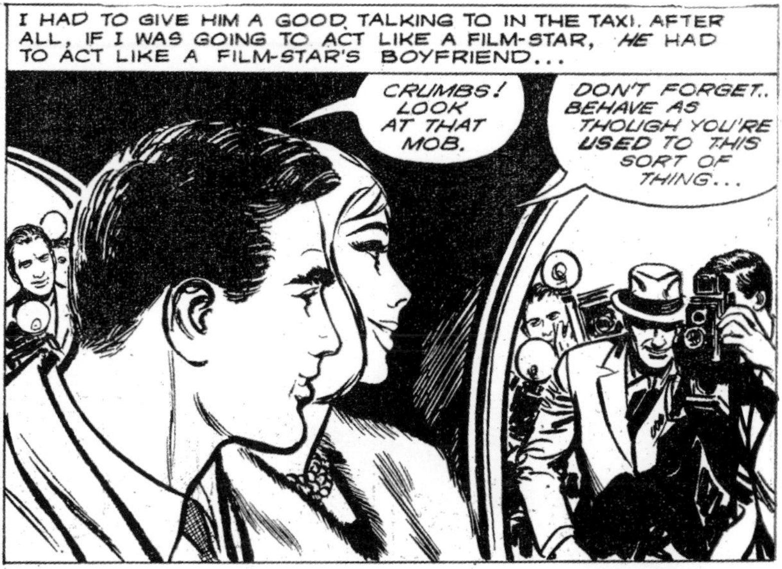
I HAD TO GIVE HIM A GOOD TALKING TO IN THE TAXI. AFTER ALL, IF I WAS GOING TO ACT LIKE A FILM-STAR, HE HAD TO ACT LIKE A FILM-STAR'S BOYFRIEND...
CRUMBS! LOOK AT THAT MOB.
DON'T FORGET.. BEHAVE AS THOUGH YOU'RE USED TO THIS SORT OF THING...

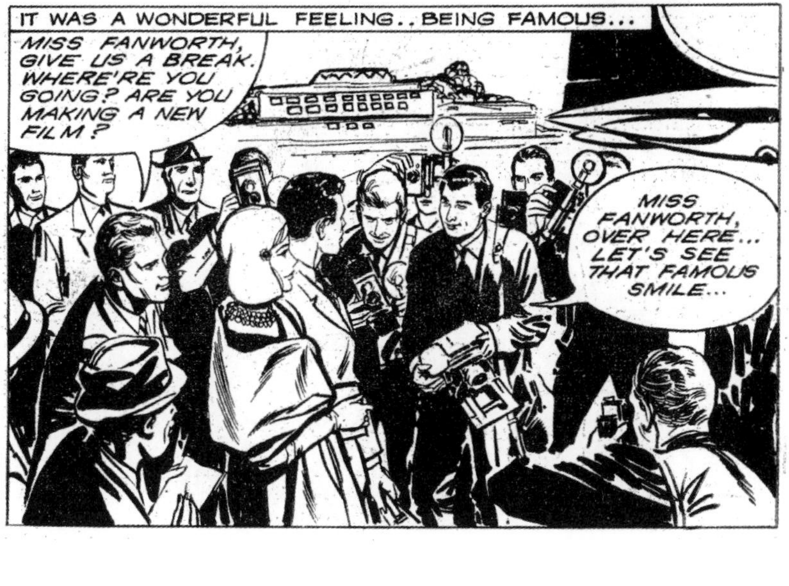
IT WAS A WONDERFUL FEELING.. BEING FAMOUS...
MISS FANWORTH, GIVE US A BREAK. WHERE'RE YOU GOING? ARE YOU MAKING A NEW FILM?
MISS FANWORTH, OVER HERE... LET'S SEE THAT FAMOUS SMILE...

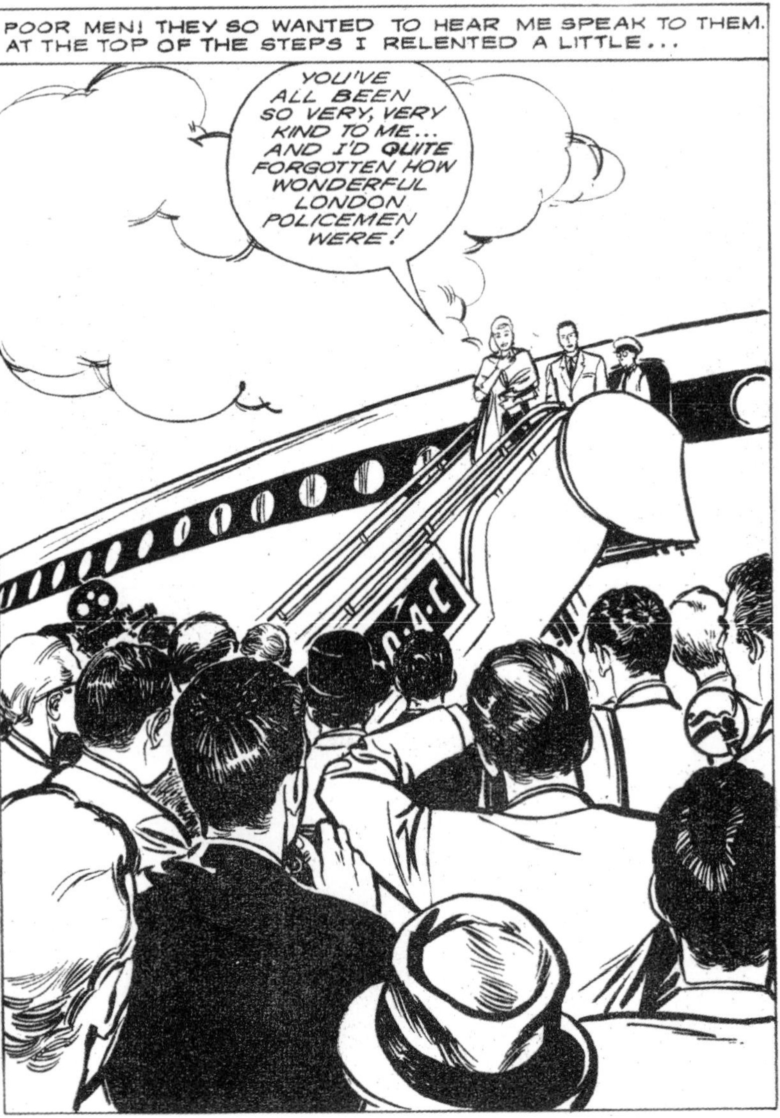
POOR MEN! THEY SO WANTED TO HEAR ME SPEAK TO THEM. AT THE TOP OF THE STEPS I RELENTED A LITTLE...
YOU'VE ALL BEEN SO VERY, VERY KIND TO ME... AND I'D QUITE FORGOTTEN HOW WONDERFUL LONDON POLICEMEN WERE!

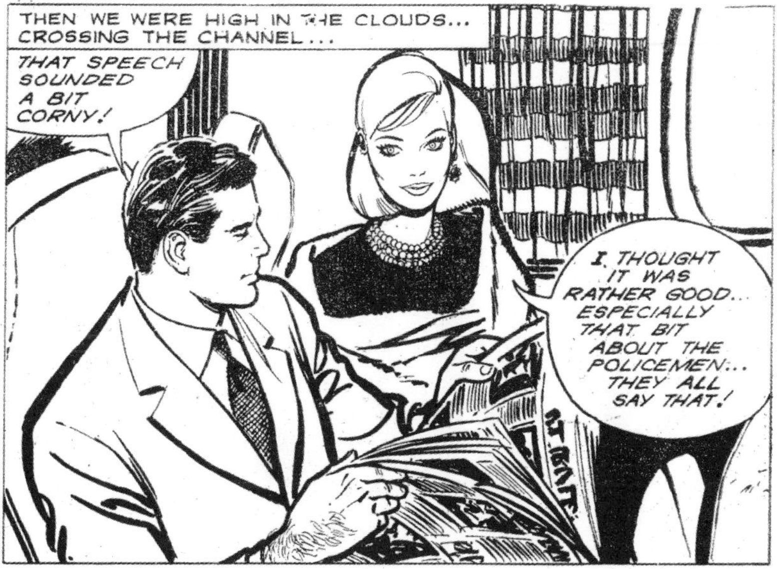
THEN WE WERE HIGH IN THE CLOUDS... CROSSING THE CHANNEL...
THAT SPEECH SOUNDED A BIT CORNY!
I THOUGHT IT WAS RATHER GOOD... ESPECIALLY THAT BIT ABOUT THE POLICEMEN... THEY ALL SAY THAT!

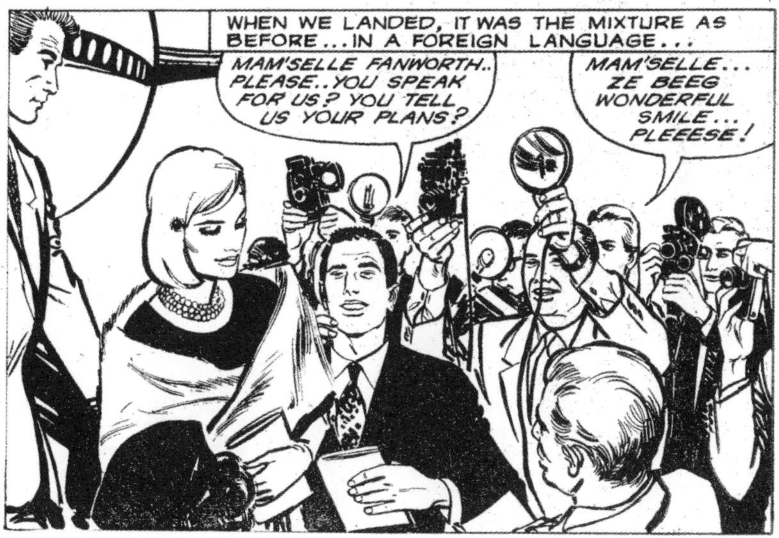
WHEN WE LANDED, IT WAS THE MIXTURE AS BEFORE... IN A FOREIGN LANGUAGE...
MAM'SELLE FANWORTH.. PLEASE.. YOU SPEAK FOR US? YOU TELL US YOUR PLANS?
MAM'SELLE... ZE BEEG WONDERFUL SMILE... PLEEESE!

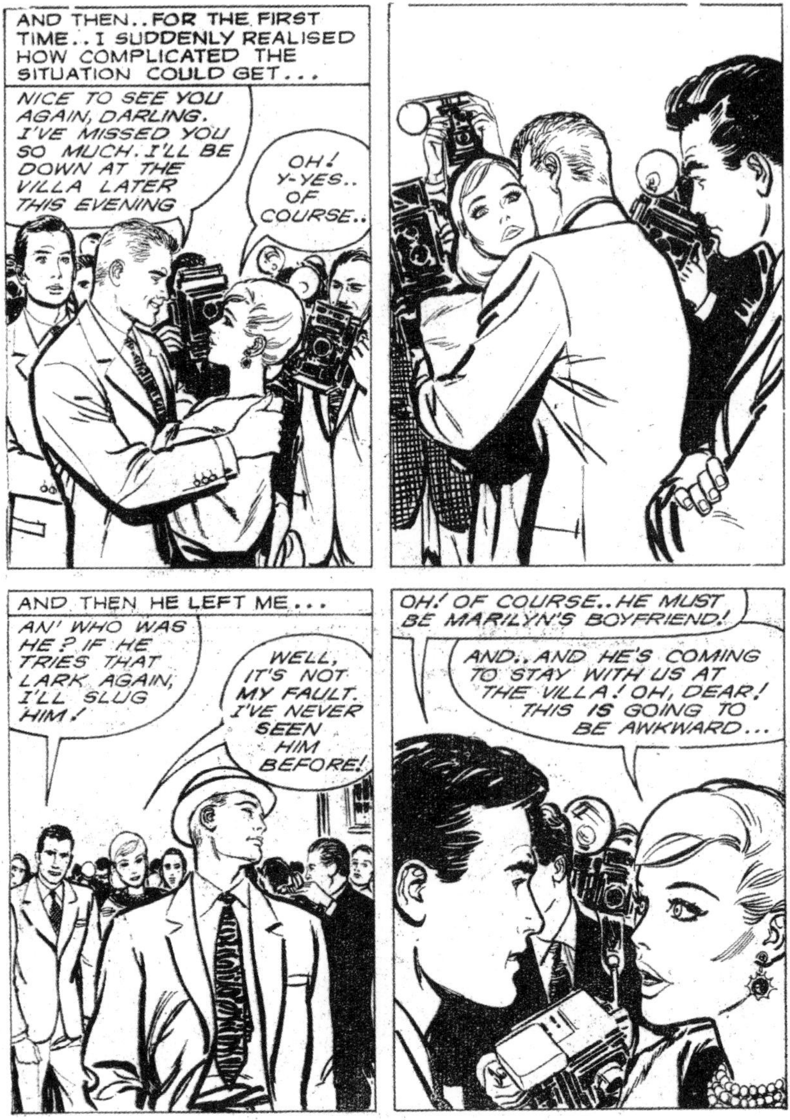
AND THEN..FOR THE FIRST TIME..I SUDDENLY REALISED HOW COMPLICATED THE SITUATION COULD GET...
NICE TO SEE YOU AGAIN, DARLING. I'VE MISSED YOU SO MUCH. I'LL BE DOWN AT THE VILLA LATER THIS EVENING
OH! Y-YES.. OF COURSE..
AND THEN HE LEFT ME...
AN' WHO WAS HE? IF HE TRIES THAT LARK AGAIN, I'LL SLUG HIM!
WELL, IT'S NOT MY FAULT. I'VE NEVER SEEN HIM BEFORE!
OH! OF COURSE..HE MUST BE MARILYN'S BOYFRIEND!
AND..AND HE'S COMING TO STAY WITH US AT THE VILLA! OH, DEAR! THIS IS GOING TO BE AWKWARD...

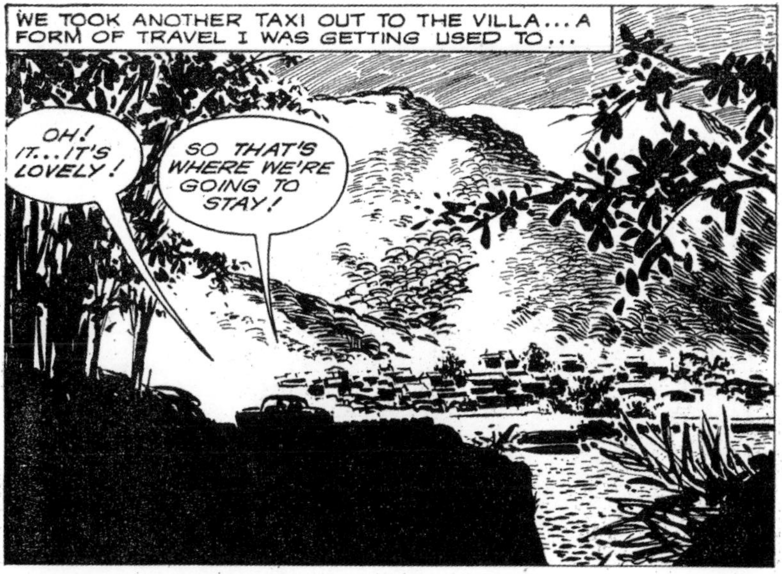
WE TOOK ANOTHER TAXI OUT TO THE VILLA... A FORM OF TRAVEL I WAS GETTING USED TO...
OH! IT...IT'S LOVELY!
SO THAT'S WHERE WE'RE GOING TO STAY!

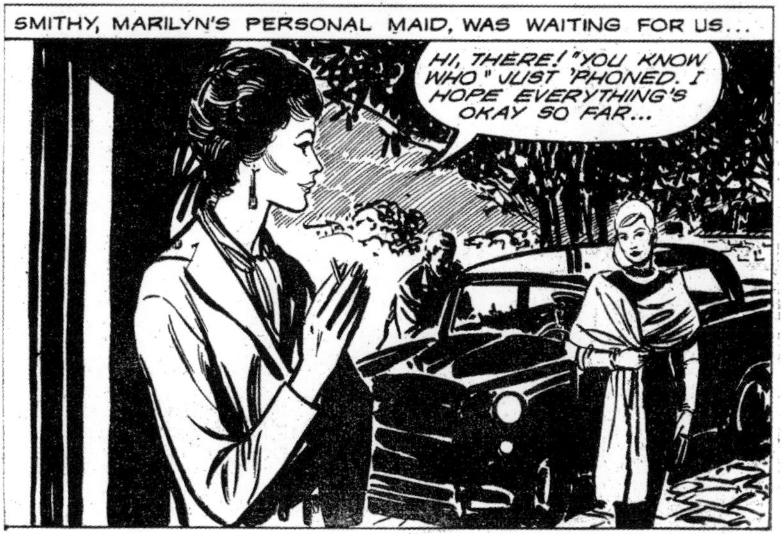
SMITHY, MARILYN'S PERSONAL MAID, WAS WAITING FOR US...
HI, THERE! "YOU KNOW WHO" JUST 'PHONED. I HOPE EVERYTHING'S OKAY SO FAR...

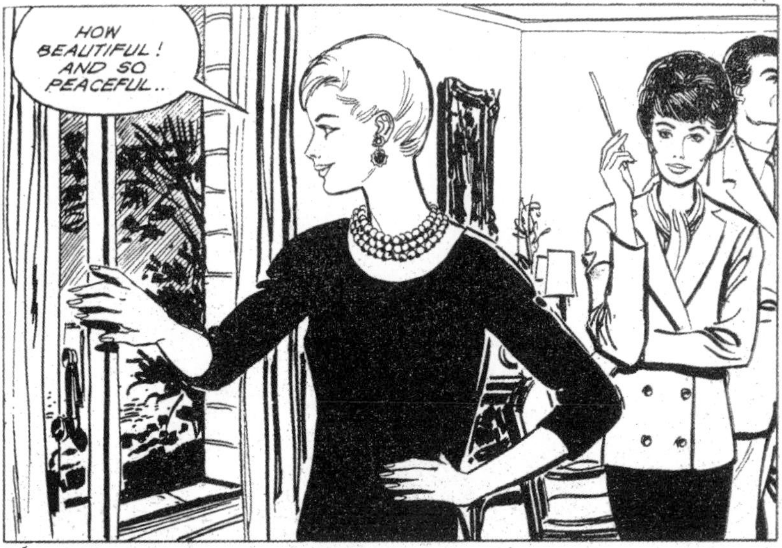
HOW BEAUTIFUL! AND SO PEACEFUL..

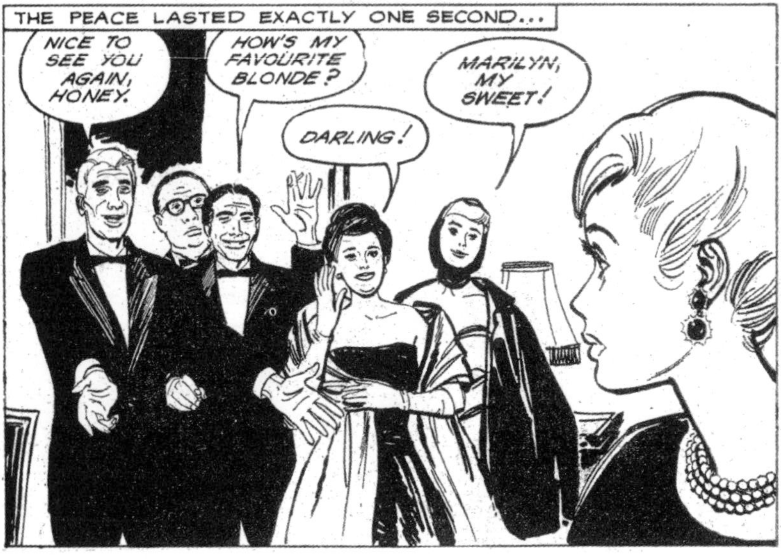
THE PEACE LASTED EXACTLY ONE SECOND...
NICE TO SEE YOU AGAIN, HONEY.
HOW'S MY FAVOURITE BLONDE?
DARLING!
MARILYN, MY SWEET!

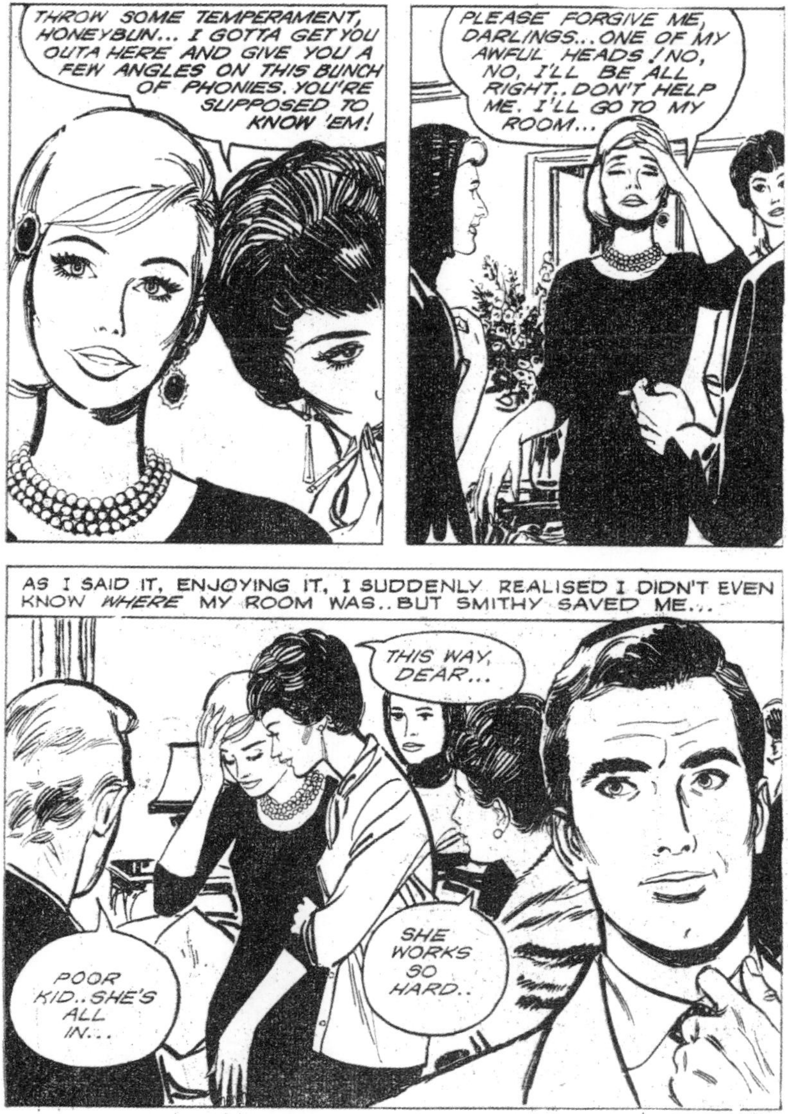
THROW SOME TEMPERAMENT, HONEYBUN... I GOTTA GET YOU OUTA HERE AND GIVE YOU A FEW ANGLES ON THIS BUNCH OF PHONIES. YOU'RE SUPPOSED TO KNOW 'EM!
PLEASE FORGIVE ME, DARLINGS...ONE OF MY AWFUL HEADS! NO, NO, I'LL BE ALL RIGHT..DON'T HELP ME. I'LL GO TO MY ROOM...
AS I SAID IT, ENJOYING IT, I SUDDENLY REALISED I DIDN'T EVEN KNOW *WHERE* MY ROOM WAS..BUT SMITHY SAVED ME...
THIS WAY, DEAR...
POOR KID..SHE'S ALL IN...
SHE WORKS SO HARD..

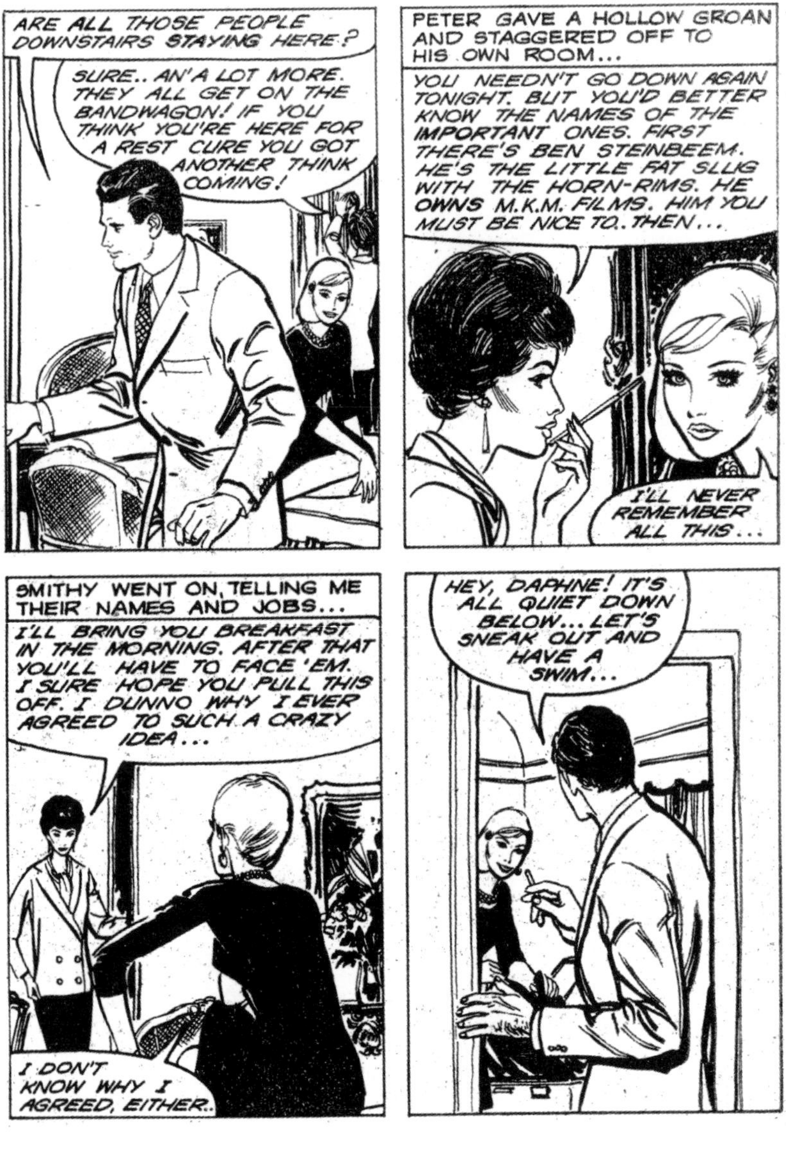
ARE ALL THOSE PEOPLE DOWNSTAIRS STAYING HERE?
SURE.. AN'A LOT MORE. THEY ALL GET ON THE BANDWAGON! IF YOU THINK YOU'RE HERE FOR A REST CURE YOU GOT ANOTHER THINK COMING!
PETER GAVE A HOLLOW GROAN AND STAGGERED OFF TO HIS OWN ROOM...
YOU NEEDN'T GO DOWN AGAIN TONIGHT. BUT YOU'D BETTER KNOW THE NAMES OF THE IMPORTANT ONES. FIRST THERE'S BEN STEINBEEM. HE'S THE LITTLE FAT SLUG WITH THE HORN-RIMS. HE OWNS M.K.M. FILMS. HIM YOU MUST BE NICE TO..THEN...
I'LL NEVER REMEMBER ALL THIS...
SMITHY WENT ON, TELLING ME THEIR NAMES AND JOBS...
I'LL BRING YOU BREAKFAST IN THE MORNING. AFTER THAT YOU'LL HAVE TO FACE 'EM. I SURE HOPE YOU PULL THIS OFF. I DUNNO WHY I EVER AGREED TO SUCH A CRAZY IDEA...
I DON'T KNOW WHY I AGREED, EITHER..
HEY, DAPHNE! IT'S ALL QUIET DOWN BELOW... LET'S SNEAK OUT AND HAVE A SWIM...

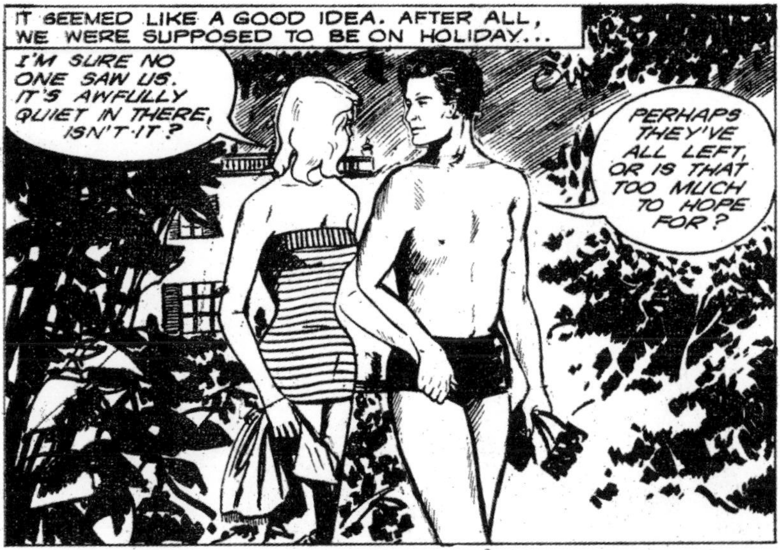
IT SEEMED LIKE A GOOD IDEA. AFTER ALL, WE WERE SUPPOSED TO BE ON HOLIDAY...
I'M SURE NO ONE SAW US. IT'S AWFULLY QUIET IN THERE, ISN'T IT?
PERHAPS THEY'VE ALL LEFT, OR IS THAT TOO MUCH TO HOPE FOR?

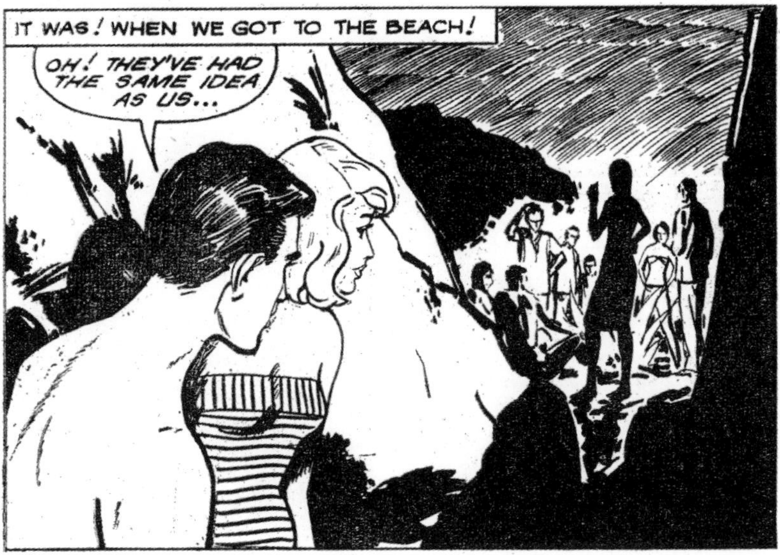
IT WAS! WHEN WE GOT TO THE BEACH!
OH! THEY'VE HAD THE SAME IDEA AS US...

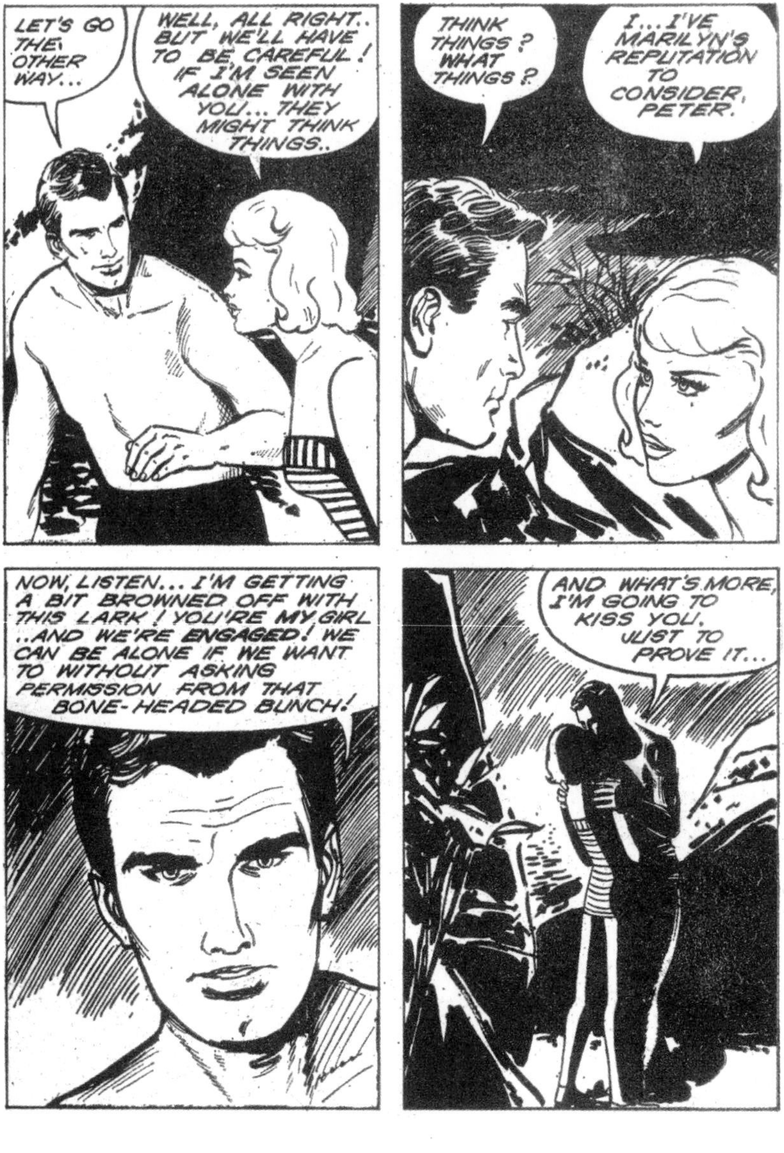
LET'S GO THE OTHER WAY...
WELL, ALL RIGHT.. BUT WE'LL HAVE TO BE CAREFUL! IF I'M SEEN ALONE WITH YOU... THEY MIGHT THINK THINGS..
THINK THINGS? WHAT THINGS?
I...I'VE MARILYN'S REPUTATION TO CONSIDER, PETER.
NOW, LISTEN... I'M GETTING A BIT BROWNED OFF WITH THIS LARK! YOU'RE MY GIRL ..AND WE'RE ENGAGED! WE CAN BE ALONE IF WE WANT TO WITHOUT ASKING PERMISSION FROM THAT BONE-HEADED BUNCH!
AND WHAT'S MORE, I'M GOING TO KISS YOU, JUST TO PROVE IT...

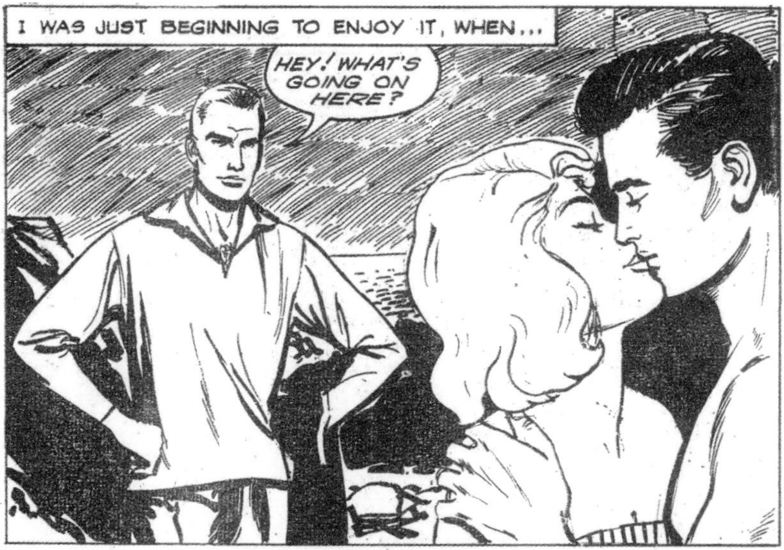
I WAS JUST BEGINNING TO ENJOY IT, WHEN...
HEY! WHAT'S GOING ON HERE?

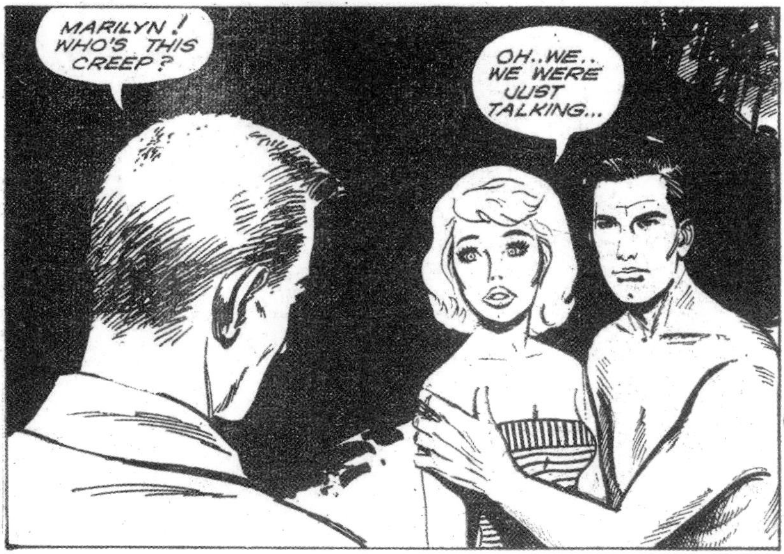
MARILYN! WHO'S THIS CREEP?
OH..WE.. WE WERE JUST TALKING...

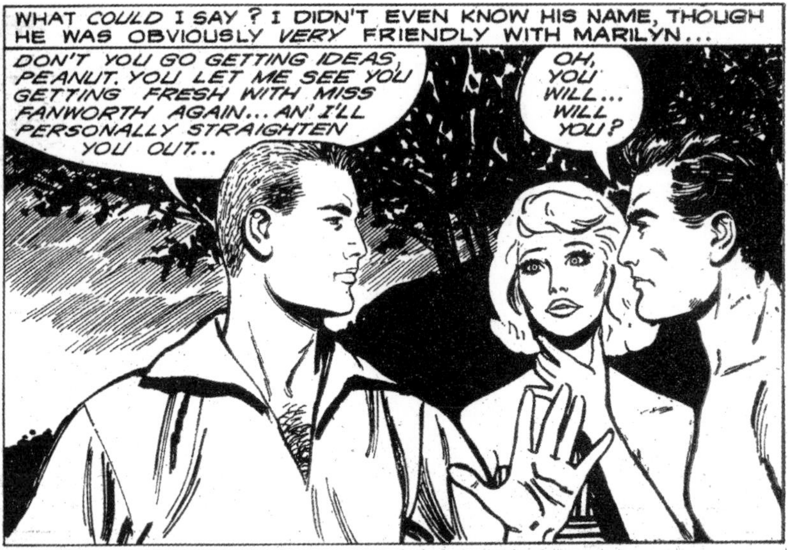
WHAT COULD I SAY ? I DIDN'T EVEN KNOW HIS NAME, THOUGH HE WAS OBVIOUSLY VERY FRIENDLY WITH MARILYN...
DON'T YOU GO GETTING IDEAS, PEANUT. YOU LET ME SEE YOU GETTING FRESH WITH MISS FANWORTH AGAIN... AN' I'LL PERSONALLY STRAIGHTEN YOU OUT...
OH, YOU WILL... WILL YOU?

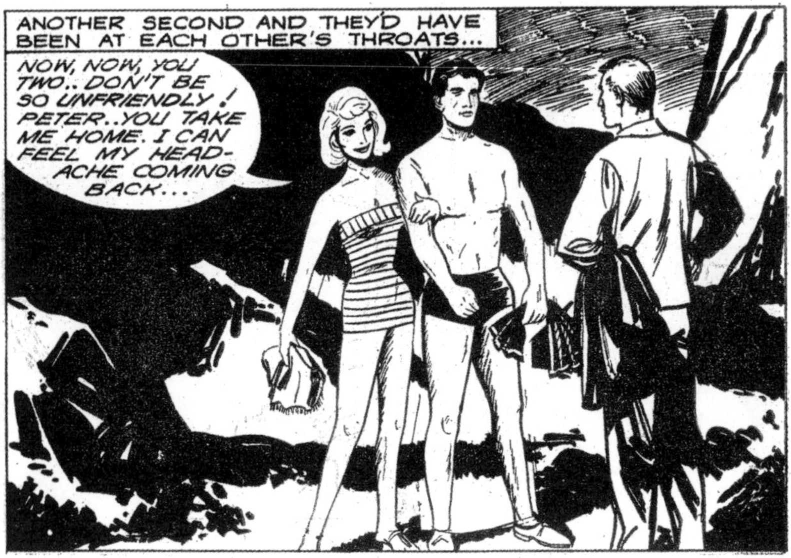
ANOTHER SECOND AND THEY'D HAVE BEEN AT EACH OTHER'S THROATS...
NOW, NOW, YOU TWO.. DON'T BE SO UNFRIENDLY! PETER..YOU TAKE ME HOME. I CAN FEEL MY HEAD-ACHE COMING BACK...

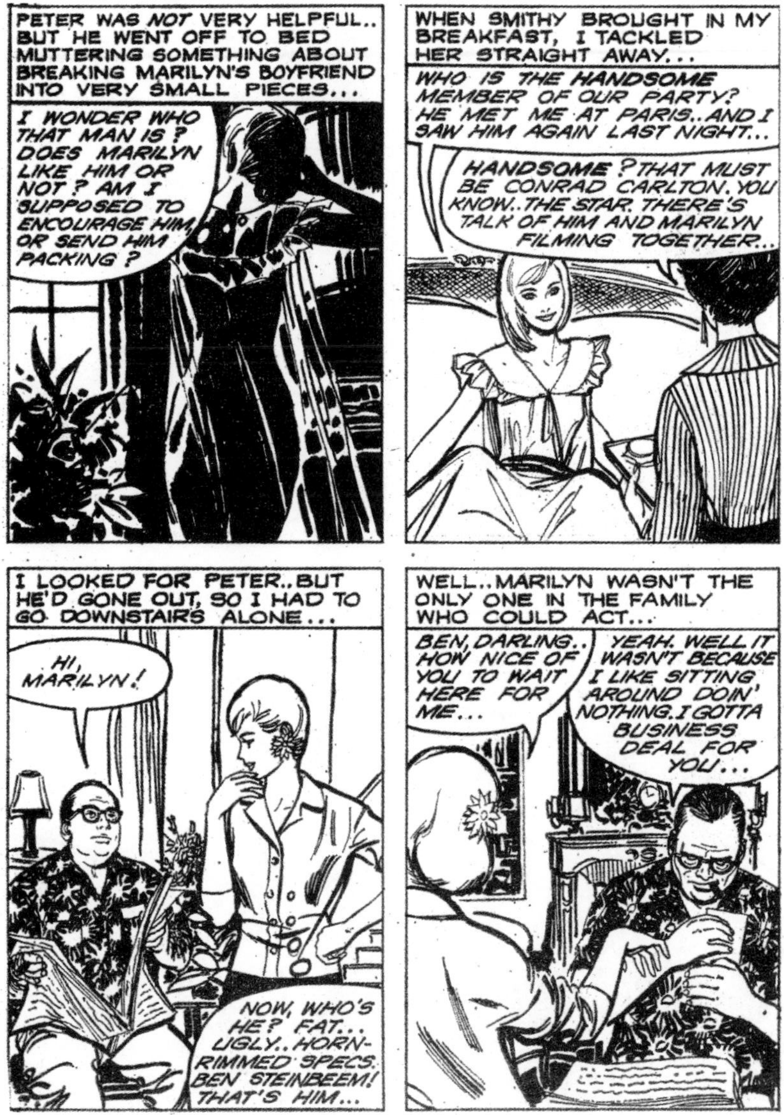
PETER WAS NOT VERY HELPFUL.. BUT HE WENT OFF TO BED MUTTERING SOMETHING ABOUT BREAKING MARILYN'S BOYFRIEND INTO VERY SMALL PIECES...
I WONDER WHO THAT MAN IS? DOES MARILYN LIKE HIM OR NOT? AM I SUPPOSED TO ENCOURAGE HIM, OR SEND HIM PACKING?
WHEN SMITHY BROUGHT IN MY BREAKFAST, I TACKLED HER STRAIGHT AWAY...
WHO IS THE HANDSOME MEMBER OF OUR PARTY? HE MET ME AT PARIS..AND I SAW HIM AGAIN LAST NIGHT...
HANDSOME? THAT MUST BE CONRAD CARLTON. YOU KNOW..THE STAR. THERE'S TALK OF HIM AND MARILYN FILMING TOGETHER...
I LOOKED FOR PETER..BUT HE'D GONE OUT, SO I HAD TO GO DOWNSTAIRS ALONE...
HI, MARILYN!
NOW, WHO'S HE? FAT... UGLY..HORN-RIMMED SPECS. BEN STEINBEEM! THAT'S HIM...
WELL..MARILYN WASN'T THE ONLY ONE IN THE FAMILY WHO COULD ACT...
BEN, DARLING.. HOW NICE OF YOU TO WAIT HERE FOR ME...
YEAH. WELL IT WASN'T BECAUSE I LIKE SITTING AROUND DOIN' NOTHING. I GOTTA BUSINESS DEAL FOR YOU...

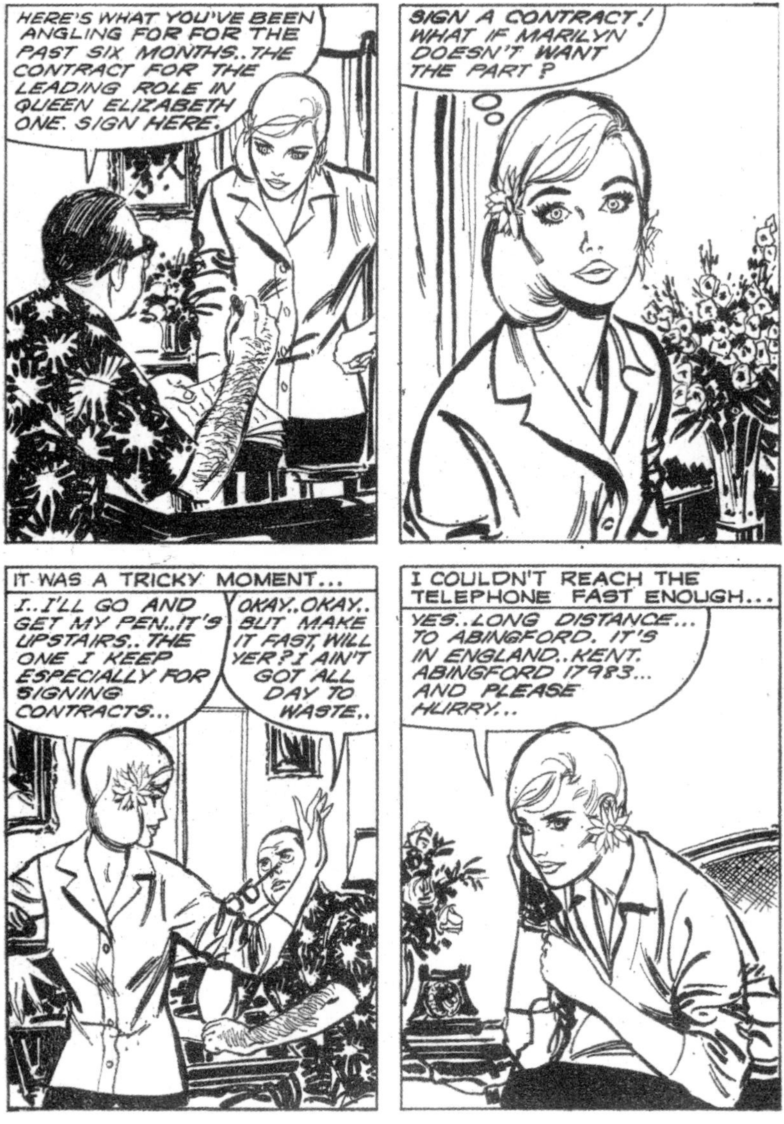
HERE'S WHAT YOU'VE BEEN ANGLING FOR FOR THE PAST SIX MONTHS..THE CONTRACT FOR THE LEADING ROLE IN QUEEN ELIZABETH ONE. SIGN HERE.
SIGN A CONTRACT! WHAT IF MARILYN DOESN'T WANT THE PART?
IT WAS A TRICKY MOMENT...
I..I'LL GO AND GET MY PEN..IT'S UPSTAIRS..THE ONE I KEEP ESPECIALLY FOR SIGNING CONTRACTS...
OKAY..OKAY.. BUT MAKE IT FAST, WILL YER? I AIN'T GOT ALL DAY TO WASTE..
I COULDN'T REACH THE TELEPHONE FAST ENOUGH...
YES..LONG DISTANCE... TO ABINGFORD. IT'S IN ENGLAND..KENT. ABINGFORD 17983... AND PLEASE HURRY...

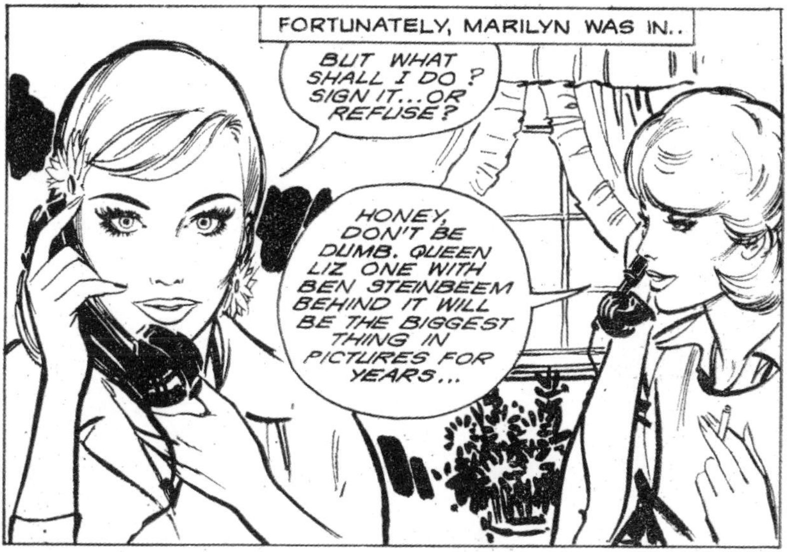
FORTUNATELY, MARILYN WAS IN..
BUT WHAT SHALL I DO? SIGN IT...OR REFUSE?
HONEY, DON'T BE DUMB. QUEEN LIZ ONE WITH BEN STEINBEEM BEHIND IT WILL BE THE BIGGEST THING IN PICTURES FOR YEARS...

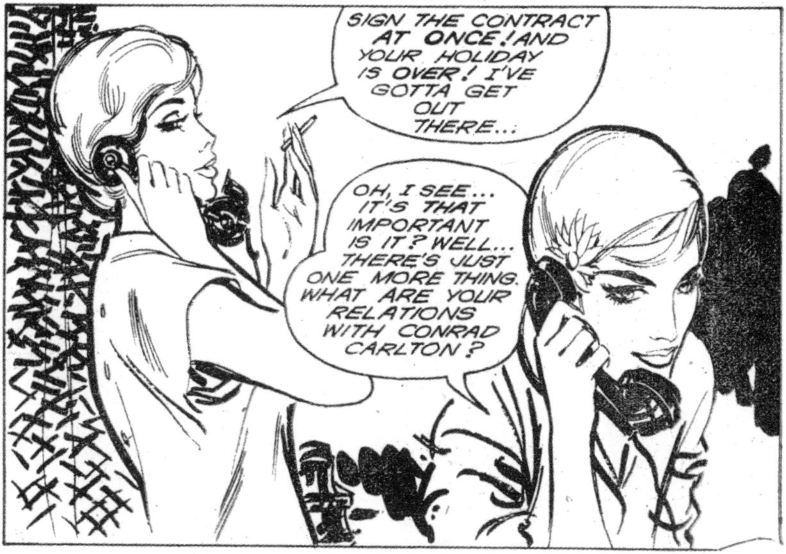
SIGN THE CONTRACT AT ONCE! AND YOUR HOLIDAY IS OVER! I'VE GOTTA GET OUT THERE...
OH, I SEE... IT'S THAT IMPORTANT IS IT? WELL... THERE'S JUST ONE MORE THING. WHAT ARE YOUR RELATIONS WITH CONRAD CARLTON?

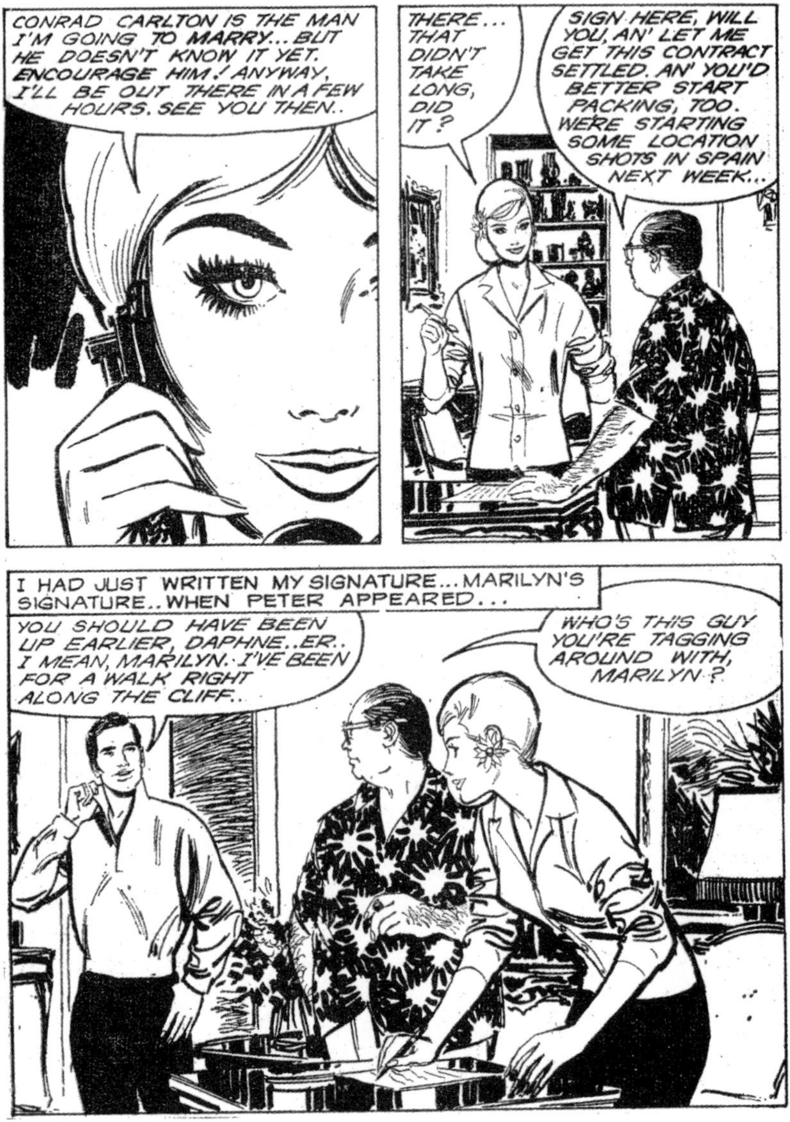
CONRAD CARLTON IS THE MAN I'M GOING TO MARRY... BUT HE DOESN'T KNOW IT YET. ENCOURAGE HIM! ANYWAY, I'LL BE OUT THERE IN A FEW HOURS. SEE YOU THEN..
THERE... THAT DIDN'T TAKE LONG, DID IT?
SIGN HERE, WILL YOU, AN' LET ME GET THIS CONTRACT SETTLED. AN' YOU'D BETTER START PACKING, TOO. WE'RE STARTING SOME LOCATION SHOTS IN SPAIN NEXT WEEK...
I HAD JUST WRITTEN MY SIGNATURE... MARILYN'S SIGNATURE.. WHEN PETER APPEARED...
YOU SHOULD HAVE BEEN UP EARLIER, DAPHNE..ER.. I MEAN, MARILYN. I'VE BEEN FOR A WALK RIGHT ALONG THE CLIFF..
WHO'S THIS GUY YOU'RE TAGGING AROUND WITH, MARILYN?

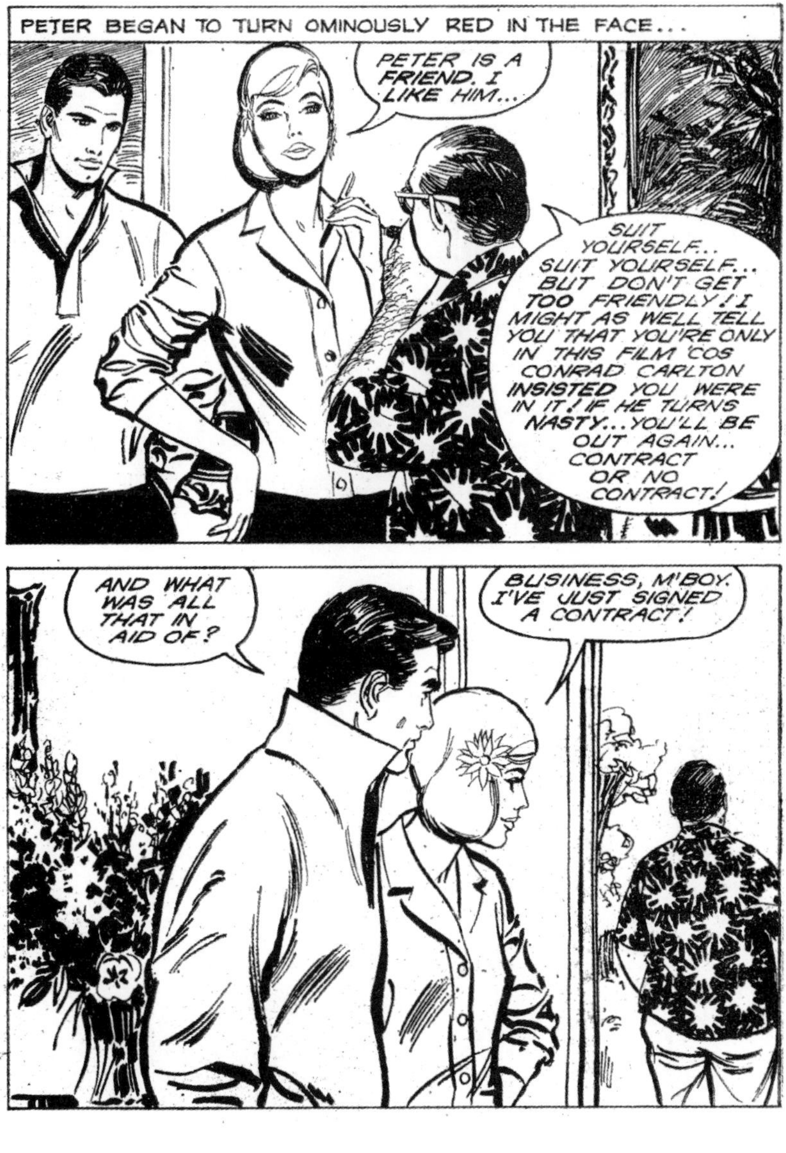
PETER BEGAN TO TURN OMINOUSLY RED IN THE FACE...
PETER IS A FRIEND. I LIKE HIM...
SUIT YOURSELF... SUIT YOURSELF... BUT DON'T GET TOO FRIENDLY! I MIGHT AS WELL TELL YOU THAT YOU'RE ONLY IN THIS FILM 'COS CONRAD CARLTON INSISTED YOU WERE IN IT! IF HE TURNS NASTY... YOU'LL BE OUT AGAIN... CONTRACT OR NO CONTRACT!
AND WHAT WAS ALL THAT IN AID OF?
BUSINESS, M'BOY. I'VE JUST SIGNED A CONTRACT!

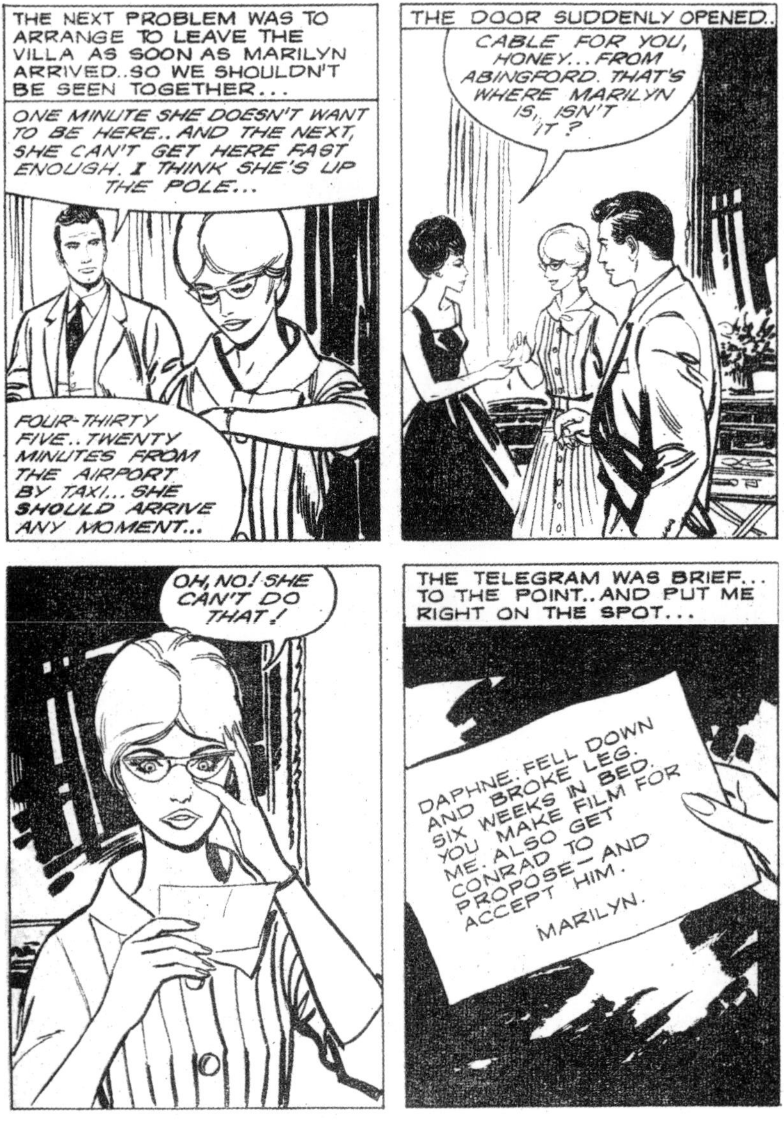
THE NEXT PROBLEM WAS TO ARRANGE TO LEAVE THE VILLA AS SOON AS MARILYN ARRIVED..SO WE SHOULDN'T BE SEEN TOGETHER...
ONE MINUTE SHE DOESN'T WANT TO BE HERE..AND THE NEXT, SHE CAN'T GET HERE FAST ENOUGH. I THINK SHE'S UP THE POLE...
FOUR-THIRTY FIVE..TWENTY MINUTES FROM THE AIRPORT BY TAXI... SHE SHOULD ARRIVE ANY MOMENT...
THE DOOR SUDDENLY OPENED.
CABLE FOR YOU, HONEY... FROM ABINGFORD. THAT'S WHERE MARILYN IS, ISN'T IT?
OH, NO! SHE CAN'T DO THAT!
THE TELEGRAM WAS BRIEF... TO THE POINT..AND PUT ME RIGHT ON THE SPOT...
DAPHNE FELL DOWN AND BROKE LEG. SIX WEEKS IN BED. YOU MAKE FILM FOR ME. ALSO GET CONRAD TO PROPOSE—AND ACCEPT HIM.
MARILYN.

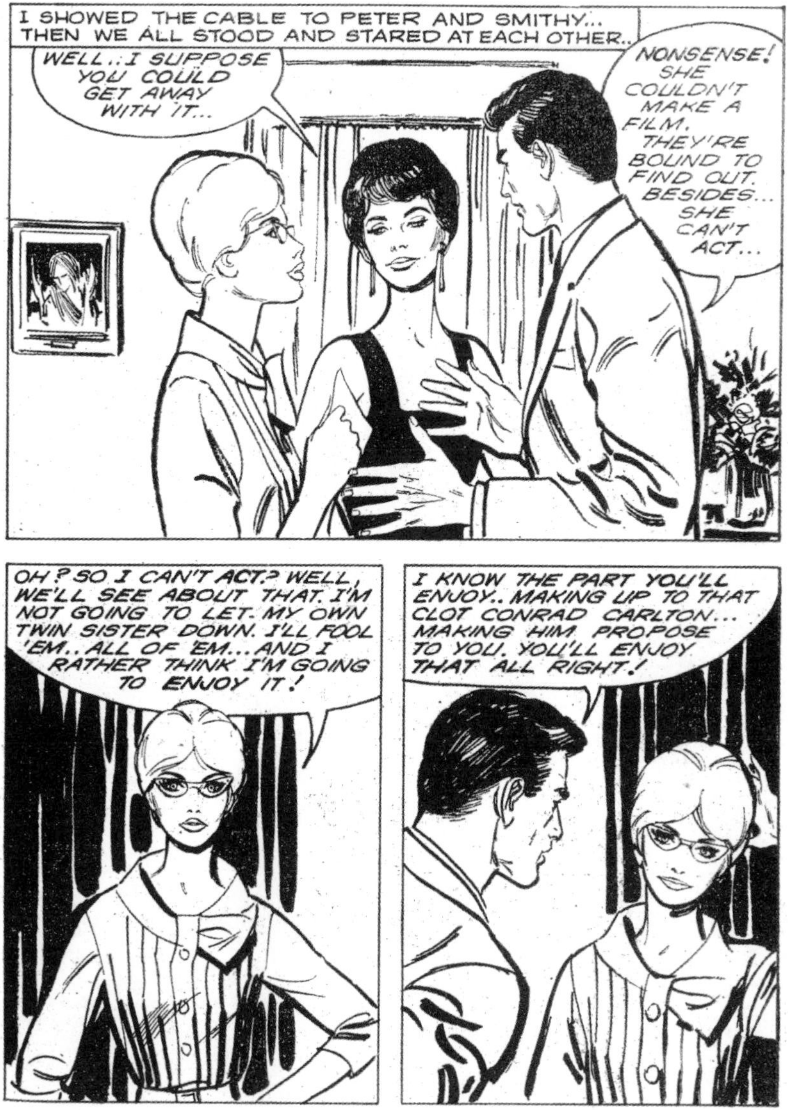
I SHOWED THE CABLE TO PETER AND SMITHY... THEN WE ALL STOOD AND STARED AT EACH OTHER..
WELL..I SUPPOSE YOU COULD GET AWAY WITH IT...
NONSENSE! SHE COULDN'T MAKE A FILM. THEY'RE BOUND TO FIND OUT. BESIDES... SHE CAN'T ACT...
OH? SO I CAN'T ACT? WELL, WE'LL SEE ABOUT THAT. I'M NOT GOING TO LET MY OWN TWIN SISTER DOWN. I'LL FOOL 'EM.. ALL OF 'EM... AND I RATHER THINK I'M GOING TO ENJOY IT!
I KNOW THE PART YOU'LL ENJOY.. MAKING UP TO THAT CLOT CONRAD CARLTON... MAKING HIM PROPOSE TO YOU. YOU'LL ENJOY THAT ALL RIGHT!

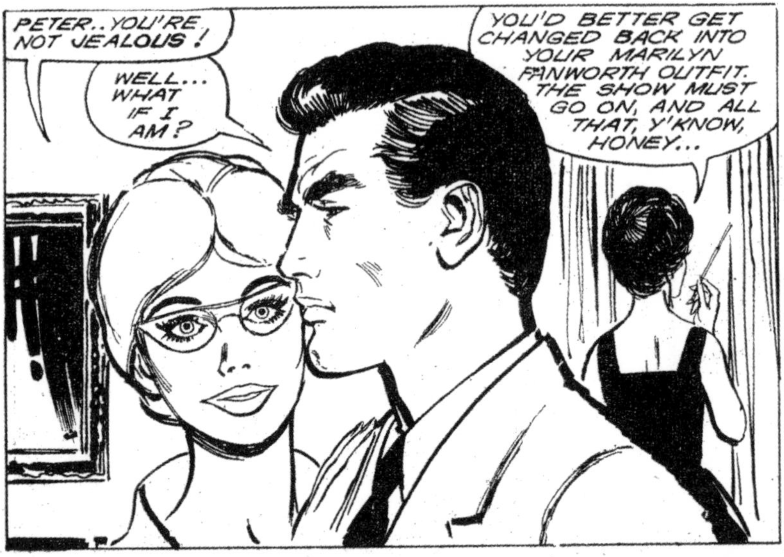
PETER..YOU'RE NOT JEALOUS!
WELL... WHAT IF I AM?
YOU'D BETTER GET CHANGED BACK INTO YOUR MARILYN FANWORTH OUTFIT. THE SHOW MUST GO ON, AND ALL THAT, Y'KNOW, HONEY...

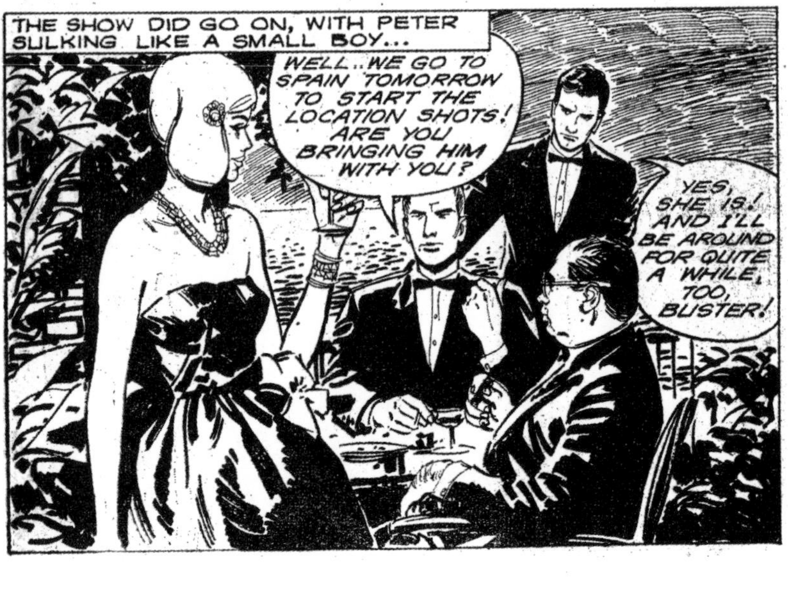
THE SHOW DID GO ON, WITH PETER SULKING LIKE A SMALL BOY...
WELL..WE GO TO SPAIN TOMORROW TO START THE LOCATION SHOTS! ARE YOU BRINGING HIM WITH YOU?
YES, SHE IS! AND I'LL BE AROUND FOR QUITE A WHILE, TOO, BUSTER!

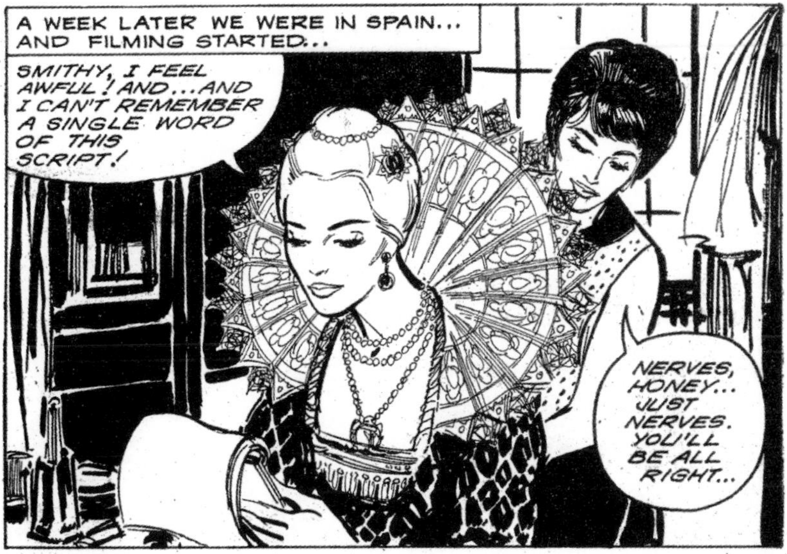
A WEEK LATER WE WERE IN SPAIN... AND FILMING STARTED...
SMITHY, I FEEL AWFUL! AND...AND I CAN'T REMEMBER A SINGLE WORD OF THIS SCRIPT!
NERVES, HONEY... JUST NERVES. YOU'LL BE ALL RIGHT...

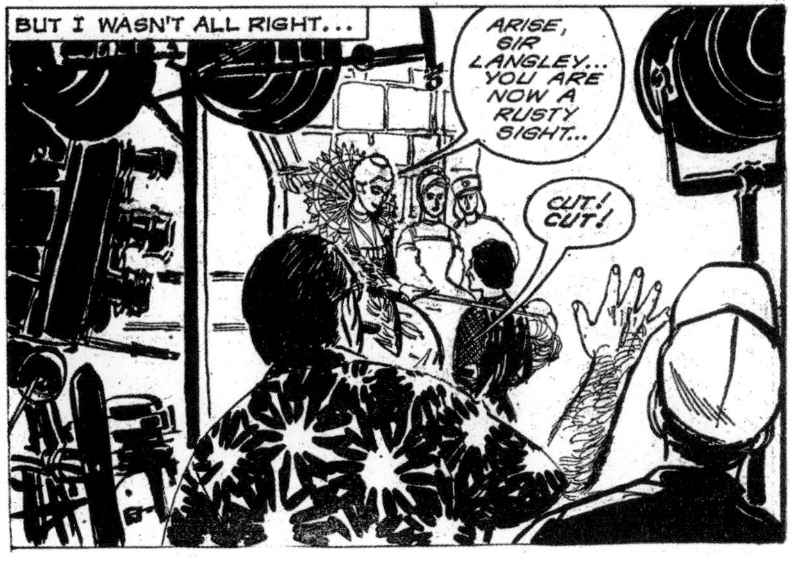
BUT I WASN'T ALL RIGHT...
ARISE, SIR LANGLEY... YOU ARE NOW A RUSTY SIGHT...
CUT! CUT!

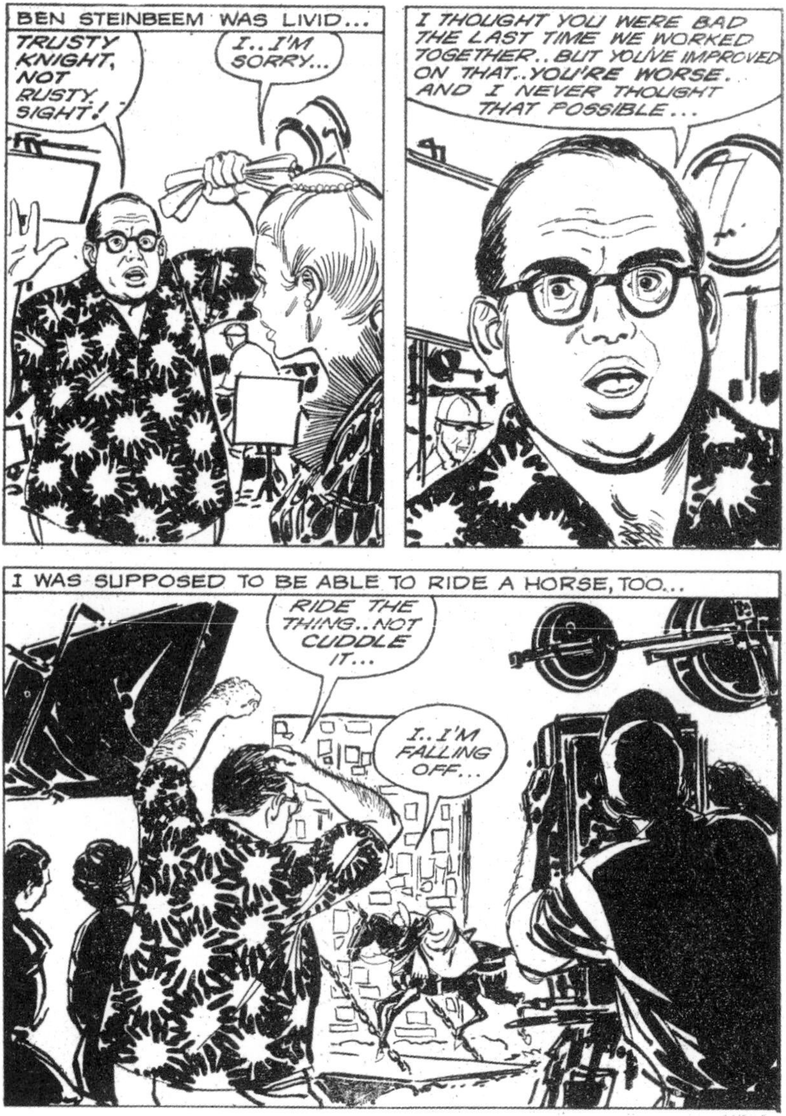
BEN STEINBEEM WAS LIVID...
TRUSTY KNIGHT, NOT RUSTY SIGHT!
I..I'M SORRY...
I THOUGHT YOU WERE BAD THE LAST TIME WE WORKED TOGETHER..BUT YOU'VE IMPROVED ON THAT..YOU'RE WORSE. AND I NEVER THOUGHT THAT POSSIBLE...
I WAS SUPPOSED TO BE ABLE TO RIDE A HORSE, TOO...
RIDE THE THING..NOT CUDDLE IT...
I..I'M FALLING OFF...

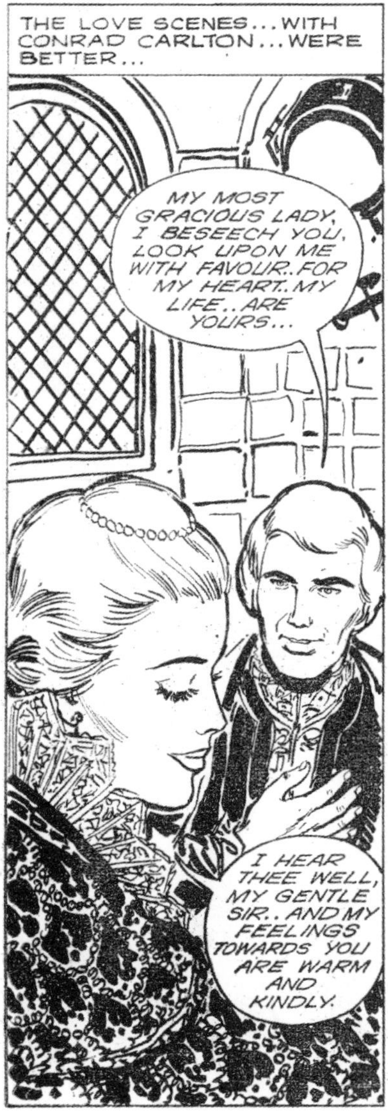
THE LOVE SCENES...WITH CONRAD CARLTON...WERE BETTER...
MY MOST GRACIOUS LADY, I BESEECH YOU. LOOK UPON ME WITH FAVOUR..FOR MY HEART..MY LIFE..ARE YOURS...
I HEAR THEE WELL, MY GENTLE SIR..AND MY FEELINGS TOWARDS YOU ARE WARM AND KINDLY.

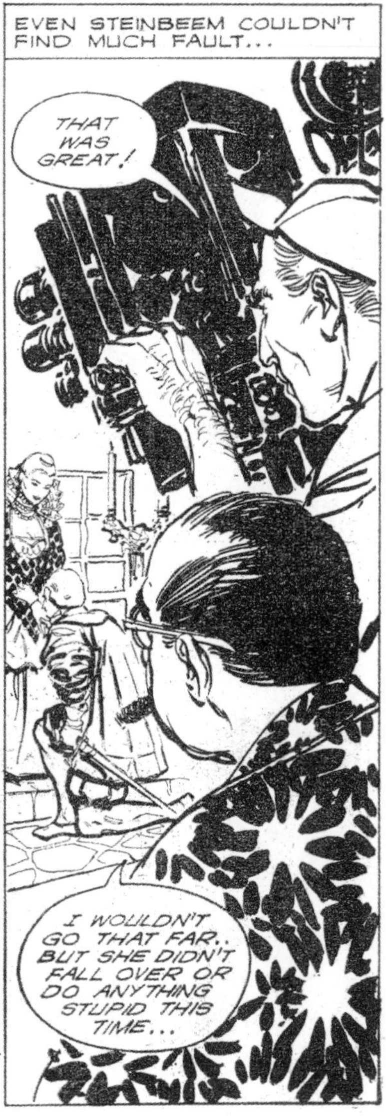
EVEN STEINBEEM COULDN'T FIND MUCH FAULT...
THAT WAS GREAT!
I WOULDN'T GO THAT FAR.. BUT SHE DIDN'T FALL OVER OR DO ANYTHING STUPID THIS TIME...

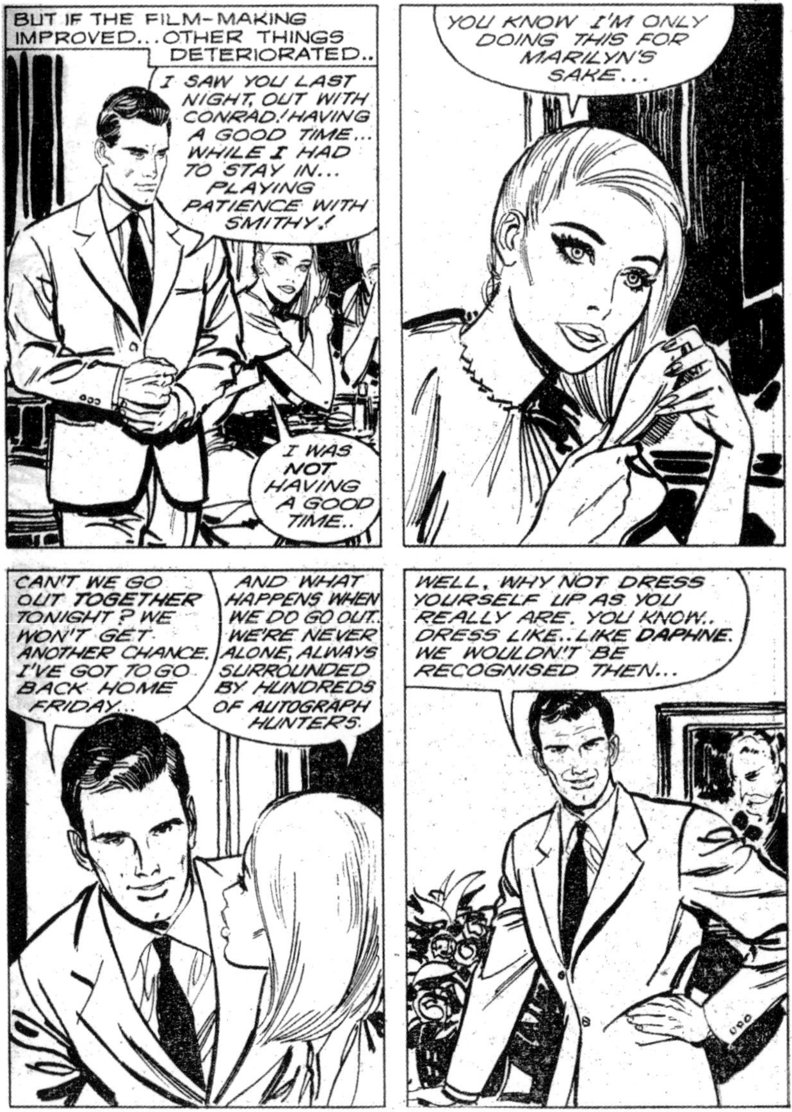
BUT IF THE FILM-MAKING IMPROVED... OTHER THINGS DETERIORATED..
I SAW YOU LAST NIGHT, OUT WITH CONRAD! HAVING A GOOD TIME... WHILE I HAD TO STAY IN... PLAYING PATIENCE WITH SMITHY!
I WAS NOT HAVING A GOOD TIME..
YOU KNOW I'M ONLY DOING THIS FOR MARILYN'S SAKE...
CAN'T WE GO OUT TOGETHER TONIGHT? WE WON'T GET ANOTHER CHANCE. I'VE GOT TO GO BACK HOME FRIDAY...
AND WHAT HAPPENS WHEN WE DO GO OUT.. WE'RE NEVER ALONE, ALWAYS SURROUNDED BY HUNDREDS OF AUTOGRAPH HUNTERS.
WELL, WHY NOT DRESS YOURSELF UP AS YOU REALLY ARE. YOU KNOW.. DRESS LIKE.. LIKE DAPHNE. WE WOULDN'T BE RECOGNISED THEN...

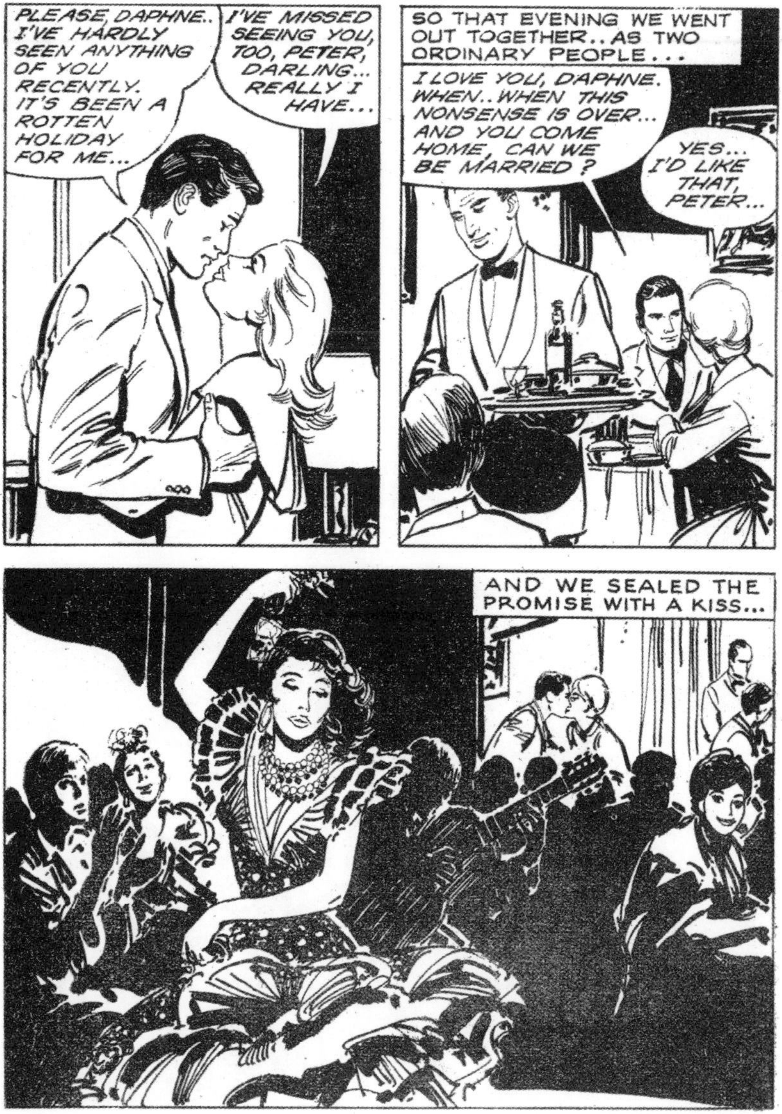
PLEASE, DAPHNE.. I'VE HARDLY SEEN ANYTHING OF YOU RECENTLY. IT'S BEEN A ROTTEN HOLIDAY FOR ME...
I'VE MISSED SEEING YOU, TOO, PETER, DARLING... REALLY I HAVE...
SO THAT EVENING WE WENT OUT TOGETHER.. AS TWO ORDINARY PEOPLE...
I LOVE YOU, DAPHNE. WHEN..WHEN THIS NONSENSE IS OVER... AND YOU COME HOME, CAN WE BE MARRIED ?
YES... I'D LIKE THAT, PETER...
AND WE SEALED THE PROMISE WITH A KISS...

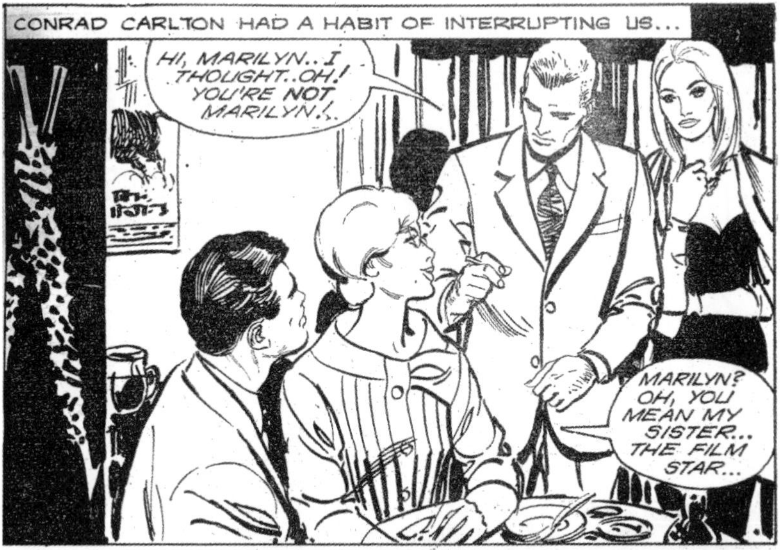
CONRAD CARLTON HAD A HABIT OF INTERRUPTING US...
HI, MARILYN.. I THOUGHT..OH! YOU'RE NOT MARILYN!..
MARILYN? OH, YOU MEAN MY SISTER... THE FILM STAR...

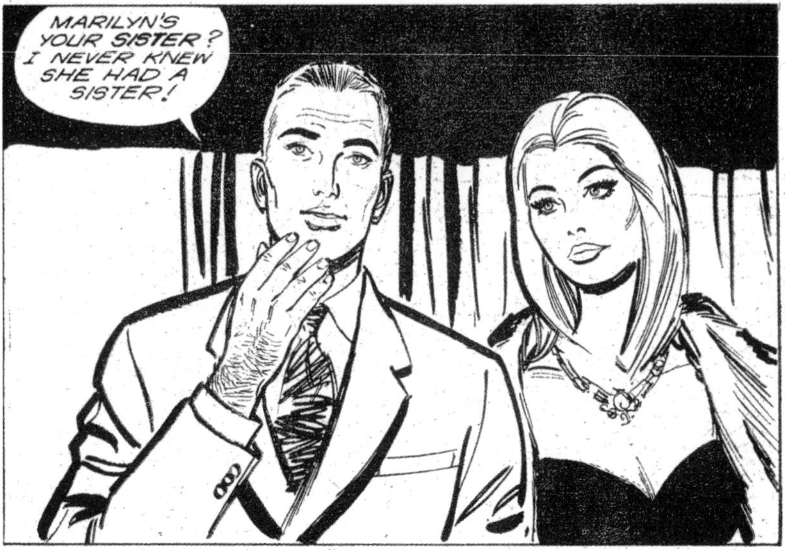
MARILYN'S YOUR SISTER? I NEVER KNEW SHE HAD A SISTER!

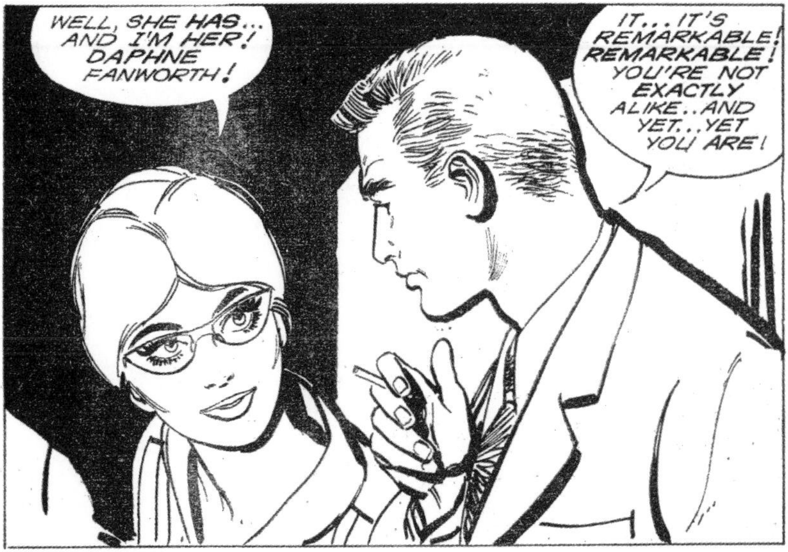
WELL, SHE HAS... AND I'M HER! DAPHNE FANWORTH!
IT...IT'S REMARKABLE! REMARKABLE! YOU'RE NOT EXACTLY ALIKE..AND YET..YET YOU ARE!

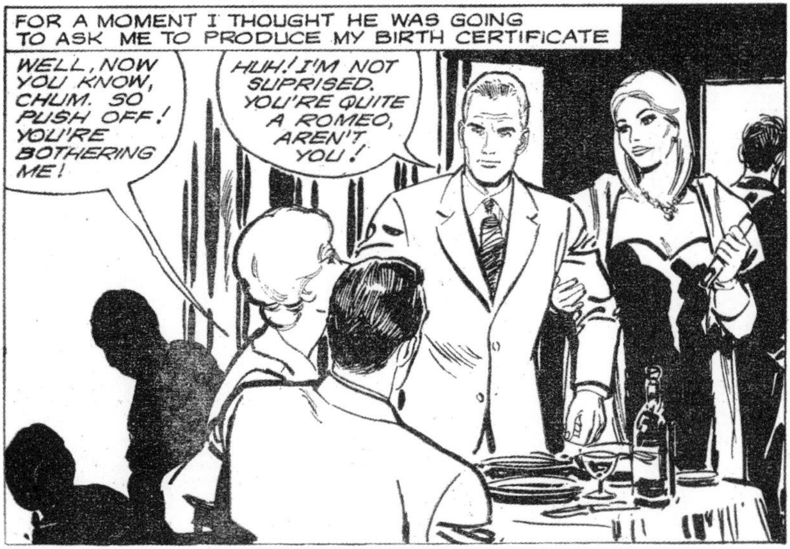
FOR A MOMENT I THOUGHT HE WAS GOING TO ASK ME TO PRODUCE MY BIRTH CERTIFICATE
WELL, NOW YOU KNOW, CHUM. SO PUSH OFF! YOU'RE BOTHERING ME!
HUH! I'M NOT SUPRISED. YOU'RE QUITE A ROMEO, AREN'T YOU!

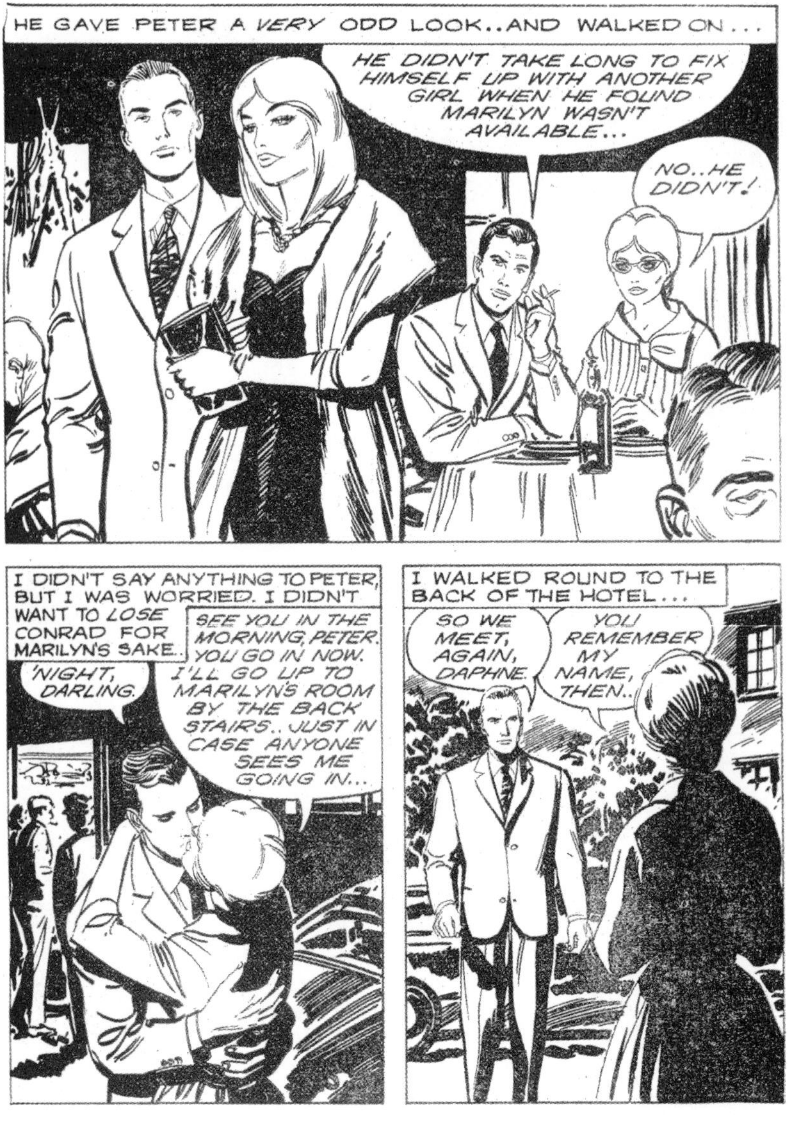
HE GAVE PETER A VERY ODD LOOK..AND WALKED ON...
HE DIDN'T TAKE LONG TO FIX HIMSELF UP WITH ANOTHER GIRL WHEN HE FOUND MARILYN WASN'T AVAILABLE...
NO..HE DIDN'T!
I DIDN'T SAY ANYTHING TO PETER, BUT I WAS WORRIED. I DIDN'T WANT TO LOSE CONRAD FOR MARILYN'S SAKE..
SEE YOU IN THE MORNING, PETER. YOU GO IN NOW. I'LL GO UP TO MARILYN'S ROOM BY THE BACK STAIRS.. JUST IN CASE ANYONE SEES ME GOING IN...
'NIGHT, DARLING.
I WALKED ROUND TO THE BACK OF THE HOTEL...
SO WE MEET, AGAIN, DAPHNE.
YOU REMEMBER MY NAME, THEN..

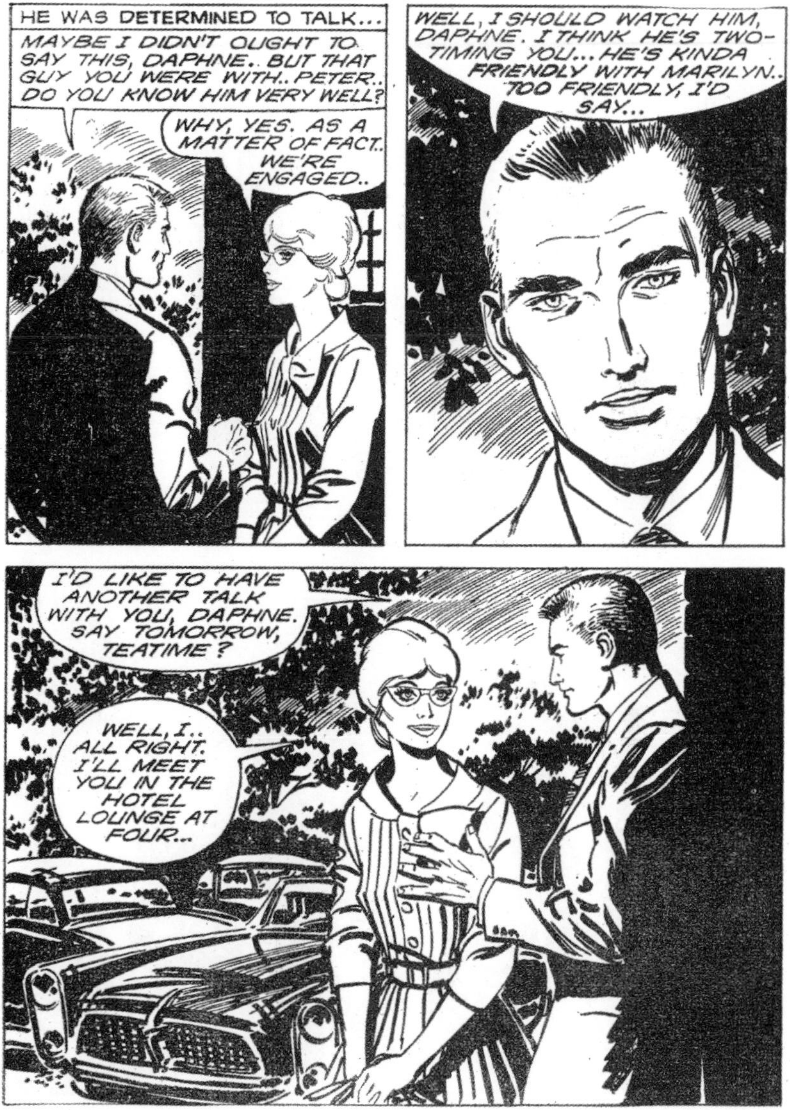
HE WAS DETERMINED TO TALK...
MAYBE I DIDN'T OUGHT TO SAY THIS, DAPHNE.. BUT THAT GUY YOU WERE WITH.. PETER.. DO YOU KNOW HIM VERY WELL?
WHY, YES. AS A MATTER OF FACT.. WE'RE ENGAGED..
WELL, I SHOULD WATCH HIM, DAPHNE. I THINK HE'S TWO-TIMING YOU... HE'S KINDA FRIENDLY WITH MARILYN.. TOO FRIENDLY, I'D SAY...
I'D LIKE TO HAVE ANOTHER TALK WITH YOU, DAPHNE. SAY TOMORROW, TEATIME?
WELL, I.. ALL RIGHT. I'LL MEET YOU IN THE HOTEL LOUNGE AT FOUR...

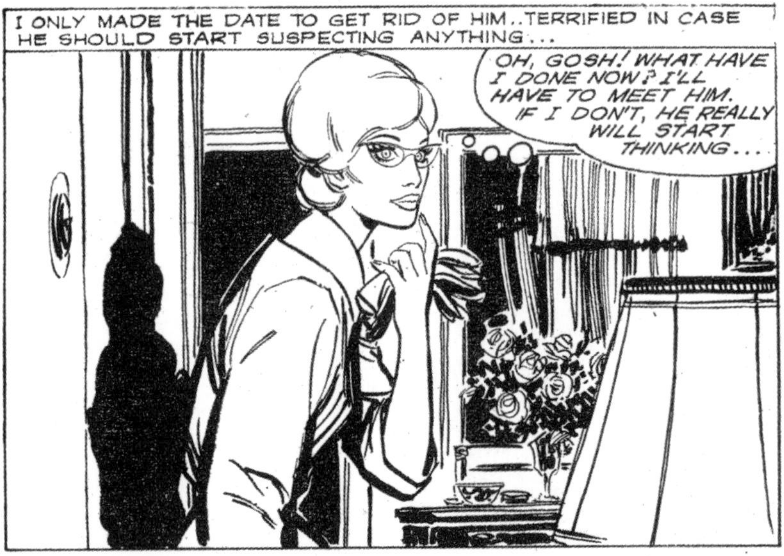
I ONLY MADE THE DATE TO GET RID OF HIM..TERRIFIED IN CASE HE SHOULD START SUSPECTING ANYTHING...
OH, GOSH! WHAT HAVE I DONE NOW? I'LL HAVE TO MEET HIM. IF I DON'T, HE REALLY WILL START THINKING...

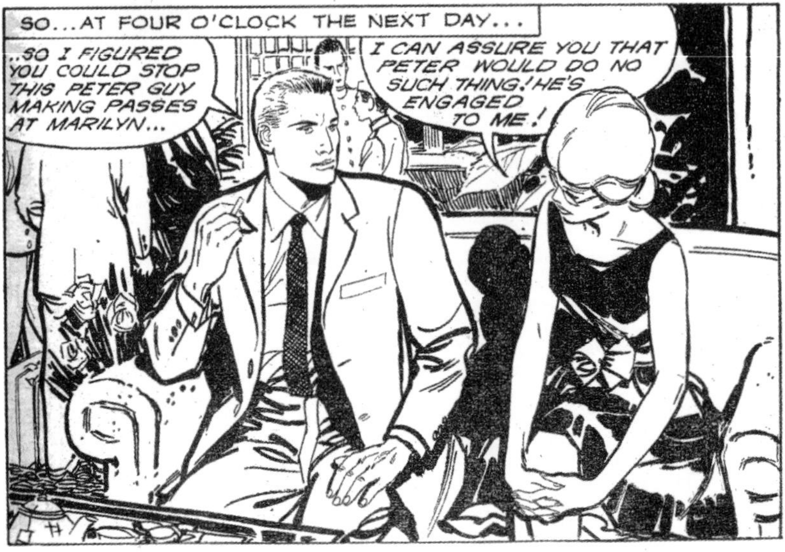
SO...AT FOUR O'CLOCK THE NEXT DAY...
..SO I FIGURED YOU COULD STOP THIS PETER GUY MAKING PASSES AT MARILYN...
I CAN ASSURE YOU THAT PETER WOULD DO NO SUCH THING! HE'S ENGAGED TO ME!

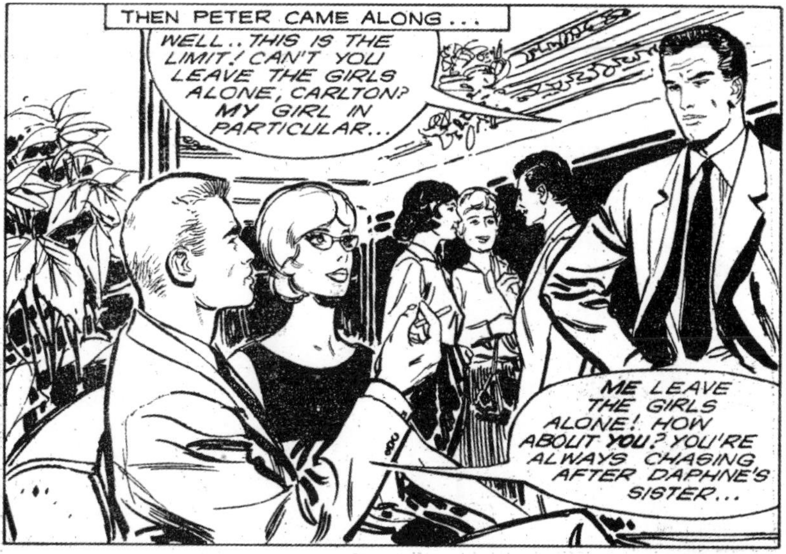
THEN PETER CAME ALONG . . .
WELL.. THIS IS THE LIMIT! CAN'T YOU LEAVE THE GIRLS ALONE, CARLTON? MY GIRL IN PARTICULAR...
ME LEAVE THE GIRLS ALONE! HOW ABOUT YOU? YOU'RE ALWAYS CHASING AFTER DAPHNE'S SISTER...

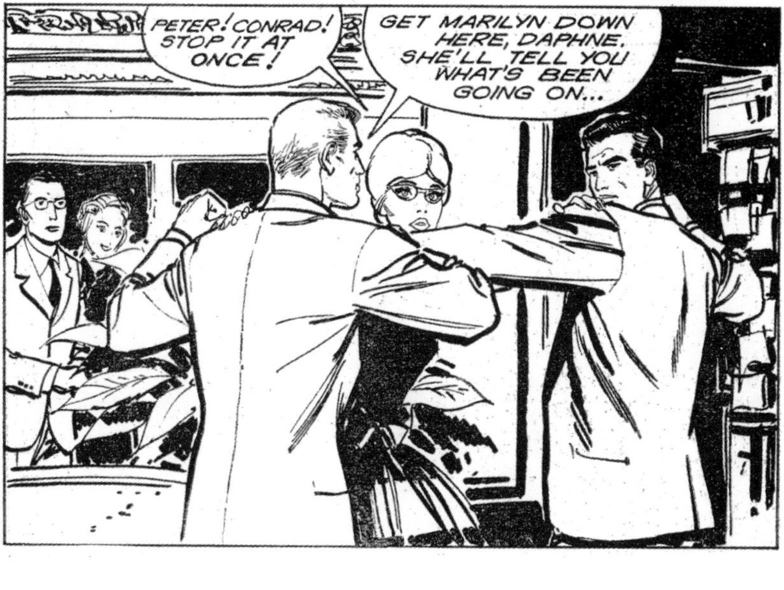
PETER! CONRAD! STOP IT AT ONCE!
GET MARILYN DOWN HERE, DAPHNE. SHE'LL TELL YOU WHAT'S BEEN GOING ON...

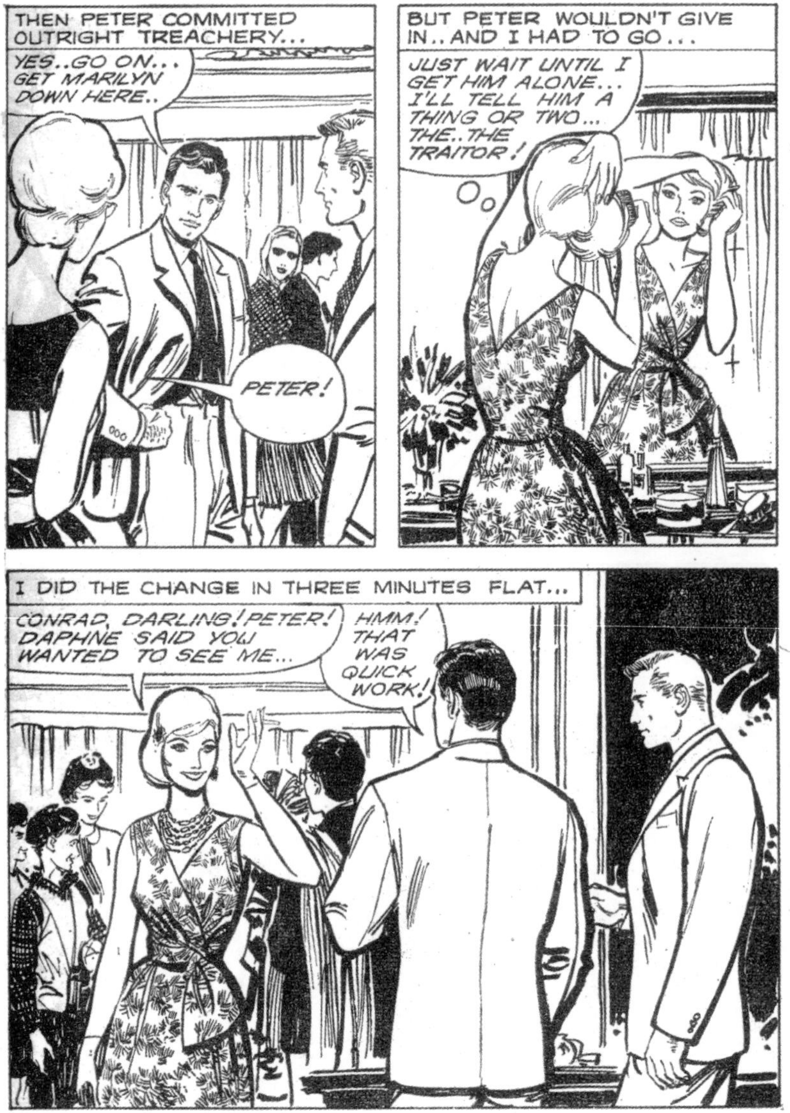
THEN PETER COMMITTED OUTRIGHT TREACHERY...
YES..GO ON... GET MARILYN DOWN HERE..
PETER!
BUT PETER WOULDN'T GIVE IN.. AND I HAD TO GO...
JUST WAIT UNTIL I GET HIM ALONE... I'LL TELL HIM A THING OR TWO... THE..THE TRAITOR!
I DID THE CHANGE IN THREE MINUTES FLAT...
CONRAD, DARLING! PETER! DAPHNE SAID YOU WANTED TO SEE ME...
HMM! THAT WAS QUICK WORK!

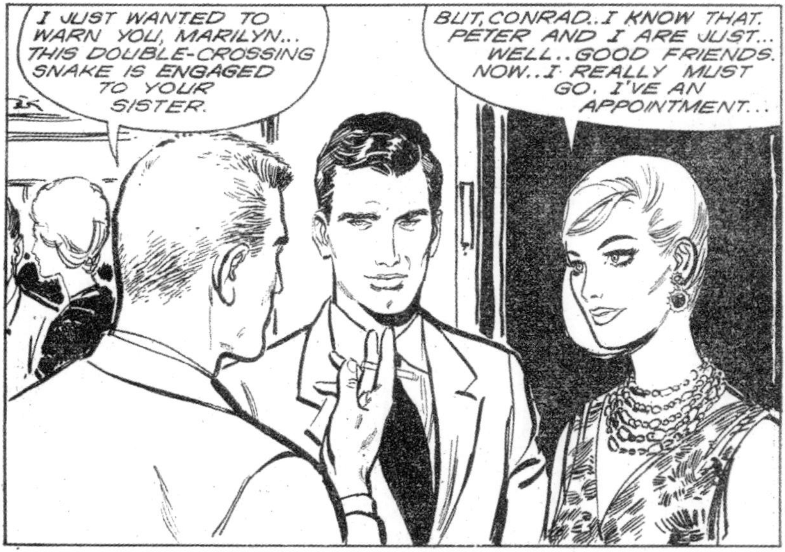
I JUST WANTED TO WARN YOU, MARILYN... THIS DOUBLE-CROSSING SNAKE IS ENGAGED TO YOUR SISTER.
BUT, CONRAD..I KNOW THAT. PETER AND I ARE JUST... WELL..GOOD FRIENDS. NOW..I REALLY MUST GO. I'VE AN APPOINTMENT...

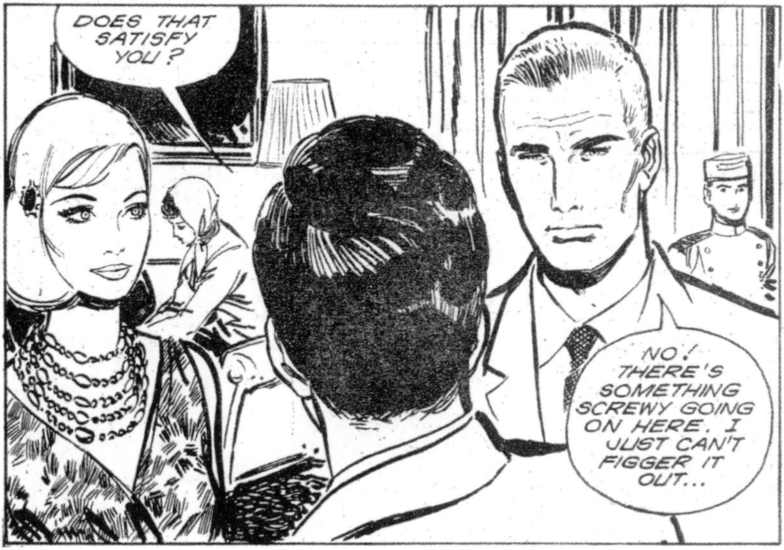
DOES THAT SATISFY YOU?
NO! THERE'S SOMETHING SCREWY GOING ON HERE. I JUST CAN'T FIGGER IT OUT...

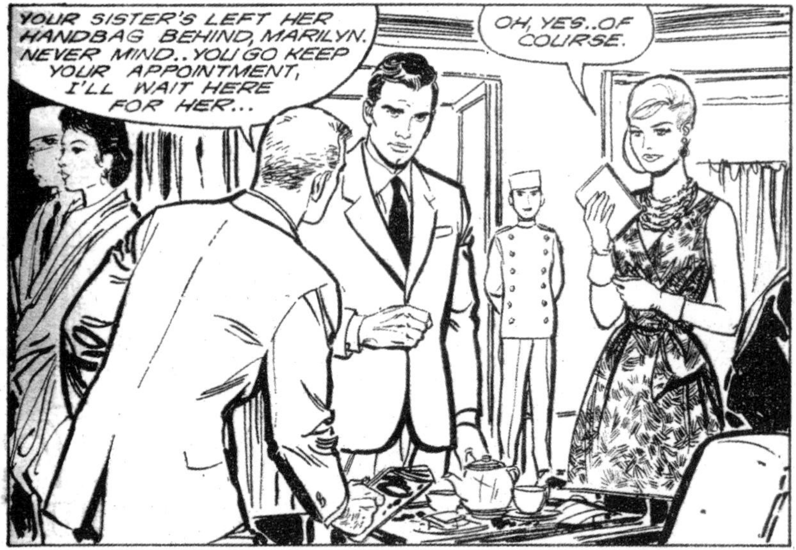
YOUR SISTER'S LEFT HER HANDBAG BEHIND, MARILYN. NEVER MIND.. YOU GO KEEP YOUR APPOINTMENT, I'LL WAIT HERE FOR HER...
OH, YES..OF COURSE.

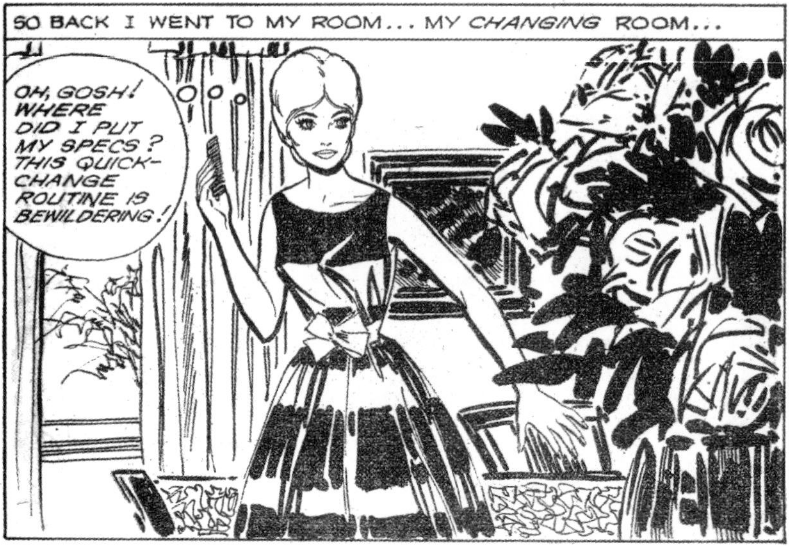
SO BACK I WENT TO MY ROOM... MY CHANGING ROOM...
OH, GOSH! WHERE DID I PUT MY SPECS? THIS QUICK-CHANGE ROUTINE IS BEWILDERING!

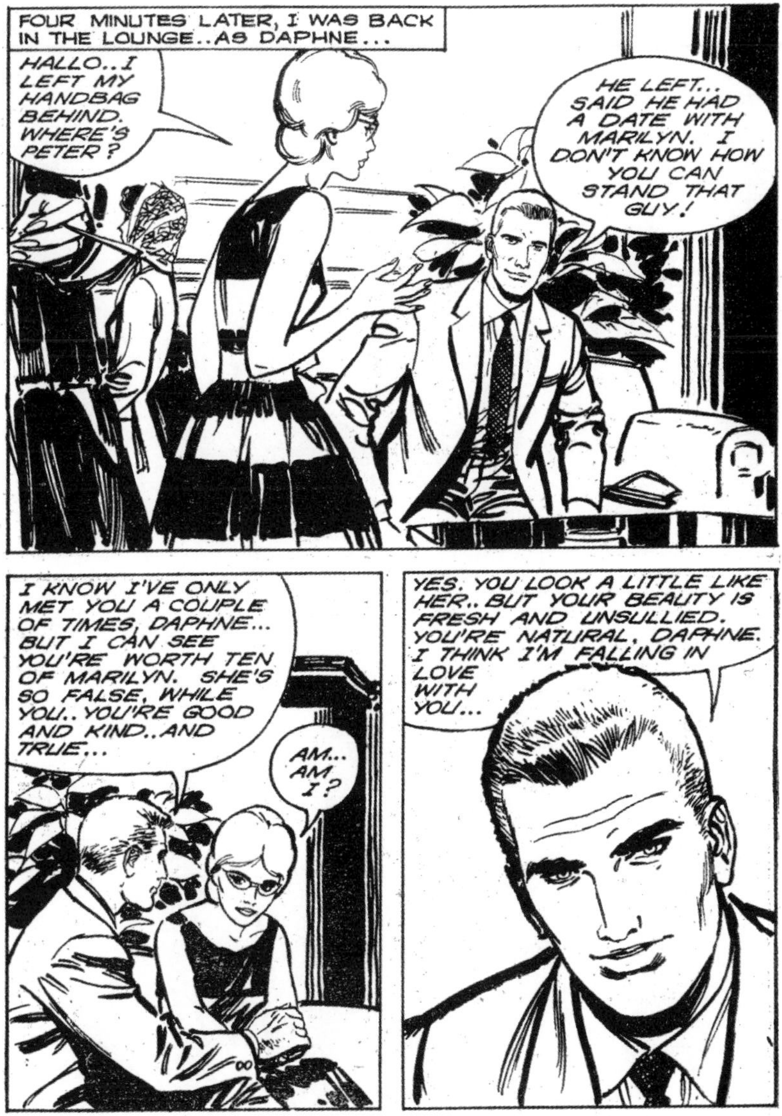
FOUR MINUTES LATER, I WAS BACK IN THE LOUNGE..AS DAPHNE...
HALLO..I LEFT MY HANDBAG BEHIND. WHERE'S PETER?
HE LEFT... SAID HE HAD A DATE WITH MARILYN. I DON'T KNOW HOW YOU CAN STAND THAT GUY!
I KNOW I'VE ONLY MET YOU A COUPLE OF TIMES, DAPHNE... BUT I CAN SEE YOU'RE WORTH TEN OF MARILYN. SHE'S SO FALSE, WHILE YOU..YOU'RE GOOD AND KIND..AND TRUE...
AM... AM I?
YES. YOU LOOK A LITTLE LIKE HER..BUT YOUR BEAUTY IS FRESH AND UNSULLIED. YOU'RE NATURAL, DAPHNE. I THINK I'M FALLING IN LOVE WITH YOU...

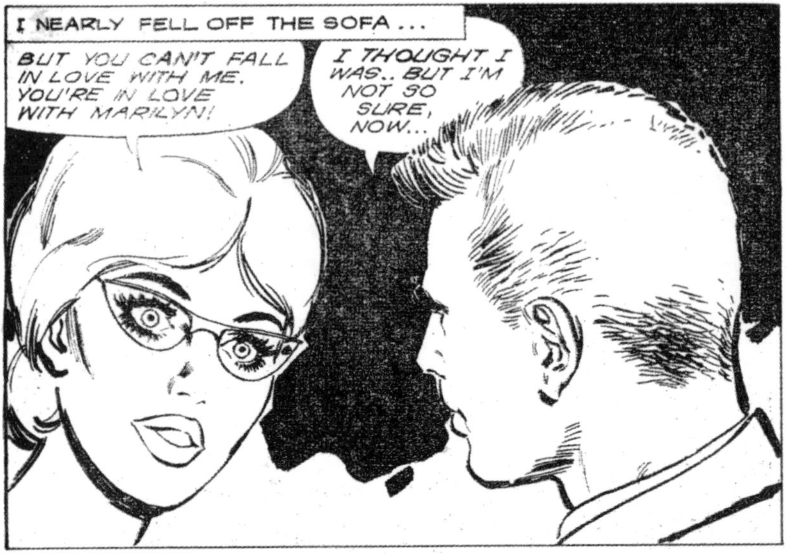
I NEARLY FELL OFF THE SOFA ...
BUT YOU CAN'T FALL IN LOVE WITH ME. YOU'RE IN LOVE WITH MARILYN!
I THOUGHT I WAS.. BUT I'M NOT SO SURE, NOW...

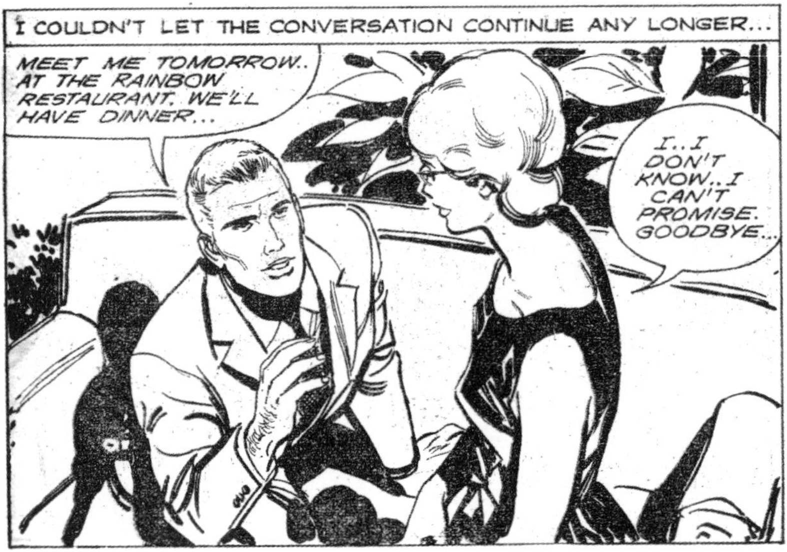
I COULDN'T LET THE CONVERSATION CONTINUE ANY LONGER...
MEET ME TOMORROW.. AT THE RAINBOW RESTAURANT. WE'LL HAVE DINNER...
I..I DON'T KNOW..I CAN'T PROMISE. GOODBYE...

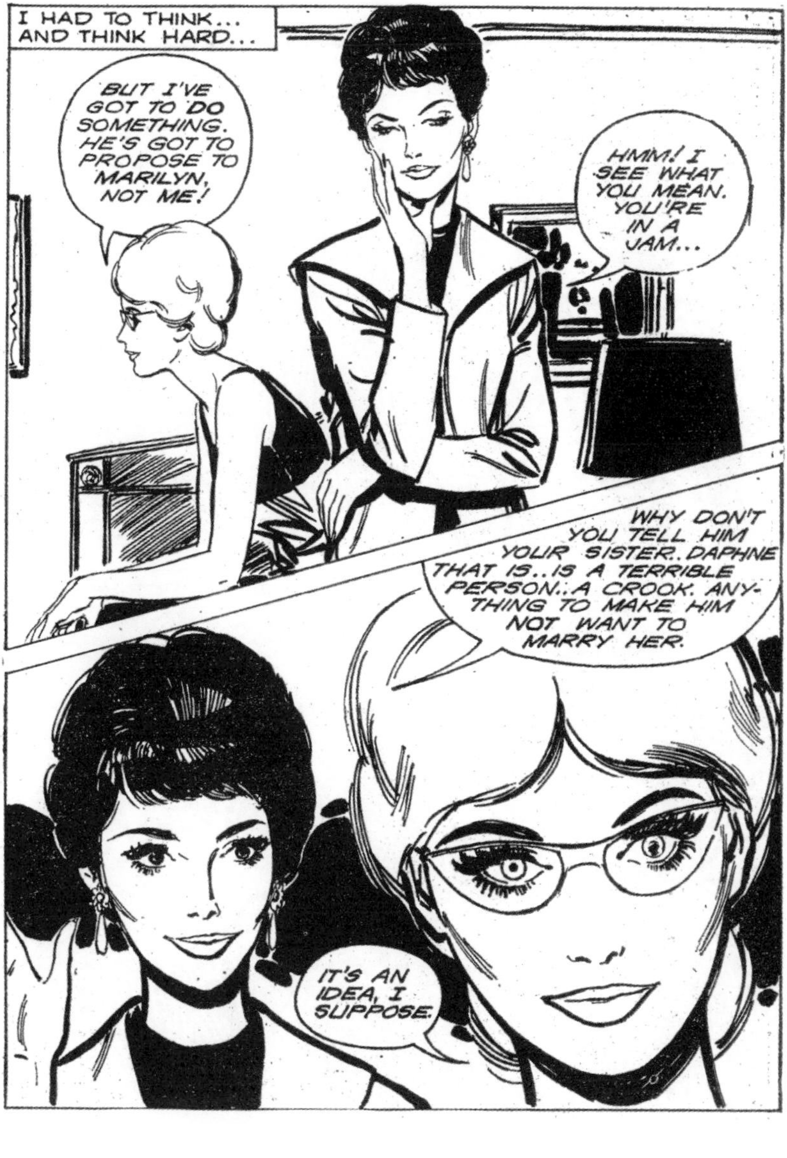
I HAD TO THINK... AND THINK HARD...
BUT I'VE GOT TO DO SOMETHING. HE'S GOT TO PROPOSE TO MARILYN, NOT ME!
HMM! I SEE WHAT YOU MEAN. YOU'RE IN A JAM...
WHY DON'T YOU TELL HIM YOUR SISTER..DAPHNE THAT IS..IS A TERRIBLE PERSON..A CROOK. ANYTHING TO MAKE HIM NOT WANT TO MARRY HER.
IT'S AN IDEA, I SUPPOSE.

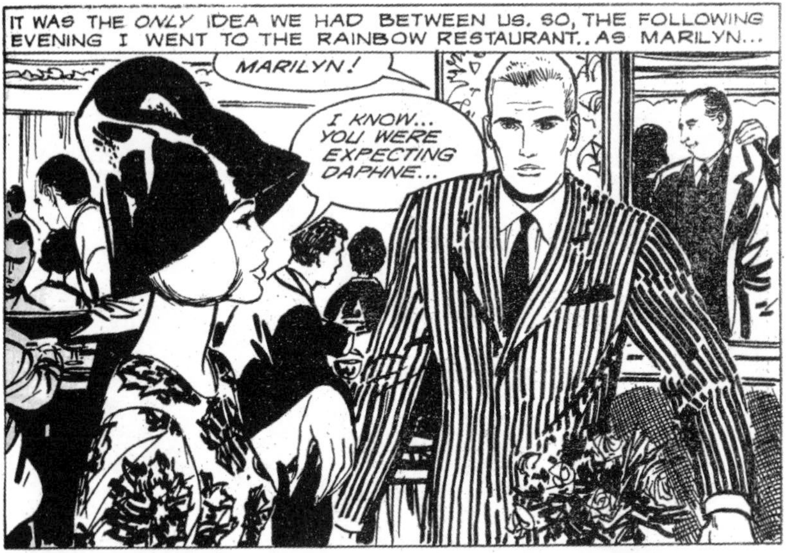
IT WAS THE ONLY IDEA WE HAD BETWEEN US. SO, THE FOLLOWING EVENING I WENT TO THE RAINBOW RESTAURANT.. AS MARILYN...
MARILYN!
I KNOW... YOU WERE EXPECTING DAPHNE...

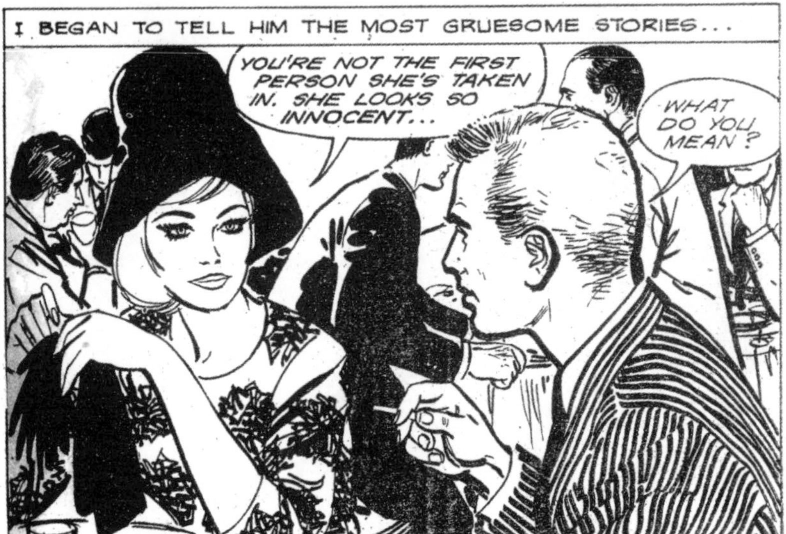
I BEGAN TO TELL HIM THE MOST GRUESOME STORIES...
YOU'RE NOT THE FIRST PERSON SHE'S TAKEN IN. SHE LOOKS SO INNOCENT...
WHAT DO YOU MEAN?

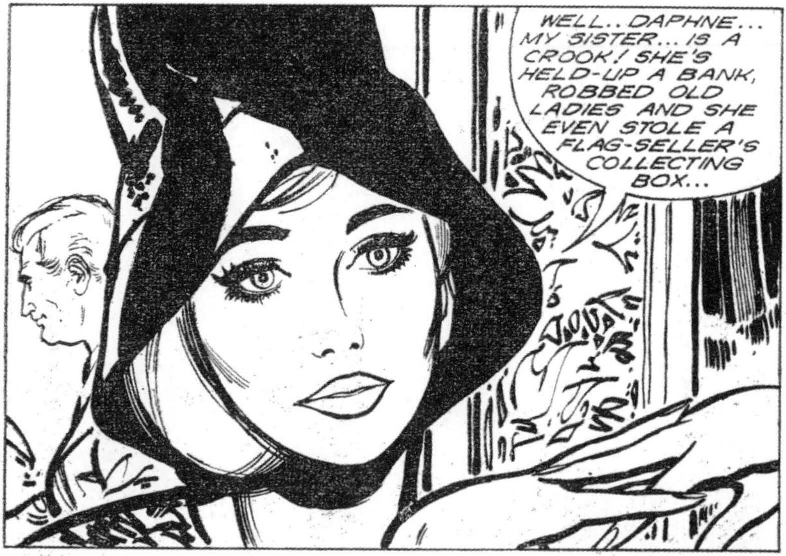
WELL...DAPHNE... MY SISTER... IS A CROOK! SHE'S HELD-UP A BANK, ROBBED OLD LADIES AND SHE EVEN STOLE A FLAG-SELLER'S COLLECTING BOX...

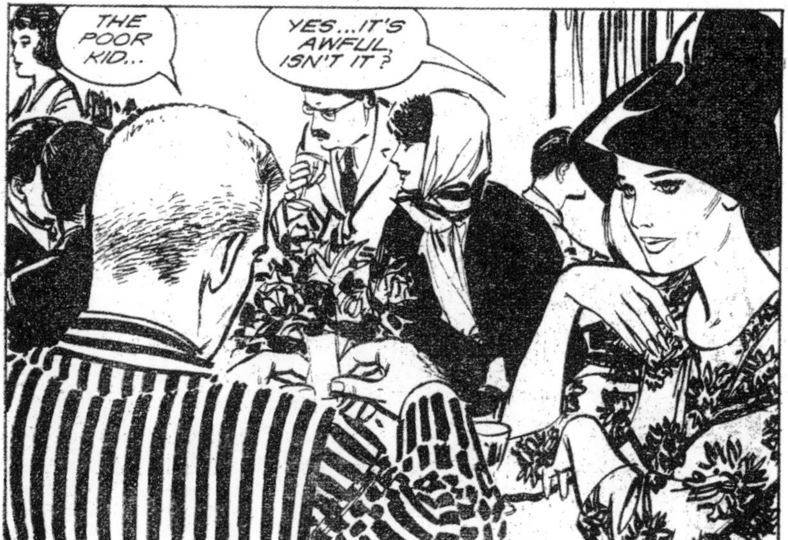
THE POOR KID...
YES...IT'S AWFUL, ISN'T IT?

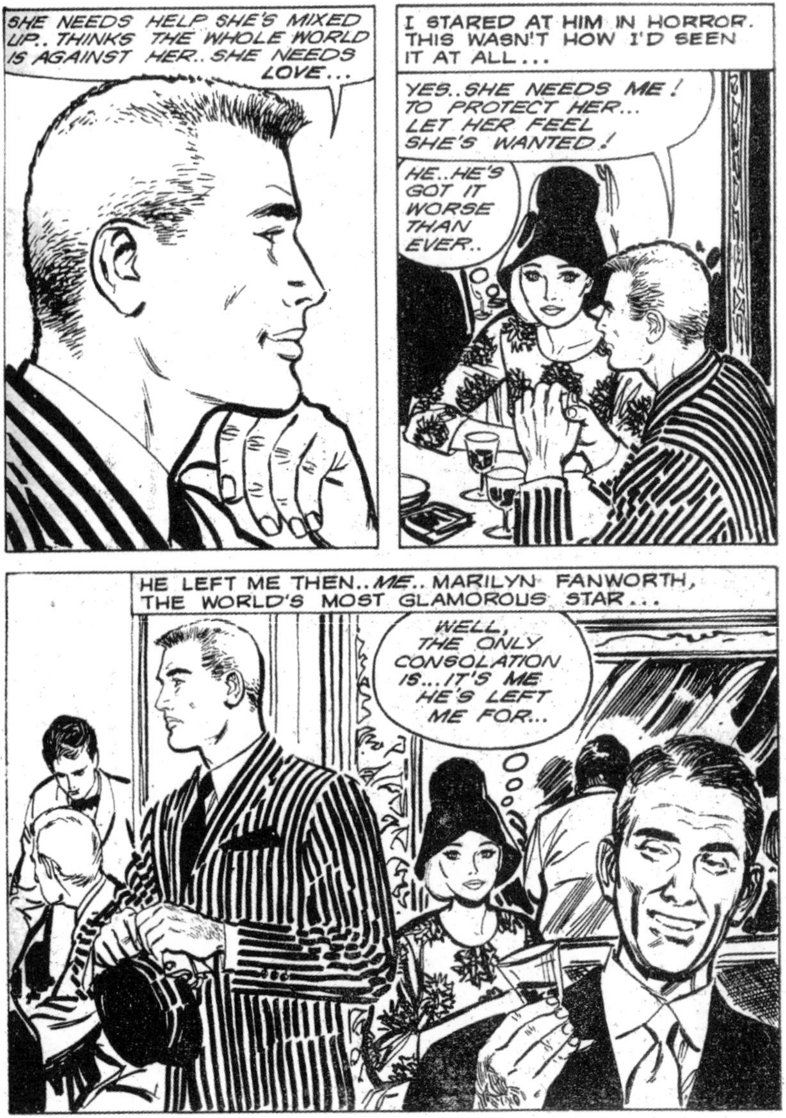
SHE NEEDS HELP. SHE'S MIXED UP.. THINKS THE WHOLE WORLD IS AGAINST HER.. SHE NEEDS LOVE...
I STARED AT HIM IN HORROR. THIS WASN'T HOW I'D SEEN IT AT ALL...
YES..SHE NEEDS ME! TO PROTECT HER... LET HER FEEL SHE'S WANTED!
HE..HE'S GOT IT WORSE THAN EVER..
HE LEFT ME THEN..ME..MARILYN FANWORTH, THE WORLD'S MOST GLAMOROUS STAR...
WELL, THE ONLY CONSOLATION IS...IT'S ME HE'S LEFT ME FOR...

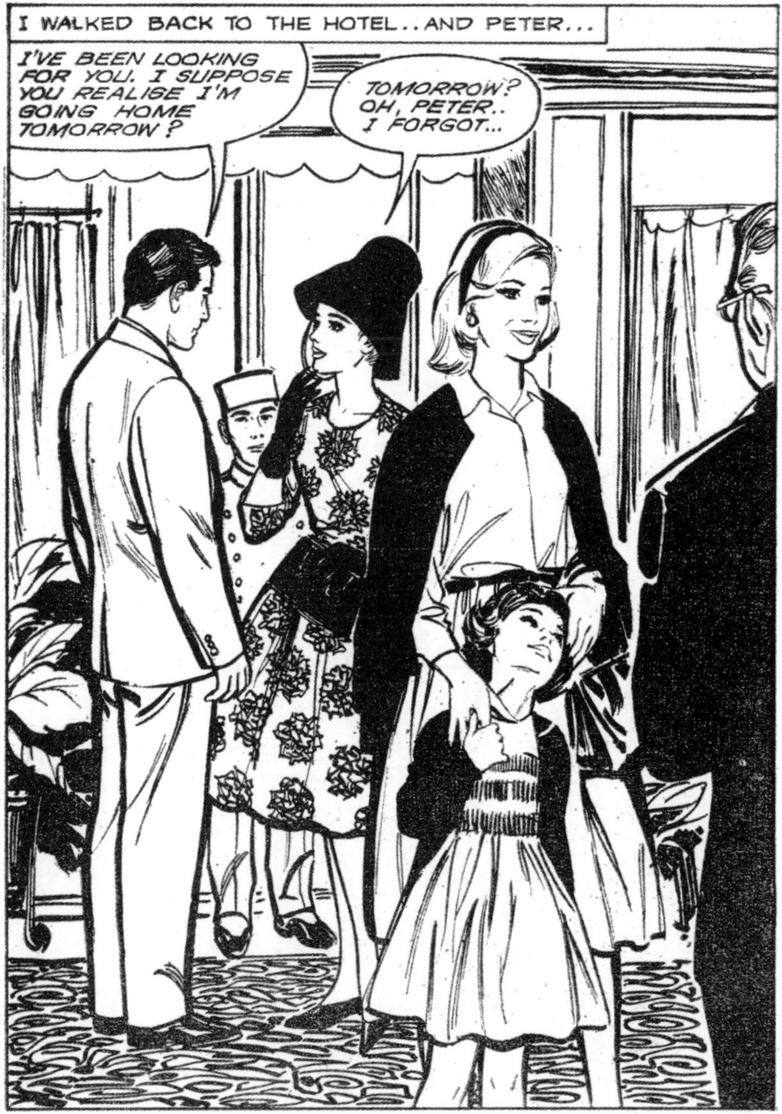
I WALKED BACK TO THE HOTEL.. AND PETER...
I'VE BEEN LOOKING FOR YOU. I SUPPOSE YOU REALISE I'M GOING HOME TOMORROW?
TOMORROW? OH, PETER.. I FORGOT...

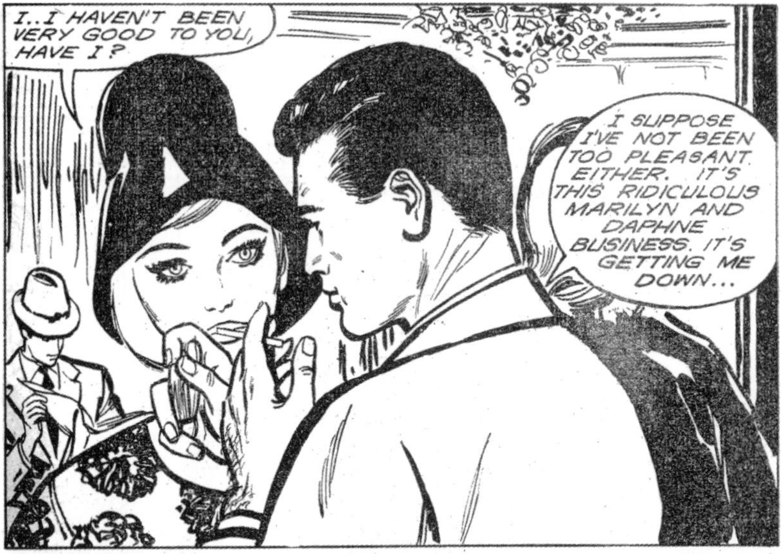
I..I HAVEN'T BEEN VERY GOOD TO YOU, HAVE I?
I SUPPOSE I'VE NOT BEEN TOO PLEASANT EITHER. IT'S THIS RIDICULOUS MARILYN AND DAPHNE BUSINESS. IT'S GETTING ME DOWN...

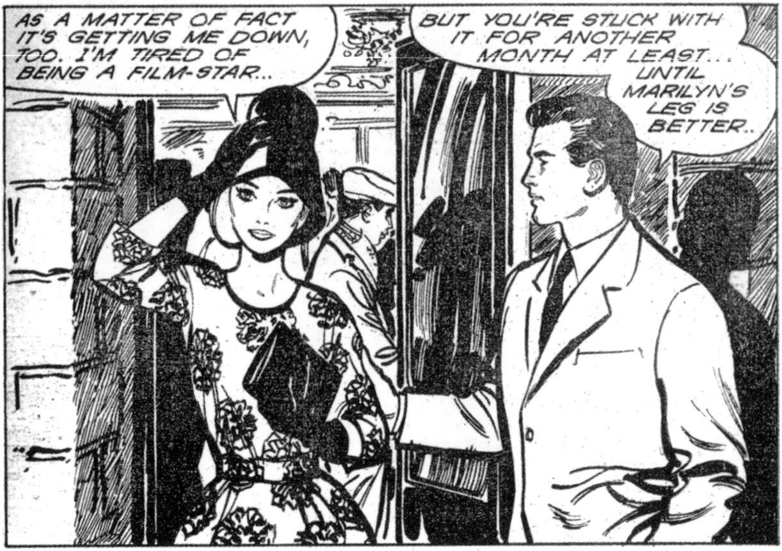
AS A MATTER OF FACT IT'S GETTING ME DOWN, TOO. I'M TIRED OF BEING A FILM-STAR...
BUT YOU'RE STUCK WITH IT FOR ANOTHER MONTH AT LEAST... UNTIL MARILYN'S LEG IS BETTER..

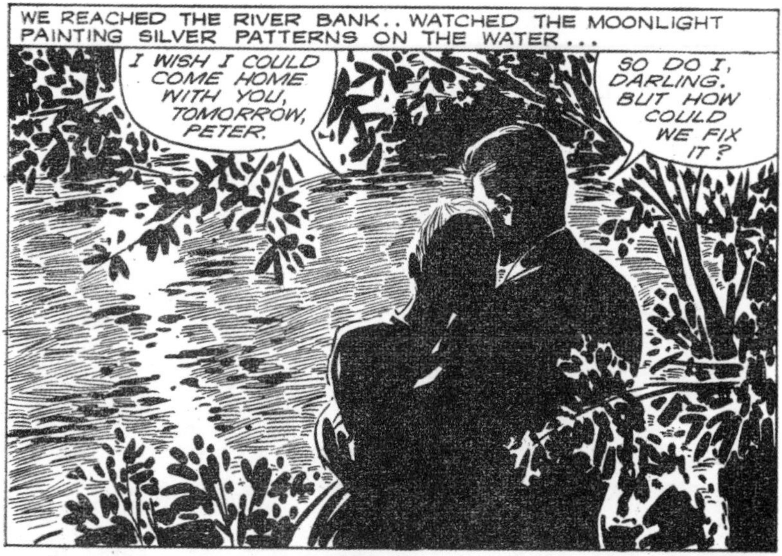
WE REACHED THE RIVER BANK.. WATCHED THE MOONLIGHT PAINTING SILVER PATTERNS ON THE WATER...
I WISH I COULD COME HOME WITH YOU, TOMORROW, PETER.
SO DO I, DARLING. BUT HOW COULD WE FIX IT?

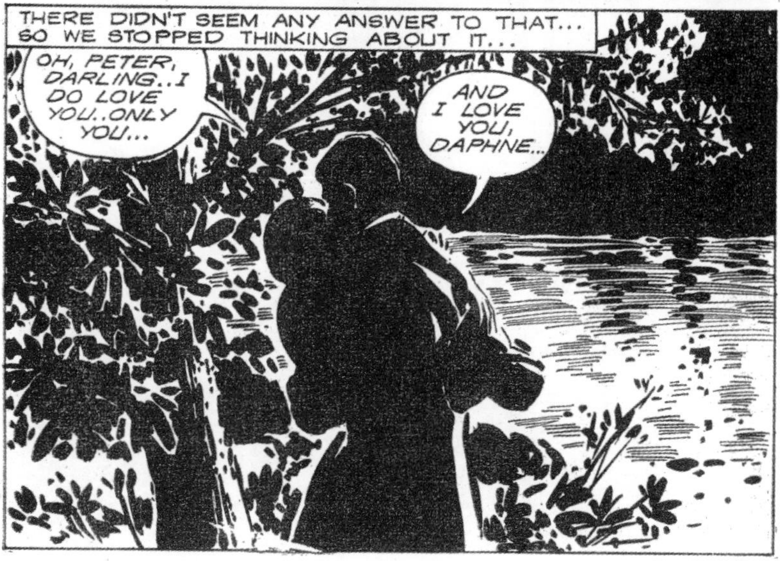
THERE DIDN'T SEEM ANY ANSWER TO THAT... SO WE STOPPED THINKING ABOUT IT...
OH, PETER, DARLING..I DO LOVE YOU..ONLY YOU...
AND I LOVE YOU, DAPHNE...

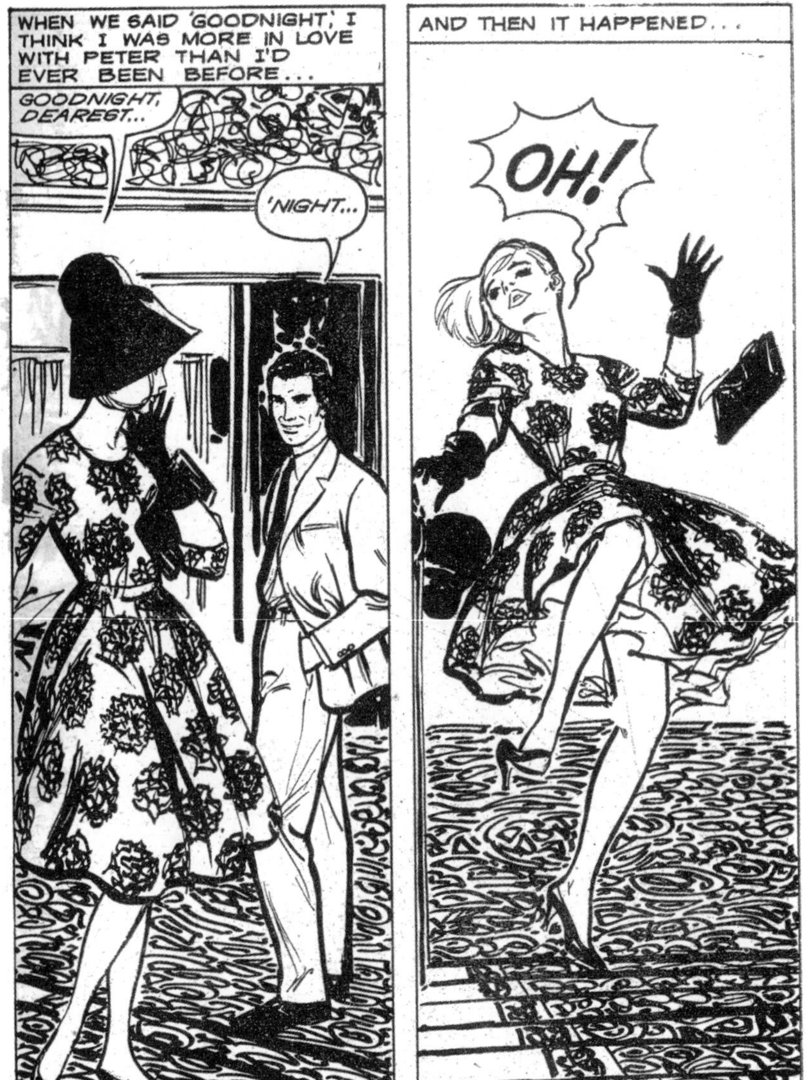
WHEN WE SAID 'GOODNIGHT,' I THINK I WAS MORE IN LOVE WITH PETER THAN I'D EVER BEEN BEFORE...
GOODNIGHT, DEAREST...
'NIGHT...
AND THEN IT HAPPENED...
OH!

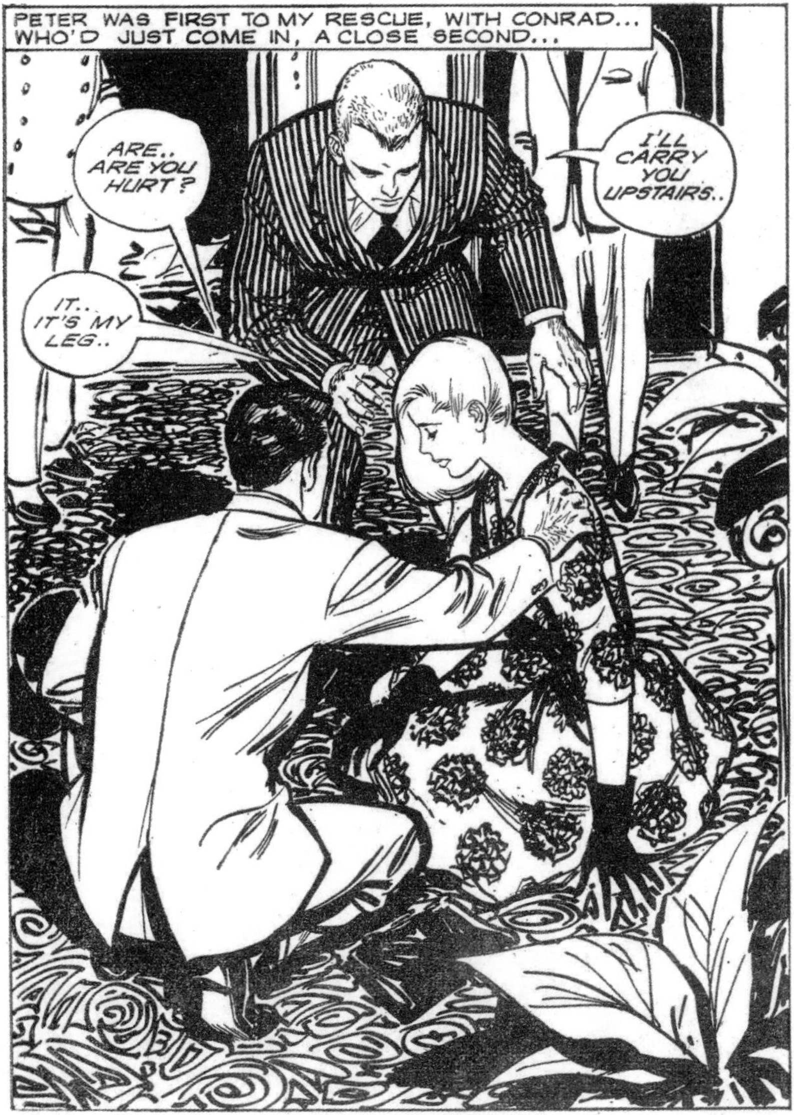
PETER WAS FIRST TO MY RESCUE, WITH CONRAD... WHO'D JUST COME IN, A CLOSE SECOND...
ARE.. ARE YOU HURT?
I'LL CARRY YOU UPSTAIRS..
IT.. IT'S MY LEG..

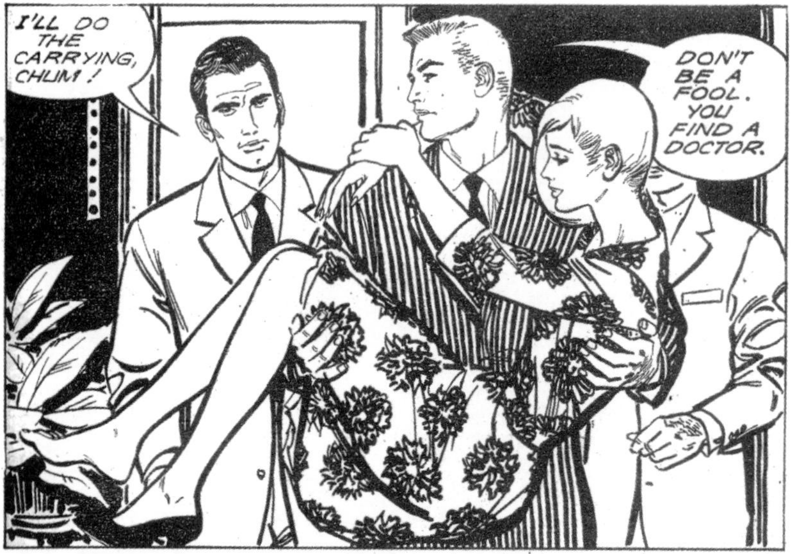
I'LL DO THE CARRYING, CHUM!
DON'T BE A FOOL. YOU FIND A DOCTOR.

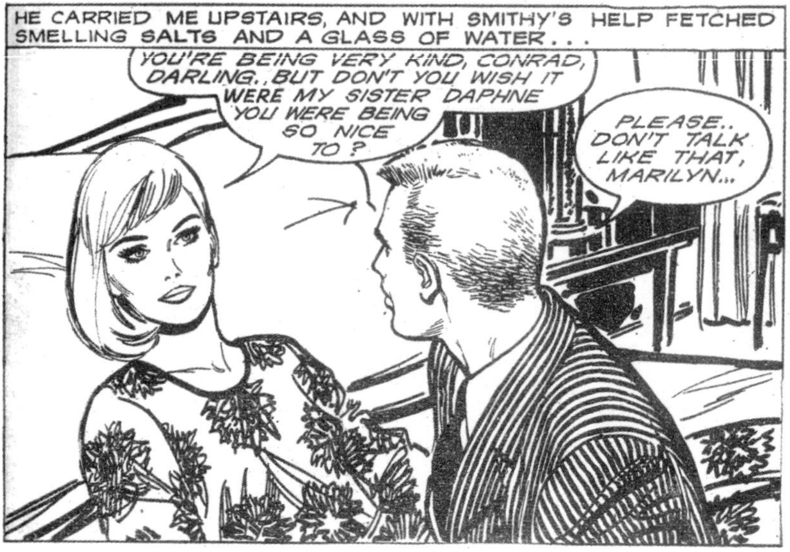
HE CARRIED ME UPSTAIRS, AND WITH SMITHY'S HELP FETCHED SMELLING SALTS AND A GLASS OF WATER . . .
YOU'RE BEING VERY KIND, CONRAD, DARLING.. BUT DON'T YOU WISH IT WERE MY SISTER DAPHNE YOU WERE BEING SO NICE TO?
PLEASE.. DON'T TALK LIKE THAT, MARILYN...

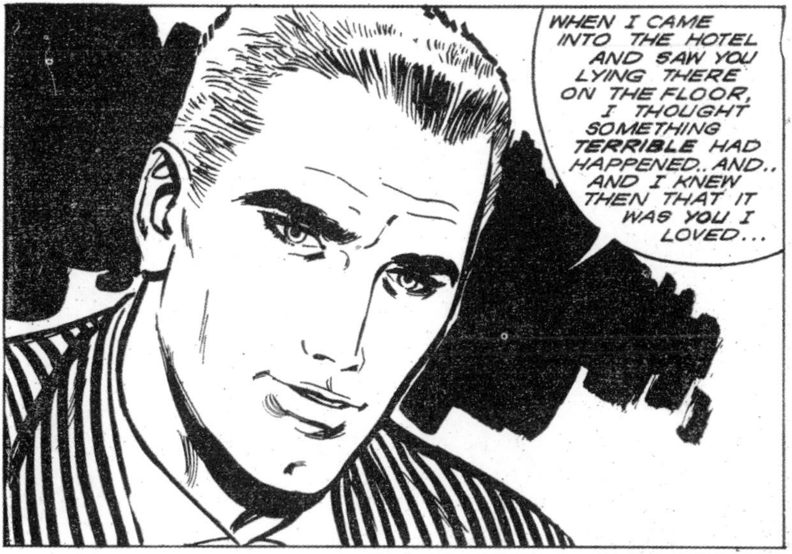
WHEN I CAME INTO THE HOTEL AND SAW YOU LYING THERE ON THE FLOOR, I THOUGHT SOMETHING TERRIBLE HAD HAPPENED.. AND.. AND I KNEW THEN THAT IT WAS YOU I LOVED...

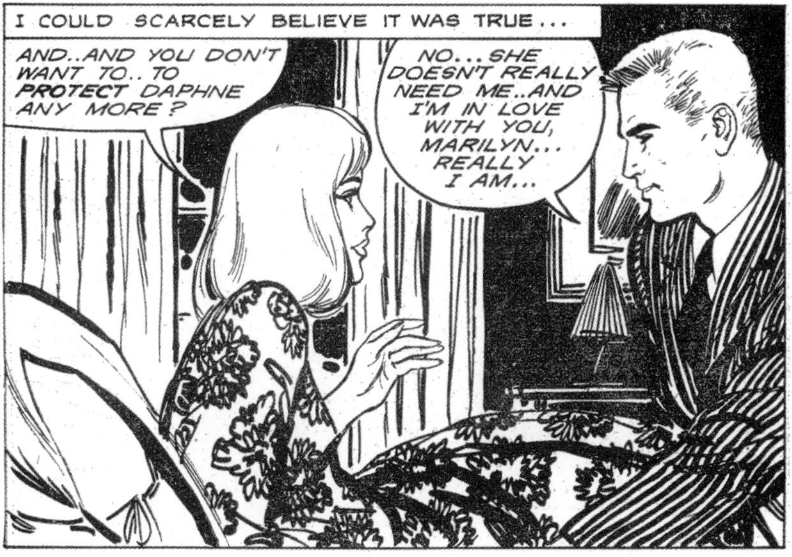
I COULD SCARCELY BELIEVE IT WAS TRUE...
AND..AND YOU DON'T WANT TO..TO PROTECT DAPHNE ANY MORE?
NO...SHE DOESN'T REALLY NEED ME..AND I'M IN LOVE WITH YOU, MARILYN... REALLY I AM...

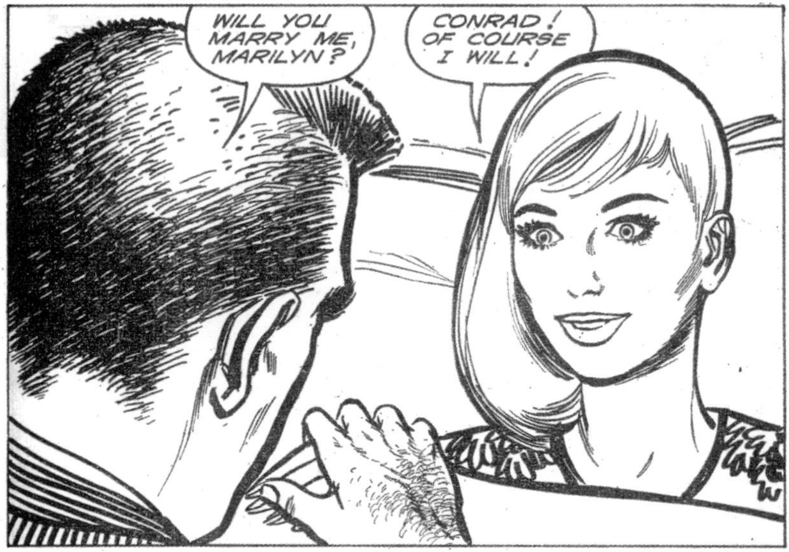
WILL YOU MARRY ME, MARILYN?
CONRAD! OF COURSE I WILL!

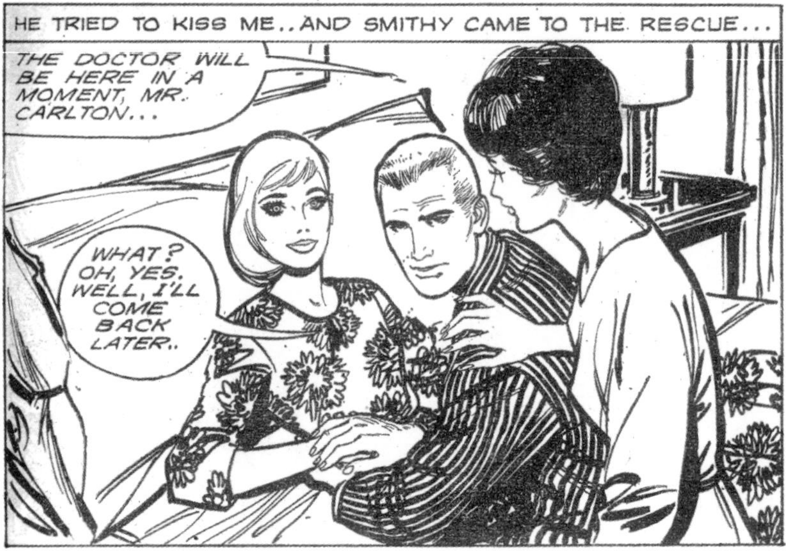
HE TRIED TO KISS ME.. AND SMITHY CAME TO THE RESCUE...
THE DOCTOR WILL BE HERE IN A MOMENT, MR. CARLTON...
WHAT? OH, YES. WELL, I'LL COME BACK LATER..

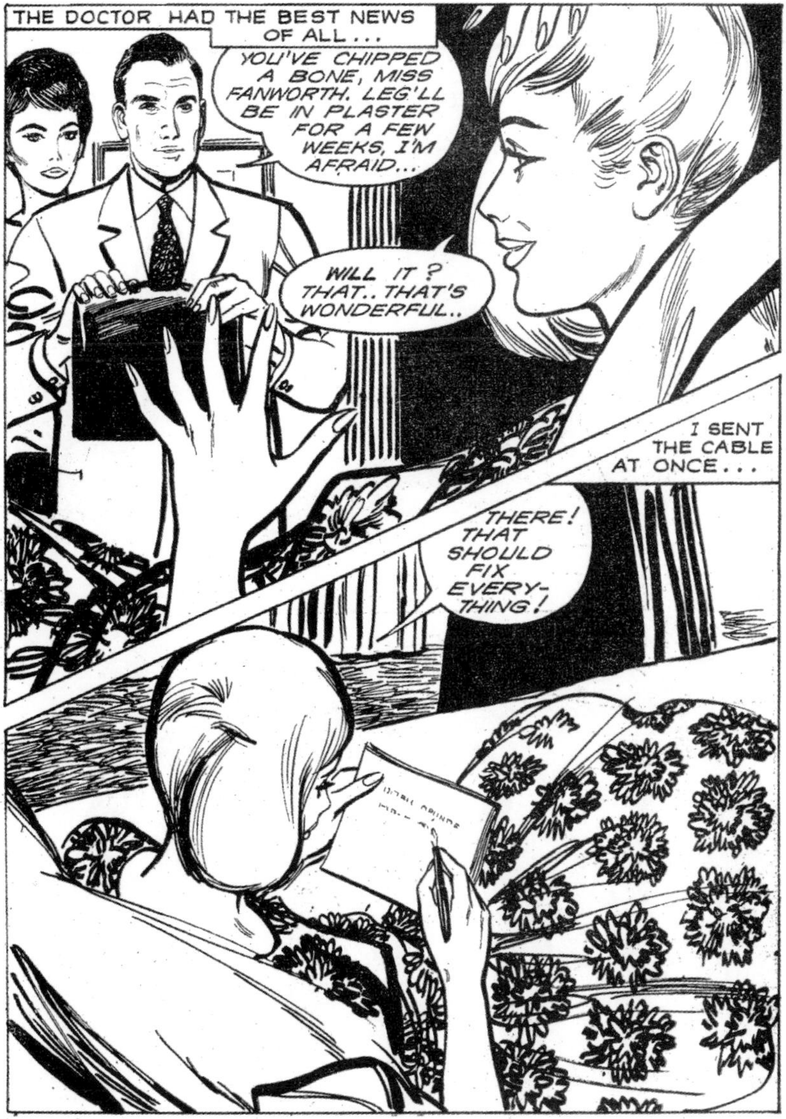
THE DOCTOR HAD THE BEST NEWS OF ALL . . .
YOU'VE CHIPPED A BONE, MISS FANWORTH. LEG'LL BE IN PLASTER FOR A FEW WEEKS, I'M AFRAID...
WILL IT? THAT.. THAT'S WONDERFUL..
I SENT THE CABLE AT ONCE . . .
THERE! THAT SHOULD FIX EVERY-THING!

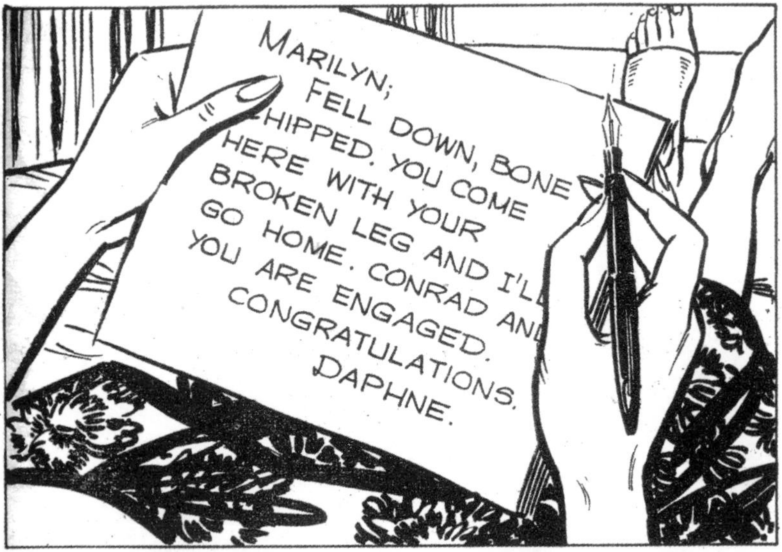
MARILYN;
FELL DOWN, BONE CHIPPED. YOU COME HERE WITH YOUR BROKEN LEG AND I'LL GO HOME. CONRAD AND YOU ARE ENGAGED. CONGRATULATIONS.
DAPHNE.

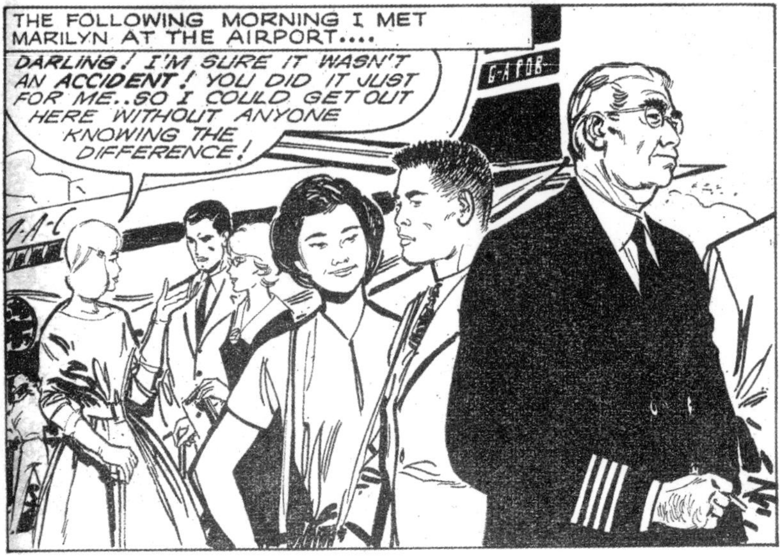
THE FOLLOWING MORNING I MET MARILYN AT THE AIRPORT....
DARLING! I'M SURE IT WASN'T AN ACCIDENT! YOU DID IT JUST FOR ME..SO I COULD GET OUT HERE WITHOUT ANYONE KNOWING THE DIFFERENCE!

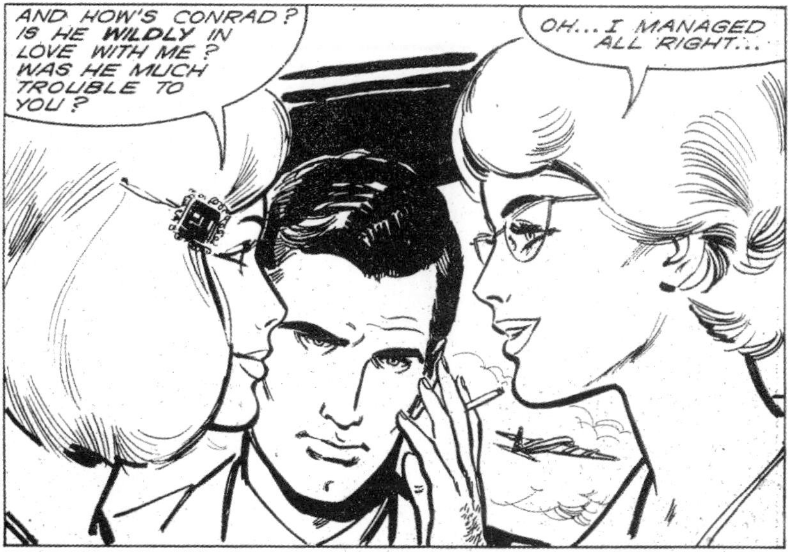
AND HOW'S CONRAD? IS HE WILDLY IN LOVE WITH ME? WAS HE MUCH TROUBLE TO YOU?
OH... I MANAGED ALL RIGHT...

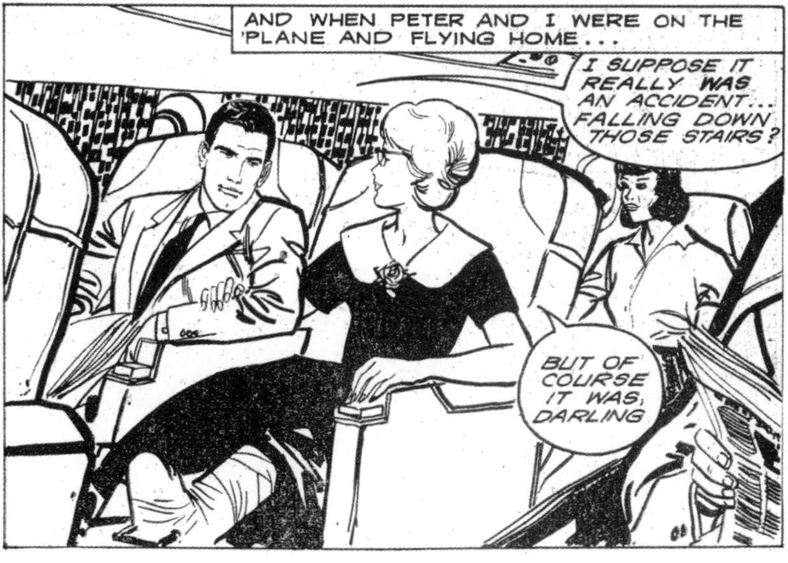
AND WHEN PETER AND I WERE ON THE 'PLANE AND FLYING HOME...
I SUPPOSE IT REALLY WAS AN ACCIDENT... FALLING DOWN THOSE STAIRS?
BUT OF COURSE IT WAS, DARLING

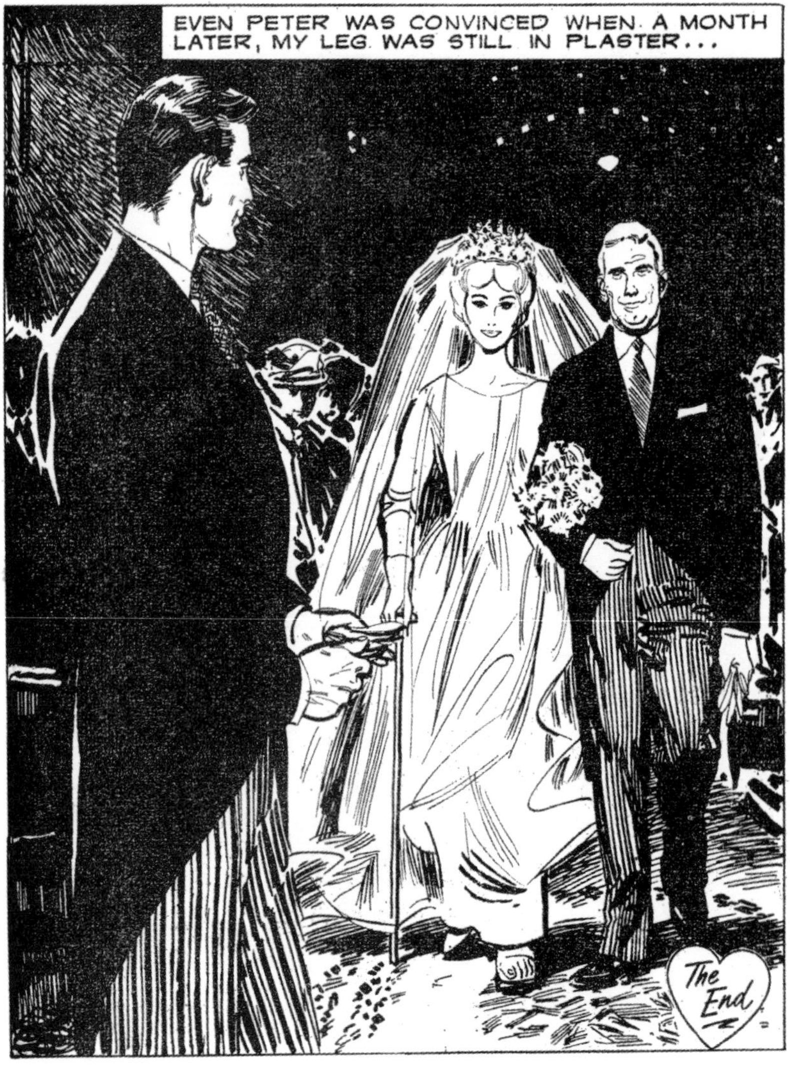
EVEN PETER WAS CONVINCED WHEN A MONTH LATER, MY LEG WAS STILL IN PLASTER...
The End

Davy of VALENTINE Talking

Here is The News...

You'll be on cloud nine every week with VALENTINE. In it are pages and pages of romantic picture-stories inspired by song titles. Look out for the ROCK AROUND THE MAILBAG page, too. I run it. It's fab !

(Davy of VALENTINE appears by kind permission of the Davy Self-Advertising Bureau.)

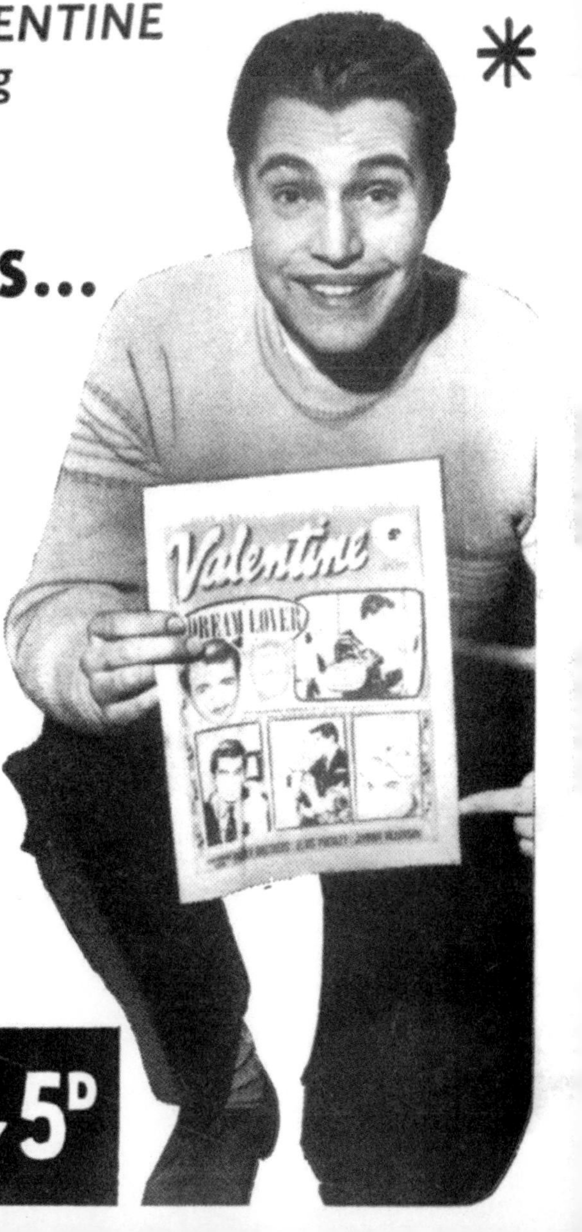
Valentine
DREAM LOVER

EVERY MONDAY 5D

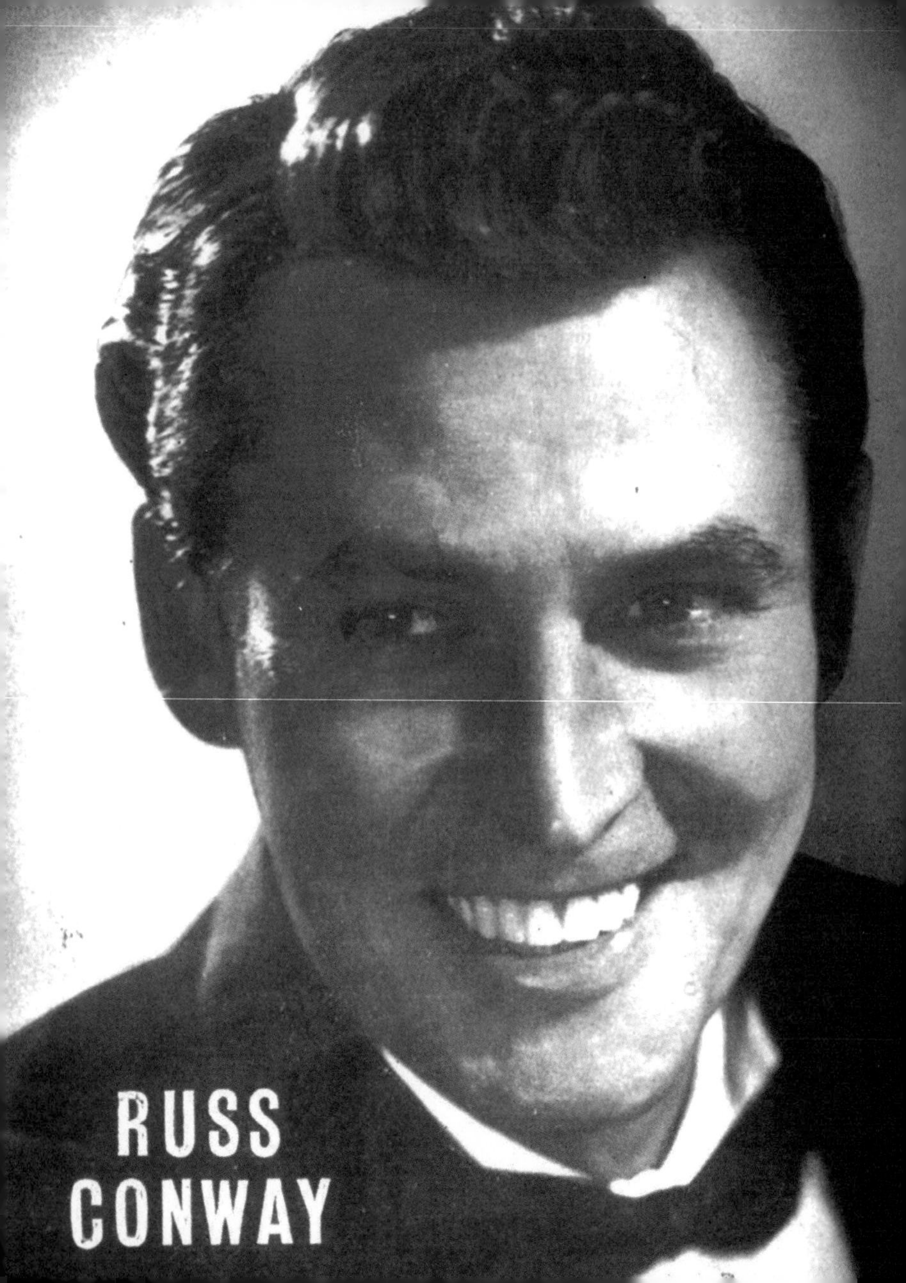
RUSS
CONWAY

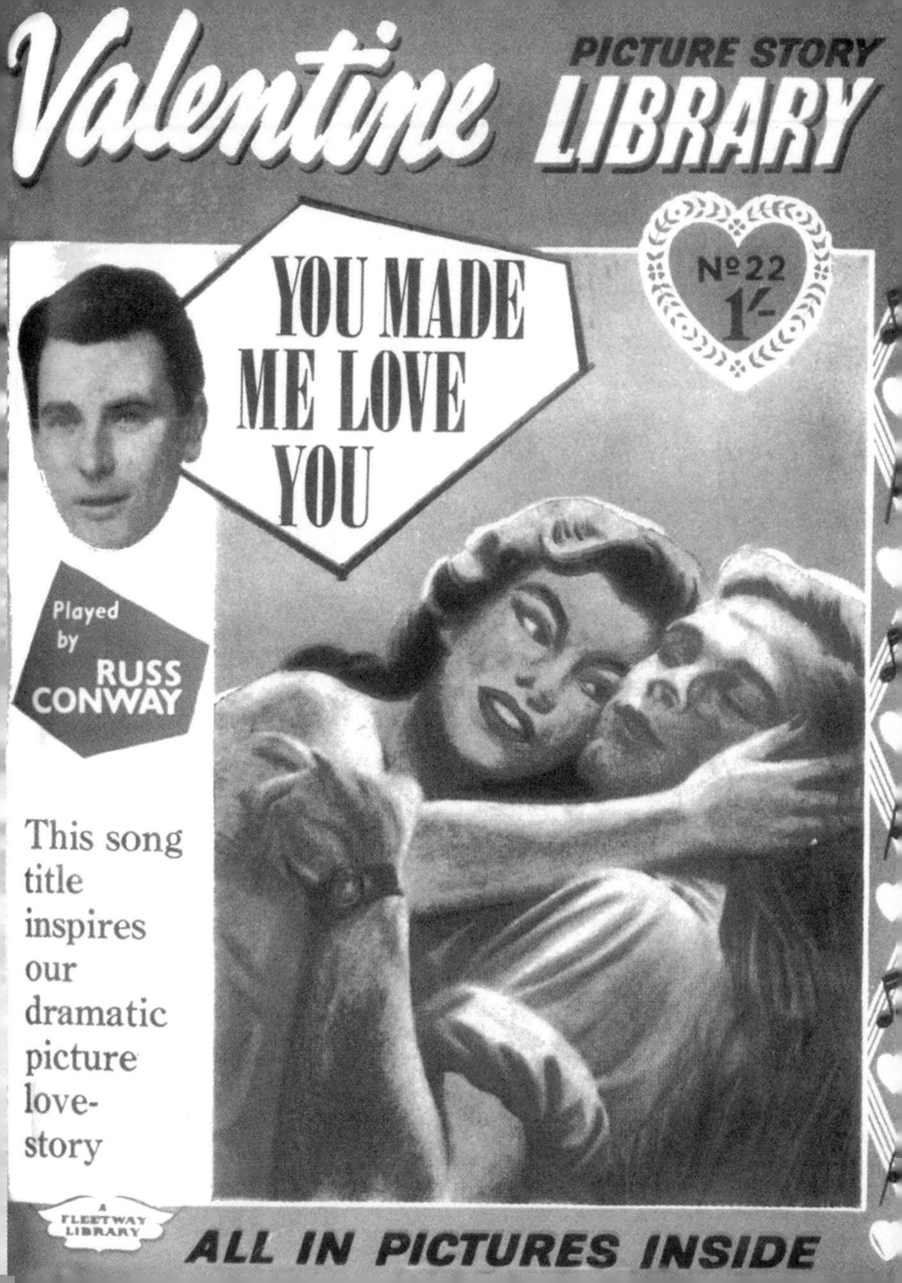
Valentine
PICTURE STORY LIBRARY
Nº22
1/-
YOU MADE ME LOVE YOU
Played by RUSS CONWAY
This song title inspires our dramatic picture love-story
A FLEETWAY LIBRARY
ALL IN PICTURES INSIDE

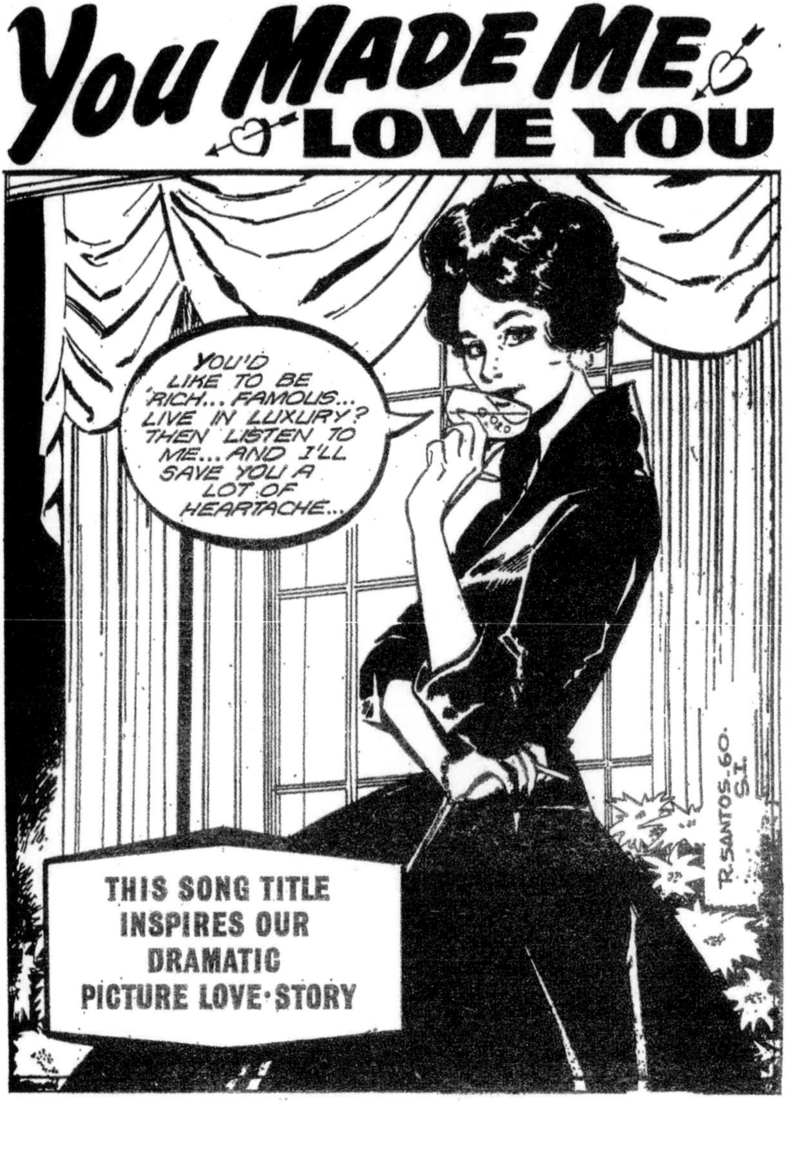
YOU MADE ME LOVE YOU
YOU'D LIKE TO BE RICH... FAMOUS... LIVE IN LUXURY? THEN LISTEN TO ME... AND I'LL SAVE YOU A LOT OF HEARTACHE...
THIS SONG TITLE INSPIRES OUR DRAMATIC PICTURE LOVE·STORY

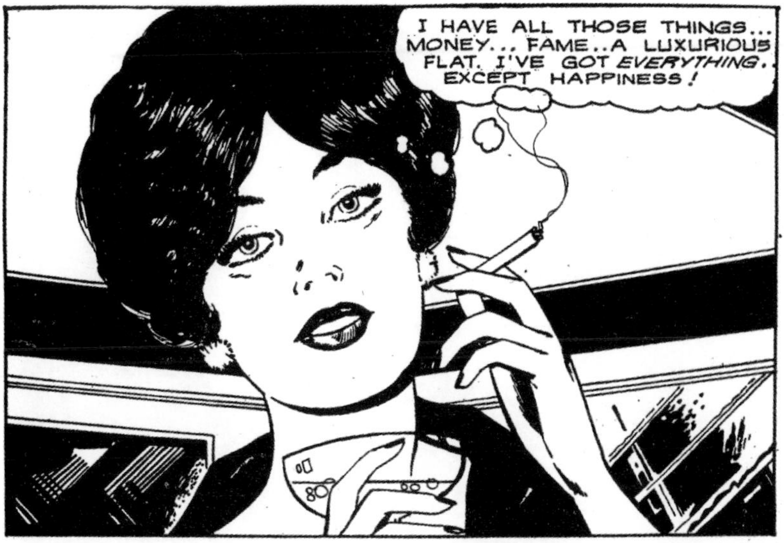
I HAVE ALL THOSE THINGS... MONEY... FAME..A LUXURIOUS FLAT. I'VE GOT EVERYTHING.. EXCEPT HAPPINESS!

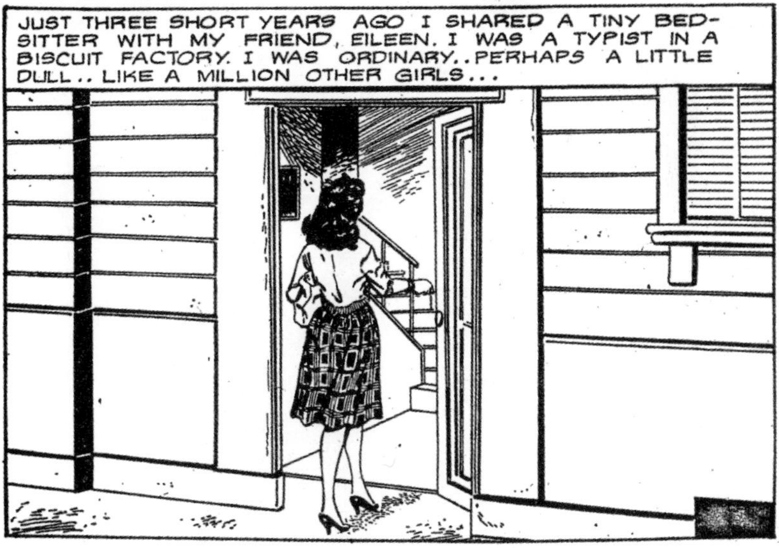
JUST THREE SHORT YEARS AGO I SHARED A TINY BED-SITTER WITH MY FRIEND, EILEEN. I WAS A TYPIST IN A BISCUIT FACTORY. I WAS ORDINARY..PERHAPS A LITTLE DULL.. LIKE A MILLION OTHER GIRLS...

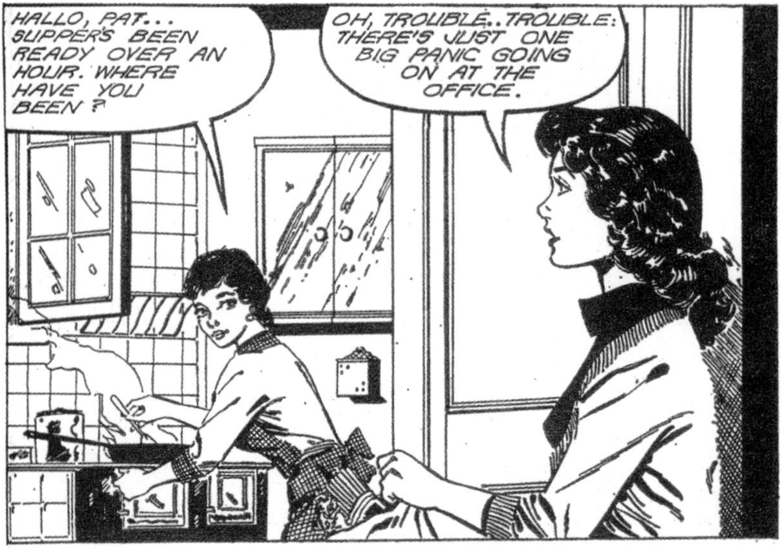
HALLO, PAT... SUPPER'S BEEN READY OVER AN HOUR. WHERE HAVE YOU BEEN?
OH, TROUBLE..TROUBLE: THERE'S JUST ONE BIG PANIC GOING ON AT THE OFFICE.

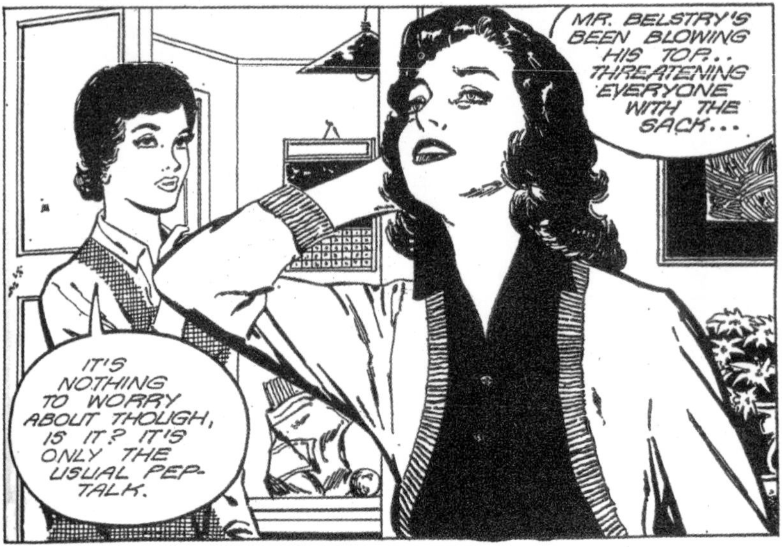
MR. BELSTRY'S BEEN BLOWING HIS TOP.. THREATENING EVERYONE WITH THE SACK...
IT'S NOTHING TO WORRY ABOUT THOUGH, IS IT? IT'S ONLY THE USUAL PEP-TALK.

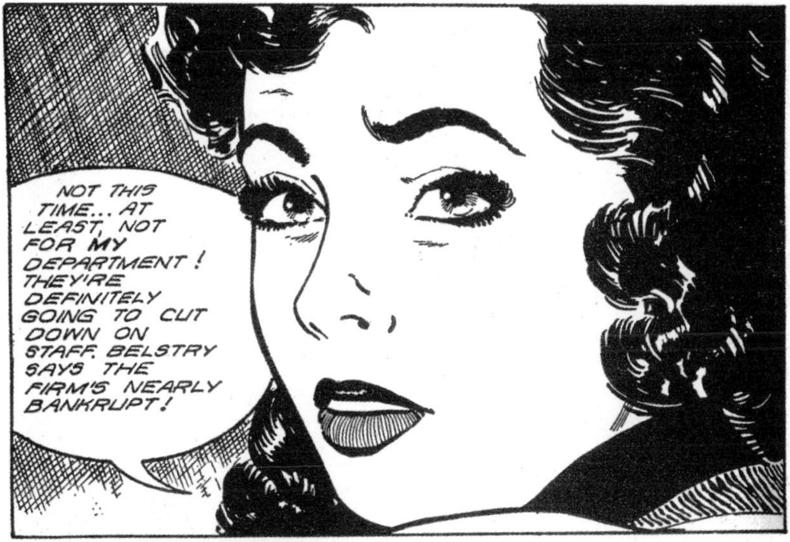
NOT THIS TIME... AT LEAST, NOT FOR MY DEPARTMENT! THEY'RE DEFINITELY GOING TO CUT DOWN ON STAFF. BELSTRY SAYS THE FIRM'S NEARLY BANKRUPT!

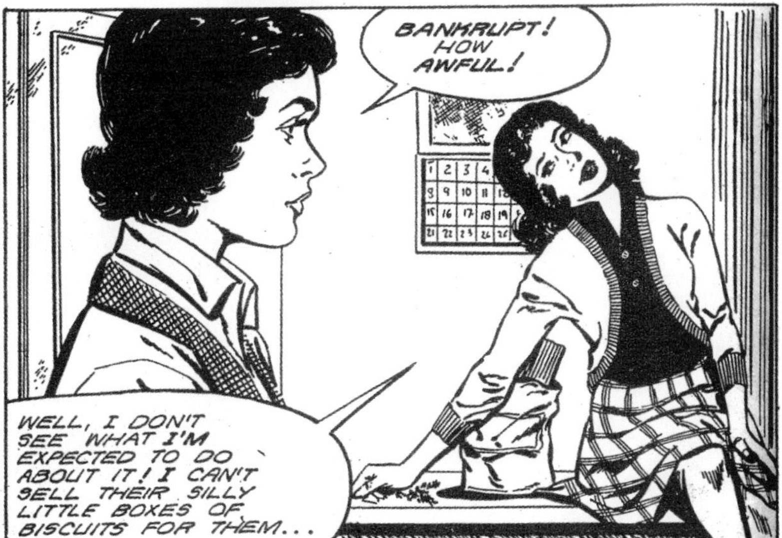
BANKRUPT! HOW AWFUL!
WELL, I DON'T SEE WHAT I'M EXPECTED TO DO ABOUT IT! I CAN'T SELL THEIR SILLY LITTLE BOXES OF BISCUITS FOR THEM...

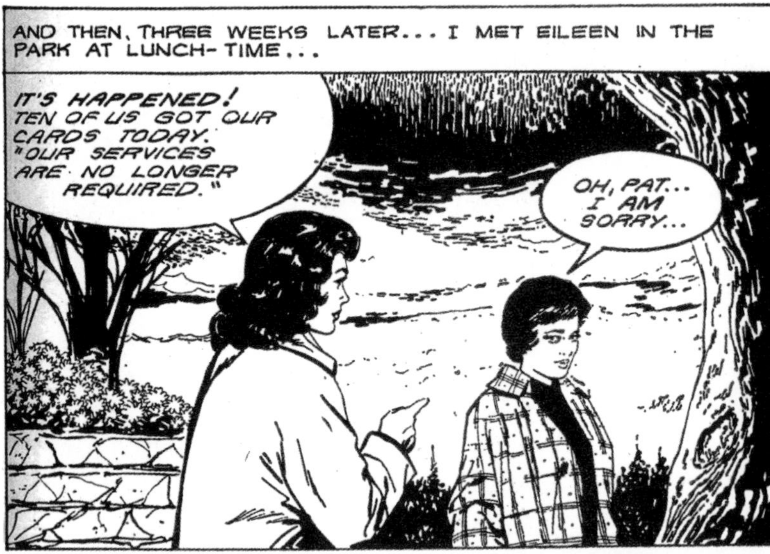
AND THEN, THREE WEEKS LATER... I MET EILEEN IN THE PARK AT LUNCH-TIME...
IT'S HAPPENED! TEN OF US GOT OUR CARDS TODAY. "OUR SERVICES ARE NO LONGER REQUIRED."
OH, PAT... I AM SORRY...

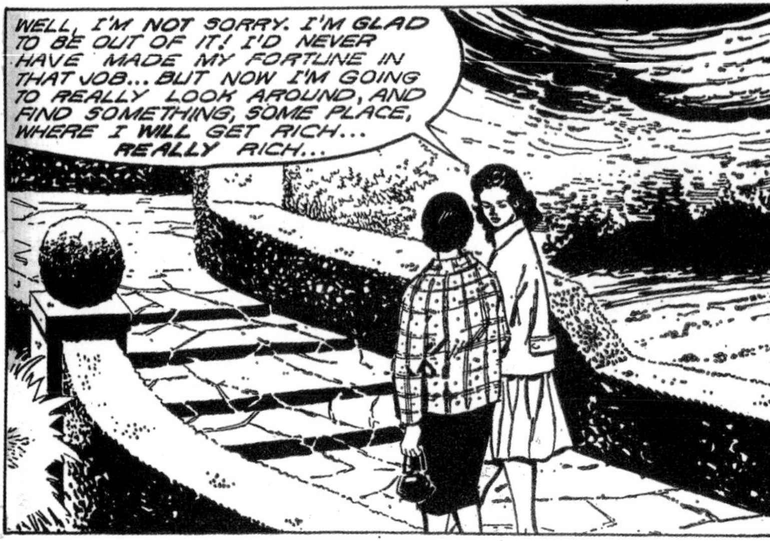
WELL, I'M NOT SORRY. I'M GLAD TO BE OUT OF IT! I'D NEVER HAVE MADE MY FORTUNE IN THAT JOB... BUT NOW I'M GOING TO REALLY LOOK AROUND, AND FIND SOMETHING, SOME PLACE, WHERE I WILL GET RICH... REALLY RICH...

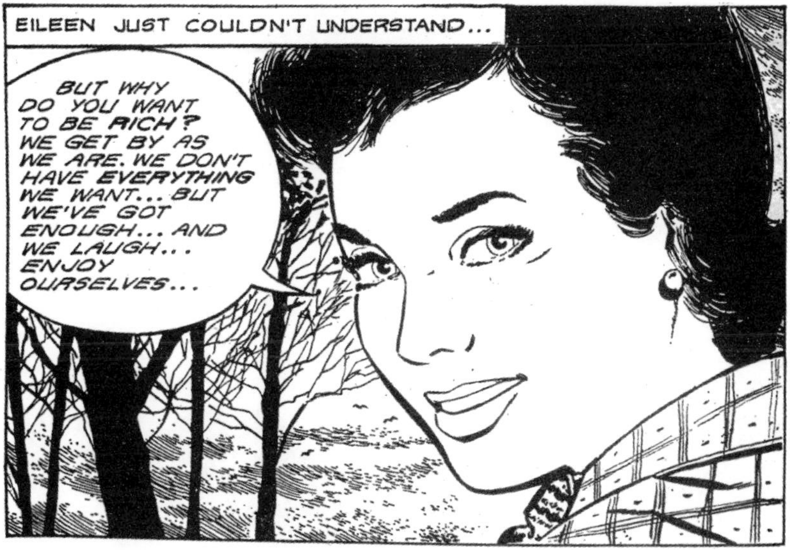
EILEEN JUST COULDN'T UNDERSTAND...
BUT WHY DO YOU WANT TO BE RICH? WE GET BY AS WE ARE. WE DON'T HAVE EVERYTHING WE WANT... BUT WE'VE GOT ENOUGH... AND WE LAUGH... ENJOY OURSELVES...

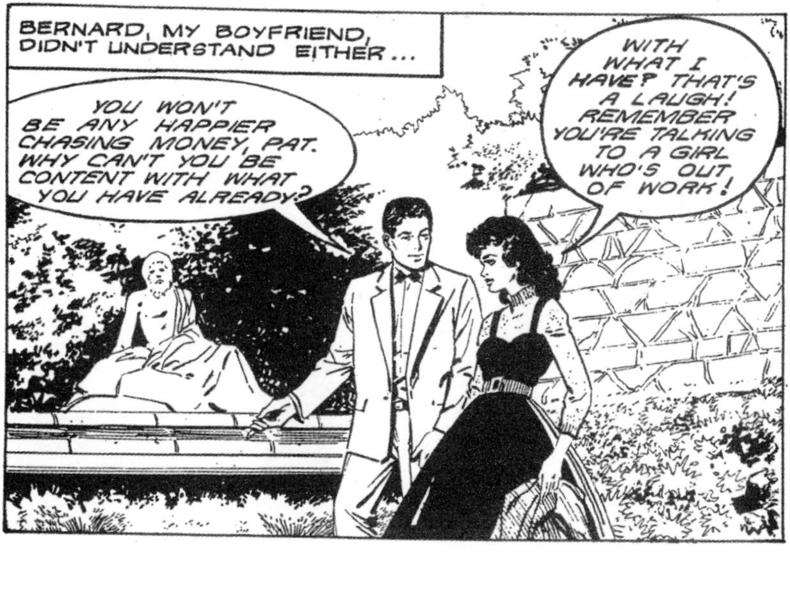
BERNARD, MY BOYFRIEND, DIDN'T UNDERSTAND EITHER...
YOU WON'T BE ANY HAPPIER CHASING MONEY, PAT. WHY CAN'T YOU BE CONTENT WITH WHAT YOU HAVE ALREADY?
WITH WHAT I HAVE? THAT'S A LAUGH! REMEMBER YOU'RE TALKING TO A GIRL WHO'S OUT OF WORK!

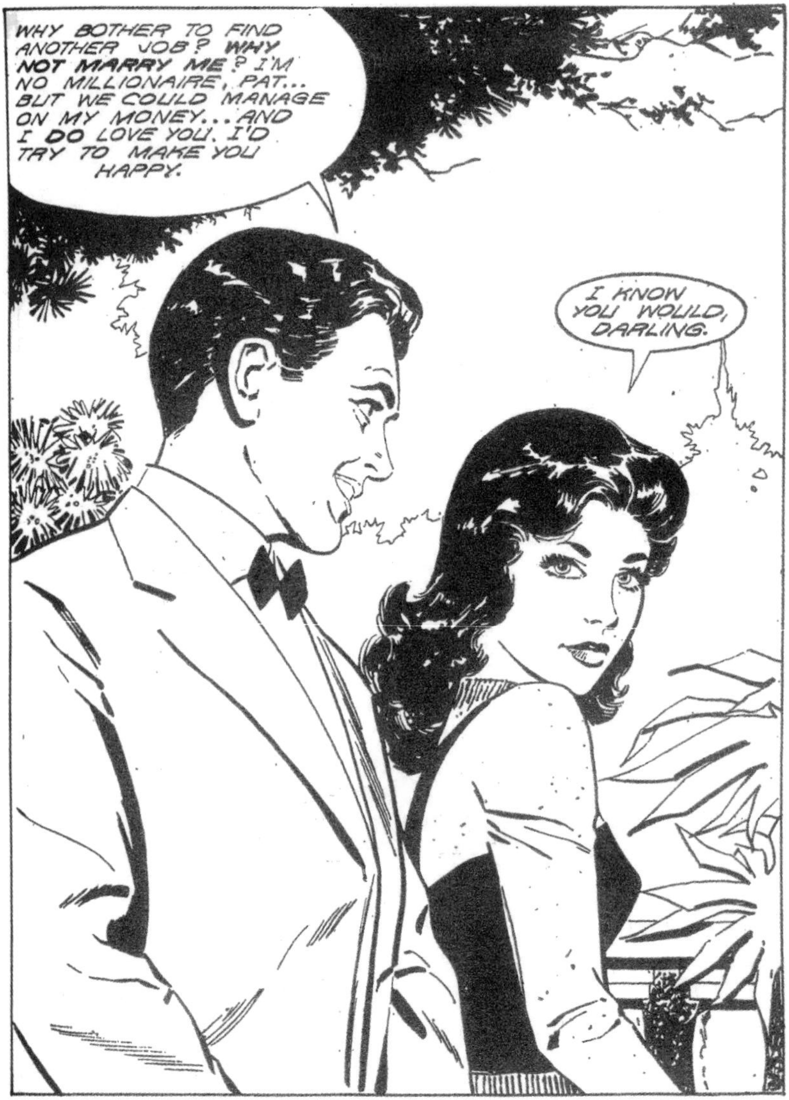
WHY BOTHER TO FIND ANOTHER JOB? WHY NOT MARRY ME? I'M NO MILLIONAIRE, PAT... BUT WE COULD MANAGE ON MY MONEY... AND I DO LOVE YOU. I'D TRY TO MAKE YOU HAPPY.
I KNOW YOU WOULD, DARLING.

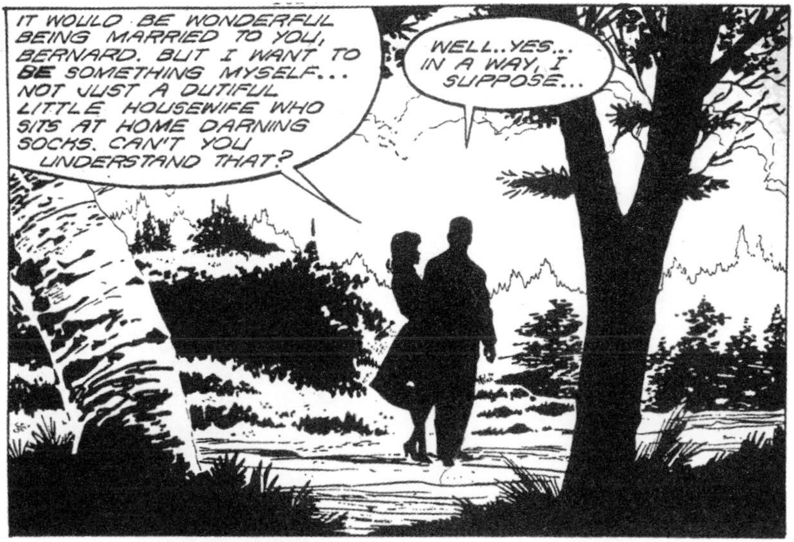
IT WOULD BE WONDERFUL BEING MARRIED TO YOU, BERNARD. BUT I WANT TO BE SOMETHING MYSELF... NOT JUST A DUTIFUL LITTLE HOUSEWIFE WHO SITS AT HOME DARNING SOCKS. CAN'T YOU UNDERSTAND THAT?
WELL..YES... IN A WAY, I SUPPOSE...

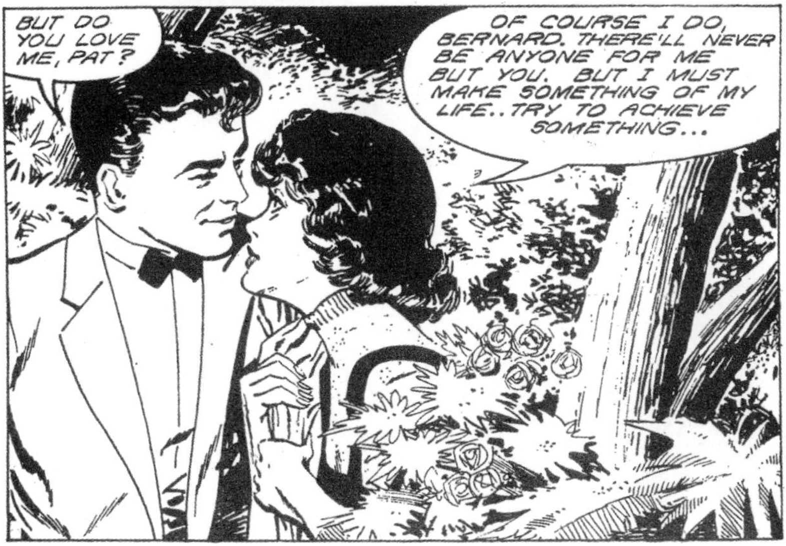
BUT DO YOU LOVE ME, PAT?
OF COURSE I DO, BERNARD. THERE'LL NEVER BE ANYONE FOR ME BUT YOU. BUT I MUST MAKE SOMETHING OF MY LIFE..TRY TO ACHIEVE SOMETHING...

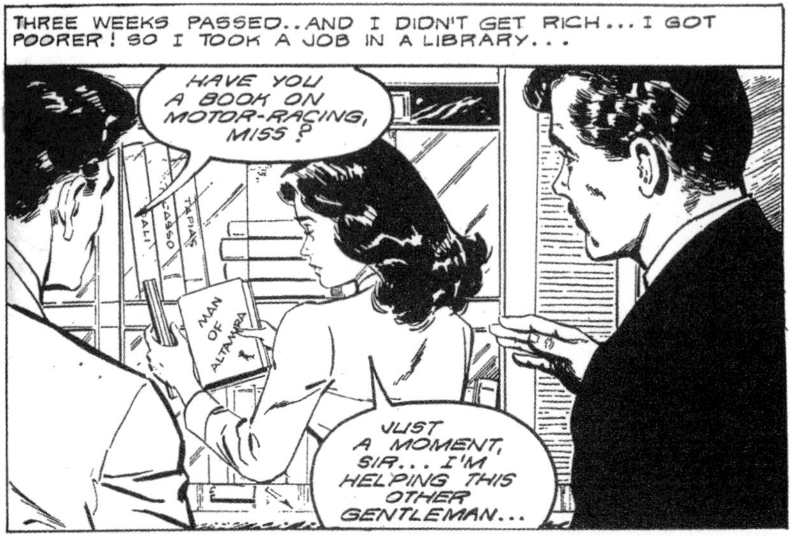
THREE WEEKS PASSED..AND I DIDN'T GET RICH...I GOT POORER! SO I TOOK A JOB IN A LIBRARY...
HAVE YOU A BOOK ON MOTOR-RACING, MISS?
DALI
PICASSO
TAPIAS
MAN OF ALTAMIRA
JUST A MOMENT, SIR... I'M HELPING THIS OTHER GENTLEMAN...

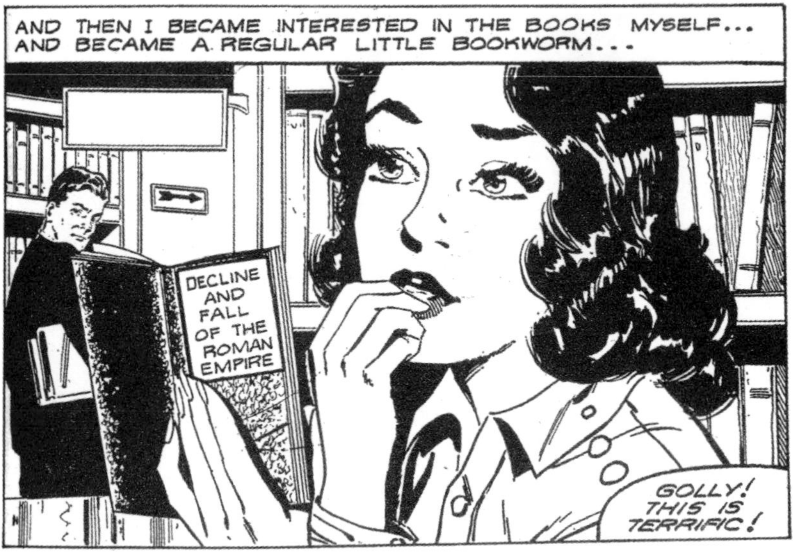
AND THEN I BECAME INTERESTED IN THE BOOKS MYSELF... AND BECAME A REGULAR LITTLE BOOKWORM...
DECLINE AND FALL OF THE ROMAN EMPIRE
GOLLY! THIS IS TERRIFIC!

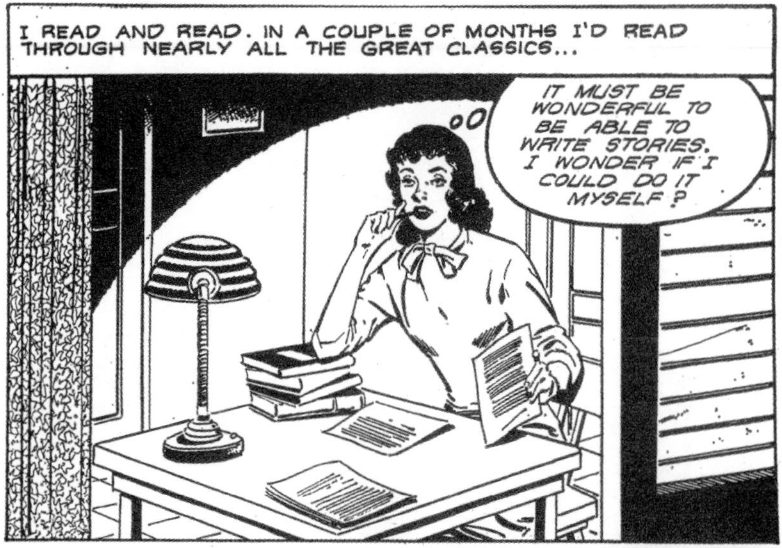
I READ AND READ. IN A COUPLE OF MONTHS I'D READ THROUGH NEARLY ALL THE GREAT CLASSICS...
IT MUST BE WONDERFUL TO BE ABLE TO WRITE STORIES. I WONDER IF I COULD DO IT MYSELF?

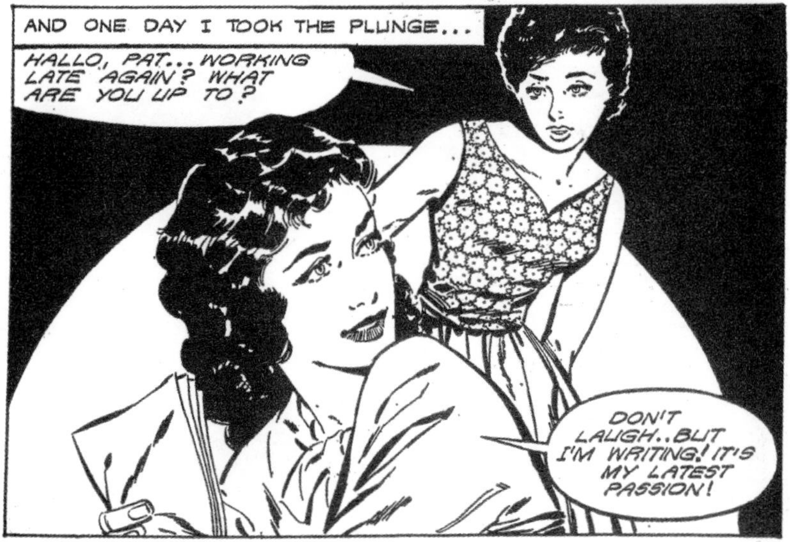
AND ONE DAY I TOOK THE PLUNGE...
HALLO, PAT... WORKING LATE AGAIN? WHAT ARE YOU UP TO?
DON'T LAUGH..BUT I'M WRITING! IT'S MY LATEST PASSION!

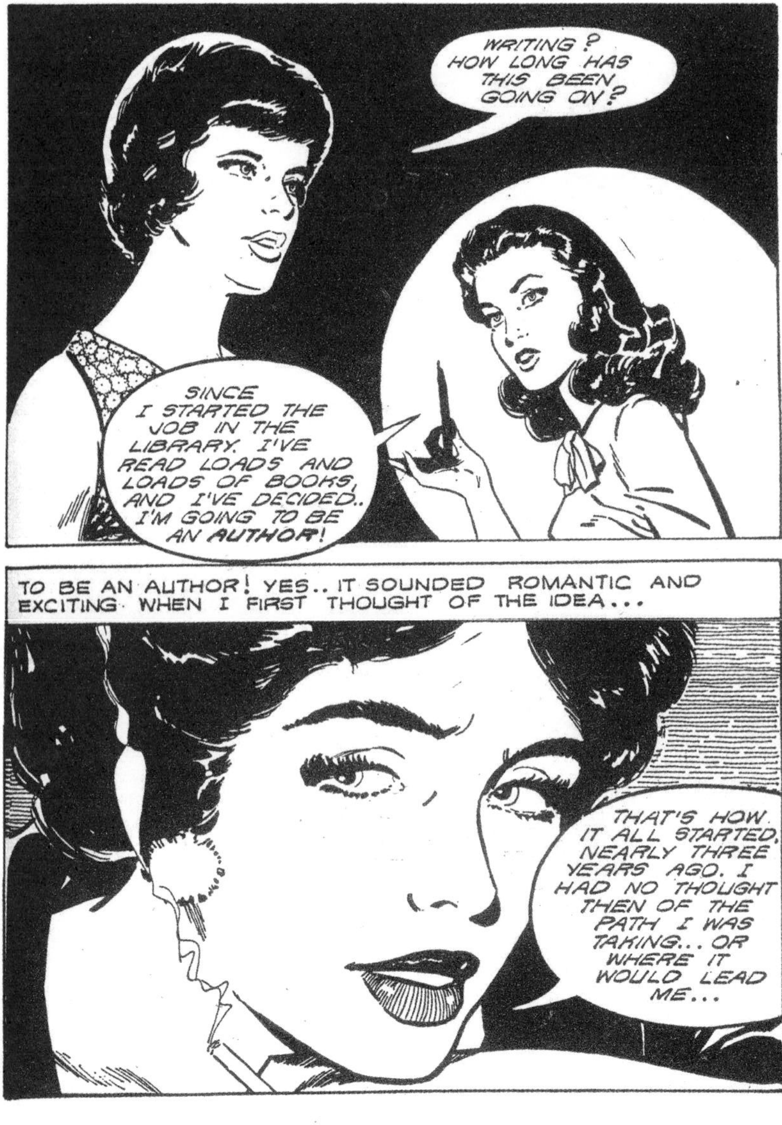
WRITING? HOW LONG HAS THIS BEEN GOING ON?
SINCE I STARTED THE JOB IN THE LIBRARY, I'VE READ LOADS AND LOADS OF BOOKS, AND I'VE DECIDED.. I'M GOING TO BE AN AUTHOR!
TO BE AN AUTHOR! YES.. IT SOUNDED ROMANTIC AND EXCITING WHEN I FIRST THOUGHT OF THE IDEA...
THAT'S HOW IT ALL STARTED, NEARLY THREE YEARS AGO. I HAD NO THOUGHT THEN OF THE PATH I WAS TAKING... OR WHERE IT WOULD LEAD ME...

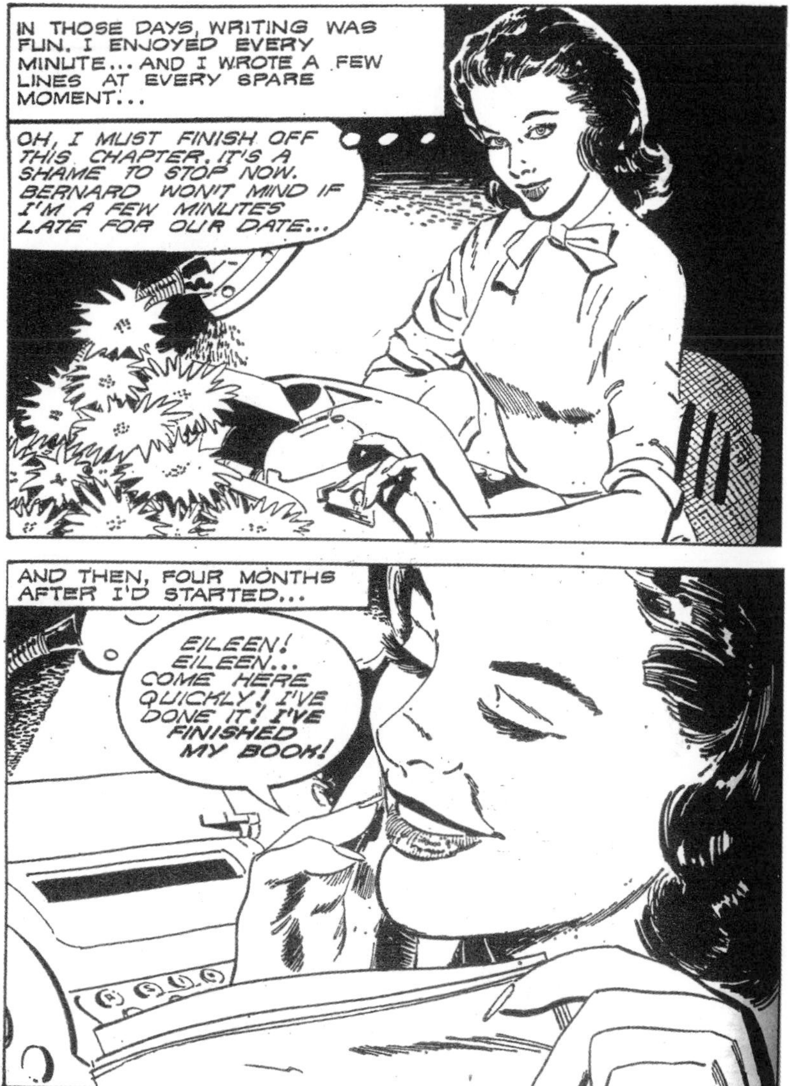
IN THOSE DAYS, WRITING WAS FUN. I ENJOYED EVERY MINUTE... AND I WROTE A FEW LINES AT EVERY SPARE MOMENT...
OH, I MUST FINISH OFF THIS CHAPTER. IT'S A SHAME TO STOP NOW. BERNARD WON'T MIND IF I'M A FEW MINUTES LATE FOR OUR DATE...
AND THEN, FOUR MONTHS AFTER I'D STARTED...
EILEEN! EILEEN... COME HERE QUICKLY! I'VE DONE IT! I'VE FINISHED MY BOOK!

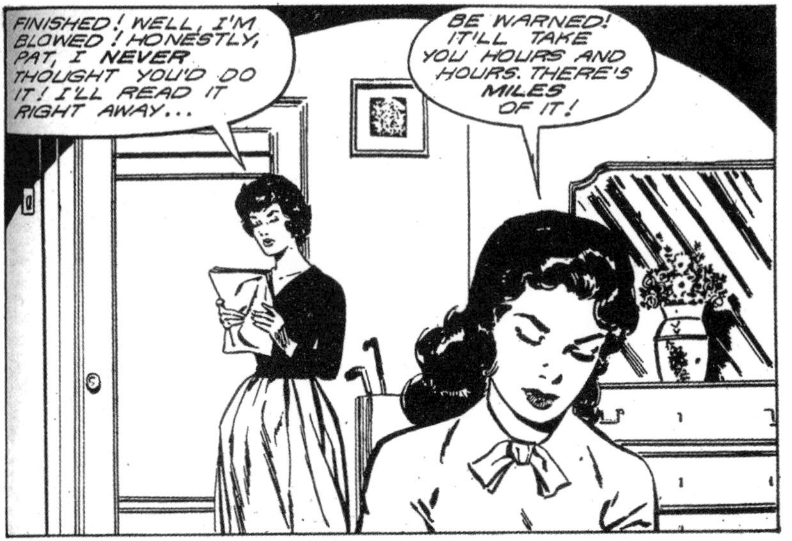
FINISHED! WELL, I'M BLOWED! HONESTLY, PAT, I NEVER THOUGHT YOU'D DO IT! I'LL READ IT RIGHT AWAY...
BE WARNED! IT'LL TAKE YOU HOURS AND HOURS. THERE'S MILES OF IT!

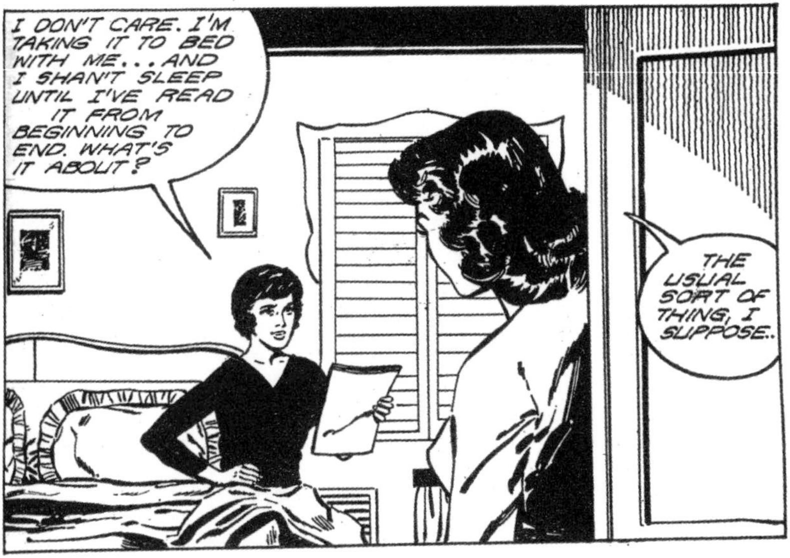
I DON'T CARE. I'M TAKING IT TO BED WITH ME... AND I SHAN'T SLEEP UNTIL I'VE READ IT FROM BEGINNING TO END. WHAT'S IT ABOUT?
THE USUAL SORT OF THING, I SUPPOSE..

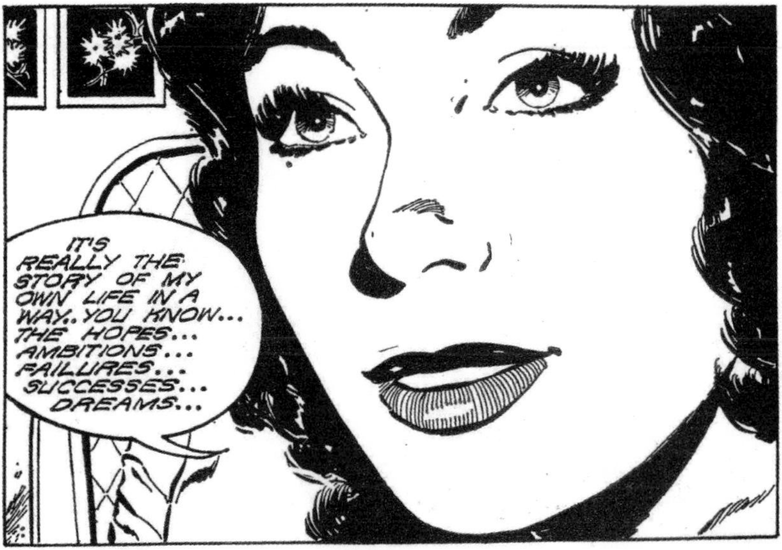
IT'S REALLY THE STORY OF MY OWN LIFE IN A WAY.. YOU KNOW... THE HOPES... AMBITIONS... FAILURES... SUCCESSES... DREAMS...

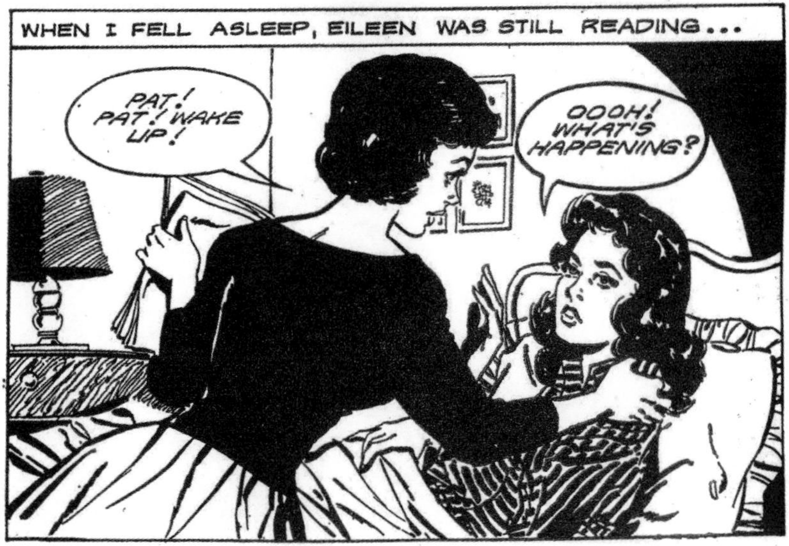
WHEN I FELL ASLEEP, EILEEN WAS STILL READING...
PAT! PAT! WAKE UP!
OOOH! WHAT'S HAPPENING?

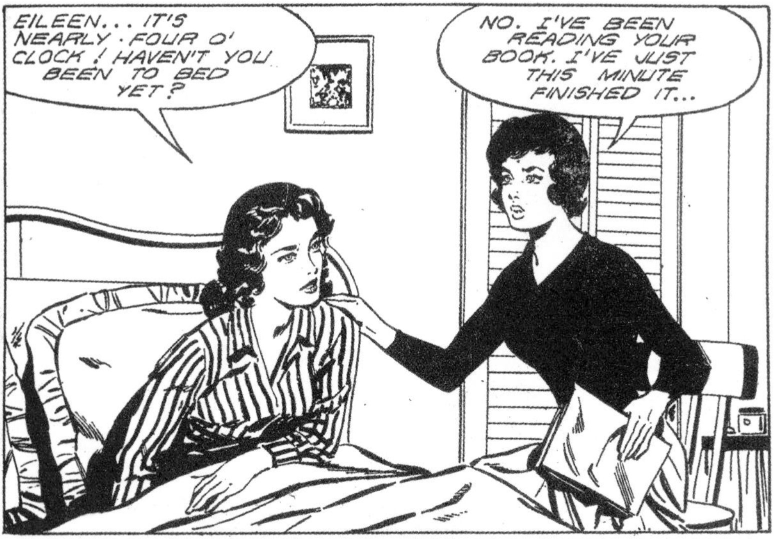
EILEEN... IT'S NEARLY FOUR O' CLOCK! HAVEN'T YOU BEEN TO BED YET?
NO. I'VE BEEN READING YOUR BOOK. I'VE JUST THIS MINUTE FINISHED IT...

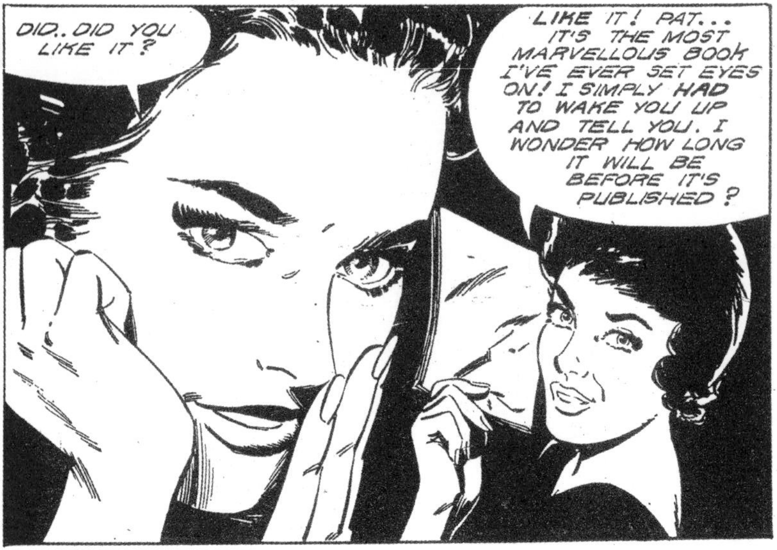
DID.. DID YOU LIKE IT?
LIKE IT! PAT... IT'S THE MOST MARVELLOUS BOOK I'VE EVER SET EYES ON! I SIMPLY HAD TO WAKE YOU UP AND TELL YOU. I WONDER HOW LONG IT WILL BE BEFORE IT'S PUBLISHED?

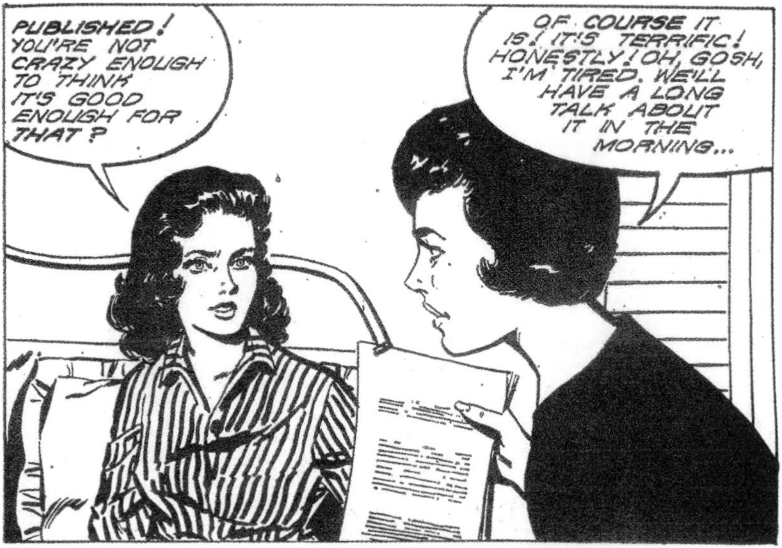
PUBLISHED! YOU'RE NOT CRAZY ENOUGH TO THINK IT'S GOOD ENOUGH FOR THAT?
OF COURSE IT IS! IT'S TERRIFIC! HONESTLY! OH, GOSH, I'M TIRED. WE'LL HAVE A LONG TALK ABOUT IT IN THE MORNING...

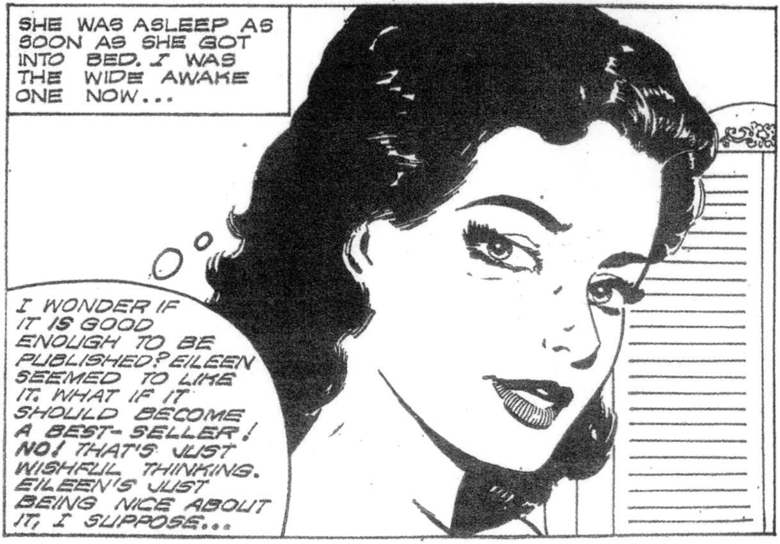
SHE WAS ASLEEP AS SOON AS SHE GOT INTO BED. I WAS THE WIDE AWAKE ONE NOW...
I WONDER IF IT IS GOOD ENOUGH TO BE PUBLISHED? EILEEN SEEMED TO LIKE IT. WHAT IF IT SHOULD BECOME A BEST-SELLER! NO! THAT'S JUST WISHFUL THINKING. EILEEN'S JUST BEING NICE ABOUT IT, I SUPPOSE...

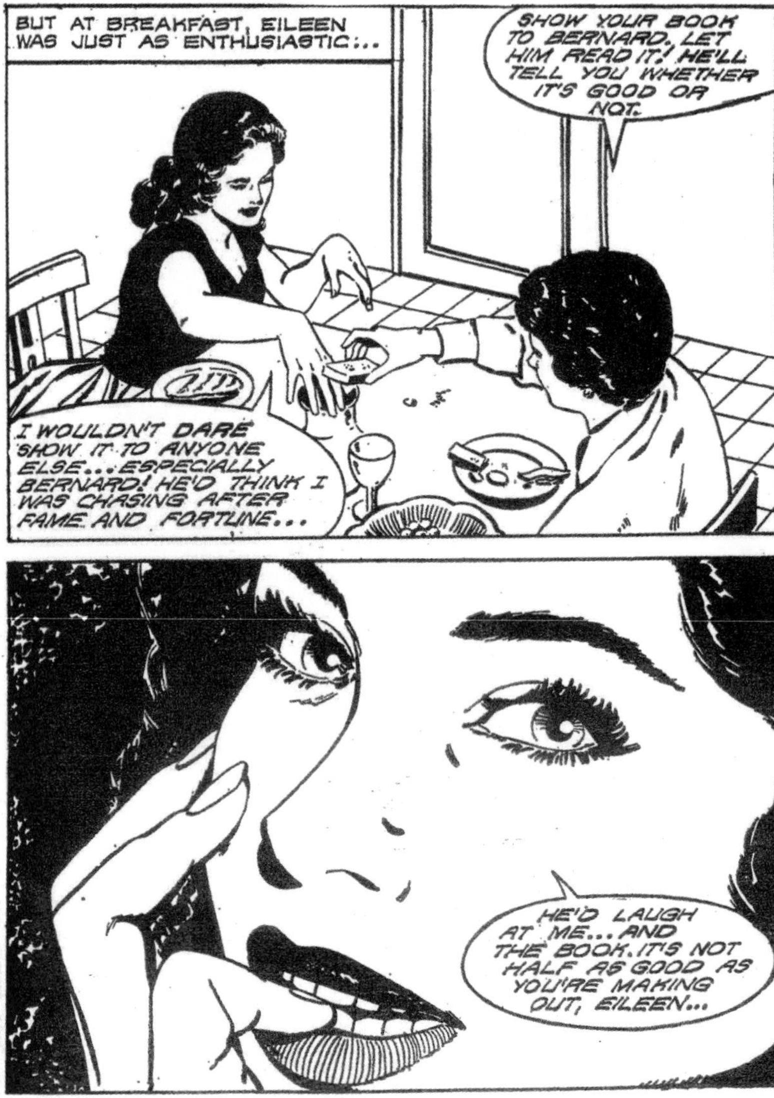
BUT AT BREAKFAST, EILEEN WAS JUST AS ENTHUSIASTIC...
SHOW YOUR BOOK TO BERNARD. LET HIM READ IT! HE'LL TELL YOU WHETHER IT'S GOOD OR NOT.
I WOULDN'T DARE SHOW IT TO ANYONE ELSE... ESPECIALLY BERNARD! HE'D THINK I WAS CHASING AFTER FAME AND FORTUNE...
HE'D LAUGH AT ME... AND THE BOOK. IT'S NOT HALF AS GOOD AS YOU'RE MAKING OUT, EILEEN...

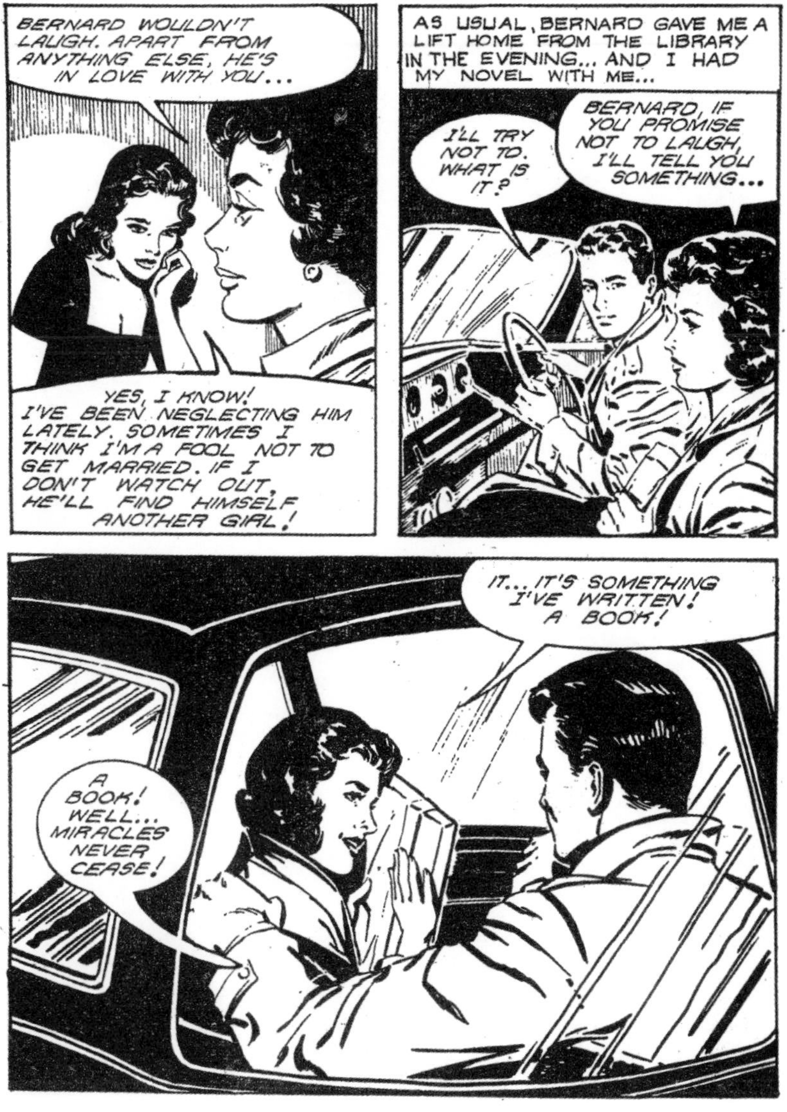
BERNARD WOULDN'T LAUGH. APART FROM ANYTHING ELSE, HE'S IN LOVE WITH YOU...
YES, I KNOW! I'VE BEEN NEGLECTING HIM LATELY. SOMETIMES I THINK I'M A FOOL NOT TO GET MARRIED. IF I DON'T WATCH OUT, HE'LL FIND HIMSELF ANOTHER GIRL!
AS USUAL, BERNARD GAVE ME A LIFT HOME FROM THE LIBRARY IN THE EVENING... AND I HAD MY NOVEL WITH ME...
BERNARD, IF YOU PROMISE NOT TO LAUGH, I'LL TELL YOU SOMETHING...
I'LL TRY NOT TO. WHAT IS IT?
IT... IT'S SOMETHING I'VE WRITTEN! A BOOK!
A BOOK! WELL... MIRACLES NEVER CEASE!

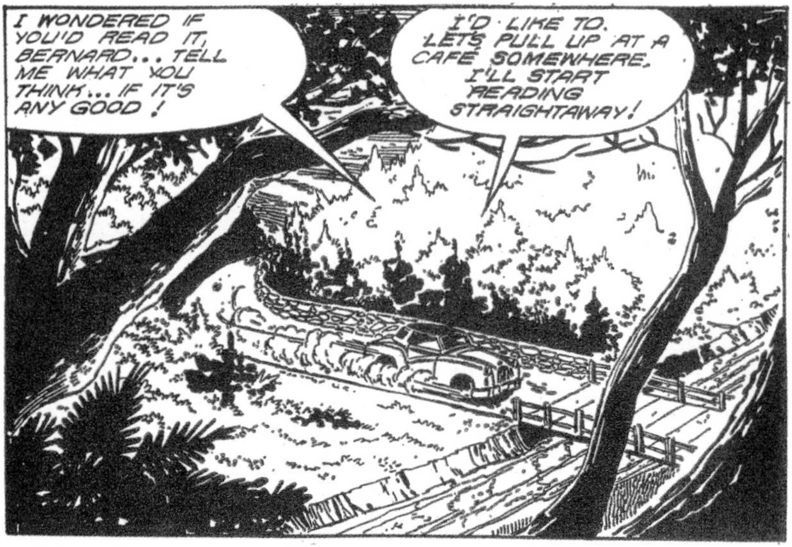
I WONDERED IF YOU'D READ IT, BERNARD... TELL ME WHAT YOU THINK... IF IT'S ANY GOOD!
I'D LIKE TO. LET'S PULL UP AT A CAFÉ SOMEWHERE. I'LL START READING STRAIGHTAWAY!

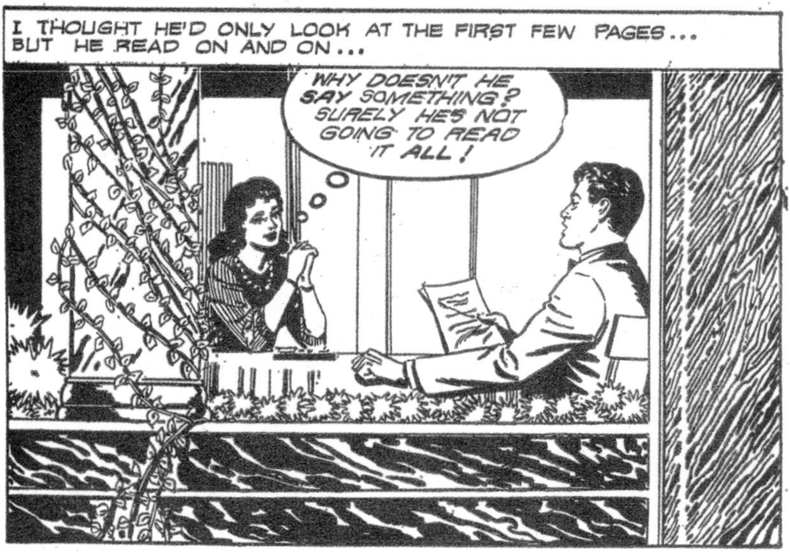
I THOUGHT HE'D ONLY LOOK AT THE FIRST FEW PAGES... BUT HE READ ON AND ON...
WHY DOESN'T HE SAY SOMETHING? SURELY HE'S NOT GOING TO READ IT ALL!

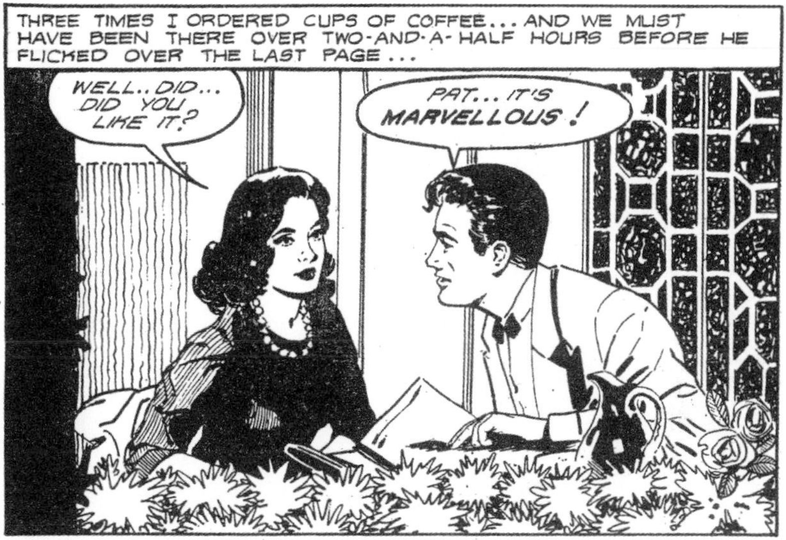
THREE TIMES I ORDERED CUPS OF COFFEE... AND WE MUST HAVE BEEN THERE OVER TWO-AND-A-HALF HOURS BEFORE HE FLICKED OVER THE LAST PAGE...
WELL.. DID... DID YOU LIKE IT?
PAT... IT'S MARVELLOUS!

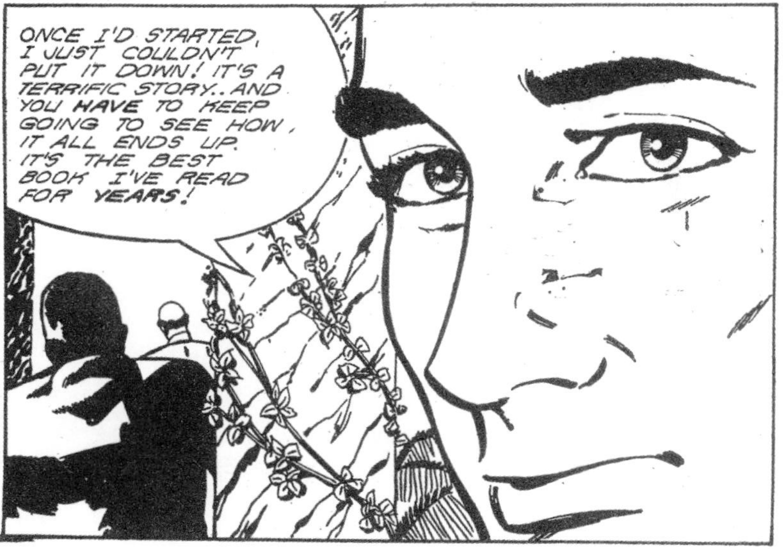
ONCE I'D STARTED, I JUST COULDN'T PUT IT DOWN! IT'S A TERRIFIC STORY.. AND YOU HAVE TO KEEP GOING TO SEE HOW IT ALL ENDS UP. IT'S THE BEST BOOK I'VE READ FOR YEARS!

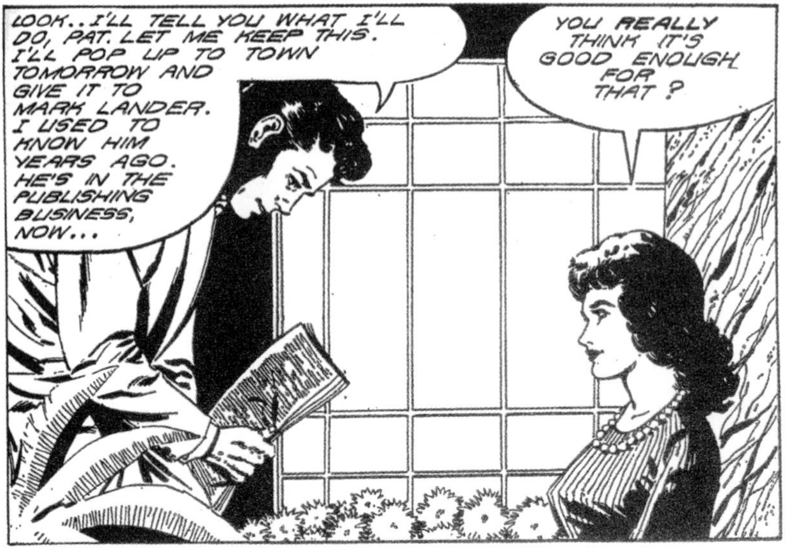
LOOK.. I'LL TELL YOU WHAT I'LL DO, PAT. LET ME KEEP THIS. I'LL POP UP TO TOWN TOMORROW AND GIVE IT TO MARK LANDER. I USED TO KNOW HIM YEARS AGO. HE'S IN THE PUBLISHING BUSINESS, NOW...
YOU REALLY THINK IT'S GOOD ENOUGH FOR THAT?

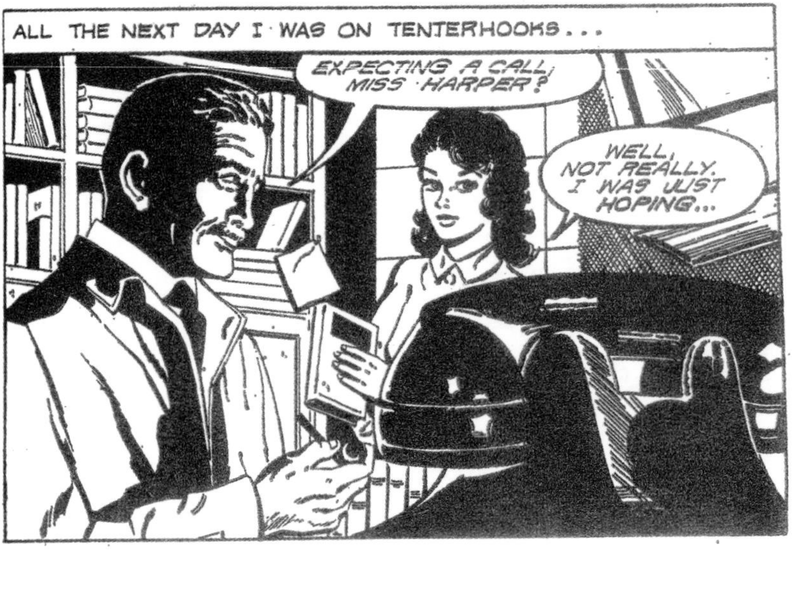
ALL THE NEXT DAY I WAS ON TENTERHOOKS...
EXPECTING A CALL, MISS HARPER?
WELL, NOT REALLY. I WAS JUST HOPING...

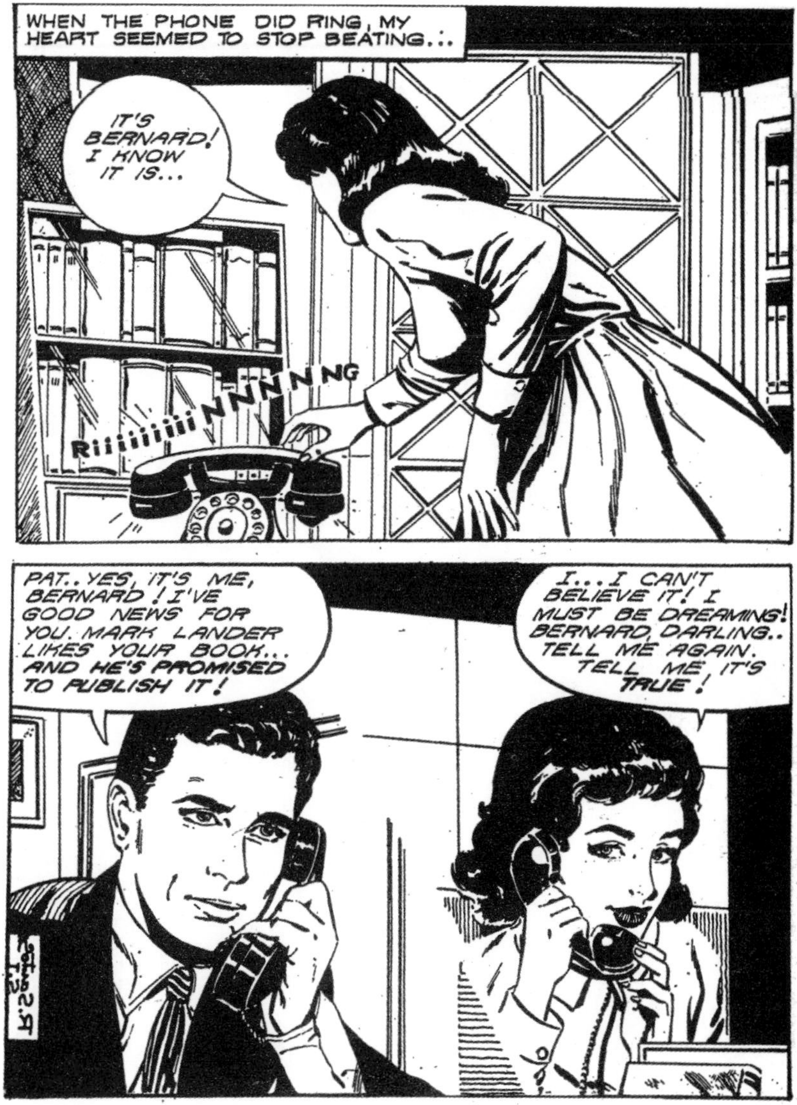
WHEN THE PHONE DID RING, MY HEART SEEMED TO STOP BEATING...
IT'S BERNARD! I KNOW IT IS...
RiiiiiiiiNNNNNNG
PAT..YES, IT'S ME, BERNARD! I'VE GOOD NEWS FOR YOU. MARK LANDER LIKES YOUR BOOK... AND HE'S PROMISED TO PUBLISH IT!
I...I CAN'T BELIEVE IT! I MUST BE DREAMING! BERNARD, DARLING.. TELL ME AGAIN. TELL ME IT'S TRUE!

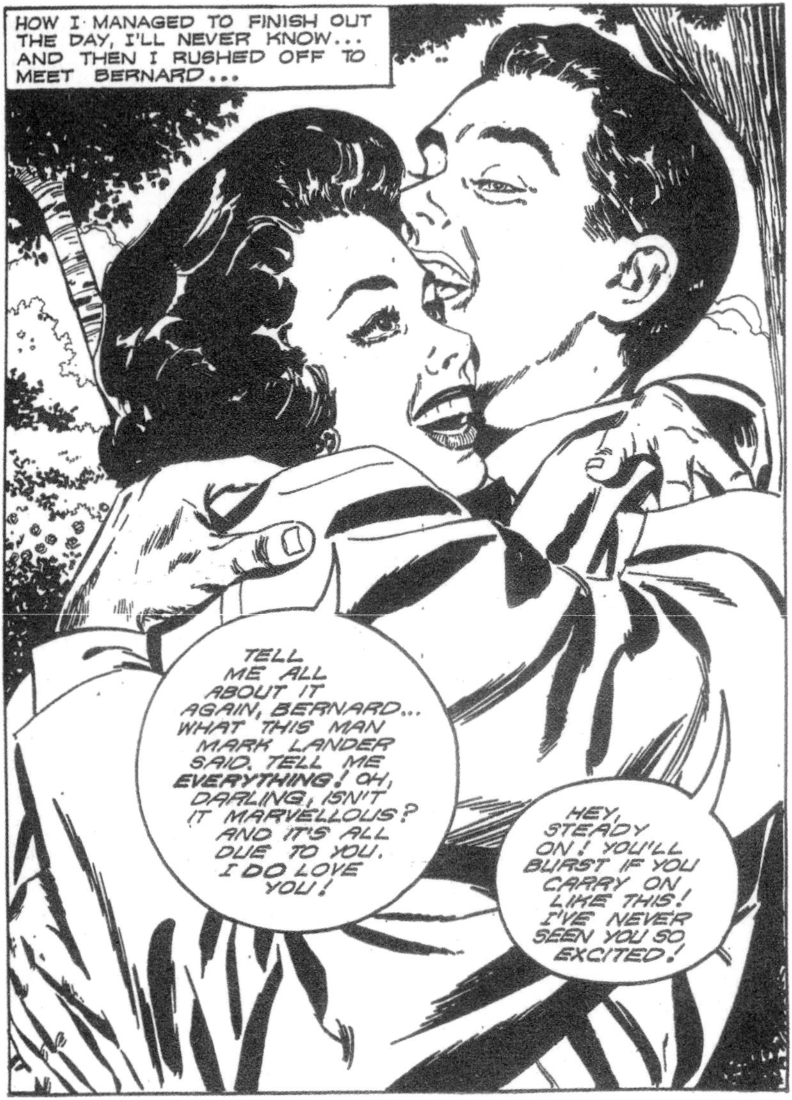
HOW I MANAGED TO FINISH OUT THE DAY, I'LL NEVER KNOW... AND THEN I RUSHED OFF TO MEET BERNARD...
TELL ME ALL ABOUT IT AGAIN, BERNARD... WHAT THIS MAN MARK LANDER SAID. TELL ME EVERYTHING! OH, DARLING, ISN'T IT MARVELLOUS? AND IT'S ALL DUE TO YOU. I DO LOVE YOU!
HEY, STEADY ON! YOU'LL BURST IF YOU CARRY ON LIKE THIS! I'VE NEVER SEEN YOU SO EXCITED!

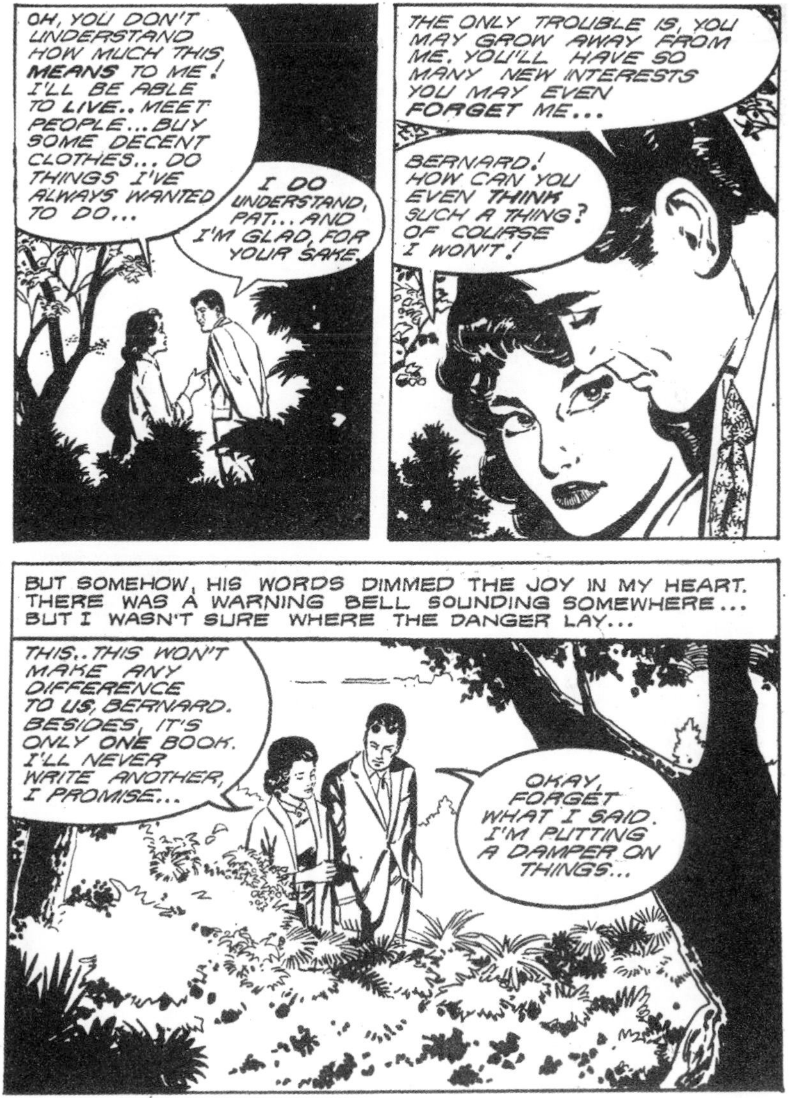
OH, YOU DON'T UNDERSTAND HOW MUCH THIS MEANS TO ME! I'LL BE ABLE TO LIVE.. MEET PEOPLE... BUY SOME DECENT CLOTHES... DO THINGS I'VE ALWAYS WANTED TO DO...
I DO UNDERSTAND, PAT... AND I'M GLAD, FOR YOUR SAKE.
THE ONLY TROUBLE IS, YOU MAY GROW AWAY FROM ME. YOU'LL HAVE SO MANY NEW INTERESTS YOU MAY EVEN FORGET ME...
BERNARD! HOW CAN YOU EVEN THINK SUCH A THING? OF COURSE I WON'T!
BUT SOMEHOW, HIS WORDS DIMMED THE JOY IN MY HEART. THERE WAS A WARNING BELL SOUNDING SOMEWHERE... BUT I WASN'T SURE WHERE THE DANGER LAY...
THIS..THIS WON'T MAKE ANY DIFFERENCE TO US, BERNARD. BESIDES, IT'S ONLY ONE BOOK. I'LL NEVER WRITE ANOTHER, I PROMISE...
OKAY, FORGET WHAT I SAID. I'M PUTTING A DAMPER ON THINGS...

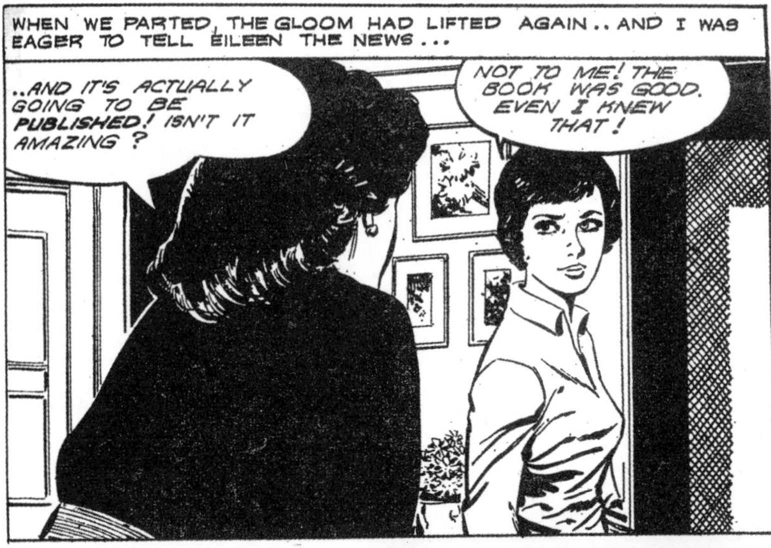
WHEN WE PARTED, THE GLOOM HAD LIFTED AGAIN.. AND I WAS EAGER TO TELL EILEEN THE NEWS...
..AND IT'S ACTUALLY GOING TO BE PUBLISHED! ISN'T IT AMAZING ?
NOT TO ME! THE BOOK WAS GOOD. EVEN I KNEW THAT !

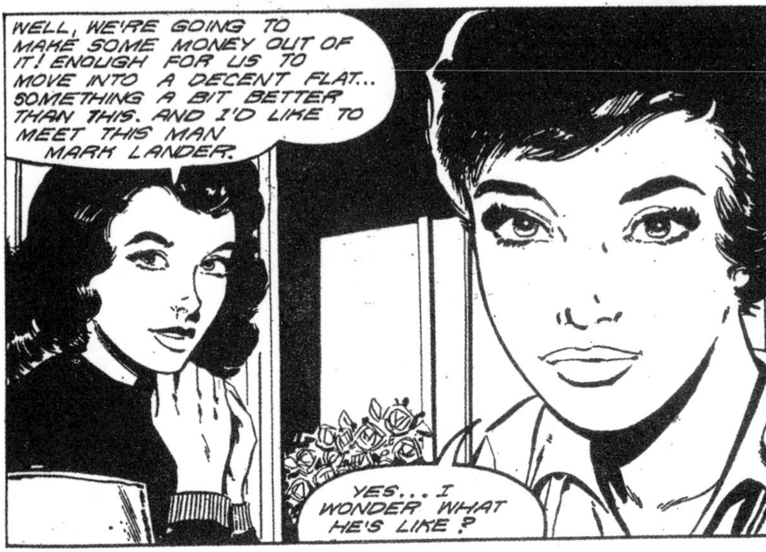
WELL, WE'RE GOING TO MAKE SOME MONEY OUT OF IT! ENOUGH FOR US TO MOVE INTO A DECENT FLAT... SOMETHING A BIT BETTER THAN THIS. AND I'D LIKE TO MEET THIS MAN MARK LANDER.
YES... I WONDER WHAT HE'S LIKE ?

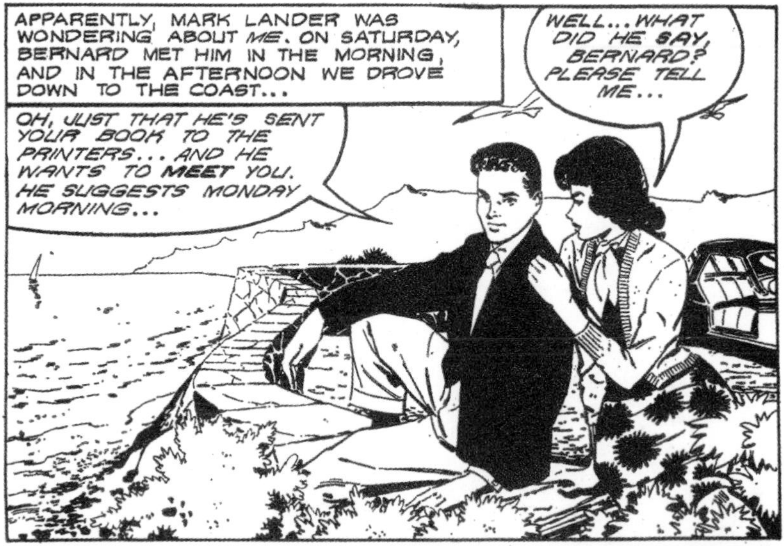
APPARENTLY, MARK LANDER WAS WONDERING ABOUT *ME*. ON SATURDAY, BERNARD MET HIM IN THE MORNING, AND IN THE AFTERNOON WE DROVE DOWN TO THE COAST...
WELL... WHAT DID HE **SAY**, BERNARD? PLEASE TELL ME...
OH, JUST THAT HE'S SENT YOUR BOOK TO THE PRINTERS... AND HE WANTS TO **MEET** YOU. HE SUGGESTS MONDAY MORNING...

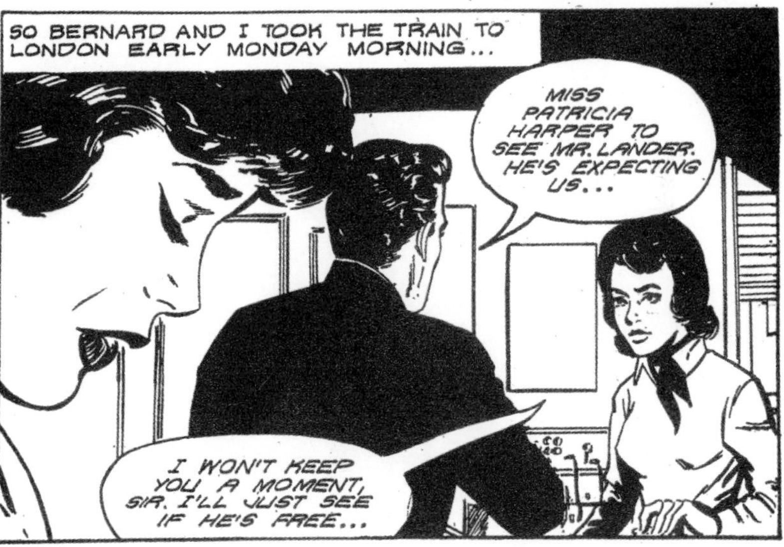
SO BERNARD AND I TOOK THE TRAIN TO LONDON EARLY MONDAY MORNING...
MISS PATRICIA HARPER TO SEE MR. LANDER. HE'S EXPECTING US...
I WON'T KEEP YOU A MOMENT, SIR. I'LL JUST SEE IF HE'S FREE...

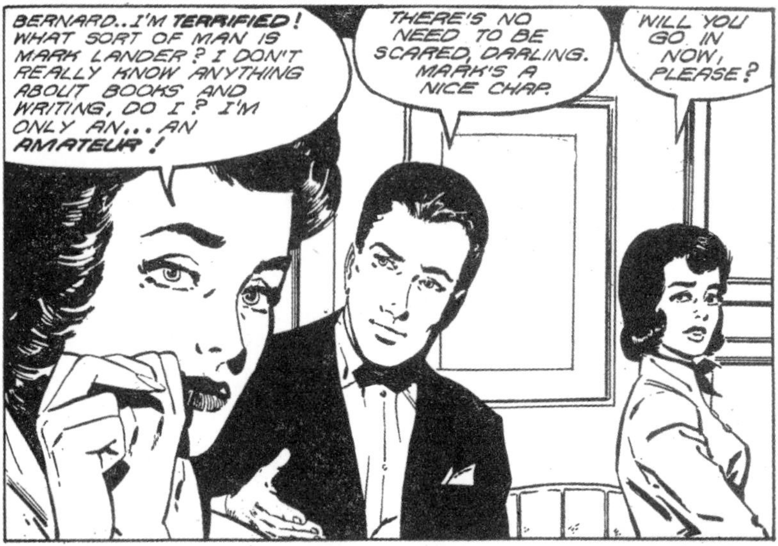
BERNARD.. I'M TERRIFIED! WHAT SORT OF MAN IS MARK LANDER? I DON'T REALLY KNOW ANYTHING ABOUT BOOKS AND WRITING, DO I? I'M ONLY AN... AN AMATEUR!
THERE'S NO NEED TO BE SCARED, DARLING. MARK'S A NICE CHAP.
WILL YOU GO IN NOW, PLEASE?

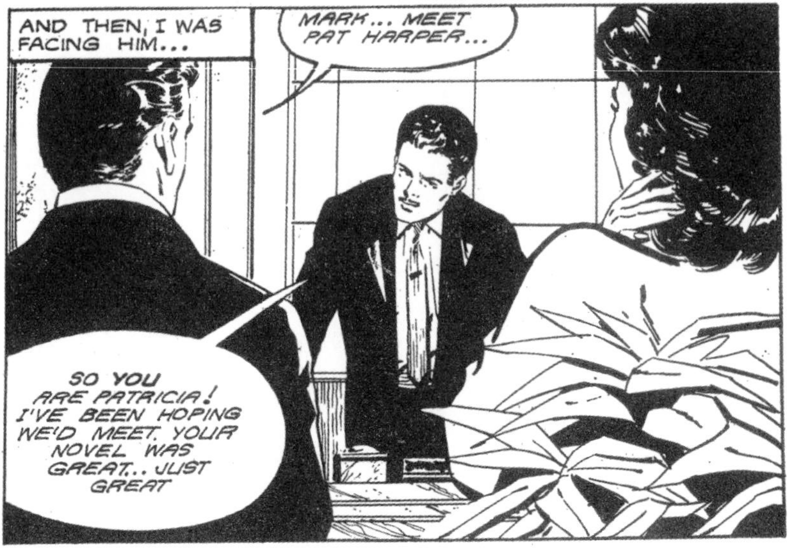
AND THEN, I WAS FACING HIM...
MARK... MEET PAT HARPER...
SO YOU ARE PATRICIA! I'VE BEEN HOPING WE'D MEET. YOUR NOVEL WAS GREAT... JUST GREAT

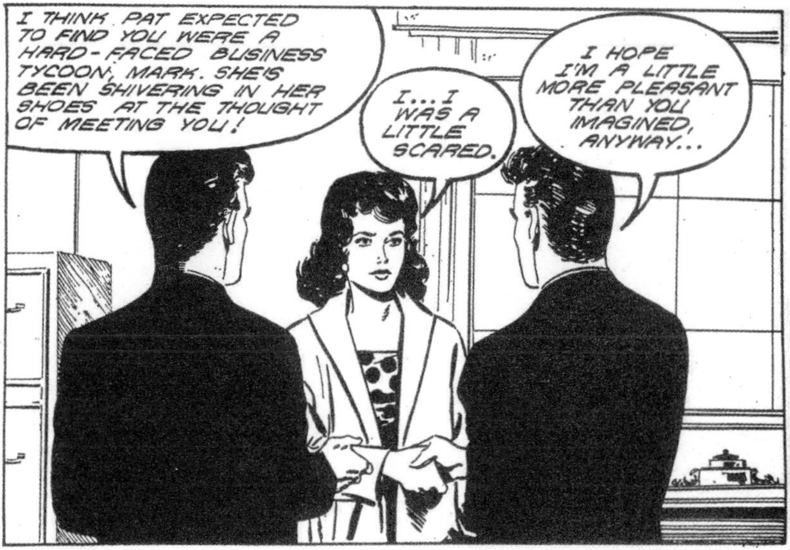
I THINK PAT EXPECTED TO FIND YOU WERE A HARD-FACED BUSINESS TYCOON, MARK. SHE'S BEEN SHIVERING IN HER SHOES AT THE THOUGHT OF MEETING YOU!
I... I WAS A LITTLE SCARED.
I HOPE I'M A LITTLE MORE PLEASANT THAN YOU IMAGINED, ANYWAY...

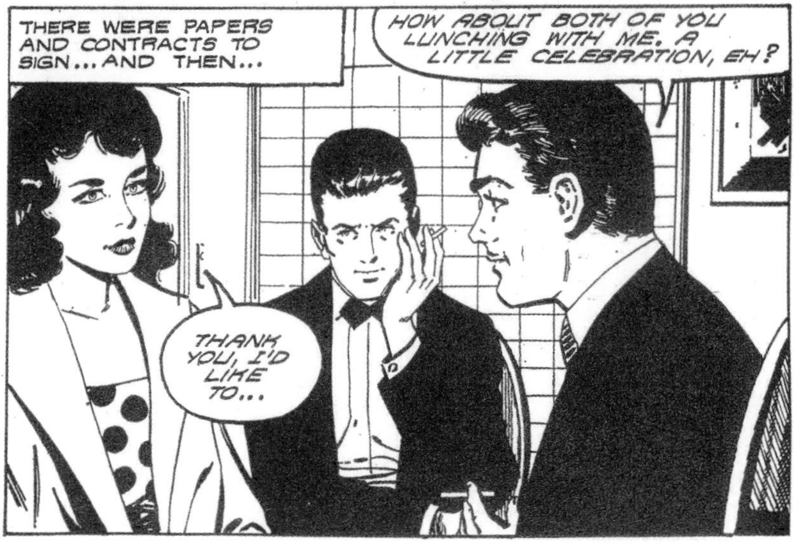
THERE WERE PAPERS AND CONTRACTS TO SIGN... AND THEN...
HOW ABOUT BOTH OF YOU LUNCHING WITH ME. A LITTLE CELEBRATION, EH?
THANK YOU, I'D LIKE TO...

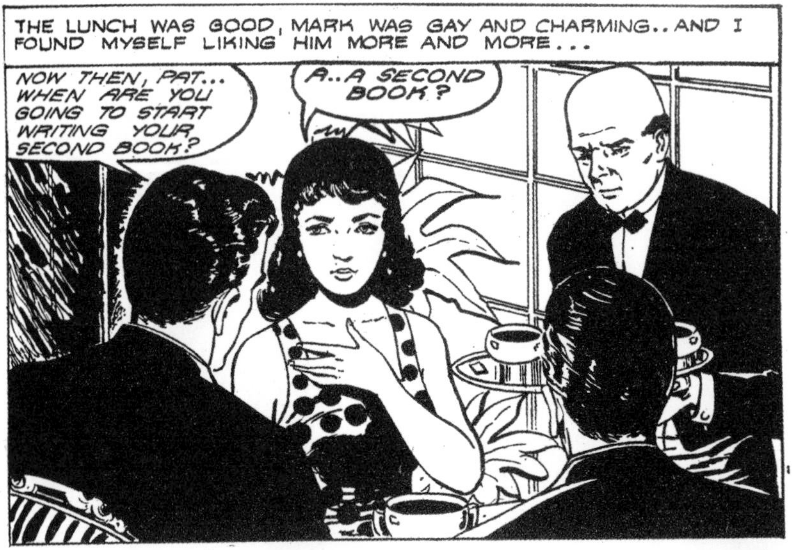
THE LUNCH WAS GOOD, MARK WAS GAY AND CHARMING.. AND I FOUND MYSELF LIKING HIM MORE AND MORE...
NOW THEN, PAT... WHEN ARE YOU GOING TO START WRITING YOUR SECOND BOOK?
A..A SECOND BOOK?

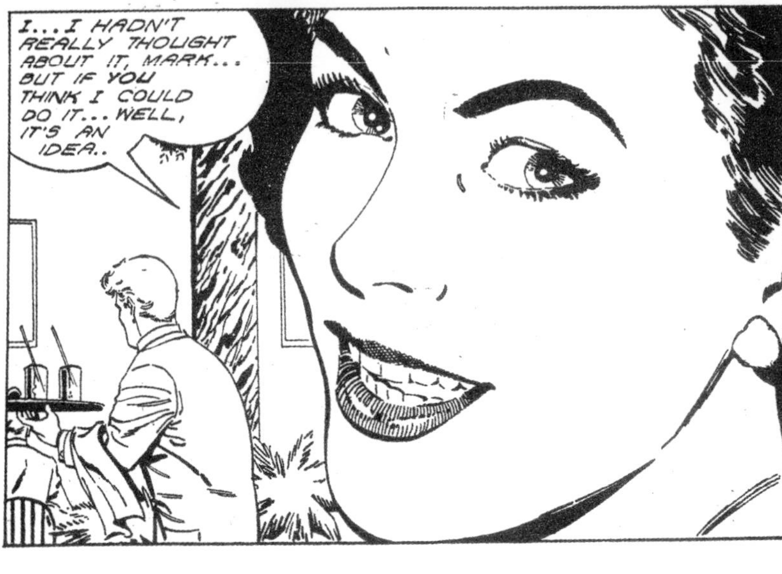
I...I HADN'T REALLY THOUGHT ABOUT IT, MARK... BUT IF YOU THINK I COULD DO IT... WELL, IT'S AN IDEA..

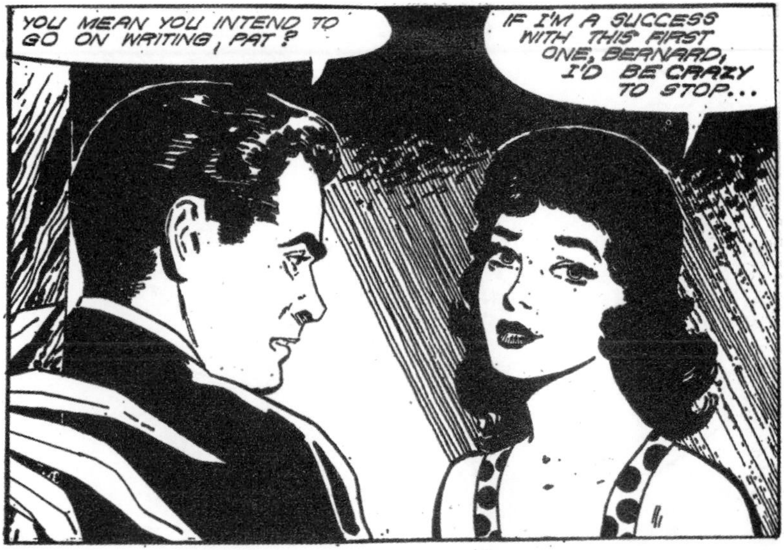
YOU MEAN YOU INTEND TO GO ON WRITING, PAT?
IF I'M A SUCCESS WITH THIS FIRST ONE, BERNARD, I'D BE CRAZY TO STOP...

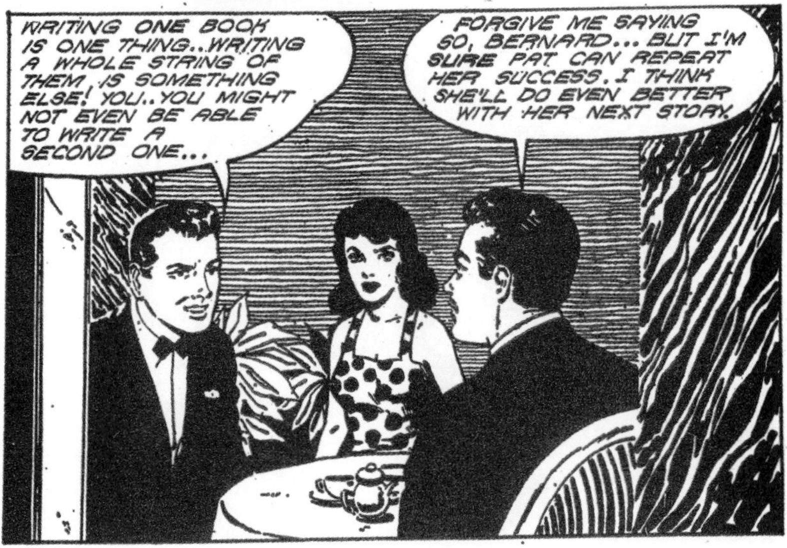
WRITING ONE BOOK IS ONE THING..WRITING A WHOLE STRING OF THEM IS SOMETHING ELSE! YOU..YOU MIGHT NOT EVEN BE ABLE TO WRITE A SECOND ONE...
FORGIVE ME SAYING SO, BERNARD... BUT I'M SURE PAT CAN REPEAT HER SUCCESS. I THINK SHE'LL DO EVEN BETTER WITH HER NEXT STORY.

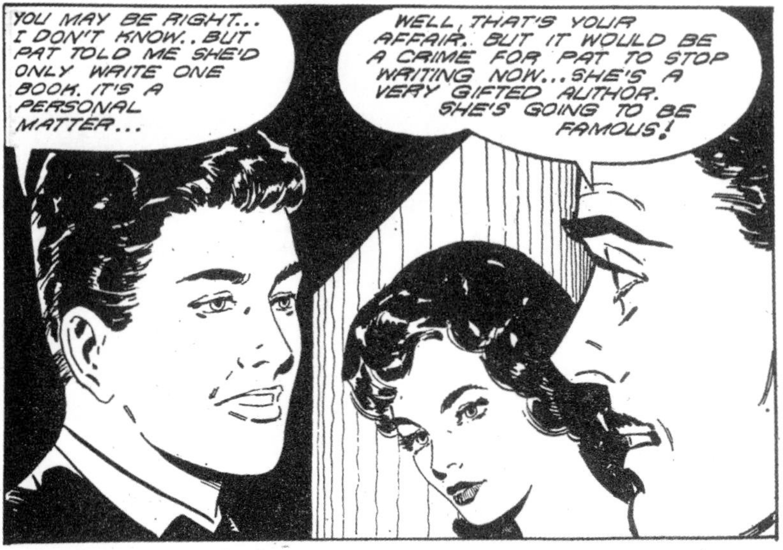
YOU MAY BE RIGHT... I DON'T KNOW.. BUT PAT TOLD ME SHE'D ONLY WRITE ONE BOOK. IT'S A PERSONAL MATTER...
WELL, THAT'S YOUR AFFAIR.. BUT IT WOULD BE A CRIME FOR PAT TO STOP WRITING NOW... SHE'S A VERY GIFTED AUTHOR. SHE'S GOING TO BE FAMOUS!

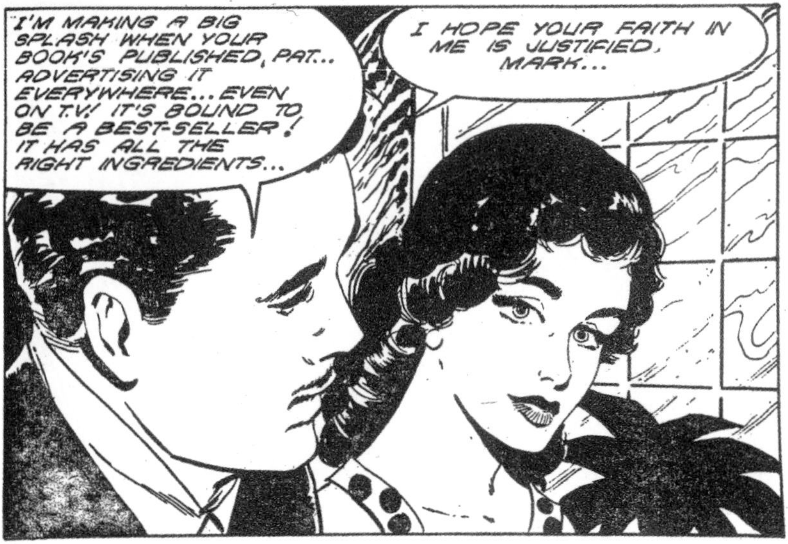
I'M MAKING A BIG SPLASH WHEN YOUR BOOK'S PUBLISHED, PAT... ADVERTISING IT EVERYWHERE... EVEN ON T.V.! IT'S BOUND TO BE A BEST-SELLER! IT HAS ALL THE RIGHT INGREDIENTS...
I HOPE YOUR FAITH IN ME IS JUSTIFIED, MARK...

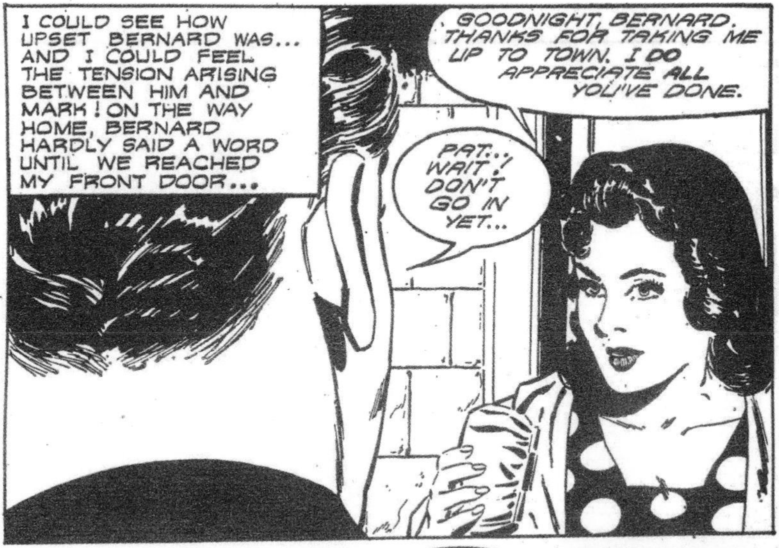
I COULD SEE HOW UPSET BERNARD WAS... AND I COULD FEEL THE TENSION ARISING BETWEEN HIM AND MARK! ON THE WAY HOME, BERNARD HARDLY SAID A WORD UNTIL WE REACHED MY FRONT DOOR...
GOODNIGHT, BERNARD. THANKS FOR TAKING ME UP TO TOWN. I DO APPRECIATE ALL YOU'VE DONE.
PAT... WAIT! DON'T GO IN YET...

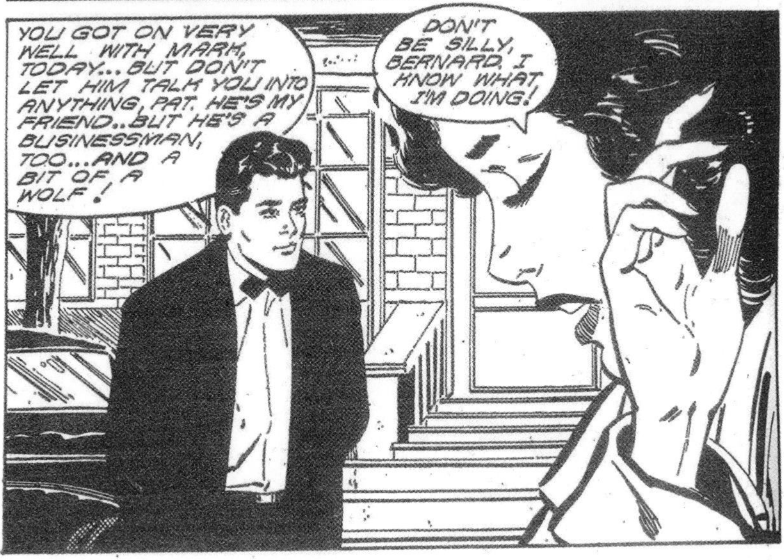
YOU GOT ON VERY WELL WITH MARK, TODAY... BUT DON'T LET HIM TALK YOU INTO ANYTHING, PAT. HE'S MY FRIEND.. BUT HE'S A BUSINESSMAN, TOO... AND A BIT OF A WOLF!
DON'T BE SILLY, BERNARD. I KNOW WHAT I'M DOING!

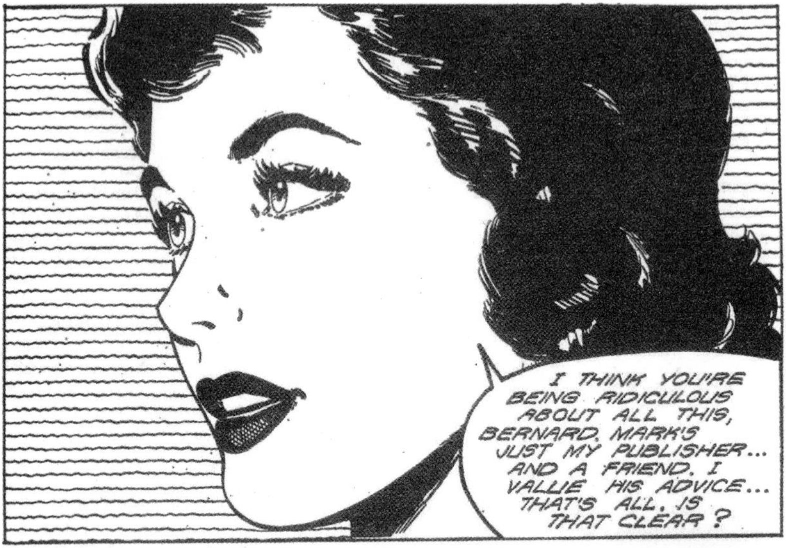
I THINK YOU'RE BEING RIDICULOUS ABOUT ALL THIS, BERNARD. MARK'S JUST MY PUBLISHER... AND A FRIEND. I VALUE HIS ADVICE... THAT'S ALL. IS THAT CLEAR ?

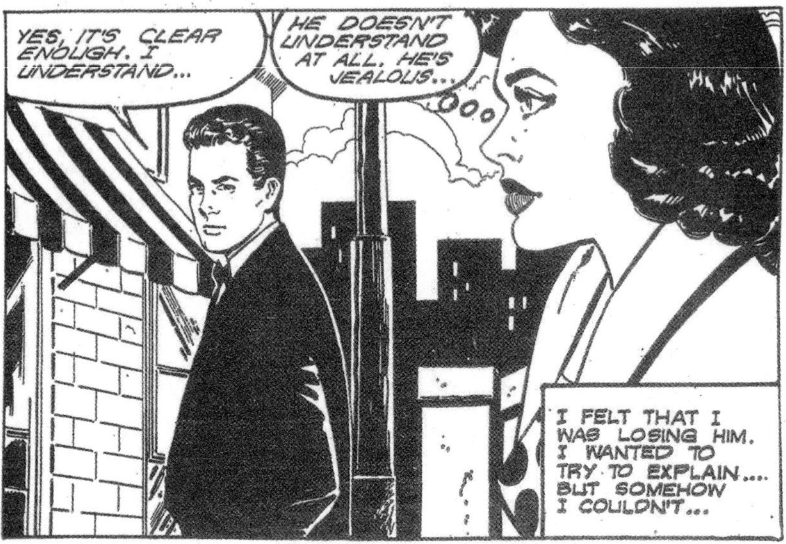
YES, IT'S CLEAR ENOUGH. I UNDERSTAND...
HE DOESN'T UNDERSTAND AT ALL. HE'S JEALOUS...
I FELT THAT I WAS LOSING HIM. I WANTED TO TRY TO EXPLAIN.... BUT SOMEHOW I COULDN'T...

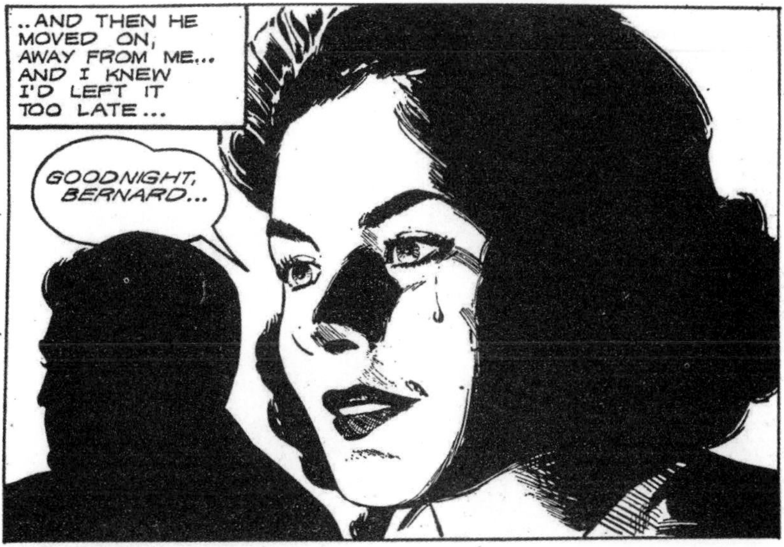
..AND THEN HE MOVED ON, AWAY FROM ME... AND I KNEW I'D LEFT IT TOO LATE...
GOODNIGHT, BERNARD...

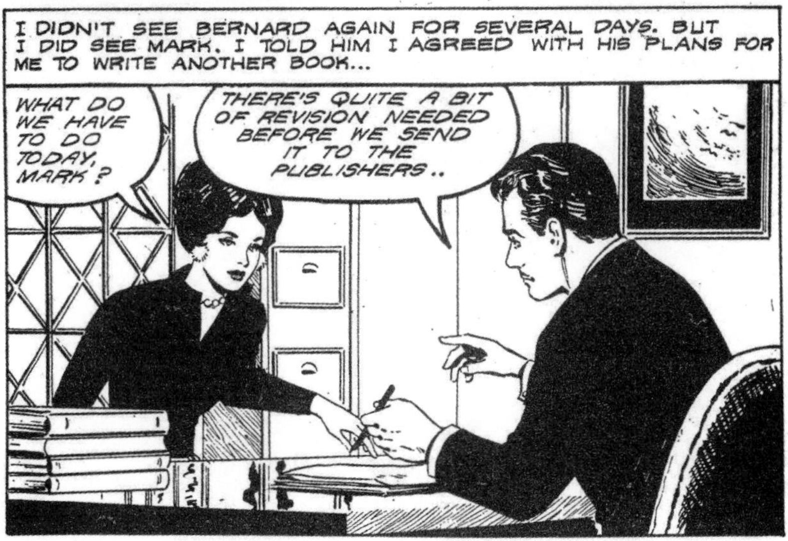
I DIDN'T SEE BERNARD AGAIN FOR SEVERAL DAYS. BUT I DID SEE MARK. I TOLD HIM I AGREED WITH HIS PLANS FOR ME TO WRITE ANOTHER BOOK...
WHAT DO WE HAVE TO DO TODAY, MARK?
THERE'S QUITE A BIT OF REVISION NEEDED BEFORE WE SEND IT TO THE PUBLISHERS..

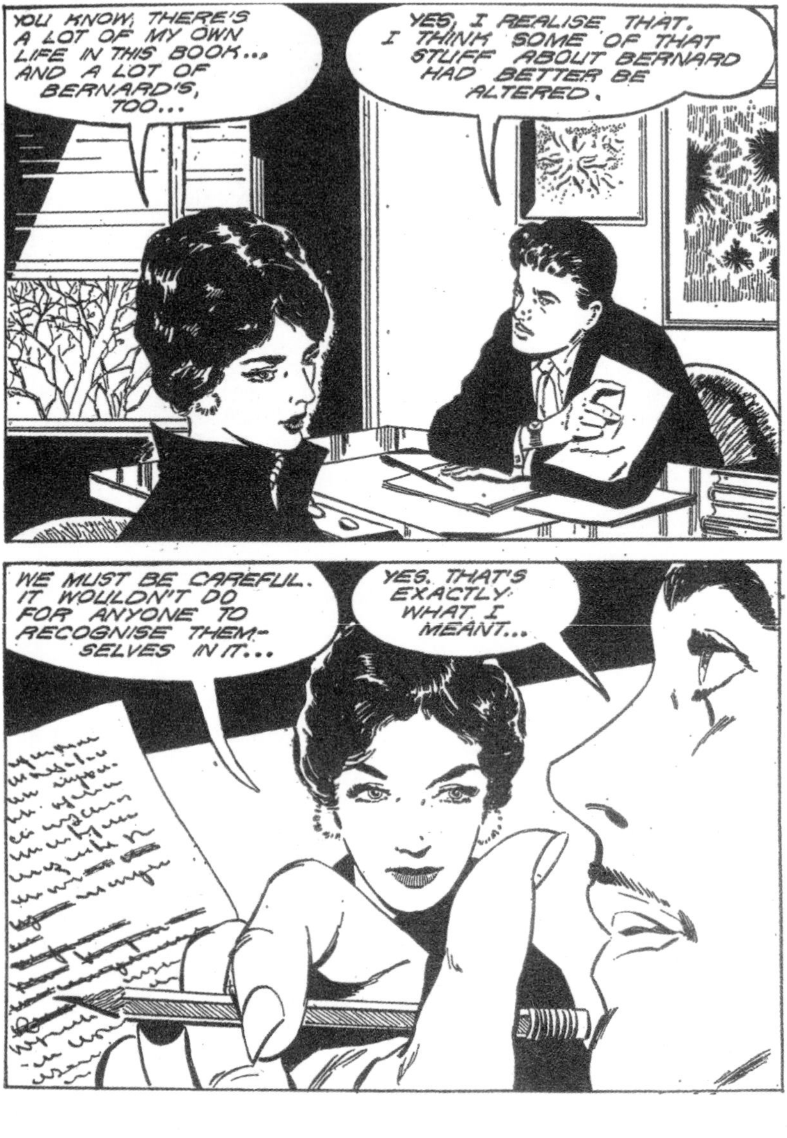
YOU KNOW, THERE'S A LOT OF MY OWN LIFE IN THIS BOOK... AND A LOT OF BERNARD'S, TOO...
YES, I REALISE THAT. I THINK SOME OF THAT STUFF ABOUT BERNARD HAD BETTER BE ALTERED.
WE MUST BE CAREFUL. IT WOULDN'T DO FOR ANYONE TO RECOGNISE THEM-SELVES IN IT...
YES. THAT'S EXACTLY WHAT I MEANT...

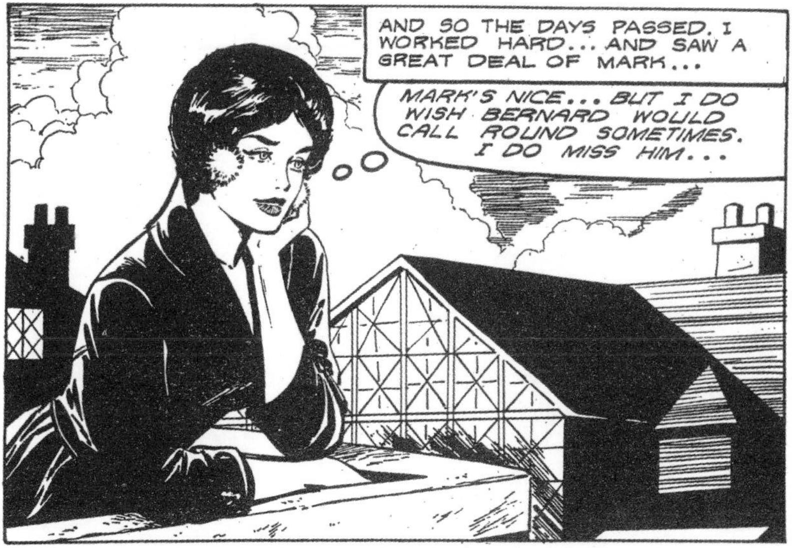
AND SO THE DAYS PASSED. I WORKED HARD... AND SAW A GREAT DEAL OF MARK...
MARK'S NICE... BUT I DO WISH BERNARD WOULD CALL ROUND SOMETIMES. I DO MISS HIM...

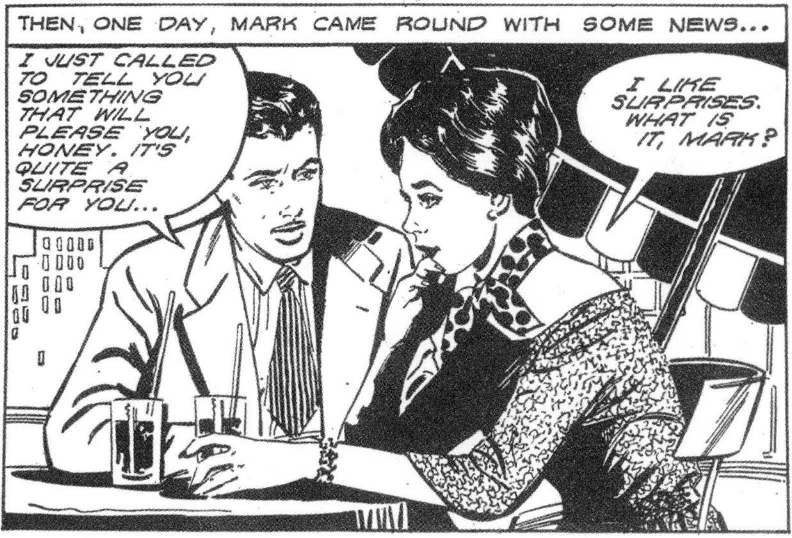
THEN, ONE DAY, MARK CAME ROUND WITH SOME NEWS...
I JUST CALLED TO TELL YOU SOMETHING THAT WILL PLEASE YOU, HONEY. IT'S QUITE A SURPRISE FOR YOU...
I LIKE SURPRISES. WHAT IS IT, MARK?

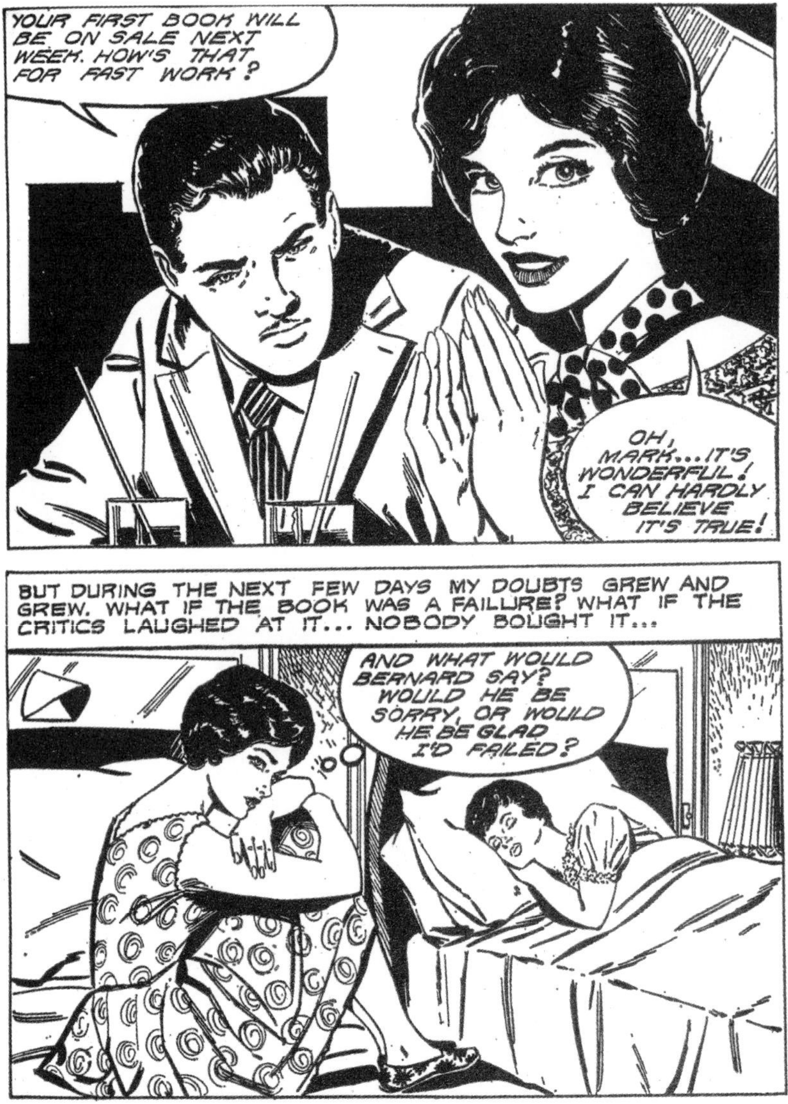
YOUR FIRST BOOK WILL BE ON SALE NEXT WEEK. HOW'S THAT FOR FAST WORK?
OH, MARK...IT'S WONDERFUL! I CAN HARDLY BELIEVE IT'S TRUE!
BUT DURING THE NEXT FEW DAYS MY DOUBTS GREW AND GREW. WHAT IF THE BOOK WAS A FAILURE? WHAT IF THE CRITICS LAUGHED AT IT... NOBODY BOUGHT IT...
AND WHAT WOULD BERNARD SAY? WOULD HE BE SORRY, OR WOULD HE BE GLAD I'D FAILED?

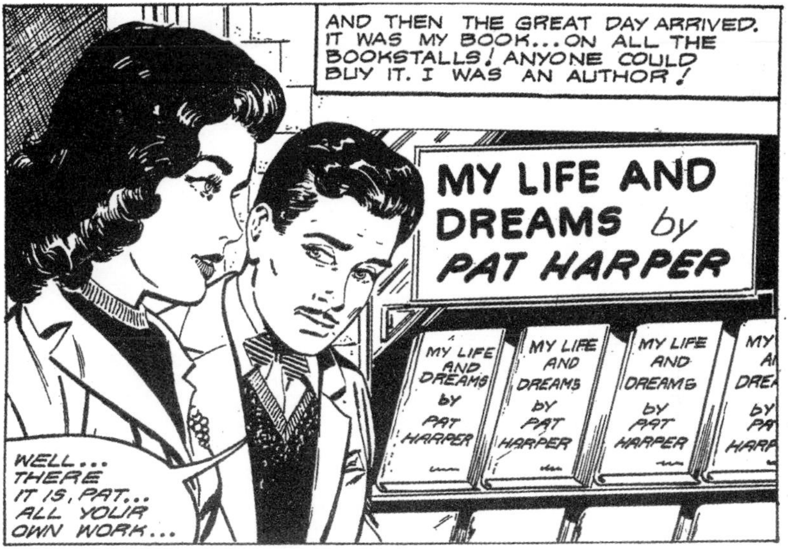
AND THEN THE GREAT DAY ARRIVED. IT WAS MY BOOK...ON ALL THE BOOKSTALLS! ANYONE COULD BUY IT. I WAS AN AUTHOR!
MY LIFE AND DREAMS by PAT HARPER
MY LIFE AND DREAMS by PAT HARPER
MY LIFE AND DREAMS by PAT HARPER
MY LIFE AND DREAMS by PAT HARPER
WELL... THERE IT IS, PAT... ALL YOUR OWN WORK...

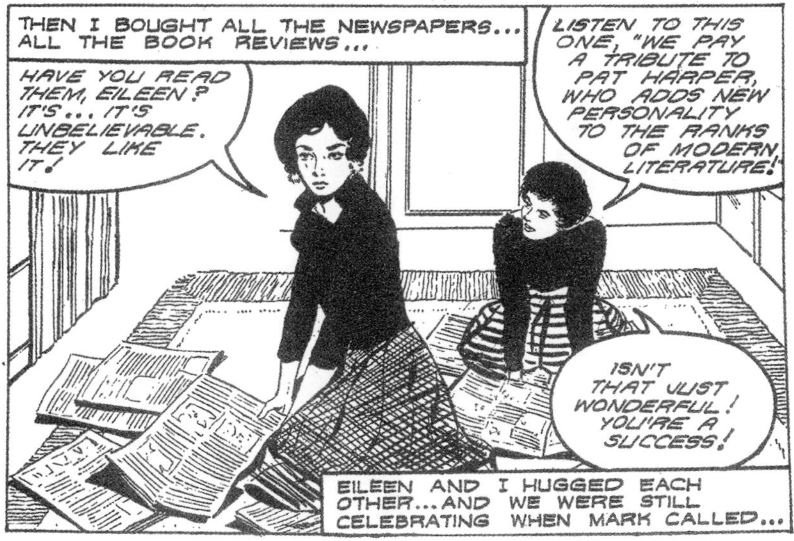
THEN I BOUGHT ALL THE NEWSPAPERS... ALL THE BOOK REVIEWS...
HAVE YOU READ THEM, EILEEN? IT'S... IT'S UNBELIEVABLE. THEY LIKE IT!
LISTEN TO THIS ONE, "WE PAY A TRIBUTE TO PAT HARPER, WHO ADDS NEW PERSONALITY TO THE RANKS OF MODERN LITERATURE!"
ISN'T THAT JUST WONDERFUL! YOU'RE A SUCCESS!
EILEEN AND I HUGGED EACH OTHER...AND WE WERE STILL CELEBRATING WHEN MARK CALLED...

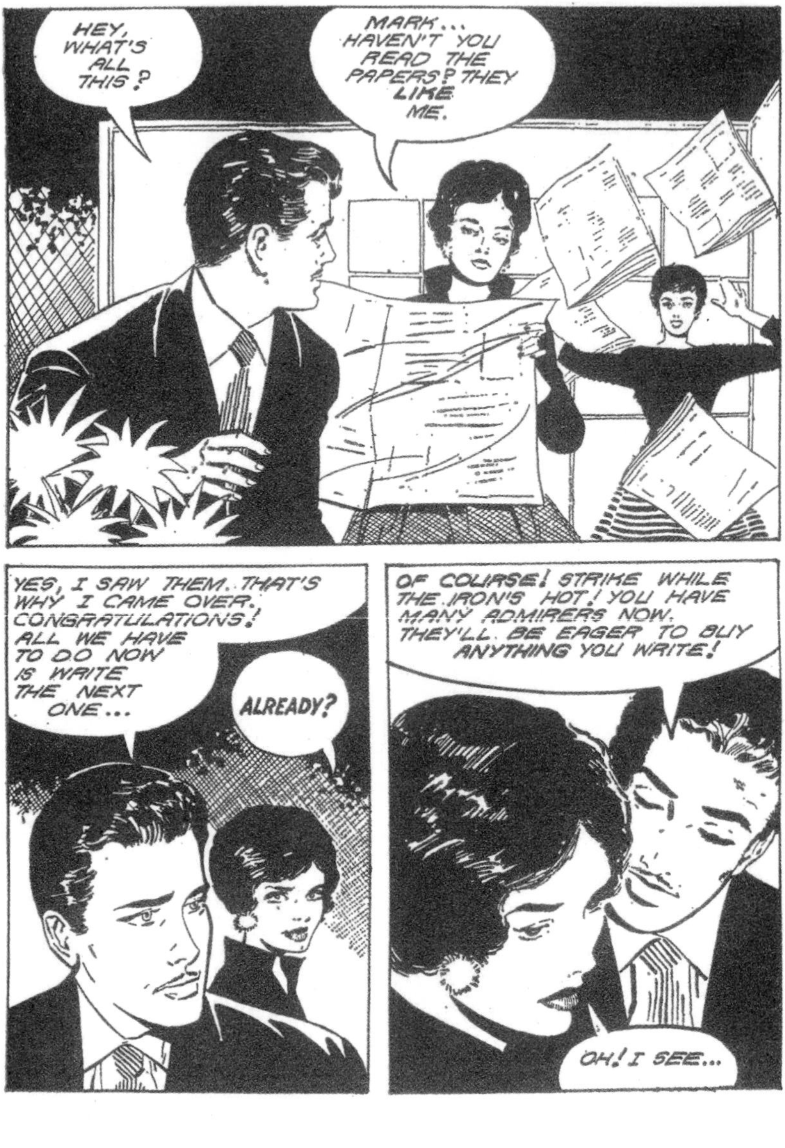
HEY, WHAT'S ALL THIS?
MARK... HAVEN'T YOU READ THE PAPERS? THEY LIKE ME.
YES, I SAW THEM. THAT'S WHY I CAME OVER. CONGRATULATIONS! ALL WE HAVE TO DO NOW IS WRITE THE NEXT ONE...
ALREADY?
OF COURSE! STRIKE WHILE THE IRON'S HOT! YOU HAVE MANY ADMIRERS NOW. THEY'LL BE EAGER TO BUY ANYTHING YOU WRITE!
OH! I SEE...

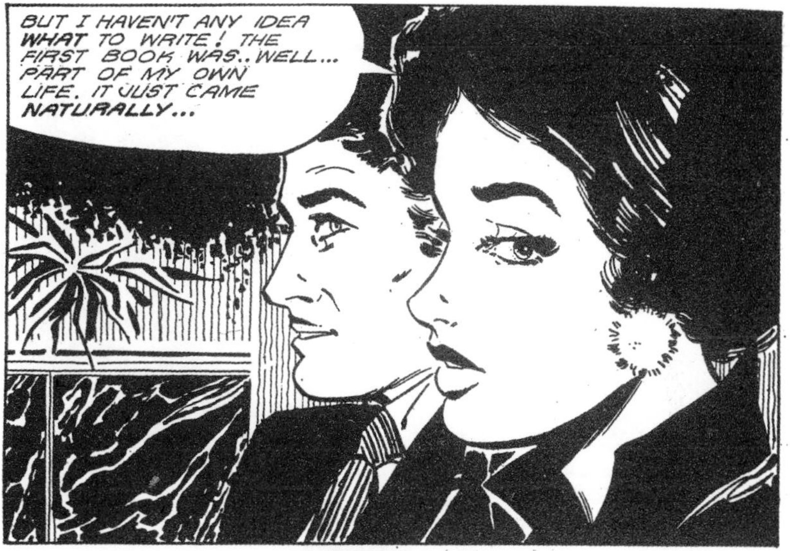
BUT I HAVEN'T ANY IDEA WHAT TO WRITE! THE FIRST BOOK WAS.. WELL... PART OF MY OWN LIFE. IT JUST CAME NATURALLY...

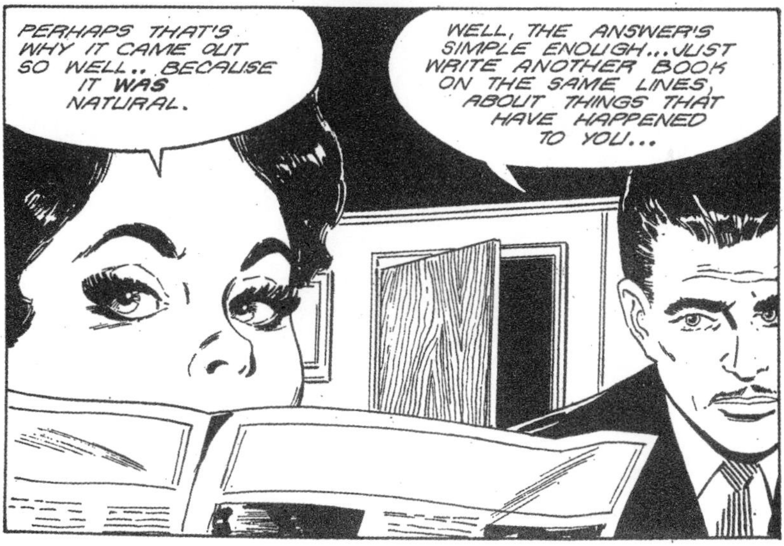
PERHAPS THAT'S WHY IT CAME OUT SO WELL.. BECAUSE IT WAS NATURAL.
WELL, THE ANSWER'S SIMPLE ENOUGH... JUST WRITE ANOTHER BOOK ON THE SAME LINES, ABOUT THINGS THAT HAVE HAPPENED TO YOU...

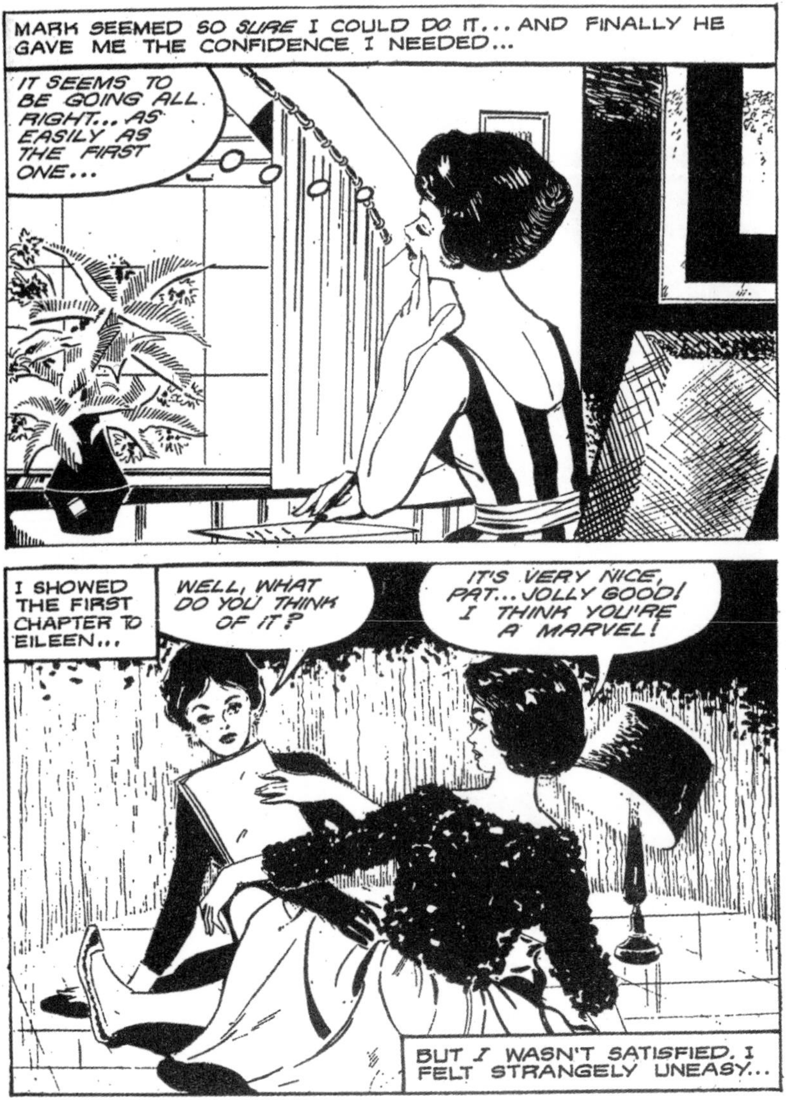
MARK SEEMED SO SURE I COULD DO IT... AND FINALLY HE GAVE ME THE CONFIDENCE I NEEDED...
IT SEEMS TO BE GOING ALL RIGHT... AS EASILY AS THE FIRST ONE...
I SHOWED THE FIRST CHAPTER TO EILEEN...
WELL, WHAT DO YOU THINK OF IT?
IT'S VERY NICE, PAT... JOLLY GOOD! I THINK YOU'RE A MARVEL!
BUT I WASN'T SATISFIED. I FELT STRANGELY UNEASY...

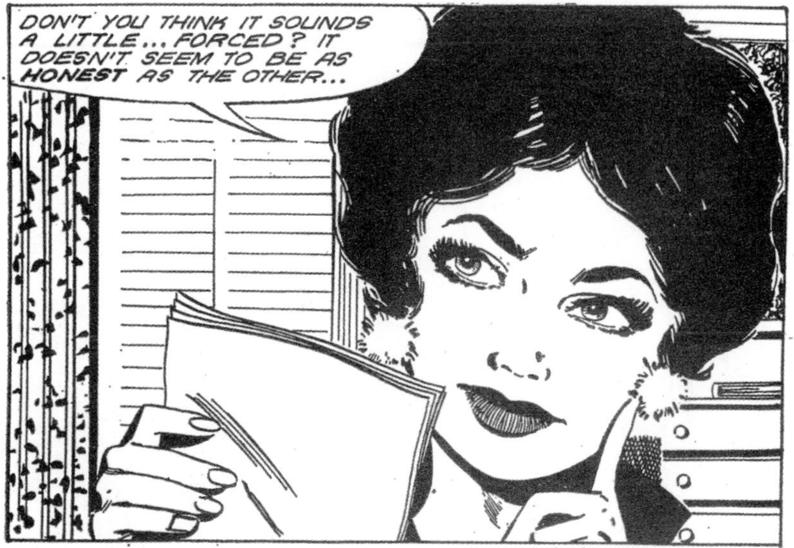
DON'T YOU THINK IT SOUNDS A LITTLE... FORCED? IT DOESN'T SEEM TO BE AS HONEST AS THE OTHER...

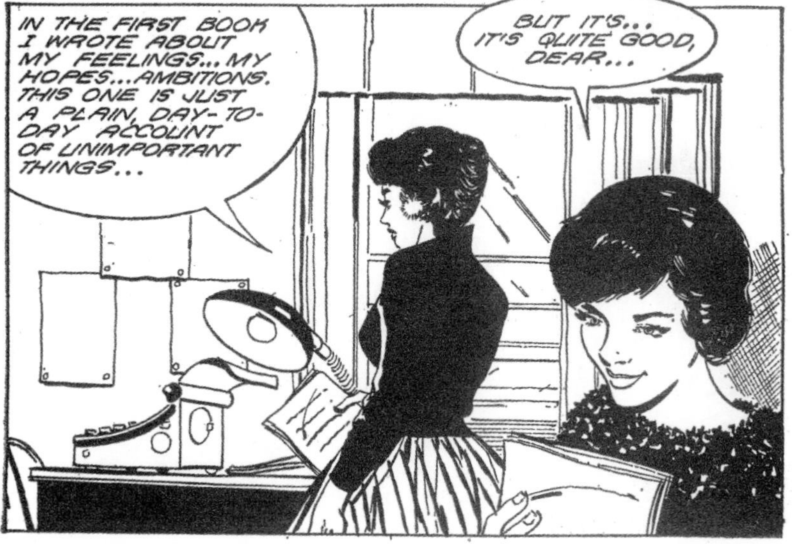
IN THE FIRST BOOK I WROTE ABOUT MY FEELINGS... MY HOPES... AMBITIONS. THIS ONE IS JUST A PLAIN, DAY-TO-DAY ACCOUNT OF UNIMPORTANT THINGS...
BUT IT'S... IT'S QUITE GOOD, DEAR...

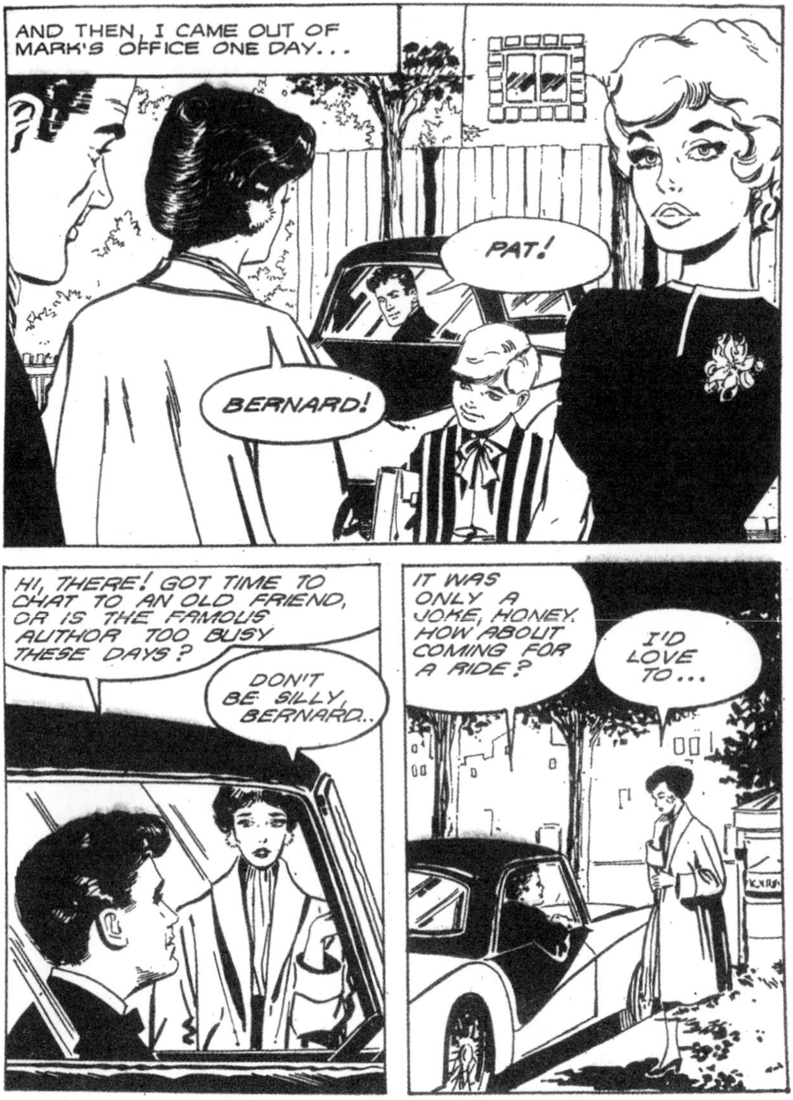
AND THEN, I CAME OUT OF MARK'S OFFICE ONE DAY...
PAT!
BERNARD!
HI, THERE! GOT TIME TO CHAT TO AN OLD FRIEND, OR IS THE FAMOUS AUTHOR TOO BUSY THESE DAYS?
DON'T BE SILLY, BERNARD..
IT WAS ONLY A JOKE, HONEY. HOW ABOUT COMING FOR A RIDE?
I'D LOVE TO...

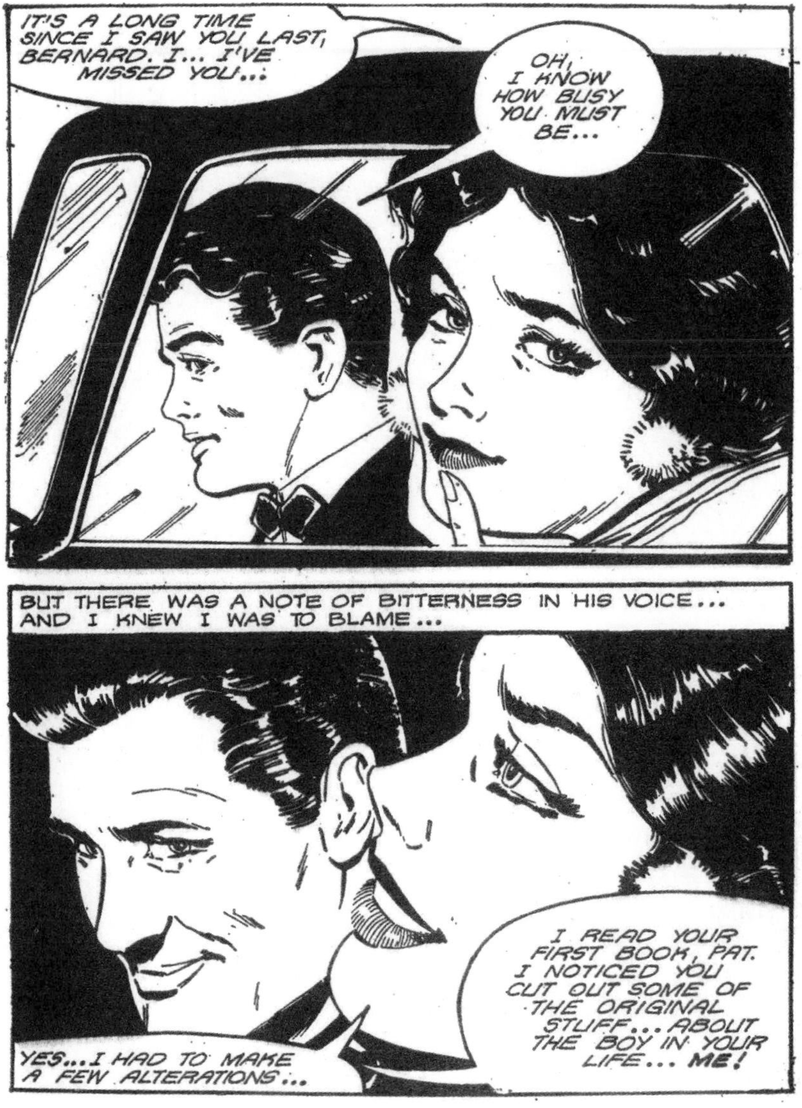
IT'S A LONG TIME SINCE I SAW YOU LAST, BERNARD. I... I'VE MISSED YOU...
OH, I KNOW HOW BUSY YOU MUST BE...
BUT THERE WAS A NOTE OF BITTERNESS IN HIS VOICE... AND I KNEW I WAS TO BLAME...
I READ YOUR FIRST BOOK, PAT. I NOTICED YOU CUT OUT SOME OF THE ORIGINAL STUFF... ABOUT THE BOY IN YOUR LIFE... **ME!**
YES... I HAD TO MAKE A FEW ALTERATIONS...

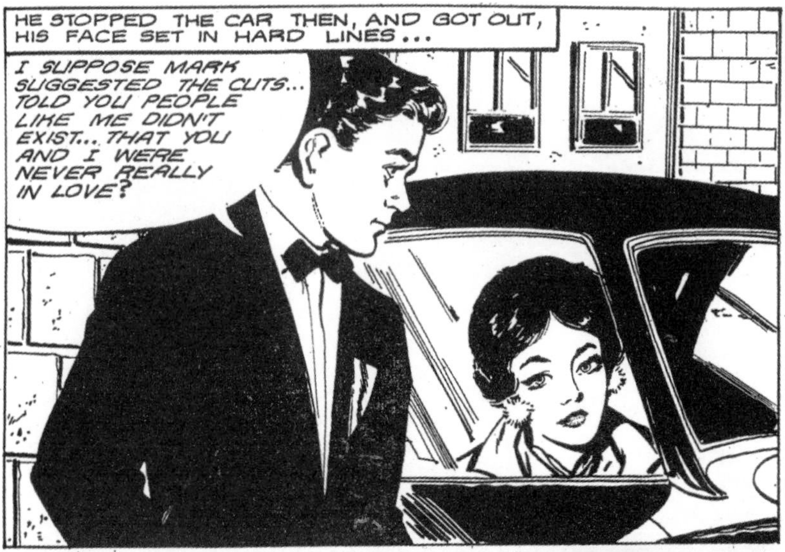
HE STOPPED THE CAR THEN, AND GOT OUT, HIS FACE SET IN HARD LINES...
I SUPPOSE MARK SUGGESTED THE CUTS... TOLD YOU PEOPLE LIKE ME DIDN'T EXIST... THAT YOU AND I WERE NEVER REALLY IN LOVE?

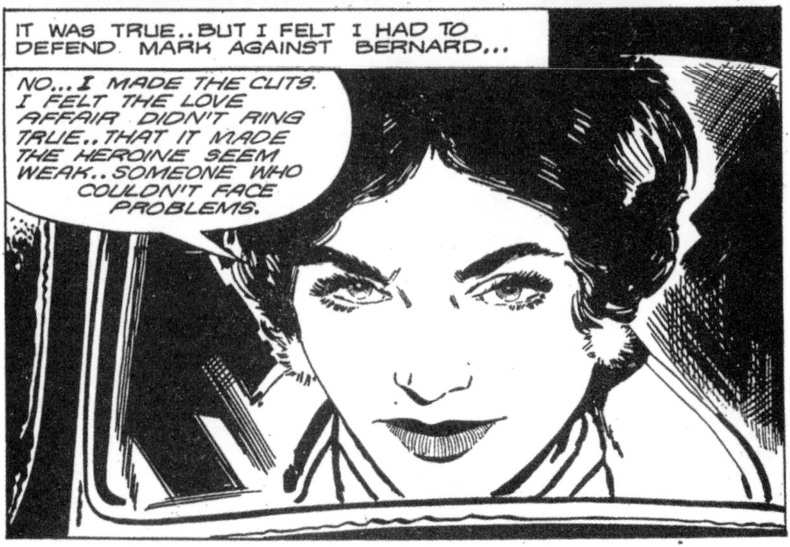
IT WAS TRUE.. BUT I FELT I HAD TO DEFEND MARK AGAINST BERNARD...
NO... I MADE THE CUTS. I FELT THE LOVE AFFAIR DIDN'T RING TRUE.. THAT IT MADE THE HEROINE SEEM WEAK.. SOMEONE WHO COULDN'T FACE PROBLEMS.

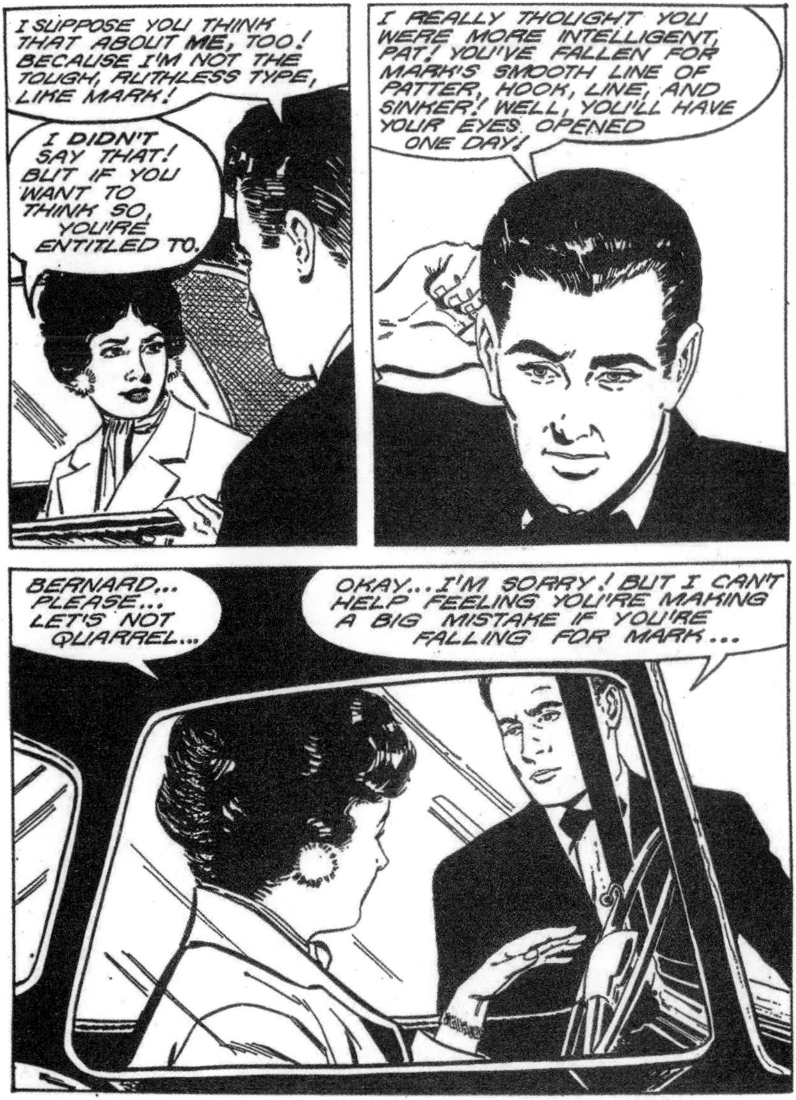
I SUPPOSE YOU THINK THAT ABOUT ME, TOO! BECAUSE I'M NOT THE TOUGH, RUTHLESS TYPE, LIKE MARK!
I DIDN'T SAY THAT! BUT IF YOU WANT TO THINK SO, YOU'RE ENTITLED TO.
I REALLY THOUGHT YOU WERE MORE INTELLIGENT, PAT! YOU'VE FALLEN FOR MARK'S SMOOTH LINE OF PATTER, HOOK, LINE, AND SINKER! WELL, YOU'LL HAVE YOUR EYES OPENED ONE DAY!
BERNARD... PLEASE... LET'S NOT QUARREL...
OKAY... I'M SORRY! BUT I CAN'T HELP FEELING YOU'RE MAKING A BIG MISTAKE IF YOU'RE FALLING FOR MARK...

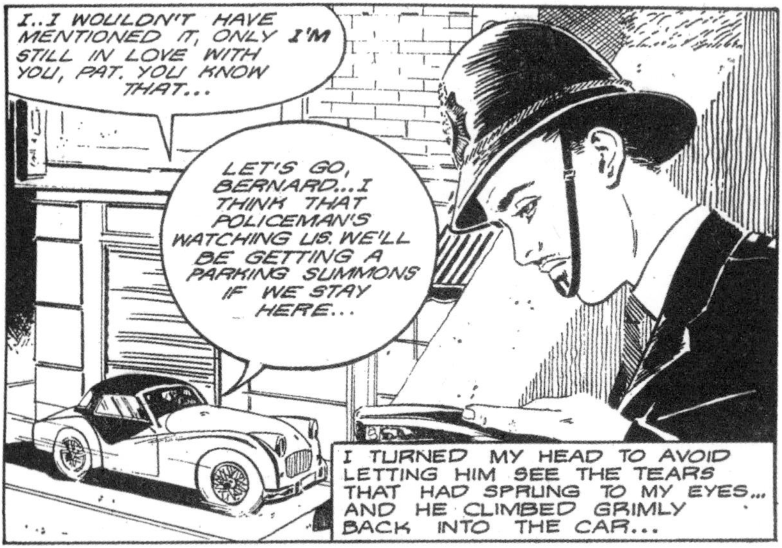
I..I WOULDN'T HAVE MENTIONED IT, ONLY I'M STILL IN LOVE WITH YOU, PAT. YOU KNOW THAT...
LET'S GO, BERNARD...I THINK THAT POLICEMAN'S WATCHING US. WE'LL BE GETTING A PARKING SUMMONS IF WE STAY HERE...
I TURNED MY HEAD TO AVOID LETTING HIM SEE THE TEARS THAT HAD SPRUNG TO MY EYES... AND HE CLIMBED GRIMLY BACK INTO THE CAR...

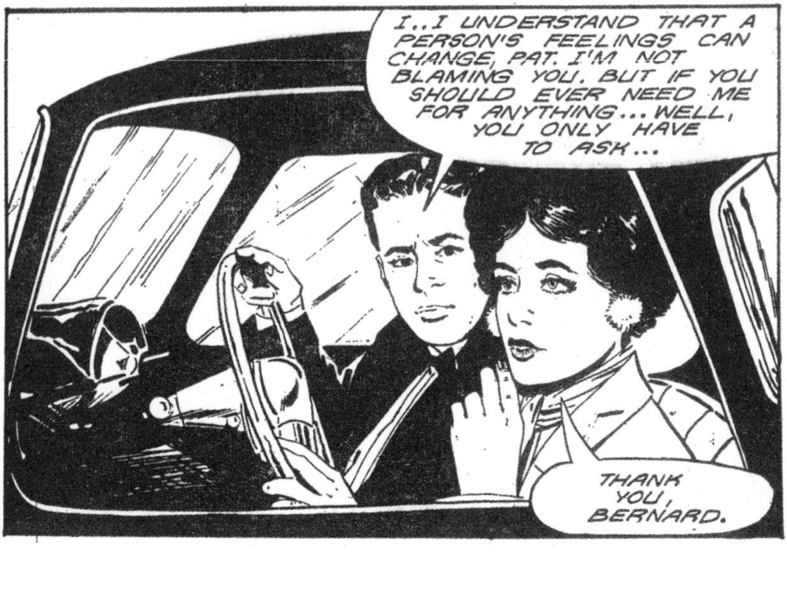
I..I UNDERSTAND THAT A PERSON'S FEELINGS CAN CHANGE, PAT. I'M NOT BLAMING YOU. BUT IF YOU SHOULD EVER NEED ME FOR ANYTHING... WELL, YOU ONLY HAVE TO ASK...
THANK YOU, BERNARD.

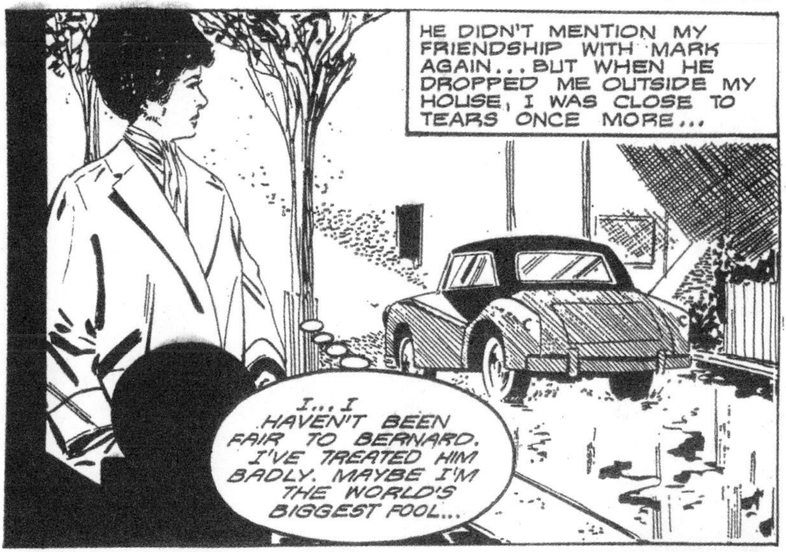
HE DIDN'T MENTION MY FRIENDSHIP WITH MARK AGAIN... BUT WHEN HE DROPPED ME OUTSIDE MY HOUSE, I WAS CLOSE TO TEARS ONCE MORE...
I... I HAVEN'T BEEN FAIR TO BERNARD. I'VE TREATED HIM BADLY. MAYBE I'M THE WORLD'S BIGGEST FOOL...

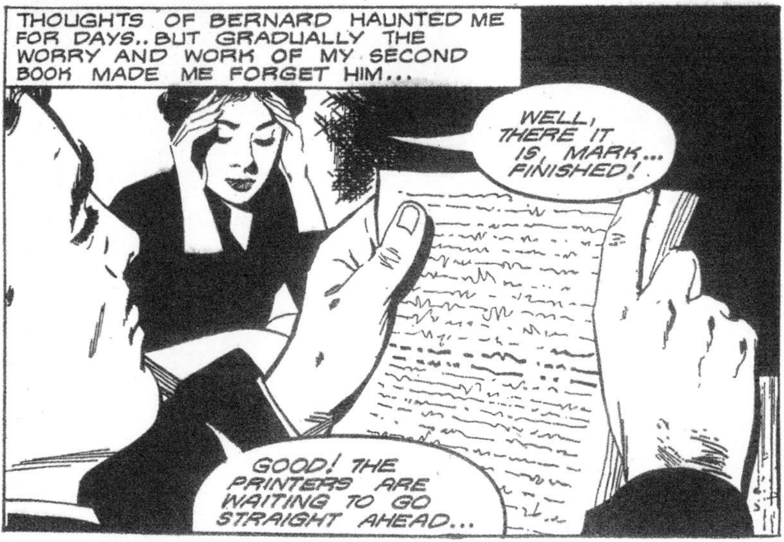
THOUGHTS OF BERNARD HAUNTED ME FOR DAYS.. BUT GRADUALLY THE WORRY AND WORK OF MY SECOND BOOK MADE ME FORGET HIM...
WELL, THERE IT IS, MARK... FINISHED!
GOOD! THE PRINTERS ARE WAITING TO GO STRAIGHT AHEAD...

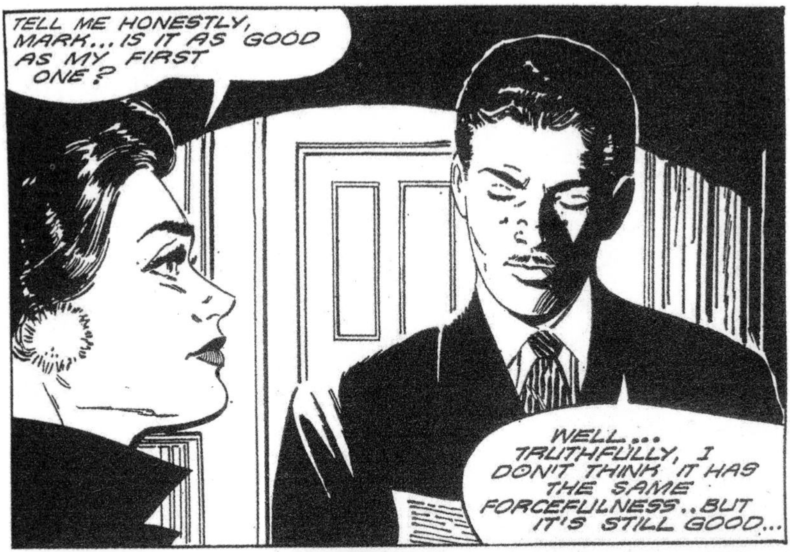
TELL ME HONESTLY, MARK... IS IT AS GOOD AS MY FIRST ONE?
WELL... TRUTHFULLY, I DON'T THINK IT HAS THE SAME FORCEFULNESS..BUT IT'S STILL GOOD...

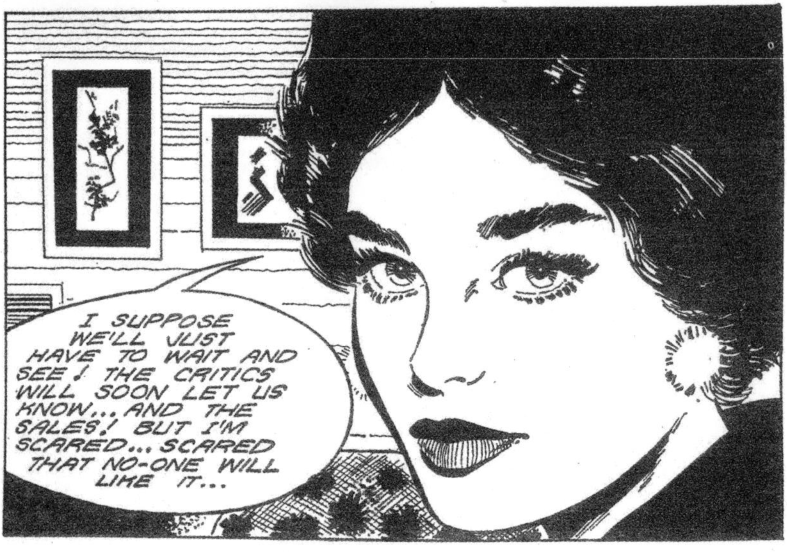
I SUPPOSE WE'LL JUST HAVE TO WAIT AND SEE! THE CRITICS WILL SOON LET US KNOW... AND THE SALES! BUT I'M SCARED... SCARED THAT NO-ONE WILL LIKE IT...

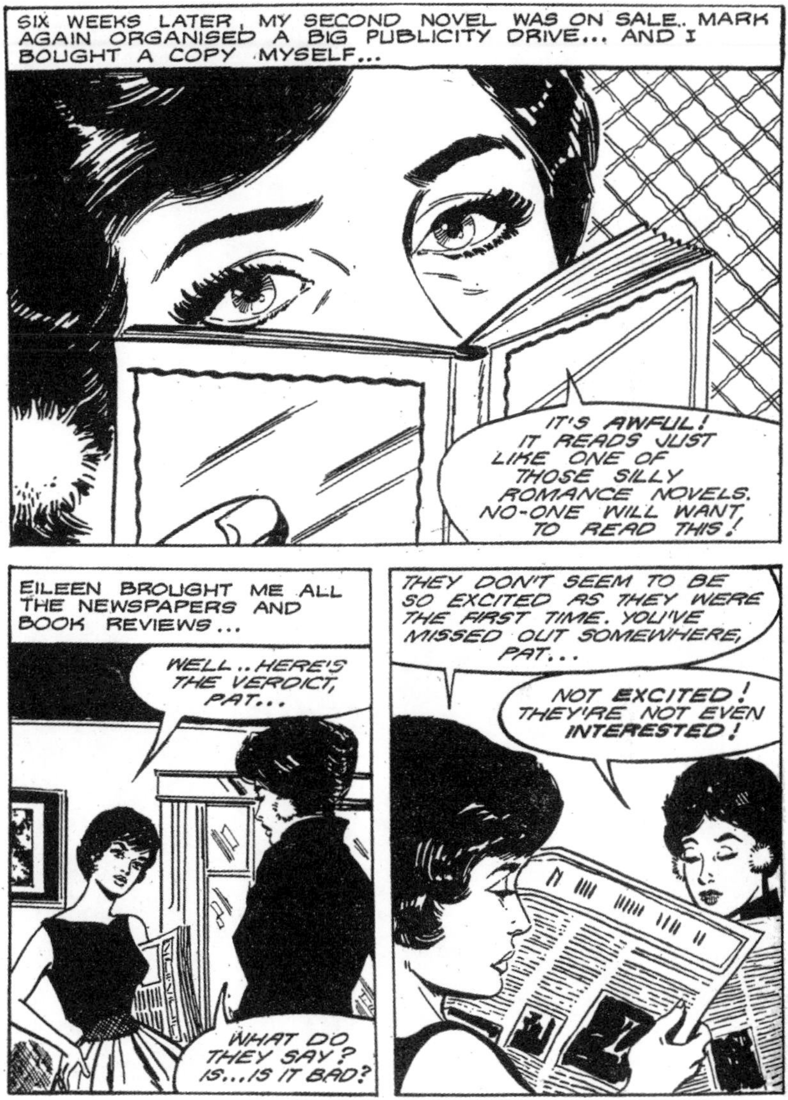
SIX WEEKS LATER, MY SECOND NOVEL WAS ON SALE.. MARK AGAIN ORGANISED A BIG PUBLICITY DRIVE... AND I BOUGHT A COPY MYSELF...
IT'S AWFUL! IT READS JUST LIKE ONE OF THOSE SILLY ROMANCE NOVELS. NO-ONE WILL WANT TO READ THIS!
EILEEN BROUGHT ME ALL THE NEWSPAPERS AND BOOK REVIEWS...
WELL.. HERE'S THE VERDICT, PAT...
WHAT DO THEY SAY? IS... IS IT BAD?
THEY DON'T SEEM TO BE SO EXCITED AS THEY WERE THE FIRST TIME. YOU'VE MISSED OUT SOMEWHERE, PAT...
NOT EXCITED! THEY'RE NOT EVEN INTERESTED!

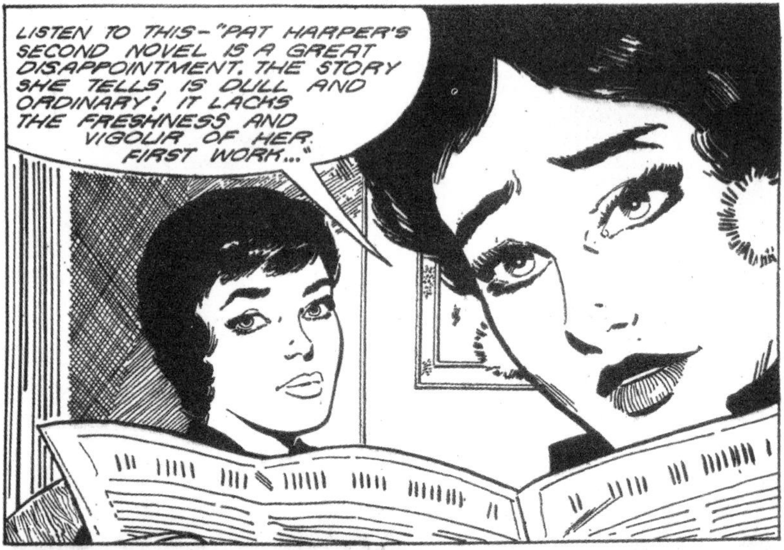
LISTEN TO THIS–"PAT HARPER'S SECOND NOVEL IS A GREAT DISAPPOINTMENT. THE STORY SHE TELLS IS DULL AND ORDINARY! IT LACKS THE FRESHNESS AND VIGOUR OF HER FIRST WORK..."

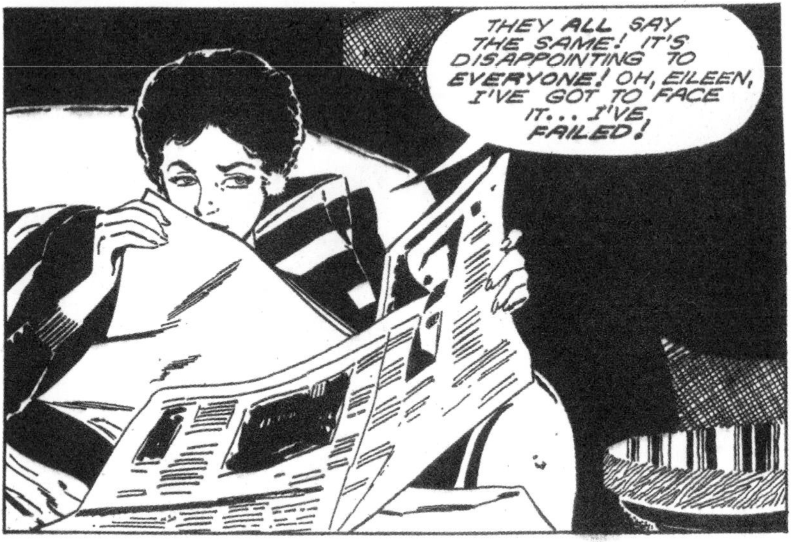
THEY ALL SAY THE SAME! IT'S DISAPPOINTING TO EVERYONE! OH, EILEEN, I'VE GOT TO FACE IT... I'VE FAILED!

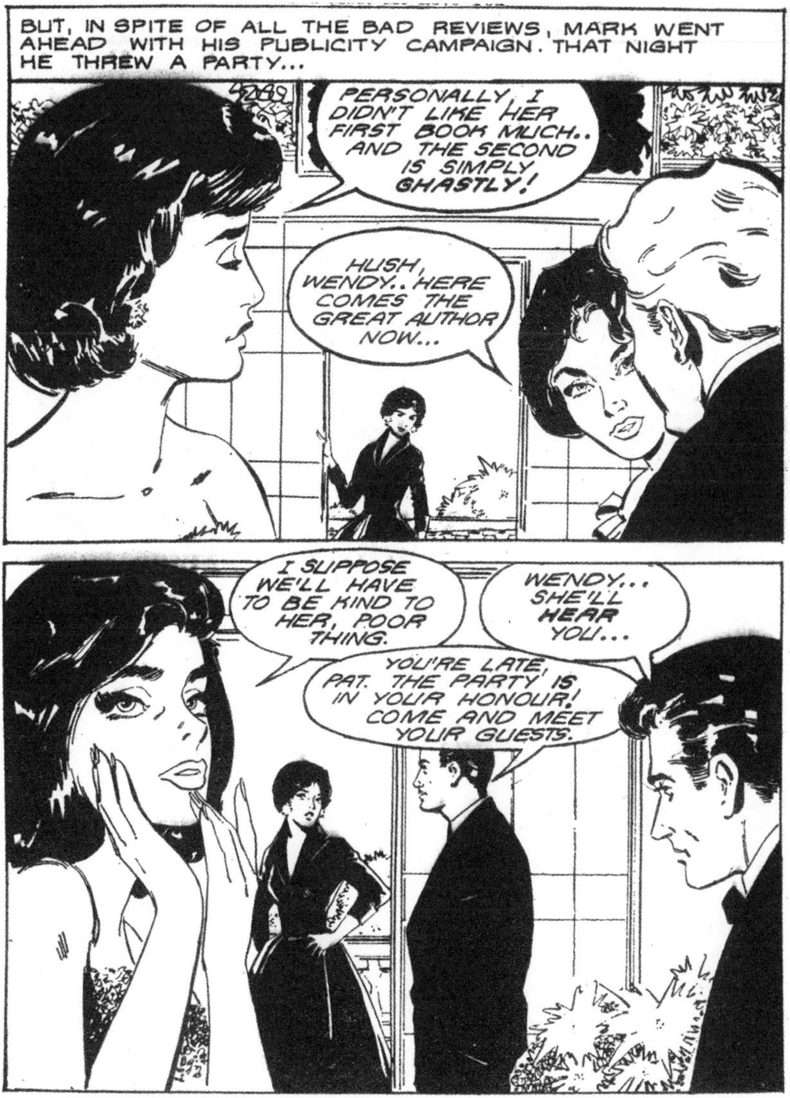
BUT, IN SPITE OF ALL THE BAD REVIEWS, MARK WENT AHEAD WITH HIS PUBLICITY CAMPAIGN. THAT NIGHT HE THREW A PARTY...
PERSONALLY, I DIDN'T LIKE HER FIRST BOOK MUCH.. AND THE SECOND IS SIMPLY GHASTLY!
HUSH, WENDY.. HERE COMES THE GREAT AUTHOR NOW...
I SUPPOSE WE'LL HAVE TO BE KIND TO HER, POOR THING.
WENDY... SHE'LL HEAR YOU...
YOU'RE LATE, PAT. THE PARTY IS IN YOUR HONOUR! COME AND MEET YOUR GUESTS.

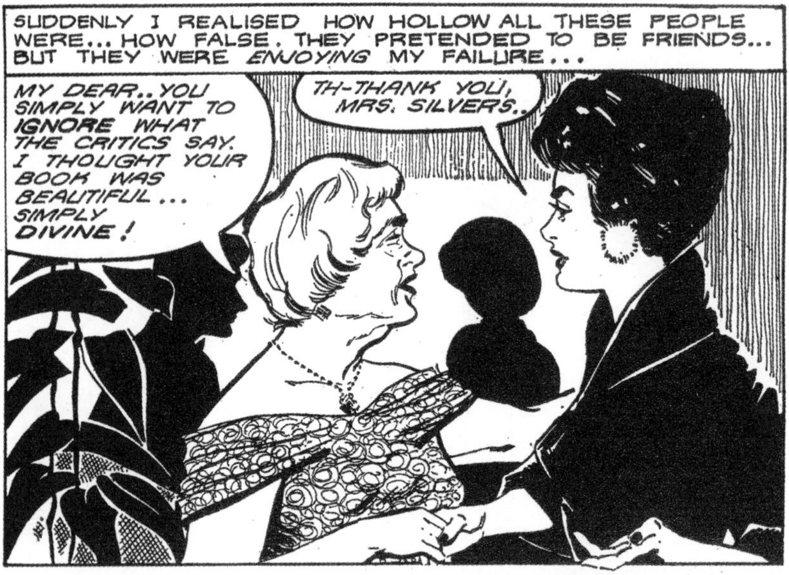
SUDDENLY I REALISED HOW HOLLOW ALL THESE PEOPLE WERE... HOW FALSE. THEY PRETENDED TO BE FRIENDS... BUT THEY WERE ENJOYING MY FAILURE...
MY DEAR.. YOU SIMPLY WANT TO IGNORE WHAT THE CRITICS SAY. I THOUGHT YOUR BOOK WAS BEAUTIFUL... SIMPLY DIVINE!
TH-THANK YOU, MRS. SILVERS..

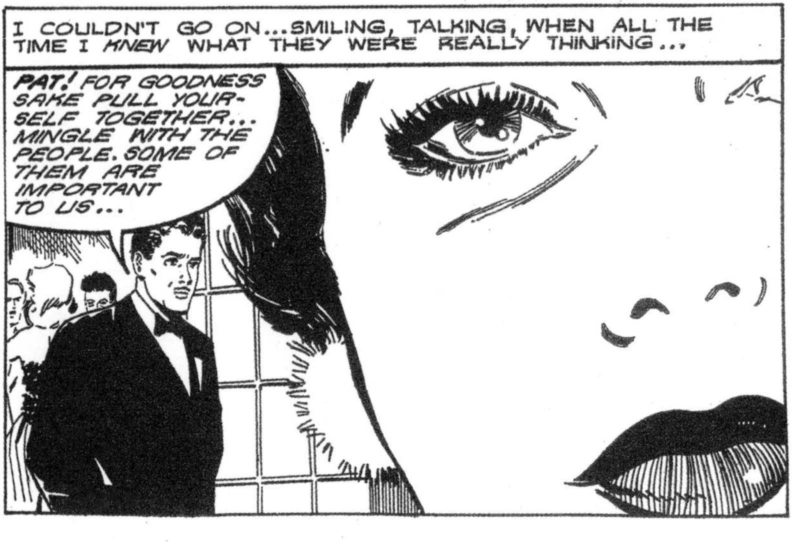
I COULDN'T GO ON...SMILING, TALKING, WHEN ALL THE TIME I KNEW WHAT THEY WERE REALLY THINKING...
PAT! FOR GOODNESS SAKE PULL YOURSELF TOGETHER... MINGLE WITH THE PEOPLE. SOME OF THEM ARE IMPORTANT TO US...

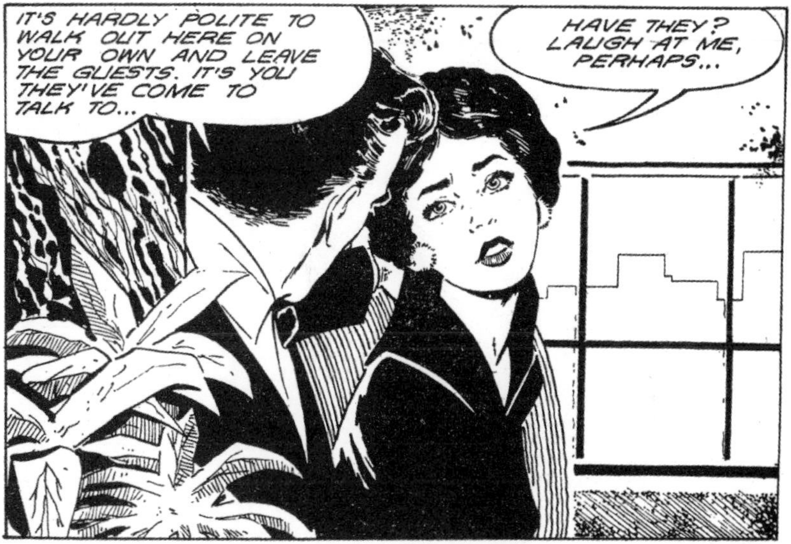
IT'S HARDLY POLITE TO WALK OUT HERE ON YOUR OWN AND LEAVE THE GUESTS. IT'S YOU THEY'VE COME TO TALK TO...
HAVE THEY? LAUGH AT ME, PERHAPS...

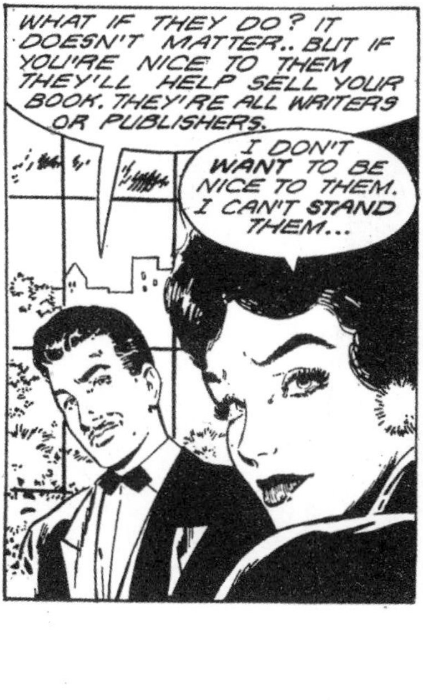
WHAT IF THEY DO? IT DOESN'T MATTER.. BUT IF YOU'RE NICE TO THEM THEY'LL HELP SELL YOUR BOOK. THEY'RE ALL WRITERS OR PUBLISHERS.
I DON'T WANT TO BE NICE TO THEM. I CAN'T STAND THEM...

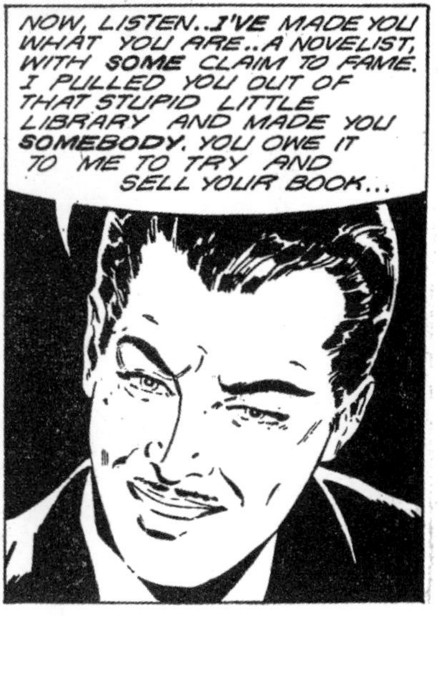
NOW, LISTEN.. I'VE MADE YOU WHAT YOU ARE.. A NOVELIST, WITH SOME CLAIM TO FAME. I PULLED YOU OUT OF THAT STUPID LITTLE LIBRARY AND MADE YOU SOMEBODY. YOU OWE IT TO ME TO TRY AND SELL YOUR BOOK...

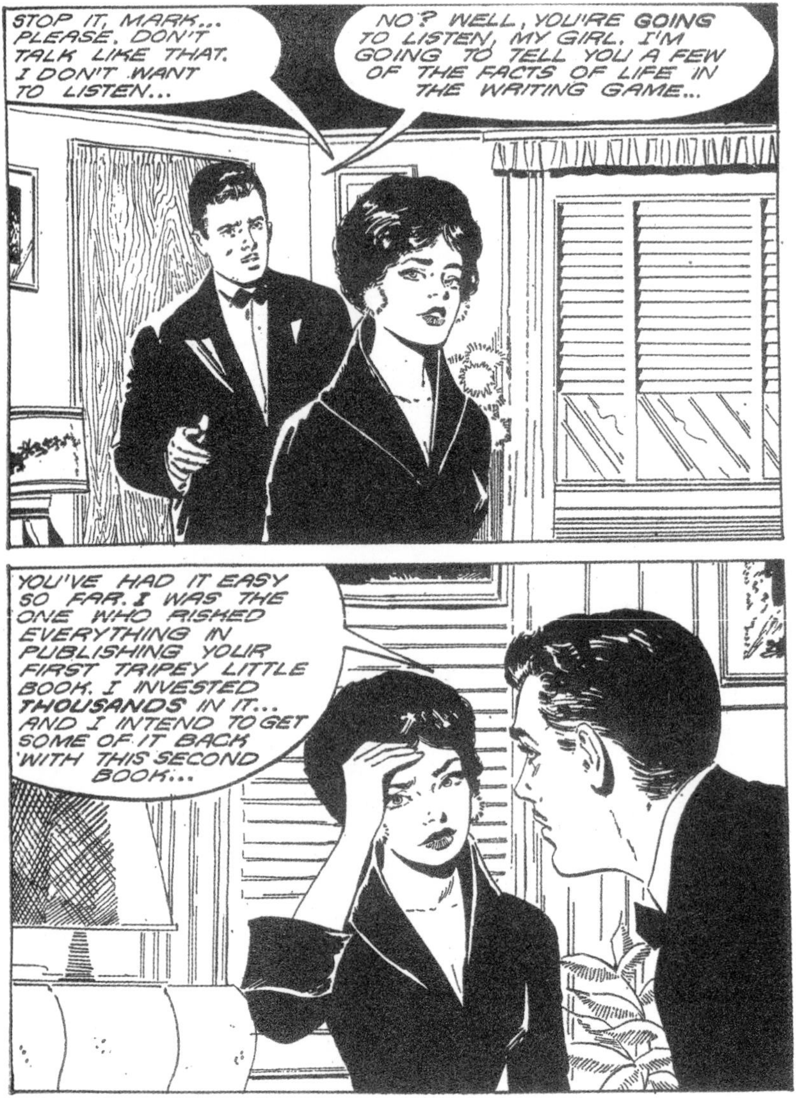
STOP IT, MARK... PLEASE. DON'T TALK LIKE THAT. I DON'T WANT TO LISTEN...
NO? WELL, YOU'RE GOING TO LISTEN, MY GIRL. I'M GOING TO TELL YOU A FEW OF THE FACTS OF LIFE IN THE WRITING GAME...
YOU'VE HAD IT EASY SO FAR. I WAS THE ONE WHO RISKED EVERYTHING IN PUBLISHING YOUR FIRST TRIPEY LITTLE BOOK. I INVESTED THOUSANDS IN IT... AND I INTEND TO GET SOME OF IT BACK WITH THIS SECOND BOOK...

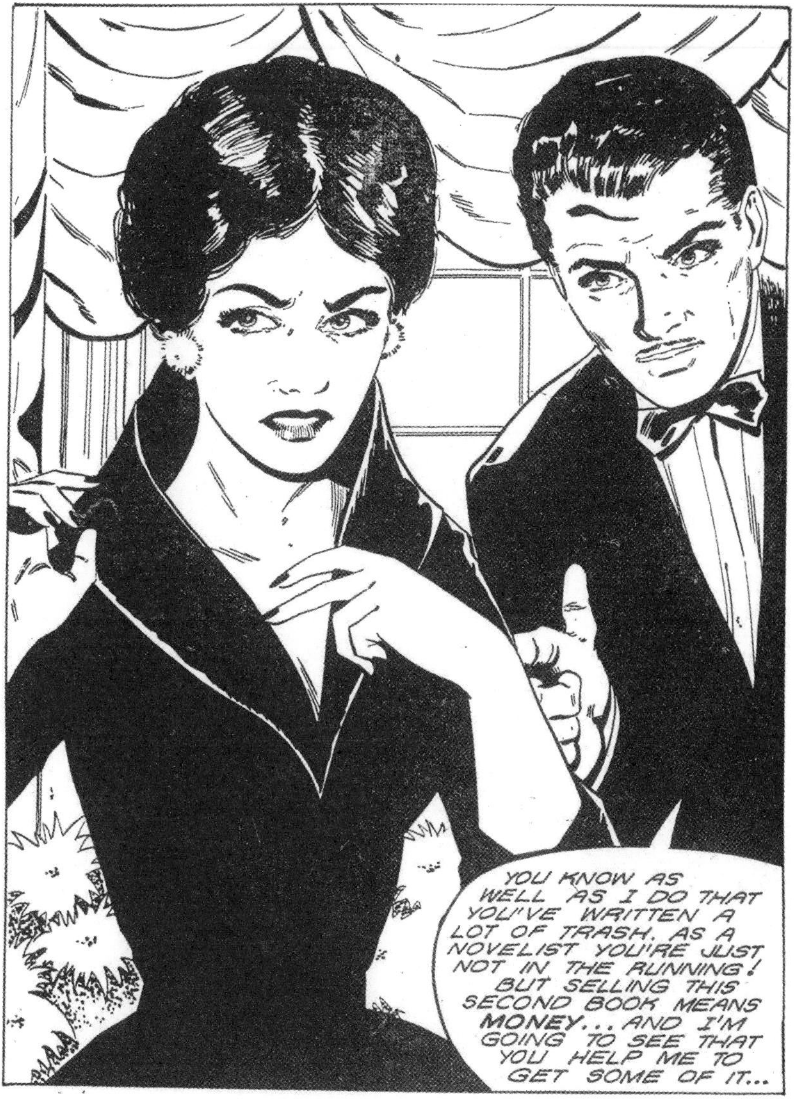
YOU KNOW AS WELL AS I DO THAT YOU'VE WRITTEN A LOT OF TRASH. AS A NOVELIST YOU'RE JUST NOT IN THE RUNNING! BUT SELLING THIS SECOND BOOK MEANS **MONEY**... AND I'M GOING TO SEE THAT YOU HELP ME TO GET SOME OF IT...

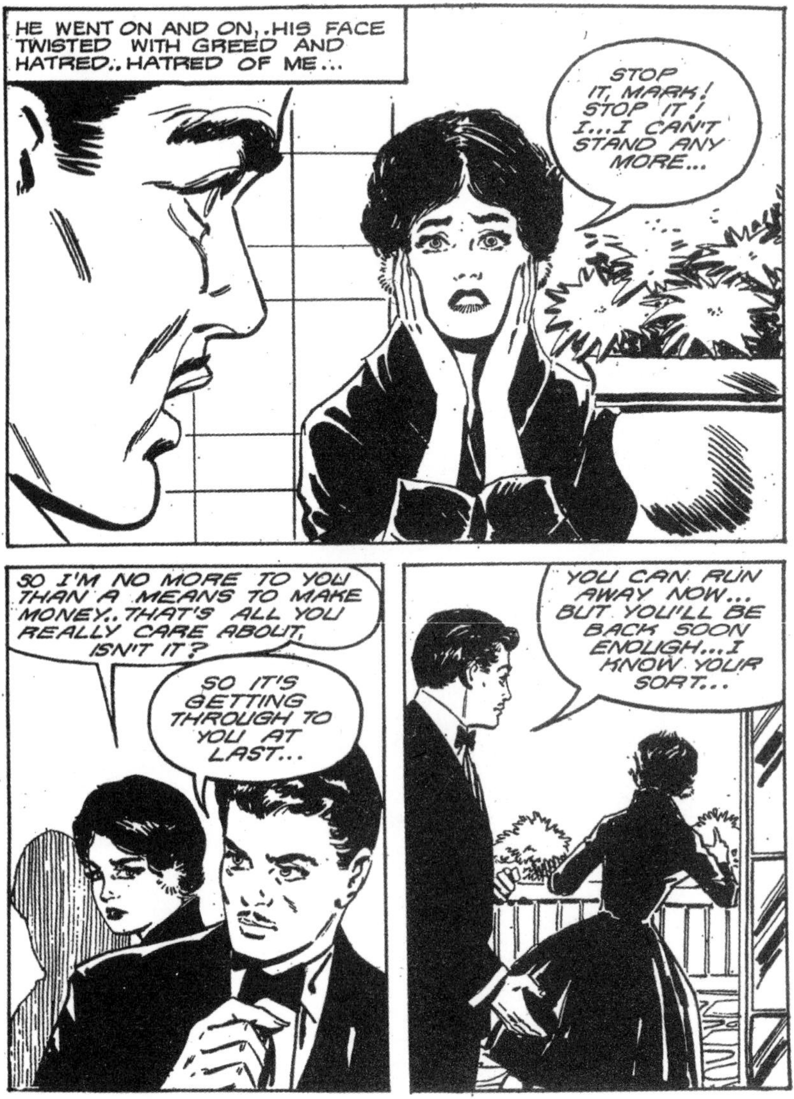
HE WENT ON AND ON, .HIS FACE TWISTED WITH GREED AND HATRED.. HATRED OF ME...
STOP IT, MARK! STOP IT! I...I CAN'T STAND ANY MORE...
SO I'M NO MORE TO YOU THAN A MEANS TO MAKE MONEY..THAT'S ALL YOU REALLY CARE ABOUT, ISN'T IT?
SO IT'S GETTING THROUGH TO YOU AT LAST...
YOU CAN RUN AWAY NOW... BUT YOU'LL BE BACK SOON ENOUGH...I KNOW YOUR SORT...

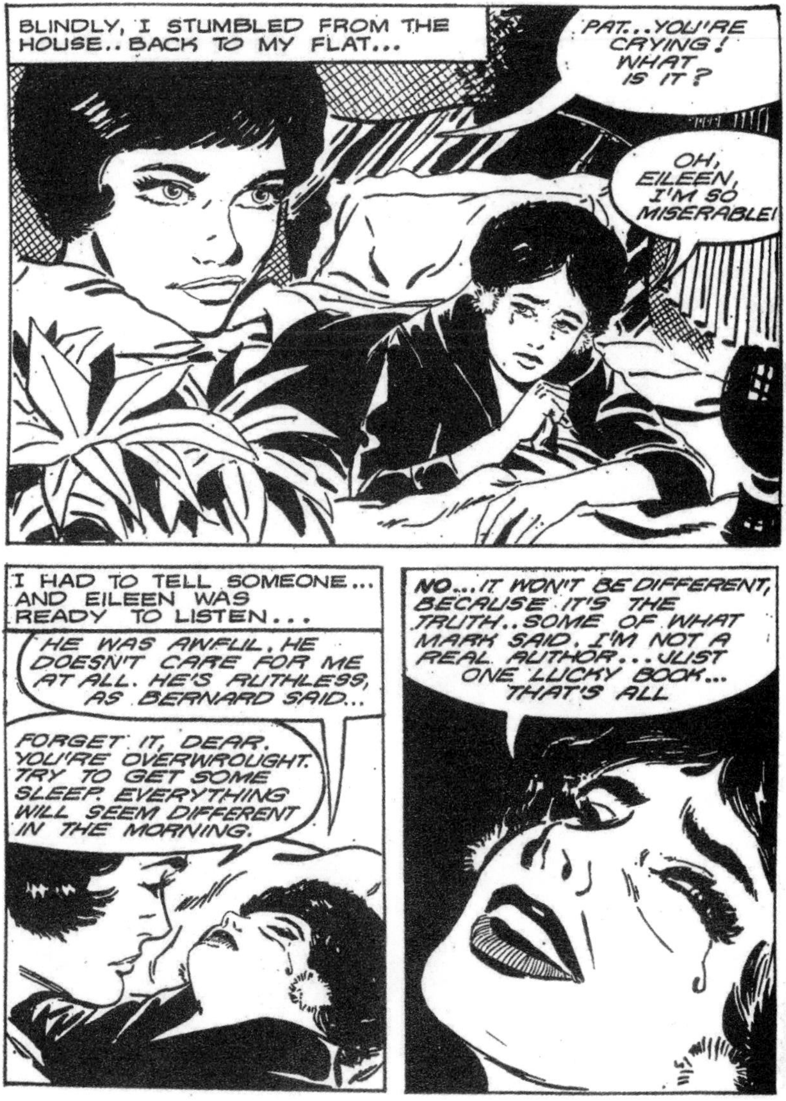
BLINDLY, I STUMBLED FROM THE HOUSE.. BACK TO MY FLAT...
PAT...YOU'RE CRYING! WHAT IS IT?
OH, EILEEN, I'M SO MISERABLE!
I HAD TO TELL SOMEONE... AND EILEEN WAS READY TO LISTEN...
HE WAS AWFUL. HE DOESN'T CARE FOR ME AT ALL. HE'S RUTHLESS, AS BERNARD SAID...
FORGET IT, DEAR. YOU'RE OVERWROUGHT. TRY TO GET SOME SLEEP. EVERYTHING WILL SEEM DIFFERENT IN THE MORNING.
NO...IT WON'T BE DIFFERENT, BECAUSE IT'S THE TRUTH..SOME OF WHAT MARK SAID. I'M NOT A REAL AUTHOR...JUST ONE LUCKY BOOK... THAT'S ALL

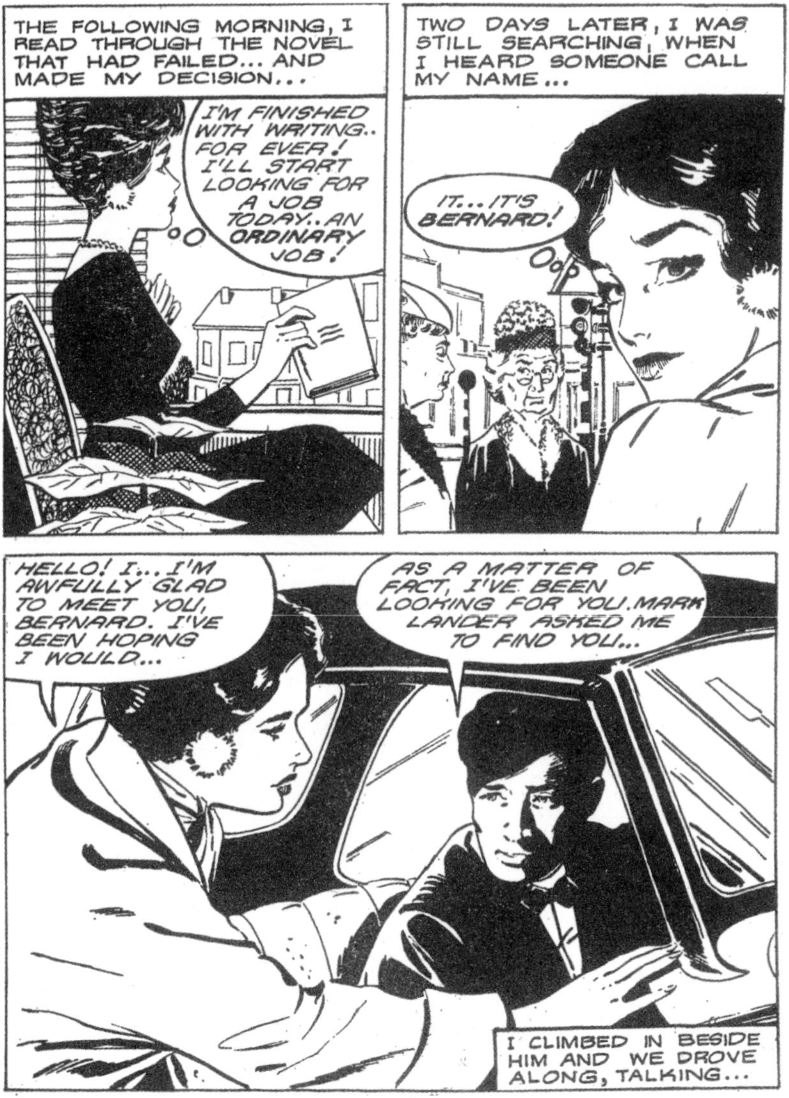
THE FOLLOWING MORNING, I READ THROUGH THE NOVEL THAT HAD FAILED... AND MADE MY DECISION...
I'M FINISHED WITH WRITING.. FOR EVER! I'LL START LOOKING FOR A JOB TODAY..AN ORDINARY JOB!
TWO DAYS LATER, I WAS STILL SEARCHING, WHEN I HEARD SOMEONE CALL MY NAME...
IT...IT'S BERNARD!
HELLO! I...I'M AWFULLY GLAD TO MEET YOU, BERNARD. I'VE BEEN HOPING I WOULD...
AS A MATTER OF FACT, I'VE BEEN LOOKING FOR YOU. MARK LANDER ASKED ME TO FIND YOU...
I CLIMBED IN BESIDE HIM AND WE DROVE ALONG, TALKING...

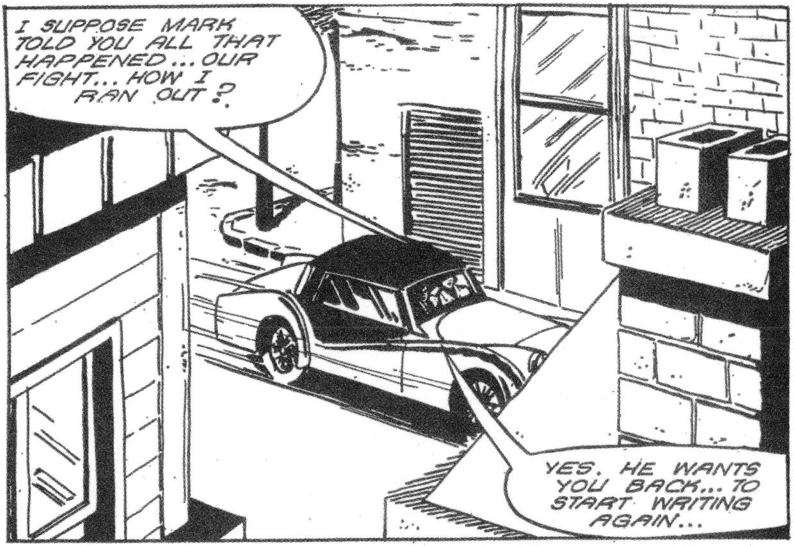
I SUPPOSE MARK TOLD YOU ALL THAT HAPPENED... OUR FIGHT... HOW I RAN OUT?
YES. HE WANTS YOU BACK... TO START WRITING AGAIN...

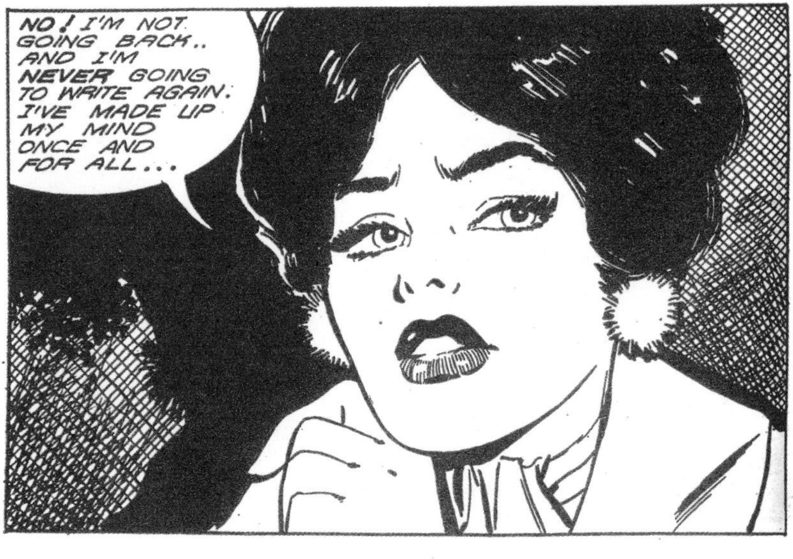
NO! I'M NOT GOING BACK.. AND I'M NEVER GOING TO WRITE AGAIN. I'VE MADE UP MY MIND ONCE AND FOR ALL...

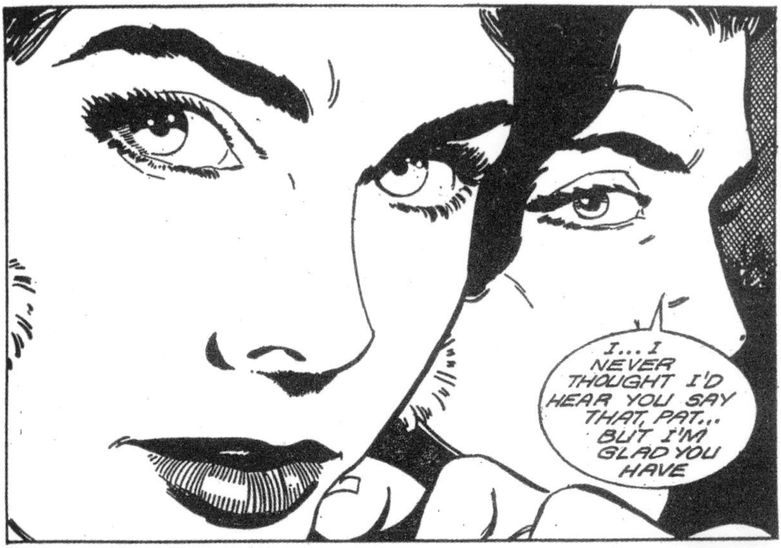
I... I NEVER THOUGHT I'D HEAR YOU SAY THAT, PAT... BUT I'M GLAD YOU HAVE

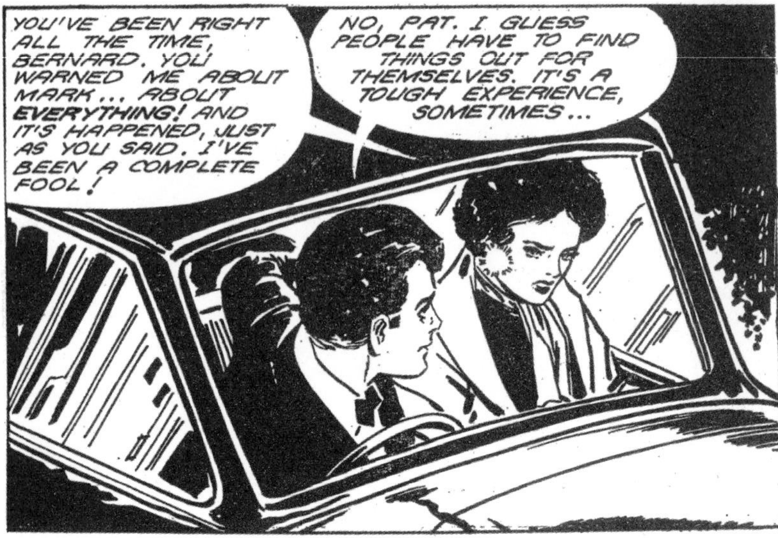
YOU'VE BEEN RIGHT ALL THE TIME, BERNARD. YOU WARNED ME ABOUT MARK... ABOUT EVERYTHING! AND IT'S HAPPENED, JUST AS YOU SAID. I'VE BEEN A COMPLETE FOOL!
NO, PAT. I GUESS PEOPLE HAVE TO FIND THINGS OUT FOR THEMSELVES. IT'S A TOUGH EXPERIENCE, SOMETIMES...

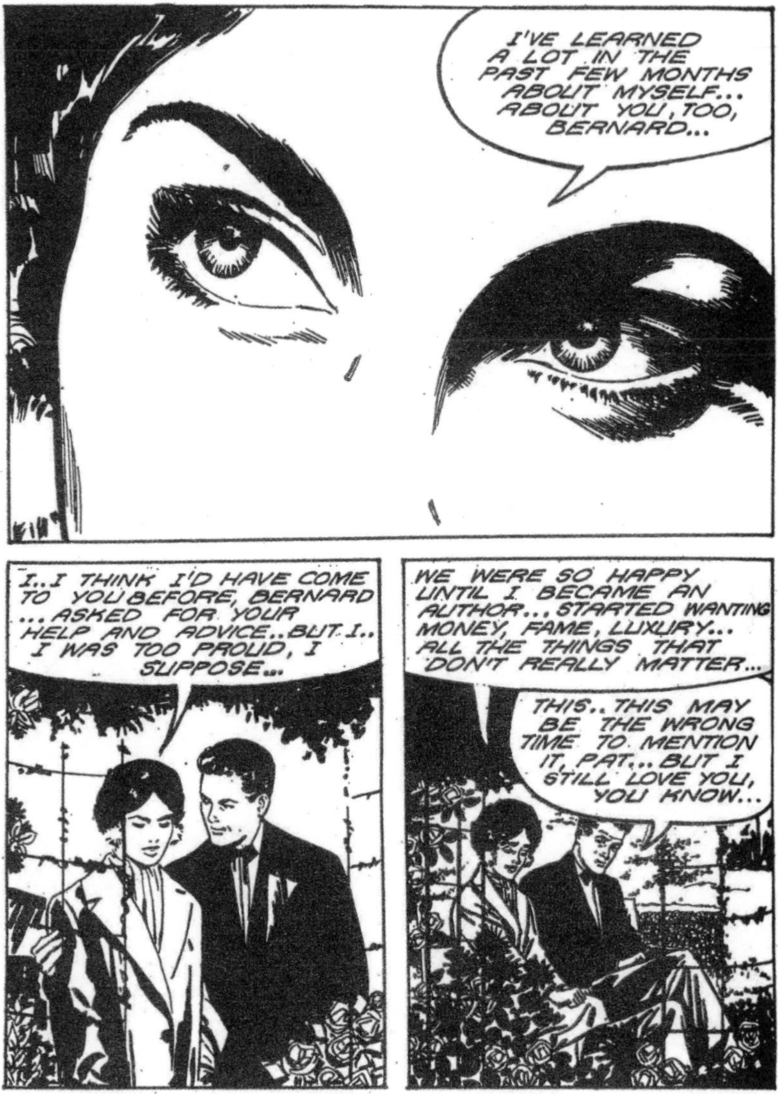
I'VE LEARNED A LOT IN THE PAST FEW MONTHS ABOUT MYSELF... ABOUT YOU, TOO, BERNARD...
I..I THINK I'D HAVE COME TO YOU BEFORE, BERNARD ...ASKED FOR YOUR HELP AND ADVICE..BUT I.. I WAS TOO PROUD, I SUPPOSE...
WE WERE SO HAPPY UNTIL I BECAME AN AUTHOR..., STARTED WANTING MONEY, FAME, LUXURY... ALL THE THINGS THAT DON'T REALLY MATTER...
THIS..THIS MAY BE THE WRONG TIME TO MENTION IT, PAT...BUT I STILL LOVE YOU, YOU KNOW...

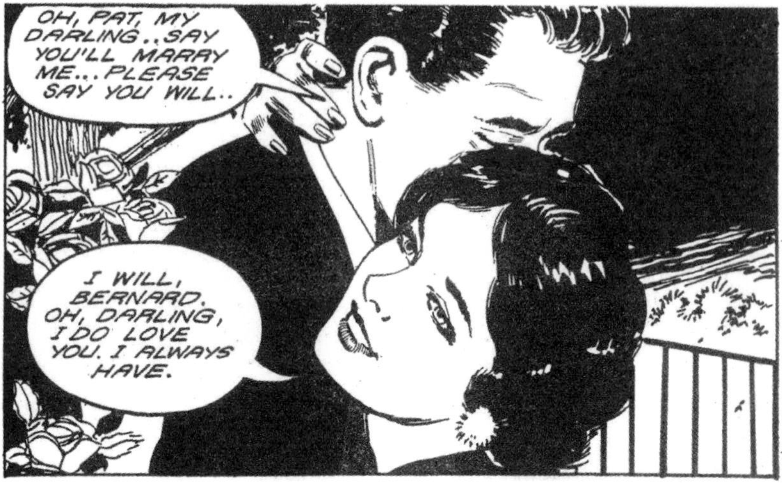
OH, PAT, MY DARLING.. SAY YOU'LL MARRY ME... PLEASE SAY YOU WILL..
I WILL, BERNARD. OH, DARLING, I DO LOVE YOU. I ALWAYS HAVE.

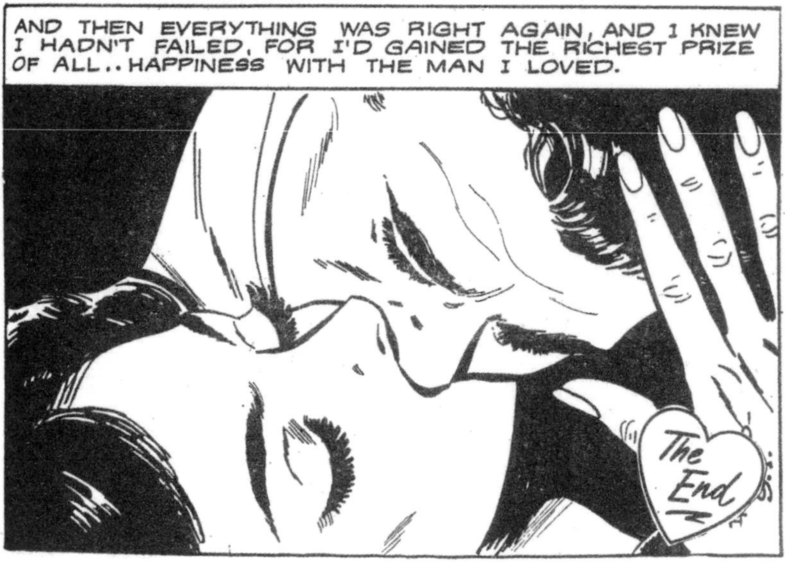
AND THEN EVERYTHING WAS RIGHT AGAIN, AND I KNEW I HADN'T FAILED, FOR I'D GAINED THE RICHEST PRIZE OF ALL.. HAPPINESS WITH THE MAN I LOVED.
The End

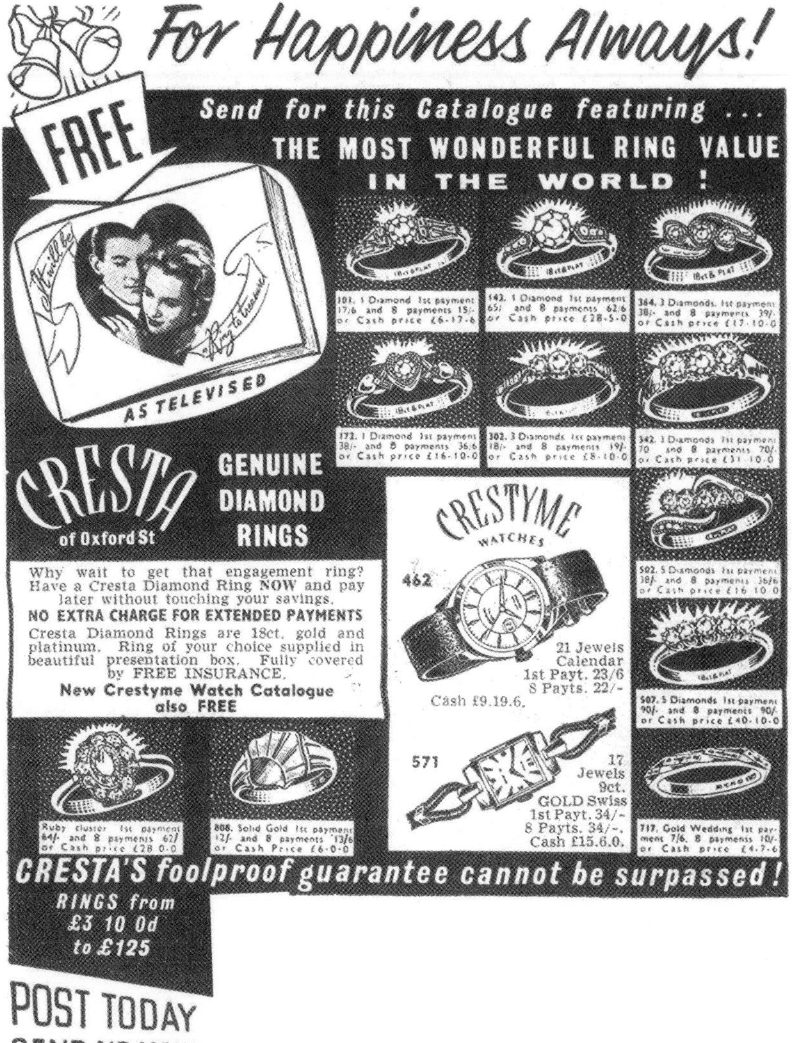
For Happiness Always!
FREE
Send for this Catalogue featuring ...
THE MOST WONDERFUL RING VALUE IN THE WORLD!
AS TELEVISED
101. 1 Diamond 1st payment 17/6 and 8 payments 15/- or Cash price £6-17-6
143. 1 Diamond 1st payment 65/ and 8 payments 62/6 or Cash price £28-5-0
364. 3 Diamonds. 1st payment 38/- and 8 payments 39/- or Cash price £17-10-0
172. 1 Diamond 1st payment 38/- and 8 payments 36/6 or Cash price £16-10-0
302. 3 Diamonds 1st payment 18/- and 8 payments 19/- or Cash price £8-10-0
342. 3 Diamonds 1st payment 70 and 8 payments 70/- or Cash price £31-10-0
CRESTA of Oxford St
GENUINE DIAMOND RINGS
Why wait to get that engagement ring? Have a Cresta Diamond Ring NOW and pay later without touching your savings.
NO EXTRA CHARGE FOR EXTENDED PAYMENTS
Cresta Diamond Rings are 18ct. gold and platinum. Ring of your choice supplied in beautiful presentation box. Fully covered by FREE INSURANCE.
New Crestyme Watch Catalogue also FREE
CRESTYME WATCHES
462
21 Jewels Calendar 1st Payt. 23/6 8 Payts. 22/-
Cash £9.19.6.
571
17 Jewels 9ct. GOLD Swiss 1st Payt. 34/- 8 Payts. 34/-. Cash £15.6.0.
502. 5 Diamonds 1st payment 38/- and 8 payments 36/6 or Cash price £16 10 0
507. 5 Diamonds 1st payment 90/- and 8 payments 90/- or Cash price £40-10-0
Ruby cluster 1st payment 64/- and 8 payments 62/ or Cash price £28 0-0
808. Solid Gold 1st payment 12/- and 8 payments 13/6 or Cash Price £6-0-0
717. Gold Wedding 1st payment 7/6. 8 payments 10/- or Cash price £4-7-6
CRESTA'S foolproof guarantee cannot be surpassed!
RINGS from £3 10 0d to £125
POST TODAY
SEND NO MONEY
NO DEPOSIT

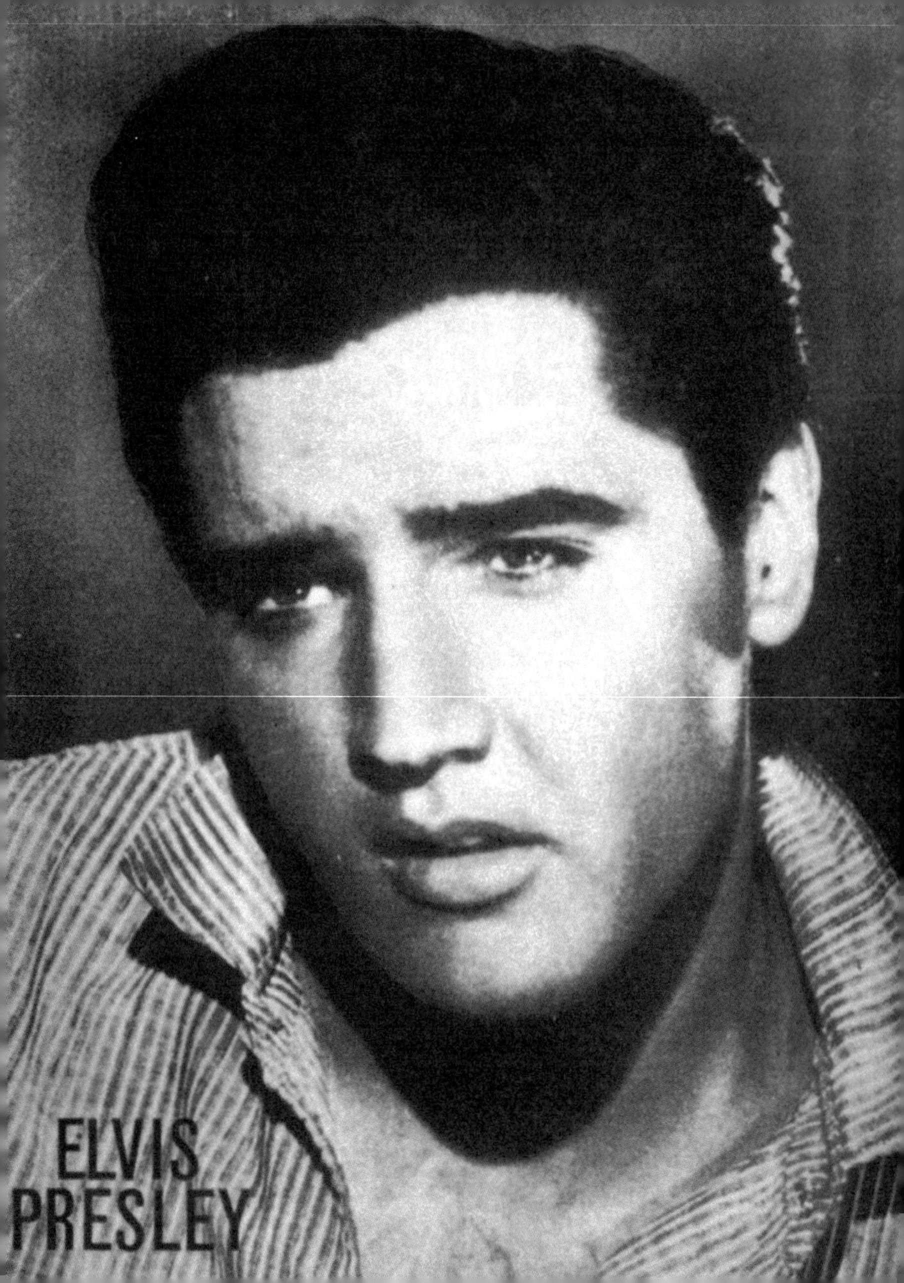
ELVIS
PRESLEY

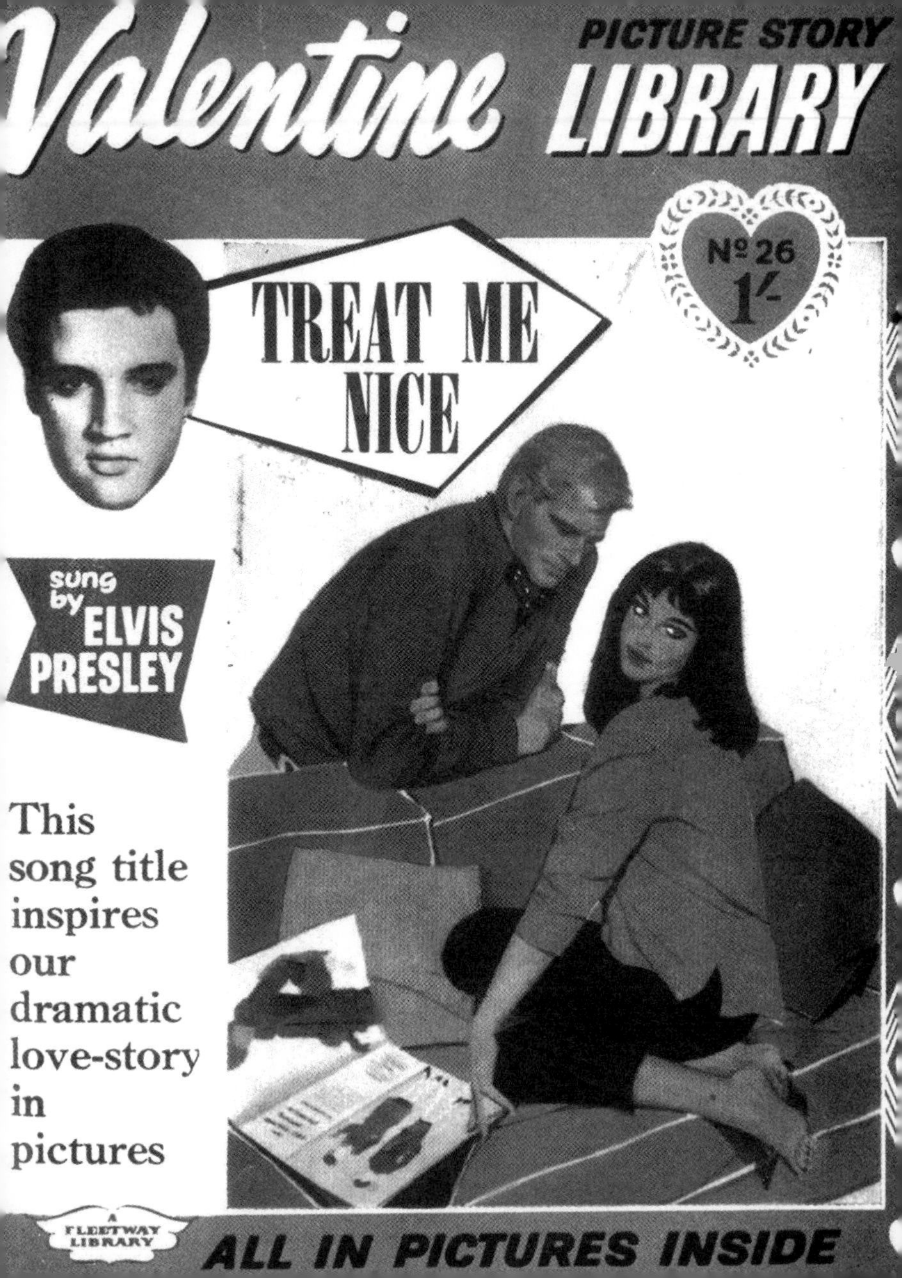
Valentine
PICTURE STORY LIBRARY
Nº 26
1/-
TREAT ME NICE
sung by ELVIS PRESLEY
This song title inspires our dramatic love-story in pictures
A FLEETWAY LIBRARY
ALL IN PICTURES INSIDE

TREAT ME NICE

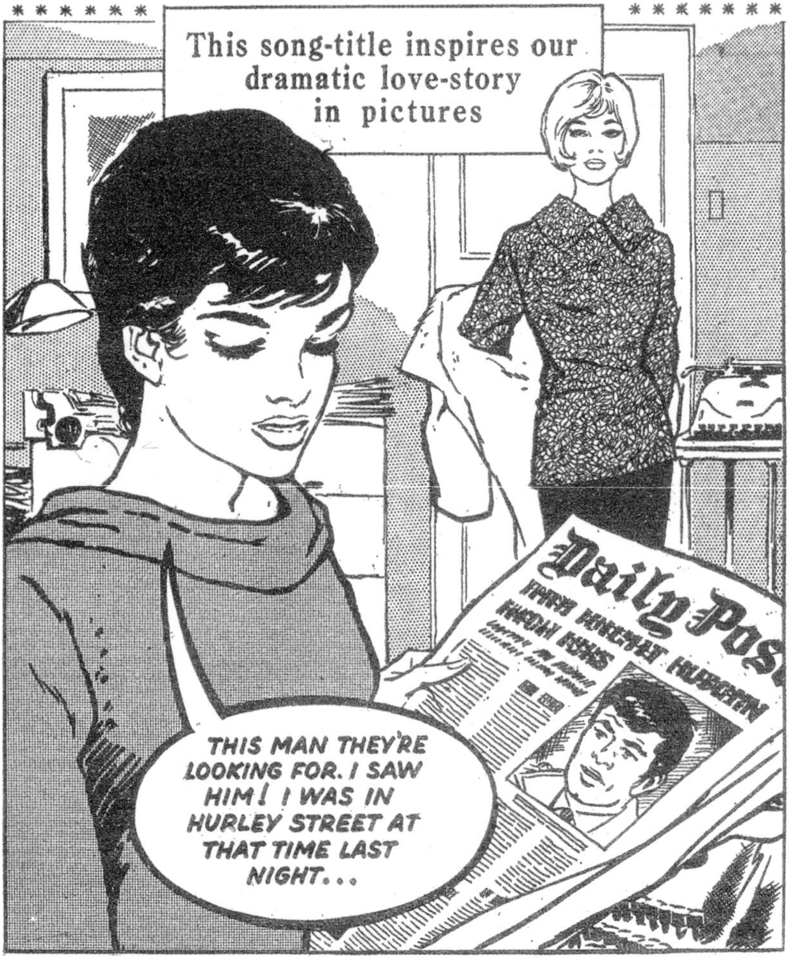
This song-title inspires our dramatic love-story in pictures
THIS MAN THEY'RE LOOKING FOR. I SAW HIM! I WAS IN HURLEY STREET AT THAT TIME LAST NIGHT...

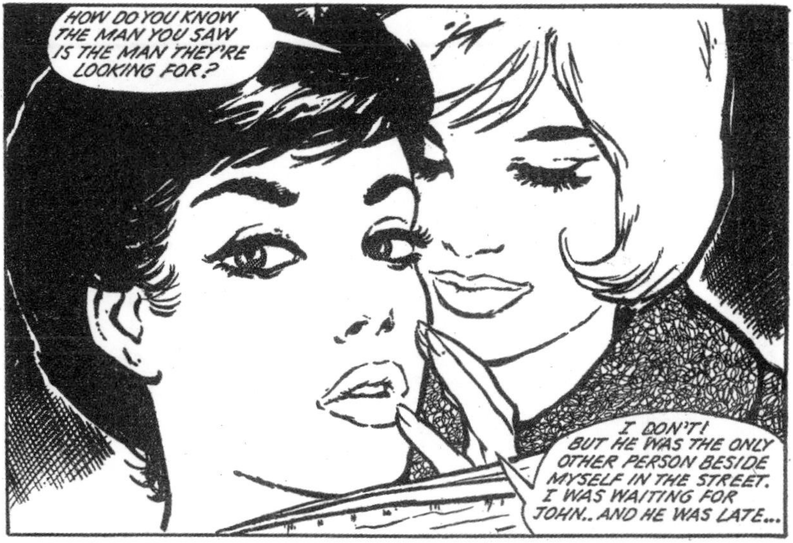
HOW DO YOU KNOW THE MAN YOU SAW IS THE MAN THEY'RE LOOKING FOR?
I DON'T! BUT HE WAS THE ONLY OTHER PERSON BESIDE MYSELF IN THE STREET. I WAS WAITING FOR JOHN.. AND HE WAS LATE...

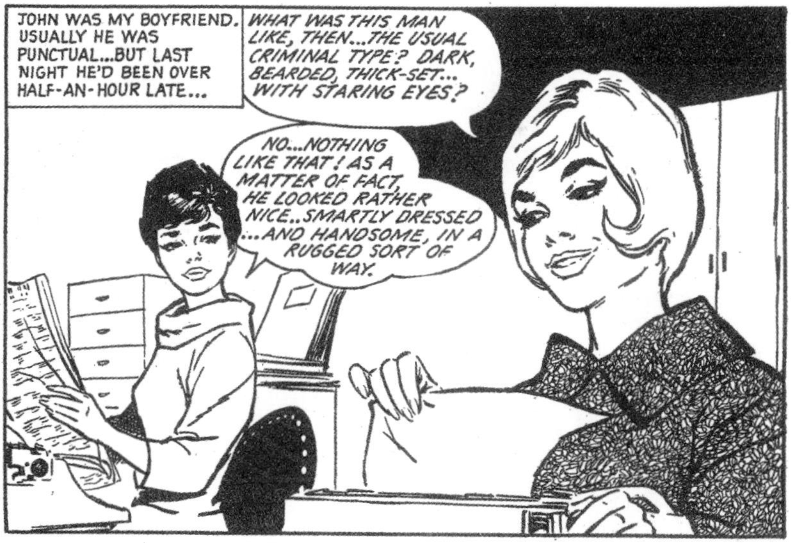
JOHN WAS MY BOYFRIEND. USUALLY HE WAS PUNCTUAL...BUT LAST NIGHT HE'D BEEN OVER HALF-AN-HOUR LATE...
WHAT WAS THIS MAN LIKE, THEN...THE USUAL CRIMINAL TYPE? DARK, BEARDED, THICK-SET... WITH STARING EYES?
NO...NOTHING LIKE THAT! AS A MATTER OF FACT, HE LOOKED RATHER NICE..SMARTLY DRESSED ...AND HANDSOME, IN A RUGGED SORT OF WAY.

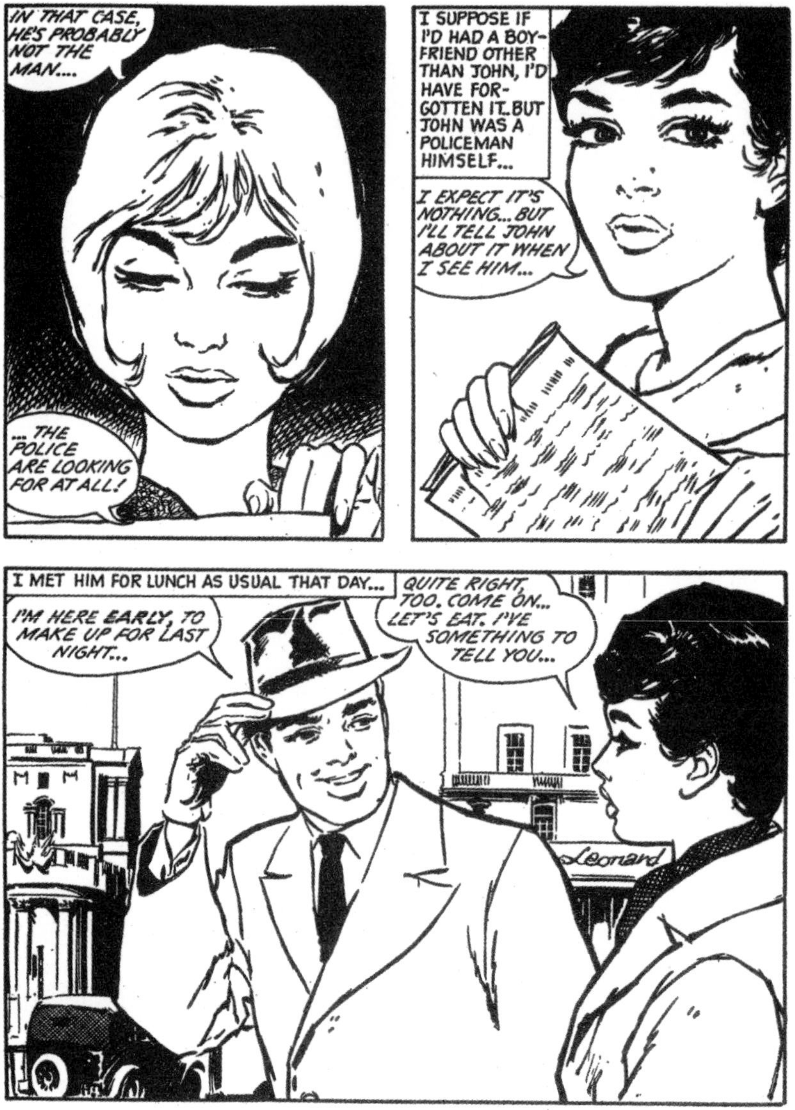
IN THAT CASE, HE'S PROBABLY NOT THE MAN....
... THE POLICE ARE LOOKING FOR AT ALL!
I SUPPOSE IF I'D HAD A BOY-FRIEND OTHER THAN JOHN, I'D HAVE FOR-GOTTEN IT. BUT JOHN WAS A POLICEMAN HIMSELF...
I EXPECT IT'S NOTHING... BUT I'LL TELL JOHN ABOUT IT WHEN I SEE HIM...
I MET HIM FOR LUNCH AS USUAL THAT DAY...
I'M HERE EARLY, TO MAKE UP FOR LAST NIGHT...
QUITE RIGHT, TOO. COME ON... LET'S EAT. I'VE SOMETHING TO TELL YOU...
Leonard

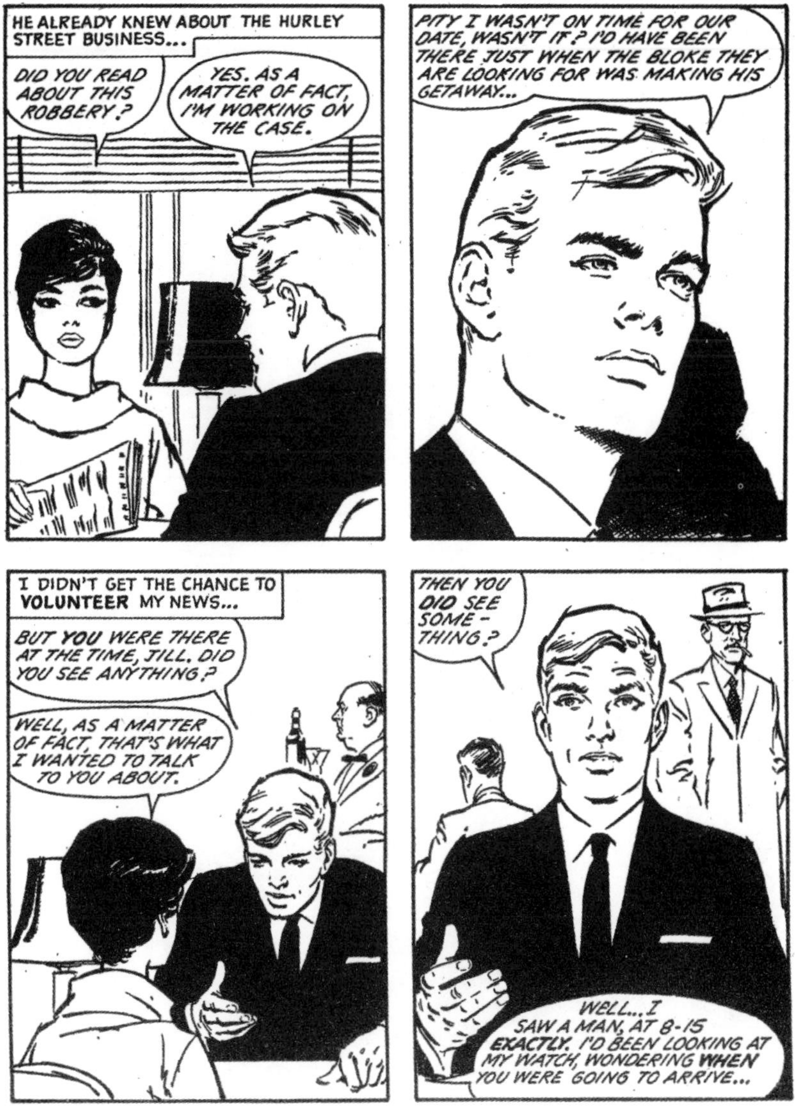
HE ALREADY KNEW ABOUT THE HURLEY STREET BUSINESS...
DID YOU READ ABOUT THIS ROBBERY?
YES. AS A MATTER OF FACT, I'M WORKING ON THE CASE.
PITY I WASN'T ON TIME FOR OUR DATE, WASN'T IT? I'D HAVE BEEN THERE JUST WHEN THE BLOKE THEY ARE LOOKING FOR WAS MAKING HIS GETAWAY...
I DIDN'T GET THE CHANCE TO VOLUNTEER MY NEWS...
BUT YOU WERE THERE AT THE TIME, JILL. DID YOU SEE ANYTHING?
WELL, AS A MATTER OF FACT, THAT'S WHAT I WANTED TO TALK TO YOU ABOUT.
THEN YOU DID SEE SOME-THING?
WELL... I SAW A MAN, AT 8-15 EXACTLY. I'D BEEN LOOKING AT MY WATCH, WONDERING WHEN YOU WERE GOING TO ARRIVE...

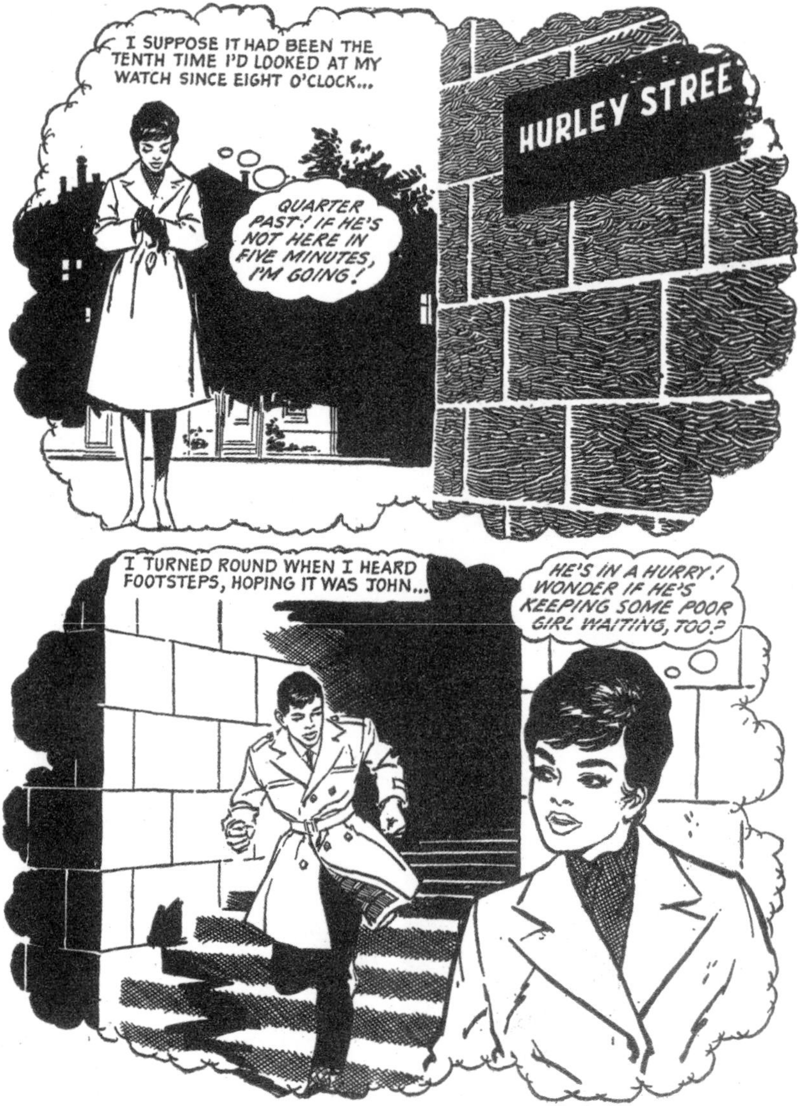
I SUPPOSE IT HAD BEEN THE TENTH TIME I'D LOOKED AT MY WATCH SINCE EIGHT O'CLOCK...
HURLEY STREE
QUARTER PAST! IF HE'S NOT HERE IN FIVE MINUTES, I'M GOING!
I TURNED ROUND WHEN I HEARD FOOTSTEPS, HOPING IT WAS JOHN...
HE'S IN A HURRY! WONDER IF HE'S KEEPING SOME POOR GIRL WAITING, TOO?

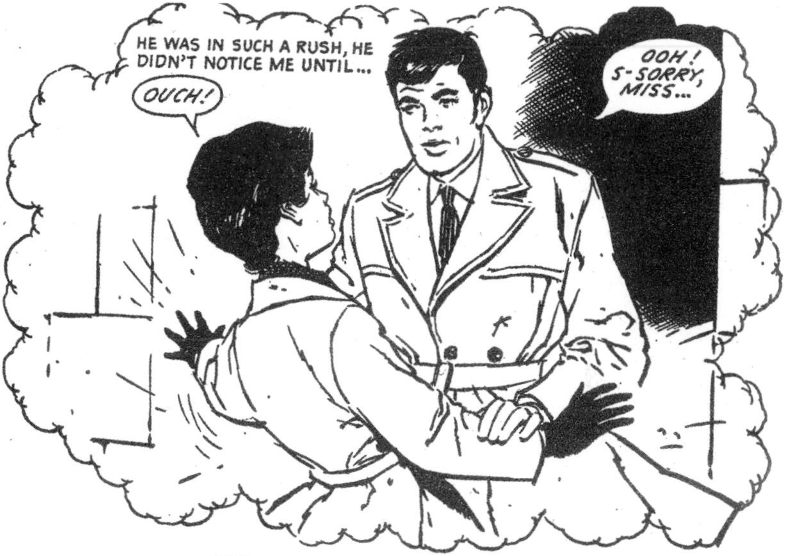
HE WAS IN SUCH A RUSH, HE DIDN'T NOTICE ME UNTIL...
OUCH!
OOH! S-SORRY, MISS...

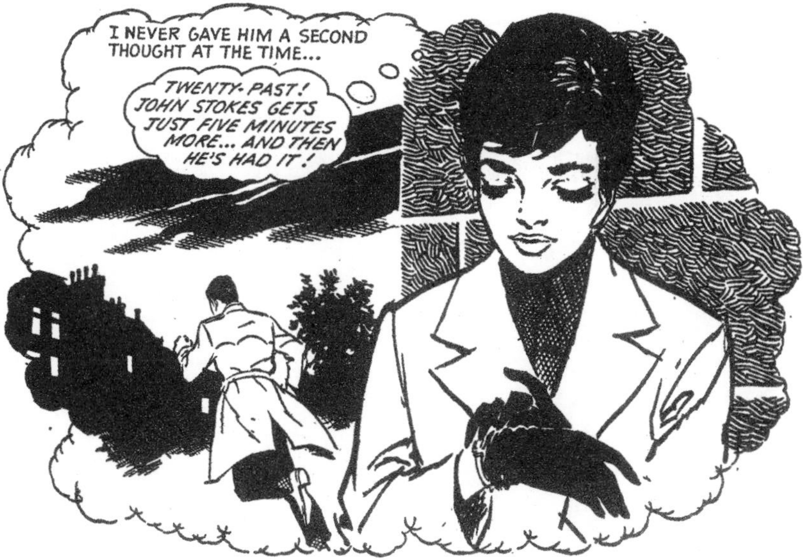
I NEVER GAVE HIM A SECOND THOUGHT AT THE TIME...
TWENTY-PAST! JOHN STOKES GETS JUST FIVE MINUTES MORE... AND THEN HE'S HAD IT!

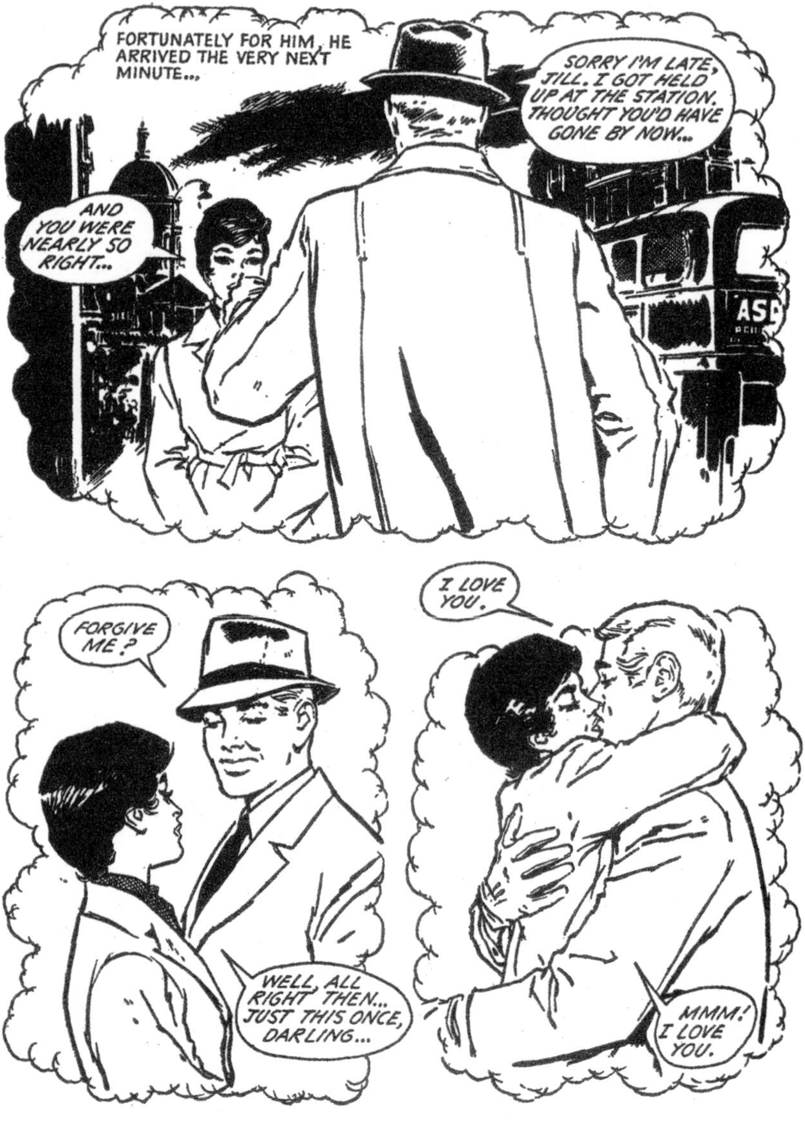
FORTUNATELY FOR HIM, HE ARRIVED THE VERY NEXT MINUTE...
SORRY I'M LATE, JILL. I GOT HELD UP AT THE STATION. THOUGHT YOU'D HAVE GONE BY NOW...
AND YOU WERE NEARLY SO RIGHT...
FORGIVE ME?
WELL, ALL RIGHT THEN... JUST THIS ONCE, DARLING...
I LOVE YOU.
MMM! I LOVE YOU.

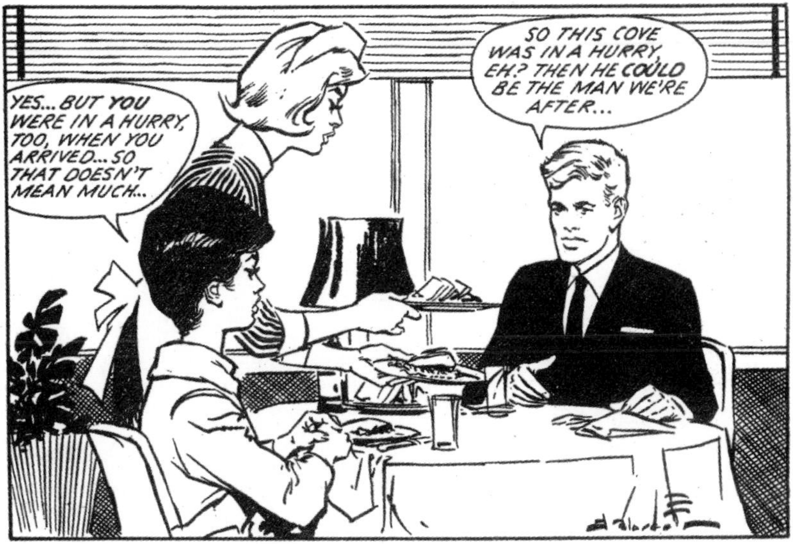
YES... BUT YOU WERE IN A HURRY, TOO, WHEN YOU ARRIVED... SO THAT DOESN'T MEAN MUCH...
SO THIS COVE WAS IN A HURRY, EH? THEN HE COULD BE THE MAN WE'RE AFTER...

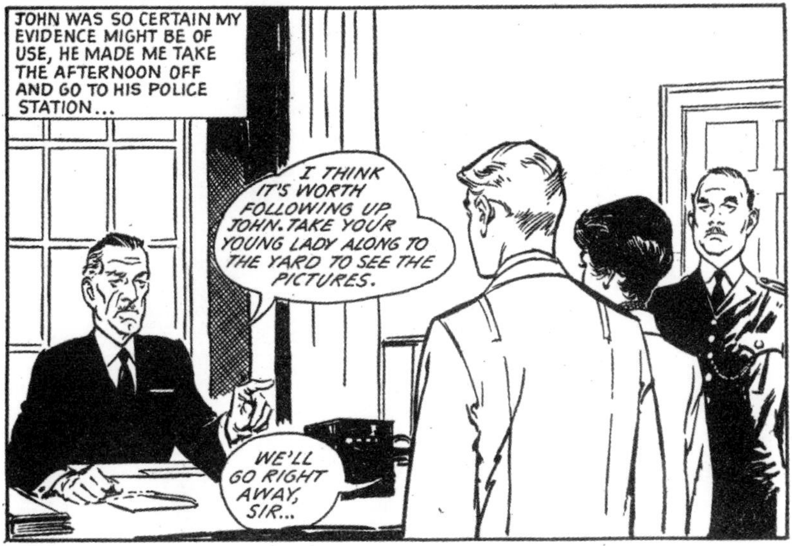
JOHN WAS SO CERTAIN MY EVIDENCE MIGHT BE OF USE, HE MADE ME TAKE THE AFTERNOON OFF AND GO TO HIS POLICE STATION...
I THINK IT'S WORTH FOLLOWING UP, JOHN. TAKE YOUR YOUNG LADY ALONG TO THE YARD TO SEE THE PICTURES.
WE'LL GO RIGHT AWAY, SIR...

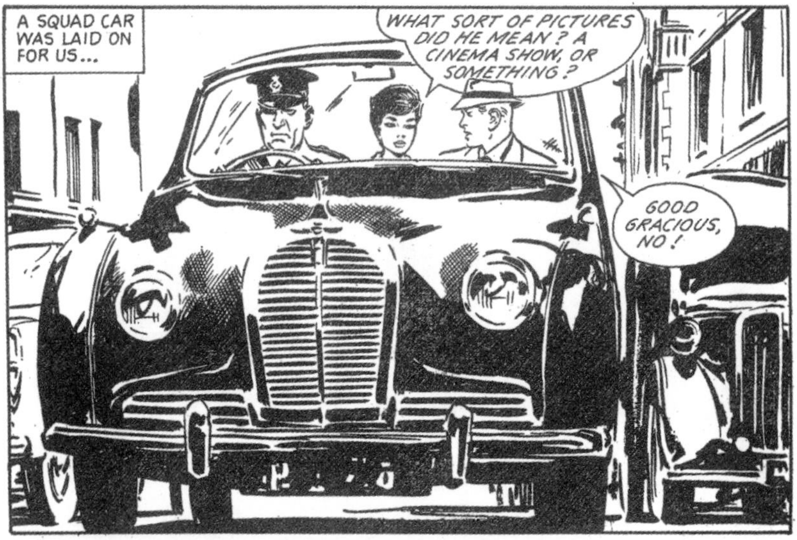
A SQUAD CAR WAS LAID ON FOR US...
WHAT SORT OF PICTURES DID HE MEAN? A CINEMA SHOW, OR SOMETHING?
GOOD GRACIOUS, NO!

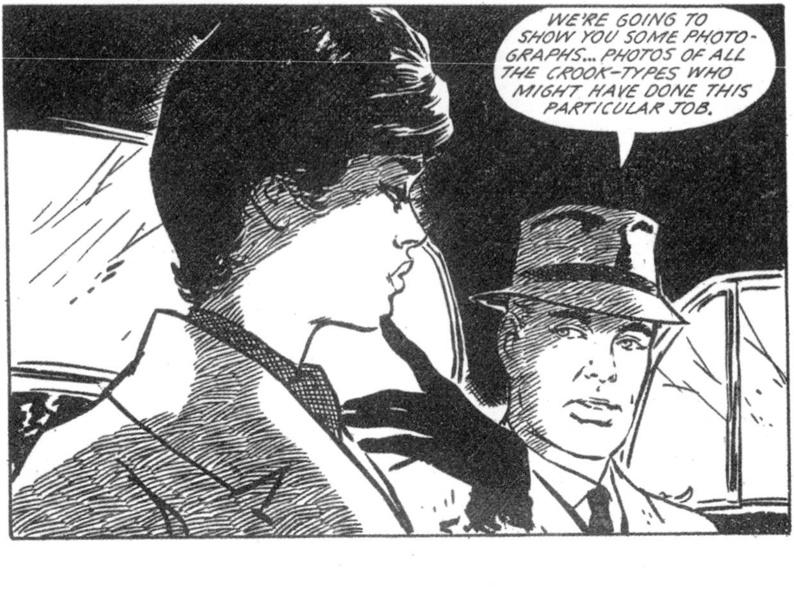
WE'RE GOING TO SHOW YOU SOME PHOTO-GRAPHS... PHOTOS OF ALL THE CROOK-TYPES WHO MIGHT HAVE DONE THIS PARTICULAR JOB.

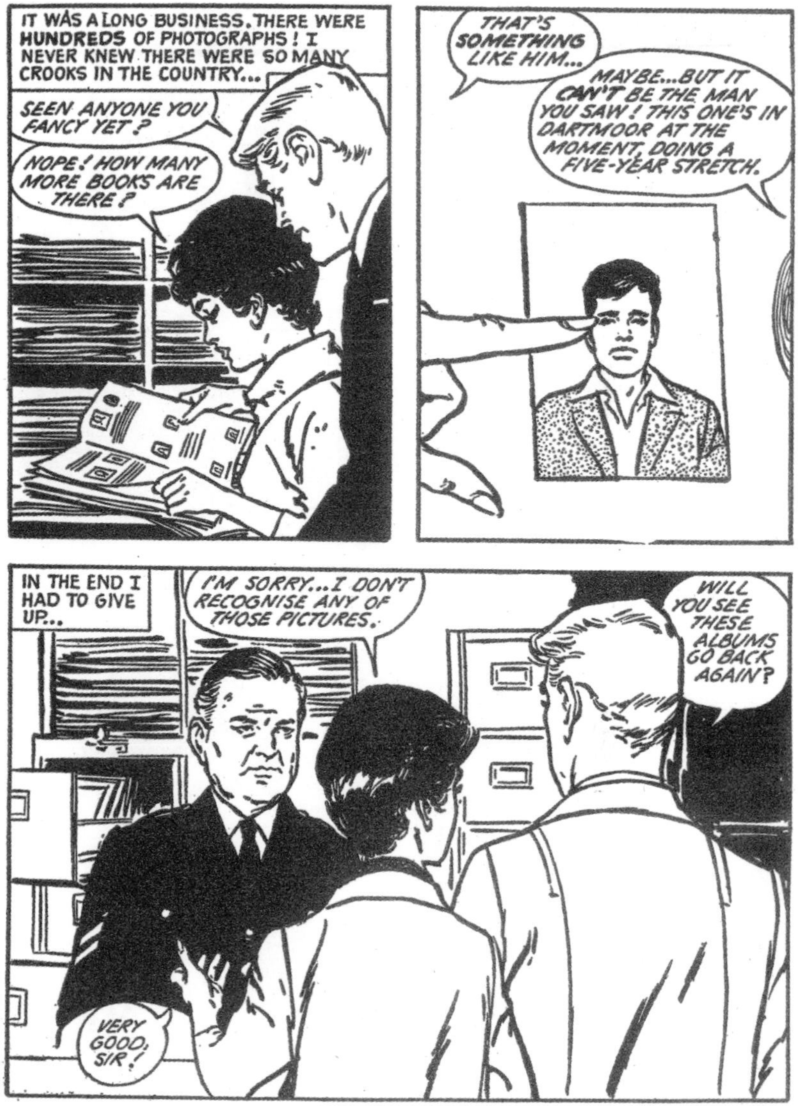
IT WAS A LONG BUSINESS. THERE WERE HUNDREDS OF PHOTOGRAPHS ! I NEVER KNEW THERE WERE SO MANY CROOKS IN THE COUNTRY...
SEEN ANYONE YOU FANCY YET ?
NOPE ! HOW MANY MORE BOOKS ARE THERE ?
THAT'S SOMETHING LIKE HIM...
MAYBE...BUT IT CAN'T BE THE MAN YOU SAW ! THIS ONE'S IN DARTMOOR AT THE MOMENT, DOING A FIVE-YEAR STRETCH.
IN THE END I HAD TO GIVE UP...
I'M SORRY...I DON'T RECOGNISE ANY OF THOSE PICTURES.
WILL YOU SEE THESE ALBUMS GO BACK AGAIN ?
VERY GOOD, SIR !

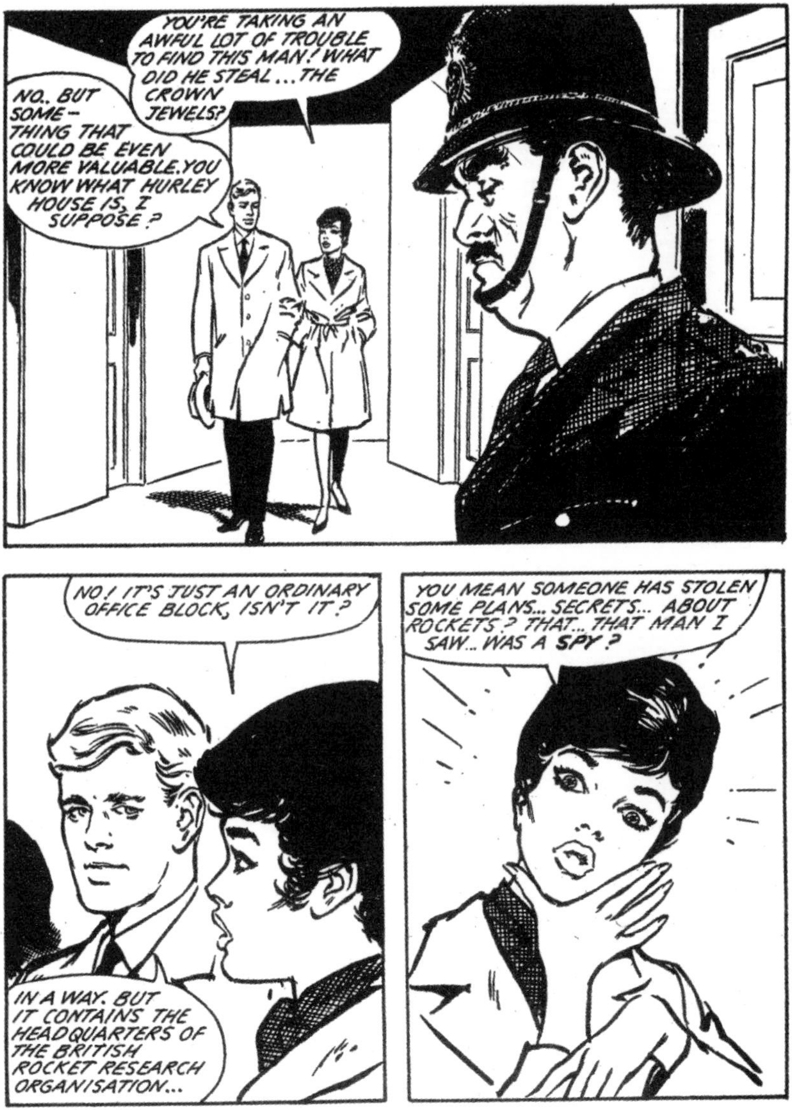
YOU'RE TAKING AN AWFUL LOT OF TROUBLE TO FIND THIS MAN! WHAT DID HE STEAL ... THE CROWN JEWELS?
NO.. BUT SOME-THING THAT COULD BE EVEN MORE VALUABLE. YOU KNOW WHAT HURLEY HOUSE IS, I SUPPOSE?
NO! IT'S JUST AN ORDINARY OFFICE BLOCK, ISN'T IT?
IN A WAY. BUT IT CONTAINS THE HEADQUARTERS OF THE BRITISH ROCKET RESEARCH ORGANISATION...
YOU MEAN SOMEONE HAS STOLEN SOME PLANS... SECRETS... ABOUT ROCKETS? THAT... THAT MAN I SAW... WAS A SPY?

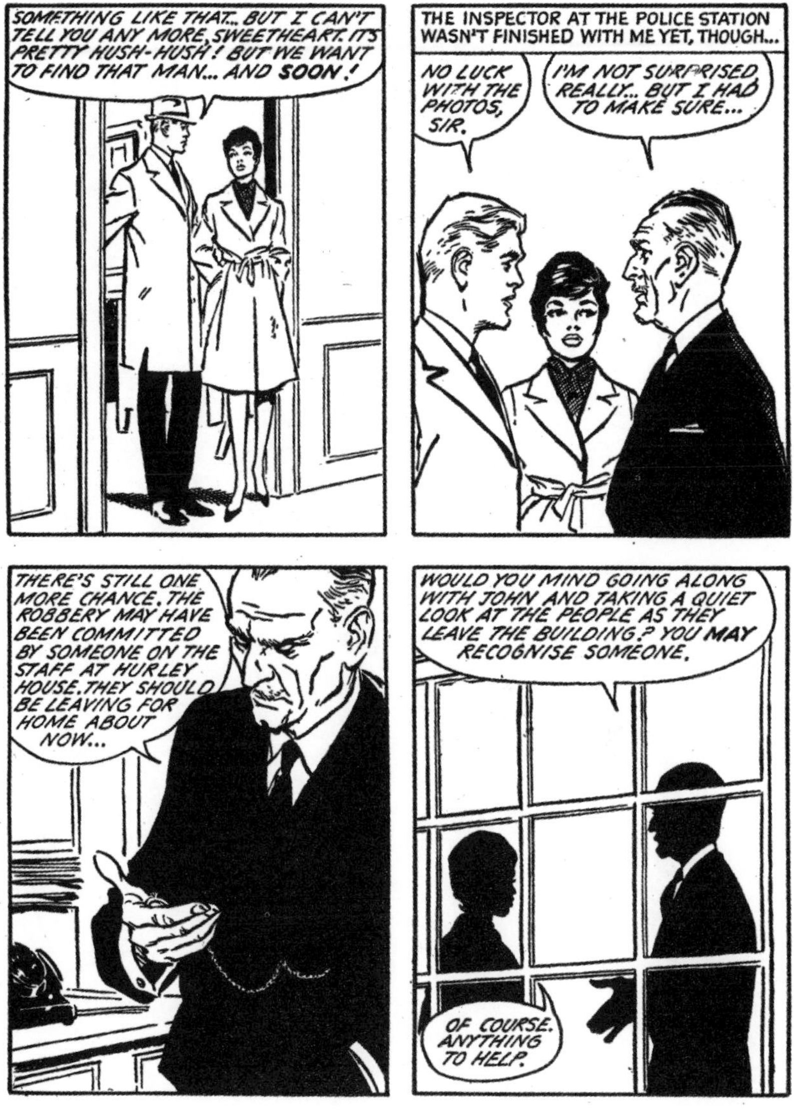
SOMETHING LIKE THAT... BUT I CAN'T TELL YOU ANY MORE, SWEETHEART. IT'S PRETTY HUSH-HUSH! BUT WE WANT TO FIND THAT MAN... AND SOON!
THE INSPECTOR AT THE POLICE STATION WASN'T FINISHED WITH ME YET, THOUGH...
NO LUCK WITH THE PHOTOS, SIR.
I'M NOT SURPRISED REALLY... BUT I HAD TO MAKE SURE...
THERE'S STILL ONE MORE CHANCE. THE ROBBERY MAY HAVE BEEN COMMITTED BY SOMEONE ON THE STAFF AT HURLEY HOUSE. THEY SHOULD BE LEAVING FOR HOME ABOUT NOW...
WOULD YOU MIND GOING ALONG WITH JOHN AND TAKING A QUIET LOOK AT THE PEOPLE AS THEY LEAVE THE BUILDING? YOU MAY RECOGNISE SOMEONE.
OF COURSE. ANYTHING TO HELP.

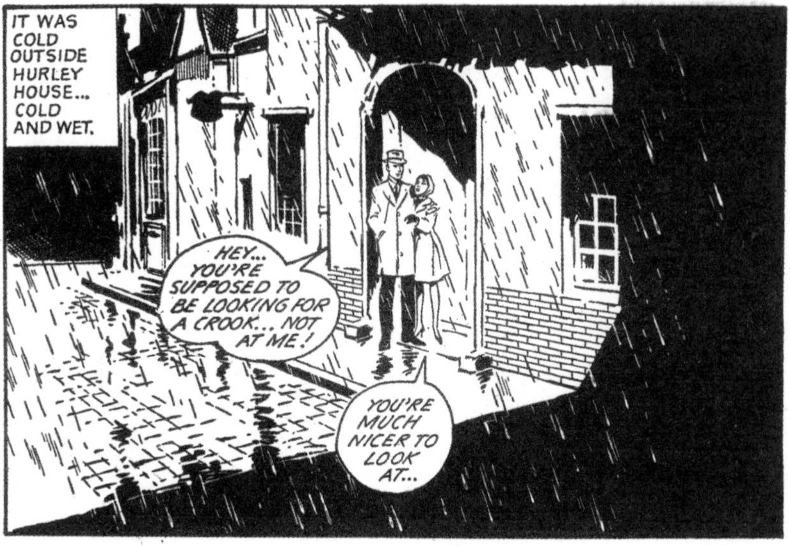
IT WAS COLD OUTSIDE HURLEY HOUSE... COLD AND WET.
HEY... YOU'RE SUPPOSED TO BE LOOKING FOR A CROOK... NOT AT ME!
YOU'RE MUCH NICER TO LOOK AT...

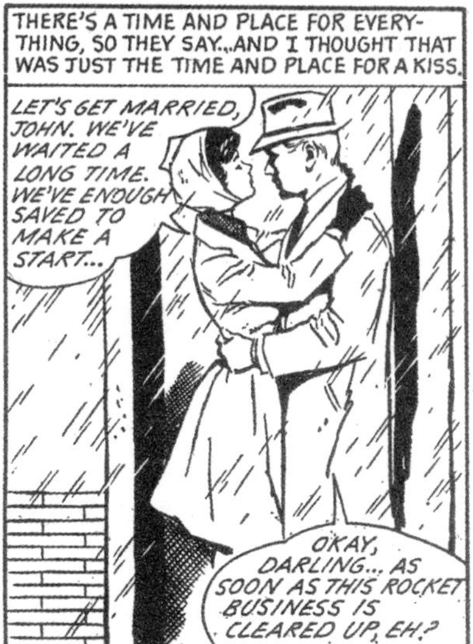
THERE'S A TIME AND PLACE FOR EVERY-THING, SO THEY SAY...AND I THOUGHT THAT WAS JUST THE TIME AND PLACE FOR A KISS.
LET'S GET MARRIED, JOHN. WE'VE WAITED A LONG TIME. WE'VE ENOUGH SAVED TO MAKE A START...
OKAY, DARLING... AS SOON AS THIS ROCKET BUSINESS IS CLEARED UP, EH?

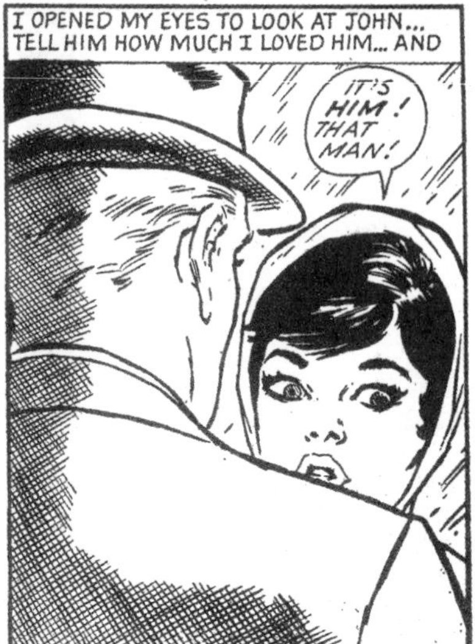
I OPENED MY EYES TO LOOK AT JOHN... TELL HIM HOW MUCH I LOVED HIM... AND
IT'S HIM! THAT MAN!

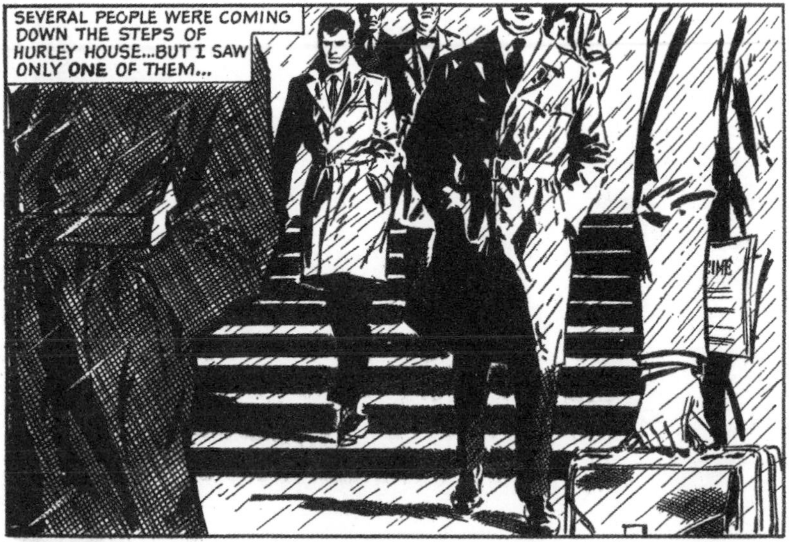
SEVERAL PEOPLE WERE COMING DOWN THE STEPS OF HURLEY HOUSE...BUT I SAW ONLY ONE OF THEM...

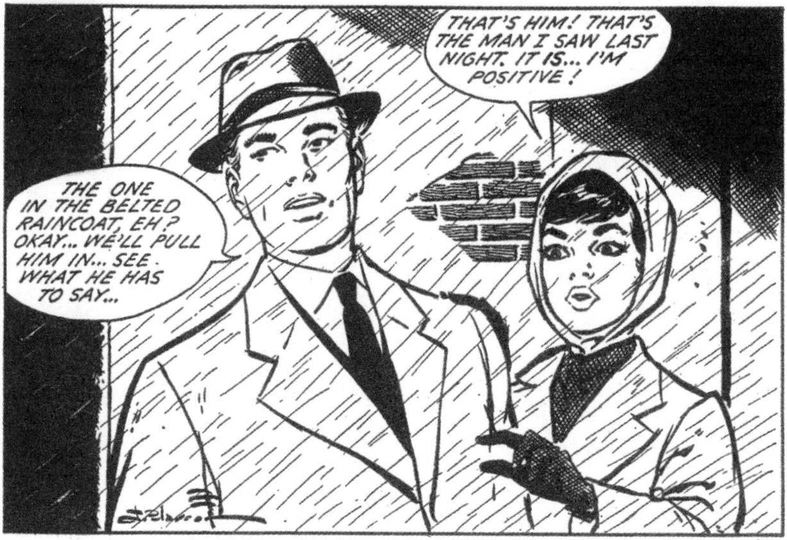
THAT'S HIM! THAT'S THE MAN I SAW LAST NIGHT. IT IS... I'M POSITIVE!
THE ONE IN THE BELTED RAINCOAT, EH? OKAY... WE'LL PULL HIM IN... SEE WHAT HE HAS TO SAY...

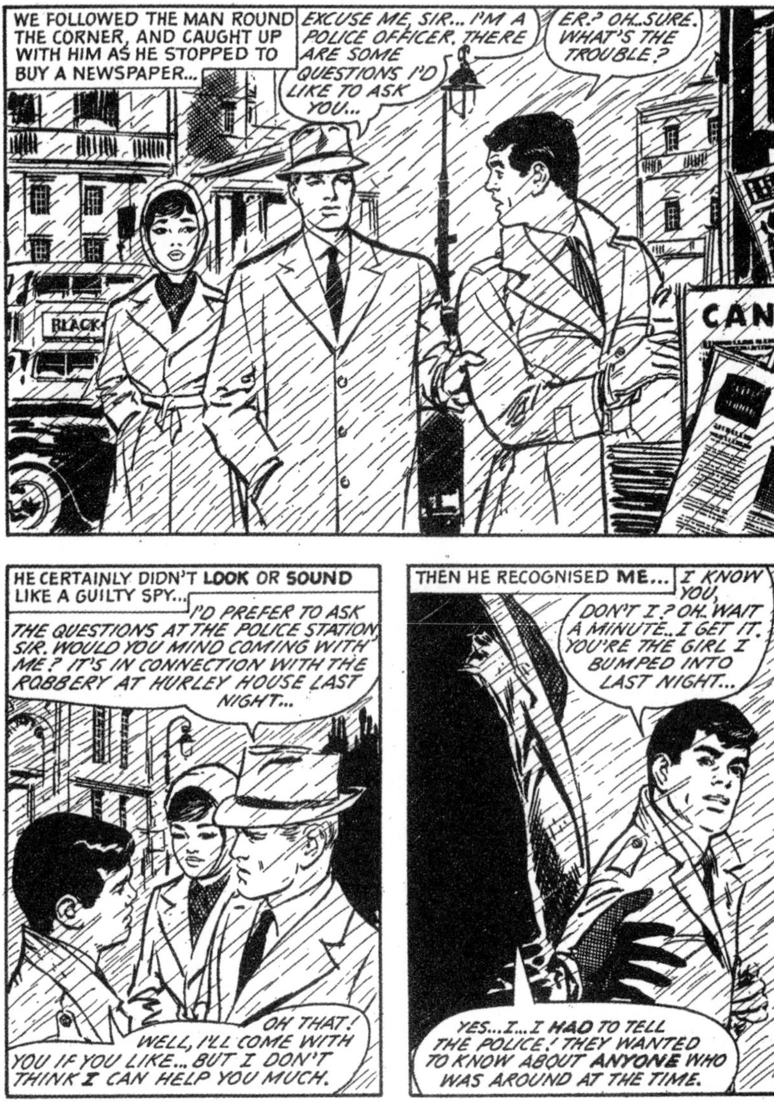
WE FOLLOWED THE MAN ROUND THE CORNER, AND CAUGHT UP WITH HIM AS HE STOPPED TO BUY A NEWSPAPER...
EXCUSE ME, SIR... I'M A POLICE OFFICER. THERE ARE SOME QUESTIONS I'D LIKE TO ASK YOU...
ER? OH..SURE. WHAT'S THE TROUBLE?
BLACK
CAN
HE CERTAINLY DIDN'T LOOK OR SOUND LIKE A GUILTY SPY...
I'D PREFER TO ASK THE QUESTIONS AT THE POLICE STATION, SIR. WOULD YOU MIND COMING WITH ME? IT'S IN CONNECTION WITH THE ROBBERY AT HURLEY HOUSE LAST NIGHT...
OH THAT! WELL, I'LL COME WITH YOU IF YOU LIKE... BUT I DON'T THINK I CAN HELP YOU MUCH.
THEN HE RECOGNISED ME...
I KNOW YOU, DON'T I? OH..WAIT A MINUTE..I GET IT. YOU'RE THE GIRL I BUMPED INTO LAST NIGHT...
YES...I...I HAD TO TELL THE POLICE! THEY WANTED TO KNOW ABOUT ANYONE WHO WAS AROUND AT THE TIME.

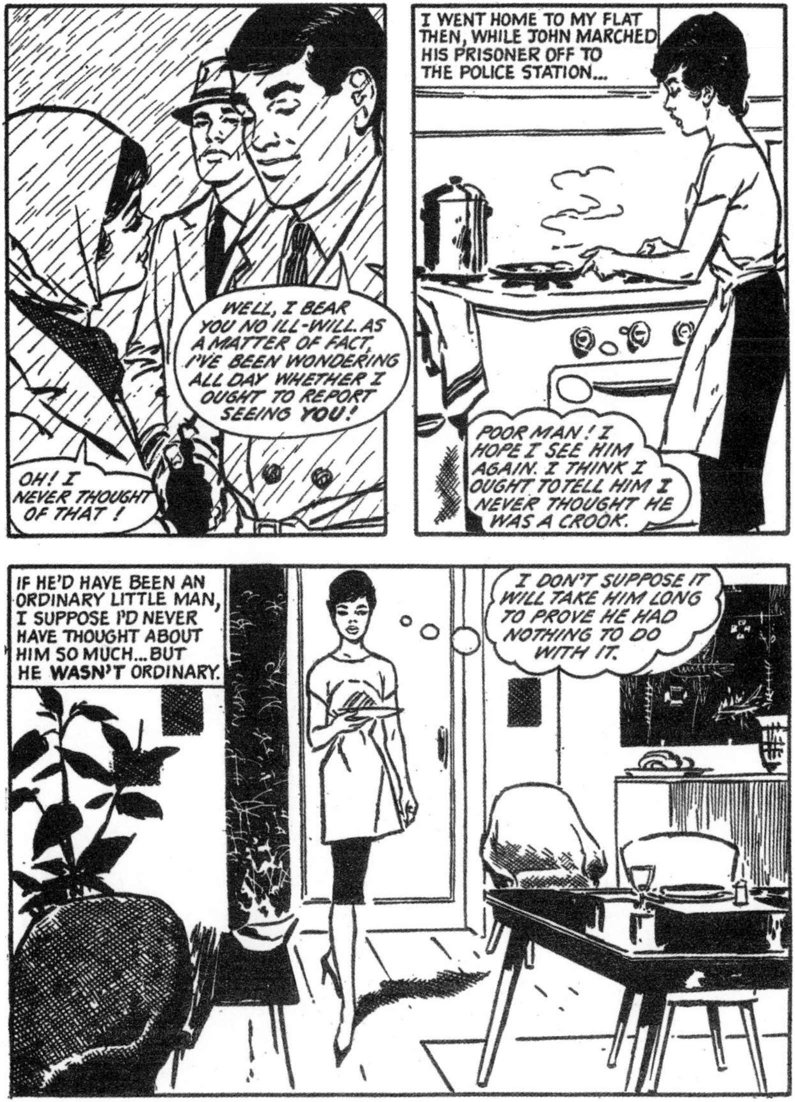
WELL, I BEAR YOU NO ILL-WILL. AS A MATTER OF FACT, I'VE BEEN WONDERING ALL DAY WHETHER I OUGHT TO REPORT SEEING YOU!
OH! I NEVER THOUGHT OF THAT!
I WENT HOME TO MY FLAT THEN, WHILE JOHN MARCHED HIS PRISONER OFF TO THE POLICE STATION...
POOR MAN! I HOPE I SEE HIM AGAIN. I THINK I OUGHT TO TELL HIM I NEVER THOUGHT HE WAS A CROOK.
IF HE'D HAVE BEEN AN ORDINARY LITTLE MAN, I SUPPOSE I'D NEVER HAVE THOUGHT ABOUT HIM SO MUCH... BUT HE WASN'T ORDINARY.
I DON'T SUPPOSE IT WILL TAKE HIM LONG TO PROVE HE HAD NOTHING TO DO WITH IT.

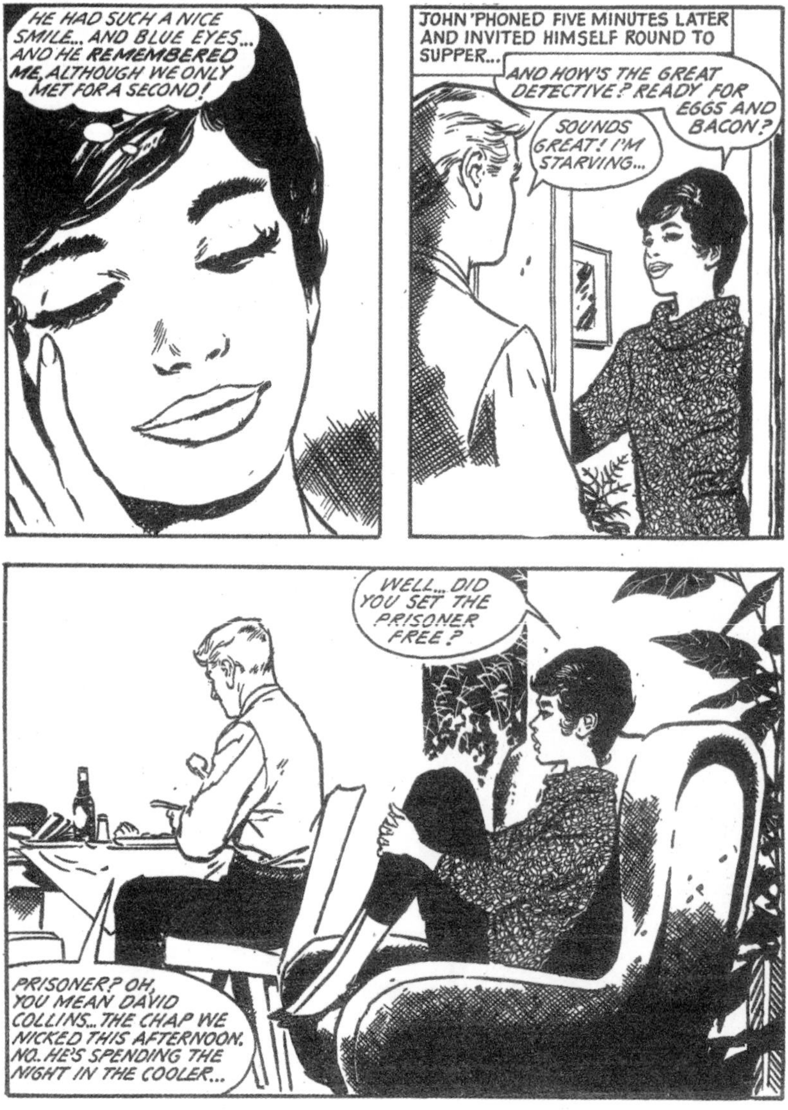
HE HAD SUCH A NICE SMILE... AND BLUE EYES... AND HE REMEMBERED ME, ALTHOUGH WE ONLY MET FOR A SECOND!
JOHN 'PHONED FIVE MINUTES LATER AND INVITED HIMSELF ROUND TO SUPPER...
AND HOW'S THE GREAT DETECTIVE? READY FOR EGGS AND BACON?
SOUNDS GREAT! I'M STARVING...
WELL... DID YOU SET THE PRISONER FREE?
PRISONER? OH, YOU MEAN DAVID COLLINS... THE CHAP WE NICKED THIS AFTERNOON. NO.. HE'S SPENDING THE NIGHT IN THE COOLER...

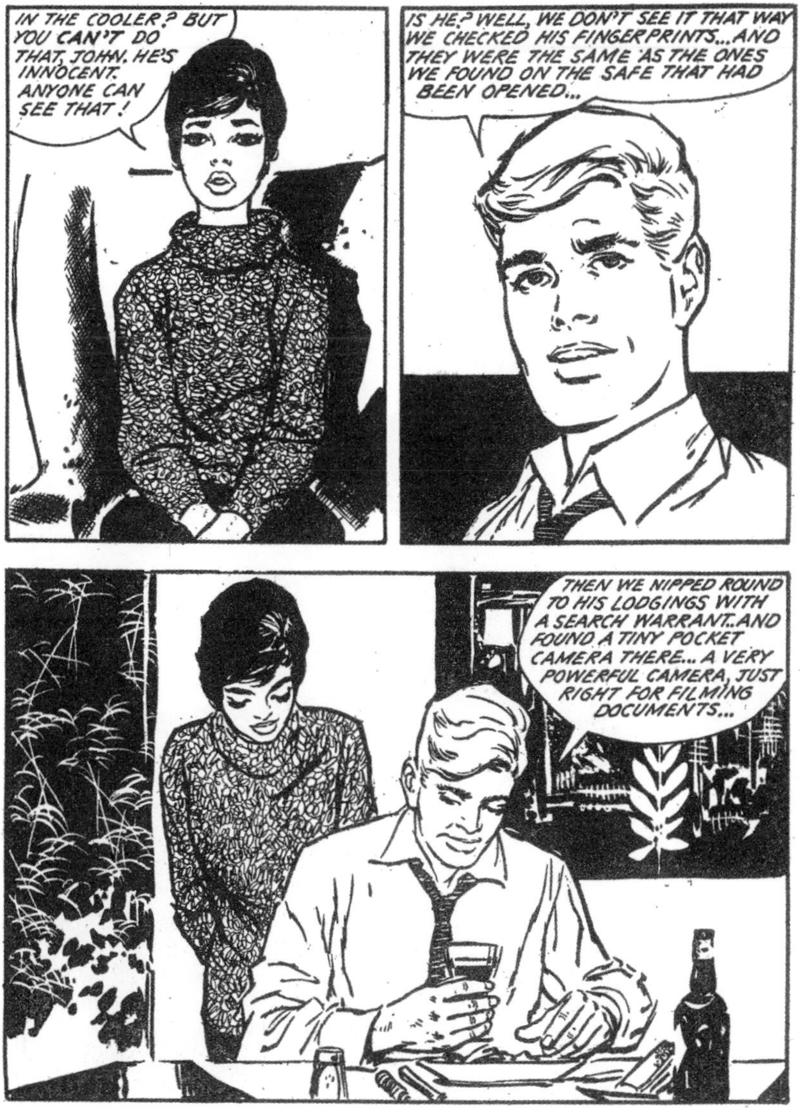
IN THE COOLER? BUT YOU CAN'T DO THAT, JOHN. HE'S INNOCENT. ANYONE CAN SEE THAT!
IS HE? WELL, WE DON'T SEE IT THAT WAY WE CHECKED HIS FINGERPRINTS...AND THEY WERE THE SAME AS THE ONES WE FOUND ON THE SAFE THAT HAD BEEN OPENED...
THEN WE NIPPED ROUND TO HIS LODGINGS WITH A SEARCH WARRANT..AND FOUND A TINY POCKET CAMERA THERE... A VERY POWERFUL CAMERA, JUST RIGHT FOR FILMING DOCUMENTS...

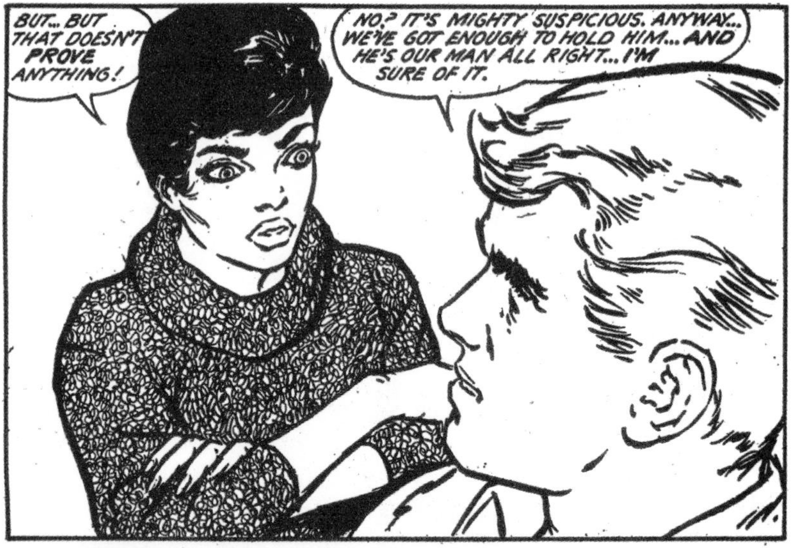
BUT... BUT THAT DOESN'T PROVE ANYTHING!
NO? IT'S MIGHTY SUSPICIOUS. ANYWAY... WE'VE GOT ENOUGH TO HOLD HIM... AND HE'S OUR MAN ALL RIGHT... I'M SURE OF IT.

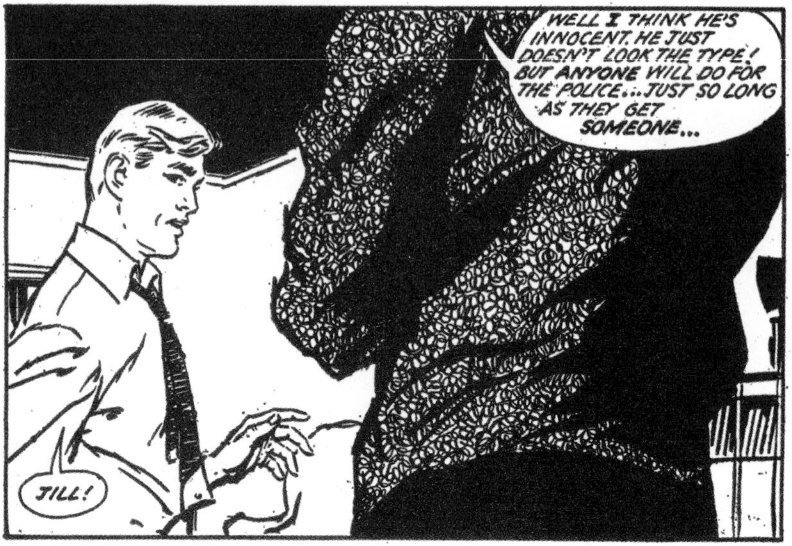
WELL I THINK HE'S INNOCENT. HE JUST DOESN'T LOOK THE TYPE! BUT ANYONE WILL DO FOR THE POLICE... JUST SO LONG AS THEY GET SOMEONE...
JILL!

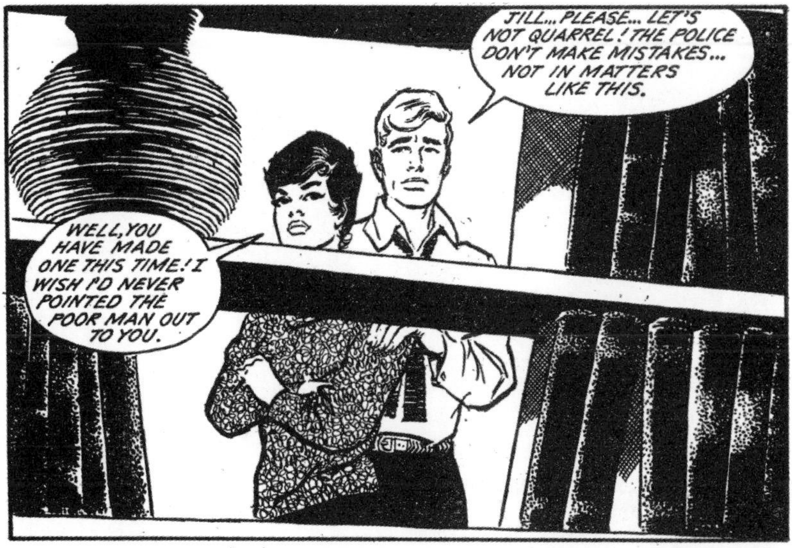
JILL... PLEASE... LET'S NOT QUARREL! THE POLICE DON'T MAKE MISTAKES... NOT IN MATTERS LIKE THIS.
WELL, YOU HAVE MADE ONE THIS TIME! I WISH I'D NEVER POINTED THE POOR MAN OUT TO YOU.

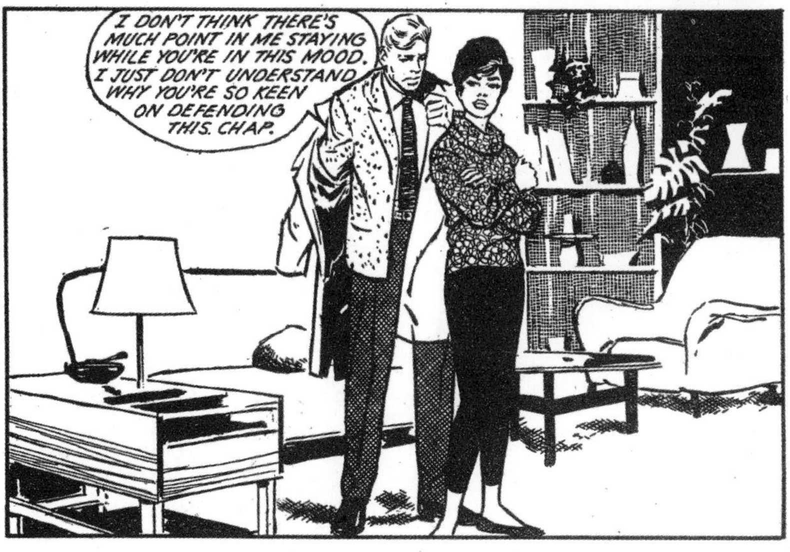
I DON'T THINK THERE'S MUCH POINT IN ME STAYING WHILE YOU'RE IN THIS MOOD. I JUST DON'T UNDERSTAND WHY YOU'RE SO KEEN ON DEFENDING THIS CHAP.

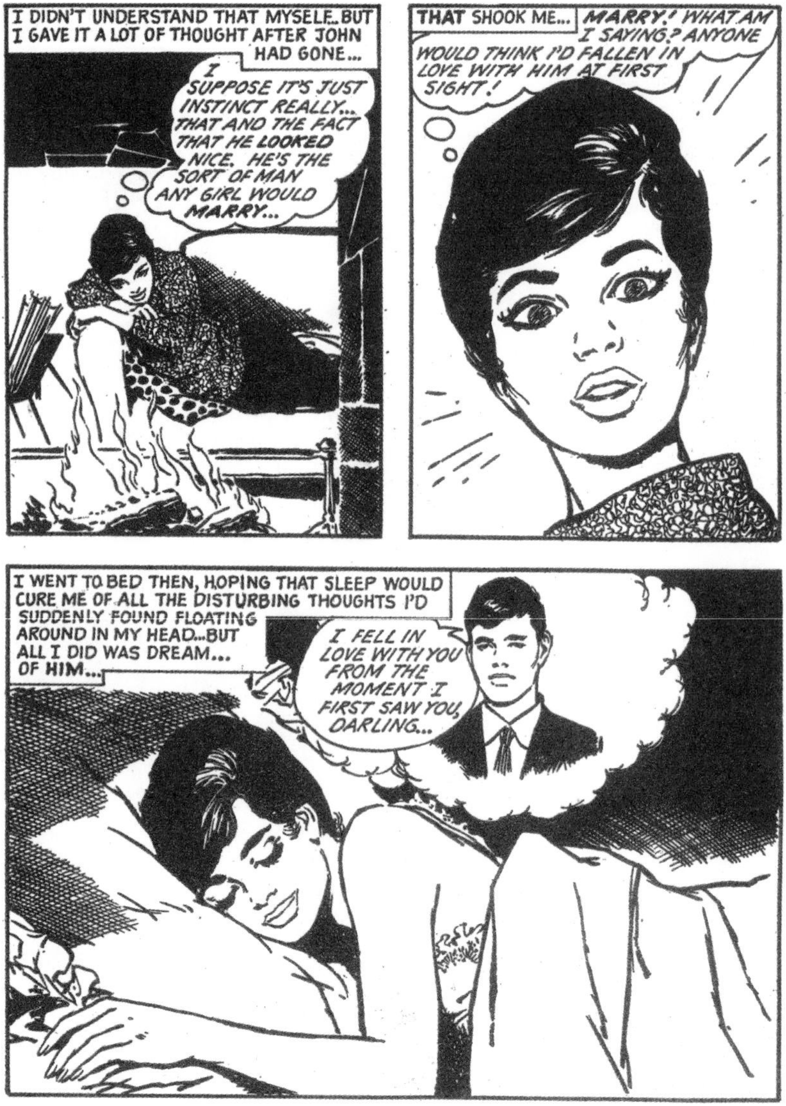
I DIDN'T UNDERSTAND THAT MYSELF... BUT I GAVE IT A LOT OF THOUGHT AFTER JOHN HAD GONE...
I SUPPOSE IT'S JUST INSTINCT REALLY... THAT AND THE FACT THAT HE LOOKED NICE. HE'S THE SORT OF MAN ANY GIRL WOULD MARRY...
THAT SHOOK ME...
MARRY! WHAT AM I SAYING? ANYONE WOULD THINK I'D FALLEN IN LOVE WITH HIM AT FIRST SIGHT!
I WENT TO BED THEN, HOPING THAT SLEEP WOULD CURE ME OF ALL THE DISTURBING THOUGHTS I'D SUDDENLY FOUND FLOATING AROUND IN MY HEAD... BUT ALL I DID WAS DREAM... OF HIM...
I FELL IN LOVE WITH YOU FROM THE MOMENT I FIRST SAW YOU, DARLING...

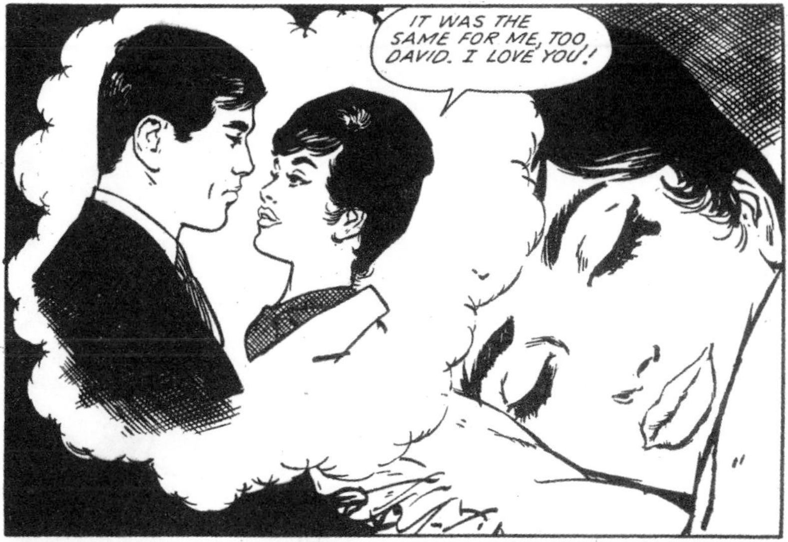
IT WAS THE SAME FOR ME, TOO, DAVID. I LOVE YOU!

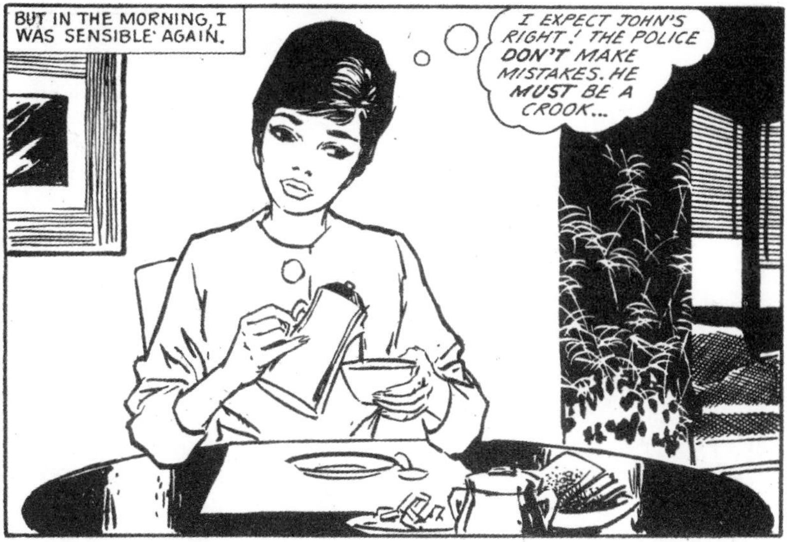
BUT IN THE MORNING, I WAS SENSIBLE AGAIN.
I EXPECT JOHN'S RIGHT! THE POLICE DON'T MAKE MISTAKES. HE MUST BE A CROOK...

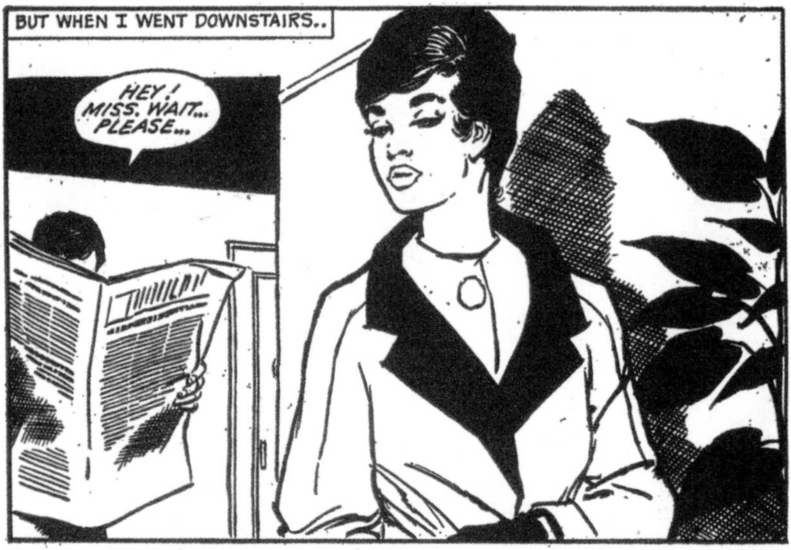
BUT WHEN I WENT DOWNSTAIRS..
HEY! MISS. WAIT... PLEASE...

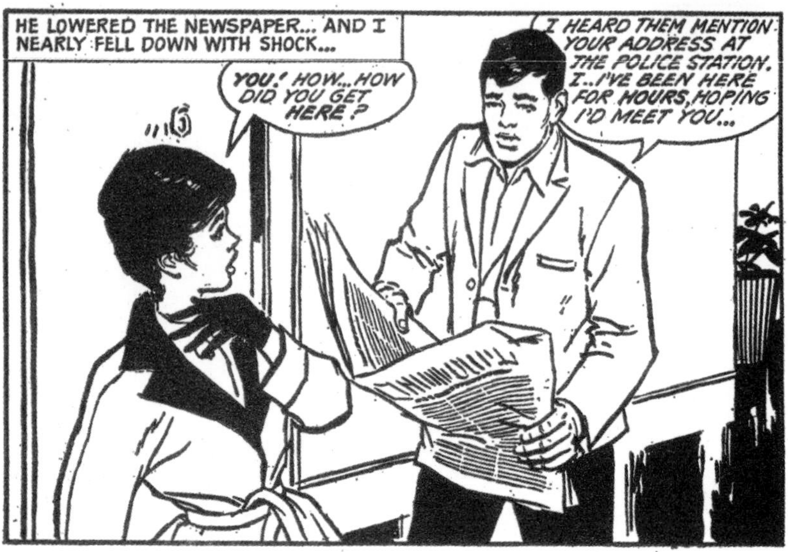
HE LOWERED THE NEWSPAPER... AND I NEARLY FELL DOWN WITH SHOCK...
YOU! HOW... HOW DID YOU GET HERE?
I HEARD THEM MENTION YOUR ADDRESS AT THE POLICE STATION. I..I'VE BEEN HERE FOR HOURS, HOPING I'D MEET YOU...

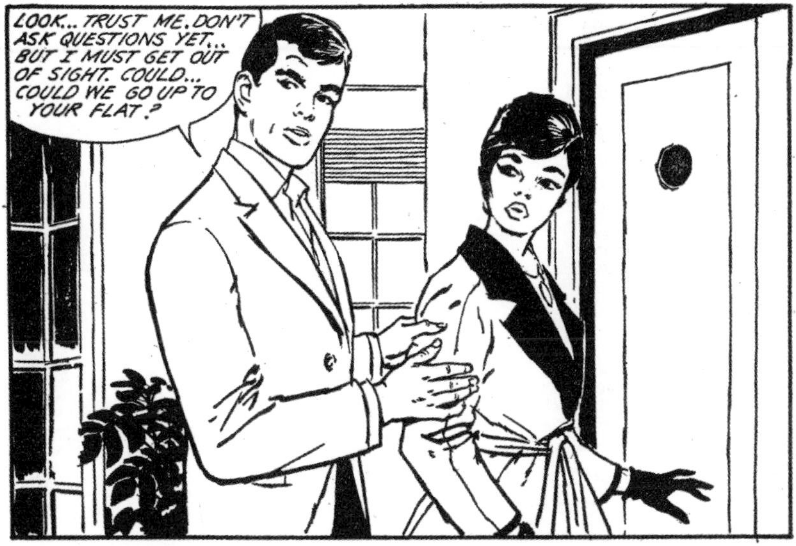
LOOK... TRUST ME. DON'T ASK QUESTIONS YET... BUT I MUST GET OUT OF SIGHT. COULD... COULD WE GO UP TO YOUR FLAT?

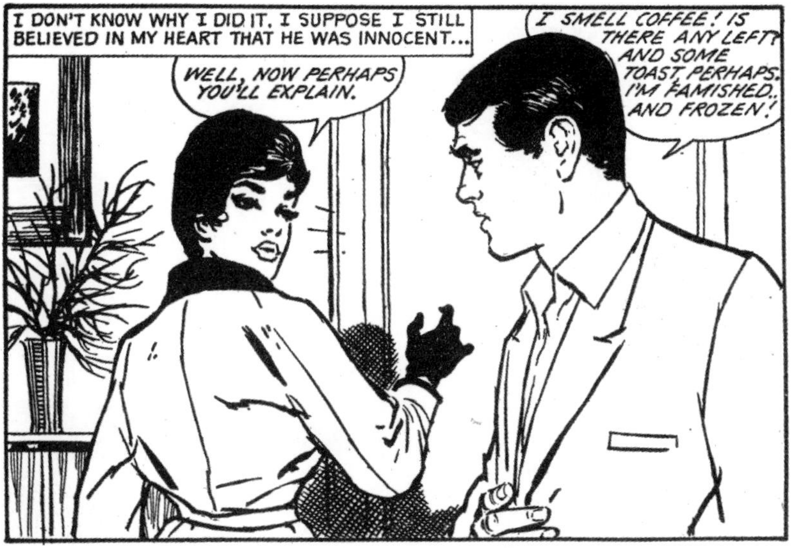
I DON'T KNOW WHY I DID IT. I SUPPOSE I STILL BELIEVED IN MY HEART THAT HE WAS INNOCENT...
WELL, NOW PERHAPS YOU'LL EXPLAIN.
I SMELL COFFEE! IS THERE ANY LEFT? AND SOME TOAST, PERHAPS. I'M FAMISHED.. AND FROZEN!

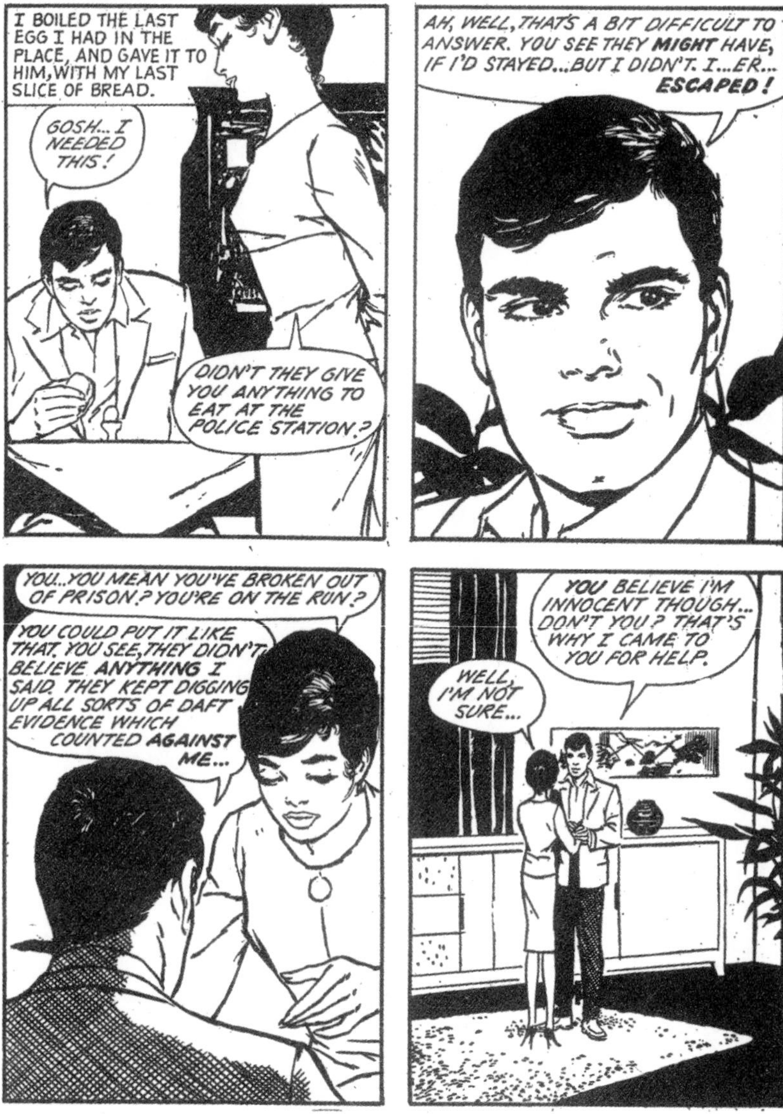
I BOILED THE LAST EGG I HAD IN THE PLACE, AND GAVE IT TO HIM, WITH MY LAST SLICE OF BREAD.
GOSH... I NEEDED THIS!
DIDN'T THEY GIVE YOU ANYTHING TO EAT AT THE POLICE STATION?
AH, WELL, THAT'S A BIT DIFFICULT TO ANSWER. YOU SEE THEY MIGHT HAVE, IF I'D STAYED... BUT I DIDN'T. I... ER... ESCAPED!
YOU... YOU MEAN YOU'VE BROKEN OUT OF PRISON? YOU'RE ON THE RUN?
YOU COULD PUT IT LIKE THAT. YOU SEE, THEY DIDN'T BELIEVE ANYTHING I SAID. THEY KEPT DIGGING UP ALL SORTS OF DAFT EVIDENCE WHICH COUNTED AGAINST ME...
YOU BELIEVE I'M INNOCENT THOUGH... DON'T YOU? THAT'S WHY I CAME TO YOU FOR HELP.
WELL, I'M NOT SURE...

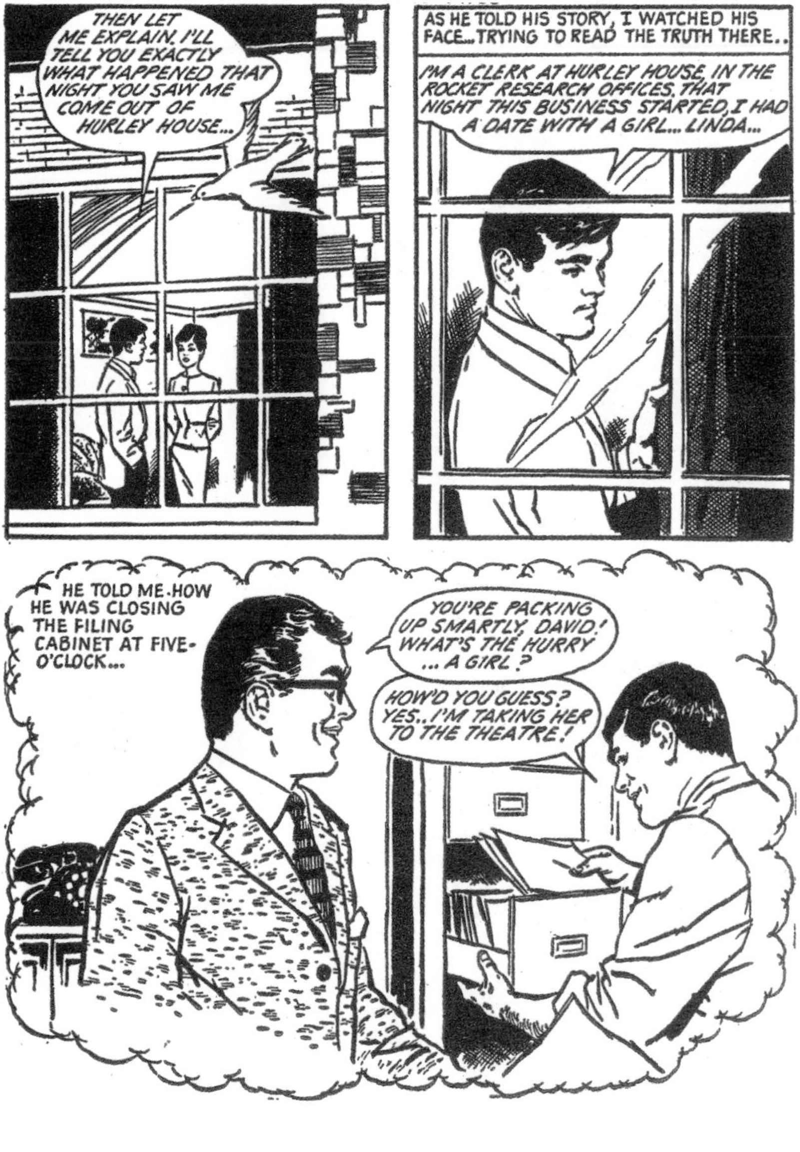
THEN LET ME EXPLAIN. I'LL TELL YOU EXACTLY WHAT HAPPENED THAT NIGHT YOU SAW ME COME OUT OF HURLEY HOUSE...
AS HE TOLD HIS STORY, I WATCHED HIS FACE...TRYING TO READ THE TRUTH THERE..
I'M A CLERK AT HURLEY HOUSE, IN THE ROCKET RESEARCH OFFICES. THAT NIGHT THIS BUSINESS STARTED, I HAD A DATE WITH A GIRL... LINDA...
HE TOLD ME HOW HE WAS CLOSING THE FILING CABINET AT FIVE-O'CLOCK...
YOU'RE PACKING UP SMARTLY, DAVID! WHAT'S THE HURRY ... A GIRL?
HOW'D YOU GUESS? YES..I'M TAKING HER TO THE THEATRE!

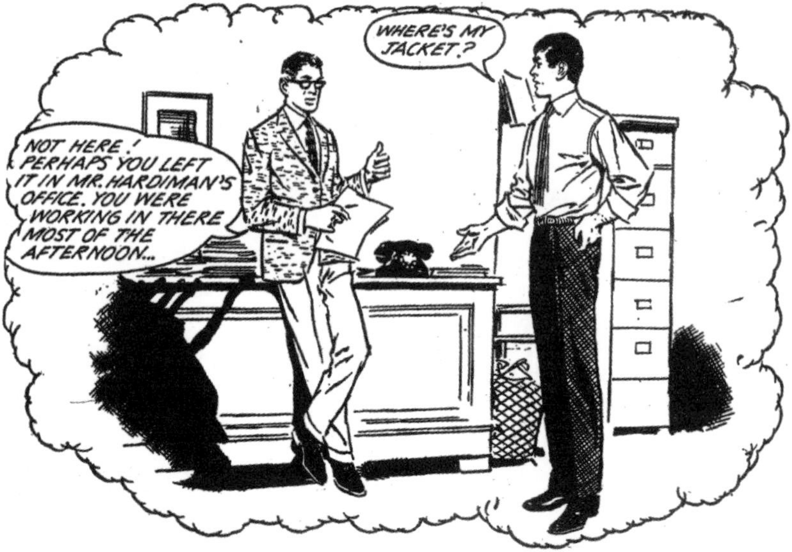
WHERE'S MY JACKET?
NOT HERE! PERHAPS YOU LEFT IT IN MR. HARDIMAN'S OFFICE. YOU WERE WORKING IN THERE MOST OF THE AFTERNOON...

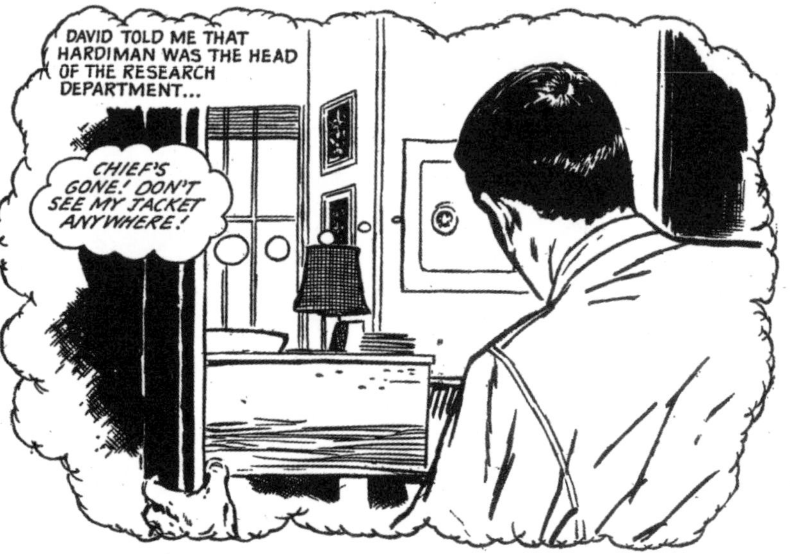
DAVID TOLD ME THAT HARDIMAN WAS THE HEAD OF THE RESEARCH DEPARTMENT...
CHIEF'S GONE! DON'T SEE MY JACKET ANYWHERE!

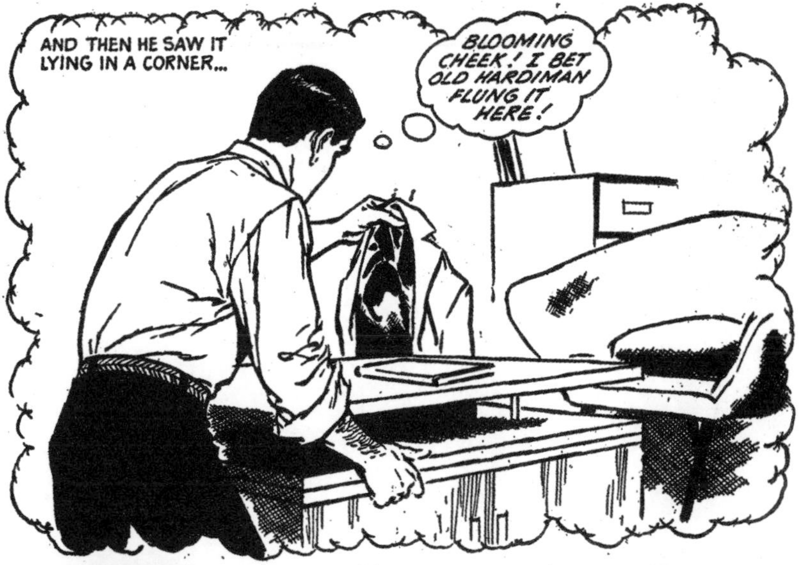
AND THEN HE SAW IT LYING IN A CORNER...
BLOOMING CHEEK! I BET OLD HARDIMAN FLUNG IT HERE!

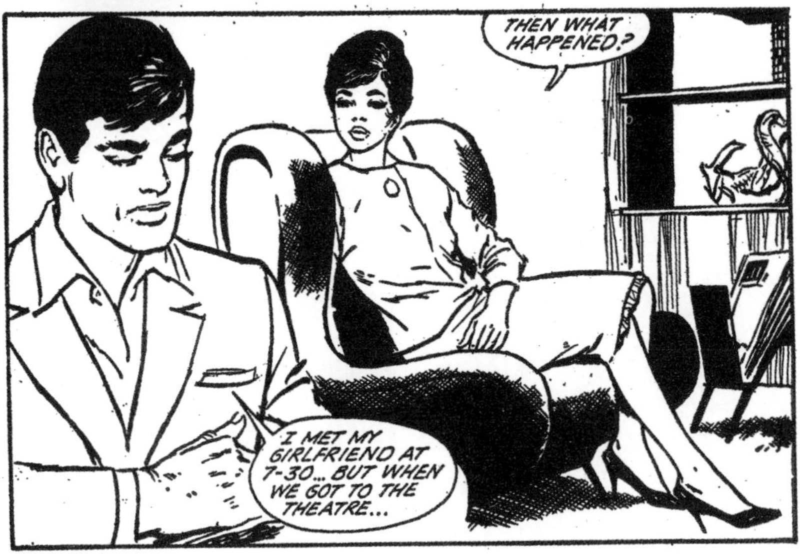
THEN WHAT HAPPENED?
I MET MY GIRLFRIEND AT 7-30... BUT WHEN WE GOT TO THE THEATRE...

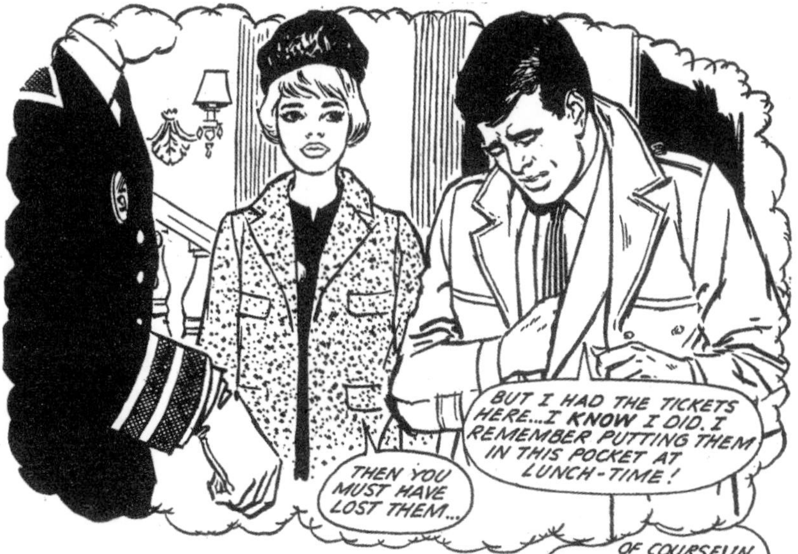
BUT I HAD THE TICKETS HERE...I KNOW I DID. I REMEMBER PUTTING THEM IN THIS POCKET AT LUNCH-TIME!
THEN YOU MUST HAVE LOST THEM...

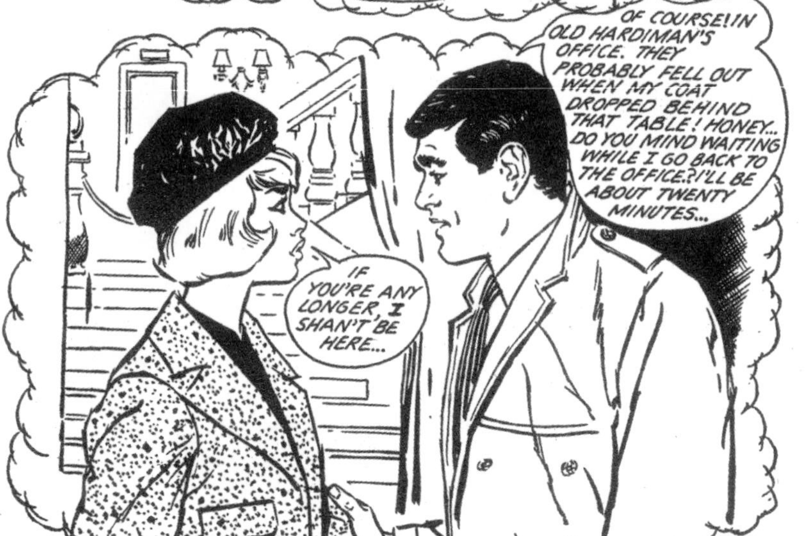
OF COURSE! IN OLD HARDIMAN'S OFFICE. THEY PROBABLY FELL OUT WHEN MY COAT DROPPED BEHIND THAT TABLE! HONEY... DO YOU MIND WAITING WHILE I GO BACK TO THE OFFICE? I'LL BE ABOUT TWENTY MINUTES...
IF YOU'RE ANY LONGER, I SHAN'T BE HERE...

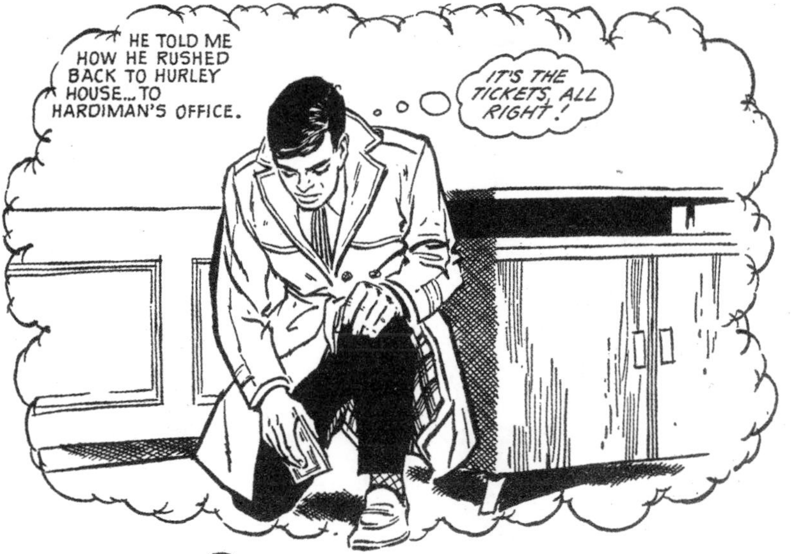
HE TOLD ME HOW HE RUSHED BACK TO HURLEY HOUSE... TO HARDIMAN'S OFFICE.
IT'S THE TICKETS, ALL RIGHT!

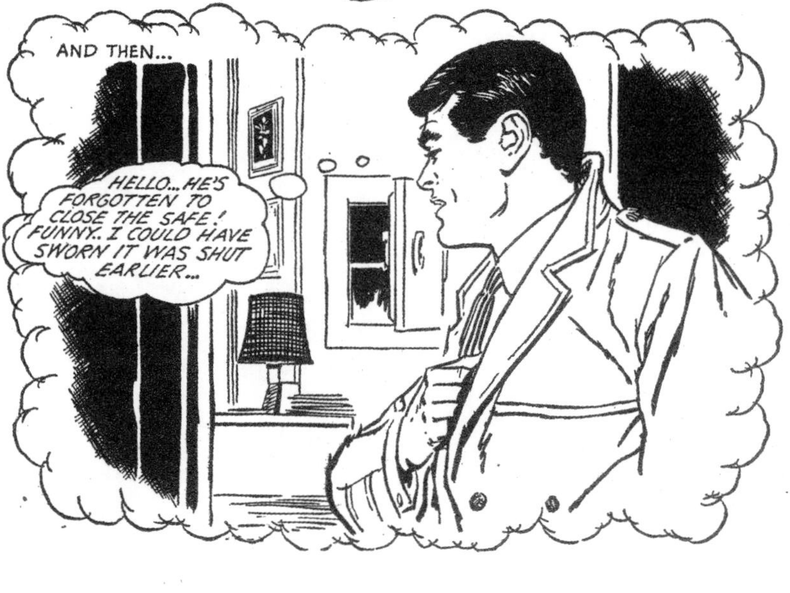
AND THEN...
HELLO... HE'S FORGOTTEN TO CLOSE THE SAFE! FUNNY.. I COULD HAVE SWORN IT WAS SHUT EARLIER...

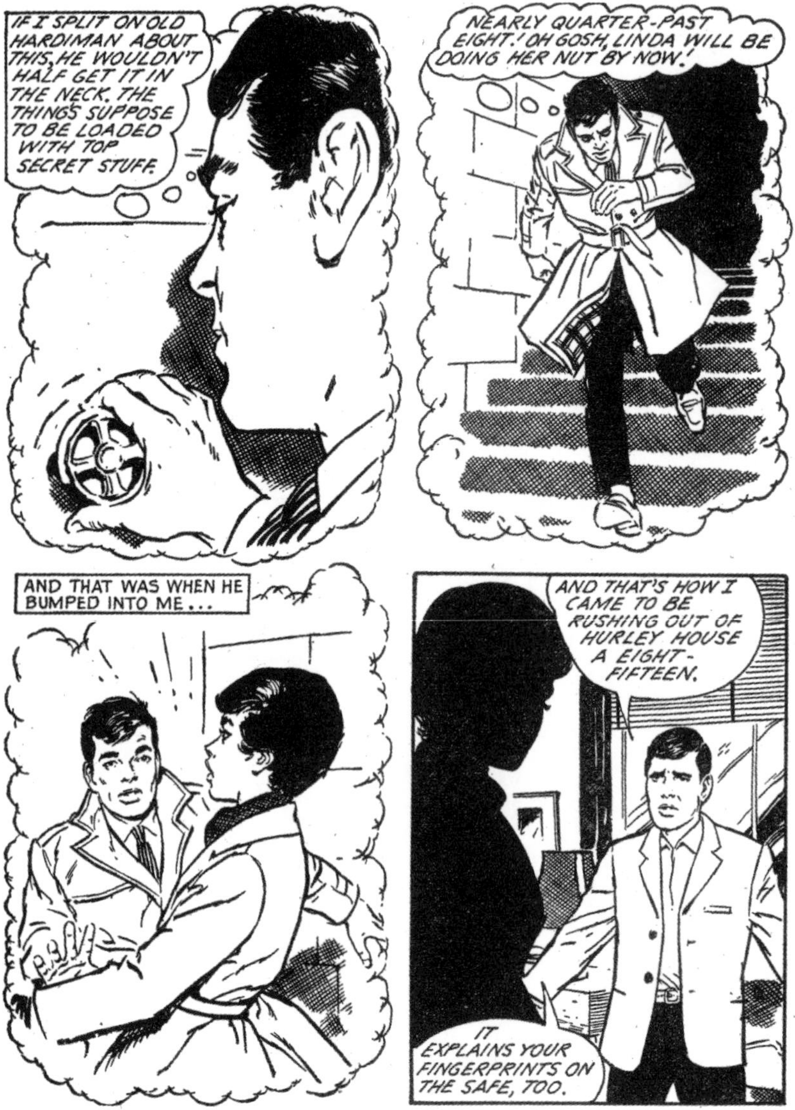
IF I SPLIT ON OLD HARDIMAN ABOUT THIS, HE WOULDN'T HALF GET IT IN THE NECK. THE THING'S SUPPOSE TO BE LOADED WITH TOP SECRET STUFF.
NEARLY QUARTER-PAST EIGHT! OH GOSH, LINDA WILL BE DOING HER NUT BY NOW!
AND THAT WAS WHEN HE BUMPED INTO ME...
AND THAT'S HOW I CAME TO BE RUSHING OUT OF HURLEY HOUSE A EIGHT-FIFTEEN.
IT EXPLAINS YOUR FINGERPRINTS ON THE SAFE, TOO.

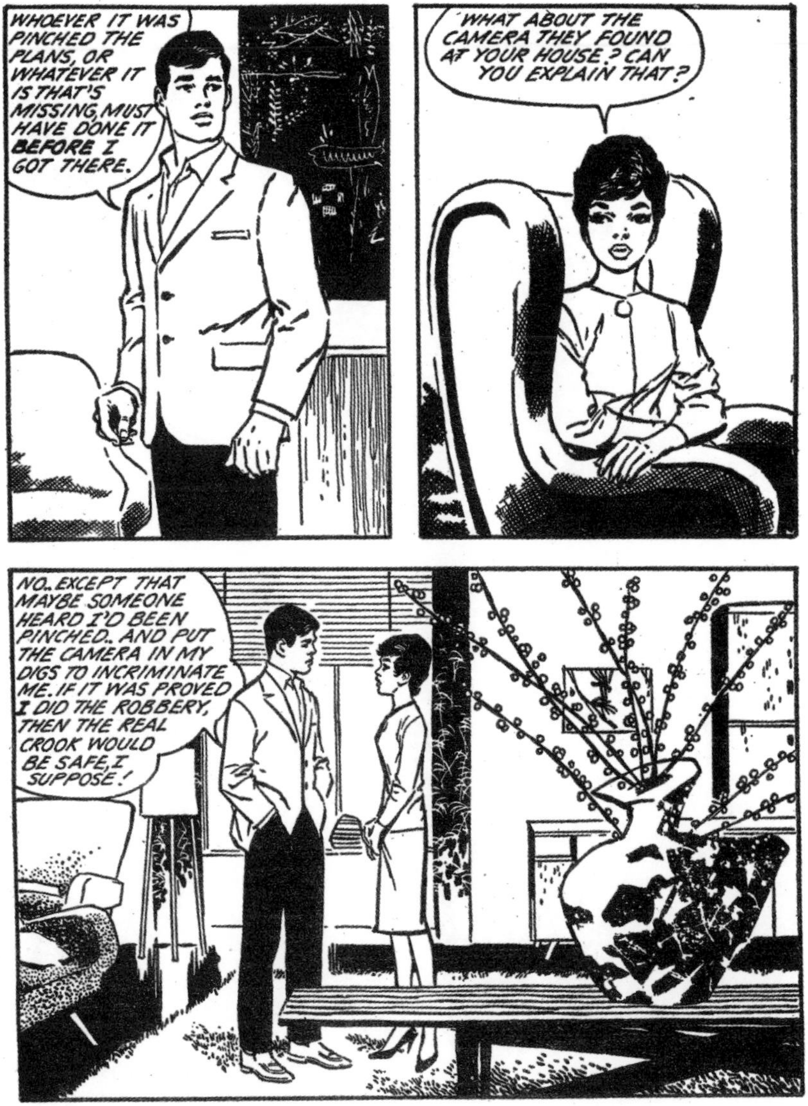
WHOEVER IT WAS PINCHED THE PLANS, OR WHATEVER IT IS THAT'S MISSING, MUST HAVE DONE IT BEFORE I GOT THERE.
WHAT ABOUT THE CAMERA THEY FOUND AT YOUR HOUSE? CAN YOU EXPLAIN THAT?
NO.. EXCEPT THAT MAYBE SOMEONE HEARD I'D BEEN PINCHED.. AND PUT THE CAMERA IN MY DIGS TO INCRIMINATE ME. IF IT WAS PROVED I DID THE ROBBERY, THEN THE REAL CROOK WOULD BE SAFE, I SUPPOSE!

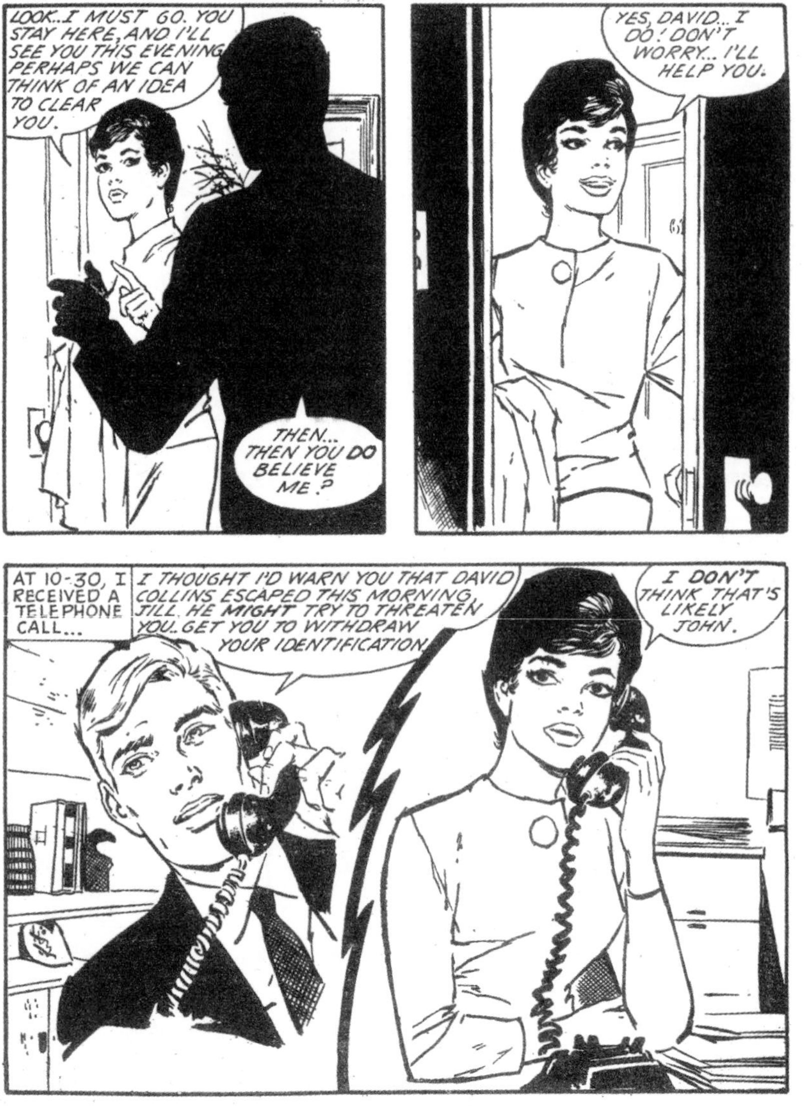
LOOK..I MUST GO. YOU STAY HERE, AND I'LL SEE YOU THIS EVENING PERHAPS WE CAN THINK OF AN IDEA TO CLEAR YOU.
THEN... THEN YOU DO BELIEVE ME?
YES, DAVID... I DO! DON'T WORRY... I'LL HELP YOU.
AT 10-30, I RECEIVED A TELEPHONE CALL...
I THOUGHT I'D WARN YOU THAT DAVID COLLINS ESCAPED THIS MORNING, JILL. HE MIGHT TRY TO THREATEN YOU.. GET YOU TO WITHDRAW YOUR IDENTIFICATION.
I DON'T THINK THAT'S LIKELY JOHN.

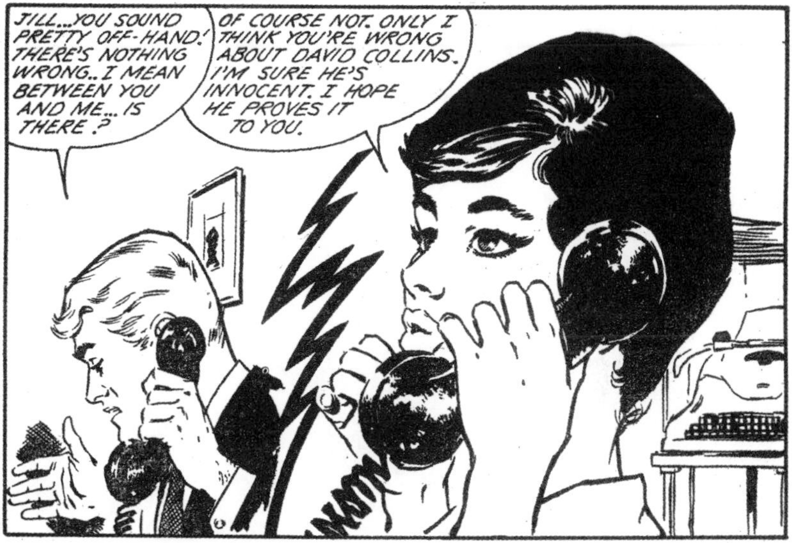
JILL...YOU SOUND PRETTY OFF-HAND! THERE'S NOTHING WRONG..I MEAN BETWEEN YOU AND ME... IS THERE?
OF COURSE NOT. ONLY I THINK YOU'RE WRONG ABOUT DAVID COLLINS. I'M SURE HE'S INNOCENT. I HOPE HE PROVES IT TO YOU.

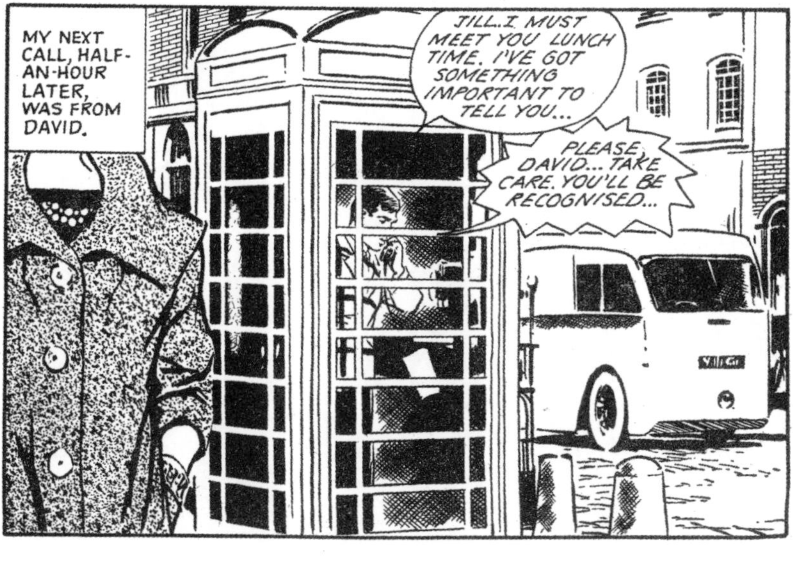
MY NEXT CALL, HALF-AN-HOUR LATER, WAS FROM DAVID.
JILL..I MUST MEET YOU LUNCH TIME. I'VE GOT SOMETHING IMPORTANT TO TELL YOU...
PLEASE, DAVID... TAKE CARE. YOU'LL BE RECOGNISED...

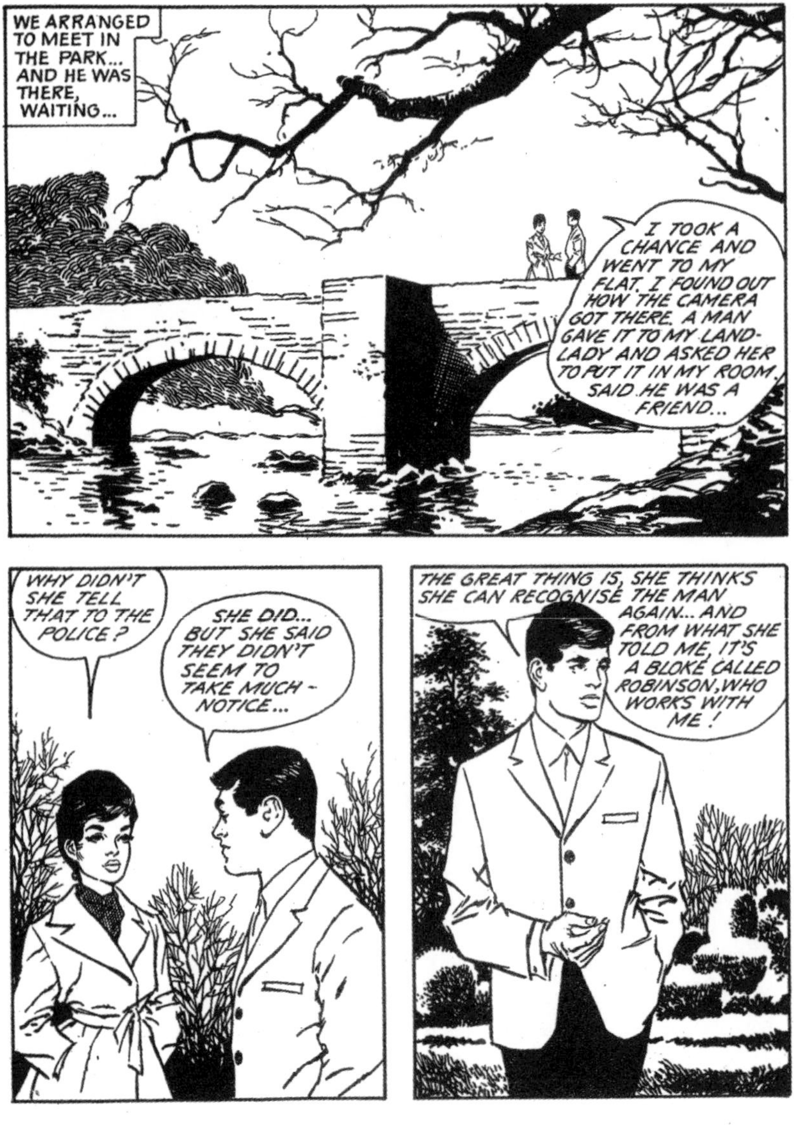
WE ARRANGED TO MEET IN THE PARK... AND HE WAS THERE, WAITING...
I TOOK A CHANCE AND WENT TO MY FLAT. I FOUND OUT HOW THE CAMERA GOT THERE. A MAN GAVE IT TO MY LANDLADY AND ASKED HER TO PUT IT IN MY ROOM. SAID HE WAS A FRIEND...
WHY DIDN'T SHE TELL THAT TO THE POLICE?
SHE DID... BUT SHE SAID THEY DIDN'T SEEM TO TAKE MUCH NOTICE...
THE GREAT THING IS, SHE THINKS SHE CAN RECOGNISE THE MAN AGAIN... AND FROM WHAT SHE TOLD ME, IT'S A BLOKE CALLED ROBINSON, WHO WORKS WITH ME!

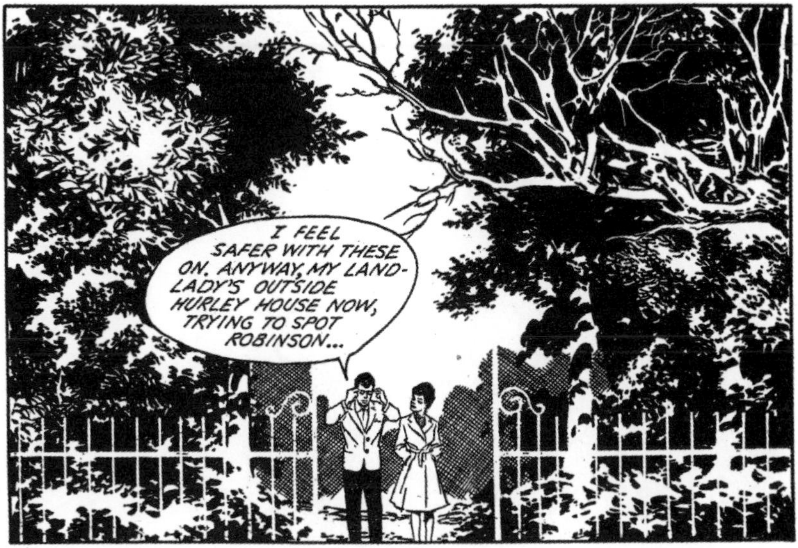
I FEEL SAFER WITH THESE ON. ANYWAY, MY LAND-LADY'S OUTSIDE HURLEY HOUSE NOW, TRYING TO SPOT ROBINSON...

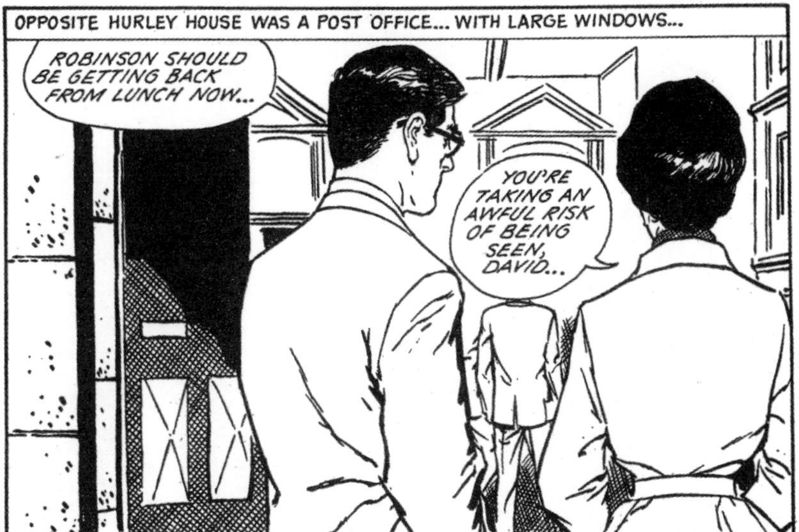
OPPOSITE HURLEY HOUSE WAS A POST OFFICE... WITH LARGE WINDOWS...
ROBINSON SHOULD BE GETTING BACK FROM LUNCH NOW...
YOU'RE TAKING AN AWFUL RISK OF BEING SEEN, DAVID...

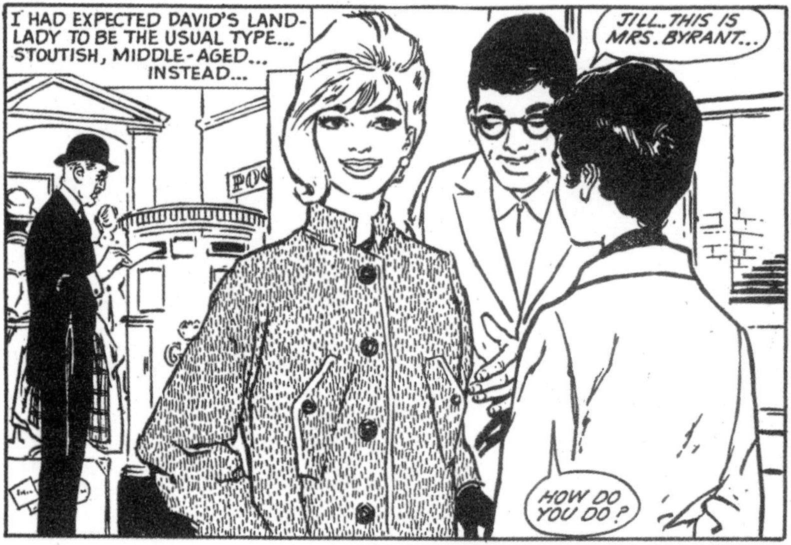
I HAD EXPECTED DAVID'S LANDLADY TO BE THE USUAL TYPE... STOUTISH, MIDDLE-AGED... INSTEAD...
JILL..THIS IS MRS. BYRANT...
HOW DO YOU DO?

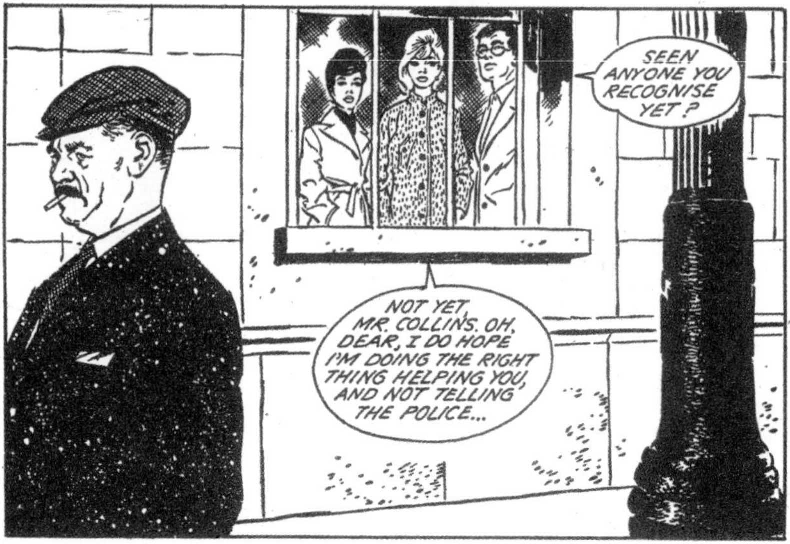
SEEN ANYONE YOU RECOGNISE YET?
NOT YET, MR. COLLINS. OH, DEAR, I DO HOPE I'M DOING THE RIGHT THING HELPING YOU, AND NOT TELLING THE POLICE...

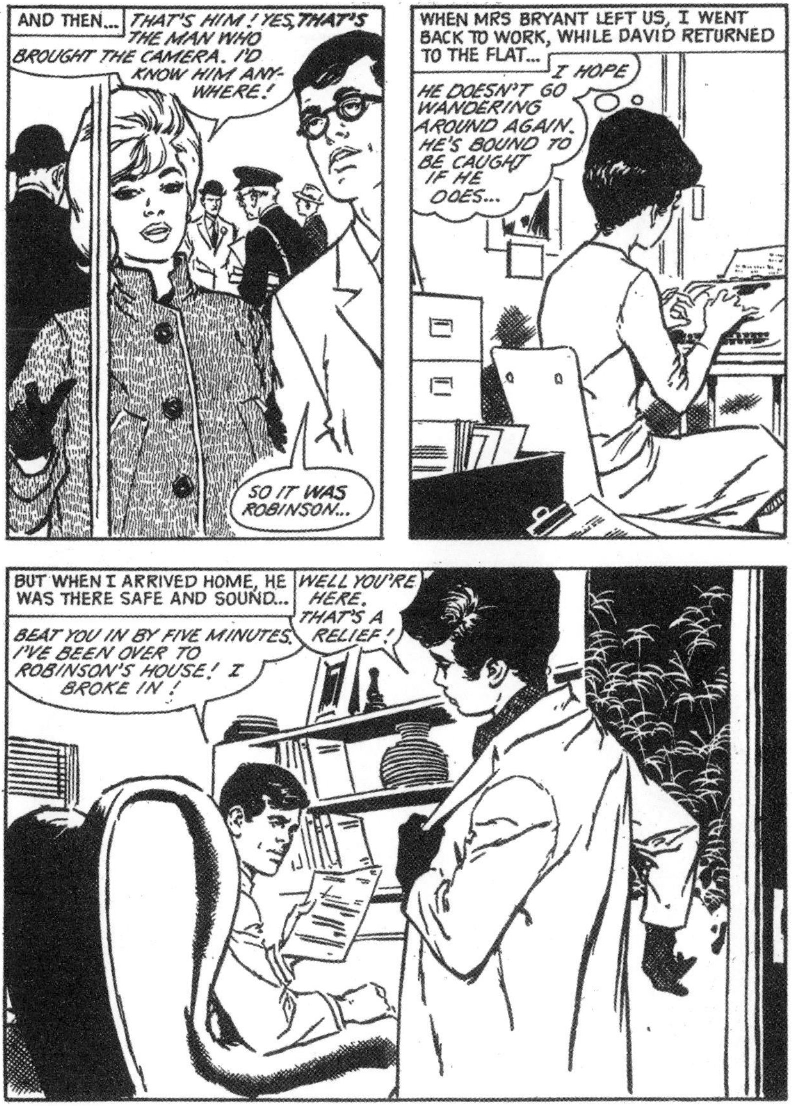
AND THEN...
THAT'S HIM! YES, THAT'S THE MAN WHO BROUGHT THE CAMERA. I'D KNOW HIM ANY-WHERE!
SO IT WAS ROBINSON...
WHEN MRS BRYANT LEFT US, I WENT BACK TO WORK, WHILE DAVID RETURNED TO THE FLAT...
I HOPE HE DOESN'T GO WANDERING AROUND AGAIN. HE'S BOUND TO BE CAUGHT IF HE DOES...
BUT WHEN I ARRIVED HOME, HE WAS THERE SAFE AND SOUND...
WELL YOU'RE HERE. THAT'S A RELIEF!
BEAT YOU IN BY FIVE MINUTES. I'VE BEEN OVER TO ROBINSON'S HOUSE! I BROKE IN!

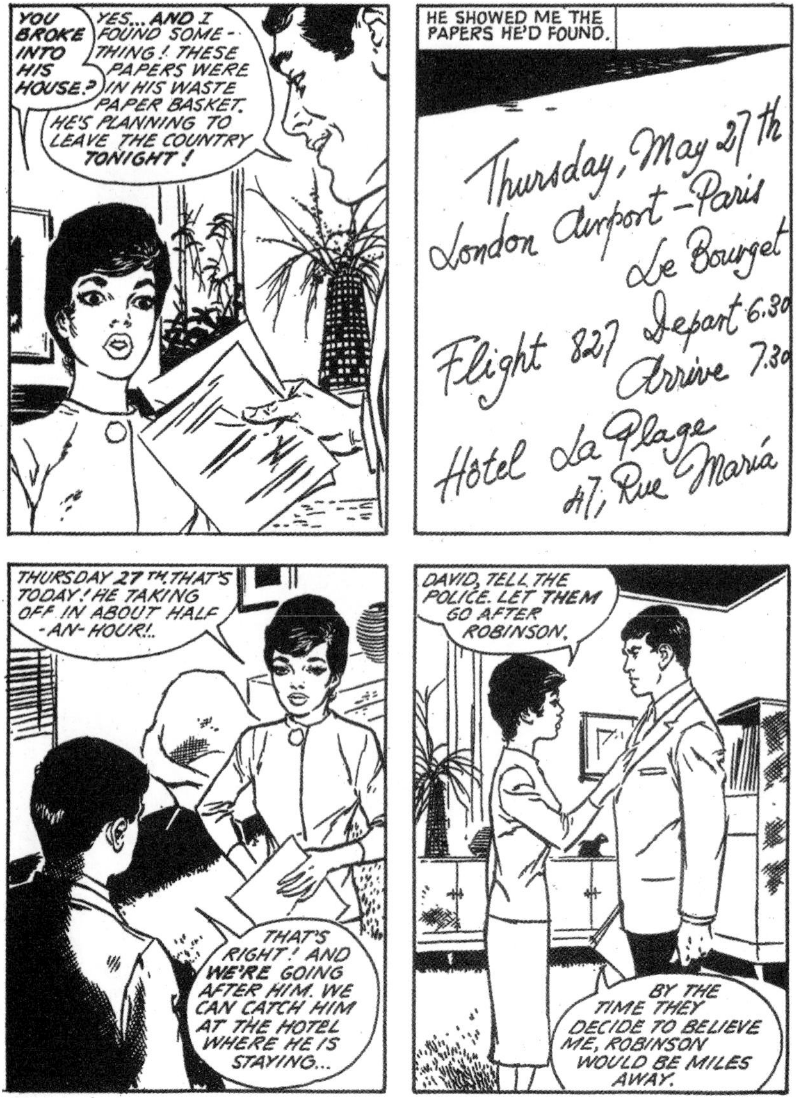
YOU BROKE INTO HIS HOUSE?
YES... AND I FOUND SOME-THING! THESE PAPERS WERE IN HIS WASTE PAPER BASKET. HE'S PLANNING TO LEAVE THE COUNTRY TONIGHT!
HE SHOWED ME THE PAPERS HE'D FOUND.
Thursday, May 27th
London Airport – Paris
Le Bourget
Flight 827 Depart 6.30
Arrive 7.30
Hôtel La Plage
47, Rue Maria
THURSDAY 27TH. THAT'S TODAY! HE TAKING OFF IN ABOUT HALF-AN-HOUR!..
THAT'S RIGHT! AND WE'RE GOING AFTER HIM. WE CAN CATCH HIM AT THE HOTEL WHERE HE IS STAYING...
DAVID, TELL THE POLICE. LET THEM GO AFTER ROBINSON.
BY THE TIME THEY DECIDE TO BELIEVE ME, ROBINSON WOULD BE MILES AWAY.

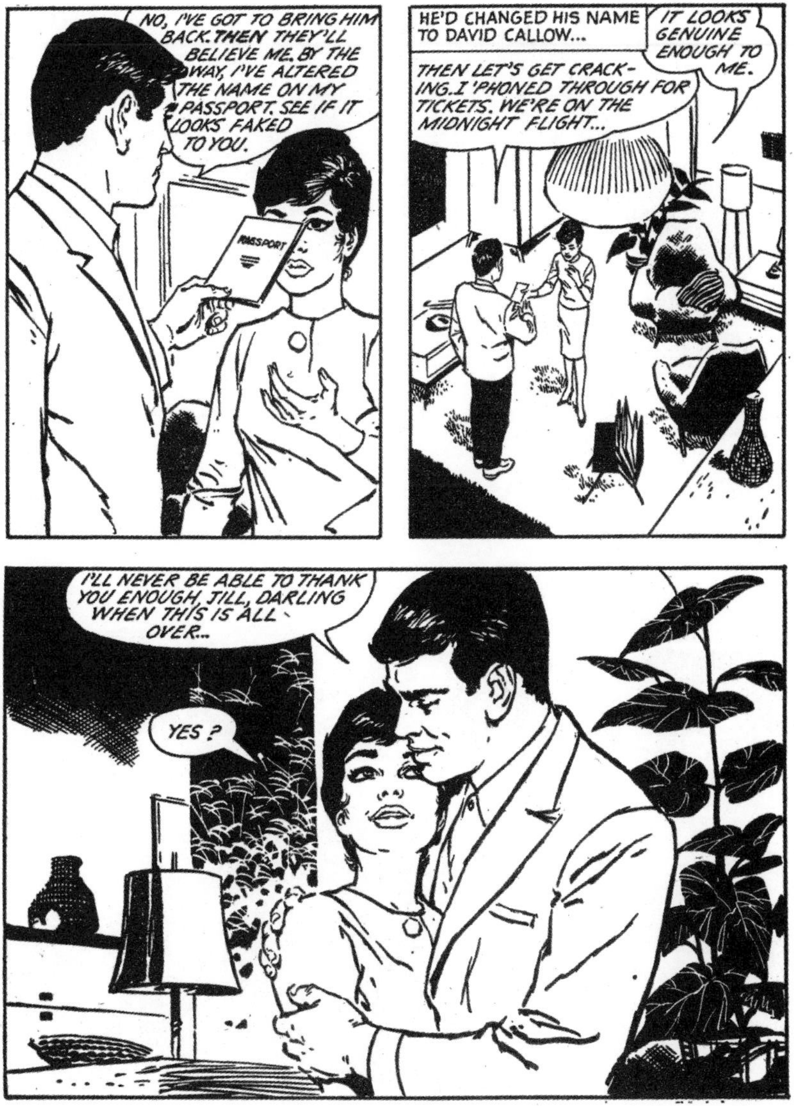
NO, I'VE GOT TO BRING HIM BACK. THEN THEY'LL BELIEVE ME. BY THE WAY, I'VE ALTERED THE NAME ON MY PASSPORT. SEE IF IT LOOKS FAKED TO YOU.
PASSPORT
HE'D CHANGED HIS NAME TO DAVID CALLOW...
IT LOOKS GENUINE ENOUGH TO ME.
THEN LET'S GET CRACKING. I 'PHONED THROUGH FOR TICKETS. WE'RE ON THE MIDNIGHT FLIGHT...
I'LL NEVER BE ABLE TO THANK YOU ENOUGH, JILL, DARLING WHEN THIS IS ALL OVER...
YES ?

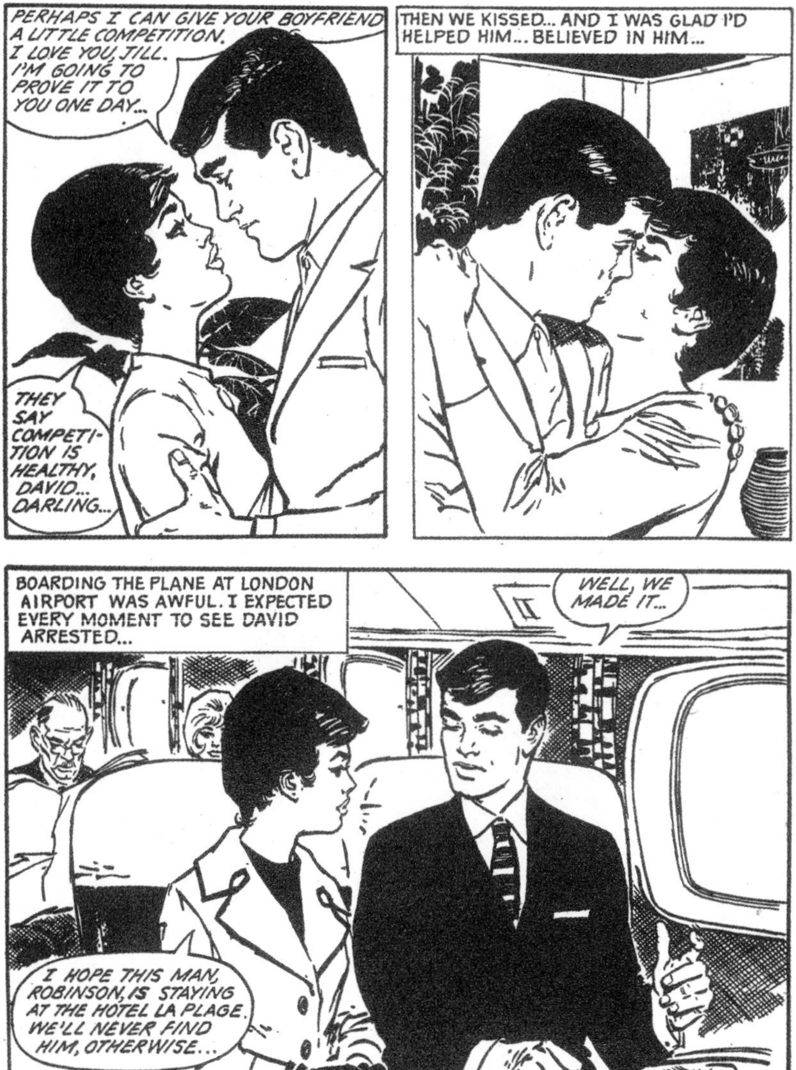
PERHAPS I CAN GIVE YOUR BOYFRIEND A LITTLE COMPETITION. I LOVE YOU, JILL. I'M GOING TO PROVE IT TO YOU ONE DAY...
THEY SAY COMPETITION IS HEALTHY, DAVID... DARLING...
THEN WE KISSED... AND I WAS GLAD I'D HELPED HIM... BELIEVED IN HIM...
BOARDING THE PLANE AT LONDON AIRPORT WAS AWFUL. I EXPECTED EVERY MOMENT TO SEE DAVID ARRESTED...
WELL, WE MADE IT...
I HOPE THIS MAN, ROBINSON, IS STAYING AT THE HOTEL LA PLAGE. WE'LL NEVER FIND HIM, OTHERWISE...

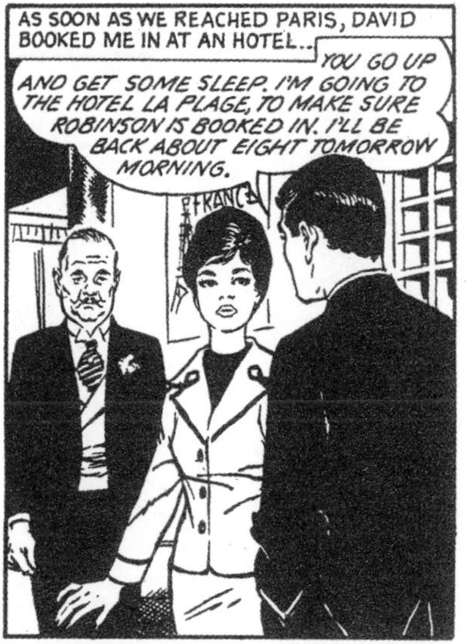
AS SOON AS WE REACHED PARIS, DAVID BOOKED ME IN AT AN HOTEL..
YOU GO UP AND GET SOME SLEEP. I'M GOING TO THE HOTEL LA PLAGE, TO MAKE SURE ROBINSON IS BOOKED IN. I'LL BE BACK ABOUT EIGHT TOMORROW MORNING.

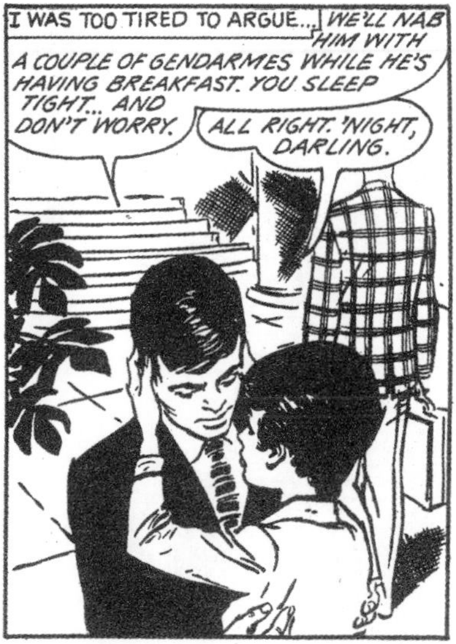
I WAS TOO TIRED TO ARGUE...
WE'LL NAB HIM WITH A COUPLE OF GENDARMES WHILE HE'S HAVING BREAKFAST. YOU SLEEP TIGHT... AND DON'T WORRY.
ALL RIGHT. 'NIGHT, DARLING.

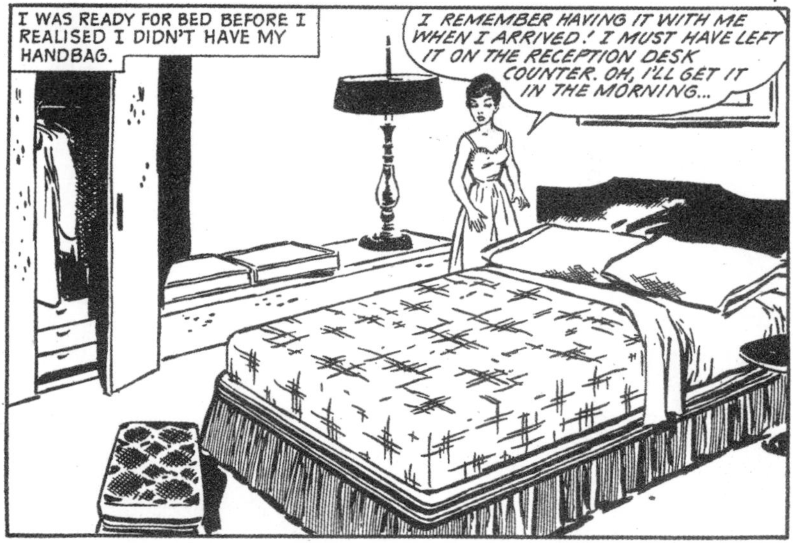
I WAS READY FOR BED BEFORE I REALISED I DIDN'T HAVE MY HANDBAG.
I REMEMBER HAVING IT WITH ME WHEN I ARRIVED! I MUST HAVE LEFT IT ON THE RECEPTION DESK COUNTER. OH, I'LL GET IT IN THE MORNING...

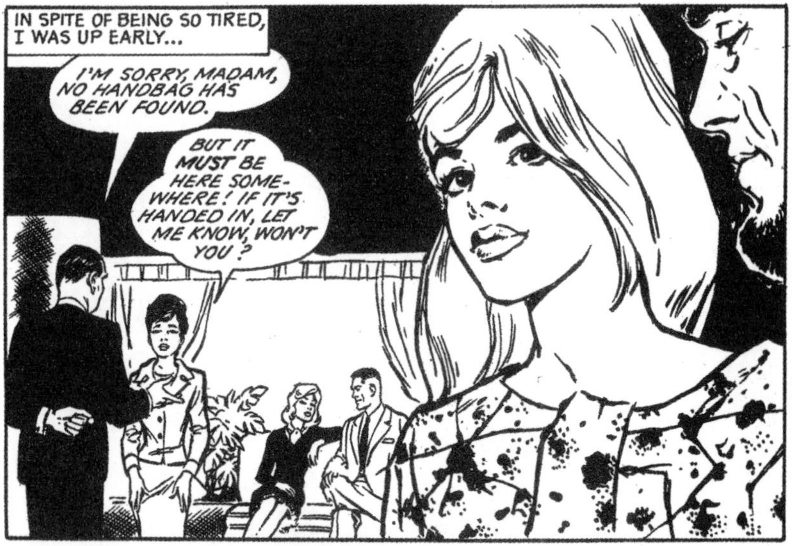
IN SPITE OF BEING SO TIRED, I WAS UP EARLY...
I'M SORRY, MADAM, NO HANDBAG HAS BEEN FOUND.
BUT IT MUST BE HERE SOME-WHERE! IF IT'S HANDED IN, LET ME KNOW, WON'T YOU?

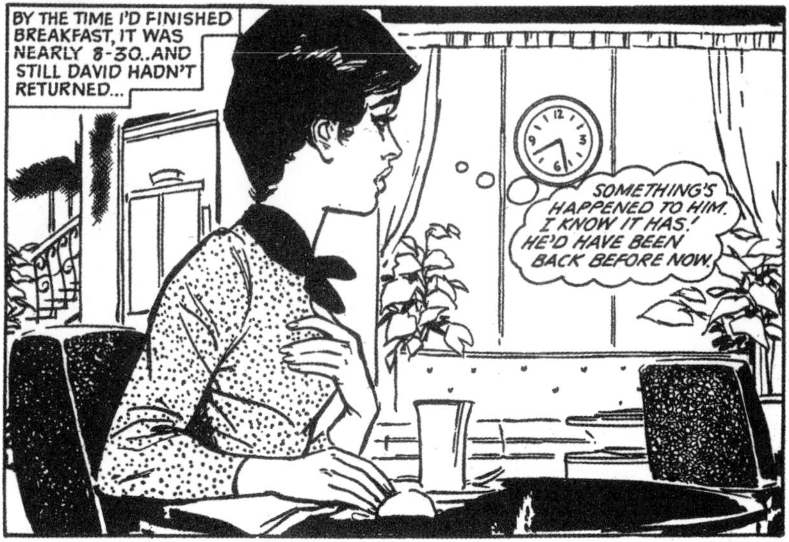
BY THE TIME I'D FINISHED BREAKFAST, IT WAS NEARLY 8-30..AND STILL DAVID HADN'T RETURNED...
SOMETHING'S HAPPENED TO HIM. I KNOW IT HAS! HE'D HAVE BEEN BACK BEFORE NOW.

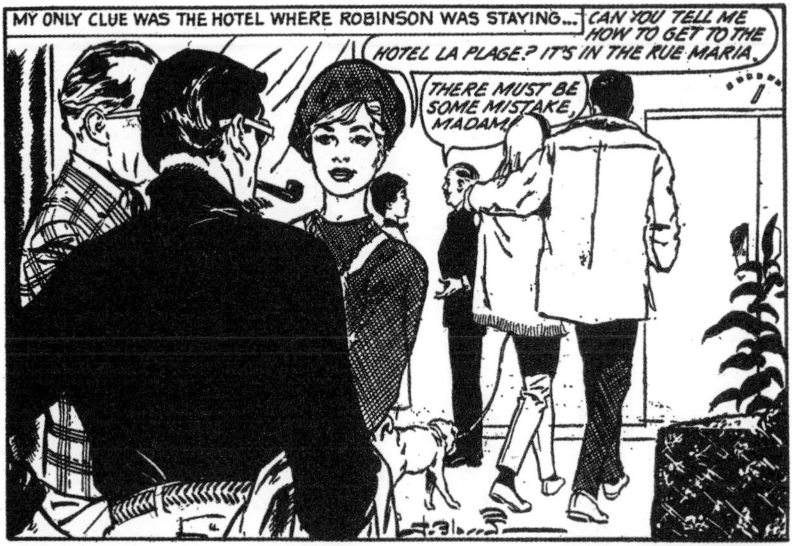
MY ONLY CLUE WAS THE HOTEL WHERE ROBINSON WAS STAYING...
CAN YOU TELL ME HOW TO GET TO THE HOTEL LA PLAGE? IT'S IN THE RUE MARIA.
THERE MUST BE SOME MISTAKE, MADAM!

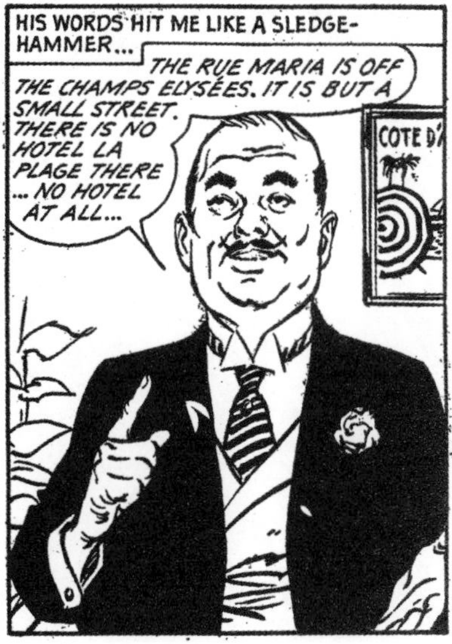
HIS WORDS HIT ME LIKE A SLEDGE-HAMMER...
THE RUE MARIA IS OFF THE CHAMPS ELYSÉES. IT IS BUT A SMALL STREET. THERE IS NO HOTEL LA PLAGE THERE ... NO HOTEL AT ALL...
COTE D'

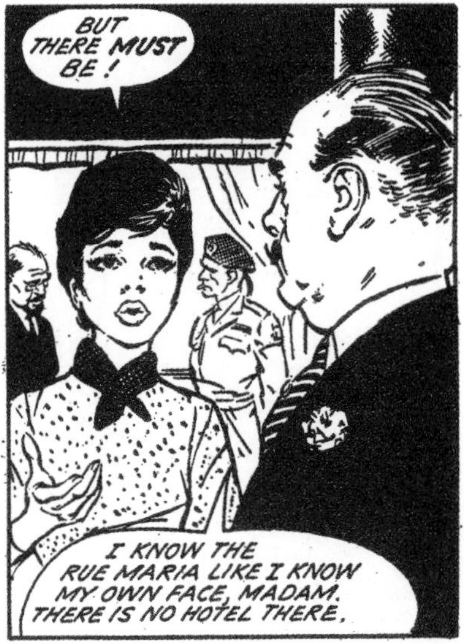
BUT THERE MUST BE!
I KNOW THE RUE MARIA LIKE I KNOW MY OWN FACE, MADAM. THERE IS NO HOTEL THERE.

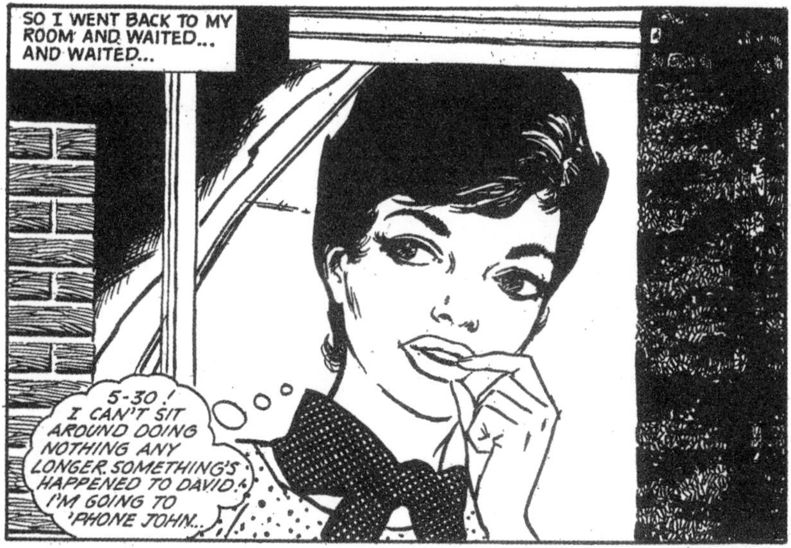
SO I WENT BACK TO MY ROOM AND WAITED... AND WAITED...
5-30! I CAN'T SIT AROUND DOING NOTHING ANY LONGER. SOMETHING'S HAPPENED TO DAVID! I'M GOING TO 'PHONE JOHN...

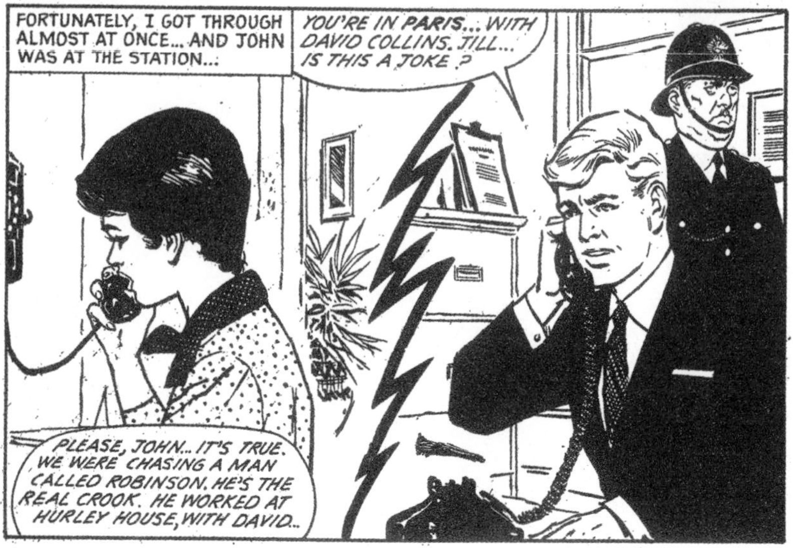
FORTUNATELY, I GOT THROUGH ALMOST AT ONCE... AND JOHN WAS AT THE STATION...
YOU'RE IN PARIS... WITH DAVID COLLINS, JILL... IS THIS A JOKE?
PLEASE, JOHN... IT'S TRUE. WE WERE CHASING A MAN CALLED ROBINSON. HE'S THE REAL CROOK. HE WORKED AT HURLEY HOUSE, WITH DAVID...

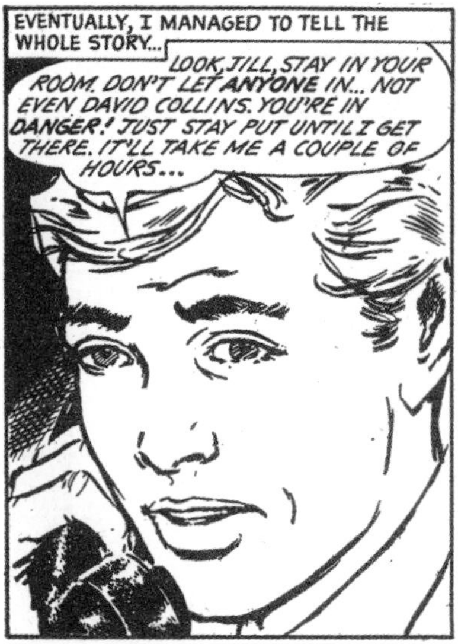
EVENTUALLY, I MANAGED TO TELL THE WHOLE STORY...
LOOK, JILL, STAY IN YOUR ROOM. DON'T LET ANYONE IN... NOT EVEN DAVID COLLINS. YOU'RE IN DANGER! JUST STAY PUT UNTIL I GET THERE. IT'LL TAKE ME A COUPLE OF HOURS...

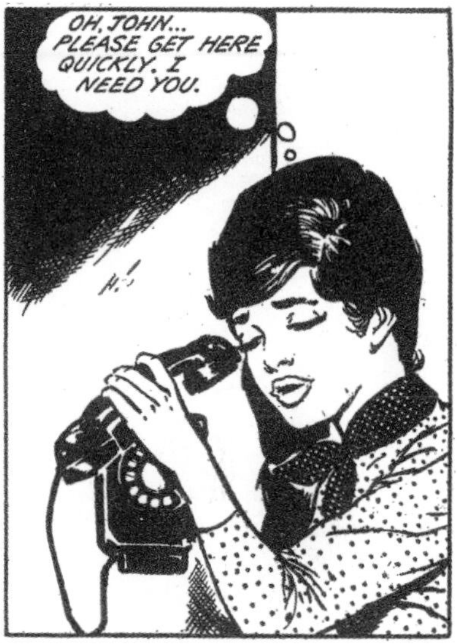
OH, JOHN... PLEASE GET HERE QUICKLY. I NEED YOU.

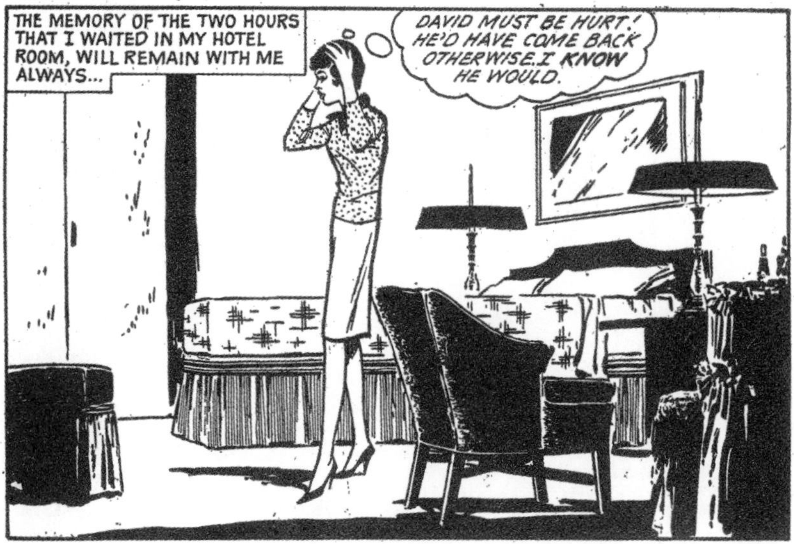
THE MEMORY OF THE TWO HOURS THAT I WAITED IN MY HOTEL ROOM, WILL REMAIN WITH ME ALWAYS...
DAVID MUST BE HURT! HE'D HAVE COME BACK OTHERWISE. I KNOW HE WOULD.

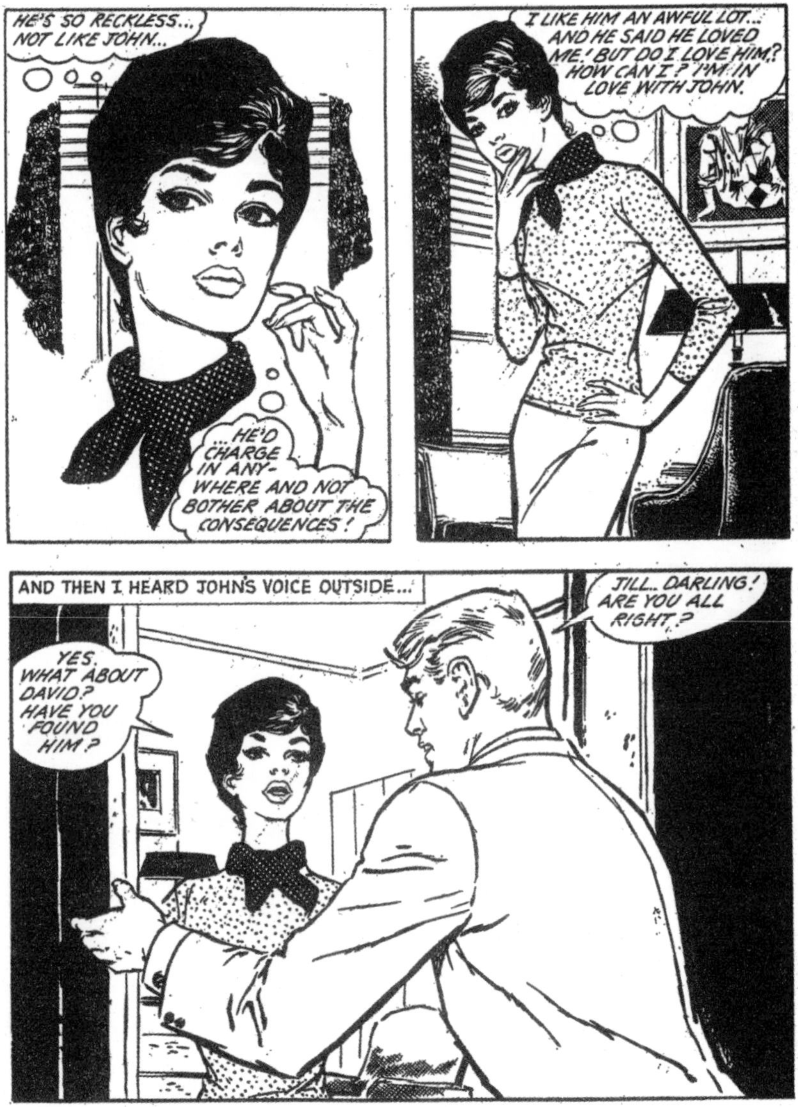
HE'S SO RECKLESS... NOT LIKE JOHN...
...HE'D CHARGE IN ANY-WHERE AND NOT BOTHER ABOUT THE CONSEQUENCES!
I LIKE HIM AN AWFUL LOT... AND HE SAID HE LOVED ME! BUT DO I LOVE HIM? HOW CAN I? I'M IN LOVE WITH JOHN.
AND THEN I HEARD JOHN'S VOICE OUTSIDE...
JILL.. DARLING! ARE YOU ALL RIGHT?
YES. WHAT ABOUT DAVID? HAVE YOU FOUND HIM?

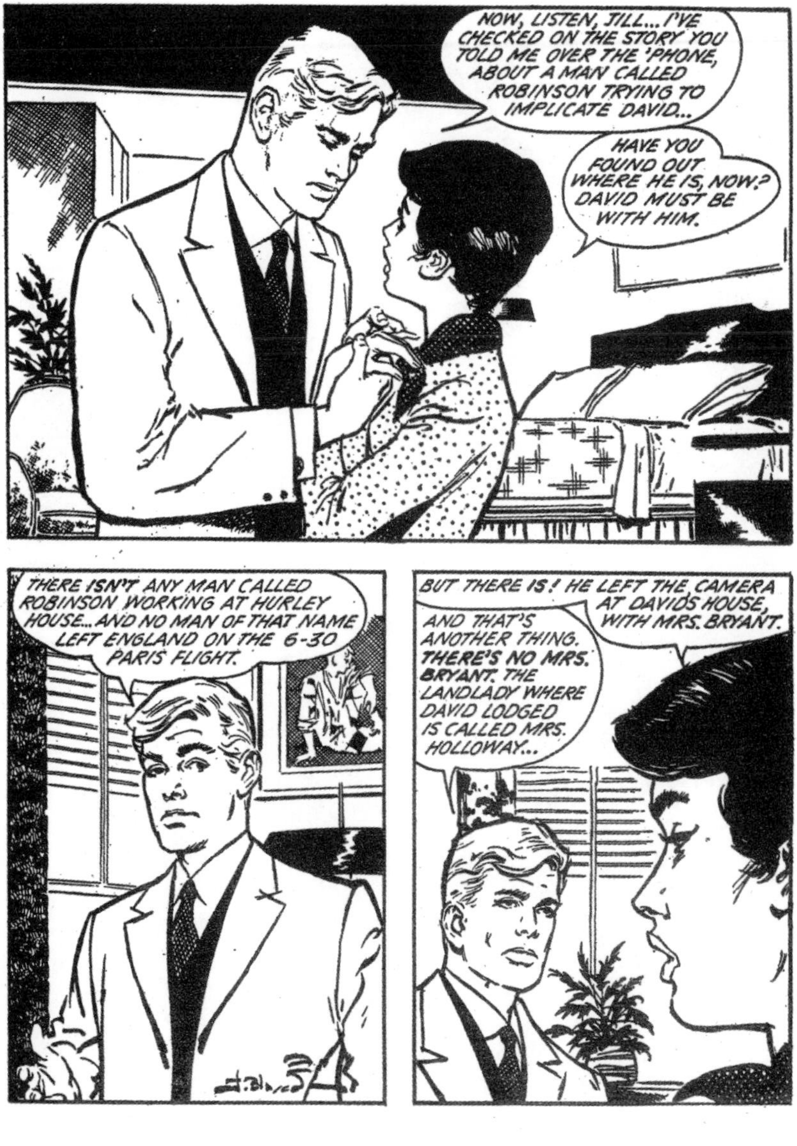
NOW, LISTEN, JILL... I'VE CHECKED ON THE STORY YOU TOLD ME OVER THE 'PHONE, ABOUT A MAN CALLED ROBINSON TRYING TO IMPLICATE DAVID...
HAVE YOU FOUND OUT WHERE HE IS, NOW? DAVID MUST BE WITH HIM.
THERE ISN'T ANY MAN CALLED ROBINSON WORKING AT HURLEY HOUSE... AND NO MAN OF THAT NAME LEFT ENGLAND ON THE 6-30 PARIS FLIGHT.
BUT THERE IS! HE LEFT THE CAMERA AT DAVID'S HOUSE, WITH MRS. BRYANT.
AND THAT'S ANOTHER THING. THERE'S NO MRS. BRYANT. THE LANDLADY WHERE DAVID LODGED IS CALLED MRS. HOLLOWAY...

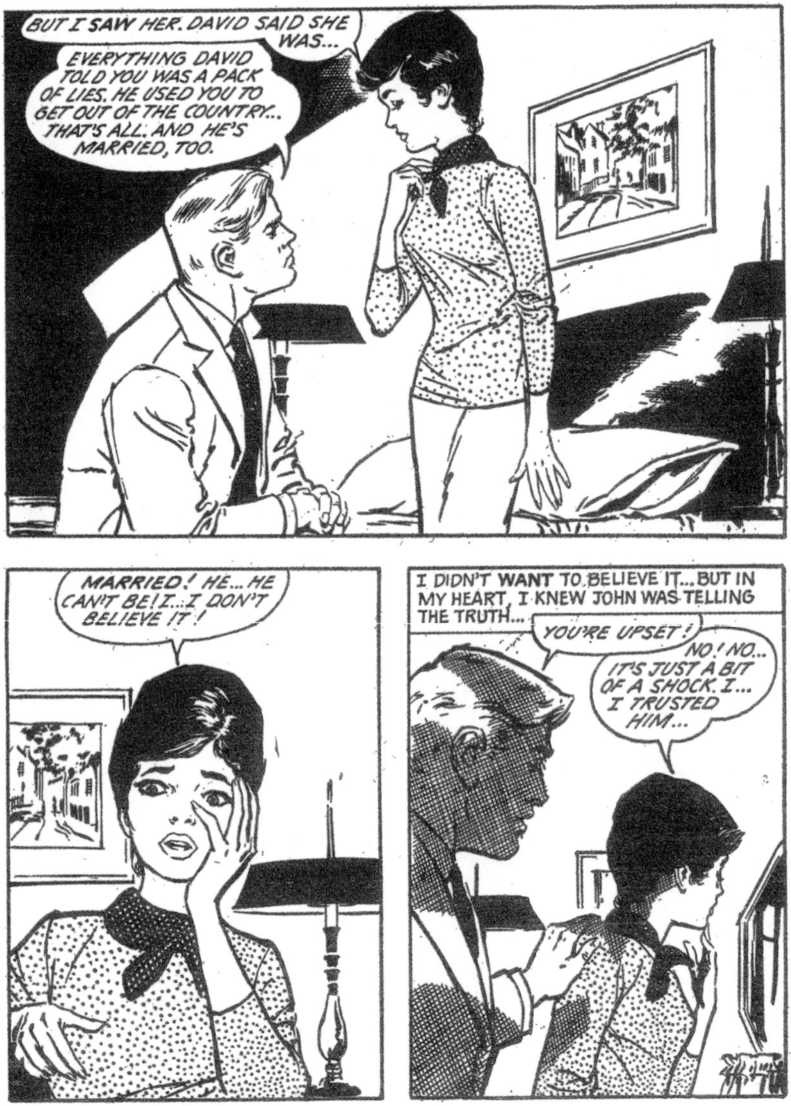
BUT I SAW HER. DAVID SAID SHE WAS...
EVERYTHING DAVID TOLD YOU WAS A PACK OF LIES. HE USED YOU TO GET OUT OF THE COUNTRY... THAT'S ALL. AND HE'S MARRIED, TOO.
MARRIED! HE... HE CAN'T BE! I... I DON'T BELIEVE IT!
I DIDN'T WANT TO BELIEVE IT... BUT IN MY HEART, I KNEW JOHN WAS TELLING THE TRUTH...
YOU'RE UPSET!
NO! NO... IT'S JUST A BIT OF A SHOCK. I... I TRUSTED HIM...

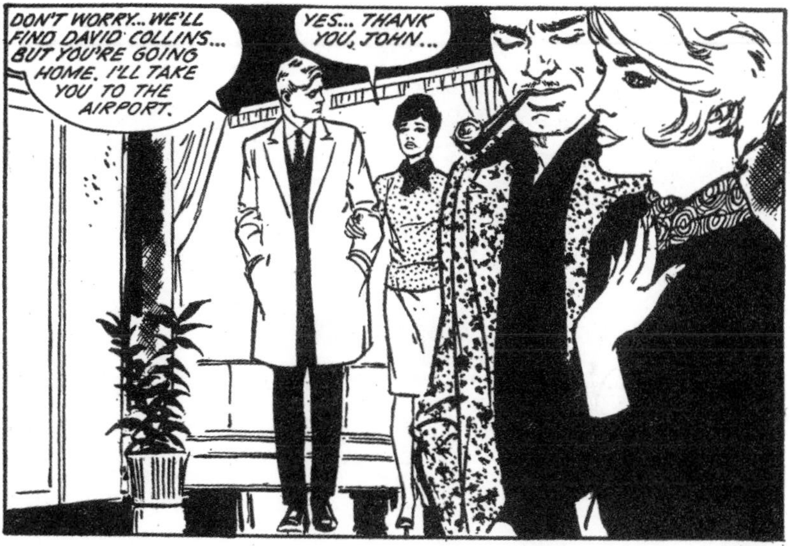
DON'T WORRY... WE'LL FIND DAVID COLLINS... BUT YOU'RE GOING HOME. I'LL TAKE YOU TO THE AIRPORT.
YES... THANK YOU, JOHN...

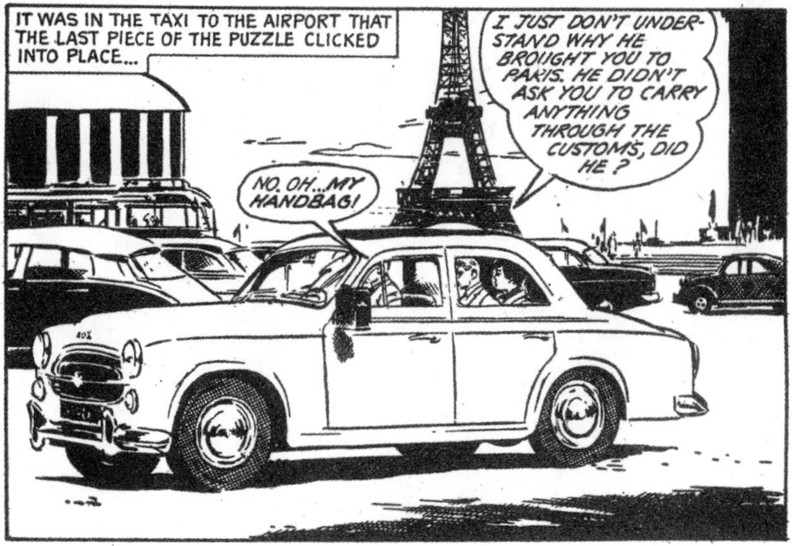
IT WAS IN THE TAXI TO THE AIRPORT THAT THE LAST PIECE OF THE PUZZLE CLICKED INTO PLACE...
I JUST DON'T UNDERSTAND WHY HE BROUGHT YOU TO PARIS. HE DIDN'T ASK YOU TO CARRY ANYTHING THROUGH THE CUSTOMS, DID HE?
NO. OH... MY HANDBAG!

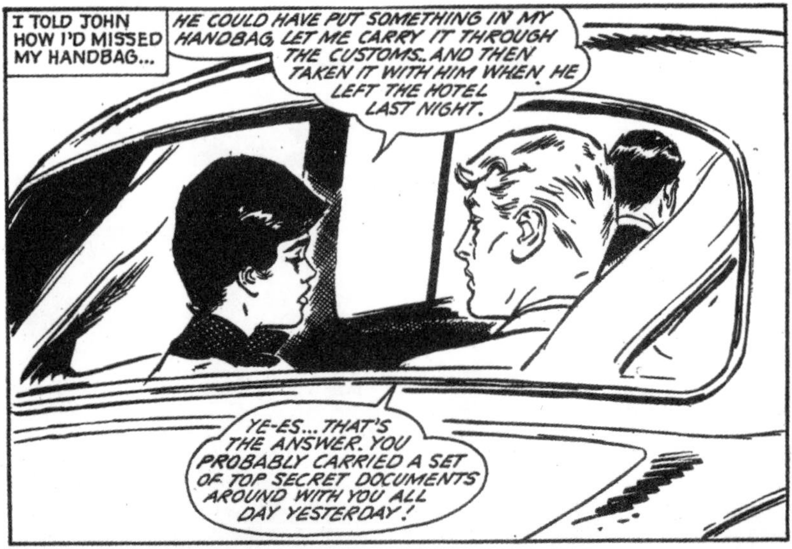
I TOLD JOHN HOW I'D MISSED MY HANDBAG...
HE COULD HAVE PUT SOMETHING IN MY HANDBAG, LET ME CARRY IT THROUGH THE CUSTOMS.. AND THEN TAKEN IT WITH HIM WHEN HE LEFT THE HOTEL LAST NIGHT.
YE-ES... THAT'S THE ANSWER. YOU PROBABLY CARRIED A SET OF TOP SECRET DOCUMENTS AROUND WITH YOU ALL DAY YESTERDAY!

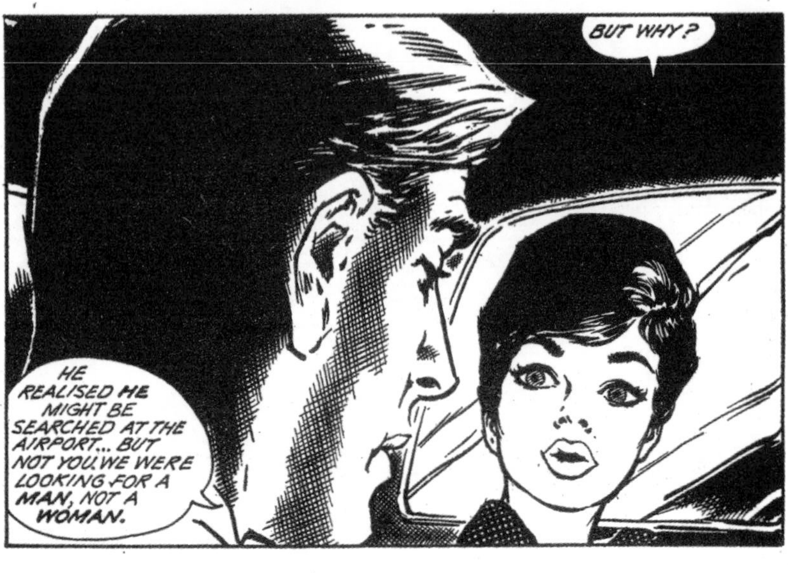
BUT WHY?
HE REALISED HE MIGHT BE SEARCHED AT THE AIRPORT... BUT NOT YOU. WE WERE LOOKING FOR A MAN, NOT A WOMAN.

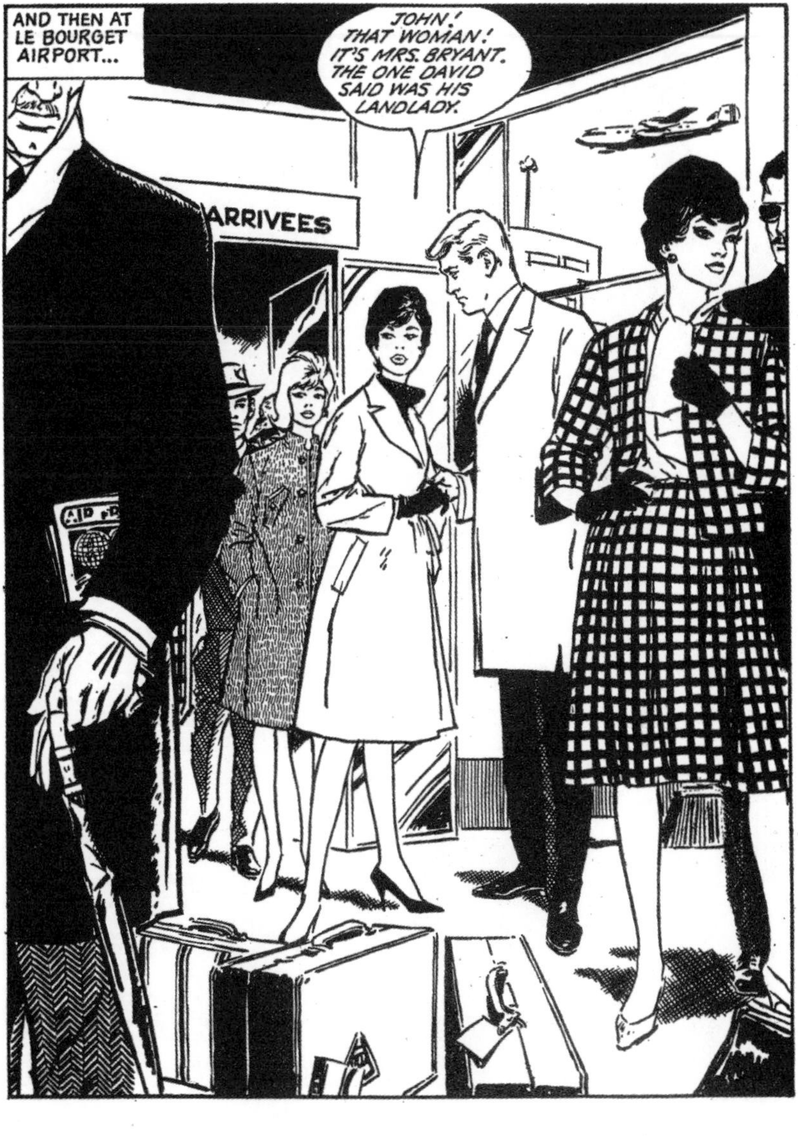
AND THEN AT LE BOURGET AIRPORT...
JOHN! THAT WOMAN! IT'S MRS. BRYANT. THE ONE DAVID SAID WAS HIS LANDLADY.
ARRIVEES

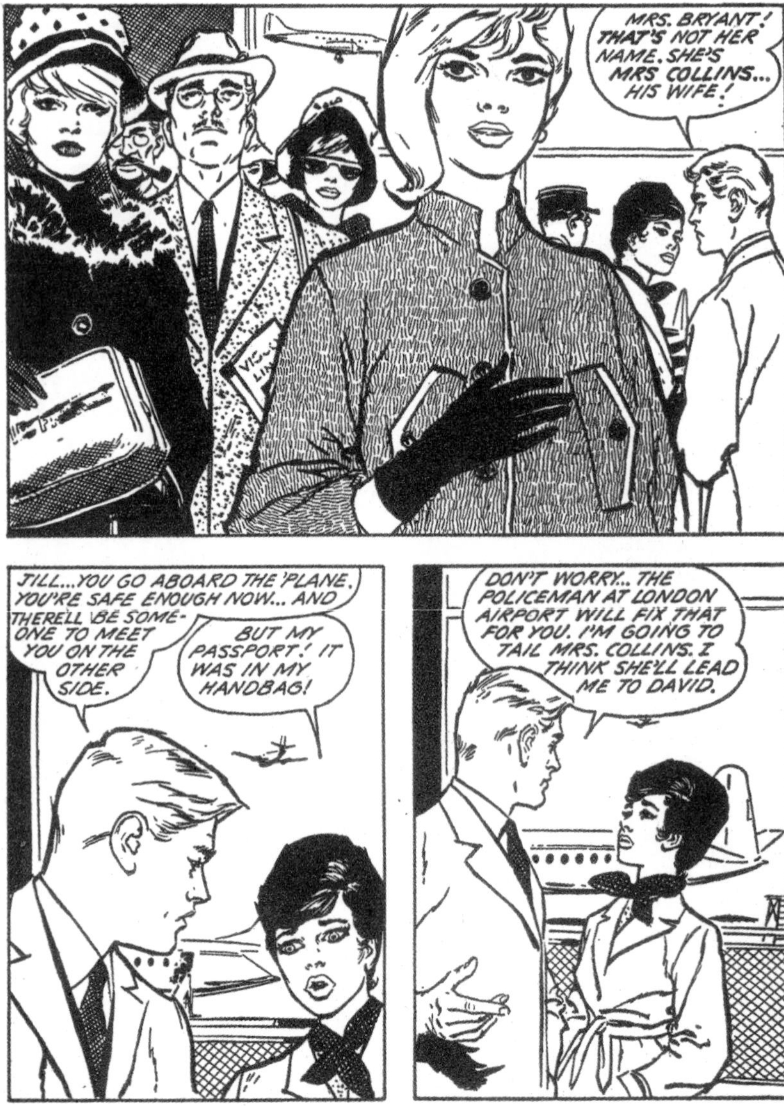
MRS. BRYANT! THAT'S NOT HER NAME. SHE'S MRS COLLINS... HIS WIFE!
JILL...YOU GO ABOARD THE 'PLANE. YOU'RE SAFE ENOUGH NOW... AND THERE'LL BE SOMEONE TO MEET YOU ON THE OTHER SIDE.
BUT MY PASSPORT! IT WAS IN MY HANDBAG!
DON'T WORRY... THE POLICEMAN AT LONDON AIRPORT WILL FIX THAT FOR YOU. I'M GOING TO TAIL MRS. COLLINS. I THINK SHE'LL LEAD ME TO DAVID.

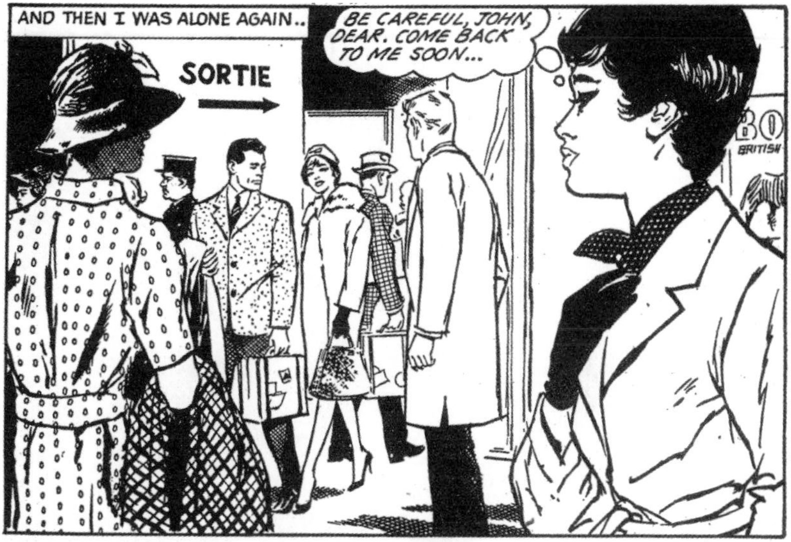
AND THEN I WAS ALONE AGAIN..
BE CAREFUL, JOHN, DEAR. COME BACK TO ME SOON...
SORTIE
BRITISH

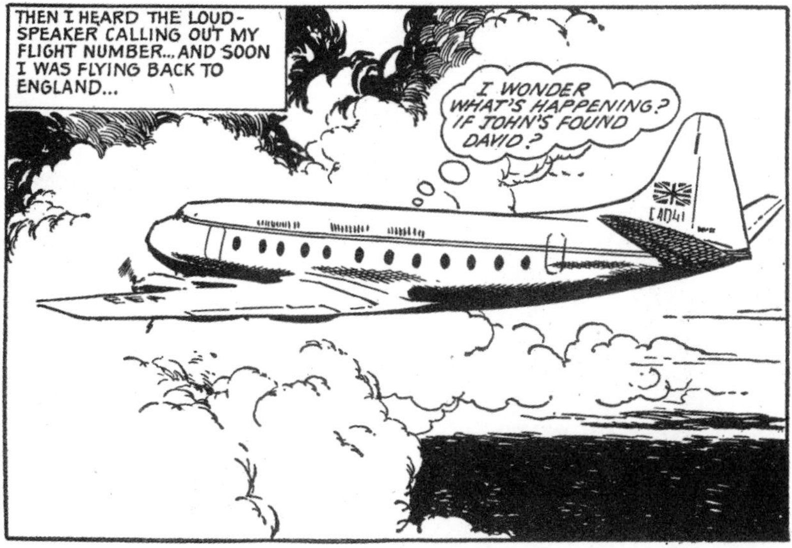
THEN I HEARD THE LOUD-SPEAKER CALLING OUT MY FLIGHT NUMBER... AND SOON I WAS FLYING BACK TO ENGLAND...
I WONDER WHAT'S HAPPENING? IF JOHN'S FOUND DAVID?

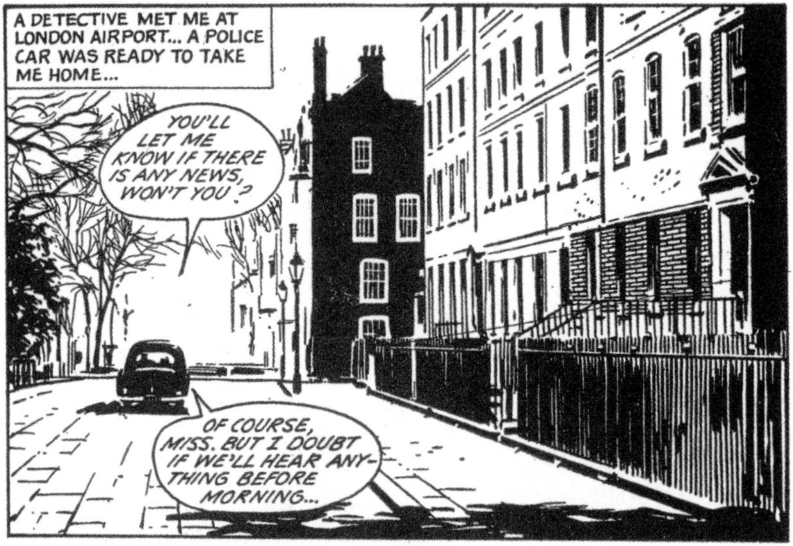
A DETECTIVE MET ME AT LONDON AIRPORT... A POLICE CAR WAS READY TO TAKE ME HOME...
YOU'LL LET ME KNOW IF THERE IS ANY NEWS, WON'T YOU?
OF COURSE, MISS. BUT I DOUBT IF WE'LL HEAR ANYTHING BEFORE MORNING...

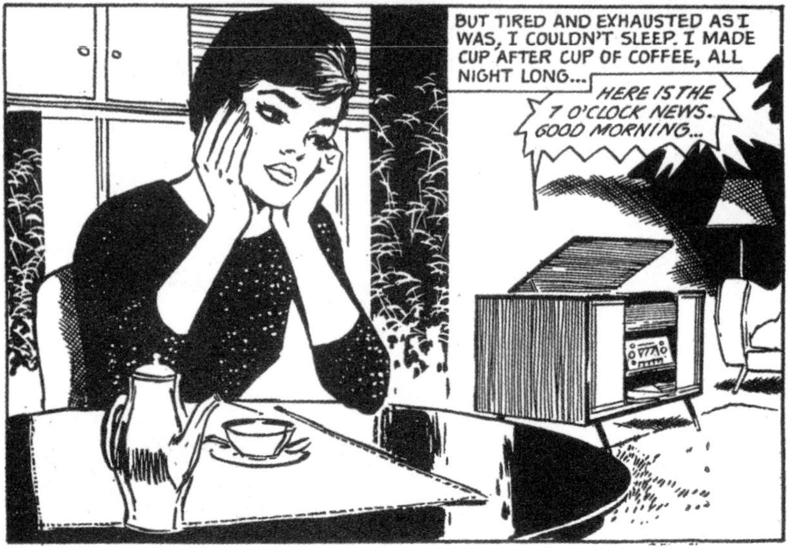
BUT TIRED AND EXHAUSTED AS I WAS, I COULDN'T SLEEP. I MADE CUP AFTER CUP OF COFFEE, ALL NIGHT LONG...
HERE IS THE 7 O'CLOCK NEWS. GOOD MORNING...

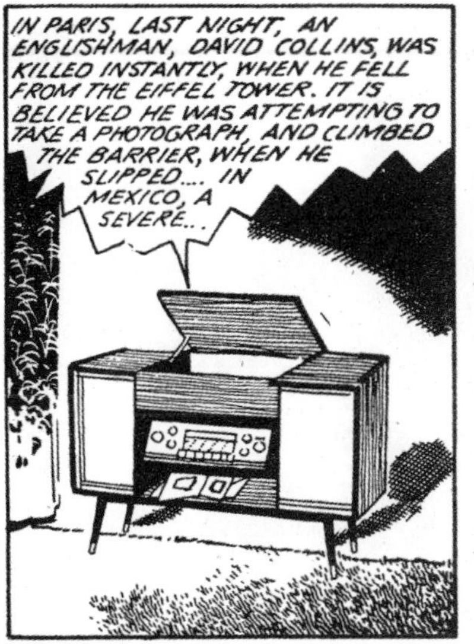
IN PARIS, LAST NIGHT, AN ENGLISHMAN, DAVID COLLINS, WAS KILLED INSTANTLY, WHEN HE FELL FROM THE EIFFEL TOWER. IT IS BELIEVED HE WAS ATTEMPTING TO TAKE A PHOTOGRAPH, AND CLIMBED THE BARRIER, WHEN HE SLIPPED.... IN MEXICO, A SEVERE...

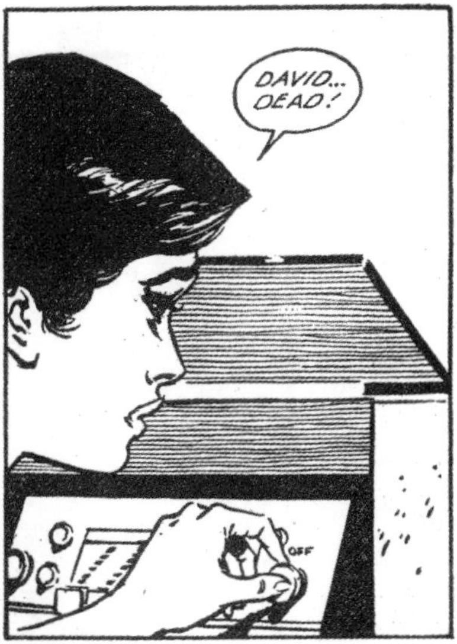
DAVID... DEAD!
OFF

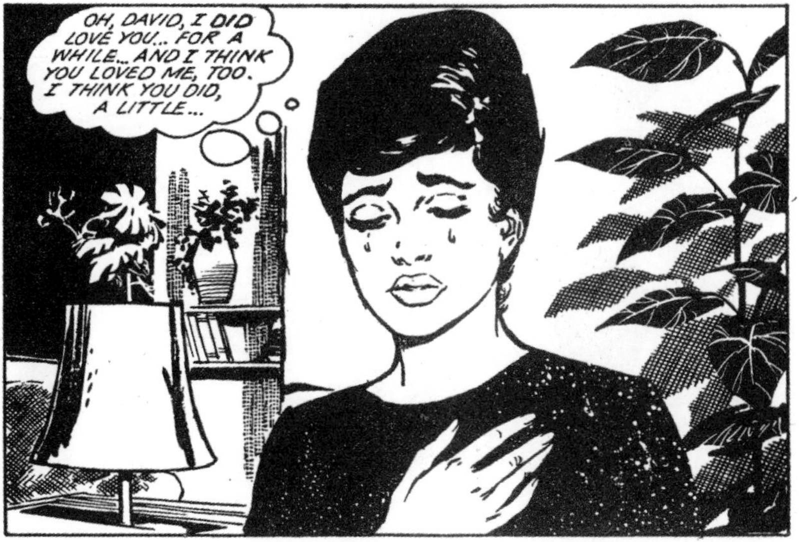
OH, DAVID, I DID LOVE YOU... FOR A WHILE... AND I THINK YOU LOVED ME, TOO. I THINK YOU DID, A LITTLE...

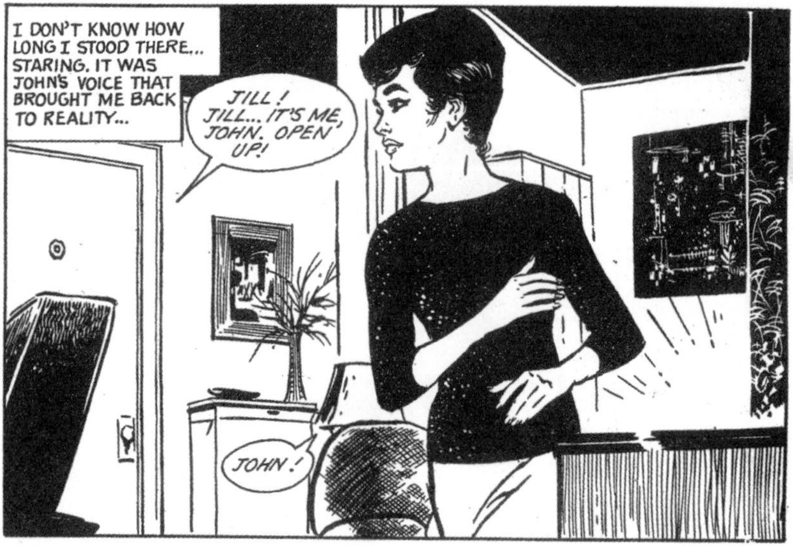
I DON'T KNOW HOW LONG I STOOD THERE... STARING. IT WAS JOHN'S VOICE THAT BROUGHT ME BACK TO REALITY...
JILL! JILL... IT'S ME, JOHN. OPEN UP!
JOHN!

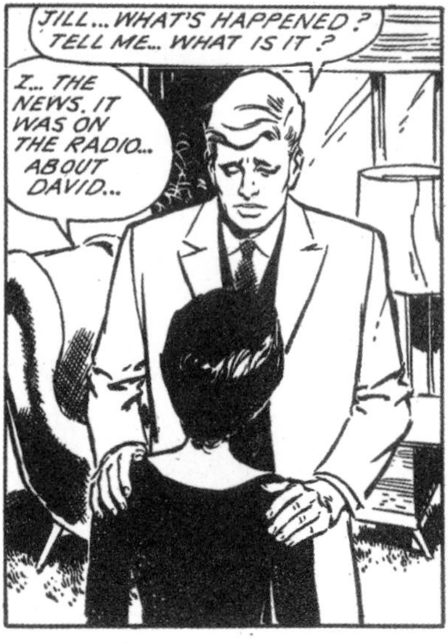
JILL... WHAT'S HAPPENED? TELL ME... WHAT IS IT?
I... THE NEWS. IT WAS ON THE RADIO... ABOUT DAVID...

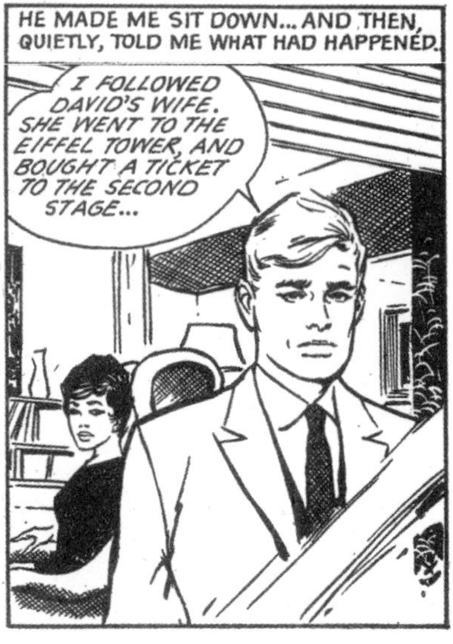
HE MADE ME SIT DOWN... AND THEN, QUIETLY, TOLD ME WHAT HAD HAPPENED.
I FOLLOWED DAVID'S WIFE. SHE WENT TO THE EIFFEL TOWER, AND BOUGHT A TICKET TO THE SECOND STAGE...

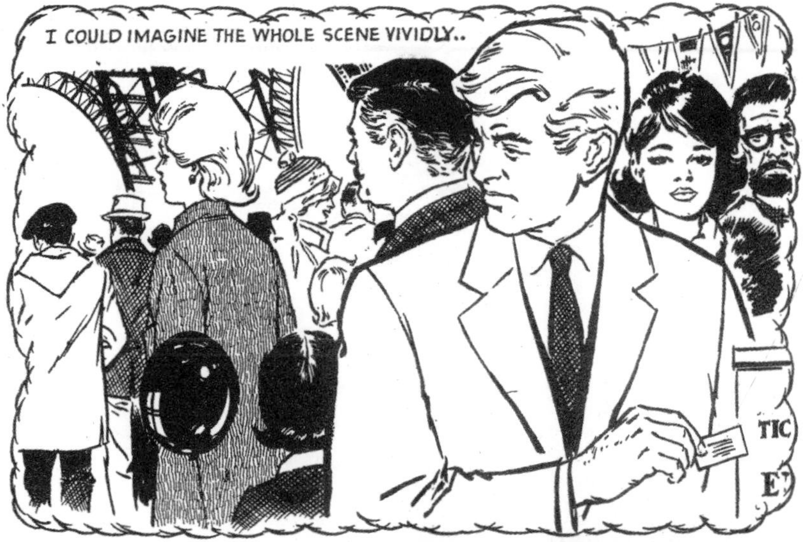
I COULD IMAGINE THE WHOLE SCENE VIVIDLY..
TIC

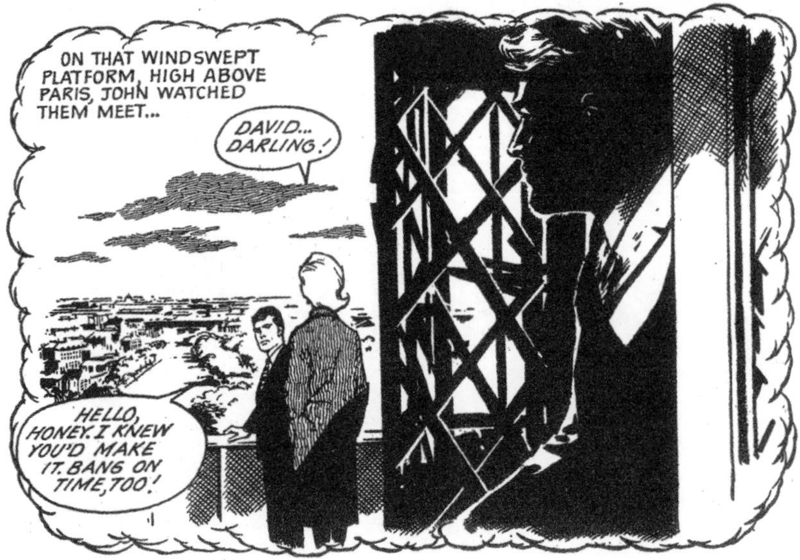
ON THAT WINDSWEPT PLATFORM, HIGH ABOVE PARIS, JOHN WATCHED THEM MEET...
DAVID... DARLING!
HELLO, HONEY. I KNEW YOU'D MAKE IT. BANG ON TIME, TOO!

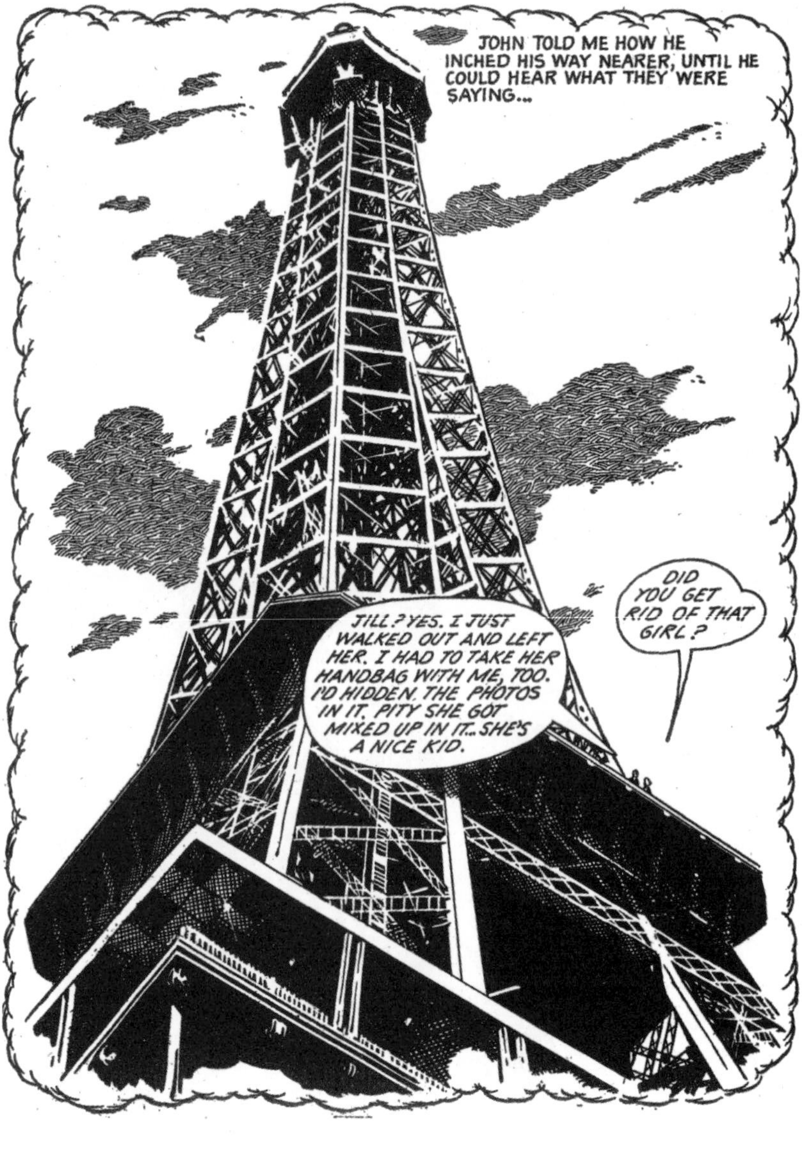
JOHN TOLD ME HOW HE INCHED HIS WAY NEARER, UNTIL HE COULD HEAR WHAT THEY WERE SAYING...
DID YOU GET RID OF THAT GIRL?
JILL? YES. I JUST WALKED OUT AND LEFT HER. I HAD TO TAKE HER HANDBAG WITH ME, TOO. I'D HIDDEN THE PHOTOS IN IT. PITY SHE GOT MIXED UP IN IT... SHE'S A NICE KID.

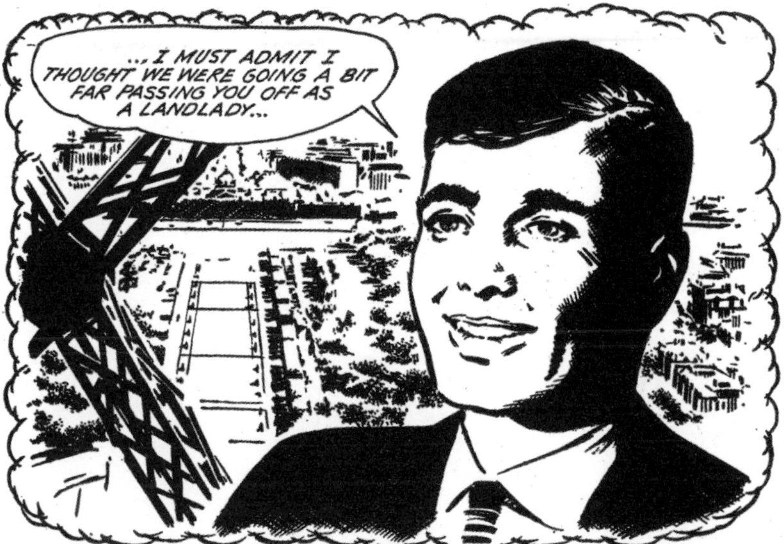
...I MUST ADMIT I THOUGHT WE WERE GOING A BIT FAR PASSING YOU OFF AS A LANDLADY...

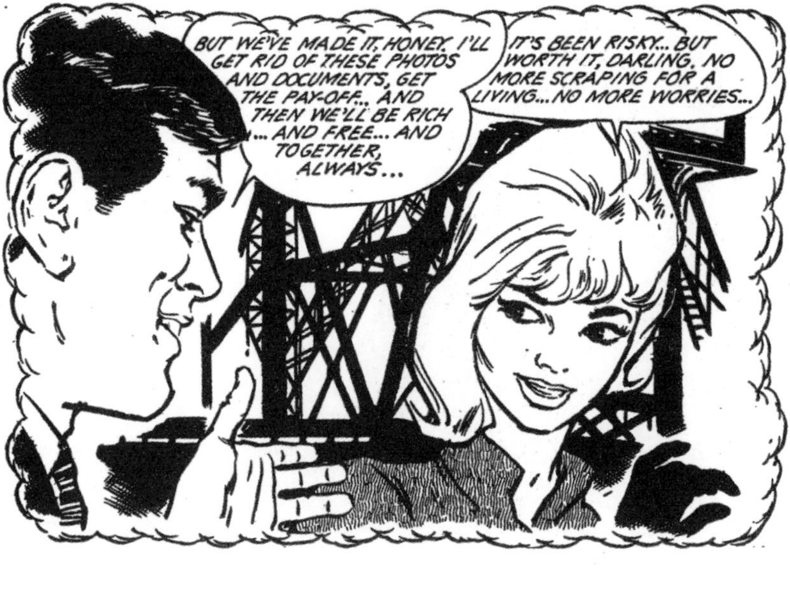
BUT WE'VE MADE IT, HONEY. I'LL GET RID OF THESE PHOTOS AND DOCUMENTS, GET THE PAY-OFF... AND THEN WE'LL BE RICH ... AND FREE... AND TOGETHER, ALWAYS...
IT'S BEEN RISKY... BUT WORTH IT, DARLING. NO MORE SCRAPING FOR A LIVING... NO MORE WORRIES...

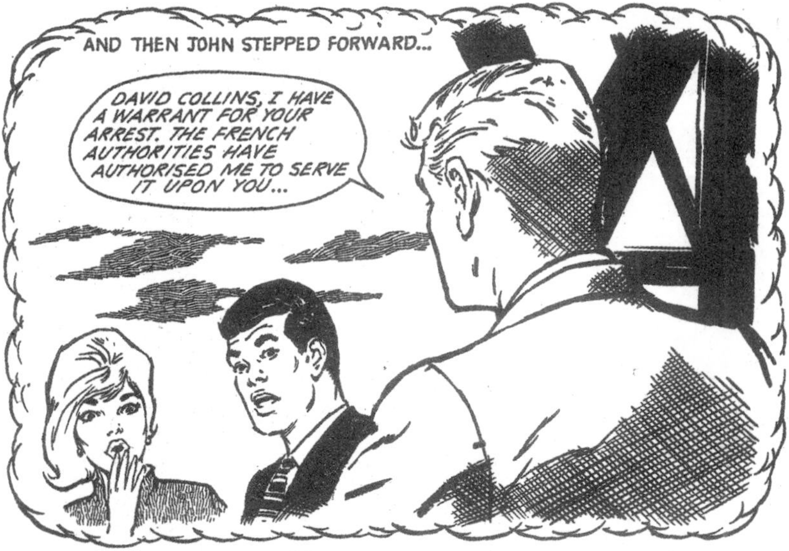
AND THEN JOHN STEPPED FORWARD...
DAVID COLLINS, I HAVE A WARRANT FOR YOUR ARREST. THE FRENCH AUTHORITIES HAVE AUTHORISED ME TO SERVE IT UPON YOU...

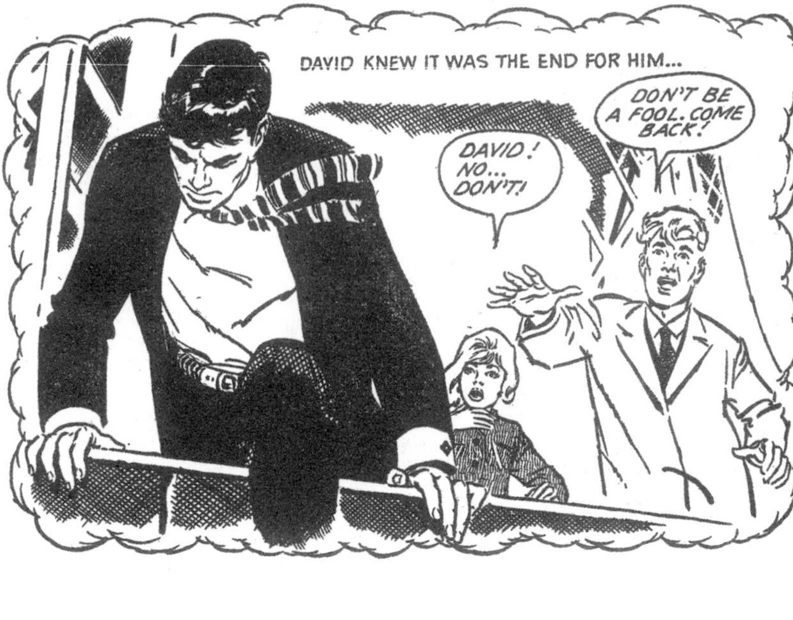
DAVID KNEW IT WAS THE END FOR HIM...
DAVID! NO... DON'T!
DON'T BE A FOOL. COME BACK!

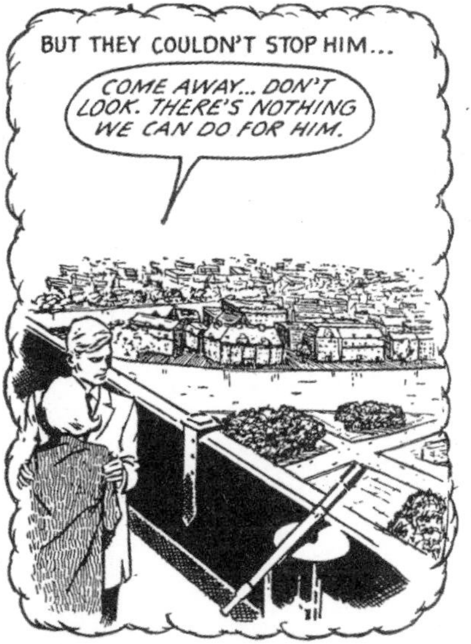
BUT THEY COULDN'T STOP HIM...
COME AWAY... DON'T LOOK. THERE'S NOTHING WE CAN DO FOR HIM.

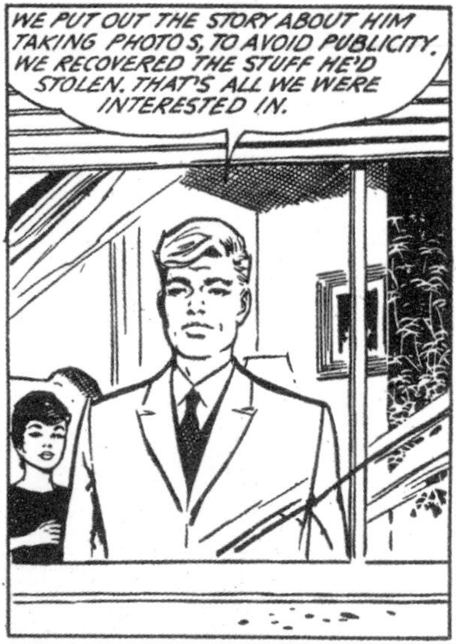
WE PUT OUT THE STORY ABOUT HIM TAKING PHOTOS, TO AVOID PUBLICITY. WE RECOVERED THE STUFF HE'D STOLEN. THAT'S ALL WE WERE INTERESTED IN.

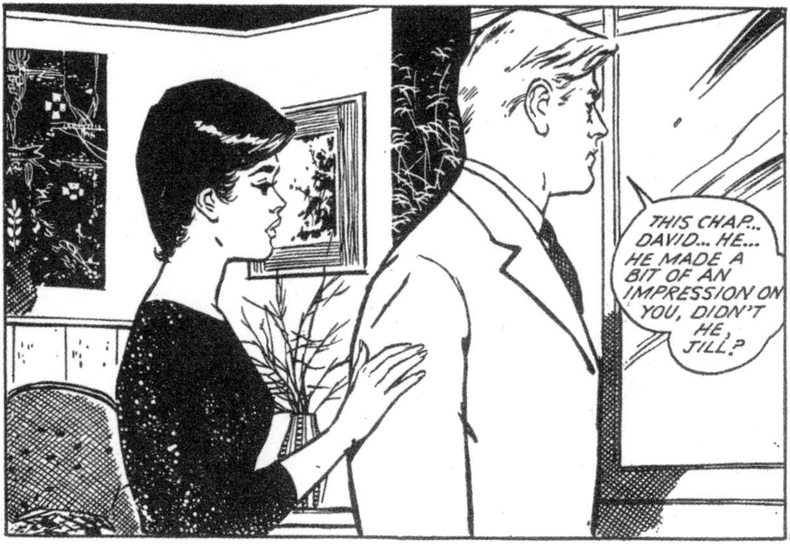
THIS CHAP... DAVID... HE... HE MADE A BIT OF AN IMPRESSION ON YOU, DIDN'T HE, JILL?

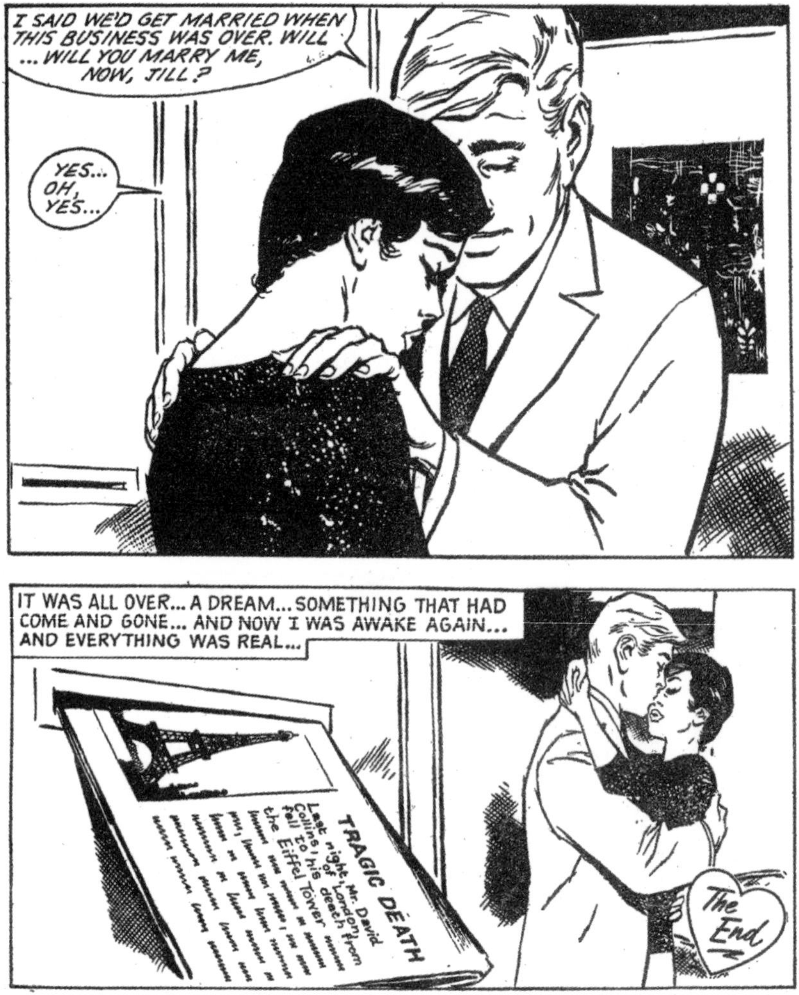
I SAID WE'D GET MARRIED WHEN THIS BUSINESS WAS OVER. WILL ... WILL YOU MARRY ME, NOW, JILL?
YES... OH, YES...
IT WAS ALL OVER... A DREAM... SOMETHING THAT HAD COME AND GONE... AND NOW I WAS AWAKE AGAIN... AND EVERYTHING WAS REAL...
TRAGIC DEATH
Last night, Mr. David Collins, of London, fell to his death from the Eiffel Tower
The End

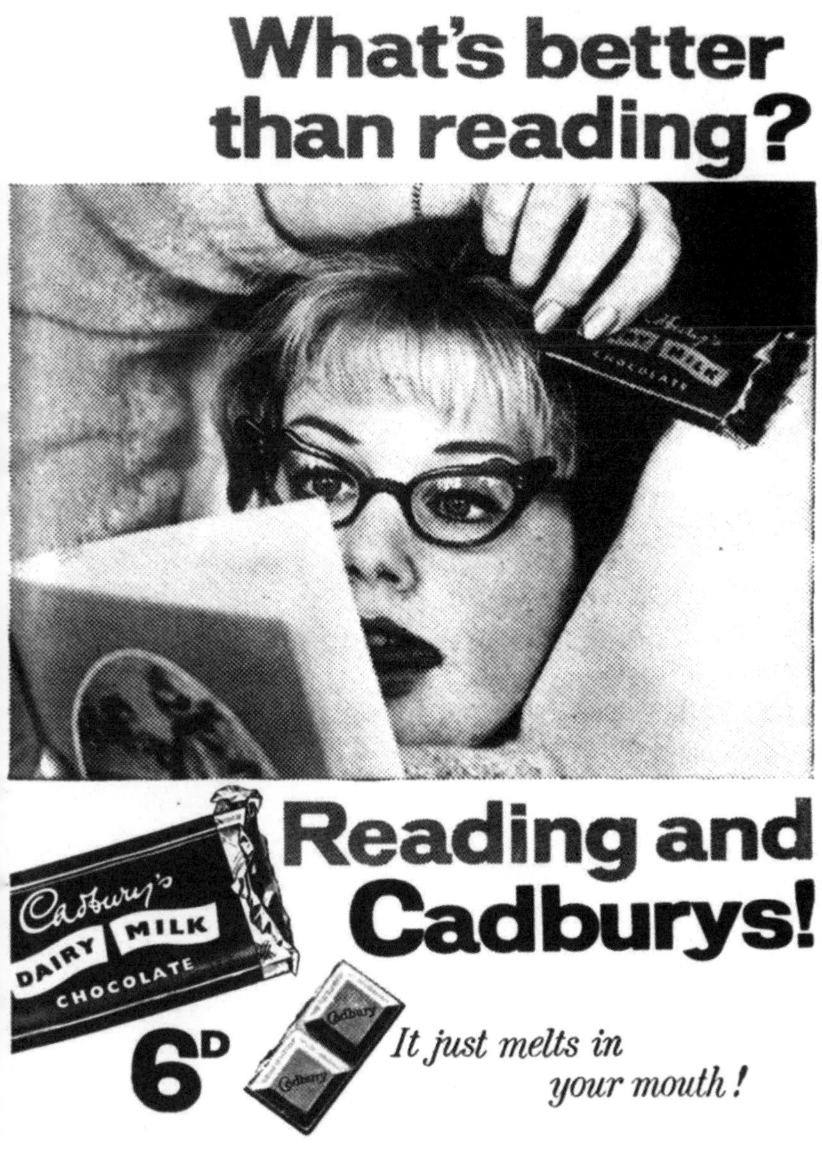
What's better than reading?
Reading and Cadburys!
Cadbury's
DAIRY MILK
CHOCOLATE
6D
It just melts in your mouth!

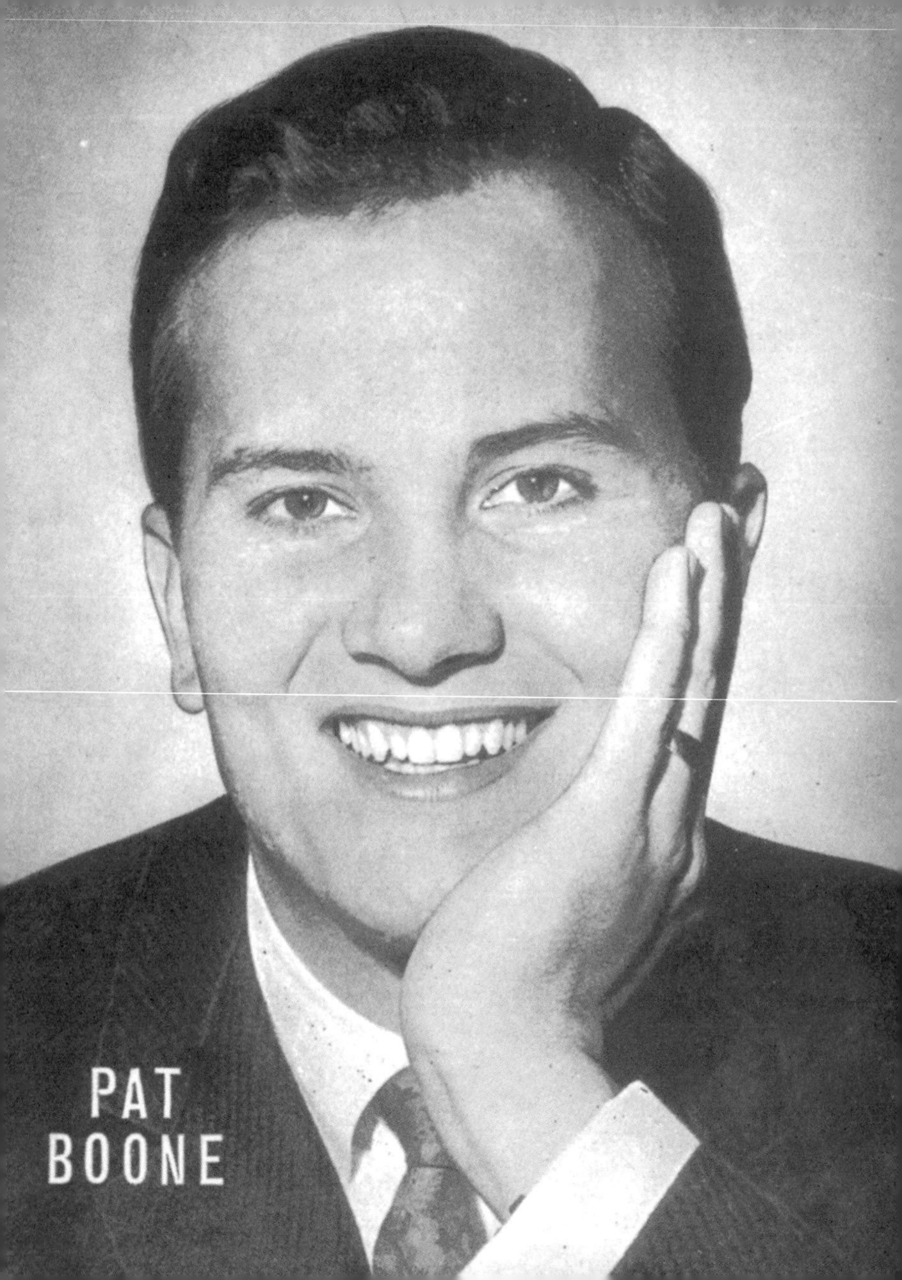
PAT
BOONE

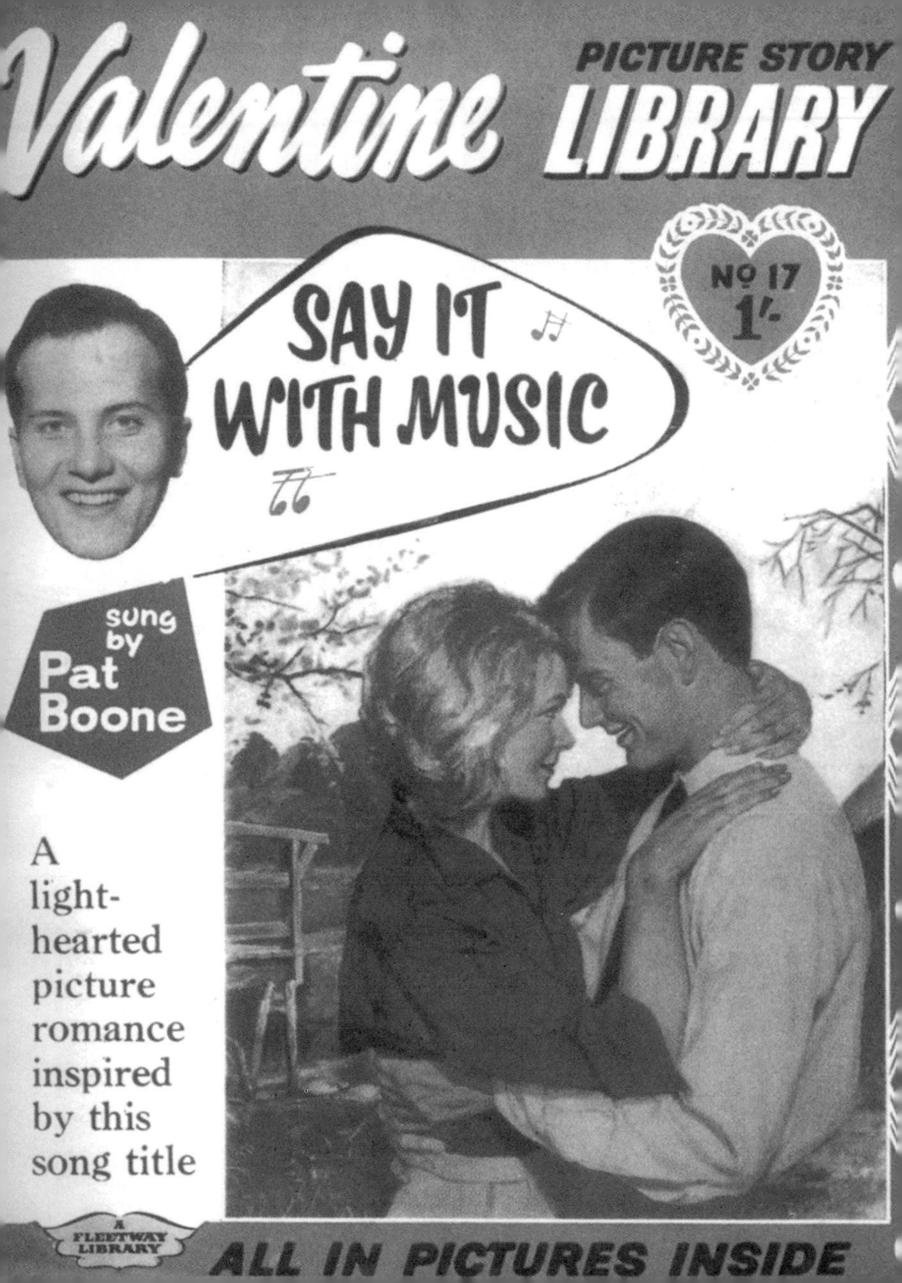

Valentine
PICTURE STORY LIBRARY
Nº 17
1/-
SAY IT WITH MUSIC
sung by Pat Boone
A light-hearted picture romance inspired by this song title
A FLEETWAY LIBRARY
ALL IN PICTURES INSIDE

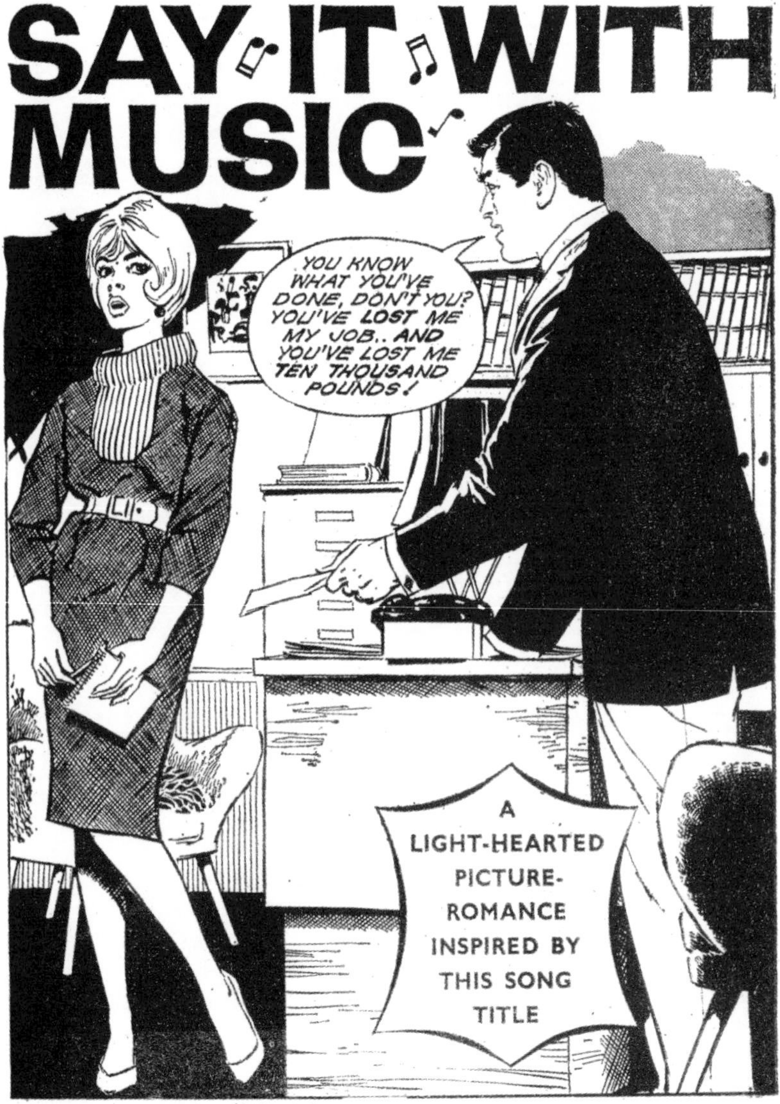
SAY IT WITH MUSIC
YOU KNOW WHAT YOU'VE DONE, DON'T YOU? YOU'VE LOST ME MY JOB.. AND YOU'VE LOST ME TEN THOUSAND POUNDS!
A LIGHT-HEARTED PICTURE-ROMANCE INSPIRED BY THIS SONG TITLE

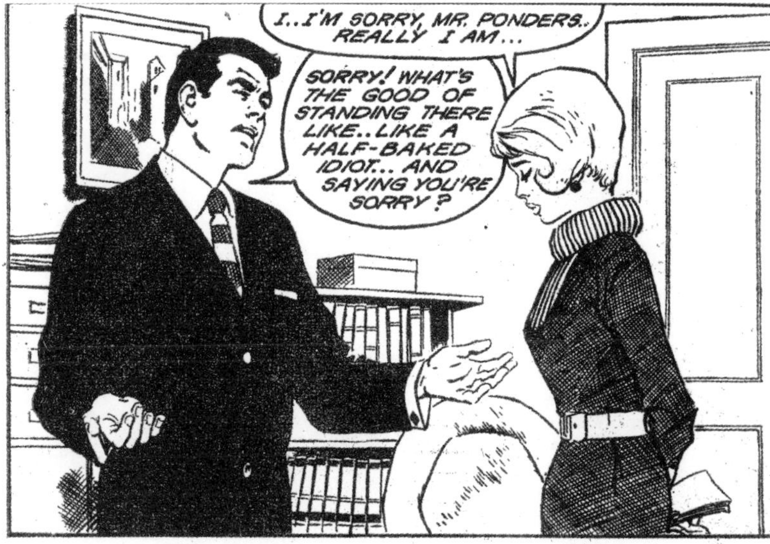
I..I'M SORRY, MR. PONDERS.. REALLY I AM...
SORRY! WHAT'S THE GOOD OF STANDING THERE LIKE..LIKE A HALF-BAKED IDIOT... AND SAYING YOU'RE SORRY?

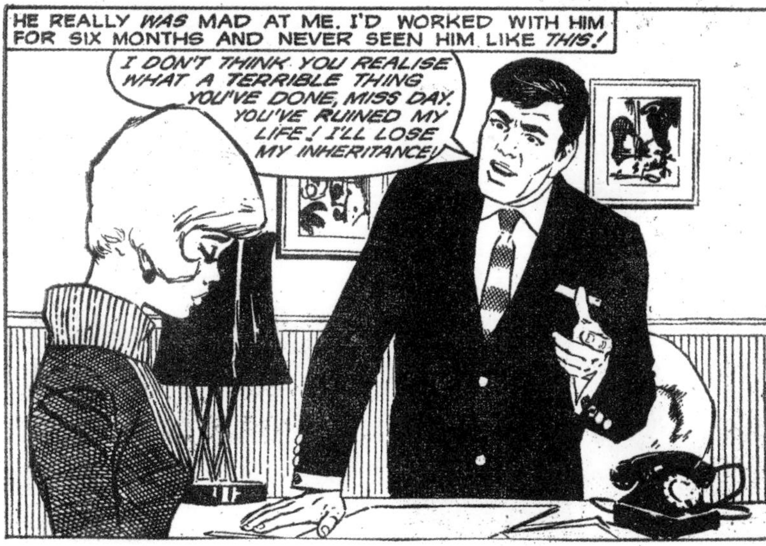
HE REALLY WAS MAD AT ME. I'D WORKED WITH HIM FOR SIX MONTHS AND NEVER SEEN HIM LIKE THIS!
I DON'T THINK YOU REALISE WHAT A TERRIBLE THING YOU'VE DONE, MISS DAY. YOU'VE RUINED MY LIFE! I'LL LOSE MY INHERITANCE!

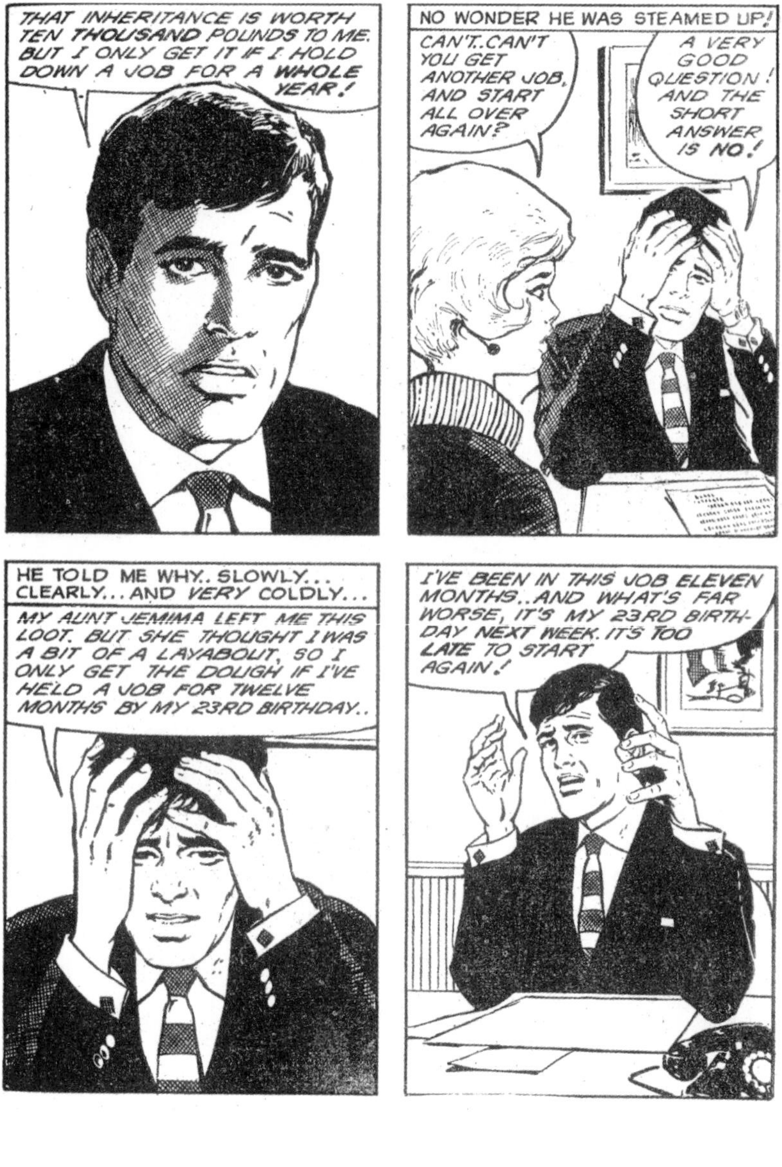
THAT INHERITANCE IS WORTH TEN THOUSAND POUNDS TO ME. BUT I ONLY GET IT IF I HOLD DOWN A JOB FOR A WHOLE YEAR!
NO WONDER HE WAS STEAMED UP!
CAN'T..CAN'T YOU GET ANOTHER JOB, AND START ALL OVER AGAIN?
A VERY GOOD QUESTION! AND THE SHORT ANSWER IS NO!
HE TOLD ME WHY.. SLOWLY... CLEARLY... AND VERY COLDLY...
MY AUNT JEMIMA LEFT ME THIS LOOT. BUT SHE THOUGHT I WAS A BIT OF A LAYABOUT, SO I ONLY GET THE DOUGH IF I'VE HELD A JOB FOR TWELVE MONTHS BY MY 23RD BIRTHDAY..
I'VE BEEN IN THIS JOB ELEVEN MONTHS..AND WHAT'S FAR WORSE, IT'S MY 23RD BIRTHDAY NEXT WEEK. IT'S TOO LATE TO START AGAIN!

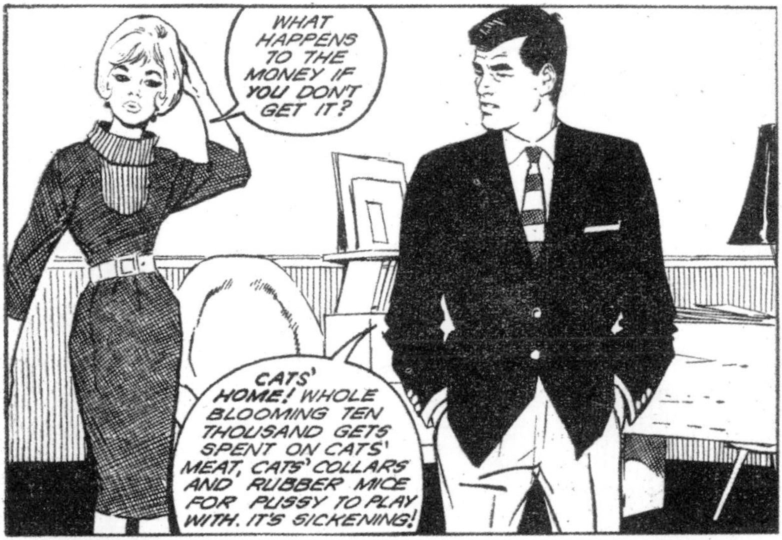
WHAT HAPPENS TO THE MONEY IF YOU DON'T GET IT?
CATS' HOME! WHOLE BLOOMING TEN THOUSAND GETS SPENT ON CATS' MEAT, CATS' COLLARS AND RUBBER MICE FOR PUSSY TO PLAY WITH. IT'S SICKENING!

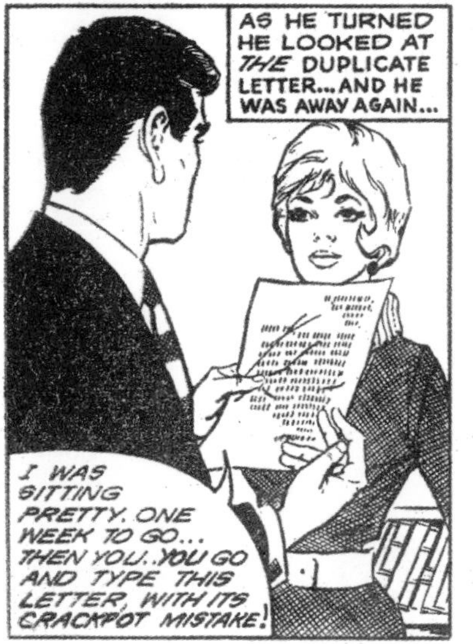
AS HE TURNED HE LOOKED AT THE DUPLICATE LETTER...AND HE WAS AWAY AGAIN...
I WAS SITTING PRETTY. ONE WEEK TO GO... THEN YOU..YOU GO AND TYPE THIS LETTER, WITH ITS CRACKPOT MISTAKE!

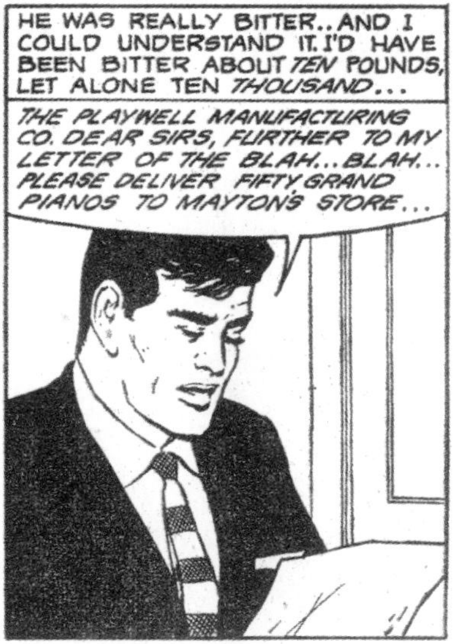
HE WAS REALLY BITTER..AND I COULD UNDERSTAND IT. I'D HAVE BEEN BITTER ABOUT TEN POUNDS, LET ALONE TEN THOUSAND...
THE PLAYWELL MANUFACTURING CO. DEAR SIRS, FURTHER TO MY LETTER OF THE BLAH...BLAH... PLEASE DELIVER FIFTY GRAND PIANOS TO MAYTON'S STORE...

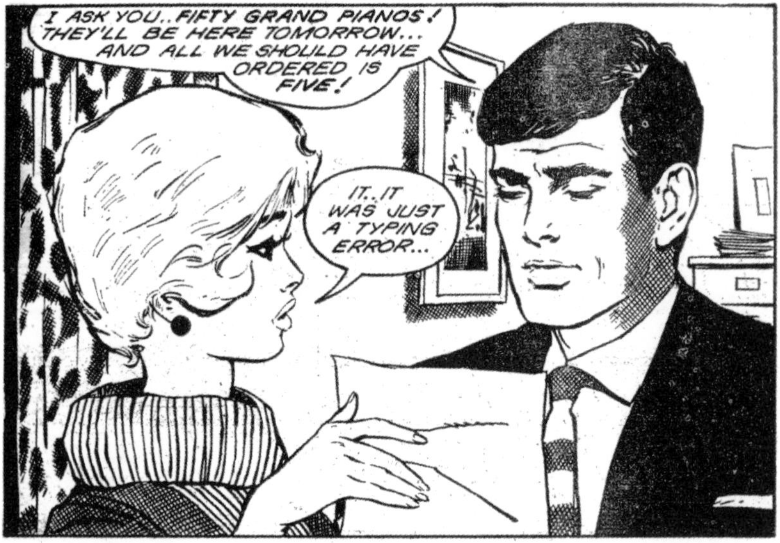
I ASK YOU.. FIFTY GRAND PIANOS! THEY'LL BE HERE TOMORROW... AND ALL WE SHOULD HAVE ORDERED IS FIVE!
IT.. IT WAS JUST A TYPING ERROR...

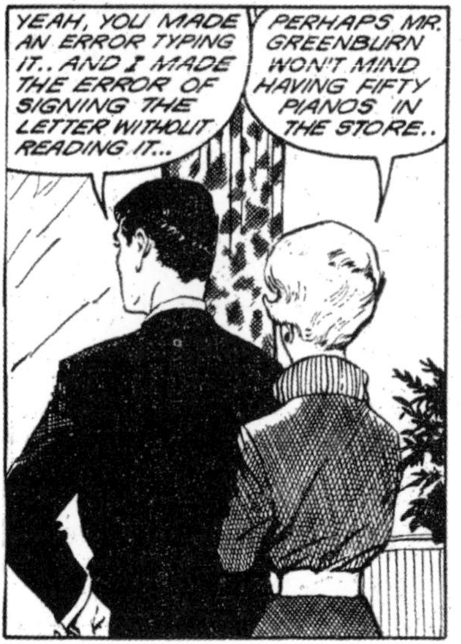
YEAH, YOU MADE AN ERROR TYPING IT.. AND I MADE THE ERROR OF SIGNING THE LETTER WITHOUT READING IT...
PERHAPS MR. GREENBURN WON'T MIND HAVING FIFTY PIANOS IN THE STORE..

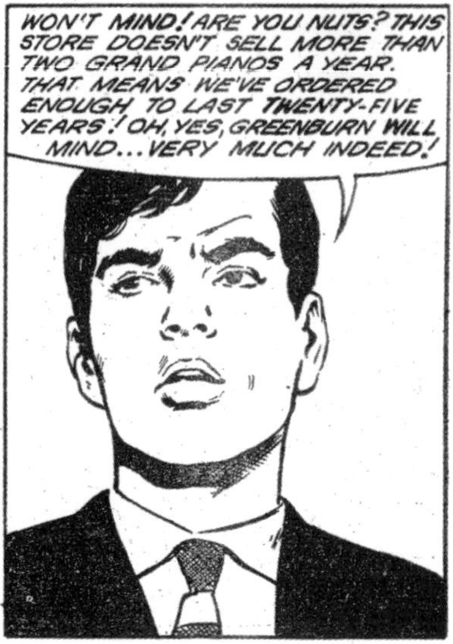
WON'T MIND! ARE YOU NUTS? THIS STORE DOESN'T SELL MORE THAN TWO GRAND PIANOS A YEAR. THAT MEANS WE'VE ORDERED ENOUGH TO LAST TWENTY-FIVE YEARS! OH, YES, GREENBURN WILL MIND... VERY MUCH INDEED!

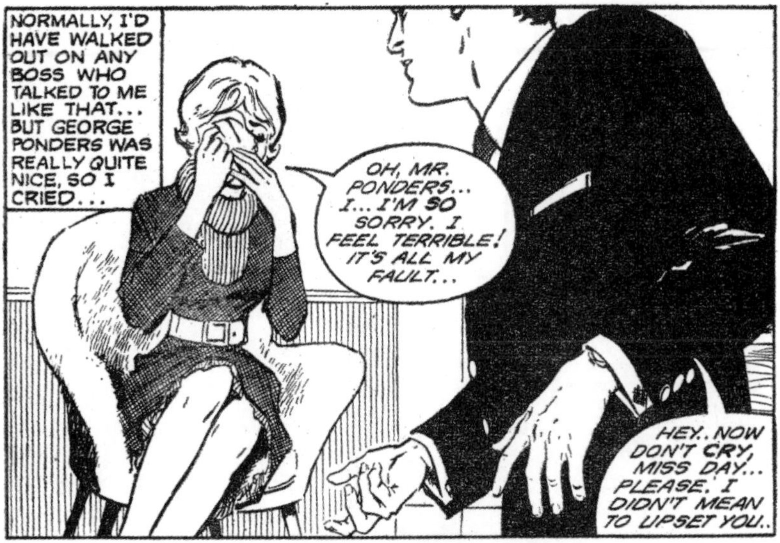
NORMALLY, I'D HAVE WALKED OUT ON ANY BOSS WHO TALKED TO ME LIKE THAT... BUT GEORGE PONDERS WAS REALLY QUITE NICE, SO I CRIED...
OH, MR. PONDERS... I... I'M SO SORRY. I FEEL TERRIBLE! IT'S ALL MY FAULT...
HEY.. NOW DON'T CRY, MISS DAY... PLEASE. I DIDN'T MEAN TO UPSET YOU..

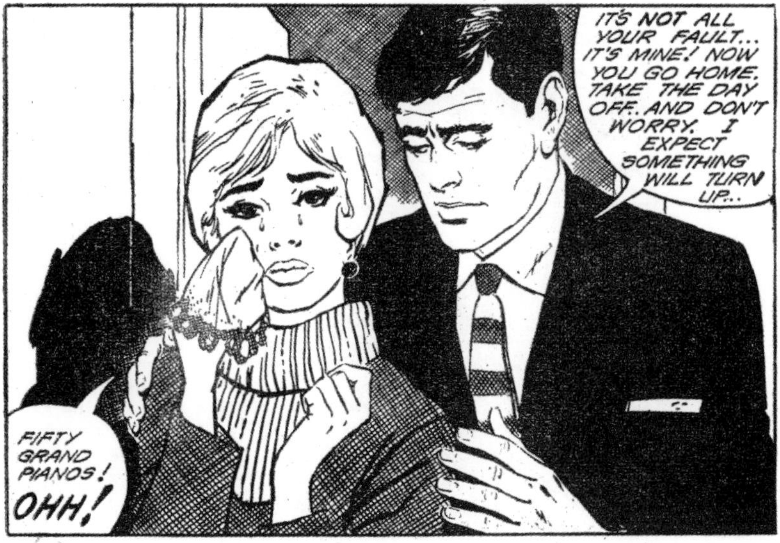
IT'S NOT ALL YOUR FAULT... IT'S MINE! NOW YOU GO HOME. TAKE THE DAY OFF. AND DON'T WORRY. I EXPECT SOMETHING WILL TURN UP...
FIFTY GRAND PIANOS! OHH!

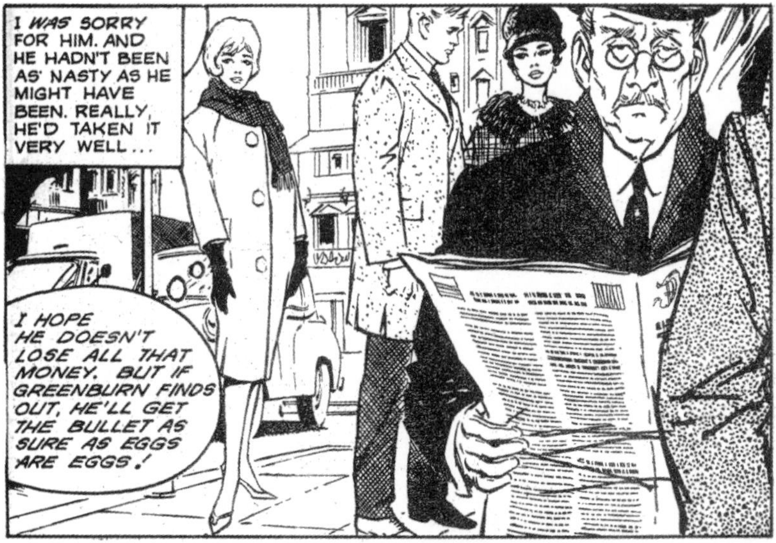
I WAS SORRY FOR HIM. AND HE HADN'T BEEN AS NASTY AS HE MIGHT HAVE BEEN. REALLY, HE'D TAKEN IT VERY WELL...
I HOPE HE DOESN'T LOSE ALL THAT MONEY. BUT IF GREENBURN FINDS OUT, HE'LL GET THE BULLET AS SURE AS EGGS ARE EGGS!

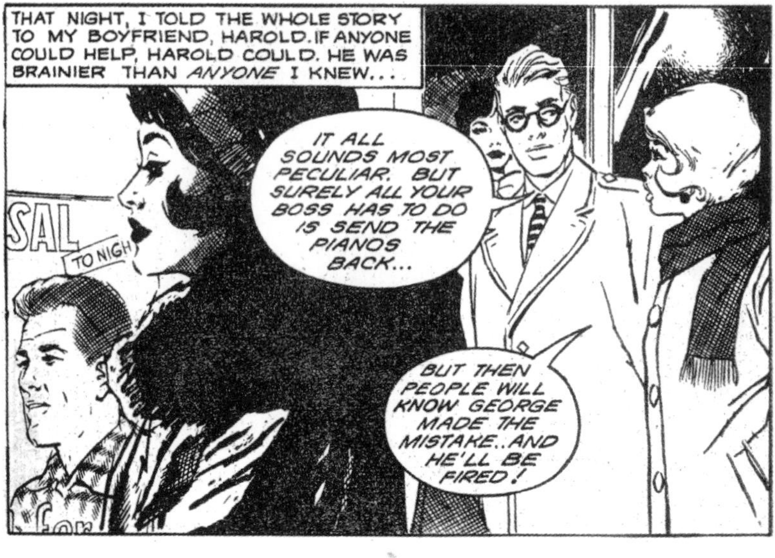
THAT NIGHT, I TOLD THE WHOLE STORY TO MY BOYFRIEND, HAROLD. IF ANYONE COULD HELP, HAROLD COULD. HE WAS BRAINIER THAN ANYONE I KNEW...
IT ALL SOUNDS MOST PECULIAR. BUT SURELY ALL YOUR BOSS HAS TO DO IS SEND THE PIANOS BACK...
BUT THEN PEOPLE WILL KNOW GEORGE MADE THE MISTAKE.. AND HE'LL BE FIRED!
SAL
TO NIGH

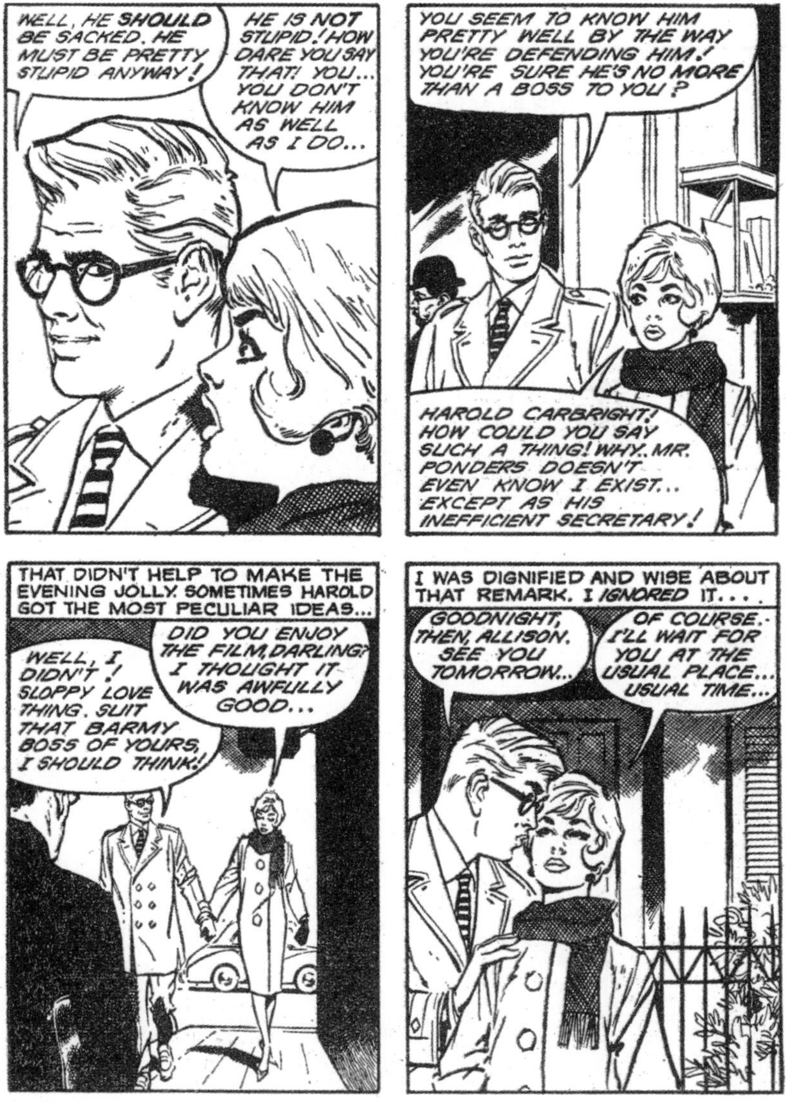
WELL, HE SHOULD BE SACKED. HE MUST BE PRETTY STUPID ANYWAY!
HE IS NOT STUPID! HOW DARE YOU SAY THAT! YOU... YOU DON'T KNOW HIM AS WELL AS I DO...
YOU SEEM TO KNOW HIM PRETTY WELL BY THE WAY YOU'RE DEFENDING HIM! YOU'RE SURE HE'S NO MORE THAN A BOSS TO YOU?
HAROLD CARBRIGHT! HOW COULD YOU SAY SUCH A THING! WHY.. MR. PONDERS DOESN'T EVEN KNOW I EXIST... EXCEPT AS HIS INEFFICIENT SECRETARY!
THAT DIDN'T HELP TO MAKE THE EVENING JOLLY. SOMETIMES HAROLD GOT THE MOST PECULIAR IDEAS...
DID YOU ENJOY THE FILM, DARLING? I THOUGHT IT WAS AWFULLY GOOD...
WELL, I DIDN'T! SLOPPY LOVE THING. SUIT THAT BARMY BOSS OF YOURS, I SHOULD THINK!
I WAS DIGNIFIED AND WISE ABOUT THAT REMARK. I IGNORED IT...
GOODNIGHT, THEN, ALLISON. SEE YOU TOMORROW...
OF COURSE. I'LL WAIT FOR YOU AT THE USUAL PLACE... USUAL TIME...

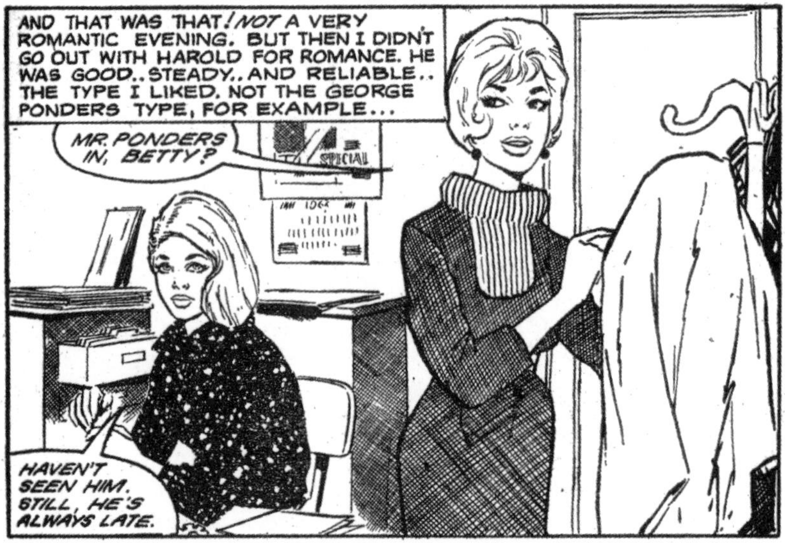
AND THAT WAS THAT! NOT A VERY ROMANTIC EVENING. BUT THEN I DIDN'T GO OUT WITH HAROLD FOR ROMANCE. HE WAS GOOD.. STEADY.. AND RELIABLE.. THE TYPE I LIKED. NOT THE GEORGE PONDERS TYPE, FOR EXAMPLE...
MR. PONDERS IN, BETTY?
HAVEN'T SEEN HIM. STILL, HE'S ALWAYS LATE.
SPECIAL

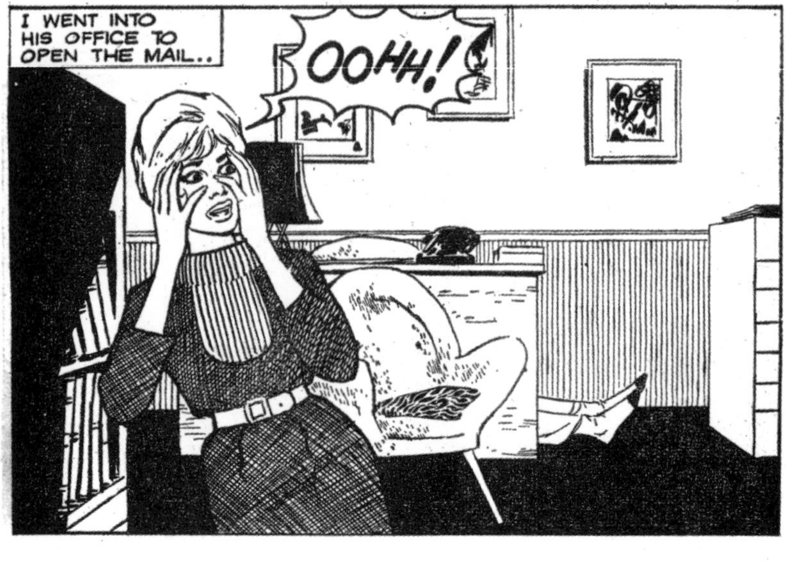
I WENT INTO HIS OFFICE TO OPEN THE MAIL..
OOHH!

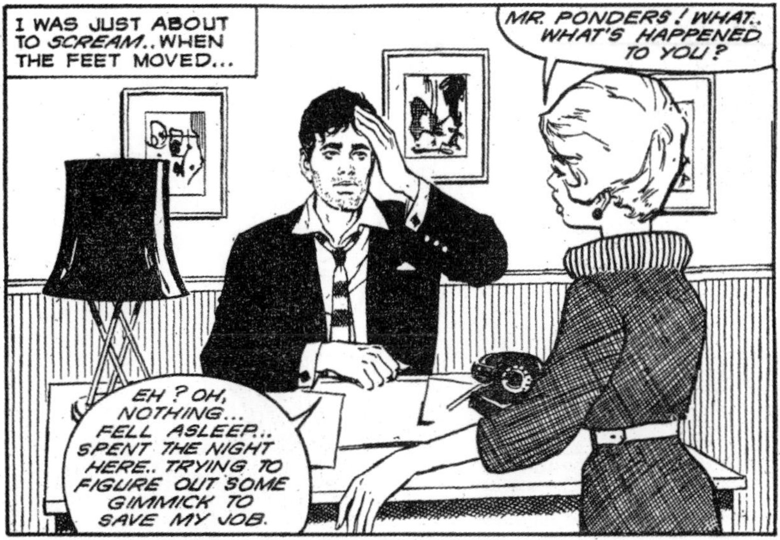
I WAS JUST ABOUT TO SCREAM.. WHEN THE FEET MOVED...
MR. PONDERS! WHAT.. WHAT'S HAPPENED TO YOU?
EH? OH, NOTHING... FELL ASLEEP... SPENT THE NIGHT HERE.. TRYING TO FIGURE OUT SOME GIMMICK TO SAVE MY JOB.

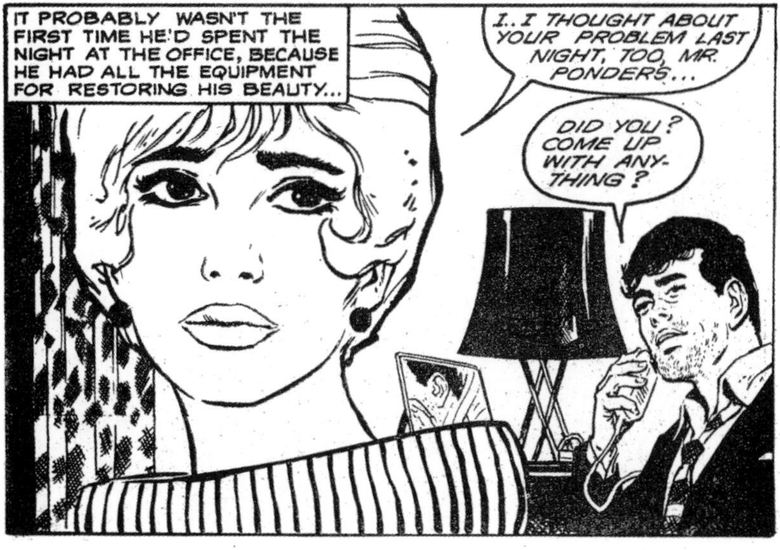
IT PROBABLY WASN'T THE FIRST TIME HE'D SPENT THE NIGHT AT THE OFFICE, BECAUSE HE HAD ALL THE EQUIPMENT FOR RESTORING HIS BEAUTY...
I.. I THOUGHT ABOUT YOUR PROBLEM LAST NIGHT, TOO, MR. PONDERS...
DID YOU? COME UP WITH ANY-THING?

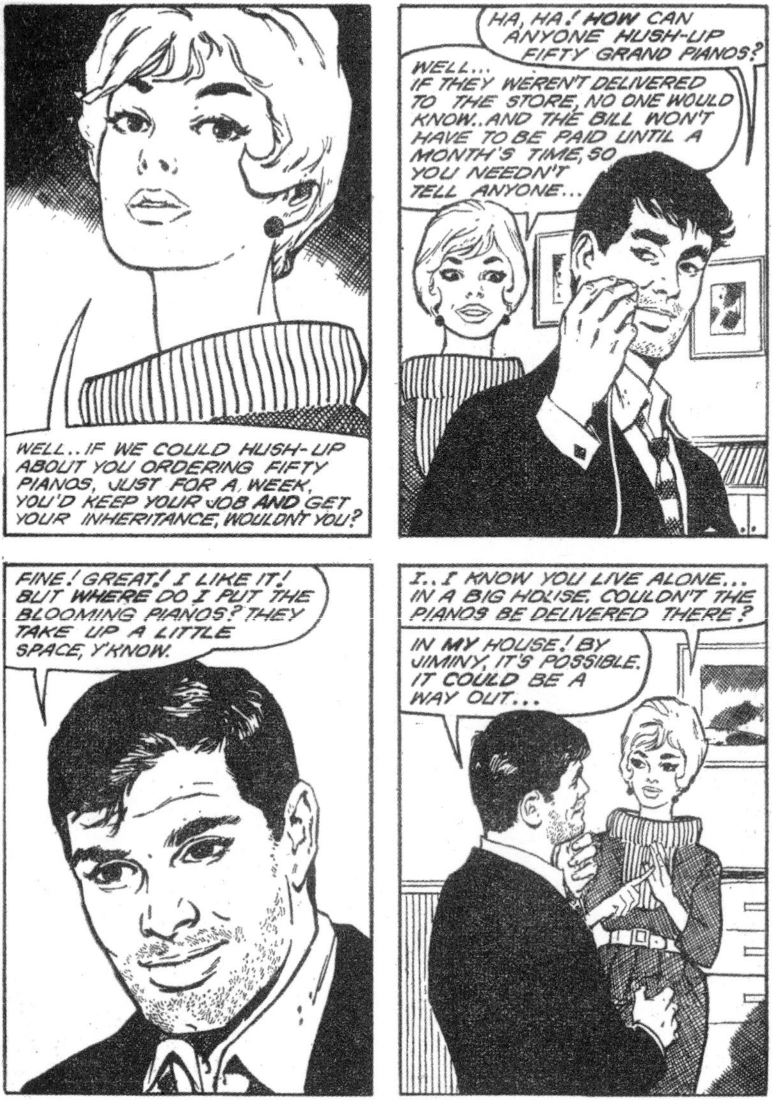
WELL.. IF WE COULD HUSH-UP ABOUT YOU ORDERING FIFTY PIANOS, JUST FOR A WEEK, YOU'D KEEP YOUR JOB AND GET YOUR INHERITANCE, WOULDN'T YOU?
HA, HA! HOW CAN ANYONE HUSH-UP FIFTY GRAND PIANOS?
WELL... IF THEY WEREN'T DELIVERED TO THE STORE, NO ONE WOULD KNOW.. AND THE BILL WON'T HAVE TO BE PAID UNTIL A MONTH'S TIME, SO YOU NEEDN'T TELL ANYONE...
FINE! GREAT! I LIKE IT! BUT WHERE DO I PUT THE BLOOMING PIANOS? THEY TAKE UP A LITTLE SPACE, Y'KNOW.
I.. I KNOW YOU LIVE ALONE... IN A BIG HOUSE. COULDN'T THE PIANOS BE DELIVERED THERE?
IN MY HOUSE! BY JIMINY, IT'S POSSIBLE. IT COULD BE A WAY OUT...

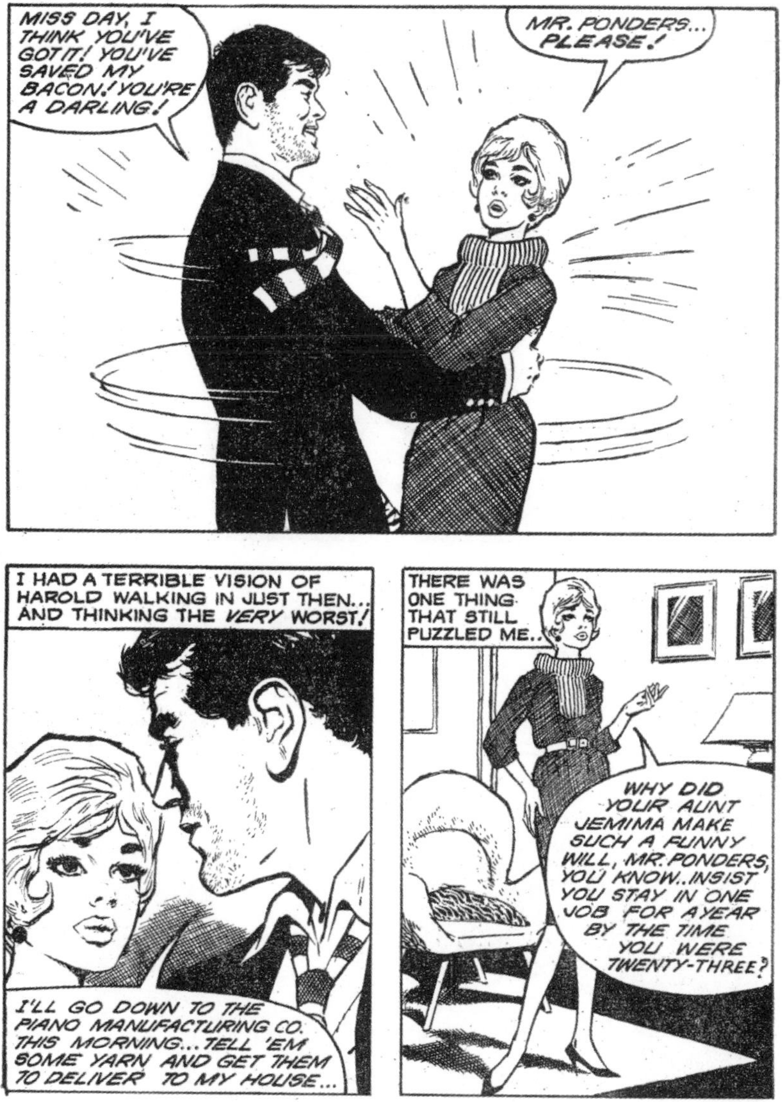
MISS DAY, I THINK YOU'VE GOT IT! YOU'VE SAVED MY BACON! YOU'RE A DARLING!
MR. PONDERS... PLEASE!
I HAD A TERRIBLE VISION OF HAROLD WALKING IN JUST THEN... AND THINKING THE VERY WORST!
I'LL GO DOWN TO THE PIANO MANUFACTURING CO. THIS MORNING... TELL 'EM SOME YARN AND GET THEM TO DELIVER TO MY HOUSE...
THERE WAS ONE THING THAT STILL PUZZLED ME..
WHY DID YOUR AUNT JEMIMA MAKE SUCH A FUNNY WILL, MR. PONDERS, YOU KNOW.. INSIST YOU STAY IN ONE JOB FOR A YEAR BY THE TIME YOU WERE TWENTY-THREE?

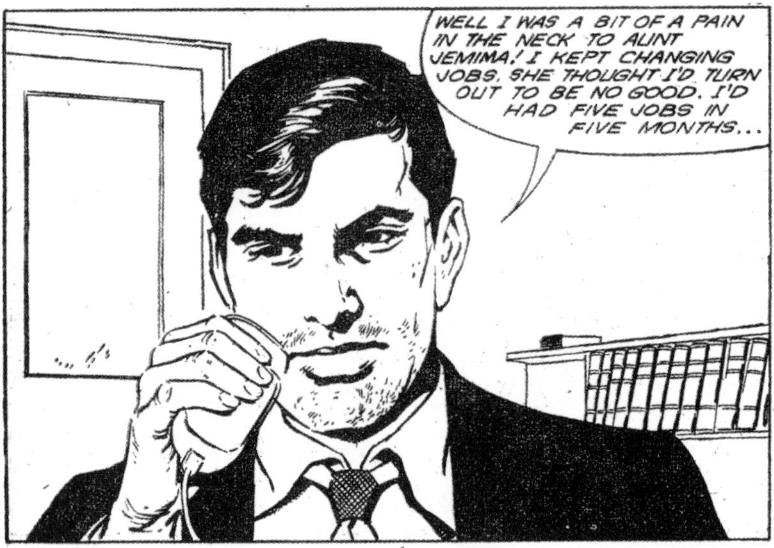
WELL I WAS A BIT OF A PAIN IN THE NECK TO AUNT JEMIMA! I KEPT CHANGING JOBS. SHE THOUGHT I'D TURN OUT TO BE NO GOOD. I'D HAD FIVE JOBS IN FIVE MONTHS...

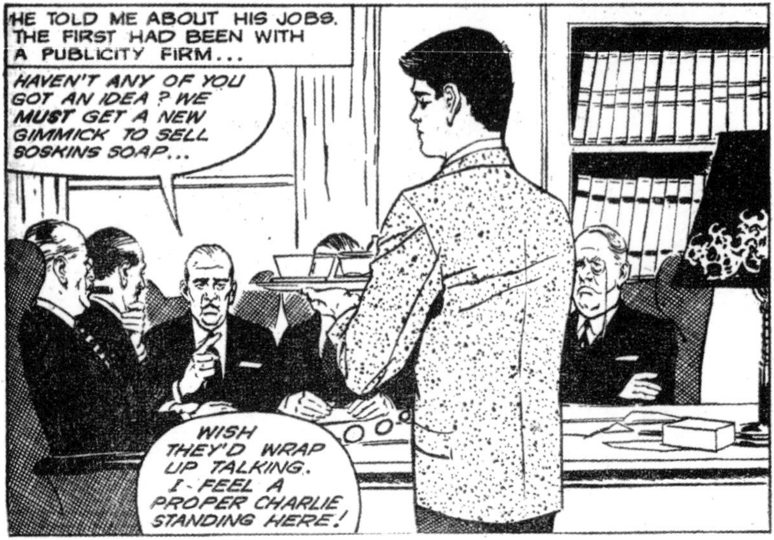
HE TOLD ME ABOUT HIS JOBS. THE FIRST HAD BEEN WITH A PUBLICITY FIRM...
HAVEN'T ANY OF YOU GOT AN IDEA? WE MUST GET A NEW GIMMICK TO SELL BOSKINS SOAP...
WISH THEY'D WRAP UP TALKING. I FEEL A PROPER CHARLIE STANDING HERE!

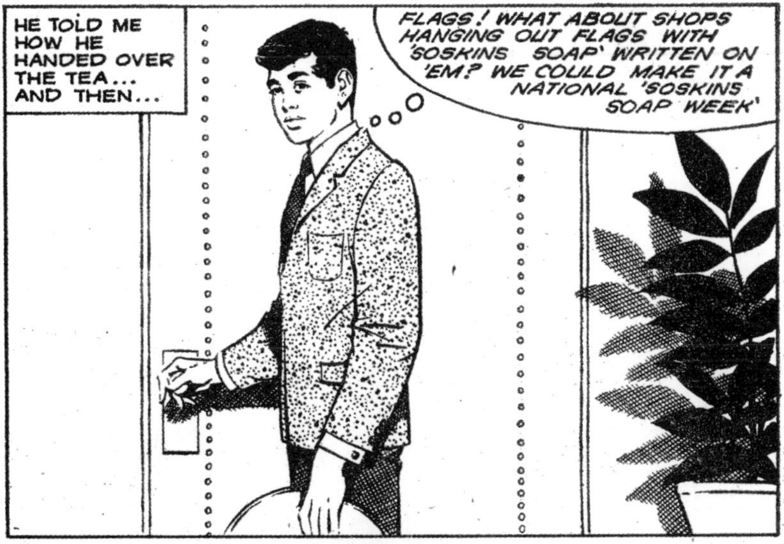
HE TOLD ME HOW HE HANDED OVER THE TEA... AND THEN...
FLAGS! WHAT ABOUT SHOPS HANGING OUT FLAGS WITH 'SOSKINS SOAP' WRITTEN ON 'EM? WE COULD MAKE IT A NATIONAL 'SOSKINS SOAP WEEK'

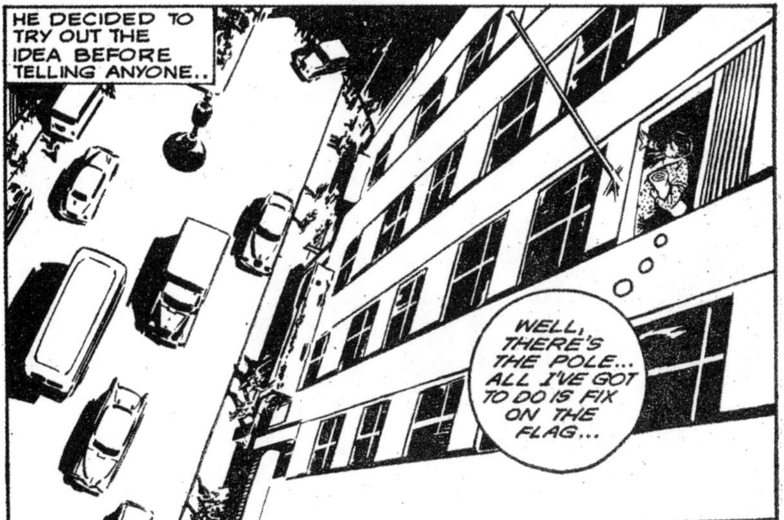
HE DECIDED TO TRY OUT THE IDEA BEFORE TELLING ANYONE..
WELL, THERE'S THE POLE... ALL I'VE GOT TO DO IS FIX ON THE FLAG...

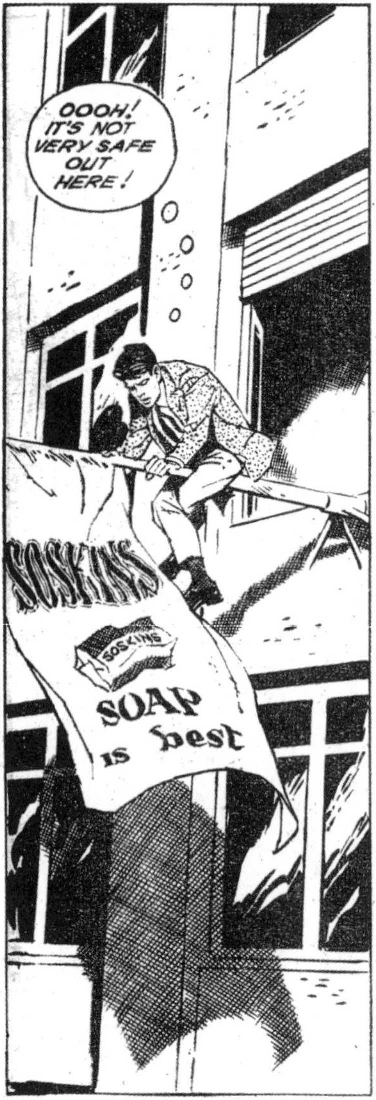
OOOH! IT'S NOT VERY SAFE OUT HERE!
SOSKINS
SOSKINS
SOAP is best

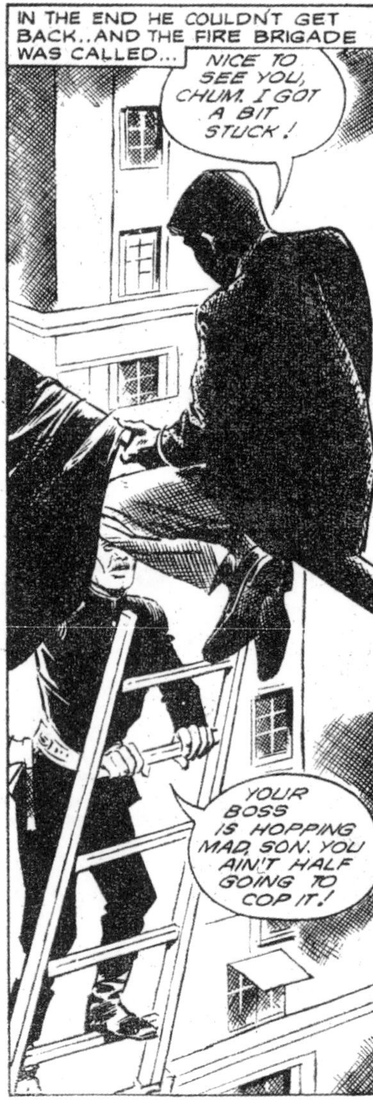
IN THE END HE COULDN'T GET BACK..AND THE FIRE BRIGADE WAS CALLED...
NICE TO SEE YOU, CHUM. I GOT A BIT STUCK!
YOUR BOSS IS HOPPING MAD, SON. YOU AIN'T HALF GOING TO COP IT!

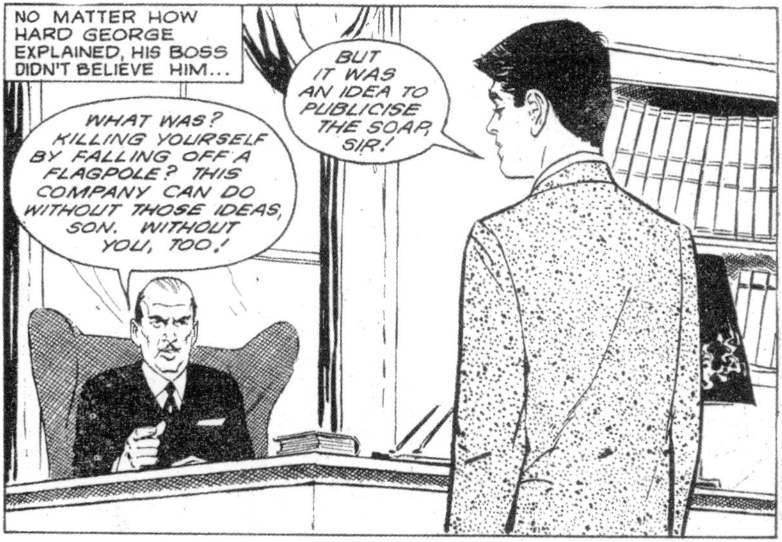
NO MATTER HOW HARD GEORGE EXPLAINED, HIS BOSS DIDN'T BELIEVE HIM...
BUT IT WAS AN IDEA TO PUBLICISE THE SOAP, SIR!
WHAT WAS? KILLING YOURSELF BY FALLING OFF A FLAGPOLE? THIS COMPANY CAN DO WITHOUT THOSE IDEAS, SON. WITHOUT YOU, TOO!

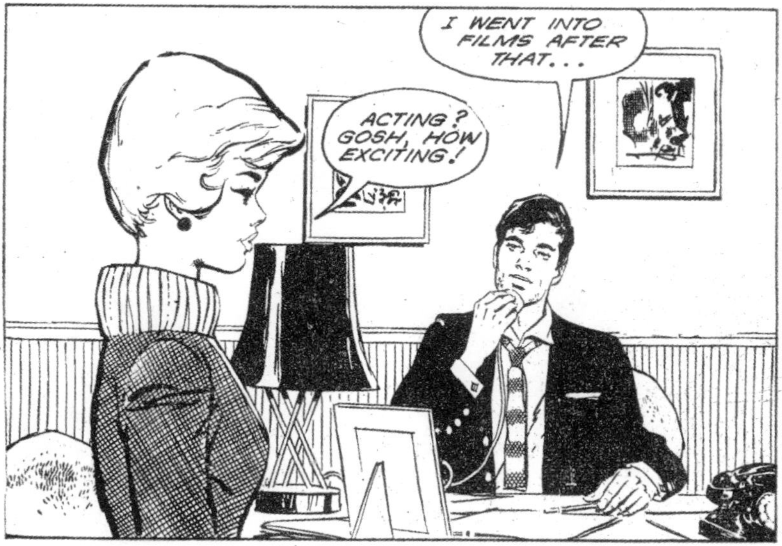
I WENT INTO FILMS AFTER THAT...
ACTING? GOSH, HOW EXCITING!

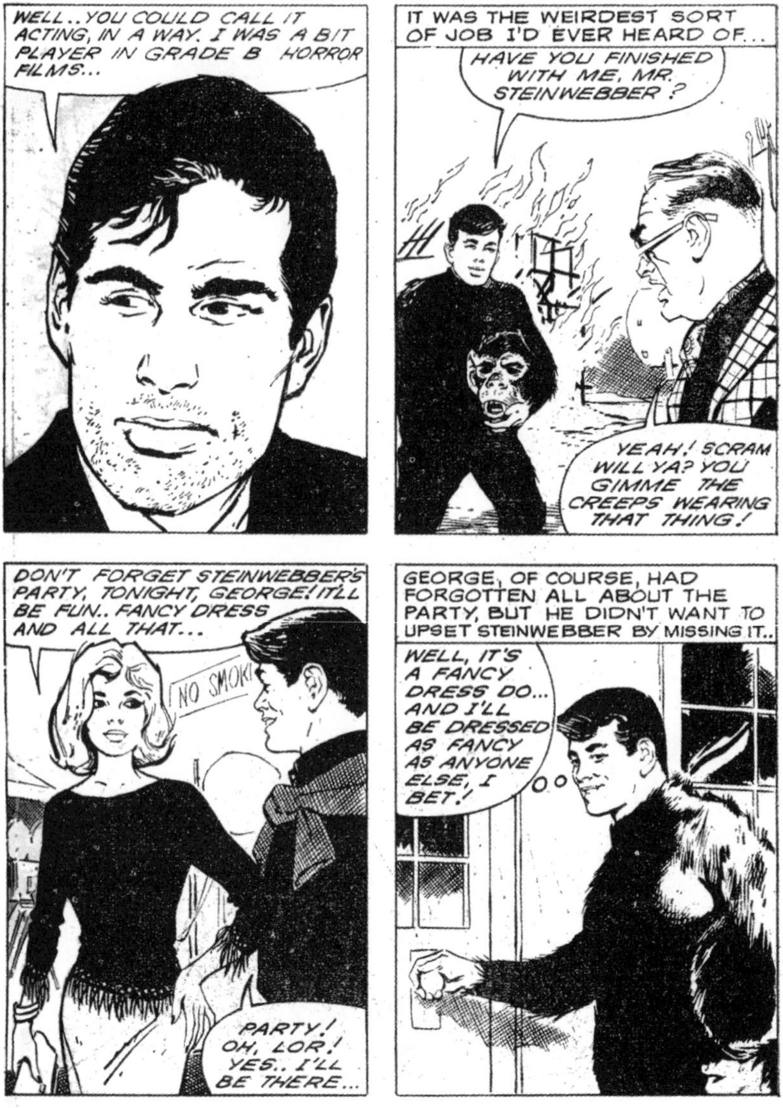
WELL..YOU COULD CALL IT ACTING, IN A WAY. I WAS A BIT PLAYER IN GRADE B HORROR FILMS...
IT WAS THE WEIRDEST SORT OF JOB I'D EVER HEARD OF...
HAVE YOU FINISHED WITH ME, MR. STEINWEBBER?
YEAH! SCRAM WILL YA? YOU GIMME THE CREEPS WEARING THAT THING!
DON'T FORGET STEINWEBBER'S PARTY, TONIGHT, GEORGE! IT'LL BE FUN.. FANCY DRESS AND ALL THAT...
NO SMOK
PARTY! OH, LOR! YES.. I'LL BE THERE...
GEORGE, OF COURSE, HAD FORGOTTEN ALL ABOUT THE PARTY, BUT HE DIDN'T WANT TO UPSET STEINWEBBER BY MISSING IT..
WELL, IT'S A FANCY DRESS DO... AND I'LL BE DRESSED AS FANCY AS ANYONE ELSE, I BET!

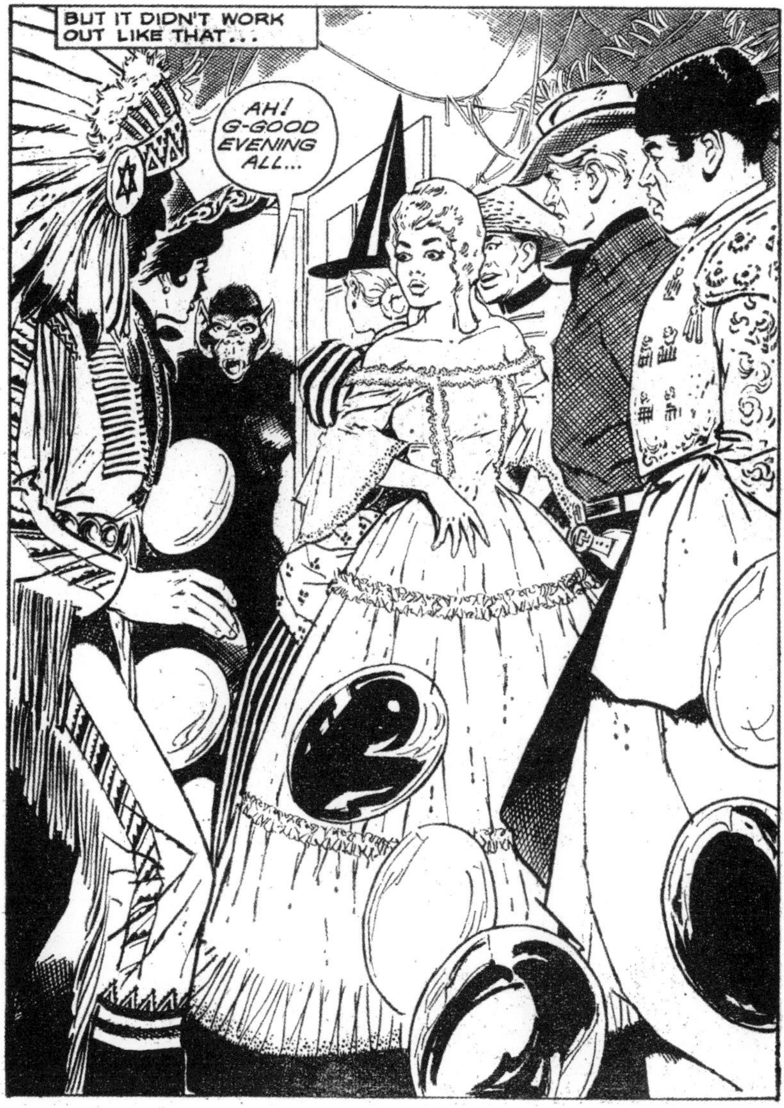
BUT IT DIDN'T WORK OUT LIKE THAT...
AH! G-GOOD EVENING ALL...

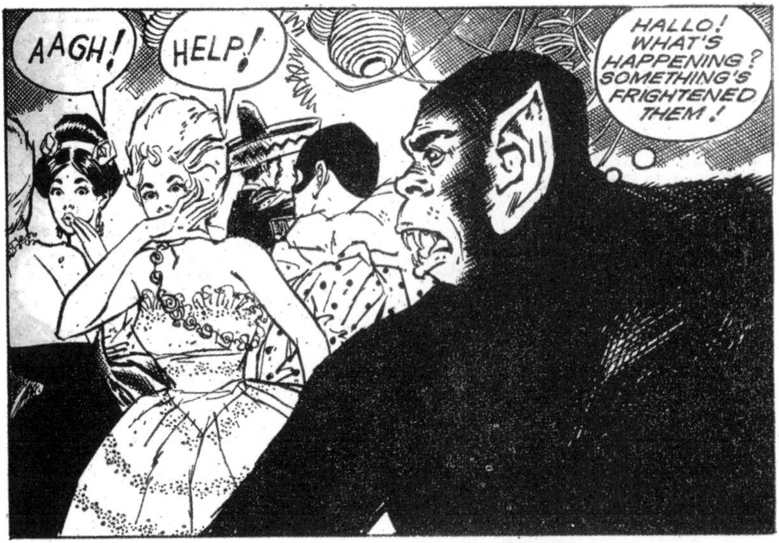
AAGH!
HELP!
HALLO! WHAT'S HAPPENING? SOMETHING'S FRIGHTENED THEM!

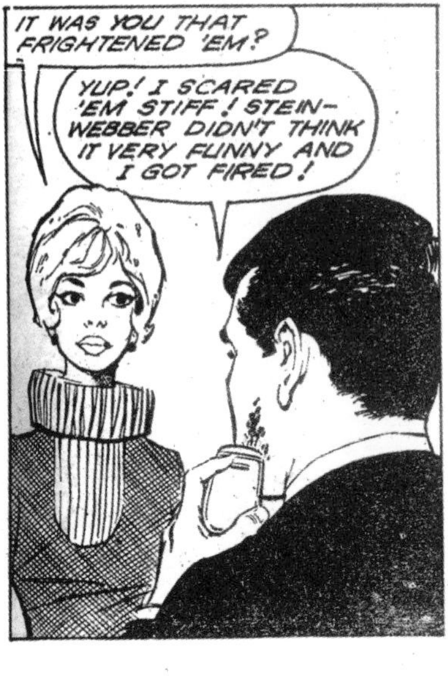
IT WAS YOU THAT FRIGHTENED 'EM?
YUP! I SCARED 'EM STIFF! STEIN-WEBBER DIDN'T THINK IT VERY FUNNY AND I GOT FIRED!

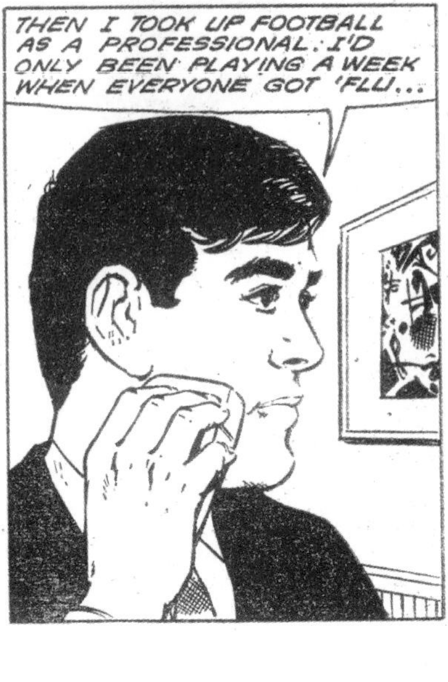
THEN I TOOK UP FOOTBALL AS A PROFESSIONAL. I'D ONLY BEEN PLAYING A WEEK WHEN EVERYONE GOT 'FLU...

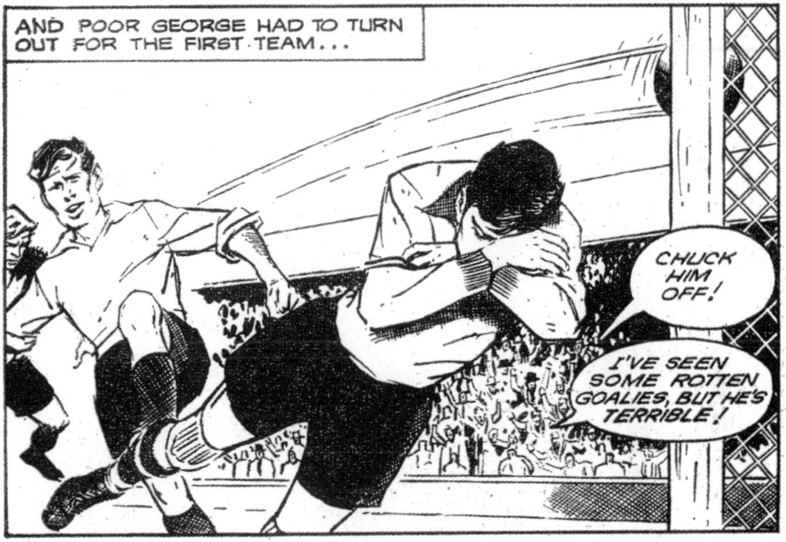
AND POOR GEORGE HAD TO TURN OUT FOR THE FIRST TEAM...
CHUCK HIM OFF!
I'VE SEEN SOME ROTTEN GOALIES, BUT HE'S TERRIBLE!

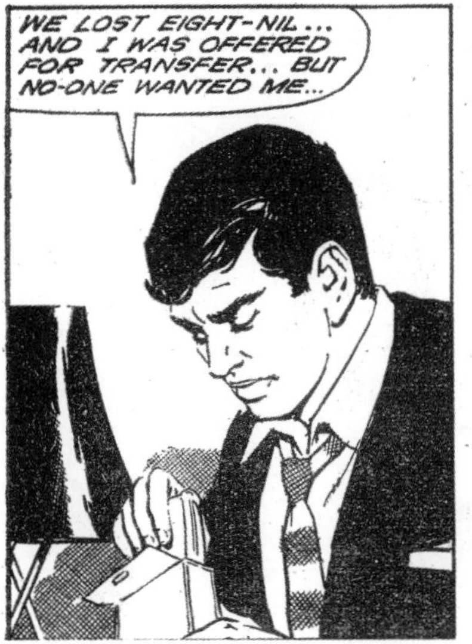
WE LOST EIGHT-NIL... AND I WAS OFFERED FOR TRANSFER... BUT NO-ONE WANTED ME...

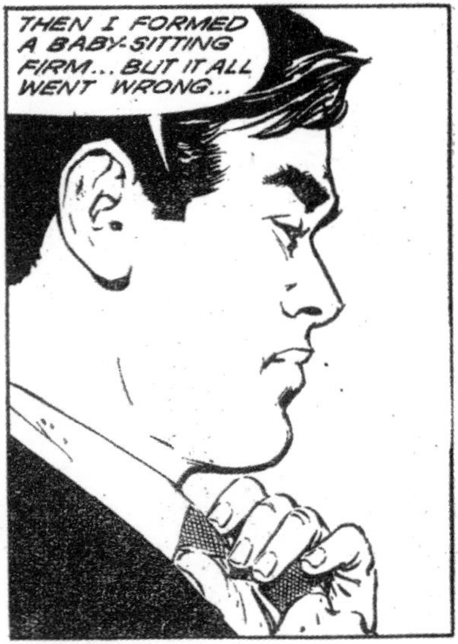
THEN I FORMED A BABY-SITTING FIRM... BUT IT ALL WENT WRONG...

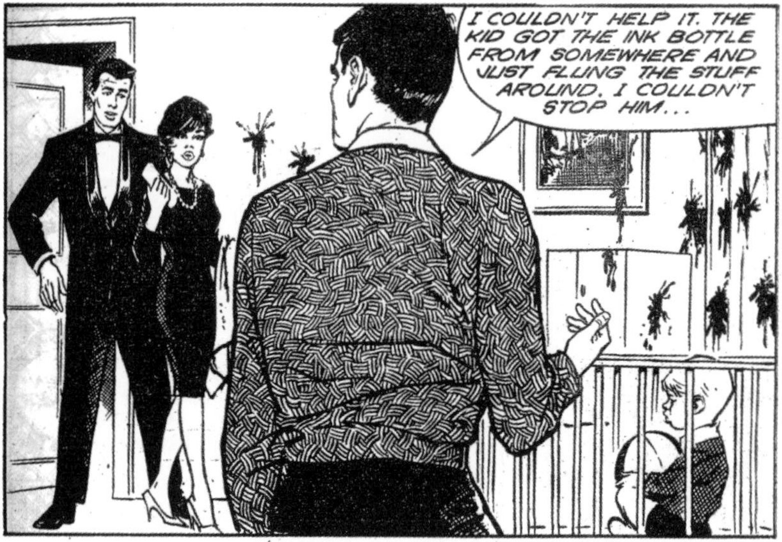
I COULDN'T HELP IT. THE KID GOT THE INK BOTTLE FROM SOMEWHERE AND JUST FLUNG THE STUFF AROUND. I COULDN'T STOP HIM...

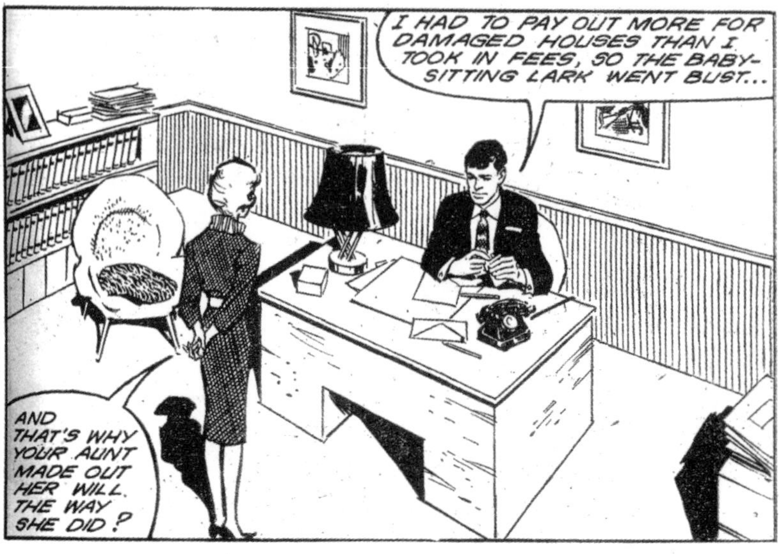
I HAD TO PAY OUT MORE FOR DAMAGED HOUSES THAN I TOOK IN FEES, SO THE BABY-SITTING LARK WENT BUST...
AND THAT'S WHY YOUR AUNT MADE OUT HER WILL THE WAY SHE DID?

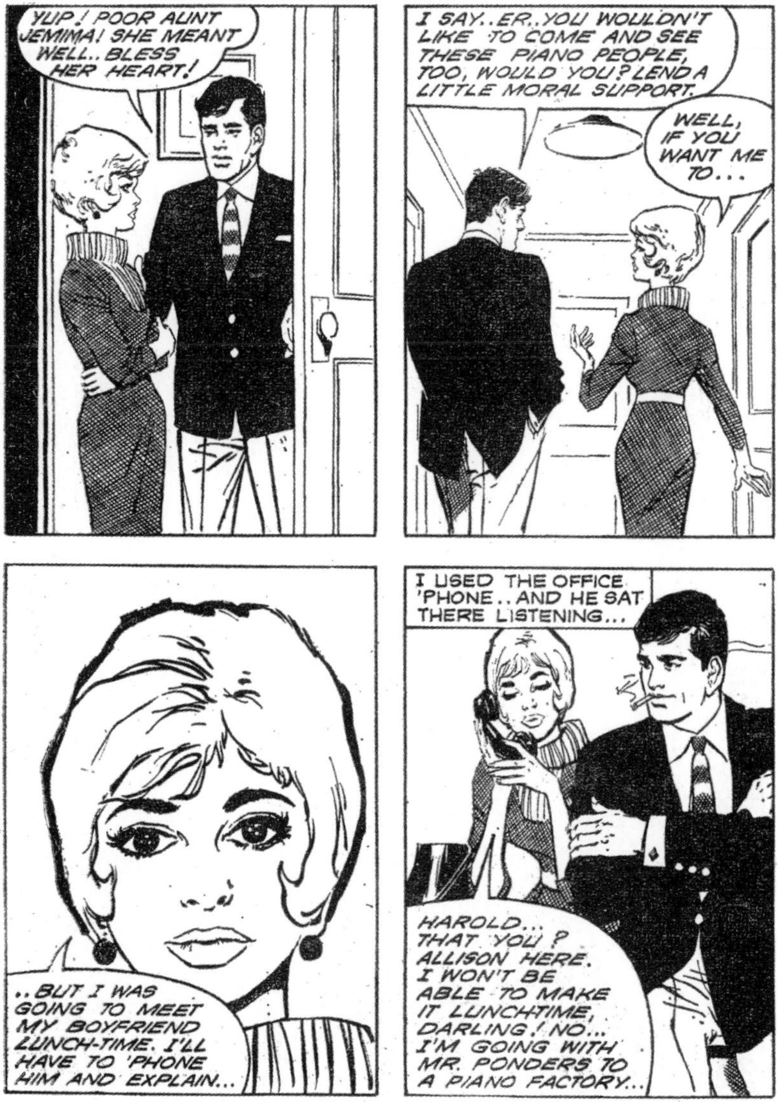
YUP! POOR AUNT JEMIMA! SHE MEANT WELL.. BLESS HER HEART!
I SAY..ER..YOU WOULDN'T LIKE TO COME AND SEE THESE PIANO PEOPLE, TOO, WOULD YOU? LEND A LITTLE MORAL SUPPORT.
WELL, IF YOU WANT ME TO...
..BUT I WAS GOING TO MEET MY BOYFRIEND LUNCH-TIME. I'LL HAVE TO 'PHONE HIM AND EXPLAIN...
I USED THE OFFICE 'PHONE.. AND HE SAT THERE LISTENING...
HAROLD... THAT YOU? ALLISON HERE. I WON'T BE ABLE TO MAKE IT LUNCHTIME, DARLING! NO... I'M GOING WITH MR. PONDERS TO A PIANO FACTORY...

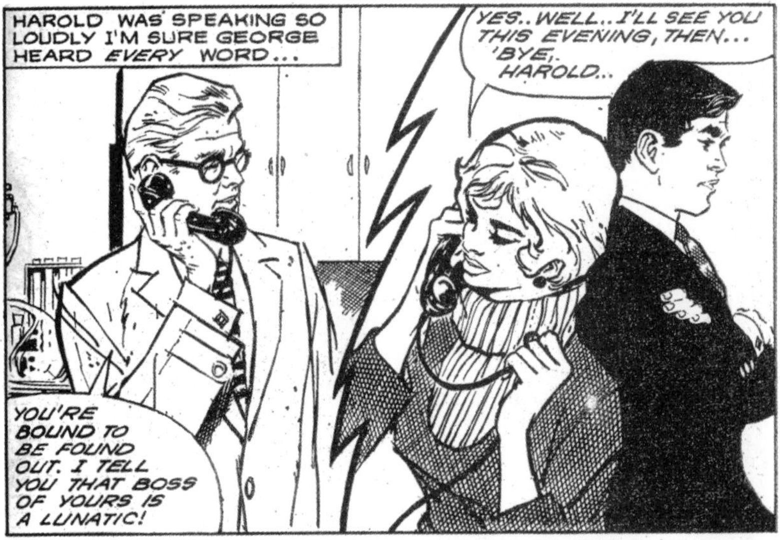
HAROLD WAS SPEAKING SO LOUDLY I'M SURE GEORGE HEARD EVERY WORD...
YES..WELL..I'LL SEE YOU THIS EVENING, THEN... 'BYE, HAROLD..
YOU'RE BOUND TO BE FOUND OUT. I TELL YOU THAT BOSS OF YOURS IS A LUNATIC!

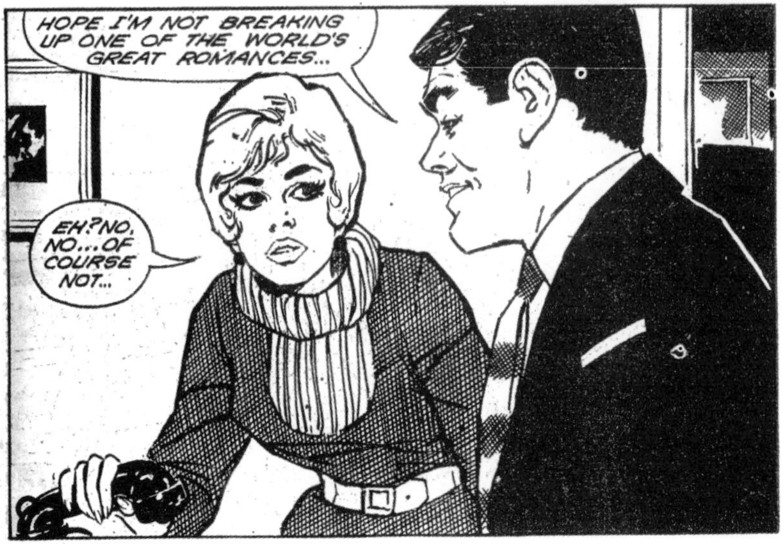
HOPE I'M NOT BREAKING UP ONE OF THE WORLD'S GREAT ROMANCES...
EH? NO, NO...OF COURSE NOT...

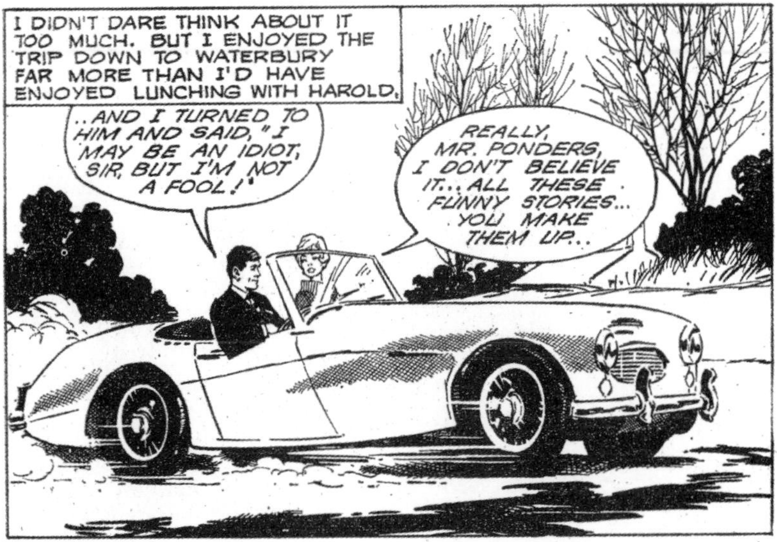
I DIDN'T DARE THINK ABOUT IT TOO MUCH. BUT I ENJOYED THE TRIP DOWN TO WATERBURY FAR MORE THAN I'D HAVE ENJOYED LUNCHING WITH HAROLD.
..AND I TURNED TO HIM AND SAID, "I MAY BE AN IDIOT, SIR, BUT I'M NOT A FOOL!"
REALLY, MR. PONDERS, I DON'T BELIEVE IT... ALL THESE FUNNY STORIES... YOU MAKE THEM UP...

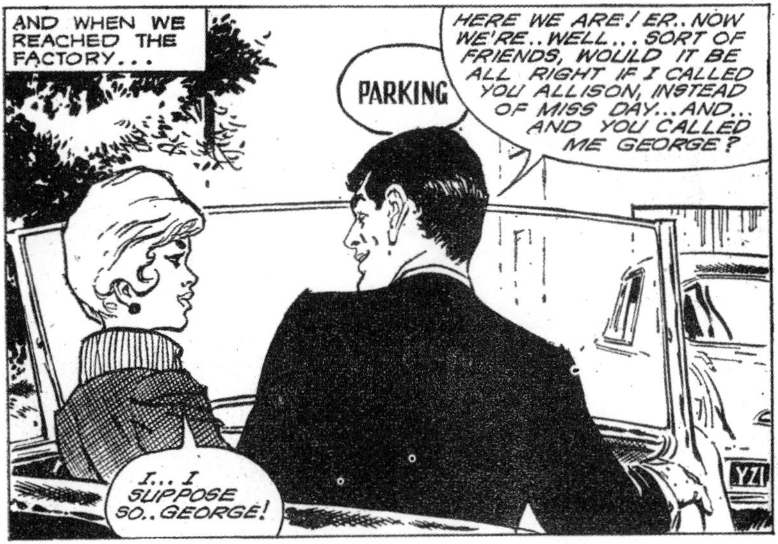
AND WHEN WE REACHED THE FACTORY...
PARKING
HERE WE ARE! ER.. NOW WE'RE... WELL... SORT OF FRIENDS, WOULD IT BE ALL RIGHT IF I CALLED YOU ALLISON, INSTEAD OF MISS DAY... AND... AND YOU CALLED ME GEORGE?
I... I SUPPOSE SO.. GEORGE!

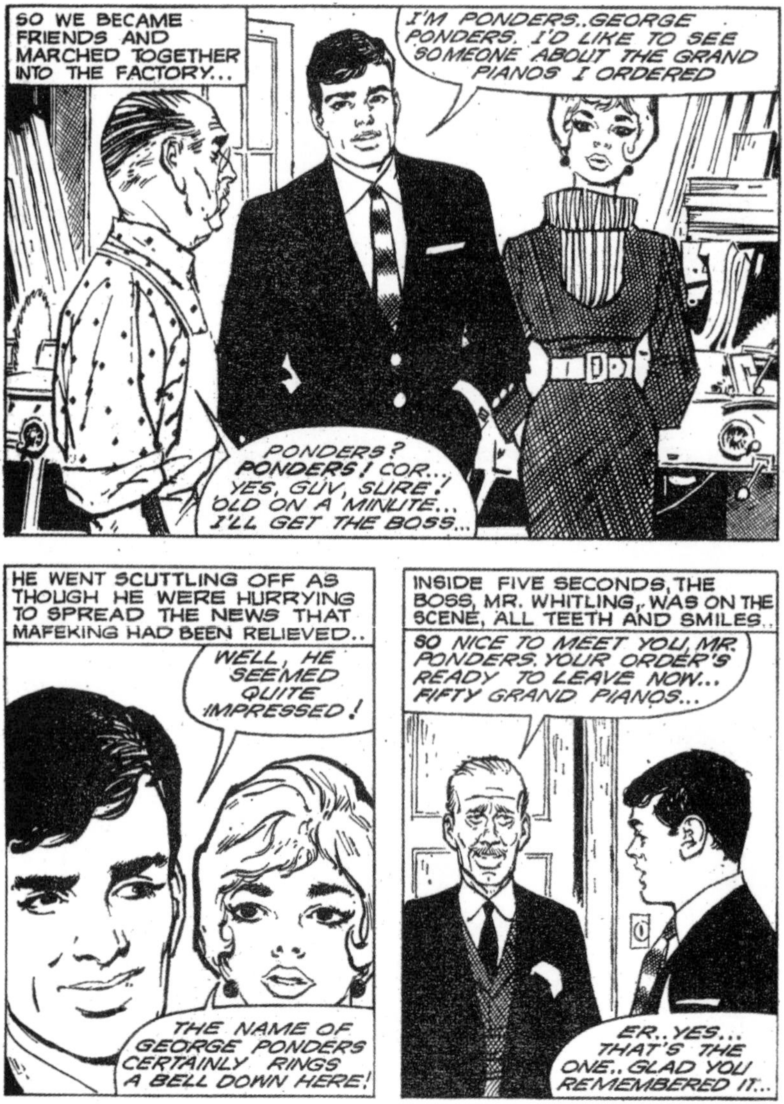
SO WE BECAME FRIENDS AND MARCHED TOGETHER INTO THE FACTORY...
I'M PONDERS..GEORGE PONDERS. I'D LIKE TO SEE SOMEONE ABOUT THE GRAND PIANOS I ORDERED
PONDERS? PONDERS! COR... YES, GUV, SURE! 'OLD ON A MINUTE... I'LL GET THE BOSS...
HE WENT SCUTTLING OFF AS THOUGH HE WERE HURRYING TO SPREAD THE NEWS THAT MAFEKING HAD BEEN RELIEVED..
WELL, HE SEEMED QUITE IMPRESSED!
THE NAME OF GEORGE PONDERS CERTAINLY RINGS A BELL DOWN HERE!
INSIDE FIVE SECONDS, THE BOSS, MR. WHITLING, WAS ON THE SCENE, ALL TEETH AND SMILES..
SO NICE TO MEET YOU, MR. PONDERS. YOUR ORDER'S READY TO LEAVE NOW... FIFTY GRAND PIANOS...
ER..YES... THAT'S THE ONE..GLAD YOU REMEMBERED IT...

REMEMBER IT? MY *DEAR* MR. PONDERS, I SHALL NEVER *FORGET* IT! MY FAMILY'S BEEN IN THIS BUSINESS OVER ONE HUNDRED YEARS AND NEVER BEFORE HAVE WE HAD ONE ORDER FOR FIFTY GRAND PIANOS. IT...IT'S ALMOST UNBELIEVABLE...

YOU'RE TELLING ME! I COULD HARDLY BELIEVE IT MYSELF WHEN *I* HEARD ABOUT IT!

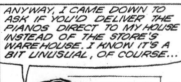

ANYWAY, I CAME DOWN TO ASK IF YOU'D DELIVER THE PIANOS DIRECT TO MY HOUSE INSTEAD OF THE STORE'S WAREHOUSE. I KNOW IT'S A BIT UNUSUAL, OF COURSE...

MY DEAR MR. PONDERS, NOTHING YOU COULD ASK WOULD SOUND UNUSUAL. FIFTY GRAND PIANOS! WE'D DELIVER THEM TO THE MONKEY HOUSE AT THE ZOO IF YOU WANTED US TO!

AND THAT WAS THAT. EVERYTHING WAS ARRANGED.

DID..DID YOU THINK THAT CHAP WAS... WELL, TAKING THE MICKEY?

HE MIGHT HAVE BEEN... BUT WHAT DOES IT MATTER? YOU'VE SAVED YOUR JOB.. AND YOUR TEN THOUSAND!

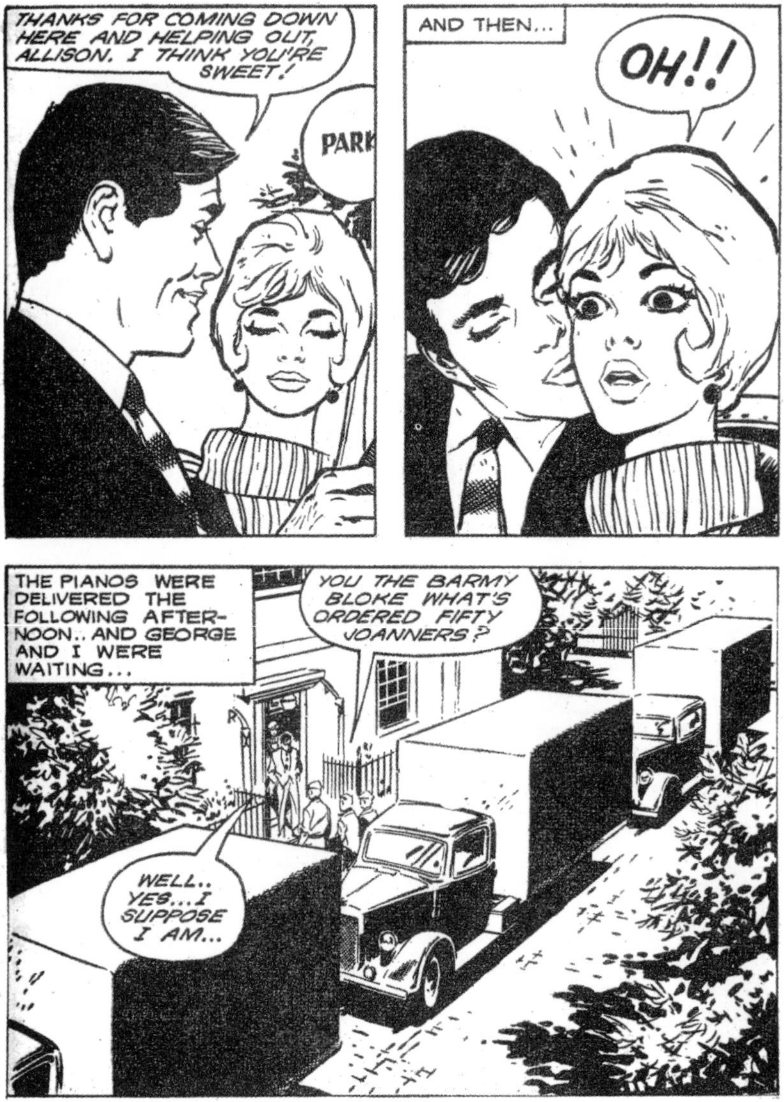
THANKS FOR COMING DOWN HERE AND HELPING OUT, ALLISON. I THINK YOU'RE SWEET!
PARK
AND THEN...
OH!!
THE PIANOS WERE DELIVERED THE FOLLOWING AFTER-NOON.. AND GEORGE AND I WERE WAITING...
YOU THE BARMY BLOKE WHAT'S ORDERED FIFTY JOANNERS?
WELL.. YES...I SUPPOSE I AM...

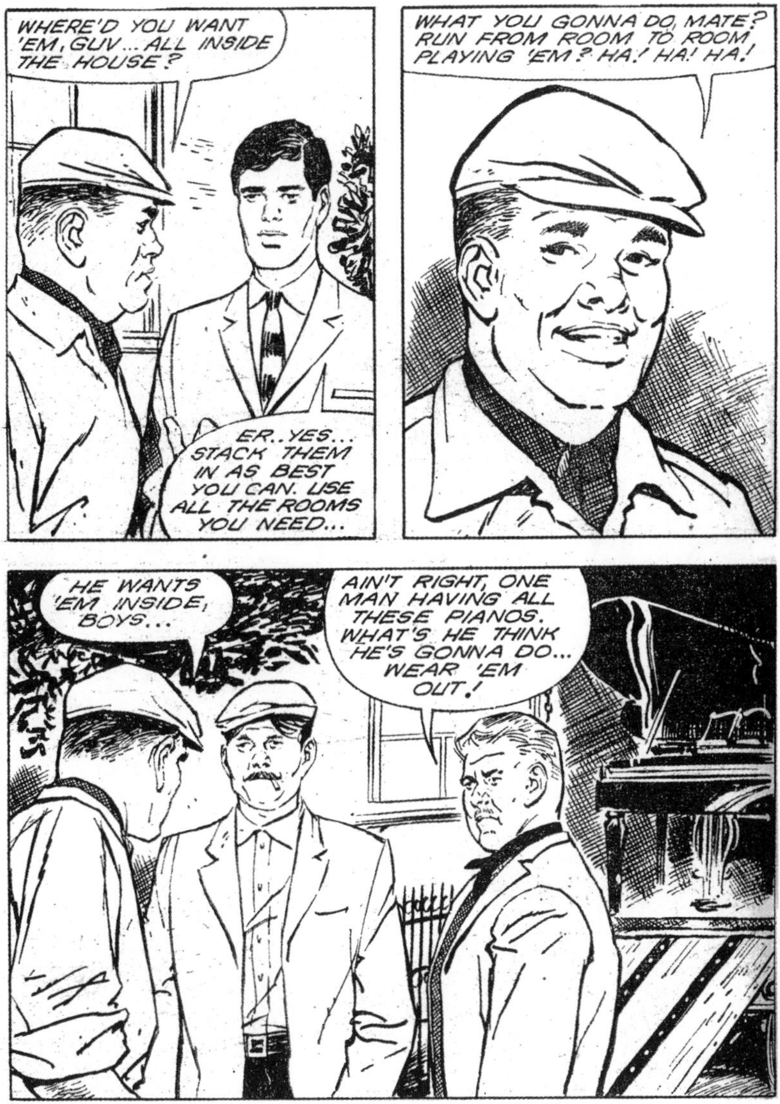
WHERE'D YOU WANT 'EM, GUV... ALL INSIDE THE HOUSE?
ER.. YES... STACK THEM IN AS BEST YOU CAN. USE ALL THE ROOMS YOU NEED...
WHAT YOU GONNA DO, MATE? RUN FROM ROOM TO ROOM PLAYING 'EM? HA! HA! HA!
HE WANTS 'EM INSIDE, BOYS...
AIN'T RIGHT, ONE MAN HAVING ALL THESE PIANOS. WHAT'S HE THINK HE'S GONNA DO... WEAR 'EM OUT!

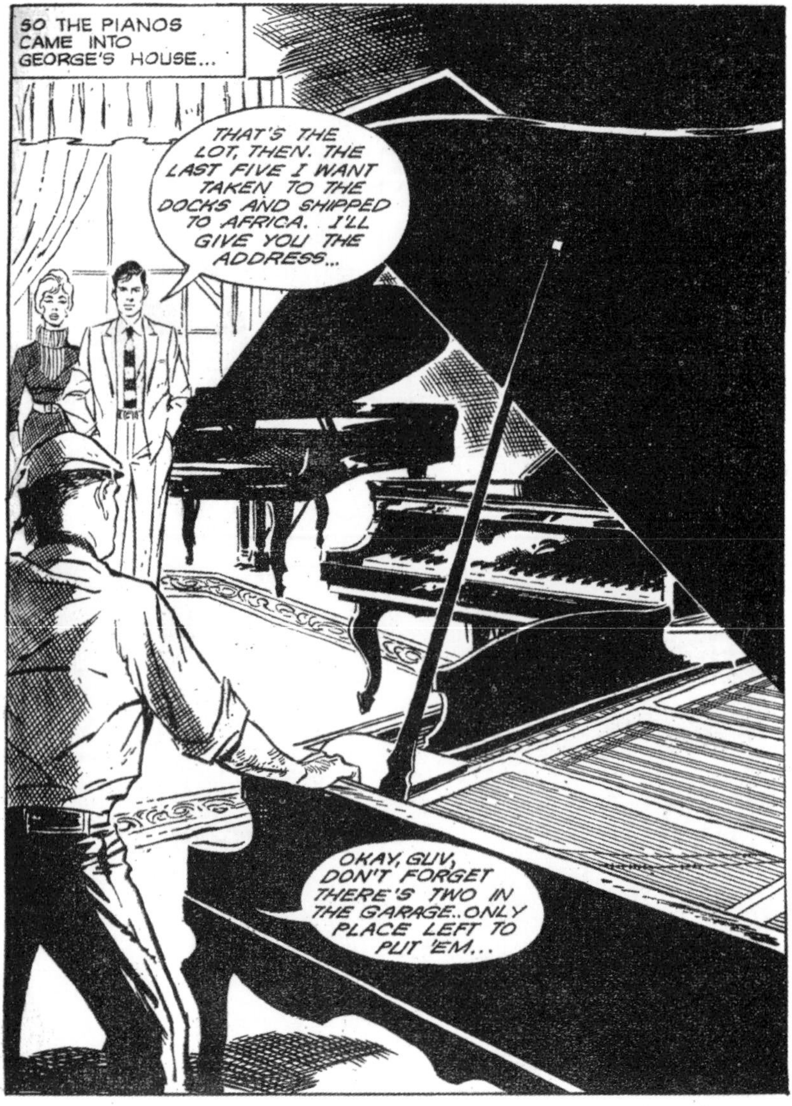
SO THE PIANOS CAME INTO GEORGE'S HOUSE...
THAT'S THE LOT, THEN. THE LAST FIVE I WANT TAKEN TO THE DOCKS AND SHIPPED TO AFRICA. I'LL GIVE YOU THE ADDRESS...
OKAY, GUV, DON'T FORGET THERE'S TWO IN THE GARAGE..ONLY PLACE LEFT TO PUT 'EM...

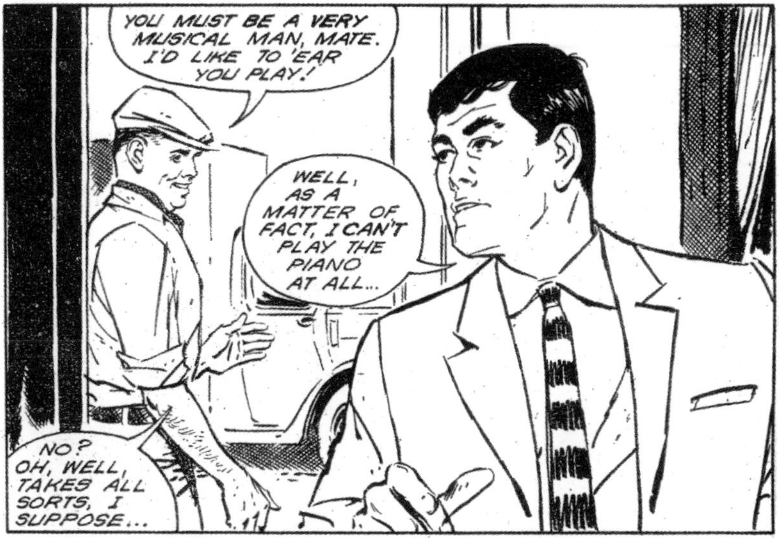
YOU MUST BE A VERY MUSICAL MAN, MATE. I'D LIKE TO 'EAR YOU PLAY!
WELL, AS A MATTER OF FACT, I CAN'T PLAY THE PIANO AT ALL...
NO? OH, WELL, TAKES ALL SORTS, I SUPPOSE...

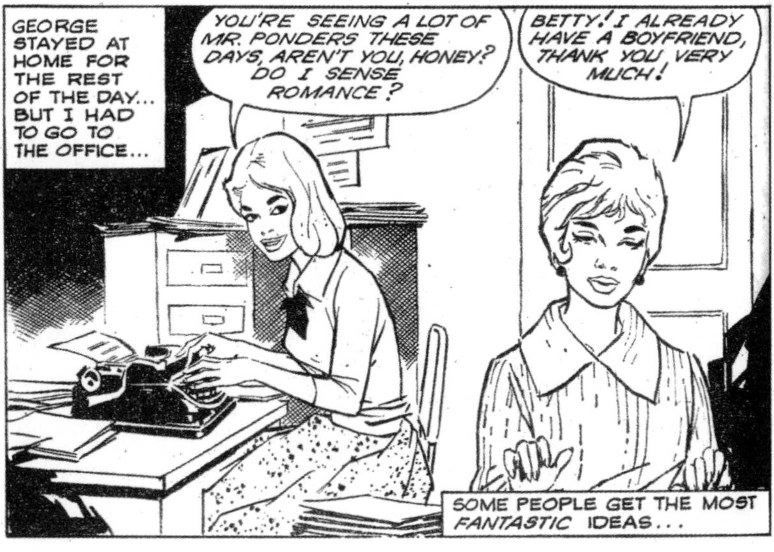
GEORGE STAYED AT HOME FOR THE REST OF THE DAY... BUT I HAD TO GO TO THE OFFICE...
YOU'RE SEEING A LOT OF MR. PONDERS THESE DAYS, AREN'T YOU, HONEY? DO I SENSE ROMANCE?
BETTY! I ALREADY HAVE A BOYFRIEND, THANK YOU VERY MUCH!
SOME PEOPLE GET THE MOST FANTASTIC IDEAS...

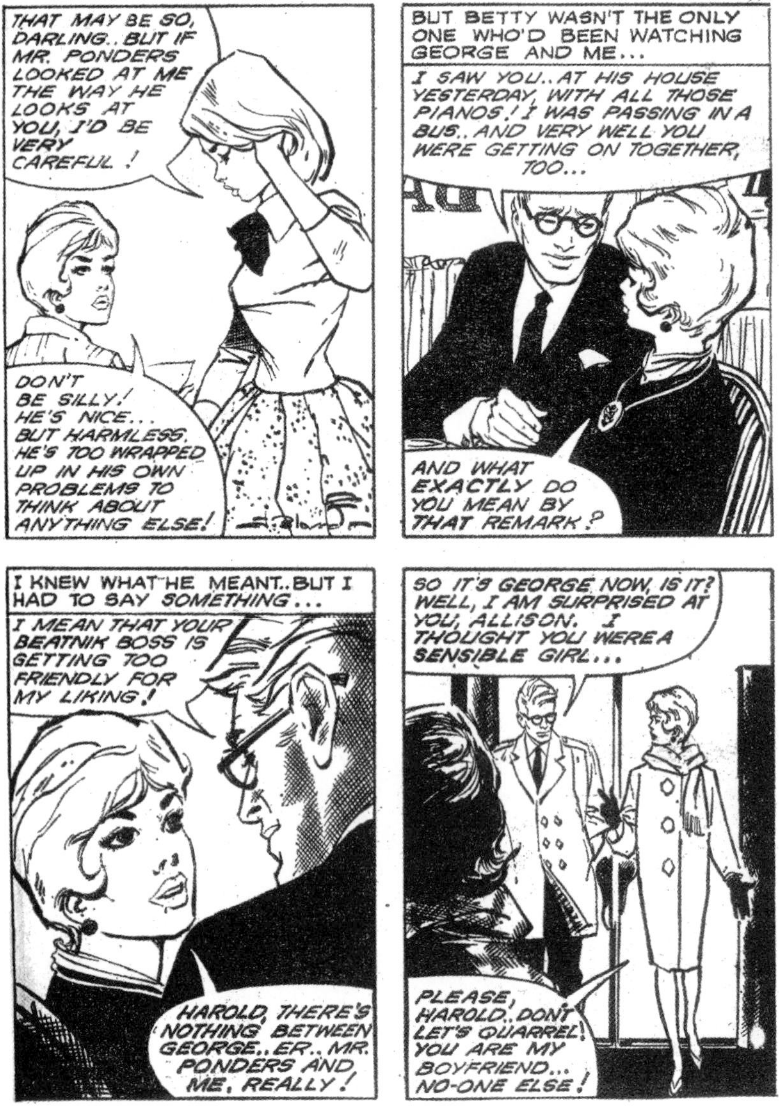
THAT MAY BE SO, DARLING.. BUT IF MR. PONDERS LOOKED AT ME THE WAY HE LOOKS AT YOU, I'D BE VERY CAREFUL !
DON'T BE SILLY! HE'S NICE... BUT HARMLESS. HE'S TOO WRAPPED UP IN HIS OWN PROBLEMS TO THINK ABOUT ANYTHING ELSE!
BUT BETTY WASN'T THE ONLY ONE WHO'D BEEN WATCHING GEORGE AND ME...
I SAW YOU.. AT HIS HOUSE YESTERDAY, WITH ALL THOSE PIANOS! I WAS PASSING IN A BUS.. AND VERY WELL YOU WERE GETTING ON TOGETHER, TOO...
AND WHAT EXACTLY DO YOU MEAN BY THAT REMARK?
I KNEW WHAT HE MEANT.. BUT I HAD TO SAY SOMETHING...
I MEAN THAT YOUR BEATNIK BOSS IS GETTING TOO FRIENDLY FOR MY LIKING!
HAROLD, THERE'S NOTHING BETWEEN GEORGE.. ER.. MR. PONDERS AND ME, REALLY!
SO IT'S GEORGE NOW, IS IT? WELL, I AM SURPRISED AT YOU, ALLISON. I THOUGHT YOU WERE A SENSIBLE GIRL...
PLEASE, HAROLD.. DON'T LET'S QUARREL! YOU ARE MY BOYFRIEND... NO-ONE ELSE!

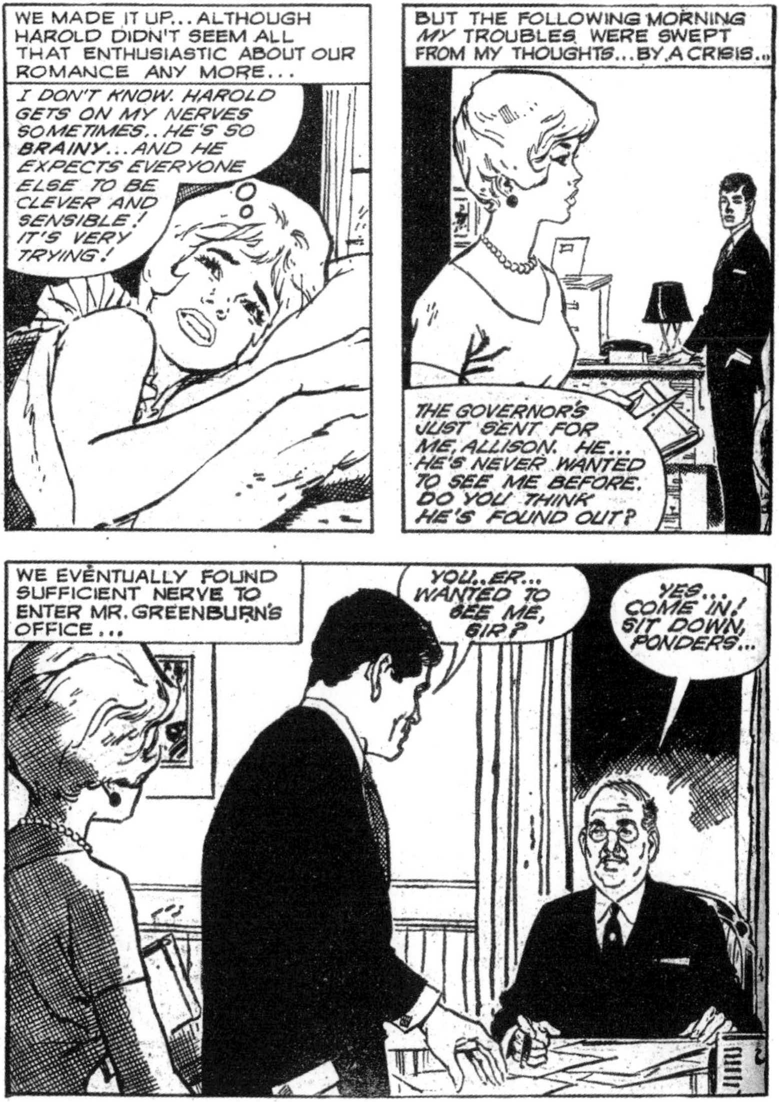
WE MADE IT UP... ALTHOUGH HAROLD DIDN'T SEEM ALL THAT ENTHUSIASTIC ABOUT OUR ROMANCE ANY MORE...
I DON'T KNOW. HAROLD GETS ON MY NERVES SOMETIMES.. HE'S SO BRAINY... AND HE EXPECTS EVERYONE ELSE TO BE CLEVER AND SENSIBLE! IT'S VERY TRYING!
BUT THE FOLLOWING MORNING MY TROUBLES WERE SWEPT FROM MY THOUGHTS... BY A CRISIS...
THE GOVERNOR'S JUST SENT FOR ME, ALLISON. HE... HE'S NEVER WANTED TO SEE ME BEFORE. DO YOU THINK HE'S FOUND OUT?
WE EVENTUALLY FOUND SUFFICIENT NERVE TO ENTER MR. GREENBURN'S OFFICE...
YOU.. ER... WANTED TO SEE ME, SIR?
YES... COME IN! SIT DOWN, PONDERS...

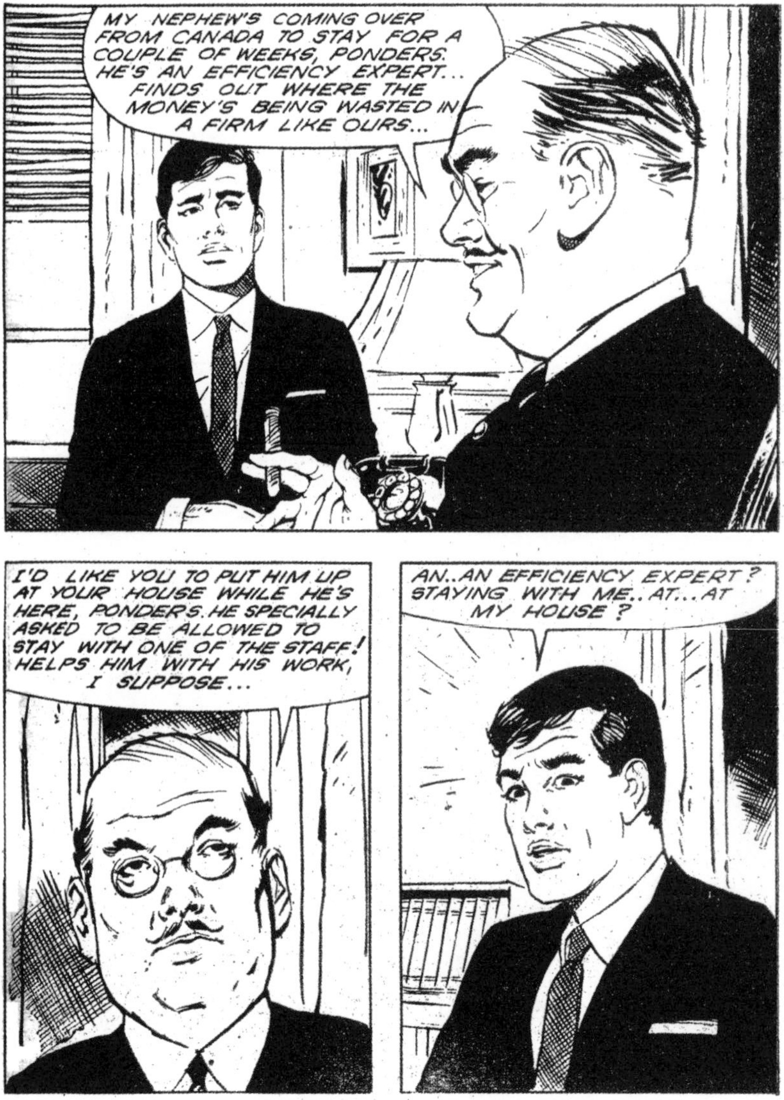
MY NEPHEW'S COMING OVER FROM CANADA TO STAY FOR A COUPLE OF WEEKS, PONDERS. HE'S AN EFFICIENCY EXPERT... FINDS OUT WHERE THE MONEY'S BEING WASTED IN A FIRM LIKE OURS...
I'D LIKE YOU TO PUT HIM UP AT YOUR HOUSE WHILE HE'S HERE, PONDERS. HE SPECIALLY ASKED TO BE ALLOWED TO STAY WITH ONE OF THE STAFF! HELPS HIM WITH HIS WORK, I SUPPOSE...
AN...AN EFFICIENCY EXPERT? STAYING WITH ME...AT...AT MY HOUSE?

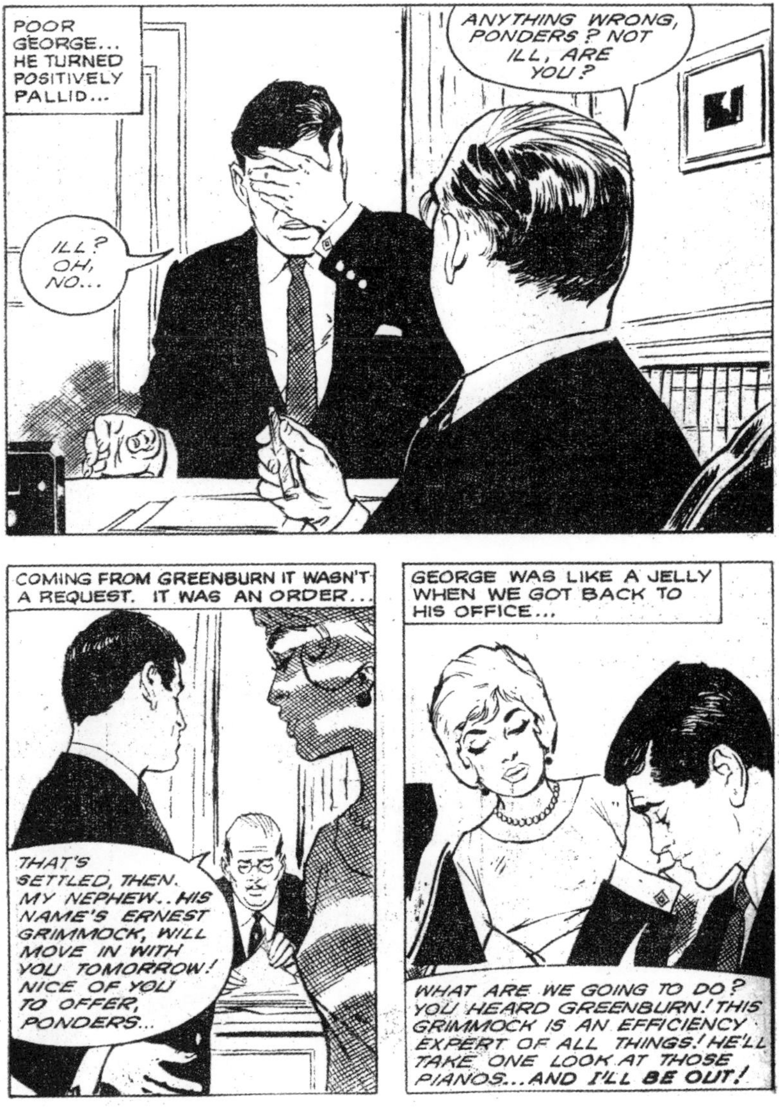
POOR GEORGE... HE TURNED POSITIVELY PALLID...
ANYTHING WRONG, PONDERS? NOT ILL, ARE YOU?
ILL? OH, NO...
COMING FROM GREENBURN IT WASN'T A REQUEST. IT WAS AN ORDER...
THAT'S SETTLED, THEN. MY NEPHEW.. HIS NAME'S ERNEST GRIMMOCK, WILL MOVE IN WITH YOU TOMORROW! NICE OF YOU TO OFFER, PONDERS...
GEORGE WAS LIKE A JELLY WHEN WE GOT BACK TO HIS OFFICE...
WHAT ARE WE GOING TO DO? YOU HEARD GREENBURN! THIS GRIMMOCK IS AN EFFICIENCY EXPERT OF ALL THINGS! HE'LL TAKE ONE LOOK AT THOSE PIANOS... AND I'LL BE OUT!

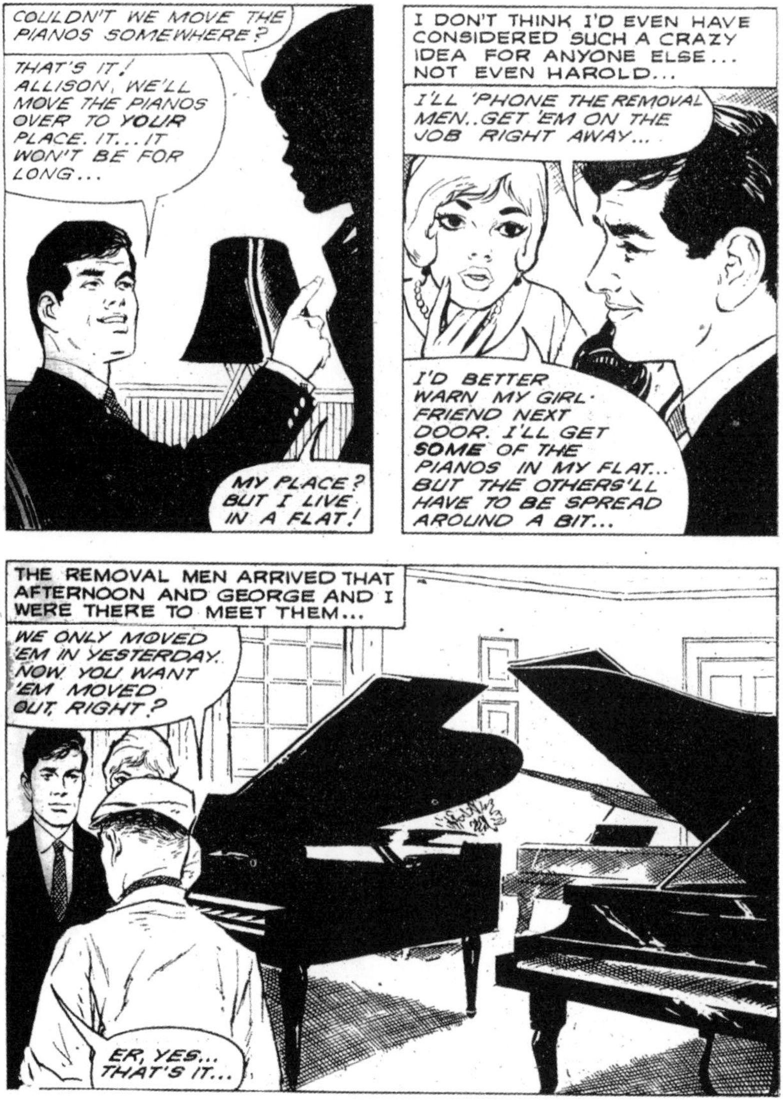
COULDN'T WE MOVE THE PIANOS SOMEWHERE?
THAT'S IT! ALLISON, WE'LL MOVE THE PIANOS OVER TO YOUR PLACE. IT... IT WON'T BE FOR LONG...
MY PLACE? BUT I LIVE IN A FLAT!
I DON'T THINK I'D EVEN HAVE CONSIDERED SUCH A CRAZY IDEA FOR ANYONE ELSE... NOT EVEN HAROLD...
I'LL 'PHONE THE REMOVAL MEN..GET 'EM ON THE JOB RIGHT AWAY...
I'D BETTER WARN MY GIRL-FRIEND NEXT DOOR. I'LL GET SOME OF THE PIANOS IN MY FLAT... BUT THE OTHERS'LL HAVE TO BE SPREAD AROUND A BIT...
THE REMOVAL MEN ARRIVED THAT AFTERNOON AND GEORGE AND I WERE THERE TO MEET THEM...
WE ONLY MOVED 'EM IN YESTERDAY. NOW YOU WANT 'EM MOVED OUT, RIGHT?
ER, YES... THAT'S IT...

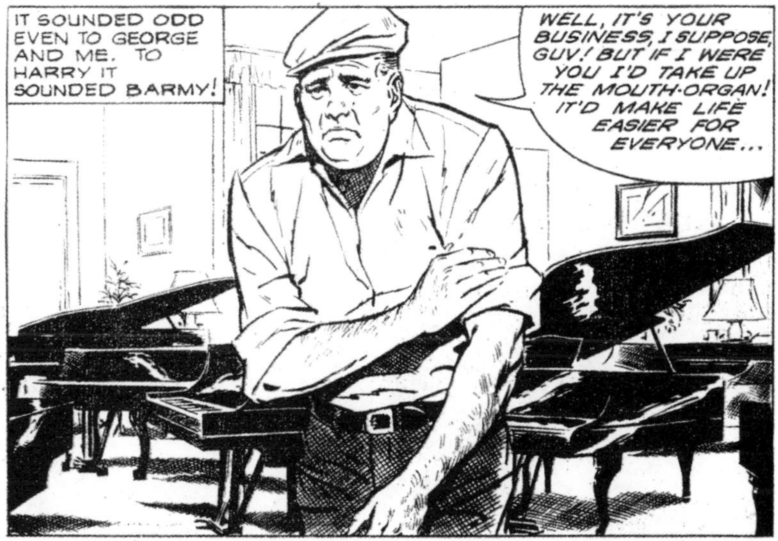
IT SOUNDED ODD EVEN TO GEORGE AND ME. TO HARRY IT SOUNDED BARMY!
WELL, IT'S YOUR BUSINESS, I SUPPOSE, GUV! BUT IF I WERE YOU I'D TAKE UP THE MOUTH-ORGAN! IT'D MAKE LIFE EASIER FOR EVERYONE...

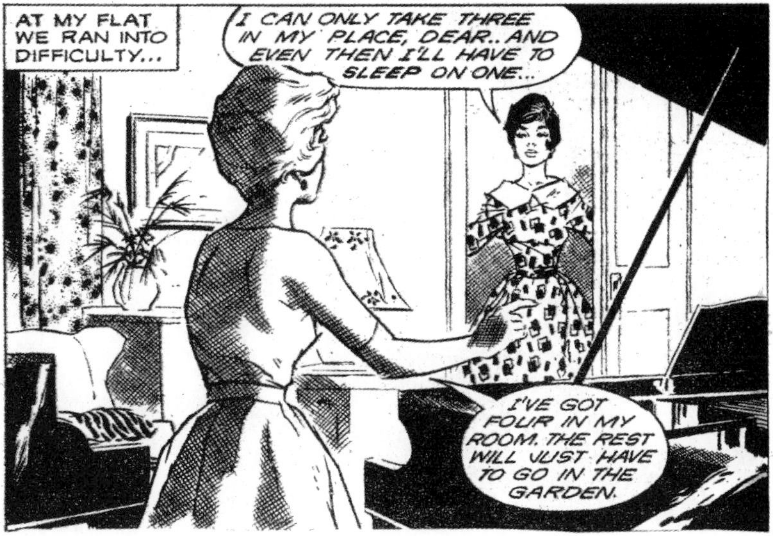
AT MY FLAT WE RAN INTO DIFFICULTY...
I CAN ONLY TAKE THREE IN MY PLACE, DEAR.. AND EVEN THEN I'LL HAVE TO SLEEP ON ONE...
I'VE GOT FOUR IN MY ROOM. THE REST WILL JUST HAVE TO GO IN THE GARDEN.

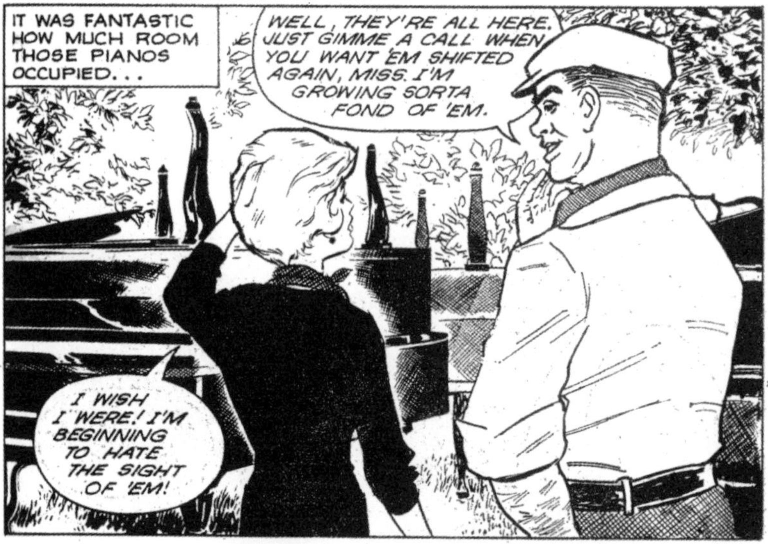
IT WAS FANTASTIC HOW MUCH ROOM THOSE PIANOS OCCUPIED...
WELL, THEY'RE ALL HERE. JUST GIMME A CALL WHEN YOU WANT 'EM SHIFTED AGAIN, MISS. I'M GROWING SORTA FOND OF 'EM.
I WISH I WERE! I'M BEGINNING TO HATE THE SIGHT OF 'EM!

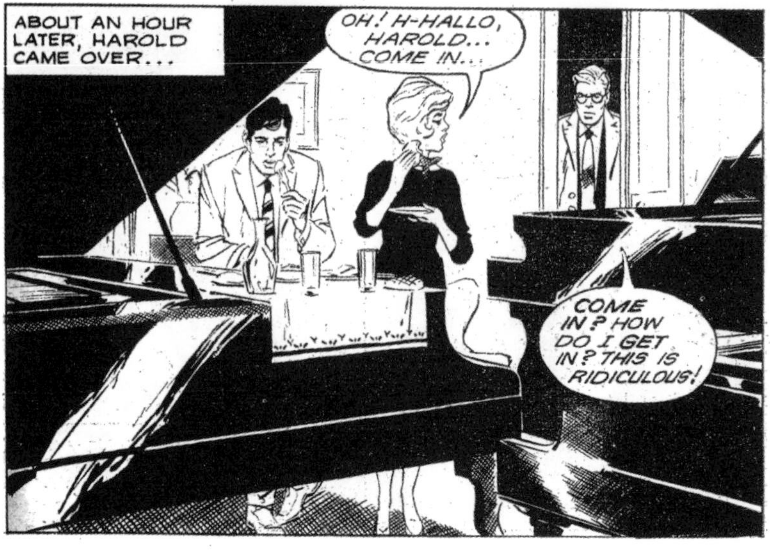
ABOUT AN HOUR LATER, HAROLD CAME OVER...
OH! H-HALLO, HAROLD... COME IN...
COME IN? HOW DO I GET IN? THIS IS RIDICULOUS!

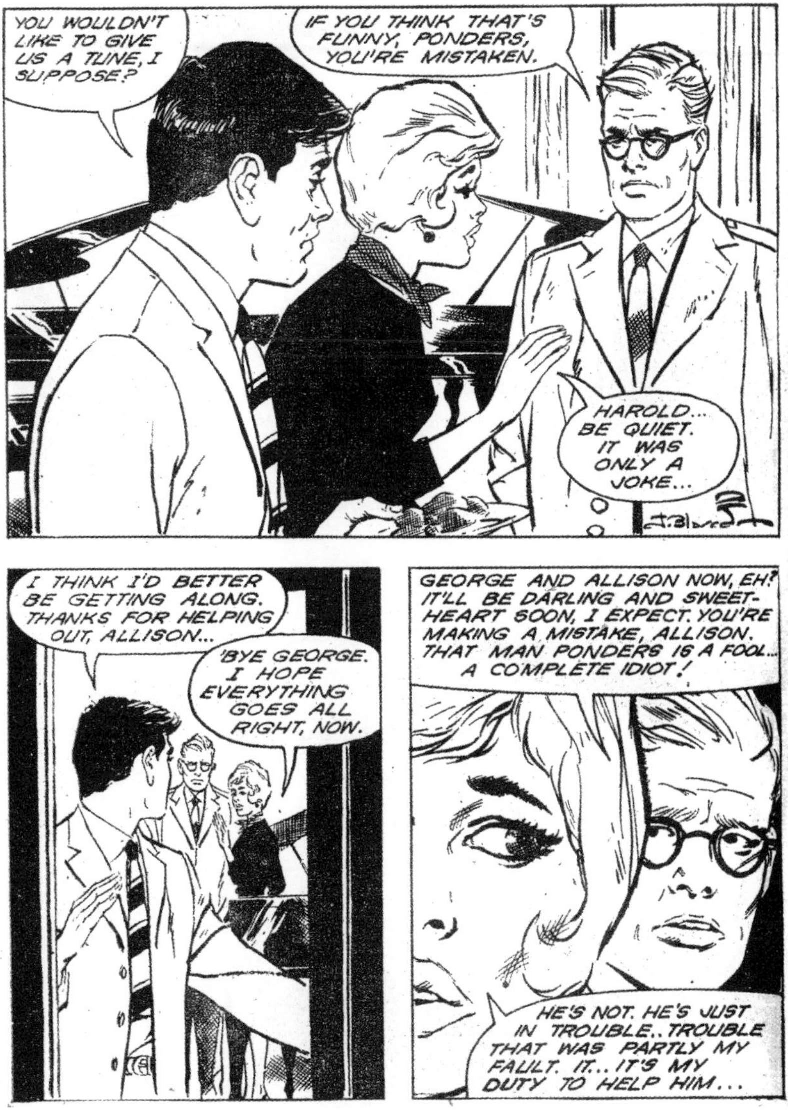
YOU WOULDN'T LIKE TO GIVE US A TUNE, I SUPPOSE?
IF YOU THINK THAT'S FUNNY, PONDERS, YOU'RE MISTAKEN.
HAROLD... BE QUIET. IT WAS ONLY A JOKE...
I THINK I'D BETTER BE GETTING ALONG. THANKS FOR HELPING OUT, ALLISON...
'BYE GEORGE. I HOPE EVERYTHING GOES ALL RIGHT, NOW.
GEORGE AND ALLISON NOW, EH? IT'LL BE DARLING AND SWEET-HEART SOON, I EXPECT. YOU'RE MAKING A MISTAKE, ALLISON. THAT MAN PONDERS IS A FOOL... A COMPLETE IDIOT!
HE'S NOT. HE'S JUST IN TROUBLE.. TROUBLE THAT WAS PARTLY MY FAULT. IT... IT'S MY DUTY TO HELP HIM...

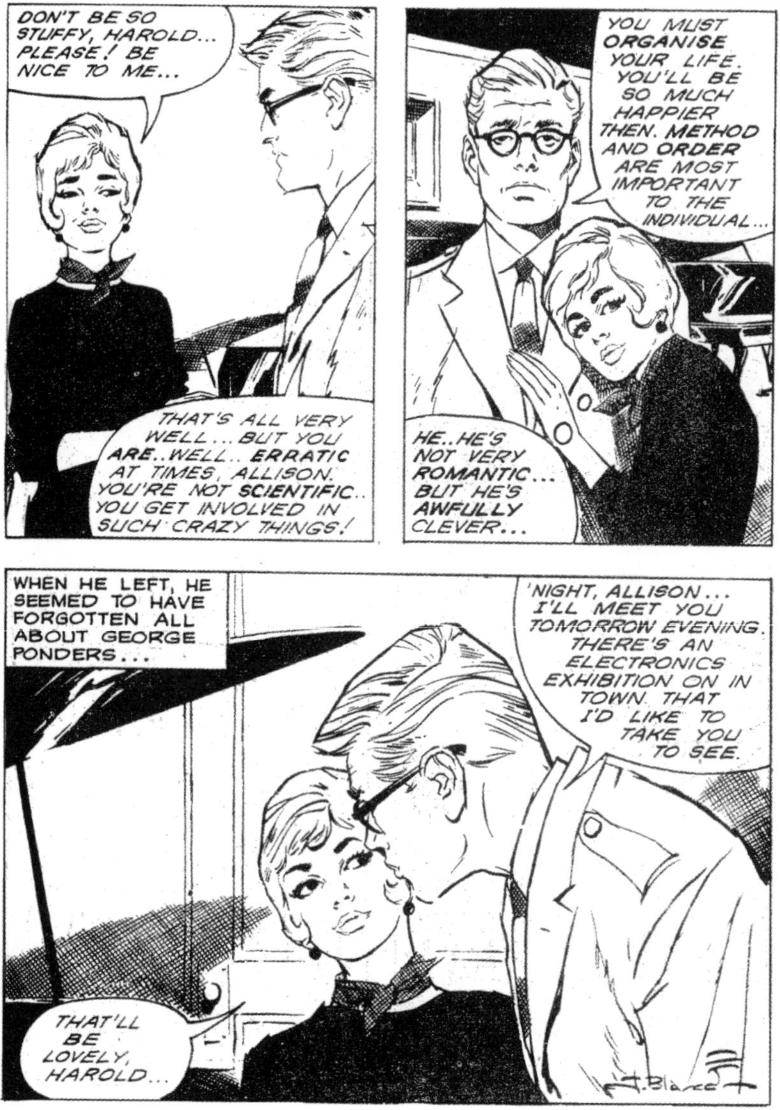
DON'T BE SO STUFFY, HAROLD... PLEASE! BE NICE TO ME...
THAT'S ALL VERY WELL... BUT YOU ARE..WELL.. ERRATIC AT TIMES, ALLISON. YOU'RE NOT SCIENTIFIC.. YOU GET INVOLVED IN SUCH CRAZY THINGS!
YOU MUST ORGANISE YOUR LIFE. YOU'LL BE SO MUCH HAPPIER THEN. METHOD AND ORDER ARE MOST IMPORTANT TO THE INDIVIDUAL...
HE..HE'S NOT VERY ROMANTIC... BUT HE'S AWFULLY CLEVER...
WHEN HE LEFT, HE SEEMED TO HAVE FORGOTTEN ALL ABOUT GEORGE PONDERS...
'NIGHT, ALLISON... I'LL MEET YOU TOMORROW EVENING. THERE'S AN ELECTRONICS EXHIBITION ON IN TOWN THAT I'D LIKE TO TAKE YOU TO SEE.
THAT'LL BE LOVELY, HAROLD...

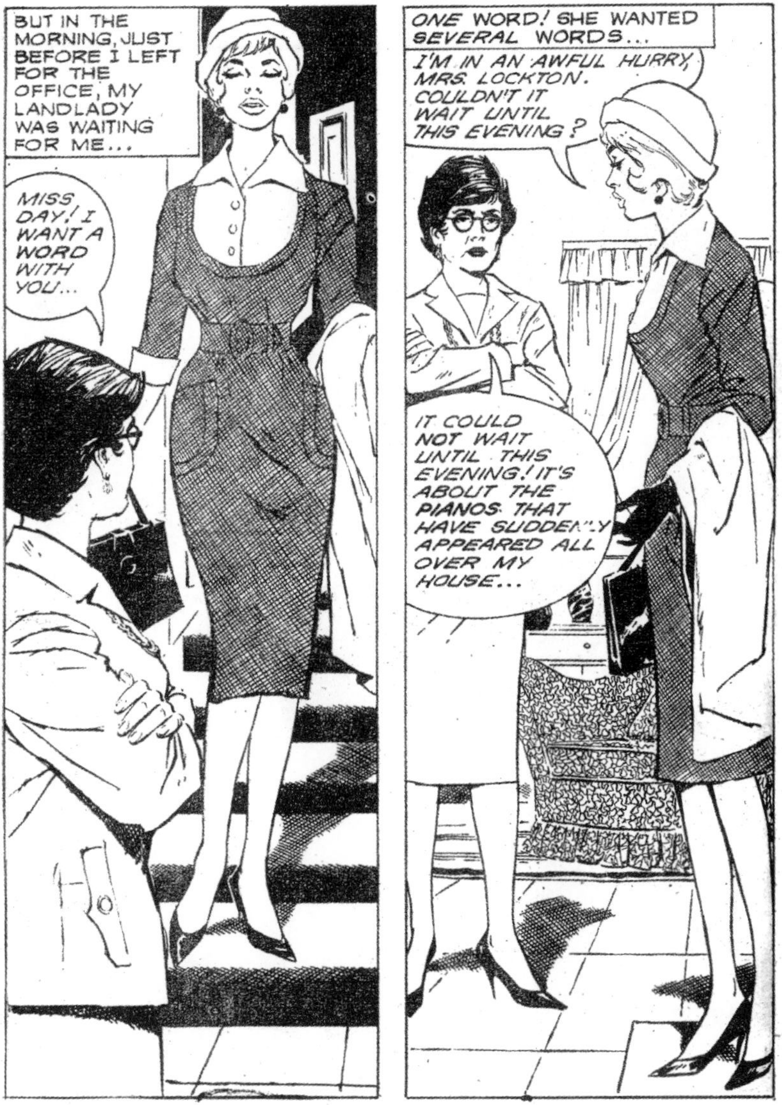
BUT IN THE MORNING, JUST BEFORE I LEFT FOR THE OFFICE, MY LANDLADY WAS WAITING FOR ME...
MISS DAY! I WANT A WORD WITH YOU...
ONE WORD! SHE WANTED SEVERAL WORDS...
I'M IN AN AWFUL HURRY, MRS. LOCKTON. COULDN'T IT WAIT UNTIL THIS EVENING?
IT COULD NOT WAIT UNTIL THIS EVENING! IT'S ABOUT THE PIANOS THAT HAVE SUDDENLY APPEARED ALL OVER MY HOUSE...

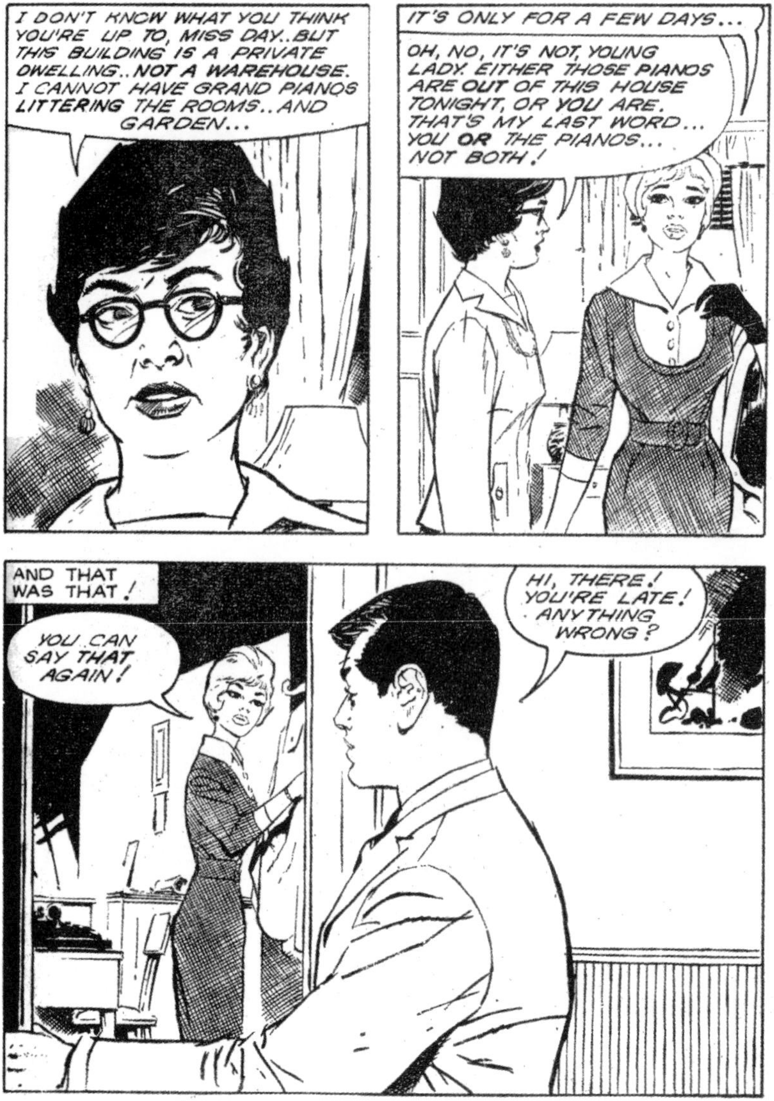
I DON'T KNOW WHAT YOU THINK YOU'RE UP TO, MISS DAY..BUT THIS BUILDING IS A PRIVATE DWELLING..NOT A WAREHOUSE. I CANNOT HAVE GRAND PIANOS LITTERING THE ROOMS..AND GARDEN...
IT'S ONLY FOR A FEW DAYS...
OH, NO, IT'S NOT, YOUNG LADY. EITHER THOSE PIANOS ARE OUT OF THIS HOUSE TONIGHT, OR YOU ARE. THAT'S MY LAST WORD... YOU OR THE PIANOS... NOT BOTH!
AND THAT WAS THAT!
HI, THERE! YOU'RE LATE! ANYTHING WRONG?
YOU CAN SAY THAT AGAIN!

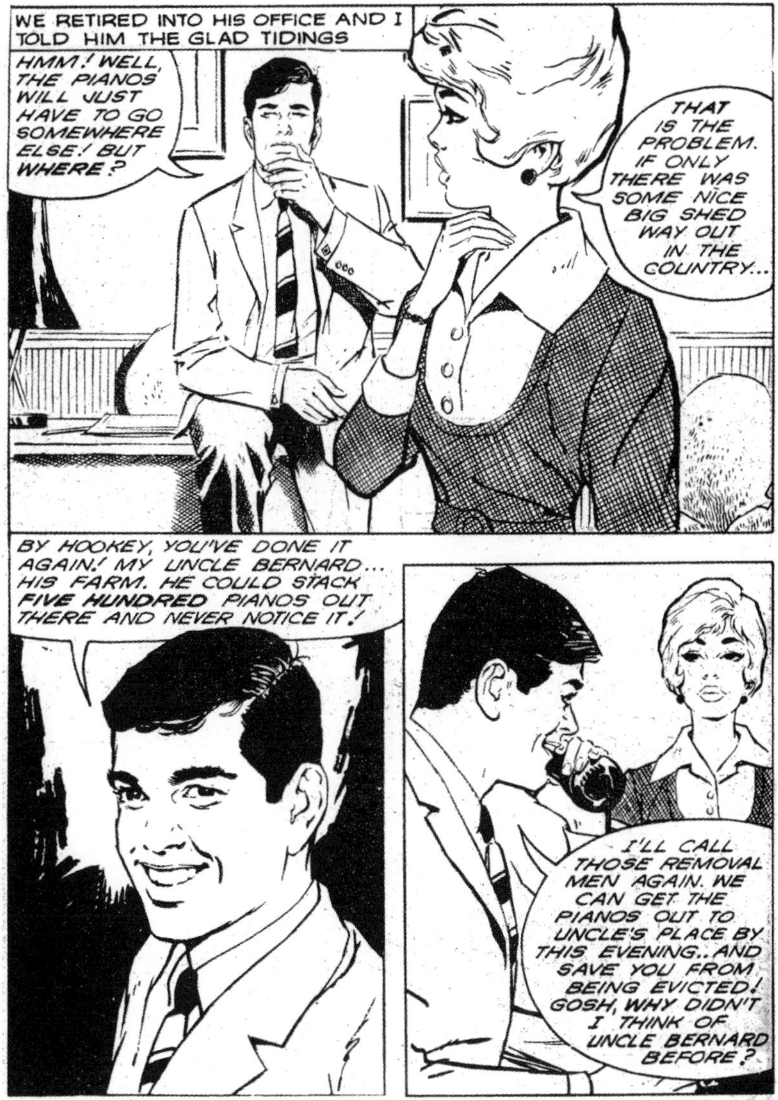
WE RETIRED INTO HIS OFFICE AND I TOLD HIM THE GLAD TIDINGS
HMM! WELL, THE PIANOS WILL JUST HAVE TO GO SOMEWHERE ELSE! BUT WHERE?
THAT IS THE PROBLEM. IF ONLY THERE WAS SOME NICE BIG SHED WAY OUT IN THE COUNTRY...
BY HOOKEY, YOU'VE DONE IT AGAIN! MY UNCLE BERNARD... HIS FARM. HE COULD STACK FIVE HUNDRED PIANOS OUT THERE AND NEVER NOTICE IT!
I'LL CALL THOSE REMOVAL MEN AGAIN. WE CAN GET THE PIANOS OUT TO UNCLE'S PLACE BY THIS EVENING.. AND SAVE YOU FROM BEING EVICTED! GOSH, WHY DIDN'T I THINK OF UNCLE BERNARD BEFORE?

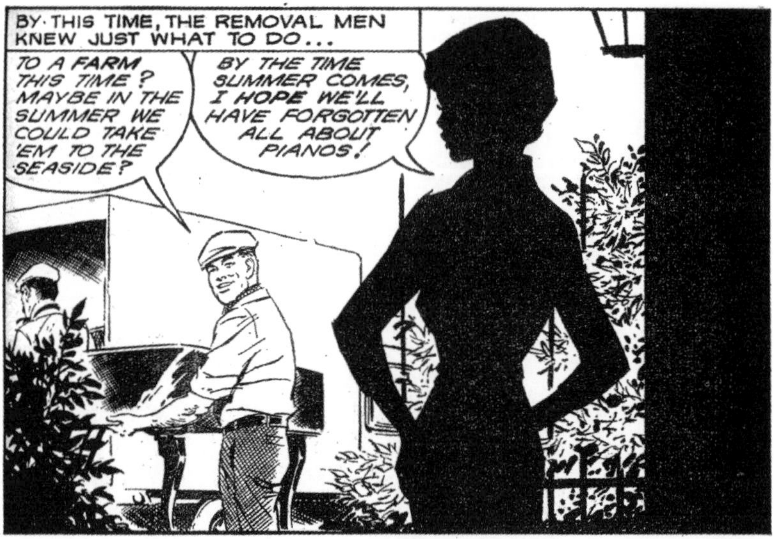
BY THIS TIME, THE REMOVAL MEN KNEW JUST WHAT TO DO...
TO A FARM THIS TIME? MAYBE IN THE SUMMER WE COULD TAKE 'EM TO THE SEASIDE?
BY THE TIME SUMMER COMES, I HOPE WE'LL HAVE FORGOTTEN ALL ABOUT PIANOS!

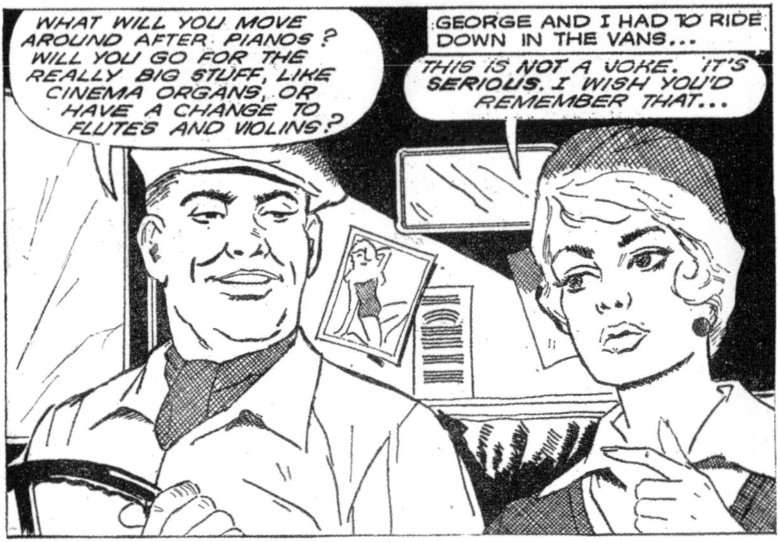
GEORGE AND I HAD TO RIDE DOWN IN THE VANS...
WHAT WILL YOU MOVE AROUND AFTER PIANOS? WILL YOU GO FOR THE REALLY BIG STUFF, LIKE CINEMA ORGANS, OR HAVE A CHANGE TO FLUTES AND VIOLINS?
THIS IS NOT A JOKE. IT'S SERIOUS. I WISH YOU'D REMEMBER THAT...

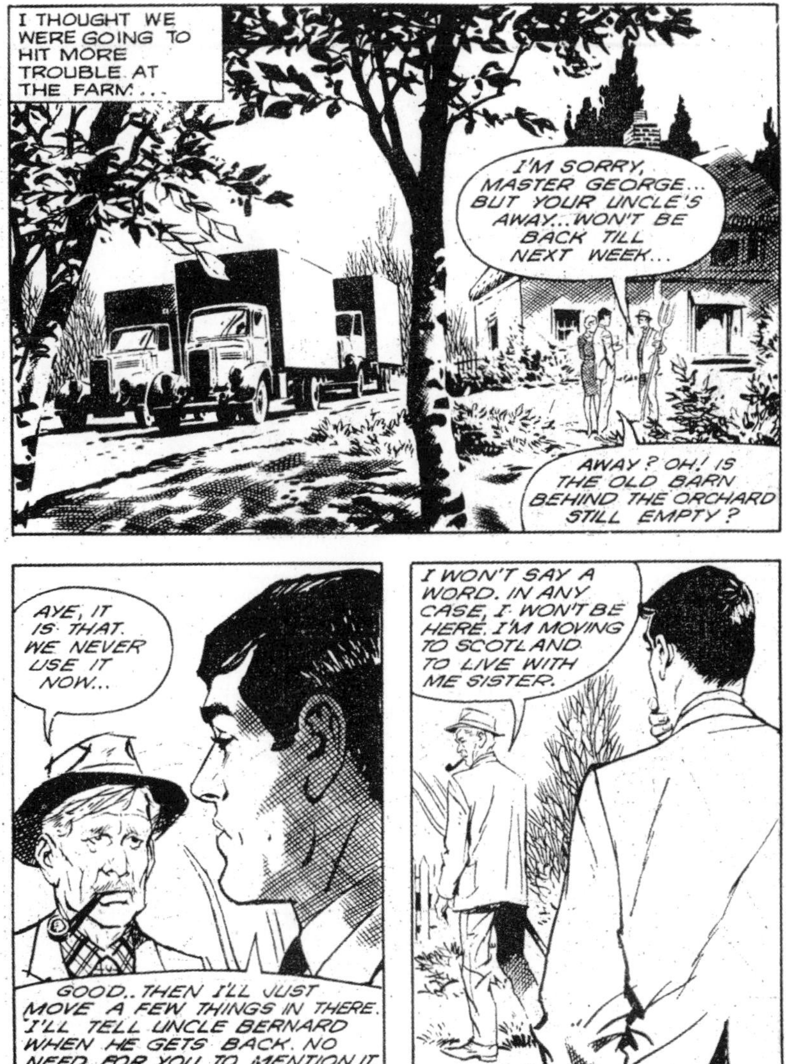
I THOUGHT WE WERE GOING TO HIT MORE TROUBLE AT THE FARM...
I'M SORRY, MASTER GEORGE... BUT YOUR UNCLE'S AWAY...WON'T BE BACK TILL NEXT WEEK...
AWAY? OH! IS THE OLD BARN BEHIND THE ORCHARD STILL EMPTY?
AYE, IT IS THAT. WE NEVER USE IT NOW...
GOOD..THEN I'LL JUST MOVE A FEW THINGS IN THERE. I'LL TELL UNCLE BERNARD WHEN HE GETS BACK. NO NEED FOR YOU TO MENTION IT FRED...I'LL..I'LL SURPRISE HIM!
I WON'T SAY A WORD. IN ANY CASE, I WON'T BE HERE. I'M MOVING TO SCOTLAND TO LIVE WITH ME SISTER.

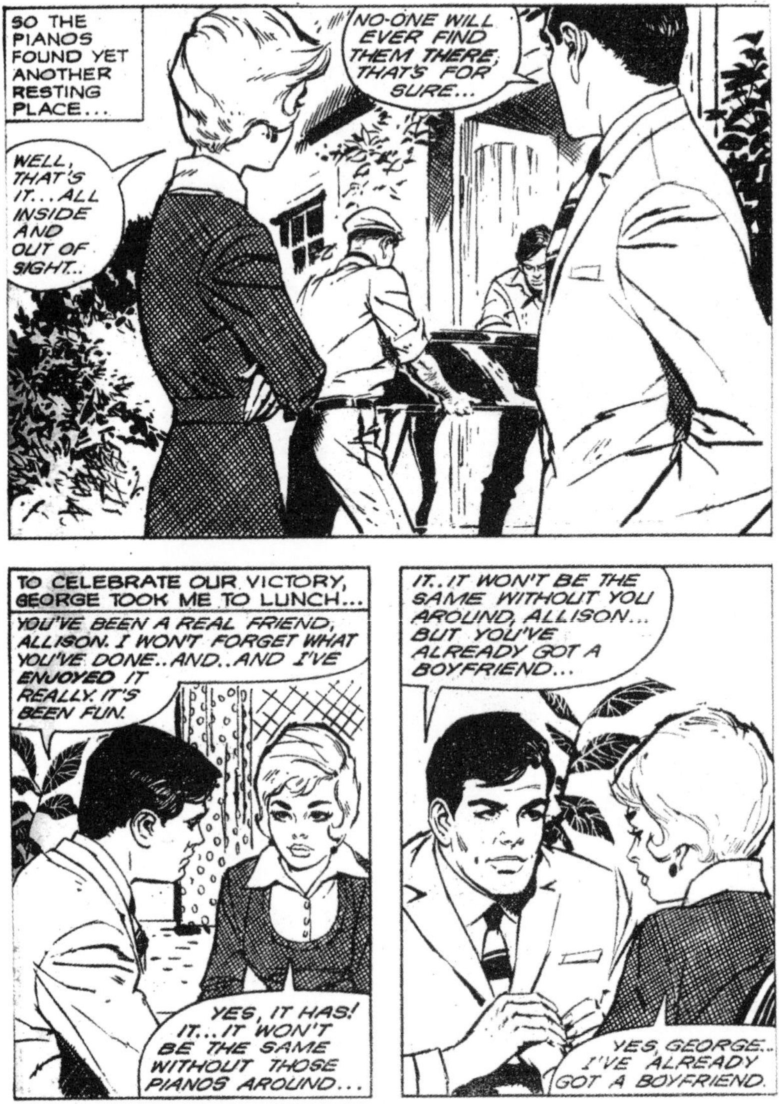
SO THE PIANOS FOUND YET ANOTHER RESTING PLACE...
NO-ONE WILL EVER FIND THEM THERE, THAT'S FOR SURE...
WELL, THAT'S IT... ALL INSIDE AND OUT OF SIGHT...
TO CELEBRATE OUR VICTORY, GEORGE TOOK ME TO LUNCH...
YOU'VE BEEN A REAL FRIEND, ALLISON. I WON'T FORGET WHAT YOU'VE DONE.. AND.. AND I'VE ENJOYED IT REALLY. IT'S BEEN FUN.
YES, IT HAS! IT... IT WON'T BE THE SAME WITHOUT THOSE PIANOS AROUND...
IT.. IT WON'T BE THE SAME WITHOUT YOU AROUND, ALLISON... BUT YOU'VE ALREADY GOT A BOYFRIEND...
YES, GEORGE... I'VE ALREADY GOT A BOYFRIEND.

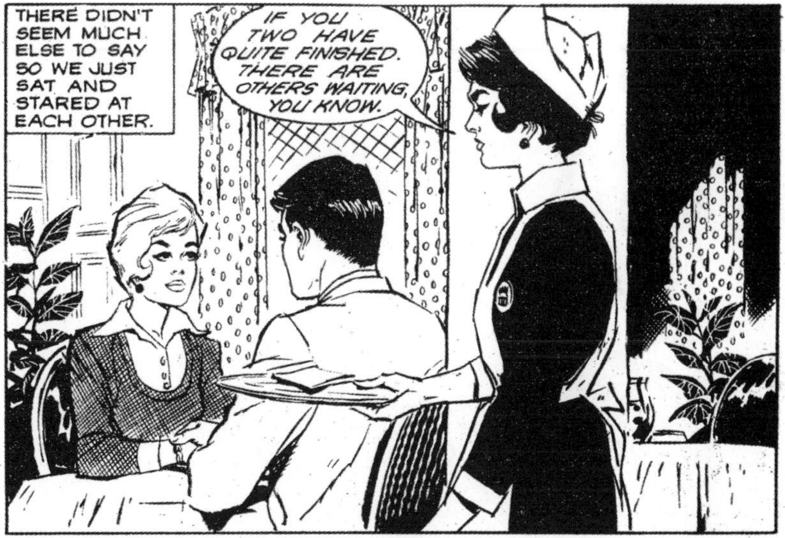
THERE DIDN'T SEEM MUCH ELSE TO SAY SO WE JUST SAT AND STARED AT EACH OTHER.
IF YOU TWO HAVE QUITE FINISHED. THERE ARE OTHERS WAITING, YOU KNOW.

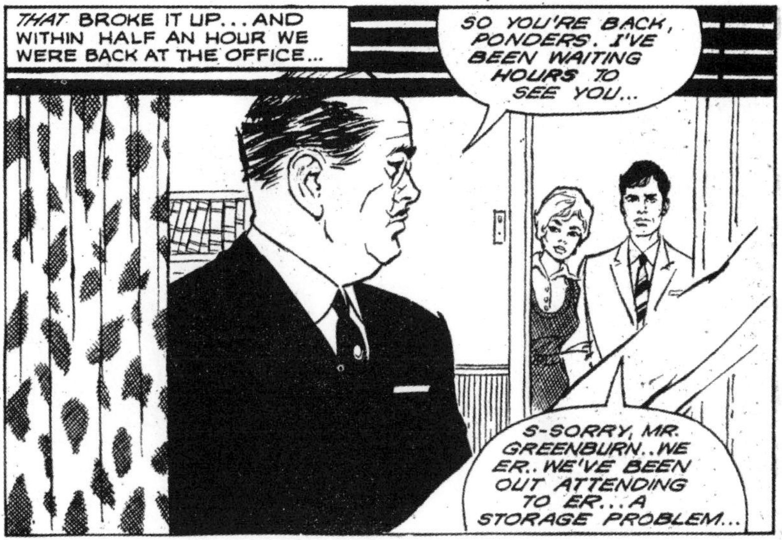
THAT BROKE IT UP... AND WITHIN HALF AN HOUR WE WERE BACK AT THE OFFICE...
SO YOU'RE BACK, PONDERS. I'VE BEEN WAITING HOURS TO SEE YOU...
S-SORRY, MR. GREENBURN.. WE ER.. WE'VE BEEN OUT ATTENDING TO ER... A STORAGE PROBLEM...

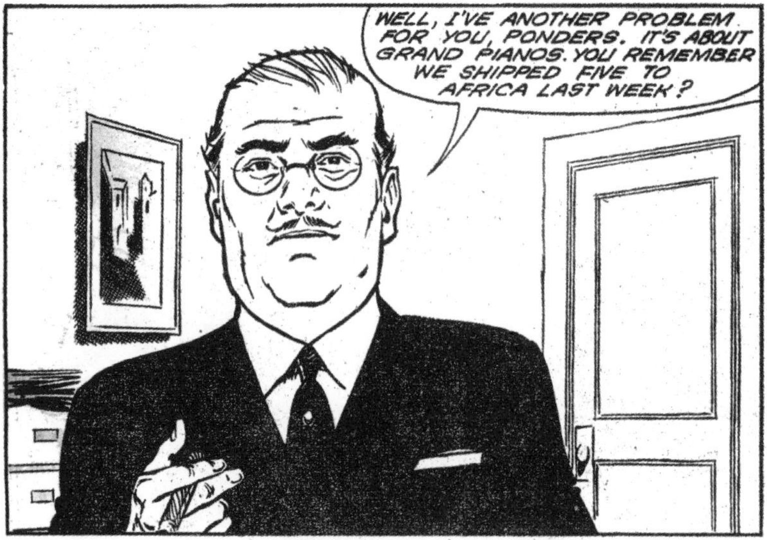
WELL, I'VE ANOTHER PROBLEM FOR YOU, PONDERS. IT'S ABOUT GRAND PIANOS. YOU REMEMBER WE SHIPPED FIVE TO AFRICA LAST WEEK?

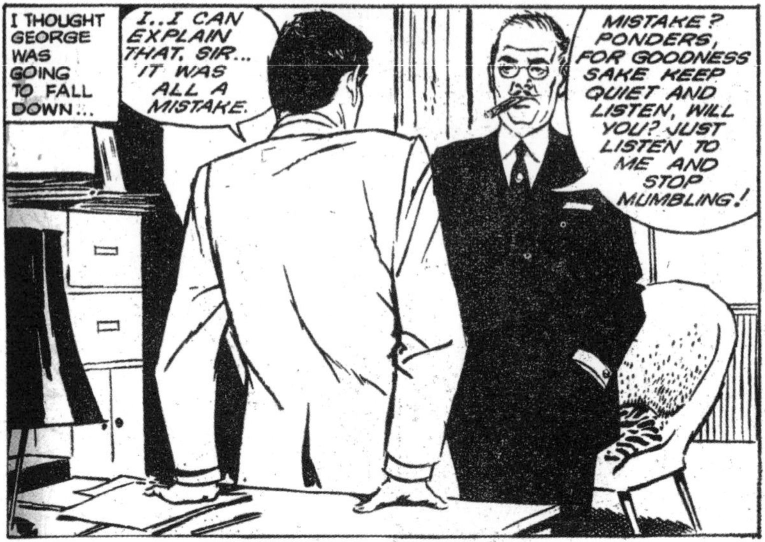
I THOUGHT GEORGE WAS GOING TO FALL DOWN...
I..I CAN EXPLAIN THAT, SIR... IT WAS ALL A MISTAKE.
MISTAKE? PONDERS, FOR GOODNESS SAKE KEEP QUIET AND LISTEN, WILL YOU? JUST LISTEN TO ME AND STOP MUMBLING!

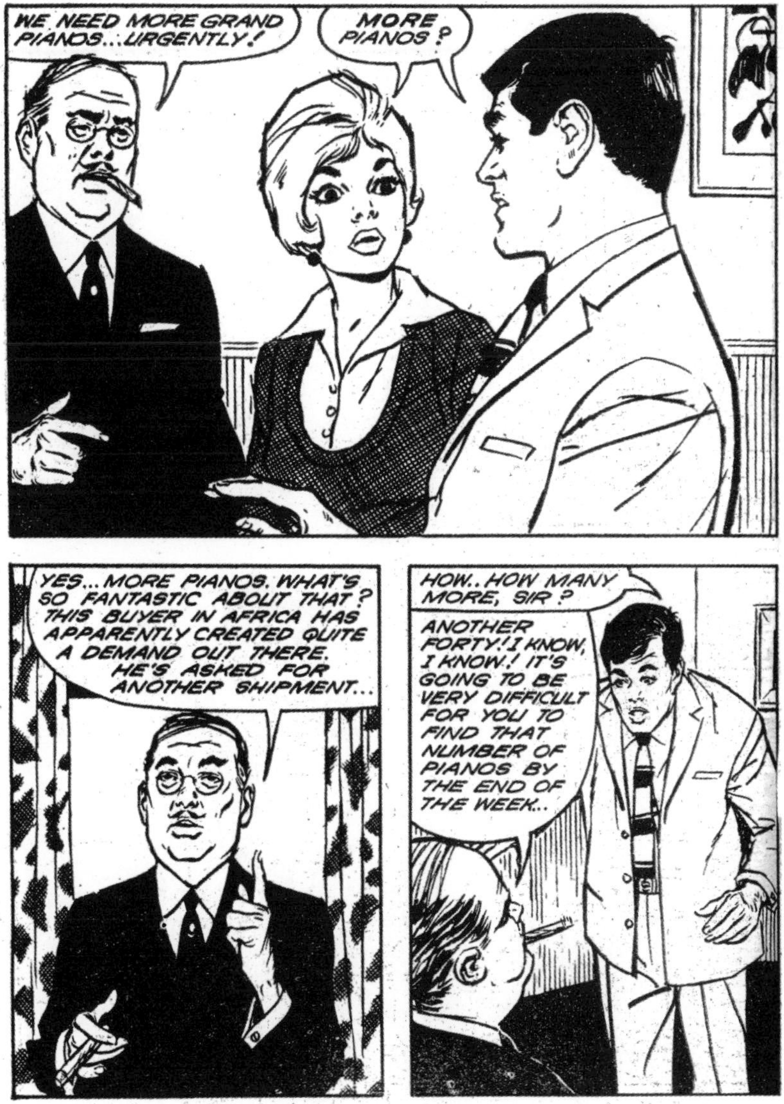
WE NEED MORE GRAND PIANOS...URGENTLY!
MORE PIANOS?
YES...MORE PIANOS. WHAT'S SO FANTASTIC ABOUT THAT? THIS BUYER IN AFRICA HAS APPARENTLY CREATED QUITE A DEMAND OUT THERE. HE'S ASKED FOR ANOTHER SHIPMENT...
HOW.. HOW MANY MORE, SIR?
ANOTHER FORTY! I KNOW, I KNOW! IT'S GOING TO BE VERY DIFFICULT FOR YOU TO FIND THAT NUMBER OF PIANOS BY THE END OF THE WEEK...

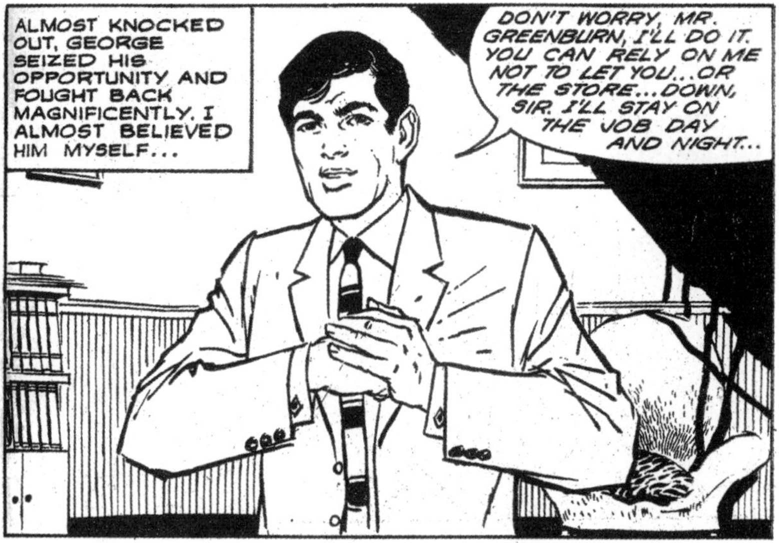
ALMOST KNOCKED OUT, GEORGE SEIZED HIS OPPORTUNITY AND FOUGHT BACK MAGNIFICENTLY. I ALMOST BELIEVED HIM MYSELF...
DON'T WORRY, MR. GREENBURN, I'LL DO IT. YOU CAN RELY ON ME NOT TO LET YOU...OR THE STORE...DOWN, SIR. I'LL STAY ON THE JOB DAY AND NIGHT...

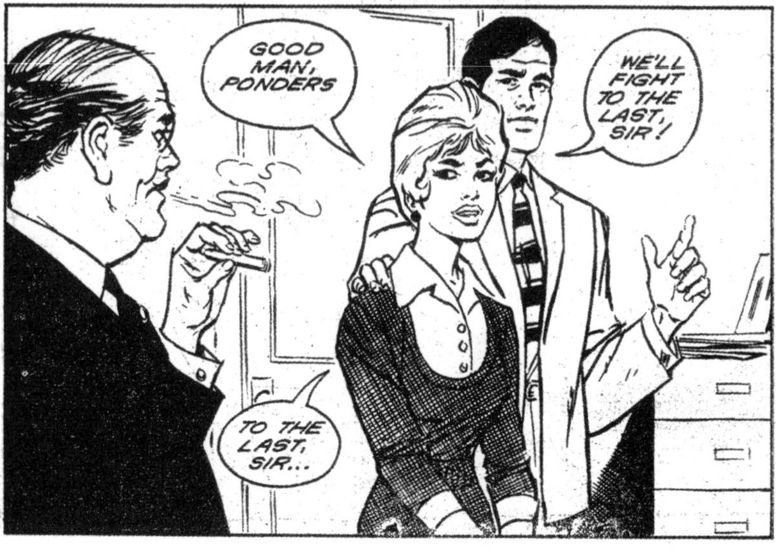
GOOD MAN, PONDERS
WE'LL FIGHT TO THE LAST, SIR!
TO THE LAST, SIR...

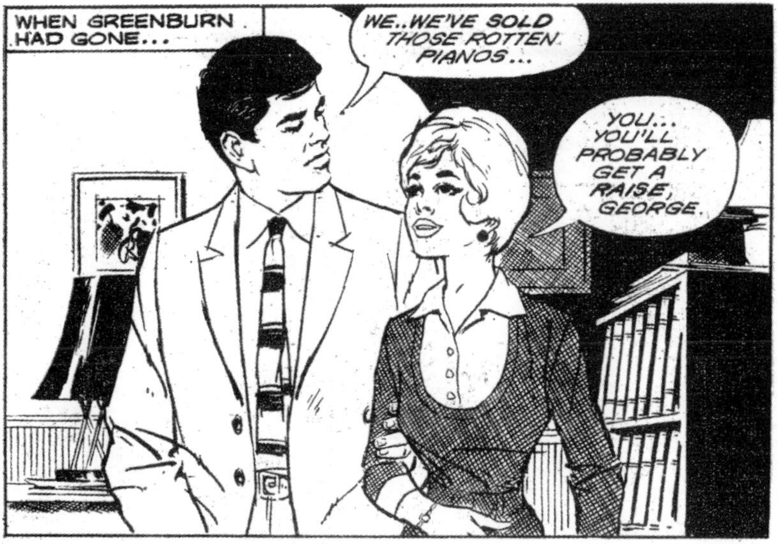
WHEN GREENBURN HAD GONE...
WE..WE'VE SOLD THOSE ROTTEN PIANOS...
YOU... YOU'LL PROBABLY GET A RAISE, GEORGE.

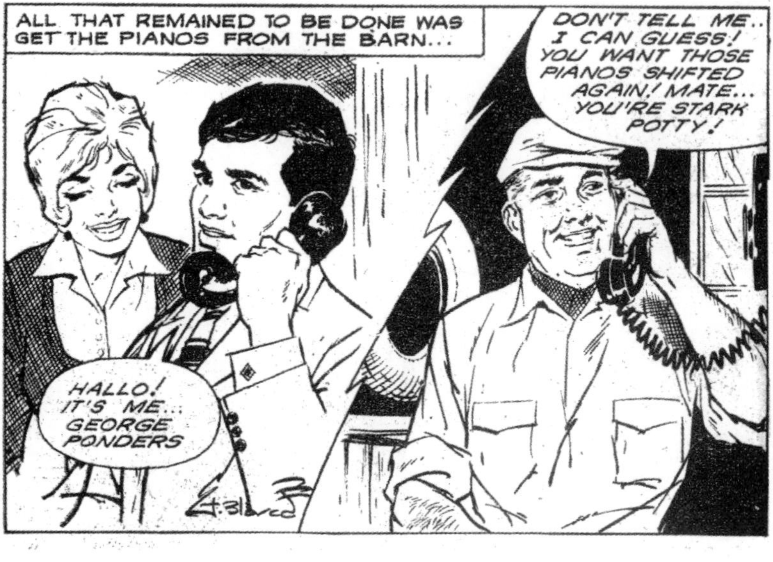
ALL THAT REMAINED TO BE DONE WAS GET THE PIANOS FROM THE BARN...
HALLO! IT'S ME... GEORGE PONDERS
DON'T TELL ME.. I CAN GUESS! YOU WANT THOSE PIANOS SHIFTED AGAIN! MATE... YOU'RE STARK POTTY!

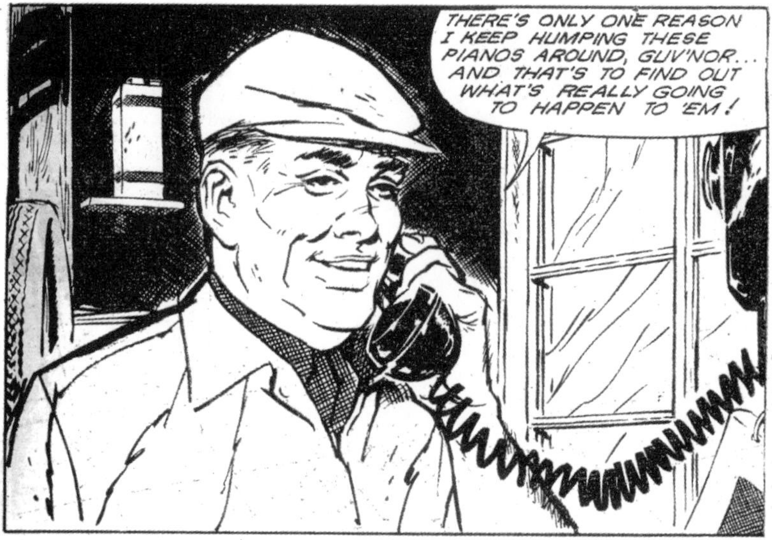
THERE'S ONLY ONE REASON I KEEP HUMPING THESE PIANOS AROUND, GUV'NOR... AND THAT'S TO FIND OUT WHAT'S REALLY GOING TO HAPPEN TO 'EM!

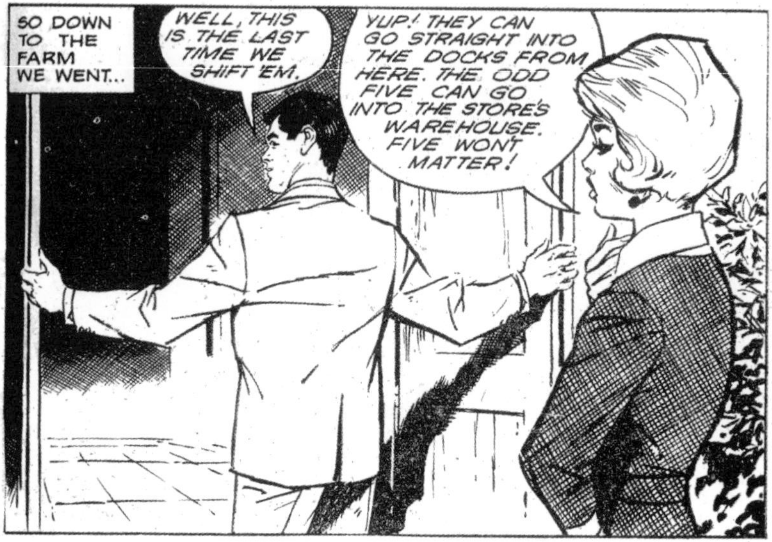
SO DOWN TO THE FARM WE WENT...
WELL, THIS IS THE LAST TIME WE SHIFT 'EM.
YUP! THEY CAN GO STRAIGHT INTO THE DOCKS FROM HERE. THE ODD FIVE CAN GO INTO THE STORE'S WAREHOUSE. FIVE WON'T MATTER!

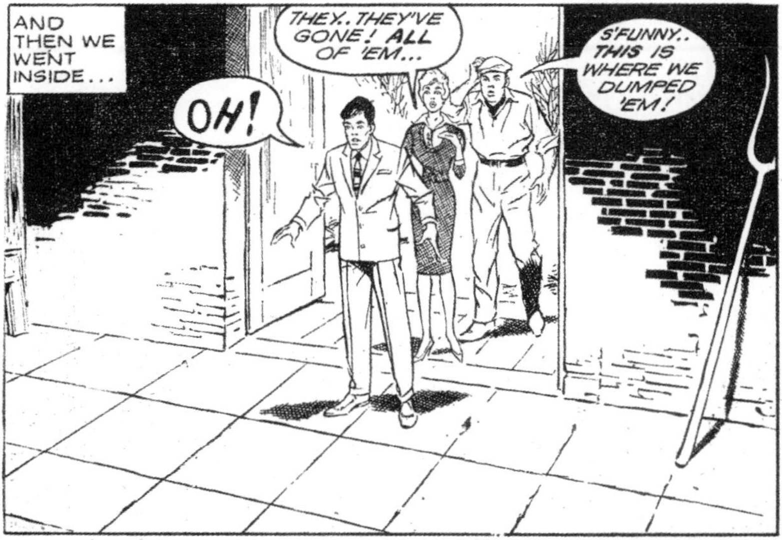
AND THEN WE WENT INSIDE...
THEY..THEY'VE GONE! ALL OF 'EM...
S'FUNNY.. THIS IS WHERE WE DUMPED 'EM!
OH!

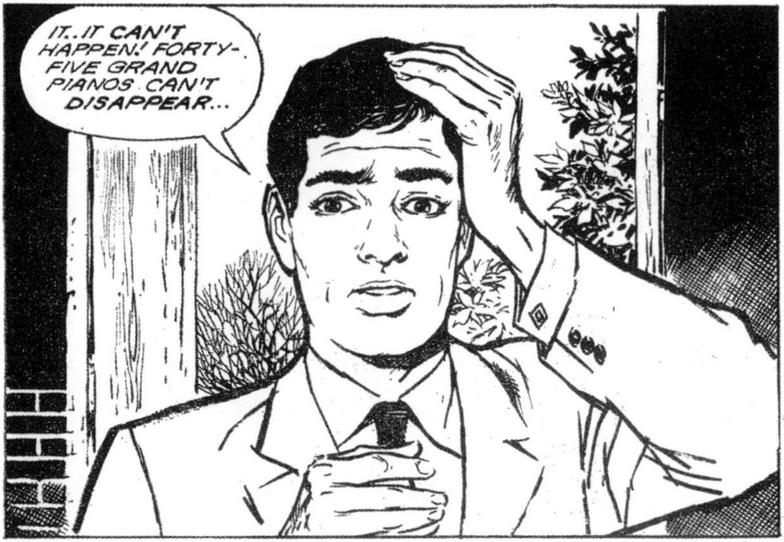
IT..IT CAN'T HAPPEN! FORTY-FIVE GRAND PIANOS CAN'T DISAPPEAR...

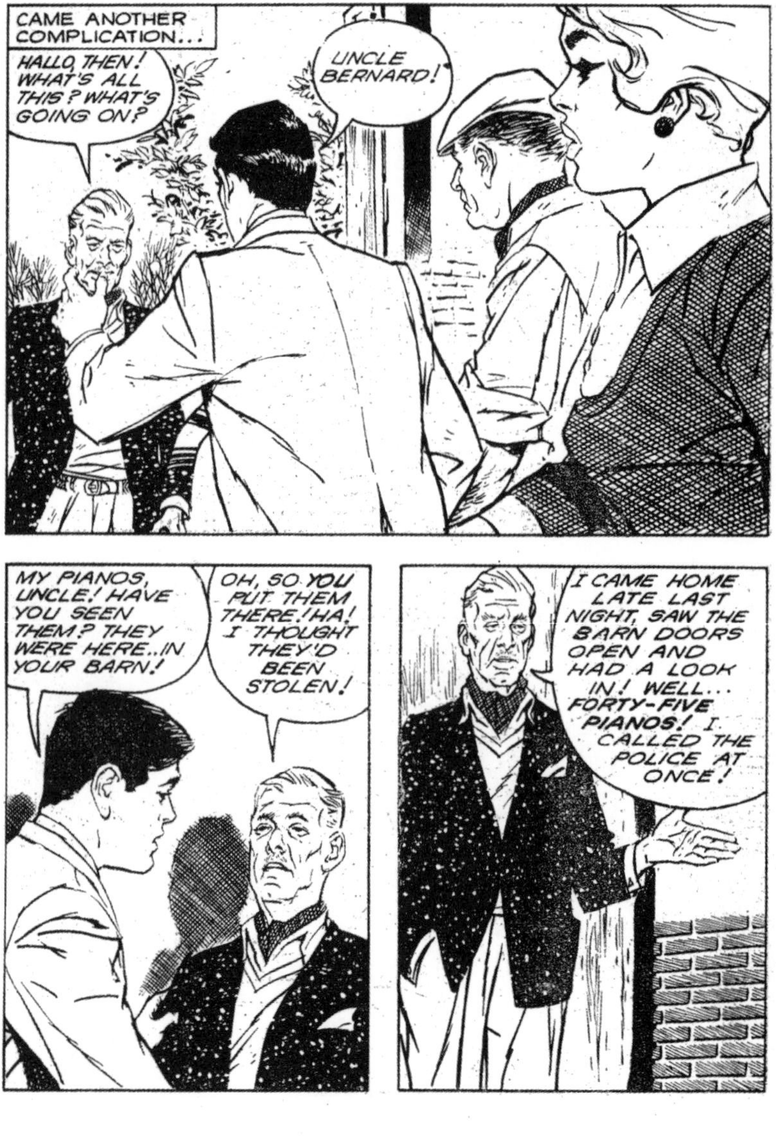
CAME ANOTHER COMPLICATION...
HALLO THEN! WHAT'S ALL THIS? WHAT'S GOING ON?
UNCLE BERNARD!
MY PIANOS, UNCLE! HAVE YOU SEEN THEM? THEY WERE HERE..IN YOUR BARN!
OH, SO YOU PUT THEM THERE! HA! I THOUGHT THEY'D BEEN STOLEN!
I CAME HOME LATE LAST NIGHT, SAW THE BARN DOORS OPEN AND HAD A LOOK IN! WELL... FORTY-FIVE PIANOS! I CALLED THE POLICE AT ONCE!

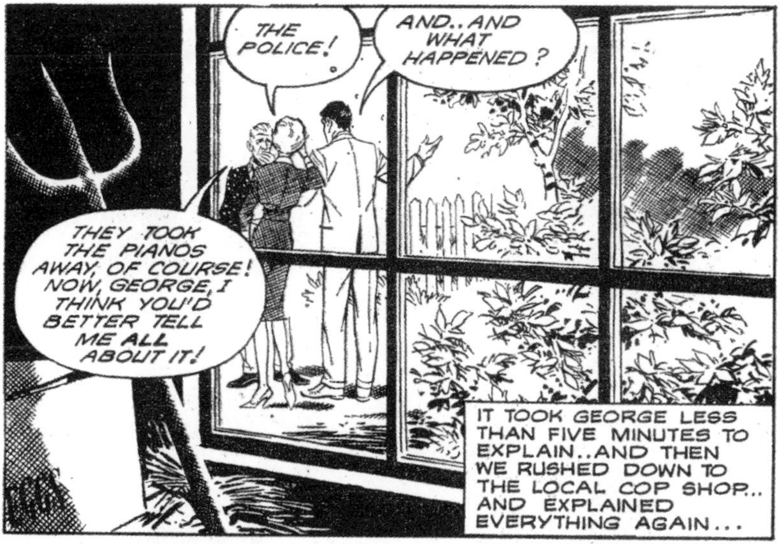
THE POLICE!
AND..AND WHAT HAPPENED?
THEY TOOK THE PIANOS AWAY, OF COURSE! NOW, GEORGE, I THINK YOU'D BETTER TELL ME ALL ABOUT IT!
IT TOOK GEORGE LESS THAN FIVE MINUTES TO EXPLAIN..AND THEN WE RUSHED DOWN TO THE LOCAL COP SHOP... AND EXPLAINED EVERYTHING AGAIN...

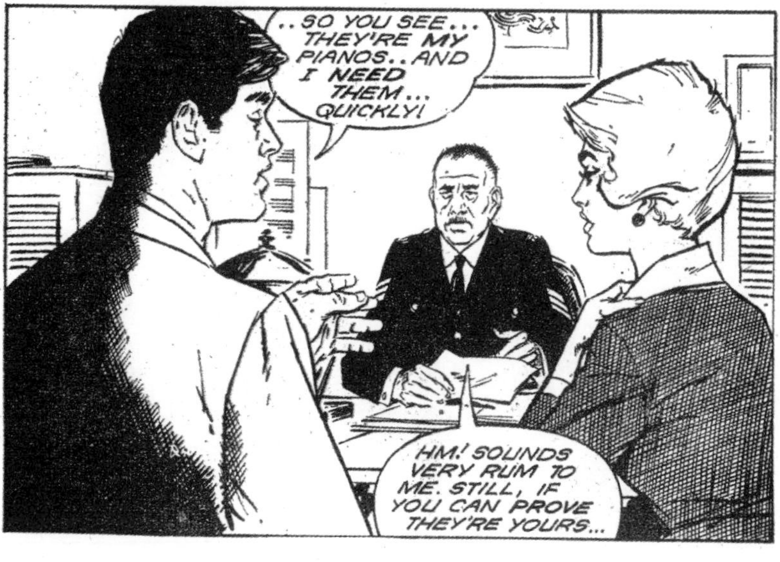
..SO YOU SEE... THEY'RE MY PIANOS..AND I NEED THEM... QUICKLY!
HM! SOUNDS VERY RUM TO ME. STILL, IF YOU CAN PROVE THEY'RE YOURS...

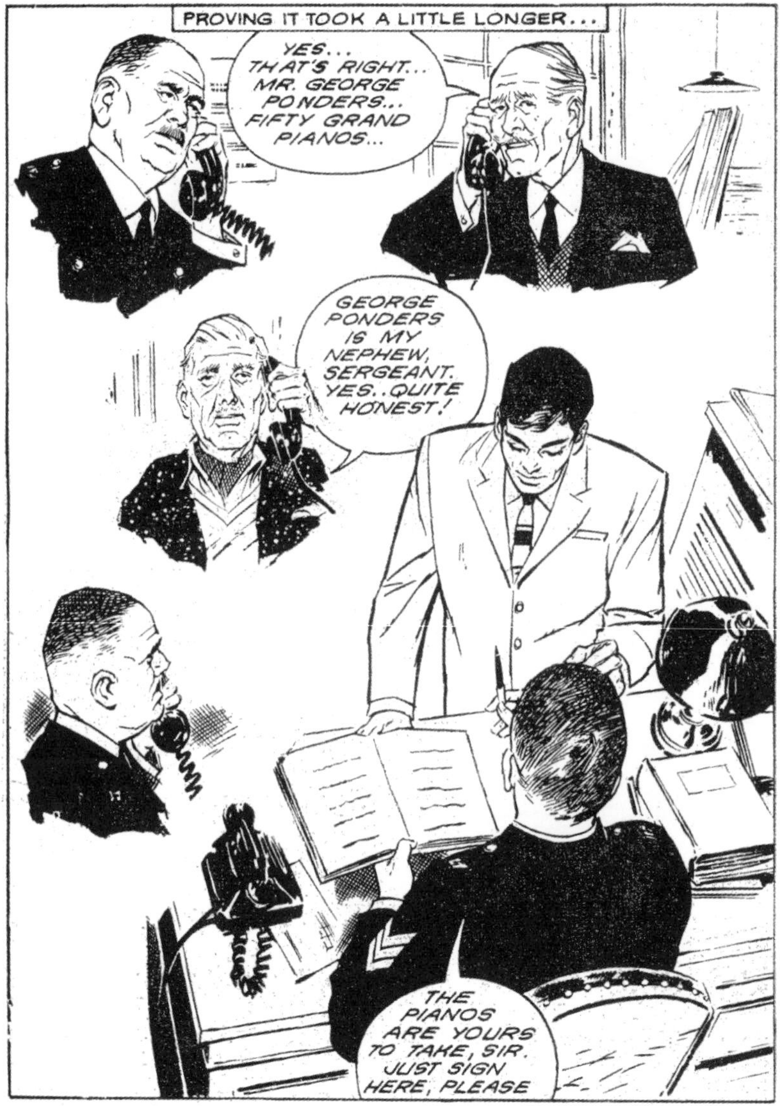
PROVING IT TOOK A LITTLE LONGER...
YES... THAT'S RIGHT... MR. GEORGE PONDERS... FIFTY GRAND PIANOS...
GEORGE PONDERS IS MY NEPHEW, SERGEANT. YES..QUITE HONEST!
THE PIANOS ARE YOURS TO TAKE, SIR. JUST SIGN HERE, PLEASE

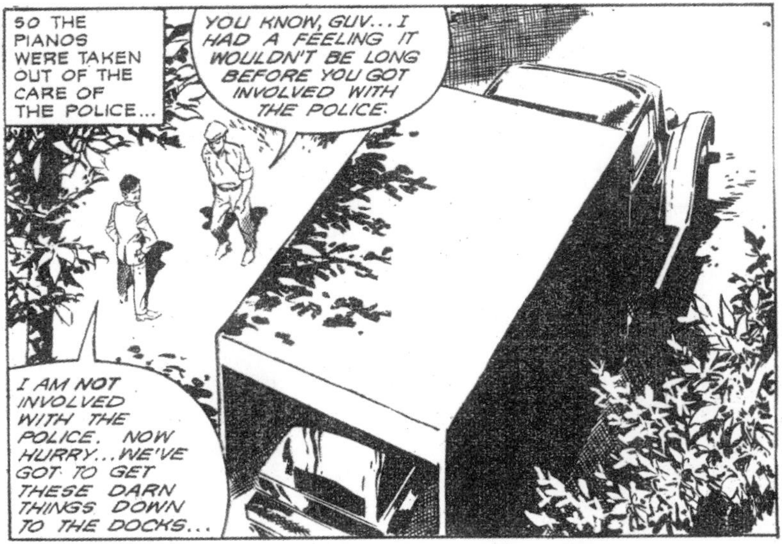
SO THE PIANOS WERE TAKEN OUT OF THE CARE OF THE POLICE...
YOU KNOW, GUV... I HAD A FEELING IT WOULDN'T BE LONG BEFORE YOU GOT INVOLVED WITH THE POLICE.
I AM NOT INVOLVED WITH THE POLICE. NOW HURRY...WE'VE GOT TO GET THESE DARN THINGS DOWN TO THE DOCKS...

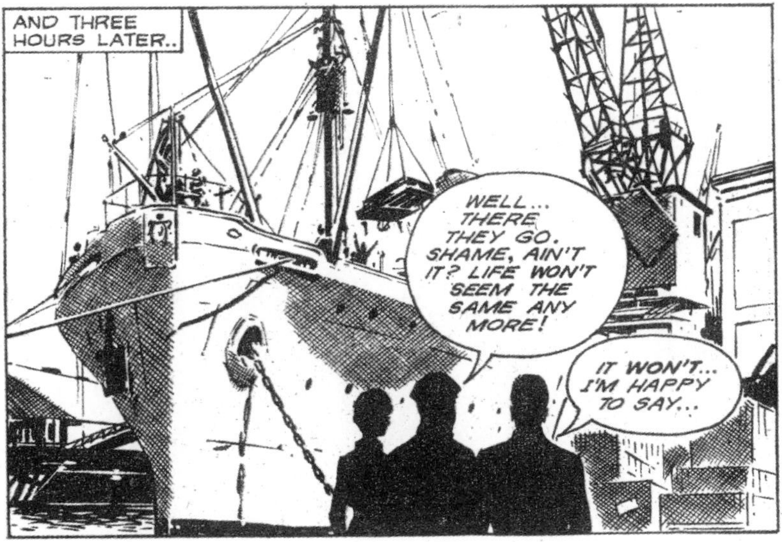
AND THREE HOURS LATER..
WELL... THERE THEY GO. SHAME, AIN'T IT? LIFE WON'T SEEM THE SAME ANY MORE!
IT WON'T... I'M HAPPY TO SAY...

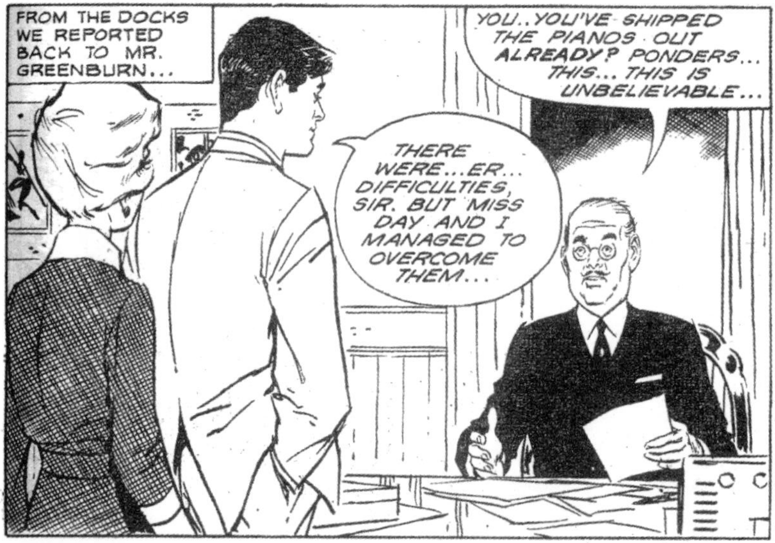
FROM THE DOCKS WE REPORTED BACK TO MR. GREENBURN...
YOU..YOU'VE SHIPPED THE PIANOS OUT ALREADY? PONDERS... THIS... THIS IS UNBELIEVABLE...
THERE WERE...ER... DIFFICULTIES, SIR. BUT MISS DAY AND I MANAGED TO OVERCOME THEM...

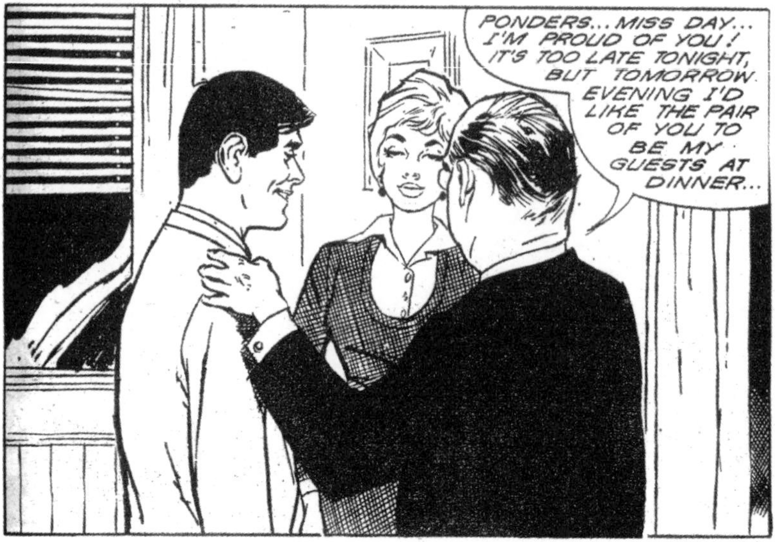
PONDERS... MISS DAY... I'M PROUD OF YOU! IT'S TOO LATE TONIGHT, BUT TOMORROW EVENING I'D LIKE THE PAIR OF YOU TO BE MY GUESTS AT DINNER...

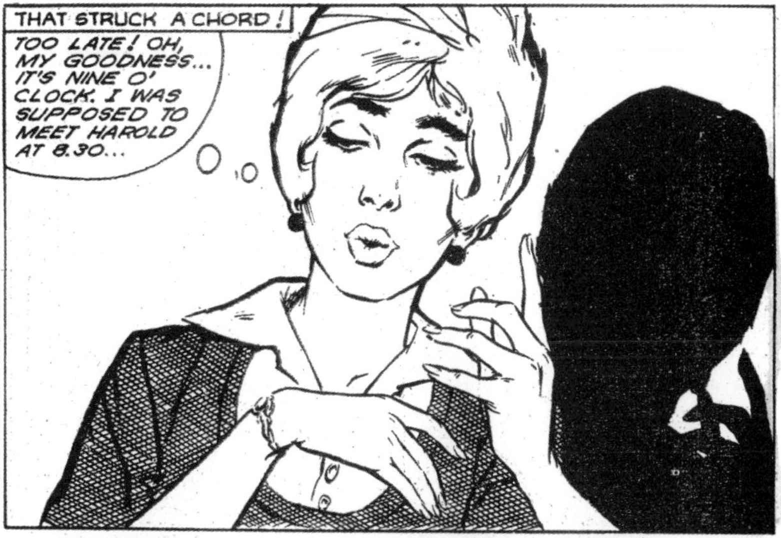
THAT STRUCK A CHORD!
TOO LATE! OH, MY GOODNESS... IT'S NINE O' CLOCK. I WAS SUPPOSED TO MEET HAROLD AT 8.30...

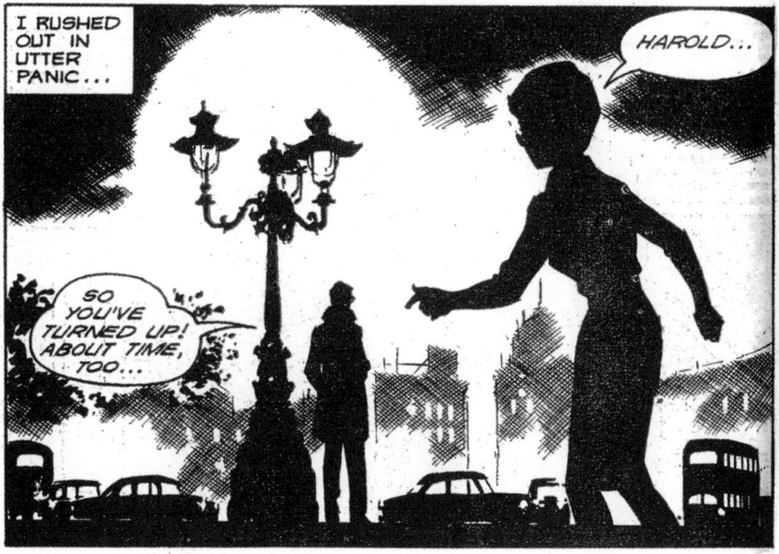
I RUSHED OUT IN UTTER PANIC...
HAROLD...
SO YOU'VE TURNED UP! ABOUT TIME, TOO...

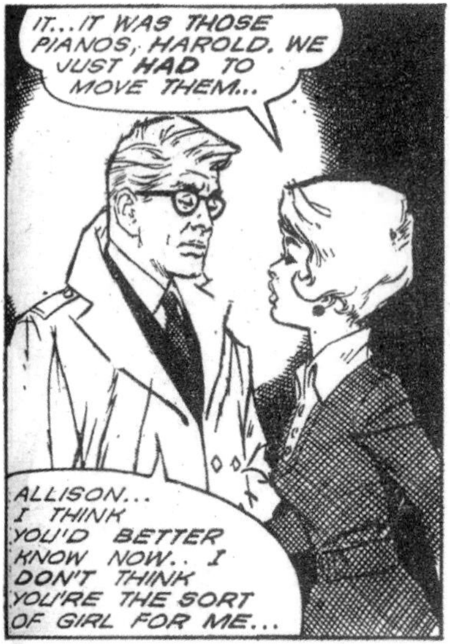
IT...IT WAS THOSE PIANOS, HAROLD. WE JUST HAD TO MOVE THEM...
ALLISON... I THINK YOU'D BETTER KNOW NOW.. I DON'T THINK YOU'RE THE SORT OF GIRL FOR ME...

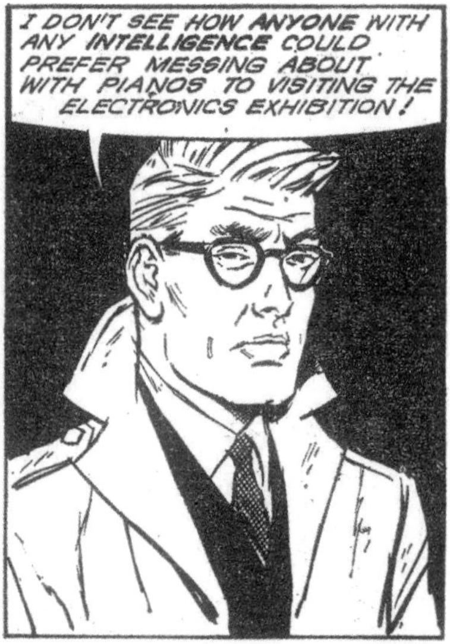
I DON'T SEE HOW ANYONE WITH ANY INTELLIGENCE COULD PREFER MESSING ABOUT WITH PIANOS TO VISITING THE ELECTRONICS EXHIBITION!

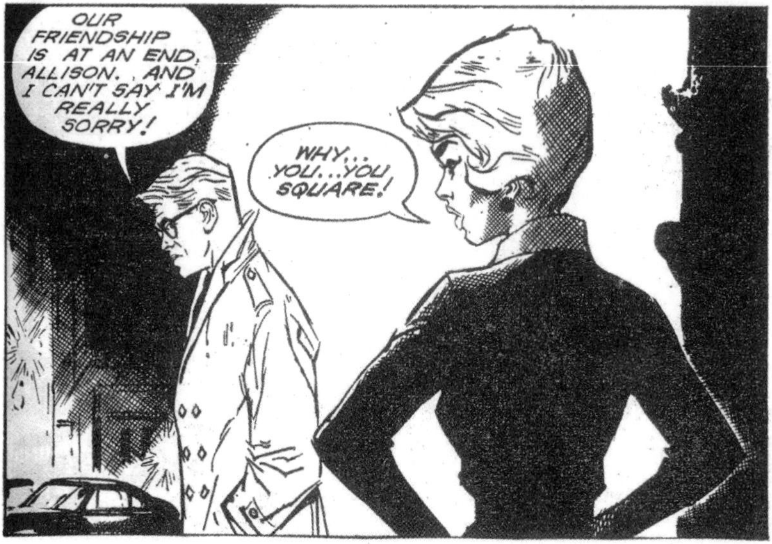
OUR FRIENDSHIP IS AT AN END, ALLISON.. AND I CAN'T SAY I'M REALLY SORRY!
WHY... YOU...YOU SQUARE!

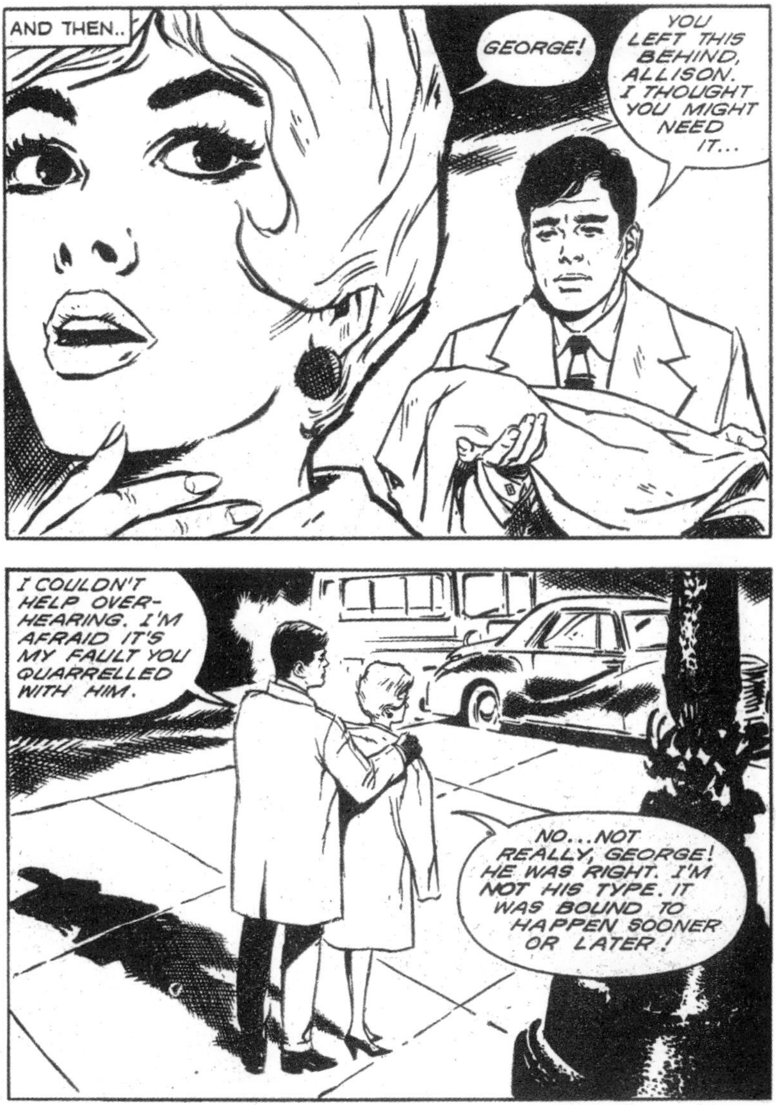
AND THEN..
GEORGE!
YOU LEFT THIS BEHIND, ALLISON. I THOUGHT YOU MIGHT NEED IT...
I COULDN'T HELP OVER-HEARING. I'M AFRAID IT'S MY FAULT YOU QUARRELLED WITH HIM.
NO...NOT REALLY, GEORGE! HE WAS RIGHT. I'M NOT HIS TYPE. IT WAS BOUND TO HAPPEN SOONER OR LATER!

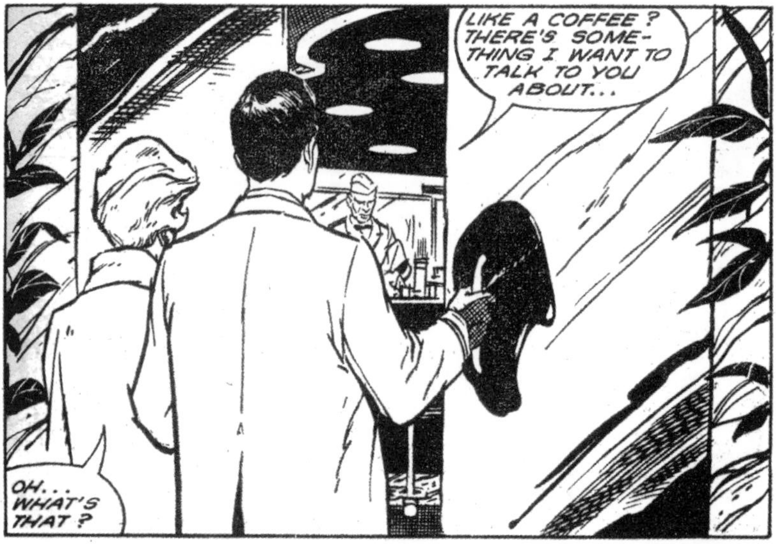
LIKE A COFFEE ? THERE'S SOME-THING I WANT TO TALK TO YOU ABOUT...
OH... WHAT'S THAT ?

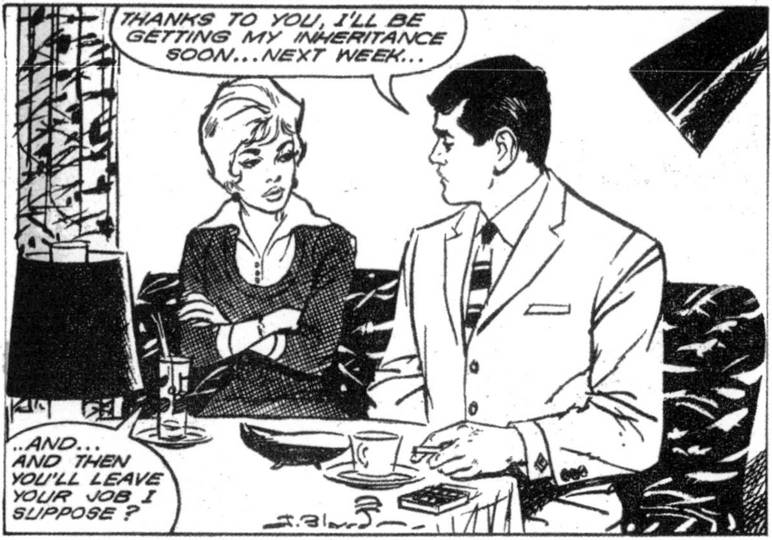
THANKS TO YOU, I'LL BE GETTING MY INHERITANCE SOON...NEXT WEEK...
..AND... AND THEN YOU'LL LEAVE YOUR JOB I SUPPOSE ?

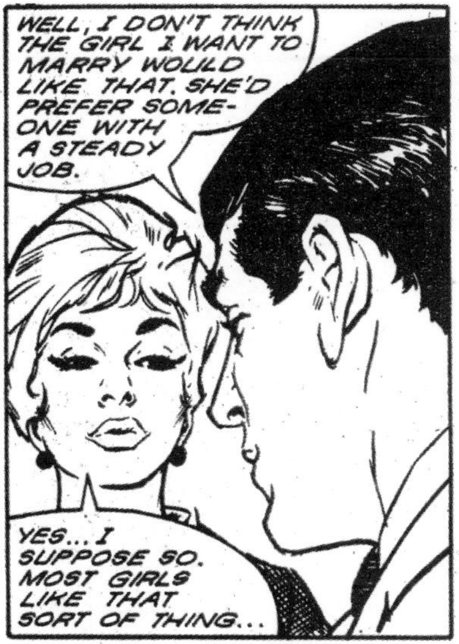
WELL, I DON'T THINK THE GIRL I WANT TO MARRY WOULD LIKE THAT. SHE'D PREFER SOME-ONE WITH A STEADY JOB.
YES... I SUPPOSE SO. MOST GIRLS LIKE THAT SORT OF THING...

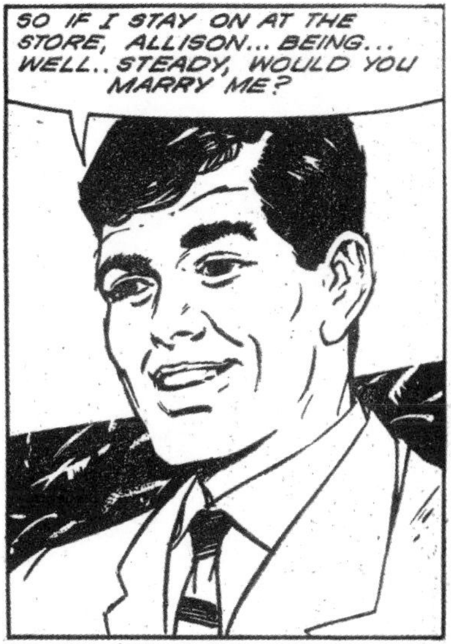
SO IF I STAY ON AT THE STORE, ALLISON... BEING... WELL.. STEADY, WOULD YOU MARRY ME?

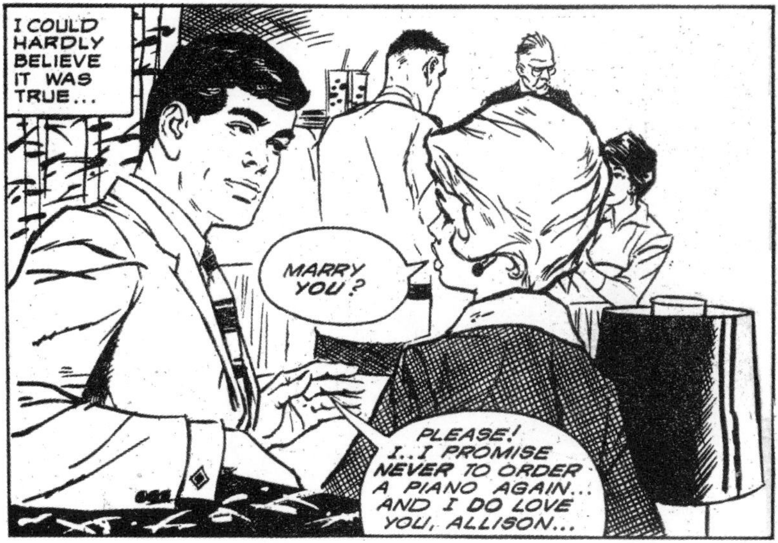
I COULD HARDLY BELIEVE IT WAS TRUE...
MARRY YOU?
PLEASE! I..I PROMISE NEVER TO ORDER A PIANO AGAIN... AND I DO LOVE YOU, ALLISON...

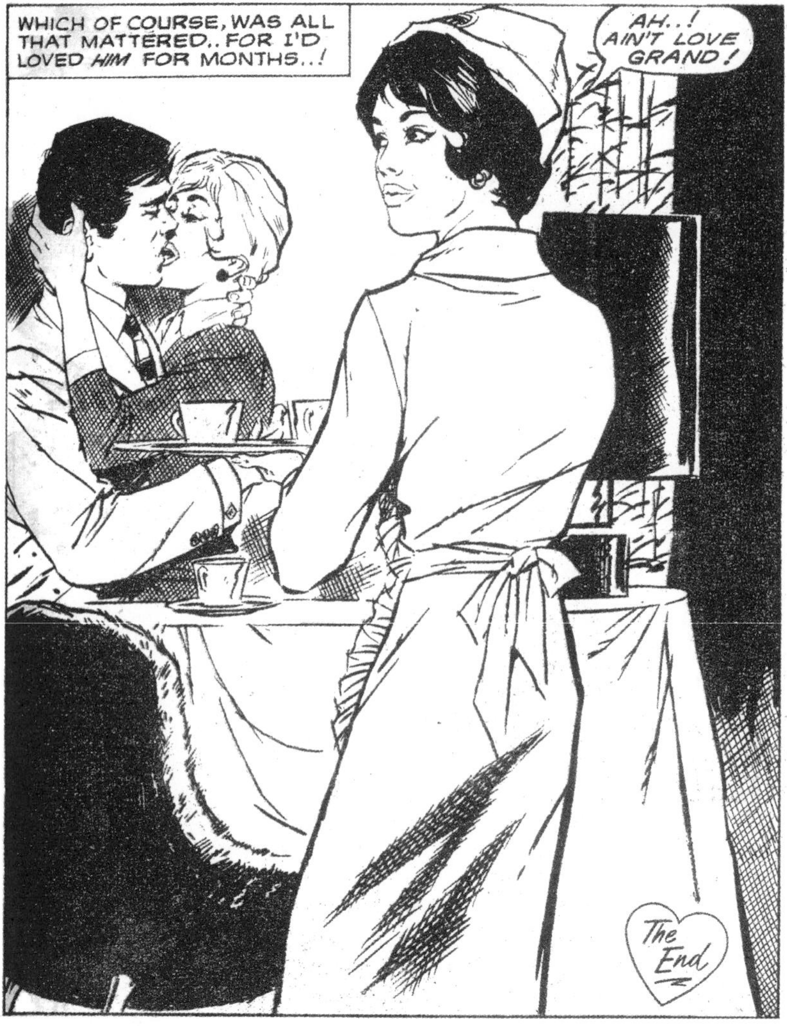
WHICH OF COURSE, WAS ALL THAT MATTERED.. FOR I'D LOVED *HIM* FOR MONTHS..!
AH..! AIN'T LOVE GRAND!
The End

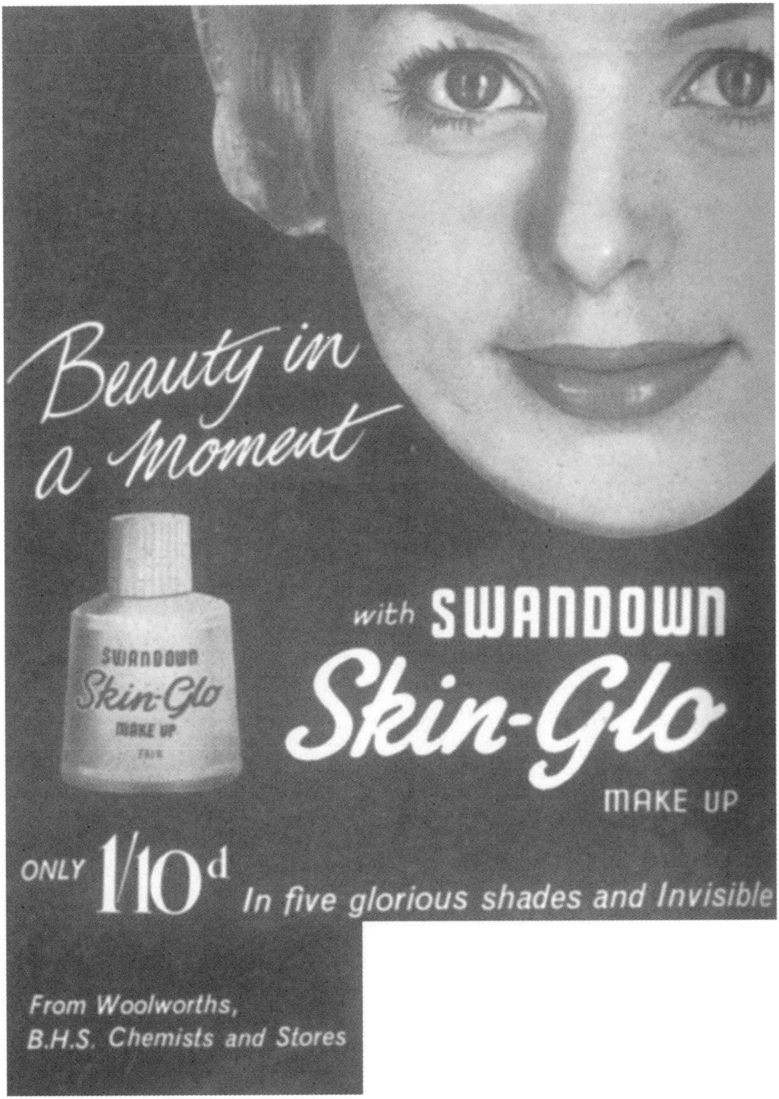

Beauty in a Moment
SWANDOWN
Skin-Glo
MAKE UP
with SWANDOWN
Skin-Glo
MAKE UP
ONLY 1/10d
In five glorious shades and Invisible
From Woolworths,
B.H.S. Chemists and Stores

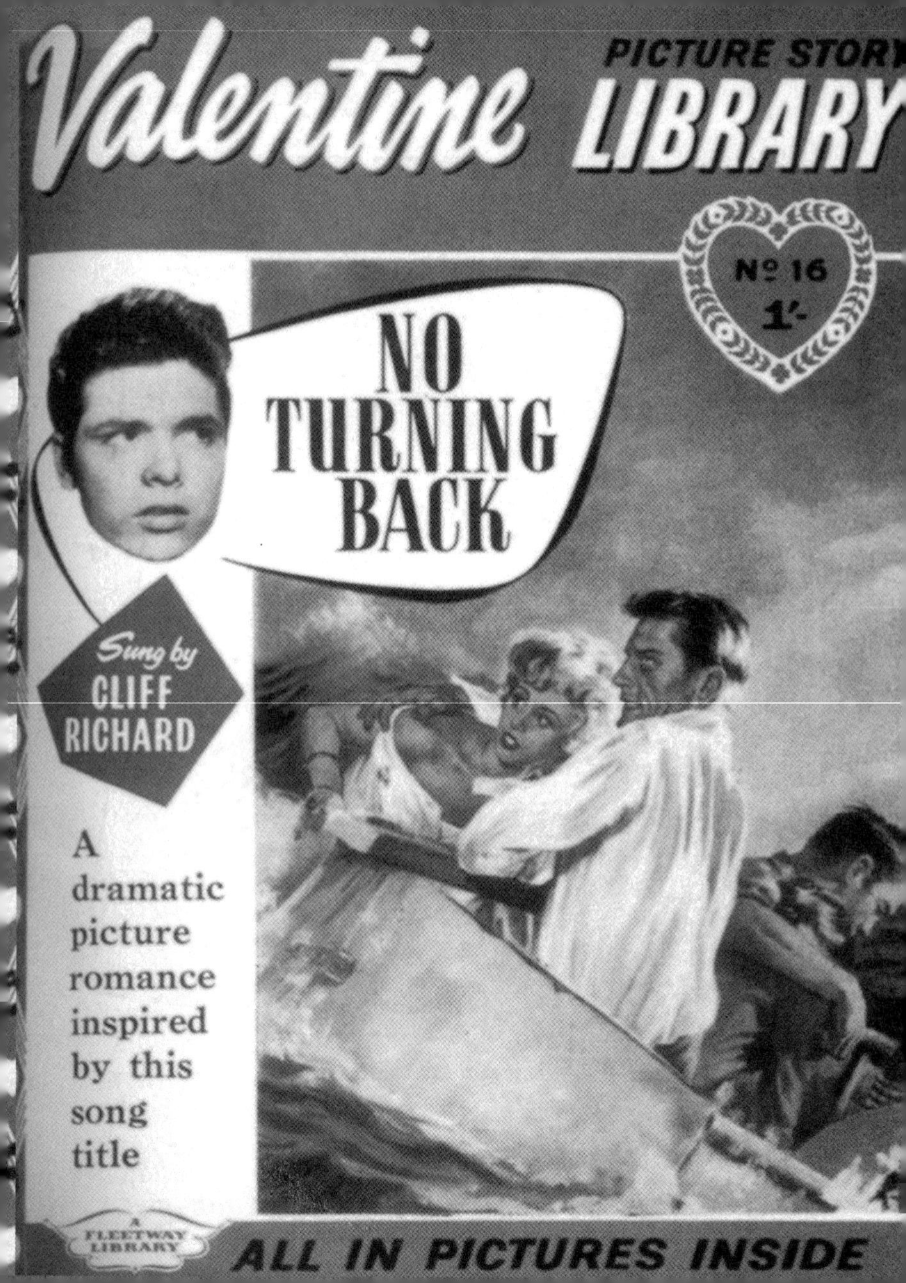

Valentine
PICTURE STORY LIBRARY
Nº 16
1/-
NO TURNING BACK
Sung by
CLIFF RICHARD
A dramatic picture romance inspired by this song title
A FLEETWAY LIBRARY
ALL IN PICTURES INSIDE

NO TURNING BACK

A dramatic picture romance inspired by this song title

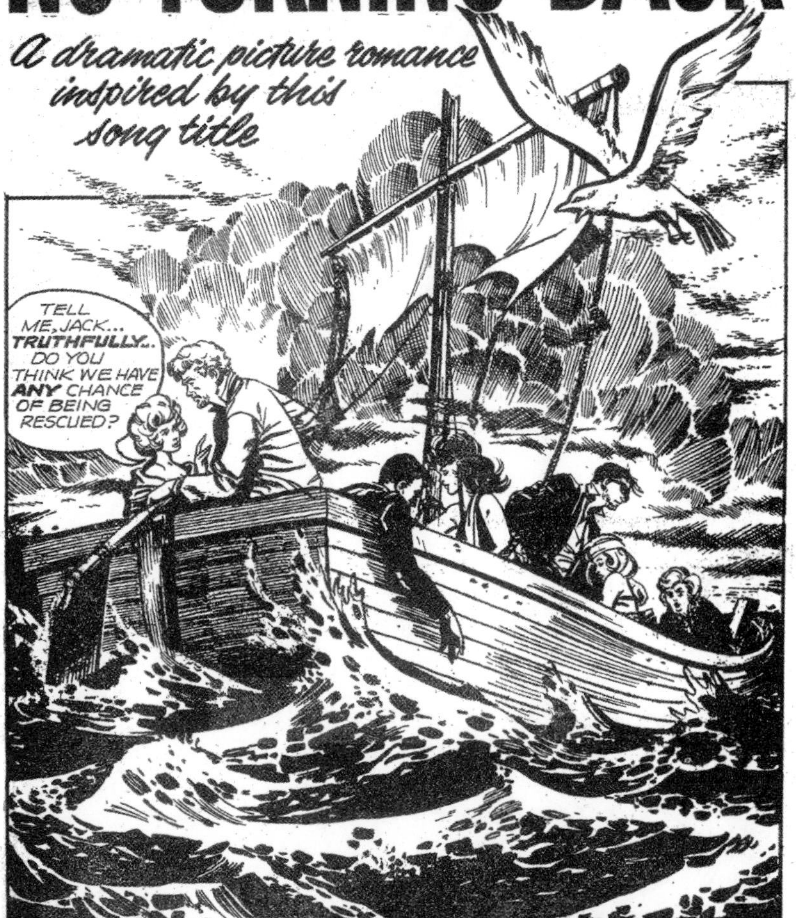
TELL ME, JACK... **TRUTHFULLY**... DO YOU THINK WE HAVE **ANY** CHANCE OF BEING RESCUED?

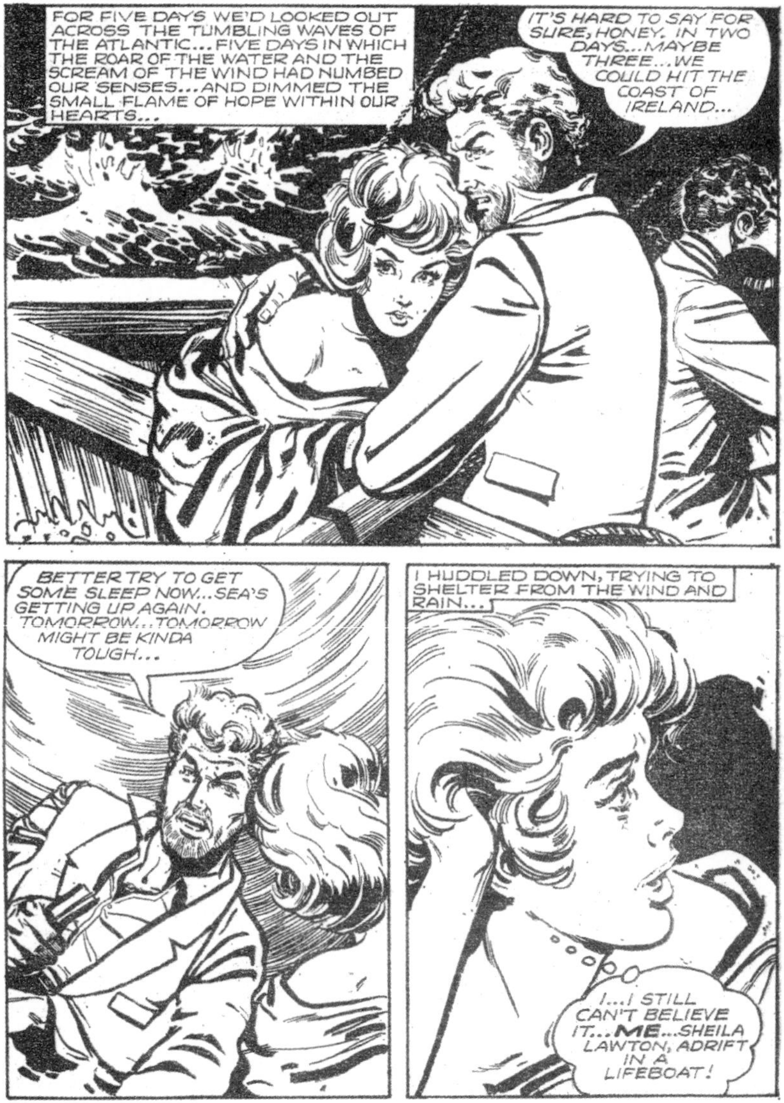
FOR FIVE DAYS WE'D LOOKED OUT ACROSS THE TUMBLING WAVES OF THE ATLANTIC... FIVE DAYS IN WHICH THE ROAR OF THE WATER AND THE SCREAM OF THE WIND HAD NUMBED OUR SENSES... AND DIMMED THE SMALL FLAME OF HOPE WITHIN OUR HEARTS...
IT'S HARD TO SAY FOR SURE, HONEY. IN TWO DAYS... MAYBE THREE... WE COULD HIT THE COAST OF IRELAND...
BETTER TRY TO GET SOME SLEEP NOW... SEA'S GETTING UP AGAIN. TOMORROW... TOMORROW MIGHT BE KINDA TOUGH...
I HUDDLED DOWN, TRYING TO SHELTER FROM THE WIND AND RAIN...
I... I STILL CAN'T BELIEVE IT... ME... SHEILA LAWTON, ADRIFT IN A LIFEBOAT!

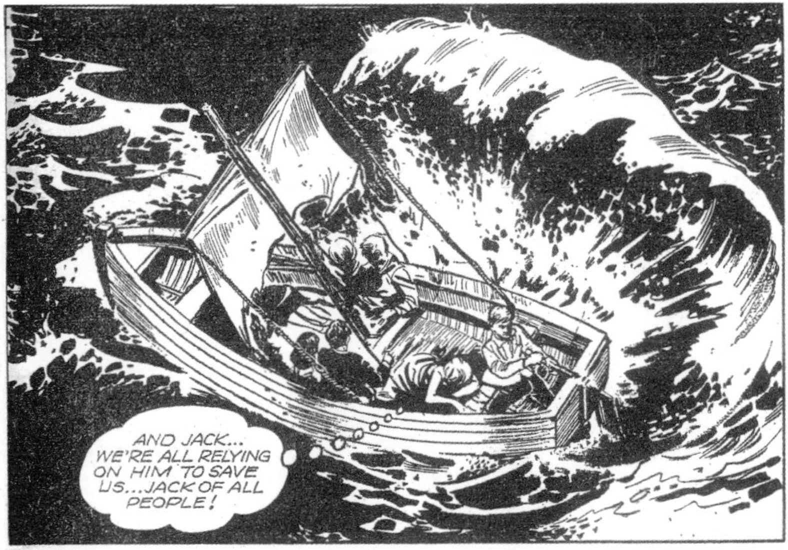
AND JACK... WE'RE ALL RELYING ON HIM TO SAVE US...JACK OF ALL PEOPLE!

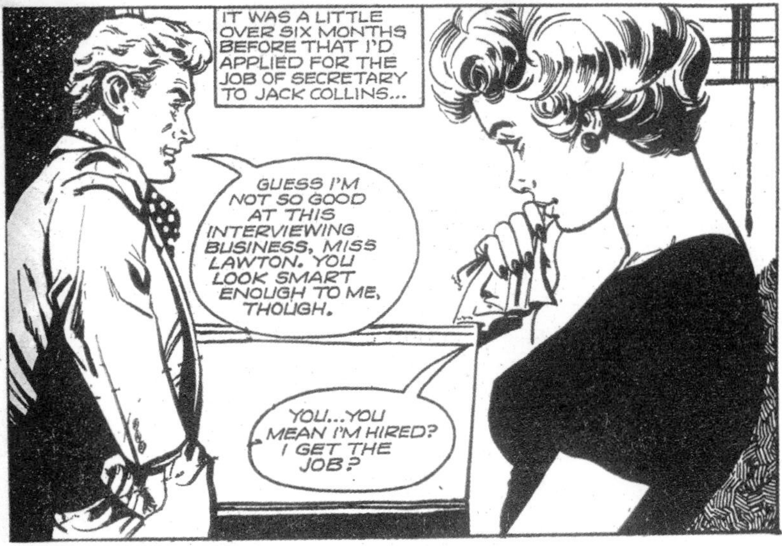
IT WAS A LITTLE OVER SIX MONTHS BEFORE THAT I'D APPLIED FOR THE JOB OF SECRETARY TO JACK COLLINS...
GUESS I'M NOT SO GOOD AT THIS INTERVIEWING BUSINESS, MISS LAWTON. YOU LOOK SMART ENOUGH TO ME, THOUGH.
YOU...YOU MEAN I'M HIRED? I GET THE JOB?

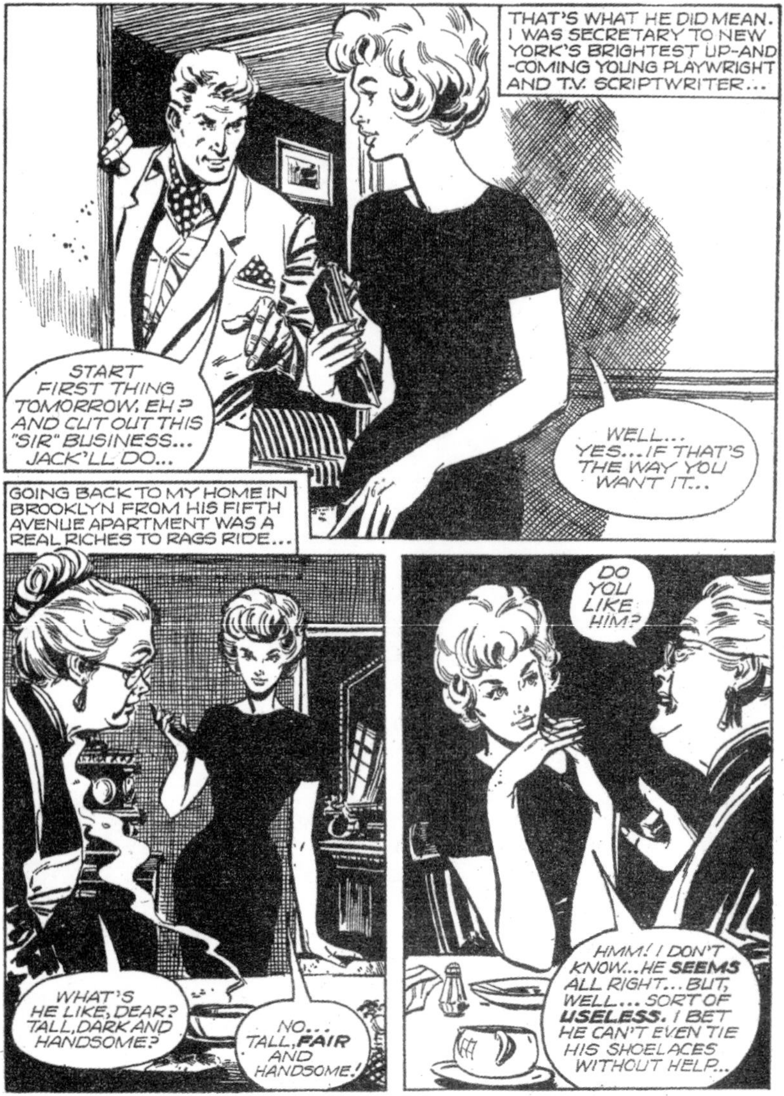
THAT'S WHAT HE DID MEAN. I WAS SECRETARY TO NEW YORK'S BRIGHTEST UP-AND-COMING YOUNG PLAYWRIGHT AND T.V. SCRIPTWRITER...
START FIRST THING TOMORROW, EH? AND CUT OUT THIS "SIR" BUSINESS... JACK'LL DO...
WELL... YES... IF THAT'S THE WAY YOU WANT IT...
GOING BACK TO MY HOME IN BROOKLYN FROM HIS FIFTH AVENUE APARTMENT WAS A REAL RICHES TO RAGS RIDE...
WHAT'S HE LIKE, DEAR? TALL, DARK AND HANDSOME?
NO... TALL, **FAIR** AND HANDSOME!
DO YOU LIKE HIM?
HMM! I DON'T KNOW... HE **SEEMS** ALL RIGHT... BUT, WELL... SORT OF **USELESS**. I BET HE CAN'T EVEN TIE HIS SHOELACES WITHOUT HELP...

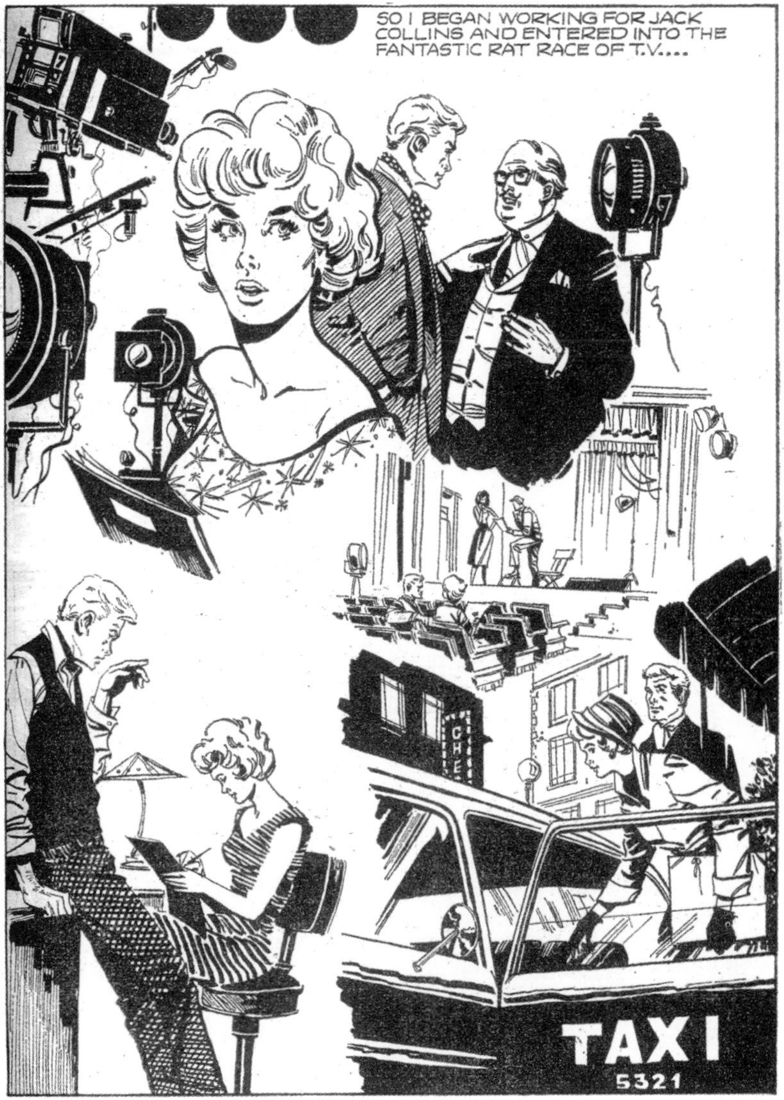
SO I BEGAN WORKING FOR JACK COLLINS AND ENTERED INTO THE FANTASTIC RAT RACE OF T.V....
TAXI
5321

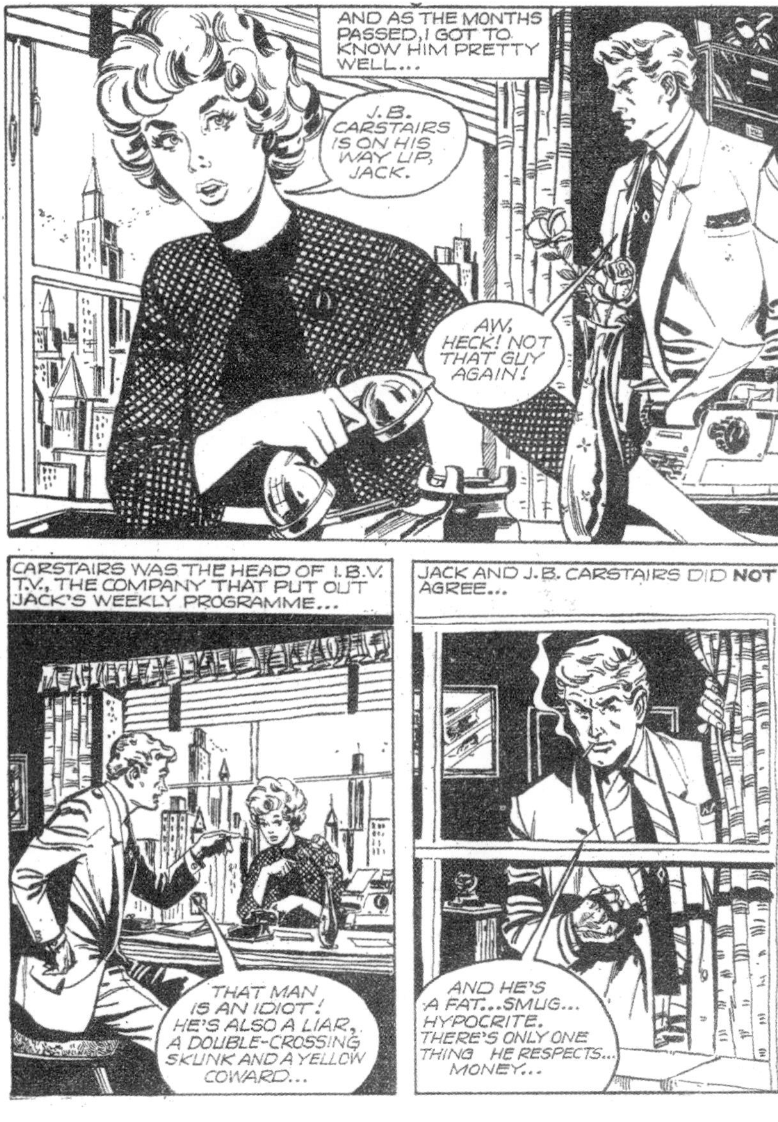
AND AS THE MONTHS PASSED, I GOT TO KNOW HIM PRETTY WELL...
J.B. CARSTAIRS IS ON HIS WAY UP, JACK.
AW, HECK! NOT THAT GUY AGAIN!
CARSTAIRS WAS THE HEAD OF I.B.V. T.V., THE COMPANY THAT PUT OUT JACK'S WEEKLY PROGRAMME...
THAT MAN IS AN IDIOT! HE'S ALSO A LIAR, A DOUBLE-CROSSING SKUNK AND A YELLOW COWARD...
JACK AND J.B. CARSTAIRS DID NOT AGREE...
AND HE'S A FAT... SMUG... HYPOCRITE. THERE'S ONLY ONE THING HE RESPECTS... MONEY...

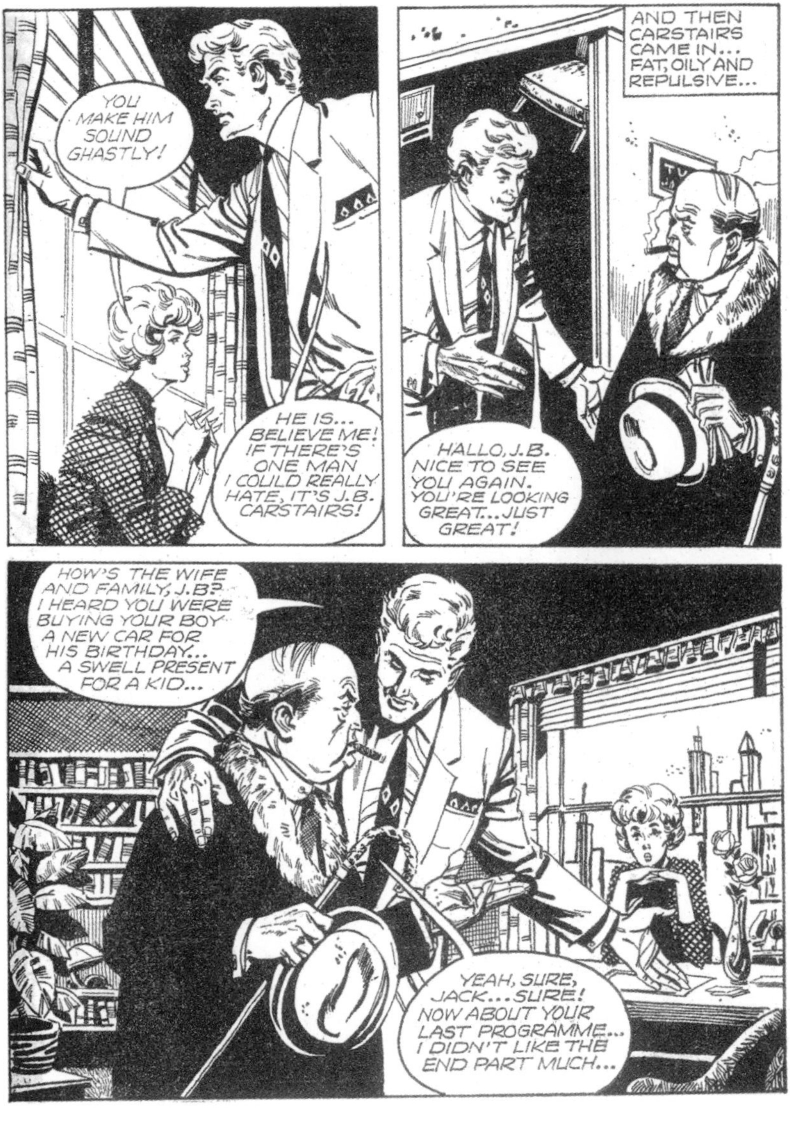
YOU MAKE HIM SOUND GHASTLY!
HE IS... BELIEVE ME! IF THERE'S ONE MAN I COULD REALLY HATE, IT'S J.B. CARSTAIRS!
AND THEN CARSTAIRS CAME IN... FAT, OILY AND REPULSIVE...
HALLO, J.B. NICE TO SEE YOU AGAIN. YOU'RE LOOKING GREAT... JUST GREAT!
HOW'S THE WIFE AND FAMILY, J.B? I HEARD YOU WERE BUYING YOUR BOY A NEW CAR FOR HIS BIRTHDAY... A SWELL PRESENT FOR A KID...
YEAH, SURE, JACK... SURE! NOW ABOUT YOUR LAST PROGRAMME... I DIDN'T LIKE THE END PART MUCH...

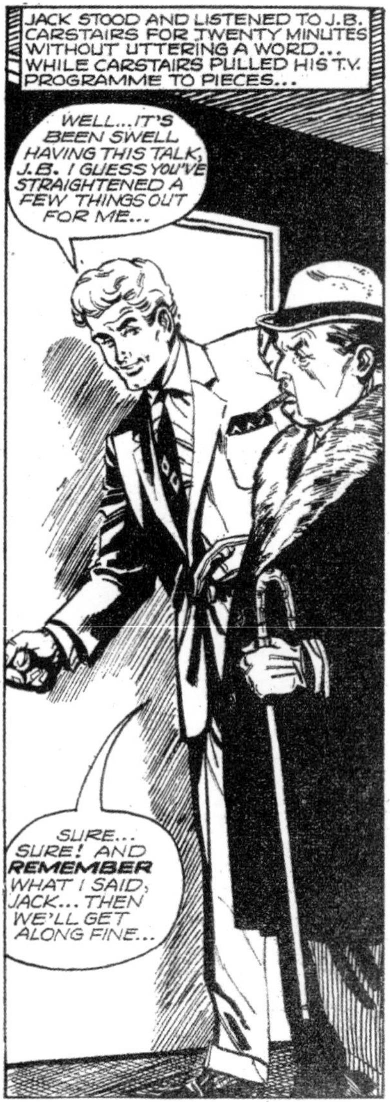
JACK STOOD AND LISTENED TO J.B. CARSTAIRS FOR TWENTY MINUTES WITHOUT UTTERING A WORD... WHILE CARSTAIRS PULLED HIS T.V. PROGRAMME TO PIECES...
WELL...IT'S BEEN SWELL HAVING THIS TALK, J.B. I GUESS YOU'VE STRAIGHTENED A FEW THINGS OUT FOR ME...
SURE... SURE! AND REMEMBER WHAT I SAID, JACK... THEN WE'LL GET ALONG FINE...

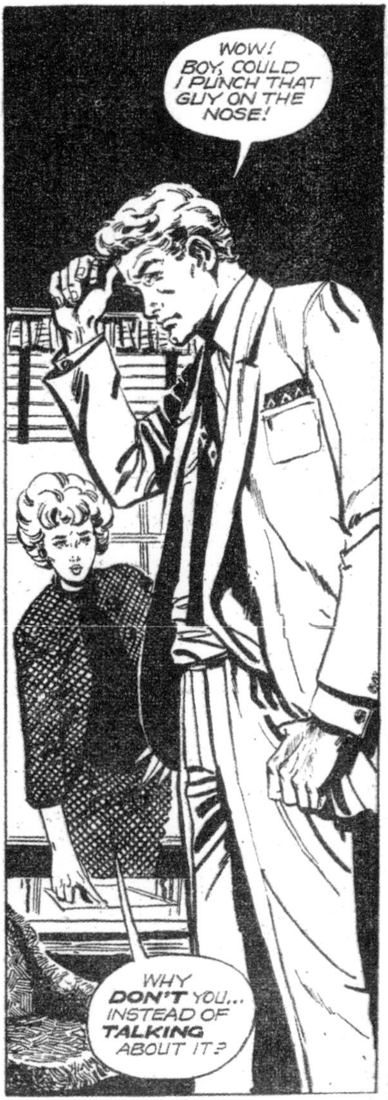
WOW! BOY, COULD I PUNCH THAT GUY ON THE NOSE!
WHY DON'T YOU... INSTEAD OF TALKING ABOUT IT?

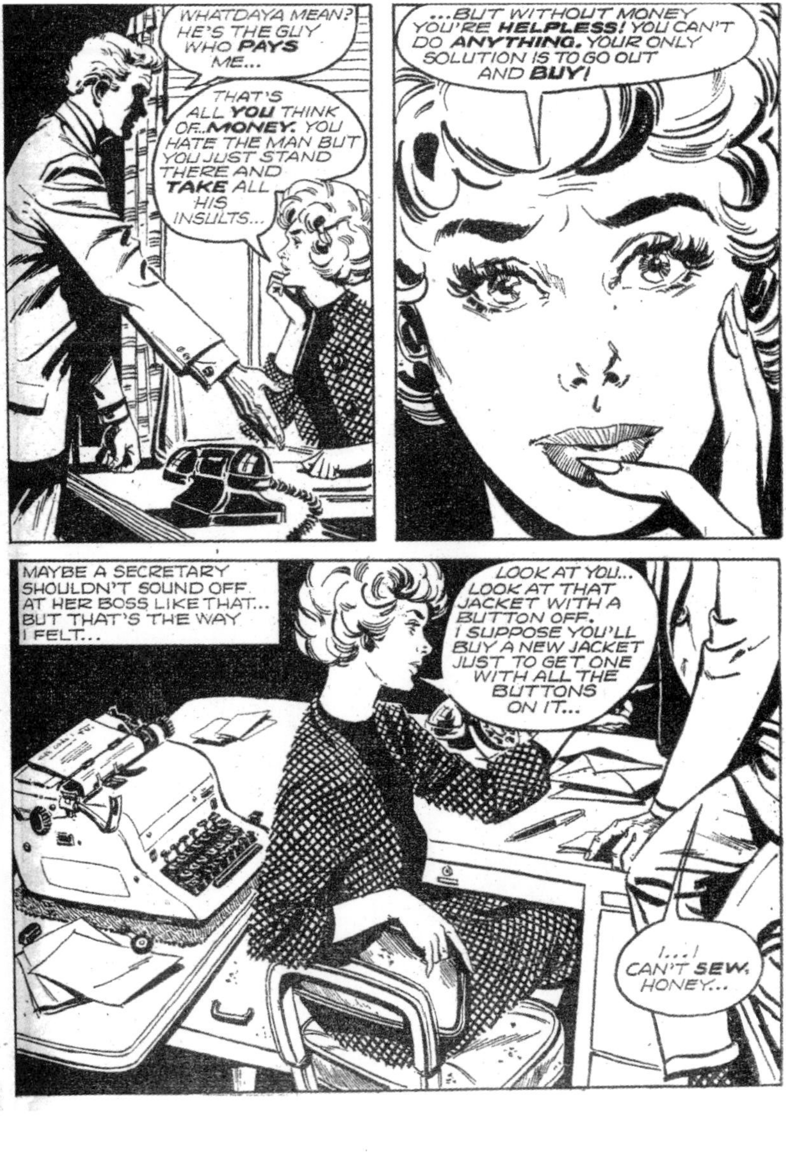
WHATDAYA MEAN? HE'S THE GUY WHO **PAYS** ME...
THAT'S ALL **YOU** THINK OF...**MONEY.** YOU HATE THE MAN BUT YOU JUST STAND THERE AND **TAKE** ALL HIS INSULTS...
...BUT WITHOUT MONEY YOU'RE **HELPLESS!** YOU CAN'T DO **ANYTHING.** YOUR ONLY SOLUTION IS TO GO OUT AND **BUY!**
MAYBE A SECRETARY SHOULDN'T SOUND OFF AT HER BOSS LIKE THAT... BUT THAT'S THE WAY I FELT...
LOOK AT YOU... LOOK AT THAT JACKET WITH A BUTTON OFF. I SUPPOSE YOU'LL BUY A NEW JACKET JUST TO GET ONE WITH ALL THE BUTTONS ON IT...
I...I CAN'T **SEW,** HONEY...

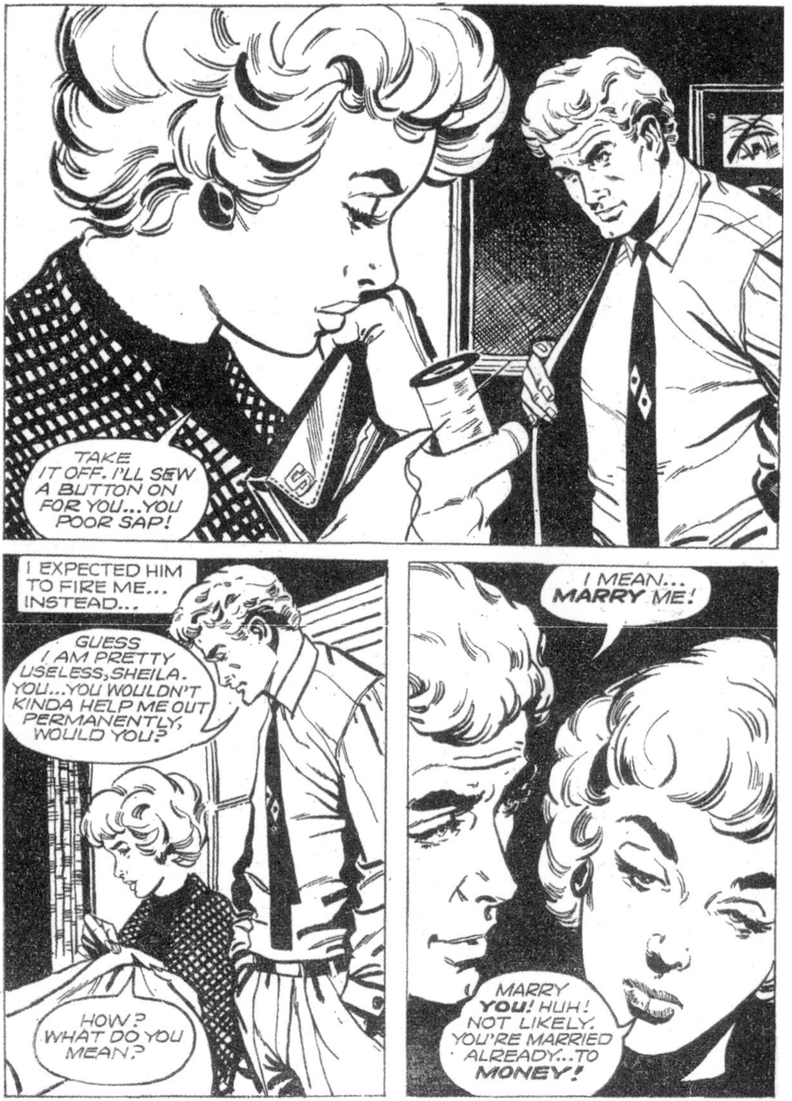
TAKE IT OFF. I'LL SEW A BUTTON ON FOR YOU...YOU POOR SAP!
I EXPECTED HIM TO FIRE ME... INSTEAD...
GUESS I AM PRETTY USELESS, SHEILA. YOU...YOU WOULDN'T KINDA HELP ME OUT PERMANENTLY, WOULD YOU?
HOW? WHAT DO YOU MEAN?
I MEAN... MARRY ME!
MARRY YOU! HUH! NOT LIKELY. YOU'RE MARRIED ALREADY...TO MONEY!

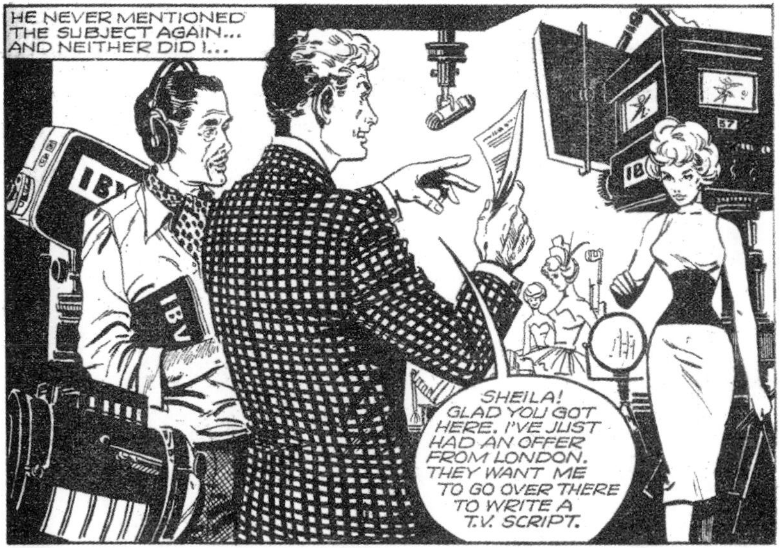
HE NEVER MENTIONED THE SUBJECT AGAIN... AND NEITHER DID I...
SHEILA! GLAD YOU GOT HERE. I'VE JUST HAD AN OFFER FROM LONDON. THEY WANT ME TO GO OVER THERE TO WRITE A T.V. SCRIPT.

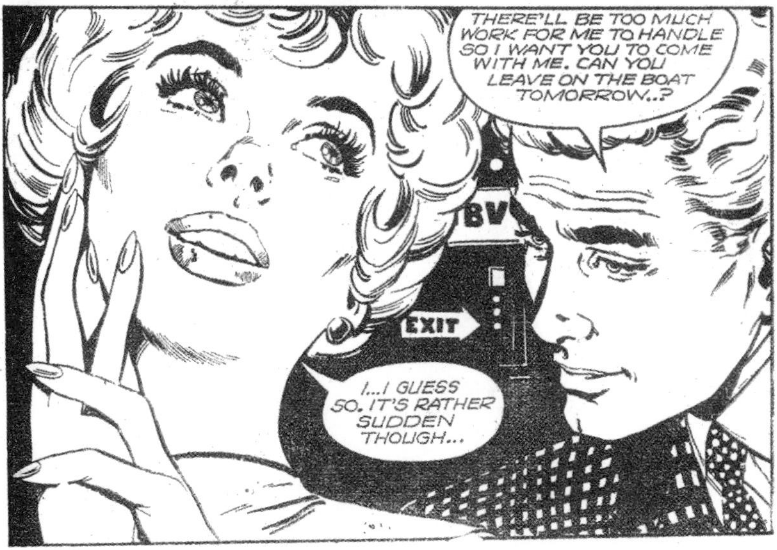
THERE'LL BE TOO MUCH WORK FOR ME TO HANDLE SO I WANT YOU TO COME WITH ME. CAN YOU LEAVE ON THE BOAT TOMORROW..?
I...I GUESS SO. IT'S RATHER SUDDEN THOUGH...

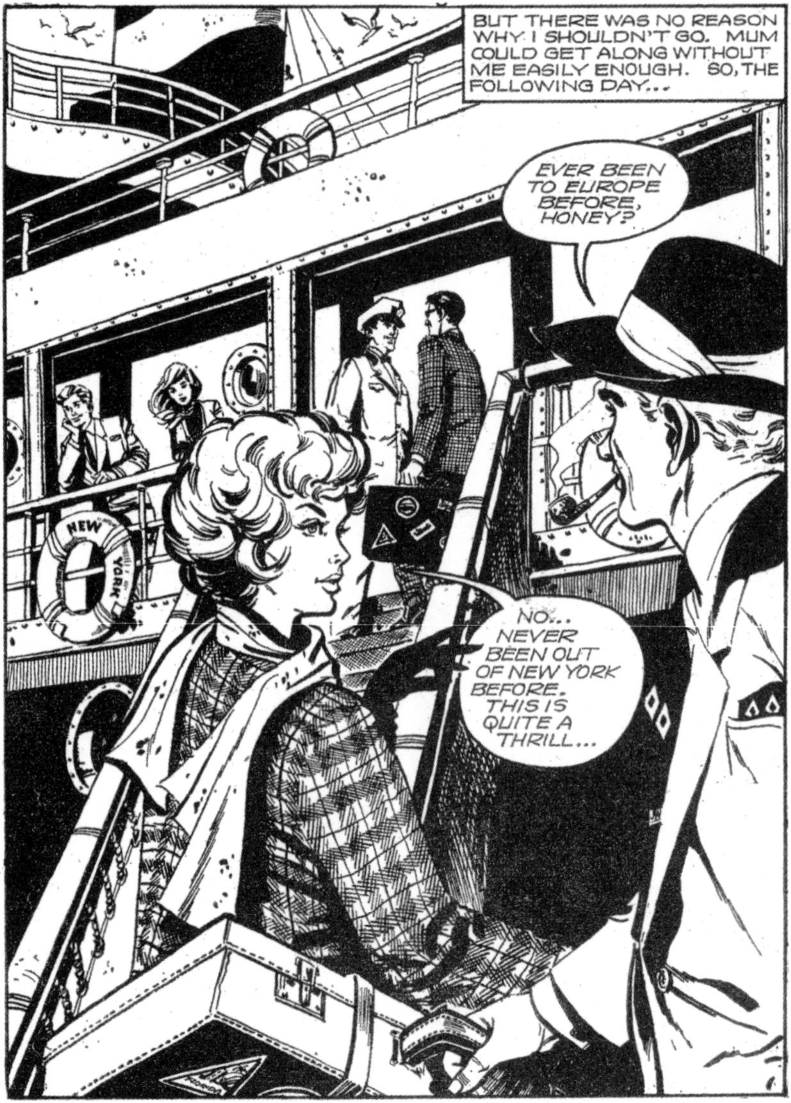
BUT THERE WAS NO REASON WHY I SHOULDN'T GO. MUM COULD GET ALONG WITHOUT ME EASILY ENOUGH. SO, THE FOLLOWING DAY...
EVER BEEN TO EUROPE BEFORE, HONEY?
NO.. NEVER BEEN OUT OF NEW YORK BEFORE. THIS IS QUITE A THRILL...
NEW YORK

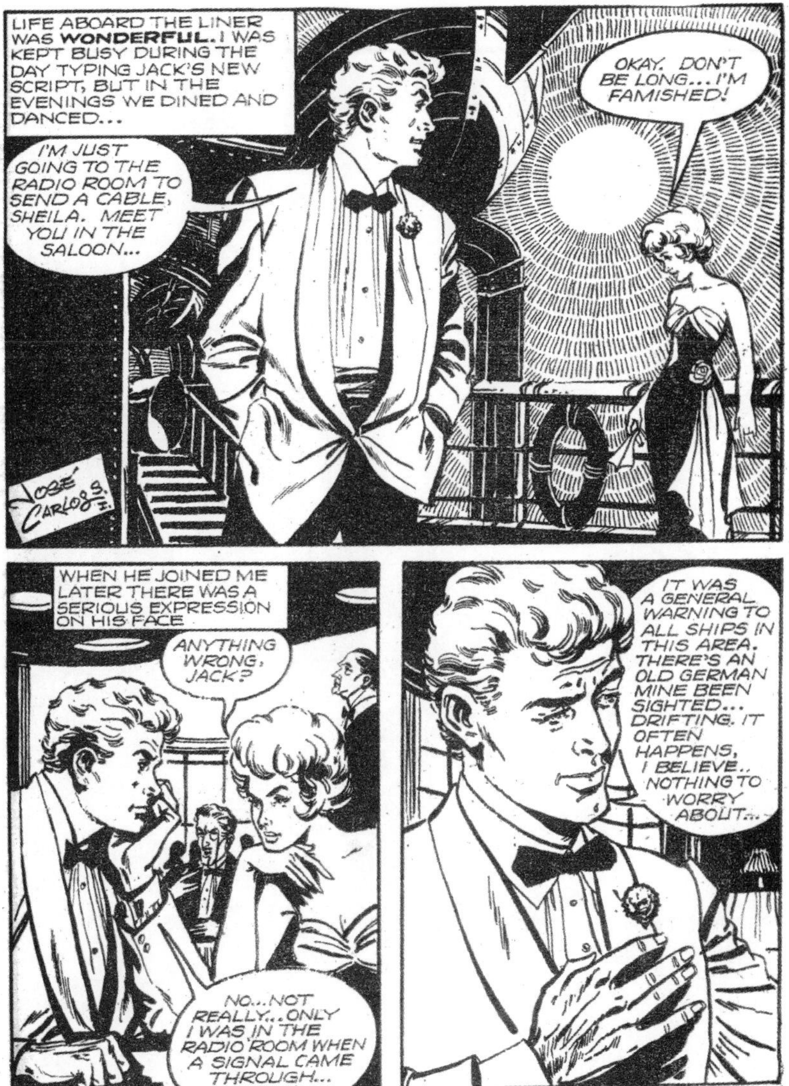
LIFE ABOARD THE LINER WAS **WONDERFUL.** I WAS KEPT BUSY DURING THE DAY TYPING JACK'S NEW SCRIPT, BUT IN THE EVENINGS WE DINED AND DANCED...
I'M JUST GOING TO THE RADIO ROOM TO SEND A CABLE, SHEILA. MEET YOU IN THE SALOON...
OKAY. DON'T BE LONG... I'M FAMISHED!
JOSÉ CARLOS S. I.
WHEN HE JOINED ME LATER THERE WAS A SERIOUS EXPRESSION ON HIS FACE
ANYTHING WRONG, JACK?
NO... NOT REALLY... ONLY I WAS IN THE RADIO ROOM WHEN A SIGNAL CAME THROUGH...
IT WAS A GENERAL WARNING TO ALL SHIPS IN THIS AREA. THERE'S AN OLD GERMAN MINE BEEN SIGHTED... DRIFTING. IT OFTEN HAPPENS, I BELIEVE.. NOTHING TO WORRY ABOUT...

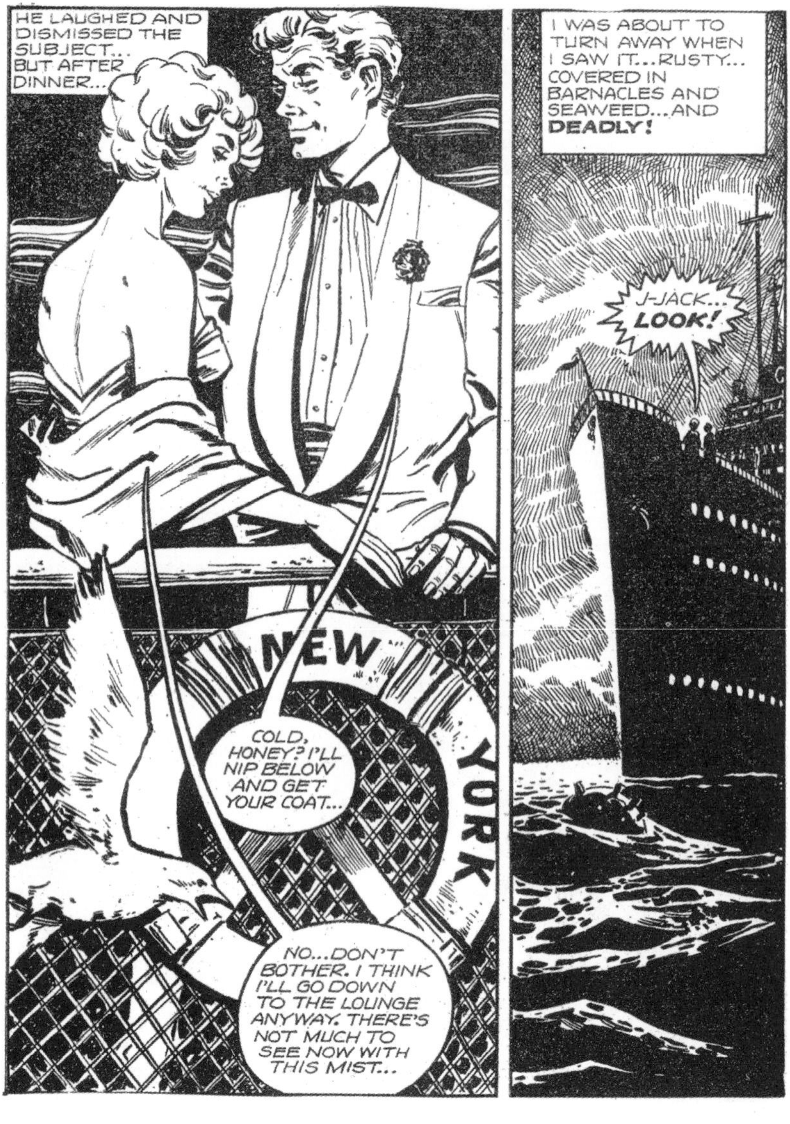
HE LAUGHED AND DISMISSED THE SUBJECT... BUT AFTER DINNER...
COLD, HONEY? I'LL NIP BELOW AND GET YOUR COAT...
NO...DON'T BOTHER. I THINK I'LL GO DOWN TO THE LOUNGE ANYWAY. THERE'S NOT MUCH TO SEE NOW WITH THIS MIST...
NEW YORK
I WAS ABOUT TO TURN AWAY WHEN I SAW IT...RUSTY... COVERED IN BARNACLES AND SEAWEED...AND **DEADLY!**
J-JACK... **LOOK!**

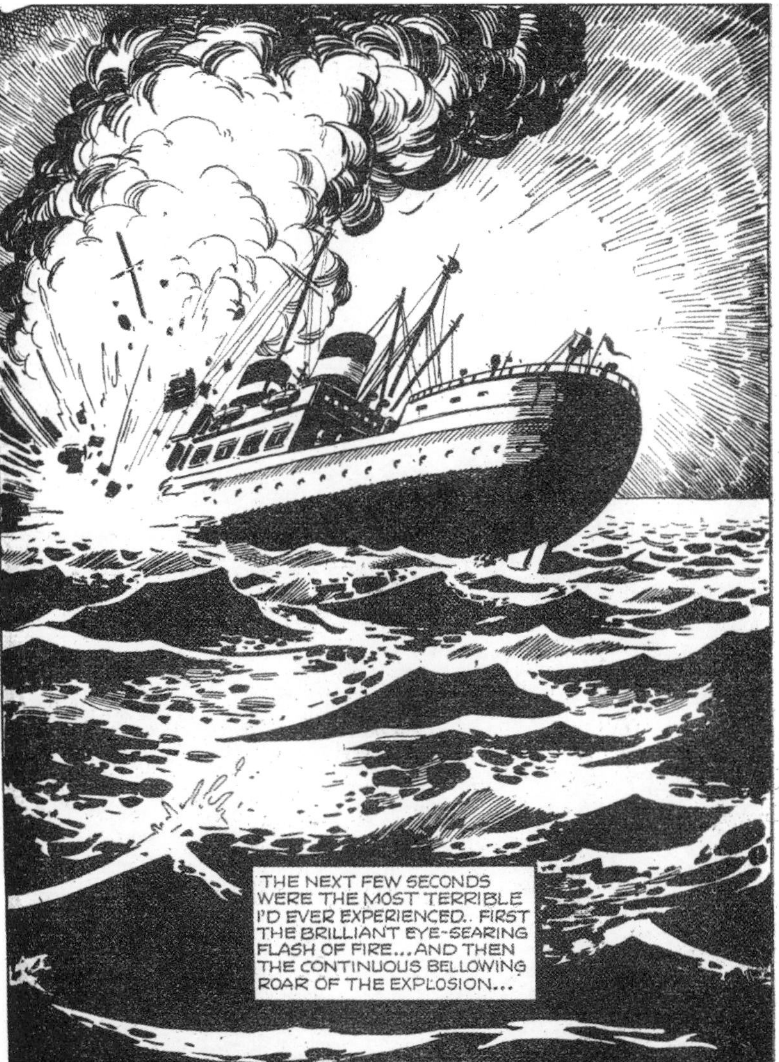
THE NEXT FEW SECONDS WERE THE MOST TERRIBLE I'D EVER EXPERIENCED.. FIRST THE BRILLIANT EYE-SEARING FLASH OF FIRE...AND THEN THE CONTINUOUS BELLOWING ROAR OF THE EXPLOSION...

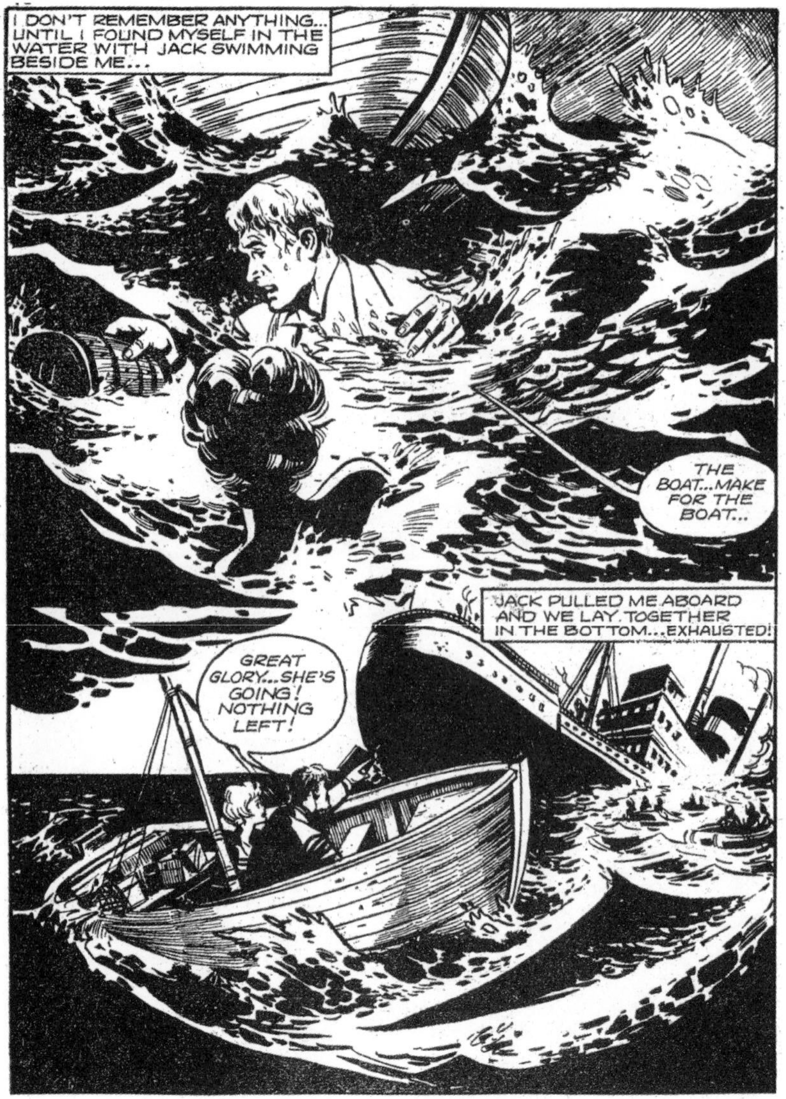
I DON'T REMEMBER ANYTHING... UNTIL I FOUND MYSELF IN THE WATER WITH JACK SWIMMING BESIDE ME...
THE BOAT...MAKE FOR THE BOAT...
JACK PULLED ME ABOARD AND WE LAY TOGETHER IN THE BOTTOM...EXHAUSTED!
GREAT GLORY...SHE'S GOING! NOTHING LEFT!

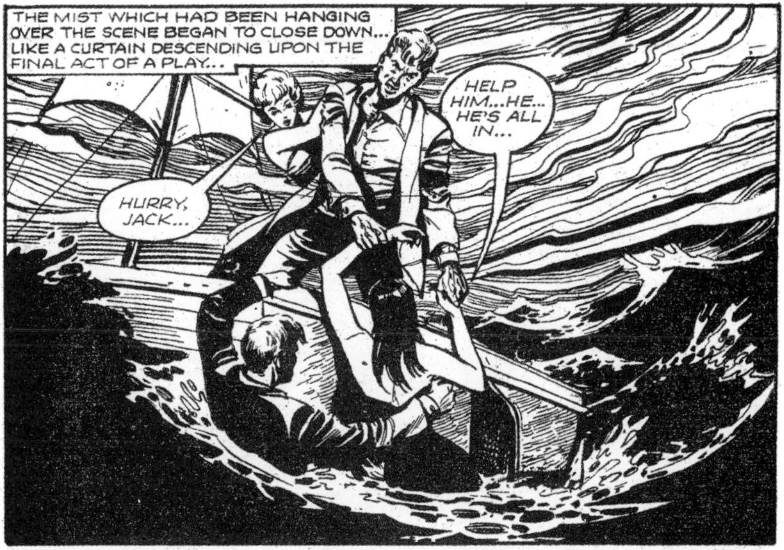
THE MIST WHICH HAD BEEN HANGING OVER THE SCENE BEGAN TO CLOSE DOWN... LIKE A CURTAIN DESCENDING UPON THE FINAL ACT OF A PLAY...
HELP HIM...HE... HE'S ALL IN...
HURRY, JACK...

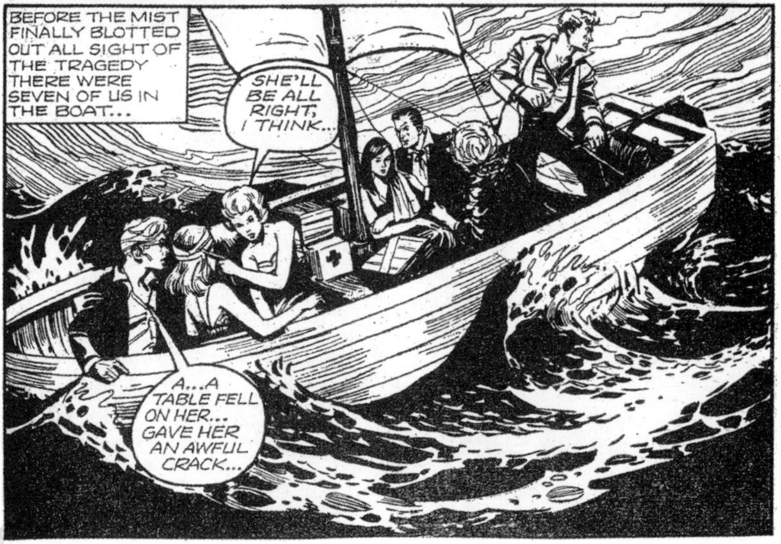
BEFORE THE MIST FINALLY BLOTTED OUT ALL SIGHT OF THE TRAGEDY THERE WERE SEVEN OF US IN THE BOAT...
SHE'LL BE ALL RIGHT, I THINK...
A...A TABLE FELL ON HER... GAVE HER AN AWFUL CRACK...

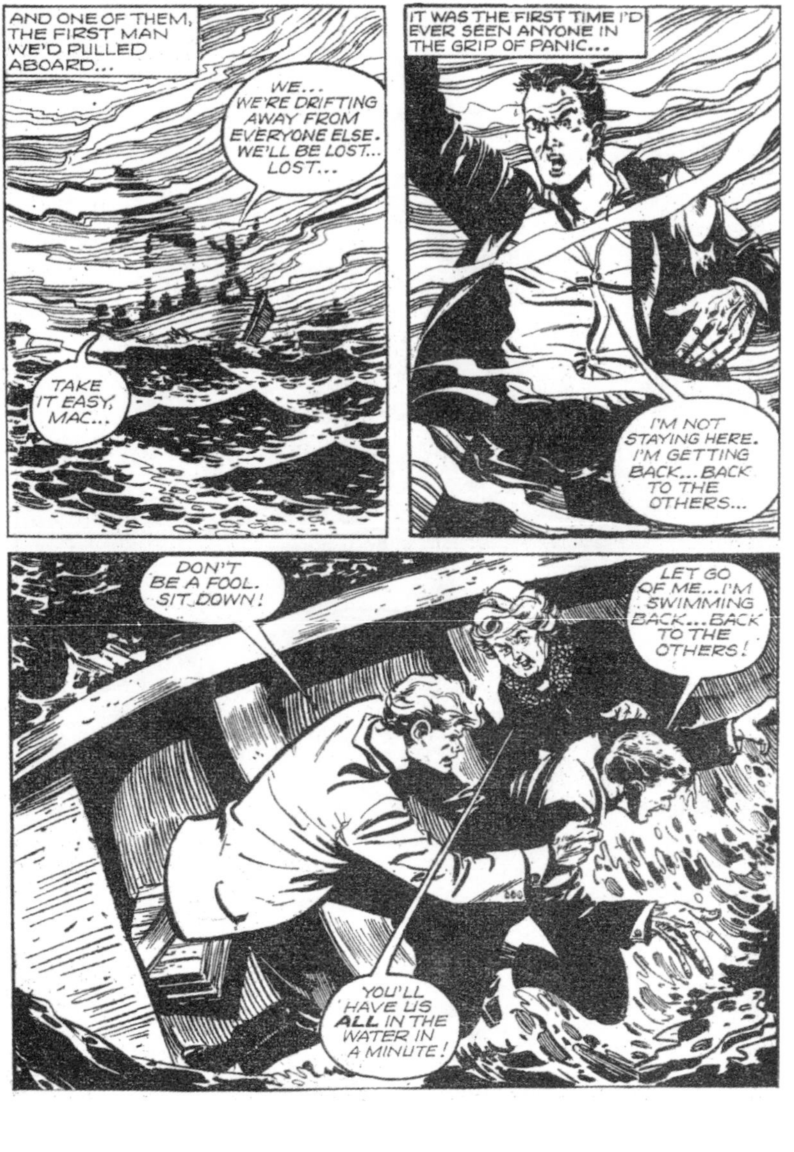
AND ONE OF THEM, THE FIRST MAN WE'D PULLED ABOARD...
WE... WE'RE DRIFTING AWAY FROM EVERYONE ELSE. WE'LL BE LOST... LOST...
TAKE IT EASY, MAC...
IT WAS THE FIRST TIME I'D EVER SEEN ANYONE IN THE GRIP OF PANIC...
I'M NOT STAYING HERE. I'M GETTING BACK... BACK TO THE OTHERS...
DON'T BE A FOOL. SIT DOWN!
LET GO OF ME... I'M SWIMMING BACK... BACK TO THE OTHERS!
YOU'LL HAVE US ALL IN THE WATER IN A MINUTE!

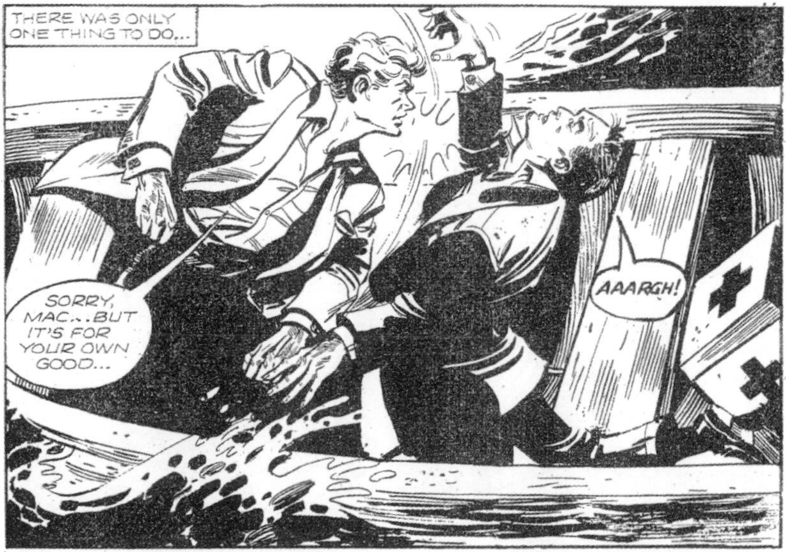
THERE WAS ONLY ONE THING TO DO...
SORRY, MAC...BUT IT'S FOR YOUR OWN GOOD...
AAARGH!

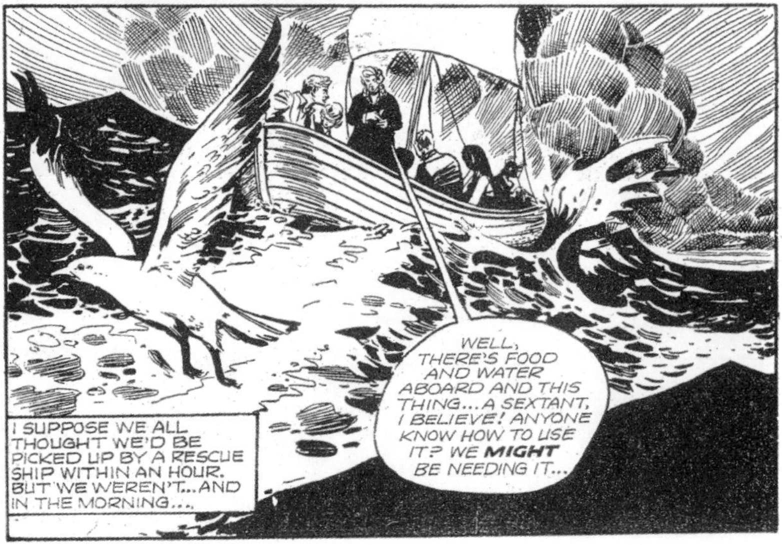
WELL, THERE'S FOOD AND WATER ABOARD AND THIS THING... A SEXTANT, I BELIEVE! ANYONE KNOW HOW TO USE IT? WE **MIGHT** BE NEEDING IT...
I SUPPOSE WE ALL THOUGHT WE'D BE PICKED UP BY A RESCUE SHIP WITHIN AN HOUR. BUT WE WEREN'T...AND IN THE MORNING....

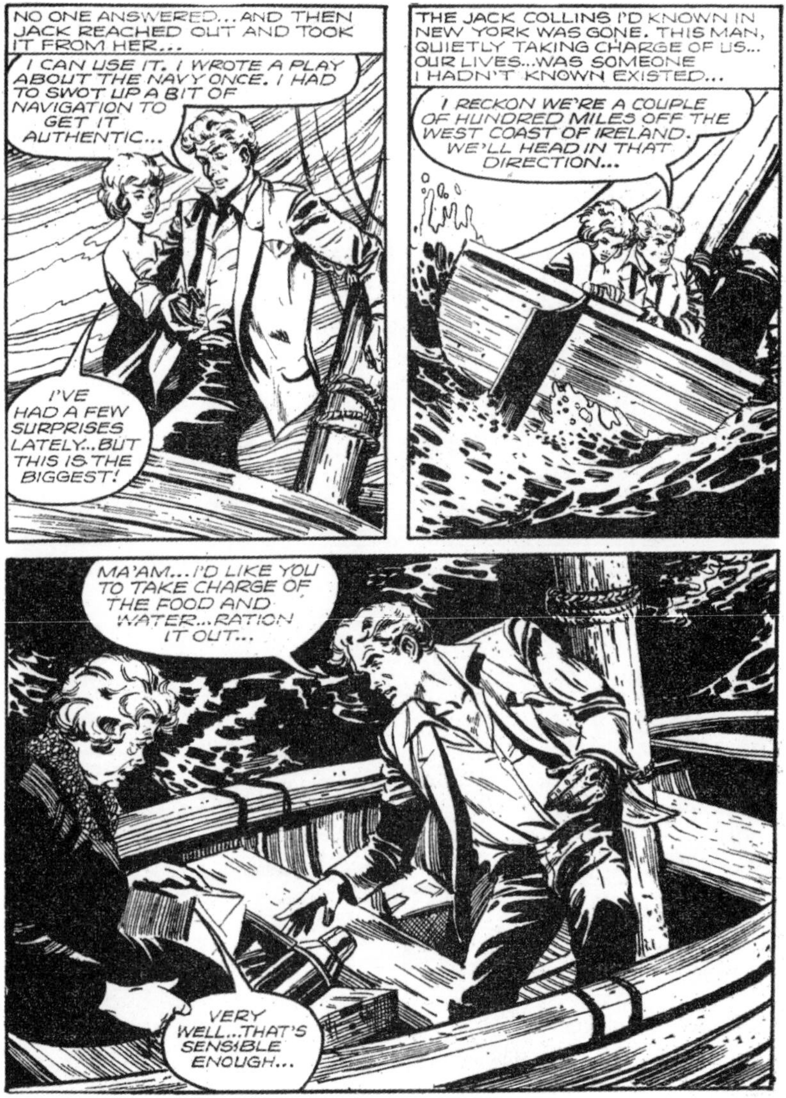
NO ONE ANSWERED... AND THEN JACK REACHED OUT AND TOOK IT FROM HER...
I CAN USE IT. I WROTE A PLAY ABOUT THE NAVY ONCE. I HAD TO SWOT UP A BIT OF NAVIGATION TO GET IT AUTHENTIC...
I'VE HAD A FEW SURPRISES LATELY... BUT THIS IS THE BIGGEST!
THE JACK COLLINS I'D KNOWN IN NEW YORK WAS GONE. THIS MAN, QUIETLY TAKING CHARGE OF US... OUR LIVES... WAS SOMEONE I HADN'T KNOWN EXISTED...
I RECKON WE'RE A COUPLE OF HUNDRED MILES OFF THE WEST COAST OF IRELAND. WE'LL HEAD IN THAT DIRECTION...
MA'AM... I'D LIKE YOU TO TAKE CHARGE OF THE FOOD AND WATER... RATION IT OUT...
VERY WELL... THAT'S SENSIBLE ENOUGH...

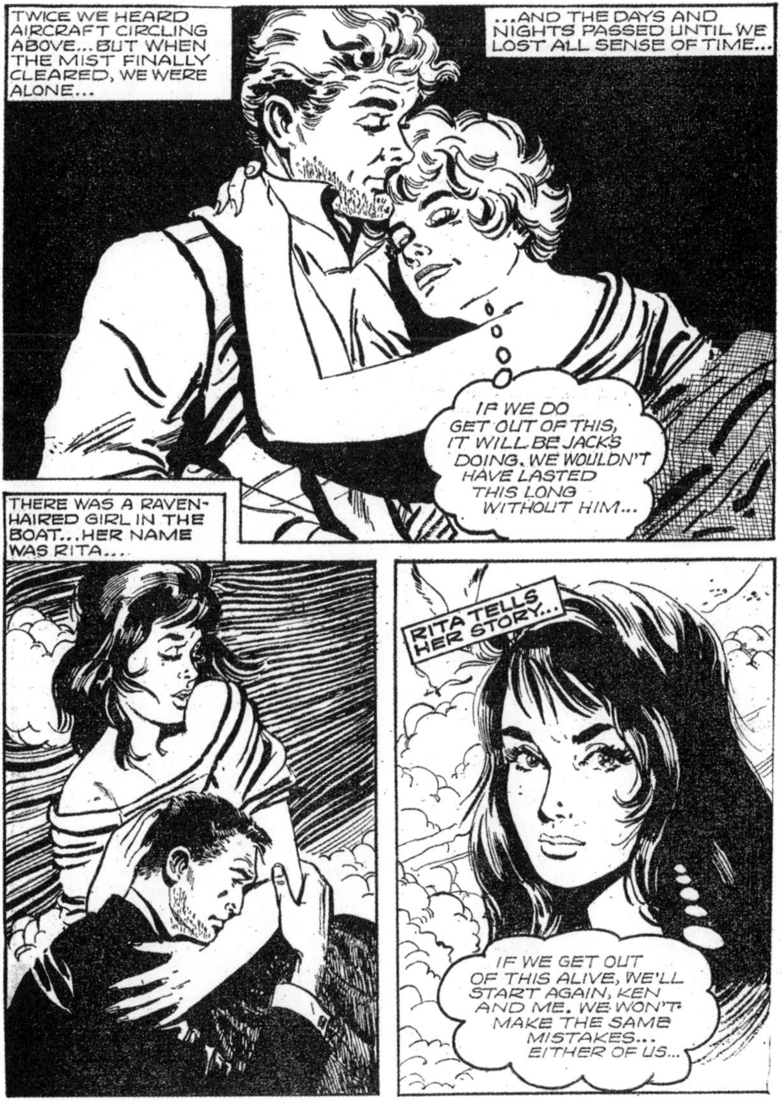
TWICE WE HEARD AIRCRAFT CIRCLING ABOVE... BUT WHEN THE MIST FINALLY CLEARED, WE WERE ALONE...
...AND THE DAYS AND NIGHTS PASSED UNTIL WE LOST ALL SENSE OF TIME...
IF WE DO GET OUT OF THIS, IT WILL BE JACK'S DOING. WE WOULDN'T HAVE LASTED THIS LONG WITHOUT HIM...
THERE WAS A RAVEN-HAIRED GIRL IN THE BOAT... HER NAME WAS RITA...
RITA TELLS HER STORY...
IF WE GET OUT OF THIS ALIVE, WE'LL START AGAIN, KEN AND ME. WE WON'T MAKE THE SAME MISTAKES... EITHER OF US...

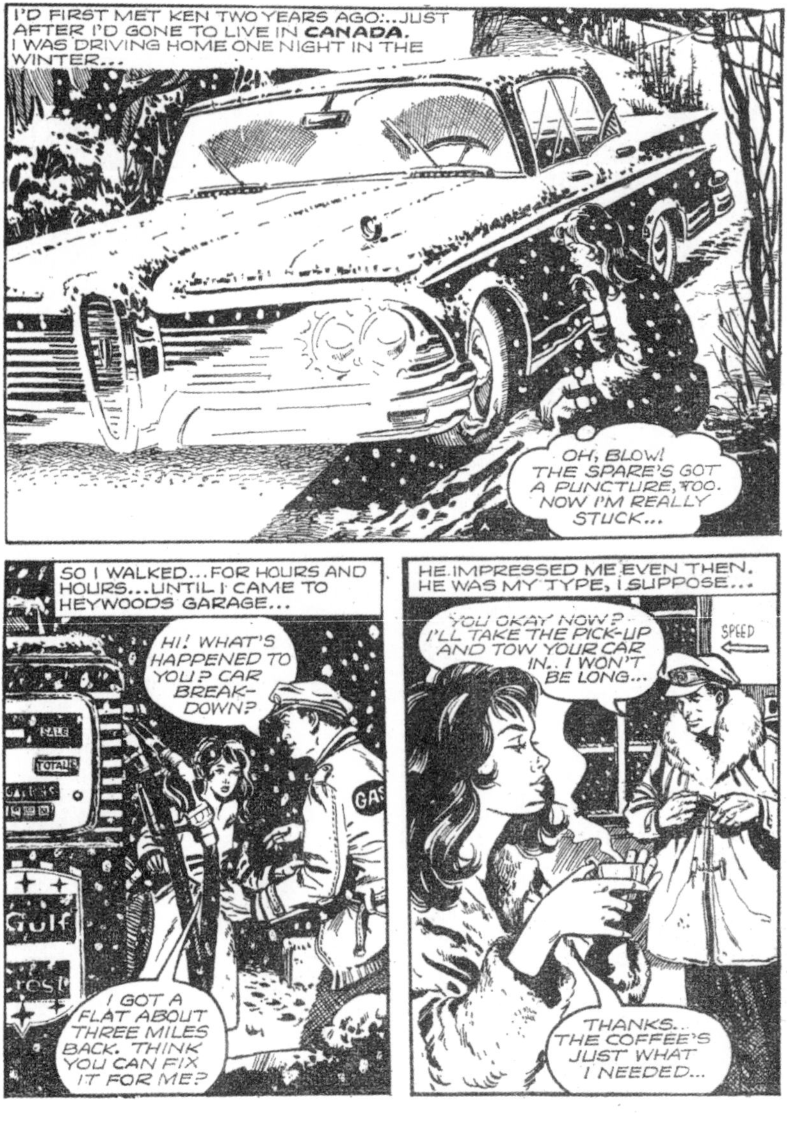
I'D FIRST MET KEN TWO YEARS AGO:..JUST AFTER I'D GONE TO LIVE IN **CANADA.** I WAS DRIVING HOME ONE NIGHT IN THE WINTER...
OH, BLOW! THE SPARE'S GOT A PUNCTURE, TOO. NOW I'M REALLY STUCK...
SO I WALKED... FOR HOURS AND HOURS... UNTIL I CAME TO HEYWOODS GARAGE...
HI! WHAT'S HAPPENED TO YOU? CAR BREAK-DOWN?
I GOT A FLAT ABOUT THREE MILES BACK. THINK YOU CAN FIX IT FOR ME?
GAS
Gulf
HE IMPRESSED ME EVEN THEN. HE WAS MY TYPE, I SUPPOSE...
YOU OKAY NOW? I'LL TAKE THE PICK-UP AND TOW YOUR CAR IN.. I WON'T BE LONG...
SPEED
THANKS... THE COFFEE'S JUST WHAT I NEEDED...

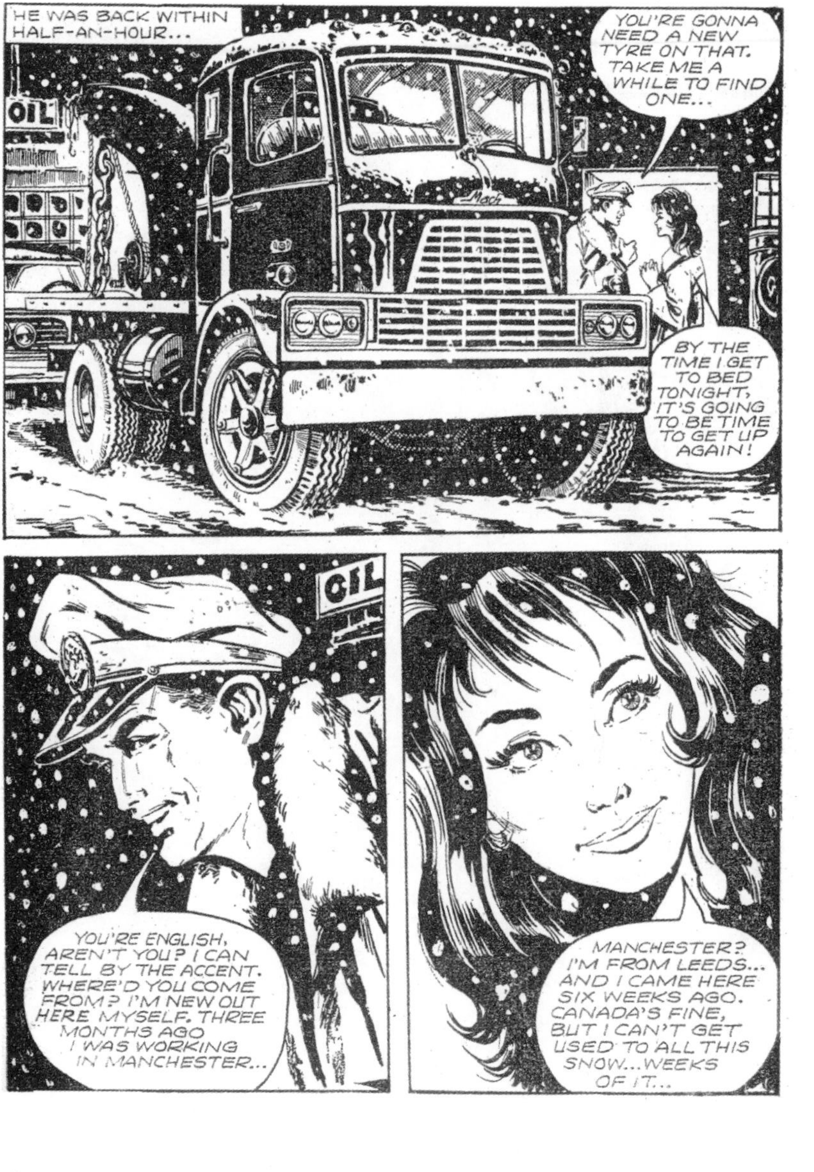
HE WAS BACK WITHIN HALF-AN-HOUR...
YOU'RE GONNA NEED A NEW TYRE ON THAT. TAKE ME A WHILE TO FIND ONE...
BY THE TIME I GET TO BED TONIGHT, IT'S GOING TO BE TIME TO GET UP AGAIN!
YOU'RE ENGLISH, AREN'T YOU? I CAN TELL BY THE ACCENT. WHERE'D YOU COME FROM? I'M NEW OUT HERE MYSELF. THREE MONTHS AGO I WAS WORKING IN MANCHESTER...
MANCHESTER? I'M FROM LEEDS... AND I CAME HERE SIX WEEKS AGO. CANADA'S FINE, BUT I CAN'T GET USED TO ALL THIS SNOW... WEEKS OF IT...

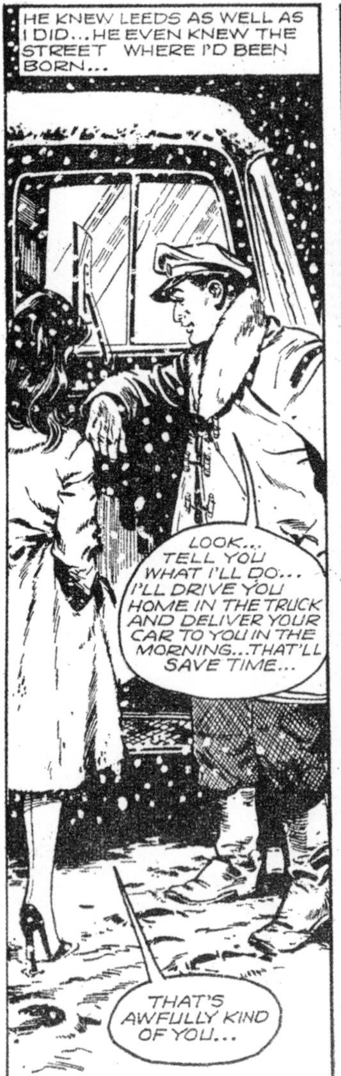
HE KNEW LEEDS AS WELL AS I DID... HE EVEN KNEW THE STREET WHERE I'D BEEN BORN...
LOOK... TELL YOU WHAT I'LL DO... I'LL DRIVE YOU HOME IN THE TRUCK AND DELIVER YOUR CAR TO YOU IN THE MORNING... THAT'LL SAVE TIME...
THAT'S AWFULLY KIND OF YOU...

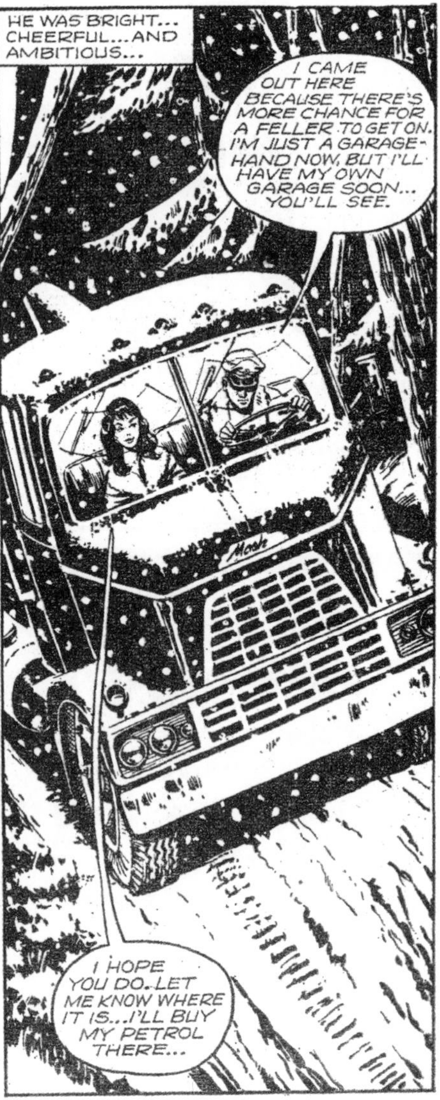
HE WAS BRIGHT... CHEERFUL... AND AMBITIOUS...
I CAME OUT HERE BECAUSE THERE'S MORE CHANCE FOR A FELLER TO GET ON. I'M JUST A GARAGE-HAND NOW, BUT I'LL HAVE MY OWN GARAGE SOON... YOU'LL SEE.
I HOPE YOU DO. LET ME KNOW WHERE IT IS... I'LL BUY MY PETROL THERE...

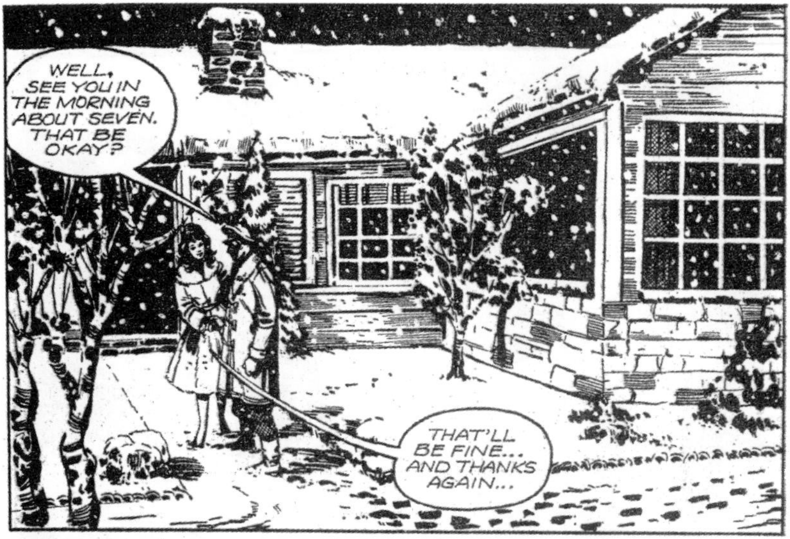
WELL, SEE YOU IN THE MORNING ABOUT SEVEN. THAT BE OKAY?
THAT'LL BE FINE... AND THANKS AGAIN...

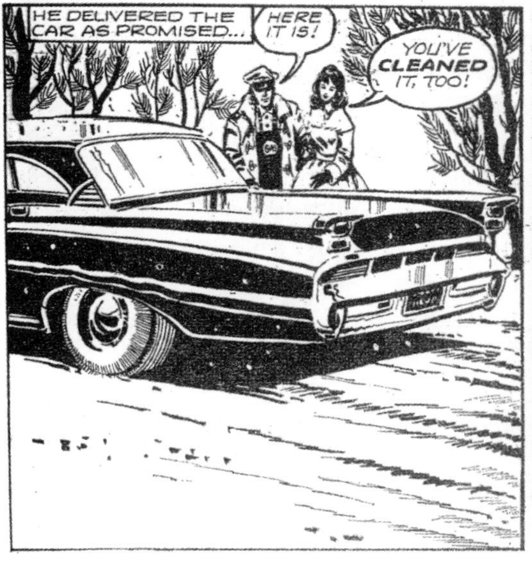
HE DELIVERED THE CAR AS PROMISED...
HERE IT IS!
YOU'VE **CLEANED** IT, TOO!

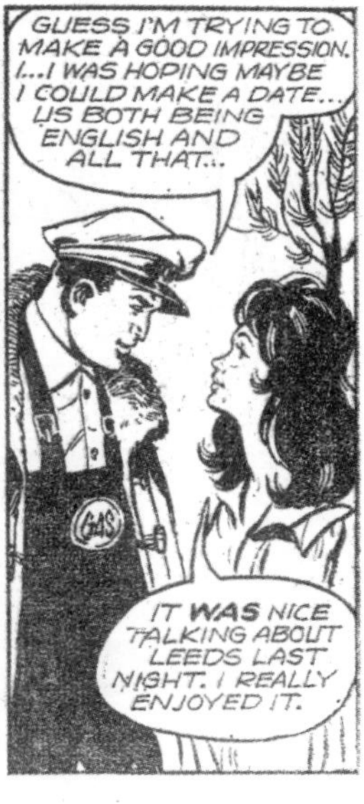
GUESS I'M TRYING TO MAKE A GOOD IMPRESSION. I...I WAS HOPING MAYBE I COULD MAKE A DATE... US BOTH BEING ENGLISH AND ALL THAT...
IT **WAS** NICE TALKING ABOUT LEEDS LAST NIGHT. I REALLY ENJOYED IT.

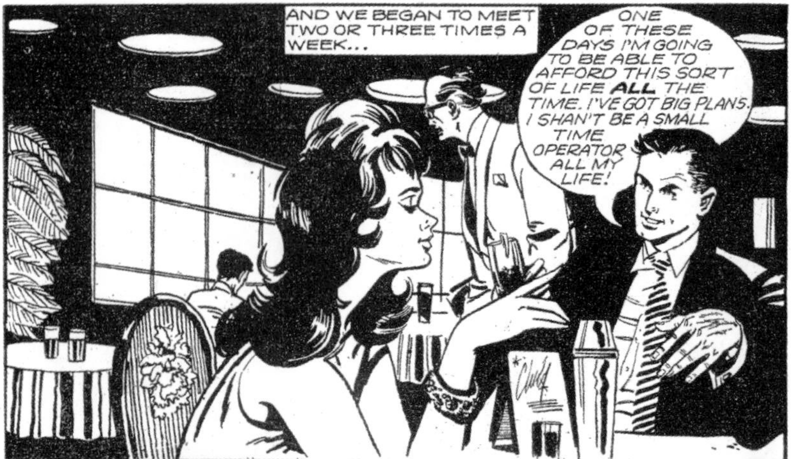
AND WE BEGAN TO MEET TWO OR THREE TIMES A WEEK...
ONE OF THESE DAYS I'M GOING TO BE ABLE TO AFFORD THIS SORT OF LIFE **ALL** THE TIME. I'VE GOT BIG PLANS. I SHAN'T BE A SMALL TIME OPERATOR ALL MY LIFE!

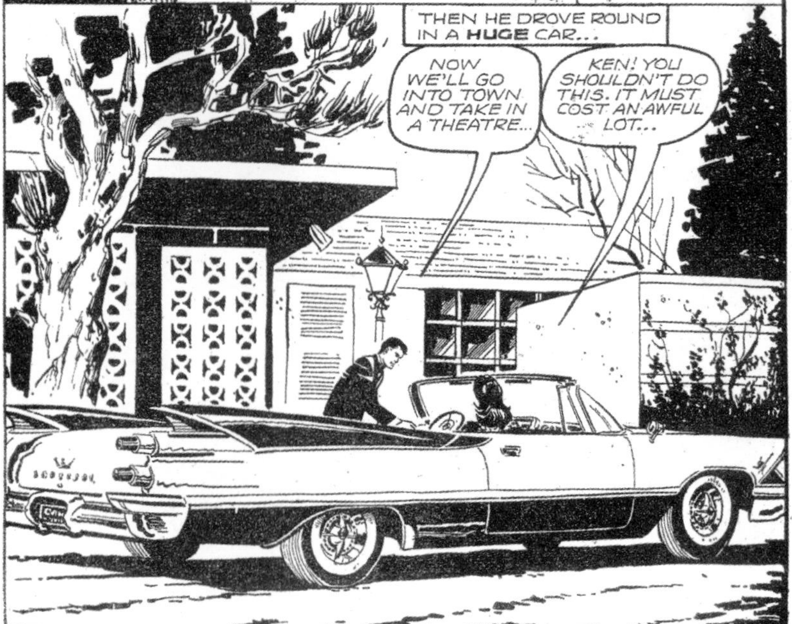
THEN HE DROVE ROUND IN A **HUGE** CAR...
NOW WE'LL GO INTO TOWN AND TAKE IN A THEATRE...
KEN! YOU SHOULDN'T DO THIS. IT MUST COST AN AWFUL LOT...

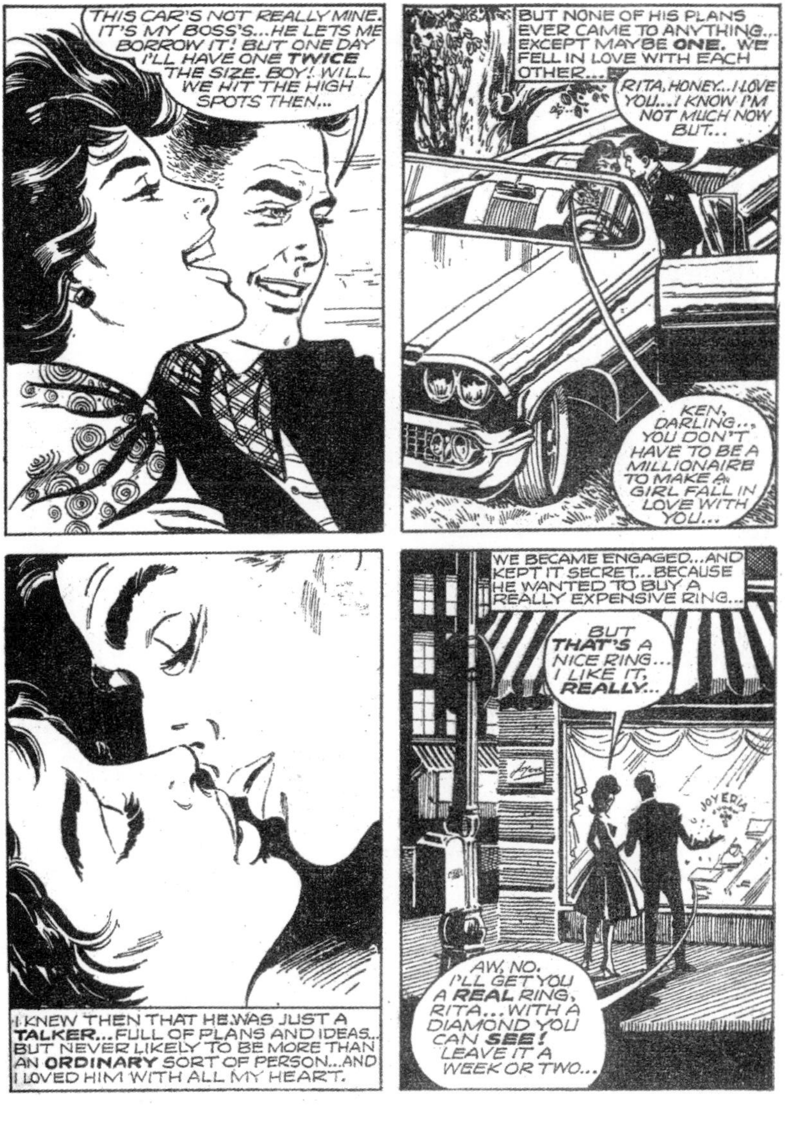
THIS CAR'S NOT REALLY MINE. IT'S MY BOSS'S...HE LETS ME BORROW IT! BUT ONE DAY I'LL HAVE ONE TWICE THE SIZE. BOY! WILL WE HIT THE HIGH SPOTS THEN...
BUT NONE OF HIS PLANS EVER CAME TO ANYTHING... EXCEPT MAYBE ONE. WE FELL IN LOVE WITH EACH OTHER...
RITA, HONEY...I LOVE YOU...I KNOW I'M NOT MUCH NOW BUT...
KEN, DARLING..., YOU DON'T HAVE TO BE A MILLIONAIRE TO MAKE A GIRL FALL IN LOVE WITH YOU...
I KNEW THEN THAT HE WAS JUST A TALKER...FULL OF PLANS AND IDEAS... BUT NEVER LIKELY TO BE MORE THAN AN ORDINARY SORT OF PERSON...AND I LOVED HIM WITH ALL MY HEART.
WE BECAME ENGAGED...AND KEPT IT SECRET...BECAUSE HE WANTED TO BUY A REALLY EXPENSIVE RING...
BUT THAT'S A NICE RING... I LIKE IT, REALLY...
JOYERIA
AW, NO. I'LL GET YOU A REAL RING, RITA...WITH A DIAMOND YOU CAN SEE! LEAVE IT A WEEK OR TWO...

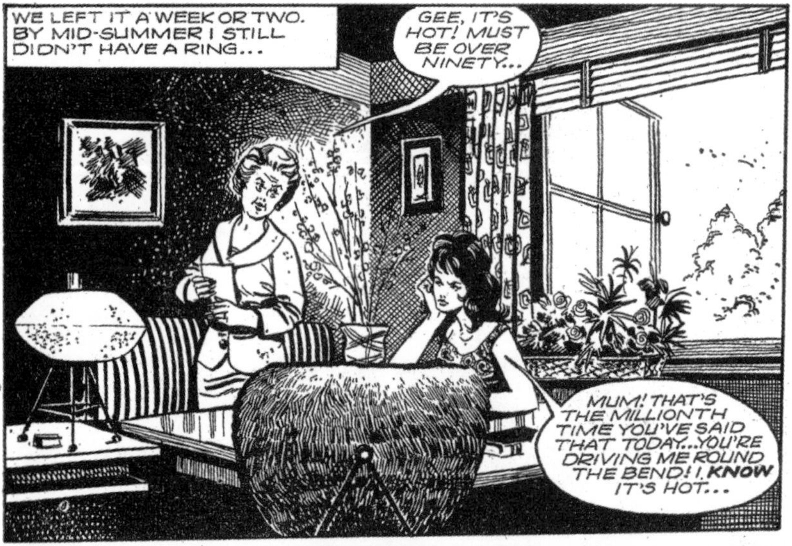
WE LEFT IT A WEEK OR TWO. BY MID-SUMMER I STILL DIDN'T HAVE A RING...
GEE, IT'S HOT! MUST BE OVER NINETY...
MUM! THAT'S THE MILLIONTH TIME YOU'VE SAID THAT TODAY...YOU'RE DRIVING ME ROUND THE BEND! I KNOW IT'S HOT...

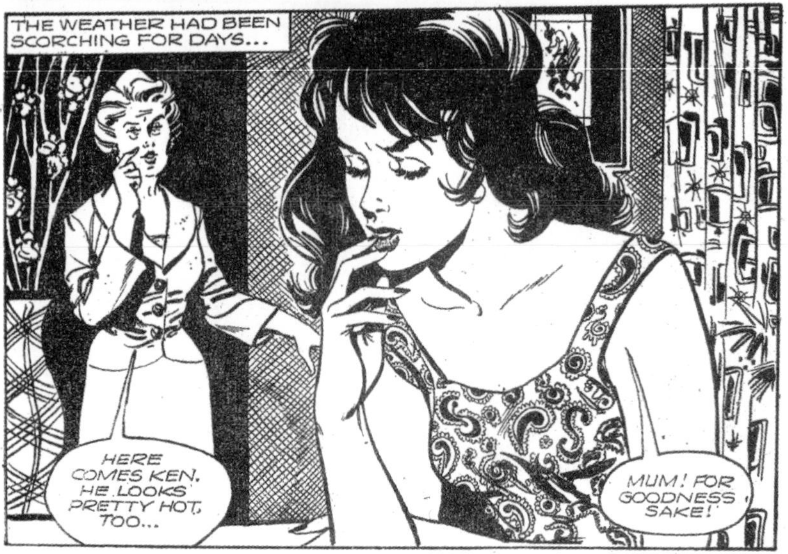
THE WEATHER HAD BEEN SCORCHING FOR DAYS...
HERE COMES KEN. HE LOOKS PRETTY HOT, TOO...
MUM! FOR GOODNESS SAKE!

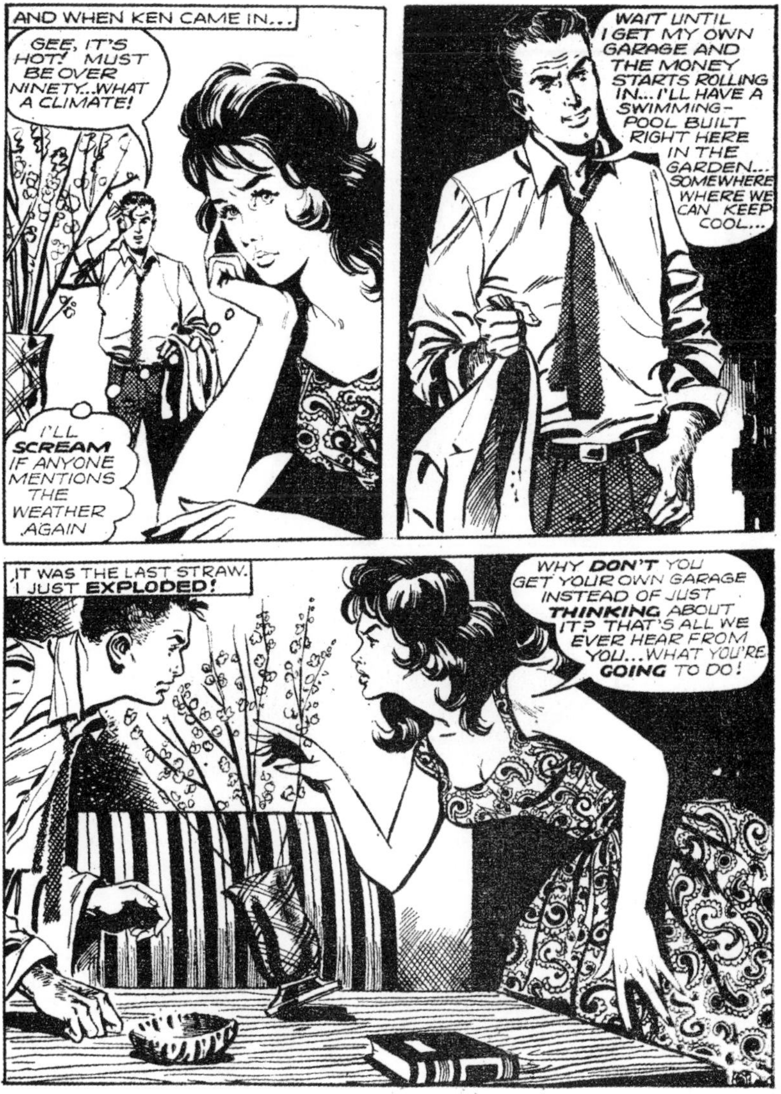
AND WHEN KEN CAME IN...
GEE, IT'S HOT! MUST BE OVER NINETY...WHAT A CLIMATE!
I'LL SCREAM IF ANYONE MENTIONS THE WEATHER AGAIN
WAIT UNTIL I GET MY OWN GARAGE AND THE MONEY STARTS ROLLING IN... I'LL HAVE A SWIMMING-POOL BUILT RIGHT HERE IN THE GARDEN... SOMEWHERE WHERE WE CAN KEEP COOL...
IT WAS THE LAST STRAW. I JUST EXPLODED!
WHY DON'T YOU GET YOUR OWN GARAGE INSTEAD OF JUST THINKING ABOUT IT? THAT'S ALL WE EVER HEAR FROM YOU... WHAT YOU'RE GOING TO DO!

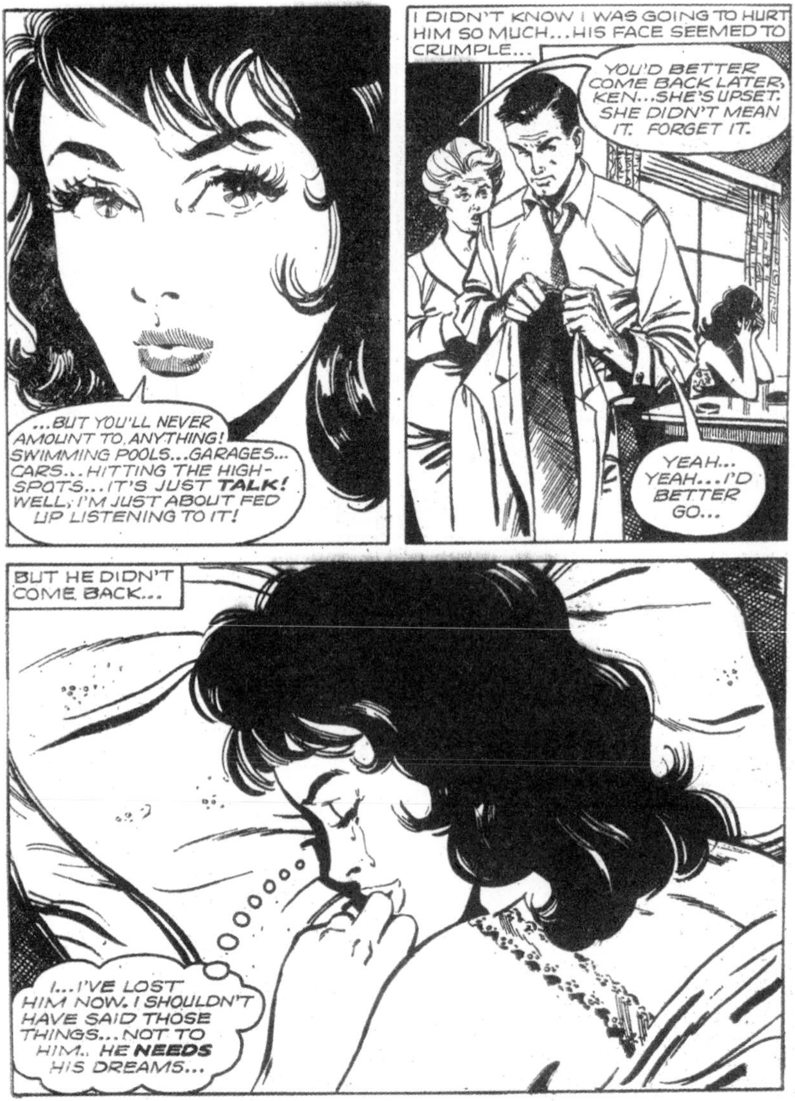
...BUT YOU'LL NEVER AMOUNT TO ANYTHING! SWIMMING POOLS...GARAGES... CARS...HITTING THE HIGH-SPOTS...IT'S JUST TALK! WELL, I'M JUST ABOUT FED UP LISTENING TO IT!
I DIDN'T KNOW I WAS GOING TO HURT HIM SO MUCH...HIS FACE SEEMED TO CRUMPLE...
YOU'D BETTER COME BACK LATER, KEN...SHE'S UPSET. SHE DIDN'T MEAN IT. FORGET IT.
YEAH... YEAH...I'D BETTER GO...
BUT HE DIDN'T COME BACK...
I...I'VE LOST HIM NOW. I SHOULDN'T HAVE SAID THOSE THINGS...NOT TO HIM.. HE NEEDS HIS DREAMS...

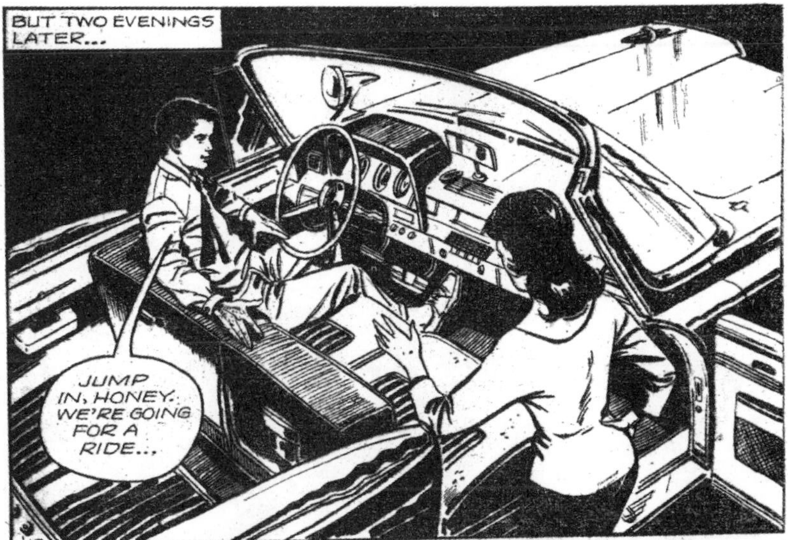
BUT TWO EVENINGS LATER...
JUMP IN, HONEY. WE'RE GOING FOR A RIDE...

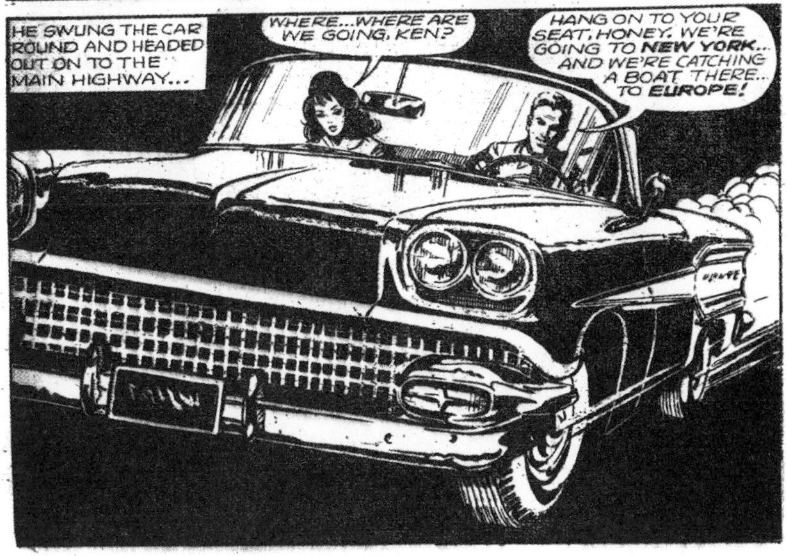
HE SWUNG THE CAR ROUND AND HEADED OUT ON TO THE MAIN HIGHWAY...
WHERE... WHERE ARE WE GOING, KEN?
HANG ON TO YOUR SEAT, HONEY. WE'RE GOING TO NEW YORK... AND WE'RE CATCHING A BOAT THERE... TO EUROPE!

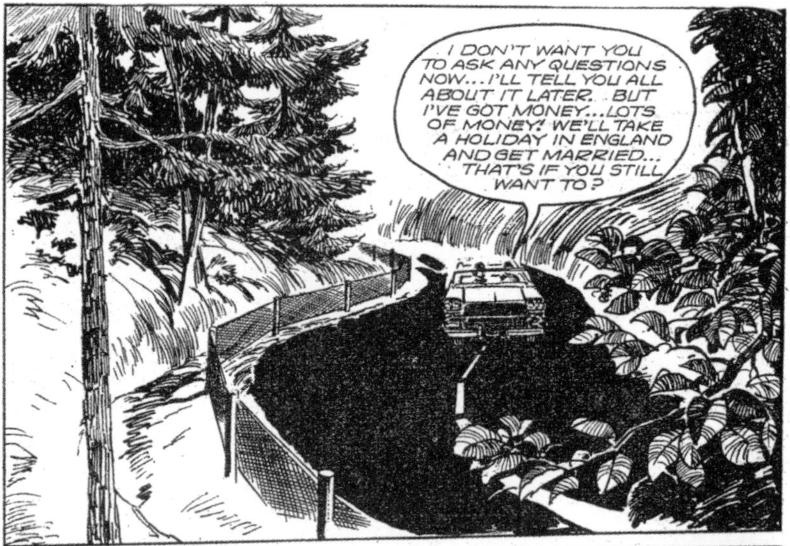
I DON'T WANT YOU TO ASK ANY QUESTIONS NOW... I'LL TELL YOU ALL ABOUT IT LATER. BUT I'VE GOT MONEY... LOTS OF MONEY! WE'LL TAKE A HOLIDAY IN ENGLAND AND GET MARRIED... THAT'S IF YOU STILL WANT TO?

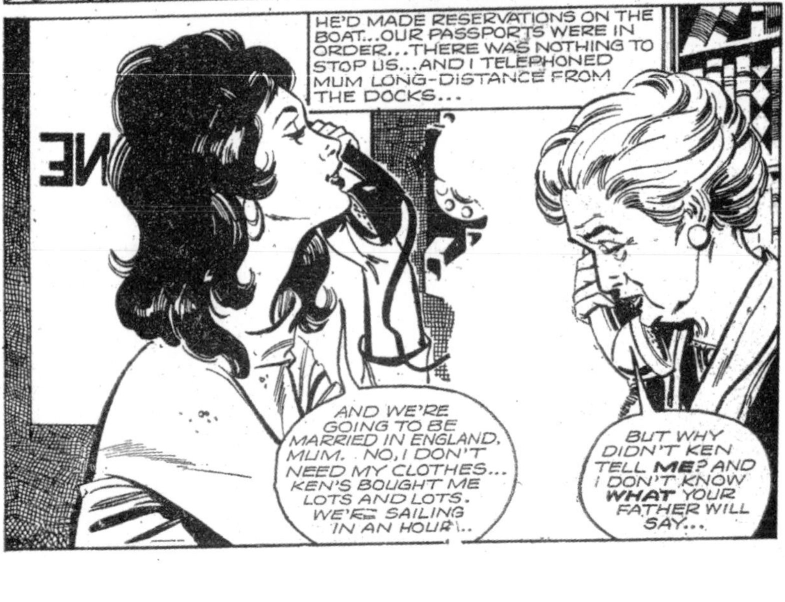
HE'D MADE RESERVATIONS ON THE BOAT... OUR PASSPORTS WERE IN ORDER... THERE WAS NOTHING TO STOP US... AND I TELEPHONED MUM LONG-DISTANCE FROM THE DOCKS...
NE
AND WE'RE GOING TO BE MARRIED IN ENGLAND. MUM. NO, I DON'T NEED MY CLOTHES... KEN'S BOUGHT ME LOTS AND LOTS. WE'RE SAILING IN AN HOUR...
BUT WHY DIDN'T KEN TELL ME? AND I DON'T KNOW WHAT YOUR FATHER WILL SAY...

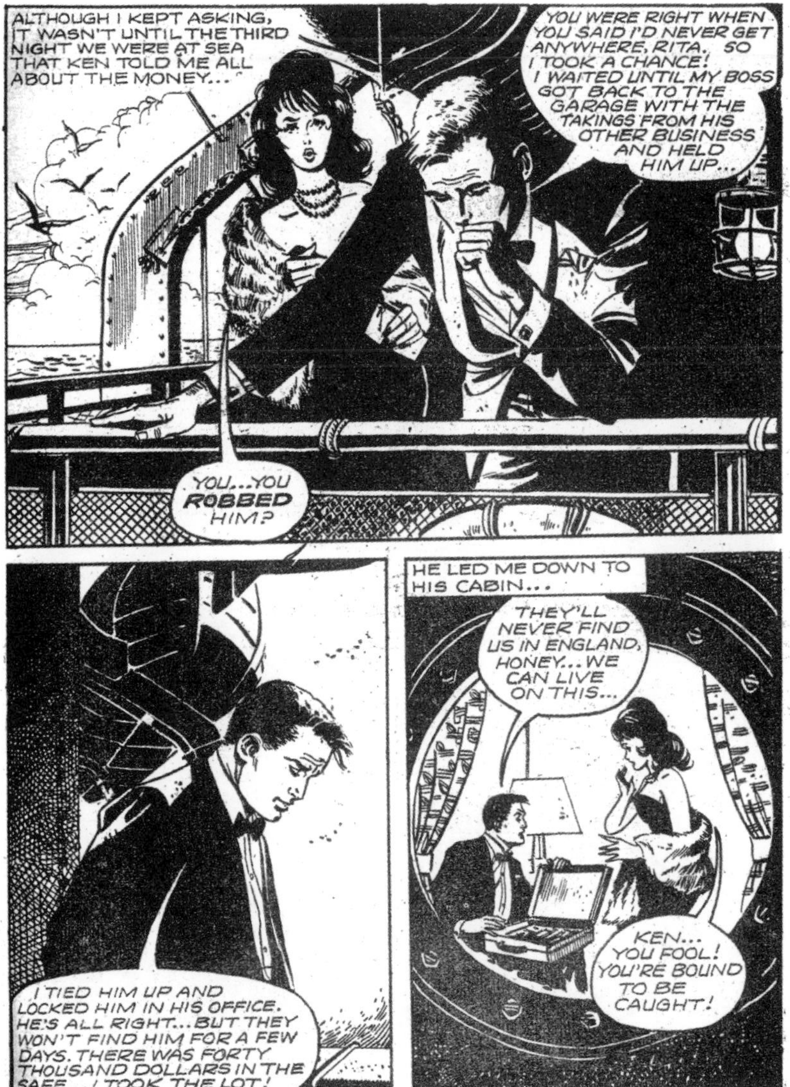
ALTHOUGH I KEPT ASKING, IT WASN'T UNTIL THE THIRD NIGHT WE WERE AT SEA THAT KEN TOLD ME ALL ABOUT THE MONEY...
YOU WERE RIGHT WHEN YOU SAID I'D NEVER GET ANYWHERE, RITA. SO I TOOK A CHANCE! I WAITED UNTIL MY BOSS GOT BACK TO THE GARAGE WITH THE TAKINGS FROM HIS OTHER BUSINESS AND HELD HIM UP...
YOU...YOU ROBBED HIM?
I TIED HIM UP AND LOCKED HIM IN HIS OFFICE. HE'S ALL RIGHT... BUT THEY WON'T FIND HIM FOR A FEW DAYS. THERE WAS FORTY THOUSAND DOLLARS IN THE SAFE... I TOOK THE LOT!
HE LED ME DOWN TO HIS CABIN...
THEY'LL NEVER FIND US IN ENGLAND, HONEY... WE CAN LIVE ON THIS...
KEN... YOU FOOL! YOU'RE BOUND TO BE CAUGHT!

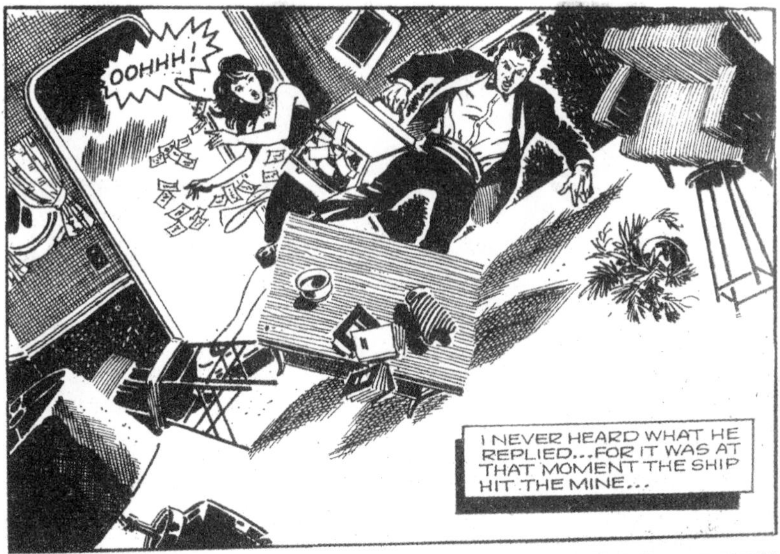
OOHHH!
I NEVER HEARD WHAT HE REPLIED...FOR IT WAS AT THAT MOMENT THE SHIP HIT THE MINE...

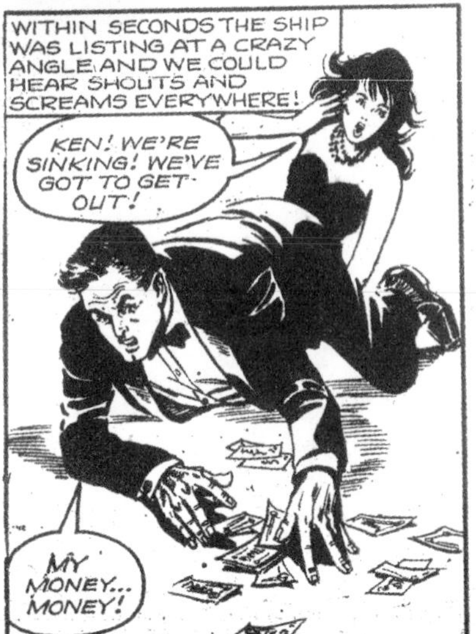
WITHIN SECONDS THE SHIP WAS LISTING AT A CRAZY ANGLE AND WE COULD HEAR SHOUTS AND SCREAMS EVERYWHERE!
KEN! WE'RE SINKING! WE'VE GOT TO GET OUT!
MY MONEY... MONEY!

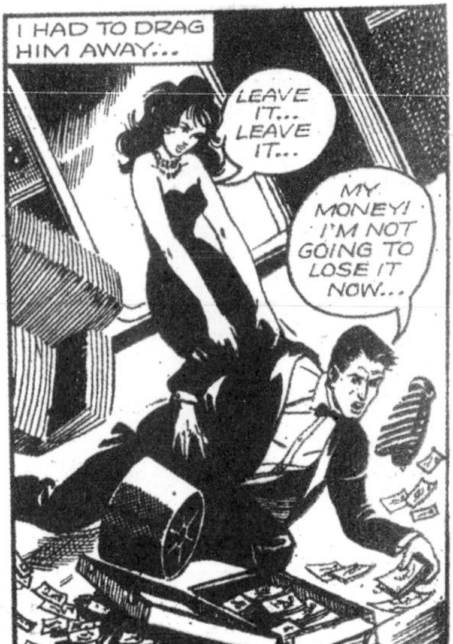
I HAD TO DRAG HIM AWAY...
LEAVE IT... LEAVE IT...
MY MONEY! I'M NOT GOING TO LOSE IT NOW...

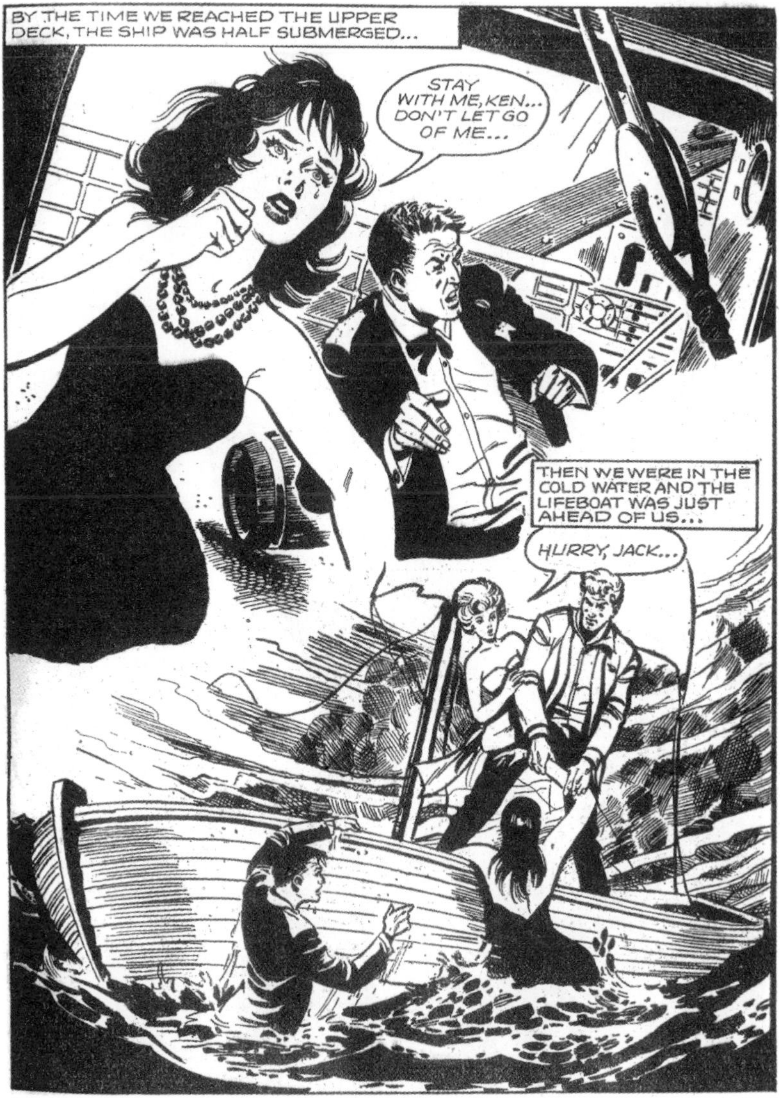
BY THE TIME WE REACHED THE UPPER DECK, THE SHIP WAS HALF SUBMERGED...
STAY WITH ME, KEN... DON'T LET GO OF ME...
THEN WE WERE IN THE COLD WATER AND THE LIFEBOAT WAS JUST AHEAD OF US...
HURRY, JACK...

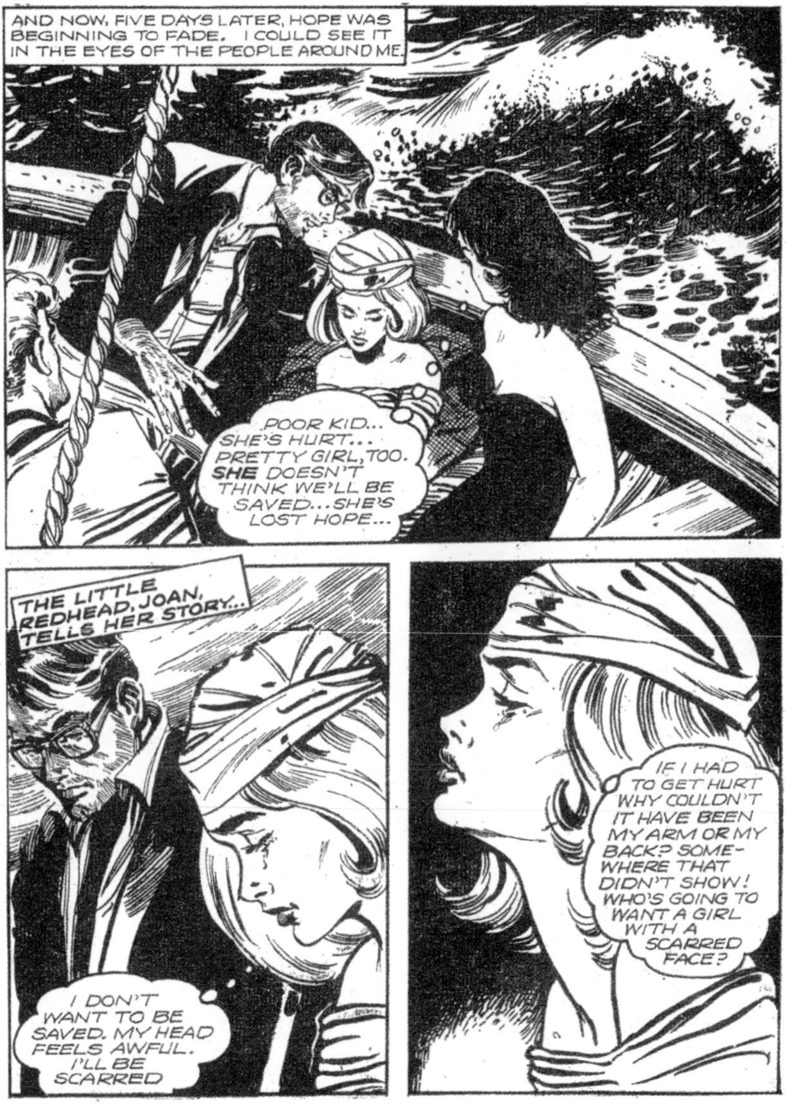
AND NOW, FIVE DAYS LATER, HOPE WAS BEGINNING TO FADE. I COULD SEE IT IN THE EYES OF THE PEOPLE AROUND ME.
POOR KID... SHE'S HURT... PRETTY GIRL, TOO. SHE DOESN'T THINK WE'LL BE SAVED... SHE'S LOST HOPE...
THE LITTLE REDHEAD, JOAN, TELLS HER STORY...
I DON'T WANT TO BE SAVED. MY HEAD FEELS AWFUL. I'LL BE SCARRED
IF I HAD TO GET HURT WHY COULDN'T IT HAVE BEEN MY ARM OR MY BACK? SOME-WHERE THAT DIDN'T SHOW! WHO'S GOING TO WANT A GIRL WITH A SCARRED FACE?

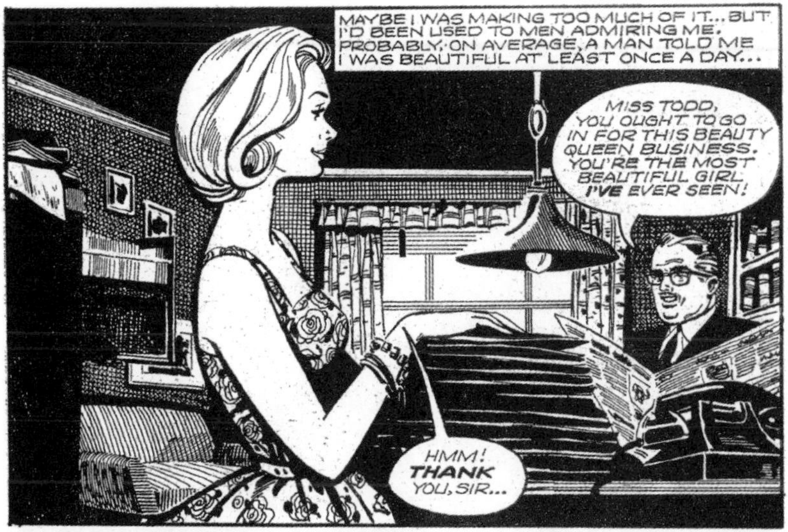
MAYBE I WAS MAKING TOO MUCH OF IT... BUT I'D BEEN USED TO MEN ADMIRING ME. PROBABLY, ON AVERAGE, A MAN TOLD ME I WAS BEAUTIFUL AT LEAST ONCE A DAY...
MISS TODD, YOU OUGHT TO GO IN FOR THIS BEAUTY QUEEN BUSINESS. YOU'RE THE MOST BEAUTIFUL GIRL I'VE EVER SEEN!
HMM! THANK YOU, SIR...

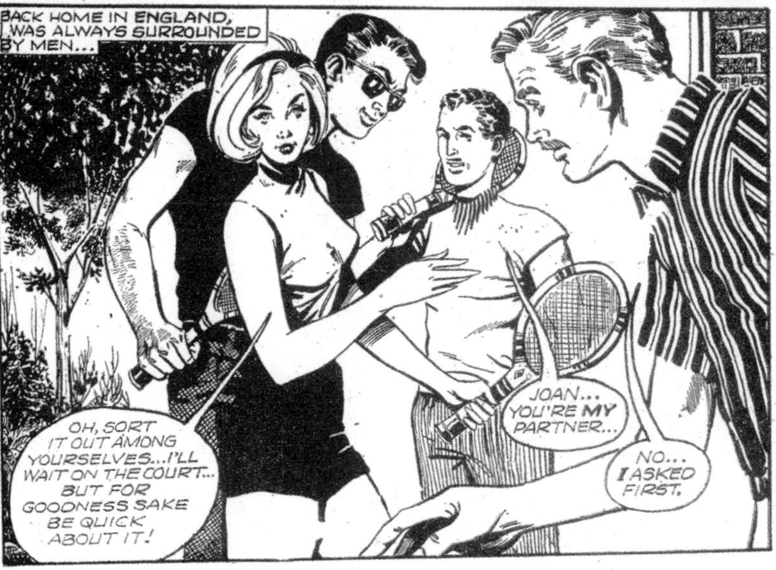
BACK HOME IN ENGLAND, I WAS ALWAYS SURROUNDED BY MEN...
JOAN... YOU'RE MY PARTNER...
NO... I ASKED FIRST.
OH, SORT IT OUT AMONG YOURSELVES... I'LL WAIT ON THE COURT... BUT FOR GOODNESS SAKE BE QUICK ABOUT IT!

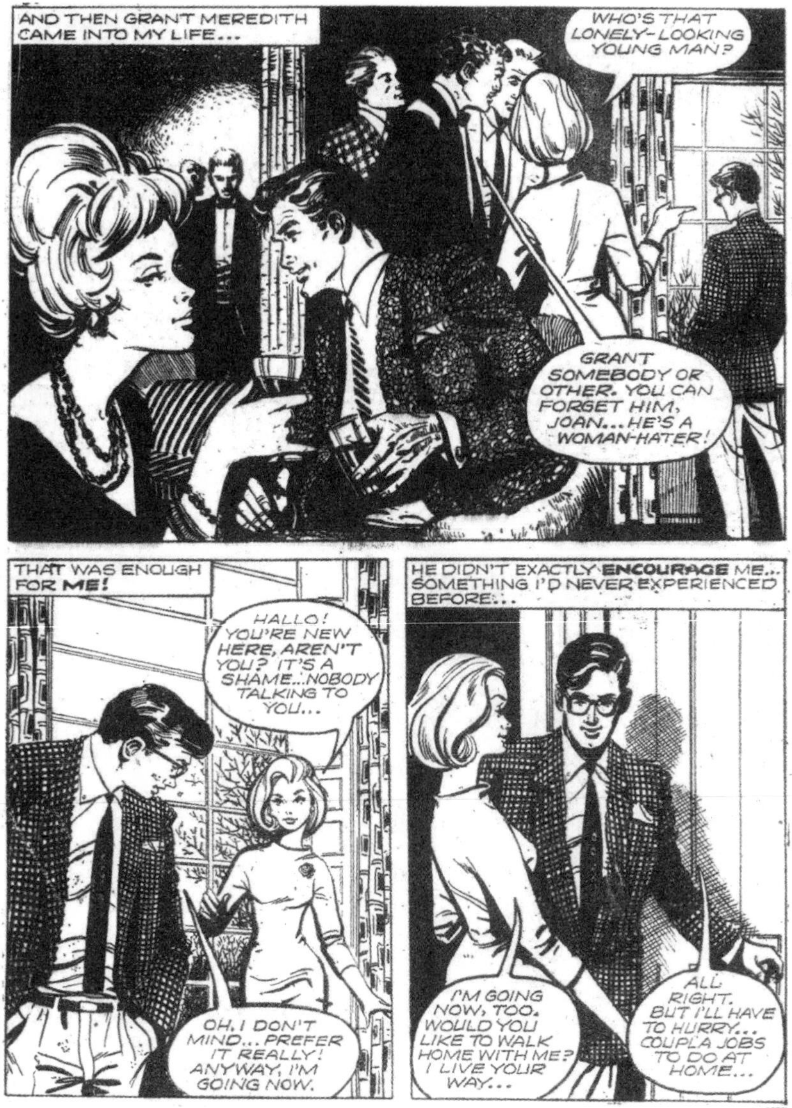
AND THEN GRANT MEREDITH CAME INTO MY LIFE...
WHO'S THAT LONELY-LOOKING YOUNG MAN?
GRANT SOMEBODY OR OTHER. YOU CAN FORGET HIM, JOAN... HE'S A WOMAN-HATER!
THAT WAS ENOUGH FOR ME!
HALLO! YOU'RE NEW HERE, AREN'T YOU? IT'S A SHAME... NOBODY TALKING TO YOU...
OH, I DON'T MIND... PREFER IT REALLY! ANYWAY, I'M GOING NOW.
HE DIDN'T EXACTLY ENCOURAGE ME... SOMETHING I'D NEVER EXPERIENCED BEFORE...
I'M GOING NOW, TOO. WOULD YOU LIKE TO WALK HOME WITH ME? I LIVE YOUR WAY...
ALL RIGHT. BUT I'LL HAVE TO HURRY... COUPLA JOBS TO DO AT HOME...

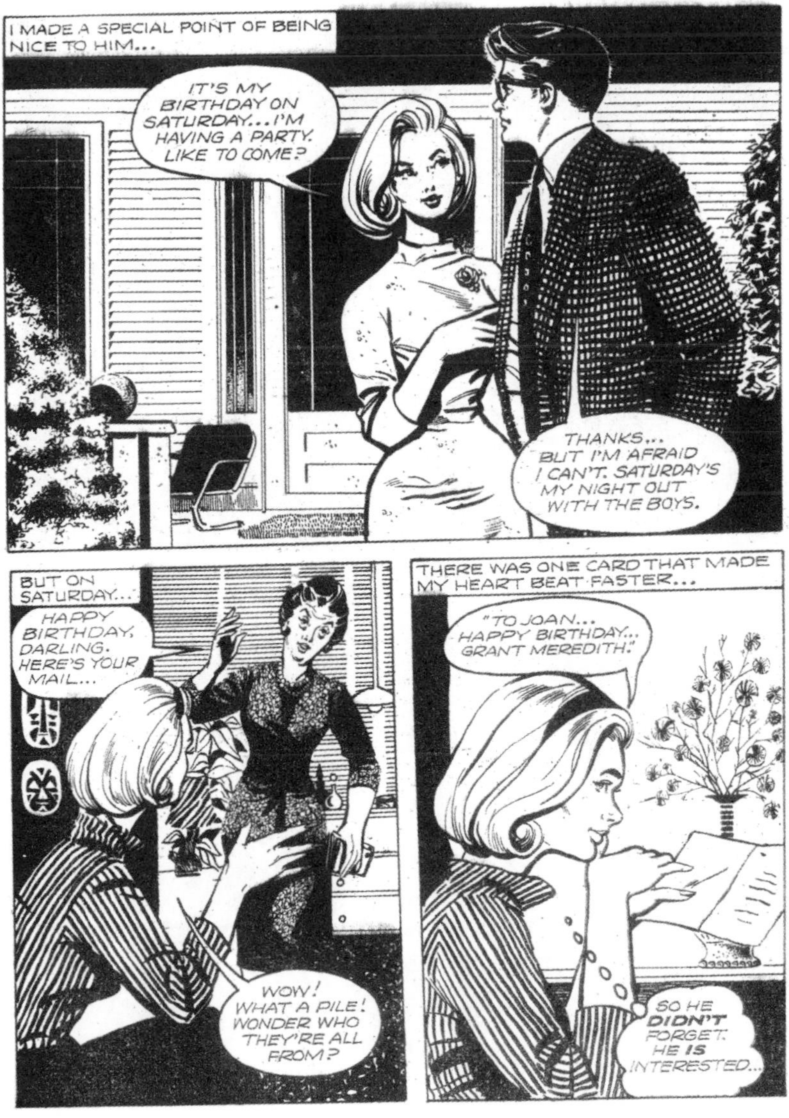
I MADE A SPECIAL POINT OF BEING NICE TO HIM...
IT'S MY BIRTHDAY ON SATURDAY...I'M HAVING A PARTY. LIKE TO COME?
THANKS... BUT I'M AFRAID I CAN'T. SATURDAY'S MY NIGHT OUT WITH THE BOYS.
BUT ON SATURDAY...
HAPPY BIRTHDAY, DARLING. HERE'S YOUR MAIL...
WOW! WHAT A PILE! WONDER WHO THEY'RE ALL FROM?
THERE WAS ONE CARD THAT MADE MY HEART BEAT FASTER...
"TO JOAN... HAPPY BIRTHDAY... GRANT MEREDITH."
SO HE DIDN'T FORGET. HE IS INTERESTED...

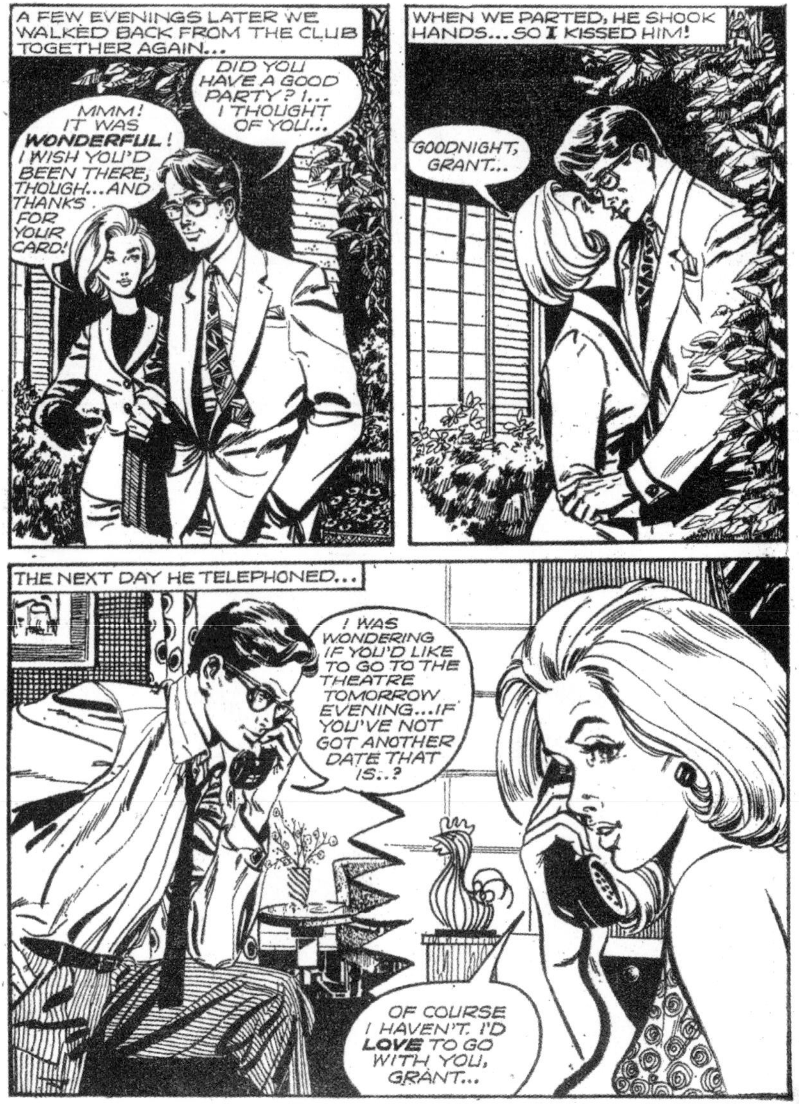
A FEW EVENINGS LATER WE WALKED BACK FROM THE CLUB TOGETHER AGAIN...
DID YOU HAVE A GOOD PARTY? I... I THOUGHT OF YOU...
MMM! IT WAS WONDERFUL! I WISH YOU'D BEEN THERE, THOUGH... AND THANKS FOR YOUR CARD!
WHEN WE PARTED, HE SHOOK HANDS... SO I KISSED HIM!
GOODNIGHT, GRANT...
THE NEXT DAY HE TELEPHONED...
I WAS WONDERING IF YOU'D LIKE TO GO TO THE THEATRE TOMORROW EVENING... IF YOU'VE NOT GOT ANOTHER DATE THAT IS..?
OF COURSE I HAVEN'T. I'D LOVE TO GO WITH YOU, GRANT...

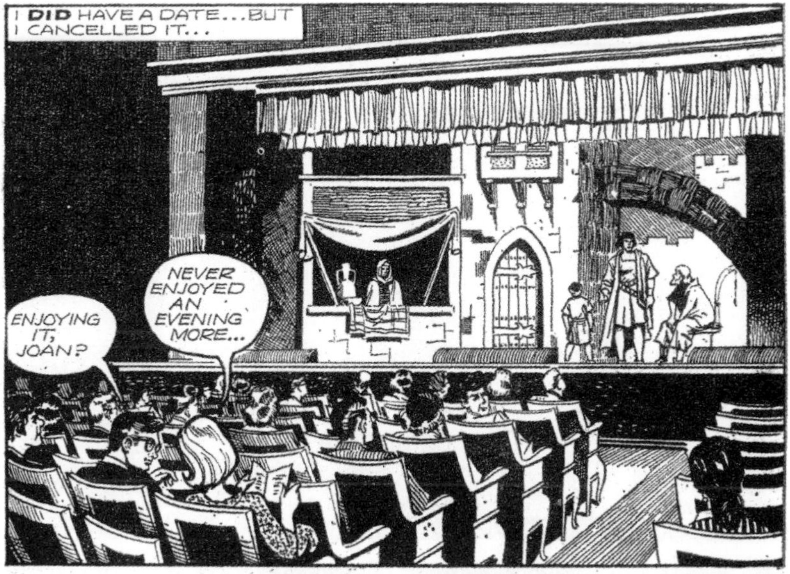
I DID HAVE A DATE...BUT I CANCELLED IT...
ENJOYING IT, JOAN?
NEVER ENJOYED AN EVENING MORE...

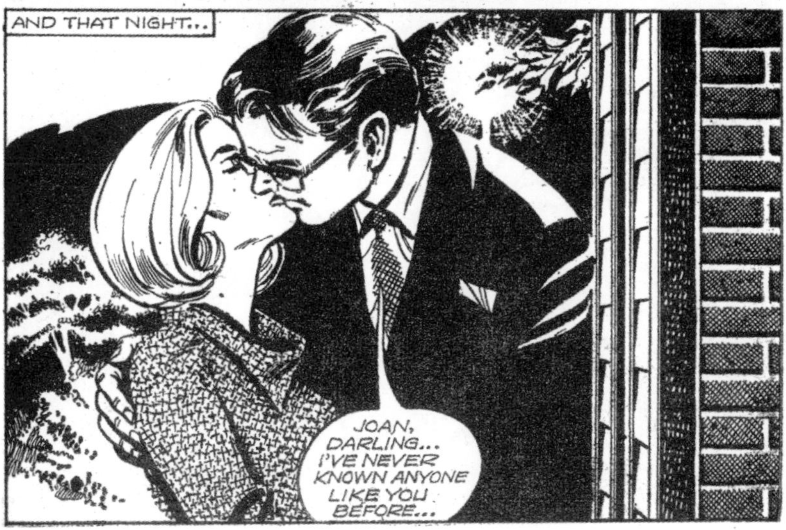
AND THAT NIGHT...
JOAN, DARLING... I'VE NEVER KNOWN ANYONE LIKE YOU BEFORE...

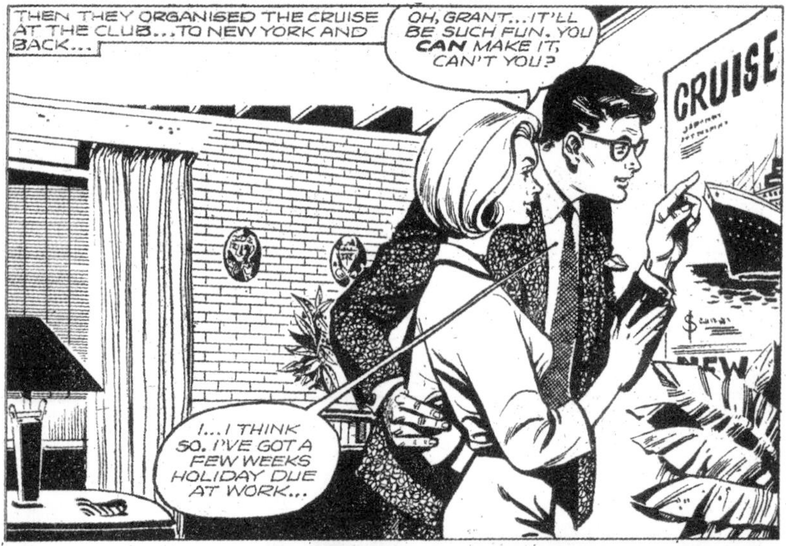
THEN THEY ORGANISED THE CRUISE AT THE CLUB...TO NEW YORK AND BACK...
OH, GRANT...IT'LL BE SUCH FUN. YOU CAN MAKE IT, CAN'T YOU?
I...I THINK SO. I'VE GOT A FEW WEEKS HOLIDAY DUE AT WORK...
CRUISE

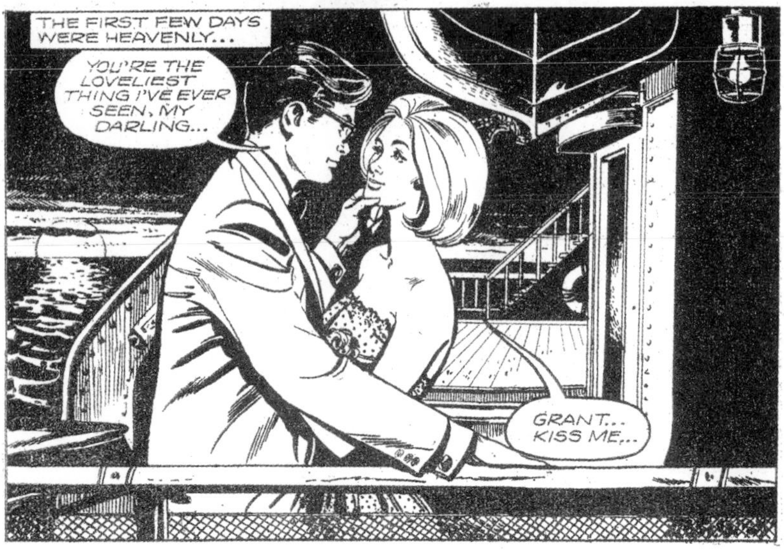
THE FIRST FEW DAYS WERE HEAVENLY...
YOU'RE THE LOVELIEST THING I'VE EVER SEEN, MY DARLING...
GRANT... KISS ME...

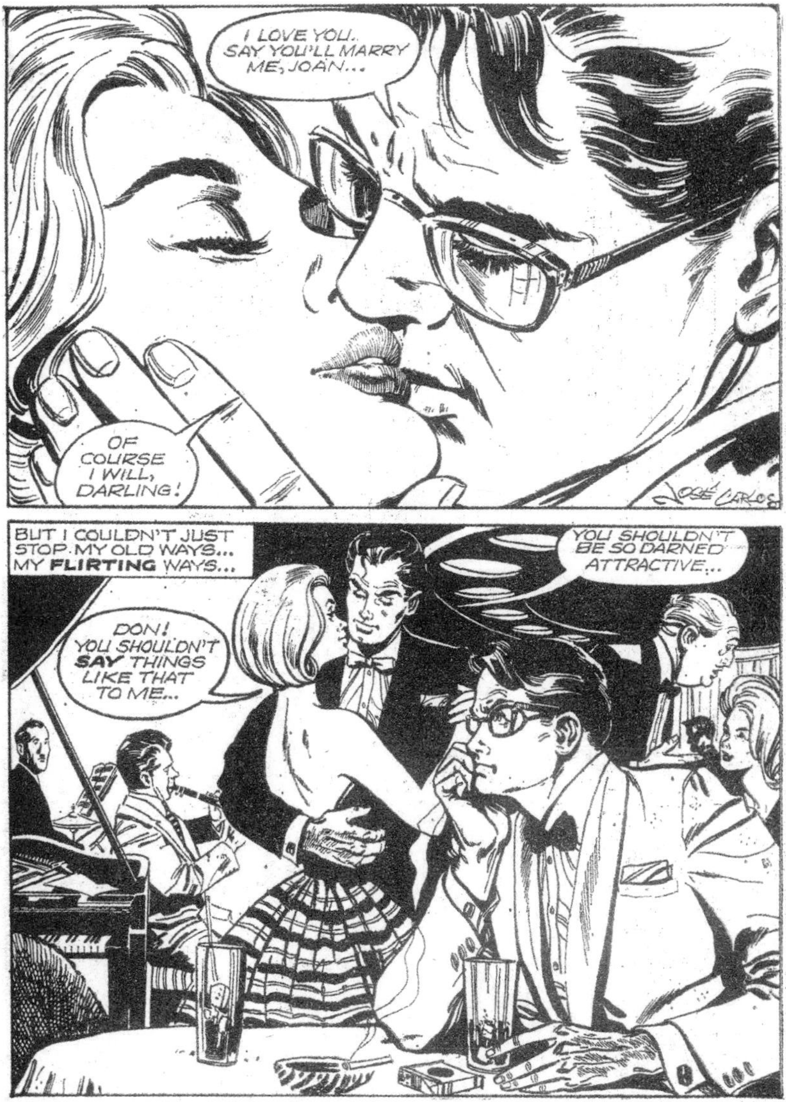
I LOVE YOU.. SAY YOU'LL MARRY ME, JOAN...
OF COURSE I WILL, DARLING!
BUT I COULDN'T JUST STOP MY OLD WAYS... MY **FLIRTING** WAYS...
YOU SHOULDN'T BE SO DARNED ATTRACTIVE...
DON! YOU SHOULDN'T **SAY** THINGS LIKE THAT TO ME...

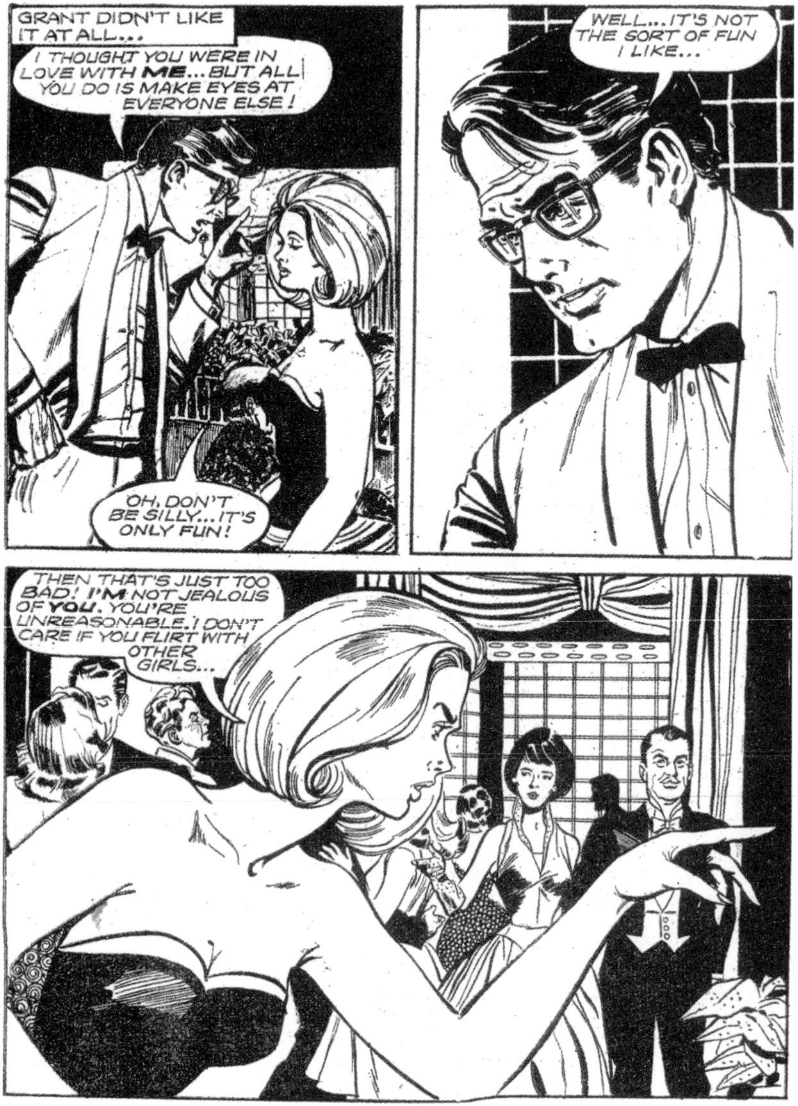
GRANT DIDN'T LIKE IT AT ALL...
I THOUGHT YOU WERE IN LOVE WITH ME... BUT ALL YOU DO IS MAKE EYES AT EVERYONE ELSE!
OH, DON'T BE SILLY... IT'S ONLY FUN!
WELL... IT'S NOT THE SORT OF FUN I LIKE...
THEN THAT'S JUST TOO BAD! I'M NOT JEALOUS OF YOU. YOU'RE UNREASONABLE. I DON'T CARE IF YOU FLIRT WITH OTHER GIRLS...

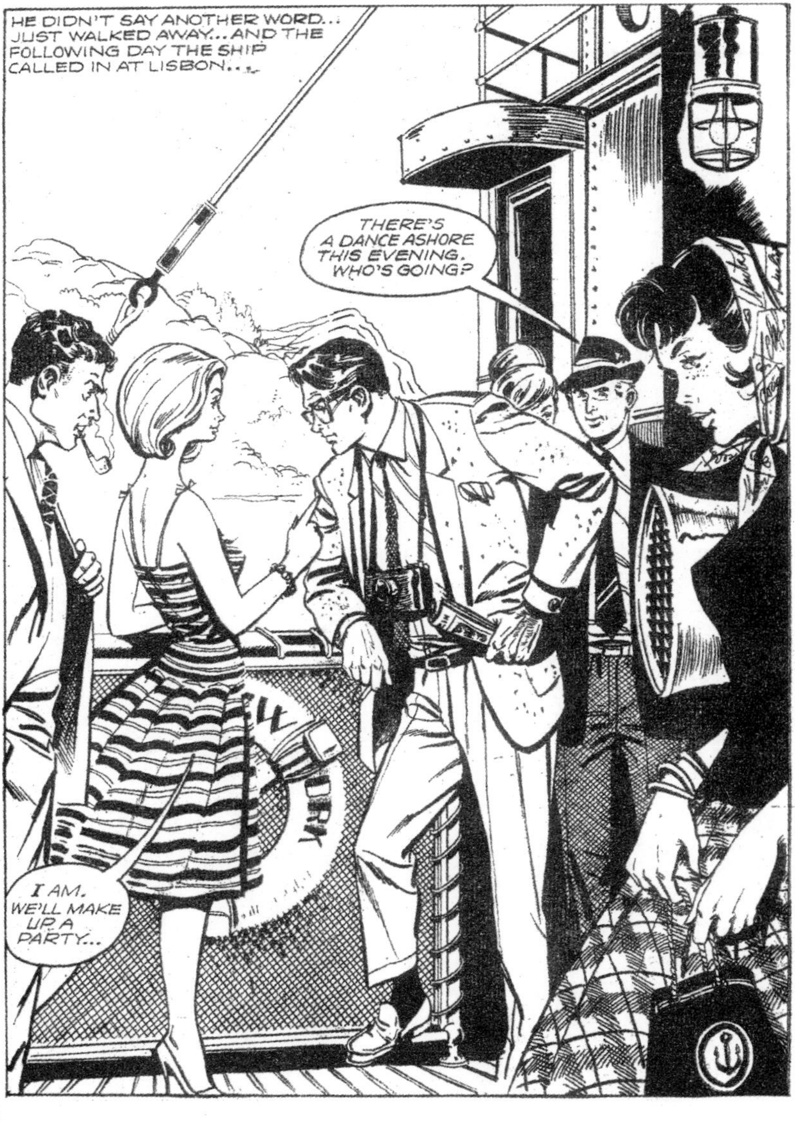
HE DIDN'T SAY ANOTHER WORD... JUST WALKED AWAY... AND THE FOLLOWING DAY THE SHIP CALLED IN AT LISBON...
THERE'S A DANCE ASHORE THIS EVENING. WHO'S GOING?
I AM. WE'LL MAKE UP A PARTY...

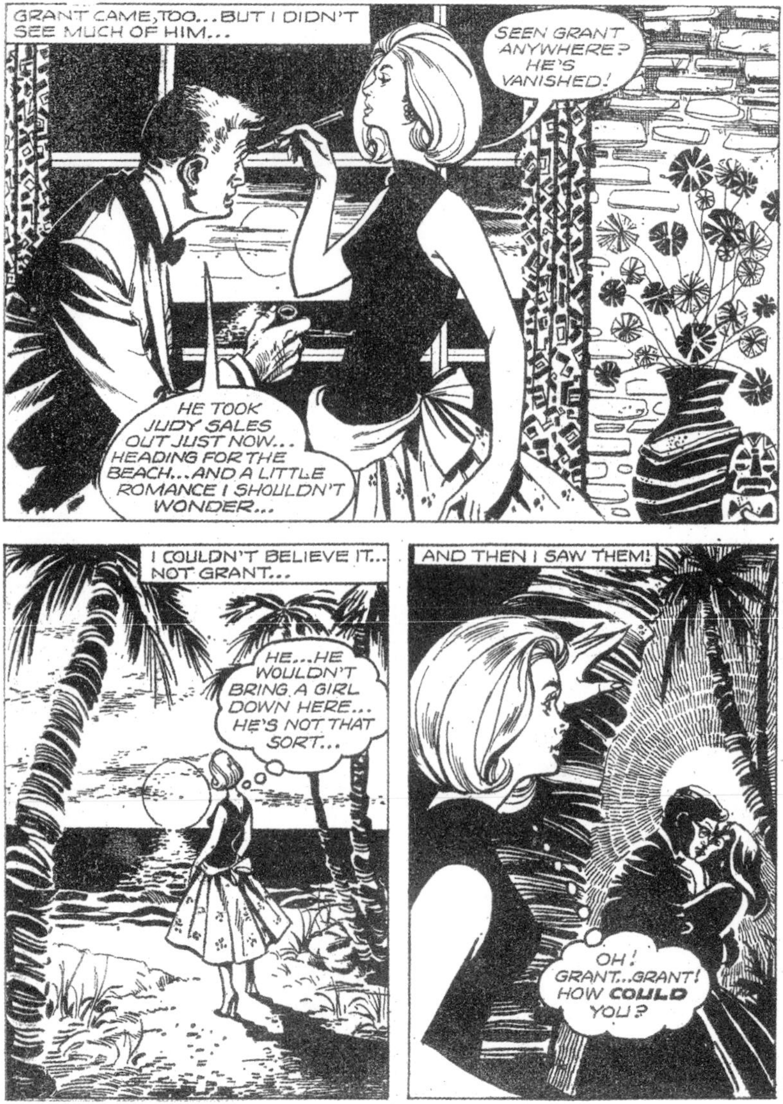
GRANT CAME, TOO... BUT I DIDN'T SEE MUCH OF HIM...
SEEN GRANT ANYWHERE? HE'S VANISHED!
HE TOOK JUDY SALES OUT JUST NOW... HEADING FOR THE BEACH... AND A LITTLE ROMANCE I SHOULDN'T WONDER...
I COULDN'T BELIEVE IT... NOT GRANT...
HE... HE WOULDN'T BRING A GIRL DOWN HERE... HE'S NOT THAT SORT...
AND THEN I SAW THEM!
OH! GRANT... GRANT! HOW COULD YOU?

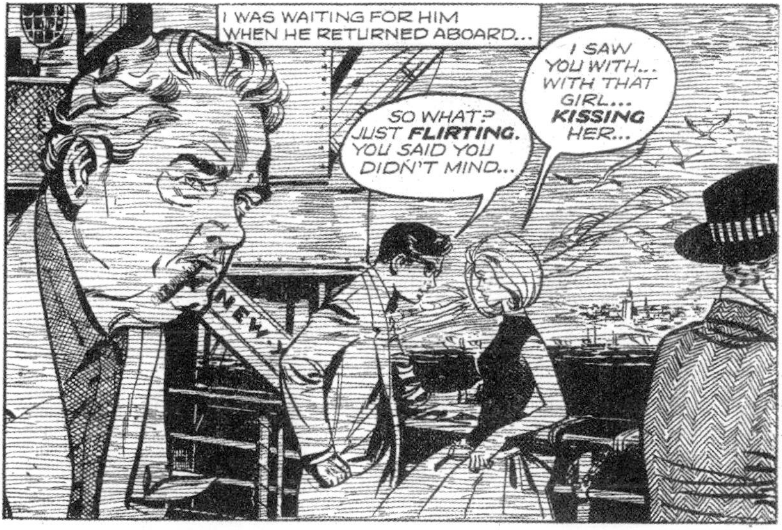
I WAS WAITING FOR HIM WHEN HE RETURNED ABOARD...
I SAW YOU WITH... WITH THAT GIRL... KISSING HER...
SO WHAT? JUST FLIRTING. YOU SAID YOU DIDN'T MIND...
NEW

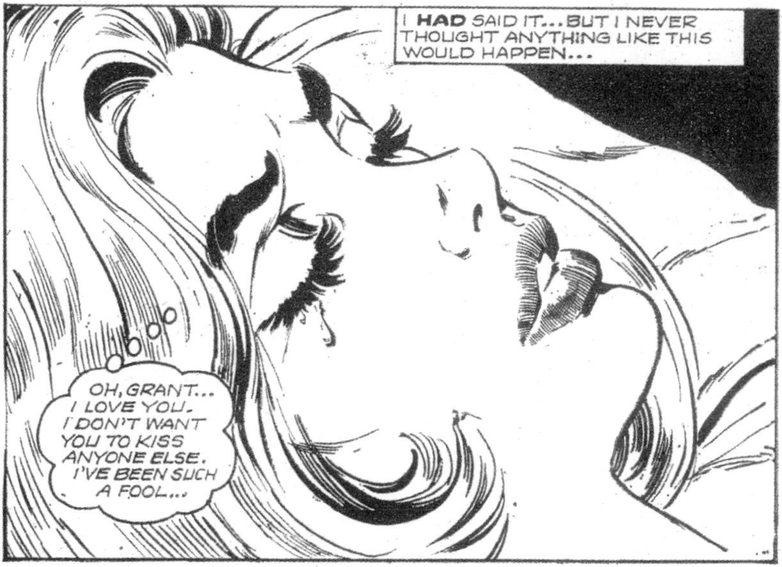
I HAD SAID IT... BUT I NEVER THOUGHT ANYTHING LIKE THIS WOULD HAPPEN...
OH, GRANT... I LOVE YOU. I DON'T WANT YOU TO KISS ANYONE ELSE. I'VE BEEN SUCH A FOOL...

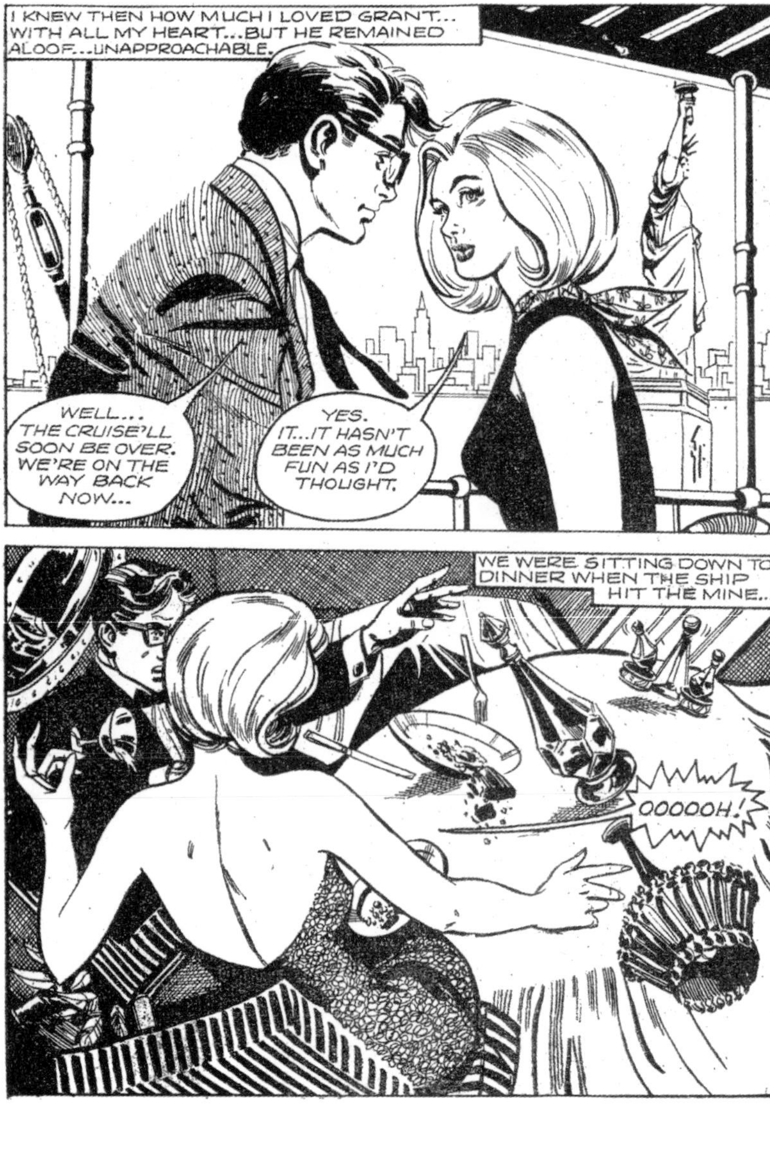
I KNEW THEN HOW MUCH I LOVED GRANT... WITH ALL MY HEART...BUT HE REMAINED ALOOF...UNAPPROACHABLE.
WELL... THE CRUISE'LL SOON BE OVER. WE'RE ON THE WAY BACK NOW...
YES. IT...IT HASN'T BEEN AS MUCH FUN AS I'D THOUGHT.
WE WERE SITTING DOWN TO DINNER WHEN THE SHIP HIT THE MINE...
OOOOOH!

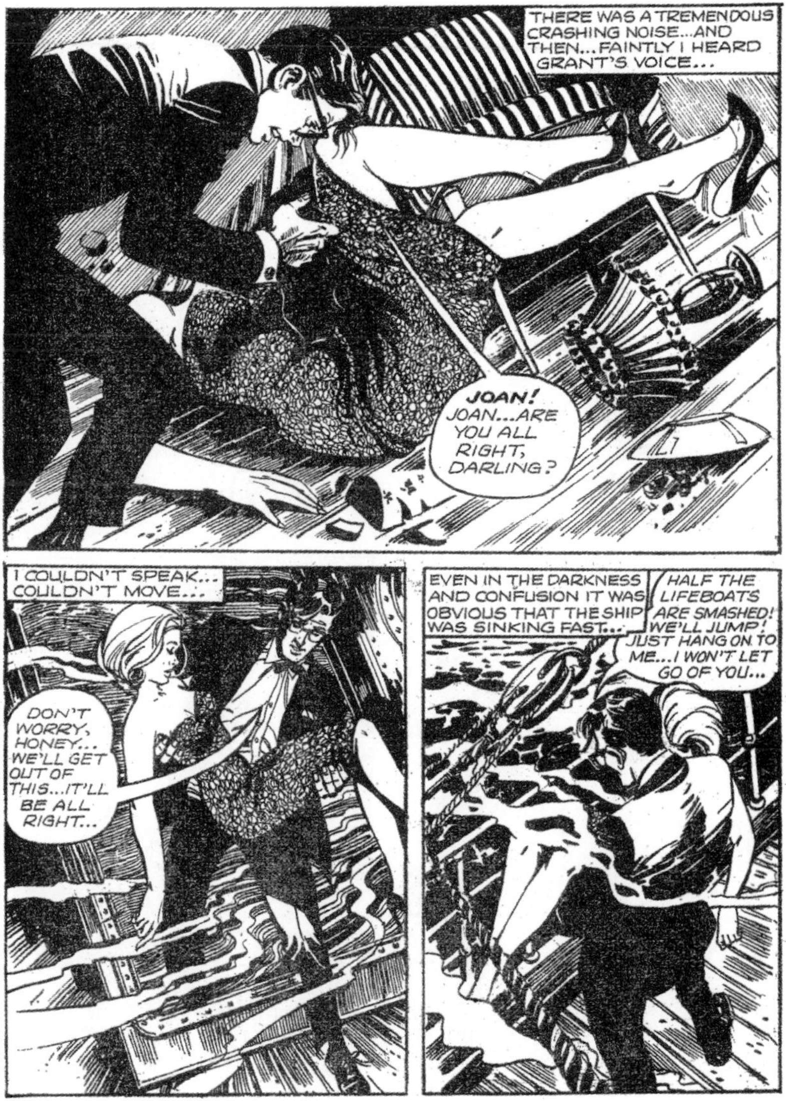
THERE WAS A TREMENDOUS CRASHING NOISE...AND THEN...FAINTLY I HEARD GRANT'S VOICE...
JOAN! JOAN...ARE YOU ALL RIGHT, DARLING?
I COULDN'T SPEAK... COULDN'T MOVE...
DON'T WORRY, HONEY... WE'LL GET OUT OF THIS...IT'LL BE ALL RIGHT...
EVEN IN THE DARKNESS AND CONFUSION IT WAS OBVIOUS THAT THE SHIP WAS SINKING FAST...
HALF THE LIFEBOATS ARE SMASHED! WE'LL JUMP! JUST HANG ON TO ME...I WON'T LET GO OF YOU...

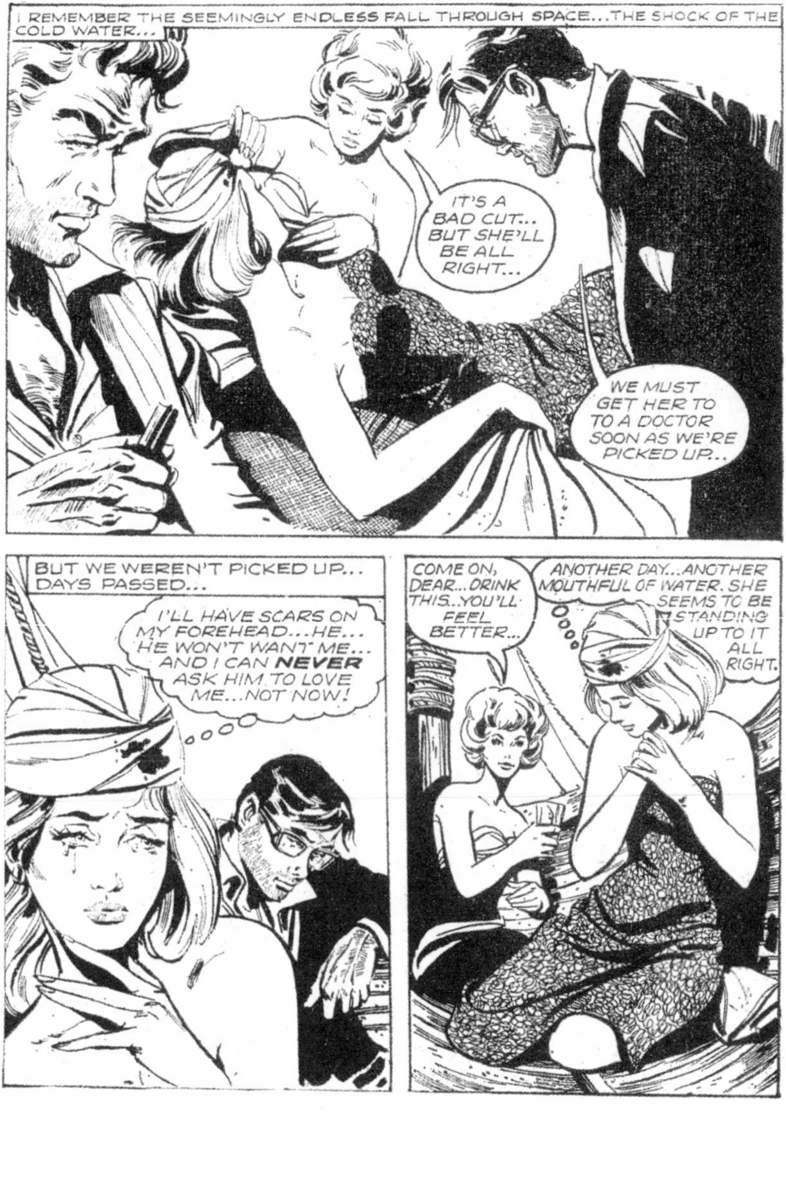
I REMEMBER THE SEEMINGLY ENDLESS FALL THROUGH SPACE...THE SHOCK OF THE COLD WATER...
IT'S A BAD CUT... BUT SHE'LL BE ALL RIGHT...
WE MUST GET HER TO TO A DOCTOR SOON AS WE'RE PICKED UP...
BUT WE WEREN'T PICKED UP... DAYS PASSED...
I'LL HAVE SCARS ON MY FOREHEAD...HE... HE WON'T WANT ME... AND I CAN NEVER ASK HIM TO LOVE ME...NOT NOW!
COME ON, DEAR...DRINK THIS...YOU'LL FEEL BETTER...
ANOTHER DAY...ANOTHER MOUTHFUL OF WATER. SHE SEEMS TO BE STANDING UP TO IT ALL RIGHT.

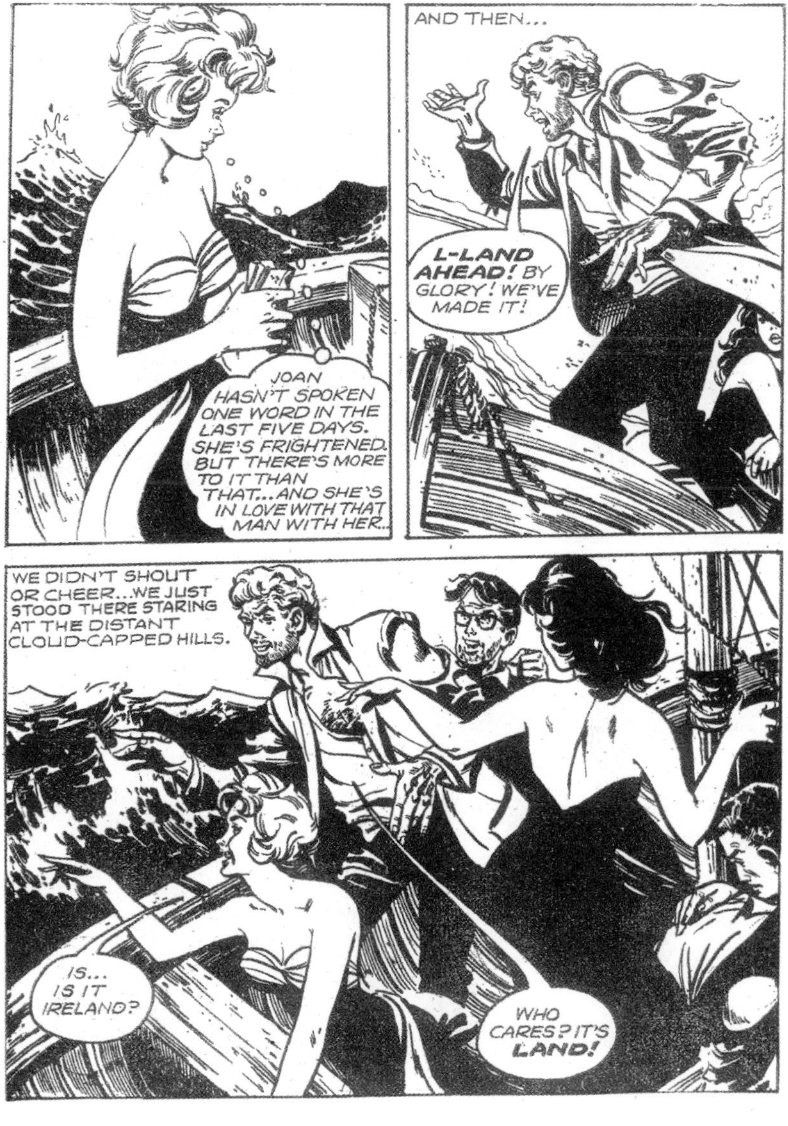
JOAN HASN'T SPOKEN ONE WORD IN THE LAST FIVE DAYS. SHE'S FRIGHTENED. BUT THERE'S MORE TO IT THAN THAT...AND SHE'S IN LOVE WITH THAT MAN WITH HER...
AND THEN...
L-LAND AHEAD! BY GLORY! WE'VE MADE IT!
WE DIDN'T SHOUT OR CHEER...WE JUST STOOD THERE STARING AT THE DISTANT CLOUD-CAPPED HILLS.
IS... IS IT IRELAND?
WHO CARES? IT'S LAND!

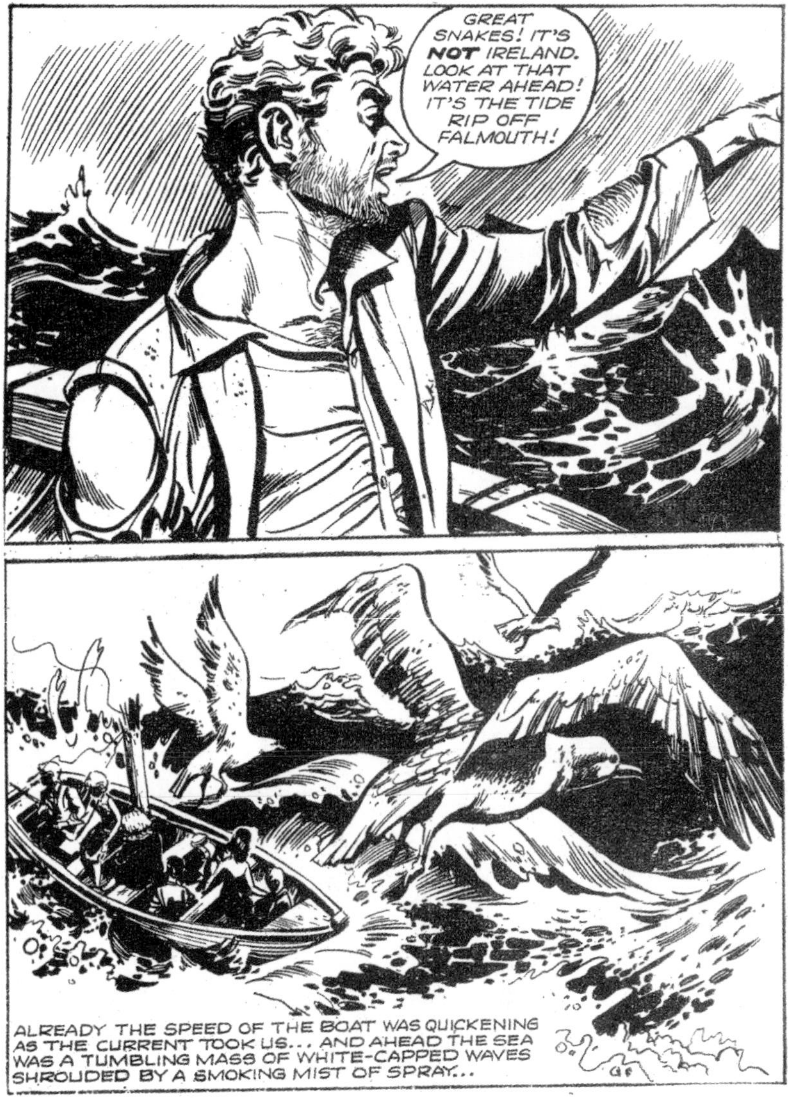
GREAT SNAKES! IT'S **NOT** IRELAND. LOOK AT THAT WATER AHEAD! IT'S THE TIDE RIP OFF FALMOUTH!
ALREADY THE SPEED OF THE BOAT WAS QUICKENING AS THE CURRENT TOOK US... AND AHEAD THE SEA WAS A TUMBLING MASS OF WHITE-CAPPED WAVES SHROUDED BY A SMOKING MIST OF SPRAY...

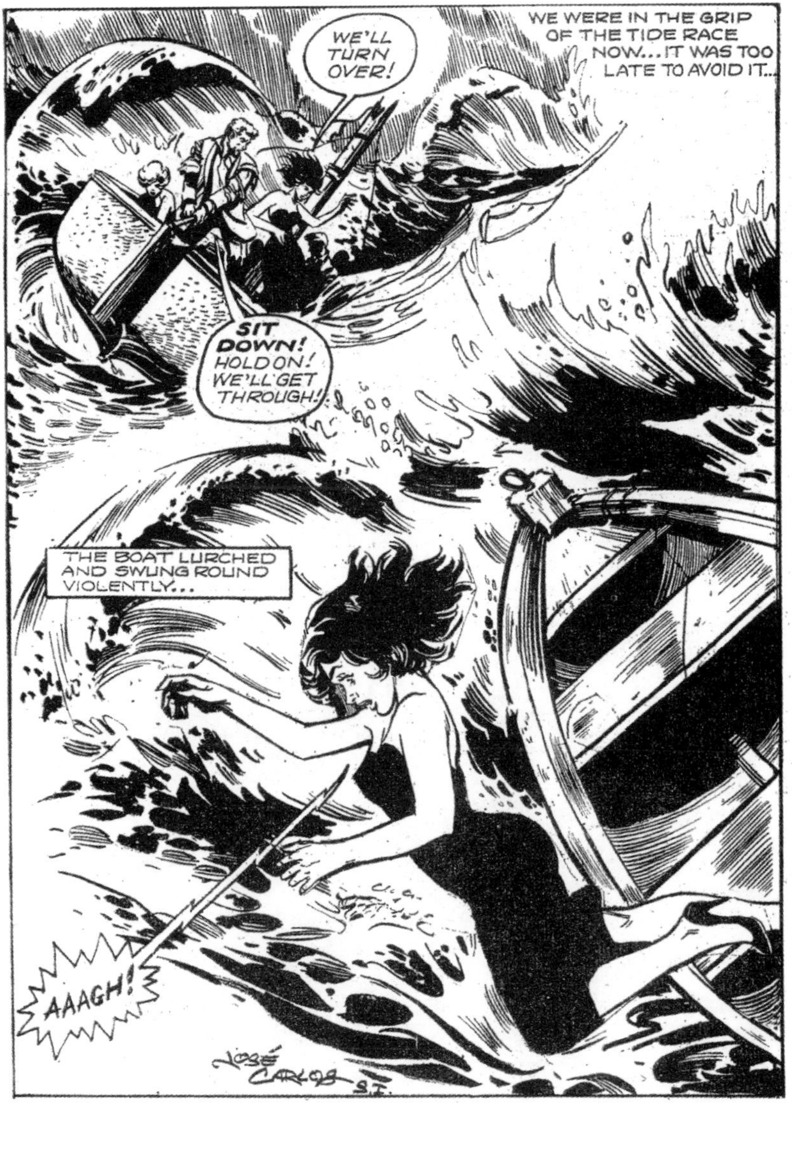
WE WERE IN THE GRIP OF THE TIDE RACE NOW... IT WAS TOO LATE TO AVOID IT...
WE'LL TURN OVER!
SIT DOWN! HOLD ON! WE'LL GET THROUGH!
THE BOAT LURCHED AND SWUNG ROUND VIOLENTLY...
AAAGH!
JOSÉ CARLOS S.I.

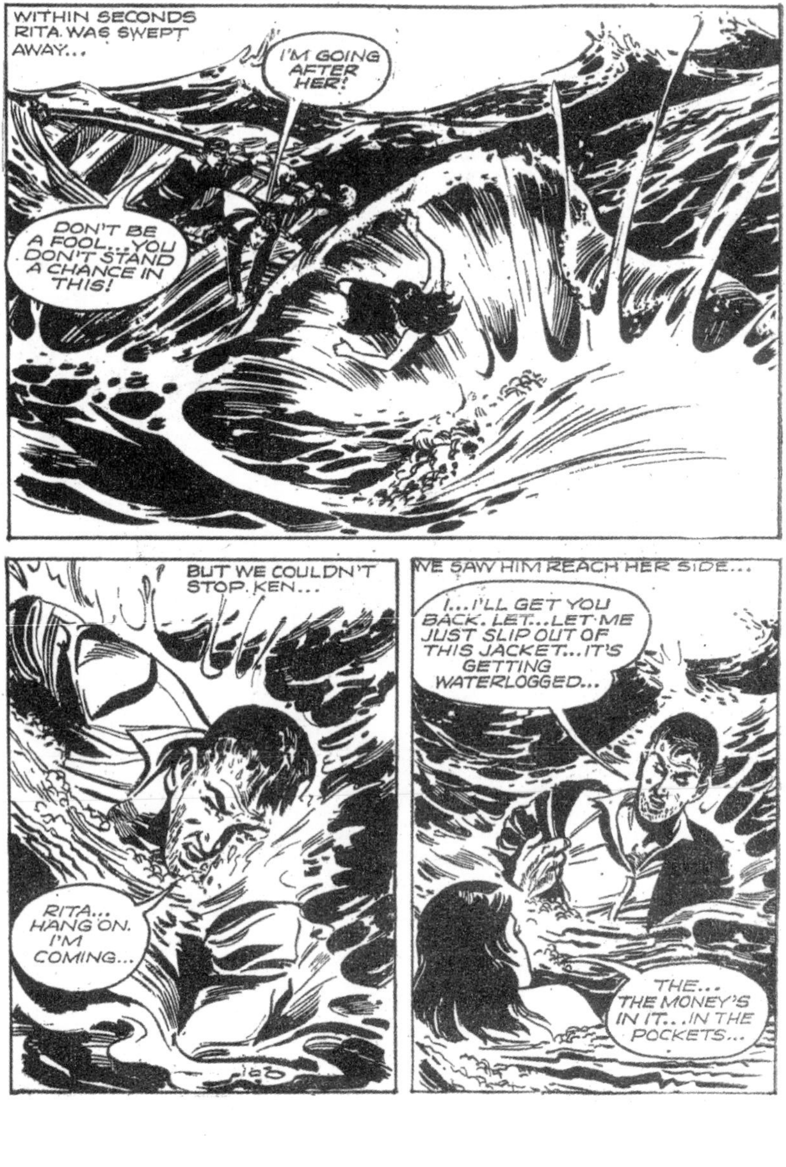
WITHIN SECONDS RITA WAS SWEPT AWAY...
I'M GOING AFTER HER!
DON'T BE A FOOL...YOU DON'T STAND A CHANCE IN THIS!
BUT WE COULDN'T STOP KEN...
RITA... HANG ON. I'M COMING...
WE SAW HIM REACH HER SIDE...
I...I'LL GET YOU BACK. LET...LET ME JUST SLIP OUT OF THIS JACKET...IT'S GETTING WATERLOGGED...
THE... THE MONEY'S IN IT...IN THE POCKETS...

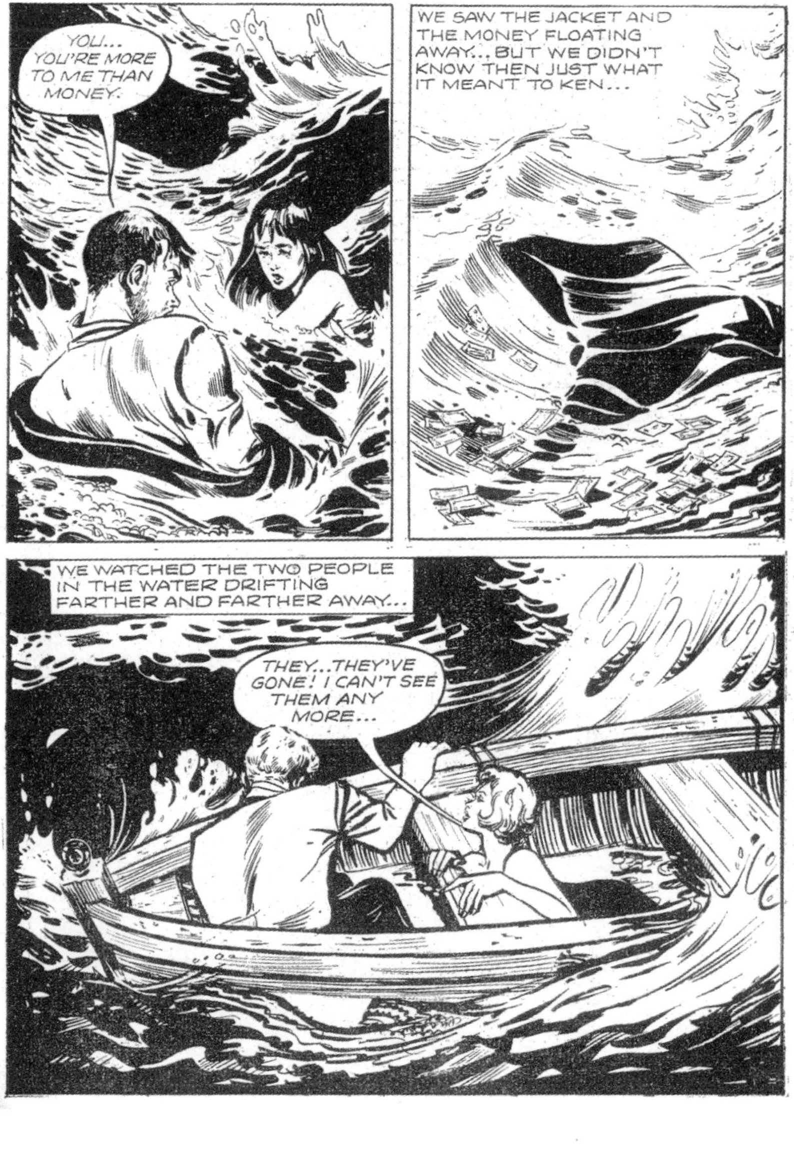

YOU... YOU'RE MORE TO ME THAN MONEY.
WE SAW THE JACKET AND THE MONEY FLOATING AWAY... BUT WE DIDN'T KNOW THEN JUST WHAT IT MEANT TO KEN...
WE WATCHED THE TWO PEOPLE IN THE WATER DRIFTING FARTHER AND FARTHER AWAY...
THEY... THEY'VE GONE! I CAN'T SEE THEM ANY MORE...

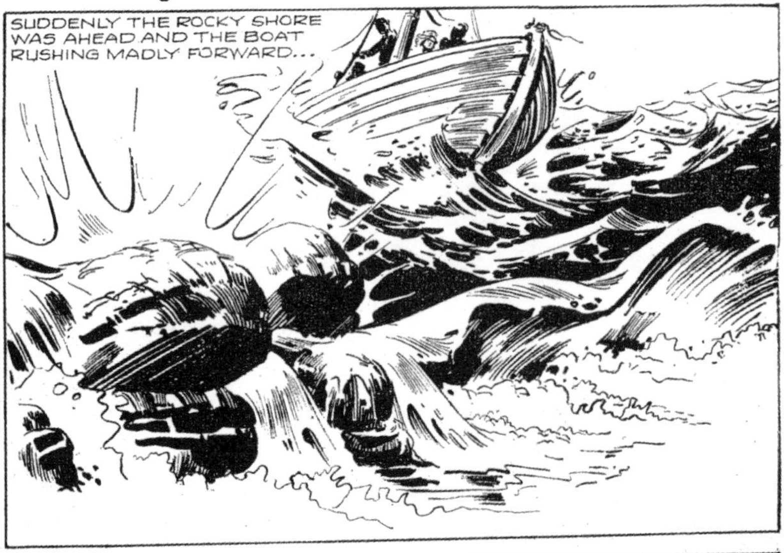
SUDDENLY THE ROCKY SHORE WAS AHEAD AND THE BOAT RUSHING MADLY FORWARD...

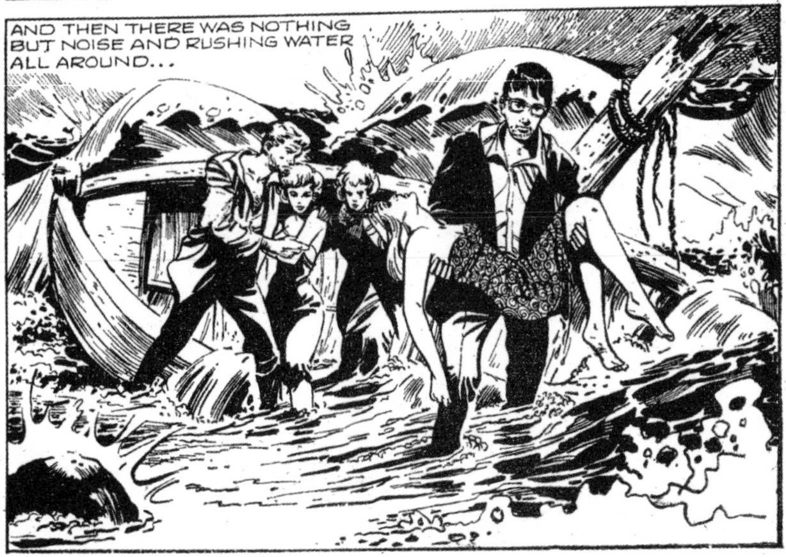
AND THEN THERE WAS NOTHING BUT NOISE AND RUSHING WATER ALL AROUND...

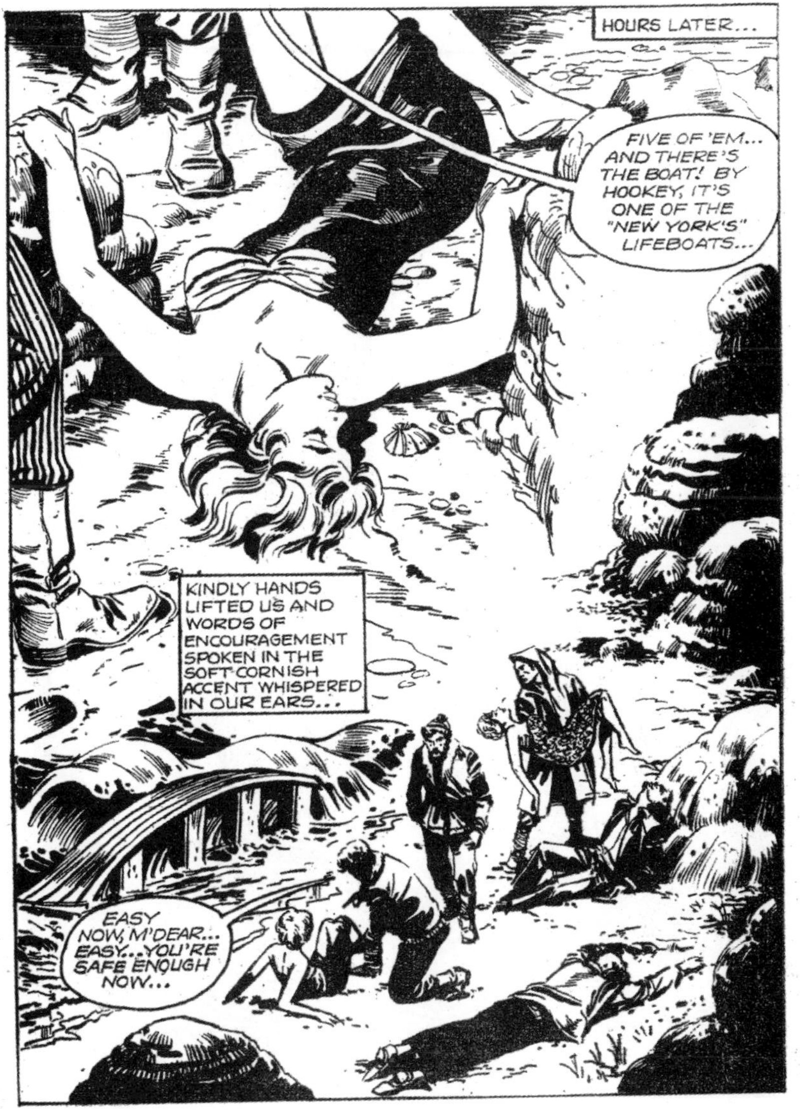
HOURS LATER...
FIVE OF 'EM... AND THERE'S THE BOAT! BY HOOKEY, IT'S ONE OF THE "NEW YORK'S" LIFEBOATS...
KINDLY HANDS LIFTED US AND WORDS OF ENCOURAGEMENT SPOKEN IN THE SOFT CORNISH ACCENT WHISPERED IN OUR EARS...
EASY NOW, M'DEAR... EASY...YOU'RE SAFE ENOUGH NOW...

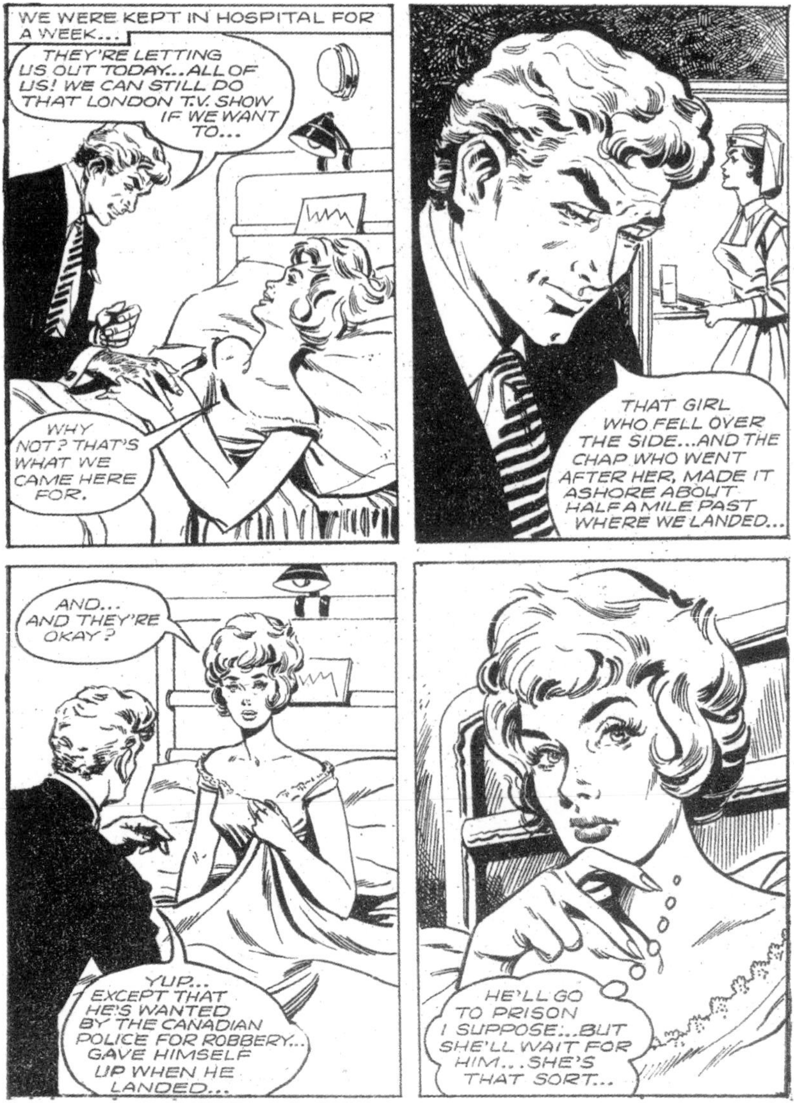
WE WERE KEPT IN HOSPITAL FOR A WEEK...
THEY'RE LETTING US OUT TODAY... ALL OF US! WE CAN STILL DO THAT LONDON T.V. SHOW IF WE WANT TO...
WHY NOT? THAT'S WHAT WE CAME HERE FOR.
THAT GIRL WHO FELL OVER THE SIDE... AND THE CHAP WHO WENT AFTER HER, MADE IT ASHORE ABOUT HALF A MILE PAST WHERE WE LANDED...
AND... AND THEY'RE OKAY?
YUP... EXCEPT THAT HE'S WANTED BY THE CANADIAN POLICE FOR ROBBERY... GAVE HIMSELF UP WHEN HE LANDED...
HE'LL GO TO PRISON I SUPPOSE... BUT SHE'LL WAIT FOR HIM... SHE'S THAT SORT...

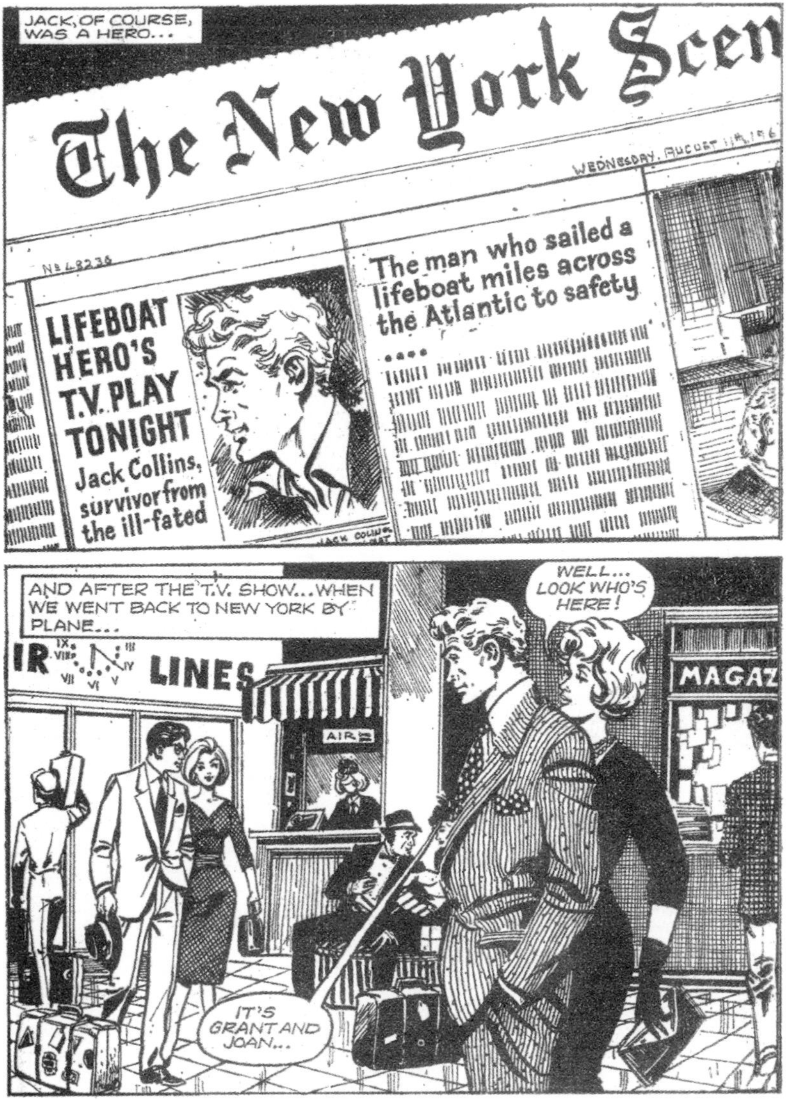
JACK, OF COURSE, WAS A HERO...
The New York Scen
The man who sailed a lifeboat miles across the Atlantic to safety
LIFEBOAT HERO'S T.V. PLAY TONIGHT
Jack Collins, survivor from the ill-fated
AND AFTER THE T.V. SHOW... WHEN WE WENT BACK TO NEW YORK BY PLANE...
IR LINES
AIR
MAGAZ
WELL... LOOK WHO'S HERE!
IT'S GRANT AND JOAN...

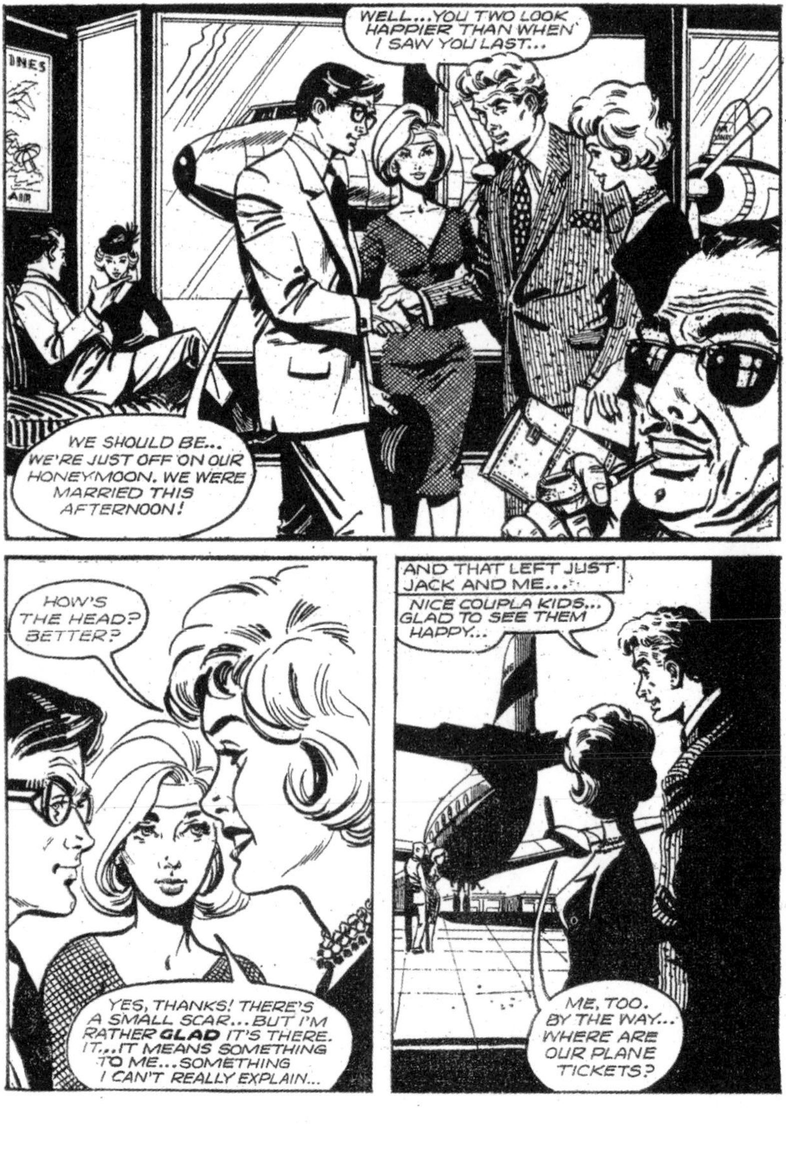
WELL...YOU TWO LOOK HAPPIER THAN WHEN I SAW YOU LAST...
WE SHOULD BE... WE'RE JUST OFF ON OUR HONEYMOON. WE WERE MARRIED THIS AFTERNOON!
HOW'S THE HEAD? BETTER?
YES, THANKS! THERE'S A SMALL SCAR... BUT I'M RATHER **GLAD** IT'S THERE. IT...IT MEANS SOMETHING TO ME...SOMETHING I CAN'T REALLY EXPLAIN...
AND THAT LEFT JUST JACK AND ME...
NICE COUPLA KIDS... GLAD TO SEE THEM HAPPY...
ME, TOO. BY THE WAY... WHERE ARE OUR PLANE TICKETS?

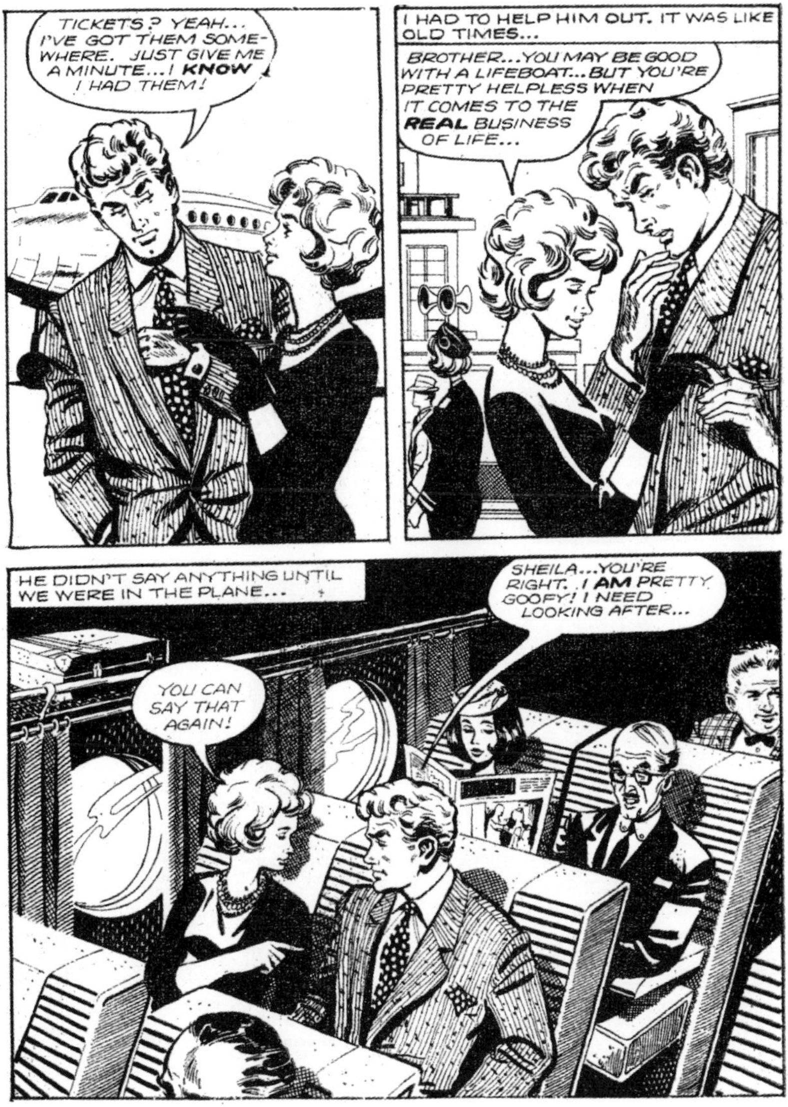
TICKETS? YEAH... I'VE GOT THEM SOMEWHERE. JUST GIVE ME A MINUTE... I KNOW I HAD THEM!
I HAD TO HELP HIM OUT. IT WAS LIKE OLD TIMES...
BROTHER...YOU MAY BE GOOD WITH A LIFEBOAT...BUT YOU'RE PRETTY HELPLESS WHEN IT COMES TO THE REAL BUSINESS OF LIFE...
HE DIDN'T SAY ANYTHING UNTIL WE WERE IN THE PLANE...
SHEILA...YOU'RE RIGHT. I AM PRETTY GOOFY! I NEED LOOKING AFTER...
YOU CAN SAY THAT AGAIN!

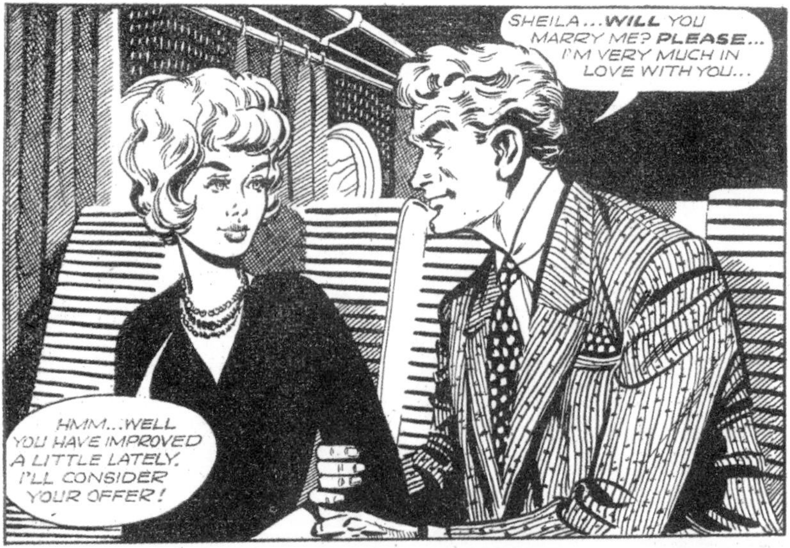
SHEILA ... WILL YOU MARRY ME? PLEASE... I'M VERY MUCH IN LOVE WITH YOU...
HMM...WELL YOU HAVE IMPROVED A LITTLE LATELY. I'LL CONSIDER YOUR OFFER!

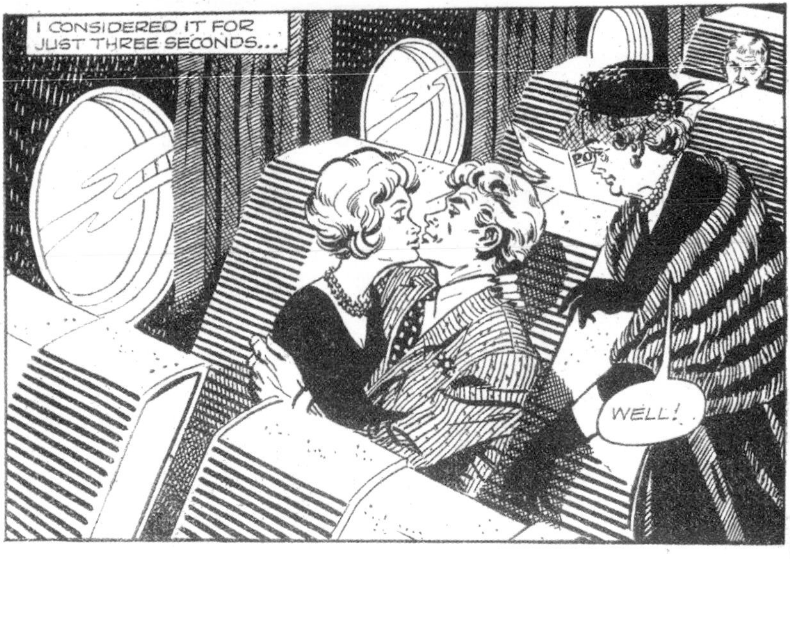
I CONSIDERED IT FOR JUST THREE SECONDS...
WELL!

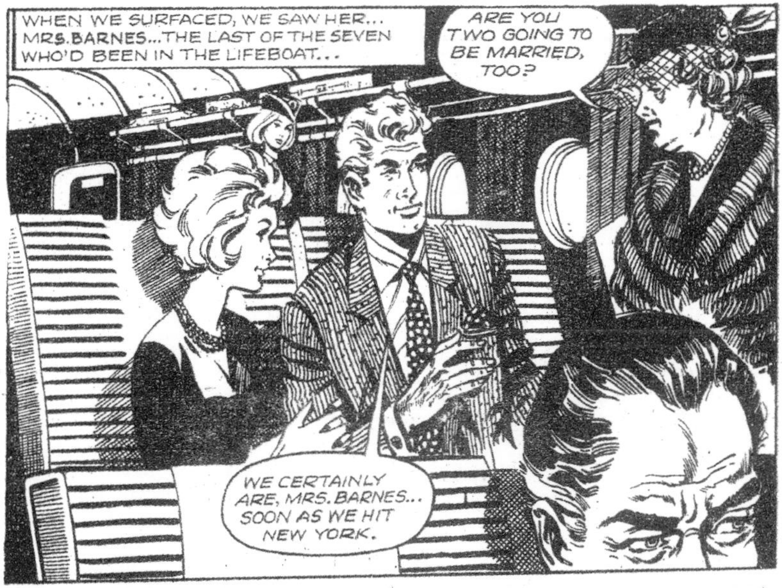
WHEN WE SURFACED, WE SAW HER... MRS. BARNES...THE LAST OF THE SEVEN WHO'D BEEN IN THE LIFEBOAT...
ARE YOU TWO GOING TO BE MARRIED, TOO?
WE CERTAINLY ARE, MRS. BARNES... SOON AS WE HIT NEW YORK.

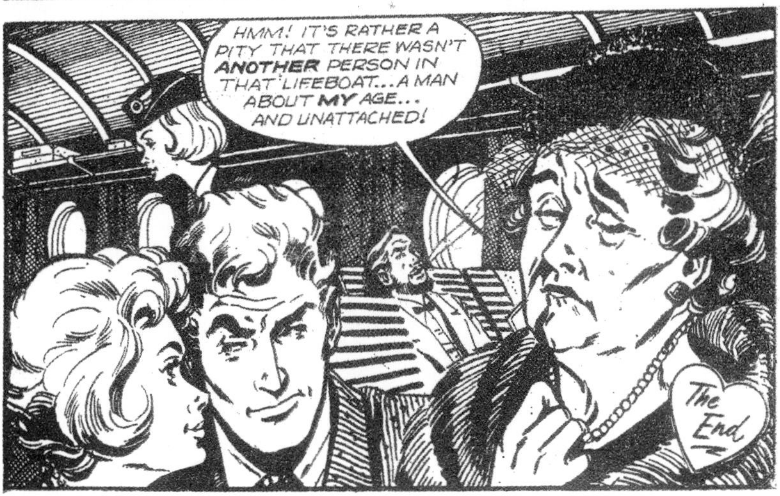
HMM! IT'S RATHER A PITY THAT THERE WASN'T **ANOTHER** PERSON IN THAT LIFEBOAT...A MAN ABOUT **MY** AGE... AND UNATTACHED!
The End

The End

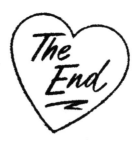

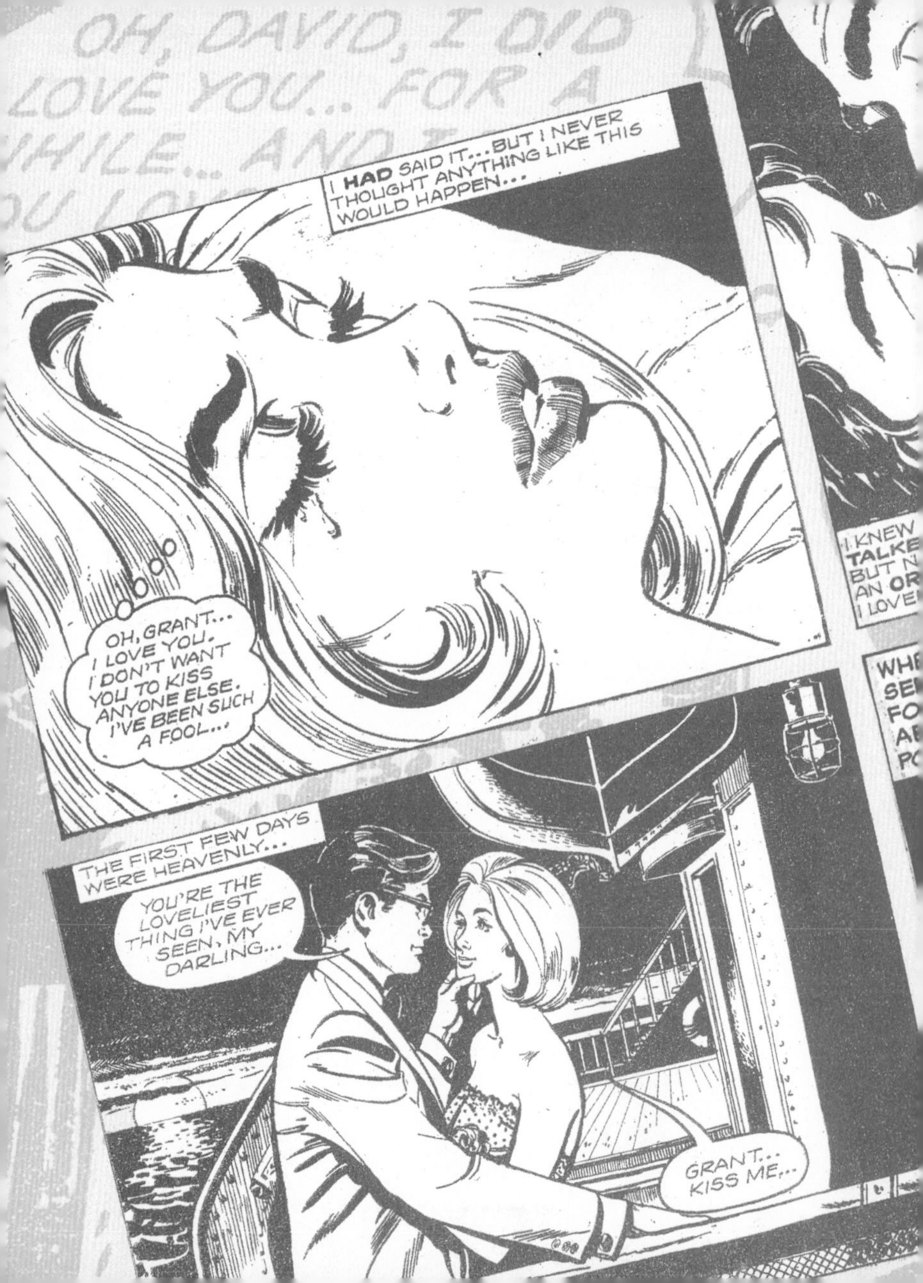
OH, DAVID, I DID
LOVE YOU... FOR A
I **HAD** SAID IT... BUT I NEVER THOUGHT ANYTHING LIKE THIS WOULD HAPPEN...
OH, GRANT... I LOVE YOU. I DON'T WANT YOU TO KISS ANYONE ELSE. I'VE BEEN SUCH A FOOL...
THE FIRST FEW DAYS WERE HEAVENLY...
YOU'RE THE LOVELIEST THING I'VE EVER SEEN, MY DARLING...
GRANT... KISS ME...

feet. The colt jerked its head up and down; the mare's ears were back and her eyes rolled. She pricked her ears once at Bruce and laid them back again.

As Bruce came up slowly the colt struggled, raised its head with white eyeballs showing, spraddled its white-footed legs, and tried to stand. It was sitting like a dog on the ground when Elsa came up, getting her breath, her hair half down. Bruce reached out and succeeded in touching the blazed face. "Gee!" he said. "Isn't he a pretty colt, Ma?"

He patted Daisy, slapped her wet neck, scratched under her mane and felt her tremble. She must have got chased hard. But there was the colt, sitting comically on the ground, and his happiness that nothing had gone really wrong bubbled out of him. "Lookit his feet," he said. "He's got four white feet, Ma. Let's call him Socks. Can I? Isn't he a nice colt, though?" He reached down to pull the colt's forelock, and the colt bobbed his head away.

Then Bruce saw his mother's face. It was quiet, too quiet. She hadn't said a word to all his jabber. Instead she was kneeling about ten feet in front of the squatting colt and staring at it. Bruce's eyes followed hers. There was something funny about the way . . .

"Ma!" he said. "What's the matter with its feet?"

He left Daisy's head and came around. The colt's pasterns looked bent—*were* bent, so that when its weight came on the front hoofs the whole pastern touched the ground. His shifting frightened the colt, and with a flopping effort it floundered to its feet and pressed against its mother. And it walked, Bruce saw, flat on its fetlocks, its hoofs sticking out in front like a comedian's too-large shoes.

Elsa pressed her lips tight, shook her head, stood up, moving so gently that she got her hand on the colt's poll. He bobbed against the pleasant scratching. You poor little broken-legged thing, she said. You poor little friendly ruined thing! Still quietly, she turned on the circle of dogs, sitting with hanging tongues out of range, even Spot staying away as if he knew he had outlawed himself. God damn you, she said, God damn your wild hearts, chasing a poor mother and a newborn colt.

To Bruce, standing with trembling lip, she said just as quietly, "Run and find Jim Enich. Tell him to bring a wagon or a democrat. And don't cry. It isn't your fault."

Bruce bit his lip and drew his face down tight, trying to keep his eyes from spilling. "It is too my fault!" he said, and turned and ran.

305

Jim Enich was a bandy-legged little man who had been a horse wrangler for Purcell for many years. He was slow, gentle, mild; there were deep creases down each side of his mouth, with a brown mole hiding in one of them. He had Bruce wait while he hitched up, and they drove down together past the picnic ground and the ballfield and the swings. Bruce's mother had the colt on the ground again, and the mare was nosing her impatiently.

Enich climbed out, walked around the mare. He squatted by the colt's head and scratched between its ears. His fingers went down to press and probe and bend the broken arch of the pasterns. He whistled tunelessly between his teeth while Bruce stood around with his feet on fire, aching to do something, ask something, but not daring to interrupt Enich's deliberate professional concentration.

Without saying anything, Enich examined the mare, still whistling.

"What do you think?" Elsa said.

"Mare's all right."

"What about the colt?"

"Lessee him try to stand up."

With one hand in the colt's topknot, he helped it to its feet. It spraddled wide, fetlocks sunk to the ground. The dropping of the weight there threw its fine, long-legged body out of proportion. Enich plucked a blade of short new grass and chewed it and shook his head.

"Ruined?" Elsa said.

" 'Fraid so."

She grimaced, and her hand tightened on Bruce's. He hadn't realized till then that he had been holding her hand. "Well, let's get them back to the barn, at least," she said.

Enich tied the colt's feet, heaved and pulled and pushed it into the wagon. It lay there with terrified white eyes rolling, and the mare toe-danced behind the endgate, butting Enich around with her nose.

"All right, gal," the wrangler said. "You can put your face right in, if you're that worried."

When they started, Daisy was left momentarily standing. She chuckled with instant apprehension, trotted quickly after the wagon, stuck her neck over the endgate and touched the colt, the breath vibrating in long wheezy solicitous nickerings in her throat.

Bruce sat between his mother and Enich, his head twisted back to watch. Every time they hit a bump and the colt's raised head thumped on the boards, he was stricken with pity and contrition.

306

"Gee whiz," he said. "Poor old Socks." He tried to reach back and touch the chestnut haunch. His mother put her arm around him to keep him from leaning too far. Absorbed in his pity for the colt, he didn't watch where they were going or notice anything ahead of them until he heard his mother say in surprise and relief, "Why, there's Bo!"

Terror tightened him rigid. He had forgotten and left Daisy out all night. It was his fault that the colt was ruined. From the narrow space between Enich and his mother he watched like a gopher from its burrow. He saw the Ford pulled up beside the barn and his father's big body leaning into it pulling out blankets and straw. There was mud from top to bottom of the car, mud all over his father's pants. The boy slid deeper into his crevice.

Then his father was at the wheel, Jim Enich was climbing down, Elsa with puckered lines in her forehead was saying that Daisy had had her colt while she was staked out, and the dogs had smelled her out and chased her and broken down the colt's feet. Pa said little. He went around and helped Enich lift the colt out onto the ground, stooped to feel its fetlocks with square muddy hands, looked once at Bruce.

"Would've been a nice colt," he said. "Damn a pack of mangy mongrels anyway." He brushed at the mud on his pants and said to Elsa, "How come Daisy was staked out?"

"I told Bruce to," she said. "The barn's so cramped for her, I thought it would do her good to stretch her legs. Then the ice went out, and the bridge, and we all forgot what we were doing . . ."

Bruce heard her trying to smooth it out and take the blame off him, but in his own mind it was perfectly clear, as it had been from the beginning. He was to blame.

"I didn't mean to leave her out, Pa," he said squeakily.

His father's somber eyes rested on him briefly, turned to the colt and then to Enich. "Total loss?" he said.

Enich shrugged.

Bruce thrust himself into it again, not wanting to, but unable to stay out. "Pa, it won't have to be shot, will it? Give it to me, I'll take care of it. I'll keep it lying down and heal its feet up."

"Yeah," his father said, and laughed, but his mother said quickly. "Jim, isn't there some kind of brace you could put on it, to hold its legs straight? I remember once at home my dad had a horse that broke a leg below the knee, and he saved it that way."

"Might try a hobble-brace," Enich agreed. He plucked a weed and stripped off the branches. "I wouldn't expect much from it, though."

307

"But it would be worth trying," she said. "Children's bones knit so quick, I should think a colt's would too."

"Would, if you could make a colt savvy he had to lay down."

"Bo," she said, "can't we try it? It seems such a shame, a lovely colt like that." She nodded at him slightly, and then both of them were looking at Bruce. He felt the tears coming up, and turned away.

"How much this hobble-brace cost?" his father said.

"Two-three dollars. Blacksmith can make it."

"All right," Bo said. "Let's go get MacDonald." He laid his hand on Bruce's shoulder. "It's your responsibility," he said. "You left Daisy out, and now you've got to take complete care of the colt."

"I will," Bruce said. "I'll take care of it every day."

Big with contrition and shame and gratitude and the sense of sudden, immense responsibility, he watched his father and Enich start for the house to get a tapemeasure. When they were almost to the kitchen door he said loudly, "Thanks, Pa! Thanks ever so much!"

His father half turned, laughed, said something to Enich. Stooping to pet the trussed colt, Bruce caught his mother's eye, started to laugh like his father and felt it turn into a sob. As he swung away he saw Spot, one of the pack that had done all this to Daisy and the colt, looking around the corner of the barn. Spot took three or four steps forward and stopped, wagging his tail inquiringly.

Very slowly (never move fast or talk loud around animals) Bruce stooped and found a stone as big as a pigeon egg. He straightened casually, brought his arm up, and threw with all his might. The stone caught Spot in the ribs. He yiped, tucked his tail, and ran. Bruce chased him, throwing clods and stones and gravel, yelling, "Get out of here! Go on, get out of here! Beat it! Go on!"

6

Chet sat in the sun on the back step, cleaning his .22. In the yard Bruce was plucking handfuls of fresh grass from the fence corners to feed into the nibbling lips of the hobble-legged colt. It was Saturday in mid-May. Flies hummed in the yard, and a swallow, skimming like an arrow, hit the tiny hole in the barn eaves and disappeared at full speed.

"Hey Brucie," Chet said. "Get your gun and let's go shoot gophers."

"I'm going to take care of Socks," Bruce said.

"Aw, come on. He can take care of himself."

"He gets excited," Bruce said. "He tries to run if I don't watch him."

Chet grunted, threw away the oiled rag, and replaced the bolt in the gun. Bruce was nutty. He'd rather stick around and watch his old colt than go out and do anything. Chet spit off the porch and went in to hang the ramrod on its nail. His mother was looking at the calendar.

"He doesn't stop to think how a person might worry," she said.

"Uh?"

"Your dad should have been home day before yesterday."

"Where's he gone? After more whiskey?"

She looked at him long and steadily, and her mouth moved as if she had something bad-tasting in it. "Chet," she said, "you don't ever talk about what Pa's doing, do you?"

"Naw. I know better'n that."

"I hope you do. Don't say anything to anybody." She laughed and shook her head. "I guess that's one trouble. A person can't talk to anybody. Where were you going?"

"Oh, out."

"Run up to the postoffice and get the mail before you go."

"Gimme two bits?"

"What for?"

"I need some cartridges. These old b-b's are no good for anything. If I saw a rabbit I'd need longs."

"All right." Chet followed her into the dining room.

"Can I have a dime for some chocolate bars too?"

"Why a dime? Won't nickels buy anything any more?"

"Well, a nickel then."

She gave him a quarter and a nickel, and as he went out he was thinking that it was kind of good to have Pa gone. He crabbed when you asked for money. Ma was better about things like that.

He was carrying the gun as he went uptown, and by the time he reached the postoffice he had picked up Bill Stenhouse and Pete Armstrong. Pete had his Daisy pump gun, and Bill had no gun at all. Chet felt both superior and magnanimous, letting them tag along.

There was no mail except a letter from Aunt Kristin, from Minnesota. In McGregor's hardware Chet bought a box of longs, and at Henderson's drug, while he took a long time deciding what kind of chocolate bar he wanted, Pete swiped a package of spearmint gum and Bill got a vial of perfume.

They clotted briefly outside, around the corner, to count their wealth and decide where they were going. "I got to take this letter home," Chet said. "Come on, I'll make Bruce lend us his old .22. He's going to stay home anyway."

He left Bill and Pete leaning on the fence looking critically at the crippled colt while he took the letter inside. "Oh, good," his mother said automatically, seeing the return address. "Nothing from Pa?"

"That was all," Chet said. "Ma, can Pete and Bill and me have a little lunch to take along hunting?"

"I suppose so. You want me to fix it?"

"I'll fix it." Chet sliced off some thick slabs of bread, buttered them, found three doughnuts gummed with powdered sugar, and dropped them all in a bag. From the cellarway he got Bruce's .22.

"Brucie," he said out the door. "Can we borrow your gun?"

"No," Bruce said. He had been quarreling with Bill and Pete, who said the colt would always be an old wreck that couldn't walk. Bruce was almost crying. "No, sir!" he said. "You leave my gun alone."

"Give you a stick of gum for the loan of it," Pete said.

"No."

"Two sticks."

"No."

"Aw, come on, Brucie," Chet said. "You aren't going to be using it."

"I'm not going to lend it, anyway."

Chet came clear out on the step. "What you want to be so stingy for? We won't hurt your old blunderbuss."

"If it's an old blunderbuss," Bruce said, "what do you want to borrow it for?"

"I'll punch your nose in a minute," Chet said. He started out, but his mother's voice stopped him.

"Let him alone," she said. "If he doesn't want to lend it, that's his right."

The three started away. "I know where you little squirts got your shanty," Chet said. "Wait and see what happens to that."

"You leave it alone!" Bruce yelled after them. "If you touch that shanty I'll drop rocks through your old boat."

"You do and you'll get your nose busted," Chet said. He walked with long, Leatherstocking strides, and the others fell into single file behind him, walking in his footprints. Bill, having no gun to occupy his hands, took out his snitched vial of perfume and began dosing his shirtfront.

A half hour later, in the exciting, growth-heavy spring wind, the three sat on pinnacles of the sandhills halfway up the bench and looked down over the river valley, the looping brown river, the willows fresh green, the valley grass a deeper, brighter green, the houses sharp-edged in the strong light. On both sides of the washed-out railroad bridge Chet saw the black dots of men moving; and the railroad itself, the double line of rails and the criss-cross of ties and the spiderweb lines of fences along the right-of-way, was drawn straight east and west along the valley.

Hooking his legs around the sandpapery stone of his pinnacle, he twisted to look back of him at the slope. The aspen came down in three bright tongues, one behind the summer cottage of Howard Palmer, one directly behind the sand hills, and one behind the shanty of Tex Davis. Tex was a cowpuncher who came and went, appearing sometimes in the spring and staying a few weeks, then disappearing again, nobody knew where. Some said he followed the rodeos and stampedes, others said he was a road agent. Chet had peeked into the one window of the shack plenty of times, but his peeks had told him nothing except that Tex was a dirty old buzzard and never swept his floor.

He turned again, looking out across the railroad to Heathcliff's place in the bottom, across Heathcliff's to Purcell's dam. The air blew across him warm and soft, and all around the bottom of the pinnacles the ground was misty purple with crocuses. He could smell sweet pea perfume floating across from the peak where Bill perched.

"There goes somebody on a bike," Bill said.

Chet looked and saw the smooth, floating motion of the wheel, the blaze of a white shirt as it caught the sun. "It must be Frankie Buck," he said. "Old Man Lipscomb must have given him Saturday off."

He took a firm grip with his legs, shot off his .22 into the air, yelled, "Hey, Frankie!" Pete and Bill yelled too, and the figure below, almost a mile away, stopped moving. The white-shirted arm waved, and they yelled to him to come up. Frankie rolled along to the gate where Angus MacLeod's road came across the tracks, and came walking his wheel through. He left both gates wide open as he started up. Chet and Bill and Pete slid down off the pinnacles and went over to Tex's shack to meet him.

He was puffing when he came up the hill, and his stockings had slid down, leaving his bowlegs bare. Frankie was adopted by Mr. Lipscomb, who ran the *Ledger*, and he had to work a lot, setting type and delivering. "Hi," he said. "What you kids doin'?"

"Horsing around," Chet said. "How come you don't have to work?"

"I have to this aft," Frankie said. "Have you shot anything?"

"Chet couldn't hit anything if we saw it," Pete said.

"Oh, couldn't I?" Chet said. He looked around for something to shoot at, found an old demijohn behind the shack, and set it up on a fence post. From fifty feet away he aimed and fired. There was a *spann-n-n-g!* but the demijohn didn't break. Pete haw-hawed.

"Well, I only had a b-b in," Chet said. "I hit it, didn't I?"

"I can do as good as that with my air gun," Pete said. He pumped his gun and shot, and again there was a noise, a higher, lighter noise, *spinn-n-n-g!* The demijohn was still intact.

"You guys are terrible," Frankie said. "Leave me have a shot, Chet."

He shot and missed. Then Bill shot and missed. Chet slipped a long into the .22 and waved them back. "Lemme show you how it's done," he said. He shot high and broke the neck off the jug. Bill and Frankie started pegging rocks at it, and in a minute it was in a dozen pieces. Inside was the dried body of a mouse.

"Lookit that," Frankie said, picking it up by the tail. "I bet he died happy."

He threw the mouse at Pete, who fell on him. They wrestled till they were both winded and lay sprawling on the warm ground.

Then they were all lying on the ground looking up into the empty, pale, sunny sky. Pete lifted his head as if that was all the strength he had left. "Gosh I'm hungry!" he said. So they ate the sandwiches and split the doughnuts and the chocolate bar and all had a drink at the spring behind the shack. On the way back, Frankie chinned himself up to the high little window and peeked in. He banged his hand against the sash, and the sash gave a little.

"Hey!" he said. "I bet we could get in here."

He pried and hammered at the sash, but it wouldn't give far enough to give him any leverage. "Stand back a minute," Chet said. "I bet I move her." He jammed the gun butt against the side, but the butt slipped, and there was a shattering tinkle of glass.

Chet pulled back and looked at the others. Bill looked scared. Frankie and Pete looked as if they didn't know how to look. "Now you've did it!" Bill said.

"Oh hell!" Chet said. He reached up the barrel and knocked another of the four lights out. In an instant the other kids were clattering and banging and pounding, and the window was a total loss.

Excitement was in them now. "Gimme a boost," Frankie said.

He jumped for the sill, but Chet pulled him down. "I busted the winda first. I get to go in first."

There was an argument, but Pete gave him a hand and he popped his head into the musty twilight of the shanty. He picked the glass out of the road, got his leg over, and slid inside to the littered floor. He was hunting plunder before Pete's face was in the window, and he had found the horse pistol before Pete was halfway inside.

With the treasure in his hand he snapped the door lock and let in a flood of sun. The pistol was an enormous single-action Colt .44 with a great arching wooden butt. It was so heavy that he needed two hands to aim it. The other kids crowded around and wanted to handle it, but he kept them off. It was his prize. And it was even loaded, five shells in it and the hammer carefully down on the empty chamber. Chet broke it and looked through the barrel. Clean.

Pete and Frankie were turning the shanty upside down looking for more, but Bill was a little scared. He said, "You ain't gonna keep it, are you, Chet?"

The word touched Chet's mind briefly: Stealing. But the gun was in his hands, ponderous, heavy, a real honest-to-goodness man-sized six-shooter. "You bet your life!" he said.

The other two, having found nothing but a rusty butcher knife and some tin dishes, were looking under the bunk. Pete lifted the mattress, and field mice dropped and scattered.

"Whee!" Frankie yelled. He leaped sideways out of a half dozen twittering, frantic mice that skittered and scurried and hid and popped out again and jumped up and down. Frankie grabbed an old alarm clock almost as he jumped, and as he alighted he turned and threw it. The thing smashed like a bomb, scattering glass and hands and wheels and springs halfway across the room.

"Oh Lordy!" Bill moaned. He stood back, but the other three kept on. Pete threw the butcher knife and it stuck quivering in the wall. Frankie skimmed a plate and cup after the clock. The mice were all out of sight by now.

"I know what," Chet said. "Here, Frankie, you take my .22. I'll use the horse pistol and Pete's got his air gun. Bill can yank the mattress up and jump back and we can all blaze at once."

Bill said, "What if old Angus MacLeod came around here and caught you? He looks after this place for Tex."

"Oh, Angus!" Chet said. "He's so tight every time he farts he whistles."

They all laughed. He looked around and saw them laughing,

and with a Dead-Eye Dick draw he yanked up the horse pistol and aimed it at the bed. "Come on, Bill," he said.

"You'd shoot me," Bill said. "I don't want to bust up Tex's shack anyway."

"You helped bust the winda," Chet said. "What are you such a sissy for?"

"I ain't a sissy."

"You sure act like one," Pete said.

"It ain't fair," Bill said. "You'd all get to shoot and I wouldn't."

"You can have second shot with my .22," Chet said. "Frankie'll shoot, and then you can."

Bill hesitated. "Well, all right," he said. "But don't any of you shoot till I get out of the way."

He walked over to the bunk, eyeing them. "Wait till I get clear out of the way, now." He stooped, still watching them, yanked the mattress over the edge, and jumped clear. Two mice dropped out of a wide hole and darted for the corner. Another one dashed from under the bed. The air rifle went off, then the .22. The mice switched back toward the bed. Chet held the pistol with both hands and pulled the trigger.

There was a tremendous roar, the gun kicked clear up over his head and almost out of his hands. The four stared. The mice had vanished, but there was a great splintered gash in the floor.

"Holy cow!" Chet said.

For a moment the damage that that one slug had done to the boards shocked them silent. How would you like to get shot with a thing like that? It would make a hole through you you could put your hand into. Bill was staring with his eyes wide and scared. "Jiminy!" he said. He looked at Chet. "I'm gonna get out of here!" he said, and bolted.

Frankie reached out a toe and scuffed at the splinters the .44 bullet had ripped from the floor. They looked at each other, almost holding their breath. Then the impulse struck them almost simultaneously. They yelled. They fired their guns into the sodden mattress. They tipped over the table and spilled magazines and candle-ends onto the floor.

"Let's burn the damn place down," Chet said. He shot the .44 into the bed again, and a mouse ran out. They cornered and killed it, ripped the mattress into the middle of the room, kicked at the mice that scattered frantically. Frankie wrenched till he got a leg off the table, and with that for a club he beat down the shelves. From the doorway the scared face of Bill watched them.

"Burn 'er down!" Chet said. "Break 'er all to pieces!" He smashed a chair against the wall and splintered one leg, threw the whole thing on the pile. Pete was bending down trying to light the mattress, soggy with winter damp. "I need some paper," he said.

The air was immediately full of crumpled sheets of paper. Pete twisted a handful, lighted the feathered end, and stuck it under the pile of broken furniture and rubbish. The flame caught, grew. Chet looked at Frankie and wet his lips. He shifted the .44 to his other hand and moved over by the door.

"You guys are gonna catch it," Bill said from outside.

"Aw bull," Chet said. He wet his lips again and watched Frankie doing a wardance around the fire. The shack was beginning to get smoky, and the smoke was exciting. Chet leaped after Frankie, waving the gun. He struck a pose by the window and stood crouching, the gun in his belt, his hand like a claw. "I'm Buck Duane," he said. "I'm the old Lone Star Ranger. Any-a you outlaws lookin' for me?"

He looked around the shack slowly, contemptuously, eyes narrowed and mouth a slit. The others were all watching. "I guess I'll just shoot your lights out anyway," Chet said, "seeing you're all too yellow to come on." He snatched for the gun in a lightning draw, but the front sight caught in a belt loop and he had to tug it loose. He fired twice into the ceiling, and Pete, by the door, pretended he was shot, clutching at his breast and staggering loosely around the floor. Frankie stuck out his foot and Pete almost fell in the fire. He arose full of wrath.

"Watch out who you go tripping."

"Oh bushwah," Frankie said.

Pete shouldered him sideways. "Bushwah nothing. You watch out who you go tripping around into fires."

"Who'll make me?"

"I'll make you."

"You and whose army?" Frankie said.

"I don't need any army."

Their hands were up, they were sparring lightly, shuffling around in the corner where the table had been. Chet coughed in the smoke. "Come on outside and settle it," he said. "We're gonna get our pants burned off in here."

The quarrelers started out just as Bill, his eyes bugging out and his jaw so loose that he could hardly speak, stuck his head inside and shouted something. "What?" Chet said. He pushed past Bill, Frankie and Pete on his heels, shouldering each other angrily in the doorway. Bill yelled again and pointed. A wagon was coming up the hill, hardly more than two blocks away, and in the wagon was Angus MacLeod and his whole family. Even as they stared

Angus was tossing the reins to his wife and jumping to the ground.

Bill and Frankie broke together around the smoking shack, Chet and Pete a step behind, hitting for the aspen coulee that came down close. After ten steps Frankie stopped, digging, and legged it back, to come after the other three in a moment pushing his bicycle on the dead run.

By the time Frankie reached the edge of the protecting brush Angus, tall, red-headed, and surprisingly fast, was around the house. He didn't even stop to look inside or put out the fire. Fists doubled, red hair blowing, he covered ground like a galloping horse, so that there never was a chance of getting the bike away. A block inside the brush Frankie wheeled it into a clump of bushes and came pounding after Chet, burdened down with his two guns. Bill and Pete were out of sight, maybe still running, maybe hiding.

The grade got steeper. Chet's mouth was dry, his eyes bulging, his chest on fire for air. Once, when the trees thinned, they heard Angus yell, and looked back to see him coming with that terrible unsuspected speed. They ducked up a side trail, raced across a stretch of level ground, slid off to the left through straggling brush, and huddled up under the bank of the watercourse, completely spent, trying to swallow the heaving of their breath. They waited, hoping that they had fooled Angus, and in a minute they heard him go thundering by. Even then they stuck where they were. Chet started to whisper to Frankie, but a sound above made him huddle close up against the bank, so close that little clods of dirt broke loose and rolled down past his cheek.

Angus was coming back. They heard his steps, heavy, not running now, and his hoarse breath. The steps went straight on down the path, and after three minutes Chet peeked through the roots on the lip of the bank and saw the farmer just disappearing into the trees. Keeping out of sight under the bank, they went back up the coulee, crossed through it onto the east side near the top, and came down through the other coulee to the sandhills. At the edge of the hills they found Bill and Pete, scared to go on any further till Angus left. They had run clear up onto the bench and then come down under the cover of the trees.

"Well, by Jeez," Chet said, "he never caught any of us."

In the low sumac between the aspen and the sandstone pillars they lay sprawling on their backs. Chet began to feel pretty good. They had got away slick as a whistle, and he still had the six-shooter, too. "Never laid a hand on a one of us," he said.

"No," Bill said, "but he's got Frankie's wheel."

Frankie sat up, was pulled down instantly. He opened his mouth and squawked. "What?"

"I seen him," Bill said. "I seen him come out of the brush pushing the bike. It's stood against the shanty now."

They all stared at Frankie. His lip trembled, and a tear popped into each eye. "What'll Mr. Lipscomb do?" Chet said.

"He'll kill me," Frankie said. He dashed his forearm across his eyes and bit his lower lip. "You don't know. When he gets mad he's just as likely to hit me with a stick of type."

On hands and knees he crawled to the very edge of the sumac. The others wriggled up and they lay in a row looking across the green slope to the shack. The smoke wasn't going up any more, but there was a smoldering pile of stuff outside, where Mrs. Mac-Leod and the kids had thrown it. Mrs. MacLeod and the children were sitting by the wagon, Angus was hitching his horses to the plow he had brought along, and Frankie's wheel was leaning against the corner of the shack.

"Oh damn!" Frankie said. He lay down in the brush with his face on his arms.

Chet, looking over the six-shooter, rolling the empty cylinder, peering down the fouled barrel, thought darkly that they ought to go right down there and throw a gun on old MacLeod and take the bike and tell him to hit the grit. He would do just that, if he had any more bullets. He would throw his gun from low on his thigh, and it would come so fast Angus wouldn't even see it. "All right, MacLeod," he'd say. "Give the kid back his bike, and don't take your time, either!"

He stole a look at Frankie. Once, on a hike, he had seen old man Lipscomb, who was the scoutmaster, get mad at Frankie and slap him so hard on the jaw that the red mark stayed there for an hour. Frankie would get hail columbia now.

Frankie raised up a little. "We got to get it back," he said doggedly. "I wouldn't dast go home without it, and I ought to be there now."

"Well, how?" Chet said.

"I ain't gonna help," Bill said. "I didn't want to bust up Tex's shack in the first place."

"You're a coward," Frankie said.

"I ain't either. I just don't want anything to do with it."

"Me neither," Pete said. "Any guy that'd shove you in the fire."

"Oh, quit arguing," Chet said. He was remembering an Indian story he had been reading in the *American Boy* where one hunter had drawn the Indians' fire while the other got away and went for help.

"Lookit," he said. "Come on over here." They all crawled to the edge again. "See? If you could get into the brush on this side, then the rest of us could go around on the other side and make a racket and get Angus chasing us and then you could dash out and get on your bike and beat it."

"I'm game," Frankie said. His face was smeared and his mouth tight. "Who's coming?"

"Not me," Bill said.

"Me neither," said Pete. "I'm not helping any guy that tries to push a guy in the fire."

Frankie half raised up. "Oh for gosh sakes," he said. "I'll smack you in the nose."

"Try it," Pete said. "I dare you. Go on and smack me."

They lay on their elbows glowering, and Chet got mad at both of them. "You can fight any old time," he said. "We got to get that wheel."

So he and Frankie went alone, Chet feeling loyal and heroic and contemptuous of the two left behind. He left his two guns with Pete, so he could run faster if Angus took after him, and he and Frankie worked back down through the coulee until they could hear the cries of Angus' two little girls playing.

"Now I'll sneak on across," Chet whispered. "You watch, and when you see the bushes jerk, get ready. Then I'll jump up and see if I can get him after me, and you grab the bike."

Stealthily he snaked through the golden bright shadows of the aspen and into the fringe of sumac. Lifting his head carefully, he could see Angus plowing the potato patch he grew on Tex's land every year, and Mrs. Angus spreading out some lunch in the shade of the wagon. None of them was within a hundred feet of the bike. He jerked the bushes, and a bush across the opening, hardly fifty feet from the shack, twitched back.

Chet drew a long breath, trying to un-knot his stomach. He waited until Angus was plowing in his direction, as far from Frankie and the bicycle as he would get. Then he jumped to his feet, yelled, waved his arms, thumbed his nose.

Angus did not hesitate a second. He dropped the reins from around his neck, turned the plow on its side, and started like a footracer for Chet. Out of the corner of his eye, before his legs could answer his command to bolt, Chet saw Frankie run crouching to the corner of the shack, and then he himself turned tail and dug for the woods.

He had gone only a few steps when Mrs. Angus yelled. He threw a scared running look over his shoulder. Angus had turned, and was trying to cut Frankie off as he pushed the wheel desperately across the bumpy ground toward the road. Chet stopped and watched, hardly breathing.

Frankie had fifty yards to go before he hit the trail and ground smooth enough to ride on, and Angus, coming down at an angle, had a good chance to cut him off. Frankie sprinted, bouncing the wheel, his bare legs and fallen stockings twinkling, but Angus was coming like a thunderbolt. Chet's heart stopped for a full two seconds as Frankie hit the road and made a running leap onto the seat. It looked as if Angus could reach out in one more stride and grab him. He had looked terribly fast before, coming uphill. Now, going down, he was all legs. He opened up clear to the neck like a clothespin, he ate up twenty feet at a stride. Frankie's head was down, his feet on the pedals were a blur, his shirt was ballooning out behind, but he did not open up any daylight between himself and Angus. One bump, one spill, and Frankie was a goner.

But he didn't spill, and he didn't let up, and even at the tracks, where he had with providential carelessness left both gates open, he pedalled right on, bumped perilously over the planks of the crossing, and legged it out the other side and up the road to town. Angus stopped at the fence.

Chet yelled, cheered, waved to Frankie far down below. When he took his eyes off the flying white figure and woke up to where he was, Mrs. Angus was only a few rods away, bearing down on him with her face puckered in anger. Like a scared antelope Chet cut for the woods. At first he didn't really fear her much. Then, a little way inside the aspen, he glanced back to see her almost upon him. She was almost as fast as Angus. Fear put a spurt of speed in Chet's legs, but he couldn't shake her. He heard her feet pounding on the path behind, close upon him. In a minute her hand might reach out . . .

Like a flash he dropped to hands and knees. Mrs. Angus' heavy knee hit him solidly, knocking his wind half out, and she went over him ponderously, grabbing for him as she fell. But Chet scrambled loose and escaped like a limping, winded fox into the brush.

When Chet got home from that expedition he hid the six-shooter in the cellar and kept his mouth discreetly shut, waiting to see what would happen. A time or two he slipped home from school at noon, when he knew his mother would be down at the post-office seeing if there was a letter from Pa, and took out the gun to snap and fondle it. But it came Monday, Tuesday, Wednesday, and nothing happened. Angus wasn't going to raise a fuss, or maybe he didn't know who to raise it at.

He and Frankie had started building an elaborate shanty in the brush by the east ford. Pete came in, over Frankie's protest, when he produced a full bag of Bull Durham stolen from his father. Bill came in too on the strength of half a raisin pie he had got from home. They camouflaged the shanty with brush, disguised the path in. And on Thursday afternoon Chet proposed that they take the six-shooter down and have some target practice. Shells for a .44 probably cost plenty, so everybody'd have to divvy in.

A quick foray under the plank sidewalk in front of the hotel turned up a dime and a good deal of tea lead. Crawling out, they scattered to their homes to see what could be raised.

In half an hour all were back. Bill had a dime. Pete had hooked seventeen cents from his father's second-best pants. Frankie had only four pennies. Mr. Lipscomb wouldn't give him any money, and he was scared to hook any. Chet had bummed a dime from his mother. Altogether they had fifty-one cents.

"I should think that'd be enough," Chet said. He shifted his pants, because the .44 was inside them and kept slipping down. On their way to the hardware store they ran into Bruce, going to mail a letter for Ma. That was the second one she had sent in two days.

"Don't you go following us," he warned Bruce.

"Why? What you gonna do?"

"None of your business. You just stay away, is all."

"I guess I can walk where I want to," Bruce said.

"You're too little to hang around with us," Chet said, and hitched his pants. The string that hung the gun around his neck was cutting into him; he walked a little spraddling to keep the pistol from banging against his stomach.

They ditched Bruce and went into the hardware. Mr. McGregor's pale egg-like bald head came forward along the dark counter. On a nail keg sat Jewel King, hugging his knees.

"Hi, Mr. King," Chet said.

"Hi, boy," King said. "Been throwing any parties lately?"

"No sir," Chet said. He wished he could forget that Mr. King was town marshal, and he wished he hadn't brought the gun along in here. It was so dark that probably the little bulge it made wasn't noticeable, but it bothered him anyway, and he crowded against the counter. "Have you got any .44 cartridges?" he said to Mr. McGregor.

Mr. McGregor bent over the counter. "You mean .45, don't you?"

"No. .44."

"That's an old-fashioned size," Mr. McGregor said. "If you really want anything that big you must want .45's. What do you want them for?"

"It's for a gun of Pa's," Chet said. "It's .44, I know."

Mr. McGregor looked across at Jewel King. His toothless mouth wrinkled up like the mouth of a paper bag. "You ever see a .44, Jewel?"

"Sure," Jewel said. "They make 'em, all right." He let his knee down and said to Chet, "You haven't got the gun handy, have you? Maybe we could tell."

Chet swallowed. Jewel King was looking at him from one side, Mr. McGregor from the other. Bruce had come in and was standing by the door. "No," Chet said. "I haven't got the gun. I just wanted some to . . . to . . ."

Jewel's hand came out suddenly and patted him around the waist, felt the gun, dragged it out, broke the string. He looked the pistol over and showed it to Mr. McGregor. Mr. McGregor nodded his head up and down. "Give themselves away every time," he said.

Jewel spoke sadly to Chet, who was standing frozen, not trying to run. "I'm sorry to do this, boy," Jewel said, "but I've got to arrest you. You stole that gun from Tex Davis' place. Didn't you?"

Chet swallowed. The door slammed and he turned his head quickly. Frankie and Pete and Bill had all skipped, and only Bruce stood inside the door.

"Yes sir," Chet said.

Mr. McGregor munched his gums together and cackled. "'Y God it's funny," he said. "Both in jail the same time. That's a funny one."

"What?" Chet said.

Jewel King looked at him soberly. "Don't you know?"

"Know what?"

"Never mind," Jewel said. "I'll have to take you over to the jail, and then I'll have to go see your mother. I don't like to see you in a mess like this, Chet. I had a pretty high opinion of you, up till now."

As they started for the door Bruce, pale and weeping, turned and fled. When they got out on the street Chet saw him streaking along the irrigation ditch toward home.

7

"He said that?"

Elsa rose slowly from the chair in the kitchen and stared at Bruce. He nodded, sniffling.

"But how could he know," she said, half to herself, "when I just got the letter today?"

"He just took hold of Chet and said, 'I'm sorry, boy, but I've got to arrest you,' and then Mr. McGregor said that about both of them at the same time. Is Pa in jail, Ma?"

Elsa put her hand in her apron pocket and felt the letter. "No," she said.

"What are they going to do to Chet?"

"Never mind," she said. "You run out and play. I'll go get Chet straightened out."

"I want to come, Ma."

She said, "You stay as far out of this as you can get. I'll be back pretty soon."

Along the ditch bank, as she went uptown, there were purple crocuses, and the primroses were just beginning to fold their petals together. A chilly little wind blew in from the river. So now everything's falling apart, she said. Now Bo's in jail in Havre and Chet's in jail at home, and we're right back where we started in Dakota, only worse now, with the kids in it.

Walking, she pulled out the letter and read it again. Two policemen had been waiting at the line, picked him up before he could get across. He was full of shame, he couldn't blame himself enough for bringing this on her. They had confiscated the car and the load and had him charged with smuggling. "I should have listened to you, Sis," he wrote, "but I wanted so damned much to get out of the hole. If I could have made a good stake at this we could have gone anywhere you wanted, and settled down to some steady business. I was just sick of living on sowbelly and beans in a dirty little jerkwater town, I guess. They've got me in jail with a nigger, but I'm not complaining. I'm no better than a nigger, the way I've made you live. I hope you won't think you have to tell the kids. If this turns out all right I'll make it up to you, that's a promise . . ."

She put the letter away again. Don't tell the kids.

At the jail she found Jewel King. "I was just going to call you," he said, "but I thought I better let Chet stew a while in the jailhouse." He chuckled, and his belly shook. "He's got guts, that kid," he said. "Most kids would of bawled, but he just sits there and grits his teeth. I like to see a kid like that."

"Do you like to see a boy steal?"

"Oh, steal," Jewel said. "This wasn't really stealing. Any kid would snitch a gun if he found it in a deserted shanty. He's just full of beans. I wouldn't of put him in the cooler only Angus MacLeod was pretty hot, said a bunch of them swiped the gun and some other stuff and then tried to burn the house down."

"Oh Lord!" Elsa said. "Did they?"

"Naw. Angus come along and put it out." Jewel fished up a bent cigar. "I wouldn't worry, Elsa. Chet wasn't the only one. We got the gun back, and if you give Angus four-five dollars damages everything's all right."

"Who are the others?"

"I don't know. Chet wouldn't tell."

"But he stole the gun himself."

"I guess so. He had it on him."

"All right," she said. "I'll give you five dollars for Angus. Chet was the ringleader. He always is. I want him to spend the night in jail."

"Oh now, that ain't necessary," Jewel said.

"I want him to stay in jail anyway," Elsa said. "I want him to learn what it means to break laws and get in trouble."

She met Jewel's queer, sidelong look steadily. "Now can I see him a minute?" she said.

He led her into the little cell back of the firehouse, where Chet slumped on a bench. He rose when the door opened, and Elsa felt a pang at the sight of his face, white and set and too old for him. Like father like son, she thought. Shame and sullenness and eagerness for sympathy and determination to act like a man whatever happened—his face said exactly the same things as Bo's letter.

"Well, Chet," she said.

"Hello, Ma."

"I never expected to see you in a jail," she said.

He stood sullenly silent. He would not, she saw, attempt to deny his guilt or plead with her. There again he was like Bo. He was what he was, and he wouldn't pretend to be anything else. Bruce would have lied, in the same situation. Chet might much more likely go clear wrong, but he'd go in his own way, with a kind of pride.

"I hope you realize what you've done," she said. "I wouldn't like to see a boy of mine grow up a thief."

She stopped then, because she didn't want to add the humiliation of tears to his punishment. "Mr. King will let you out in the morning in time for breakfast," she said. "You come home and eat and get ready for school."

Chet turned and sat down on the bench, and to keep from crying herself she brushed past Jewel and went outside. "I'd rather spend the night in there myself than make him do it," she said.

"Yeah," Jewel said. "Well, I'll see that Diamond Dick gets back home all right. Don't worry about the jail. That's a good clean jail. No bugs or anything."

"Will he have to sleep on that bench? I didn't see any bed."

"Bed in the firehouse part," he said. "He'll be okay."

"All right." She looked hard at Jewel. "But don't you be too easy on him. Don't give him the idea that what he's done is smart, or manly, or anything. I want him to know that being in jail is a disgrace."

So now there would be waiting again, as it seemed to her she had waited all the time she had known Bo. Now there would be sitting day after day busying herself with little unimportant things, but jumping at the slightest noise, running to the window at the slightest flash of movement along the south road. There would be getting through the day somehow, anyhow, getting the boys to bed, sitting in the evenings to do fancy work or to read, and her ears twice as alert as in daylight, her mind twice as receptive to frettings and worry. There would be dragging off to bed with the worries waiting for her to lie down, hanging over her like mosquitoes on a warm night.

There would be the escapes she had used before, the daydreams and the memories of childhood that sometimes were so similar that they confused her: pictures of quiet streets, apple trees heavy with fruit or white with blossoms in a green back yard, her children scuffling leaves under the maples and running to greet Bo when he came down the sidewalk on a summer evening, coming from work with his coat on his arm and the six-o'clock sun on his face. That dream expanded indefinitely: neighbors dropped in for root-beer and whist, Bo told stories, did card tricks, sang songs, kept them all laughing. There were good nights of tenderness and love, and in the mornings Bo's voice singing a fool song.

She didn't want much. Yet it seemed to her sometimes as if life had conspired to keep from her exactly that one thing that she desired, and as if her husband and her children, who were the single indispensable part of her day-dreams, should be the ones to destroy what she had been working for.

One night she sat reading a novel that someone had loaned her. It was all about castaways on a cannibal island, and war with wooden swords between the tribes, and it was romantic and exciting and a little silly, but she kept at it because if she didn't she would have to think. Once her head lifted: it sounded like some-one out behind. But there had been too many of those false alarms lately. Her ears were like the ears of a dog pricking in sleep at phantasmal noises.

Then she heard it again, distinctly. She stood up just as the door between dining room and kitchen opened and Bo's grinning face looked in.

She dropped the book and ran to him, was swept into his bearhug. When he set her down and she could look at his face his eyes were sly and warm.

"Hi, Mama," he said. "How've you been?"

"Oh, all right," she said. She had him by the arms, looking him over. There was something different about him, something gayer and younger. His clothes . . .

"Why, you've got a new suit," she said.

"Like it?"

"It's lovely. But what . . . I thought . . . How did everything come out?"

"Did you think they'd hang me?" His laugh was so open and amused that she stared. There was no such shame as she had expected, no hangdog look of creeping home in disgrace, and she realized instantly, though the idea had never entered her head before, that she had been counting on that, expecting to steer him with it as she had steered Chet.

"What happened over there?" she said.

He laughed again. "They had to turn me loose. Didn't have any business pinching me in the first place. The American prohibition law isn't in effect yet, see? They pinched me on the wrong side of the line. The cops just got all snarled up about what their job was. So after they'd kept me in jail a week or so they had to give me back the car and the load."

"But how could they be so stupid? If there wasn't any law . . ."

"They don't know what the law is yet, that's their trouble. Neither did I. I was piping pretty small till my lawyer put me wise. He was a smart little shyster." He shook her fondly by the shoulders and narrowed his eyes, grinning. "Want to see something?"

"Sure. What?"

"Where's the lantern?"

"I'll get it. What've you got?"

"Wait and see." With an air of great secrecy he lighted the lantern.

"And you didn't have to pay a fine or anything?" she said, going out.

"Nary a nickel. Go on, keep moving, right on out to the shed."

The shed doors were open, but Bo muffled the lantern so that she could see nothing. "Open your mouth and shut your eyes," he said.

"You're just like a child," she said. "Unexpected returns, and surprises, and mysteries. What is this?"

"Now you can open."

She opened. There was a car in the shed that was not the old Ford. It was new, expensive looking. Bo had turned on the headlights, which burned with a white brilliance against the shed wall and reflected back on the gleaming dark green of the body.

"My goodness!" Elsa said. "Where did you get this?"

"Bought it."

"Bought it! With what?"

"With seventeen hundred dollars."

"*What?*"

"Take it easy," he said. "There's plenty more where that came from."

"Well, I just don't understand," she said. She inspected the mysterious dials on the dashboard, wiggled the gear-shift knob, read the name on the plate: Essex. It was by all odds the finest car she had ever seen. The seats were grained leather, the top was black and rakish as a taut sail. "A new suit and a car that cost seventeen hundred dollars," she said. She lifted the blankets in the back of the car and looked under. "And another load!"

"And that isn't all," Bo said. "Come on back inside."

He shut off the headlights and locked the shed doors. On the way to the house he laid his arm across her shoulders and shook her again. "Got your eyes bugging out, haven't I?"

"You've mystified me enough," she said. "I give up. Now tell me, quick."

Inside the kitchen he blew out the lantern with a sharp puff of breath and let the chimney down. In the light of the lamp on the table his eyes were bright as a cat's.

"I had almost two thousand when I left here," he said.

"And you've spent it all."

"Don't get ahead of yourself. I put fifteen hundred in a Havre bank and got a load and started back. That's when they pinched me and took me back to Havre. And in jail I met a guy that put me wise."

"The nigger?"

He looked at her in disgust. "No, not the nigger! All he did was teach me to play coon-can. This was a guy that got pinched in a gambling raid. After I got through talking to him, and they let me out, I went out and traded old Lena in on this boat, and moved the load from one to the other, and bought some more to fill this one up, and there she is."

"But if it cost seventeen hundred . . ."

326

"I got four hundred and fifty for Lena," Bo said, "and I gave them two-fifty cash. We owe a thousand on her."

"But what are we going to use it for? I'd feel silly, riding around this town in a car like that."

"Maybe you won't be riding around this town," Bo said. "This boat will go twice as fast as old Lena, and she holds half again as much. She'll pay for herself before you can spit twice."

"You're going on running whiskey," Elsa said.

He nodded, watching her. "Till I get so far ahead I can afford to get out," he said. "You know what we're going to do?"

"I can imagine."

"We're going to move."

"Where to?"

"One of the Montana towns. Havre or Great Falls."

"And leave the homestead, and this house, and the stock . . ."

"Hell with all of it," Bo said. "The hell with this little burg, too. Soon as that prohibition law goes into effect in the States there'll be millions to be made. There is now. Some of the states are already dry, and there's always a market in a dry state. We're going to run whiskey where there's money to pay for it in wholesale lots."

Elsa stood quietly, everything in her sagging, as if she had worked all day and saw more work ahead that had to be done before she could rest. "I wish . . ."

"Uh?"

"What if they *had* convicted you in Havre?"

"They didn't," Bo said. "And they won't ever get the chance again, not as long as I've got a fast car."

His eyes were steady on hers, as if he dared her to raise an objection, as if he had arguments and statistics and proofs to counteract anything she could say. She sighed and gave it up. Bo seemed to feel the moment when her resistance disintegrated. He swung around the kitchen as if shaking the whole thing from his back, and yelled for food. While she got him something he sat at the table, natty and citified in his new clothes (he told her that he had stopped out on the bench and changed, so as to come in with all flags flying) and watched her slyly. His hand was in his coat pocket. Absently, when she set the food before him, he picked up her left hand and looked at it, bent the knuckles tentatively forward and back, smoothed out the skin. "Nice little hand you've got there."

"Nice and red and rough."

"No," he said. "You've got nice hands."

"Now what do you want?" she said.

"Just want to prettify it a little," Bo said. He brought a small package out of his pocket. Inside the paper was a jeweler's plush box, and inside the box was a tiny gold watch. She looked at it, at him, back at it, and suddenly she was crying. Bo came around the table and put his arm around her, whispering into her hair. "Take it easy," he whispered. "I just wanted you to know how much . . . I appreciate . . . you've been swell."

She said no more that night about the whiskey business she had been determined to steer him out of. She couldn't. Instead, she sat and listened to him talk about what they were going to do and see, the money they were going to make. He opened up the future like a Christmas package for her delight, and he was so delighted himself that she couldn't be otherwise.

"We've been stuck in this backwater too long," he said. "You're going back where there are lawns and trees and cement sidewalks and automobiles that make that one out there look like a donkey cart. You're going to have a fur coat and nice clothes—and you aren't going to make them yourself, either. The kids are going to a high school and I'm smoking nothing but two-for-a-quarter cigars, starting now. We've been chasing pipedreams too long. This is the time we make it go."

8

For a week they were a wonder. When Bo drove the Essex downtown and parked it a crowd gathered. Boys ran their hands over the finish, men lifted the hood and bent in over the motor, stood back respectfully when Bo climbed in and stepped on the self-starter. They examined it from front to rear, their faces closed, their eyes veiled. They kicked the tires. They listened to the idling motor. They unscrewed the radiator cap and looked in. They asked, casually, how fast she'd go and how good she was on hills. They commented on her lines, her color, her mechanical perfections. Some said oh hell, she wasn't anything but a cheap Hudson, but they watched like the others when she went by.

In that week Elsa had a thousand things to do. There was the house to clean out, clothes to pack, books to box. Bo sold the two cows to Hank Freeze, on the north bench. The horses he couldn't sell, so he left them with the oldest Heathcliff boy to keep for half the increase. For the house there was no market at all; George McKenna at the store finally agreed to try to sell it for them.

The wholesale sell-out brought up the question of Bruce's colt. It was getting no better. As it grew it threw more weight on the broken legs, and its walk was the same floundering lunge it had had when they found it in the bend. Jim Enich came over to see

Bo about it, and with Bruce hanging anxiously on the fringes of their talk they looked the colt over.

Bo's eyes went to Bruce, rubbing the colt's neck under the long sorrel mane. He drew Enich aside, but Bruce left his pet and followed. Patting his pockets, Bo pretended to hunt for something. "Run inside and get me a couple cigars."

Bruce looked suspiciously from one to the other, hesitated, then turned and darted away.

"Worth anything at all?" Bo said.

Enich spat. "Hide."

Bo breathed angrily through his nose. "I never should have let the kid get attached to it," he said. "He's all wrapped up in it now."

"It ain't a very pleasant thing to do," Enich said. "I'll take it off your hands, if you want. The hide's worth about three bucks."

Bruce came running back with the cigars, his eyes swinging from one face to the other. Bo cleared his throat. "Well," he said, "Jim's willing to make a deal for your colt."

"Couldn't we . . . ?" Bruce said. "Couldn't we take him along? Ship him, or something?"

"No," Bo said. "We couldn't do that. He'll be better off here. Jim'll take care of him for you. He'll give you three dollars for him."

"Oh gee!" Bruce said. "I don't want to sell Socks!"

"Well, it's either sell him or give him away," Bo said. He squatted down and put his hand on the boy's shoulder. "Look," he said. "Maybe we'll be coming back here sometime. Your colt couldn't get along running with the herd over at Heathcliff's. So you'd better sell him to Jim, and if we come back you can buy him back."

"And he'll still be mine?"

"Sure thing," Enich said.

Bruce broke loose from his father and went over to the colt. He reached up and hugged it around the neck, and it nuzzled his shirt, leaving flecks of moisture on the cloth. The boy reached up to whisper something private in the colt's ear. Then he turned and said, "All right, I'll sell him to you, Mr. Enich. He'd rather stay with you than anybody else. He knows you."

He took Enich's three silver dollars and held them uncertainly in his hand. "Can I come and see him before we go?" he said.

"I'm taking him out to the ranch," Enich said. "That's pretty far."

Over his head Bo made a motion at Enich, and Enich went out to drive his wagon around in back. In ten minutes he pulled out again, the half-raised head of the trussed colt showing above the endgate. Bruce ran after the wagon, rubbing the sorrel's nose, the tears shaking big down his face, until almost the east ford. There he stood waving, seeing through a blur of crying the high-wheeled wagon and the sorrel hide and the blazed white nose and one rolling scared eye over the endgate as the wagon went on down the trail and around the curve behind the willows.

They gave Spot to the Chance boys. Old Tom was wheeled away one morning in a doll buggy by three excited little girls who had dressed his languid, sleepy gray body in petticoats and tucked him under the covers, where he lay in a most uncatlike position, flat on his back, and purred like a teakettle.

"I hate to see old Tom go," Elsa said. "He was such a comfortable, sleepy old cat."

"Except when a dog got after him," Chet said. "Remember when Chapman's airedale treed him in the barn? He went right up in the air and came down on that old airedale's back with his claws digging like sixty. He rode him clear up past Van Dam's."

"He wasn't so sleepy out hunting, either," Bruce said. "Remember when we saw him dive into the river on top of the mudhen?"

That was the way of their uprooting. "Remember the time . . . ?" Five years in that town had made it home. Elsa wondered if her boys would have the same homesick memories of that barren little river-bottom village as she had of the maple-lined streets and the creamery and the white-steepled church in Indian Falls. Home was a curious thing, like happiness. You never knew you had had it until it was gone.

You never knew either how many people you thought of with kindness, the people who now met you on the street as you went about pulling up all the little roots that had gone down in five years, and shook your hand, and said don't forget us, don't get so prosperous over there in the States that you never remember your old friends . . .

There was no time for regrets. Maybe this whiskey business, for all its illegality, was as good as anything they could have chosen. There were no places on earth any more where opportunity lay new and shining and untouched. The old days when people used to rush to Dakota or California or Alaska in search of easy wealth were gone forever; she and Bo together had tried one or two of those worn-out dreams, to their sorrow. But if he could do as well as he said he could at this business, and then get out, he at least would have been preserved from his own irritability and restlessness and bad temper.

So she went carefully pulling up the little roots that gave with a slight unwilling tug, and left the future to Bo. He was so sure of it.

In the sun-slanting, dew-fresh morning they stood for the last time on the porch, the loaded car nosing the front fence. Not even the rush of packing had ruffled Bo's temper this time. He locked the door, tossed the key in his hand, looked at Elsa, puckered his lips in a jigging whistle, and winked. He rubbed his finger down the door-frame.

"Goodbye, Old Paint," he said. Elsa was looking through the front window at the bare room, its raw floor showing inside the frame of painted border. The mantel Bo had put in with the intention of some day building a fireplace under it was empty of knickknacks, the picture of three white horses floating-maned against a background of storm was gone, and only its clean oval shape remained on the wall.

She touched Bo's arm. "Let's try," she said. "Let's try awful hard this time."

They went out to the car, the boys half hysterical with excitement, singing loudly, "Goodbye, Old Paint, I'm leavin' Cheyenne, I'm leavin' Cheyenne, I'm goin' to Montana, Goodbye, Old Paint . . ."

"You want to wake up the whole town?" Bo said. He shoved them into the back seat, where they squirmed their way neck-deep into the luggage. Their heads stuck out like the heads of young owls in a nest.

"Open your mouth and I'll drop in a mouse," Bo said.

They had to leave the key with George McKenna, out on the east edge of town. At the low swampy spot that had been made into the dumpground the road split, leaving the dump like an island in the middle, and as they bumped over the right-hand fork they smelled the foul stench from the garbage and bones and offal thrown out there.

"Pee-you!" Elsa said, and held her nose. The boys echoed her. "Pee-you! Pee-you-willy!" They clamped their noses shut and pretended to fall dead.

"I better get to windward of that coming back," Bo said.

They left the key with McKenna, shook hands with him twice (he was very affable now that Bo had paid up the long-standing grocery bill) and started back, really leaving now. The things they saw as they passed had the sharpness of things seen for the last time. They noticed things they had never consciously noticed before, the way the hills came down into the river on the north like three folds in a blanket, the extreme height of the stovepipe on the Chinaman's shack below Poverty Flat. The boys chanted at everything they saw, "Goodbye, Old Chinaman, Goodbye, Old Whitemud River, Goodbye, Old Dumpground, Goodbye."

"Hold your noses," Bo said. He eased the car into the windward fork around the dump. "Somebody sure dumped something rotten."

He stared ahead, bending forward a little, and Elsa heard him swear under his breath. The car jumped ahead over the bumpy trail.

"What?" Elsa said. She looked at his set face, the dark look of anger in it. Then she saw too, with a hard, flinching pain, and closed her lips tight over her teeth. Hurry, she said. Oh, hurry, get by before he sees it!

But the boys were not missing anything. They were half standing, excited by the burst of speed and the reckless bouncing. She knew he saw it before she heard him cry out; she could feel his seeing it like a bright electric shock, the way she had once felt the pain of a woman in the travelling dentist's chair when the dentist dug a living nerve out of the woman's tooth and there was a livid tableau, the woman sitting with face lifted, half rising from the chair, the dentist scrambling stupidly on hands and knees looking for the wire of pain he had dropped. Then she heard Bruce's cry.

"Oh!" he said. "It's Socks! Ma, it's Socks! Stop, Pa, there's Socks!"

His father drove grimly ahead, not turning or speaking, and Elsa shook her head. Bruce screamed, and neither of them turned or spoke. And when he dug down into the luggage, burrowing in and hiding his head, shaking with long smothered sobs, there was no word in the car except Chet's "Gee whiz, he still had his hobbles on!"

So they left town, and as they wound up the dugway to the bench none of them had the heart to look back on the town they were leaving, on the flat river bottom green with spring, its village snuggled in the loops of river. Their minds were all on the bloated, skinned body of the colt, the sorrel hair left below the knees, the iron braces still on the broken front legs.

Wherever you go, Elsa was thinking, whenever you move and go away, you leave a death behind.

VI

It was two
o'clock in the
morning when Bo
hit the outskirts of
Great Falls. Through
the uncurtained front of
the car the air was cold, with
a faint remembrance of leaf-fires
in its smell. Across the river on his
left, the high stack of the copper
smelter went up like a great dark lamp
chimney above the huddled houses of
Little Chi. Downriver he could see a glow
of light from the power station on Rainbow Falls.

Bumping across the cartracks, easing the car over
a rutted intersection, feeling the built-up springs sink
heavily, clear down, on a slow bump, he swung left to avoid
the main streets. His headlights, knocked out of line somewhere on the trip, glared along front porches, fences, up into
the thinning color of the maples. Then the street, the alley, the
turn, the branches of the crabapple tree over the garage, and he
swung in, dimming the lights and climbing out stiffly to fumble
among his keys. From Govenlock to Great Falls, on that kind of
road, was all you wanted to drive.

For a moment, standing inside in the glow of the dimmed lights,
he wondered if he ought to unload, but the weariness of driving
ached in his shoulders, and he snapped the padlock on the garage
doors, opened the wire gate in the fence, and went up to the back
door.

He heard the bell ring far inside the house, and as he waited
under the frosty, star-spiked sky a little wind stirred the creeper
over the back porch trellis. Probably Elsa would be scared to
death. She always jumped a yard when the doorbell rang.

The window above him opened, and her voice called down,
"Who is it?"

"Me," Bo said.

"Oh good!" she said. "Just a minute."

The key turned in the kitchen door and he stepped inside, still
in the dark. His hands reached out and felt her, pulled her close.
She was in her nightgown. "Mmmmm!" he said, and kissed her.
She snapped on the light.

333

"I bet you're tired," she said. "Do you want something to eat?"

"I might use a sandwich at that. How've you been?"

"All right. Chet got his nose broke."

"Fighting?"

"He's out for football, gone clean crazy about it. I never see him from morning till night except when he drags home after dark with half the skin off him."

"That won't hurt him," Bo said. He sat with his overcoat on, his legs sprawled wide, watching her pad around the kitchen. The way the silk lay close to hips and breasts made him stir with a comfortable, warm unease. Silk nightgowns, big house, gas stove, electric lights, icebox, lawn and trees. You couldn't kick.

"Heimie come over after his stuff?" he said.

"Yes. Day before yesterday."

"Pay you?"

"No. He said he'd see you when you came back."

Bo grunted.

"I wish you didn't have to work with that crowd," she said.

"They've got contacts. It would have taken me a long time to work in here alone."

"You'd have made more."

"Once I got in. But we weren't doing anything very wonderful till the last few months. Besides that, if you work with those guys a little you're safer. They'd as soon stool you off as look at you."

She went to the icebox, and he saw the corrugated metal interior, a package of sliced bacon, bottles of milk, oranges, a roast of some kind, a glass-covered dish of butter.

"Quite a bit different from the old cellar hole," he said. The fat richness of the food, the clean crinkled metal, the kitchen with white woodwork and linoleum floor, filled him with a sense of luxurious prosperity. Elsa ought to like it. She'd been hollering for a nice home for fifteen years.

"Yes," she said. "Only I never had to be afraid that anyone would come and take the cellar hole away from me."

"For God's sake," he said disgustedly, and filled his mouth with bread. "You wouldn't be satisfied if you were a calf and your ma was giving liquid gold."

"Oh, I'm satisfied," she said. "I've got everything I could want here, sure enough." She started out into the hall.

"Where you going?"

"To get a kimono. It's chilly."

"Heck with it," Bo said. He reached out and pulled her onto his lap, eating with one hand while with the other he caressed

334

the creased softness of her stomach. "You feel pretty nice through silk," he said.

Elsa laughed. "I should think you'd be too tired to feel anything."

"Never too tired," Bo said. "Is there any hot water?"

"I think so."

"Hot dog," he said. "Hot running water, bath tub six feet long, and a chicken in a silk nightgown. I'd have been home hours ago if I'd thought of that."

She smiled, arching away from his arm, and he saw that she was very glad to have him home, that she liked his hand on her, that the beauty parlor he had made her go to had done things for her hair and skin. He bit her. "You hit the grit," he said. "I'll be along before you can say Ishmael Rabinowitz."

When he woke in the morning he lay watching the sun that lay like a wide yellow board under the blind. There were noises downstairs—Elsa getting the kids off to school. He stretched luxuriously in the wide bed, kicked the covers off and inspected his white feet, his heavy, white-skinned calves with the black hair worn nearly off where the garters went around.

"Old piano legs," he said, but he liked his legs, the way the muscles hardened into flat plates when he wiggled his feet.

Chet, with the whole middle of his face bandaged, came in and stood looking at him, eyes solemn over the gauze. "Hi, Pa."

"Hi," Bo said. "Who you been mixing it with, Jess Willard?"

"Football," Chet said. "I got my nose broke."

"Somebody must've kicked pretty high."

"Oh, you don't kick in football. Just once in a while."

"What do they call it football for?"

"Because . . . I don't know." Chet's eyes wandered around the bedroom. He seemed at once indifferent and ill at ease.

"Pa."

"What?"

"Could I have four dollars?"

Bo stared. "You don't want much. What are you planning to do, go into business?"

"I want a football. If I had one of my own I could practice around after school."

"Yuh," Bo said. He swung his legs over the edge of the bed and sat in his nightshirt, looking at Chet. It didn't take long to give a kid millionaire ideas. A year ago a dime would have looked like a fortune to this one.

"I might make the first team next year," Chet said. "I'd be a sophomore, and if I gained ten pounds or so and got so I could throw passes good I could . . ."

"You could get your behind in a sling," Bo said. "Do all the other kids get busted up the way you do?"

"This isn't anything," Chet said. He passed his fingers tenderly over the taped gauze. "Sloppy Johnson bust his collarbone last week. He's on the team."

"So if you could have a football and practice a lot maybe you could get on the team and break a leg," Bo said. He laughed, tickled at the solemn earnestness of this little squirt with the patched face. "Hand me my pants," he said. He fumbled in the pants, found the wallet, leafed off a five-dollar bill. "I'll want change."

"You bet," Chet said. "Thanks, Pa, a lot. I'll bring the change after school."

He scooted out, went downstairs like a falling safe. Bo laughed. It was a good feeling to give a kid something when he wanted it that much. Sitting on the bed leisurely pulling on his socks, he thought, I'll give it to him, too. I'll have it to give all of them. Give me another few months, let the roads stay open a few weeks longer . . . He began dressing more purposefully. He had to see Heimie, get a half dozen things, get things organized so he could pull out tomorrow. And if Heimie wanted part of this load he'd have to be satisfied with two or three cases. There was more in it the other way.

"Got anything to eat for a starving Armenian?" he said in the kitchen.

"Oh, a few odds and ends." She took bacon and toast from the oven and set them before him. "How many eggs?"

"Make it three. I've got a lot to do."

"Going to unload?"

"No. I'm leaving it right there. I'll be pulling out again in the morning."

"Where?"

"Right on down to Nebraska."

She turned to watch the frying eggs, but he could see by the set of her shoulders and the angle of her head that she was going to protest.

"I'm scared of that trip," she said. "It's so long."

"That's why there's more money in it."

"And more risk," she said.

"That's the chance you take," Bo said. "I want to get this sold and get back to Govenlock for another load before the roads get too bad. Then we can live off the fat of the land the rest of the winter."

He wolfed his breakfast, wiped his mouth, kissed her, and went out, walking fast. At the drugstore on the corner he bought four two-for-a-quarter cigars and turned into Central Avenue, letting the fragrant smoke fill his mouth. At the door of Chapell's Garage he slowed, looking in. Frank Chapell was burning waste in the office stove.

"Mornin'," he said. "Thought you was out of town."

"Was," Bo said.

"Anything stirring up north?"

"Quiet as a church."

"Same here," Frank said. "Anything I can do for you?"

Bo gave Chapell a cigar. "I'm looking for a Wyoming license plate. Got any?"

"Might have."

Chapell looked under the bench at the rear of the shop. "Pair of Utahs, pair of Oregons, couple sets of Montanas."

"It's better when there's only one plate. Couldn't pick me up one, could you?"

"When you want it?"

"This afternoon."

"Come around sometime after three," Frank said. "I think I can smouge you one."

From Chapell's Bo went to Strain's Department Store and found a floor walker. "I want to buy a clothes dummy," he said.

The floor walker looked baffled. "You mean a regular dummy? Window dummy?"

"Yes."

"I'll get the manager."

"I'd rather have a dead one," Bo said, and laughed at the floor walker's startled face.

He waited for the manager, waited again while that polite gentleman looked back among the invoices to see what dummies cost, and finally bought one for sixteen dollars, twice what he thought it was worth. Across the street at Gill's Hardware he bought two boxes of large-headed roofing nails, and with those in his overcoat pockets walked the last block and a half to the Smoke House, guarded by its wooden Indian and flanked on either side of the door by peephole slot machines saying "Adults Only."

Heimie Hellman was eating breakfast at the counter with his overcoat and hat on, and while he ate the shine from the barber-shop next door sat jackknifed on a portable stool and shined his yellow shoes. Bo, coming in the door, let his lip curl slightly.

Ladies' man, probably pimp. He was too God damned elegant in his yellow shoes and tan silk shirt and velvet-collared coat.

Heimie looked over, lifted his head and half shut his eyes and opened his mouth, the whole gesture like an act. He lifted a hand, and as Bo slid onto a stool beside him, he tossed a quarter to the shine, who grinned and went.

"Well," Heimie said. "How they hanging?"

"Okay."

Heimie shook his head in an admiration that might have been ironic. "How do you do it?" he said. "Every other guy I know has been knocked over at the line one time or another. You just go up and come back like you was driving in the park." He smiled at Bo, thumping a cigarette on the counter gently. "You must have a rabbit's foot," he said.

"I just happen to know roads the law never heard of," Bo said. "Things moving here?"

"Little slow yet. We'll start turning it over when people begin buying for Christmas."

Bo looked down the counter and watched the waiter draw a cup of coffee. "You won't want anything for a while then."

"What did you bring?"

"White Horse and Haig and Haig."

"You can't get what good Scotch is worth around here," Heimie said. "Most of our customers are pikers, 'sa fact. Rather rot their guts out than pay for good stuff."

"Yeah," Bo said. "Well, I guess I can get rid of it."

Through hands cupped to light the cigarette Heimie watched him. "Running it on down?"

"I didn't say," Bo said. "I could spare you two or three cases if you wanted them. Probably I'll be making another trip before Christmas. Let me know what you want and I'll bring it then."

"How soon'll that be? The rush might start quicker than we expect."

Leaning over, Bo dropped the cigar butt in a spittoon. "I could get it to you within two weeks."

Heimie frowned, tapping his fingers on the counter. He looked at himself in the mirror and took off his hat to smooth his beetle-shell hair. "Two weeks is pretty late," he said.

"That's as quick as I can make it."

"Well," Heimie said, "we might have to draw on somebody else. I thought you'd have some plain stuff this trip."

"Send somebody up," Bo said contemptuously. "Somebody that always gets knocked over at the line, with a lot of your hooch aboard."

Heimie shrugged. "Maybe two weeks will do. But I'll give you a tip about running that Scotch south."

"I didn't say I was running it anywhere."

"Just the same," Heimie said, "I know damn well you didn't think you could sell a whole load of White Horse and Haig and Haig in this burg." He smiled and tapped a finger on Bo's chest. "If you do go south, stay away from Sheridan," he said. "They're getting tough as hell around there. Prohis at all the bridges and ferries, stopping every suspicious car. Friend of mine was knocked over down there last week with a new Marmon and a thousand dollar load."

"Well," Bo said, "I guess we'll let the guys around Sheridan worry about that." He slid off the stool. "Do you think you can move two or three Scotch, or shall I unload them myself?"

Motioning to the waiter, Heimie slid a half dollar down the counter and stood up, tightening the overcoat across his chest. He walked to the door with Bo, his head bent. "What's it going to come at?"

"It's up. Cost me eight dollars a case more at Govenlock this time. I'll have to pass that on."

"That would make it sixty-two," Heimie said. He stood picking his teeth, looking down across the shoulder of the wooden Indian. A boy of twelve or so, standing on tiptoe before the eyepiece of one of the "Adults Only" slot machines, jerked his head away and pretended to be interested in the window full of pipes and razor blades and tins of tobacco.

"I've been thinking," Heimie said. "You take a lot of chances running it on down. You get a better price, sure, but with Wyoming hot you take chances. What about making a deal for the whole load?"

"I've got other customers I have to take care of," Bo said. "I thought you couldn't sell Scotch in this town anyway."

"Little water'll do wonders to the price of Scotch," Heimie said. "Brings it down where pikers can buy it."

"That'll lose you customers, too, in the long run." Bo reached out another cigar and bit off the end. "No, I guess I better stick with the arrangements I already made."

"I'll take the whole load," Heimie said. "That saves you a lot of trouble. I'll take the whole load at the old price, fifty-four a case."

"I'd be a sucker," Bo said. "I can sell it for seventy-five in wholesale lots."

"Not here in town."

"What does that matter? I can sell it for that—got it sold."

"Well, I can't pay any price like that," Heimie said. "I can't get that selling it by the bottle."

That, Bo knew, was a lie. Heimie had been getting seven and eight a bottle for watered Scotch for six months, ever since people's stored-up liquor had begun to run out. And at Christmas time he'd hike the price.

"I might make it sixty," Heimie said. "But I wouldn't stand to make anything much. Customers kick like steers even at the old price."

"We'd better let it slide," Bo said. "You can have the three cases if you want."

"Fifty-four?"

"Sixty-two. I can't absorb that eight-buck raise."

Heimie considered. "All right. Can you bring them over to the house tonight?"

"Can't you come after them?"

"I'm tied up. Got to see a guy from Kalispell out at the tourist park. Matter of fact, you might be interested in what's in the wind."

Bo waited, but Heimie apparently was not going to say what was in the wind, so Bo shrugged. "All right," he said. "I'll be over around nine."

As he went down the street he cursed Heimie's deviousness. He might just as well have said in the beginning that he wanted the whole load—at a cut price, on credit!—instead of beating around the bush with bear stories about Wyoming being hot, and maybe they'd have to draw on somebody else for stuff. At the same time, there was just enough possibility that Wyoming was hot so that it would pay to be careful. There was only one decent road south unless you went clear over into Dakota and then down. And ever since the Federals got organized they had been making trouble. It might be a good idea to go clear around Sheridan, at that.

Then he thought of having to unload the whole car, just to take three cases over to that damned lazy Heimie. If it wasn't for the certainty that Heimie would stool on anybody who told him off, he would have liked to back out even on the three cases.

He unloaded, put the rear cushion in, threw three sacks of sand in the back end along with Heimie's three cases, to bring the built-up springs down, and went in to lunch. While they were eating the dummy arrived over the shoulder of a grinning delivery boy. "Just put her on the couch," Bo said. He went into the hall and called Elsa. "Here's your dummy," he said.

"My what?"

"Your dummy. Come on in here."

"What on earth are you talking about?" she said. "I haven't ordered anything." She came into the room and stopped. "Now what?"

"Look," Bo said, boxing his ankles and scuffing his toe. "I didn't know how you'd feel about it, so I didn't say anything about it before, but this girl wants to ride down to Nebraska with me."

"Take that silly look off your face and tell me," Elsa said.

"No fooling. She wants a ride. Only she hasn't got any clothes to wear."

Elsa laughed. "Where did you get this thing?"

"This is camouflage," Bo said. "It's too easy to spot a car with one man in it, travelling fast. Henriette here is coming along to look after me."

"But anyone could tell in a minute . . ."

"Put a veil on her. Just seeing us go by, nobody is going to spot her."

"You're like a little kid playing detective," Elsa said. "I'll bet anything you're doing this because it tickles your funny bone. You'll be talking to her all the way down."

"Why not?" he said. "Put some classy duds on her and she'll be worth talking to."

"Well, I'll see."

She went upstairs, and in a few minutes came down with an armful of clothes. "She'll have to wear hand-me-downs," she said. "I'm not giving away any of my good clothes to a girl no better than she should be."

"She'll need an overcoat."

"I can fix that all right."

She dressed the dummy quickly, while he stood watching. "No underwear?" he said. He whistled, wagging his head. "How about the veil?"

"I'll have to cobble one."

She found a small black hat and dug out of the sewing machine some black net. When she had the dummy veiled and pushed back on the couch Bo cackled. "That's the goods," he said. "Put her behind sidecurtains and guys'll be flirting with her."

Elsa looked at him and shook her head. "For a man in a dangerous business, you try more fool kid tricks than anyone I ever saw," she said.

At nine that night he pulled up in front of the house Heimie and his outfit had rented the month before. It was an old house that had formerly had some connection with a silver smelter. The two-hundred-foot stack, all that still stood of the smelter, soared out of the bottom of the lot close to the river.

Bo sat in the car, in the shadow of the overgrown lilac bushes, looking the place over. It was a good house, way off the main track. The only thing Heimie would have to watch would be kids prowling around in the summertime. But it was extra good as far as the smell was concerned. Heimie had never said he was running a still, but it was plain enough.

His feet crunched in broken glass and rubbish in the path. The house was completely dark. When he tapped with the heavy brass knocker the noise echoed inside. He waited.

"Who is it?" a voice said through the door.

"Mason."

The bolt was shot, and the door opened. "You got the stuff here?" the man inside said.

"In the car."

"Just a minute, I'll help you." The man stepped back and shut the basement door, from which a little light and a strong smell of mash came up. "Heimie said you'd be along," he said, coming out on the porch. "He wants you to wait till he gets back."

"When'll he be here?"

"He ought to be along pretty quick."

They took a case apiece inside, and Bo went back for the third. The man locked the door and took Bo's arm. "Come on down here."

He led Bo down the basement steps, the light brightening as they went, the mash smell thickening. The furnace, like a great octopus, hid the source of the light. When they got around it Bo saw a row of oak kegs, two oak barrels with boards across them to form a table, two men sitting against the wall with glasses in their hands. The light came over a low partition, where the still must be.

One of the men, the small dark one, made a motion with his glass. "Hi," he said. The other slouched back against the wall and barely nodded. He had a heavy-jawed face with a smudge of black beard, and he looked tough. The one who had brought him downstairs, now that he saw him in the light, he recognized. Beans McGovern, a small-time thug.

"Got it snug down here," Bo said, and shook off his overcoat.

"Furnace makes it nice," McGovern said. "Have a drink?"

"Thanks."

"This is Joe Underwood," McGovern said, waving at the heavy-jawed man. "Used to work out of Butte. This is Blackie Holmes. Bo Mason." He poured a glass from a jug and handed it across the boards.

Underwood was watching Bo steadily. He had a slight cast in one eye. Bo was instantaneously reminded of the cop who had been killed in Little Chi a week before. This was the kind of cookie that might have done that sort of job. At best he was a bouncer. At worst he might be a hatchet man.

"Heimie tells me you just been north," McGovern said. He squatted on a keg and tipped it back carefully against the wall.

Bo nodded.

"Still doing the old land office business in Govenlock?"

"They got a warehouse big as a freight yard," Bo said. "And their ideas are getting as big as the warehouse. Hiked the price of Scotch eight bucks a case this time."

"There wasn't any raise last time I was up there," Underwood said. He spoke flatly, without lifting his voice or changing his position against the wall, but there was a challenge there, a hard deliberate will to pick a fight. The thought that he might be in a trap, that Heimie might have fixed all this up, made Bo slow to answer. He sipped his drink, getting a look all around through half-closed eyes over the rim of the glass. He moved a little so that his back was to the furnace. "When were you up there last?" he said.

"Ten days ago."

"They raised it on the first, they said."

"I hadn't heard about it from anybody else," Underwood said.

Bo deliberately drained his glass and put it down. "Then you haven't been talking to the people that know."

McGovern cut in. "Heimie says you're slick at getting back and forth."

"I manage to make a few trips," Bo said.

"Sixteen loads without a knock-over," McGovern said. "You must have all the cops fixed."

"I was talking with a prohi that works the Chinook territory," Underwood's flat voice said. "He was telling me he chased a guy a month or so ago, so close he could hear the guy banging over the bumps up ahead, running without lights, and then all of a sudden the guy vanished. The prohi tried every crossroad for ten miles up and down, no go. Just evaporated."

Bo looked at him steadily. This bird knew something. His tone, however, had got less nasty since McGovern had cut in a minute ago. Still it wasn't good. Something was behind that first tone, and behind this little probing, apparently aimless, conversation. "That was me," Bo said. "That sonofabitch cost me three cases in break-age."

Blackie Holmes squirmed his back against the wall. "What did you do, take a disappearing powder?"

"I missed a bridge," Bo said. "I was loaded so heavy behind I just sailed out flat as an airplane and lit in the bottom on all four wheels. Blew out every tire. So I sat there while the prohi ran up and down a while, and then I came in on the rims."

McGovern wagged his head and spat at the base of the furnace. "Lucky!" he said.

"That was the one time," Bo said, his eyes steady on Underwood, "when I took advice about a road. From a guy at the warehouse in Govenlock. He wouldn't be a friend of your prohi friend from Chinook, would he?"

He held Underwood's eye, or tried to, but Underwood had the advantage of the slight cast. It was hard to tell whether he was looking at you or past you. "I don't keep track of any prohi's friends," Underwood said.

After a minute Bo took his eyes off him. He had lost the feeling of being in a trap, but he was surer than ever that this Underwood was not only dangerous, but was deliberately making himself look dangerous. It was perfectly possible that Underwood was the stool who was responsible for all the knock-overs at the line. He was in the business, he would have hot tips on who was coming through, and when.

McGovern raised a hand. "Somebody on the door?" he said.

He went upstairs fast, his sneakers thudding softly on the treads. Bo heard the door open. Steps came down the stairs, and Heimie appeared around the furnace, ducking his head and shuddering his shoulders together.

"Jesus, it's getting cold," he said. "Hi, Bo. Hi, boys. How's every little thing?"

"Can't kick," Bo said. Underwood nodded. Holmes raised his glass. Heimie rubbed his hands together, reached up and felt the furnace pipe over his head, stood reaching with both hands against the warm tin. "I just been talking to Bill Burman from Kalispell," he said. "You remember, I told you this morning I was going to see him."

Bo nodded.

"He's a bright boy," Heimie said. "Made me a proposition sounds pretty good."

"Better take it then," Bo said. Heimie took his hands from the pipe, flapping and slapping them from loose wrists. He moved around jerkily, smiling.

"He's got a lot of know-how," he said. "There's only one way this racket can be made to pay big and keep on paying big. This'll interest you, Bo."

Bo waited. He looked at Underwood, slumped down, almost lying, against the wall, his face in shadow.

"This is how Bill lays it out," Heimie said, "and it ain't bushwah. The Federals are getting tough, and the state and city are beginning to work with 'em. You can pay off the city and maybe some of the state, but the Federals are hard to get at, and every once in a while they're going to knock you over. Lose your car, lose your load, pay a big fine. There's no percentage in it."

"Not unless you stay out of their way," Bo said.

"Yeah," said Heimie, "but you can't. So Bill lays out a proposition for some big-time distribution that's a honey. We've got the connections here, see? Here and in Havre. Bill's got 'em in Kalispell and Helena. That's four good towns. We can work into Butte later, after we get organized. We have a bunch of guys to bring it in from the line, we have another bunch to truck it around where it's needed. When one town gets loaded up we drain it off to the others. Take about ten guys, we could supply the whole state with stuff. Anybody gets in a jam, we spring him, hire a lawyer that can play all the cards. How's that sound?"

"Sounds all right for the guys that don't take the chances," Bo said.

"It's all right for everybody," Heimie said. "Look what you get: You get protection in town, and that'll be foolproof. And if the state or Federals gets hot and you get knocked over, the organization pays your lawyer, pays your fine, sets you up to a new car and puts you back to work. You can't lose."

"How much would a man make?" Bo said. "That's the angle I'm interested in."

"That'd have to be figured out."

"It looks like a guy could make about twice as much alone."

Heimie put his hands up to the pipe again, took them down to remove his overcoat. He had changed clothes since morning, and the shirt he wore now was whitest silk. When he opened his coat to smooth out his shirttails Bo saw the blue embroidered butterfly on the shirt pocket. "A guy alone could make more," Heimie said, "until he got knocked over. Then he could lose about five times as much. And it's a cinch that any man working alone is going to get knocked over oftener than if he works with us." His eyes strayed over to Underwood, sprawling against the partition, and Underwood met his look.

Bo sat still, as if considering. They made it clear enough. The

345

threat was doubly underlined. Rising and stretching, Bo smiled into Heimie's pale, widow's-peaked face. "Yeah," he said. "It sounds like a good layout. You want me to come in, is that it?"

"You'd be doing yourself and us both a favor," Heimie said. "When you planning to get going?"

"Right away. We've already got this place for a depot. Bill's got another in Kalispell. We've got everything we need except the organization, and that shouldn't take long."

"Well, you let me know," Bo said. "When you get things moving, call me up."

"I'm asking you in right now," Heimie said. "There's a beautiful chance to get rid of this Scotch of yours in Helena. Bill could move it like water down a drain."

Bo let his eye drift over the others as he reached out a cigar. Underwood was sitting up. Holmes had his glass to his lips, watching Heimie over the rim. McGovern was slouched against a barrel, watching.

"I couldn't come in with this load," Bo said. "I've got this promised. Suppose I think it over and let you know next week."

The point of Heimie's widow's peak moved down, then back, and he shrugged. "There's such a thing as waiting too long."

"I guess I'll have to take that chance," Bo said. "I can't go back on the promises I've already made."

For a moment they looked at each other, then Heimie shrugged again. With his overcoat thrown around his shoulders like a cape he followed Bo up the stairs and into the dark hall. The cold pushed in in a solid, moving mass as Heimie shot the bolt and opened the front door.

"There's one thing I want to know before I do anything," Bo said. "That's about this Underwood cookie."

"What about him?"

"He's a stool."

He could not see Heimie's face, but Heimie's low laugh filled the hall. "He knows which side his bread is buttered on," he said. "You don't need to worry about him."

"Far as I'm concerned," Bo said, "a stool pigeon is like a clay pigeon. He can fly any way he's pushed."

"I said don't worry," Heimie said. "I've got enough on that bruiser to make him be a good dog."

"Yeah," Bo said. "Well, long as you're sure."

"If that was what bothered you, why don't you come in now and get on the gravy boat?"

In the dark Bo stood for a minute silent. "I'll have to see you

346

about that next week," he said. "And I'll have to have the dough for these three now. I need it."

Without a word Heimie shut the door, snapped on a little blue light, and counted out the money. He laughed. "Anything you ask for you get," he said. "That's the way this new outfit works."

"That's a good start," Bo said. "Well, see you next week."

"You going to be in town all week?"

"Yeah," Bo said. "I'll be around."

"I'll call you if anything hot comes up."

"Okay."

He went out down the rubbishy path, the night very dark, with a chilly, searching wind. His eyes were narrowed and his blood hot with rage. Come in with us little shyster crooks or get run out of business. Come in and be our errand boy, driving a truck in our transfer business. Take all the chances for little piddling wages and we'll bail you out of the hoosegow when you get caught! Wasn't it a dandy! Why, the dirty little pimping son of a bitch . . .

But it would pay to be careful. It would pay to be careful as hell. Underwood had been planted there to scare him, but if he didn't scare then Underwood might be used for other things. It was complicated and dangerous, and by the time he pulled into the garage he had decided not to leave the next morning as he had planned. It wasn't too far-fetched to believe that Heimie might try to stool him off. That might happen either at home or on the road, but he had to take that chance. He'd better lie low for a day and slip out when the coast looked clear.

2

From the back door Bo looked out across the yard, across the alley to the back hedge of a house on the next street, up to the corner where the street light had just come on, dim and popping in the November dusk. There was no one in sight; the fresh and slightly smoky air made him anxious to start. He had already been lying around the house too long, just because of Heimie and his gang of two-by-four toughs. The car was loaded, the Wyoming plate installed, the dummy in the front seat.

He went back into the kitchen and picked up his overcoat. "Guess I'll be going," he said. Elsa dried her hands and left the sink to call the boys in from the front room.

They came out, Chet tossing his new football. "Goodbye, Pa," they said, like parrots. Bo looked at them, Chet husky, stringy with muscle, the younger one thin, puny actually, with staring hungry eyes and spindly legs.

"So long, kids," he said. "You mind your mother now, while I'm gone."

As they stood looking at him he had a feeling that they were a thousand miles away, unreachable; they were strangers who studied him critically and without affection. He reached back into his hip pocket and got the wallet. "Brucie, you didn't get anything to match Chet's football. What do you want?"

"I don't know," Bruce said. A wavering grin split his face and he threw a quick, triumphant look at Chet. "A Boy Scout hat, maybe."

"You aren't old enough to be a scout," Chet said.

"Well, I can wear a scout hat, can't I?"

"How much this hat cost?" Bo said.

"I don't know."

"Here," Bo said, and laid a five dollar bill in Elsa's hand. "Get him his hat. That'll make everything even."

He stooped and kissed both boys, and under his hands their slight bodies were stiff and unemotional. Obscurely baffled, he roughed their hair once, put his arm around Elsa, and led her to the door. He kissed her long and hard, the boys watching. "I'll be about a week," he said. "Don't worry, now. All I have to do is unload and turn right around and come back. I'll be hightailing it all the way."

"Goodbye," she said. "Please be careful."

He squeezed her arm and ducked out under the trellis, and she followed to close the garage doors after him. As he drove out the alley he saw her standing with her hand on the door, watching after him, and the picture struck him as somehow pathetic. These trips were pretty hard on her.

And that was the last he thought about his family. He let them slide out of his mind, concentrated on getting out of town, covering ground. If Heimie had posted any prohis on the road they'd be tired of it and gone by now, after a day and a half. Just the same, he wouldn't go down the good road to Helena and Three Forks. He'd cut over the Little Belt Mountains and hit Livingston that way. It was a bad road to run with a load on, but it was shorter.

"How about it?" he said to the dark dummy at his side. "Want to take a little trip through the mountains?" He nudged her, and she tilted stiffly against the side. "Okay," he said. "You don't have to be scared of me, chicken."

Out of town, past street lamps and houses, the road clear now and deserted, planing into whiteness under the lights, the weeds brittle in the passing glare along the roadside, the country ahead and aside and behind all dark and lost and only the ribbon of glare-lighted road slipping visible into invisible, real into unreal. The driver of an automobile on a lonely road is a set of perceptions mounted in the forehead of a mechanical monster. The air that comes through the sidecurtains is the air of another planet, the only real world is the narrow cabin from which he sees unreal shapes writhe by, fences and trees and bridge rails, the mouths of culverts jammed with tumbleweed, the snaky road with its parallel-and-then-unparallel lines, the ruts of rainy drivers still unerased and serpentining between the even boundaries of the grade. Those flashes of the unreal world become before long completely absorbing; the eye clings to them, is filled and satisfied by them; the brain asks no other business than to see. A car approaches with glaring lights, and the world broadens momentarily into an alley of pasture and creek bottom and three sleeping horses behind a three-strand fence, and then dark again, the headlights fingering the unknown sides of the world as it slips by. I see, said he, the elephant is very like a wall, like a board fence, like a man with a flashlight in an immense dark barn, like a moving picture reel unwinding too fast, catching fire, going black again. I see, said he, the elephant. I see . . .

The Essex rides heavily, rolling with the dips like a laden barge. The speedometer shows, on this stretch of fairly smooth grade, forty miles an hour. The ammeter, with the lights on, reads minus five. In the cold night the motor sounds sweet, sounds contented and purring. And the eyes sit above the wheeling car, immensely lofty and percipient, watching the irregular unravelling of the road. The hands are loose on the wheel, the body relaxed. The lights of a car a good distance behind glint in the cop-spotting rear-view mirror, and the hand reaches up to turn the mirror sideways.

A hundred and seventy-five miles to Livingston by this road, fifty less than by Helena, but a steep pull over Kings Hill Pass and a bad road down the other side. Seven o'clock when he started: budget eight hours to Livingston. With luck he might better it.

The streets of Belt, a few men on the sidewalk before a poolhall, their breath white under the arc light; a block of stores, square false fronts, then shacks, weeds, sweet clover fields, the town dump, the highway again. Little towns were all alike. You could be dropped into any one of them anywhere and swear you'd lived there one time or another.

As he swung into the little village of Armington, the lights from the car behind glinted again in the mirror, and a tiny, watchful alertness awakened in his mind. The outskirts, the dump, the foot pressing down harder on the round button of the accelerator, and the eyes watchful in the readjusted mirror. Then the brakes, the hard shuddering stop, the craning from the dark cabin to see which of the two forks, and the swing to the right, leaving the hard high-crowned road. Now the perceptive apparatus mounted in the forehead of the beast tightened and quickened, because those lights behind might mean a chase, and a chase on this unmarked trail was dangerous. There was every chance that when you came to a bridge there would be a plank out, or the bridge itself gone, or that the approach on either side might have a chuckhole hell-deep that would drop your heavy breakable load like a jug into a quarry, snap your brittle and overloaded springs, break an axle. The speedometer now, even with the lights behind to drive him on, read only twenty-five.

He watched the mirror, saw the lights break into the open around a hill, saw them move on past the forks and on down the main highway. His breath came easier, and he eased up on the throttle. False alarm.

No more towns now till Neihart, up in the mountains forty miles or so, and beyond Neihart nothing till White Sulphur. He crossed a creek, and after ten minutes crossed it again. A hundred yards further on he recrossed it on a wobbly log bridge. The road tilted under the lights. He was starting to climb. On his left he saw a hill blacker than the sky. He shifted his weight in the seat and took a new grip on the wheel.

"Wouldn't be so bad," he said to the silent dummy, "if there was any way of knowing what's up ahead of where your lights hit. Keeps you on a strain all the time. Or are you interested?"

"Sure," the dummy said. "Get it off your chest."

"It's the worst part of this business," Bo said. "You have to make time, and you're always having to do it on roads that'll break your neck if you go over twenty. Still you got to do thirty or thirty-five on them. You can't stop anywhere and take a snooze because somebody might come snooping around. Sometimes you have to drive thirty hours at a stretch, and every damn mile of it full of bends and chuckholes and narrow bridges and mud. It's the roads that make this business tough. Give me good roads and I'd make two thousand a month without turning a hair."

"You don't say," said the dummy.

Bo's foot smacked on the brake pedal, the loaded tonneau surged up behind him, the dummy lurched sideways. He shifted, crawled through a wash, flattened out again, reached out to straighten the tipped dummy.

"I've learned a hell of a lot about automobiles since I got into this, though," he said conversationally. "One time I broke an axle in Wolf Creek Canyon above Helena, and I had to cache the load in the sagebrush and tear down the rear end and walk back to where I could telephone for a new ax, and then I had to put her in and reload. And I only lost seven hours altogether."

"You're good," the dummy said. "Why don't you post these things up on a billboard?"

"The hell with you. Another time I broke a spring leaf and didn't know it till it slipped in against the brake drum and locked me tighter than a clam. And over by Havre I blew a gasket and had to pull the head in the middle of the night by the light of a candle and a box of safety matches."

"My word!" the dummy said.

Bo, leaning over the wheel, peering into the unreal darkness ahead, trying to jump his vision ahead of the lights, anticipate the curves, guess the bumps, his foot tender yet insistent on the throttle-head, saw his own face dimly reflected in the windshield, and thumbed his nose at it.

"You're a pretty smart girl," he said to the dummy. "But you don't know how much I've made in the last six months, just by being able to get over roads better than most, and patch up a car better than most, and stay awake longer than most."

"I couldn't begin to guess," the dummy said. "A million?"

"Just give me time," Bo said. "Give me a little more time."

"Well, how much have you made?"

His eyes and his mechanical hands and feet still busy, Bo let his mind turn into an adding machine. Sixteen loads, and he must have averaged five or six hundred dollars profit a load. That was around eight thousand, and expenses and breakage and a little fixing of a deputy or two would knock off about fifteen hundred. Say sixty-five hundred, and he owned this car and this load, and here was thirty cases of Scotch all arranged for at seventy-five a case. He'd come back from Omaha with a cold two thousand in his jeans, and his bank balance of cash was already over four thousand.

"It's better than picking gooseberries at a dime a quart," he said. "If they leave me alone for a year I'll be in the money good and plenty."

"I wish I'd ever meet them after they got into the money instead of when they're just going to get in," the dummy said. "Every guy I meet is right on the edge of making a killing. I'm jinxed, I guess."

"Stick around," Bo said. "Stick around a year."

"Uh-huh," the dummy said. "And what about Heimie Hellman

and his little band of Boy Scouts? Are you going to play ball with that outfit?"

With a wrench of the elbows Bo pulled the Essex around a hook in the road. His headlights, bursting into space, touched a steep wall with small black spruces toe-nailed into it, and his nose, joining his perceptive faculties for the first time, sniffed at the balsamy smell. He was in the pass. The motor labored. He shifted into second and gave it a good goose before shifting back.

"I don't know," he said. "I don't know what about that bunch. They can make trouble if they try."

"But you don't think they'll try," said the dummy. "You'll say 'Boys, you're going to make me uncomfortable if you try any squeeze plays,' and then they'll back away and say, 'Beg pardon, we wouldn't want to put you out.'"

"Yeah, like hell," Bo said.

"Well, what are you going to do?"

"I don't know," Bo said. "If I buck 'em, they stool me off, and if I try stooling them off to protect myself I run into a lot of cops and prosecutors Heimie and his gang own."

"And if you play ball with them," the dummy said, "you don't get anything but wages out of it, and you're all tied in with a bunch of pimps and strongarm men."

"Yeah," he said. "Suppose you take a nap. I can think of people I'd rather talk to."

"And if you try to buck them," the dummy said, "you haven't got enough customers without using Heimie's outlets, even if you could keep out of the law's way."

"I guess I could get customers," Bo said. "I guess good straight stuff at a fair price would take Heimie's customers away from his watered-down Scotch and rotgut moon."

"And some guy like Underwood might take you away from the bosom of your family, too," the dummy said. "Those guys wouldn't stop at murder. How long would you last? You make me laugh. You and your big money. You know what I think?"

"I don't know that I care," he said.

"I think they've got you," the dummy said. "I think this is your last trip on your own."

"Oh, shut up!" he said. "I'll be running whiskey when you're back in some department store window showing off your legs."

"You'll be running it for Heimie," she said. "You and your big ideas of being your own boss. Bushwah. You'll be taking orders from that pimp in the embroidered shirts."

"Shut up!" he said again, and for a half hour he drove in silence, sullenly, his mind edging up to the problem, finding a wall, blowing up in anger, edging up again at a different point. But it was all wall. His eyes strained out through the windshield, splashed and pebbled now with muddy water from a wash he had forded. The world unrolled in steep blackness beyond the fleeting glow of the lights, and the beam picked up an occasional timbered or rocky slope, a bank rose perpendicularly on his right and the road narrowed to two rocky ruts that apparently ended dead against the mountain. I see, said he, the elephant is very like a wall. I see, I see . . .

If you could only know what was on the other side of the light's beam, if you could see far enough ahead to take the strain off, you could make two thousand a month without turning a hair. His mind crept out toward the wall again, and he jerked it away. Through the slits in the sidecurtains came the strong smell of pines, and the Essex labored on the grade.

Entering Neihart, up in the pine woods, he eased up on the throttle, looking for a garage where he might get gas, a café where he could wash away the fuzzy feeling in his head with a cup of coffee. There was only one garage, with two gas drums on wooden supports and another drum marked "Oil." As he pulled in he caught the reflection from the headlights of a car parked against the side, facing out. He swung a little to bring his lights on it. Empty.

A man came to the door holding a lantern shoulder high. "Gas," Bo said, and climbed out, shutting the door on the shrouded dummy.

"You bet," the man said. He took a five-gallon can and began to fill it at one of the drums. "How many?"

"She'll hold five all right."

"You bet." He concentrated on the pour from the drum's spout. "Just closin' up. Don't many people come through this late."

Bo grunted, standing by the door to block off the man's view of the dummy.

"You're the third in the last hour," the man said. "Funny how some nights they come all in a covey and some nights I sit from supper time till eleven and not a one shows up."

"The others go on through?"

"One did. The other's right here against the wall. Couple fellas in it. Went on over for a cup of coffee."

His mind instantly alert and suspicious, Bo dug a couple of silver dollars from his pocket and laid them in the garage man's hand. Two men, driving a back road at night, parking nose out by a garage wall, didn't look good. It looked like law, either law or another bootlegger. And a bootlegger wouldn't leave his car like that. He watched the café across the street, but there was only the shadow of the counter man moving up and down behind the dirty window.

He took his change, gathered his overcoat around his hips, and slid in. "Come again," the garage man said. Bo pulled away. The trail climbed steadily, second gear much of it, and many curves, the roadbed deeply washed, exposing the solid rock in places. It was no road to make time on, but he rode the throttle anyway. Whoever was waiting back there was asleep at the switch, there was that to be thankful for.

But at the top of a long swinging hairpin he looked back and saw the moving lights of a car.

He swore, clicked off the dash light in order to see better. The road climbed up and up and up, a rocky shelf in the mountain's side. Sometime soon he should hit the top of the pass and start down, and on the other side it was better, not so steep or crooked. But he had to make the pass first: on this side, with a load on, he was at a disadvantage.

When he next looked back the lights were out of sight, but at the next bend he saw them burst around a corner, already closer, coming up on him like a house afire. He swore and slid the Essex into low, got a start over a steep pitch, slipped into second and stayed there, gunning it, the speedometer needle trembling around thirty. His arms and shoulders were set like cement. "By God," he said to the dummy, "if that's the law they're going to have a ride."

Skidding on a curve, he felt the weight of the car haul him sideways, settle, come back to center. The tires shot gravel like bullets up under the fenders. Then there was a flattening, a dropping, the road ahead tilted flat, tilted down. He shifted and settled himself. It was a horserace now. With one eye on the mirror he counted, waiting for the lights. He was up to thirty-eight when they blazed over the rim, diffused among the pines. That settled it. They hadn't lost much, if any. And nobody would drive as fast as he was driving without good reason, on that road.

He felt in his overcoat pocket for a box of roofing nails. "Looks like we've got to give these prohis a headache," he said to the dummy.

Driving with one hand, he ripped the end out of the box and shook into his palm a heavy weight of nails, big-headed, an inch and a half long. He unbuttoned the sidecurtain all down one side, losing time in doing so, and when he was ready he saw that the lights had gained more.

"Well, let's see if you can be slowed down a little!" he said. With a twisting, upward heave he threw the handful of nails back over the car's top, so that they would land in the center of the road. Another handful, then another, then another, until he had emptied the box and gathered up all the loose nails in his lap. Then he threw the box out the window and started crowding it again.

"It'll take a little while," he told the dummy. "The nails'll plug their own holes for a while. But pretty soon they start ripping the tube, and then those guys are going to have a nice long walk."

"You're pretty cagey," the dummy said. "You got out of that better than I thought you would."

"Let's hold the celebrating for a while," Bo said. "We may have to sow a few more seeds of kindness."

The light was still behind them, growing, snuffing out again, seeming not to move very fast, but keeping up, not more than a half mile behind. The road levelled out, and he took the stretch at a run, hitting it up to fifty, pouring his weight recklessly on the throttle. At the slightest beginning of a bend he eased up. The quickest way to get nabbed was to wreck yourself.

He could see no lights now. The road swung left, then right, and his own lights showed him rounded grassy hills instead of the rocks and pines of the pass. He was getting down. He watched the mir-ror, waiting for the flash. None came.

"You must have got 'em," the dummy said.

"Maybe."

He kept looking back, but all the way down out of the hills the road behind was black, part of that unknown and unreal world the single lighted reality of the Essex hurtled through. It was all right. Those cookies were sitting on their running board right now cuss-ing. And he hadn't even hit a bump hard enough to shift the load or break a bottle.

Still, he had been chased, and the pit of his stomach was even yet a small, pulsating, sensitive hole. He breathed his lungs full and yelled aloud, letting off pressure. After a while he began to sing.

When he had sung himself normal again he slid down in the seat, pulled the gas lever down, and rested his throttle foot, wig-gling it to limber the ankle. "I wonder," he said to the dummy, "if those prohis were tipped off by our friend Heimie."

"He'd have had to work fast."

"It doesn't take long to put in a telephone call," Bo said. "Only thing is, how would he know what road I was taking, and when I was leaving?"

"He could have had your house watched," the dummy said. "And for that matter, remember the lights that followed you down to the fork past Armington? Suppose one of Heimie's boys was in that, just tailing you to see which road you took? Once you were on this road you couldn't get off."

"By God," Bo said, "there might be something in that."

"But if that's the way it was," the dummy said, "those guys in Neihart would have known within a few minutes when you'd be there. Wouldn't you expect them to be parked across a bridge waiting to stop you?"

"Yes," Bo said. "I would. I don't savvy this business at all. You'd say those guys were chasing us, wouldn't you?"

"They weren't out driving for their health."

"No. So they must just have got careless and let me get through and then tried to catch me."

He began snapping up the sidecurtain, hearing through the opening the noise of the tires, the flip and pop of pebbles, the swish of running rubber. It would have been the easiest thing in the world for him to blow a tire himself hitting that road the way he had. A last look behind showed him only the empty face of the dark, and he buttoned himself in.

He came to a fork and stopped. There were no signs, but the main travelled road led on. The other must cut off to Harlowtown. There was only one thing to do, when he didn't know the country. He took the main road.

His watch said a quarter of one. He must be more than half way to Livingston. He might make Billings for breakfast. Or he might, if he found the road good that way, cut down through Yellowstone and angle across Wyoming until he hit the Lincoln Highway. That would put him a long way around Sheridan, just on the chance Heimie's tip had been worth anything.

"How about it?" he said. "Want to see Yellowstone Park, baby?"

"It wouldn't be open," the dummy reminded him.

"We could circle around it. There's a road down the west side. Or there's one cuts over into Wyoming near the east entrance, around Cody. That'd be better."

"Save your plans till we get past Livingston," the dummy said. "Once we're that far we're past anything Heimie might have had up his sleeve, and then we can really make it a honeymoon."

Bo settled back, relaxed into the torpor of driving, the unthinking suspension of mind; became once more the set of faculties in the forehead of the beast, eyes and ears for the road and the motor, hands for the steering. He noticed that they were in a flat of some kind, probably a river valley. Thin willows slid by, the road became wallowed sand. He shifted as a precaution, and a moment later came to a peering stop as the road disappeared and became merely two planks with two-by-four flanges, a skimpy skeleton of a bridge walking a foot above the deep sand of the riverbed. It was hardly wider than a railroad track, but perfectly safe and solid if taken easy. He eased out onto the planks. It was like driving on an extended grease rack.

The new sensation jogged him, and he sat up. "This is one way to make a road," he said to the dummy. "Damn if it isn't a pretty good idea, long as nobody's coming the other way."

He peered out, trying to see if there was water underneath, but all he could see was dimly luminous white sand and the occasional dark blob of willows. But he stared so persistently, trying to make out what it was he was crossing, that he almost ran into the obstruction in the road.

His foot slapped on the brake, the Essex halted with its nose almost against the barrier, and in the light he saw the stack of railroad ties three feet high laid across the planks. A trap. He knew it instantly, coldly, furiously, even before he saw the shadows start up from beside the road. Before he heard their shout he had slammed the Essex into reverse and was backing up, tightrope-walking the narrow planks, driving blind, by ear, by feel, his breath stilled in his chest and one arm rigid across the wheel, the other ripping the sidecurtain out so that he might lean out and crane, steering by the gleam, the glimmer of his tail light. He felt the tires start up on the low flange of two-by-four and then pinch down again, but his foot on the throttle didn't relax. The car roared full speed backward into the dark along the car-track road.

The figures which had leaped from the roadside were running after him. Out of the very periphery of his vision he saw one stumble and go headlong off the runway, and he heard them yelling. The first shot throbbed in his ears, but it didn't mean anything. All that meant anything was the tight wire of plank unreeling under his left hind wheel. If he could hold her on it, get back to the road, he had a chance yet. They would lose time getting to their car, wherever it was. He could run back to the Harlowtown fork, cut down on that . . .

Lights blazing, he was a beautiful target, but he didn't dare switch them off. He needed their glow. Pink flashes stabbed the dark, but the running figures were dropping behind, and his blood leaped. Another hundred feet, and he would have outrun them, even in reverse. Then a quick turn, a dash back to the forks . . .

The wheel kicked out of his hand, numbing his locked wrist, and the front wheels were wrenched up and sideways, swerving the car, bucking it up over the flange, dropping it down awkwardly angled across the tracks. There was a heavy crunch from the shifting load, and for a moment the car hung uncertainly, about to go over, before it settled back.

Before it had quite settled Bo was on the ground, crouching. The Essex sat with its front wheels high, the tires still revolving slowly. The headlights burned like furious eyes up into the black. He heard the pound of feet sodden in the sand, and with no more than a second's hesitation he turned and ran.

3

He came so quietly that she didn't hear him at all. She simply looked up and he was there, his face blackened with new beard, his overcoat ripped from one pocket halfway to the hem. In the instant when their eyes met it crossed her mind that if he had not been her husband she would have been frightened to death at his face.

"Bo . . . ?"

He sat down and stared at her. His trousers, she saw, were also ripped, and there were scabbed scratches on hands and wrists. He made a disgusted sound and spread his hands. "Kapoot," he said. "Gone. Load, car, everything."

She said the thing that was instantaneous in her mind. "But they didn't catch *you!*"

His stare was almost contemptuous. "They weren't after me. They could have had me if they'd half tried."

"I don't understand," she said.

"It wasn't the law."

"Then who?"

"Hijackers."

He had straightened it out in his mind on the way back. The pieces fitted. First that car tailing him out of Great Falls, seeing which road he went. Then the two waiting in Neihart, letting him go by, closing in behind him. Then the barricade. It was neatly planned, and far enough away from everything so that there was no chance of anyone blundering by and spoiling it.

"I should have caught on in Neihart," he said. "That's where I saw the car parked against the garage." He rubbed his emory-paper jaw, the story coming out past the tips of his teeth. "I still thought they were law, then. By Christ, I don't know what was the matter with me. I ought to have my head examined."

"But . . ." she began, and even that one word of expostulation or lack of understanding made him furious.

"Does it stand to reason that two cops would sit in a town waiting for me, knowing I was coming in a few minutes, and then go

358

over for a cup of coffee and let me slide right on by? Does that sound like sense?"

"No," she said. "I just . . ."

"It isn't sense," he said. "Those guys didn't want me there, either. They just wanted to let me past so I could run down into their little trap. They weren't taking any chances of me getting away, I'll say that for them."

"But how could they know so well?" Elsa said. "It sounds as if they knew every minute what you were going to do."

"They did."

"But who could have?"

"There's only one son of a bitch in Montana that could have known or guessed that much."

"Heimie?"

"Heimie."

"Now what?" she said, watching him steadily. "Are they after you?"

"I don't know. I doubt it."

"What will we do if they are?"

"I don't think they are. I think this is Heimie's little way of inducing me to come in with his crowd."

"You won't," she said.

"I don't know. If we want to stay in this town we may have to."

"Then let's not stay in this town!" Elsa said. There were tears in her eyes. "I don't want to see you mixed up with those people. They're criminals, they'd rob and murder and do anything. You don't want to go in with them, Bo. You know you don't."

"You're exactly right," Bo said. "But what are we going to do?" He stood up impatiently, fingering the gash in his overcoat, his eyes vague and troubled. "I don't know," he said. "I've got to figure it out. All I know is that if there's a good chance to get even with that little silk-shirted bastard I'm going to."

"You'll get yourself killed."

"Not if I'm careful."

She shivered and half turned. "You didn't tell me how you got away."

"No," Bo said, his words heavy as iron. "I didn't tell you and I'm not going to." The fury in him broke out, and he swung around shouting. "How would I get away? I ran like a God damned jackrabbit. I plowed through sand and tore through brush and walked a thousand miles and hooked a ride on a home-steader's wagon. How the hell would I get away? Fly?"

"I'm sorry," she said quietly. It didn't do to question him when he was sore. Whenever anything went wrong he butted against it like a ram, and the worse it went the more violent and stubborn he got, and though he generally got through, the effort outraged something deep and furious in him. He would never learn to climb over or go around. He had to butt right through, and when he got his head hurt he was untouchable.

But the car gone, and the whole load, two or three thousand dollars gone as surely as if they had taken the sum in hundred dollar bills and touched a match to them. It served her right. She had been thinking of that bank balance almost in the same terms Bo had. She had been seeing ultimate security and emancipation in it. It was just as well for her to learn that security was not there, that the whole thing could disappear like mist touched by the sun.

"I'm going to bed," Bo said. "If anybody calls or comes around, I'm out of town and you don't know when I'll be back."

Three days later he hunted up Heimie in the Smoke Shop. Heimie, elegant in a lavender silk shirt, pinstripe suit, yellow shoes, had a greeting as mellow as syrup. He led Bo into the back room and sent the counter man for a bottle.

"You made a quick trip," he said.

"What makes you think I've been anywhere?" Bo said, and stared at Heimie hard. Heimie shrugged and let it go.

The bottle came and Heimie poured two shots. "Here's how," he said. Bo drank, watching him. It would have been a pleasure to reach across the table and slap that light secretive smile off Heimie's mouth, but it wouldn't do. You had to know when somebody had you, or you'd wash out fast.

Heimie's smile deepened. He twirled the whiskey glass slowly. "Thought any more about that proposition?" he said.

"I'm willing to listen."

"Ah," Heimie said. "That's what I've been wanting to hear. You're too valuable a man to waste your talents working alone." Steadily smiling, inviting Bo to make a double meaning out of that if he chose, he leaned his impeccable elbows on the table and dropped his voice. "What is it you want to know, now?"

"I want to know what the proposition is," Bo said impatiently. "How do I know whether it's any good or not?"

"You want to go on hauling down from the line?"

"That's my racket," Bo said. "I don't want anything to do with any still, if that's what you mean."

"Beans can handle that all right." Heimie pursed his lips, thinking. "What would you say to a proposition like this: You haul down to us here, whole loads. You don't have to fuss around with deliveries or collections or anything. Just whole loads, dump them off and you're clean. *And* protected."

"What would I get out of it?"

"What's it worth?"

"I can make six hundred a load at least, hauling for myself."

"But you take chances," Heimie said. "You take a lot more chances. Law all over the place, and getting thicker. And they have to pinch somebody, see? They're fixed not to pinch our boys, so they have to make their reputations on the stragglers and lone wolves. It's a good setup to be in on."

"How much?" Bo said.

"What about two hundred a load?"

"Don't make me laugh."

"That's high pay, boy, for a job that's safe as a church."

"But it isn't high enough," Bo said, "and it isn't as safe as you make out. What if I got hijacked?"

He watched Heimie's face closely, but Heimie didn't tumble. His face was still smiling, faintly amused.

The organization will take that chance, not you," Heimie said. "But I don't think it's much of a risk." He grew more confidential, huddling across the table and squinting as he figured in his head. "Now look," he said, "you're the best man I know at getting in and out with stuff. We can use you, and you can use us. We'd be suckers to work against each other, but that's what we'd be doing if you didn't come in. But two hundred a load—well, make it two fifty—is damn good for what you'd be doing."

"We aren't getting anywhere," Bo said heavily. "Now I'll make *you* a proposition. I'm willing to come in, on any kind of terms that gives me a decent cut. I'll haul down from Govenlock for you for fifteen bucks a case, no less, you putting up the money for the stuff and paying me cash on the nose when I bring it in. You guarantee protection, and let me be the judge of when it's safe to make a trip. And if I don't haul for anybody but you, you'd have to furnish me a car."

"Say, now, wait a minute!" Heimie had his hands up, warding off imaginary blows. "Fifteen a case? And protection? *And* a car? You want a gold mine."

"That's what you've got," Bo said. "Why shouldn't I want one?"

"You've got an exaggerated idea of how much there is in this business," Heimie said, still playfully. He took out a pencil and figured on an envelope. "Make it twelve a case, and you furnish the car, and it's a go."

"Couldn't do it," Bo said.

"Fifteen a case would be four hundred and fifty a load."

"That's a whole lot less than I'm making now."

Heimie shook his head, at first slowly, then emphatically. "We couldn't afford that kind of money."

"Listen," Bo said. "This is a business deal, isn't it?"

"What else?"

"And I'm going to be a kind of hired man in it."

"Not exactly."

"Exactly," Bo said. "And I'll be doing the hard and the dangerous part, and you know it damn well. So I'm worth wages enough to keep me interested in working hard for you, and it's up to you to put up the car. You don't ask a truck driver to furnish his own hack."

"Suppose we did put up a car," Heimie said after a pause. "Would you haul for twelve?"

"Fifteen."

"Then I guess we can't get together." Heimie's voice grew crisp. "Twelve a case, and we'll put up a car. That's as deep as we can go. Take it or leave it?"

For a moment Bo hesitated. He didn't like it at any price, but there wasn't much else he could do. "Okay," he said finally. "I'll take it."

4

Toward the end of May Bo came home from town with his special look of excited secrecy, his air of being possessed by great schemes, which could only be divulged little by little, with suspense and the aggravation of Elsa's curiosity. He began by asking, quite casually, if she wanted to go on a little trip.

"Up to Govenlock?" she said.

"No. A real trip."

"Sure. Where?"

"Yellowstone, maybe. Salt Lake City. All around."

"You mean—just for the trip?"

"Sure."

"Kids too?"

"Kids too."

"That would be wonderful!" she said. "Can we afford it?"

Bo's wink was almost grim. "I'm going to see that we can afford it. This is where I catch up a little on Heimie and his outfit."

"Oh," she said, and her animation faded. "You mean we'll be hauling a load."

"For the love of Mike," he said, "did you think we could go off touring just for the fun of it?"

"Some people do."

"Some people are richer than we are, too. Come on out in the garage, I want to show you something."

He took her out and showed her: an auto tent, folding beds that hooked to the running boards, a food box bolted to the right front fender, with shelves and boxes and a lid that folded down for a table. "Everything the very latest," he said. "This is due to be a trip in style."

"But the kids," she said. "What if we should get caught?"

"That's just it. With the kids along we wouldn't even get stopped. No prohi is stopping families on a tour. He'd lose his job the first time he searched some big shot's car."

She was silent, and her eyes came up to meet his. "It's so much like *using* them," she said.

He snorted. "They'd have the time of their lives. We'd camp out, see some scenery, take it easy. There isn't a chance for a hitch."

"Where would we be hauling to?"

Bo smiled, his lips tight across his teeth. "Heimie wants to open up some new territory. Salt Lake City, especially. And I've been such a good dog he's sending me. It's only incidental that if I get knocked over down there he'd wash his hands of me and not know anything about any agreement. But that's all right."

"Why?" she said. "Why would you go?"

"Because I can get even with the son of a bitch," Bo said. "I'm taking his load in the car, all right, but I'm hooking on a trailer of my own."

"That's double-crossing him."

"You're damned right," Bo said. "The old double-x, just what he pulled on me."

He pulled her back to the house, talking all the time. "I'm going up to Govenlock day after tomorrow. You'll have to pack up and store what stuff we've collected. We've lived in this house long enough. Can you be ready soon as the kids are out of school?"

"I guess so," she said, "but . . ."

"But nothing. This is going to be the nicest trip you ever had."

"I know it would be fun for me. I was thinking about the kids."

"I'll bet you a hundred dollars they'd stow away if we tried to leave them behind."

She laughed uncertainly. "I guess they would, at that." Her laugh died, and she threw him a pained and anxious look. "I keep thinking of that dummy you took along once," she said. "Now you're taking all of us for the same reason. We'll all be camouflage."

He looked at her with such utter lack of comprehension that she gave up.

They pulled out in broad daylight, with the neighbors out to see them off, going publicly like any tourists, their lunch box high on the right fender, the rest of that whole side wedged with suitcases in the luggage carrier, the tent and camp beds strapped on the iron grill back of the spare tire. In the tonneau the boys' heads stuck up through a mountainous load. Bo laughed as he packed them in. "Whiskey to right of them, whiskey to left of them, whiskey on top of them gurgled and thundered," he said. Sixteen cases of whiskey, camping equipment, food, and four people were in the car. They sat on dynamite and waved goodbye to the neighbors and pulled out boldly through the town on the road to Fort Benton, and at Fort Benton, back in a dusty alley behind a warehouse, they picked up the loaded trailer carrying fourteen more cases of whiskey, and crossed the Missouri and started south. The detour to Fort Benton took them almost a half day out of their way, but it made the trailer safe. Eventually, that night, they wound up in the pass above where Bo had been hijacked in November.

The next night, after slogging all day through heavy gumbo mud, they camped in the clear evening with the sun pink on the Crazy Mountains east of them, and the next day they were in Yellowstone, one loaded car among dozens of dusty loaded cars, one family of tourists among the hundreds who peeked into the smoking caverns of geysers and tossed chocolate bars to bears and strung out behind the road construction gangs on dusty unsurfaced grades through the timber. All of that was fun. Elsa never failed to wave at cars they met or passed; they rarely failed to wave at her, and the feeling of being free and open and in society again, part of a good-natured fraternity of gypsies, pleased her almost more than the scenery.

Yellowstone took them exactly one day. In spite of his belief that he was taking it easy, seeing the sights, Bo pushed the Hudson along. A half hour was enough for the canyon, fifteen minutes apiece sufficed for two or three of the more notable geysers, ten minutes was enough to stop and feed some old robber bear. Elsa and the boys looked enviously at parties starting out on horseback, at enticing trails leading off to Mount Washburn or Cody or the Tetons. For all that, they were outside the boundaries of the park by seven the next morning, and that night they were creeping through heavy construction again on the edge of Blackfoot, Idaho.

The roadbed was almost impassable, the detours worse. When they were within sight of the trees of the town they hit a chuckhole that rocked them clear to the axle. Bo winced and gritted his teeth, and the boys whooped from the back seat, pushing the shifted load back off them.

"Smell anything?" Bo said.

Elsa sniffed. "No."

"I do," Chet said.

"God damn!" Bo said. He stopped the car and got out, sniffing over the load. "Busted one, that's sure," he said finally. "But it would be like hunting for a needle in a haystack."

"What can you do?"

"Nothing, now. If we get to a good out-of-the-way camp I can unload."

Ahead of them the late sun burned through the tops of a long line of Lombardy poplars, and the roadside was deep green and cool-smelling with alfalfa. "This is a pretty town," Elsa said. "I don't know when I've seen a town so green."

"Irrigation," Bo said.

There were ditches along the road, a wide canal running off across the meadow toward the north. When they pulled past the big U.S. ROYAL CORD scroll bearing the history of Blackfoot, Elsa said, "It would be nice if we could camp here somewhere, it's so cool and green," and five minutes later, when they came to the town tourist park, green-lawned under a canopy of trees, Bo looked at her once and pulled in. Broken bottle or no broken bottle, this was too pleasant a camp ground to miss.

They found a spot under the trees near the irrigation ditch, and after supper Bo rummaged a little in search of the broken bottle. But the load was too solid, and he didn't dare unload completely now, with tourists pulling in every few minutes and settling down for the night. A car was parked and a tent went up hardly fifty feet away. All he could do was settle everything back in and tuck quilts and blankets in tightly all around, to keep the smell as muffled as possible. By nine o'clock they were in bed.

It was barely daylight when Bo sat up abruptly, creaking the iron framework of the bed. "Hey!" a voice was saying outside the tent. "Hey, wake up!"

He poked his head through the tent flap. A man on a horse was outside, and as the horse moved, its feet splashed in the sodden grass. "What's the matter?" Bo said, wide awake now, his mind stiff with the prospect of the law.

"Ditch has busted loose," the man said. "There's already two inches of water running through here. You better pack up and get out or your car'll bog down." In the gray light he kicked his horse closer. "With that trailer, you might have trouble," he said. "I can get you a team after while if . . ."

His nostrils pinched in, dilated once. Bo, sitting up to get shoes on, saw his attention wander. That God damned smell . . .

"Thanks," he said. "We'll get out of here right now." He shouted to the boys and shook Elsa. As the rider turned away, looking back over his shoulder, Bo said, "How's the road to Ashton?"

" 'Sall right. Might be some snow up high, but the road's open."

"Thanks," Bo said again. He swung on Elsa the minute he let the tent flap fall. "Hustle!" he said. "We've got to get out of here damn fast."

"Ashton?" Elsa said, still only half awake. "Isn't that back up in Idaho?"

"Yeah."

"But . . ."

"Let it go!" Bo hissed. "That damn snooper smelled us, see? We've got to move."

He set his feet down and felt cold water as high as his ankles. The thought of the slippery lawn, the soaked topsoil, under the heavy wheels of the overloaded Hudson made him want to knock somebody down. The Hudson was no good in mud anyway. Too much power, too much weight. A lighter car would walk right through mud that would mire this elephant . . .

In ten minutes they were packed, the tent and beds and blankets thrown in hastily, any which way, on the load. Bo slid in and stepped on the starter.

"You get out and be ready to push," he said to Chet and Bruce. Elsa climbed out too, and the three braced themselves in water that flowed in a silvery sheet over the whole lawn. It had been almost fifteen minutes since the rider had left. He would have had time to get a cop and come back, if he was the kind that would turn you in. Five minutes more might be too many to delay. They had to make it out the first time or they were sunk.

A gravelled driveway circled the park, fifty or sixty feet to their left. If they could make that . . . Bo leaned out the window. "Push like the devil," he said. "Now!" He let out the clutch and felt the Hudson strain, roll. At the first sign of spinning he eased up, feeding only enough gas to keep the car moving. He heard one of the boys yell and fall down, but he kept easing it, inching it, heavy and lumbering, toward the drive. Ten feet, fifteen, three car lengths. It was like driving a loaded wagon over thin ice. The minute the wheels started to spin in mud instead of on grass, they would be in to the hubs.

The lawn sloped slightly downward, a barely perceptible dip, and then upward again to the drive. He would have to run for it. He stepped down on the throttle, felt the clumsy car spin and swerve, but gain momentum. As long as it was downhill it was all right. But he had to gun it up that slope. In fury he stamped down on the accelerator and went roaring, throwing mud and water, skidding and whipping back into line, his hind wheels digging in and his speed slowing, slowing, until he barely crept for all the noise of the motor and threshing of the wheels. His front wheels made the gravel, he swung left to ease the hill, and his hind wheels spun, dug, found something solid and pushed him two feet, spun again. Elsa and the boys came panting, threw themselves against the fenders, and gradually, painfully, inch by inch, the car crept up on hard surface until one wheel caught. Elsa jumped aside to avoid the trailer. Bruce was flat on his face in the mud, his upraised forehead spattered. Chet trotted triumphantly alongside.

Bo started again before they were half into the car. "Keep your eye peeled," he said over his shoulder. "If you see any cars behind us, you tell me."

"If he believed that Ashton business we may be all right," he said to Elsa, "but if he didn't we may have to run for it."

She looked at him with her mouth set, turned her head and looked at the boys, muddy and wet, crowding their faces against the spattered back window. They didn't look scared, they weren't bothered by what might happen. They were only excited. She sighed.

"There's a car!" Bruce said. Chet crowded him aside to see better, and they fought for the window.

"Nope," Chet said. "It's turned off again."

They clung precariously balancing on their knees while Bo drove fast down the straight road to Pocatello. On smooth stretches he took it up to sixty, and gravel spanged under the fenders, the tires whined on little curves, the trailer behind wove from side to side, the car rocked with a monumental, dangerous weight on the punished springs.

"Whoopee!" Chet yelled. He grabbed for the top brace to steady himself. Bruce, a little white around the eyes, yelled in echo, and they both screeched hysterically, drunk with excitement and speed, until Bo turned and yelled at them to shut up.

"Sit down," Elsa said quietly. "I don't think there's anybody coming now." She looked back a long time. The road was clear as far as she could see, and a white curtain of dust blew eastward to meet the sun. "You can slow down," she said to Bo. "I'm sure it's all right."

Bo let the Hudson back down to forty, looked once at her, and pressed his lips together. "That could have been bad," he said. "Scare you?"

"Yes."

So that, her mind was saying, is the end of any pretense that this is a picnic trip. Now at least we aren't trying to fool ourselves any more.

It was a day when, having started wrong, they could not do anything right. After the first hundred miles, which they made before breakfast because Bo would not stop until he was clear of possible pursuit, they made bad time. At breakfast Bruce cut himself deeply with the butcher knife, and in his surprise and pain swore furiously out loud, and Bo slapped him end over end. An hour after they had started again it clouded over and began to rain, a slow, insistent, misty drizzle. At three o'clock, after a cold lunch huddled in the car, they were descending a dugway into a river valley. A yellow delivery truck was coming up the grade toward them, hogging the road. Bo rode the horn, pulled the Hudson as far over toward the edge as he dared, and bent, swear-ing, to peer through the streaming windshield. At the last minute the truck saw them, swerved, skidded, slewed around, and shot by in second gear, and at the instant the soft clay shoulder of the bank began to give under the Hudson's rear wheels. Bo swung in and stepped on the throttle, but the weight of the car bore them down, the trailer slipped half over the edge and pulled at them, and in the end they stuck there, two wheels over the edge and the Hudson balanced precariously on its universal housing like a bal-ancing rock.

Very carefully they climbed out the upper side into the rain. Bo's jaw was set, his whole face smouldering. He went to the edge and looked down, walked rapidly up to the next curve and looked back. When he came back to Elsa he was already shooting out orders. "Chet, you run on over to that farm, see, over there on the river. See if they've got a team to pull us out of here. Bruce, you go up to the curve and watch for cars. The minute you see one, wave and yell." To Elsa he said, "There's a sheepshed or some-thing right below us. We can maybe camp there tonight, but first we got to get this damn load off and ditch it."

He was lifting a sack out of the upper side, and Elsa moved to help him. He went plowing down the slope with the sack, and even before she could get another out of the wedged load he was back. His energy was enormous. Put him in a tight spot, she thought, let him get into a place where something serious might happen, and he didn't even waste time swearing. An intense and terrible concentration came upon him. He was driven, furious, violent, but his violence got things done. In twenty minutes he cleaned out the car and cached the sacks in the sagebrush, and in another twenty he had the trailer emptied, had unhooked the coupling, and pulled the trailer by hand up onto the road. No cars or wagons had showed up. Bruce still stood huddled under a blanket at the upper curve.

"You and Bruce go down and start a fire if you can," Bo said. "I'll wait and see if Chet had any luck."

So she took blankets and quilts and went through the rain to the shed. It was open on one side, and the floor was paved with dry and trampled sheep dung, but the roof was decently sound. With damp paper and a loose board she got a fire going and hung the blankets around to dry out. Bruce stood chattering and shivering beside the little blaze, and the sight of his misery epitomized so completely her own disillusion and discomfort that she laughed.

"Well," she said. "How do you like touring?"

They looked at each other. Bruce's solemn face cracked, grinned, and they stood giggling at each other. When Chet and Bo came in to report that the farmer was gone for the day and no one had come by on the road, they were sitting half dressed drying out their clothes and eating a chocolate bar and laughing as if at some uproarious joke.

Late in the afternoon a passing wagon pulled the car off the edge, and that night, in the persistent rain, Bo lugged the sacks one by one over to the sheepshed and reloaded. Early the next afternoon they rolled around the base of Ensign Peak and looked upon the city of the Saints.

"Gee," Bruce said, standing up to see better. "This is a big town."

"Isn't it nice?" Elsa said. "It's like all the towns through here, so green and nice."

Bo stirred and sat up behind the wheel, filling his eyes with wide streets, gutters running with clean mountain water, trees in long rows down the parkways. "This is something like," he said. "There ought to be plenty doing in a town this size."

They coasted slowly through the traffic, swung eastward up a broad avenue leading to the mountains that went up sheer from the edge of the city. A gas station attendant told them there was camping in any of the canyons, and following his directions they climbed a long hill to a ledge under the steep bare peaks, from which they could look back on the city like a green forest below them, and beyond that the white salt flats and the cobalt water of Great Salt Lake far to the west.

"Quite a town," Bo said. "There'd be some point living in a town like this. This makes Great Falls look pretty dumpy."

"Onward and upward," Elsa said. "Excelsior!" As long as they had lived together they had lived in little towns, with only that one bad year in Seattle to break the pattern, and as long as they had lived together he had hated the little burgs. He wanted to get into the big time. The few months he had spent in Chicago, a cocky youngster from the sticks in the incredible metropolis, had been a scented memory all these years. The very name of a big city lighted a fire in him. "Why don't we move on down?" she said.

She said it as a joke, to twit him about the way he itched for somewhere else, but the serious stare he turned on her said that he did not think it was so funny, or even so impossible.

In the next three days she could see the idea working in him, see the progress from speculation to conviction to enthusiasm. Everything he saw and did in the city fed that fire. The three names which Heimie had given him, a shine-parlor operator, a head bellhop, and a brakeman on the D. and R.G.W., were all names that meant solid business. There was a whiskey famine. A reform administration, an active city prohibition force called the Purity Squad, and a consistent record of prosecutions and convictions for bootlegging had steered the whiskey supply to other points. The shine parlor man thought he could use four cases. The bellhop could definitely use two cases immediately, and probably more tomorrow. The brakeman could dispose of three cases as soon as they could be delivered. And all three had their fingers on the places which were good outlets for whiskey. That night Bo loaded the car with the five cases he had definitely sold, and after dark buried the rest of the load deep under the oak brush. Then he took the whiskey and his family to town, treated the four of them to a show and a sticky ice cream orgy in a confectionery store, and drove them home all singing under an incredible round moon that tipped the valley with light like an underwater forest. In his pocket was a roll of three hundred and seventy-five dollars.

In the next two days his brakemen outlet got busy, and before he was through moved twelve cases. The bellhop and the shine parlor man moved another four between them. None of them had even blinked at his asking price of eighty dollars a case. On the fourth day, by dropping the price five dollars a case, Bo unloaded all he had left on the brakeman and the bellhop and was clean.

"My God!" he said to Elsa. "Look at the bead on that." He sat in the tent on a folding stool and spread the money on the bed, smoothed every bill out, separated them into piles of fives and tens and twenties. He got out an envelope and began to figure—his old game. She had seen him, when other figuring palled, sit for three hours computing the ultimate fate of a hundred dollars left in the bank to bear interest at four percent computed semi-annually for a hundred years. He had once even bought a copy of Coffin's *Interest Tables* just for the fun of looking up things like that.

Now he stopped figuring to count out five hundred and sixty dollars, the cost of Heimie's sixteen cases, and laid it aside. Heimie's profit on that was twenty-two fifty a case. He multiplied it neatly, laid out another three hundred and fifty. That left him fourteen hundred and forty-five as his own share. He counted it to make sure, bundled up Heimie's roll and put a rubber band around it, figured again. His own net profit was nine hundred and fifty-five dollars.

"Holy cats," he said. "I could sell whiskey in this town as fast as I could haul it in. I guess you're not going to have as long a vacation as you figured on."

"Well," she said, a little tartly, "we might take two or three days to see the place. You said Heimie didn't expect you back for two weeks."

"Yeah," he said. "Sure, we can stay a while and look around." He looked at the brown canvas wall, his fingers tapping lightly on the bed. "Say!" he said, "did it ever occur to you . . . ?"

"What?"

Excitement lifted him to his feet. His head lifted, eyes narrowed, he stood hefting the roll of bills in his palm. "Could you get along here for a week or so, you and the kids?"

"For a week? Why?"

"Because," Bo said, "I'm going back up to Canada after another load."

"But why can't we all go?"

"I want to crowd it. Heimie expects me to take two weeks. All right, I'll take two weeks. But in the meantime I'll haul in a load on my own hook."

"It's his car," she said, "and you're supposed to be working for him."

"Yeah," Bo said, "and he owes me a car and a load of Scotch."

In the glare of the gasoline lantern his eyes were glowing slits. Elsa noticed again how the upward curve at the outer edge of his eyebrows gave him a curiously devilish look. "Besides," he said, "I've got a feeling our dealings with Heimie are almost over."

"I don't know," she said. "If you make this trip you'll be as bad as Heimie."

"Oh for hell's sake!" he said, and turned away. In a moment he

371

was back, not to argue, because his mind was made up, but to pursue another strand of the idea. "I might take Chet along. You and Bruce could stay here and be comfortable."

"How comfortable do you think I could be with him along on a trip?"

"He came down this last trip, didn't he?"

"I was along," she said. "I'll tell you right now, Bo, you can't take him. I wish you wouldn't go yourself."

He tossed the roll impatiently in his hand and stared at her. "We'd sure get rich if we followed your line," he said. "I can make us fifteen hundred bucks cold."

"I'm not thinking about that," she said stiffly. "I'm thinking of what you'll get yourself into. What'll you do afterward? Go back, or stay down here, or what? And if you stay down here what'll you do with Heimie's car? Steal it?"

"I'd just as soon."

"Oh you fool!" she said. "You'll get shot dead in some alley some day." Tears gathered on her lashes and she shook them off. "Go ahead," she said. "Put yourself on Heimie's level, take all the chances you want. But you can't take Chet."

"All right," he said. "I won't take Chet."

Just at evening, seven days later, Bo bumped off the road into the campsite under the maples. He was red-eyed, sleepless, unshaven, weary, but he had thirty-five cases on the car and trailer, and the car was a brand new Hudson Super-Six, a mighty seven-passenger behemoth that even under the mud and dust gleamed with an expensive luster. He had not broken a bottle, had a spot of trouble, or been so much as looked at suspiciously, and he was loose from Heimie for good. Heimie's Hudson he had left at Fort Benton. At first he had been tempted, he said, to keep all of Heimie's roll, drive the car over a bridge somewhere, and make out to have killed himself. He could have changed his name and they could have started out as Mr. and Mrs. Johnson, or Mr. and Mrs. Davis, with a nice fat bankroll. But he had got thinking of what Elsa would say to that, and in the end he had sent Heimie a cashier's check for his share of the first load, and had left his car in a Fort Benton garage with a message that he was through, quitting the business and going back to Dakota.

Now, he said, they could really roll. Now their hands were untied and the world ahead of them.

During the ten days in which he was disposing of the second load he bought clothes, two new suits and three pairs of shoes and two Panama hats. He sent Elsa into town to outfit the boys and herself, and in the evening, a two-bit cigar in his mouth and the top of the new, washed, polished car down to air their prosperity to the world, he drove them all out to Saltair and blew the lid in a Coney Island spree. He tossed silver dollars to the boys whenever they ran out of money, he took them over the roller coaster, through the Fun House, into the restaurant where they had lobster which none of them either liked very well or knew how to eat. Once or twice he looked critically at Elsa's dress, and on the way in, driving with the cool night wind stirring their hair above the plate-glass wind wings, he told her she'd better go in tomorrow and get something dressy. The stuff she'd bought was all right for every day, but she ought to have something snappy to step out in.

"Isn't this all right?" she said. "Just camping the way we are, I should think this would do. It's a nice little dress."

"Sure it's a nice little dress," he said. He fished for a cigar. "It would do all right in Great Falls, but you can't step out in it around here. You're in the big leagues, Mama. You're out of the bush leagues now."

"Can I have a house to live in?" she said. "Now that we're rich and can have new clothes and a new car and can throw money around at resorts, can I have a house? I'd like to be dry when it rains, and have a bath out of something besides a pail for a change."

"Tomorrow," he said, "we'll go house hunting. And we won't be hunting any little dump, either."

"When we're poor," she said, "you're as miserly as old Scrooge, and when we make a few dollars you throw it around with both hands. You need a manager."

"Only thing I need a manager for," he said, "is to add up my money for me. I get so I can't add that high after while." He blew a whiff of expensive smoke into the air and put his arm around her, driving one-handed like a young buck stepping out on a flapper date, and when she stabbed him in the ribs to make him quit playing the fool he quelled her with a smoke screen.

VII

Long afterward,
Bruce looked back
on the life of his
family with half-amused
wonder at its rootlessness.
The people who lived a
lifetime in one place, cutting
down the overgrown lilac hedge
and substituting barberry, changing
the shape of the lily-pool from square
to round, digging out old bulbs and
putting in new, watching their trees grow
from saplings to giants that shaded the house,
by contrast seemed to walk a dubious line between
contentment and boredom. What they had must be
comfortable, pleasant, worn smooth by long use; they did
not feel the edge of change.

It was not permanence alone that made what the Anglo-
Saxons called home, he thought. It was continuity, the flux of
fashion and decoration moving in and out again as minds and
purses altered, but always within the framework of the established
and recognizable outline. Even if the thing itself was paltry and
dull, the history of the thing was not.

If one subscribed to the idea of home at all, one would insist
on an attic for the family history to hide in. His mother had felt
so all her life. She wanted to be part of something, an essential
atom in a street, a town, a state; she would have loved to get
herself expressed in all the pleasant, secure details of a deeply-
lived-in house. She was cut out to be a wife and mother as few
women were. Given half a chance, she would have done well at it.

But look, he said, at what she had to work with. Twelve houses
at least in the first four years in Salt Lake, each house with its
taint from preceding tenants, each with its own invulnerable atmosphere and that spiritual scent that the Chinese call the *fêng
shui*. Twelve houses in four years, in every part of the city. They
moved in, circled around like a dog preparing to drop its haunches,
and moved out again, without any chance of ever infusing any
house with the quality of their own lives.

He remembered some of those houses: the first one, the preten-
tious place with the two cement urns like enormous pustules
flanking the front walk. To that place his father brought ball

players for beer-busts after the games, not for any commercial purpose but because he liked ball players and because now, feeling prosperous and meeting players who had been famous once in the big leagues, he liked to expand and play glad-hand host. That was about all there was left of that house in Bruce's memory: the brown men laughing with glasses in their hands, and his father circulating around with a pitcher. That house held them five months.

Then an abrupt declension in style. Perhaps Bo Mason had been knocked over or had lost a load or got in trouble somehow. Bruce never knew. But the second house was a ratty old place on the edge of a weedy field. The front door, decorated down its sides with lozenges of colored glass, had a bullet hole through it at the level of Bruce's eyes. In the back yard was a barren pear tree, and the lawn was mangy and run down. In this house, during the spell of hard times, his father started selling liquor by the drink. Bruce remembered coming home from high school and going into the kitchen to avoid the people crowding the parlor. Once in a while, when there was a rush, he had to serve drinks. He hated it. So did his mother. There was almost always a quarrel after one of those afternoons. Then the Purity Squad raided the house next door and poured barrels of stinking mash out the second-story windows, and Bo Mason moved out quick. He never went back to the speakeasy business, perhaps because Elsa objected too much. Before long he was running liquor in from the coast.

A house by the municipal playground, a good one, with big trees and a wide back lawn, a house his mother liked and wanted to stay in. That was the year when a woman named Sarah Fallon boarded with them while she studied beauty culture, and Bruce remembered the dimes he used to earn every afternoon massaging her incipient double chin. The feel of that soft, moist skin clung to his fingers yet, a sharper memory than any other he had of the house. They moved from there because his father got suspicious of the pious Mormons next door. A man who drove a big car and came in and out with suitcases a good deal, but never seemed to have any regular working hours, was too likely to get the neighbors talking. You couldn't stay too long in one place.

So they moved, and moved again. A brick bungalow up on the avenues overlooking the long wooded sweep of the city; a two-story frame house where they boarded a ball player's wife and family one summer; another undistinguished bungalow; an old adobe house almost as old as the city, but cool and pleasant under its locust trees. They melted and flowed together in the mind, a montage of houses, crowding the recollections of four years. An apartment in a big brick block, a little doll house near a gully where the mocking birds sang madly on moonlit nights, a vague and telescoped memory of some time spent living with an automobile salesman on a chicken ranch south of town . . .

What other houses? What else? They blurred and ran together. Things like the places you had lived got lost. They had importance in one context, but in the daily process of living they dwindled. There was school to take Bruce's time, there was the constant impatient agonized wish that he would ever start growing, get some muscle, get to be an athlete like Chet. There was the habit of walking on tiptoe all the way to school to develop his calves, the secret exercises in the basement to harden his neck and arms. There were his envy and pride, oddly mixed, when Chet did something spectacular and got his name in the papers, and his moral horror when he found that Chet and all his gang of big-chested boys smoked cigarettes and played penny ante poker.

There was his pride in his grades at school, his caddying at the golf club and his growing interest in the game of golf. There were his fear of girls, his tormenting dreams, his adolescent agonies, his constant furious expenditure of energy in the effort to be a top scholar, an officer in the ROTC. His whole private life took up his time, and the life in his home he noticed only when it irritated or balked him. Moves from one house to another meant to him only the necessity of finding new cross-lot ways to school.

It was only in retrospect that the moves had any significance, only when he thought of what his mother's life must have been all that time; and even there, he realized, his memories were probably colored by a sentimental pity that had little relation to his mother's real feelings. She never complained, except humorously, about the life she led. Probably much of the time she was almost contented except for her constant nagging worry that Bo would get into trouble that he couldn't get out of. But there was nothing really unhappy about her life, in spite of its rootlessness, until the spring when Chet was seventeen.

2

It was cool in the locker room after the sun outside, and it felt good just to sit and feel the tiredness run down his arms and legs. His spikes scratched a little on the cement floor as he hunched his shoulders to lean forward with elbows on knees. His mind was full of visions.

They would have that one in the papers all right. Through the open windows he could hear the last ragged yell for West High, and the babble of voices and clack of spikes coming down the hall. The cheers he had got as he trotted off at Muddy's wave, not even stopping to lean into the huddle and give three for his beaten opponents, were still sweet in his ears, but he did not look up as the doors slammed open and the team swarmed in. Hands hit his back, knocking him further down in his slump on the bench, but he paid no attention. His eyes were fixed on the floor in a steady, completely-faked look of despondency or exhaustion.

Hands seized his bowed head and roughed it, and he looked up as if mad. Muddy Poole, the coach, stood there grinning. "Great stuff, Chet," he said. "You really got in there and pitched that one."

Chet glowered, then winked. "Guess I smacked a couple too, didn't I?" he said. He could see the newspapers now. "Mason Holds West to Three Hits." "Chet Mason, star portsider of East High, held the strong West team to three meager bingles yesterday while his mates were collecting eight off the combined offerings of Rudd and Jenkins to win, 5-0. Two of East's hits were rousing doubles by Mason which drove in three runs . . ."

Muddy shook his two hands at him and went in behind the lockers. Shoes were dropping all over the room, bodies were squirming out of sweat shirts and pants, somebody yelled as a flipped sock garter spatted against his skin, and in an instant there was a towel fight in the aisle, Pinky DeSerres and Jerry Knowlton cracking them off like bullwhips. Pinky took refuge behind Chet, using him as a shield, and Chet watched his chance to smack him a beauty across the rump. He saw the red mark start and swell almost before the yelping Pinky was out in the aisle again and being chased toward the shower room.

Van Horsley, the catcher, came out from the lockers in jock strap and socks. His face was waggling in astonishment. "Looky," he said. "Look what that potlicker Rudd almost did to me when he beaned me in the fifth."

He pulled his supporter down and showed the aluminum crotch guard, dented as if someone had hit it with a mallet.

"Oh well," Chet said. "Nothing there to get hurt."

"Yeah," Van said. "I guess I can take care of myself. What've you got you're so proud of?" He ripped Chet's buttons and ducked the return kick.

"Come on," he said, reappearing with a towel. "You can't sit around here all afternoon and gloat. There's a couple hot numbers waiting outside."

"I got a date."

"I know it," Van said. "She's waiting with my date by the gym door."

"She is, ha?" Chet said. He dug a sweaty towel from his locker and started for the showers. "Well, let her wait."

But he took only a short shower, and he was dressed before Van.

The girls were sitting on the steps in the afternoon sun, amusing themselves by tossing scraps from scattered lunch boxes to the seagulls that coasted with cocked heads over the lawn. Laura Betterton, slim and quick, brown-haired, brown-eyed, waved her hand at Chet and started over. She was older than the high school girls, wasn't a high school girl at all, but a student at a business college downtown. "Oh Chet," she said, "I think it was just simply *swell!*"

Chet looked at her, looked away vaguely. "Oh, I don't know," he said. "West's not so hot. L.D.S. is the tough one in this league."

"But only three hits!" Laura said. Her enthusiasm embarrassed him.

"Been feeding the gulls?" he said.

"Yes. Aren't they tame?"

"Show you something."

He scouted around till he found a scrap from a lunch box, tied a length of string on it, and walked onto the lawn. Three gulls hung over his head, crying, and he made elaborate gestures of protecting his head from droppings. The three watching him laughed. "Watch him now," Chet said. He tossed out the scrap, keeping hold of the string, and a gull swooped and grabbed and flapped up again. Chet let him get about fifteen feet up before he pulled the string. The gull turned almost a complete somersault, a startled squawk was yanked out of him along with the scrap, and in a confusion of feathers and indignant cries he lit out straight for Great Salt Lake.

They were all laughing. "I think you're mean," Laura said.

"My hero!" Van said.

"Aw, shut up."

"I thought you were the hero," the other girl said. She was taller than Laura, rather thin, with a bright spot of rouge on each cheekbone.

"Sure," Chet said. "Van got heroically injured in the front line trenches."

"What do you mean, trenches?" Van said. He was burbling with secret laughter, and his girl's face wore a sly, sidelong smile that she couldn't quite conceal. Laura was looking at Chet and didn't seem to be listening.

Van, Chet was thinking, was a real slicker. His hair was always Sta-combed back, he could toss the old bull around, his suit was pretty snazzy, pinch-waisted coat with four pearl buttons set close together under the breastbone, bell-bottom pants with straight-across pockets and a broad belt band. The next suit Chet got was going to be one like that, even if his old man did call them "four-button pimp suits." There was no percentage in going around looking like an old sack of laundry. You had to have style, like Van. Van had a stripped-down Ford bug, too.

"Where we going?" Van's girl said.

Chet looked at Laura, and she took his hand and tucked it under her elbow. "I don't care," she said.

"I'm hungry," Van said. "Let's go have a dog."

"I know what," Chet said. "You got your car, Van?"

"Yeah."

"Let's go out to Saltair."

"Is it open?"

"Sure. Opened the fifteenth. I'm going to work out there soon as school's over. We can get in anywhere for nothing. I know all the guys."

"I ought to call home," Laura said.

"Okay," Chet said. He looked at Van's girl. "How about you?"

"I ain't got no home," she said, and puckered her face into a gamin's grin.

"Me neither," Van said. "Come on, let's go over to Mad Maisie's and get a dog and call."

Ten minutes later they piled into Van's red bug, a home-made racing car with a souped-up carburetor and a Rajah head and a Ruxtell axle. It had no muffler, no top, no fenders, no windshield, no seats except folded blankets.

Chet and Laura were in the back cockpit. They went down South Temple as if propelled by rockets, slowed a little crossing the business section, and swung out past the fair grounds and the airport on the Saltair Speedway. The speedway was a dirt road, but smooth and straight across the salt flats. Chet and Laura ducked further down out of the tearing wind, their eyes close to the sign scrawled in white paint across the red metal: "No mugging aloud." They looked at each other and smiled, and he slid his arm around her. Her hair blew across his face, tickling, as she relaxed against him.

Van was horsing the bug all over the road, unable to see much for the glare of the dropping sun, and pretending not to be able to see anything at all. He drove on the left side, held his course in the face of approaching cars until his girl shrieked, and then swung wildly toward the right-hand ditch. Other cars almost went off the road avoiding him, drivers turned and yelled, and one car even started to turn around in the road.

"Hey!" Chet said. "He's after you."

Van looked back, raised his eyebrows, and yanked down the gas lever. The bug tore up the straightaway, the wide-open exhaust roaring so loud that no one could hear what anyone else yelled. They hung onto the bucking seats and laughed. By the time they reached the salt works the other car had dropped back out of sight.

"Safe at last!" Van yelled. He pulled his girl over to him and hugged her, let go the wheel to use both arms, grabbed it again just as the bug was careening toward the ditch. Laura was frowning. "He's crazy!" she shouted, close to Chet's ear, and he nodded. He had been a little scared himself when the other car started to chase them. The old man would raise some hell if he wound up in jail.

There were not many people at the Moorish pavilion built on piles out into the lake. It was too early in the season, and the Coney Island of the West was having a moderately dull Saturday afternoon. Chet took them around to the bathing houses, winked at the attendant, and got them all in for a swim free. At the hot dog stand he ordered four hot dogs and got eight.

Laura hung onto his arm above the elbow, and he liked the way her hand didn't go more than halfway round his muscle. On the roller coaster a little later she hung onto him in panic, and he scared her pants off, he told Van afterward, by standing up on the first steep pitch.

They toured the Fun House, rolling drunkenly in front of distorting mirrors, yelling encouragement when Van's girl got caught in a whole battery of air blasts and had her skirts blown up around her ears. Her efforts to keep them down were not very successful, and Van dug Chet with an elbow. "Did you see that?" he hissed. "No pants!"

"Not bad!" Chet said. He hadn't seen anything, because he had been watching Laura edge along the walk with her dress clutched down in both hands so that only the hem blew. Van's girl was standing at the other end laughing. "That's a dirty trick," she said, but she was still laughing when they went outside.

The sun was flat along the lake, and the heavy brine sloshed against the piles. From the left came the shriek of a girl on the roller coaster, and the roar of a car avalanching down the first incline. Ahead of them the barker was just helping two couples out of the square-ended barge at the mouth of the Tunnel of Wonders. He saw Chet and waved.

"Hi," Chet said. "Packin' 'em in?"

"Not so fast. Hasn't really got going yet."

"How about a ride?"

The boy looked right and left across the pavilion. "Get in," he said. "I'll shoot you through."

Van's girl pretended to hesitate. "Are there any blow-holes in there?" She looked at the watery tunnel, the water dotted with wrappers from candy bars, gum, Eskimo Pies, popcorn.

"What's the diff?" Van said. "It's dark in there."

"That might be worse," she said, and stepped into the barge. The look she flashed back over her shoulder at Van made Chet shift his feet. Van was getting there, all right. He was a little uncomfortable with Laura at his elbow. She wasn't any little cheap chippy like Van's squaw, but just for a minute he almost wished she was. You could get away with plenty in that tunnel with a swamp angel like Gladys.

They slid smoothly, silently, into the mouth of the *papier maché* tunnel. The opening was a blurred glow behind them, and then as the flume curved the glow was gone and they moved in velvet blackness.

"Eeee!" Gladys said. "This is spooky!"

Sitting in the rear seat, Chet couldn't see either Van or Gladys, couldn't even see Laura a foot away. He felt for her hand, got it, felt her crowd against him. His lips felt stiff. Up ahead he heard rustling, a giggle, soft exciting noises. Van's voice, an insinuating whisper with a burble of laughter in it, said, "How'd you like to walk home from here, baby?" and Gladys' voice said, "I could swim, I guess."

"That's what the mermaid thought," Van said. "You know what happened to her." The voices stopped, and there were only the soft noises that Chet listened to with held breath, trying to interpret them. He swallowed and leaned sideways until his lips felt Laura's hair. She turned up her face and they kissed. In the hot velvet black the kiss lengthened and tightened, and their bodies crowded together. An alcove with a dim red light and a phosphorescent death's head broke them apart momentarily. The barge crawled on, around another bend. In just a minute the surprise lights would flash on. Chet kept his arm around Laura's waist but raised his head, focussing on the dark ahead. Van's activities up there fascinated him. Would the lights catch them dead to rights? He squinted so that he wouldn't be blinded when it happened.

The gray tunnel walls leaped instantly out of the dark, the square ends of the barge were there, the water with floating papers and bits of popcorn, and the two: Their heads jerked apart as if pulled by ropes, and Gladys' hands grabbed downward. Chet saw the white gleam of skin, heard Van's startled grunt, and then the light went off and dropped them into blackness blacker than before.

"What the hell!" Van said. "That's kind of hard on the heart."

Chet laughed out loud, and startled them all with the thunderous reverberation in the tunnel. "I thought that'd catch you," he said.

"You might have said something, if you knew it was coming," Gladys snapped.

"Oh bushwah," Chet said. He was a little disappointed. They had only been necking, then. But her skirt was up over her knees. Van must have been giving her a working over.

Laura's body moved against his, and he bent to kiss her again. There was a light throbbing all through her, as if she were shivering. He slipped his hand up over the swelling of her breast, and when her hand came up again to push it down he whispered, "It's all right. There's nothing but little red lights from now on. There's three or four minutes more."

She let his hand stay, and he forced her up against him in a fierce embrace, forgetting the soft noises from the front seat. When they coasted around the last bend into the growing glow of light he was taken by surprise. He straightened and looked at Laura. In the half dark her eyes had a curious shine, and her lips were parted. Before she shifted over on the seat and with a pat or two made herself demure she squeezed his hand once, hard. On the front seat Van and Gladys untangled.

"Holy cow!" Van said. "Let's go around again."

"Want to go again?" Chet said. Laura shook her head at him quickly.

"Oh, come on," Van said. "I never got much of a look at the wonders last time."

Laura rose teetering and stepped out on the platform, clinging to Chet's hand. He looked back at Gladys and Van in the barge. "You go ahead," he said. "We'll meet you."

"Where?"

"At the car?"

"All right. When?"

"I don't care. Say an hour?"

"Okay," Van said. He dug thirty cents out and held it up to the barker, and Gladys settled herself on the seat, tilting her head away from him to look at him with her sidelong smile.

Alone, Chet stood a little uneasily watching Laura. The shine was gone from her eyes. She looked quiet, almost severe. "What do you want to do?" he said.

"Couldn't we go somewhere and just talk?"

"How about going swimming again? We could float around and have a regular old gab fest."

"All right," she said. "It was hot in that tunnel."

Lights were on all over the resort, an umbrella of white dazzle. The potted palms moved a little in the first night wind; the cement floor of the pavilion was still radiating warmth from the sun. At the bathing concession the attendant was just closing his shutters.

"Sorry, Chet," he said. "I got to be checked in and have everything closed up by nine."

"Hell, you could let us go out," Chet said. "I don't need any lifeguard."

The boy hesitated. "Come on," Chet said. "It's no skin off you. I'll be quiet."

"Oh, all right," the boy said. He looked curiously at Laura as he passed out two keys with rings of elastic on them, two towels, and two gray cotton bathing suits. "You'll have to undress in the dark," he said. "I can't leave any lights on."

"That's okay," Chet said. He held the gate open for Laura and raised his hand to the attendant. "I'll do as much for you some day," he said.

Going back through the rows of dressing rooms Laura clung to Chet's arm. "Are you sure it's all right? We could have gone and sat in the car."

"Sure it's all right. Everybody hangs together out here. It's okay."

He found her dressing room for her with the help of a match, and by the door he pulled her to him and kissed her again. "You're pretty nice," he said.

"Am I?" Her head was back, cocked, and her eyes glinted a little in a flake of light wavering across from the pavilion. "You're pretty nice yourself."

"Like me better than anybody?"

"Oh," she said, shivering. "Much!" She stood on tiptoe, pecked him with a kiss, and whipped laughing inside the dressing room before he could grab her. He was remembering the soft resilience of her body all the way over to his own room. She had a nice shape, more roundness to her, a better armful than any of these high school kids. She was a woman, not any little half-baked kid. There was no percentage in playing around with kids.

They went barefoot together out the long pier. To their right the pavilion was a blaze of light, the Moorish minarets lifting like green mushrooms from the glare, people moving around, the sound of barkers and the roar of the roller coaster and the yells of girls in the shake-up concessions coming loud and yet unimportant across the oily water. The air was cool, but when they slipped down the stairs and into the brine it felt warm, almost lukewarm, with a slippery, half-sticky feel to it from the salt.

For a while they floated quietly, the buoyant water holding them cradled, their feet lifting helplessly high in the water. Paddling himself like a canoe, Chet came close to Laura's vague pale shape. Heavy-sounding as cement, the water slopped against the salt-crusted piles under the pier.

"This is nice," Laura said. "This is ever so much nicer than sitting in the car."

"This is a pretty good place," Chet said. "It's fun working out here."

They drifted and paddled. "Wonder what Van and Gladys are doing now?" Chet said.

Laura said nothing for quite a while. "Do you like Gladys?" she said finally.

"I guess so. I don't know. Why?"

"I think she's cheap."

"Yuh, I guess she is, a little." He rowed himself around in a circle and came back to position with his feet pointing toward Laura. "She's probably giving Van quite a workout in that tunnel."

"That's just it," Laura said. Her voice was sharp. "I don't think a place like that is decent. They just fix it so all sorts of things can go on, and people like Van and Gladys like it."

"Oh well," Chet said. "Van can take care of himself. He's a pretty handy boy with the women."

They were silent again, floating under the blurred noises of the pavilion. "Chet," Laura said.

"Uh?"

"You're not like that, are you?"

"Like what?"

"Like Van. Chasing girls all the time just to see what he can get. Picking the cheapest ones because they're easy."

"I picked you," Chet said. "Not for that reason, though."

"I know you're not like that," she said. She waded toward him, the brine shining around her white shoulders. "You're clean," she said, standing close to him and speaking with a shiver in her voice. "Just to look at you I could tell you were clean. Just to look at your hands."

"My hands?" he said stupidly.

"You've got beautiful hands," she said. "So big and long and square. I noticed them before I ever knew you, when I just saw you at a ballgame."

Chet laughed self-consciously. "Big hands are a help playing ball."

She reached out and took one, stroking it. "The skin is just like satin on them," she said. "Like a girl's skin. I think you can judge people by their hands, don't you? Better than by their faces. I watch the hands of people down at school. Most of them are skinny, like claws, or else big fat wads of things."

Her voice in the dark praising him, flattering him; the feel of her fingers moving on the skin of his hands, their skins touching with the slightly-sticky, slightly-slippery feeling of the salt water on them, excited him. He pulled her close, hard against him. "You're . . . beautiful," he said. The word was hard to get out.

Playfully she leaned back against his encircling arms and swayed as if she were in a hammock, and every movement brushed her body against his. He licked his lips, tasting salt, and cringed away a little from the intimate kiss of their skins under water.

"How old are you anyway, Chet?" she said.

"Nineteen," Chet said. He had lied about his age so consistently at school, because he hated being the youngest member of the football team, that he almost believed it himself.

"Only nineteen," she said, almost as if disappointed. "I'm twenty-one, did you know that?"

"I could tell you weren't any punk kid," he said. "These little high school flappers give me a pain."

"They're no worse than the boys," she said. "They all go around pretending to be so grown up, necking and fooling around. They've got no more intention of getting married than the man in the moon."

"Married!" Chet said. The word was like the word "beautiful," a solemn and importunate and scary sound. "There's plenty of time to get married," he said.

She had stopped swinging, and seemed to be searching his face, but in the dim light that flaked off the water he couldn't see her well. Then her head turned. "I never thought very much . . ." he was saying, before he realized that she was crying.

"Good hell," he said. "What's the matter, Laura?"

She continued to cry silently, standing with her face twisted away from him, and he gathered her unprotestingly close. "You shouldn't cry," he said. "What's wrong?"

"I just . . . keep thinking . . . how impossible it is," Laura said. She wiped her eyes on her upper arms to keep from getting salt in her eyes.

"How impossible what is?"

"You're only nineteen."

"What difference does that make?"

"You won't want to get married for a long time," she said, the words strangling out sideways, ending in a wail. "If I can't marry you I don't ever want to get married!"

Chet swallowed, standing very still, his arms like wood around her. "Well, good hell," he said. "I love you, you know that, don't you?"

She was hard against him again, her fingers clenched on his arms. "Oh, I do!" she said. "I do, and I love you too, Chet. Terribly. I love you more than anything in the whole world."

Chet lifted his head and looked over her white cap at the thick, glimmering water and the lights curving up along the roller coaster scaffolding in an intricate tracery that wavered in reflection toward him across the moving surface. "Aw honey," he said, and patted her back.

"Chet," she said, and put her face in the hollow of his shoulder. "I'm such a baby. I've been thinking and thinking, and I didn't know how you felt, whether you thought of me the way I did of you. A girl can't go on forever not knowing. I hate my home, and school, and everything but you. The only fun I have is watching you play ball and being proud of you, and seeing you afterwards."

Chet swelled his chest, got self-conscious, and pushed her backward with it until she half laughed. He swung her around in the water like a pinwheel, and his strength seemed like something superhuman, something that could break down anything, tear things up by the roots, give him whatever he wanted. "I tell you what," he said. "Soon as I'm out of school I'll get a job and we'll save, and pretty soon we'll get married. We don't have to wait till I'm twenty-one. I could pass for twenty-one most places."

"Oh, Chet," she said, her breath against his skin. "Oh, Chet!"

They stood in the deep shadow of the pier, their bodies locked together. Laura made tiny whimpering noises as he kissed her, breaking her mouth away and bringing it back eagerly. A chill not from the water shook Chet till his teeth chattered. With one hand he unbuttoned the shoulder strap of her suit.

Above them, as they stood in water to their shoulders, the noise of merrymakers in the concessions drifted unmeaningly, and the light splintered and shook over the moving water.

"Where can we go?" he whispered. "Up on the pier?"

Her hands pushed against his chest and she waded backward, stooping for the fallen suit around her ankles. "No," she said. "No, Chet, not now, I don't want to, please!

"*Please,* Chet," she said, as he reached for her again. He stopped, watching her pull the dark suit on again. She came up to him, ran her hands up and down his sides, pulled them away with a little laugh and put them behind her. "Oh Chet," she said, "you'll think I'm one of those like Gladys."

"Bushwah," Chet said sullenly. "You couldn't be like Gladys if you tried. But I don't see why you won't. We love each other, don't we?"

"If we didn't I'd be so ashamed I could die," Laura said. "If I didn't know we'd be married, sometime soon . . ."

"It can't be too soon for me," Chet said.

She laid her head against his shoulder, and instantly the blood leaped up in his veins, hot and throbbing. "That'll be lovely," she said with a little sigh.

"Then why not? There's nobody around. It's dark up there. Come on."

"No, no please."

"Why not?"

"Chet," she said.

"What?"

"You don't carry anything around with you, do you?"

"What do you mean?"

"Those . . . protection."

"Oh," he said. "No. But . . ."

"See?" she said. "I knew you didn't. I knew you were clean. So you see, it wouldn't be safe, Chet." She laid her hand on his arm. "Please wait."

"Oh, all right," he said. "But you're driving me crazy."

They climbed the ladder to the pier. Walking back to the dressing rooms he had his arm around her under the suit, and by the time they reached her door they were stammering, stopping every five feet to kiss passionately. "Why not in here?" he said.

She beat her fists against his chest, but there was laughter in her voice, and she punctuated every four words with a kiss. "You great big impatient bullying thing!" she said. "Can't you even wait till I get used to the idea of being engaged?"

"No."

387

"Well, you'll have to," she said, and whisked in the door. He jumped after her, but the latch had clicked. A dim foot and ankle poked out below the swinging door. "Here," she said. "You can kiss my big toe."

Chet stooped and took her ankle, caressed it a moment, bent and bit her big toe savagely. She squealed, smothered the sound quickly.

"That'll teach you," he said, and stalked off. But while he was dressing he was thinking how he had almost had her. Jeez, it was hard to imagine that it had been him out there in the water with her, and her suit off . . . But it was all right anyway. She thought he was the clear goods, and now that they were engaged it was going to be hunky-dory, no fooling. And she was a real woman, none of your fifteen-year-old hallway flappers, and Jesus, Jesus, it was wonderful.

It was already too late, he knew, to meet Van and Gladys at the car. They'd probably be off somewhere in the dark getting in their licks. He and Laura would have to ride home on the train, but that would be all right too, sitting on the steps of the open car with the wind off the salt flats, and the smell of the flats that was like no other smell on earth, a stink almost, so that the first time you smelled it you held your nose, but it grew on you, and before long you found yourself sniffing it, liking it, a salt, exciting, sea-smell that was wonderful to take in great gulps when you were driving or riding the train at night. And now there'd be Laura right next, snuggling against him with her head on his shoulder.

Engaged, he said. Holy cats.

Back in his mind was a door that he could open any time he wanted to but he didn't want to now. Behind the door was a sign, and it said in big letters—but he didn't look at the letters because what was the point?—"Chet Mason isn't nineteen, he's only seventeen." He didn't open the door and he didn't look at the sign, but he knew it was there and he knew what it said.

3

The papers had it. Chet sat at breakfast eating by feel, his eyes pasted to the sport page of the *Tribune*. That had all that about the stingy East southpaw and about only two West runners reaching second, and about his two doubles. But what held his attention longest was the Sports Chatter column. Bill Talbot, the manager of the Salt Lake Bees, had seen the game from the stands, and had remarked to the reporter that he had seldom seen a high school pitcher with more promise. A good curve ball, the reporter said. But it wasn't the curve that interested Talbot. Anybody could learn to throw a hook. "The kids you want to watch," he said, "are the ones that can throw a baseball a mile a minute and keep it up all afternoon. When their fast one hops, you want to watch them extra close. This kid's fast one hops."

Spooning his breakfast food automatically, Chet looked through the wall, which opened suddenly to show him trying out on a green diamond with the Bees, striking out the head of the lineup one—two—three while Bill Talbot stood on the third base line watching. He saw the headlines at the end of a season, when Mason was announced as the standout pitcher in the Coast League with a record of twenty-five won and six lost. He saw the Big League scouts coming, heard the prices they quoted to Talbot, saw his picture on a sport page snapped at the top of his windup with his spikes in the air, and underneath the legend, "Seventy-five Thousand Dollar Beauty goes to Cardinals." He saw himself playing ball with Collins and Sisler and Ruth and Schulte. He saw himself starting a game in the World Series, and the headlines and the chatter about that: "Miller Huggins, masterminder for the New York Yanks, has his work cut out for him to think up some magic to counteract the stuff his Yanks will have thrown at them today via the good left arm of Chet Mason, brilliant young freshman hurler who this season set a record for strikeouts in the National League . . ."

He pushed the cereal bowl away and reached for a roll. His mother, clearing up the rest of the dishes, looked at him and smiled. "Got it memorized?"

"Oh, bushwah," Chet said. He grinned and waved the paper in her face. "See what Bill Talbot said? Did you get an eyeful of that 'promise' stuff? You'll grin out of the other side of your face when I'm pitching in the big leagues and drawing down twenty-five thousand a year and splitting a World Series melon every fall."

He didn't know his father had come into the room until he heard him grunt. "Maybe you'd better get out of short pants before you start swallowing all of Bill Talbot's guff," he said. "What was the matter with those guys yesterday? All sick?"

"I was just throwin' it past 'em," Chet said.

His father laughed and looked across at his mother. "Modest, isn't he?"

"Terrible," she said. "But I guess he must have been just a little bit good."

"Just a little bit my eye," Chet said. "I was terrific. My fast one was hopping four inches."

"You know me, Al!" his father said.

"Well, it was."

389

"How about those six bases on balls?"

"I didn't walk six guys."

His father's big blunt hand came down and took the paper and held it in front of his nose. "Bases on balls, off Mason, six," he read from the box score. Chet took the paper and read it for himself. "They must have got it wrong," he said. "Even if this is right, how about those eleven strikeouts?"

"I don't care how many you strike out. If you walk six guys you put six possible runs on base."

"None of 'em got past second."

"But they might have," his father said. "Six walks are as good as six singles."

"Well, the umpire was blind in both eyes," Chet said. "You had to groove it or it was a ball."

"Now we've got an Alibi Ike around the place," Bo Mason said. He chopped out a laugh from down below his belt. "Come on out in the yard," he said. "Let's see this hot one of yours."

"You couldn't hang onto it," Chet said. "It takes a good catcher to catch me."

"I was catching guys faster than you when you were nothing but a vague idea," his father said, "and doing it with my bare hands."

"You won't need the mitt then," Chet said.

His father looked at him. "Come on, Smarty," he said. "Get that pillow and a baseball and get out and let's see what you've got."

Chet dug the mitt, his own glove, and a ball from the hall closet. "Bo," Elsa said as they went past her, "I don't think you've played catch with the kids for ten years."

Chet winked. "This'll be the last time. I'm going to blow him over backwards."

He would show the old man whether or not he had a fast one. They laid down a folded dishtowel from the clothesline for a plate, and Chet stepped off the distance. He put his toe on an imaginary rubber, took an easy windup, and lobbed one over. It plunked into his father's mitt and came back smartly. For a few minutes they tossed the ball back and forth, warming up. "All right," his father said. "Let one go."

Chet wound up and threw. The ball smacked into the mitt with a flat, wet-leather sound. The return throw stung. "High and outside to a right hander," his father said. "Ball one. Come on now, quit babying them."

Chet pitched again, a perfect waist-high strike. "Okay," his father said. "Pitch to me."

He held his mitt for a target, low and inside. Chet threw him a hook that broke a little late, and he had to move the mitt six inches. "Hit where I call for 'em," his father said. "Never mind the roundhouse stuff."

He moved the mitt thereafter only when he had to to stop a pitch, and Chet threw at the target, really trying to put it squarely in the pocket, bearing down as if the bases were loaded and nobody out. He walked the first imaginary batter, struck out the next two, walked another, and everything he threw his father took handily, peppering the ball back with a sharp wrist throw.

"You must have had a pretty fair peg to second when you were playing ball," Chet said.

"Fair," his father said drily. "I used to stand on home plate and throw balls into a barrel in center field on the first bounce."

He pulled off the mitt, examined his pink palm, and tossed the mitt to Chet. "That's enough," he said, and took a cigar from his leather case. He squinted at Chet speculatively, and Chet, wondering what the old man thought of his pitching, looked off down the street as if expecting someone.

"Your fast one is pretty fast," his father said. "You're no Walter Johnson, but you can burn one in. But it doesn't hop as much as you think."

"I can't get a good toehold without spikes. It was hopping yesterday."

"Forget the alibis," his father said, watching him steadily. "What I'm telling you I'm telling you for your own good. You might make a ball player. You've got the build and you've got an arm. But it's awful easy to think you're Christy Mathewson when you're only some little busher. You'll never make a class-A league till you buckle down to throwing baseballs at a knothole in a barn. You're wild as a steer."

"Well, I'll practice up and pitch me a no-hitter with no walks next time," Chet said. He grinned, but his father did not grin back.

"And forget to be so proud of what the papers say," his father said. "You'd have got knocked out of the box yesterday if those kids didn't all step in the bucket. They're scared of a fast ball. Throw 'em up that way to a hitter and he'll lose your ball for you."

"You just think they step in the bucket. That's a heavy-hitting outfit."

"I know they step in the bucket," his father said, "because I was there. I was sitting right beside Bill Talbot. One or two heavy hitters who weren't scared of a fast one, and you'd have had half a dozen runs scored against you, with all those walks. You got to remember one thing about a fast ball. If a guy even meets it it's likely to go for two or three bases."

"Yeah," Chet said, a little sullenly. The old man could never say anything without sounding as if he was daring you to contradict him. Well, maybe he knew a lot of baseball and maybe he didn't.

He tossed the ball up and caught it, wishing the old man would go on inside or somewhere and get this catechism over, when the other thought cut into his mind like a car cutting into a stream of traffic. Chet Mason, it said, is not nineteen. He's only seventeen. But just the same in two or three years he may be playing in the big leagues, and this morning, now, he is engaged to a woman twenty-one years old. This is not, he said, any punk kid you're dishing up free advice to. It's about time you got next to that notion.

But it was funny about the old man being at the game yesterday.

"Pa," he said, "can I have the car for a couple hours this afternoon?"

"What for?"

"Van and I have got a line on summer jobs at the Magna smelter. They put you on the bull gang or something, but what you really do is play ball for them. We have to get out and see a guy about it."

That about the smelter job was true enough, but it was not true that he and Van had to see anyone. The smelter man was coming up to school to interview four or five team members on Monday. Chet's lips had gone over the lie smoothly, but he felt sullen and defensive under his father's eyes. He hated to be made to explain.

"What's the matter with the streetcar?"

"You can't take a streetcar to Magna."

"You can't take the car either," his father said. "I need it myself."

"But Jeez, I want that job, Pa!"

He felt aggrieved, as if his father were keeping him from a real appointment. His mother, out on the back porch and listening, looked at his father.

"Why not?" she said. "If it's a chance to play ball . . ."

"Maybe we can all drive out," Bo said.

Chet opened his mouth, shut it, fished up another excuse. "But I have to pick up Van, and we may have to hunt all over Magna for this fella. We haven't got a regular appointment, he just said come out any time and see him." He shot a look at his father's suspicious face. "I know you," he said. "If you had to wait around for me ten minutes you'd be sore as a boil."

His mother laughed. "That touched you, Papa," she said.

His father was staring at him somberly. "If I let you have it," he said, "I want it understood that you don't go over forty and that you're back here by four o'clock. I've got a delivery to make."

"Okay," Chet said.

"Remember now," his father said, and went inside.

"Good gosh," Chet said to his mother. "You'd think that car was made of solid gold. Other guys can get their dads' cars when they need them."

"You're getting it," she reminded him. "It's Van more than anything that makes Pa careful. He thinks Van is wild. Is he?"

"No," Chet said. "He's all right."

"He looks like a kind of girl-chaser. You don't want to get mixed up that way."

"Well, I'm not."

His mother smiled. "You don't have to bite my head off. You didn't get enough sleep last night. Can't you try to get in earlier?"

"I couldn't," he said. "We were with Van and his girl and we had to wait for them for an hour."

"What'd you do after the game?"

"Just went out to Saltair and fooled around."

"That's one thing that made Pa grumpy," Elsa said. "He went to the game and thought you were real good, and he was expecting to talk it all over with you last night. And then you didn't come home. He was proud of you yesterday, Chet."

"He sure doesn't act like it."

"That's just his way," she said. "He's been around a lot more than you have, and he knows what it takes to be a good ball player, and how a boy can be ruined by getting off to the wrong kind of start. He thinks if you'd quit smoking and train more you'd make something big out of baseball."

"Well," Chet said. "If this smelter job pans out I can get some experience this summer, anyway."

He went down to the drug store and bought the *Telegram* and the *Deseret News*, read their accounts of the game, clipped them both carefully, along with the one from the *Tribune*, and brought his scrap book up to date. At one o'clock, before the family were more than half through dinner, he got the keys and drove out of the garage. But he didn't head either for Van's house or for Magna. He headed for South State Street and Laura.

She met him at the door, and her smile so clearly asked him to remember last night that he slipped into the hall and took her in his arms. She leaned back and put her finger on her lips. "Come in and meet the folks," she said aloud.

He had never been in her house, only in the hall at night. It was not, he saw now, a very good house. Neither it nor her family looked prosperous. Her father looked him over pretty sharply, put out a big rough workman's hand, and sat back. Her mother was excessively fat, almost as broad as she was tall, and fully as thick as she was broad. Her mouth disappeared in great buttery cheeks. The two kids in the kitchen were her brother Jim, about twelve, and her sister Connie, eight. It seemed funny that Laura should be so grown up and still have brothers and sisters as little as that.

"Chet's the fellow that pitched the three-hitter yesterday," Laura said. Her father raised his eyebrows, but he didn't say anything.

"I saw what Bill Talbot said about you," Laura said.

"Oh well," Chet said. "You can't believe all that stuff. I just had a lucky day. I walked so many guys that a few solid hits would've sunk me."

He waited for a denial of this from any of the Bettertons, but none came. "Going to play ball this summer?" Laura's father asked.

"I'm talking to a fellow on Monday about a job at Magna, playing in the Copper League."

"I thought you'd be working at Saltair," Laura said.

"Not if this other job turns up."

"Would it pay more?"

"Quite a bit more, I think," Chet said. "I'll know Monday."

He was getting uncomfortable. He kept stealing looks at Mrs. Betterton, the fattest woman he had ever seen. The parlor seemed warm. His eye flicked around looking for ashtrays as he thought of lighting a cigarette. There weren't any ashtrays. Mormons, he supposed. He had never thought to ask Laura.

"I've got the car," he said to Laura. "Want to take a little ride?"

"Fine," she said. "When's dinner, Mom?"

"About three. I got a chicken, so you'd better get back."

Laura threw Chet a peculiar pleading look and went into the hall. "Well, goodbye," Chet said in the parlor. "It's been nice to meet you."

They stood up and watched him out, and he had a feeling of relief when he and Laura got into the air. "Do they know?" he said.

"No."

"They seemed to be looking me over pretty sharp."

"They always do that," Laura said. "They're so darned afraid I'll start going with somebody they don't like. They just sit and stare at people I bring home."

The edge in her voice warned him to shut up about her family. Maybe she was ashamed of them. It would make you squirm, all right, to walk along the street with that fat woman and have everybody turn and stare.

"When we get married," Laura said, "I want to move clean away from Salt Lake."

"I don't know why not," Chet said. "It's a dump, far as I'm concerned." He opened the door of the car for her, and she stopped dead still.

"My goodness!" she said. "What is it, a Lincoln?"

"Cad."

"Gee!" She admired it as she got in, sat down almost uncomfortably on the leather and looked at the dashboard. "I didn't know you were rich," she said.

"We're not."

"But a Cadillac!"

"My old man just likes good cars," Chet said.

"Well, he must be able to afford them," Laura said. "What does he do, Chet? You never told me anything about your family."

Chet sat pumping up the gas tank, his eyes fixed on the radiator cap across the gleaming hood. "He fusses around with mines," he said. He couldn't have told why he gave that answer. It made the old man sound richer than the Cadillac did.

"Oh," Laura said. Chet locked the pump and stepped on the starter. The motor purred.

"Where do you want to go?"

"I don't care."

"Up a canyon?"

"All right."

She moved over closer to him, and he dropped one hand to squeeze her knee. "Still love me?"

"Um," she said, and smiled her intimate, inviting, remember-last-night smile.

"You were pretty stingy last night."

"Was I?"

"You bet your cockeyed hooley you were."

"Maybe that's the way I am."

"Maybe that's a pretty lowdown way to be."

She looked up at him sideways. "Did you suffer?"

"I didn't sleep all night."

Her laugh rang out, and two girls walking along the sidewalk looked up with envy in their faces. Laura patted his arm. "Poor itty-bitty baby," she said. "It suffered."

"But I'm not going to suffer any more," Chet said. He watched her with excitement mounting in his blood to see if she'd say anything to that. But she only smiled and dug her fingers into his muscle.

They drove up on the east bench and started out toward Big Cottonwood. At Thirty-Third South Chet hesitated, pulled the Cadillac over to the curb. He looked Laura steadily in the eyes. "I want to stop in the drug a minute," he said.

If she understood she made no sign. But after what had happened last night she ought to understand. She did understand, by the Lord. She was just pretending to be dumb and bashful. Exultation carried him out of the car and up to the door of the drug store. It was only after he got inside that the fear of the bald-headed clerk almost stopped him. He looked at the candy counter for a minute, and then, covering up the unease with a swagger, he went back to the furthest, most intimate corner.

It was already three-thirty by the dashboard clock when they came down out of the canyon. Laura, although she sat close, seemed miles away, her face still and her eyes remote. Chet kept stealing looks at her, a little ashamed because he had shown up his own inexperience, a little afraid she was distant because she was disappointed in him. He gnawed his lip.

"Still love me, honey?" he whispered.

Her smile this time was slow and deep, and it thrilled him so that he could hardly sit still. "Ummm," she said. That was better. He was still shaky from her tears up on the mountainside, from her passionate clinging and her stumbling words. He wouldn't think badly of her, he mustn't! He knew it was only because she loved him so much, because she loved him till it choked her to look at him . . .

"Me too," he said, sitting rigidly behind the wheel. His eye lighted on the clock. A quarter to four. Laura had missed her dinner, and he would be late with the car. God damn. Something was always getting in the way. He didn't want to take her home now. It would have been perfect to go somewhere to eat and then go up the canyon again in the evening, with plenty of time and everything dark all around, and the lights winking down the valley.

"I guess you're late to that chicken dinner," he said.

"I guess so."

396

"What'll we do tonight?"

"I don't care. Can you come down?"

"Sure."

"The folks will be going to meeting at six thirty."

They were Mormons all right, then. "Don't you go?" he said.

"I haven't gone for a year," she said. "They think I'm a lost soul." Her eyes flicked up to his, and she turned her face to lay her cheek against the seat. "I guess I am."

"I guess you're not."

"Sometimes I think I could almost die, living at home," Laura said. "They're both suspicious all the time, and Pa's grouchy, and the kids are always getting into trouble and stealing things. I almost hated to have you meet them. You're so strong and clean and you don't know what all that nagging can mean."

"It won't be for long," Chet said. He drove like a lord, weaving the Cadillac through the Sunday afternoon traffic, conscious of his hands and wrists on the wheel. He was glad she liked his hands. Great big old paws, he said. Mentally he flexed one, feeling how it could go almost around a baseball. "You won't have to live in that much longer," he said.

He turned into State Street and up toward her house. As she got out of the car she hesitated, her brown eyes searching his face. "You *do* love me, don't you?" she said. "We *are* engaged."

"We're married," Chet said. "All but paying the preacher."

Secretly she grabbed his hand and bent over to kiss it. She was biting her lips when she looked up. "You're wonderful!" she said breathlessly. "Oh darling, I think you're perfect!"

He watched her run up the sidewalk. Then he swelled his chest and cramped the car around. She was his woman, and she thought he was perfect, and she was wonderful herself. The way she'd hardly made any fuss up there on the mountain, never pretended or made him coax . . . Oh sweet patootie, he said, and wished it was six thirty.

That made him think of his father and look at the clock. Twenty minutes past four. He'd be a half hour late. The rest of the way home his mind struggled between the need of inventing excuses for the old man and the need of remembering with wonder how fiercely Laura had met his lovemaking in that pocketed hollow under the maples and the sumac just leafing with high spring. Almost as if she were afraid he'd get up and run, as if she were scared she had to hold him to keep him . . .

His father was waiting on the back porch, his watch in his hand, his face like a thundercloud. "Is this your idea of four o'clock?" he said.

"We ran into some construction," Chet said. "I'm sorry, Pa. I got home as quick as I could."

"It isn't quick enough," his father said. "When I say four I mean four, not twenty minutes to five."

"It's only four thirty," Chet said.

"Let's not waste any more time," Elsa said quietly. "We can still make it down by five."

She motioned for Chet to go inside, but he remained standing by the porch. He wasn't going to run from the old man's blustering. The hell with him. He watched his father carry the suitcase down the steps and put it in the car, watched his mother settle herself. His father's head bent to look at the dashboard, then jerked up. His hard eyes looked across the lawn at Chet. "I thought you said you were going to Magna."

"I did."

"You did like hell," his father said. "I'm getting sick of your lies. You haven't driven but thirty-three miles, and it's more than that to Magna and back."

"I don't care how far it is," Chet said. "That's where we went."

"And I say that's a lie!"

"Don't call me a liar," Chet said.

"Why God damn you . . . !" His father opened the door and started to get out, but Elsa's hand was on his arm.

"Bo."

His lips together, his breath snorting through his nose, Bo looked at Chet, standing defiantly by the porch rail. "The next time you want a car to chariot some cheap floozie around," he said, "don't come to me. This is the last time."

"That's all right with me," Chet said. He locked eyes with his father, who swore and jerked the car into reverse. On the way out he backed off the twin strips of red concrete that served as a drive, and gouged up a stretch of lawn. Chet didn't even bother to laugh. He just looked contemptuously until they were out of sight.

4

On Monday he got his job at Magna, twenty dollars a week and a five dollar bonus to every player when they won a game. "You don't have to do much but play ball," the man from the smelter said. "Mornings you'll putter around, do whatever the foreman of the bull gang finds for you. Lots of the guys spend half the morning in the can. But we want you to play ball for keeps. You'll go to practice at three every afternoon, and twice a week you'll play.

We're making it plenty easy for you so we can walk away with that league this summer."

It was pretty nifty, Van and Chet agreed. If they won most of their games they would make close to a hundred a month. They were on the gravy boat. Plenty of dough to spend.

Chet was already back-tracking on the marriage business, postponing it in his mind. You couldn't really bank on it, he told Laura. It wouldn't pay to go getting themselves in a hole.

But it was not really money that was making him cautious. It was the sign behind the door in his mind, the sign that said, "Chet Mason isn't nineteen, he's only seventeen." It was easy to forget that when he was with Laura, but it kept coming back when he lay in bed and thought about things before sleeping.

There was one more week of school, one more game in the high school league. Two days before he was to pitch against L.D.S., Laura came up to school after practice, and she and Chet and Van went over to Mad Maisie's for a root beer. They were sitting there smoking cigarettes just off the edge of the school grounds when Muddy Poole came by. The next day both Chet and Van were dropped from the squad.

That was a blow, no matter how the two tried to swagger it off. It made them celebrities of a kind, got them kidded in the halls, even made them the center of a righteous and indignant group. Muddy ought to have more loyalty to the school than to throw off his first-string battery right before a crucial game. If East lost this one, and West took Granite, then L.D.S. would win the championship. Muddy ought to be able to overlook smoking. What was a cigarette anyway?

All that was pleasant enough, but still Chet was sullen when he went up to the field and sat in the bleachers to watch the game. He didn't even bother to hunt up Van. Obscurely he hoped that something would go wrong, that the team would get in a hole and Muddy would have to come up in the stands and ask him to get in there and save the day. At the end of the second inning he saw his father come down the cement steps and find a seat, and before the end of an inning rise and go out again. Probably he had found out from somebody why Chet wasn't pitching. Now there'd be a big blowup at home.

God damn, Chet said, and sat glumly watching his team pound the L.D.S. pitcher for three runs in the third and two in the fourth. Hench, a little squirt with not half the stuff Chet had, settled down after giving up one run in the first, and had yielded only four hits by the time Chet got disgusted and left.

"It serves you right," his father said at supper that night. "It serves you damn well right. You had a chance, and you blew it. Maybe it'll teach you something."

"Rub it in," Chet said.

"Maybe I need to rub it in. Maybe if it isn't rubbed in it'll run right off your thick hide."

"Oh, let it drop," Chet said. "It isn't worth making all this fuss about."

"It doesn't matter to you, uh?"

Chet raised his eyes. "Not very much."

"No," his father said. His voice was acid with contempt. "I guess it wouldn't, at that. The only thing that'd matter to you is running around with this flapper of yours every night till one-two o'clock."

"Don't you call her a flapper!" Chet said.

His father looked at him a moment. "All right, she isn't a flapper. She just doesn't know when to go home to bed. Hasn't she got anybody to tell her she can't stay out all night every night?"

"Oh, all night!"

"Two last night," his father said. "One-thirty the night before. Three the night before that. You haven't been in before midnight for a week."

"Oh bushwah."

"Yes, bushwah. You haven't."

"Bo," Elsa said. To Chet she said, "You have been staying out awful late. It's not good for you while you're growing, and you don't get your studying done."

"I do my studying at school," Chet said. "And for gosh sake, I'm through growing."

"Well," she said smiling. "We'd like to see you once in a while. You might stay home one night a week."

"Okay, okay," he said. "I'll stay home tonight. I'll sit here and twiddle my thumbs till ten o'clock and go to bed."

He had a date with Laura, but he was so mad at his family for grinding him down, and so sore about the game, that he just called her instead, sitting in the hall from eight fifteen till nine o'clock with his lips confidentially close to the mouthpiece and his voice secret and soft. When he finally hung up he stretched elaborately and yawned. "Well, it's almost nine," he said. "Time for big athletes to go beddy bye."

His father did not rise to his sarcasm, and his mother only said, smiling, "I guess it wouldn't do you any great harm."

So he went, and for an hour lay imagining how it would have been if L.D.S. had cracked down on Hench right at the beginning, and the sub catcher had let a pitch through him and allowed a run to come in, and the whole battery had fallen apart, and runs had kept coming across, so that Muddy had to come leaping up in the stands and get Chet and Van right down in their street clothes to save the day. He could hear the crowd yelling, nine for Mason, nine for Horsley, and he saw himself toeing the rubber in street shoes, rolling up his sleeves and going to it, and the succession of strikeouts, his fast one burning in there so fast that Van shook his mitt hand and grinned when he tossed the old apple back. Not a hit, not a walk, after his appearance in the fifth. Not an L.D.S. runner to reach first, while East whittled away at the big lead and got two here, one there, till they tied it up. It would have been something to come up in the eighth or ninth with the score tied and slam one down the right field line for two or three bases, driving Van in from second with the winning run, and have Van wait at home to shake his hand and pound him on the back. Then the two of them would walk off with the crowd yelling. Muddy would have to come up and stick out his hand and admit that when he threw them off the squad he threw away his ball club, and then they would have shaken hands and lighted up a cigarette right in his face.

But instead of that East had won seven to two, the sub catcher hadn't made a single error, and Hench had held L.D.S. to six hits. The little pipsqueak.

Then graduation, he and Bruce graduating together, the assembly hall full of parents and all the little high school girls running around halls and lawns in their first formals, the long meeting when you sat and waited your turn to go up on the stage and get your football sweater, walking across and taking it from Muddy's hand and going back and sitting down while the applause died for you and started for the next one. Muddy couldn't cheat him out of that sweater, anyway. He'd earned that one, catching that fourth quarter pass and beating Provo six to nothing, and taking a kickoff eighty yards against Brigham City, and completing seven passes for three touchdowns against Granite. He'd earned that one, and plenty. And he sat in the row of athletes holding the sweater box in his lap, wondering if just maybe they'd give him a baseball letter too. He'd earned that too, the potlickers. East wouldn't have taken the championship if he hadn't won three games for them. But probably Muddy would hold a grudge and not even read his name off.

The football candidates were finished, the basketball team had gone up one after another, the midget basketball team had climbed the stage to the accompaniment of polite clapping and snickers from the audience. Bruce was one of the little guys. He looked puny and skinny, even though he had suddenly started to grow in the last year and had shot up a couple of inches. Chet felt a little ashamed that his brother was such a runt. Probably he could have done all right in high school if he'd been bigger. He wasn't bad at anything for his size.

The Superintendent of Public Instruction was introduced, and stood up to present the silver loving cup representing the baseball championship to Muddy Poole. Muddy made a little speech, it was all due to the fellows, they had got in there and worked like mad and played the game clean and hard, and sat down. The names of the baseball team started, and the line where Chet sat began to shift as boys worked their way out to the aisles. Chet crossed his hands on his football sweater box and sat still. He almost caught himself breaking into a whistle. Van, down the row, turned and winked.

Then Muddy read off Van's name. Van shot a look at Chet, stood up, marched down the aisle, and was given a sweater. Muddy read off others: Longabaugh, Mackay, Mason. Chet stood up and marched. Muddy, his face perfectly straight, held out the box and said without moving his lips, "I ought to charge you ten bucks for this, you stinker." Chet grinned, conscious of the audience at his back, the row of teachers and dignitaries along the stage. "Horse collar," he said, in the same stiff-lipped deadpan whisper. Muddy shoved the box hard in his belly, as a quarterback tucks the ball into the arms of a halfback coming around on a reverse, and Chet put his head down and made a play of running it off-stage for a touchdown. There were some smiles, some looks of formal surprise on the faces along the stage, some laughter from the audience. Chet skinned back into his seat over the crowded legs. Muddy was all right, a good guy.

That was the cream of the assembly, as far as Chet was concerned, but there were a lot of other awards, pins for publications and opera and glee club and student offices. Chet was up twice more, for opera and glee club, and then once again with the glee club when it sang. Then the speakers, the valedictorian and the salutatorian and the Superintendent of Schools and the Commencement speaker, and the long queues forming for the passing out of the diplomas, and that was the end of that.

That was the end of school, of stinking chem labs, of physics classes where you experimented with the laws of the pendulum, swinging plumb-bobs on strings down the stairwell from the third floor to the basement, so that girls going into the door of the girls' gym could be bopped with them. Now was the end of practices after school, of showers in the steamy old shower room and towel fights between the lockers, of snake dances through the streets to celebrate victories, of operas in the old Salt Lake Theater where you sang tenor leads in *Mademoiselle Modiste* or *The Red Mill*. This was the end of lunches on the lawns while the gulls flew over crying, of butts snitched behind the corner of Mad Maisie's, of hot dogs and mustard and rootbeer over her messy counter, of toting a gun in ROTC drills and marching on hot spring days up through the lucerne toward the mountains, a whole battalion breaking ranks sometimes and tearing through the alfalfa when a racer snake slid from under the file-closer's feet, all of them chasing the swift snake while the student officers yelled their heads off and howled commands that nobody minded and tossed around demerits that nobody listened to, and the commandant started back from Company A to see what was the matter.

Now was the end of a lot of things. He held the rewards of the year in his hands and lap, sat among his fellows as he could now no longer, in quite the same way, sit among them. He was through school, grown up. It had been all right, but he didn't want any more of it. Bruce said he was going on to college. Let him be the grind of the family. There was more fun in the world than that. There was his ball-playing job this summer, the possibility in the future of a tryout with the Bees, and the big leagues ahead.

And in back of the hall somewhere, back where the first sharp spats of clapping started whenever his name was called to go up for an award, was Laura, and Laura was somehow the symbol of the end of all this. He turned his head and looked at the boys along the row, whispering together, snickering, telling jokes. Kids. Nothing but kids.

His mother and father and Bruce were standing together near the arc light under the row of little planted maples when he came out with Laura. For a moment he would have slipped away if he could have. But the crowd was shoving behind him. He took Laura's arm. "Come on," he said, "you want to meet my folks?"

"Oh gee!" Laura said. She made quick dabs at her hair and peeked into her compact mirror. "Do I look all right?"

"You look swell."

"I'm scared," she said. "What if they don't like me?"

"If they don't, that's their tough luck."

He was a little nervous himself, for fear his old man would make some break, be grouchy about something. But it was all right. His father was dressed up fit to kill, black and white shoes, Panama hat, diamond in his tie, and his mother wore her best dress, the one that had cost eighty dollars and had been bought over her protests when the old man had a fit of generosity. Chet was glad she had it, anyhow. It looked nice. And you could always depend on Ma to be kind. She smiled at him and took Laura's hand, and it was all right. His father kidded them. Didn't Laura feel a little funny, going around with a Big Shot? She'd be lucky to kiss the hem of his garments now. He took off his Panama and clapped it on Chet's head. "How's the head size?" he said.

"All right."

"Good," his old man said. He kept looking out over the crowd, standing big and broad as a bridge pier while the crowd swirled around him. He seemed abstracted, almost embarrassed. His eyes met Chet's, wandered away, came back again. "Well, you've got more education now than either your mother or I had," he said to Chet and Bruce. "Let's see what you can do with it."

They looked at him and moved their lips, murmuring something.

"It's a big night for both of you," Elsa said. "I'm proud of you both." She turned to Laura. "They're pretty good boys, both of them, even if they are so homely," she said, and her smile asked Laura into the family, made her part of the circle.

"Homely!" Laura said. "I think they're two of the best looking boys in school."

"Now my head size is going up," Chet said.

Bruce kept looking at Laura. "I hate to be classed with him," he said. "He looks like something you'd find in a rat trap. Like old second-hand cheese."

"I could think of something you look like," Chet said, "but I'm too polite to mention it here."

"You look a good deal alike to me," Elsa said. "How does that suit you?"

"Rotten," Bruce said.

"Lousy," said Chet. He reached over and took a poke at Bruce. "So you graduated from high school!" he said. "When you gonna get your first long pants?"

"Horse collar," Bruce said.

They were all grinning, and it was a good feeling to be standing there all dressed up, something accomplished, everybody friendly and horsing around. "Mama," Bo Mason said, "maybe we ought to take these young fry out to celebrate. Where shall we go?"

"Where do they want to go?" Elsa said.

"Where do you want to go?" Chet said to Laura.

"Gee," she said, "I ought to go home, really."

"Oh bushwah. How about a show?"

"It's pretty late, isn't it?"

"Not late at all," Bo Mason said. "I often stay out after ten."

"Well, all right," she said, laughing.

"Haven't you got a girl, Bruce?" Elsa said. "Wouldn't you like to take somebody?"

"No, I guess not."

"Bruce's scared of girls," Chet said. He tucked Laura's arm boldly under his. "There's a half dozen chase him around all the time, but he dowanna."

"Go lay a nice rough firebrick," Bruce said.

They went to the movies, and after the movies they stopped for ice cream, and on the way back to the car they passed a shooting gallery and Bruce and Chet and their father shot for kewpie dolls. Bruce won, and his father looked at him in something like amazement. "He's been practicing up all spring on the rifle team," Chet said.

"Yeah," his brother said. "And even when I'm out of practice I'll take you on any old time."

"This seems funny," Elsa said. "Remember back in Dakota when you won me a lot of kewpies and pennants and things at the carnival in Devil's Lake?"

"I was shooting a little better that day," Bo said.

"I guess. That was the day you won the state traps championship."

"Really?" Laura said.

"He just looks that way," Chet said, and poked his father's shoulder, solid as a wall. "He used to be a shooter and a ball player and all sorts of things. Never think it to look at him now."

His father let loose a stinging cuff that just grazed Chet's ear, and they sparred on the sidewalk, horsing around like kids, until Chet got self-conscious and quit. His father's iron arm stuck out to jolt him one. "Get on any time," his father said, holding the arm out straight. "Do some trick bar stuff. Chin yourself. Let me know when you do, though, so I don't forget you're there and drop you."

"Gee," Laura said later, when he took her in. "I think your family's swell. Your dad is a good egg."

"He's all right," Chet said.

"And your mother's so sweet. I just love her."

"So do I," Chet said. "See you tomorrow?"

"After class?"

"Okay, I'll meet you there."

He went back to the car and got in, and on the way home they all sang. It was funny, Chet thought as he got into bed. It was darned funny how the old man changed. One minute he was the damnedest old crab on earth, ordering you around and bawling you out, and the next he was a hell of a good guy. You could depend on Ma to be right in there, any time, even if she felt lousy, but you could never tell about the old man.

He guessed that the old man was pretty proud of his kids tonight, maybe that explained it. He stewed around and raised hell, but he wanted you to be something all the time, and because he had never got past the eighth grade himself he thought education was the clear stuff. That was a laugh. He ought to go into a study hall sometime. Still, it was sort of nice to know that the old man was proud of you. It made you feel as if everything was all right. As he dropped off to sleep he had a curious feeling that his old man's pride was somehow the best thing in the whole day.

Now summer, the best part of the year. Rising at six thirty you could hear the birds making a great clatter in the back yard, and see robins running, their heads cocking sideways to listen, their beaks digging down hard and their legs bracing, and the night-crawlers coming out of the grass stretching and hanging on. You could smell the morning smell of sprinkled lawns, and hear from across the street the whir of a lawnmower, and as you ate breakfast alone in the kitchen the *Tribune* thudded on the front porch and you went to get it, propping it against the milk bottle as you ate.

You went out tiptoeing, so as not to wake the family, and your chest couldn't hold all the air it wanted, and at the corner, in the first light of the sun just breasting the Wasatch, you leaned against a tree and had your first cigarette of the day. In the early morning the sounds that at mid-day were an indistinct and blurred overtone were distinct and clear. The rumble of a truck coming down the unpaved hill past the old brewery, the even clop of a milk-horse, the whistling of the little sheeny opening his doors and running down his awning half way up the block, the thud of a flat wheel on the streetcar as it came around the upper curve and started down toward your corner. As you swung aboard your nose gave up the whiff of honey locust it had been smelling and smelled instead the familiar dust-and-ozone-and-oil smell of the streetcar, and you went to find a seat between the men with lunchpails like your own on their laps.

At Third South and State you got off to join the other guys waiting for the smelter truck. If merchandise was being unloaded into the sidewalk doors of Auerbach's store, you ran hurdle races over bales and cartons. If you got there early, and there was nothing else to do, you could horse the deaf-and-dumb newspaper vendor who came up to wave his papers in your face and make his ungodly noises. "Umwaooo! Umiayah!" When you just stood looking across the street and pretended you didn't hear, he would get furious, thrust a paper right under your nose, almost jump up and down. Then you could act surprised, eye him coldly, say "What?", put one hand up around your ear. You could always get a laugh from people going by, and it sure made the old guy mad.

Work at the mill was a joke. Half the time you couldn't have found anything to do if you'd wanted to. You just sat and threw the old bull around, or chucked rocks at tin cans, or went up to the roofless backhouse and read a magazine until somebody hammered on the door and threatened to tip you over if you didn't get the hell out.

About three you went out and peppered the ball around, held battery practice, batting practice, infield practice, fungoed out flies. Generally you got up a game of rounders for the last half hour before the five-thirty truck pulled out. On the way in to town you could generally talk the driver into stopping at Otto's, on Thirty-Ninth South, for a pitcher of home brew, the whole gang of you storming into Otto's parlor to guzzle his cold black beer, pouring some into a saucer for the cat and watching him get tight, hanging around till the truck driver got scared he'd be called for staying on the road too long.

You got home about six thirty in time for a shower before supper, while Bruce crabbed at you for not getting home in time to do your share of lawn mowing, and your old man sat on the porch reading the *Telegram* and going out once in a while to move the sprinkler around the lawn. If you didn't have a date with Laura, you telephoned her until someone wanted the phone. It made the old man sore sometimes to have you hang onto the phone for an hour, but what the hell.

It was a swell life, and he was pitching good ball, never got into trouble once except when Tooele rooters started shooting a mirror into his eyes from the stands. That made him so mad he blew up entirely, walked two men, allowed three hits, and wild-pitched another run home before the manager jerked him. All the Dagoes and Greasers and Wops and Bohunks in the Tooele stands razzed the hell out of him, giving him the old hip-hip as he walked off. But that was the only time anything had gone wrong. He had won two games, saved another for Pearson, and lost only that one, and his team was tied for the lead at six won and two lost. It was a swell life.

The best part of it was the secret part, the nights with Laura at Lagoon, at Saltair, at movies—times when they borrowed Van's bug, or went out with Van and some girl and drank beer, coming home loud and late, parking under the poplars of some dark street and growing quiet, necking. It was hard to find anywhere to go to make love really. The cockpit of a bug was no place, especially if you were really in love and your girl didn't like the idea of being jammed up in a seat and maybe some snooper or cop come by and flash a light on you. Laura was always cautious when Van was around anyway. She thought he talked too much.

Then they moved. It made little difference to Chet except that now he had to walk two blocks to the carline. But it made a difference when his mother broke down and had to go up in the mountains to Brighton for a rest. That meant he was camping in the house with Bruce and his father, and when Bruce went up to Brighton too to live in a tent below the inn, then Chet and his father were the only ones left. They got their own meals or ate out: because of his father's business they had never had a maid or a cook. After a while, when Chet had got home too late, and the supper his father had fixed was all cold and the old man mad about it, they quit making believe they were keeping house. Chet left before his father was up, came home often to find the house empty, went out again to see Laura and came home late, and often for two days at a time they didn't even see each other. The old man couldn't stay around the house much. It gave him the jim-jams, so that often he stayed out till midnight just to avoid being in the place alone.

"The damn place is like a morgue," he said. "I wish to hell your mother would get well."

"So do I," Chet said. "You going up Sunday to see her?"

"Yes."

"Maybe I'll come along," Chet said. He really ought to. She'd been up there two weeks and he hadn't even written her a letter. He'd been going to, but then Bruce went up, and there didn't seem any point in a letter as long as he was there. "Maybe Laura could come along," he said. "Is that all right?"

"Can't you go anywhere without her in your hip pocket?"

"I don't see that it'd be so awful to take her along."

"All right, take her along. Only don't forget you're going up there to see your mother, not squire your Laura around."

"Don't worry," Chet said. "I guess I appreciate Ma as much as you do."

5

The sun was slow coming over the mountains. The bedroom in the log lodge was cold, and she dressed shivering. But there was always a fire in the huge rock fireplace on the mezzanine where she had breakfast, and when she went out on the second-floor balcony and around the corner into the early sun she stepped from cool to warm instantly, as if the bar of shadow the corner threw was an insulating wall. There was a dewy smell of balsam fir, and the air was so high and pure that it made her lightheaded.

Sitting on the balcony in the mornings, waiting for Bruce to come up from his camp, she could see out over the whole little settlement, the old collapsing frame hotel, the glint of Silver Lake beyond it, the Twin Lakes foot trail a brown line against the green mountainside. It was fun to sit and look up a half mile, past timberline, to the snow that still lay in northern crevices, and to let her eyes swing around the whole circular rim of the divide, over the fir and aspen that floored the cirque, over the peaks sharp and clean between her and the farther sky. A smoke always went up from the girls' camp on Lake Katherine, a straight feather among the trees, and sometimes there was a distant rumble of blasting from Park City, nine miles over the divide. Chipmunks ran along the top rail of the balcony looking for peanuts or crumbs: the first time she got one to come into her lap for a nut she laughed aloud for the pure joy of having made friends with something.

She felt guilty for having so much fun. Poor Bo and Chet were batching down in town in the heat, the house probably a mess, nobody to get their meals. She ought to go back down and take care of them. But she didn't really want to. The way she lived up here—everything done for her, the balsam smell good in her nostrils even while she slept, reading a little and walking a little and napping a little in the afternoons—was a condition so unusual and pleasant that the thought of breaking it off was like Sunday-morning awakening to a lazy sleeper. Let it go on a little while longer.

Bruce came whistling along the road and stopped under the balcony to look up at her, his face a thin brown wedge. He had a camera on a strap over his shoulder, and a loose, almost-empty knapsack in his hand. "Howdo, Modom," he said. "Feeling pretty spry?"

"Spry as a cricket," she said. "I think every morning is more wonderful than the last one."

"How'd you sleep?"

"Like a log."

"Eat a good breakfast?"

"Enormous," she said, and patted her stomach.

"Lessee your tongue."

She stuck her tongue out, leaning over the balcony rail, and he squinted up at it. "I guess you're all right," he said. "Want to go for a walk?"

"I was just hoping you would. It's such a lovely morning."

"I know a good trail up around the edge of Mount Majestic. Once you get up the slope you walk along under the aspens for a mile or so. It's pretty nice, only it's a little far."

"Let's go," she said. "I feel as if I could walk all day."

Up the long trail through the firs they walked slowly. In openings along the trail the columbines were pure and tall and white, sometimes a space of half an acre solidly white with them. Farther up, as they climbed a brown rooty path around the flank of the mountain, the columbines were not so large, not so tall, but their petals were touched with the palest blue and pink, like the blush of blood through a transparent skin.

"It's the altitude," Bruce said. "When you get up high they get that tinge."

"I know I shouldn't pick any," Elsa said. "But do you suppose one each would matter?"

"I guess not," he said seriously. "They only reproduce from seed, and a lot of old dames come up here and pick an armful and then there aren't any more."

"I don't want to be an old dame, then, I guess," she said.

"Here." He picked her one of each color, and she folded them into her book, amused at his solemn air of being the personal caretaker of the whole mountain, and very fond of him.

They came over a steep hump that had her warm and breathless, her legs tired, and before them lay a level trail cut through the aspen. Through the thin trees on the lower edge of the trail she could look over a long oceanic roll of ridges and peaks, a forested valley stretching southward, the blue glimmer of water. Clouds like cottonwool coasted over the peaks on the Alta side, snagged on spines of rock, blew eastward in frayed strings.

"Those are the Ontario Lakes," Bruce said, pointing. "The valley is Bonanza Flat."

Elsa sat down on a stone, filling her eyes with green and blue distance. The sun through the thin aspen leaves was warm, the earth was fragrant with bark and mould and bitter leaf smell.

"Oh dear!" she said. "I don't ever want to go back."

"How'd a cabin be right here?" Bruce said. "With that view in your eye? You could ski on over to Park City when you needed supplies in winter, and stay the year around."

"You build it sometime and I'll come be your housekeeper."

"I'd like to," Bruce said. "Don't ever think I wouldn't." His eyes, she thought, were strangely dark and brooding. You could never

410

tell what he was thinking. He steered you off when you got close.

"What made you say that?"

"What?"

"What you just said."

"I don't know," he said. "I'd like it. Wouldn't you?"

"It might be a pretty hard life."

"That kind of a hard life is easier than a lot of other kinds," he said. He stared down over the twinkling trees, flowing like bright water down the slope into Bonanza Flat. "Last time I came across here it was raining cats and dogs," he said, and Elsa understood that he had changed the subject. That was all he was going to say about that other, whatever it was.

"When was that?" she said.

"Last year. That was the day after we spent the night in the Park City jail."

"What?"

"Sure. We went over to a ballgame, walked over along the old tramway, and in the afternoon it rained so we couldn't walk back. We didn't have any money, so we asked a cop what to do and he let us sleep in the jail."

"For goodness sake," she said. "You never told me about that."

"Sure I did."

"You never did." She shivered her shoulders. "That's the last place I'd ever want to sleep," she said. "I'd rather walk in the rain."

"It was all right. The cockroaches were a little bad."

Arms hooked around his hunched-up knees, he looked down across the valley, and Elsa watched him with pity, knowing that what had been in his mind a minute before was sullenness about his father's business, bitterness that the days weren't always like this. She couldn't have told how she knew what was in his mind. Perhaps that reference to jail. There had been a shadow on her own thoughts, instantly, at that word.

"Well," she said, "shall we walk some more?"

"I don't care. How do you feel?"

"Maybe we'd better start back," she said. "Pa may come up to have Sunday dinner with us, and it's getting on toward eleven now."

It was a curious feeling for Elsa to come down the trail and see Bo and Chet pitching horseshoes beside the inn, with Laura watching. She saw them objectively, as she would see strangers. Bo big and dark, getting a little heavier, his Panama on the back of his head and the diamond glittering in his tie when he turned sideways in the sun; Chet not as tall, but broad, very deep in the chest, his arms heavy and muscular under his rolled-up sleeves. Almost in surprise she thought, "Why, he's really a very handsome boy!" Everything about him looked clean and strong. And there was Laura along. That was getting to be quite a romance—almost too much time spent on one girl.

Laura turned and saw her, waved. The horseshoe pitchers stopped.

"Hi, Ma," Chet said. "How you feeling?"

She kissed him, then Bo, put out her hand to Laura. "Oof, we've walked a long way," she said, and sat down on the step to fan herself.

"You're up here for a rest," Bo said, frowning. "You don't want to overdo it."

"I'm having a lovely rest," she said. "How do you two get along at home?"

"I never see this guy from one week's end to the next," Bo said.

"Oh horse," Chet said. "I'm home more than you are."

"Neither one of us wears the place out living in it," Bo said. "When you going to get well and come home, Mama?"

"I don't know. The doctor said two months, but I feel fine now, rested as can be."

"You look better, I think," Laura said. "I noticed it right away. Lots better."

"Really?" Elsa said. "I'm glad I don't look worse. That would be pretty hard on my family."

"When do they eat around this place?" Chet said.

"It ought to be pretty quick now. Did you make a reservation?"

"I'd better go do that," Bo said, but Elsa rose. "I'll do it. I have to go tidy up anyway. You want to come with me, Laura?"

"Sure," Laura said.

A very quiet girl, Elsa thought. Yet there was something there she vaguely disliked. As if her quiet were put on, as if it wasn't quite her own face she wore. Or maybe the hungry way she looked at Chet, or the very slight dissatisfied wrinkle between her eyes.

While she took off her walking dress Elsa could see her in the mirror. "How's Chet been pitching?" she said. "I don't see the paper very often up here."

"He's done swell," Laura said. "He's only lost one game."

"Fine," Elsa said with her mouth full of hairpins. She shook her hair down and brushed it hard.

Laura sat with her hands in her lap, nervously swinging her foot. "You've got beautiful hair," she said.

"It's the one thing I ever had that doesn't seem to fade or wear out," Elsa said. She looked at Laura in the mirror, saw her hungry eyes, the look almost of weeping around the mouth. "Don't you feel well?" she said, turning.

Laura wet her lips. "Oh yes, I feel all right."

"I thought for a minute you might be ill," Elsa said. To her dismay the girl jumped up from the bed and threw her arms around her, her face twisted.

"Oh Mrs. Mason!" she said.

"Why, what is it?"

"I wish I had a mother like you!" Laura said. She buried her face in Elsa's shoulder and clung when Elsa tried gently to break her loose.

"Let's be sensible," she said. "You have your own mother."

"But she isn't like you!" Laura wailed. "She's always after me for something, and suspicious of me, and she isn't pretty at all. She's *fat!*"

"Well," Elsa said. "I'm sure she's . . ."

"You don't know," Laura said. She turned and sat on the bed again, dabbing at her averted eyes. She said without looking up, "You just don't know how it is to have a family that's vulgar and bullying. I see how pleasant everything is in your family, and how kind you are, and how they all love you and you love them, and how nice Mr. Mason is, and I can't help it. I wish I had a family like yours."

"Why you poor child," Elsa said. The thought of anyone's envying their family life was so wild that she wanted to laugh. "We have to be satisfied with what we have," she said. "Maybe your mother is tired, or overworked." She watched Laura's bent head. "Maybe you're poor," she said. "I know all about that. It's hard to keep pleasant when things go wrong all the time."

"We aren't poor," Laura said sullenly. "We have enough. But we're just not kind like you, we don't get along. I don't know why it is."

"Love is a thing that works both ways," Elsa said quietly. "We have to give other people a chance to love us before we find them lovable, sometimes."

Laura stood up and tried to laugh. "I'm silly. I don't know what got the matter with me all of a sudden."

Elsa went back to putting up her hair, watching the girl in the mirror. She was a rather helpless, pretty thing, and obviously unhappy. But her unhappiness was obscurely annoying too. There was the edge of spite in it, the eagerness to blame someone else for her misery, that would have made one want to shake her if she had been one's own. She turned and faced the girl squarely. "Is it because you're in love with Chet?" she said. "Don't your family like him?"

"Oh, they like him all right."

"But you *are* in love with him," Elsa said.

Laura nodded, keeping her head down.

"How does Chet feel about it?"

Laura nodded again, unwilling to meet Elsa's eyes.

Elsa sighed. "There's no reason you shouldn't go together, as long as you aren't foolish about it. When you're both old enough to get married you probably won't even like each other any more, but if you do nobody will try to stop you from marrying in a few years."

Laura lifted tragic eyes, but said nothing, and Elsa frowned. "You children aren't serious, now?"

Her eyes full of utterly disproportionate terror, Laura pushed herself back on the bed. "I . . . that is . . . I don't know . . ."

Elsa took her hand and pulled her to her feet. "Good heavens, don't be afraid of me! I didn't mean to scare you. I just wanted to be sure you and Chet weren't going to be foolish about waiting. Waiting isn't too hard, when you can see each other all the time. Nobody's trying to keep you apart, child."

"Oh Mrs. Mason!" Laura said, and began to cry. "I'm so unhappy!"

Elsa stood waiting, but the girl said no more, so Elsa said it herself, the words heavy and sodden and hard to lift. "You and Chet haven't got in trouble, have you?"

"No," Laura said. "Oh no, nothing like that."

"Well then, everything will turn out all right. You've got your whole lives ahead of you. You shouldn't be unhappy, at your age."

But she was thinking as they went downstairs that Laura had been playing some kind of double game, had been trying to say something she was afraid to say, and at the same time had been angling for sympathy, trying to ingratiate herself by appearing miserable and picked on, as if to justify that other thing that she hadn't dared to say.

Poor child, she thought automatically. Kids in love gave themselves endless troubles for nothing. But she didn't like the idea of Chet's being involved with this girl as deeply as he apparently was. He was too young, he didn't know enough. She had hardly phrased her automatic pity for Laura before the phrase had twisted itself in her mind into something else: Poor Chet.

She watched Chet at dinner, kept glancing up to intercept looks between him and Laura. They did not act like kids out for a good

414

time. They were sober, their eyes and their occasionally-touching hands eloquent of secrets. The thing was obviously serious, but how serious it was hard to tell. But two children like that! she thought. Chet was only seventeen. Still, he was in deep. He wasn't full of horseplay the way he ordinarily was, he hardly laughed at all except with his sly, sidelong look at Laura. There was something brooding and almost deadly in the way the two looked at each other.

Oh Lord! she said, why are they so intent on ruining their own lives?

After dinner Bo was playing the slot machines while Laura and Bruce watched, and she crooked her finger at Chet. As they walked away she felt Laura's eyes on her back. Everything that happened, the slightest incident, was significant to those two, pertinent to some guarded secret of their own.

"Let's sit down," she said. The mezzanine was empty. The other guests were all out on the porch, their voices a dim buzzing through the doors. Finding it hard to begin, not knowing exactly what she had brought him up here to say to him, Elsa took his hand.

"You've got paws just like your father's," she said. "It doesn't seem any time at all since they were making mud pies."

Chet said nothing. He waited.

"Chet," she said. "What about Laura?"

She could feel the stiffness of his body through his hand. His eyes were veiled as if she were an enemy. "What about her?"

"She talked to me a little before dinner, up in my room."

Instantly there was life in the veiled eyes. "What did she say?"

"What could she have said?"

The eyes went dull again. "I don't know," he said, and shrugged slightly.

"She said she was in love with you," Elsa said.

Chet tried to laugh. "Good," he said. "She never told me that."

"Oh Chet!" his mother said, and stood up impatiently. "You needn't try to duck and hide from me. I just want to talk to you openly and see if I can't give you some good advice."

"People are always awful free with advice," Chet said.

"Have I been?"

"You're always worrying about what time I come in, and stuff like that. You can't get over thinking of me as a kid."

"I was thinking more about your health than anything else."

"Oh, my health! I'm healthy as a horse. No guy wants to be mothered and babied around. I've got to grow up sometime."

"Not too soon," she said softly. "Not so soon you spoil your whole life by it. I'm not trying to hold you back, Chet. You're old for your age, in some ways. But you're still only seventeen, and you can ruin your life by getting too serious with a girl too soon. I'm just asking you to remember that you aren't really a man till you're twenty-one. Lots of boys aren't till later than that."

His ears were pink, his brows pulled down in a black frown. At least she had got the mask off him, she thought wearily. But it didn't do any good.

"I can look after myself," he said. "I know enough to come in out of the rain." He said it angrily, but he did not quite meet her eyes, and she read him as if he were an eight-year-old trying to bluster his way out of trouble. Underneath that anger he was uncertain and scared. He knew he was in deep.

"We're getting altogether too serious," she said lightly. "I didn't bring you up here to croak at you. I just wanted to remind you to keep yourself free and clean. If you want to be a ball player you'll have to be free for a few years, Chet."

"Yeah," he said. "I don't know what got you thinking I wasn't going to be."

"Laura."

"Oh," he said. He looked past her, the dull and sullen look on his mouth. "Shall we go on down again?" he said.

For a moment Elsa looked at him feeling that she wanted to cry. He was just like Bo, as stubborn and immovable as a wall, as unwilling to admit a mistake. What he did was right. It had to be. Out of her anger and irritation came a curious desire to reach out and hug him, but that would have been as embarrassing and bothersome to him as her attempt to give advice. She turned and went downstairs. She did not want to be an interfering mother, but she was determined that if there was anything she could do to prevent his making a fool of himself she would do it, short of actual compulsion.

"What about speaking to Bill Talbot about Chet?" she asked Bo out on the porch later. "Couldn't you get him a chance to try out with the Bees? He's been doing so well out in the Copper League."

"He isn't ready for any Double-A league," Bo said. "When's he's ready, they'll be after him themselves. Besides, you don't try out in the middle of the summer. They look over the young guys in the spring, in training camp."

"But . . ."

"What do you want him pushed so fast for?" Bo said, irritated. "Let him grow up a little. He'd just blow his chance."

"Bo," she said, "I wish you'd talk to Bill, just the same."

416

His brows drew down, and he turned to stare. "What's on your mind?"

With her eyes she indicated Chet and Laura leaning over the balcony rail. Chet was pointing at something, and Laura was bent close to him, trying to see. "I think it would do Chet a lot of good to get away from Salt Lake for a while," Elsa said. "Bill's a good friend of yours. He'd do it for you as a favor. Even if we had to pay Chet's expenses . . ."

Bo jerked his head at the oblivious two. "You think . . . ?"

"I don't know. I'm afraid they're both pretty far gone."

"At seventeen!" he said, and snorted through his nose.

"It doesn't do any good to talk to him," Elsa said. "I've tried. If you tried you'd just make him bull-headed. But if you could get Bill to let him go along with the team, maybe pitch for batting practice or something . . ."

"Yeah," Bo said. "Well, I'll see. But I wouldn't expect too much. Bill's the best judge of when he wants to look anybody over."

They looked at each other, and both laughed. It was funny, in a way, how they schemed on one end of a balcony while Chet and Laura plotted heaven only knew what on the other. "I guess they never get too old to need taking care of," Elsa said. "How's business going?"

"Yesterday," Bo said, "I bought another thousand bucks worth of U. S. Steel."

"How much does that make?"

He winked. "Mama," he said, "we may not be as rich as we'd be if we played the market right, but we've got eighteen thousand dollars' worth of stock in that safety deposit box, and we own every nickel's worth of it."

"Eighteen thousand," Elsa said. It seemed an enormous sum.

"I figured up our assets the other day," Bo said. "We're worth pretty close to thirty thousand, counting everything. Give me time to multiply that by ten and we'll retire."

Elsa smiled. "Remember when you first started you said you'd make a few trips and get a stake and get into some business. Then you got knocked over and had to make it up. Then Heimie spoiled things for you in Great Falls and we had to make *that* up. But you always said when you got ten thousand dollars ahead you'd get out of this business, Bo."

"You know what the interest on ten thousand would amount to?" Bo said. "Even if you had it in seven percent preferred stock you'd only get seven hundred a year off it. How long could you live on seven hundred?"

"But you've got more than ten thousand. You've got two or three times that much."

"You never figure right when you're down," Bo said. "Ten thousand looks like a million from where we used to be. But you can't get into any kind of business with only that kind of capital. You got to put up dough."

"But you'll have to get out sometime," she said. "It isn't fair to the kids. Bruce'll be going to college this fall. What if you got into trouble and all his friends knew what you did? What if all Chet's friends knew it?"

"What do you want?" he said, eyeing her somberly. "Want me to sit on my tail and let what we've got dribble away?"

"You know what I want. I want you to find some business that we don't have to be ashamed of. The kids feel it, Bo. They don't like to bring their friends around the house. They have to lie about what you do. It isn't fair to them."

"Well, I'm keeping my eyes open," he said. "You can't just rush into a thing blind."

He moved impatiently and stood up at the rail to watch two boys ride hell-for-leather around the trail and out of sight into the woods. "Ho hum," he said. "Here I thought you'd be excited at the idea of another thousand socked away."

"Did it ever occur to you," she said, her eyes on his, "that there are things that would make me feel better than any amount of money?"

6

The game had started when Bo got there. He slipped the usher a half dollar and moved down to a box on the first base line. At the end of the fourth Bill Talbot came out of the dugout to take a turn coaching at first, and Bo waved to him. After the third out Bill came over.

"How's tricks?" he said.

"Can't complain. Looks like you got a ball club this year."

"They look pretty good, don't they?" Bill said. "You never saw a bunch of guys hit like these kids. If we had the pitching we'd be in first place by ten games."

"You're only three games off the pace. You can make that up."

"I got my fingers crossed," Bill said. "Anything stirring in your league?"

"Nothing except a favor I want to ask. Maybe you can't do it, I don't know."

"What is it?"

"You know that kid of mine."

"The pitcher? I been seeing his name in the Copper League. Doing all right."

"Doing pretty good," Bo said. "I went out and caught him in the back yard one day. He's got a fast one that whistles, and a pretty good hook."

Bill bowed himself to spit carefully in the dust and then erase the spit with his spikes. "What's the favor?"

"I was wondering if you could take the kid along on a road trip."

Bill shook his head. "Got my quota. We can't have any extras on the payroll after the middle of May."

"Trouble is," Bo said, and bit the end off a cigar, "trouble is, the damn kid's got a crush on a girl and I'd like to shake him loose till he cools off, and there's nothing he'd leave her for but maybe baseball."

Bill opened his mouth to laugh, raised his cap to cool his bald head, slipped it back on again. "You don't want me to put him on the team then."

"He isn't ready for that, hell no."

"Tell you what," Talbot said. "Would he come as batboy, do you think?"

"I don't know. I should think so."

"He wouldn't get any money, only expenses. But you could tell him I'll be looking him over. He could work out with the boys, nobody'd fuss about that."

"I should think that would do it," Bo said. He lighted the cigar and chuckled out a cloud of blue smoke. "It would do him good to be a batboy. He thinks he's ready to pitch to Ruth right now."

"Tell him to come down and see me," Bill said. "I'd like to get a longer look at him, for a fact. We need pitchers so bad that even a green one with stuff looks pretty interesting. He might set himself up for a tryout next spring."

"Good," Bo said. "You leave next Monday?"

"Gone for two weeks, then back for two, then gone for three. He could go this trip or wait till the August one. What about his smelter job?"

"If I know him," Bo said, "he'll throw that overboard in a minute. And the sooner he's got out of here the better."

He watched Bill go back to the coach's box at first, and after another inning he rose and went home. He felt so good about the way he had used his influence to give Chet a chance and at the

419

same time to get him away from Laura that he got out a bottle of Scotch and wrapped it up and put it aside for Chet to take down to Bill when he went.

His slight fear that Chet would stick up his nose at a batboy's job lasted only the first minute of their conversation. Chet saw the possibilities all right.

"Jeez, let me at him!" he said. "Did he say I could work out with them?"

"Yeah. He wants a look at your stuff. But he has to put you on as batboy because his quota's full. You keep your eyes open and your mouth shut and try training a little and you might get a break out of this, boy. Bill's short of pitchers."

Chet looked up at the ceiling and cracked his knuckles together. "Maybe somebody'll get hurt and they'll have to put me in a game," he said.

"You won't get in any games," Bo said shortly. "You're not on the team, for one thing. For another, you wouldn't last a third of an inning. But you might learn something."

"If I don't I'll kiss a pig," Chet said. "Can I take the car now?"

Bo laughed. "Don't let any grass grow under you. Yeah, if you get it back here by seven."

"Okay."

"What'll you do about the smelter?"

"That can fry," Chet said. "I can't pass this up just to pitch in that league."

"Then what'll you do all winter? Sit around on your tail?"

"That shows how much you know about it," Chet said. "I already lined up a job at the International Harvester. I'm going to play basketball for 'em this winter."

"Okay, okay," Bo said. The kid had enough ambition. Wean him away from his Laura and he'd do all right. "You better get along," he said. "Give this bottle to Bill."

Chet took it, stood in the doorway jingling loose change in his pocket, looked up once, then out the door. "Well, thanks, Pa," he said uncomfortably, and went out.

He was back promptly in an hour. "All fixed," he said, and took a basketball shot at the top of a lamp with a sofa cushion. The lamp teetered and started to fall, and he leaped to grab it. "Caught him and half the team at dinner," he said. "Bill said I could stick around till the end of the season if I wanted."

"I never saw anybody quite so overjoyed at getting a job as batboy," Bo said.

"Stick around, boy," Chet said. "I'll be on that team when it starts training next spring."

A few minutes later Bo heard him talking on the telephone in the hall. He held his paper still, listening. "Yeah," Chet was saying. "Bill wants to look me over this summer. No fooling. Yeah, Monday night. No, just to look me over, sort of a preliminary tryout. That's what I was thinking, you bet your life. I'll do what I can. Old John can't go on catching forever. His legs are all shot. I don't know why not. I'll sure talk you up, anyway. Tell 'em I can't pitch to anybody but you . . ."

Bo waggled the paper and grinned to himself. Big Shot, he said softly. The batboy getting jobs for his friends. He looked at his watch and got up. That half case was due down on South Temple at seven thirty.

After his father had gone out Chet wandered restlessly around the house. Jeezie Kly, it was all right. Two months with the Bees, sitting in the dugout with them, eating with them in diners and hotels, meeting players from all the other clubs, guys like Lefty O'Doul and Chief Bender and Walter Mails. There was the guy with the fast one. Old Bill Talbot was no bush leaguer, for that matter. He'd been one of the best outfielders in the business in his day, and he was still good enough at forty to hit over three hundred and play a good left field more than half the games. He'd been up in the big time a long while, and he knew them all, Ruth and Hornsby and Walter Johnson and Grover Alexander and Casey Stengel and Sisler and Collins and all of them. You ought to be able to learn plenty just sitting and listening to Bill.

It was darn nice of Bill to take him along—though probably he thought he'd get his money back in a year or so when Chet made the team and strengthened the pitching staff. It was nice of the old man to speak to Bill, for that matter. Every once in a while he cropped up with something like this that made you think he was all right for sure. Like the night he took them all out on the night of graduation. Laura was still talking about what a good egg he was.

Well, he said, you made up for plenty this time. This'll make you a good egg for a long time.

He had a date with Laura at nine, but he'd stick around now till the old man came home, just on the chance that he could get the car. Laura was going to feel bad about his going, but after all he'd only be away two weeks, and then back for two, and then away three. He went into the hall to call her up. Her eyes would stick out on stems.

The doorbell rang, a faint muffled tinkling in the kitchen. Chet looked through the window in the front door, but whoever was ringing was off to the side and he couldn't see anything. He turned the knob, and the door swung in hard against his chest, pushing him against the wall.

"Say, what in . . ." he said.

He was looking into the muzzle of a gun.

The man holding the gun came around the door and let two others in behind him. Pushing Chet into the front room he took a quick look in bedrooms and kitchen to make sure no one else was at home. He came back and patted Chet's pockets perfunctorily and motioned him over into a chair. "You sit down and take it easy," he said. "This is a raid. Want to tell us where it is and save yourself trouble?"

"I don't know what you're talking about," Chet said.

The other two men were already in the kitchen. Chet heard the feet of one go thumping down the cellar stairs. Because he could do nothing else, he sat in the chair while they went methodically through the house and cellar. All the time they were below Chet sat still under the eyes of the officious detective with the gun, his ears strained to hear any sound of moving. The preserve cupboard that his father had built so that it looked like a solid wall out from the furnace room, with a little six by six room back of it packed with liquor, bottles, labels, seals, alcohol, would be a find if they had sense enough to try to move the shelves. But the two came upstairs with nothing in their hands but a sack and some straw bottle sheaths. The three of them stood looking at Chet. "Where's your old man?" one said.

"He's out of town."

"Went kind of suddenly, didn't he?" the man with the gun said sarcastically. "I saw him this afternoon."

Chet shrugged.

"Hell with the old man," the second man said. "Where do you keep the whiskey? You'll get off easier if you spill it."

"What whiskey?" Chet said.

"Oh for Christ sake," the first man said. "Don't be as stupid as you look. You aren't pulling anything off."

The blood had drained from Chet's face. He could feel his skin dead and stiff on his bones. "Go to hell," he said flatly.

The tableau of the three glaring at him was interrupted by a jerk from the little hook-nosed man in the middle. He held up a hand. "Shhh!" he said. In the garage beside the house a motor was cut. A car door slammed.

"Round in front, you, Ted," the man with the gun whispered. "Joe and I'll wait for him at the back door."

Chet wet his lips. He ought to jump and shout a warning. But the deputy had his gun out again. The old man wouldn't have a chance to run for it, and he might get shot. He closed his mouth, but he couldn't stay sitting down. As the back door opened he saw the deputy spring forward, his gun out. "I got you!" he said. He was so excited that his mouth frothed. "Don't you make a move, I got you, by God!"

Caught entirely unaware, Bo stood in the doorway, the sack of whiskey he had been unable to deliver in his arms. His eyes shot from the deputy with the gun to Chet, standing white and still in the other doorway. His lips came together and he breathed once, audibly, through his nose.

"All right," he said. "You're Tom Mix. You got me. What do you want?"

The deputy grabbed the sack and Bo let it go in contempt. It crashed on the floor with a thudding clink of smashed glass. The deputy, showing his teeth, let it lie there. "You're under arrest," he said. "Possession and transportation."

Bo's voice was perfectly controlled, the voice of a good citizen annoyingly bothered by officious officers. "Since when have you started arresting people for having a little liquor around for their own private use?"

"Own use my ass," the deputy said. "Come on, you too." He motioned to Chet, took a pair of handcuffs from his pocket and shook them.

Bo's eyes went narrow and black. "He's got nothing to do with whatever you're charging me with," he said. "He's just a kid."

"Would you like to handle this?" the deputy said. He handcuffed the two of them together, and for just an instant their eyes met, Chet's smoky, sullen, a little scared, Bo's bleak and gray. "Don't worry, kid," Bo said. "This smart bastard is just showing off. You'll be out of this in an hour."

"That's all right," Chet said. He went along out to the deputies' car, feeling his chained hand brush against his father's as he walked, and his whole mind was emptied as if water had washed through it.

7

For an hour after lunch she had been sitting on the balcony with two women from Salt Lake, one a dancing instructor at the university, the other the wife of a professor. They were very pleasant women, easy to know, their voices quiet. The things they talked about let her for a little while look into a world that had been completely closed to her. The professor's wife had been reading a book by a man named Sinclair Lewis.

"You must read it," she told Elsa. "It's priceless. I should think every Rotarian in the country would be squirming."

"I think it's rather pathetic," the dancing instructor said. "After his boy has run off and married the girl, you remember, Babbitt has to accept it and give the two his blessing. When he said that about never having been able once in his life to do what he really wanted to do, I could have wept."

"The Civil War didn't abolish slavery," Mrs. Webb said. "We're all slaves to something, just like Babbitt. I hate to think of what somebody might write about college professors, plugging along with their minds half on their work and half on a promotion. There are a thousand things George would like to do, but there he goes on reading themes and getting up lectures and going through the same old grind year after year, just getting acquainted with his students' minds and then having them pass the course and vanish. I should think that must be the worst feeling on earth, teaching freshmen in college. You'd never meet any minds but seventeen-year-old ones. Eventually your own mind must freeze at that level."

"Have you noticed George deteriorating?" the instructor said.

"I notice he never gets his book done. That's where my slavery comes in. He's a slave to his classes and I'm a slave to the duty of driving him in to work on his book." She smiled at Elsa. "What's your husband a slave to?"

"I don't know," Elsa said. "Cigars, maybe."

She could have come much closer than that, but it wouldn't do. Any consideration of his slavery or her own had to be kept for the nights when sleep wouldn't come and the thoughts went around in their circular paths, pacing the mind like animals caged. Neither she nor her thoughts had any place in the society of these women who could talk shop freely and openly, criticize their husbands because nobody would dare to think for a moment that their husbands were not respectable and estimable men. You criticized in public only when you hadn't really much to object to.

For an instant, sitting in the sweet afternoon sun with these women who read books, went to plays, knew music, moved in an atmosphere of ideas, she felt a pang of bitter black envy. It had never occurred to her why the world of criminals and lawbreakers was called the underworld, but it was clear now. You were shut out, you moved in the dark underneath, and if you came up for a brief time, as she was doing now, you knew, better than these women who accepted you in friendship as something you were not, that you were an uneasy visitor in a place where you didn't belong. Under other circumstances these women might really have been her friends. They could have played bridge or Mah Jong in the evenings, visited at each other's houses, loaned each other books, gone to plays or movies or musicals together.

"That's dreadfully true," she said. "That about the slavery."

The mail truck from Salt Lake came up across the bridge and stopped under the balcony. A boy carried the mail sack inside.

"There's what I'm a slave to," the instructor said. She put away her petit point and stood up. "I just exist from one mail to the next. If the truck broke down some day and didn't get here at least with my newspaper I think I'd die."

She went down after her mail, and the professor's wife held out the Lewis book. "Would you like to read this? I think you'd like it."

"Why thank you," Elsa said. "My son and I have been reading things aloud in the evenings. He'll be going to the university this fall."

She riffled the pages, wondering when Bruce was coming up. He generally came around three, after he had gone through all his rituals of being a good camper. She stood up to look down the road, and it was then that she saw the Cadillac coming. It pulled into the parking lot and Bo got out, and she could tell from the very way he walked that something was wrong.

"Excuse me," she said to Mrs. Webb, and laid the book down in her chair. "Here comes my husband . . ."

In her room she heard him through in silence. "Well," she said when he was done, "I guess I'd better start packing my things."

"Do you think you ought to?" Bo said. "The doc said a couple months, at least."

"Did you come up just to tell me to stay on here?" she said. Then she saw that he was hurt. He had run to her the minute he got into trouble, and he had come to take her back, but he didn't like to be told why he had come. "I wouldn't think of staying," she said. "I feel worlds better. A month has been more than enough."

"I want you to stay right here if you think you need to," Bo said. "There's no point in coming down if you're going to get all run down again."

Out of the weariness that had come back on her, Elsa smiled. "We'll be moving again, I suppose."

"I guess we'll have to."

He sat on the bed and watched her put her clothes in the bags. He was nervous and fidgety, stood up to look out the window, lit a cigar, let it go out, lit it again. "That damned show-off prohi," he said. "Waving a gun around as if he was catching horse thieves. I wish to hell Chet hadn't been there."

Elsa turned sharply. "Was Chet there?"

"Didn't I tell you?" Bo said. "They took him down to the station with me, but they let him loose right away. It was just that prohi trying to get himself a reputation. I don't think he'd ever made a raid before."

Elsa only half heard him. She wanted to say "Oh my God!" and sit down on the bed and cry. Instead she said, quietly, "How did Chet take it?"

"All right. He was pretty white. He just kept his mouth shut till they turned him loose."

"Have you seen him since?"

"No. I didn't get out till eleven-thirty. They didn't take the car, because they didn't have any evidence I'd been transporting in it, so I gave Chet the keys. When I got back this morning the car was in the garage and Chet was gone. I suppose he went to work, or else out to make some arrangements."

"Arrangements for what?"

"I guess I didn't tell you that, either. I saw Bill Talbot and he's taking Chet along this trip."

So it was better, she thought. That would keep him from thinking too much about it. But it was bad enough to have had him dragged off to jail. "That's the part I hate worst about this business," she said. "To have the boys get mixed up in it . . ."

"Do you think I like it?"

"You could have prevented it if you'd quit a long time ago."

His face flushed darkly. "Kick me," he said. "I'm down."

"That isn't fair," she said, almost crying.

"Is it fair to gouge me when I'm down? I'd have done anything to prevent that, if I could have."

"Bo," she said, "let's not fight. I'm sorry. I'm just sick about Chet, that's all."

So you've given up again, her mind said. You've backed away when you knew you were right. You used to have more spirit than that.

Will you go on, she said, will you keep on backing away until your children are both blackened by this dirty business, or driven to something worse? She looked at Bo, his face haggard, almost old, the faint lines of bitterness and violence deepened around his mouth. He was miserable too, as miserable as she was.

But then why! she said. He could have got out of this business years ago.

What is your husband a slave to, Mrs. Mason? To himself, Mrs. Webb, to himself. To his notion that he has to make a pile, be a big shot, have a hundred thousand dollars in negotiable securities in his safety deposit box, drive a Cadillac car, have seven pairs of shoes with three-dollar trees for each pair, buy three expensive Panamas during a summer and wear a diamond worth fifteen hundred dollars in his tie. He doesn't know, he wouldn't know, what to do with money when he has it. Would he ever think of going to the theater, or reading a good book, or taking a trip somewhere just for the trip? He gave up reading books ten years ago, and even when he goes to a movie he goes only to kill three hours . . .

"Chet'll be all right," he said. "I wouldn't worry about him, Else."

"I hope so," she said. "He's more sensitive than you think, though. He has to show off a lot, and pretend he's older than he is. He lives on the admiration of his pals. And if this gets in the paper it'll hurt his pride so bad. . . . Is it in the paper?"

"Not very big," Bo said. "It's there, though."

"Poor Chet," she said.

"We'll have to stop at Bruce's camp," she said. "Maybe we could let him stay up here."

"Moving, we could use him," Bo said.

"Well, we'll see." She took one bag and Bo the other. At the top of the stairs Elsa remembered Mrs. Webb and the book. "I have to run up again," she said. "I'll meet you in the car."

Up on the balcony she spoke to Mrs. Webb. "I'm sorry," she said. "I guess I won't be able to read your book after all. My husband just came up and I have to go down with him."

"I hope it isn't anything serious," Mrs. Webb said.

"No. Nothing serious. I may come back in the next few days. I . . . hope so. It's been a wonderful place."

"If you don't," Mrs. Webb said, "don't forget to come and call. I'd love to see you. Did I give you my address?"

"Yes," Elsa said. "I hope you'll come and see me too."

Mrs. Webb put out her hand. "It's been ever so nice to know you," she said. "Be easy on yourself. You don't want to get sick again."

"I feel almost as if I were leaving home," Elsa said. "Will you say goodbye to Miss Sorenson for me?"

She broke away and went, and on the stairs she met Miss Sorenson and had to go through it again. Miss Sorenson had the paper under her arm, and as she got into the car Elsa thought miserably that now, probably, up there in the sun on the balcony, the two would read that news item, not very big but there all right, and know her for what she was. Next to her worry about how Chet was taking everything, that was the most miserable of many miserable thoughts. The only consolation was that the address she had given Mrs. Webb would be useless after a day or two. So even if Mrs. Webb missed that item in the paper, and came to call, she would find only blank windows and a closed door. At the very least, the underworld could hide.

She found more to worry about than even her worse anxieties could have anticipated. When, at the end of a week that left her sick and spent, she sat down in the afternoon with all of it settled, Chet gone, Bruce off with a friend's family on a tour of the southern parks, Bo downtown making the last of his undercover arrangements that would get him off lightly with a fine, she felt as if she had gone through an earthquake, and the world was still tipsily rocking. Moving hadn't helped any, either. Her curtains weren't up yet, there were boxes still unpacked in the kitchen, the linen was piled on top of the bed in the spare bedroom. The house, like her own life, was upside-down, but she couldn't do any more now. She just wanted to sit and cry. Even the realization of how burnt-out she felt sent a twinge through her, and she rested her forehead on her hand. Ah Chet, Chet, she said, blinking the tears. She had cried enough already, she thought in wonder, so that she shouldn't be able to cry any more.

She looked up at the uncurtained room. It was a pleasant enough room, far pleasanter than many she had lived in, but the windows were streaked, the shades hung a little crookedly in their brackets, the rug wasn't down yet and the furniture was arranged anyhow. It struck her as a cold room, an unlived-in room, as unfriendly to its new occupants as a barn. Whenever she moved anything the sound echoed. Outside, in the stretch of vacant lots that went for a half block down the street, children were yelling, and cars went up and down on the new pavement, but the sounds too were remote and indifferent. She was shut up here in this half-lived-in house, hidden behind its dirty windows, in isolation as complete as if she lived in Labrador.

The mantel clock said four o'clock. It would be pleasant, she thought, to have somebody drop in (her eyes took in the amount

428

of cleaning and straightening still necessary, and she retreated from her wish, then came back to it again. What difference did the condition of the house make? They had moved in only yesterday. Whoever would be coming would be a close friend). They would have a glass of iced tea and a cookie or cake, and sit and talk a while. It would be a relief to talk. For five days she hadn't talked to anyone but furious people, sullen people, stubborn people, tearful people. She had had to play peace-maker to the whole bunch of them when she would rather have gone to her room and cried.

Somebody to talk to. What if Mrs. Webb came around?

Don't be stupid, she said. You couldn't talk to her, or to anyone except Bo or Bruce, and Bruce is gone for a week and Bo is still mad enough to fly off the handle at a word. You can sit and let it simmer inside you, that's all you can do.

Now, she said, you really know what it is to be uprooted. You're as homeless as a tramp on a park bench. You've pulled away from all your family and you're alone in a room that isn't really yours. You have a father, a step-mother who used to be your best friend, a sister, a brother, uncles and aunts and cousins, but you don't know any of them any more except maybe Kristin.

Psycho-social isolation, her mind said. That was what Bruce had said about the way they lived, one day when they were talking in the parlor by the fire. She had laughed then at the big words, and at the half-playful venom with which he spat them out. Something he had got in school—another mysterious world that she saw only in reflections and heard only in echoes, through her children. Psycho-social isolation.

"Well, whatever you call it," she said to the empty room, "I hate it!"

And oh, Chet, Chet, she said, why did you let it hit you so hard? You were strong enough to bear burdens and strains and fatigue. Why weren't you strong enough to bear shame?

She rose and wandered around the room, picked up the metal elephant on the mantel, brushed the dust on it experimentally, set it down again. There was a box of stationery, two or three bottles of ink, some pens and pencils in a carton on the other end of the mantel, waiting for time when she could put them away. The clock said four-twenty. Bo wouldn't be home till six, probably. She took paper, pen, and ink and went into the dining room. Somebody to talk to. The best she could do was Kristin, fifteen hundred miles away. Sitting with the pen in her hand she found herself crying again, her eyes running over without effort or strain or sobs, as if she were too tired to cry properly, but had to sit and simply drip from the eyes. And she knew she couldn't write it, even to Kristin.

All she could do was think it, wonder why Chet had thrown up the whole works, even the trip with the ball team, even the chance he had been dreaming about for two or three years. Why he should be so humiliated and shamed that he would run off that way, take Laura with him, be so sullen and unapproachable when the police finally brought them back . . .

But she knew, really. He wouldn't have anything to do with anything his father had ever touched. He had meant that runaway as a final pulling-up of all the roots—he had meant never to come back. He had it in his mind that he couldn't ever face anybody he knew, now. If he appeared at the ball park with the team he was afraid the people in the stands who knew him would say, "There's Chet Mason. His old man got pinched for bootlegging a while back. He's got a nerve, showing his face around."

But to get married! she said. At seventeen! To run across the state line into Wyoming and lie about his age four years, and with only a few dollars in his pockets. To hate his father so bad he would do anything like that, give up his whole ambition, just to get away . . .

Oh Lord, she said, and leaned her head on her hand. The whole business was mixed up and confused, but the confusion couldn't eliminate the certainty of what had happened. It couldn't make her forget the fury Laura's father had been in, the way he gobbled and strangled over the telephone when the runaway had first been discovered, and the way Bo had shouted back at him. He would blame Chet himself, and be hard as nails with him, but he wouldn't let Laura's father blame him.

And all that argument, and Chet so sullen that he wouldn't speak, and Laura shut up in her house and kept even from telephoning. She tried to think of what she might have said to Kristin if she had written, how she would have told about all that, even the buggy whip that Mr. Betterton had used on Laura, and how she had had to be peace-maker, calm Bo down, finally go down herself in a taxi and insist that Laura be allowed to come up and talk with her privately. She would have said how she had urged them both to submit to annulment, save trouble by letting the proceedings go through. They couldn't fight it anyway. All they could do would be to make themselves and everybody else unhappier than they were. It was best to pretend that they hadn't been for two days man and wife. They could go back to work and save their money and get married again after a few years, and it would be better.

Talking like that, all the time with Chet's sullen face before her, and Laura twisting her hands, crying, so frightened of her father that she wailed, and said she had to get away, she couldn't go back, why couldn't people have left them alone? But it was Chet she worried about. He was too grim and silent, he too obviously hated Bo, and even if this was smoothed over she knew there would be other things, that Chet wouldn't stay now.

It was Laura, she would have had to say to Kristin, who finally weakened. Chet would have stood up in court and shouted that they had lived together, and that the marriage shouldn't be annulled. It was Laura who listened when she told them how hard life could be without enough money, how a few years spent saving now might make all the difference later. It was Laura who accepted the promise of help later, and agreed to let their fathers cancel the marriage. And it was Laura who convinced Chet.

Not, Elsa said bitterly, his mother. His mother couldn't convince him of anything. Only his girl could, and she only because she was so scared, poor thing.

And what Chet had said when he finally agreed: "I'm doing this for you, Mom, not for him, and I'm never going to live at home again." She hadn't had the heart to tell Bo that. It would have made him boiling mad, but it would have hurt him too. And she hadn't pointed out to Bo (and this she couldn't have said to Kristin at all) that it was the whiskey business that was the cause of the whole trouble. She knew what his answer would have been: What could he do? He had to make a living somehow, didn't he? How was he going to make up the loss brought on by this last raid? Christ Almighty, did she think he *liked* having the law in his hair all the time? Let him get a little ahead, and he'd quit, sure, but how could he quit now? And could he help it if the prohi making the raid was a hysterical damn fool and pinched the kid? Did she think *he* liked it?

Elsa pushed away the pen and ink and stood up. There wasn't any of it you could tell Kristin. It was nothing that could be told. All you could do was shut your mouth and make the best of it. But the mere thought of making the best of it, reconciling yourself to the thought that your son went white with hatred when his father talked to him, that he had blown all his chances and might never pick them up again, that his sullenness might drive him to any sort of foolish and reckless act, made her bite her lips. Like the last two nights Chet had been home. Drunk both nights, she knew. But what could she say? What could she do? What argument could she have used to move him, brace him up, give him the feeling that his whole life wasn't ruined? He was so sure it was. First, his mind seemed to say, Bo had spoiled his life at home for him, and now he had spoiled the only other life that had been open. All right, with both spoiled he would go to hell as fast as possible. It was silly, it was childish, but it was unstoppable, unless Chet came to himself, got a decent job up in Idaho where he'd gone, got on his feet again and hooked up with another ball team, something to give him confidence in himself and the world again . . . This trouble was only a moment, if he looked at it straight. There was his whole life ahead of him.

She thought of what Bruce had said one day at Brighton. He had amazed her then, as he sometimes did, with the things that went on in his mind. People, he had said, were always being looked at as points, and they ought to be looked at as lines. There weren't any points, it was false to assume that a person ever *was* anything. He was always becoming something, always changing, always continuous and moving, like the wiggly line on a machine used to measure earthquake shocks. He was always what he was in the beginning, but never quite exactly what he was; he moved along a line dictated by his heritage and his environment, but he was subject to every sort of variation within the narrow limits of his capabilities.

It was too complicated an idea for her, but it seemed to her now that if she could bring herself to look at Chet as a line and not as a point she might even be able to laugh. If she could only look back and fix her mind on escapades of his childhood. He was always getting into scrapes, having the neighbors over for drinks during the flu epidemic in Whitemud, stealing that gun from Tex Davis' shack and thinking how big and tough he was with a man-sized forty-four, getting into trouble years ago back at that home in Seattle, when she had had to take the boys out and go home to Indian Falls . . .

She shut her mind on that too. There was danger in looking at people as lines. The past spread backward and you saw things in perspective that you hadn't seen then, and that made the future ominous, more ominous than if you just looked at the point, at the moment. There might be truth in what Bruce said, but there was not much comfort.

Chet came home, but not because he wanted to. A week after he and Van went up into Idaho they got drunk in Idaho Falls and were thrown in the bullpen for the night. When they were released next day and asked to get out of town they decided to hit for Ashton, up in the high timber country, to see if anything was stirring in the sawmills or placer mines. Ten miles out of Idaho Falls they hit a pile of gravel and rolled over. Van, wedged behind the wheel, had three broken ribs, a broken collar bone, and a badly skinned face. Chet, thrown clear, broke his right arm in two places. A passing motorist took them back to Idaho Falls, where they spent all their remaining money for doctor bills. As soon as Van was able to travel, they came back to Salt Lake on the train, their fare paid by Van's mother.

For almost two weeks Chet stayed sullenly at home, hardly going out of the house except to the drugstore for newspapers and magazines. All morning he sat with the paper, all afternoon with a magazine, his feet propped on a chair and his sling adjusted across his stomach. Even to his mother he said nothing about his marriage or what had come after it, nothing about how the accident had happened, nothing about what he was going to do when his arm knitted. He did not, so far as any of them saw, have any communication with Laura. Nobody ever saw him use the telephone or write any letters.

At the end of two weeks, when his arm was out of the cast, he asked his mother for a little money. She had none at hand except a few dollars left from the household allowance, but she gave him that without asking questions. He counted it. Eleven dollars.

"Can you get me a little more?" he said. "Ten dollars or so?"

"Are you going away again, Chet?"

He nodded. "For good," he said.

"Where?"

"I don't know."

"Will you write? Promise."

"I'll write," he said. "Don't think I'm blaming you, Mom. You've been swell. I'll write to you."

That night she asked Bo for twenty dollars. He looked up in surprise, because she rarely asked him for money beyond her allowance. But he didn't ask what she wanted it for. Without a word he dug it out of his wallet and she slipped it under the base of the lamp by Chet's bed.

The next morning, after Bo had gone downtown, Chet came into the kitchen with his suitcase packed. She wanted to hold him, hang onto him, beg him not to go, to stay and get a job in town and forget all that had happened, but his face was so somberly still that she didn't. She was as helpless to keep him with her now as she had been to prevent the whole debacle that had driven him into himself.

433

"Goodbye, Chet," she said, and felt his arms tighten around her. There was that comfort at least; he loved her, nothing that had happened had alienated him from her. "You've got so little money," she said. "Why don't you wait and I'll get some more."

"I wouldn't want more," Chet said. "I'll take enough of his money to get me out of town, and that's all."

"You're bitter," she said, searching his eyes. "Don't hold things against your dad. He feels bad that things worked out the way they did. And if you get in any trouble, or even if you don't, write to him. He'd be pleased to help you, Chet. Do you know that?"

"I guess he won't have the chance," Chet said. "I'm not going to get into any trouble."

"But you'll write . . . him too."

He squeezed her hands, the grip of his left hand hard, that of his right weaker, feeble from the recent injury. "Take care of yourself," he said. "I'll let you know where I land."

And there he went, Elsa thought, there he went, this time for good.

Three months later, from Rapid City, South Dakota, she got a postcard. Chet and Laura were married again.

VIII

From his
window on the
third story Bruce
could look out over
a flat acreage of lights
climbing upward to the
signboards and the tall mills
along the Mississippi. The river
itself was a sunken black channel
with firefly lights moving mysteriously
along its bottom, and against the glow
of the St. Paul side he saw the superstructure of
the bridge he crossed every morning on his way to class.

He had picked the highest room he could find, because
he hated the flat country. The sky came down too close all
around, like a smothering tent, and an eye that wanted to
look out was constantly interrupted by buildings, trees, the
swell of low hills. Even outside the city, where he had gone
hopefully on walks, he had found no place high enough to give
him a view, no place flat enough to let him see more than a quarter
of a mile. The upper-floor room helped some. It gave him a
chance at night to pretend that the lights he looked down on were
much farther away than they really were, and to cultivate his
nostalgia for the high benches around Salt Lake with the forty-
mile valley wide open below him, the state road a string of
distended yellow lights on down toward the Jordan narrows, the
slag dumps at Magna and West Jordan belching gobbets of fire
on the black slope of the Oquirrhs.

He was homesick and almost terrifyingly alone. He ought to go
out to a movie, or get busy on torts. There were plenty of things
to do if he could bring his mind to them, but instead he went and
sat on the window sill, opened the sash to let in a blast of cold
January air, and sat looking out.

Bruce Mason, he said. Bruce Mason, first year law. There was
something almost cosmically ironical about his choice of profession. He remembered what Bill Levine, a friend of his father's,
had said when he heard it. That big gross animal with the
shrunken legs, sitting in his wheel chair all day with a sanctimo-
nious look on his face, a look that said, "See, I'm a cripple, I have
to sell taffy and nuts on the street for a living. A nickel for a bag
of nuts will help keep life in a body that the world has miserably

misused!" And under cover of the taffy and nuts he would arrange you a woman, sell you a stolen car, get you a bottle or a case, give you a card to the hop joints in Plum Alley, play procurer and pimp with his patient, resigned smile that covered a lewdness as deep and stinking as the pit.

"There's nothing like a lawyer in the family," he had said. "Eh Harry?"

Bruce shut the window and stood up. And what, he said, would you do if you became a public prosecutor and found yourself prosecuting your old man? Would you send him to McNeil Island for two years for conspiracy to evade the prohibition law? That would make a nice little problem in family loyalty and public duty. Would you sprinkle dust on Polynices' head, or leave him for the wolves?

If I only understood better, he said. If I really knew what I think, what I am, what he is and mother is and Chet is, how everything got off on the wrong foot. If I knew how and why mother has stood it for over twenty-five years, I might know something.

He got out his mother's last letter, delivered that morning, written three days before. It was a good letter, but it told him nothing of what he wanted to know. Everything that was tangled or thwarted or broken in the family relationships was carefully held back.

If a man could understand himself and his own family, Bruce thought, he'd have a good start toward understanding everything he'd ever need to know. He laid his mother's letter down and sprawled his legs under the desk. The book on torts was at his elbow. He tossed it over on the cot and reached for a notebook.

"This is not a journal," he wrote. "It is not notes for a novel, not a line-a-day record of the trivia my mind dredges up. Call it an attempt to understand."

Understand what? he said. Where do I begin? With myself, my father, his father, his grandfather? When did the germ enter? Where did the evil come in?

"I suppose," he wrote, "that the understanding of any person is an exercise in genealogy. A man is not a static organism to be taken apart and analyzed and classified. A man is movement, motion, a continuum. There is no beginning to him. He runs through his ancestors, and the only beginning is the primal beginning of the single cell in the slime. The proper study of mankind is man, but man is an endless curve on the eternal graph paper, and who can see the whole curve?

"What is my father? What is my mother? What is my brother?

What am I? Those sound like fatuous questions, but they occupy our whole lives. Suppose I said my father is a bootlegger who lives in Salt Lake City, is easily irritated, has occasional spells of intense good spirits? Suppose I said he wears a diamond like a walnut in his tie and another as big as a pickled onion on his finger, that he pays a hundred dollars apiece for his suits. Those are observable characteristics. Or suppose I said that all his life he has been haunted by the dream of quick wealth and isn't quite unscrupulous enough to make his dream come true, that he is a gambler who isn't quite gambler enough, who has a streak of penuriousness in him, a kind of dull Dutch caution, so that he gambles with one hand and holds back a stake with the other. He might have made a mint playing the market before the crash; instead he bought gilt-edged stocks outright and made less. Suppose I labelled him: a self-centered and dominating egotist who insists on submission from his family and yet at the same time is completely dependent on his wife, who is in all the enduring ways stronger than he is. Suppose I listed his talents: a violent stubbornness that butts through things and often overcomes them, immense energy (generally in the wrong causes), a native tendency to be generous that is always being overcome by his developing greediness and his parsimonious penny-pinching. Add a vein of something like poetic talent, a feeling for poetry of a certain sort, as witness his incredible performance last summer of quoting, after a lapse of almost thirty years, pages and pages of Burns that he had learned in the Wisconsin woods.

"When I have put that down, I have perhaps sketched a character, I have done the sort of thing a novelist probably does before writing his book. But I have not even scratched the surface of Harry Mason. Everything I have listed is subject to contradiction by other characteristics, open to qualification in degree and kind; everything has a history that goes back and back toward a vanishing point. His history is important. It is important to know that he ran away from home at fourteen, and why; that he worked in the woods and on the railroad; that he was disappointed in his ambition to be a big league ball player. It is valuable to remember that all his ancestors as far back as I know anything about them were pioneers, and that he was born when almost all the opportunities for pioneering were gone. It is necessary to look at his father, about whom I know nothing except that the Andersonville prison spoiled his disposition. Probably it didn't spoil his disposition at all, but only let out something that was already there. It would be as accurate to say that the strain of living outside the law has soured my father's temper. Actually he has always had it. It's like the tar in tar paper. When it's new and fresh the tar is distributed, the paper holds it. Under conditions of sun or rain or exposure the tar begins to lump or ooze out. The process of growing older is perhaps a simple process of breaking down cell walls, releasing things that have for a while been bound up in the firmness of young muscle.

"And how far back beyond one ought to go, and how infinitely much one could fill in to the bare outline of two generations! I can't, obviously, make even a beginning. What bred that evil temper and that egotism and that physical energy and that fine set of senses and that manual dexterity and that devotion to pipe-dreams into Harry Mason, into his violent old father, into the generations hidden down below the eroded surface of the present?

"To know what Harry Mason is, as of January, 1931, I should have to know every thought, accident, rebuff, humiliation, triumph, emotion, that ever happened to him and all his ancestors, and beyond that I should have to weigh him against a set of standards to which I was willing to subscribe. That would be understanding, but that kind of understanding can only happen instantaneously in the mind of God."

So where do I start? he said. He had been writing furiously for three quarters of an hour, but he hadn't even come to a starting point. Nothing in the whole texture of his life or his family's life was arbitrary, yet he could approach it only by being arbitrary. There were too many things he couldn't know.

All right, he said, I'll start with the things I do know.

"I suppose I have always hated him, probably not always with justice. Most children whose fathers are not completely house-broken must have that same hatred in greater or less degree. Yet if a father is housebroken he is less than God, and open to contempt. It must be a hard thing to be a father. To get away with it, a man should have both strength and patience, and patience my father never had. I know that I hold things against him that were my fault, times when I whined or disobeyed or didn't listen, but still, to have one's nose rubbed in one's own excrement, or have his collarbone broken by his father's knocking him end over end across the woodbox, are humiliations that a child cannot easily forget or forgive. It helps not at all to know that your father is often sorry and ashamed after a blow-up.

"When the child is a cry-baby, as I was, the situation gets worse, because the cry-baby runs to his mother and there arises a combination of mother and child against father. (I wonder what cry-

438

babyishness in a child becomes as the child matures? What is the connection between uncontrolled bawling in a child and uncontrolled rage in a man? It is curious to think that maybe my father as a child was a cry-baby.)

"My hatred of him seems to arise from two things: his violence to me, and his inability or unwillingness to see that he was misusing my mother. It is possible that she has never thought herself misused, though I know she has always hated the liquor business, and has thought that Chet with another kind of start would have done better.

"Add to those reasons my own adolescent snobbishness. I was ashamed of the old man all the time I was in college. I was envious of boys whose fathers were respectable, companionable, understanding, everything that mine was not. I hated the flashiness he put on in his clothes, I hated what I saw as boorishness in his manners. I don't believe we've had a friendly and open conversation since I was twelve, and I know he hasn't kissed me since at least that long ago. I think he has been afraid to.

"It used to drive me crazy, wondering why mother stayed with him. I have asked her a dozen times why she didn't leave him. I'd get a job and support her. She always said that I didn't understand. Understand what? There's only one thing she could have meant, that she loved him. That, and her belief that loyalty to your own actions is the highest virtue, are the only reasons she would have stayed. She made her bed, and she'll lie in it till she dies in it. That kind of loyalty, without love, would be stupider than I think any action of mother's could be, but even without love, it is more admirable than anything the old man can show. I don't think he has ever faced the consequences of an act; he shuts his eyes and gets mad.

"Chet's the same way, only he never did have a bad temper. It was only when the old man pushed him around that he got hard and mulish. Somehow the tar missed him; and though it seems a mad thing to say, I think he is weaker for not having it. When things go wrong for him he broods. He was that way at Christmas, having trouble with Laura, thinking about how he had to come crawling back last year and ask charity from the family. It's a pity that he couldn't have stayed with baseball, but once he got his back up he wouldn't admit his mistake about Laura. If he had, he wouldn't be out of work now, and he wouldn't have had to take that blow in his pride. I could have cried, almost, at Christmas, the way he's got so gentle with me. He used to be always horsing around and sparring at me and kidding me. Now he's Big Brother, obviously proud of me, taking me on as an equal and in some ways, painfully, as a superior. And there was that graduation present he bought me just after he'd come back, when he didn't have a dime and was still looking for work and was still raw from having to ask the old man to help him out. I know he stole the money for that cigarette lighter from the baby's bank, and that Laura found him out and they had a fight.

"That was a nasty time for him, and I don't imagine it's much better now, driving a taxi. I remember how he was when he came back, after the mine closed down and he lost his job. All day he'd sit in the front room learning to play a Hawaiian guitar, twanging away on 'The Rosary,' a sick tune if there ever was one, sitting there all alone, wrapped in some kind of personal isolation, while the baby cried and Laura scolded and mother tried to keep things smooth . . . There's a defeat in that picture that I hate, because Chet is a good fellow. He'd give you his shirt in zero weather. I guess he missed the old man's selfishness, too—and in a way that too weakens him. I hate to see him whipped before he's twenty-four, hopelessly practising a home course in taxidermy, and fooling with that damned guitar.

"And the dreams, the hopelessly rosy dreams. I remember just after I'd gone back for the holidays, when we were taking a shower together and harmonizing in the bathroom. He thought we could work up some songs, go in for a vaudeville act, try to get on the Pantages circuit. He actually had got himself believing it was possible. It isn't, even though he can sing. I don't know why it's impossible, but I know it, and I knew it then. It all belongs with the taxidermy and the dead magpies in the basement and the glue and paper and feathers, and the interminable damned guitar twanging 'The Rosary.'

"That's a defeat that the old man is at least partly responsible for. Mother's is another.

"Yet it's important to remember that he isn't a monster, as I used to think he was. He doesn't tramp on people out of meanness. They get in his road, that's all, or he's tied to them and drags them along with him. He can even be kind, and I guess that now I think of it I can see why mother loved him once and maybe still does. I saw that when she got sick a year ago.

"When she came out that morning with the queer look on her face and said that she'd found a big lump in her breast, their eyes jumped to meet each other, and it seemed to me that all of a sudden I could see what living together twenty-five years can do to two people. They asked and answered a dozen questions in that one look.

"I remember her operation, too, the way the old man woke me

440

at six in the morning to go to the hospital. He probably hadn't slept much. But he couldn't stand it down there. He held her hand while they gave her the ether—and I suppose I was jealous that she wanted him, not me—but the minute they began getting ready, and Cullen came out of the washroom with his scrubbed hands in the air for a nurse to pull the gloves on, the old man lurched out as white as chalk. Once or twice during the operation I saw his face looking in the operating room door, but it never stayed more than a second or two, and when Cullen came back with the slides and said it was malignant, that it meant radical surgery, we had to hunt for two or three minutes to find the old man. He was sitting out on the fire escape, gray clear to the lips. He just nodded when Cullen told him, and he never made a move to come in again. If he had he probably would have fainted, because it was like a butcher's block.

"Afterwards he visited her twice a day, brought her candy, filled her room with flowers. He even tried to talk to me about her and get me to say she would probably be all right now, wouldn't she? There wasn't anything left for cancer to grow in, was there? I'm afraid I didn't give him much help. I didn't think then, and I don't now, that she has more than a fifty-fifty chance of its not coming back. I suppose I acted cold, but it was only because I was talking to him. I agonized over it enough, because I love my mother, and respect her, more than anyone I have ever met, and that's not anything a psychologist can grin about. Why shouldn't I? There's a positive flame in her, a curious little bright flame that never goes down.

"But the old man was good to her then. He wouldn't have talked her into going to visit Kristin if he had been thinking only of himself. Maybe he thought that she might not live long, that he owed her a visit home. He suggested that she go through Hardanger and see the people they'd known when they were first married, and just before she left, when Chet and Laura and the baby came in from the mine, he agreed without a whimper to take them in. Give him credit: he's kept them ever since, even if he has grumbled.

"She enjoyed that trip. Nobody in Hardanger recognized her at first, and she had fun being mysterious and letting recognition dawn on them. They gave her the keys to the town, apparently. That must be a curious feeling, to go back after twenty-five years and see all your friends grown gray and fat and bald, and count the stones in the graveyard, and know that you've grown older along with everything else. Anyway she enjoyed it, and she came back in better health.

"Maybe she'll get by. Maybe there's a chance that after I finish here I can get her to break loose from that life. She deserves some friends, she deserves a rest. She's had too long a vacation from any sort of normal woman's life.

"It's an almost marvellous fact that a dozen years of living among bootleggers and pimps and bellhops and all the little scummy riffraff on the edge of the criminal class hasn't touched her—simply hasn't touched her. Neither has the constant sacrifice she has had to make of her own wishes and her own life. It's almost comical to see how completely those small-time thugs respect her. She has been the repository of the confessions and woes of half a dozen kept women, she's been within smelling distance of a dozen stinking episodes, she has had for companions altogether too many foul-mouthed, unscrupulous, lying, cheating, vicious people, but all they have succeeded in doing is to make her kindly-wise. For all her yielding and her self-sacrificing, there is something in her that doesn't give when it's pushed at. She only gives up her wishes, never herself."

Bruce stretched his cramped fingers and looked up. This could go on all night and he would be no closer to what he was after. Probably when he read over what he had written he wouldn't even agree with half of it. He picked up his mother's letter again. No mention of how the double-family arrangement was going now, nothing about how the old man was behaving. Chet had finally agreed to go back to the business school, which he had started once and then dropped. His father was looking at a little sporting goods shop down on Second South, with the idea that he might buy it and set Chet up as manager. They hadn't said anything to Chet yet, and it was still only an idea, but she hoped it would come about. Chet was sick now, in bed. A week ago they had driven up to watch the ski jumping at Ecker Hill, and Chet had helped push some people out of the snow, and had got overheated and caught cold. He was running a little fever, and if he didn't get over it by tomorrow she was going to send him down to the hospital. The baby was fine, it was wonderful to have a child around the house again.

Without moving from the desk, Bruce scribbled off a letter. He had been hitting the books pretty solidly since he came back. Examinations came up next week, but he wasn't worrying too much. Maybe he'd go over to see Kristin one of these days. She was one of the great cookie-makers, and whenever he got tired of cafeteria food he liked to go over and have an orgy at her house. Also her kids were nice kids and George was a good quiet sensible

442

sort of guy. A little home atmosphere was good after a few weeks of grinding. Too bad Chet was sick. "Give him an enema," he said, "from me."

Feet clumped on the hall linoleum and knuckles rapped at his door.

"Come in," Bruce said.

It was Brucker, the fellow from the floor below, a graduate student in economics. "Just got sick of sitting on my tail," he said, peering in. "You busy?"

"No. Come on in."

His visitor flopped on the cot. "If I ever again hear the words Malthus, Mill, Pareto, or Marx," he said, "I'll puke."

"That's something I've been meaning to ask you," Bruce said. "Who is this guy Marx?"

Brucker stared at him. "You go to hell."

"Come on, tell me about him. What'd he write?"

"I'll strangle you," the economist said. "I'm in no mood to be toyed with."

Bruce laughed. "By the end of next week there won't be a sane man in the house."

"There isn't one now," Brucker said. "Boyer is down in his room lying on the bed playing with his toes, cackling like a madman. Nicholson has clutched his books unto his breast and rushed into the night toward the library so as to avoid a fine. Hadley has chucked the whole works and gone hunting a woman. How do you manage to stay up in this attic dungeon and crack the books?"

"One way is to send your only good pants to the cleaner's so you can't go out. Or maybe you have two pairs of pants."

"Three," Brucker said. "All of them so thin on the backside you can read a newspaper through them. That's why I'm studying economics."

"Come on out and let the wind blow through them," Bruce said. "I've got to mail a letter."

They went down the two flights of stairs and Bruce opened the door. Brucker sniffed. "What's that smell?" he said suspiciously.

"I don't smell anything."

"By God, I do believe it's fresh air," the economist said.

As they walked to the corner, their collars up against the still cold, a messenger boy on a bicycle passed them. Under the arclight his face looked blue. He had a muffler wrapped around his ears and his cap crammed down over it. "Brrr!" Brucker said. "I'll never again send a telegram in the winter time. It's cruelty to animals."

They sprinted from the corner back to the house, yelling, racing each other in an unpremeditated burst of energy up the stairs. At the top they met the messenger, his nose red and leaking. "Mason live up here?" he said.

"Yeah," Bruce said, surprised. "Here."

He watched the boy take the yellow envelope out of his hat. The single hall bulb threw his shadow hulking down the wall of the stairway. "Got a telegram with a money order attached," he said. "You sign right here."

"A money order?" Bruce said. He looked at Brucker and frowned. The shadow of the runty messenger heaved on the wall as the boy extended the book. Bruce looked at it without reaching out. The certainty was like ice in his throat. He looked again at Brucker. His voice came out of his tight throat in a dry, difficult whisper.

"My brother's dead!" he said.

2

He had been playing with Chet and a bunch of other kids in the loft of Chance's barn, back in Whitemud, and Chet had slid down the hay on top of him and they had had a fight. Chet had thumped him unmercifully, got him down and tried to make him holler enough, but he wouldn't holler enough, even when Chet bent his arm back in a hammerlock and he felt his shoulder heaving out of joint. "I'll give you an enema!" he kept screaming. "God damn you, just wait, I'll give you an enema!"

"Friend or enema?" Chet said. He put his grinning face down close to Bruce's and twisted his arm harder. "Come on, friend or enema?"

"Enema!" Bruce screamed. "Do you hear me, enema!"

Chet's face began to fade, the grin dwindled and sobered until the face hanging above him was serious and frowning, thinning away, going . . .

"Chet," his mother's voice said, and without surprise Bruce saw that she was there and that the kids had gone. "Chet, I wish you'd try not to scowl so. You look as if you didn't have a friend in the world."

"I'll give him an enema!" Bruce screamed. He opened his eyes and saw the row of green chair backs, the blue night lights, the sprawling figures of sleepers, the pale gleam of bunched pillows half falling off the arms into the aisle. Outside there was a thin and watery light, not yet strong enough to be called daylight, but not quite darkness. His mouth was bitter with the taste of coal smoke, and his throat was sore.

In the curious unreality of the chair car, less real than the dream

444

he had just awakened from, he straightened himself, lifted his aching shoulder from its cramped position. Half stupefied, he rose and rocked back between the sleepers to the men's room, rinsed his mouth, washed his face and hands, looked at himself in the mirror. His face was pale and floating, his tie twisted, and for a long time he stood stupidly wondering where he'd got the overcoat. It wasn't his. He didn't own one. He had got around to combing his hair before the realization came to him, not suddenly, but as a dull transition from not-knowing to knowing. Brucker's coat. He remembered Brucker, solicitous, almost anguished, and himself wandering down the hall, shaking off Brucker's hands, standing with his back to the top of the stairs while the messenger boy's scared face went on down and the fact of death lay in the hall like a heavy foul smell. Then Brucker putting him on the twelve-fifteen later, pressing his overcoat on him, shaking his hand hard, wringing it, his face stiff with sympathy. A good guy, a good friend.

He moved a spittoon with his foot so that he could sit down on the leather bench by the window. The pane was so streaked that he could barely see out. What he could see looked like Nebraska. Farms, windmills, occasional trees, fields and fences, a strip of ghostly highway and a car on it, its lights still on. He put his hand in his overcoat pocket, felt the paper, drew it out yellow and crumpled, read it again.

"Chester passed away this morning wiring you train fare love. Harry Mason."

Harry Mason, Bruce thought. Not "Dad." Not "Father." Harry Mason. As if he didn't dare use any familiar word, or were so confused he didn't know quite what he was doing. Or as if the loss of his one son had made him realize what a bottomless gulf lay between himself and the other. A stiff and formal telegram. Chester passed away this morning . . .

Oh Jesus, Bruce said, poor mother!

Tears squeezed between his lids, and at the sound of a step in the aisle he rose quickly and washed his face again. The brakeman looked through the curtain, nodded, and went on. Bruce went back to his seat and lay down, his eyes close to the smeared window, staring out across the flat land. It couldn't be Nebraska. It had to be Minnesota or Iowa. They weren't due in Omaha till sometime around six. Then a thousand miles of Nebraska and Wyoming and Utah. He'd get into Salt Lake at the worst possible time, two or three in the morning.

Chet is dead, he said. Your brother has died suddenly, and you are on your way back to his funeral. Your father has sent you a telegram and a money order. You change at Omaha to the Union Pacific and you will arrive very early in the morning in Salt Lake. You will see your mother with the knife in her. You will see Chet's wife, whom you do not much like, parading her grief, and his little girl bewildered and whimpering. You will also see your father, whom you hate, and how will he be taking it? He always liked Chet better than you, even though he treated him harder.

And Chet, he said, is dead. His life is finished at twenty-three, before it had a chance to begin. Never, he said. Not ever. He was, and now is not.

Suddenly he was flooded by memories of terrifying clarity, he and Chet trapping muskrats together on the river in Canada, playing soldier down in the burnouts on the homestead, singing together in school cantatas, getting into fights over the Erector set, swimming in the bare-naked hole down by where Doctor O'Malley's tent used to be pitched, playing map games on the long ride down from the Canadian border to Utah. The smell of gasoline from the auxiliary can in the hot grove near Casper, the mourning doves that cooed all that morning from the cottonwoods, and the ledge up behind, where they killed the rattlesnake. The pride he had felt, the tremendous exuberant exultation, when Chet caught the pass in the last quarter to beat Provo, and himself running out on the field hysterical with "school spirit," pushing through players slimed with black mud from head to foot, only their eyes unmuddied, to grab Chet's hand and pound him on the back, and the way Chet had grinned almost in embarrassment behind his mask of mud, still holding the ball in his big muddy hands . . .

It had never seemed that he and Chet had much in common, that they had ever run together much. Chet had been above and beyond him, with the big gang. But there were thousands of ties, millions, so many that he was amazed and saddened. They were brothers, something he had never really considered before.

Had been, he said. Had been brothers. That was all gone. Everything that had force to make them brothers was already done. If he wanted to find a brother now he had to find him in the past, in recollections that he hadn't even known were there.

He bit his lips together and bent his forehead against the cold windowpane. But he did not cry much. His eyes were dry when they ran through the shacktowns and suburbs of Council Bluffs and across the river and into Omaha.

For two hundred miles across Nebraska he thought of nothing except how clean the Union Pacific kept its trains. At Kearney he

446

bought a newspaper and read it through painstakingly, knowing what he was looking for and completely aware that it was not there. People died everywhere, all the time. Why should anyone in Omaha take note that Chet Mason had died suddenly in Salt Lake City? Who was Chet Mason that anyone should mark his death? Yet the strange lethargy that held him, the torpor waiting on complete realization, did not believe that slip of yellow paper in his overcoat pocket, and the absence of any notice in the paper was almost comforting. He knew he would not believe Chet was dead until he had more proof than the telegram.

At North Platte he bought another paper. At Cheyenne he bought another. From Cheyenne clear on across the plateau to Rock Springs he sat in the club car playing poker with three drummers, and won eighty cents. When they hiked the ante he left the game and went back to his seat to try to sleep. Out past the panes of double glass the moon silvered the empty waste of the Wyoming Plateau, and the telegraph poles were like the ticking second-hand of a watch, the muted racket of the wheels the grinding of a remorseless mechanism carrying him closer and closer to the time when he had to wake up.

When the train swung out of the canyon in a long curve and backed into the yards at Ogden he roused himself and got off for a cup of coffee. Forty miles to go. In the station washroom he washed and combed his hair, and at the newsstand he bought a Salt Lake paper.

He didn't look into it until the train started again. Then he went back to the men's room and sat down. He found it immediately, a little three-inch story on the local page, and the fact that Chet was not stuck away in a column of nameless and unimportant deaths brought him an instant of fierce pride. "Former High School Athlete Dies," it said. So Chet was not entirely unknown. Some of the people reading that three-inch notice would recall games he had starred in, plays he had made spectacularly.

Why try to fool yourself? he said. Why pretend that Chet was anything, amounted to anything? Why back up your grief by making believe Chet mattered to anyone outside his family? He mattered to you, isn't that enough? Does he have to be important to other people before you'll think him worth a tear?

But those three inches of type helped, nevertheless. He was more calm when he stepped off the train than he had been all day, and when he saw his mother, alone, coming toward him with her face twisting toward tears, he did not break down. He spread his arms and she came into them.

447

"Ah, Bruce," she said.

He held her tightly, looking over her head at the people moving toward the exits. "Mom," he said.

She was back out of his arms, shaking tears from her eyes, trying to smile. "You've got an overcoat," she said. "I imagined you coming through in this cold weather without either hat or coat."

"I borrowed it," he said. "Where's Pa?"

His mother looked at him. "He . . . couldn't come." Bruce put his arm around her and led her toward the exit. "Let's not talk," he said. "Let's not try to explain anything."

"I came down in a taxi," she said. "Your dad is terribly broken up. He's like a madman. Just walks and walks. He hasn't slept at all."

She took a handkerchief out of her purse and fumbled with it while he called a cab. In the car she held his hand hard without saying anything. Bruce stared stonily at the back of the driver's neck.

At home Bo Mason met them at the door, shook Bruce's hand, stared into his face a moment, and swung around to disappear into his bedroom. He did not come out again, but later, as he lay sleeplessly staring upward in the bed that he and Chet had shared during the Christmas vacation less than a month ago, Bruce heard a sudden cry from the room down the hall, a smothered scream and the thud of feet heavy on the floor, and his mother's voice saying, "Bo, Bo, please! Bo, you mustn't! Get back into bed, please." After that there was a sound that made Bruce grit his teeth in the dark, the sound of his father sobbing, a muffled, uncontrolled weeping, a little shameful and completely shattering.

When Bruce got up his father had already gone. "He had to get out," his mother said. "He can't stand to be still a minute."

She waited on Bruce at breakfast, even tried to butter his toast. She was pale but perfectly composed. On an impulse, while he was eating, he reached out and covered her hand with his. "Mom," he said, and his smile was so great a strain that it hurt. "You're taking it like a Trojan."

"What else can you do?" she said.

"Would it help to tell me about it?"

"If you like," she said, her eyes steady and clear. "I guess there are . . . two or three things I ought to tell you."

"Where are Laura and the baby?"

"That's part of it," she said. "Laura left him, you know. She took the baby and left to live with her family just a few days after you went back."

"But you said in your letters . . ."

"I didn't want to bother you with it," she said. "I thought it might straighten out."

"They were fighting pretty much at Christmas," Bruce said. "Did she . . . when he got sick . . . ?"

"When he got bad. It went so fast. He was only in the hospital two days. Afterwards she went all to pieces. She's in bed now."

"It's a little late, isn't it?" he said. "She might have shown a little of that when it would do some good."

Her eyes were steady and very blue. "You're thinking about your dad too."

"Maybe I am. Maybe I'm thinking about myself. Everybody but you."

"Don't," she said. He watched her, thinking that there was a dignity, a nobility almost, in the clean bony curve of her temple, the way her hair went back from her forehead, the way her mouth could be firm without being hard or bitter. "Please don't even hint anything like that to your dad," she said. "That's what makes him crazy, almost. He blames himself for everything." She shook her head. "I don't know," she said. "It's everybody's fault. Chet's too. We tried to do something for him, tried to get him to go to business school. He started for a while, you know, and then he quit. I found out after three weeks that he'd never been near the place after the first few days, and had got his tuition money back."

"What was he doing?"

"It's such an unhappy, tangled mess," she said, and shook her head again. "Chet was having trouble with Laura, and she kept throwing it up to him that she was working and all he could do was drive a taxi, and I think . . ." She laughed a little as if in pain. "I've never talked to you like this. I think she wouldn't let him come to bed with her. For a long time. You know how Chet was. He got sullen and swore he'd find somebody else, and they had a fight."

Very carefully Bruce said, "Was he running around with another woman, then?"

"You mean about the tuition money."

"Yes."

"He didn't have any other woman," she said. "He just . . ." Her face flushed, and she bit her lips. "That taxi job was no good," she said. "It threw him in with a lot of no-good people."

There were tears in her eyes. "He never did get a decent break," Bruce said.

"Oh, let's be honest," she said, almost violently. "Chet was a good boy, he always was, but he was impulsive, and I'm afraid he

449

was a little weak. He made a lot of mistakes, but you couldn't blame him for them because he *was* such a nice boy really. He just . . . I guess Chet didn't have much backbone." She stared at him, her eyes bright with the tears that swam in them. "It hurts me to say it, and I don't say it to blame him," she said. "He *was* decent, and generous, wasn't he? But he didn't have much backbone. He got hurt too easily."

"It might take a lot of backbone to live with Laura," Bruce said.

"Oh, let's not blame her either," she said. "Chet had bad luck. If he'd been stronger he could have come out of it, but it whipped him." She turned her face half away and sat with her hand pressed against her mouth.

Bruce stood up and went around the table to put his hand on her shoulder. "It sounds like sentimental hypocrisy," he said slowly, "but maybe Chet's better off. Maybe he couldn't ever have got back."

"You know what he said to me just before he died?" she said. "I talked to him just an hour or two before, when he came out of the coma. He knew then that he was going to die, and I think he was almost glad. It was as if just then he was more peaceful than he'd been any time in years. Just as I was leaving he took hold of my hand and said, 'I'm leaving you the dirty work, Mom. I'm sorry.' That was the last thing he ever . . .'"

Bruce's jaws were locked, but he couldn't break down. The old man was already doing too much of that, throwing more strain on her. Chet, sick and lost, had already done too much of that. He stood with his face stiff and dry as paper, with his hand on her shoulder.

"Bruce," she said, "do you believe in a Heaven, a hereafter? That we might see Chet again?"

For a long minute he did not reply. When he did he almost whispered, he was so afraid of taking something away from her. "No," he said.

"I guess I don't either," she said. "Ever since he died I've been wondering if I still believed that, but I really don't. It's too much to wish for. It would be too good. I guess I've about come to believing that anything we wish for too much is bound never to happen. Probably it's better that way."

"What can I do?" Bruce asked later. "Are there any arrangements I can take care of?"

"Everything's done."

"Would you like to go down with me, to see him?"

"No," she said. "I've said goodbye. I'd rather you saw him alone."

"I don't like to leave you."

"You go," she said. "I'll be all right. I'll be getting lunch."

"Why don't we go out to eat?"

"It's better when I have something to do," she said.

He took a streetcar to the funeral parlor, spoke Chet's name to the girl in the office, and was directed to the third room on the right. His feet dragged in the deep carpet. Panic mounted in him as he passed the first door, the second. Quick glances, as if he shouldn't look in at all, showed him empty rooms like sitting rooms. The third door was also open. He came up to it slowly, stopped outside, and looked in.

He had had no previous acquaintance with death, and he did not know how it can make an outsider of a living person. From the moment he looked in the door he was ill at ease, an intruder, and the emotion that made him move on tiptoe was not so much grief or fear as embarrassment. Chet lay fully dressed, ready for burial, on the wheeled table under the windows. There were three or four baskets of flowers in the room, and the quiet was so deep that his own breathing bothered him.

For a long time he stood beside Chet simply looking. This was the end of it, then. This was the way you said goodbye, when he was already beyond all goodbyes, beyond hearing you when you said you wished you'd been a better brother, had understood better, had given him a hand when you could. Now that it was too late you wished you could tell him how you'd felt about that cigarette lighter at graduation, when you knew really, without his ever saying so, that he was desperate and sick and lonely, down to his last dime and quarreling with his wife and ashamed of having come crawling back. You wished you believed that he could understand you now as you stood thinking it, how you had really felt that gift, how you had known he was reaching out for you, trying to indicate a love that neither you nor he could ever indicate, and how you were really his friend and brother, you'd stick to him as he was asking you to. This was the way it was, all of it too late. There was that in death which made the living humble and ashamed.

He reached out and touched one of the stiff inhuman hands. "So long, boy," he said softly, and backed out. He was so shaken that he had to go into one of the empty rooms and stand looking out into the dirty snow for a long time before he dared go out through the hushed office and into the street.

The funeral was set for two-thirty. At twelve-thirty Bruce and his mother sat down to lunch alone. "It's probably no use waiting for Pa," she said. "He couldn't eat anyhow."

In the middle of the meal he came in, his eyes bloodshot, his face sallow and sagging, his hands curiously fumbling and helpless. He sat down and began eating as if he tasted nothing.

"Anybody call?" he said.

"Harry Birdsall," Elsa said. "And Mrs. Webb, a woman I met up at Brighton that summer. I haven't heard from her since. It was nice of her to call now."

"None of Chet's friends?"

"No," she said. "Now Bo, don't . . ."

He was already standing, half shouting. "What's the matter with them? Don't they *care*?"

"They probably don't even know," she said. "Please, Bo."

"Why don't they know?" he shouted. "It's been in the papers, hasn't it? The funeral's been listed in the papers. There won't be ten people there."

"They'd all come if they knew," she said. "Chet had lost touch, that's all, he'd been away so long."

He sat down again, heavily, the outburst dying in a kind of groan. He stared down at the dishes on the table, picked up his fork, laid it down again. His eyes came up to Elsa's with a glazed, terrified glare.

"He didn't have a friend in the world," he said.

"Please!" she said again, and put her hand on his. She shot a look at Bruce that asked him to say something, start some conversation, and Bruce grabbed at the first lie he could think of.

"I saw Ham Roberts downtown this morning," he said. "He didn't know, but he's coming. He was pretty badly shocked to hear . . ."

His father's dull voice cut in on him. "I went down to the mortuary," he said. "There were no more flowers there than there were yesterday. Three or four little handfuls."

His face twisted, he stood up again holding the napkin in shaking hands. "I'm going back down now," he said. "If there aren't any more flowers there now I'm going to buy three hundred dollars' worth!"

He had lurched into the hall and got his hat and coat and gone before either of them could speak. The outside door slammed. Bruce looked at his mother. She had her hand over her face.

Salt Lake City
Feb. 14, 1931

Dear Bruce,

I suppose that by now you must be taking the examinations you missed by coming home. I hope everything goes well—I know it will. It has been very quiet and lonely here since you left. Neither of us has much heart to do anything. Your dad is better, but he still wakes me sometimes sweating and screaming. He blames himself so much. He's wanted for a long time to do something for Chet and get him back on his feet, but he never did know what it should be, until the sporting goods store came up. He wanted that for Chet, because he thought even an inside job, if it was handling guns and sporting equipment, would suit him. I think it would have, myself. There are so many things we would do, and so many we wouldn't, if we could do it over.

We're leaving Salt Lake for a while to go to Los Angeles. I think it is a good idea, your dad is so miserable here, and everything reminds us both too much of what has happened. We have enough money put away so that we can afford a vacation. Pa is blessing his stars he bought his stocks outright instead of on margin. Everybody we know is losing money hand over fist, and getting sold out. We've lost some, but not everything by any means. I wish . . . but I guess you know what I wish without my telling you.

I'm sending a sweater and some cigarettes for your birthday. We'll go within a week, I think. As soon as we get settled anywhere I'll send you a postcard.

Be careful of yourself, Bruce, and don't work too hard. I know what you're likely to do when there's nobody there to boss you around. It's just possible that when you come back we may be living permanently in Los Angeles. Your dad talks that way sometimes. He has visions of an orange ranch, but probably those are like the other visions. I guess I must be getting cynical about visions. Still, it would be pleasant to have a home in an orange grove, wouldn't it? I'll keep my fingers crossed.

All my love,
Mother

Los Angeles, March 12, 1931

Dear Bruce,

Well, put the vision of the orange grove away with the others. That would have been too tame for Pa anyhow. He's got a new bug now. In the last couple of weeks he's been feeling much better, and just sitting around has made him nervous. But one thing seems to be pretty well settled. He's going to get out of the liquor business. I suppose I should be glad, and of course I am, that he's pulling out, but what he's probably going into now doesn't make me exactly happy. He's been having conferences for a week with a couple of men from Reno, one of them a Frenchman named Laurent and the other a Basque whose name I can't even pronounce, much less spell. They've got a big deal brewing to open a gambling place in Reno.

Honestly, Bruce, when he comes to me with his plans I don't know what to say. He wants to be encouraged, but how can I encourage him to open a gambling house? I guess I hurt his feelings. I said it looked to me like jumping out of the frying pan into the fire. Then he got mad and said I'd been after him long enough to quit the whiskey business, I ought to be tickled to death.

Maybe I want too much, I don't know. Everything that attracts him seems to be on the wrong side of the law. Of course gambling is legal in Nevada, but there are so many other things that go along with gambling that even though we don't have that fear hanging over our heads all the time we may have something just as bad. Still, it may be some improvement. The trouble is, he'd have to put into it most of what we've saved in the last ten years, and your dad isn't as good a plunger as he used to be. He gets thinking about what might happen if things went wrong, and he goes half crazy worrying. But I think he's about ready to plunge, so I suppose I'd better start getting reconciled to gambling. It isn't a business to be very proud of, but at least its legal, and Pa thinks it will make us a lot of money. If it will, he'll be happy, and that's something. But sometimes I wish we lived on a salary of a hundred dollars a month and never had any hope of more. We might be a whole lot more comfortable in our minds.

So now when he comes around and asks me for the thousand dollars' worth of Utah Power and Light preferred stock he gave me for Christmas two years ago I guess I won't make much of a fuss. He's already been hinting that he'll need them. He can have them, for all of me. I never did think of them as mine, and he never did think he was really giving them to me. The only thing I wanted them for was for you or Chet, and if you get to the point where you need them I'll get them back. Just to tease him, I'm going to make him sign a note for them, or cut me into the profits of the gambling house, or something. Do it all up with legal red tape. I must be getting mean in my old age.

454

You've been good about writing. And we're both anxious for the time when school is out, so we can get acquainted with our family lawyer.

All love,
Mother

Reno, April 8, 1931

Dear Bruce,

Pretty soon you won't be able to keep track of us at all, we move around so fast. We came on up here to look over the proposition your dad's got on the fire. It was really a nice trip, and I wished all the time that you could have been along. We drove up the coast as far as Monterey, and then over to Merced and up to Yosemite just for the fun of it, to see the gorge in the snow. We stayed all night at the Ahwahnee Hotel (ten dollars apiece per day. I never felt so extravagant!). The snow was going in the canyon, but the cliffs were marvellous and the waterfalls looked as if they burst right out of a glacier. From Yosemite we went back to Merced and then up to Sacramento and the Emigrant Pass and on to Tahoe. There was a lot of snow there, higher than the car in the pass, but the sun was as warm as late spring, and it was lovely. We stopped in another fancy hotel there, where most of the people came down to dinner in tuxedos and evening gowns. I tried to get Pa to stop somewhere else, but when he gets a streak like that there's no holding him, so we dressed up as well as we could and played millionaire. I swear that if your dad had had a tuxedo he would have worn it all the time we were there, breakfast and all. Yesterday afternoon we came down here to Reno and this morning your dad is out looking things over. He's all excited about the deal now. So many divorcees are around, most of them with too much money to spend and too much time to kill, so that the night clubs and gambling houses run twenty-four hours a day. But it's a big gamble. Each of the three will have to put up between fifteen and twenty thousand, cash, and that's a lot of money for us. It will mean selling most of our stock when it's low. Even if we make money, I doubt if this gambling is going to do your dad any good. He thinks it would be pretty dandy to roll in money and hobnob with movie stars and prize fighters, but he wouldn't be comfortable in that kind of company, and I think he knows it at bottom. It's a funny thing, but I keep remembering how contented and good-natured he was all the time he was building that house on the homestead. He went around whistling, and he could get absorbed in his job for hours. Ever since we

455

started making money more than five dollars at a time he acts as if somebody were behind him all the time. But how can you tell him that you think he'd have been three times as happy if he'd stayed a carpenter? And what good would it do now?

He's having fun laying plans, anyway. We'll live in this tourist cottage for a while, but when things get moving he'll buy a lot up on Tahoe or Donner Lake and build us a summer house where I'll stay all the time and he'll come up when he's off shift. It's only a couple of hours up there from here. When he's resting from looking at catalogues of roulette wheels and chuck-a-luck cages and wheels of fortune and crap tables, he's already started looking at motor boat catalogues. The summer home of the well-known millionaire sportsman Harry Mason is already taking shape.

Oh Lord! I guess my main impulse is to laugh. But I'd be glad of a place on Tahoe, so I can't laugh too loud. I don't think I'd do very well as the Madame of a gambling joint.

Sometimes the way we live reminds me of Bill Glassner. Remember him? He used to come around the house a good deal four or five years ago. His whole stock of conversation was "Never a dull moment, eh Bo?" When he got drunk he used to imagine that he was somebody named Scissor-Bill who had pushed Buffalo Bill Cody in the Platte. Never a dull moment, no fooling.

Anyway, if we do build a place on Tahoe, you might have a nice summer. I don't know why you couldn't ask a friend or two from Salt Lake to come down. That might be one blessing of being out from under the law. We could have friends again.

Now I sound like your dad, laying little plots and plans. But maybe this will turn out. It's funny what a few weeks free from pressure will do. I'm ashamed sometimes at how good I feel, when I think of Chet. Laura, I hear, has bought a car with Chet's little insurance money, and has a job as a stenographer. I don't know why she shouldn't buy a car, but it made your dad mad. He thought she owed that to little Anne. But I don't know. Hard as it is to get used to the idea that Chet is dead, I can't help thinking that we owe the living more than we do the dead. I must always have thought that. When my mother died I could have died too, because I loved her more than anyone, but there were Erling and Kristin and Dad and even me, and we were all alive and needed to live. Laura is still young, and has her own way to make now, and she ought to be the best judge of how to do it. Chet is at peace finally. I try to keep remembering that. Pa and I don't talk about it much any more. He's afraid, somehow.

Here comes Pa now. I suppose we're going out and dine in style at some night club. I'd rather get groceries and cook meals here, but he has to throw his money around for a little while longer. By the time the place opens he'll have a fit of stinginess and I'll probably be taking in washing. Never a dull moment.

All my love,
Mother

4

When Bruce drove west in June, after the frenzy of examinations and the rush to clear out his room, settle his bills, pack the Ford, have a last round of beers with the Law Commons boys, he drove directly from rainy spring into deep summer, from prison into freedom. That day was the first bright warm day in two weeks, and the year was over, he was loose. He watched the sun drink steam from the cornfields, heard the meadowlarks along the fences, the blackbirds in the spring sloughs. Even the smell of hot oil from the motor could not entirely blot out the lush smell of growth.

It was the end of his first year away from home, and he was going back. Ahead of him was the long road, the continental sprawling hugeness of America, the fields and farmhouses, the towns. Northfield, Faribault, Owatonna, Albert Lea, and then west on Highway 16—Blue Earth, Jackson, Luverne, and the junction of Big Sioux and Missouri. Then Sioux City, Yankton, Bridgewater, Mitchell, Chamberlain, Rapid City, the Badlands and the Black Hills breaking the monotonous loveliness of the Dakota plain. Then the ranges and the echoing names: Spearfish, Deadwood, Sundance, the Wyoming that was Ucross and Sheridan and Buffalo and Greybull and Cody, the Yellowstone of dudes and sagebrushers, the Idaho that was the Mormon towns along the Snake: St. Anthony, Rexburg, Sugar City, Blackfoot, Pocatello, and the Utah of Cache Valley and Sardine Canyon and the barricade of the Wasatch guarding the dead salt flats and the lake.

The names flowed in his head like a song, like the words of an old man telling a story, and his mind looked ahead over the long road, the great rivers and the interminable plains, over the Black Hills and the lovely loom of the Big Horns and the Absaroka Range white against the west from Cody.

It was a grand country, a country to lift the blood, and he was going home across its wind-kissed miles with the sun on him and the cornfields steaming under the first summer heat and the first bugs immolating themselves against his windshield.

But going home where? he said. Where do I belong in this?

Going home to Reno? I've never been in Reno more than six hours at a time in my life. Going home to Tahoe, to a summer cottage that I haven't ever seen, that isn't even quite completed yet? Or going home to Salt Lake, only to go right on through across the Salt Desert and the little brown dancing hills, through Battle Mountain and Wells and Winnemucca and the dusty towns of the Great Basin that are only specks on a map, that have no hold on me? Where do I belong in this country? Where is home?

Maybe it's Minnesota, because my mother came from here. Certainly I picked Minnesota as a school to go away to, partly because it seemed that I knew it some, having a grandfather in Indian Falls and an aunt and uncle and cousins in Minneapolis, and second and third cousins, and great-aunts and great-uncles, in a dozen towns where Norwegian is still spoken as much as English. Does that make Minnesota home? Maybe I'm going away from home, not toward it.

Or maybe I've never been home. Maybe I'd recognize the country along the Rock River where the old man came from, maybe I'd feel it the minute I saw it. Or maybe I belong back in some Pennsylvania valley, where the roots first went down in this country, where the first great or great-great grandfather broke loose from his Amish fireside and started moving rootless around the continent.

He bounced into the streets of Faribault talking to himself. On a corner he saw a young man squiring two dressed-up girls—altogether too dressed up for this hour of the morning—across the intersection. The earnestness of the young man's attempt to be scrupulously impartial, to offer an arm to each, to keep his head turning on a metronome swing from one to the other, made Bruce laugh.

"There were two pretty maidens from Faribault," he said, and nursed the rhymes along as he edged the Ford through the morning traffic and out onto the highway again.

> *There were two pretty maidens from Faribault*
> *Who agreed they would willingly share a beau.*
> *But one beau to a pair*
> *Was no better than fair.*
> *It was worse than just fair, it was taribault.*

Nuts, he said. You ought to go into the Christmas card business. But thereafter he made up limericks for every town he passed through, intoxicating himself on names.

> *A maiden from Alibert Lea*
> *Thought her knee had been bit by a flea.*

She lifted her skirt
To see what had hurt,
But it wasn't a flea, it was me.

It was me, he said, just a boll weevil lookin' for a home. Do I belong in Minnesota? Do I belong in Albert Lea where Kristin went to school? Do I belong in Minneapolis where I go to school and have relations? If I did I wouldn't be so glad to get out of here.

Or is it North Dakota? he said. That's where I was born. Grand Forks, North Dakota, behind the bar in a cheap hotel. I ought to go back some day and put up a fence around that old joint and charge admission to see the birthplace of the great man. What would Jesus Christ have amounted to if he'd been born in a commercial hotel in Grand Forks, North Dakota, instead of in a barn in Bethlehem? Suppose his earliest visitors had been barflies with whiskey breaths instead of sheep and kine with big wondering eyes and breaths of milk and hay? Suppose the Gifts had been brought by drummers instead of wise men?

In a minute he was back on limericks again.

A Jesus from Grand Forks, No. Dak.
Went hunting his home with a Kodak.
There were plenty of mansions
And suburban expansions,
But no home, either No. Dak. or So. Dak.

Well, where is home? he said. It isn't where your family comes from, and it isn't where you were born, unless you have been lucky enough to live in one place all your life. Home is where you hang your hat. (He had never owned a hat.) Or home is where you spent your childhood, the good years when waking every morning was an excitement, when the round of the day could always produce something to fill your mind, tear your emotions, excite your wonder or awe or delight. Is home that, or is it the place where the people you love live, or the place where you have buried your dead, or the place where you want to be buried yourself? Or is it the place where you come in your last desperation to shoot yourself, choosing the garage or the barn or the woodshed in order not to mess up the house, but coming back anyway to the last sanctuary where you can kill yourself in peace?

Still feeling good, bubbling with the sun and wind and the freedom of movement, the smell of the burning oil in the motor like a promise of progress to his nostrils, he let himself envy the people who had all those things under one roof. To belong to a clan,

459

to a tight group of people allied by blood and loyalties and the mutual ownership of closeted skeletons. To see the family vices and virtues in a dozen avatars instead of in two or three. To know always, whether you were in Little Rock or Menton, that there was one place to which you belonged and to which you would return. To have that rush of sentimental loyalty at the sound of a name, to love and know a single place, from the newest baby-squall on the street to the blunt cuneiform of the burial ground . . .

Those were the things that not only his family, but thousands of Americans had missed. The whole nation had been footloose too long, Heaven had been just over the next range for too many generations. Why remain in one dull plot of earth when Heaven was reachable, was touchable, was just over there? The whole race was like the fir tree in the fairy-tale which wanted to be cut down and dressed up with lights and bangles and colored paper, and see the world and be a Christmas tree.

Well, he said, thinking of the closed banks, the crashed market that had ruined thousands and cut his father's savings in half, the breadlines in the cities, the political jawing and the passing of the buck. Well, we've been a Chrstmas tree, and now we're in the back yard and how do we like it?

How did a tree sink roots when it was being dragged behind a tractor? Or was an American expected to be like a banyan tree or a mangrove, sticking roots down everywhere, dropping off rooting appendages with lavish fecundity? Could you be an American, or were you obliged to be a Yankee, a hill-billy, a Chicagoan, a Californian? Or all of them in succession?

I wish, he said, that I were going home to a place where all the associations of twenty-two years were collected together. I wish I could go out in the back yard and see the mounded ruins of caves I dug when I was eight. I wish the basement was full of my worn-out ball gloves and tennis rackets. I wish there was a family album with pictures of us all at every possible age and in every possible activity. I wish I knew the smell of the ground around that summer cottage on Tahoe, and had a picture in my mind of the doorway my mother will come through to meet me when I drive up, and the bedroom I'll unload my suitcases and books and typewriter in. I wish the wrens were building under the porch eaves, and that I had known those same wrens for ten years.

Was he going home, or just to another place? It wasn't clear. Yet he felt good, settling his bare arm gingerly on the hot door and opening his mouth to sing. He had a notion where home would turn out to be, for himself as for his father—over the next range, on the Big Rock Candy Mountain, that place of impossible loveliness that had pulled the whole nation westward, the place where the fat land sweated up wealth and the heavens dropped lemonade . . .

> On the Big Rock Candy Mountain
> Where the cops have wooden legs,
> And the handouts grow on bushes,
> And the hens lay soft-boiled eggs,
> Where the bulldogs all have rubber teeth
> And the cinder dicks are blind—
> I'm a-gonna go
> Where there ain't no snow,
> Where the rain don't fall
> And the wind don't blow
> On the Big Rock Candy Mountain.

Ah yes, he said. Where the bluebird sings to the lemonade springs and the little streams of alcohol come trickling down the rocks. The hobo Heaven, the paradise of the full belly and the lazy backside. That was where his family had been headed for all his life. His father had never gone off the bum. That Bo Mason who had gone bumming in his youth out from Rock River, seeing the big towns and resting his bones in knowledge boxes and jungling up by some stream where the catfish bit on anything from a kernel of corn to a piece of red flannel, was simply an earlier version of the Bo Mason who now fished for big money in a Reno gambling joint and rested his weekend bones among the millionaires on Lake Tahoe.

So when, he said, do we get enough sense to quit looking for something for nothing?

He looked up the straight road running clean and white westward between elms and wild plum thickets, cleaving the wide pastures and fields. The sky to the west was a clear blue, not as dark as it would be beyond the Missouri, and paling to a milky haze at the horizon, but clean and pure and empty, as if there were nothing beyond, or everything. If he hadn't known that beyond the rise limiting his view there was western Minnesota and then Dakota and Wyoming and Idaho and Oregon, if he had been moving through waist-high grass with nothing in his mind but the dream and the itch to see the unknown world, he could easily enough have been a chaser of rainbows. It was easy to see why men had moved westward as inevitably as the roulette-ball of a sun rolled that way. What if the ball settled in the black, on the odd, on number 64? There were so many chances, such lovely possibilities. And if you missed on the first spin you could double and try

461

again, and keep on doubling till you hit it. You could break the bank, you could bust the sure thing, you could, alone and unarmed, take destiny by the throat.

Oh yes, he said. If you don't recognize limits. But that's all over now. That went out with the horse car.

Oh lovely America, he said, you pulled the old trick on us again. You looked like the Queen of Faery, and your hair smelled of wind and grass and space, and your eyes were wild. Oh Circe, mother of all psycho-analysts, you can shut the gates of the sty now. We are all fighting for the trough, and the healing fiction is fading like a dream. Oh Morgain, bane of all good knights, click the iron in the stone, for we know now that what we took for fairy was really witch, and it is time we planned our dungeon days while making friends with the rats and spiders. Oh Belle Dame sans Merci, do you enjoy our starved lips in the gloam?

The music from behind the moon was silent, the lemonade springs were dry, along with half the banks in America. The little streams of alcohol that used to come trickling down the rocks were piped now into the houses of the great, and the handout bushes didn't bear any more and the hens had the pip and the bulldogs had developed teeth and the cinder dicks had x-ray eyes and the climate had changed. So what did you do, if you didn't want to get caught as Bo Mason had been caught, pumped full of the dream and the expectation and the feeling that the world owed you something for nothing, and then thrown into a world where expectations didn't pay off?

He sang again,

> *You're in the army now*
> *You're not behind the plow*
> *You'll never get rich,*
> *So marry the witch,*
> *You're in the army now.*

Oh beautiful, he said, for spacious skies, for amber waves of grain, for purple mountain majesties, and penury, and pain.

Don't you think, he said, that this has gone about far enough? Who are you to philosophize about the problems of a nation? For all the part you or your family have taken in this nation's affairs, you might as well have been living like Troglodytes in a cave. Who are you to mouth phrases, when you don't even belong to the club?

All right, he said, I'll shut up. But I'd still like to join the club, in spite of the Ford Motor Company and the Standard Oil of Indiana and the murder of Sacco and Vanzetti and the emptiness of Main Street. I don't want to bet my wad. I just want to ante.

462

Oh let us sing, he said, of Lydia Pinkham . . .

Nuts to Lydia Pinkham. Let us sing. Oh what? Of man's first disobedience, and the fruit of that forbidden tree whose mortal taste? No. Arms and the man, who first, pursued by Fate, and haughty Juno's unrelenting hate? Arma virumque canuts. Let us sing of purple mountain majesties. That's what we've always been best at, the land.

The roadside cabins with Simmons beds, Flush toilets, Private showers,
The barns and cribs and coops and sheds, the houses buried deep in flowers,
The towns whose names are Burg and Ville, whose maximum speed is Twenty Mi.
Whose signs point in to the business block to lure the tourists who might shoot by.
"We love our children. Please drive slow." We're also proud of our hybrid corn.
"Registered Rest Rooms. Road maps free. Snappy Service—Just toot your horn."
Ma's Home Cooking and Herb's Good Eats, Rotary every Thursday noon,
Lions Friday. Then straggling streets, the foot on the throttle, the outskirts soon
And the corn again, and the straight flat road, and the roadside split with the wedge of speed,
And the wind of a hurrying car ahead blowing the flat green tumbleweed.
The kids by the roadside who yell and wave. Texaco. Conoco. Burma-Shave:

> *Blighted romance*
> *Stated fully.*
> *She got mad when*
> *He got woolly.*

I'll take it, he said. I love it, whatever good that does. Even if I don't know where home is, I know when I *feel* at home.

At the next service station where he stopped he felt it even stronger, the feeling of belonging, of being in a well-worn and familiar groove. He felt it in the alacrity with which the attendant shined up his windshield and wiped off his headlights and even took a dab at the license plates, in the way he moved and looked, in the quality of his voice and grin. Anything beyond the Missouri was close to home, at least. He was a westerner, whatever that was. The moment he crossed the Big Sioux and got into the brown country where the raw earth showed, the minute the grass got sparser and the air dryer and the service stations less grandiose and the towns rattier, the moment he saw his first lonesome shack on the baking flats with a tipsy windmill creaking away at the reluctant underground water, he knew approximately where he belonged. He belonged where the overalls saw the washtub less often, where the corduroy bagged more sloppily at the knees, where the ground was bare and sometimes raw and the sand-devils whirled across the landscape and the barns were innocent of any paint except that advertising Dr. Peirce's Golden Medical Discovery. The feeling came on him like sun after an overcast day, and in pure contentment he limbered his knees and slouched deeper against the Ford's lefthand door.

At sunset he was still wheeling across the plains toward Chamberlain, the sun fiery through the dust and the wide wings of the west going red to saffron to green as he watched, and the horizon ahead of him vast and empty and beckoning like an open gate. At ten o'clock he was still driving, and at twelve. As long as the road ran west he didn't want to stop, because that was where he was going, west beyond the Dakotas toward home.

5

The summer cottage nestled back in a bay in the tall cedars and pines on the east slope of the Big Rock Candy Mountain. The water in front, beyond the strip of gravelly beach, was in the mornings clear emerald, and sometimes at moonset clear gold. Strung out along the shores were the summer homes of the wealthy and comfortable, and of the not-so-wealthy and not-so-comfortable who wished to appear so. A few miles up the road toward the summit was the monument to the Donner Party, symbol of all the agony in the service of dubious causes, archetype of the American saga of rainbow-chasing, dream and denouement immortalized in cobble-rock and granite, its pioneer Woman and unconsciously ironic portrait of endurance and grief.

In the cottage, still not finished, its bedrooms only partly partitioned off, its windows still stopped with bent nails, its yard littered with a half-raked-up mess of shavings, nail kegs, ends of two-by-fours, and chips, Bruce and his mother lived for a while a summer idyll.

His mother was proud of the cottage. "Pa built most of it himself," she said. "He had some carpenters put up the studding and the frame, but he sheathed the whole thing, and shingled the roof, and framed the windows and doors, and even made all the inside doors and cupboards, in his spare time. He's been working like a horse every minute—too much, but I think he liked it. Didn't you, Papa?"

"There's still plenty to do," his father said. "You can take off your shirt any time and fall to. Soon as we finish up the inside here we can start landscaping."

He was heavier than when Bruce had last seen him. His cheeks sagged a little, his mouth was rarely without a cigar in it, his columnar neck had softened and whitened, and he had obviously been cultivating a hearty laugh. His plans for the cottage were grandiose. What they had here was just a beginning, turn out to be the servants' wing when they got steaming along. This big room here, with the fireplace, would stay the main living room, but sooner or later they'd build a wing straight off the back, and another wing off that to make a sort of enclosed court—pave it with flagstones for outdoor dining, looking out on the lake. The kitchen and storeroom and laundry room could be built off the other way, where the view was blocked by the woods. Then they'd have some guy come up and plow the yard up and dump on loam, and sow a lawn, and shine the whole grounds up, put in plenty of shrubs and flowers, maybe a little stone terrace. Make it the snappiest place on the lake.

"What do you want to do, make a mansion out of it?" Bruce said. "What's the matter with pine needles for a yard?"

"Hell with that," his father said. "This isn't just any old shanty in the woods. This is a house. Once we get the driveway scraped off and gravelled we can live up here most of the winter, put in a woodburning furnace. If it gets too cold we can run over to the coast for a couple of months of the year."

"Well," Bruce said. "Give me my orders. I haven't done anything with my hands for so long I've about forgotten how."

Thereafter the two of them worked every morning, nailing in window stops, fitting shutters to the outside frames, lining the interior with wallboard. Bruce protested at the wallboard. "What can you do with it after it's in?" he said. "You can only paint it, and then it'll look like a cheap imitation of a town house. Why not leave the studs showing? It looks more like what it is, then."

"You don't know the seat of your pants from ten cents a week," his father said amiably. "How can you make a room look like anything as long as it's unfinished? You want this place to look like the homestead?"

"That's all right up in the woods."

"Not for me," his father said. "You can build yourself a ratty little shack somewhere if you want. I'm making this one snappy."

"Why not make it really finished, then? Plaster it, put on mould-ings, cover the floors, lay in parquetry, go in for indirect lighting and picture windows."

His father made a sound of disgust. He wanted a snappy place, not a shack. But he wasn't going to blow his whole roll on it, either. He'd use his own labor and wallboard instead of lath and plaster, and he would get, Bruce assured him, exactly what he wanted—a compromise, a half-baked thing.

Elsa stayed out of it. She told Bruce that she was saying nothing whatever about how the house should be made unless Bo asked her. He was having so much fun puttering that she'd rather let him jazz the whole place up than protest. He loved building things, it took his mind off Chet and business. Not that he had many busi-ness worries. The gambling house was coining money, even with expenses over twenty thousand a month. "He's in the money," she said. "That's where he's always wanted to be. Let him play with it any way he wants. It isn't worth an argument. The lake is so lovely no kind of house can spoil it."

"It's just silly, that's all," Bruce said. "Wallboard isn't necessary at all, but he spends a couple hundred dollars for it that he might have put into something good. Then he has to buy panel strips to cover the cracks. Then he has to buy paint. He just builds up a lot of unnecessary expense. First thing you know he'll be putting in crystal chandeliers."

His mother smiled. "I wouldn't be surprised. What harm does it do?"

Bruce shrugged and let it go. But he couldn't keep from arguing again when his father came out from town with a five-gallon pail of brown paint. "Good Lord," he said, "what do you want to paint it for? Those shakes will weather the loveliest soft gray in about two years."

But within an hour he was swinging a paint brush, and he swung it rebelliously for the next week, putting two coats of oak-leaf brown over the shakes that he would much rather not have touched. He was maliciously pleased at how bad it looked, but his father found nothing wrong with it. He came out, looked it over with approbation, and produced a pail of white for the trim. "How's your painting arm?" he said.

Bruce shrugged. "Now that the place is ruined this far, we might as well finish it."

His father shot him a quick, suspicious glare. "Oh, ruined!" he said. "You got a lot of funny ideas in college. Don't colleges believe in paint?"

"Not in the wrong places. But I'll paint it. It needs it now, as far as that goes." He ducked out of the argument, because every word he said betrayed to the old man the chasm that separated them. It wasn't worth it. He kept his mouth shut when it came time to mix saffron and green shingle stain for the roof. He didn't even open it to squawk at the line of round niggerhead stones that his father one Sunday laid neatly along the edge of the drive, and he was not at all surprised when his father came out the next morning with a paint bucket and painted them all white.

"Give him another week and he'll be putting blue spots on them," he told his mother. "The more he works on this place the more it looks like Camp Cozy."

"He's a good carpenter," his mother said, as if that settled something.

"Sure he's a good carpenter. He's a heck of a good carpenter. He's a cabinet maker. But why doesn't he stick to carpentry or cabinet making, and let somebody whose taste isn't all in his mouth design things? Why does he have to add all these nightmares?"

"He said the stones would outline the drive so people coming in wouldn't run off."

"Who's coming in?" he said. "Once a week, maybe, somebody from Reno. Every other day a delivery truck. What if they did run off? They've got reverse gears on their cars."

She laughed at him. "You're butting your head against a wall," she said. "He'll do it the way he wants, no matter what you or anybody else says."

"And we get blamed for his taste. People drive by and look at the place and hold their noses and say, 'Holy cats, look at the monstrosity.'"

"Do you care?" she said curiously. "Even if it were as bad as you say, which it isn't, would you care? Does it matter that much to you what people think?"

"I don't know. It just makes me mad. The way he has of putting his fingerprints on everything. This place ought to be yours, and look it, not his."

"Ah Bruce," she said. "You're hard on your father."

The expression he saw in her face surprised him. "I'm sorry," he said. "I'm an intolerant lout. Let's go for a swim."

It wasn't worth an argument. His mother was right. And with the old man gone from noon until almost midnight they had the place to themselves. They could swim, fish, putt around the lake in the motor boat. The boat had a mast step in it, and in a few afternoons Bruce cobbled a mast out of a cedar pole, got an old sail from a camper down the lake, and improvised a rig. He was no sailor, but it was fun to come ghosting into the bays over the water that shifted cobalt to emerald, and to hear the silence along **the** forested shore. A motor was all right, it was a lazy man's way to go boating or fishing. He supposed it matched his old man, somehow. But a sail, even a clumsy and inefficient one, was better. A canoe was better. Even a rowboat was better. The more labor-saving the machinery the less the pleasure. But not for Bo Mason. He believed in modern improvements. Anything that wasn't the latest was an old granny system. He had even come to the point now where an unpaved road was a personal insult, and a detour a deliberate conspiracy to spoil his day. Considering the roads he had driven on in his time, that was quite a step.

His father's was a curious state of mind, Bruce reflected. He and his mother would probably have been content to sit on the pine needles and watch the lake. They would never have finished the cottage inside, or painted it outside, or lined up the driveway, or projected any landscaping. They liked the present, they preferred the static, but for the old man today was only a time in which to get steamed up about tomorrow. The world went forward as a wheel turns, and if you didn't keep up with it you were an old fogy. Your bank account got bigger, your needs became more and more elaborate, your appetites required stronger and stronger stimulation, your ideas of what was your just due became more grandiose. Even the gastro-intestinal tract, he said. Even the amount of laxatives you take to keep your bowels open. Last year one Feenamint, this year two Ex-Laxes, next year three Seidlitz powders. By God, it was laughable. Oh for the tomorrow when you have graduated to Pluto Water. Oh for the day of the daily enema.

Yet he enjoyed those weeks. He liked working with tools, he liked fishing, swimming, sailing. He liked the days when they all went down to Reno. He had fun playing nickels on the chuck-a-luck cage, methodically playing the odd and doubling when he lost. He took pleasure in the two or three dollars he won every time he went in, and he even got a certain rueful enjoyment out of the cleaning the game took him for when it finally took him.

He played the slot machines and had beers at the bar and watched the crowds mill through the place, jamming up by the crap tables and the Wheel of Fortune and the roulette wheels, thinning out toward the back where the intent games of poker and blackjack and panguingui went on, thinning out still more at the very back, where deadpan Chinamen and professional gamblers sat endlessly playing faro.

He met dozens of gamblers, shills, bouncers. Prize fighters and movie stars and tourists and shrill women surged through the place night and day. When one of the janitors of the club died of a heart attack in the little back room among his brooms and brushes, his father offered him the job, twelve dollars a day for pushing a broom eight hours among the multitudinous feet. He might have taken that job if his mother had not asked him to pass it up.

It took only a few visits to the club to understand his father's excitement about the place. There was excitement merely in the stacks of silver dollars on the tables, in the flat chants of the dealers, in the screeches of touring school teachers when they hit the jackpot on a slot machine or won two dollars at craps. There was excitement in the three or four "floor managers," his father among them, who went constantly through the crowd keeping an eye out for pickpockets or slot machine sluggers. The afternoon when a much-advertised fugitive from justice passed a stolen traveler's check at the cashier's window and was picked up at the door by a pair of bouncers, relieved of his shoulder gun, and led off to jail, was a fine and thrilling afternoon.

There was something not so thrilling about what was done with the men who were occasionally caught cheating or slugging a machine. Bruce had seen them two or three times being led quietly downstairs by a pair of husky bouncers, and he had seen the bouncers come back after about fifteen minutes and quietly mingle with the crowd again. None of the tinhorns ever came up. When he asked his father what went on down there his father said the bouncers beat hell out of them and tossed them out into Douglas Alley by a back door.

He could see how the big money, the quick money, the easy money, could take hold on his father. He did not know how deeply it had taken hold until one afternoon when a photographer and a reporter from a magazine came to shoot and investigate the place. Bruce saw his father shouldering through the crowd with his glad-hand smile, his hearty laugh, escorting the photographer around. He saw him laughing with self-conscious playfulness when the photographer stood him up at the edge of the crowd and took a shot of him, summer jacket, stickpin, smile and all. When the article appeared only a couple of weeks later Bo Mason loomed over the crowd, his chin up, his smile gleaming, his hand up in a gesture of greeting or fellowship. The Big Shot. The instant he saw it Bruce was reminded of the night he and Chet graduated from high school and Chet came up to get his football sweater. The same look, the same inability to keep the gratified and self-gratulatory smile off the mouth, the same playing for the gallery. He hated that picture and the things it reminded him of. He didn't want to think of Chet that way.

In July Bruce's mother reminded him that if he wanted to have friends come and stay a while she would be glad to have them, so he wrote to Joe Mulder in Salt Lake, and later in the month Joe and his sister came down. Bruce half expected to have his father object to putting them up. It had happened before. What was the idea of asking everybody in the world to come see you, eat up twenty dollars' worth of food, burn up a lot of gas, cost you a lot of money and waste your time? Let them stay at a hotel if they wanted to stop over. But this time his father even seemed to want them. Perhaps being free of the fear of the law let him loosen up; perhaps he merely was proud of himself and his place and wanted to show off. Anyway, to Bruce's half-cynical surprise, he put himself out. He was jovial at table, he took the visitors for boat rides, he personally escorted them through the club and showed them how to shoot craps, he made booming wisecracks to the dealer so that people looked over at him, and Bruce saw them whisper to each other. Must be the boss. Look at him toss out the bucks, there! Big shot, obviously.

Joe and his sister were delighted. They whirled through Reno like a pair of sand devils. They loved the gambling, they were tickled by the way you could go up to any cop and ask where the nearest speakeasy was and have him direct you. There was no city or state liquor law, and the city cops didn't have any percentage in enforcing federal laws. They loved the mineral springs where Bo took them all swimming, they were full of admiration for how rich Bo Mason was, and they laughed themselves helpless at his wisecracks. Even Bruce, grudgingly, admitted that he was really funny when he got wound up. The night after the swimming Bo was still expansive. He took them out to Steamboat Springs, set them up to dinner, flirted with Helen Mulder and kidded her pink, crooked a lordly finger at the soulful-eyed Mexican with the guitar who was singing sweet sad sentimental songs to the diners, and had him over to sing Helen's favorites. For every song he tossed the Mexican a silver dollar, and for an hour afterward, after he had gone to sing hopefully at other tables, the Mexican kept looking back at the Mason table, showing his teeth and eyes, flirting at a distance with the girl there, hoping that the big man with the diamond would crook his finger again. That was quite an evening. Bo stooped to dance—a thing he had not done in twenty-five years—and he cut his shift at the club.

For a good many weeks there was nothing wrong with that summer. The jazzy excitement of Reno could be sluffed off in the lake's quiet, the hangover of too many cigarettes and too late hours could be dissipated simply by lying under the pines and watching the shifting color of the lake that Mark Twain called the most beautiful in the world. There were books to read and good long hours of puttering with tools, the hands busy and the mind quiet.

The club was still doing well, though the fantastic take of the early summer had fallen off. The prize fight crowd which had come in to watch the Baer-Uzcudun fight, and the Basque sheepherders who had come in in droves to bet money on their woodchopping countryman against the Livermore butcher boy, had flocked out again. Rings still went into the Truckee regularly, and the court house pillars still acquired new smears of lipstick from the grateful mouths of pilgrims, and the kids who planted dimestore rings in the river and then fished them out again to sell to gullible tourists still did a fair business. The town was good, but not as good as it had been. Business at the club fell off just enough to make Bo sit down occasionally to his figuring, to make him curse the neon company that charged twelve hundred dollars for a sign, to make him chew his lips over the two men who came in one afternoon with plenty of money in their pockets and played dimes on the chuck-a-luck cage. In one afternoon they took four hundred dollars out of the game with their little penny-ante bets, and it made Bo mad. There were several things like that. The faro game had a streak of losing, until Bo had half a mind to take faro out of the club entirely. There wasn't enough percentage in favor of the house. A smart gambler could win at it, and most of the people who played it were professionals as slick as the dealers. Yet in the long run you couldn't afford to close out the monte games and lose those professionals.

Increasingly Bo left the finishing of the cottage to Bruce, and even when he did work on the place he was likely to be jerky and irritable, to burst into an inordinate flood of swearing if he made a mistake or couldn't get a joint to fit or hurt his hands. He complained of headaches and sleeplessness.

"Why don't you just rest when you come up here?" Elsa said. "You're down there too much, and then you come up here and work instead of resting. Just sit around and take it easy, or go fishing."

"Yeah," he said. "I'd better do that. No use getting myself run down."

But he couldn't sit still. The first morning he tried it he read the paper for an hour and sat for a half hour more on the porch. By ten thirty he was out in the yard making a bench out of two short lengths of log and a wide slab of pine. It would, he said, make a nice place for anyone to sit down under the trees if they wanted to lazy around in the yard.

Every night the faro game was in the red when checks were counted after the midnight change of shifts. After a week, following a talk with Laurent, Bo fired one of the dealers, a little cold-eyed man who had been a boxer, and hired a dealer newly arrived from one of the gambling boats outside the twelve-mile limit off Long Beach. O'Brien, the dismissed dealer, was sore. He called Bo names and got abusive and violent, until Bo had him thrown out of the place by a couple of shills.

"The God damned guy," he said later up at the lake. "He's been losing at that table ever since he went in there. We pay those cookies twenty bucks a day. That ought to be plenty to make them want to work for the house. What does he want, for Christ sake? I wouldn't be surprised if he'd been chiseling all the time."

"Well, he's fired," Elsa said. "I wouldn't worry about him."

"I'm not worrying about him. The hell with him. I'm worrying about that monte game. We're making money on everything else. If we made money on that we'd be in clover. It takes the profits from two crap tables to pay for that damn thing."

"Doesn't it work in streaks?" she said. "Won't it start winning again sometime?"

"That's what I'm talking about!" he said. "Sure it will. It's got to. But this streak has gone on for three weeks. Can't you understand what I'm telling you?"

"You needn't get mad at me," she said. "I'm not making it lose. I should think if you're going to be a gambler you'd have to make up your mind to take what the luck brings."

In his glare there was something like pity for anyone who could make a remark like that.

The next afternoon Bruce was sitting in a bathing suit on the gunwale of the boat, repairing the cobbled rigging, when his mother came down to the shore. "Can you drive me into town this afternoon?" she said. "I hate to take you away from the lake on such a nice day, but I've got to go in."

"Sure," he said. "Need some groceries?"

He was bending down twisting a wire tight with pliers, and when she didn't answer he looked up. Her face wore a deprecatory grimace, and her eyes were puckered at the corners.

"I've got to see the doctor," she said.

He laid down the pliers. "What for?"

"I'm sorry," she said, and he saw that she was embarrassed. "I didn't tell you. The lumps have been coming back, and I'm taking x-ray treatments. I'd have gone in with Pa, only he went early, and I'd have had to wait till midnight to get back."

"You needn't worry about that," he said. "I'm not doing anything." He turned to pull the boat further up on the sand. When he stood up and turned she was still standing there, looking at him.

"You should have told me," he said. "How long have you been taking treatments?"

"Since about April." Her eyes puckered still more, and she put her arm around him as they walked up the cottage. "I hate to be a worry and a bother and an expense," she said.

"Nuts to that. Do the treatments work?"

"They take the lumps away, all right, but others keep coming, up in my armpit. They're all just in the skin. I go in once a month. I hate it. They cost like anything."

"Forget what they cost. Don't they give you bad effects?"

"They knock me out a little sometimes." She laughed. "I fainted once. Scared your dad half to death."

"I should think." He opened the screen door for her and shook his fist under her nose. "From now on," he said, "don't you hide things like that from me. You need me to keep you looking after yourself."

She paused on the steps, her blue, clear eyes searching his. Then she patted his hand lightly. "Don't you start worrying," she said. "It's just little nodules under the skin."

But when she went into her bedroom to dress before going into town he sat on the couch and stared into the black empty fireplace and felt the heavy beating of his own pulse. In the one minute when he looked into her eyes by the door he had seen that she knew she was going to die.

6

Three people were in the doctor's office. There would be at least a half hour to wait. "There isn't any use of your waiting around," Elsa said. "I can sit here and read a magazine and you can come back in an hour or so."

"Well," he said, "I've got a few things to buy." He looked at her uncertainly, thinking that there wasn't much chance to talk to the doctor about her as long as she was here. He could go over to the club and see what the old man knew. "I'll just be a little while," he said.

At the club the crowd was even thicker than usual. He pushed his way through it to the cashier's window, leaned on the ledge to look around. His father was not in sight. The cashier, a young Basque who played football for St. Mary's, raised his eyebrows and lifted his head in recognition.

"My dad around anywhere?" Bruce said.

"I thought he went home," the cashier said. He shook his head slightly, as if to say, half-smiling, "Too bad!"

"What for?"

The cashier fished for a cigarette. "You didn't see it, then."

"See what?"

"Come on in," the cashier said. He clicked the lock and pushed the door open. Puzzled, Bruce went in and shut the door after him. "What happened?"

"I thought probably you'd seen it," the cashier said. "Little mixup. O'Brien came around with a gun and a pair of brass knucks."

"The faro dealer?"

"Was. Your dad canned him, that's what he was mad about. He got a few drinks in him and came over to clean up."

"What'd he do?"

The cashier seemed embarrassed. "Knocked the old man down," he said. "Right over in front of the slot machines. Old man wasn't expecting anything. They were just standing there arguing a little when O'Brien let one fly." He looked at Bruce sidelong. "Give them an even break, your old man'd bust him in two," he said. "He wasn't expecting anything."

"Don't apologize," Bruce said. "A guy half his size knocked him down."

"Knocked him kicking," the cashier agreed. "Hung a shiner on him big as a plate. Course he's younger than the old man, and in better shape. Couple shills grabbed O'Brien and took him down cellar, but Pete's a pretty good friend of O'Brien's. I imagine they just opened the door and turned him loose in the Alley."

"Yeah," Bruce said. He looked out through the grilled window at the milling people, men with straw hats on the backs of their heads, coats over their arms; dealers in long eyeshades bending, reaching, leaning back to let their mouths go loose on the interminable chants. Right over in front of the slot machines, right in the middle of the crowd, with a couple of hundred people around, the Big Shot had been knocked silly by a little bantam who came to his shoulder. It was funny. It made him want to laugh right out loud.

But he didn't laugh right out loud. He was ashamed and furious, and he hated the apologetic cashier who really wanted to laugh, who was outside it and could laugh, but who didn't quite dare laugh in the face of the boss's son.

"You think he went back up to the lake?"

"I don't know," the cashier said. "He left here with a towel over his eye. I supposed he was going to a doc. If I had that eye I sure wouldn't be around at work for a day or two."

"I suppose I'd better get on back and see how he's doing," Bruce said. He nodded to the cashier and let himself out.

In the hot bright street the traffic was thick. Cars coated with dust from the desert nosed into the curb to let out women in bloomers and wrinkled blouses and men in creased plus-fours. But the traffic and the blare of horns and the heat and the hot tourists and the light blazing up from the sidewalk were out beyond Bruce, beyond arm's length, and between them and his eyes was the image he had had ever since he stepped out of the office, the image of his father, summer jacket, stickpin, heavy dark face, Big Shot air, going down kicking under O'Brien's fist, and the surprised look on his face, the purpling skin, the expression of heavy struggling impotence and rage and consternation. It was not a pretty image; it made him crawl. In spite of the heat, he walked very fast back to the doctor's office.

His mother was not in the waiting room. He peeked through the door and saw her sitting in a muslin gown, one shoulder bare, with her breast pressed against a little window in the wall. She turned her head at his step, and smiled at him, making a little face.

"How's it going?" he said.

"All right. I'll be through in about ten minutes."

"I'll wait outside here."

Lips smiling, eyes puckered, she made her deprecatory face again. "I'm a nuisance."

"You're terrible," he said. "I don't see how I stand you."

He went out and sat down, tried to read a magazine, put it down to stare at the white wall. His father's humiliation was as raw in his mind as if he himself had been knocked down. He found himself hating O'Brien. A damned little hard-eyed chiseler, a borderline gangster, a brainless tough guy. Yet the old man had probably earned what he got. He couldn't fire anybody without insulting him. He'd sit at home and worry about the monte game and work himself into a fury, and probably snoop around when O'Brien was on shift, and make his suspicions perfectly plain, and then finally he would take out all his dissatisfaction on O'Brien, make him the goat. You could hardly blame the dealer for getting sore.

So maybe this is better than bootlegging, he said. So this is legal and no cops knock on your door late at night. But you play around with the same cheap people, the same flashy men with big rolls, the same cheap squaws. You get yourself into a situation where somebody swings on you or takes a shot at you in the alley, and when you get up off the floor with your eye pickled and the crowd gaping at you you haven't even got a sense of outraged virtue to lean on. All you've got is the officious sympathy of flunkeys who will dust off your clothes and get a towel for your eye and laugh after you're gone, and you know they're laughing because anybody likes to see a big shot taken for a ride.

He got up from the chair and looked in the door again. His mother sat patiently, her forehead against the wall, her mutilated breast exposed to the healing eye of the window.

God damn, he said miserably.

On the way to the lake she lay back in the seat with her eyes closed, her face paper-white and pinheads of perspiration on her upper lip. The smell of ozone clung in her hair. Bruce drove fast, looking at her now and again, afraid that she had fainted, but when he said, "You feel all right, Mom?" she opened her eyes and smiled and said, "Sure, I'm all right. I just feel a little weak is all."

"You go to bed when we get back, and stay there."

Her only reply was a mild, withdrawn smile, as if the effort of moving her lips were almost too great, and in a kind of terror he started up the long, swinging grade. The smell of ozone that clung to her was like the odor of disease, and looking at her he felt that with that mild smile on her face and her eyes closed she was contemplating the battleground of her own body, warring cells going crazy, multiplying, proliferating, spreading and crowding out the healthy cells, leaving her less and less of herself. A body completely replaced itself in seven years, but that was done to pattern, according to a plan. This was something else, an insane crowding of formless hostility, a barbarian invasion, blotting out the order and the form and the identity, transforming it into a shapeless thing that was not his mother at all, but an unidentified colony of cells, functionless and organless and hopeless. For one blasted moment he stared at her in panic, almost expecting her to bulge and puff and swell, lose her features, change into a grotesque horror before his eyes.

She sat with closed eyes, her lips together, breathing quickly but softly through her nose. The crowsfeet of laughter were not gone even in repose from the corners of her eyes.

The new LaSalle was in the garage when they pulled up under the pines. The good mountain smell came down across the cove, and the lake wrinkled under the wind. Stepping down to help his mother from the car, Bruce set his foot on one of the white stones with which his father had lined the drive, and he swore under his breath. "Feel all right, or do you want to rest a minute?" he said.

476

"I'm all right." She stepped out and stood straight. "It never lasts very long." She looked along the curve of bright lake shore where the slant sun glittered off the water and glanced on the red-brown trunks of the trees flanking the house. "It would be pretty hard not to feel all right up here," she said. "It was hot in town, that was all."

"Bed for you anyway," he said, and steered her up the steps. He was hoping that the old man would be off in bed or somewhere. But the first thing he saw as they stepped into the living room was his father, sitting in the big chair by the window, a white pad over one eye and his other eye glaring at them, bloodshot and furious. He said nothing when they came in, but jerked in his chair.

"Bo!" Elsa said. She broke from Bruce's hand and crossed the room, laid a hand on Bo's head above the bandage. He flinched irritably away. "What happened?" she said.

"Isn't it clear enough what happened?" he said. "I got a black eye."

"Oh." She stood for a moment, steadying herself by a chair back. "Have you been to a doctor? Have you had it fixed?"

"Did you think I patched this thing on myself?"

"Come on," Bruce said, and took her arm again. "You're feeling pretty rocky yourself. You go and lie down."

But she held back. "Bo," she said. "Who?"

He jerked around in the chair again and his one visible eye glared out the window. His teeth were bitten together, almost chattering. Here we go, Bruce thought almost wearily. He's been humiliated and now he's mad, and he'll take it out on anybody within reach. He pulled at his mother's arm.

"You're supposed to lie down."

"But your dad is hurt," she said. "Let me be a minute."

"Go and lie down!" Bruce said, suddenly furious. His mother looked at him, glanced at Bo, frowned as if a pain had hit her, and went silently into the bedroom. Bruce, turning from watching her go, found his father's bloodshot eye fixed hard on him.

"What in Christ's biting you?" his father said.

"She's sick," Bruce said. "She just had a treatment and I thought she was going to faint all the way home. She's in no shape to doctor anybody, or even talk to anybody."

His father glared a moment longer, then turned away with a grunt.

"If there's anything you need done to your eye," Bruce said, "I'll do it."

His father didn't bother to answer.

For almost a week the old man sat around the cottage reading the papers, figuring, sprawling back in the chair while Elsa fixed poultices for the injured eye. By the third day the soreness was gone, but the flesh from his cheekbone to his nose was swollen and purple, with a streak of dull yellow along the upper eyelid. Every time he looked in a mirror he swore, and when he got up on the fourth morning and found that the other eye had developed sympathetic purple and yellow streaks he was untouchable for hours. He got the idea that sunlight was good for it, and sat in the yard with his face tilted back, but if a delivery truck came into the drive, or walkers passed along the lake front, he turned his head away, or raised a newspaper in front of his face, or went inside.

Bruce was cynically amused. "He looks like one of those obscene colored baboons," he said. "A sensitive baboon who can't stand his own looks."

"That's not a very nice thing to say."

Bruce shrugged.

"You don't feel a bit sorry for him, do you?" she said.

"I guess not."

She shook her head, and her voice was almost pleading. "There's nothing shameful about being knocked down by a person half your age."

"And half your size," he said.

"O'Brien used to be a prize fighter," she said, "and your dad is pretty close to sixty years old, did you realize that?"

"I can't help it," Bruce said. "If he's sixty he ought to be the sort of person of sixty that you just don't hit in the eye."

She shook her head, her mouth sad. "You're hard. I guess I don't understand how you can be that hard."

He knew he ought to stop. He was hurting her, and he didn't want to. But he kept on anyway. "Maybe I'm getting even," he said. "Maybe I remember once when he broke my collarbone knocking me over the woodbox, and once when he rubbed my nose in my own mess."

She was looking at him startled, close to tears. "I knew you remembered that," she said. "You never forget anything, do you? You never make allowances for hot temper or anything."

"Forget it," Bruce said. "I don't really hold that against him. I just get sick and tired of all his airs and his self pity."

"Sometime you'll learn," she said. She turned away and began pushing the carpet sweeper over the rug, talking straight ahead of her, not at him. "Some day you'll learn that you can't have people exactly the way you want them and that a little understanding is all you need to make most people seem halfway decent. What you don't understand is that your dad is ashamed to death."

478

"What you don't understand," Bruce said, "is that I'm ashamed too."

She turned, and their eyes met for a moment. "Yes," she said finally. "Of course. So am I. But I'm more sad than ashamed. I know your father better than you do, and I know that just one thing, one little disgrace like that, is about all that's needed now to make an old man of him. He isn't young any more. Everything goes down from here. I don't think it ever occurred to him before that he wasn't just as young and just as strong as he ever was."

"What that means," Bruce said, "is that he'll come to you all the more to be babied."

He knew he ought to be slapped, but his mother merely looked at him with her eyes clouded. Then she turned again and took up the handle of the cleaner. "I babied you too," she said. "I couldn't have lived with you if I hadn't."

On Sunday a long convertible pulled up in the drive and the Frenchman, Laurent, slid his fat stomach from behind the wheel. Bruce, down on the shore sawing up driftwood, saw him waddle up on the porch and go in, and he deliberately stayed away until Laurent was gone. Then he took the bucksaw up to the garage, got a bottle of beer from the icebox, and came through the living room to the front porch with it. His mother and father were talking in the living room. "Yes," his father said, "but they've got to honor their notes. If they don't, we can collect from whoever signs them. That part of it's all right."

"Wouldn't they think there was something wrong if you both . . ."

"We've got the books. We can prove it to them, can't we? We've been making money."

"I should be getting dinner," she said, as Bruce went through the front door. "You hungry, Bruce?"

"Not so hungry I can't wait a while. I'll wait out here."

From the porch he watched the lake between sips of beer. A speedboat cut across the cove leaving an emerald and white wake, and after three or four minutes the waves began to slap on the beach. It was a good place, a quiet place, a lovely place—but he was already getting a little restless. Doing nothing all summer was a little wearing. He should have got a job. Still, it was the middle of August now. In another month he'd be threading the Ford into the sun's eye across the desert.

So you're capable of staying in one place two months and a half before you get jumpy, he said. You're the guy who was looking for a home. He shifted himself comfortably and let it go. The hell with a home. You had to get out and do something, not just vegetate and sail and saw wood.

His parents were still talking inside; it was an hour before his mother called him to dinner. The old man, sitting at the dining room table, had a pencil and paper and was figuring. He figured until he had to move to make way for a plate.

"No," he said. "I'd be a sucker to get out just when things are rolling smooth."

"What's up?" Bruce said. "Are we planning to move?"

"Laurent's got an offer for his third interest," his mother said. "Some gamblers from Denver want to buy in."

"Doesn't he want to sell?"

"He isn't sure. Pa got talking with him and figured that he might sell if Laurent didn't want to."

"I thought the place was making money."

His father's face across the table was heavy and thoughtful. The discolored flesh around his eye made him look as if he were wearing a mask. "I don't know," he said. "I'm damned if I do. It's made money so far, but there's no telling what it'll do in winter. It's bound to fall off."

"What would you do if you sold?"

"How do I know?" his father said irritably. "I could find something, I guess."

Out of the corner of his eye Bruce caught his mother's glance, and bent to his food. Her look and the expression on the old man's face were equally clear. The club was getting him down. He'd been scared of it from the beginning, it was too big a gamble, he wasn't up to gathering the gold off the Big Rock Candy Mountain once he got there. It weighed him down, it worried him, the excitement it gave him was tinged with fear. He was riding a tiger, and he knew he wasn't the man to do it. It was a sure thing the old man wanted, not a gamble.

But that, Bruce said to himself, wasn't the biggest reason why the old man was toying with this chance to get out while he was still ahead. As much as anything else, it was that eye, the humiliation of going back after ten days of hiding and having the dealers and shills and steady customers look at him sideways. It was the fear he had of coming back a soiled big shot.

Like Chet, Bruce said. Just exactly like Chet. He'd blow this money-making club in a minute to save his pride, only he'd never admit why he was doing it. After working up—or down—to something like this all his life he'd sell out just because a little tinhorn hit him in the eye.

"How much has the place made in the last six months?" he said.

"It's only been running four," his father said. "I don't know exactly. We put in fifteen thousand apiece. These Denver guys are offering eighteen for a third interest. It's worth more than that. I expect I'm ahead about eight thousand in four months, if I could sell my third for twenty thousand."

"Rate of twenty-five thousand a year for each of you," Bruce said. "You can't gripe at that, except when you come to pay your income tax."

His father laughed. "Income tax!" he said.

"Have you ever paid an income tax?"

"No," his father said, "and I don't intend to."

"Some day they'll haul you off to the pen for three years."

"They've got to catch me first," his father said.

Bruce buttered his roll and laid his knife down. "I'll bet there isn't a family like ours in the United States," he said. "You've never paid an income tax. Did either of you ever vote?"

"I never did," his mother said. "Isn't that awful? I never knew enough about it to make the effort."

"I guess I voted once," Bo said. "Back in Dakota. How long ago? Twenty-five years? Nearer thirty, I guess."

"Ever serve on a jury?"

"No."

"There we are," Bruce said. "Two of us have never voted, and the other one voted once, thirty years ago. We never lived in any house in the United States for more than a year at a time. Since I was born we've lived in two nations, ten states, fifty different houses. Sooner or later we're going to have to take out naturalization papers."

"And now we might move right out of here," his mother said, "just about the time we get the cottage finished up. Wouldn't that be typical? Let's not sell this place, Bo, even if you do sell out of the club."

"This is headquarters," Bo said. "I've paid taxes on this already. That ought to make us permanent residents."

"Do you think you will sell out of the club?" Bruce said.

"If I got a good enough offer I might. I've got a feeling this whole racket is going to be a flash in the pan."

Bruce laughed. "Here we go round the prickly pear," he said.

"What?"

"Nothing."

His mother rose to clear the table for dessert, and he saw her wince. "What's the matter?" he said.

"Oh, my darned hip!"

"What's the matter with your hip?"

"I don't know. Rheumatiz, I guess. I must be getting old."

She made her special face and limped like an old crone into the kitchen. Across the table Bruce's eyes met his father's, and he saw the question there that he knew must be in his own. And the fear.

Thereafter he had two things to watch, one working in his father and one in his mother. His father's problem he did not worry about. It made no great difference to him whether the old man sold the club or not, except as it might affect his mother. But his mother's condition was another thing. Once he had noticed that she was hiding a pain, he couldn't seem to look up without catching her wincing or favoring one side—the same right side always. Her appetite was like a bird's, and she got out of breath easily.

"Maybe it's the altitude," he said. "Maybe this is too high for you."

"Oh, it isn't anything. I'm getting old and rickety, that's all."

But he watched her, and he saw that now in the afternoon she lay down for a rest, something she had never done as far back as he could remember. And when the old man powdered up his discolored cheek and went into town he heard her ask him to bring out some sleeping pills. The fear that made him sensitive to her least gesture of weariness or pain made him pretend with her. He kidded her about her rheumatiz, told her that all she needed was a little exercise, like a nice dip in the lake. When she took him up he was horrified and wouldn't let her. The lake was getting too cold. Finally he compromised on a mild walk, but when they came back she was out of breath, weak, her mouth set in a hard line. They had walked less than a mile.

"Your hip?" he said.

"I guess I'm not much good any more."

"You're going in and see the doctor."

"Oh, fiddlesticks," she said. "It's nothing but a little stitch. Probably I've got an abscessed tooth or something."

"It wouldn't do any harm to find out."

"All right," she said. "If it will make you feel better I'll go, next time I go in."

She lay down and rested for an hour while he sat in the sun and whittled aimlessly. At five-thirty his father came back. "Well," Bruce said. "Sell the gold mine?"

His father hesitated on the step as if debating whether to sit down and talk or go inside. "I can make a deal, I think, if I want to. Where's your mother?"

"Lying down."

"Sick?" His father's face turned sideways to look at him with a fixed, almost vacant expression.

"Her hip's hurting her."

The old man chewed his lip and took off his hat. His hair, Bruce noticed, was getting thin, and he was almost white above the ears. "What the devil you suppose that is?" he said. "It just seemed to come on all of a sudden."

"I know what I'm scared it is," Bruce said.

His father's eyes wandered away. He tapped his hat against his trouser leg. His lips moved slightly, and he blinked his eyes.

"I'm taking her in to the doctor tomorrow," Bruce said. "There just isn't any point in not finding out."

"Yeah," his father said. He flapped the hat against his leg. "Yeah. Well. . . ." He went up the steps and into the house. Bruce followed him, almost as if he were guarding his mother, keeping people who were worrying about selling gambling houses from bothering her with their problems.

She was still, apparently, lying down. They went together down the little hall between the partitions and looked in the door of her bedroom. She lay face downward on the bed, and as they looked they could see her body writhe.

"Mom!" Bruce said. He jumped to the bed and knelt, his arm over her shoulder. "Mom, for God's sake!"

Her shoulder stiffened. For a moment she kept her face in the pillow. Then she turned it and smiled, and he saw that her cheeks were wet. "I'm a baby," she said.

Bruce looked at his father, irresolute at the foot of the bed. The old man wet his lips and came closer. "Maybe," he said, "maybe you ought to take a couple aspirin."

She smiled again, and as she shifted on the bed the smile froze whitely against her teeth. "I've taken . . . six," she said.

"Damn it," Bruce said wildly. "Why didn't you call me?"

"I couldn't seem to . . . make much noise."

Without saying goodbye or where he was going, Bruce went out of the bedroom, walking fast, running as he hit the back steps. The Ford was blocked into the garage by the LaSalle, so he took the LaSalle. As he roared out the drive he saw his father run to the front door to look after him. At the paved highway he didn't even bother to wonder which way he was going to turn. He just turned. There were cottages, stores, little centers for groceries and boats and fishing tackle, in both directions on that side. He let the LaSalle out, and was startled at how fast it leaped under him, how smoothly it ran, with hardly a sound except an eager low humming. His foot was almost to the floor when he saw the first store, and he rode the brakes through the loose gravel of the turn-out. A man came running out of the service station with a pail in his hand, as if he were going to a fire.

Bruce leaned out the window and shouted. "Know of a doctor close around here?"

"Might try the C.C.C. Camp," the man said. "Know where it is?"

"No."

"Go right on. Exactly seven tenths of a mile, I measured it. There's a sign . . ."

He took his foot off the running board and Bruce slammed the car into second. The gravel spattered. Bruce's hand went onto the horn and stayed there as he swung around a party of girls parked at the roadside with a flat tire. They started to flag him down, and stood with upraised arms and opened mouths as he roared by. At exactly seven tenths of a mile a road wriggled off into the timber, and he tramped on the brakes and careened in. Back in the timber a half mile he came to four long low barracks, one of them with a flagpole in front. A man in army uniform was sitting at a desk inside.

"Is there a doctor here?" Bruce said.

"Not right now," the officer said. "He went into Carson this afternoon. Ought to be back by now."

"Damn!" Bruce said. He was panting as if he had run all the way from the cottage. "You haven't got any morphine or anything here, have you?"

"The doctor'd have to give you that," the officer said. He rose from behind the desk. "What's the matter?"

"My mother's in a hell of a pain," Bruce said. He looked at the officer and saw that the officer thought he was out of his head. It wasn't worth explaining. "Could you ask the doctor to come over when he gets back, if he comes in the next hour?"

The officer nodded, then lifted his hand and made a motion of shooting a revolver at the door. "Here he is now," he said.

Bruce was at the car door before it could open. "Can you come over and look at my mother?" he said. "She's had cancer—carcinoma—had an operation for it. Now she's got awful pains in her hip. I don't know what they are. She's been taking x-ray treatments . . ."

"Wait a minute," the doctor said. He was in army uniform like the man in the headquarters building. "I'll get my bag."

He stepped out and walked with what seemed callous slowness into the building. In five minutes he came out, closing his black bag. "You lead," he said. "I'll follow along."

484

"I can take you and bring you back."

"No thanks. I'll drive my own."

To the officer, standing before the building, he said, "Tell that lousy cook to keep my dinner warm, Harry."

She was still in pain when they got back. Bo Mason sat at the head of the bed holding her hand, looking helpless and clumsy. He got up when the doctor came in, and stumbled against the chair. The doctor set his bag where Bo had been.

"Hello," he said to the woman on the bed. "Having a little pain, eh?"

To Bruce he said, "Can you put a tablespoon in a pan of water and boil it a couple minutes?"

Bruce went out, and his father followed him. "Where'd you find him?" he said.

"C.C.C. Camp."

"Couldn't you get anybody better than that? He's probably some horse doctor."

"I don't give a damn," Bruce said. "He can give her a shot of something. I was just looking for somebody quick, and he was the quickest." He filled a pan with water and threw a spoon into it. Leaving it on the burner, he went back into the bedroom. The doctor had his mother bare to the waist and was pressing with his finger tips under her arm, feeling down the scarred side, over the bulge of her hip bone. Bruce turned away. But when the doctor had covered her again, without comment, and gone into the kitchen to sterilize a needle, and came back with a hypodermic full of brownish liquid, he watched, because that was what he had got the doctor for. The needle stabbed in, a slight bump of liquid swelled under the skin.

"That will fix you for a while," the doctor said. "You'll sleep a good while, probably. Then you'd better go in and see somebody in town."

She nodded. "If she wakes up," the doctor said to Bruce, "give her some orange juice or broth or milk, anything. If she doesn't wake up for a long time don't worry."

He pulled the quilt across her. "I wouldn't even bother to undress," he said. "You're getting sleepy already."

"I can feel it in my tongue."

"You'll feel it all over in a minute," he said. He went out and held the door open for Bruce and his father, shut it quietly.

"How long since her operation?"

"A year and a half," Bruce said.

"Umm."

"What is it?" Bo Mason said. "What could be giving her pains like that way down in her hip? She's awful hard to hurt. I never saw her cry for pain in my life before. . . ."

His voice was almost babbling. The skin of his face was slack. The doctor shrugged and shook his head.

"You'd better get her in to a specialist," he said. "I wouldn't want to say, but my guess would be that it's a secondary growth. When that stuff gets so far along it breaks off and the bloodstream carries it around. You say she's been short of breath?"

"For the last month or so," Bruce said.

"Sounds like lungs too. Probably she'll have to be tapped."

"Has she got a chance?" Bo said.

The doctor looked at him a moment. "I doubt it," he said.

She slept until past noon the next day, and when she finally awoke, fuzzy-tongued and drowsy-eyed, she had apparently been dreaming. Her mouth was drooping and sad. That evening she asked Bo if they could go back to Salt Lake.

"Salt Lake?" he said. "What for?"

"I want to," she said.

"I don't know why you'd want to go back to that smoky hole for the winter when we could go to L.A. or somewhere."

"Bo," she said. "Couldn't we? Even if you don't sell your share in the club, couldn't we?" She took his hand and held it, watching his face. "That's where Chet is," she said, and Bruce saw that it shamed her to have to tell him. She was going to die and they all knew it. The next morning, his face gray and haggard, Bo went down and without a word to anyone closed the deal for his share of the club.

Bruce closed up the cottage by himself, refusing to let his mother get up. His father had gone down to the coast, vaguely on business, and would meet them in Salt Lake. It was clear enough what he was going for. With the club sold, the notes of the Denver gamblers laid away to mature, the move back to Salt Lake coming up, his mind frayed and undone, he turned naturally and immediately back to whiskey. It would give him something to do, it would bring in a little cash.

"By hell, it would make me laugh if it didn't make me want to kill him," Bruce said to his mother. "What if we get raided in Salt Lake? That would be a fine help to getting you well, wouldn't it? Why couldn't he wait till you got back on your feet, at least?"

"He'd just sit around and stew himself to death if he didn't have something to keep him busy," she said. "I don't care. He's better off doing something, even that."

486

She was thinner, a week had made her thinner, and her cheeks looked sunken, but her eyes were still a sudden and incredible blue, unmisted by sickness. "You're not going to be too comfortable going across in the Ford, either," he said. "He might have thought of that."

She shook her head and smiled. "Don't worry about me. You help us get moved and then you go back to school and be the head of the class."

"Head of the class," Bruce said. "I've been head of the class quite a lot, haven't I?"

"You have," she said, and the pride in her voice made him crawl. "You've got a good head. You can be an important man if you try, Bruce."

"Will you promise to come and live at the White House?" he said. With a fury that was close to tears he went back to his half-finished packing. There were only two possibilities that he would go back to school this fall. One was that she would die before school opened. The other was that he would deliberately leave her to die with only the old man for company. He would have cut his throat before he would have agreed to either.

They were packed for two days, waiting, before they had word from Bo. He wired from Salt Lake that he had taken an apartment and that they should come on. In the afternoon a truck came and got their freight. The next morning at six, with the woods all around them showing the first fall color and the lake a sheet of pure emerald and the eastern sky so pure and blue it hurt the eyes, they started down the Big Rock Candy Mountain for home, for Salt Lake City, for the spot where the dead was buried and the living would die, and there was for Bruce none of the exhilaration that had blown him westward in June, though he was now more truly than then going home.

IX

All through
September she
lay dying in the
dark little apartment,
in the bedroom through
whose open windows in the
morning Bruce could smell the
bitter tang of the winter pall of
smoke, coming down now, settling
in the evenings and lasting until the
valley breeze cleared it out about noon.
Through those windows, when he came in
at six or seven o'clock to find his mother
wide awake, awake for no one knew how many
hours, maybe all night, he could see the thin
morning sun touching the back lawn of the apartment
house opposite, and the yellowing leaves of the hickories
along the sidewalk, like sunlight cut into long ovals.

But no sun touched the bedroom. It was gloomy even at
mid-day, and more than once Bruce felt like kicking the windows
out of their frames, tearing down the curtains, pushing the wall
out to let one sweep of sun and light cleanse the room. The very
air in the place was the color of patience and pain. The old man
might at least, he thought, have found her a pleasant room to die
in.

He told her so, obliquely. "A pleasant room to be sick in," he
put it, but she smiled at him from the bed, trying to braid her
long hair with fingers that tired after a few motions. "It's a nice
enough room," she said. "It could be more cheerful, but then your
dad never did have much of an eye for what made a house pleasant."

"No," Bruce said. "Here, let me do that."

He took the rope of hair from her and braided it, found a
rubber band for the end of each braid, and lifted her while he
smoothed out sheets and pillow. "Now what for breakfast?" he
said. "How about some ham and eggs this morning?"

Her smile was like the smile of a very old, very wise, very gentle
grandmother. "Maybe some orange juice," she said.

"Nothing else?"

"I'm not hungry, really."

Seeing how thin she had grown, he said miserably, "You need

to eat to get your strength back," and he saw in her eyes, the bright, incredibly blue eyes, unmarked and clear, that she was smiling inside herself at the idea of getting her strength back. If she pretended not to know that she was going to die, she did it to spare him, not herself.

"No milk?" he said. "Some milk toast, maybe?"

"No thanks. Just some orange juice. Don't go to any trouble."

"I'll bring you in an orange and you can peel it yourself," he said. He took the tray from the bed table and went into the kitchen. Orange juice, when she had hardly eaten anything for ten days! He squeezed a big glass of orange juice, poured a glass of milk just in case it might tempt her, opened the icebox door and got out some grape juice for the same reason, scooped a dish of bright jello. The icebox was full of invalid's dishes that he had made and never got her to eat. He ought to give it up, he thought, lifting the tray. He ought to quit urging her to eat, let the weariness take her, shorten it for her. But how could he? She didn't want it that way. She wouldn't deliberately shorten her agony one second.

Play it out till the whistle blows, he said bitterly, and hardened his mouth at that football-field stupidity that was here somehow present in his mother and that he could neither fight against nor condemn. Sixty to nothing against you and the other team with a first down on your five yard line, but play it out, break your neck on that last tackle in the end zone. That was the way she had done it all her life, and there was no changing her.

His father was in the sickroom when he came back, standing near the door looking big and uneasy and out of place, his lips forming the platitudes that were all he could ever say to her now. How you feeling this morning? Having any pains? And, stooping to look out the window, Nice day again outside.

He moved aside when Bruce came with the tray. His eyes were bloodshot and wandering. "There you are," Bruce said. "Let's see you clean that tray."

She laughed. "My goodness, I can't eat all that."

Bo Mason wagged his head, and Bruce hated him for his fumbling bulk, his stupid, vague embarrassment. "You want to eat," he said, and catching Bruce's eye he almost flushed.

At least he feels it, Bruce said. At least he feels frozen out. Nobody wants him around, and he knows it. And by God he's earned it.

"Well," the old man said, and looked out the window again. "Going to be a nice day." He moved toward the door. "Anything you want from town?"

"Are you going down already?" she said. "You haven't had breakfast yet."

"I can get something downtown."

"There's plenty of stuff here," Bruce said. "I'll fix something in a minute."

Nothing to do, he thought. No place to go. But he has to rush out of here before breakfast, just so he can hang around cigar stores and hotel lobbies all day.

He watched his mother sip her orange juice. "Come on," he said, "let's get out of here and let Mom eat in peace." He went into the kitchen and started breakfast. He was just putting the toast in the toaster when he heard his mother in the bedroom, and ran in. Leaning back against the pillow wiping her lips, she gave him a weak, apologetic smile. "I'm sorry," she said. "I couldn't keep it down."

"Feel all right now?"

She nodded, and he took the pail into the bathroom. Not even her orange juice this morning. Worse and worse.

"Pa," he said when he came back, "I think we ought to get a nurse for Mom, till she gets back on her feet."

"You're better than any nurse," his mother said. "Unless you get tired of taking care of me." She wiped her lips, puckered her eyes at him. "You're stuck in this apartment too much," she said. "But I don't need a nurse. I guess I can still do a few things for myself."

"And tire yourself all out," Bruce said. "I don't know how to take care of you right."

"You take care of me beautifully," she said. "A nurse would be expensive, too."

"Only six dollars a day."

"Six dollars a day!" his father said. He seemed suddenly angry, the indecision and helplessness dissolved in violence. "My God, doesn't that show you? The minute anybody gets sick there's ten million vultures waiting to pounce. What makes a nurse worth six dollars a day?"

"See?" Elsa said. "It's out of the question. Now why don't both of you go out and get some fresh air? You don't want to stick around with me all day."

"Yeah?" Bruce said. "What if you got a pain?"

"I guess I could stand it. Maybe you could pull the telephone close, and if I need anything I could call Mrs. Welch."

"What does she know about giving hypos?" He looked at his father, and it was with difficulty that he kept his voice down. "If

490

you were sick yourself you'd think a nurse was worth six dollars a day," he said.

His father threw up his hands and walked to the door. "Fifteen dollars a shot for x-rays," he said. "The doctor coming here three or four times a week at five bucks a throw. Medicine to buy. Syringes to buy. God Almighty, we're not made of money. We have to eat, too, you know. I'll play nurse myself, if we need a nurse."

"You'd be a lot of good," Bruce said between his teeth.

"Please!" Elsa said. "I don't need a nurse, Bruce. Really. We're getting along just fine."

The old man came over to the bed, stooped to kiss her. His face was sober and tired and his eyes redder than ever. "Don't think I don't want you to have the best care," he said. "It's just so damned quiet now, all out-go and no income. How'd it be if I got some good woman who could cook and clean and do things for you?"

"No," she said. "I'm an awful expense. I'm sorry."

He stared at her with whipped, bewildered eyes, rolled his shoulders, winced. "I've got a damn boil coming on my back," he said. "Every time I move it half kills me."

"Oh dear!" she said. Her instant sympathy, the spectacle of her lying there in the bed she would die in, crucified by unbearable pain every few hours, and wasting sympathy on a great booby's boil made Bruce so furious he couldn't stay in the room. When his mother called him to fetch iodine and a bandage he brought them sullenly, looking sideways at his father's milk-white body stripped to the waist, the angry red swelling between his shoulder blades, and his mother propped on one weak arm, all her attention and strength focussed on painting and dressing the boil. He couldn't stand it. He escaped again.

Boils, he said. Wouldn't it be just like him to have boils, the dirtiest, messiest kind of affliction he could get, and then come running to let his half-dead wife waste her strength babying him! Oh my God, he said, if he was only the one on that bed, and she the one on her feet!

And he knew that that too was wrong. It would have been obscene to see him have to bear the things she bore.

When his father came out, shouldering himself gingerly into his coat, Bruce went out into the hall with him and confronted him there. "Mom just simply has to have a nurse," he said. "I can't do the things to make her comfortable that a nurse could."

His father sighed. "If you can tell me how we can afford six dollars more a day . . ."

"Go in debt!" Bruce said. "She's dying in there, can't you get that through your head?"

His father's eyes were glassy. He looked dazed, as if he had not slept for a long time. The outburst of irritability a few minutes ago had gone completely. "None of it can save her," he said. "That's just it. Do you think if she had a chance I wouldn't do everything, spend every cent we've got?"

"All right," Bruce said. "She's dying, so let's let her die. I'll cut out the orange juice. That'll save fifty cents a day."

For an instant, watching his father's hand clench, he thought they were going to have a fight there in the hall. He stood up to it, so furious himself that his stomach was a sick fluttering. Then the dark face of the old man twitched, his hands loosened, and without a word he turned and went out.

"You mustn't be too hard on your dad," his mother said later. "He never was any good in sickness, his own or anybody else's."

"No," Bruce said. "Witness his boils."

"Boils are painful," she said. "There's hardly anything worse than a boil."

"You're having a little pain yourself," he said. "Why should you have to tend that big baby? What does he do for you when a pain hits you, except stand around looking helpless?"

"He wants to help," she said. "He just can't stand to see anybody in pain, that's all. It drives him frantic. I remember when I scalded my arm, he was ten times more scared than I was. He almost cried."

"If he wants to help so bad," Bruce said, "why won't he let me get a nurse? If he's so broke he can't afford a nurse for a couple weeks he ought to apply for charity." He went to the window and tried to make the shade roll higher, to let in a little more light. "Broke!" he said. "He's rolling in money. Twenty or thirty thousand dollars, and he can't even . . . !" He turned on her. "You're going to have a nurse, whether he'll pay for her or not."

"Bruce," she said strongly, "I won't let you spend your money for a nurse. It's silly. I don't need one."

He made a bitter mouth at her. "Do you think you wouldn't have one now if I had any money? I haven't got ten dollars to my name."

He went out to wash the dishes and clean up the house, and when he came back she was in pain. She didn't want a hypo. It wasn't bad yet. But he gave her one anyway. "The object of a hypo," he said, "is to keep you from having any pain at all."

"You'll make a dope-head of me."

"I guess we can take that chance."

A few minutes after the hypo she dropped off into a heavy

sleep, and when she awoke, an hour or so after noon, he got her to drink a little grape juice. She wasn't hungry enough to take more.

For a while he read to her. He had filled a shelf with books from the library, but they were law books, history, things she wouldn't have liked or understood. So he started again on *South Wind*, which he had half finished, and she lay quietly like a dutiful child being read to. When he came to Miss Wilberforce his mother giggled.

He lowered the book to his lap. "Like it?" he said, pleased.

"It's good," she said. "That Miss Wilberforce reminds me of Edna Harkness. You remember Edna."

"Sure. I didn't know she was a drunkard, though."

"Edna was lonesome," she said. "She used to sit alone drinking until she couldn't stand it, and then she'd come over to our house to cry. She tried to commit suicide there once."

"What for?"

"She was in love with somebody—not Slip, he was just a piece of saddle-leather as far as she was concerned—but another man, a Catholic. He wouldn't marry her unless she turned Catholic, and if she turned Catholic then she couldn't get a divorce from Slip. She used to take off her clothes too, sometimes."

"In Whitemud?"

"It sounds funny, doesn't it? Three or four times. She kept saying she wasn't ashamed of her shape. She was so dreadfully afraid of getting old and homely." Smiling, she shook her head. "Poor Edna."

Seeing the life he had known as a small boy now strangely re-focussed through his mother's eyes, remembering Edna Harkness as a somewhat sallow and sagging woman married to a Texas cowpuncher, Bruce felt for a moment the strangeness of that past, those almost-twenty-three years that were behind him now, irrecoverable, but more real than many things that happened in the present. Edna Harkness, with troubles that were silly and self-begotten, coming to his mother for sympathy and consolation. They had always come that way, every lost sheep they had ever known had fed on her.

While he groped back in that past, watching his mother's face, he saw the sweat pop in tiny beads on her forehead and lip as if it were something squeezed through porous cloth, and saw her lips even in the midst of a wry smile for poor Edna go white and stiff. The blue eyes looked straight upward. Bruce dropped the book and stood up.

"Pain?"

She nodded, still in the throes. Her legs moved slightly under the spread.

"How long?"

"It's been coming on for a little while."

"Why in God's name didn't you tell me?" he said.

"I didn't want to interrupt. I thought it might go away." She grunted, a startled sound as if someone had knocked the wind out of her, and rolled half on her side.

Full of the anger and panic that came over him when he saw her stricken with the pain, he ran into the kitchen, flipped on a burner on the stove, dissolved a codine tablet in a half teaspoon of water and held it over the blaze. In a moment the water sizzled around the edges, the tablet dissolved brownly, the mixture bubbled. Then fit the syringe together, draw the cooled mixture into it, press out the air bubbles carefully, and hurry back to the bedroom, for your mother is in agony and this little weapon will straighten her cramped body, put her to sleep for a while, stall off the pain until next time, until this evening maybe.

The first paroxysm had passed, and she lay on her back again. "Arm or leg?" he said.

"Make it . . . leg," she said, and stiffened. He tore back the covers, found an unpunctured spot above her knee, a clear patch on the blue-punctured skin, swabbed with the wad of alcohol-soaked cotton, laid the needle against her skin, slanting, and jabbed. The codine made a tiny bluish bump under the skin, and the needle-hole wept one colorless tear as he swabbed again and covered her.

"Feeling better?"

"In a minute." Her smile was so strained that he bent over her. "Why don't you cry?" he said. "It'd be easier."

She let out a shuddering breath, as if exhaling the pain with the air. "I guess I've forgotten how," she said, quite seriously. "I try sometimes. I can't."

For a few moments he stood over her watching. The tightness went gradually out of her face, the forehead smoothed out. "Want to take a little sleep?" he said.

She nodded, and he opened the window, pulled the shades down, straightened the sheet under her chin, kissed her, and went out. In the other room he tried to read, but he couldn't concentrate. Once, reading through a discussion of riparian rights, his eyes distinctly saw, in print, the words: "Codine at nine o'clock. Codine again at two. Only five hours between pains now." Tiptoeing to the half-open door, he saw that his mother was asleep.

On an impulse he slipped into the hall and up to the apartment of Mrs. Welch, the only person they knew in the building.

"I wonder if you could do me a favor?" he said. "Are you going to be busy for the next hour or two?"

"No," she said. "What is it?" She was a fat, comfortable woman, too sympathetic and too-continuously ready to weep, but she would do.

"Could you sit with mother? She's asleep, and ought to sleep a couple of hours. I have to go uptown for a few minutes."

"Why sure," she said. She gathered up her magazine and came along, and Bruce put on his coat and went out into the air.

Dr. Cullen sat at his desk twirling a swab stick between his palms. "Anything wrong at home?"

"There's nothing much very right."

"Mother worse?"

"Oh, I don't know!" Bruce said. "About the same, I guess. Maybe she's worse. The codine doesn't seem to have the effect it used to. She had to have a hypo at nine and another one at two."

"Yes," the doctor said. "We have to expect that." He scribbled a prescription on the pad and tore it off, holding the sheet by the corners and blowing on it gently so that it rotated. His face was smooth and impassive, and his voice was the careful, flat, guarded voice Bruce remembered from the operating room.

"How is she eating?"

"Not at all. She can't even keep fruit juice down now."

"Um," Cullen said. He blew the prescription sheet. "If you want to," he said, "we can feed her by bowel. It would mean prolonging her life a week, two weeks."

"Would it make her any stronger?" Bruce said. "Would it help her stay stronger right to the end, even if she has to be full of dope, so she won't just dwindle away . . . ?"

He felt his face twisting, and forced himself to look straight at the doctor. "It's that dwindling that's hard to watch," he said. "She gets smaller and thinner every day."

"Bowel feeding would help that," Cullen said. "You couldn't do it very well, though."

"That's what I came to see you about," Bruce said. It was difficult to talk. The office was too padded, too quiet, the doctor's voice too carefully controlled. He knew Cullen liked and admired his mother, and that made it harder to talk to him. "I spoke to the old man this morning about a nurse," he said. "He says it's too expensive." With fascinated helplessness he heard himself shouting. "I can't stand to sit around there and watch her die *cheaply!"* he said. "She's got to have a nurse. I'll mortgage any money I ever make . . ."

"No," Cullen said. "I wouldn't want to see you do that." He looked out the window, and Bruce dabbed furiously at his wet eyes. Crying, sitting here bawling like a baby . . .

"I know a woman," the doctor said, turning. "I'll send her over tonight. And don't worry about the bill. I'll have Miss Ostler pay it and then add it to my bill. Your father can think I'm a hold-up man."

"Thanks," Bruce said. He took out his handkerchief and blew his nose. "I'm sorry I blew up. I just get so . . ."

Cullen rose and laid the prescription in Bruce's hand. "What are you going to do," he said. "Afterwards?"

"I don't know. Go back to school, I suppose, if I can find any way to work it out."

"Coming back here to practice after you get your degree?"

"I hadn't thought much about it."

"Don't," the doctor said.

"What?" Bruce said.

"I'm a busy-body," Cullen said. "I'm giving you advice. I've known your family for a good many years, and I can't help knowing a few things. Give yourself a chance. Get away from all that history."

"I suppose that's right," Bruce said.

"I might as well say my piece out," Cullen said. "Stop me if you want." He paused, and Bruce made a little motion with his hand. "Your mother is an exceptional woman," Cullen said. "I don't imagine she ever had any opportunities at all, but she's arrived at something without them. She's wise and brave and decent. But she's going to die, and there's nothing we can do for her except make her comfortable. When she does, clear out, and if there ever comes a time when your father wants to use you, live on you, get anything from you, keep out of it. He could spoil your life."

He laid his hand on Bruce's shoulder. "I'll drop by in the morning," he said as he went.

Bruce stayed in the room for five minutes with his back to the hallway, looking out the windows into the paved court. Even though you knew it, even though you were watching it every day, it came hard to hear the doctor say she would die. He remembered looking at the pictures of her lungs with the roentgenologist, the scientific finger pointing out the blurred and darkened places in the web of ribs and organs that was his mother. "She's doomed," the x-ray man said that day, and his big voice, too big for so small a man, boomed in the hollow office. He could hear it now.

The nurse and another patient came in. "Oh, I'm sorry," she said. "I thought Dr. Cullen had finished with you."

"He has," Bruce said. He brushed by her and went out.

The coming of Miss Hammond, the nurse, changed the quality of living in the apartment; it gave to his mother's dying a dignity it had not had before, a professional neatness, an air of propriety and authority. Miss Hammond was a neat and efficient and tireless young woman. She took complete charge of the place, cooked the meals, made the beds, fed and bathed and changed her patient. She even, when Bo Mason came in the next morning to have Elsa dress his boil, took charge of that too, in spite of his grumbling and distrust.

From the moment she came in the door Bruce knew he had an ally. Her first look around, with its covert criticism of the respectable gloom of the rooms, and the immediacy with which his mother liked her, cheered him up. And when his father had gone out, he saw her fussing with the blinds in the bedroom, trying to coax them up, as he had, to let a little light and sun in.

"It's no use," he said. "The place is like a dungeon. There's no help for it."

She smiled a little as she looked at him, her lips curving slowly, a pleasant, cheerful face. "Some flowers might help," she said.

Bruce looked from her to his mother and back. "My God," he said. She had lain in the gloom for three weeks, and he had never once thought to bring her flowers.

"Bruce has been stuck inside with me so much," his mother said. "He's hardly had a chance to poke his nose outside."

"Don't alibi me," he said. "I ought to be kicked." He looked at Miss Hammond and laughed. "I'll be back in an hour or two," he said.

In ten minutes he was on his way up Mill Creek Canyon. He had little money to buy flowers, and it would take twenty dollars' worth to brighten up that bedroom. But there were other things. Ahead of him the steep scarp of the Wasatch rose like a mighty wall, and on all the slopes, in every erosion gully, the oak-brush lay like a tufted, green-bronze blanket. He could see the tufts, tender and soft as wool, clear on down past Olympus and Twin Peaks, on down to the long ramp of Long Peak, running down to the point at the Jordan Narrows. In one gash down the side of Long Peak, ten miles away, lay a tongue of brilliant scarlet.

Ahead of him the sharp V of the canyon mouth opened, and in it, only an occasional tree at first, but higher up more and more, the ripe maples bloomed, fiery as poinsettias. He parked the car in a side road on the flat above the Boy Scout camp, and started up the rocky slope.

High up, his arms full of branches of sumac and maple and yellow aspen, he sat down and smoked a cigarette. West of him the view opened, framed in the V of the canyon—the broad valley still green with truck gardens and alfalfa, the petit point of orchards, the broad yellow-and-white band of the salt marshes, and beyond that band the cobalt line of the lake, the tawny Oquirrhs on the south end feathered with smoke from the smelters. At the right, just visible, was the end of Antelope Island, yellow-gold in the blue and white distance, and far beyond that, almost lost in the haze, the tracery of the barren ranges on the far side, almost seventy miles away.

He picked a leaf from the sheaf of branches beside him and chewed the bitter stem, his eyes on that view. He had seen it dozens of times, from the top of Olympus, from the saddle of Twin, from the westward rim of the Wasatch at a dozen different points, but looking at it now he narrowed his eyes and thought, as a man stopped by a noise in the heavy dusk of the woods might stop and peer in search of what had startled him. There was something lost and long forgotten stirring in the undergrowth of his memory. Something far back, as far back as Saskatchewan. That sweep of flat land below the abrupt thrust of the mountains, the notched door through which he saw it . . .

Then he had it. The Bearpaws, the picnic they had taken from the homestead when he was very young, the afternoon on the wooded shelf beside the spring, with the whole Montana plain under them. His mother had carried armfuls of leaves back with her from that picnic, in love with their cool feel and the memories they stirred in her of Minnesota. Maple leaves, pointed like a spread hand. And he himself, then as now, had been smothered by a memory, had been groping all afternoon to remember something from still another time in the mountains when he was very young indeed, barely out of infancy. This haunting sense of familiarity, this dream within a dream . . .

For a moment his brain whirled. Memory was a trap, a pit, a labyrinth. It tricked you into looking backward, and you saw yourself in another avatar, smaller and more narrow-visioned but richer in the life of the senses, and in that incarnation too you were looking back. You met yourself in your past, and the recognition was a strong quick shock, like a dive into cold water.

If you could pass that door, if you could look back through many funneling memories instead of one or two, you might be able to escape the incommunicable identity in which you lay hidden. You might remember your mother's memories, or your father's, contain within yourself the entire experience of your family, going back and back in time, a succession of diminishing images like the images in double mirrors, go back and beyond in time as the ranges went back and beyond in distance past the cobalt line of the lake.

He was not Bruce Mason, but a girl of eighteen named Elsa Norgaard, and he was sick in his mind to escape from the prison that home had become. And he was a boy named Harry Mason, running away from home at fourteen, the world wide ahead of him and at his back a house full of hatred and bad treatment.

He opened his eyes wide and breathed his lungs full and shook his head to clear it. He felt drunk, dizzy, but he thought he knew something that he hadn't known before. That was the way it went. The dog-wolf killed its young, the young wolves turned on the strength which begot them. You hate your father and I'll hate mine, in a circling, spiralling continuity up from the time-hazed past. You honor your mother, I'll honor mine. The varieties of family experience, he said, and thought of Proust, the sick man, crawling backward among the obscenities of recollection, and of Samuel Butler, so cursed in his heritage that he would never marry and have children to dominate and tyrannize over.

Sick and cursed, he said. As sick as Proust and as cursed as Butler. But he didn't exactly understand what he meant by it, and his mind shied away, wary after that tottering moment when memory had opened under him like a gulf and the solidities of the known world, the comfortable assumptions of his own identity, had slipped out of reach and left him poised on the brink of the unknowable.

Carefully, his mind as cautious and deliberate as his feet, he started climbing down the rocky slope with the bundle of brilliant leaves in his arm.

2

October first was his mother's birthday. On that morning, because he had time now to go and come as he wanted, he went downtown and with part of his few dollars bought her a quilted satin bed jacket. She had visitors sometimes. She ought at least to look nice, as if she were being taken care of.

When he gave it to her she looked as if she were going to cry.

She fumbled with the wrapping, and when she had it open her fingers lay on the satin quietly. "Bruce, you shouldn't have," she said. "I won't . . ."

"Hush," he said. "You needed it. And I couldn't let your birthday go by. There's something important about birthdays."

"I guess I haven't forgotten how to cry after all," she said, and squeezed his hand.

At eleven she had a bad pain, and the hypo, morphine now instead of codine, put her almost immediately to sleep. Miss Hammond went out for a walk and Bruce read. When she came back she said immediately, "I've got a suggestion, if you won't think I'm butting in."

"No. What?"

"I was just talking to the landlord. There's an apartment vacant on the other side, much lighter than this, with plenty of sun."

"Is it clean? Ready to move into?"

"It's just been all cleaned and redecorated."

"I'll go see about it," he said. "Will you help? If it's all right, could we do it alone?" He paused, looking at the bedroom door. "How about moving her?"

"If you carried her. It would be much pleasanter on the other side."

In ten minutes he was back. The new apartment was five dollars a month more, but he would let the old man worry about that. "Come on," he said. "Let's get this done before she even wakes up."

At five his father wandered in, stood in the door of the stripped apartment staring. "What's going on?" he said.

Coming out of the kitchen with the last bags of condiments, odds and ends, spices, groceries, Bruce said, "We're moving downstairs and across the hall." He half expected his father to be enraged at the way all initiative had been taken from him, all decision in his own house, but the old man simply moved aside as he came through the door, stood a little stooping with the pain of his boil, his face slack and tired.

"Sunnier down there?" he said.

"A lot." Bruce stopped with his arms full, willing for just that minute to let him back into her family. "Did you remember Mom's birthday?"

"Birthday? Is it her birthday?"

"Today," Bruce said.

"I forgot, I guess," his father said.

"You could do something nice for her."

500

The quick, suspicious look stopped him. His father, for all his fumbling helplessness now, was no fool. He knew he was an outsider, but he wouldn't be pushed around and told what to do. Bruce started to go on, but his father stopped him. "What?" he said.

"It'd be nice if she had some flowers when she moved in. I'd have got some, only I didn't have any money."

His father's answer was so prompt and hearty that it surprised him. "I'll get some," he said. "You got all the stuff down?"

"We'll be through in about fifteen minutes."

As if his tiredness had left him suddenly, the old man went down the steps and outside. When he came back he had his arms full of flowers, a great sheaf of gladioli, a bundle of bronze and yellow chrysanthemums, a potted geranium and a big potted fern. He gave them up gingerly to Miss Hammond, walked all through the apartment looking it over, stepped into the sleeping porch, glassed on three sides, with venetian blinds for privacy, where the sick woman would be put.

"It's better, don't you think?" Bruce said.

"Yes," the old man said. "Is your mother asleep?"

"She was a few minutes ago. The hypo before lunch laid her out."

"Yuh," his father said. His eyes were vague, wandering, looking anywhere but at Bruce, and his cheeks were thinner than Bruce ever remembered them. He looked sick himself. "Have you noticed about her lately?" he said. "That dope is getting her. She's so far off all the time, as if she didn't know where she was."

"I haven't noticed it."

"No?" His father jingled change in his pocket. "Well . . ." He turned toward the door. "We might as well bring her down."

She was awake, but still dreamy and thick-tongued. Her face and throat were wet with perspiration, and the pillow case under her head was soaked. As they entered, all three at once, she turned her head to smile, a smile in which sweetness and wry apology were mixed. She held one braid in her hand, back on the pillow.

Bo approached tiptoeing, and the way he moved made Bruce mad. Why did he have to act as if she lay there with candles at head and feet and the death-house hush already in the room? He stooped to kiss her, and she made a face. "I'm ashamed," she said. "I sweat so, and my hair gets so sour. I couldn't have a shampoo could I, Miss Hammond?"

"I'm afraid not," the nurse said. "I'll get a towel and dry it for you."

"I'll get you some perfume tomorrow," Bo said. "Make you smell like a flower garden." He picked up the quilted jacket that lay on the foot of the bed. "Where'd this come from?"

"Bruce gave it to me. Isn't it lovely?"

"Yuh." His eyes wandered. Stymied again, Bruce thought. Too slow to think of her birthday himself, but resentful of having anyone else do it. "You're having quite a birthday," he said. "Moving, and everything."

"Moving?"

"Didn't you know?"

"No. Moving where?"

The vague and wandering look on his face gave way to a look sly and sidelong. His eyes caught Bruce's. At least I'm in on this, they said. Here's one thing you haven't shut me out of. "We've got a little surprise for you," he said, and the "we" was a clear insistence on his right to have a place in his own family. But the sick woman's eyes, Bruce noticed, turned away from him, turned to Bruce himself, for an explanation, and that was triumph of a sort.

Miss Hammond came in with a bath towel, unbraided the damp hair, helped the sick woman to sit up, and began drying her hair, rubbing handfuls of it between folds of the towel until it stood out all around her head. It was like a light in the room, like the brilliant leaves, curling and dry now, that were still banked in a vase between the windows. Miss Hammond began smoothing the hair down with a brush, but when she took hold of it to rebraid it Bo Mason said, quite unexpectedly, "Leave it down a while. Let her look pretty for her birthday."

"Pretty!" she said drowsily. "I'll bet I look pretty!"

"You do," Bruce said, and now he was trying just as his father had to intrude on something that was between the other two. Her prettiness had been the old man's, not his. All his own memories of her were worn like an old tintype, the shadow of pain and resignation lying behind the calm face so that many times he had had the impression that his mother's face was sad, though there was nothing tangible to base that impression on. Her mouth did not droop, her eyes had light crowsfeet of laughter at the corners, there were no bitter lines. "You do look pretty," he said in a kind of desperation, hating his father for seeing and saying it first. "You've got a glow on you."

"It's her hair," Miss Hammond said. "She's got lovely hair."

"It's because everybody is so nice to me," Elsa said. "If you baby me I might cry."

Miss Hammond held the jacket for her to slip her arms into,

502

tied the foolish pom-pom strings at the wrists. *"Doesn't* she look pretty!" she said. Elsa made another face, the color higher in her cheeks, as if they had caught a reflection from the gorgeous hair.

"Well," Bo said. "Ready to move?"

"Where are we going?" She looked at Miss Hammond with crinkling eyes. "All my life he's been moving me around," she said. "I can't even get sick and stay quietly in bed. He has to move me within a month."

"You'll like this move," Bo said. Again Bruce felt a twinge of irritation at the way the old man butted in and took credit for something he would never have thought of for himself. Then he remembered that he hadn't thought of it either. Miss Hammond had thought of it. He lifted the dried leaves from the vase and stuck them crackling into the waste basket.

"Bruce!" his mother said. "My nice leaves!"

"They're all dead. There's something better where you're going." His eyes held his father's in ironic renunciation of his part in the birthday change. Let him have it. He couldn't hold it anyway. And at least he was being pleasant, he had had the inspiration or the good luck to call his wife pretty, and bring a bloom on her. Let him have it, as long as she was pleased.

"How are we going to do this?" she said. "Is it far?"

"Just a step," Bo said. "I'll carry you."

"Carry me! I can walk."

"In a pig's eye," he said. "Here."

He bent over, and as the coat tightened across his broad back he stopped as if paralyzed. A grunt of pain escaped him, and her eyes jumped to his face in alarm. "What is it?"

"My God damned boil!" he said between his teeth. He straightened up carefully, moving his shoulders as if to tempt the pain into revealing its location. Bruce stepped forward.

"You'd better not," he said. "I'll carry her."

But his father blocked his way. "I'll take her," he said. "Keep your shirt on."

He bent again, slowly. "Bo," Elsa said, "do you think you'd better? There's no need to hurt yourself."

"I'll carry you!" he said harshly. "Take hold of my neck."

She put her arms around his neck. "I'm pretty heavy," she said anxiously. Bruce, watching, saw his father set his teeth and lift, saw the pain hit him and his mouth tighten. And he saw something else. The sick woman's body came up lightly, easily, and the old man staggered a little as a man expecting another step in the dark staggers when his foot finds none. Bruce knew. He had lifted her in bed. She had wasted away to nothing. But he saw in the instant of his father's lifting that the old man hadn't known, that he was surprised and shocked.

His right arm was under her knees, and her white feet trailed out from the nightdress. Her arms were around his neck, her hair falling down the back of his coat.

"Okay," the old man said grimly. "Here we go." He shot one look at Bruce, a look with pain and triumph and horror in it, and stepped out through the door, swinging her feet carefully to avoid bumping them. Miss Hammond darted ahead to make the bed ready. Bruce followed behind.

"Hurting you?" Bo said.

"No," she said. "How about you?"

He stepped carefully down the stairs. Over his shoulder Elsa's face twitched with something that might have been pain, and Bruce smiled at her with stiff lips. "Just like a bride over the threshold," he said. That was what he had been planning to say as he himself carried her into the new apartment. He hated the sight of his father's broad back with her hair shawled across it.

In the new living room she exclaimed aloud. The sun, just setting, came full through the west window, flushing the perfect gladioli against the curtains. "Oh," she said. "The sunny side!"

Steadily, without pausing, Bo carried her into the glassed porch, and Bruce saw her hand come down to brush the petals of the geranium as she was carried by it. Carefully Bo laid her on the bed, and Miss Hammond drew the sheet up around her waist, leaving her shoulders propped high.

"There!" Bo said. "How do you like it?"

Her eyes went over the neat room, the geranium and the green delicacy of ferns against the venetian blinds. Her fingers touched the crisp sheet at her waist, and the cry that was wrenched from her was like an accusation.

"I told you I'd cry!" she said, and put her hands over her face.

3

That night Bruce sat reading a dull and blundering volume of history while his mother and father talked in the glassed porch. He heard their voices, and even more clearly the pauses in their talk. Miss Hammond sat under the other lamp stitching at one of her patient's nightgowns. Once she glanced up and said, "What are you studying so hard?"

"History."

"What for? Going back to school?"

"Sometime, maybe." He saw her lower her head again, embarrassed at having come too close to the thing they all avoided.

His eyes were on the white jamb of the door through which the voices of his father and mother came low and intimate. What could they find to talk about so long?

In a few minutes his father came to the door of the sickroom. "I guess she wants to get to sleep," he said to Miss Hammond.

The nurse went in, came out after awhile and nodded to Bruce, and he went in and took his mother's hand. "Well," he said. She squeezed his hand and shook it lightly. Her hair was braided again for the night, and the shaded bedlamp threw shadows on her face so that it looked pinched and starved. "It's been a lovely day," she said.

"I'm glad. You look better than you have for quite a while."

"I feel better," she said. "You must be tired from moving." She lay for a while looking quietly past and beyond, at the wall or at nothing. "Where's everyone going to sleep down here?" she said. "You've given me the nicest place, and Pa says there's only one other bedroom."

"He'll be in that. I'll sleep in the murphy bed in the living room, and Miss Hammond's got a cot set up in the dining room."

"She can't be comfortable on a cot. Isn't there anything . . . ?"

"I tried to make her take the murphy. She won't."

Her hand held his, patted it, as if unwilling to give it up. "Well, goodnight, then," she said.

"Goodnight." He stooped to kiss her. Trust the old man to sit and talk and tire her out completely. She hardly had strength to turn over in bed. The old brainless fumbling . . .

"Sleep tight," he said, and left her.

Miss Hammond closed the door all but a crack, so that the light would not bother her, and then the three sat in the living room, the old man with his hands on his knees, vacant and unoccupied, his body slumped in the chair. He looked old and dissipated and sick, his face dark, with black bags under his eyes. Bruce watched him covertly, saw him put up a hand to rub his face, heard the rasp of bristles under the big square hand.

> *He looked like a man with a foot in the grave*
> *And scarcely the strength of a louse . . .*

The lines jumped to his mind, and with them the memory, clear and sharp, of the family around the stove in the little parlor in Whitemud, his mother darning, he and Chet hugging their knees on the floor to hear their father read Robert W. Service. Liking it, he said. Lapping it up, fascinated and impressed, loving him then, briefly, absorbing images and inflections and words that would never leave the mind, that would always be a part of his memory of the time when they had lived in one house for five years. It was incredible that at times, in his childhood, he had watched the dark face of his father with love and admiration and trust . . .

His eyes went rubbering round the room
And he seemed in a sort of daze . . .

"She's gone," his father said. Bruce lowered his book and looked up. His father's face was ghastly, and his mouth worked. "You can see it just to look at her," he said. "She's so quiet, she's got no interest in anything."

Bruce said nothing, and Miss Hammond, after one quick look, dropped her head over her mending. "All but her eyes," the old man said. With a puzzled face he looked directly at Bruce for the first time. "You'd never know it by her eyes," he said. "They're just as bright and clear . . . You'd never know she'd been sick a day."

He rubbed his palm across his face again. "What're you reading?"

Bruce held up the book.

"Studying, uh? Yeah." The momentary interest flickered out. "It's the dope," he said. "She's hopped up all the time. She can hardly make herself listen to what you're saying."

"Maybe she didn't want to," Bruce said. "She's weak. She hasn't got the strength to talk much."

His father stood up. His trousers were bagged and wrinkled, and there were cigar ashes on his sleeve. He started to say something, closed his mouth, shot a look of quick hard suspicion at Bruce, and wandered over to the dining room table, through the sliding doors. He swung around.

"How long?" he said.

Bruce shook his head. "I asked Cullen. He can't tell. He says if she didn't have a heart like a horse she'd be gone now."

The old man moistened his lips. "Yuh," he said vaguely. He stayed with his finger tips touching the table, turned again. "Do you think I . . ." He stopped, took his fingers off the wood, and went through the hall to his own bedroom, shutting the door behind him.

Bruce drew a deep breath, looked once at Miss Hammond's troubled face, and opened the book again.

He awoke late. Miss Hammond had his place set at the breakfast table, but the other dishes were all washed and put away. His father was not around.

"My dad gone uptown already?" he said as he came in from the bathroom.

"He's gone away," Miss Hammond said. She went to the cupboard and got an envelope. "He left this, and said he'd be gone three or four days."

"Well what in hell!" Bruce said. He opened the envelope. There were some bills in it. Forty dollars. "Did he say where he was going?"

"No. I gathered it was business. He had to go, he said."

"Yeah!" Bruce said, starting for the bedroom. "Is mother awake?"

"Yes. She seems to know all about it."

At the door of the porch Bruce checked himself. He couldn't rush in there in a fury and demand an explanation. For a moment he stood gnawing his lip, and glancing back at Miss Hammond he saw with absolute clearness the nurse's complex of bewilderment and sympathy and desire to stay back out of family troubles. But even while he was looking at her he forgot her. So the old man had skipped. He put his teeth together and went into the porch.

"Hi," he said. Her smiling face turned toward him, but in the first glance he knew that something had happened to her. She was worse. There was no brightness in her. He came up and laid his hand on her forehead, cool and moist as putty. "How is it this morning?" he said. "I was a pig. I slept till eight thirty."

"Good," she said, as if her mouth were almost too tired to form the word. Her smile was only a crinkling of the lines around her eyes.

"Miss Hammond says Pa's gone," he said, watching her, seeing in her face how close the end was now, how she seemed to grope in a mist, make an effort to look out from somewhere, like a person looking backward from the moving observation car of a train. The wrinkles deepened around her eyes, that was all.

"He's been shut up too long," she said.

"I don't see . . ." he began, but she stopped him.

"Don't blame him," she said. "He just . . . wasn't made for it."

"He must have had an excuse," he said. "He's always got an excuse."

His mother smiled. "He went for a load. He had to be doing something."

"Did he tell you first?"

"He told me last night. Patton's got some stuff waiting for him in Los Angeles. He'll be back in a few days."

He said nothing more, but he saw in her face everything he needed to know. She wouldn't last those three days, and the old man had known it. She had said her goodbyes and sent him out knowing she wouldn't live till his return, and she lay there now ready at any time, living only by physiological habit. That was the change he had seen when he came in. There had been an air of resistance in her before. Something (the old man's cowardice?) had broken the brightness and will in her.

"Shall I read to you?" he said.

"Yes. Would you?"

Even while he read with an automatic voice, using only the top of his mind, the floor of his mind was uneasy with rage and contempt and wonder. To pull out, to run, to leave her when he knew she was dying, to go after a load of whiskey, worry himself into a fifteen hundred mile trip on the pretense that he was getting low on money, couldn't afford to stay off the job any longer . . . At his wife's funeral he would probably take orders for cases of Scotch. Oh the God damned contemptible selfish cowardly heartless old bastard!

"Yes?" his mother said. He looked up, confused, and realized that he had stopped reading.

"Sorry," he said, and picked up the story where he thought he must have broken off.

Now for two days he watched and waited with sick and hopeless certainty, his mother farther and farther away, withdrawing deeper into herself and the numbing morphine.

It was obscene and unjust the way she had to die. Loving her as he did, he was offended a dozen times a day by the sour smell of her sweat in the sickroom and the horror of the noises she made in breathing. It outraged him that she could not die sweetly and quietly, with her family around her, wrapped in love and the sense of a life that had fruited and borne. Instead, she lay most of the time like a stranger, her hair soaked and her skin clammy, running down like an old cheap clock, with her husband gone and one son miserably dead and the other unable to reach her.

In the times when she roused from her doped coma, Bruce sat with her, sometimes reading, though he was sure she didn't listen except to the sound of his voice. But she was altogether better awake than asleep. Her breathing was easier, and far away as she was, her words had sometimes a strange oracular wisdom, a tolerance untouched by personal feeling, as if she had withdrawn far enough not to be moved any more, far enough to see her life as a wry comedy, the world as a goldfish tank in which fishes of all sizes and shapes and colors went after food, made love, nosed with incomprehensible and unimportant compulsions up and down, up and down, against the glass walls, or lay suspended among the water plants, insulated from watchers by the different element they lived in.

"Did you know," she said to Bruce on the second afternoon, "that your dad is keeping another woman?"

"No," he said slowly. "I did not!"

She smiled. "For quite a while now," she said, and made her little face, the lines deepening around her eyes. "He had her in Reno. Now he's got her here."

"How do you know?"

"I can smell her," she said. She shook her head at him slightly. "I shouldn't have told you. You'll take it hard."

The biting edges of his teeth were set precisely together. He felt the little trench along the edge of the incisors, and his mind said, accurately and scientifically, Faulty occlusion. But through his teeth he said aloud, "Why shouldn't I take it hard? Why shouldn't you?"

"I don't," she said. "I don't seem to care. I can't blame him. I haven't been any good as a wife for a long time."

That intimacy outraged him, as he had been outraged during adolescence to see them kissing. He sat very still and said nothing.

"Bruce," she said, and took hold of his fingers. "Don't blame him too much. There's something in him that has to have a woman to lean on. He's leaned on me all his life, but he can't now."

"When you get sick," he said. "When you can't take care of his boils and wipe his nose and listen to his troubles, he abandons you and finds some slut . . ."

"No," she said. She smiled at him wearily, wiser than he would ever be, not bothered either by her husband's weakness or her son's hatred, not part of it any more, withdrawing, smiling remotely on the pillow with her braids down across her shoulders. "Don't," she said.

."Oh my God!" He stood up, blinded by the pressure that in a moment would be tears. Abruptly he left her, motioned at Miss Hammond as he went through the living room with averted face, and shut himself in the bathroom.

During that day workmen had installed a neon sign on the front of the apartment house across the street, and with the apartment darkened the bluish echo of its light lay on the walls. Miss Hammond was lying down, and Bruce stretched out on the murphy bed, forcing his mind away from the snoring breath in the sickroom, forcing himself to think of anything, everything, that there was life in—the sensuous shape and texture of the world, the nights and days and hours and moments when the burden was removed and a man was himself and himself only, wrapped in his own bright identity beyond which there was nothing. He thumbed them over like pictures from an old album, discarding these because there was a shadow on them, laying others aside to be looked at more carefully. His mind adjusted itself, re-focussed, as the eyes adjust to the parallax of a stereopticon lens, and in the timelessness of memory the pictures sprang into three dimensions, permanent and ineradicable, the things that had life in them instead of death.

The sky was a wonder to him then, the immense blackness and the lustrous stars, on a night when his parents took him out to a neighbor's after dark, put him to sleep in a strange bedroom, and out of his sleep pulled him lost and groping and clinging to slumber, to load him into the buggy. There, cradled in his mother's lap, he opened his eyes fully and saw the wonder, the black roof with the glory streaming through its rents, and the miracle of a night sky would always be with him; there would never be another night of his life when the sight of the stars would not have in it some of that first awe and wonder, when his jaded perception would not borrow freshness from that original bright image in the eyes of a star-gazing child.

That was one. That was one of many. They were not all visual images, he discovered, sorting them out. There were smells and sounds and old tunes sung over and over until they gathered to themselves all the associations of the places and times in which they had been sung.

His mother's snoring breath went up catchily, grating in the sick lungs to its tremulous climax, paused, came out in the windy sigh. Bruce shut his mind on it, turned away, fled, just as he had lain still and pretended to sleep as a child, when the windstorms blew the slatted curtains and tubs and buckets began tumbling in the homestead yard: he had lain snug and warm, hearing the padding of feet and his father's grumbling, and he had known he should get up to help, but the sheets were warm, the bed was comfortable, sleep lay just around the corner where he had left it . . .

There was the smell of hot chokecherry patches, hillsides hot under the sun, and spice and bark and leaf mold and the fruity

odor of the berries, and the puckery alum tang of a ripe cluster
stripped into the mouth, the feel of the pits against the palate—
the free and wild and windy feeling of late summer on the bench
hills, and the odor of the berry patch through it like a theme.
It was an odor that he had never quite found again, though
dozens of times, in the canyons, on sunny streets under the lines
of Lombardy poplars, in warehouses, in stores, he had stopped,
sniffing, his nose assailed by a tantalizing fragrance that was almost
it but not quite. That smell, or its ghost, could bring him out of
reverie or talk or concentration deep as a well, and leave him for
a moment free from time, eager and alive and excited, in search
of an odor that was more than a memory, that was a permanent
reality.

And the songs:

The Bugle Song on the bank of the coulee among the early
summer blossoming of primrose and cactus and buttercup, with the
ghostly mountains far down across the heat-scorched plain; the song
that had always meant, and meant now, all romantic yearning, all
nostalgia for the never-never and the wonderful; that still, in spite
of all he had learned since, could have an instant effect on him,
choke him up, clog his tear ducts, make him, driving alone on an
open road singing to himself, wipe his hand across his eyes and
laugh with self-conscious shame.

A childhood-hunter, a searcher for old forgotten far-off things
and battles long ago, a maunderer. He knew it. Yet the words of
life were in those songs and those smells and the green dreams
of childhood; in his life there had been the death of too many
things.

He shifted in the bed, realizing that not anything he had been
thinking of had cut off the sound of his mother's breathing. Oh
Christ, he said. I wish . . .

He sat up. The light had gone on in the bedroom, and the
breathing was broken. In three steps he was through the door, the
fear like a hand clenched in his shirt. His mother lay moving her
head weakly from side to side, her forehead puckered, her face and
neck wet.

"Will you turn . . . on the light?" she said.

He stared at her. She was looking straight up into the brightness of the lamp.

"Sure," he said, from a dry mouth. "I should have put a string
on that switch." He rattled the metal pull of the lamp. "Better?"

She did not answer directly, but moved her hand toward the
water glass. The bewildered look was fading from her face. He
helped her take a sip of water, wiped her face with a towel, turned

511

her pillow. When Miss Hammond appeared in the doorway he told her to go and lie down again. He would sit up a while. It was still early.

His mother lay back, the light stark on her sunken cheeks and wet skin. "It was so dark," she said fuzzily. "I thought everyone . . . had gone."

"Try to go back to sleep," he said. "I'll sit here with you a while."

Her fingers found his and clung, and with her hand alternately clenching and relaxing on his she appeared to doze. The agonized fight for breath went on. After a few minutes he pulled off the light. The neon blue fluttered for a moment through the venetian blinds, steadied to a pale laddered glimmer. The tires of passing cars whispered and hissed in the rainy street.

This is it, Bruce said, sitting still, sitting quietly, unwilling to shift his cramped body for fear of disturbing her. Any breath may be her last one.

He bent his head on his hand and let himself slump, tired, ready to fall asleep but fighting sleep and hating his tiredness because they were treachery, because she was dying now, tonight. At any minute the worn heart might go, the breathing shiver to a stop.

He listened to the breaths, up and up and up, painfully, and the wheezy escape of the hard-won air. Miss Hammond came out on tiptoe and laid a sweater across his shoulders, and he pulled it around him, aware that it was chilly. The traffic was less on the street, but the neon light drifted in steadily, like vague blue smoke, a slight tremor in the shadowy room. He heard the court-house clock strike eleven, then twelve. The breathing faltered, strengthened, slowed, went on.

The vitality, he said, is lowest during the early morning hours. If she lived past three, she might last another day, stubbornly clinging to the life she had already given up. He found himself hoping that she would die, now, and the imminence of the thing he had been watching and fearing for weeks made him move cautiously, straighten his slumped and aching back, thrust one chilled hand into his pocket.

His mother moved. Her fingers tightened, and her voice, flat and muffled, said, "You're a good boy, Bruce."

He sat thinking of that, thinking of the times for years back when he had been selfish or thoughtless, of the girls he had chased and dated four or five nights a week, never remembering that his mother might be alone, that the old man went off to prowl with his friends or deliver whiskey, leaving her in an empty house.

512

He remembered the few times he had taken her anywhere, to movies, for drives in the canyons, to dinner, and those times seemed so pitifully few and mean that he writhed. You're a good boy, Bruce.

Yes, he said, twenty years too late, and overpaid in advance, fifty times in advance, and now paid with gratitude on her death bed.

Oh Jesus, he said, let her die.

The clock, heavy and solemn over the sleeping city, gathered itself and struck once. The sound aroused the sick woman. She struggled up on one elbow, her hand hard on Bruce's fingers. Her head turned to the right, then to the left.

"Which . . . way?" she said.

"It's all right, Mom," he said, and pushed her gently back, pulling the covers to her chin. She lay still, immediately back in the drugged coma, and he sat on in the straight chair, listening to her fighting, impossible breath, holding his own breath when the snore labored to its peak, relaxing again when it was released, counting her breaths, almost, because at any point in the difficult scale her heart might quit like a tired horse in the harness.

The vitality is lowest during the early morning hours. One fifteen, or thereabouts, and the minutes crawling, and his mother retreating breath by breath. Which . . . way?

His nodding head jerked up. The *ah-ah-ah-ah-ah*—had stopped, snagged, at the top of the scale. The long pause between inhalation and exhalation was slow, was too long. He yanked on the light.

"Miss Hammond!"

She came instantly, it seemed, was shoving him away from the bedside. In the shouting silence he saw her seize his mother's shoulders, put a finger in her mouth, jerk it out again to grab a spoon from the table and with the handle pry against his mother's tongue, pulling it back out of her throat. The legs under the covers moved slightly, the clogged breath gave easily, in three little sighs, and he was staring into the sick face of Miss Hammond, the spoon in her hand free now, and his mother's eyes closing, very slowly.

He saw the tears come into Miss Hammond's eyes as she groped without looking to lay the spoon on the table. The covers were disarranged over his mother's body, and the nightgown was pulled aside. He saw her breast, the unmutilated one, like a lumpy mummified thing, the nipple retracted, pulled in as if by a terrific suction, and the skin blue-black and withered over her whole side.

"Oh my God," Miss Hammond was saying, "Oh my God."

He turned, blind and terrified, and fled.

When he came in again, the light was on in both front room and porch. Miss Hammond looked up quickly. He could not meet her eyes for more than an instant, because behind her was the lighted porch, and his mind went around that door and stopped at the foot of the bed.

Instead of going in, he went to the telephone and called long distance, waiting with the blank wall before his eyes and the receiver against his ear, fixing his mind on the efficient buzzings, the unknown voices speaking crisply, the long regular unmusical ringing on the other end. Death travelled fast. In three minutes he could spread death. He waited, the receiver humming at his head.

What would the old man say? Would he pretend grief, he with his cowardice and his kept slut? Maybe she was with him. That would make it just dandy. She could ride back with him, consoling him all the . . .

"Hello," he said, breaking in on the voice at the other end. It was a man's voice, probably Patton's. "Hello," he said. "This is Bruce Mason. Is my father there?"

"Yeah," the voice said surlily, and then quickly, as if remembering, "Yeah, sure. Hold it just a minute."

He waited again. Through the open line he could hear steps coming. He looked straight at the yellow wall, his tongue like an unbendable rod in his mouth. "Hello?" his father's quick voice said. "Hello, Bruce? What is it? Is . . . ?" There was a rattling noise, and then his father's voice again, quick and anxious. "Hello? Dropped the damn phone. What's the matter?"

"She's dead," Bruce said. "Two hours ago. I thought you'd want to know."

There was no answer for so long that he dropped his lips to the mouthpiece to say "Hello, hello," but as he did so he heard the sigh of his father's breath, distorted and rasping over the wire, and then his voice, quiet, almost a whisper. "Yeah. I'll be right home."

"All right," Bruce said. "I'll make the arrangements."

There was another pause, only a kind of panting coming through the receiver. "Was it bad?" his father said. "Did she . . . was she in pain?"

Bruce raised his head. On impulse, out of pure contempt, he lied. "No," he said. "She just went to sleep."

The nurse moved aside, and he stepped past her into the porch. His mother lay with the sheet up to her chin. Her hands, folded on her stomach, made a little draped mound under the sheet.

Her hair had been dried and re-braided, and her face was wiped clean of any expression, even the lines rubbed away as an artist might erase lines from a sketch. It was a younger face that lay there, a face completely calm, a prettier face actually than he had known. But it was not his mother. His mother had been wiped away with the lines that living had left on her. She was the shading, not the face itself. In this wax image there was none of her patience, none of her understanding and sympathy, none of her kindness, none of her dignity. This corpse was a thing you could bury without regret, put into the ground beside your brother's body; and the other things, the qualities that had been mystically your mother, you buried within yourself, you became a grave for her as you were a grave for Chet, and you carried your dead unquietly within you.

On the evening of the next day he sat reading in the deserted apartment. He had gone grimly through his duties, half grateful for something to do, half appreciating why the race made a ritual of death. He had bought a casket, feeling that if he left that to his father his father would throw away hundreds of dollars in a useless sacrifice to his own shame and fear. He had talked to Cullen, signed the death certificate, gone to the cemetery and seen the sexton about the grave lot next to Chet's. After dinner he had said goodbye to Miss Hammond.

Tomorrow, probably around noon, his father should be back. The funeral was set for three. If the old man was late that was his bad luck. He could be shown where she was buried, that would be all he deserved.

He looked at the clock on the end table by the sofa. Ten fifteen. He might go to bed, but he knew he couldn't sleep, even though he was exhausted. He moved the light closer and opened the book again.

At eleven thirty he stopped reading to listen. Someone was fumbling at the door. He stood up just as his father opened the door and came in, and in the silent apartment, with the fact of death between them, they confronted each other.

His father's face was like a dirty dough mask. The unhealthy bags under his eyes had swollen and darkened, his cheeks sagged, his eyes were furtive and haunted. For a moment he stood with his hand on the knob, moistening his lips with his tongue.

"You got back quick," Bruce said.

"I . . ." The old man closed the door and took a step or two into the room. His eyes darted past Bruce toward the door of the porch. Without the door to hang to he staggered a little, and put his hand down on the arm of the sofa, lowering himself into it heavily. "I . . . got lost," he said. His lips moved in the parody of a smile, and his eyes went secretly past Bruce toward the porch door again.

"You couldn't have stayed lost very long. I wasn't expecting you till tomorrow."

"I don't know what was the matter," his father said, rubbing his hand back and forth on the arm of the couch. "I was dazed, I guess. I've been over that road a hundred times." He shook his head. "I left right after you called."

Bruce watched him, wondering if he were quite right in the head. He must have driven like a madman.

"Down around Yermo somewhere," his father said. "I got out on some God-forsaken road with sand to the running boards. Just ran around in circles in the desert. Didn't know where I was. Dazed, I guess." He took out his watch, looked at it, turned it over in his hand two or three times, put it back in his pocket. His eyes came up to Bruce fleetingly, wavered away again.

"I'll get you something to eat," Bruce said. He wondered how long they would play this game of steering away from mentioning her death. The old man came back from a trip and they passed banalities back and forth and had a snack to eat. In the kitchen he almost smiled. The old man was out again, like a bum who has been thrown out of jail and stands with the bars in his hands, wishing he was back in the warmth and light getting three meals a day.

"What . . . time did she pass away?" his father said behind him.

Even that, Bruce thought. Even "pass away." But there was such a strained harsh quality in the old man's voice that he turned around. The watch was in his father's hand again.

"A little after one," Bruce said. "About one fifteen." He saw the spasm cross the dark heavy face, the harsh lines contracting as if at a sudden pain.

"That was twelve fifteen in L.A.," the old man said. He turned the watch over slowly in his hand, looked at the face. He looked back at Bruce, swaying a little, breathing rapidly through his half-open mouth. "Look," he said, and passed over the watch with its dangling chain.

The watch said fourteen minutes past twelve.

"I was in bed," the old man said, and his tongue came out to touch his upper lip. "I heard it stop. I thought it needed winding, but it didn't. It wouldn't start again."

The blank terror in his eyes made Bruce look away, down at the watch. He shook it, held it to his ear.

"That won't do any good," his father said. "I tried everything."

His face contorted again, twisted, softened. He sat down on a kitchen chair and put his face in his hands, and his body shook. After a minute, unwillingly, not knowing exactly why he did it, Bruce laid a hand on the wide, shaking shoulder.

"It's no good now," he said. "We just have to stand it."

That was all he could think of to say. He did not believe in his father's grief. It was not grief, but self-pity and superstitious fear. With his hand on the heavy shoulder, troubled and embarrassed, he kept thinking, "You might have given her a little of this while she was alive."

5

Bo Mason could not stand to stay in the place Elsa had died in. The door of the porch seemed to bother him. His eyes were always wandering to it with the vague, groping, puzzled expression that was now very frequent on his face. Every night he had nightmares, and on the fourth day they moved across the street.

Bruce, shrugging, carried their little household accumulation across. This move was all of a piece with the rest. The old man couldn't bear to think of her dead, pitied himself for being left, couldn't bring himself to mention her except in roundabout euphemisms like "passing away," and now couldn't stand to be near the room she had died in. It made little difference to Bruce. In January, if he got back the scholarship he had written about, he would be pulling out for school again, and he would not be coming back.

He felt so little established in that barren apartment that he didn't even unpack his suitcases completely, but left them propped open on chairs in the bedroom. And this was what it finally came to. For thirty years his mother had tried to break the old man to family life, had wanted to make something rooted and continuous that would bridge the dissonant generations, and in the end, with her death, it came down to an apartment in which he and his father, the survivors, lived together in perpetual armed suspicion, with half-packed suitcases in the bedroom ready for instant flight.

He got a few jobs through friends at the university, typing theses and reading papers, and the money from those jobs he hoarded like a miser. There would be little enough to live on once he broke away, and he would ask nothing from the old man. Meantime, if he was keeping the house, he was entitled to anything he could save out of the expense money. He pinched nickels and dimes like a houswife hoarding for Christmas, spent little and went out little. In the time he had free from his jobs he sat in the apartment and read, read with lunch, read with dinner, read in bed, woke to read with breakfast. His friends he never called, even Joe Mulder; they would have tried to take him out and cheer him up. When he saw his father watching him, he made no sign, buried himself in a book, until the old man put on his new black hat and went out. For whole days, sometimes, there were not twenty words between them.

October slipped into the shortening, smoky days of November, and the color faded from the scarp of the Wasatch. In the afternoons the sun hung like a monstrous orange over the Oquirrhs, and the night air was bitter with smoke. On one such night Bo Mason tried to blunder through the barrier of suspicion that lay between him and his son.

He had come home for dinner, which was unusual, and after dinner, instead of going out again, he sat in the living room looking at a magazine. Every few minutes he looked over as if inviting conversation, but Bruce kept still. Finally his father said, slapping the magazine down on his lap, "By God, I don't see what a man can do."

"What's the trouble?" Bruce said.

"Everything's the trouble," the old man said. "Nobody's got a dime, there's no business, the place is dead as a doornail. There isn't a damn thing stirring, not a thing."

"Haven't you got enough from the sale in Reno to hold you till things pick up?"

"That wouldn't last," the old man said. "I've only got six thousand out of that so far. The rest is tied up in notes. And with nothing coming in you can't live on the interest on a few thousand."

Bruce shrugged.

"I've been talking with some guys down at the Newhouse," his father said. "They've got a proposition they want me to come in on."

Something stirred in Bruce like a quick wind moving the leaves and then dying again. The old man was repeating the performance he had gone through with his wife every time a new bug hit him, asking advice, coming around and hinting and opening it up little by little. Only it wasn't advice he wanted. It was justification, encouragement.

"What sort of proposition?" Bruce said.

For a moment his father's eyes were quick and clear, the vague look gone from them. "A mine," he said. "Looks like a pretty good thing."

518

"A lot of mines look like pretty good things," Bruce said. "Only when you take a good look you find that the good things have been blown into them with a shotgun."

"All right," his father said. "You know it all."

"I don't know anything about it," Bruce said. He felt himself flushing, and for a moment their dislike was hard and ugly, in the open. "I'd just be suspicious of any mining deal, on principle. The Utah Copper and the International and the Apex and all the other big mines have got every prospect in the state tagged, just waiting till it will pay them to open them up."

"This mine," his father said, "isn't even in Utah. It's in Nevada. And it's got gold enough in it to be damn well worth looking at."

"Then look at it," Bruce said. "I wasn't trying to knock it. I'm just suspicious of any kind of scheme that's going to make you rich overnight."

"Uh," his father said. The groping look had come back, and two little dewlaps of skin sagged below his jaw. He fumbled in his inside coat pocket and brought out a bundle of papers. "This is a fairly low-grade lead," he said. "It'd take money to develop it, need a stamp mill and one thing and another. But it's a big lead, a vein twenty feet wide. We can get this fellow's claim and options on four claims joining it."

"Have you had an assay?"

"Four ounces of gold to the ton," the old man said. "Some silver, some lead."

"How do you know the samples came out of that hole?"

"Paul Dubois has been down looking it over. He knows a sound mine when he sees one."

"What do they want of you?"

"Want me to come in for a third. We could put up three or four thousand apiece, enough for some development. Then we incorporate and capitalize for a hundred thousand or so, sell enough stock to put in the mill. Once it gets producing we can either work it ourselves or sell out for a fat price to some big outfit."

"Make a million dollars," Bruce said. He laughed. "I'd sure want to take a good geologist down with me before I dove in a hole like that. And I'd want to know about water, and transportation, and a lot of other things."

"There isn't time for much of that," his father said. "Hartford Consolidated is snooping around. They had a prospector out there last month. And there's a tunnel going in on the other side of the hill, about three miles off. If we want to get the jump, we've got to move fast."

When Bruce sat looking at him silently, the old man's brows drew down and his face darkened. "I suppose you'd say it was dangerous."

"When somebody wants you to jump quick," Bruce said, "there's a good chance there's something fishy. But it's your funeral. Have you got the three or four thousand?"

"I'm not so hard up I couldn't raise three thousand," his father said. "I could sell some stock. The damn stuff's never going to come up again anyway. I've still got some Firestone and some U. S. Steel."

"Suit yourself," Bruce said. "I'm no gambler, and I don't know beans about mines."

The old man put the papers back into his pocket. Bruce had never made a move to look at them. "Well, we'll see," his father said. He was wearing the black tie he had bought for the funeral, and there was a stain on it. Picking up his hat, he started for the door. "I may be out pretty late," he said.

The door closed, and Bruce sat thinking. If the old man started playing the wildcat mines he'd be cleaned in a year. He was not a good gambler. He was careful and suspicious to a point, and then he opened up like a grain chute in an elevator. Anybody who got past his first caution could pump him like a well.

And I don't give a damn if they do, he said. Remembering the miserly unwillingness of his father to get a nurse, he tightened his lips across his teeth. Not so hard up he couldn't raise three thousand. And now mourning! he said. Now it's a black felt hat and a black tie, and an armband probably, if he could get anybody to sew one on him.

Oh yes, he said, sitting furiously with his hands tight on the book. You can't come back and accuse me of anything. I wear black to commemorate my bereavement! I have put the cross above my door and tossed the salt over my left shoulder and spun three times round and said the words. My dead can't touch me. I have fulfilled the forms, buried the body deep in the ground, spread flowers on the earth, paid the sexton for perpetual care of the grave lot. And I have bought a new black hat and a black tie.

I hope, he said to the barren walls of the apartment, they roll him for everything he's got and leave him stranded in the gutter without carfare to the poorhouse.

In the last week of November, when the leaves were pulpy in the gutters and piled high on the curbings waiting for the trash trucks, Bruce borrowed a shotgun and went duck shooting up on

Bear River Bay with a carful of friends. For just that one day, in spite of cold and chilblains and a raw, wet wind, he felt liberated and happy. It was so much positive joy to crouch uncomfortably in the blind waiting for the swift flights to come over, listening to the sodden boom of an automatic up the marshes; so much fun to leap upright in the tules and slap the padded butt to his shoulder, follow the speeding ducks with the muzzle, lead them a little, let go and be thumped by the recoil. It was so much fun to see a racing long-necked duck fold suddenly and fall like a stone that he wondered at himself. Why should it be fun to kill ducks? What possible joy was it to spread death, when you had yourself lived with death too much, and hated the very word? But he could not deny that it gave him a hot bright pleasure.

Maybe it was just the fun of knowing you were a fairly decent shot. The ducks were scared, and flew fast. Not everybody could hit a target the size of a saucepan, moving sixty miles an hour.

And that was something he had learned from his old man. At least in the business of killing his instruction had been good. But even that reflection couldn't spoil the fun of being outdoors, getting the wind on him, seeing the brown tules emerge from the mist and the gray channels of water open up as the light grew.

He thought of Chet, lost and miserable, the heart taken out of him, his health shot, trying to learn taxidermy in the last months of his life, going out in his off hours to the salt marshes and shooting small birds, fussing with them on the bench in the basement, working in patient protective abstraction with wadding and glue and pins, the mailorder taxidermy book open beside the crows and magpies and snipe he had brought home. Chet had always loved to hunt. For an instant, in the cold circle of tules under the sky like cold lead, he felt naked and alone and scared, and he would have given anything to have Chet there with him, just for an hour, just to say hello, just to lend him the gun for a shot or two.

Chet had been too soft, not soft like his mother, but weak. His mother, soft and gentle as she was, had beaten the old man in a way. It was he who ran at the last minute. Because she knew how to renounce without giving up herself, she could win just by being herself in spite of everything. Chet couldn't. There was enough of the old man in him to spoil him, enough of his mother to soften him, not enough of either to save him.

What about you? he said. What have you got? But he knew without asking. He had got enough of the old man's hardness to armor him. He was as hard as his father—harder. The old man could still bluster, but he wasn't what he used to be. He was whipped, and he knew it. His wife had whipped him, without ever meaning to and without realizing it, and his one remaining son was going to whip him further.

It was a curious thing that once he got away from Salt Lake for a day he could see how in a way his mother's life, which had shut her off from everything she wanted to have, had forced her to become what she wanted to be. The older she grew the richer she became in herself, and the older and more affluent the old man became, the more he deteriorated. He lost friends where she gained them, he weakened as she grew stronger, he lowered himself year by year . . .

Going home after dark that night, his chilled feet aching with a hard constricting pain, he leaned back in the seat contentedly, thinking of that day, only a month or so away now, when he could pull out for good. The thirty-four dollars he had put away would get him there. Once there, he could make out somehow. There was always some way you could make it, something you could do to live if you wanted to live. You could wash dishes, scrub floors, fire furnaces, wait table, do something. You could renounce everything but the essentials, and the essentials included only a minimum to eat and wear.

He was asleep when they reached Salt Lake, and awoke only when the car pulled up in front of a drugstore on Third South and State while Joe went in for some cigarettes. Bruce stretched, yawned, moved the pile of ducks a little with his aching feet. He looked out at the crowds coming from the movies, swarming into the drug for a snack. The clock on the Sears Roebuck store said ten fifteen. He yawned again.

He shut his mouth so sharply against the yawn that it hurt his jaw. His father was coming down State Street, strolling, and with him was a woman holding the leash on an ugly Boston bull. The pup's wide chest was clothed in a red and blue sweater, and his legs strained as he surged against the thong.

So that, Bruce thought, is what he's been keeping. He watched her. Youngish—early thirties, probably. Hennaed. Small, well-made, mounted on heels four inches high, her legs and ankles the kind of legs and ankles he had seen on dozens of women of her kind, small-boned and rounded, the calf muscles bunching a little as she walked. That was what the old man picked when he wanted a woman. With a quarter of a century of a good woman behind him, he could pick up a sleazy little chippy like that. He watched her pull together the collar of her black fur coat, laughing a little as the dog pulled her off balance. Then he slouched down in the seat for fear his father would glance sideways and recognize him in the parked car.

That night he fell into bed after a hot bath, too tired for anger and weary of anger anyway, sick for the time when he could leave. There was his own life to live, and none of it lay here any more. In the morning he looked into the other bedroom. Either his father had not come home, or was already gone. The kitchen table was still cluttered with dirty dishes, a piece of kippered salmon had been left out of the refrigerator and was curling on a plate, a half bottle of milk stood out. Sourly he washed up before getting his own breakfast, and after breakfast he started sweeping up the other rooms. On the end table in the living room he found the letter left out for him. It was from Minnesota, and it said that no scholarships were available at the mid-year. If he chose to come on, some work could perhaps be found for him, and in view of his record of the past year Doctor Aswell had offered to take him on as an assistant. That would pay two hundred dollars for the semester. Other things would perhaps turn up if he were on the ground.

He rattled the letter and read it again, lifted his head to look out into the bare branches of the hickories. It was not as good as he had hoped for, but it was good enough. In a pinch he could almost live on two hundred for the semester.

Hi de ho! he said. He was loose, he was free. He might even leave a little early and stay with Kristin for a few days before school opened. In a month, at most, he could shed the whole dead weight of the past and start over.

He felt too good to read. His fingers itching to pack, he estimated the cleaning bill he would have to run up in order to leave with his clothes in shape, calculated the date he would have to send the laundry so as to get it back the day before he left. And in the middle of those calculations he thought of his mother's clothes. He hadn't had the heart to go through them and sort them out, lay aside a pile for the Salvation Army, give her better things to her friends. It was stupid to keep them in the closet till the moths destroyed them. That was the sort of sentimental, useless gesture his father might make.

He went to the hall closet and opened the door, but the instant emanation, the something of his mother that emerged, made him pause. He put out his hand and touched a house dress, neatly starched and pressed, left that to finger the silk of what had once been her best dress. She was in these clothes, somehow. She was in them as she had not been in the body the undertakers wheeled out that night. These were things her taste had selected. Her spirit as well as her body had worn them, and they had in them something of her plainness, something of her simple dignity. It was hard to destroy this too, to give away every fragrant remnant of what she had been.

But there was her fur coat, there were two or three good dresses, some shoes, a good many things that some of her friends would appreciate and use. It was only decent to divide her among people who had liked and respected her. The coat, for instance, could be sent to Laura, who had moved to California.

He rattled the hangers down the rod, frowned, slipped them back one by one, looking. Then he lifted the clothes back to see the hooks on the wall. The fur coat was not there, though he had put it there himself only a couple of weeks ago.

For a second he stood furious and incredulous. He yanked the hangers sideways, thumbing through them with shaking hands. The best dress was gone, the black velvet. Two pairs of the best shoes were gone. There was no sign of the quilted bed jacket he had given her on her birthday. And that slut on the corner last night had been wearing a black fur coat, seal with a squirrel collar, and it was only the best things, the new things, that were missing.

The closet swam in a red mist. He was shaking so hard that he had to feel his way out, and when he found a chair and sat down on it he hung onto it with both hands. The red mist lay over the whole room; his sight was bloody with it. In that moment, if his father had been in the room, he would have tried to kill him, and he knew it. Even if he wasn't in the room . . .

He jumped up and rummaged through his father's dresser, found the .38 that the old man carried on trips, broke the cylinder and found it loaded in five chambers, the hammer down carefully on the empty sixth. It was a heavy, solid satisfaction to his palm, it was iron and it was murderous.

Putting on his coat, he slipped the gun into the side pocket and went out, and all the way down the hall and stairs and into the hazy brightness of the morning street he moved with his jaw locked like a trap and a singular quietness in his muscles, as if he waited for something. The red smear of mist was still before his eyes.

He started walking up West Temple toward town, heading for the New Grand Hotel where his father sometimes hung out. His hand was in his coat pocket, holding the sag of the gun.

After all these years, he said. After twenty years of hating him!

He noticed that the morning was fine. The smoky air lay over him soft as feathers, the sunlight was diffused and mellow. Trucks were working down the street picking up heaps of leaves still sodden from the rains. His eyes were very sharp: things fixed themselves on his senses. He had a curious feeling that his mind was a steel plate, a mirror, which reflected impressions without absorbing them.

Quick tears stung his eyes as suddenly as if he had had acid flung in his face, and he bent his head, still walking, still with his fingers curled under the weight of the .38.

Ahead of him was the hotel, and he closed his fingers hard around the gun. Now! his mind said. If he's there . . . His body was curiously light, a steel framework, as if he were not solid, as if he were invisible, and he did not hear his own steps on the tile floor as he crossed the lobby to the desk.

"I'm looking for my father," he said to the clerk. "Harry Mason."

"Yeah," the clerk said. He stood up and looked up and down the lobby. "He was in here a while ago. Seems to me I saw him just a few minutes back."

He beckoned a bellhop. "Seen Harry Mason around?"

"Not for a while," the bellhop said. "He was sittin' over by the windows for a while, talkin' to a woman, and then a couple guys come in. I guess they all went out together."

"Thanks," Bruce said. "I'll look somewhere else."

He went across the open lobby again, and as he turned sideways to avoid a man coming in the door he saw the clerk and bellhop watching him. He took his hand out of his pocket, put it back again because the gun showed through the cloth.

On the street he hesitated, his mind carefully numb to everything except the simple question of where his father might be. As if he were bearing a message, as if he had no personal interest in his father but had to find him for someone else, he went up a block and pushed open the door of the cigar store. Two men were leaning against the counter, but his father was not there. He looked toward the back room, but the door was half closed and he could see nothing. The man behind the counter recognized him and spoke. "Looking for your dad?"

"Yeah."

"I think he's gone out of town. He was in this morning, said something about going to Nevada to look at a mine."

"Oh," Bruce said. An instant sickness, a feeling as if he might faint, made him put his hand on the counter. "Well, thanks," he said, and turned away.

"Anything wrong?" the clerk said.

"No."

So it would have to wait. On the sidewalk again, breathing

deeply, he felt his body come back to him, heavily, a tired weight of flesh. He took his sweating hand off the gun and rubbed it on his coat, and without much thought of why he went, he turned back toward home.

In the apartment he sat down and looked fixedly at the half-filled bookcase. Somebody would have to take those books back to the library. He imagined the landlord coming in sourly, looking around the place, wondering what to do first in this apartment, what to do with the property of the dead man and his jailed son, picking up a book and seeing the library stamp on it, laying out a stack to send back, looking into the closets, shaking his head at the burdens people laid on him . . .

This is the end of that, Bruce said. They will hang a considerable amount of reading when they hang me. He took the gun out and laid it on the table. Beyond him the open closet door yawned, and with petulant haste he got up to slam it shut.

For some time he sat looking at the gun, the blued steel, the brown wooden butt gracefully and powerfully arched. I thank you, he said, for teaching me to shoot. But he felt the closet door behind him, and he broke a cigarette taking it from the pack. Everything material that was left of his mother was in the closet, and he heard it talking to him.

I held no grudge, it said. Why should you? Your father was lonely, lonelier even than you, probably, because he's old and you're young. He had to have a woman to lean on and to reassure him that he was a man, and strong. And the clothes were no good to me, they might as well have been given to someone.

"But my God!" he said aloud. "To that slut!"

You don't know, the closet behind him said. You never met her. Maybe she's good for him, better than I was.

He picked up the gun and went into his bedroom. His suitcases sat open on their chairs. There was all that, the whole life he had planned for himself, the studies he wanted to finish, the career he wanted. Did you blow things like that, blow your mother's faith and pride in you, blow every chance you had to live down your old man's life and make something useful of yourself, just for the pleasure of ridding the earth of him?

He went into his father's room, slowly, and put the gun back in the drawer. He knew he couldn't do it now. He had known it, actually, from the time of that momentary sickness in the cigar store. If he could have done it in a rage it would be done now, but the minute he started thinking about it it was impossible. Back in his own room again he began frantically throwing clothes into the suitcases, dirty ones and clean ones together, shirts and socks and handkerchiefs and pajamas jammed in with shoes and laundry, cramming them in as if he had only minutes to catch a train. He was still cleaning the dresser drawers when he heard the front door open.

In the flash of returning rage he wished for the gun. He saw his father in the red haze, framed by the door, and he saw himself shooting him down, felt the hard jumping kick of the gun in his wrist, saw the heavy black-hatted figure stagger and slump, one hand hanging to the jamb . . .

He turned and went on with his packing, and from the living room heard his father's voice. "How was the hunting?"

"Fair," he said without turning. "I got seven."

"Ha," his father said. "A duck feed. I haven't had a duck feed for two-three years."

"I gave three to the fellow I borrowed the gun from," Bruce said, "and two to the boy who loaned me the boots. There's two in the icebox."

"You can't have a duck feed on two ducks," his father said. "What did you give them all away for?"

"To pay my debts," Bruce said. The old man came into the bedroom behind him.

"Packing up?" he said. "Where you going?"

"I'm pulling out for Minneapolis," Bruce said, turning. His father was staring at him with quick, prying eyes, the little dewlaps of skin below his jowls giving him a pugnacious, bulldog look.

"I thought school didn't start till the middle of January or so."

"It doesn't. I'll go visit Kristin."

"You make up your mind pretty sudden, don't you?"

"I got a letter," Bruce said. "They'll give me a little job. There's nothing to stick around here for."

Standing with one hand on the lid of the suitcase, he set himself. In a minute he wouldn't be able to do this patter-chorus any longer, and then they would be out in the open. There was a light trembling in his legs, and his face was stiff.

"No," his father said after a pause. "I guess not." He wandered to the dresser, fingered the corner of a pile of handkerchiefs. He turned around. "Need any money?"

Bruce's lips flattened against his teeth. "Not from you," he said.

Now they were looking at each other as they had wanted to look for twenty years without either of them daring. The trembling came up inside him, came up and outward, and he clenched his hands to keep them steady. He saw the dark face before him go darker.

"What the hell is eating you?" his father said. "Nobody's been holding you here."

"Nobody could," Bruce said.

He saw the symptoms of his father's quick and growing anger, the old old symptoms, remembered from his cradle, it seemed to him, the way his head wagged back and forth, the way his teeth came together, the way he snorted through his nose and his eyes got hard and boring.

"I'll tell you what's eating me," he said, and it was as if he were sitting on his voice, holding it down. "It's the same thing that's been eating me ever since I was old enough to walk. You've never been a decent father to me . . ."

"What?" the old man said. "What are you talking about?" He was in a shaking rage, but Bruce's voice, coming like a sharp thin blade, cut him off, stabbed him with the accumulated grievances of his whole life.

"You never were a decent father to Chet," he said. "You broke him before he ever had a chance to get started. You never were a decent husband to mother . . ."

Both his father's hands were over his head. "Shut up!" he shouted. His whole head shook, and his hands came down in a pounding gesture. "Shut up! What in Christ's name are you saying?"

The abrupt, wide-shouldered lurch with which he swung away said that he was not going to stand and listen to any more damned nonsense, but in an instant he had pivoted as if in a dance step and come back. His voice was a harsh rattle. "How haven't I been a decent father? How did I break Chet?"

"You cowed us both from the time we were out of diapers," Bruce said, the shaking like an ecstasy inside him. "You bullied and stormed and never tried to understand that you were dealing with children. You kept on running whiskey when you knew all of us hated it and suffered for it. You made Chet ashamed in front of his friends, and you chased him into finding friends he didn't need to be ashamed in front of. You led mother a dog's life all the time she was married to you."

The rage had disappeared from his father's face, and he looked tired, weak, flabby. "You too, I suppose," he said.

"I went through college being ashamed of you," Bruce said. "Lying about you on questionnaires and registration forms. Father's profession—rancher, cattle buyer, veterinary! Other people could respect their fathers. I couldn't. All I could do was . . ."

His father's voice was so like a groan that he stopped, out of breath and panting. The old man's face twisted, the loose flesh puckered in a wild grimace. "Oh Jesus God," he said, "I had to make a living, didn't I? I had to support you, didn't I? You lived on me all the time you were having such troubles being ashamed of me, didn't you?"

"I paid my own tuition and most of my expenses for four years," Bruce said. "I worked from the summer when I was thirteen. Remember? When I worked at the news company and didn't even know that checks should be cashed, and kept them every week in a cigar box till the manager told me to cash them so he could keep his books straight? And why do you suppose I worked? I worked so I could get free from you at the earliest possible minute. Even at thirteen. If it hadn't been for mother I'd have been free of you five or six years ago."

The rage tried to come back into his father's face, but he saw that it wasn't real rage; it was an attempt, lost from the beginning, to generate a passion and bully him down, and Bruce closed his mouth over the cold words. It was as if he stepped back, watching the old man's contorted features trying to be the old fighting domineering face, and failing.

The old man acted as if he were strangling. He swung around again, swung back. His face was black with dark blood, and a distended vein beat in his temple. In two steps he came close to Bruce and seized his arm.

"Bruce," he said, "I hope you make a success. I hope you make a lot of money and get everything you want." His hand was shaking Bruce's arm, and his breath, tainted with stale tobacco (the old, stale father-smell, remembered and constantly renewed down the years), beat against Bruce's face. "I hope you have all the luck in the world," he said, and shook his arm, dropped it. "But I never want to see you again!"

He turned away, for good this time, but not before Bruce saw the tears in his eyes. As he went out the door, walking fast and cramming the black hat on his head, his shoulders were almost as wide as the opening, but they looked bleak and strengthless and strangely forlorn.

It was not until the fast hard steps had diminished and gone down the hall that Bruce felt his own face wet. There was a hard agony in his throat and chest, and when he turned again to his packing he did it wearily, without enthusiasm, and in his mind was a dull wonder that the break with the father he hated could make him almost as miserable as the death of the mother he had loved.

Late in the afternoon he took his suitcases to the Ford, came back for the books that would have to be returned to the library on the way, and closed the door of the partment, leaving his key on the table inside. There was his whole life ahead, but he went toward it without eagerness, went almost unwillingly, with a miserable sense that now he was completely alone.

"I was just standin' there, see?" the desk clerk said. "Right in front of Joe Vincent's. This big Duke guy was chewin' a toothpick out in front, talkin' to Imy Winckelman—you know, the lightweight. Then these four soldiers come by. By God, that Duke must hate soldiers like poison. First thing I know I see Duke saunter up behind and kick one of the soldiers' ankles together so he almost falls down, and when he staggers, Imy is right there to be bumped into, and Imy shoves the soldier, and first thing any of the soldiers know they're gettin' the hell beat out of them. I saw Duke slough one and give him the boots, and Imy was standin' in the doorway sluggin' with two others, and the fourth one jumps on Duke's back and starts battin' his ears off. Duke must of shook him twenty feet, right on his head. By the time you could spit twice there was nothin' but old Army Store duds around."

The telephone rang, and he picked it up wearily. "Winston Hotel. Yeah, he's right here." He held the phone dangling. "You, Harry." He waved the phone at the booth to the right of the desk and Bo went in and pulled the door shut. Probably Dubois. It was about time.

"Hello," he said.

Dubois' voice crackled in the earpiece. "Talk a little slower," Bo said.

"I say I just got back," Dubois said. "Thought I'd call you up and put you wise."

"Well, how is it? How're things going down there?"

"They're making progress," Dubois said. "It's a tough place to get going. They practically have to pack things in and out on their backs."

"I know all that," Bo said. "What I want to know is when do they start taking out ore?"

The voice crackled and fizzed. Bo's left arm was growing numb again, propped on the shelf. He changed hands in the tight booth and put the receiver to his right ear. "Talk a little slower," he said.

". . . about three weeks," Dubois said. "But there's one thing down there I don't quite like the looks of."

"Oh Christ," Bo said. "What is it this time?"

"You know those options we hold?"

"I ought to."

"Well, they aren't enough."

"What do you mean, they aren't enough?"

"Janson's got us surrounded, did you know that?"

"How can he have us surrounded when we own that whole strip?"

"Not on the west," Dubois said. "And that's where the payoff is going to be. Creer's got his tunnel in three hundred feet now, and if you ask me, he's got something. And where'd we be if he struck it and bought up those options of Janson's? We ought to get Janson out of there before somebody gives him the idea he's got something valuable."

Bo stared at the corrugated metal wall of the booth, its green paint flaking off and its surface scratched with addresses, names, numbers, doodle-marks. "How much dough would that mean?"

"I smelled around," Dubois said. "I'd be willing to bet we could pick up the whole block for two thousand."

"Yeah," Bo said. "Where would we get the two thousand?"

"Hell, we can raise that," Dubois said. "Three ways, that's only seven hundred apiece. The way I figure it, it's a good gamble."

"Maybe it's a good gamble," Bo said, "but I tell you, Paul, I'm all tied up."

Dubois was laughing at the other end. "Hock your overcoat," he said. "We just can't afford to pass it up, the way I figure it. If Creer or one of the big outfits picks them off they'll buy us out at their price, you watch. Or freeze us out."

Bo moistened his lips and shook his left arm hard. "Have they moved any ore at all?"

"Getting a shipment out in a week or two. They've been in the vein for three or four days, and it looks good."

"A week or two," Bo said. "Tomorrow. Next month. By Jesus I wish something would ever happen today, instead of next week. Where are you now?"

"Over at the Newhouse."

"Going to be there a while?"

"Yeah."

"I'll be over," Bo said, and hung up.

"I'd hate to tangle with him," the clerk was saying. "He's a tough monkey."

Old Fat Hodgkiss, one of the permanent roomers, was rubbing his bald head. "I wish he'd come around in front of here and pick on somebody," he said. "I could use a little excitement." He yawned his chins tight, relaxed them again. Mrs. Winter, the "widow" on the second floor, passed through the lobby and gave them all a bright smile. Getting skinnier every day, Bo thought. A bird could perch on her hipbones.

"Going over town?" Bo said.

"Yes."

"Guess I'll give you a break and walk along," he said. To Dobson, the clerk, he said, "If Mrs. Nesbitt comes in, you haven't seen me."

The clerk raised a weary hand. "What makes you think she'd be looking for you?" he said. Fat Hodgkiss laughed.

The afternoon street was bright after the lobby. Mrs. Winter pegged along beside Bo, swinging her handbag. "What's the matter?" she said. "You and Elaine still on the outs?"

"Don't talk about that squaw," he said. He was feeling, clear down his left side and into his leg, the barely-perceptible numb tug, the feeling as if he had been lying down and had put half his nerves to sleep. But no prickling, no itch of returning sensation when he walked or when he shook the fingers of his left hand. He was remembering what Elaine had said to him the last time he mentioned it: "For the love of Mike, quit belly-aching. What you need to do is go out and do something. You're just rotting on your own bones."

"How you feeling?" he said to Mrs. Winter. "Any better?"

"I always feel better in the spring," she said. "I cough myself purple all winter, and then in the spring I'm better."

"It's a hell of a town," Bo said. "Deader than a dead fish."

"How's your mine going?"

"How'd you know I had a mine?"

"You told me."

"Did I? I'm just on my way over to see my partner about it now."

"Something stirring?"

"Maybe."

"Oh, I hope so," Mrs. Winter said. "Waiting is the worst job there is." She looked at him under her mascaraed lashes. "Especially when you're having trouble with your lady friend."

"I said to skip her!"

Mrs. Winter paid no attention. "Maybe she's tired of waiting too. Some women are like that. She'll be all right when you get your break and the mine comes in."

"Maybe she'll be all right," Bo said. "But she won't be in on the mine."

Mrs. Winter swung her handbag. In the bright sun the lines showed through the paint on her face. "This is where I go in," she said, stopping by an entrance. She lifted her peaked face and breathed deeply. "Smell that air!" she said. "Spring's wonderful. Everything turns out right in the spring. First thing you know you'll be right back on top of the world."

"How much you charge for a course in cheering-up?" Bo said, kidding her.

For just a moment her eyes were blank and cold as stone, and he found himself thinking that she looked a little like Emmy Schmaltz in the funny paper. Then she waved her handbag at him playfully. "It's just my nature," she said. "I'm just a ray of sunshine."

Dubois was shaving when Bo knocked and came in. He twisted around and waved the razor at a chair and tilted his head back to get at his throat, shooting his underlip out and squinting his eyes.

"What's all this new come-on for more dough?" Bo said.

"Be with you in a minute," Dubois said. "Look in the bag there, there's a map."

Bo opened the gladstone on the bed, lifted up shirts and socks, found a folded paper. He spread it out. There were angling plats laid out with names printed on them: Siskiyou, Magpie, Bozo, Alma, Pieut, Rosebud, Independent. Across the top of the map was a long arrow, and under it a double-lined box. "Being a sketch map of the Loafer Hills or Hobo District (unsurveyed) lying to the northwest of Winnemucca, Nevada. This is not a transit map, nor official as being absolutely accurate in all details, but believed to be approximately representative of the district. Black stars indicate approximately points where ore has been discovered to date."

In the rectangle marked Della Mine, checked with red pencil, there were two black stars, and further to the right, at a large square marked Galway Gulch Town Sight, a red arrow led off the map to the margin, which read, "Call on Mr. Janson, he will show you correct location."

"What's there new about this?" Bo said.

Dubois washed the razor and dabbed his throat with a towel. "See all those blanks around the Della, up toward the ridge? Those are the ones Janson holds options on. He's a long ways away, clear over in the Big Fortune, there, but he's right next door to Creer, see? And Creer's tunnel is going to turn something up. If we get to Janson before he catches on to what Creer's got, we ought to be able to buy him out cheap. He's got options on half of Nevada."

"You're sure you didn't give him the idea you wanted them bad."

"Do I look silly? I never cracked my mouth to Janson." He slapped the towel over the rack. "How I figure it, after looking the place over again, is that the vein comes right down here through Creer's property, and maybe across the corner of the Big Fortune, and then right through the hill." His finger made a wiggly line across the plats. "That means that probably all but the top one of those optioned properties is good, see? We ought to get that block of stuff for at least a half mile west."

"Wills' doodlebug said the lead bent off north from the Della."

Dubois smiled. "You know that doodlebug. I saw him demonstrate it once out on Exchange Street and it made a noise like a jackpot right in front of the Copper Bank."

"Well, he wasn't so far wrong," Bo said, and laughed. He watched Dubois slip a tie into his collar. "How soon would we have to pick up this stuff?"

"I'd say quick," Dubois said. "The minute we start hauling ore out of there, and Creer hits anything, Janson'll be wise. We ought to get down there before the first of the month."

Bo looked out the window at the flag flying from the postoffice building. "By God I don't see where I can raise seven hundred right away," he said. The fury that lay always just under the surface, the balked, frustrated sense of waiting forever for something to happen, the hatred he had for the hard times, the clothes getting shabby, the way he had to cross the street when he saw O'Brien coming, because he owed O'Brien a ninety dollar hotel bill from last year, lashed him to his feet. "Four thousand bucks I've poured into that God damned hole!" he said. "Next week it'll get moving, next month it'll make us rich. Only first we have to dig up another seven hundred apiece. I can't raise it. I'm broke."

Dubois stood pursing his lips and frowning. "You got to expect things like that in the mining game. It's a slow racket, till you hit it right. Considering what that seven hundred may mean to you this time next year, it doesn't amount to a hill of beans."

It was just possible, Bo thought, that Dubois was bleeding him and keeping him stringing along. His hands tightened, and he felt the numbness under the left thumb. But Dubois was in it as deep as anybody. He straightened his fingers again, feeling shaky. "I don't know," he said, and sat down on the bed, pushing the gladstone bag aside. "If something doesn't break pretty soon I don't know what I'll do."

"Try a loan," Dubois said. "Ninety days ought to clear it. How about one of the boys over on the exchange?"

"They wouldn't lend me a dime."

He saw Dubois looking at him queerly. "You really hard up?" Dubois said. "You really scratching bottom?"

"I've been scratching the bottom for three months," Bo said. "Nothing coming in, everything going out. Whiskey business is gone. I used to be able to depend on that to pull me out of a hole." He hesitated, realizing that he sounded too broke. "Oh, I've got it. I've got collateral from here to Winnemucca. It's the cash that crowds me. Nick Williams owes me four thousand—notes due two months ago. But Nick sells out of Reno and ties himself all up in a gambling boat off Long Beach, and I have to wait till he gets wheeling again."

He glanced at Dubois' face to see how he was taking it. "What makes me the maddest is that God damn Patton in L.A.," he said. "Did I tell you what that son of a bitch did?"

"No."

"We used to do a lot of business together," Bo said. "Plenty of times I've trusted him for three or four thousand. He kept on running a little booze, beating the liquor taxes. There was money in it, if he was careful. A year ago I sent him down a certified check for twenty-five hundred, to get me some stuff off the boat. I was sick, had a kind of stroke or something. Left me all numb down this side. So I sent him the money and was going after the stuff as soon as I felt a little better. Next I hear they've picked up his speedboat, and the grand jury indicts him on a conspiracy charge, and there goes my twenty-five hundred. Patton skips his bond and hits for the Philippines. Not a God damned word out of him since."

"Tough," Dubois said.

"I hope it's tough," Bo said. "Now you want seven hundred."

"It isn't me that wants it," Dubois said. "I just think we'd be damn fools to let that possibility slide."

Bo rose. His legs were tired, and he was filled with abrupt rage at the thought that he didn't even have a car any more, and would have to walk all the way back up to First South. "Well," he said, "I don't know. I don't know whether I can raise it or not."

"If you can't," Dubois said, "why I suppose Clarence and I might scratch it up. I'd rather see us all even, though."

"I'll go take a gander around," Bo said.

"I'm going back down in about a week. Want to go along?"

"Yeah," Bo said. "I would."

"Okay. I'll let you know."

Back in his room, Bo lifted the blind a little, dug in the desk drawer for the bundle of papers, and hunched down to go through them all carefully. Nick Williams' notes—due not two months ago, but a year and a half ago. If he wasn't so washed out he'd go down to the coast and take that four thousand out of that tinhorn's hide. He'd been over a year paying the other fifteen thousand, dribbling it out five hundred at a time so that you could never do anything with it, you never felt that you'd got your money. And then welch on the last four thousand, sell out and beat it. Four thousand. That would put him on his feet again if he could get it.

Carefully he laid the papers to one side and wrote a letter to Nick putting it up to him strong. But he knew when he sealed the envelope that there wasn't much chance. The fellow who had signed Williams' notes, the vice-president of a Las Vegas bank, had blown his brains out six months ago down in Needles. One chance in a thousand that Williams would honor his obligations, and how could you sue a guy living twelve miles off shore beyond the law?

He laid the letter on the bed and went back to the papers. Cards, addresses scrawled on envelopes, some of which he no longer remembered the significance of; slips for safety deposit boxes he no longer had; receipts for payments in a building and loan association he had been cleaned out of in 1931; a deposit book on a defunct bank. He threw them all in the waste basket, went on. A Nevada fishing license, two years old. A tax receipt for the cottage on Tahoe.

Picking it up in the fingers of his awkward left hand, he looked at it. He had almost forgotten he owned that place. Two thousand he must have sunk into that, and there was the boat, the motor, his shotgun and deer gun, equipment like stoves and refrigerators and furniture, a lot of it almost new.

Holding the slippery paper down hard, he scratched a note to a real estate shark in Reno. He would sell the whole place, just as it stood, two-car garage, boat, motor, guns, furniture, for . . . He stopped, thinking. How much? Nobody would want to put two thousand into a summer cottage in times like these. Fifteen hundred? He wrote in the figures, putting a long firm bar on the five. Fifteen hundred cash. It was worth a damn sight more. He'd paid a hundred and twenty-five for the boat alone, and that much more for the motor.

"What I want," he wrote, "is quick action. At the price I'm asking, you ought to be able to move it in a week. I'm clearing out everything I've got a finger in in Nevada, and I'm willing to take a loss."

Still holding the opened pen, he pawed through the rest of the papers. Junk. His certificate of stock—only a notarized paper signed by both Wills and Dubois—showing that he had four thousand dollars, a third interest, in the Della Mine in the Loafer Hills district in Nevada. The insurance policy, only five hundred dollars, and he wouldn't have got that, with his blood pressure where it was, if it hadn't been for Hammond. The deed to the cemetery lot, and the receipt for the payment for perpetual care. Those he put together and put back into the desk.

Two possibilities, Williams and the Tahoe place, and only the Tahoe place worth much even as a possibility. If they both came through he'd be set. He should have been riding Nick's tail every week for the last year and a half. But he just hadn't felt well enough. He shook his fingers, trying to get a tingle. No dice.

If neither of them came through, he was in the hole. His diamonds had gone a year ago, when he was raising money to send to Patton. His watch? He took it out and looked at it. Fifteen dollars maybe, at a hock shop. He looked around the room. Suitcases? Maybe fifteen more. Overcoat? He might get five. He had paid ninety six months ago. He took his check book out of his coat and looked at the last stub. A hundred and three dollars left. He might as well close that out. There was no use paying a damned bank a dollar a month on an account like that.

Anger made him rock in the chair. Twelve hundred shot when the bank blew. The damned bankers sitting behind their mahogany taking your money and losing it for you. But he figured that dead account anyway. Eventually, when the Bank Examiner and the rest of them got through and got theirs, he might get another twenty or thirty percent of that. Forty or fifty altogether.

Forty or fifty? he said. I ought to get a hundred percent plus interest for all the time they've had it!

But maybe a couple of hundred more from the bank sometime. Next week. Next month. Next year.

Damn it to hell, he said. By rights he had six thousand dollars, over eight thousand counting what Patton skipped with. Only he didn't have it, any of it. And what if nothing paid off? Where was he going to raise seven hundred?

Maybe he ought to try selling out of the Della. It was a comer, it looked good. Somebody might take his four thousand interest off his hands clean.

And then what? Sit around on his can and eat up the four thousand and then what?

You didn't have a chance, not a show. You were sixty-one years old, sick, broke. Everybody you trusted snaked on you, beat it for the Philippines or the twelve-mile limit with your money. The woman you kept in style for two solid years turned iceberg as soon as the money got tight, cold-shouldered you in the lobby, wasn't in when you came around, even had the God damned gall to stay on in the same hotel and act like you were somebody she'd met once but didn't quite like.

By Jesus, it was . . . ! Some day, he thought with his eyes narrowing, he'd kill that bitch. Nice as pie as long as he had the dough, and as soon as he slipped a little she was out hustling some other sugar daddy.

The bitch, the dirty blood-sucking gold-digging squaw. Some day he would kill her, so help him.

But he couldn't hang onto the rage. It seeped out of him, leaked away, left him sitting slumped and tired, thinking: Sixty-one years old, and sick and broke and alone. Who gives a damn about you now? They were all your friends when you had it. Now where are they? There isn't a soul cares whether you live or die.

Bruce, maybe? he said. Bruce had written a couple of times in the year and a half since he left. Maybe he'd got over the way he felt after Sis. . . . He tightened his muscles, staring hard at the wall, feeling the tears come hot and acid into his eyes. He put his forehead down on his arm and ground his teeth.

After a minute he raised his head again, thinking of Bruce in Minnesota. He worked after classes and then worked all summer. He might have something, he might be willing to help his old dad when he got in a hole. *He* had sent money back to Rock River, hadn't he, long after he'd run away from there. And they'd never done a damn thing for him, not a tenth as much as he'd done for Bruce. He took out another sheet of paper and unscrewed the pen.

But he found himself writing almost with his breath held back, almost pleadingly, and he hadn't even the will to tear the letter up and throw it away. He had told Bruce he never wanted to see him again, and he didn't, the ungrateful whelp. But he was writing, and he kept on writing, and as he wrote the vision of the Della grew brighter. If they could just get that into production, capitalize and get a smooth organization going. It was a sure thing, a dead immortal cinch, a gold lead as good as anything ever dug up in Nevada. But it took money to get it started, for the mill and everything. He had four thousand in it, and when it got going he'd get it back twenty times. But meantime the whole thing might fizzle for the lack of a few hundred dollars. If Bruce wanted to come in, he'd cut him in share and share alike for whatever he put up. It wasn't too far-fetched to say that a few hundred now might put him on Easy Street the rest of his life, and he'd be helping his dad at the same time. The main thing was to get that mine going, so he could get back on his feet. He wasn't feeling too good, that stroke or whatever it was had left his left side numb. He might not live very long, and that was another reason why Bruce ought to get in on this while he could. He'd get the whole third share anyway, in the course of a few years.

Writing that made him feel better, more optimistic. And he felt better toward Bruce. He was a good enough kid. Bright as a whip. It was Elsa's death that had put him off that way, made him bitter. He was doing all right now, going to be a good lawyer sometime.

Ought to send him something, he thought. Some little present, just to show him that his old man still wished him well. He dug the loose change from his pocket, counted the two dollars and forty-five cents in his palm, thought of the hundred and three dollars in the bank, looked in his wallet and found two fives and a two. Maybe he'd better take it easy. He had to eat, himself.

Then he noticed the pen on the desk. It was a good pen, cost seven fifty when he bought it. He took it up and wrote at the bottom of the letter, "I'm sending you a little present, something you may be able to use in school." He carried the pen to the wash bowl, squirted the ink in a blue stream against the porcelain, drew the bulb full of water two or three times, wiped it off carefully with toilet paper. It looked practically new. He shined the point clean and rummaged in the closet till he found a shoe box from which he cut strips to make a little carton. When he went down to the desk after stamps he felt better than he had for quite a while, and he straightened his tie at the mirror by the desk before he left the hotel.

Looking pretty seedy, he thought. Coat all out of press, pants baggy. You got down and forgot to watch your appearance. You'd never get back on your feet looking like a tramp. People had to be able to look at you and see that you were a responsible looking guy. Dubois, with his little thin look, asking if you were really scraping bottom. You couldn't take chances on things like that. They hurt your reputation.

In a tavern just off State Street he had a quick beer, standing straight in front of the bar and looking at himself in the mirror. From the tavern he went straight to the shine parlor of Joe Ciardi, his old whiskey outlet.

"Look," he said, almost before Joe could say hello. "I need a press job. Got a closet I can sit in?"

"Sure thing," Joe said. "Got a date?"

"I've been so damn busy I haven't had time to wipe my nose," Bo said. "Just looked in a mirror and saw I looked like a bum."

He sat down with a magazine in the curtained closet. After a minute he pulled off his shoes and opened the curtain and beckoned to the colored shine and slid the shoes across the tiles to

540

him. Sitting in his shirt tails, he remembered that he still wore his hat, and took it off. Pretty sloppy. He opened the curtain again and whistled at Joe and sailed the hat toward him. "Might as well shoot the works," he said.

Joe, smoothing the trousers on the goose, caught the hat and hooked it over a blocking form. He took the wallet from the hip pocket of the pants and cleaned the side pockets of change. "This for me?" he said.

"Some of it's for you if you ever get done," Bo said.

"What the hell," Joe said. "I got to use the goose, not magic. I think you got a date."

"I got half a dozen dates. Get busy and don't talk so much."

He was impatient waiting, but he didn't feel as tired as he had that morning. When he stood in front tying his tie he found himself whistling. There was a spot on the tie, and he fixed it so the vest covered it. The newly-creased trousers were warm on his legs, the coat fitted smoothly across his shoulders again. He looked in the mirror steadily while the shine gave him an unnecessary brush-off, and he tipped the shine a dime.

Then he cut diagonally across the street to the building which housed Miller and Weinstein, Tailors.

Louis Miller, sidling, peering near-sightedly, came around the immaculate counter in front of the dressing rooms. Bo gauged exactly the cordiality of his greeting. It was all right. Miller would sell him anything in the store. He ought to. He'd got cash on the nose for enough clothes in the last ten years.

"Ah," Louis said. "Mr. Mason. What can I do for you?"

"Like to look at some of your rolls of burlap," Bo said.

"Yes!" Louis Miller said. "Any special color?"

"I don't know. Gray. Blue."

Miller put his hand up to the door of one glass-fronted case. "You don't want just anything," he said.

"Did you ever know me to want just anything?" Bo said. "I want a *suit*."

The fawning agreement of Miller's smile warmed him clear down. "Now right back here," Louis said, "I have something I think you like."

When he left at five-thirty, Bo had ordered a ninety-dollar suit, had stood while Louis gave him the old line during the measurements. You are a wise man to have suits tailored to measure. You are a hard man to fit. So big up here.

And he carried with him to the sidewalk six of Louis' best ties, telling Louis offhand to put them with the bill. He had felt of his bare head and asked Louis if he had any hats. Louis did not. Bo toyed with the idea of going somewhere else and getting one, but gave it up because he didn't have a charge account at any haber-dasher's and would have to pay cash. The hat could wait till Joe polished up the old one.

It was only when he started walking that he remembered he didn't have anyone to see or anywhere to go except the hotel.

In the lobby of the Winston, after dinner, he sat smoking a cigar, the first one he had bought for two weeks. His legs were crossed, one glittering shoe swinging slightly. The cigar was sweet and fragrant in his mouth after the sour pipe he had been smoking.

"You look all spiffed up," the clerk said. "Isn't that a new tie?"

"That's a new three-dollar tie."

"Must have cleaned up."

Bo winked. "Killed a Swede," he said, and lay back on the back of his neck. By now all three of those letters were on the way. One of them was sure to turn up something. A man didn't have any-body but himself to blame if he let a little hard luck get him down. Keep up the appearance, that was the thing. The world looked like a different place with your shoes shined and your pants pressed.

The scratching of the dog's claws made him turn his face toward the door. The bulldog came in, tugging at the leash, his wide chest pushing close to the floor, and then she came, letting the door go behind her and tinkling a little laugh as the dog pulled her off balance. Bo saw her face freeze slightly as she saw him. He re-mained where he was, sprawling in the chair.

"Hi, Good-looking," he said.

He noticed that she stopped the dog all right when she wanted to. That was another of her God damned poses, that little game of being dragged along helplessly behind the pup, and laughing, and getting herself noticed. Now she hauled the pup short with a curt jerk of the leash and stood looking Bo over.

"Well, if it isn't Baby Harry, named after his father's chest," she said. "I thought you'd left town."

Bo motioned to the next chair. "Sit down."

"What for?"

"Not for anything. Can't you sit down and pass the time of day?"

She glanced from him to the clerk, and he could see her wonder-ing what was up. They hadn't been on speaking terms for ten days, ever since she threw that cheap-john stuff at him and he cussed her out. "I'm a pretty busy woman," she said.

"Yeah," Bo said. "So I've heard."

542

As if a hinge had given away, she sat down suddenly on the arm of the other chair. Her eyes were hard. "What do you mean by that?"

"You've been too busy to talk to me," Bo said, and shrugged.

"Who *could* talk to you?" she said. "The minute anybody opens their mouth you jump right down their throat about something. I don't have to take that kind of treatment."

"No," Bo said. "I guess not."

She was giving him the once-over, obviously wondering why he had asked her to sit down and talk. Let her wonder. He didn't know himself, exactly. While he was looking up at her from under his eyebrows, she put out her finger and touched the new tie. "Mmm," she said. "New tie."

"Check."

"Handsome."

"Glad you like it."

She looked around the lobby, humming a little song. The bull-dog sniffed at Bo's glittering shoes, and she jerked the leash. "So you're not really mad at me," she said.

"No," he said, watching her. "No, I'm not mad at you."

She slid off the arm of the chair onto the cushion, bent to un-snap the dog's leash. "Heard anything from Dubois?"

"I saw him this morning."

"You look as if something nice had happened," she said.

"Something nice has."

"Oh, I'm so glad!" she said. (He saw her fix her face for that one.) "What?"

Now she was wondering just how nice she ought to be, esti-mating the value of what had happened, trying to guess whether he was worth making a play for and taking back on. The bitch. But she was good looking, you couldn't deny it. The meat was put on her bones just right.

"Oh, come on," she said, and leaned a little forward. "You know I'd be glad to hear anything nice that had happened to you."

Whatever game it was he had been playing—and he didn't know himself why he was sitting here gassing with her—was swallowed in the enormous angry contempt he felt. "Especially if you thought I'd made some dough," he said.

She was no longer leaning forward. "Now don't start that **again!**" she said.

"It's true, isn't it?"

"No, it's not true," she said. "You think you put me up so damned handsome, and I ought to stick around while you let loose

543

of nickels one by one! You talk about all the money you spent on me. All the money you ever spent on me you could put you know where, and it wouldn't clog you either."

There was nothing in the whole lobby but her spiteful face. He wanted to reach out and slap it bloody. The blood came heavy and slow into his own face, a smothering weight of it. "You thought when you came in here I'd made a killing, didn't you?" he said. "So you thought maybe you'd snuggle up and play sisters again. Well, you can go to hell. Maybe I've made a killing and maybe I haven't . . ."

She stood up. "I don't give a damn whether you have or not," she said. "You could be rolling in gold and you'd still be nothing but a filthy old goat to me!"

"If I was rolling in gold . . ." he said, but she cut him off, whiplashed him.

"You could go roll in the manure for all I care. It wouldn't make you smell any different!"

She started for the stairs, turned with set face to whistle up the dog, and disappeared. Bo worked his hands. He was standing, ready to leap after her, knock her down, kick her apart, beat her damned good-looking weasel face in. He breathed loudly, heard himself gasping for air, and sat down again.

The clerk was looking at his nails behind the desk. In the doorway off to the side Mrs. Winter stood as if not quite sure she should come in at all. She must have come in the back way while they were shouting at each other. Furiously fumbling for a match to re-light his cigar, he ignored her, but she came over and sat down anyway.

"Oh dear!" she said.

He grunted.

"I don't see why she has to be that way," Mrs. Winter said. When he didn't answer she turned the handbag over in her lap and picked with her painted nails at the patterned alligator leather. "Don't be downhearted about her," she said. "It'll all come around."

"If you think I'm downhearted about her," he said through his teeth, "take another think!"

She smiled and patted his knee. "That's the way. Don't let her bother you. Just between you and me . . ." She leaned her skinny face toward him.

"Just between you and me what?"

"Just between you and me," Mrs. Winter said, "she's a bitch."

He grunted again. The anger had ebbed away, leaving the old dead weariness. Mrs. Winter smiled at him coaxingly. "You need a drink," she said. "Come on up to my room and I'll buy you one."

"Oh, I guess not, thanks."

"Come on. You'll feel better after a shot."

He let her lead him up to her room on the second floor. He had not been in her room before. It was fussed up, he noticed. Curtains on the windows with tie-backs on them, woman's junk around. Mrs. Winter got a bottle out of the bureau drawer and rinsed out the two bathroom glasses. She poured two stiff slugs and passed him one.

"Success," she said. "Everything you ever wanted."

"Mud in your eye," he said automatically, and tossed it off. It went down smoothly, warmly, and he raised his eyes from the glass to see Mrs. Winter's birdlike face smiling a birdlike smile at him.

"Feel better?" she said.

"Yeah," he said. "Good Scotch."

"Have another." She poured him one, and they sat on the edge of the bed and drank. This old crane of a Winter, he was thinking, was all right, even if she could hide behind a toothpick. By the third drink he was telling her about the Della, Patton, Nick Williams, the closed bank and the bankrupt building and loan association, the notes and the debts and the possibilities.

"It's hard," she said. "Once you've been up it's harder to climb back after a streak of bad luck. You're all alone, too, aren't you?"

"All alone," he said. "Got one boy left. He's studying law in Minneapolis." He felt for his wallet. "Want to see his picture?"

He showed her the frayed newspaper photograph of Bruce with a golf bag over his arm, taken one day three or four years ago when he had been the medalist in a golf tournament.

"He looks like you," Mrs. Winter said.

"He's a bright kid," Bo said, folding the picture back. "I haven't seen him for a couple years, almost. Away at school." The weariness had left him, but he felt sad. Everybody gone. Sis dead, Chet dead. "I had another boy," he said. "Good ball player. He'd have made the big leagues with any kind of breaks. Died of pneumonia a little over three years ago."

"And your wife too," Mrs. Winter said. "I know how it is. My husband died four years ago last April. I've just never seemed to belong anywhere since."

Bo heaved himself off the creaking bed. "I better run along," he said. "Thanks for the drinks."

But Mrs. Winter was in front of him, her peaked face working. "Don't go," she said. "Please don't go!"

"Why not?"

She twisted her twiggy fingers together. Her rings hung loosely, upside down, above the bony knuckles. "I don't know," she said. "I just. . . . I don't know."

"Lonesome?"

She nodded. "I guess. Lonesome as hell. I been through the mill. I just sort of feel like you've been too, you know how it is."

"Baby," Bo said softly, "I'm not worth the try. I'm broke. I'm an old man, and I'm sick, and I'm broke. You'd be wasting your time. I couldn't give you a thing."

"I don't want anything," she said. "It's just tonight. I feel as if everybody'd gone away and left me. I wish you'd stay."

For some reason he kissed her, and felt her bony body crowd him, shivering. A sound that he meant for a laugh half strangled him. Not a soul in the whole damned town who wanted you except an old consumptive whore, and the hell of it was you liked it. "Look," he said. "Think I'm a piker all you want. But I'm so strapped I couldn't even afford two dollars. What little I've got I've got to keep to eat on till something breaks."

"I don't care about the two dollars," she said.

He thought briefly of Elaine up on the fourth floor, bedded down in her silk pajamas reading a magazine in bed, soft and warm and ten years younger than this poor old skin, and the thing that rose in him was quick and light as a bubble and bitter as a curse.

"Okay," he said.

She was surprisingly passionate. Her thin arms were like a vise, her fingers like birds' claws. For a while, for ten minutes, he was powerful, he felt his own weight and the undiminished strength of his body, but afterward he lay spent and breathing hard beside her, and when he got up quietly and got into his clothes and went down the night-lighted hall to his own room he was old and tired, and the numbness was back in his side and arm.

2

The sky that morning was like blue water with a white surf of clouds rolling eastward under a high wind, though no wind blew down on the city and the campus trees stirred only to the shrill of the seventeen-year locusts. Standing in the long line of gowned figures, waiting for the officials and the president and the visiting dignitaries to head the procession, Bruce sweated under the black serge and the heavy square of the mortar board. He opened the gown to let in some air, and as he did so his hand came close to the

546

inner pocket of his coat, where the letters were. He reached in to feel them.

There was no use to worry himself about what the last letter said and the others hinted. All those letters meant was that the old man wanted to squeeze some money out of him.

Yes? he said. Then why did you telephone Joe Mulder in Salt Lake to go and see him, and tell Joe to lend him some money if he needed it, and send the bill to you?

Because you were worried, he said. Sure you were worried. You are now. But you don't believe it, anyway. If he's down and out, you'll give him what you can, but you're not going to give him money just to throw down a worthless mine shaft.

How much had he sent, anyway, since the first letter came in April? More than he could afford to send, anyway. You're a sucker, he said. You let yourself be gouged because you have a sneaking feeling of guilt, God knows why. And you don't even quite believe Joe when he writes that the old man is all right, a little worn looking, but all right. But of course he's all right. You'd have heard if he wasn't.

And that damned stock. That was what really bothered him. Either that was a very shrewd way of pumping him for money, or it meant something. Why should the old man send on a paper indicating that he had put forty-seven hundred dollars into that mine, with the note: "Hang onto this stock, Bruce. Some day it will make you a lot of money. It's all I've got left to give you. Good luck and don't worry about me. I'm at the end of my rope, that's all."

He looked up as the gowned line stirred and murmured. The president came down the steps of Northrop. At least this silly rigmarole was beginning. It irritated him to have to stand in a hot gown for two or three hours while they went through a lot of medieval mummery. He ought to be doing something, either getting on down and starting work in George Nelson's office, or hitting for Salt Lake to see what he could do there.

No sir, he said. I won't go running out there on a wild goose chase. If he needs money to live he knows he can get it from Joe. If he's sick, Joe will see that he gets into a home or a hospital. There's nothing else I can do. I'm a fool to take that much trouble.

It was the eighth of June. His father's last letter had been written on the first. If he had made up his mind before he wrote that letter, why hadn't anything happened by now? It wasn't going to happen, that was why. Joe would telegraph or call if anything did, and Joe had sent no word except the airmail letter dated the fourth. The whole thing was a squeeze play. Talk about losing your pride! The Big Shot stooping to use a trick like that worthless stock!

He tried to be angry, but all he could feel was a baffled sense of frustration, of pain and regret and loss. To get mad was to kick the old man when he was down, and whether he meant that last letter or not, he was down.

The procession began to shuffle forward. He shuffled with it, still thinking, still bothered, and he forgot to hook up the throat of his gown until the officious man ahead of him turned around and motioned. Ah yes, the forms, he said, and walked shufflingly, tipping his head back to watch the clouds wheel over before the unheard, unfelt upper-air wind.

He saw the young woman a long way away, coming up along the procession as if looking for someone, moving against the stream and searching the faces under the flat black caps. He almost chuckled, thinking what a job it would be to locate any one particular face in that half mile of people all dressed alike. She came on, peering, not waiting for the line to come past her, but walking fast herself, and when she got nearer he saw that it was Mary Trask, the secretary of the Law School, and then he knew that she was looking for him.

He stepped out of line, aware that heads turned to watch him, and with a frozen quiet that was like walking in sleep he went to meet her. She was agitated, half out of breath.

"Oh, I was afraid I wouldn't catch you till you got in," she said. "Can you come?"

"Telephone?" Bruce said.

"Yes. They tried at your room and the landlady told them you were at the exercises so they called the school." They were already walking fast away from the line, across the clipped and manicured carpet of lawn under the still trees, with the locusts' noise loud as a wind in the branches but not a leaf stirring. Mary glanced up at his face. "I'm afraid it's something bad," she said. "I wouldn't have come, only they said it was a matter of life and death."

Bruce said nothing. He was locked tight, everything inside him put away and the doors slammed shut.

Except for a couple of stenographers the office was empty. Mary let him in behind the hinged door and picked up the telephone. He saw her turn aside to avoid meeting his eyes, and there was relief in her voice when she got the operator. "This is the Law School," she said. "Mr. Mason is here now."

Silently she handed the instrument to Bruce, and he stood listen-

548

ing to the far-off buzz, the half-heard monosyllables of the operator, the click of connections. In a minute now death would walk its slack wire from Salt Lake City to Minneapolis, that buzzing and those monosyllables and the mechanical clicks would jell down into their real meaning, and Joe's voice would be saying . . .

"Hello!" he said.

"One moment please."

It seemed to him that half his life had been spent going through this monotonous ritual of death. Long distance calls, telegraph messages, a flying trip to Salt Lake. He was like a vaudeville performer caught in an act he loathed but forced to go on through endless repetitions, starting at the same stale cues, going into his dance at the same habitual moments.

"Hello," Joe's voice said. "Hello?"

Bruce stiffened. "Hello," he said. "Hello, Joe. What is it? Has he . . . ?"

"It's hell," Joe said. "You all right?"

"I'm all right."

"He's dead," Joe said. "Shot himself this morning in the hotel lobby."

There was no shock in the words. Bruce was braced so hard that nothing could have moved him then. "Yeah," he said.

"It's worse than you think," Joe said. "He shot a woman too."

"Oh Jesus," Bruce said. "Dead?"

"Yes. I didn't get her name. Maybe you'd know who she was. One of our workmen lives in that hotel. He heard about it just a minute after it happened, and I went right over. There wasn't much I could do, so I started calling you."

"Yeah," Bruce said. "Yeah, thanks, Joe. Can you do me a favor?"

"Anything."

"Have him taken up to the mortuary."

"I already did. The one where Chet and your mother were."

"Good," Bruce said. He started to ask what about the police, saw Mary Trask's pained face as she listened, and said only, "I'll be there tomorrow night. Have to drive. I haven't got the money for a plane or train. Take me about thirty-six hours."

"Hell," Joe said. "Hold it two hours and I'll wire you some money. You can't drive right through."

"I'd better drive," Bruce said. "Look for me sometime before midnight tomorrow."

He hung up. The two stenographers were sitting behind their typewriters, watching and listening, Mary Trask was looking as if she might cry. The noise of the locusts rasped through the opened windows. "I'm sorry," Mary said. "Is there anything . . . ?"

"Yes," Bruce said. "If you would." He stripped off the gown and mortar board and laid them on a desk. "Could you return these for me? They're paid for. Somebody comes around to collect them, I think."

"Of course," she said. "I'll fix it about the graduation. The dean will be back after the exercises, and I'll see about a degree *in absentia*."

"That's good of you," he said. "Thanks very much."

"And you're going to drive straight through to Salt Lake?"

He nodded.

"I couldn't help hearing," she said, confused. "I could lend you some money."

"No thanks, I'd rather drive." He was already through the gate into the outer office.

"Who?" Mary said, following him. "Who was it?"

"My father," Bruce said. "He's dead."

He went outside. The last ragged end of the procession was disappearing into the building. He stood a moment on the edge of the grass to look in his wallet. Ten dollars, and his last check from the school wouldn't be out for three or four days. He'd have to get some from George Nelson. This part too was familiar—the things to do, the mechanical completion of necessary details. Get the money—fifty ought to do it for the time being. Get a tank of gas. Stop by his room for some clothes? No. He would get along with what he was wearing, buy a shirt or two when he got there. Even while he planned the campaign he was hitting for the car, parked off at the edge of the campus, and within ten minutes he was in his uncle's office explaining, his voice cold, his insides still frozen hard against any feeling whatever.

His uncle asked few questions. He wrote a check and cashed it from the safe, made a note of two or three things that Bruce wanted him to do, shook his hand, told him not to worry about the job. He could come back and go to work any time he got through out there. He stood in the doorway hanging onto Bruce's hand, his earnest, good-natured face puckered.

"I haven't seen your father since about 1912," he said. "More than twenty years. I liked him then. I'm sorry."

"Thanks," Bruce said. "He was down and out. Maybe it's better the way it is." He broke his hand away. "Thanks for everything. I've got to run. I ought to be back in a week or so."

He couldn't stand and listen to George talk about twenty years ago and what the old man had been like then. He had heard it before, from both him and Kristin—the grudging, half-willing

550

admiration they had had for him in spite of their disapproval. There were other compulsions on him. Within an hour of the time Joe Mulder called, while the graduates were still listening to the Commencement Address, he was pushing the Ford down through the traffic toward Northfield, seeing his own frozen face in the windshield and thinking of nothing except drive, cut around that truck, unreel the miles, hit the trunk line west and push it. A body did not keep forever. He was going home to bury the last of his family, straighten out the last tangles that the old man in his desperation had wound himself up in. Straighten out the police, straighten out the funeral arrangements, get the sexton to dig a third grave beside the others in the half-rod of ground known as lot 6, block 37. He was going home again, the next to last time, and there was no doubt where his home was, because part of him was already buried in those two graves and in two days another part—admit it—would be buried in the third.

Now the old familiar catalogue of cities, towns, villages, the old perennial bee-line pilgrimage across the great valley hammocked between Appalachians and Rockies, the familiar feel of the throttle's round button under his sole and the green June tumbleweed blowing flat on each side under the speed-whipped wind.

But no quiet in the mind this time, no limericks, no idle speculation to pass the miles, no fine free feeling of space and air. Only the disbelief, like the disbelief he had had going back for Chet's funeral, only the endless prodding and the endless repudiation and the everlasting no. He had not believed in that first death because there had been practically no warning, because he had never met death close, because he had a boy's feeling that nothing of his could die. Now he refused to believe in his father's death because of the manner of it.

How? he said, in God's name how? In one of those rages that sent him berserk? Then why the letters with their increasing hopelessness, why the pitiful sheet of paper showing that he had poured his last forty-seven hundred dollars into a worthless hole in the ground, and his hopes and his life with them?

But plan it? Make up his mind to shoot that woman and then himself? Do it coldly and deliberately? Bo Mason, who believed in tomorrow as he believed in himself, deliberately scheme to commit murder and suicide on a tomorrow? That called for a cold-bloodedness, a calculation, he had never possessed.

Revenge? Self-pity? Despair?

If he could once convince himself about how it had happened, he could believe it. He knew it was true, he was on his way to bury his father, but he still couldn't believe that last violence. Somehow he had always thought that violence stopped short of finalities for the old man. It had always been at least part show, for an effect, to compel obedience or bully someone down. There was no point in bullying if you were going to die immediately. There was a desperation in this last act that would probably never be quite credible.

The afternoon waned ahead of him down the long straight road, moving faster than he moved, flattening, sinking, going dusky. Sky and earth were a bowl over a disc, then two planes, the upper lighter than the lower, between which he moved. He turned on his lights and unwrapped the sandwich he had bought the last time he stopped for gas.

This too was familiar, the feel of the car's motion, oil-smell and night-smell, the sweet muffled roar of the motor, the phantasmagoria of half-seen shadows, trees, buildings, outside the running headlights. It was old and familiar and even comfortable, and all he had to do was to keep the hard hot accelerator button under his foot, keep the white center line of the highway just off his left front wheel. The dawn too would be familiar, the slow lightening of the sky until the two planes became again disc and bowl: the windless pale light just barely not darkness, the horses standing in the pastures, the cars cutting along the road with lights still on, the clatter and smoke of the Los Angeles Limited coming behind him, catching him, passing him, the shades down on the dark pullmans, the observation car with windows palely alight, an early-rising passenger on the rear platform watching the vanishing point of steel.

It was all familiar. It seemed to him, yawning, scratchy-eyed, that there was the whole rhythm of his life in it, that all through his remembered life the days had gone under him like miles, that he and his whole family had always been moving on toward something that was hidden beyond where the road bent between the hills. As he shifted to ease his aching back he thought of the old man, always chasing something down a long road, always moving on from something to something else. At the very end, before that fatal morning, he must have looked down his road and seen nothing, no Big Rock Candy Mountain, no lemonade springs, no cigarette trees, no little streams of alcohol, no handout bushes. Nothing. The end, the empty end, nothing to move toward because nothing was there.

He began to see, dimly, why his father had shot himself, and half to believe that he had.

"You can't go down there now," Joe said. "You haven't had any sleep in two days. Let it wait till morning."

"I'd better go," Bruce said. "I don't think I could sleep anyway till I did." He looked at the clock in the kitchen, and yawned so wide he couldn't see the hands. Joe, watching him from across the table, pulled the corners of his mouth down.

"I feel all right," Bruce said. "I'd better get it over." It was only nine-forty. A bath had helped, the clean shirt and underclothes and socks borrowed from Joe had helped. He could stay awake another hour or two. And until he got down to that hotel and got a few things straight he wasn't going to be comfortable.

Beside him on the porcelain top of the kitchen table was yesterday's paper, the front page, with a two-column story and a picture of Elaine Nesbitt holding the leash on a straining bulldog. "S.L. MINING MAN KILLS WOMAN, SELF," the headline said. He read the story through again, trying to get that "how" straight in his mind, but what the newspaper said didn't help much. Harry Mason, local mining man, had met Elaine Nesbitt in the lobby of the Winston Hotel at nine in the morning. They had quarreled some time previously over mining interests in which both were interested, according to James Dobson, the hotel clerk. They quarreled again in the lobby, and Mrs. Nesbitt, pretty auburn-haired widow, struck Mason with her handbag and ran out toward the side entrance. Mason jerked a gun from his coat pocket and followed. Dobson, trying to grapple with him, was thrown against the desk. He heard the outside door slam, then two shots. When he got to the door Mason was slumped against the radiator with a bullet through his head. He was still breathing, but died within ten minutes. There was a bullet hole through the door, and outside Mrs. Nesbitt lay face down, shot through the heart.

So it was rage, blind berserk fury.

But he read on, and it wasn't so clear. According to Desk Sergeant Walter Hill, Mason had come in three days previously to get a permit to carry a gun. He had mining interests in Nevada, and was accustomed to carry considerable sums on his person. In granting the permit, the sergeant had asked him if he had any criminal record, a routine question, and Mason had said jokingly "Not yet." At the time he had seemed calm.

"I've just got to go down there," Bruce said. "It shouldn't take more than an hour or two."

"Want me to go along?" Joe said.

"You're already mixed up in this enough."

"That's all right," Joe said. "I'd be glad to come along, if you want."

Bruce shook his head, tore the story out of the newspaper and folded it into his pocket.

He remembered the hotel, a dark little semi-respectable place on First South. The lighted shelf above the entrance looked dingy, and the door opened hard. There was no one in the lobby except the clerk behind the desk. Bruce's eyes darted past the desk, spotted the hall leading to the side entrance, and the radiator's dull gilt gleaming in the desk light. He locked his insides as if he were trying not to vomit.

"I'm Bruce Mason," he said to the clerk. "I just got in."

The clerk had a cast in one eye. The other one jumped, startled, in his pale face. He came out from behind the desk, hurrying. "Oh yeh," he said. "I'll get Dobson. He was on when . . . Just wait here a minute."

He ran up the stairs two at a time, and Bruce stood still by the desk. In this dingy little lobby, yesterday morning, the thing had been done. He moved toward the side entrance. The carpet down the little hall had been taken up, and he saw the unpainted boards and the splintered tack holes. Against this radiator, within reach of his hand, his father had stood, in what desperate frenzy, and spattered his brains against this wall. He shut his jaw and turned away, and as he turned he saw the bullet-hole in the panel of the door.

Steps were coming, and he went back to the desk. A short man with a bald spot came down and shook his hand. "I been expecting you," he said. "Your dad left some papers and things. Want to look at them now?"

"I might as well."

The little man looked at him sidelong. "It's a hell of a thing," he said. "You seen the papers? You know how it happened?"

"Let it go," Bruce said. "I've seen the paper." For all his need to settle the tiniest detail, the facial expression even, of that last furious minute of his father's life, he did not want to talk to the clerk. It had to come without any coloring. But the lobby had told him nothing. The radiator was a radiator, nothing more, and even the stains of his father's blood on it, if there had been any, would not have made this thing any more believable.

"I never had any idea he was feeling that way," Dobson said as they went upstairs. "Oh, I knew he was having a little trouble about money, and he'd had a spat or two with Elaine, but Jesus . . ." He turned down the hall, unlocked the door of a room. "The cops told me to keep it locked," he said, "but you can go in."

Bruce stood half in the door. "Would you mind?" he said. "Could I look things over alone?"

"Sure." Dobson hesitated. "I don't want to push, or anything, but Harry owed me twenty dollars. If he had any insurance or anything I wonder . . ."

"I'll fix it up," Bruce said. "Did he owe anything else, do you know?"

"I know he owed something to O'Brien, from the Cantwell Hotel. O'Brien came around here trying to collect once or twice. I think he owes some rent here, too."

"Well, I'll go through things and see what's here," Bruce said.

"And he owed for a suit of clothes," Dobson said. "He wasn't hardly cold before that Jew Miller was calling up wanting to know where he was going to get his money."

"Where is the suit?"

"He was wearing it."

"All right," Bruce said. He closed the door and looked around. The bed was made, the closet door open. Inside the closet there was a suit and a pair of black shoes and a bundle of neckties, several of which had apparently never been worn. On the dresser, under a silver shaving mug, was a large envelope addressed to Bruce Mason.

Then he had known he was going to do it. It hadn't been done in a rage. The letters and the worthless stock certificate were not blackmail or begging. As he sat down on the bed with the heavy envelope in his hand he felt as if he were going to be sick.

The envelope contained an insurance policy for five hundred dollars and a receipt book showing that his father had made monthly payments, the last one on June first. Clipped together there were five pawn tickets with pencilled scribblings on the backs. The tickets said overcoat, suitcase, watch, suitcase, suitcase. There was a map with red markings in the corner, showing the location of the Della Mine. There were the three letters that Bruce had written during the last two months, in answer to his father's. His own handwriting looked incongruous and strange to him now, seen as his father had seen it.

And what about the letters? he said. Nothing in them but little bread-and-butter checks and a lot of smug free advice. Take a brace, keep your chin up, you're not licked yet, why not get a job at something, any kind of job, till you get a stake again, instead of waiting and depending on this mine? He held the three letters in his hand hating himself.

The last thing he looked at was a certificate of ownership for the cemetery lot, together with a sexton's receipt and another receipt showing that perpetual care had been bought and paid for.

He sat on the bed weighing the papers in his hands. No note. The letter written on June first was the last. He had known that long before that there wasn't anything left.

The shaving mug on the dresser caught his eye, and he reached to lift it down. The metal was tarnished, one side was dented, the inscription on the side was worn almost away, but he held it up to the light and read it:

Champion of North Dakota
Single Traps
Harry Mason, 1905

That was the final sum, the final outcome, of the skill and talents and strength his father had started with. One dented silver mug, almost thirty years old. One pair of worn shoes, one worn suit, a dozen spotted neckties, a third interest in a worthless mine, a cemetery lot with perpetual care. A few pawn tickets, a few debts, a few papers, an insurance policy to bury him and a cemetery lot to bury him in, that last small resource hoarded jealously even while the larger and hopeful resources were squandered.

Quietly he set the mug down, folded pawn tickets and papers into the envelope, and stood up, thinking of the radiator downstairs, the little hall with the carpet taken up, the door with the bullet hole. His father had wasted himself in a thousand ways, but he had never been an incompetent. Even in that last despair, that last shattered minute when rage led him to include the woman in his plan of death, he had done a workmanlike job. He killed the woman with one shot through the door, and he killed himself cleanly with another. There were so many things the old man could do a good job on. He had had a knack for versifying and story-telling, he was a dead shot with any kind of gun, he could take an automobile apart and put it back together in the dark, he was a carpenter, a cabinet-maker, he was strong as a bull, stubborn as a mule, single-minded as a monk. And all of that wasted in the wrong causes, all of that coming to its climax with a neat and workmanlike job of murder and suicide.

There was a light knock on the door, and he swung around, stuffing the papers into his coat as if he had stolen them. A tall and very thin woman stood there, looking at him with a soft, almost dewy expression in her eyes. Her mouth twitched. "You're his son," she said.

"I heard you were here," she said. "I had to come and see you. I'm Mrs. Winter, I live just down the hall."

"I see," he said, wondering what she had to do with it, where she came in. Another of his father's women?

"You look like your picture," Mrs. Winter said. "He showed it to me once."

"You mean he had a picture of me?"

"In his wallet."

That shamed him too. The man he had hated all his life carried a picture around in his wallet, showed it to people, perhaps with pride. Everything in this bare, cheap little room shamed him.

"Did you see much of him . . . before?" he said.

She had started to cry, without noise. "He was just desperate," she said. "He told me a month ago he was going to do it, and he was so violent and hard you couldn't come near him. He told me a couple of weeks ago he was going to do it the next day."

"What stopped him then?" Bruce said. His imagination was on ahead of her, seeing the despair and hopelessness and desperation coming face to face with the final violence, and shying away, weakening.

"I don't know," she said. "I did what I could. I got a friend of mine with a car and we all went out to the lake and drove around all afternoon, and I talked to him. I told him he'd get back on his feet, but he just looked out the window and gritted his teeth. I kept him up as late as I could that night, but when he left I was scared to death. Then I saw him the next morning, and I was so relieved!"

"Yes," Bruce said.

"I thought he was all over it," Mrs. Winter said. "The last three or four days before it happened he was just as sweet, just as gentle and smiling, you'd have thought all his troubles had been settled. And all the time he had that gun he'd got the permit for."

"I guess," Bruce said, "that nobody could have done anything to stop him. You were good to try."

"I liked him," Mrs. Winter said. "He was honest."

Honest? Bruce said. Honest? Well, maybe, with everyone but himself. He could cheat himself, and fool himself, and justify himself, every time. But those last few days? he said. Those three or four days when he went around quiet and smiling and gentle, with the pawn-shop gun in his pocket? He was honest with himself then, for perhaps the first and last time. Everything was over for him then. Even the last act, then, must have seemed unimportant.

He put out his hand to Mrs. Winter. "Thank you for being his friend," he said. "I guess he didn't have many, at the last."

"Everybody turns against you when you're down," she said. "I know." With her face bent she went with short quick steps down the hall and turned in a door.

And there was one version. Harry Mason, that old lush who hung around the Winston lobby and sponged meals and five-dollar loans from anybody he could collar, that old broken-down Big Shot who still dreamed of fantastic wealth out of a Nevada gold mine, was to one woman at least an honest man, a kind man, a misunderstood man, an unhappy man.

Oh most certainly an unhappy man, he said, and stood in the open door of his father's room with the tears hot and sudden in his eyes, thinking of that picture in the wallet and of those three or four days when he was kind and gentle and smiling, with a gun in his pocket.

At eleven thirty he fell into bed at Joe's and lay sleepless for hours, his eyes burning up into the darkness and his hands and feet feeling immense, swollen, elephantine from the quarts of coffee he had drunk on the road. He threshed it all through and cried hard racking sobs into the dark, and when he finally fell asleep he slept until noon.

Then there was the undertaker to see, and the discovery, this third time he had used him, that the undertaker was an old whiskey customer of his father's. He laid out the things taken from Bo Mason's clothes—a wallet with five dollars in it, a handful of change, an address book, some keys, a couple of pencils—and talked sadly and thoughtfully, drumming with his finger tips on the desk. He had seen Harry around occasionally. No idea he was hard up or in trouble. It was a terrible and mysterious thing. Couldn't have been money only, because Harry had plenty of friends who would have been glad to see him through a bad spot. He'd have given him a loan himself, if he'd known. He was full of friendship and sympathy and careful avoidances, he made no effort to sell Bruce an expensive casket, he loaned him a car to run errands in. Bruce wanted to despise him for his profession and his careful talk, but he couldn't despise him. He was too genuinely helpful.

While he was talking in the office a woman came into the hushed parlor, and through the door, in a tearful whisper, asked if she could see Mr. Mason, asking as if she expected not to be allowed to. She looked at Bruce once, then ignored him, but as she was starting down the hall she turned to look again, stared steadily with an anguished pucker between her eyes. Her face was vaguely familiar.

"Aren't you," she said, coming back a few steps. "You aren't . . . Bruce?"

"Yes."

In an instant she was in his arms, hanging onto him, sobbing, her ravaged and repaired face close to his, crying out that it was terrible, oh my God it was terrible, why did he do it, why did he ever get mixed up with that woman, oh my God she couldn't believe it. She would have come to him, she would have left her family and everything else, and had told him so, but not while Elsa was alive, she wouldn't have hurt Elsa for anything in the world, but she could have kept him from that woman, and my God, Bruce, she wished she had, she wished she had.

Leaning back a little, Bruce said yes, and no, and yes. She mustn't take it so hard, there was nothing anyone could do now, nobody was to blame.

She clung to him for a little while, got control of her babbling and her tears, wiped her eyes, blew her nose, looked at him yearningly, and finally went down the hall, and he never did find out who she was or where he had known her or what connection there had ever been between her and his father.

Next there was the insurance man, Hammond. He too shook Bruce's hand, asked him about his studies, wanted to know where he was going to hang up his shingle. He too kept his face closed and his mouth discreet, looked up the policy and found that sixty dollars had been borrowed on it. That would have to be deducted from the claim.

"I got Harry this policy after he got sick a couple years ago," he said. "Pretty hard to get it through the office. He wasn't well, he wasn't well at all. Had some kind of stroke, blood pressure way up."

He filled in blanks and asked questions, shook his head as he waited for the ink to dry. Words of condolence, of sympathy, were on the tip of his tongue, and Bruce knew it. The man might even be grieved at Bo Mason's death. But it was not a death you could talk about. All Hammond could say was "Yes sir, I've known Harry for almost fifteen years." That seemed to express what it was possible to express under the circumstances. He repeated it when he shook Bruce's hand in farewell and assured him that the policy would come right through, two weeks or so at the most. A graying and not-too-prosperous business man, he stood shaking Bruce's hand thoughtfully, saying Yes sir, he'd known Harry for fifteen years.

Not, Bruce thought angrily on his way out, "Yes sir, Harry was a swell guy, one of the best, his death is a loss." Not that. Not even "Yes sir, Harry and I have been friends for fifteen years." It took courage to say to the son of a murderer and suicide that you

559

liked him, that he was your friend. It took courage even to talk about the manner of his death. The best you could say was . . .

Damn them, he said, if they can't say anything good about him why don't they keep their mouths shut?

The minister who said the few ritual words in the funeral parlor was obviously embarrassed. He clearly found it difficult to say much over the body of one who had lived and died by violence, and though he was bound to ask God's grace on this poor sinner, he did it only with half a heart, and spent most of his ten minutes on the afflictions that are visited upon mankind, the trials that come in life, the unhappiness that burdens us from the cradle to the grave. Man is born to sorrow as the sparks fly upward. This little family, for instance, had been grievously stricken. Within three years the mother, the son, and now the father had been struck down. He prayed that God's mercy would be with them all, and with the young man who survived.

As he halted on, avoiding direct reference to Bo Mason, making solemn generalities in the solemn padded parlor, talking about a man he had not known, and lamenting for a family he had never heard of until today, Bruce could feel him all the way wanting to make the body of this Bo Mason the subject of a sermon on the wages of sin, holding back because the offices he was conducting prohibited any ill-speaking of the dead; and so, morally indignant and yet unable to speak his mind, limping through his solemn and meaningless ten minutes. As he talked, Bruce's mind worked in ironic counterpoint:

This man whom today we consign to the grave, this Harry Mason, was a man whom I and many others have condemned. We have sat in judgment on him, and we have found him guilty of violence, brutality, wilfulness. He was frequently inconsiderate of others, he was obtuse about other people's wishes. He was a man who never knew himself, who was never satisfied, who was born disliking the present and believing in the future. He was not, by any orthodox standard, a good husband or a good father. He chafed against domestic restraints, ruled by violence instead of love, forced his wife and children to live a life they despised and hated. He broke the law, he blasphemed, he served Mammon, he was completely incapable of anything remotely resembling social responsibility, and with dedicated selfishness he went after the Big Money. He wore out his wife and broke her heart, he destroyed one son and turned the other against him. At the end he degenerated into a broken old man, sponging a bare living and sustaining himself on a last gilded and impossible dream; and when he could no longer bear the indignities which the world heaped upon him, and when the dream broke like a bubble, he sought some way, out of an obscure and passionate compulsion to exonerate himself, to lay the blame onto another, the woman who had been his mistress. He shot her and then turned the gun upon himself, thus ending his life appropriately and fittingly, in violence. God may have mercy on this Harry Mason, but he may also wreak justice. God's will be done.

Yet this Harry Mason, violent and brutal and unthinking, this law-breaker and blasphemer, kept for over a quarter of a century the love of as good a woman as ever walked, my mother, and when he appeared to abandon her just before her death, he did so because the prospect of her death was intolerable to him, because in spite of his bullying and self-willed spirit he loved and cherished her, and he knew that the best of himself would die when she died.

This same father who broke the spirit and spoiled the chances of his older son took a very great pride in that son's exploits, had dreams for him as golden as his dreams for himself, shook with nightmares for months after that son died. This same father who turned his second son into an animate cold hatred carried a photograph of that son in his wallet to the morning of his death. This same selfish fortune-hunter was so little cold and calculating that in his last years he was a sucker for the really calculating, the women and promoters who drained off his money and left him sick and broke in a second-rate hotel. This Harry Mason, this anti-social monster, could be nobly generous on occasion, could be affectionate, could weep like a child.

It is of that child that we should be talking and thinking while we sit here in judgment over the body of Harry Mason, that child with a quick mind and talented hands, a child off on the wrong foot and unable to see that he was wrong, a child with tremendous self-reliance and tremendous energy and a tremendous drive toward the things that seemed to him good. If he went wrong, he was mistaken, not vicious; or if vicious, his viciousness was merely the product of the balking of his will. And let us remember that at the end he did not run or try to hide from himself, he saw himself for a little while honestly, and only the last minute of rage which led him to kill the woman too prevented his death from being a thing almost humble. As it was, he saw near at hand two people who had wronged and betrayed and disgraced him, and as his last act he killed them both.

Harry Mason was a child and a man. Whatever he did, any time, he was a completely masculine being, and almost always he was a child, even in his rages. In an earlier time, under other circumstances, he might have become something the nation would have elected to honor, but he would have been no different. He would always have been an undeveloped human being, an immature social animal, and the further the nation goes the less room there is for that kind of man. Harry Mason lived with the woman who was my mother, and whom I honor for her kindness and gentleness and courage and wisdom. But I tell you at his funeral, and in spite of the hatred I have had for him for many years, that he was more talented and more versatile and more energetic than she. Refine her qualities and you would get saintliness, but never greatness. His qualities were the raw material for a notable man. Though I have hated him, and though I neither honor nor respect him now, I can not deny him that.

Into the grave. Into lot 6, block 37, beside Elsa Mason and Chester Mason, and let the bodies of the united family unite more intimately in the deep earth than they ever did in life. There is the makings of a man in that family, and more of it than I ever thought will have to come out of the tissues of my father.

The preacher stopped. Bruce had not heard him for several minutes. Now he saw him fold his hands and bend his head. From the pews behind, where a sprinkling of acquaintances, nondescript pall-bearers recruited from his father's old intimates, banker and broker and bootlegger and pimp, sat and listened to the preacher's words, there came a light sniffle. The attendants came to the edge of the curtains and stood ready. The minister finished his short prayer, the chapel organ began to cough and mourn. Dry-eyed, Bruce stood up and stepped three steps forward to where the coffin lay open. He had not yet brought himself to look at his father's body.

The heavy square hands were crossed on the neatly-pressed coat-front. The thinning hair was brushed back, and the right temple, where the bullet had entered, was so smoothly patched with wax that only a knowing eye could have detected it. The mouth was gentle, almost humorously curved; the jaw was blunt and strong. Whatever violence had been in the face had been erased.

But what he noticed most strongly, before the attendants stepped forward and lowered the lid of the casket, was the enormous, powerful arch of his father's chest, and the width of the shoulders in the satin-lined box.

As he followed the handful of people out through the entrance into the sun of the court, he could feel no grief for his father, nor for his mother and brother whose graves were grassy beside the new raw hole at the cemetery. He could think only of the brightness of the sun, an excessive sparkling brightness, as if there were some meaning in it, or a blessing, and he saw the sweep of the spring-green slopes up to the worn peaks above Dry Canyon. His past was upon him, the feeling he had had two or three times that he bore his whole family's history in his own mind, and he remembered the time when he had gone with his mother and father on a picnic to the Bearpaw Mountains, the wonder and delight of his childhood, and the shadow behind it of the things that his mind had caught from infancy, from other times, from some dim remoteness that gave up its meaning slowly and incompletely. He remembered the great snake his father had killed by the roadside, and the gopher that had come slimy and stretched from the snake's mouth, and the feeling he had had then was like the feeling he had now: it was a good thing to have been along and seen, a thing to be remembered and told about, a thing that he and his father shared.

Perhaps that was what it meant, all of it. It was good to have been along and to have shared it. There were things he had learned that could not be taken away from him. Perhaps it took several generations to make a man, perhaps it took several combinations and re-creations of his mother's gentleness and resilience, his father's enormous energy and appetite for the new, a subtle blending of masculine and feminine, selfish and selfless, stubborn and yielding, before a proper man could be fashioned.

He was the only one left to fulfill that contract and try to justify the labor and the harshness and the mistakes of his parents' lives, and that responsibility was so clearly his, was so great an obligation, that it made unimportant and unreal the sight of the motley collection of pall-bearers staggering under the weight of his father's body, and the back door of the hearse closing quietly upon the casket and the flowers.

AMERICAN CENTURY SERIES

AC 1 *The Hoosier School-Master* by Edward Eggleston
AC 2 *The Magnificent Ambersons* by Booth Tarkington
S 3 *The Harbor* by Ernest Poole
AC 5 *The Flush Times of Alabama and Mississippi* by Joseph Baldwin
S 6 *Ivory, Apes, and Peacocks* by James Gibbons Huneker
AC 7 *The Higher Learning in America* by Thorstein Veblen
AC 8 *The Shame of the Cities* by Lincoln Steffens
S 9 *Company K* by William March
AC 10 *The Influence of Seapower upon History* by Alfred T. Mahan
S 11 *A Daughter of the Middle Border* by Hamlin Garland
AC 12 *How the Other Half Lives* by Jacob Riis
S 13 *His Fifty Years of Exile (Israel Potter)* by Herman Melville
AC 14 *Barren Ground* by Ellen Glasgow
S 15 *Hospital Sketches* by Louisa May Alcott
S 16 *A Traveler from Altruria* by William Dean Howells
AC 17 *The Devil's Dictionary* by Ambrose Bierce
S 18 *Moon-Calf* by Floyd Dell
S 19 *The Big Rock Candy Mountain* by Wallace Stegner
S 20 *The Octopus* by Frank Norris
AC 21 *Life on the Mississippi* by Mark Twain
S 22 *Troubadour* by Alfred Kreymborg
S 23 *The Iron Heel* by Jack London
S 24 *Georgia Scenes* by A. B. Longstreet
S 25 *The Grandissimes* by George W. Cable
S 26 *The Autocrat of the Breakfast Table* by Oliver Wendell Holmes
AC 28 *The Jeffersonian Tradition in American Democracy* by Charles Wiltse
AC 29 *The Narrative of Arthur Gordon Pym* by Edgar Allan Poe
AC 30 *A Connecticut Yankee in King Arthur's Court* by Mark Twain
AC 31 *Theodore Roosevelt and the Progressive Movement* by George E. Mowry
AC 32 *The Autobiography of an Ex-Coloured Man* by James Weldon Johnson
AC 33 *Jack London: Short Stories*
AC 34 *Jefferson* by Albert Jay Nock
AC 35 *America Goes to War* by Bruce Catton
AC 36 *Hemingway and His Critics: An International Anthology* edited and with an Introduction by Carlos Baker
AC 37 *Stars Fell on Alabama* by Carl Carmer
AC 38 *Writers in Crisis: The American Novel, 1925–1940* by Maxwell Geismar
AC 39 *The Best of Simple* by Langston Hughes
AC 40 *American Social Thought* edited by Ray Ginger
ACW 41 *William Dean Howells* edited by Rudolf and Clara Marburg Kirk
ACW 42 *Walt Whitman* edited by Floyd Stovall
ACW 43 *Thomas Paine* edited by Harry Hayden Clark
AC 44 *American Moderns: From Rebellion to Conformity* by Maxwell Geismar
AC 45 *The Last of the Provincials: The American Novel, 1915–1925* by Maxwell Geismar
ACW 46 *Edgar Allan Poe* edited by Hardin Craig and Margaret Alterton
ACW 47 *Jonathan Edwards* edited by Clarence H. Faust and Thomas H. Johnson

ACW 48 *Benjamin Franklin* edited by Frank Luther Mott and Chester E. Jorgenson
AC 49 *Indian Tales* by Jaime de Angulo
AC 50 *A Time of Harvest* edited by Robert E. Spiller
AC 51 *The Limits of Language* edited by Walker Gibson
AC 52 *Sherwood Anderson: Short Stories* edited and with an Introduction by Maxwell Geismar
AC 53 *The World of Lincoln Steffens* edited by Ella Winter and Herbert Shapiro, with an Introduction by Barrows Dunham
AC 54 *Mark Twain on the Damned Human Race* edited and with an Introduction by Janet Smith
AC 55 *The Happy Critic and Other Essays* by Mark Van Doren
AC 56 *Man Against Myth* by Barrows Dunham
AC 57 *Something in Common and Other Stories* by Langston Hughes
AC 58 *Writers in Transition: Seven Americans* by H. Wayne Morgan
AC 59 *The Lincoln Nobody Knows* by Richard N. Current
AC 60 *The Disinherited* by Jack Conroy, with an Introduction by Daniel Aaron
AC 61 *Eisenhower As President* edited by Dean Albertson
AC 62 *Rebels and Ancestors* by Maxwell Geismar
AC 63 *Mount Allegro* by Jerre Mangione
AC 64 *Thoreau: People, Principles, and Politics* edited and with an Introduction by Milton Meltzer
AC 65 *The Big Sea* by Langston Hughes
AC 66 *The Golden Age of Homespun* by Jared van Wagenen, Jr.
AC 67 *The Senate Establishment* by Joseph S. Clark and Other Senators
AC 68 *I Wonder As I Wander* by Langston Hughes
AC 69 *Science in Nineteenth-Century America: A Documentary History* edited and with an Introduction by Nathan Reingold
AC 70 *The Course of the South to Secession: An Interpretation* by Ulrich Bonnell Phillips
AC 71 *American Negro Poetry* edited and with an Introduction by Arna Bontemps
AC 72 *Horace Greeley* by Glyndon G. Van Deusen
AC 73 *David Walker's Appeal* edited and with an Introduction by Charles M. Wiltse
AC 74 *The Sentimental Years* by E. Douglas Branch
AC 75 *Henry James and the Jacobites* by Maxwell Geismar
AC 76 *The Reins of Power* by Bernard Schwartz
AC 77 *American Writers in Rebellion* by H. Wayne Morgan
AC 78 *Policy and Power* by Ruhl Bartlett
AC 79 *Wendell Phillips on Civil Rights and Freedom* edited by Louis Filler
AC 80 *American Negro Short Stories* edited and with an Introduction by John Henrik Clarke
AC 81 *The Radical Novel in the United States: 1900–1954* by Walter B. Rideout
AC 82 *A History of Agriculture in the State of New York* by Ulysses Prentiss Hedrick
AC 101 *Fabric of Freedom: 1763–1800* by Esmond Wright
AC 102 *The New Nation: 1800–1845* by Charles M. Wiltse
AC 103 *The Stakes of Power: 1845–1877* by Roy F. Nichols
H 13 *Mark Twain and the Russians* by Charles Neider
H 26 *Citizen Toussaint* by Ralph Korngold
H 27 *Digging Up America* by Frank C. Hibben
H 33 *Free World Colossus* by David Horowitz